To Kathryn and Kyndra

PREFACE

This 2010 Supplement reflects changes in professional standards through August 2009. It begins with the current version of the ABA Model Rules, as extensively amended by the ABA House of Delegates in 2002, 2003 and also amended in 2009. We have also updated the appendices to the Model Rules, giving a state-by-state analysis of rules on client confidences, imputed disqualification and when a written fee agreement is required.

As always, we have retained the ABA Model Code of Professional Responsibility (1970) and the ABA Canons of Ethics (1908), both as amended, for their help in showing the history of the current Rules. We also include the California Rules of Professional Conduct and related statutes, and the new New York Rules of Professional Conduct as illustrations of different approaches to the issues.

Federal regulation of lawyers remains important, and this Supplement continues to include the SEC regulations implementing obligations on lawyers imposed by the Sarbanes–Oxley Act, the statute regulating practice by former Federal Government lawyers, and the IRS regulations on tax shelter opinions.

On the subject of judicial ethics we have reprinted the 2007 ABA Model Code of Judicial Conduct, as well as the corresponding California Code and selected federal statutes relating to judges.

We hope that students and faculty alike will find these materials up to date and useful in their study of professional responsibility. We thank, in particular, Stephanie Arrache, Chapman Law School, Class of 2010, for her research assistance.

T.D.M.

R.D.R.

October 2009

TABLE OF CONTENTS

TABLE OF CONTENTS

FOUNDATION PRESS

MODEL RULES
OF PROFESSIONAL CONDUCT
and
OTHER SELECTED STANDARDS

Including California and New York Rules

on

PROFESSIONAL
RESPONSIBILITY

THE AMERICAN BAR ASSOCIATION
MODEL RULES OF PROFESSIONAL CONDUCT
August, 2003

The ABA House of Delegates adopted the Model Rules of Conduct on August 2, 1983. They were amended over the years and were subject to substantial modifications in August, 2001, and February and August, 2002, in response to changes proposed by the ABA Commission on Evaluation of the Rules of Professional Conduct, popularly called "Ethics, 2000." Only a year later, in August, 2003, the ABA amended Rule 1.6 and Rule 1.13 in response to the Enron collapse. This version reflects all of these changes. The editors' footnotes to Rule 1.6 and Rule 1.13 show what these Rules looked like just before the post-Enron changes.

Contents

PREAMBLE: A LAWYER'S RESPONSIBILITIES

[1] A lawyer, as a member of the legal profession, is a representative of clients, an officer of the legal system and a public citizen having special responsibility for the quality of justice.

[2] As a representative of clients, a lawyer performs various functions. As advisor, a lawyer provides a client with an informed understanding of the client's legal rights and obligations and explains their practical implications. As advocate, a lawyer zealously asserts the client's position under the rules of the adversary system. As negotiator, a lawyer seeks a result advantageous to the client but consistent with requirements of honest dealings with others. As an evaluator, a lawyer acts by examining a client's legal affairs and reporting about them to the client or to others.

[3] In addition to these representational functions, a lawyer may serve as a third-party neutral, a nonrepresentational role helping the parties to resolve a dispute or other matter. Some of these Rules apply directly to lawyers who are or have served as third-party neutrals. See, e.g., Rules 1.12 and 2.4. In addition, there are Rules that apply to lawyers who are not active in the practice of law or to practicing lawyers even when they are acting in a nonprofessional capacity. For example, a lawyer who commits fraud in the conduct of a business is subject to discipline for engaging in conduct involving dishonesty, fraud, deceit or misrepresentation. See Rule 8.4.

[4] In all professional functions a lawyer should be competent, prompt and diligent. A lawyer should maintain communication with a client concerning the representation. A lawyer should keep in confidence information relating to representation of a client except so far as disclosure is required or permitted by the Rules of Professional Conduct or other law.

[5] A lawyer's conduct should conform to the requirements of the law, both in professional service to clients and in the lawyer's business and personal affairs. A lawyer should use the law's procedures only for legitimate purposes and not to harass or intimidate others. A lawyer should demonstrate respect for the legal system and for those who serve it, including judges, other lawyers and public officials. While it is a lawyer's duty, when necessary, to challenge the rectitude of official action, it is also a lawyer's duty to uphold legal process.

[6] As a public citizen, a lawyer should seek improvement of the law, access to the legal system, the administration of justice and the quality of service rendered by the legal profession. As a member of a learned profession, a lawyer should cultivate knowledge of the law beyond its use for clients, employ that knowledge in reform of the law and work to strengthen legal education. In addition, a lawyer should further the public's understanding of and confidence in the rule of law and the justice system because legal institutions in a constitutional democracy depend on popular participation and support to maintain their authority. A lawyer should be mindful of

deficiencies in the administration of justice and of the fact that the poor, and sometimes persons who are not poor, cannot afford adequate legal assistance. Therefore, all lawyers should devote professional time and resources and use civic influence to ensure equal access to our system of justice for all those who because of economic or social barriers cannot afford or secure adequate legal counsel. A lawyer should aid the legal profession in pursuing these objectives and should help the bar regulate itself in the public interest.

[7]   Many of a lawyer's professional responsibilities are prescribed in the Rules of Professional Conduct, as well as substantive and procedural law. However, a lawyer is also guided by personal conscience and the approbation of professional peers. A lawyer should strive to attain the highest level of skill, to improve the law and the legal profession and to exemplify the legal profession's ideals of public service.

[8]   A lawyer's responsibilities as a representative of clients, an officer of the legal system and a public citizen are usually harmonious. Thus, when an opposing party is well represented, a lawyer can be a zealous advocate on behalf of a client and at the same time assume that justice is being done. So also, a lawyer can be sure that preserving client confidences ordinarily serves the public interest because people are more likely to seek legal advice, and thereby heed their legal obligations, when they know their communications will be private.

[9]   In the nature of law practice, however, conflicting responsibilities are encountered. Virtually all difficult ethical problems arise from conflict between a lawyer's responsibilities to clients, to the legal system and to the lawyer's own interest in remaining an ethical person while earning a satisfactory living. The Rules of Professional Conduct often prescribe terms for resolving such conflicts. Within the framework of these Rules, however, many difficult issues of professional discretion can arise. Such issues must be resolved through the exercise of sensitive professional and moral judgment guided by the basic principles underlying the Rules. These principles include the lawyer's obligation zealously to protect and pursue a client's legitimate interests, within the bounds of the law, while maintaining a professional, courteous and civil attitude toward all persons involved in the legal system.

[10]   The legal profession is largely self-governing. Although other professions also have been granted powers of self-government, the legal profession is unique in this respect because of the close relationship between the profession and the processes of government and law enforcement. This connection is manifested in the fact that ultimate authority over the legal profession is vested largely in the courts.

[11]   To the extent that lawyers meet the obligations of their professional calling, the occasion for government regulation is obviated. Self-regulation also helps maintain the legal profession's independence from government domination. An independent legal profession is an important force in preserving government under law, for abuse of legal authority is more readily

challenged by a profession whose members are not dependent on government for the right to practice.

[12] The legal profession's relative autonomy carries with it special responsibilities of self-government. The profession has a responsibility to assure that its regulations are conceived in the public interest and not in furtherance of parochial or self-interested concerns of the bar. Every lawyer is responsible for observance of the Rules of Professional Conduct. A lawyer should also aid in securing their observance by other lawyers. Neglect of these responsibilities compromises the independence of the profession and the public interest which it serves.

[13] Lawyers play a vital role in the preservation of society. The fulfillment of this role requires an understanding by lawyers of their relationship to our legal system. The Rules of Professional Conduct, when properly applied, serve to define that relationship.

SCOPE

[14] The Rules of Professional Conduct are rules of reason. They should be interpreted with reference to the purposes of legal representation and of the law itself. Some of the Rules are imperatives, cast in the terms "shall" or "shall not." These define proper conduct for purposes of professional discipline. Others, generally cast in the term "may," are permissive and define areas under the Rules in which the lawyer has discretion to exercise professional judgment. No disciplinary action should be taken when the lawyer chooses not to act or acts within the bounds of such discretion. Other Rules define the nature of relationships between the lawyer and others. The Rules are thus partly obligatory and disciplinary and partly constitutive and descriptive in that they define a lawyer's professional role. Many of the Comments use the term "should." Comments do not add obligations to the Rules but provide guidance for practicing in compliance with the Rules.

[15] The Rules presuppose a larger legal context shaping the lawyer's role. That context includes court rules and statutes relating to matters of licensure, laws defining specific obligations of lawyers and substantive and procedural law in general. The Comments are sometimes used to alert lawyers to their responsibilities under such other law.

[16] Compliance with the Rules, as with all law in an open society, depends primarily upon understanding and voluntary compliance, secondarily upon reinforcement by peer and public opinion and finally, when necessary, upon enforcement through disciplinary proceedings. The Rules do not, however, exhaust the moral and ethical considerations that should inform a lawyer, for no worthwhile human activity can be completely defined by legal rules. The Rules simply provide a framework for the ethical practice of law.

[17] Furthermore, for purposes of determining the lawyer's authority and responsibility, principles of substantive law external to these Rules determine whether a client-lawyer relationship exists. Most of the duties flowing from the client-lawyer relationship attach only after the client has

requested the lawyer to render legal services and the lawyer has agreed to do so. But there are some duties, such as that of confidentiality under Rule 1.6, that attach when the lawyer agrees to consider whether a client-lawyer relationship shall be established. See Rule 1.18. Whether a client-lawyer relationship exists for any specific purpose can depend on the circumstances and may be a question of fact.

[18] Under various legal provisions, including constitutional, statutory and common law, the responsibilities of government lawyers may include authority concerning legal matters that ordinarily reposes in the client in private client-lawyer relationships. For example, a lawyer for a government agency may have authority on behalf of the government to decide upon settlement or whether to appeal from an adverse judgment. Such authority in various respects is generally vested in the attorney general and the state's attorney in state government, and their federal counterparts, and the same may be true of other government law officers. Also, lawyers under the supervision of these officers may be authorized to represent several government agencies in intragovernmental legal controversies in circumstances where a private lawyer could not represent multiple private clients. These Rules do not abrogate any such authority.

[19] Failure to comply with an obligation or prohibition imposed by a Rule is a basis for invoking the disciplinary process. The Rules presuppose that disciplinary assessment of a lawyer's conduct will be made on the basis of the facts and circumstances as they existed at the time of the conduct in question and in recognition of the fact that a lawyer often has to act upon uncertain or incomplete evidence of the situation. Moreover, the Rules presuppose that whether or not discipline should be imposed for a violation, and the severity of a sanction, depend on all the circumstances, such as the willfulness and seriousness of the violation, extenuating factors and whether there have been previous violations.

[20] Violation of a Rule should not itself give rise to a cause of action against a lawyer nor should it create any presumption in such a case that a legal duty has been breached. In addition, violation of a Rule does not necessarily warrant any other nondisciplinary remedy, such as disqualification of a lawyer in pending litigation. The Rules are designed to provide guidance to lawyers and to provide a structure for regulating conduct through disciplinary agencies. They are not designed to be a basis for civil liability. Furthermore, the purpose of the Rules can be subverted when they are invoked by opposing parties as procedural weapons. The fact that a Rule is a just basis for a lawyer's self-assessment, or for sanctioning a lawyer under the administration of a disciplinary authority, does not imply that an antagonist in a collateral proceeding or transaction has standing to seek enforcement of the Rule. Nevertheless, since the Rules do establish standards of conduct by lawyers, a lawyer's violation of a Rule may be evidence of breach of the applicable standard of conduct.

[21] The Comment accompanying each Rule explains and illustrates the meaning and purpose of the Rule. The Preamble and this note on Scope

provide general orientation. The Comments are intended as guides to interpretation, but the text of each Rule is authoritative.

RULE 1.0: TERMINOLOGY

(a) "Belief" or "believes" denotes that the person involved actually supposed the fact in question to be true. A person's belief may be inferred from circumstances.

(b) "Confirmed in writing," when used in reference to the informed consent of a person, denotes informed consent that is given in writing by the person or a writing that a lawyer promptly transmits to the person confirming an oral informed consent. See paragraph (e) for the definition of "informed consent." If it is not feasible to obtain or transmit the writing at the time the person gives informed consent, then the lawyer must obtain or transmit it within a reasonable time thereafter.

(c) "Firm" or "law firm" denotes a lawyer or lawyers in a law partnership, professional corporation, sole proprietorship or other association authorized to practice law; or lawyers employed in a legal services organization or the legal department of a corporation or other organization.

(d) "Fraud" or "fraudulent" denotes conduct that is fraudulent under the substantive or procedural law of the applicable jurisdiction and has a purpose to deceive.

(e) "Informed consent" denotes the agreement by a person to a proposed course of conduct after the lawyer has communicated adequate information and explanation about the material risks of and reasonably available alternatives to the proposed course of conduct.

(f) "Knowingly," "known," or "knows" denotes actual knowledge of the fact in question. A person's knowledge may be inferred from circumstances.

(g) "Partner" denotes a member of a partnership, a shareholder in a law firm organized as a professional corporation, or a member of an association authorized to practice law.

(h) "Reasonable" or "reasonably" when used in relation to conduct by a lawyer denotes the conduct of a reasonably prudent and competent lawyer.

(i) "Reasonable belief" or "reasonably believes" when used in reference to a lawyer denotes that the lawyer believes the matter in question and that the circumstances are such that the belief is reasonable.

(j) "Reasonably should know" when used in reference to a lawyer denotes that a lawyer of reasonable prudence and competence would ascertain the matter in question.

(k) "**Screened**" **denotes the isolation of a lawyer from any participation in a matter through the timely imposition of procedures within a firm that are reasonably adequate under the circumstances to protect information that the isolated lawyer is obligated to protect under these Rules or other law.**

(*l*) "Substantial" when used in reference to degree or extent denotes a material matter of clear and weighty importance.

(m) "Tribunal" denotes a court, an arbitrator in a binding arbitration proceeding or a legislative body, administrative agency or other body acting in an adjudicative capacity. A legislative body, administrative agency or other body acts in an adjudicative capacity when a neutral official, after the presentation of evidence or legal argument by a party or parties, will render a binding legal judgment directly affecting a party's interests in a particular matter.

(n) "Writing" or "written" denotes a tangible or electronic record of a communication or representation, including handwriting, typewriting, printing, photostating, photography, audio or video-recording and e-mail. A "signed" writing includes an electronic sound, symbol or process attached to or logically associated with a writing and executed or adopted by a person with the intent to sign the writing.

Comment

Confirmed in Writing

[1] If it is not feasible to obtain or transmit a written confirmation at the time the client gives informed consent, then the lawyer must obtain or transmit it within a reasonable time thereafter. If a lawyer has obtained a client's informed consent, the lawyer may act in reliance on that consent so long as it is confirmed in writing within a reasonable time thereafter.

Firm

[2] Whether two or more lawyers constitute a firm within paragraph (c) can depend on the specific facts. For example, two practitioners who share office space and occasionally consult or assist each other ordinarily would not be regarded as constituting a firm. However, if they present themselves to the public in a way that suggests that they are a firm or conduct themselves as a firm, they should be regarded as a firm for purposes of the Rules. The terms of any formal agreement between associated lawyers are relevant in determining whether they are a firm, as is the fact that they have mutual access to information concerning the clients they serve. Furthermore, it is relevant in doubtful cases to consider the underlying purpose of the Rule that is involved. A group of lawyers could be regarded as a firm for purposes of the Rule that the same lawyer should not represent opposing parties in litigation, while it might not be so regarded for purposes of the Rule that information acquired by one lawyer is attributed to another.

[3]   With respect to the law department of an organization, including the government, there is ordinarily no question that the members of the department constitute a firm within the meaning of the Rules of Professional Conduct. There can be uncertainty, however, as to the identity of the client. For example, it may not be clear whether the law department of a corporation represents a subsidiary or an affiliated corporation, as well as the corporation by which the members of the department are directly employed. A similar question can arise concerning an unincorporated association and its local affiliates.

[4]   Similar questions can also arise with respect to lawyers in legal aid and legal services organizations. Depending upon the structure of the organization, the entire organization or different components of it may constitute a firm or firms for purposes of these Rules.

Fraud

[5]   When used in these Rules, the terms "fraud" or "fraudulent" refer to conduct that is characterized as such under the substantive or procedural law of the applicable jurisdiction and has a purpose to deceive. This does not include merely negligent misrepresentation or negligent failure to apprise another of relevant information. For purposes of these Rules, it is not necessary that anyone has suffered damages or relied on the misrepresentation or failure to inform.

Informed Consent

[6]   Many of the Rules of Professional Conduct require the lawyer to obtain the informed consent of a client or other person (e.g., a former client or, under certain circumstances, a prospective client) before accepting or continuing representation or pursuing a course of conduct. See, e.g., Rules 1.2(c), 1.6(a) and 1.7(b). The communication necessary to obtain such consent will vary according to the Rule involved and the circumstances giving rise to the need to obtain informed consent. The lawyer must make reasonable efforts to ensure that the client or other person possesses information reasonably adequate to make an informed decision. Ordinarily, this will require communication that includes a disclosure of the facts and circumstances giving rise to the situation, any explanation reasonably necessary to inform the client or other person of the material advantages and disadvantages of the proposed course of conduct and a discussion of the client's or other person's options and alternatives. In some circumstances it may be appropriate for a lawyer to advise a client or other person to seek the advice of other counsel. A lawyer need not inform a client or other person of facts or implications already known to the client or other person; nevertheless, a lawyer who does not personally inform the client or other person assumes the risk that the client or other person is inadequately informed and the consent is invalid. In determining whether the information and explanation provided are reasonably adequate, relevant factors include whether the client or other person is experienced in legal matters generally and in making decisions of

the type involved, and whether the client or other person is independently represented by other counsel in giving the consent. Normally, such persons need less information and explanation than others, and generally a client or other person who is independently represented by other counsel in giving the consent should be assumed to have given informed consent.

[7] Obtaining informed consent will usually require an affirmative response by the client or other person. In general, a lawyer may not assume consent from a client's or other person's silence. Consent may be inferred, however, from the conduct of a client or other person who has reasonably adequate information about the matter. A number of Rules require that a person's consent be confirmed in writing. See Rules 1.7(b) and 1.9(a). For a definition of "writing" and "confirmed in writing," see paragraphs (n) and (b). Other Rules require that a client's consent be obtained in a writing signed by the client. See, e.g., Rules 1.8(a) and (g). For a definition of "signed," see paragraph (n).

Screened

[8] This definition applies to situations where screening of a personally disqualified lawyer is permitted to remove imputation of a conflict of interest under Rules 1.11, 1.12 or 1.18.

[9] The purpose of screening is to assure the affected parties that confidential information known by the personally disqualified lawyer remains protected. The personally disqualified lawyer should acknowledge the obligation not to communicate with any of the other lawyers in the firm with respect to the matter. Similarly, other lawyers in the firm who are working on the matter should be informed that the screening is in place and that they may not communicate with the personally disqualified lawyer with respect to the matter. Additional screening measures that are appropriate for the particular matter will depend on the circumstances. To implement, reinforce and remind all affected lawyers of the presence of the screening, it may be appropriate for the firm to undertake such procedures as a written undertaking by the screened lawyer to avoid any communication with other firm personnel and any contact with any firm files or other materials relating to the matter, written notice and instructions to all other firm personnel forbidding any communication with the screened lawyer relating to the matter, denial of access by the screened lawyer to firm files or other materials relating to the matter and periodic reminders of the screen to the screened lawyer and all other firm personnel.

[10] In order to be effective, screening measures must be implemented as soon as practical after a lawyer or law firm knows or reasonably should know that there is a need for screening.

CLIENT–LAWYER RELATIONSHIP

RULE 1.1: COMPETENCE

A lawyer shall provide competent representation to a client. Competent representation requires the legal knowledge, skill, thoroughness and preparation reasonably necessary for the representation.

Comment

Legal Knowledge and Skill

[1] In determining whether a lawyer employs the requisite knowledge and skill in a particular matter, relevant factors include the relative complexity and specialized nature of the matter, the lawyer's general experience, the lawyer's training and experience in the field in question, the preparation and study the lawyer is able to give the matter and whether it is feasible to refer the matter to, or associate or consult with, a lawyer of established competence in the field in question. In many instances, the required proficiency is that of a general practitioner. Expertise in a particular field of law may be required in some circumstances.

[2] A lawyer need not necessarily have special training or prior experience to handle legal problems of a type with which the lawyer is unfamiliar. A newly admitted lawyer can be as competent as a practitioner with long experience. Some important legal skills, such as the analysis of precedent, the evaluation of evidence and legal drafting, are required in all legal problems. Perhaps the most fundamental legal skill consists of determining what kind of legal problems a situation may involve, a skill that necessarily transcends any particular specialized knowledge. A lawyer can provide adequate representation in a wholly novel field through necessary study. Competent representation can also be provided through the association of a lawyer of established competence in the field in question.

[3] In an emergency a lawyer may give advice or assistance in a matter in which the lawyer does not have the skill ordinarily required where referral to or consultation or association with another lawyer would be impractical. Even in an emergency, however, assistance should be limited to that reasonably necessary in the circumstances, for ill-considered action under emergency conditions can jeopardize the client's interest.

[4] A lawyer may accept representation where the requisite level of competence can be achieved by reasonable preparation. This applies as well to a lawyer who is appointed as counsel for an unrepresented person. See also Rule 6.2.

Thoroughness and Preparation

[5] Competent handling of a particular matter includes inquiry into and analysis of the factual and legal elements of the problem, and use of methods

11

and procedures meeting the standards of competent practitioners. It also includes adequate preparation. The required attention and preparation are determined in part by what is at stake; major litigation and complex transactions ordinarily require more extensive treatment than matters of lesser complexity and consequence. An agreement between the lawyer and the client regarding the scope of the representation may limit the matters for which the lawyer is responsible. See Rule 1.2(c).

Maintaining Competence

[6]   To maintain the requisite knowledge and skill, a lawyer should keep abreast of changes in the law and its practice, engage in continuing study and education and comply with all continuing legal education requirements to which the lawyer is subject.

RULE 1.2: SCOPE OF REPRESENTATION AND ALLOCATION OF AUTHORITY BETWEEN CLIENT AND LAWYER

(a) Subject to paragraphs (c) and (d), a lawyer shall abide by a client's decisions concerning the objectives of representation and, as required by Rule 1.4, shall consult with the client as to the means by which they are to be pursued. A lawyer may take such action on behalf of the client as is impliedly authorized to carry out the representation. A lawyer shall abide by a client's decision whether to settle a matter. In a criminal case, the lawyer shall abide by the client's decision, after consultation with the lawyer, as to a plea to be entered, whether to waive jury trial and whether the client will testify.

(b) A lawyer's representation of a client, including representation by appointment, does not constitute an endorsement of the client's political, economic, social or moral views or activities.

(c) A lawyer may limit the scope of the representation if the limitation is reasonable under the circumstances and the client gives informed consent.

(d) A lawyer shall not counsel a client to engage, or assist a client, in conduct that the lawyer knows is criminal or fraudulent, but a lawyer may discuss the legal consequences of any proposed course of conduct with a client and may counsel or assist a client to make a good faith effort to determine the validity, scope, meaning or application of the law.

Comment

Allocation of Authority between Client and Lawyer

[1]   Paragraph (a) confers upon the client the ultimate authority to determine the purposes to be served by legal representation, within the limits imposed by law and the lawyer's professional obligations. The decisions

specified in paragraph (a), such as whether to settle a civil matter, must also be made by the client. See Rule 1.4(a)(1) for the lawyer's duty to communicate with the client about such decisions. With respect to the means by which the client's objectives are to be pursued, the lawyer shall consult with the client as required by Rule 1.4(a)(2) and may take such action as is impliedly authorized to carry out the representation.

[2] On occasion, however, a lawyer and a client may disagree about the means to be used to accomplish the client's objectives. Clients normally defer to the special knowledge and skill of their lawyer with respect to the means to be used to accomplish their objectives, particularly with respect to technical, legal and tactical matters. Conversely, lawyers usually defer to the client regarding such questions as the expense to be incurred and concern for third persons who might be adversely affected. Because of the varied nature of the matters about which a lawyer and client might disagree and because the actions in question may implicate the interests of a tribunal or other persons, this Rule does not prescribe how such disagreements are to be resolved. Other law, however, may be applicable and should be consulted by the lawyer. The lawyer should also consult with the client and seek a mutually acceptable resolution of the disagreement. If such efforts are unavailing and the lawyer has a fundamental disagreement with the client, the lawyer may withdraw from the representation. See Rule 1.16(b)(4). Conversely, the client may resolve the disagreement by discharging the lawyer. See Rule 1.16(a)(3).

[3] At the outset of a representation, the client may authorize the lawyer to take specific action on the client's behalf without further consultation. Absent a material change in circumstances and subject to Rule 1.4, a lawyer may rely on such an advance authorization. The client may, however, revoke such authority at any time.

[4] In a case in which the client appears to be suffering diminished capacity, the lawyer's duty to abide by the client's decisions is to be guided by reference to Rule 1.14.

Independence from Client's Views or Activities

[5] Legal representation should not be denied to people who are unable to afford legal services, or whose cause is controversial or the subject of popular disapproval. By the same token, representing a client does not constitute approval of the client's views or activities.

Agreements Limiting Scope of Representation

[6] The scope of services to be provided by a lawyer may be limited by agreement with the client or by the terms under which the lawyer's services are made available to the client. When a lawyer has been retained by an insurer to represent an insured, for example, the representation may be limited to matters related to the insurance coverage. A limited representation may be appropriate because the client has limited objectives for the representation. In addition, the terms upon which representation is undertaken may exclude specific means that might otherwise be used to accomplish the client's

objectives. Such limitations may exclude actions that the client thinks are too costly or that the lawyer regards as repugnant or imprudent.

[7]   Although this Rule affords the lawyer and client substantial latitude to limit the representation, the limitation must be reasonable under the circumstances. If, for example, a client's objective is limited to securing general information about the law the client needs in order to handle a common and typically uncomplicated legal problem, the lawyer and client may agree that the lawyer's services will be limited to a brief telephone consultation. Such a limitation, however, would not be reasonable if the time allotted was not sufficient to yield advice upon which the client could rely. Although an agreement for a limited representation does not exempt a lawyer from the duty to provide competent representation, the limitation is a factor to be considered when determining the legal knowledge, skill, thoroughness and preparation reasonably necessary for the representation. See Rule 1.1.

[8]   All agreements concerning a lawyer's representation of a client must accord with the Rules of Professional Conduct and other law. See, e.g., Rules 1.1, 1.8 and 5.6.

Criminal, Fraudulent and Prohibited Transactions

[9]   Paragraph (d) prohibits a lawyer from knowingly counseling or assisting a client to commit a crime or fraud. This prohibition, however, does not preclude the lawyer from giving an honest opinion about the actual consequences that appear likely to result from a client's conduct. Nor does the fact that a client uses advice in a course of action that is criminal or fraudulent of itself make a lawyer a party to the course of action. There is a critical distinction between presenting an analysis of legal aspects of questionable conduct and recommending the means by which a crime or fraud might be committed with impunity.

[10]   When the client's course of action has already begun and is continuing, the lawyer's responsibility is especially delicate. The lawyer is required to avoid assisting the client, for example, by drafting or delivering documents that the lawyer knows are fraudulent or by suggesting how the wrongdoing might be concealed. A lawyer may not continue assisting a client in conduct that the lawyer originally supposed was legally proper but then discovers is criminal or fraudulent. The lawyer must, therefore, withdraw from the representation of the client in the matter. See Rule 1.16(a). In some cases, withdrawal alone might be insufficient. It may be necessary for the lawyer to give notice of the fact of withdrawal and to disaffirm any opinion, document, affirmation or the like. See Rule 4.1.

[11]   Where the client is a fiduciary, the lawyer may be charged with special obligations in dealings with a beneficiary.

[12]   Paragraph (d) applies whether or not the defrauded party is a party to the transaction. Hence, a lawyer must not participate in a transaction to effectuate criminal or fraudulent avoidance of tax liability. Paragraph (d) does not preclude undertaking a criminal defense incident to a general retainer for

legal services to a lawful enterprise. The last clause of paragraph (d) recognizes that determining the validity or interpretation of a statute or regulation may require a course of action involving disobedience of the statute or regulation or of the interpretation placed upon it by governmental authorities.

[13]   If a lawyer comes to know or reasonably should know that a client expects assistance not permitted by the Rules of Professional Conduct or other law or if the lawyer intends to act contrary to the client's instructions, the lawyer must consult with the client regarding the limitations on the lawyer's conduct. See Rule 1.4(a)(5).

RULE 1.3: DILIGENCE

A lawyer shall act with reasonable diligence and promptness in representing a client.

Comment

[1]   A lawyer should pursue a matter on behalf of a client despite opposition, obstruction or personal inconvenience to the lawyer, and take whatever lawful and ethical measures are required to vindicate a client's cause or endeavor. A lawyer must also act with commitment and dedication to the interests of the client and with zeal in advocacy upon the client's behalf. A lawyer is not bound, however, to press for every advantage that might be realized for a client. For example, a lawyer may have authority to exercise professional discretion in determining the means by which a matter should be pursued. See Rule 1.2. The lawyer's duty to act with reasonable diligence does not require the use of offensive tactics or preclude the treating of all persons involved in the legal process with courtesy and respect.

[2]   A lawyer's work load must be controlled so that each matter can be handled competently.

[3]   Perhaps no professional shortcoming is more widely resented than procrastination. A client's interests often can be adversely affected by the passage of time or the change of conditions; in extreme instances, as when a lawyer overlooks a statute of limitations, the client's legal position may be destroyed. Even when the client's interests are not affected in substance, however, unreasonable delay can cause a client needless anxiety and undermine confidence in the lawyer's trustworthiness. A lawyer's duty to act with reasonable promptness, however, does not preclude the lawyer from agreeing to a reasonable request for a postponement that will not prejudice the lawyer's client.

[4]   Unless the relationship is terminated as provided in Rule 1.16, a lawyer should carry through to conclusion all matters undertaken for a client. If a lawyer's employment is limited to a specific matter, the relationship terminates when the matter has been resolved. If a lawyer has served a client over a substantial period in a variety of matters, the client sometimes may assume that the lawyer will continue to serve on a continuing basis unless the

lawyer gives notice of withdrawal. Doubt about whether a client-lawyer relationship still exists should be clarified by the lawyer, preferably in writing, so that the client will not mistakenly suppose the lawyer is looking after the client's affairs when the lawyer has ceased to do so. For example, if a lawyer has handled a judicial or administrative proceeding that produced a result adverse to the client and the lawyer and the client have not agreed that the lawyer will handle the matter on appeal, the lawyer must consult with the client about the possibility of appeal before relinquishing responsibility for the matter. See Rule 1.4(a)(2). Whether the lawyer is obligated to prosecute the appeal for the client depends on the scope of the representation the lawyer has agreed to provide to the client. See Rule 1.2.

[5]   To prevent neglect of client matters in the event of a sole practitioner's death or disability, the duty of diligence may require that each sole practitioner prepare a plan, in conformity with applicable rules, that designates another competent lawyer to review client files, notify each client of the lawyer's death or disability, and determine whether there is a need for immediate protective action. Cf. Rule 28 of the American Bar Association Model Rules for Lawyer Disciplinary Enforcement (providing for court appointment of a lawyer to inventory files and take other protective action in absence of a plan providing for another lawyer to protect the interests of the clients of a deceased or disabled lawyer).

RULE 1.4: COMMUNICATION

(a) **A lawyer shall:**

(1) **promptly inform the client of any decision or circumstance with respect to which the client's informed consent, as defined in Rule 1.0(e), is required by these Rules;**

(2) **reasonably consult with the client about the means by which the client's objectives are to be accomplished;**

(3) **keep the client reasonably informed about the status of the matter;**

(4) **promptly comply with reasonable requests for information; and**

(5) **consult with the client about any relevant limitation on the lawyer's conduct when the lawyer knows that the client expects assistance not permitted by the Rules of Professional Conduct or other law.**

(b) **A lawyer shall explain a matter to the extent reasonably necessary to permit the client to make informed decisions regarding the representation.**

Comment

[1]   Reasonable communication between the lawyer and the client is necessary for the client effectively to participate in the representation.

Communicating with Client

[2]   If these Rules require that a particular decision about the representation be made by the client, paragraph (a)(1) requires that the lawyer
promptly consult with and secure the client's consent prior to taking action
unless prior discussions with the client have resolved what action the client
wants the lawyer to take. For example, a lawyer who receives from opposing
counsel an offer of settlement in a civil controversy or a proffered plea bargain
in a criminal case must promptly inform the client of its substance unless the
client has previously indicated that the proposal will be acceptable or unacceptable or has authorized the lawyer to accept or to reject the offer. See Rule
1.2(a).

[3]   Paragraph (a)(2) requires the lawyer to reasonably consult with the
client about the means to be used to accomplish the client's objectives. In
some situations—depending on both the importance of the action under
consideration and the feasibility of consulting with the client—this duty will
require consultation prior to taking action. In other circumstances, such as
during a trial when an immediate decision must be made, the exigency of the
situation may require the lawyer to act without prior consultation. In such
cases the lawyer must nonetheless act reasonably to inform the client of
actions the lawyer has taken on the client's behalf. Additionally, paragraph
(a)(3) requires that the lawyer keep the client reasonably informed about the
status of the matter, such as significant developments affecting the timing or
the substance of the representation.

[4]   A lawyer's regular communication with clients will minimize the
occasions on which a client will need to request information concerning the
representation. When a client makes a reasonable request for information,
however, paragraph (a)(4) requires prompt compliance with the request, or if
a prompt response is not feasible, that the lawyer, or a member of the
lawyer's staff, acknowledge receipt of the request and advise the client when a
response may be expected. Client telephone calls should be promptly returned
or acknowledged.

Explaining Matters

[5]   The client should have sufficient information to participate intelligently in decisions concerning the objectives of the representation and the
means by which they are to be pursued, to the extent the client is willing and
able to do so. Adequacy of communication depends in part on the kind of
advice or assistance that is involved. For example, when there is time to
explain a proposal made in a negotiation, the lawyer should review all
important provisions with the client before proceeding to an agreement. In
litigation a lawyer should explain the general strategy and prospects of
success and ordinarily should consult the client on tactics that are likely to
result in significant expense or to injure or coerce others. On the other hand,
a lawyer ordinarily will not be expected to describe trial or negotiation
strategy in detail. The guiding principle is that the lawyer should fulfill
reasonable client expectations for information consistent with the duty to act

in the client's best interests, and the client's overall requirements as to the character of representation. In certain circumstances, such as when a lawyer asks a client to consent to a representation affected by a conflict of interest, the client must give informed consent, as defined in Rule 1.0(e).

[6] Ordinarily, the information to be provided is that appropriate for a client who is a comprehending and responsible adult. However, fully informing the client according to this standard may be impracticable, for example, where the client is a child or suffers from diminished capacity. See Rule 1.14. When the client is an organization or group, it is often impossible or inappropriate to inform every one of its members about its legal affairs; ordinarily, the lawyer should address communications to the appropriate officials of the organization. See Rule 1.13. Where many routine matters are involved, a system of limited or occasional reporting may be arranged with the client.

Withholding Information

[7] In some circumstances, a lawyer may be justified in delaying transmission of information when the client would be likely to react imprudently to an immediate communication. Thus, a lawyer might withhold a psychiatric diagnosis of a client when the examining psychiatrist indicates that disclosure would harm the client. A lawyer may not withhold information to serve the lawyer's own interest or convenience or the interests or convenience of another person. Rules or court orders governing litigation may provide that information supplied to a lawyer may not be disclosed to the client. Rule 3.4(c) directs compliance with such rules or orders.

RULE 1.5: FEES

(a) A lawyer shall not make an agreement for, charge, or collect an unreasonable fee or an unreasonable amount for expenses. The factors to be considered in determining the reasonableness of a fee include the following:

(1) the time and labor required, the novelty and difficulty of the questions involved, and the skill requisite to perform the legal service properly;

(2) the likelihood, if apparent to the client, that the acceptance of the particular employment will preclude other employment by the lawyer;

(3) the fee customarily charged in the locality for similar legal services;

(4) the amount involved and the results obtained;

(5) the time limitations imposed by the client or by the circumstances;

(6) the nature and length of the professional relationship with the client;

(7) the experience, reputation, and ability of the lawyer or lawyers performing the services; and

(8) whether the fee is fixed or contingent.

(b) The scope of the representation and the basis or rate of the fee and expenses for which the client will be responsible shall be communicated to the client, preferably in writing, before or within a reasonable time after commencing the representation, except when the lawyer will charge a regularly represented client on the same basis or rate. Any changes in the basis or rate of the fee or expenses shall also be communicated to the client.

(c) A fee may be contingent on the outcome of the matter for which the service is rendered, except in a matter in which a contingent fee is prohibited by paragraph (d) or other law. A contingent fee agreement shall be in a writing signed by the client and shall state the method by which the fee is to be determined, including the percentage or percentages that shall accrue to the lawyer in the event of settlement, trial or appeal; litigation and other expenses to be deducted from the recovery; and whether such expenses are to be deducted before or after the contingent fee is calculated. The agreement must clearly notify the client of any expenses for which the client will be liable whether or not the client is the prevailing party. Upon conclusion of a contingent fee matter, the lawyer shall provide the client with a written statement stating the outcome of the matter and, if there is a recovery, showing the remittance to the client and the method of its determination.

(d) A lawyer shall not enter into an arrangement for, charge, or collect:

(1) any fee in a domestic relations matter, the payment or amount of which is contingent upon the securing of a divorce or upon the amount of alimony or support, or property settlement in lieu thereof; or

(2) a contingent fee for representing a defendant in a criminal case.

(e) A division of a fee between lawyers who are not in the same firm may be made only if:

(1) the division is in proportion to the services performed by each lawyer or each lawyer assumes joint responsibility for the representation;

(2) the client agrees to the arrangement, including the share each lawyer will receive, and the agreement is confirmed in writing; and

(3) the total fee is reasonable.

Comment

Reasonableness of Fee and Expenses

[1] Paragraph (a) requires that lawyers charge fees that are reasonable under the circumstances. The factors specified in (1) through (8) are not exclusive. Nor will each factor be relevant in each instance. Paragraph (a) also requires that expenses for which the client will be charged must be reasonable. A lawyer may seek reimbursement for the cost of services performed in-house, such as copying, or for other expenses incurred in-house, such as telephone charges, either by charging a reasonable amount to which the client has agreed in advance or by charging an amount that reasonably reflects the cost incurred by the lawyer.

Basis or Rate of Fee

[2] When the lawyer has regularly represented a client, they ordinarily will have evolved an understanding concerning the basis or rate of the fee and the expenses for which the client will be responsible. In a new client-lawyer relationship, however, an understanding as to fees and expenses must be promptly established. Generally, it is desirable to furnish the client with at least a simple memorandum or copy of the lawyer's customary fee arrangements that states the general nature of the legal services to be provided, the basis, rate or total amount of the fee and whether and to what extent the client will be responsible for any costs, expenses or disbursements in the course of the representation. A written statement concerning the terms of the engagement reduces the possibility of misunderstanding.

[3] Contingent fees, like any other fees, are subject to the reasonableness standard of paragraph (a) of this Rule. In determining whether a particular contingent fee is reasonable, or whether it is reasonable to charge any form of contingent fee, a lawyer must consider the factors that are relevant under the circumstances. Applicable law may impose limitations on contingent fees, such as a ceiling on the percentage allowable, or may require a lawyer to offer clients an alternative basis for the fee. Applicable law also may apply to situations other than a contingent fee, for example, government regulations regarding fees in certain tax matters.

Terms of Payment

[4] A lawyer may require advance payment of a fee, but is obliged to return any unearned portion. See Rule 1.16(d). A lawyer may accept property in payment for services, such as an ownership interest in an enterprise, providing this does not involve acquisition of a proprietary interest in the cause of action or subject matter of the litigation contrary to Rule 1.8(i). However, a fee paid in property instead of money may be subject to the requirements of Rule 1.8(a) because such fees often have the essential qualities of a business transaction with the client.

[5] An agreement may not be made whose terms might induce the lawyer improperly to curtail services for the client or perform them in a way contrary to the client's interest. For example, a lawyer should not enter into an agreement whereby services are to be provided only up to a stated amount when it is foreseeable that more extensive services probably will be required, unless the situation is adequately explained to the client. Otherwise, the client might have to bargain for further assistance in the midst of a proceeding or transaction. However, it is proper to define the extent of services in light of the client's ability to pay. A lawyer should not exploit a fee arrangement based primarily on hourly charges by using wasteful procedures.

Prohibited Contingent Fees

[6] Paragraph (d) prohibits a lawyer from charging a contingent fee in a domestic relations matter when payment is contingent upon the securing of a divorce or upon the amount of alimony or support or property settlement to be obtained. This provision does not preclude a contract for a contingent fee for legal representation in connection with the recovery of post-judgment balances due under support, alimony or other financial orders because such contracts do not implicate the same policy concerns.

Division of Fee

[7] A division of fee is a single billing to a client covering the fee of two or more lawyers who are not in the same firm. A division of fee facilitates association of more than one lawyer in a matter in which neither alone could serve the client as well, and most often is used when the fee is contingent and the division is between a referring lawyer and a trial specialist. Paragraph (e) permits the lawyers to divide a fee either on the basis of the proportion of services they render or if each lawyer assumes responsibility for the representation as a whole. In addition, the client must agree to the arrangement, including the share that each lawyer is to receive, and the agreement must be confirmed in writing. Contingent fee agreements must be in a writing signed by the client and must otherwise comply with paragraph (c) of this Rule. Joint responsibility for the representation entails financial and ethical responsibility for the representation as if the lawyers were associated in a partnership. A lawyer should only refer a matter to a lawyer whom the referring lawyer reasonably believes is competent to handle the matter. See Rule 1.1.

[8] Paragraph (e) does not prohibit or regulate division of fees to be received in the future for work done when lawyers were previously associated in a law firm.

Disputes over Fees

[9] If a procedure has been established for resolution of fee disputes, such as an arbitration or mediation procedure established by the bar, the lawyer must comply with the procedure when it is mandatory, and, even when it is voluntary, the lawyer should conscientiously consider submitting to it. Law may prescribe a procedure for determining a lawyer's fee, for example, in

representation of an executor or administrator, a class or a person entitled to a reasonable fee as part of the measure of damages. The lawyer entitled to such a fee and a lawyer representing another party concerned with the fee should comply with the prescribed procedure.

RULE 1.6: CONFIDENTIALITY OF INFORMATION*

(a) A lawyer shall not reveal information relating to the representation of a client unless the client gives informed consent, the disclosure is impliedly authorized in order to carry out the representation or the disclosure is permitted by paragraph (b).

(b) A lawyer may reveal information relating to the representation of a client to the extent the lawyer reasonably believes necessary:

(1) to prevent reasonably certain death or substantial bodily harm;

(2) to prevent the client from committing a crime or fraud that is reasonably certain to result in substantial injury to the financial interests or property of another and in furtherance of which the client has used or is using the lawyer's services;

(3) to prevent, mitigate or rectify substantial injury to the financial interests or property of another that is reasonably certain to result or has resulted from the client's commission of a

* Editors' Note: The text reflects Rule 1.6 as amended in August, 2003. What follows below is the text of Rule 1.6 as amended by the ABA House of Delegates in August, 2002, and Comment [14] to Rule 1.6 that was deleted in 2003.

RULE 1.6: CONFIDENTIALITY OF INFORMATION

(a) A lawyer shall not reveal information relating to the representation of a client unless the client gives informed consent, the disclosure is impliedly authorized in order to carry out the representation or the disclosure is permitted by paragraph (b).

(b) A lawyer may reveal information relating to the representation of a client to the extent the lawyer reasonably believes necessary:

(1) to prevent reasonably certain death or substantial bodily harm;

(2) to secure legal advice about the lawyer's compliance with these Rules;

(3) to establish a claim or defense on behalf of the lawyer in a controversy between the lawyer and the client, to establish a defense to a criminal charge or civil claim against the lawyer based upon conduct in

which the client was involved, or to respond to allegations in any proceeding concerning the lawyer's representation of the client; or

(4) to comply with other law or a court order.

Comment * * *

Withdrawal

[14] If the lawyer's services will be used by the client in materially furthering a course of criminal or fraudulent conduct, the lawyer must withdraw, as stated in Rule 1.16(a)(1). After withdrawal the lawyer is required to refrain from making disclosure of the client's confidences, except as otherwise permitted by Rule 1.6. Neither this Rule nor Rule 1.8(b) nor Rule 1.16(d) prevents the lawyer from giving notice of the fact of withdrawal, and the lawyer may also withdraw or disaffirm any opinion, document, affirmation, or the like. Where the client is an organization, the lawyer may be in doubt whether contemplated conduct will actually be carried out by the organization. Where necessary to guide conduct in connection with this Rule, the lawyer may make inquiry within the organization as indicated in Rule 1.13(b).

crime or fraud in furtherance of which the client has used the lawyer's services;

(4) to secure legal advice about the lawyer's compliance with these Rules;

(5) to establish a claim or defense on behalf of the lawyer in a controversy between the lawyer and the client, to establish a defense to a criminal charge or civil claim against the lawyer based upon conduct in which the client was involved, or to respond to allegations in any proceeding concerning the lawyer's representation of the client; or

(6) to comply with other law or a court order.

Comment

[1] This Rule governs the disclosure by a lawyer of information relating to the representation of a client during the lawyer's representation of the client. See Rule 1.18 for the lawyer's duties with respect to information provided to the lawyer by a prospective client, Rule 1.9(c)(2) for the lawyer's duty not to reveal information relating to the lawyer's prior representation of a former client and Rules 1.8(b) and 1.9(c)(1) for the lawyer's duties with respect to the use of such information to the disadvantage of clients and former clients.

[2] A fundamental principle in the client-lawyer relationship is that, in the absence of the client's informed consent, the lawyer must not reveal information relating to the representation. See Rule 1.0(e) for the definition of informed consent. This contributes to the trust that is the hallmark of the client-lawyer relationship. The client is thereby encouraged to seek legal assistance and to communicate fully and frankly with the lawyer even as to embarrassing or legally damaging subject matter. The lawyer needs this information to represent the client effectively and, if necessary, to advise the client to refrain from wrongful conduct. Almost without exception, clients come to lawyers in order to determine their rights and what is, in the complex of laws and regulations, deemed to be legal and correct. Based upon experience, lawyers know that almost all clients follow the advice given, and the law is upheld.

[3] The principle of client-lawyer confidentiality is given effect by related bodies of law: the attorney-client privilege, the work product doctrine and the rule of confidentiality established in professional ethics. The attorney-client privilege and work product doctrine apply in judicial and other proceedings in which a lawyer may be called as a witness or otherwise required to produce evidence concerning a client. The rule of client-lawyer confidentiality applies in situations other than those where evidence is sought from the lawyer through compulsion of law. The confidentiality rule, for example, applies not only to matters communicated in confidence by the client but also to all information relating to the representation, whatever its source. A lawyer

may not disclose such information except as authorized or required by the Rules of Professional Conduct or other law. See also Scope.

[4] Paragraph (a) prohibits a lawyer from revealing information relating to the representation of a client. This prohibition also applies to disclosures by a lawyer that do not in themselves reveal protected information but could reasonably lead to the discovery of such information by a third person. A lawyer's use of a hypothetical to discuss issues relating to the representation is permissible so long as there is no reasonable likelihood that the listener will be able to ascertain the identity of the client or the situation involved.

Authorized Disclosure

[5] Except to the extent that the client's instructions or special circumstances limit that authority, a lawyer is impliedly authorized to make disclosures about a client when appropriate in carrying out the representation. In some situations, for example, a lawyer may be impliedly authorized to admit a fact that cannot properly be disputed or to make a disclosure that facilitates a satisfactory conclusion to a matter. Lawyers in a firm may, in the course of the firm's practice, disclose to each other information relating to a client of the firm, unless the client has instructed that particular information be confined to specified lawyers.

Disclosure Adverse to Client

[6] Although the public interest is usually best served by a strict rule requiring lawyers to preserve the confidentiality of information relating to the representation of their clients, the confidentiality rule is subject to limited exceptions. Paragraph (b)(1) recognizes the overriding value of life and physical integrity and permits disclosure reasonably necessary to prevent reasonably certain death or substantial bodily harm. Such harm is reasonably certain to occur if it will be suffered imminently or if there is a present and substantial threat that a person will suffer such harm at a later date if the lawyer fails to take action necessary to eliminate the threat. Thus, a lawyer who knows that a client has accidentally discharged toxic waste into a town's water supply may reveal this information to the authorities if there is a present and substantial risk that a person who drinks the water will contract a life-threatening or debilitating disease and the lawyer's disclosure is necessary to eliminate the threat or reduce the number of victims.

[7] Paragraph (b)(2) is a limited exception to the rule of confidentiality that permits the lawyer to reveal information to the extent necessary to enable affected persons or appropriate authorities to prevent the client from committing a crime or fraud, as defined in Rule 1.0(d), that is reasonably certain to result in substantial injury to the financial or property interests of another and in furtherance of which the client has used or is using the lawyer's services. Such a serious abuse of the client-lawyer relationship by the client forfeits the protection of this Rule. The client can, of course, prevent such disclosure by refraining from the wrongful conduct. Although paragraph (b)(2) does not require the lawyer to reveal the client's misconduct, the lawyer

may not counsel or assist the client in conduct the lawyer knows is criminal or fraudulent. See Rule 1.2(d). See also Rule 1.16 with respect to the lawyer's obligation or right to withdraw from the representation of the client in such circumstances, and Rule 1.13(c), which permits the lawyer, where the client is an organization, to reveal information relating to the representation in limited circumstances.

[8] Paragraph (b)(3) addresses the situation in which the lawyer does not learn of the client's crime or fraud until after it has been consummated. Although the client no longer has the option of preventing disclosure by refraining from the wrongful conduct, there will be situations in which the loss suffered by the affected person can be prevented, rectified or mitigated. In such situations, the lawyer may disclose information relating to the representation to the extent necessary to enable the affected persons to prevent or mitigate reasonably certain losses or to attempt to recoup their losses. Paragraph (b)(3) does not apply when a person who has committed a crime or fraud thereafter employs a lawyer for representation concerning that offense.

[9] A lawyer's confidentiality obligations do not preclude a lawyer from securing confidential legal advice about the lawyer's personal responsibility to comply with these Rules. In most situations, disclosing information to secure such advice will be impliedly authorized for the lawyer to carry out the representation. Even when the disclosure is not impliedly authorized, paragraph (b)(4) permits such disclosure because of the importance of a lawyer's compliance with the Rules of Professional Conduct.

[10] Where a legal claim or disciplinary charge alleges complicity of the lawyer in a client's conduct or other misconduct of the lawyer involving representation of the client, the lawyer may respond to the extent the lawyer reasonably believes necessary to establish a defense. The same is true with respect to a claim involving the conduct or representation of a former client. Such a charge can arise in a civil, criminal, disciplinary or other proceeding and can be based on a wrong allegedly committed by the lawyer against the client or on a wrong alleged by a third person, for example, a person claiming to have been defrauded by the lawyer and client acting together. The lawyer's right to respond arises when an assertion of such complicity has been made. Paragraph (b)(5) does not require the lawyer to await the commencement of an action or proceeding that charges such complicity, so that the defense may be established by responding directly to a third party who has made such an assertion. The right to defend also applies, of course, where a proceeding has been commenced.

[11] A lawyer entitled to a fee is permitted by paragraph (b)(5) to prove the services rendered in an action to collect it. This aspect of the rule expresses the principle that the beneficiary of a fiduciary relationship may not exploit it to the detriment of the fiduciary.

[12] Other law may require that a lawyer disclose information about a client. Whether such a law supersedes Rule 1.6 is a question of law beyond the

scope of these Rules. When disclosure of information relating to the representation appears to be required by other law, the lawyer must discuss the matter with the client to the extent required by Rule 1.4. If, however, the other law supersedes this Rule and requires disclosure, paragraph (b)(6) permits the lawyer to make such disclosures as are necessary to comply with the law.

[13] A lawyer may be ordered to reveal information relating to the representation of a client by a court or by another tribunal or governmental entity claiming authority pursuant to other law to compel the disclosure. Absent informed consent of the client to do otherwise, the lawyer should assert on behalf of the client all nonfrivolous claims that the order is not authorized by other law or that the information sought is protected against disclosure by the attorney-client privilege or other applicable law. In the event of an adverse ruling, the lawyer must consult with the client about the possibility of appeal to the extent required by Rule 1.4. Unless review is sought, however, paragraph (b)(6) permits the lawyer to comply with the court's order.

[14] Paragraph (b) permits disclosure only to the extent the lawyer reasonably believes the disclosure is necessary to accomplish one of the purposes specified. Where practicable, the lawyer should first seek to persuade the client to take suitable action to obviate the need for disclosure. In any case, a disclosure adverse to the client's interest should be no greater than the lawyer reasonably believes necessary to accomplish the purpose. If the disclosure will be made in connection with a judicial proceeding, the disclosure should be made in a manner that limits access to the information to the tribunal or other persons having a need to know it and appropriate protective orders or other arrangements should be sought by the lawyer to the fullest extent practicable.

[15] Paragraph (b) permits but does not require the disclosure of information relating to a client's representation to accomplish the purposes specified in paragraphs (b)(1) through (b)(6). In exercising the discretion conferred by this Rule, the lawyer may consider such factors as the nature of the lawyer's relationship with the client and with those who might be injured by the client, the lawyer's own involvement in the transaction and factors that may extenuate the conduct in question. A lawyer's decision not to disclose as permitted by paragraph (b) does not violate this Rule. Disclosure may be required, however, by other Rules. Some Rules require disclosure only if such disclosure would be permitted by paragraph (b). See Rules 1.2(d), 4.1(b), 8.1 and 8.3. Rule 3.3, on the other hand, requires disclosure in some circumstances regardless of whether such disclosure is permitted by this Rule. See Rule 3.3(c).

Acting Competently to Preserve Confidentiality

[16] A lawyer must act competently to safeguard information relating to the representation of a client against inadvertent or unauthorized disclosure by the lawyer or other persons who are participating in the representation of

the client or who are subject to the lawyer's supervision. See Rules 1.1, 5.1 and 5.3.

[17]   When transmitting a communication that includes information relating to the representation of a client, the lawyer must take reasonable precautions to prevent the information from coming into the hands of unintended recipients. This duty, however, does not require that the lawyer use special security measures if the method of communication affords a reasonable expectation of privacy. Special circumstances, however, may warrant special precautions. Factors to be considered in determining the reasonableness of the lawyer's expectation of confidentiality include the sensitivity of the information and the extent to which the privacy of the communication is protected by law or by a confidentiality agreement. A client may require the lawyer to implement special security measures not required by this Rule or may give informed consent to the use of a means of communication that would otherwise be prohibited by this Rule.

Former Client

[18]   The duty of confidentiality continues after the client-lawyer relationship has terminated. See Rule 1.9(c)(2). See Rule 1.9(c)(1) for the prohibition against using such information to the disadvantage of the former client.

RULE 1.7: CONFLICT OF INTEREST: CURRENT CLIENTS

(a) Except as provided in paragraph (b), a lawyer shall not represent a client if the representation involves a concurrent conflict of interest. A concurrent conflict of interest exists if:

(1) the representation of one client will be directly adverse to another client; or

(2) there is a significant risk that the representation of one or more clients will be materially limited by the lawyer's responsibilities to another client, a former client or a third person or by a personal interest of the lawyer.

(b) Notwithstanding the existence of a concurrent conflict of interest under paragraph (a), a lawyer may represent a client if:

(1) the lawyer reasonably believes that the lawyer will be able to provide competent and diligent representation to each affected client;

(2) the representation is not prohibited by law;

(3) the representation does not involve the assertion of a claim by one client against another client represented by the lawyer in the same litigation or other proceeding before a tribunal; and

(4) each affected client gives informed consent, confirmed in writing.

Comment

General Principles

[1]   Loyalty and independent judgment are essential elements in the lawyer's relationship to a client. Concurrent conflicts of interest can arise from the lawyer's responsibilities to another client, a former client or a third person or from the lawyer's own interests. For specific Rules regarding certain concurrent conflicts of interest, see Rule 1.8. For former client conflicts of interest, see Rule 1.9. For conflicts of interest involving prospective clients, see Rule 1.18. For definitions of "informed consent" and "confirmed in writing," see Rule 1.0(e) and (b).

[2]   Resolution of a conflict of interest problem under this Rule requires the lawyer to: 1) clearly identify the client or clients; 2) determine whether a conflict of interest exists; 3) decide whether the representation may be undertaken despite the existence of a conflict, i.e., whether the conflict is consentable; and 4) if so, consult with the clients affected under paragraph (a) and obtain their informed consent, confirmed in writing. The clients affected under paragraph (a) include both of the clients referred to in paragraph (a)(1) and the one or more clients whose representation might be materially limited under paragraph (a)(2).

[3]   A conflict of interest may exist before representation is undertaken, in which event the representation must be declined, unless the lawyer obtains the informed consent of each client under the conditions of paragraph (b). To determine whether a conflict of interest exists, a lawyer should adopt reasonable procedures, appropriate for the size and type of firm and practice, to determine in both litigation and non-litigation matters the persons and issues involved. See also Comment to Rule 5.1. Ignorance caused by a failure to institute such procedures will not excuse a lawyer's violation of this Rule. As to whether a client-lawyer relationship exists or, having once been established, is continuing, see Comment to Rule 1.3 and Scope.

[4]   If a conflict arises after representation has been undertaken, the lawyer ordinarily must withdraw from the representation, unless the lawyer has obtained the informed consent of the client under the conditions of paragraph (b). See Rule 1.16. Where more than one client is involved, whether the lawyer may continue to represent any of the clients is determined both by the lawyer's ability to comply with duties owed to the former client and by the lawyer's ability to represent adequately the remaining client or clients, given the lawyer's duties to the former client. See Rule 1.9. See also Comments [5] and [29].

[5]   Unforeseeable developments, such as changes in corporate and other organizational affiliations or the addition or realignment of parties in litigation, might create conflicts in the midst of a representation, as when a company sued by the lawyer on behalf of one client is bought by another client represented by the lawyer in an unrelated matter. Depending on the circumstances, the lawyer may have the option to withdraw from one of the representations in order to avoid the conflict. The lawyer must seek court

approval where necessary and take steps to minimize harm to the clients. See Rule 1.16. The lawyer must continue to protect the confidences of the client from whose representation the lawyer has withdrawn. See Rule 1.9(c).

Identifying Conflicts of Interest: Directly Adverse

[6] Loyalty to a current client prohibits undertaking representation directly adverse to that client without that client's informed consent. Thus, absent consent, a lawyer may not act as an advocate in one matter against a person the lawyer represents in some other matter, even when the matters are wholly unrelated. The client as to whom the representation is directly adverse is likely to feel betrayed, and the resulting damage to the client-lawyer relationship is likely to impair the lawyer's ability to represent the client effectively. In addition, the client on whose behalf the adverse representation is undertaken reasonably may fear that the lawyer will pursue that client's case less effectively out of deference to the other client, i.e., that the representation may be materially limited by the lawyer's interest in retaining the current client. Similarly, a directly adverse conflict may arise when a lawyer is required to cross-examine a client who appears as a witness in a lawsuit involving another client, as when the testimony will be damaging to the client who is represented in the lawsuit. On the other hand, simultaneous representation in unrelated matters of clients whose interests are only economically adverse, such as representation of competing economic enterprises in unrelated litigation, does not ordinarily constitute a conflict of interest and thus may not require consent of the respective clients.

[7] Directly adverse conflicts can also arise in transactional matters. For example, if a lawyer is asked to represent the seller of a business in negotiations with a buyer represented by the lawyer, not in the same transaction but in another, unrelated matter, the lawyer could not undertake the representation without the informed consent of each client.

Identifying Conflicts of Interest: Material Limitation

[8] Even where there is no direct adverseness, a conflict of interest exists if there is a significant risk that a lawyer's ability to consider, recommend or carry out an appropriate course of action for the client will be materially limited as a result of the lawyer's other responsibilities or interests. For example, a lawyer asked to represent several individuals seeking to form a joint venture is likely to be materially limited in the lawyer's ability to recommend or advocate all possible positions that each might take because of the lawyer's duty of loyalty to the others. The conflict in effect forecloses alternatives that would otherwise be available to the client. The mere possibility of subsequent harm does not itself require disclosure and consent. The critical questions are the likelihood that a difference in interests will eventuate and, if it does, whether it will materially interfere with the lawyer's independent professional judgment in considering alternatives or foreclose courses of action that reasonably should be pursued on behalf of the client.

Lawyer's Responsibilities to Former Clients and Other Third Persons

[9]   In addition to conflicts with other current clients, a lawyer's duties of loyalty and independence may be materially limited by responsibilities to former clients under Rule 1.9 or by the lawyer's responsibilities to other persons, such as fiduciary duties arising from a lawyer's service as a trustee, executor or corporate director.

Personal Interest Conflicts

[10]   The lawyer's own interests should not be permitted to have an adverse effect on representation of a client. For example, if the probity of a lawyer's own conduct in a transaction is in serious question, it may be difficult or impossible for the lawyer to give a client detached advice. Similarly, when a lawyer has discussions concerning possible employment with an opponent of the lawyer's client, or with a law firm representing the opponent, such discussions could materially limit the lawyer's representation of the client. In addition, a lawyer may not allow related business interests to affect representation, for example, by referring clients to an enterprise in which the lawyer has an undisclosed financial interest. See Rule 1.8 for specific Rules pertaining to a number of personal interest conflicts, including business transactions with clients. See also Rule 1.10 (personal interest conflicts under Rule 1.7 ordinarily are not imputed to other lawyers in a law firm).

[11]   When lawyers representing different clients in the same matter or in substantially related matters are closely related by blood or marriage, there may be a significant risk that client confidences will be revealed and that the lawyer's family relationship will interfere with both loyalty and independent professional judgment. As a result, each client is entitled to know of the existence and implications of the relationship between the lawyers before the lawyer agrees to undertake the representation. Thus, a lawyer related to another lawyer, e.g., as parent, child, sibling or spouse, ordinarily may not represent a client in a matter where that lawyer is representing another party, unless each client gives informed consent. The disqualification arising from a close family relationship is personal and ordinarily is not imputed to members of firms with whom the lawyers are associated. See Rule 1.10.

[12]   A lawyer is prohibited from engaging in sexual relationships with a client unless the sexual relationship predates the formation of the client-lawyer relationship. See Rule 1.8(j).

Interest of Person Paying for a Lawyer's Service

[13]   A lawyer may be paid from a source other than the client, including a co-client, if the client is informed of that fact and consents and the arrangement does not compromise the lawyer's duty of loyalty or independent judgment to the client. See Rule 1.8(f). If acceptance of the payment from any other source presents a significant risk that the lawyer's representation of the client will be materially limited by the lawyer's own interest in accommodating the person paying the lawyer's fee or by the lawyer's responsibilities to a payer who is also a co-client, then the lawyer must comply with the require-

ments of paragraph (b) before accepting the representation, including determining whether the conflict is consentable and, if so, that the client has adequate information about the material risks of the representation.

Prohibited Representations

[14]   Ordinarily, clients may consent to representation notwithstanding a conflict. However, as indicated in paragraph (b), some conflicts are nonconsentable, meaning that the lawyer involved cannot properly ask for such agreement or provide representation on the basis of the client's consent. When the lawyer is representing more than one client, the question of consentability must be resolved as to each client.

[15]   Consentability is typically determined by considering whether the interests of the clients will be adequately protected if the clients are permitted to give their informed consent to representation burdened by a conflict of interest. Thus, under paragraph (b)(1), representation is prohibited if in the circumstances the lawyer cannot reasonably conclude that the lawyer will be able to provide competent and diligent representation. See Rule 1.1 (competence) and Rule 1.3 (diligence).

[16]   Paragraph (b)(2) describes conflicts that are nonconsentable because the representation is prohibited by applicable law. For example, in some states substantive law provides that the same lawyer may not represent more than one defendant in a capital case, even with the consent of the clients, and under federal criminal statutes certain representations by a former government lawyer are prohibited, despite the informed consent of the former client. In addition, decisional law in some states limits the ability of a governmental client, such as a municipality, to consent to a conflict of interest.

[17]   Paragraph (b)(3) describes conflicts that are nonconsentable because of the institutional interest in vigorous development of each client's position when the clients are aligned directly against each other in the same litigation or other proceeding before a tribunal. Whether clients are aligned directly against each other within the meaning of this paragraph requires examination of the context of the proceeding. Although this paragraph does not preclude a lawyer's multiple representation of adverse parties to a mediation (because mediation is not a proceeding before a "tribunal" under Rule 1.0(m)), such representation may be precluded by paragraph (b)(1).

Informed Consent

[18]   Informed consent requires that each affected client be aware of the relevant circumstances and of the material and reasonably foreseeable ways that the conflict could have adverse effects on the interests of that client. See Rule 1.0(e) (informed consent). The information required depends on the nature of the conflict and the nature of the risks involved. When representation of multiple clients in a single matter is undertaken, the information must include the implications of the common representation, including possible effects on loyalty, confidentiality and the attorney-client privilege and the

advantages and risks involved. See Comments [30] and [31] (effect of common representation on confidentiality).

[19] Under some circumstances it may be impossible to make the disclosure necessary to obtain consent. For example, when the lawyer represents different clients in related matters and one of the clients refuses to consent to the disclosure necessary to permit the other client to make an informed decision, the lawyer cannot properly ask the latter to consent. In some cases the alternative to common representation can be that each party may have to obtain separate representation with the possibility of incurring additional costs. These costs, along with the benefits of securing separate representation, are factors that may be considered by the affected client in determining whether common representation is in the client's interests.

Consent Confirmed in Writing

[20] Paragraph (b) requires the lawyer to obtain the informed consent of the client, confirmed in writing. Such a writing may consist of a document executed by the client or one that the lawyer promptly records and transmits to the client following an oral consent. See Rule 1.0(b). See also Rule 1.0(n) (writing includes electronic transmission). If it is not feasible to obtain or transmit the writing at the time the client gives informed consent, then the lawyer must obtain or transmit it within a reasonable time thereafter. See Rule 1.0(b). The requirement of a writing does not supplant the need in most cases for the lawyer to talk with the client, to explain the risks and advantages, if any, of representation burdened with a conflict of interest, as well as reasonably available alternatives, and to afford the client a reasonable opportunity to consider the risks and alternatives and to raise questions and concerns. Rather, the writing is required in order to impress upon clients the seriousness of the decision the client is being asked to make and to avoid disputes or ambiguities that might later occur in the absence of a writing.

Revoking Consent

[21] A client who has given consent to a conflict may revoke the consent and, like any other client, may terminate the lawyer's representation at any time. Whether revoking consent to the client's own representation precludes the lawyer from continuing to represent other clients depends on the circumstances, including the nature of the conflict, whether the client revoked consent because of a material change in circumstances, the reasonable expectations of the other clients and whether material detriment to the other clients or the lawyer would result.

Consent to Future Conflict

[22] Whether a lawyer may properly request a client to waive conflicts that might arise in the future is subject to the test of paragraph (b). The effectiveness of such waivers is generally determined by the extent to which the client reasonably understands the material risks that the waiver entails. The more comprehensive the explanation of the types of future representa-

tions that might arise and the actual and reasonably foreseeable adverse consequences of those representations, the greater the likelihood that the client will have the requisite understanding. Thus, if the client agrees to consent to a particular type of conflict with which the client is already familiar, then the consent ordinarily will be effective with regard to that type of conflict. If the consent is general and open-ended, then the consent ordinarily will be ineffective, because it is not reasonably likely that the client will have understood the material risks involved. On the other hand, if the client is an experienced user of the legal services involved and is reasonably informed regarding the risk that a conflict may arise, such consent is more likely to be effective, particularly if, e.g., the client is independently represented by other counsel in giving consent and the consent is limited to future conflicts unrelated to the subject of the representation. In any case, advance consent cannot be effective if the circumstances that materialize in the future are such as would make the conflict nonconsentable under paragraph (b).

Conflicts in Litigation

[23]　Paragraph (b)(3) prohibits representation of opposing parties in the same litigation, regardless of the clients' consent. On the other hand, simultaneous representation of parties whose interests in litigation may conflict, such as coplaintiffs or codefendants, is governed by paragraph (a)(2). A conflict may exist by reason of substantial discrepancy in the parties' testimony, incompatibility in positions in relation to an opposing party or the fact that there are substantially different possibilities of settlement of the claims or liabilities in question. Such conflicts can arise in criminal cases as well as civil. The potential for conflict of interest in representing multiple defendants in a criminal case is so grave that ordinarily a lawyer should decline to represent more than one codefendant. On the other hand, common representation of persons having similar interests in civil litigation is proper if the requirements of paragraph (b) are met.

[24]　Ordinarily a lawyer may take inconsistent legal positions in different tribunals at different times on behalf of different clients. The mere fact that advocating a legal position on behalf of one client might create precedent adverse to the interests of a client represented by the lawyer in an unrelated matter does not create a conflict of interest. A conflict of interest exists, however, if there is a significant risk that a lawyer's action on behalf of one client will materially limit the lawyer's effectiveness in representing another client in a different case; for example, when a decision favoring one client will create a precedent likely to seriously weaken the position taken on behalf of the other client. Factors relevant in determining whether the clients need to be advised of the risk include: where the cases are pending, whether the issue is substantive or procedural, the temporal relationship between the matters, the significance of the issue to the immediate and long-term interests of the clients involved and the clients' reasonable expectations in retaining the lawyer. If there is significant risk of material limitation, then absent informed

consent of the affected clients, the lawyer must refuse one of the representations or withdraw from one or both matters.

[25]   When a lawyer represents or seeks to represent a class of plaintiffs or defendants in a class-action lawsuit, unnamed members of the class are ordinarily not considered to be clients of the lawyer for purposes of applying paragraph (a)(1) of this Rule. Thus, the lawyer does not typically need to get the consent of such a person before representing a client suing the person in an unrelated matter. Similarly, a lawyer seeking to represent an opponent in a class action does not typically need the consent of an unnamed member of the class whom the lawyer represents in an unrelated matter.

Nonlitigation Conflicts

[26]   Conflicts of interest under paragraphs (a)(1) and (a)(2) arise in contexts other than litigation. For a discussion of directly adverse conflicts in transactional matters, see Comment [7]. Relevant factors in determining whether there is significant potential for material limitation include the duration and intimacy of the lawyer's relationship with the client or clients involved, the functions being performed by the lawyer, the likelihood that disagreements will arise and the likely prejudice to the client from the conflict. The question is often one of proximity and degree. See Comment [8].

[27]   For example, conflict questions may arise in estate planning and estate administration. A lawyer may be called upon to prepare wills for several family members, such as husband and wife, and, depending upon the circumstances, a conflict of interest may be present. In estate administration the identity of the client may be unclear under the law of a particular jurisdiction. Under one view, the client is the fiduciary; under another view the client is the estate or trust, including its beneficiaries. In order to comply with conflict of interest rules, the lawyer should make clear the lawyer's relationship to the parties involved.

[28]   Whether a conflict is consentable depends on the circumstances. For example, a lawyer may not represent multiple parties to a negotiation whose interests are fundamentally antagonistic to each other, but common representation is permissible where the clients are generally aligned in interest even though there is some difference in interest among them. Thus, a lawyer may seek to establish or adjust a relationship between clients on an amicable and mutually advantageous basis; for example, in helping to organize a business in which two or more clients are entrepreneurs, working out the financial reorganization of an enterprise in which two or more clients have an interest or arranging a property distribution in settlement of an estate. The lawyer seeks to resolve potentially adverse interests by developing the parties' mutual interests. Otherwise, each party might have to obtain separate representation, with the possibility of incurring additional cost, complication or even litigation. Given these and other relevant factors, the clients may prefer that the lawyer act for all of them.

Special Considerations in Common Representation

[29] In considering whether to represent multiple clients in the same matter, a lawyer should be mindful that if the common representation fails because the potentially adverse interests cannot be reconciled, the result can be additional cost, embarrassment and recrimination. Ordinarily, the lawyer will be forced to withdraw from representing all of the clients if the common representation fails. In some situations, the risk of failure is so great that multiple representation is plainly impossible. For example, a lawyer cannot undertake common representation of clients where contentious litigation or negotiations between them are imminent or contemplated. Moreover, because the lawyer is required to be impartial between commonly represented clients, representation of multiple clients is improper when it is unlikely that impartiality can be maintained. Generally, if the relationship between the parties has already assumed antagonism, the possibility that the clients' interests can be adequately served by common representation is not very good. Other relevant factors are whether the lawyer subsequently will represent both parties on a continuing basis and whether the situation involves creating or terminating a relationship between the parties.

[30] A particularly important factor in determining the appropriateness of common representation is the effect on client-lawyer confidentiality and the attorney-client privilege. With regard to the attorney-client privilege, the prevailing rule is that, as between commonly represented clients, the privilege does not attach. Hence, it must be assumed that if litigation eventuates between the clients, the privilege will not protect any such communications, and the clients should be so advised.

[31] As to the duty of confidentiality, continued common representation will almost certainly be inadequate if one client asks the lawyer not to disclose to the other client information relevant to the common representation. This is so because the lawyer has an equal duty of loyalty to each client, and each client has the right to be informed of anything bearing on the representation that might affect that client's interests and the right to expect that the lawyer will use that information to that client's benefit. See Rule 1.4. The lawyer should, at the outset of the common representation and as part of the process of obtaining each client's informed consent, advise each client that information will be shared and that the lawyer will have to withdraw if one client decides that some matter material to the representation should be kept from the other. In limited circumstances, it may be appropriate for the lawyer to proceed with the representation when the clients have agreed, after being properly informed, that the lawyer will keep certain information confidential. For example, the lawyer may reasonably conclude that failure to disclose one client's trade secrets to another client will not adversely affect representation involving a joint venture between the clients and agree to keep that information confidential with the informed consent of both clients.

[32] When seeking to establish or adjust a relationship between clients, the lawyer should make clear that the lawyer's role is not that of partisanship normally expected in other circumstances and, thus, that the clients may be

required to assume greater responsibility for decisions than when each client is separately represented. Any limitations on the scope of the representation made necessary as a result of the common representation should be fully explained to the clients at the outset of the representation. See Rule 1.2(c).

[33] Subject to the above limitations, each client in the common representation has the right to loyal and diligent representation and the protection of Rule 1.9 concerning the obligations to a former client. The client also has the right to discharge the lawyer as stated in Rule 1.16.

Organizational Clients

[34] A lawyer who represents a corporation or other organization does not, by virtue of that representation, necessarily represent any constituent or affiliated organization, such as a parent or subsidiary. See Rule 1.13(a). Thus, the lawyer for an organization is not barred from accepting representation adverse to an affiliate in an unrelated matter, unless the circumstances are such that the affiliate should also be considered a client of the lawyer, there is an understanding between the lawyer and the organizational client that the lawyer will avoid representation adverse to the client's affiliates, or the lawyer's obligations to either the organizational client or the new client are likely to limit materially the lawyer's representation of the other client.

[35] A lawyer for a corporation or other organization who is also a member of its board of directors should determine whether the responsibilities of the two roles may conflict. The lawyer may be called on to advise the corporation in matters involving actions of the directors. Consideration should be given to the frequency with which such situations may arise, the potential intensity of the conflict, the effect of the lawyer's resignation from the board and the possibility of the corporation's obtaining legal advice from another lawyer in such situations. If there is material risk that the dual role will compromise the lawyer's independence of professional judgment, the lawyer should not serve as a director or should cease to act as the corporation's lawyer when conflicts of interest arise. The lawyer should advise the other members of the board that in some circumstances matters discussed at board meetings while the lawyer is present in the capacity of director might not be protected by the attorney-client privilege and that conflict of interest considerations might require the lawyer's recusal as a director or might require the lawyer and the lawyer's firm to decline representation of the corporation in a matter.

RULE 1.8: CONFLICT OF INTEREST: CURRENT CLIENTS: SPECIFIC RULES

(a) A lawyer shall not enter into a business transaction with a client or knowingly acquire an ownership, possessory, security or other pecuniary interest adverse to a client unless:

(1) the transaction and terms on which the lawyer acquires the interest are fair and reasonable to the client and are fully

disclosed and transmitted in writing in a manner that can be reasonably understood by the client;

(2) the client is advised in writing of the desirability of seeking and is given a reasonable opportunity to seek the advice of independent legal counsel on the transaction; and

(3) the client gives informed consent, in a writing signed by the client, to the essential terms of the transaction and the lawyer's role in the transaction, including whether the lawyer is representing the client in the transaction.

(b) A lawyer shall not use information relating to representation of a client to the disadvantage of the client unless the client gives informed consent, except as permitted or required by these Rules.

(c) A lawyer shall not solicit any substantial gift from a client, including a testamentary gift, or prepare on behalf of a client an instrument giving the lawyer or a person related to the lawyer any substantial gift unless the lawyer or other recipient of the gift is related to the client. For purposes of this paragraph, related persons include a spouse, child, grandchild, parent, grandparent or other relative or individual with whom the lawyer or the client maintains a close, familial relationship.

(d) Prior to the conclusion of representation of a client, a lawyer shall not make or negotiate an agreement giving the lawyer literary or media rights to a portrayal or account based in substantial part on information relating to the representation.

(e) A lawyer shall not provide financial assistance to a client in connection with pending or contemplated litigation, except that:

(1) a lawyer may advance court costs and expenses of litigation, the repayment of which may be contingent on the outcome of the matter; and

(2) a lawyer representing an indigent client may pay court costs and expenses of litigation on behalf of the client.

(f) A lawyer shall not accept compensation for representing a client from one other than the client unless:

(1) the client gives informed consent;

(2) there is no interference with the lawyer's independence of professional judgment or with the client-lawyer relationship; and

(3) information relating to representation of a client is protected as required by Rule 1.6.

(g) A lawyer who represents two or more clients shall not participate in making an aggregate settlement of the claims of or against the clients, or in a criminal case an aggregated agreement as to guilty or nolo contendere pleas, unless each client gives informed consent, in a writing signed by the client. The lawyer's disclosure shall include the existence and nature of all the claims or pleas involved and of the participation of each person in the settlement.

(h) A lawyer shall not:

(1) make an agreement prospectively limiting the lawyer's liability to a client for malpractice unless the client is independently represented in making the agreement; or

(2) settle a claim or potential claim for such liability with an unrepresented client or former client unless that person is advised in writing of the desirability of seeking and is given a reasonable opportunity to seek the advice of independent legal counsel in connection therewith.

(i) A lawyer shall not acquire a proprietary interest in the cause of action or subject matter of litigation the lawyer is conducting for a client, except that the lawyer may:

(1) acquire a lien authorized by law to secure the lawyer's fee or expenses; and

(2) contract with a client for a reasonable contingent fee in a civil case.

(j) A lawyer shall not have sexual relations with a client unless a consensual sexual relationship existed between them when the client-lawyer relationship commenced.

(k) While lawyers are associated in a firm, a prohibition in the foregoing paragraphs (a) through (i) that applies to any one of them shall apply to all of them.

Comment
Business Transactions Between Client and Lawyer

[1]   A lawyer's legal skill and training, together with the relationship of trust and confidence between lawyer and client, create the possibility of overreaching when the lawyer participates in a business, property or financial transaction with a client, for example, a loan or sales transaction or a lawyer investment on behalf of a client. The requirements of paragraph (a) must be met even when the transaction is not closely related to the subject matter of the representation, as when a lawyer drafting a will for a client learns that the client needs money for unrelated expenses and offers to make a loan to the client. The Rule applies to lawyers engaged in the sale of goods or services related to the practice of law, for example, the sale of title insurance or investment services to existing clients of the lawyer's legal practice. See Rule 5.7. It also applies to lawyers purchasing property from estates they represent. It does not apply to ordinary fee arrangements between client and lawyer, which are governed by Rule 1.5, although its requirements must be met when the lawyer accepts an interest in the client's business or other nonmonetary property as payment of all or part of a fee. In addition, the Rule

does not apply to standard commercial transactions between the lawyer and the client for products or services that the client generally markets to others, for example, banking or brokerage services, medical services, products manufactured or distributed by the client, and utilities' services. In such transactions, the lawyer has no advantage in dealing with the client, and the restrictions in paragraph (a) are unnecessary and impracticable.

[2] Paragraph (a)(1) requires that the transaction itself be fair to the client and that its essential terms be communicated to the client, in writing, in a manner that can be reasonably understood. Paragraph (a)(2) requires that the client also be advised, in writing, of the desirability of seeking the advice of independent legal counsel. It also requires that the client be given a reasonable opportunity to obtain such advice. Paragraph (a)(3) requires that the lawyer obtain the client's informed consent, in a writing signed by the client, both to the essential terms of the transaction and to the lawyer's role. When necessary, the lawyer should discuss both the material risks of the proposed transaction, including any risk presented by the lawyer's involvement, and the existence of reasonably available alternatives and should explain why the advice of independent legal counsel is desirable. See Rule 1.0(e) (definition of informed consent).

[3] The risk to a client is greatest when the client expects the lawyer to represent the client in the transaction itself or when the lawyer's financial interest otherwise poses a significant risk that the lawyer's representation of the client will be materially limited by the lawyer's financial interest in the transaction. Here the lawyer's role requires that the lawyer must comply, not only with the requirements of paragraph (a), but also with the requirements of Rule 1.7. Under that Rule, the lawyer must disclose the risks associated with the lawyer's dual role as both legal adviser and participant in the transaction, such as the risk that the lawyer will structure the transaction or give legal advice in a way that favors the lawyer's interests at the expense of the client. Moreover, the lawyer must obtain the client's informed consent. In some cases, the lawyer's interest may be such that Rule 1.7 will preclude the lawyer from seeking the client's consent to the transaction.

[4] If the client is independently represented in the transaction, paragraph (a)(2) of this Rule is inapplicable, and the paragraph (a)(1) requirement for full disclosure is satisfied either by a written disclosure by the lawyer involved in the transaction or by the client's independent counsel. The fact that the client was independently represented in the transaction is relevant in determining whether the agreement was fair and reasonable to the client as paragraph (a)(1) further requires.

Use of Information Related to Representation

[5] Use of information relating to the representation to the disadvantage of the client violates the lawyer's duty of loyalty. Paragraph (b) applies when the information is used to benefit either the lawyer or a third person, such as another client or business associate of the lawyer. For example, if a lawyer learns that a client intends to purchase and develop several parcels of land,

the lawyer may not use that information to purchase one of the parcels in competition with the client or to recommend that another client make such a purchase. The Rule does not prohibit uses that do not disadvantage the client. For example, a lawyer who learns a government agency's interpretation of trade legislation during the representation of one client may properly use that information to benefit other clients. Paragraph (b) prohibits disadvantageous use of client information unless the client gives informed consent, except as permitted or required by these Rules. See Rules 1.2(d), 1.6, 1.9(c), 3.3, 4.1(b), 8.1 and 8.3.

Gifts to Lawyers

[6] A lawyer may accept a gift from a client, if the transaction meets general standards of fairness. For example, a simple gift such as a present given at a holiday or as a token of appreciation is permitted. If a client offers the lawyer a more substantial gift, paragraph (c) does not prohibit the lawyer from accepting it, although such a gift may be voidable by the client under the doctrine of undue influence, which treats client gifts as presumptively fraudulent. In any event, due to concerns about overreaching and imposition on clients, a lawyer may not suggest that a substantial gift be made to the lawyer or for the lawyer's benefit, except where the lawyer is related to the client as set forth in paragraph (c).

[7] If effectuation of a substantial gift requires preparing a legal instrument such as a will or conveyance the client should have the detached advice that another lawyer can provide. The sole exception to this Rule is where the client is a relative of the donee.

[8] This Rule does not prohibit a lawyer from seeking to have the lawyer or a partner or associate of the lawyer named as executor of the client's estate or to another potentially lucrative fiduciary position. Nevertheless, such appointments will be subject to the general conflict of interest provision in Rule 1.7 when there is a significant risk that the lawyer's interest in obtaining the appointment will materially limit the lawyer's independent professional judgment in advising the client concerning the choice of an executor or other fiduciary. In obtaining the client's informed consent to the conflict, the lawyer should advise the client concerning the nature and extent of the lawyer's financial interest in the appointment, as well as the availability of alternative candidates for the position.

Literary Rights

[9] An agreement by which a lawyer acquires literary or media rights concerning the conduct of the representation creates a conflict between the interests of the client and the personal interests of the lawyer. Measures suitable in the representation of the client may detract from the publication value of an account of the representation. Paragraph (d) does not prohibit a lawyer representing a client in a transaction concerning literary property from agreeing that the lawyer's fee shall consist of a share in ownership in the property, if the arrangement conforms to Rule 1.5 and paragraphs (a) and (i).

Financial Assistance

[10]   Lawyers may not subsidize lawsuits or administrative proceedings brought on behalf of their clients, including making or guaranteeing loans to their clients for living expenses, because to do so would encourage clients to pursue lawsuits that might not otherwise be brought and because such assistance gives lawyers too great a financial stake in the litigation. These dangers do not warrant a prohibition on a lawyer lending a client court costs and litigation expenses, including the expenses of medical examination and the costs of obtaining and presenting evidence, because these advances are virtually indistinguishable from contingent fees and help ensure access to the courts. Similarly, an exception allowing lawyers representing indigent clients to pay court costs and litigation expenses regardless of whether these funds will be repaid is warranted.

Person Paying for a Lawyer's Services

[11]   Lawyers are frequently asked to represent a client under circumstances in which a third person will compensate the lawyer, in whole or in part. The third person might be a relative or friend, an indemnitor (such as a liability insurance company) or a co-client (such as a corporation sued along with one or more of its employees). Because third-party payers frequently have interests that differ from those of the client, including interests in minimizing the amount spent on the representation and in learning how the representation is progressing, lawyers are prohibited from accepting or continuing such representations unless the lawyer determines that there will be no interference with the lawyer's independent professional judgment and there is informed consent from the client. See also Rule 5.4(c) (prohibiting interference with a lawyer's professional judgment by one who recommends, employs or pays the lawyer to render legal services for another).

[12]   Sometimes, it will be sufficient for the lawyer to obtain the client's informed consent regarding the fact of the payment and the identity of the third-party payer. If, however, the fee arrangement creates a conflict of interest for the lawyer, then the lawyer must comply with Rule. 1.7. The lawyer must also conform to the requirements of Rule 1.6 concerning confidentiality. Under Rule 1.7(a), a conflict of interest exists if there is significant risk that the lawyer's representation of the client will be materially limited by the lawyer's own interest in the fee arrangement or by the lawyer's responsibilities to the third-party payer (for example, when the third-party payer is a co-client). Under Rule 1.7(b), the lawyer may accept or continue the representation with the informed consent of each affected client, unless the conflict is nonconsentable under that paragraph. Under Rule 1.7(b), the informed consent must be confirmed in writing.

Aggregate Settlements

[13]   Differences in willingness to make or accept an offer of settlement are among the risks of common representation of multiple clients by a single lawyer. Under Rule 1.7, this is one of the risks that should be discussed before

undertaking the representation, as part of the process of obtaining the clients' informed consent. In addition, Rule 1.2(a) protects each client's right to have the final say in deciding whether to accept or reject an offer of settlement and in deciding whether to enter a guilty or nolo contendere plea in a criminal case. The rule stated in this paragraph is a corollary of both these Rules and provides that, before any settlement offer or plea bargain is made or accepted on behalf of multiple clients, the lawyer must inform each of them about all the material terms of the settlement, including what the other clients will receive or pay if the settlement or plea offer is accepted. See also Rule 1.0(e) (definition of informed consent). Lawyers representing a class of plaintiffs or defendants, or those proceeding derivatively, may not have a full client-lawyer relationship with each member of the class; nevertheless, such lawyers must comply with applicable rules regulating notification of class members and other procedural requirements designed to ensure adequate protection of the entire class.

Limiting Liability and Settling Malpractice Claims

[14] Agreements prospectively limiting a lawyer's liability for malpractice are prohibited unless the client is independently represented in making the agreement because they are likely to undermine competent and diligent representation. Also, many clients are unable to evaluate the desirability of making such an agreement before a dispute has arisen, particularly if they are then represented by the lawyer seeking the agreement. This paragraph does not, however, prohibit a lawyer from entering into an agreement with the client to arbitrate legal malpractice claims, provided such agreements are enforceable and the client is fully informed of the scope and effect of the agreement. Nor does this paragraph limit the ability of lawyers to practice in the form of a limited-liability entity, where permitted by law, provided that each lawyer remains personally liable to the client for his or her own conduct and the firm complies with any conditions required by law, such as provisions requiring client notification or maintenance of adequate liability insurance. Nor does it prohibit an agreement in accordance with Rule 1.2 that defines the scope of the representation, although a definition of scope that makes the obligations of representation illusory will amount to an attempt to limit liability.

[15] Agreements settling a claim or a potential claim for malpractice are not prohibited by this Rule. Nevertheless, in view of the danger that a lawyer will take unfair advantage of an unrepresented client or former client, the lawyer must first advise such a person in writing of the appropriateness of independent representation in connection with such a settlement. In addition, the lawyer must give the client or former client a reasonable opportunity to find and consult independent counsel.

Acquiring Proprietary Interest in Litigation

[16] Paragraph (i) states the traditional general rule that lawyers are prohibited from acquiring a proprietary interest in litigation. Like paragraph

(e), the general rule has its basis in common law champerty and maintenance and is designed to avoid giving the lawyer too great an interest in the representation. In addition, when the lawyer acquires an ownership interest in the subject of the representation, it will be more difficult for a client to discharge the lawyer if the client so desires. The Rule is subject to specific exceptions developed in decisional law and continued in these Rules. The exception for certain advances of the costs of litigation is set forth in paragraph (e). In addition, paragraph (i) sets forth exceptions for liens authorized by law to secure the lawyer's fees or expenses and contracts for reasonable contingent fees. The law of each jurisdiction determines which liens are authorized by law. These may include liens granted by statute, liens originating in common law and liens acquired by contract with the client. When a lawyer acquires by contract a security interest in property other than that recovered through the lawyer's efforts in the litigation, such an acquisition is a business or financial transaction with a client and is governed by the requirements of paragraph (a). Contracts for contingent fees in civil cases are governed by Rule 1.5.

Client–Lawyer Sexual Relationships

[17] The relationship between lawyer and client is a fiduciary one in which the lawyer occupies the highest position of trust and confidence. The relationship is almost always unequal; thus, a sexual relationship between lawyer and client can involve unfair exploitation of the lawyer's fiduciary role, in violation of the lawyer's basic ethical obligation not to use the trust of the client to the client's disadvantage. In addition, such a relationship presents a significant danger that, because of the lawyer's emotional involvement, the lawyer will be unable to represent the client without impairment of the exercise of independent professional judgment. Moreover, a blurred line between the professional and personal relationships may make it difficult to predict to what extent client confidences will be protected by the attorney-client evidentiary privilege, since client confidences are protected by privilege only when they are imparted in the context of the client-lawyer relationship. Because of the significant danger of harm to client interests and because the client's own emotional involvement renders it unlikely that the client could give adequate informed consent, this Rule prohibits the lawyer from having sexual relations with a client regardless of whether the relationship is consensual and regardless of the absence of prejudice to the client.

[18] Sexual relationships that predate the client-lawyer relationship are not prohibited. Issues relating to the exploitation of the fiduciary relationship and client dependency are diminished when the sexual relationship existed prior to the commencement of the client-lawyer relationship. However, before proceeding with the representation in these circumstances, the lawyer should consider whether the lawyer's ability to represent the client will be materially limited by the relationship. See Rule 1.7(a)(2).

[19] When the client is an organization, paragraph (j) of this Rule prohibits a lawyer for the organization (whether inside counsel or outside

counsel) from having a sexual relationship with a constituent of the organization who supervises, directs or regularly consults with that lawyer concerning the organization's legal matters.

Imputation of Prohibitions

[20]   Under paragraph (k), a prohibition on conduct by an individual lawyer in paragraphs (a) through (i) also applies to all lawyers associated in a firm with the personally prohibited lawyer. For example, one lawyer in a firm may not enter into a business transaction with a client of another member of the firm without complying with paragraph (a), even if the first lawyer is not personally involved in the representation of the client. The prohibition set forth in paragraph (j) is personal and is not applied to associated lawyers.

RULE 1.9: DUTIES TO FORMER CLIENTS

(a) A lawyer who has formerly represented a client in a matter shall not thereafter represent another person in the same or a substantially related matter in which that person's interests are materially adverse to the interests of the former client unless the former client gives informed consent, confirmed in writing.

(b) A lawyer shall not knowingly represent a person in the same or a substantially related matter in which a firm with which the lawyer formerly was associated had previously represented a client

> **(1) whose interests are materially adverse to that person; and**

> **(2) about whom the lawyer had acquired information protected by Rules 1.6 and 1.9(c) that is material to the matter;**

unless the former client gives informed consent, confirmed in writing.

(c) A lawyer who has formerly represented a client in a matter or whose present or former firm has formerly represented a client in a matter shall not thereafter:

> **(1) use information relating to the representation to the disadvantage of the former client except as these Rules would permit or require with respect to a client, or when the information has become generally known; or**

> **(2) reveal information relating to the representation except as these Rules would permit or require with respect to a client.**

Comment

[1]   After termination of a client-lawyer relationship, a lawyer has certain continuing duties with respect to confidentiality and conflicts of interest and thus may not represent another client except in conformity with this Rule. Under this Rule, for example, a lawyer could not properly seek to

rescind on behalf of a new client a contract drafted on behalf of the former client. So also a lawyer who has prosecuted an accused person could not properly represent the accused in a subsequent civil action against the government concerning the same transaction. Nor could a lawyer who has represented multiple clients in a matter represent one of the clients against the others in the same or a substantially related matter after a dispute arose among the clients in that matter, unless all affected clients give informed consent. See Comment [9]. Current and former government lawyers must comply with this Rule to the extent required by Rule 1.11.

[2]   The scope of a "matter" for purposes of this Rule depends on the facts of a particular situation or transaction. The lawyer's involvement in a matter can also be a question of degree. When a lawyer has been directly involved in a specific transaction, subsequent representation of other clients with materially adverse interests in that transaction clearly is prohibited. On the other hand, a lawyer who recurrently handled a type of problem for a former client is not precluded from later representing another client in a factually distinct problem of that type even though the subsequent representation involves a position adverse to the prior client. Similar considerations can apply to the reassignment of military lawyers between defense and prosecution functions within the same military jurisdictions. The underlying question is whether the lawyer was so involved in the matter that the subsequent representation can be justly regarded as a changing of sides in the matter in question.

[3]   Matters are "substantially related" for purposes of this Rule if they involve the same transaction or legal dispute or if there otherwise is a substantial risk that confidential factual information as would normally have been obtained in the prior representation would materially advance the client's position in the subsequent matter. For example, a lawyer who has represented a businessperson and learned extensive private financial information about that person may not then represent that person's spouse in seeking a divorce. Similarly, a lawyer who has previously represented a client in securing environmental permits to build a shopping center would be precluded from representing neighbors seeking to oppose rezoning of the property on the basis of environmental considerations; however, the lawyer would not be precluded, on the grounds of substantial relationship, from defending a tenant of the completed shopping center in resisting eviction for nonpayment of rent. Information that has been disclosed to the public or to other parties adverse to the former client ordinarily will not be disqualifying. Information acquired in a prior representation may have been rendered obsolete by the passage of time, a circumstance that may be relevant in determining whether two representations are substantially related. In the case of an organizational client, general knowledge of the client's policies and practices ordinarily will not preclude a subsequent representation; on the other hand, knowledge of specific facts gained in a prior representation that are relevant to the matter in question ordinarily will preclude such a representation. A former client is not required to reveal the confidential information learned by the lawyer in

order to establish a substantial risk that the lawyer has confidential information to use in the subsequent matter. A conclusion about the possession of such information may be based on the nature of the services the lawyer provided the former client and information that would in ordinary practice be learned by a lawyer providing such services.

Lawyers Moving Between Firms

[4]   When lawyers have been associated within a firm but then end their association, the question of whether a lawyer should undertake representation is more complicated. There are several competing considerations. First, the client previously represented by the former firm must be reasonably assured that the principle of loyalty to the client is not compromised. Second, the rule should not be so broadly cast as to preclude other persons from having reasonable choice of legal counsel. Third, the rule should not unreasonably hamper lawyers from forming new associations and taking on new clients after having left a previous association. In this connection, it should be recognized that today many lawyers practice in firms, that many lawyers to some degree limit their practice to one field or another, and that many move from one association to another several times in their careers. If the concept of imputation were applied with unqualified rigor, the result would be radical curtailment of the opportunity of lawyers to move from one practice setting to another and of the opportunity of clients to change counsel.

[5]   Paragraph (b) operates to disqualify the lawyer only when the lawyer involved has actual knowledge of information protected by Rules 1.6 and 1.9(c). Thus, if a lawyer while with one firm acquired no knowledge or information relating to a particular client of the firm, and that lawyer later joined another firm, neither the lawyer individually nor the second firm is disqualified from representing another client in the same or a related matter even though the interests of the two clients conflict. See Rule 1.10(b) for the restrictions on a firm once a lawyer has terminated association with the firm.

[6]   Application of paragraph (b) depends on a situation's particular facts, aided by inferences, deductions or working presumptions that reasonably may be made about the way in which lawyers work together. A lawyer may have general access to files of all clients of a law firm and may regularly participate in discussions of their affairs; it should be inferred that such a lawyer in fact is privy to all information about all the firm's clients. In contrast, another lawyer may have access to the files of only a limited number of clients and participate in discussions of the affairs of no other clients; in the absence of information to the contrary, it should be inferred that such a lawyer in fact is privy to information about the clients actually served but not those of other clients. In such an inquiry, the burden of proof should rest upon the firm whose disqualification is sought.

[7]   Independent of the question of disqualification of a firm, a lawyer changing professional association has a continuing duty to preserve confidentiality of information about a client formerly represented. See Rules 1.6 and 1.9(c).

[8]   Paragraph (c) provides that information acquired by the lawyer in the course of representing a client may not subsequently be used or revealed by the lawyer to the disadvantage of the client. However, the fact that a lawyer has once served a client does not preclude the lawyer from using generally known information about that client when later representing another client.

[9]   The provisions of this Rule are for the protection of former clients and can be waived if the client gives informed consent, which consent must be confirmed in writing under paragraphs (a) and (b). See Rule 1.0(e). With regard to the effectiveness of an advance waiver, see Comment [22] to Rule 1.7. With regard to disqualification of a firm with which a lawyer is or was formerly associated, see Rule 1.10.

RULE 1.10: IMPUTATION OF CONFLICTS OF INTEREST: GENERAL RULE

(a) While lawyers are associated in a firm, none of them shall knowingly represent a client when any one of them practicing alone would be prohibited from doing so by Rules 1.7 or 1.9, unless

(1) the prohibition is based on a personal interest of the disqualified lawyer and does not present a significant risk of materially limiting the representation of the client by the remaining lawyers in the firm; or

(2) the prohibition is based upon Rule 1.9(a) or (b) and arises out of the disqualified lawyer's association with a prior firm, and

(i) the disqualified lawyer is timely screened from any participation in the matter and is apportioned no part of the fee therefrom;

(ii) written notice is promptly given to any affected former client to enable the former client to ascertain compliance with the provisions of this Rule, which shall include a description of the screening procedures employed; a statement of the firm's and of the screened lawyer's compliance with these Rules; a statement that review may be available before a tribunal; and an agreement by the firm to respond promptly to any written inquiries or objections by the former client about the screening procedures; and

(iii) certifications of compliance with these Rules and with the screening procedures are provided to the former client by the screened lawyer and by a partner of the firm, at reasonable intervals upon the former client's written request and upon termination of the screening procedures.

(b) When a lawyer has terminated an association with a firm, the firm is not prohibited from thereafter representing a person with interests materially adverse to those of a client represented by the

formerly associated lawyer and not currently represented by the firm, unless:

> **(1) the matter is the same or substantially related to that in which the formerly associated lawyer represented the client; and**

> **(2) any lawyer remaining in the firm has information protected by Rules 1.6 and 1.9(c) that is material to the matter.**

(c) A disqualification prescribed by this rule may be waived by the affected client under the conditions stated in Rule 1.7.

(d) The disqualification of lawyers associated in a firm with former or current government lawyers is governed by Rule 1.11.

Comment

Definition of "Firm"

[1]   For purposes of the Rules of Professional Conduct, the term "firm" denotes lawyers in a law partnership, professional corporation, sole proprietorship or other association authorized to practice law; or lawyers employed in a legal services organization or the legal department of a corporation or other organization. See Rule 1.0(c). Whether two or more lawyers constitute a firm within this definition can depend on the specific facts. See Rule 1.0, Comments [2]–[4].

Principles of Imputed Disqualification

[2]   The rule of imputed disqualification stated in paragraph (a) gives effect to the principle of loyalty to the client as it applies to lawyers who practice in a law firm. Such situations can be considered from the premise that a firm of lawyers is essentially one lawyer for purposes of the rules governing loyalty to the client, or from the premise that each lawyer is vicariously bound by the obligation of loyalty owed by each lawyer with whom the lawyer is associated. Paragraph (a)(1) operates only among the lawyers currently associated in a firm. When a lawyer moves from one firm to another, the situation is governed by Rules 1.9(b) and 1.10(a)(2) and 1.10(b).

[3]   The rule in paragraph (a) does not prohibit representation where neither questions of client loyalty nor protection of confidential information are presented. Where one lawyer in a firm could not effectively represent a given client because of strong political beliefs, for example, but that lawyer will do no work on the case and the personal beliefs of the lawyer will not materially limit the representation by others in the firm, the firm should not be disqualified. On the other hand, if an opposing party in a case were owned by a lawyer in the law firm, and others in the firm would be materially limited in pursuing the matter because of loyalty to that lawyer, the personal disqualification of the lawyer would be imputed to all others in the firm.

[4]   The rule in paragraph (a) also does not prohibit representation by others in the law firm where the person prohibited from involvement in a matter is a nonlawyer, such as a paralegal or legal secretary. Nor does

paragraph (a) prohibit representation if the lawyer is prohibited from acting because of events before the person became a lawyer, for example, work that the person did while a law student. Such persons, however, ordinarily must be screened from any personal participation in the matter to avoid communication to others in the firm of confidential information that both the nonlawyers and the firm have a legal duty to protect. See Rules 1.0(k) and 5.3.

[5] Rule 1.10(b) operates to permit a law firm, under certain circumstances, to represent a person with interests directly adverse to those of a client represented by a lawyer who formerly was associated with the firm. The Rule applies regardless of when the formerly associated lawyer represented the client. However, the law firm may not represent a person with interests adverse to those of a present client of the firm, which would violate Rule 1.7. Moreover, the firm may not represent the person where the matter is the same or substantially related to that in which the formerly associated lawyer represented the client and any other lawyer currently in the firm has material information protected by Rules 1.6 and 1.9(c).

[6] Rule 1.10(c) removes imputation with the informed consent of the affected client or former client under the conditions stated in Rule 1.7. The conditions stated in Rule 1.7 require the lawyer to determine that the representation is not prohibited by Rule 1.7(b) and that each affected client or former client has given informed consent to the representation, confirmed in writing. In some cases, the risk may be so severe that the conflict may not be cured by client consent. For a discussion of the effectiveness of client waivers of conflicts that might arise in the future, see Rule 1.7, Comment [22]. For a definition of informed consent, see Rule 1.0(e).

[7] Rule 1.10(a)(2) similarly removes the imputation otherwise required by Rule 1.10(a), but unlike section (c), it does so without requiring that there be informed consent by the former client. Instead, it requires that the procedures laid out in sections (a)(2)(i)–(iii) be followed. A description of effective screening mechanisms appears in Rule 1.0(k). Lawyers should be aware, however, that, even where screening mechanisms have been adopted, tribunals may consider additional factors in ruling upon motions to disqualify a lawyer from pending litigation.

[8] Paragraph (a)(2)(i) does not prohibit the screened lawyer from receiving a salary or partnership share established by prior independent agreement, but that lawyer may not receive compensation directly related to the matter in which the lawyer is disqualified.

[9] The notice required by paragraph (a)(2)(ii) generally should include a description of the screened lawyer's prior representation and be given as soon as practicable after the need for screening becomes apparent. It also should include a statement by the screened lawyer and the firm that the client's material confidential information has not been disclosed or used in violation of the Rules. The notice is intended to enable the former client to evaluate and comment upon the effectiveness of the screening procedures.

[10]   The certifications required by paragraph (a)(2)(iii) give the former client assurance that the client's material confidential information has not been disclosed or used inappropriately, either prior to timely implementation of a screen or thereafter. If compliance cannot be certified, the certificate must describe the failure to comply.

[11]   Where a lawyer has joined a private firm after having represented the government, imputation is governed by Rule 1.11(b) and (c), not this Rule. Under Rule 1.11(d), where a lawyer represents the government after having served clients in private practice, nongovernmental employment or in another government agency, former-client conflicts are not imputed to government lawyers associated with the individually disqualified lawyer.

[12]   Where a lawyer is prohibited from engaging in certain transactions under Rule 1.8, paragraph (k) of that Rule, and not this Rule, determines whether that prohibition also applies to other lawyers associated in a firm with the personally prohibited lawyer.

RULE 1.11: SPECIAL CONFLICTS OF INTEREST FOR FORMER AND CURRENT GOVERNMENT OFFICERS AND EMPLOYEES

(a) Except as law may otherwise expressly permit, a lawyer who has formerly served as a public officer or employee of the government:

(1) is subject to Rule 1.9(c); and

(2) shall not otherwise represent a client in connection with a matter in which the lawyer participated personally and substantially as a public officer or employee, unless the appropriate government agency gives its informed consent, confirmed in writing, to the representation.

(b) When a lawyer is disqualified from representation under paragraph (a), no lawyer in a firm with which that lawyer is associated may knowingly undertake or continue representation in such a matter unless:

(1) the disqualified lawyer is timely screened from any participation in the matter and is apportioned no part of the fee therefrom; and

(2) written notice is promptly given to the appropriate government agency to enable it to ascertain compliance with the provisions of this rule.

(c) Except as law may otherwise expressly permit, a lawyer having information that the lawyer knows is confidential government information about a person acquired when the lawyer was a public officer or employee, may not represent a private client whose interests are adverse to that person in a matter in which the information could be used to the material disadvantage of that person. As used in this Rule, the term "confidential government information" means information that has been obtained under governmental authority and which, at the time this Rule is applied, the government is prohibited by law from disclosing to the public or has a legal privilege not to disclose and which is not otherwise available to the public. A firm with which that lawyer is associated may undertake or continue representation in the matter only if the disqualified lawyer is timely screened from any participation in the matter and is apportioned no part of the fee therefrom.

(d) Except as law may otherwise expressly permit, a lawyer currently serving as a public officer or employee:

(1) is subject to Rules 1.7 and 1.9; and

(2) shall not:

(i) participate in a matter in which the lawyer participated personally and substantially while in private practice or nongovernmental employment, unless the appropriate government agency gives its informed consent, confirmed in writing; or

(ii) negotiate for private employment with any person who is involved as a party or as lawyer for a party in a matter in which the lawyer is participating personally and substantially, except that a lawyer serving as a law clerk to a judge, other adjudicative officer or arbitrator may negotiate for private employment as permitted by Rule 1.12(b) and subject to the conditions stated in Rule 1.12(b).

(e) As used in this Rule, the term "matter" includes:

(1) any judicial or other proceeding, application, request for a ruling or other determination, contract, claim, controversy, investigation, charge, accusation, arrest or other particular matter involving a specific party or parties, and

(2) any other matter covered by the conflict of interest rules of the appropriate government agency.

Comment

[1] A lawyer who has served or is currently serving as a public officer or employee is personally subject to the Rules of Professional Conduct, including the prohibition against concurrent conflicts of interest stated in Rule 1.7. In addition, such a lawyer may be subject to statutes and government regulations regarding conflict of interest. Such statutes and regulations may circumscribe the extent to which the government agency may give consent under this Rule. See Rule 1.0(e) for the definition of informed consent.

[2] Paragraphs (a)(1), (a)(2) and (d)(1) restate the obligations of an individual lawyer who has served or is currently serving as an officer or

employee of the government toward a former government or private client. Rule 1.10 is not applicable to the conflicts of interest addressed by this Rule. Rather, paragraph (b) sets forth a special imputation rule for former government lawyers that provides for screening and notice. Because of the special problems raised by imputation within a government agency, paragraph (d) does not impute the conflicts of a lawyer currently serving as an officer or employee of the government to other associated government officers or employees, although ordinarily it will be prudent to screen such lawyers.

[3] Paragraphs (a)(2) and (d)(2) apply regardless of whether a lawyer is adverse to a former client and are thus designed not only to protect the former client, but also to prevent a lawyer from exploiting public office for the advantage of another client. For example, a lawyer who has pursued a claim on behalf of the government may not pursue the same claim on behalf of a later private client after the lawyer has left government service, except when authorized to do so by the government agency under paragraph (a). Similarly, a lawyer who has pursued a claim on behalf of a private client may not pursue the claim on behalf of the government, except when authorized to do so by paragraph (d). As with paragraphs (a)(1) and (d)(1), Rule 1.10 is not applicable to the conflicts of interest addressed by these paragraphs.

[4] This Rule represents a balancing of interests. On the one hand, where the successive clients are a government agency and another client, public or private, the risk exists that power or discretion vested in that agency might be used for the special benefit of the other client. A lawyer should not be in a position where benefit to the other client might affect performance of the lawyer's professional functions on behalf of the government. Also, unfair advantage could accrue to the other client by reason of access to confidential government information about the client's adversary obtainable only through the lawyer's government service. On the other hand, the rules governing lawyers presently or formerly employed by a government agency should not be so restrictive as to inhibit transfer of employment to and from the government. The government has a legitimate need to attract qualified lawyers as well as to maintain high ethical standards. Thus a former government lawyer is disqualified only from particular matters in which the lawyer participated personally and substantially. The provisions for screening and waiver in paragraph (b) are necessary to prevent the disqualification rule from imposing too severe a deterrent against entering public service. The limitation of disqualification in paragraphs (a)(2) and (d)(2) to matters involving a specific party or parties, rather than extending disqualification to all substantive issues on which the lawyer worked, serves a similar function.

[5] When a lawyer has been employed by one government agency and then moves to a second government agency, it may be appropriate to treat that second agency as another client for purposes of this Rule, as when a lawyer is employed by a city and subsequently is employed by a federal agency. However, because the conflict of interest is governed by paragraph (d), the latter agency is not required to screen the lawyer as paragraph (b) requires a law firm to do. The question of whether two government agencies

should be regarded as the same or different clients for conflict of interest purposes is beyond the scope of these Rules. See Rule 1.13 Comment [9].

[6]   Paragraphs (b) and (c) contemplate a screening arrangement. See Rule 1.0(k) (requirements for screening procedures). These paragraphs do not prohibit a lawyer from receiving a salary or partnership share established by prior independent agreement, but that lawyer may not receive compensation directly relating the lawyer's compensation to the fee in the matter in which the lawyer is disqualified.

[7]   Notice, including a description of the screened lawyer's prior representation and of the screening procedures employed, generally should be given as soon as practicable after the need for screening becomes apparent.

[8]   Paragraph (c) operates only when the lawyer in question has knowledge of the information, which means actual knowledge; it does not operate with respect to information that merely could be imputed to the lawyer.

[9]   Paragraphs (a) and (d) do not prohibit a lawyer from jointly representing a private party and a government agency when doing so is permitted by Rule 1.7 and is not otherwise prohibited by law.

[10]   For purposes of paragraph (e) of this Rule, a "matter" may continue in another form. In determining whether two particular matters are the same, the lawyer should consider the extent to which the matters involve the same basic facts, the same or related parties, and the time elapsed.

RULE 1.12: FORMER JUDGE, ARBITRATOR, MEDIATOR OR OTHER THIRD–PARTY NEUTRAL

(a) **Except as stated in paragraph (d), a lawyer shall not represent anyone in connection with a matter in which the lawyer participated personally and substantially as a judge or other adjudicative officer or law clerk to such a person or as an arbitrator, mediator or other third-party neutral, unless all parties to the proceeding give informed consent, confirmed in writing.**

(b) **A lawyer shall not negotiate for employment with any person who is involved as a party or as lawyer for a party in a matter in which the lawyer is participating personally and substantially as a judge or other adjudicative officer or as an arbitrator, mediator or other third-party neutral. A lawyer serving as a law clerk to a judge or other adjudicative officer may negotiate for employment with a party or lawyer involved in a matter in which the clerk is participating personally and substantially, but only after the lawyer has notified the judge or other adjudicative officer.**

(c) **If a lawyer is disqualified by paragraph (a), no lawyer in a firm with which that lawyer is associated may knowingly undertake or continue representation in the matter unless:**

   (1) **the disqualified lawyer is timely screened from any participation in the matter and is apportioned no part of the fee therefrom; and**

(2) written notice is promptly given to the parties and any appropriate tribunal to enable them to ascertain compliance with the provisions of this rule.

(d) An arbitrator selected as a partisan of a party in a multimember arbitration panel is not prohibited from subsequently representing that party.

Comment

[1]   This Rule generally parallels Rule 1.11. The term "personally and substantially" signifies that a judge who was a member of a multimember court, and thereafter left judicial office to practice law, is not prohibited from representing a client in a matter pending in the court, but in which the former judge did not participate. So also the fact that a former judge exercised administrative responsibility in a court does not prevent the former judge from acting as a lawyer in a matter where the judge had previously exercised remote or incidental administrative responsibility that did not affect the merits. Compare the Comment to Rule 1.11. The term "adjudicative officer" includes such officials as judges pro tempore, referees, special masters, hearing officers and other parajudicial officers, and also lawyers who serve as part-time judges. Paragraphs C(2), D(2) and E(2) of the Application Section of the Model Code of Judicial Conduct provide that a part-time judge, judge pro tempore or retired judge recalled to active service, shall not "act as a lawyer in a proceeding in which the judge has served as a judge or in any other proceeding related thereto." Although phrased differently from this Rule, those Rules correspond in meaning.

[2]   Like former judges, lawyers who have served as arbitrators, mediators or other third-party neutrals may be asked to represent a client in a matter in which the lawyer participated personally and substantially. This Rule forbids such representation unless all of the parties to the proceedings give their informed consent, confirmed in writing. See Rule 1.0(e) and (b). Other law or codes of ethics governing third-party neutrals may impose more stringent standards of personal or imputed disqualification. See Rule 2.4.

[3]   Although lawyers who serve as third-party neutrals do not have information concerning the parties that is protected under Rule 1.6, they typically owe the parties an obligation of confidentiality under law or codes of ethics governing third-party neutrals. Thus, paragraph (c) provides that conflicts of the personally disqualified lawyer will be imputed to other lawyers in a law firm unless the conditions of this paragraph are met.

[4]   Requirements for screening procedures are stated in Rule 1.0(k). Paragraph (c)(1) does not prohibit the screened lawyer from receiving a salary or partnership share established by prior independent agreement, but that lawyer may not receive compensation directly related to the matter in which the lawyer is disqualified.

[5] Notice, including a description of the screened lawyer's prior representation and of the screening procedures employed, generally should be given as soon as practicable after the need for screening becomes apparent.

RULE 1.13: ORGANIZATION AS CLIENT*

(a) A lawyer employed or retained by an organization represents the organization acting through its duly authorized constituents.

* Editors' Note: **The text reflects Rule 1.13 as amended in August, 2003. What follows below is Rule 1.13 as amended by the ABA House of Delegates in August, 2002.**

RULE 1.13: ORGANIZATION AS CLIENT

(a) A lawyer employed or retained by an organization represents the organization acting through its duly authorized constituents.

(b) If a lawyer for an organization knows that an officer, employee or other person associated with the organization is engaged in action, intends to act or refuses to act in a matter related to the representation that is a violation of a legal obligation to the organization, or a violation of law which reasonably might be imputed to the organization, and is likely to result in substantial injury to the organization, the lawyer shall proceed as is reasonably necessary in the best interest of the organization. In determining how to proceed, the lawyer shall give due consideration to the seriousness of the violation and its consequences, the scope and nature of the lawyer's representation, the responsibility in the organization and the apparent motivation of the person involved, the policies of the organization concerning such matters and any other relevant considerations. Any measures taken shall be designed to minimize disruption of the organization and the risk of revealing information relating to the representation to persons outside the organization. Such measures may include among others:

(1) asking for reconsideration of the matter;

(2) advising that a separate legal opinion on the matter be sought for presentation to appropriate authority in the organization; and

(3) referring the matter to higher authority in the organization, including, if warranted by the seriousness of the matter, referral to the highest authority that can act on behalf of the organization as determined by applicable law.

(c) If, despite the lawyer's efforts in accordance with paragraph (b), the highest authori-ty that can act on behalf of the organization insists upon action, or a refusal to act, that is clearly a violation of law and is likely to result in substantial injury to the organization, the lawyer may resign in accordance with Rule 1.16.

(d) In dealing with an organization's directors, officers, employees, members, shareholders or other constituents, a lawyer shall explain the identity of the client when the lawyer knows or reasonably should know that the organization's interests are adverse to those of the constituents with whom the lawyer is dealing.

(e) A lawyer representing an organization may also represent any of its directors, officers, employees, members, shareholders or other constituents, subject to the provisions of Rule 1.7. If the organization's consent to the dual representation is required by Rule 1.7, the consent shall be given by an appropriate official of the organization other than the individual who is to be represented, or by the shareholders.

Comment

The Entity as the Client

[1] An organizational client is a legal entity, but it cannot act except through its officers, directors, employees, shareholders and other constituents. Officers, directors, employees and shareholders are the constituents of the corporate organizational client. The duties defined in this Comment apply equally to unincorporated associations. "Other constituents" as used in this Comment means the positions equivalent to officers, directors, employees and shareholders held by persons acting for organizational clients that are not corporations.

[2] When one of the constituents of an organizational client communicates with the organization's lawyer in that person's organizational capacity, the communication is protected by Rule 1.6. Thus, by way of example, if an organizational client requests its lawyer to investigate allegations of wrongdoing, interviews made in the course of that investigation between the lawyer and the client's employees or other constituents are covered by Rule 1.6.

This does not mean, however, that constituents of an organizational client are the clients of the lawyer. The lawyer may not disclose to such constituents information relating to the representation except for disclosures explicitly or impliedly authorized by the organizational client in order to carry out the representation or as otherwise permitted by Rule 1.6.

[3] When constituents of the organization make decisions for it, the decisions ordinarily must be accepted by the lawyer even if their utility or prudence is doubtful. Decisions concerning policy and operations, including ones entailing serious risk, are not as such in the lawyer's province. However, different considerations arise when the lawyer knows that the organization may be substantially injured by action of a constituent that is in violation of law. In such a circumstance, it may be reasonably necessary for the lawyer to ask the constituent to reconsider the matter. If that fails, or if the matter is of sufficient seriousness and importance to the organization, it may be reasonably necessary for the lawyer to take steps to have the matter reviewed by a higher authority in the organization. Clear justification should exist for seeking review over the head of the constituent normally responsible for it. The stated policy of the organization may define circumstances and prescribe channels for such review, and a lawyer should encourage the formulation of such a policy. Even in the absence of organization policy, however, the lawyer may have an obligation to refer a matter to higher authority, depending on the seriousness of the matter and whether the constituent in question has apparent motives to act at variance with the organization's interest. Review by the chief executive officer or by the board of directors may be required when the matter is of importance commensurate with their authority. At some point it may be useful or essential to obtain an independent legal opinion.

[4] The organization's highest authority to whom a matter may be referred ordinarily will be the board of directors or similar governing body. However, applicable law may prescribe that under certain conditions the highest authority reposes elsewhere, for example, in the independent directors of a corporation.

Relation to Other Rules

[5] The authority and responsibility provided in this Rule are concurrent with the authority and responsibility provided in other Rules. In particular, this Rule does not limit or expand the lawyer's responsibility under Rule 1.6, 1.8, 1.16, 3.3 or 4.1. If the lawyer's services are being used by an organization to further a crime or fraud by the organization, Rule 1.2(d) can be applicable.

Government Agency

[6] The duty defined in this Rule applies to governmental organizations. Defining precisely the identity of the client and prescribing the resulting obligations of such lawyers may be more difficult in the government context and is a matter beyond the scope of these Rules. See Scope [18]. Although in some circumstances the client may be a specific agency, it may also be a branch of government, such as the executive branch, or the government as a whole. For example, if the action or failure to act involves the head of a bureau, either the department of which the bureau is a part or the relevant branch of government may be the client for purposes of this Rule. Moreover, in a matter involving the conduct of government officials, a government lawyer may have authority under applicable law to question such conduct more extensively than that of a lawyer for a private organization in similar circumstances. Thus, when the client is a governmental organization, a different balance may be appropriate between maintaining confidentiality and assuring that the wrongful act is prevented or rectified, for public business is involved. In addition, duties of lawyers employed by the government or lawyers in military service may be defined by statutes and regulation. This Rule does not limit that authority. See Scope.

Clarifying the Lawyer's Role

[7] There are times when the organization's interest may be or become adverse to those of one or more of its constituents. In such circumstances the lawyer should advise any constituent, whose interest the lawyer finds adverse to that of the organization of the conflict or potential conflict of interest, that the lawyer cannot represent such constituent, and that such person may wish to obtain independent representation. Care must be taken to assure that the individual understands that, when there is such adversity of interest, the lawyer for the organization cannot provide legal representation for that constituent individual, and that discussions between the lawyer for the organization and the individual may not be privileged.

[8] Whether such a warning should be given by the lawyer for the organization to any constituent individual may turn on the facts of each case.

Dual Representation

[9] Paragraph (e) recognizes that a lawyer for an organization may also represent a principal officer or major shareholder.

(b) If a lawyer for an organization knows that an officer, employee or other person associated with the organization is engaged in action, intends to act or refuses to act in a matter related to the representation that is a violation of a legal obligation to the organization, or a violation of law that reasonably might be imputed to the organization, and that is likely to result in substantial injury to the organization, then the lawyer shall proceed as is reasonably necessary in the best interest of the organization. Unless the lawyer reasonably believes that it is not necessary in the best interest of the organization to do so, the lawyer shall refer the matter to higher authority in the organization, including, if warranted by the circumstances, to the highest authority that can act on behalf of the organization as determined by applicable law.

(c) Except as provided in paragraph (d), if

(1) despite the lawyer's efforts in accordance with paragraph (b) the highest authority that can act on behalf of the organization insists upon or fails to address in a timely and appropriate manner an action or a refusal to act, that is clearly a violation of law, and

(2) the lawyer reasonably believes that the violation is reasonably certain to result in substantial injury to the organization,

then the lawyer may reveal information relating to the representation whether or not Rule 1.6 permits such disclosure, but only if and to the extent the lawyer reasonably believes necessary to prevent substantial injury to the organization.

(d) Paragraph (c) shall not apply with respect to information relating to a lawyer's representation of an organization to investigate an alleged violation of law, or to defend the organization or an officer, employee or other constituent associated with the organization against a claim arising out of an alleged violation of law.

(e) A lawyer who reasonably believes that he or she has been discharged because of the lawyer's actions taken pursuant to paragraphs (b) or (c), or who withdraws under circumstances that require or permit the lawyer to take action under either of those paragraphs,

Derivative Actions

[10] Under generally prevailing law, the shareholders or members of a corporation may bring suit to compel the directors to perform their legal obligations in the supervision of the organization. Members of unincorporated associations have essentially the same right. Such an action may be brought nominally by the organization, but usually is, in fact, a legal controversy over management of the organization.

[11] The question can arise whether counsel for the organization may defend such an action. The proposition that the organization is the lawyer's client does not alone resolve the issue. Most derivative actions are a normal incident of an organization's affairs, to be defended by the organization's lawyer like any other suit. However, if the claim involves serious charges of wrongdoing by those in control of the organization, a conflict may arise between the lawyer's duty to the organization and the lawyer's relationship with the board. In those circumstances, Rule 1.7 governs who should represent the directors and the organization.

shall proceed as the lawyer reasonably believes necessary to assure that the organization's highest authority is informed of the lawyer's discharge or withdrawal.

(f) In dealing with an organization's directors, officers, employees, members, shareholders or other constituents, a lawyer shall explain the identity of the client when the lawyer knows or reasonably should know that the organization's interests are adverse to those of the constituents with whom the lawyer is dealing.

(g) A lawyer representing an organization may also represent any of its directors, officers, employees, members, shareholders or other constituents, subject to the provisions of Rule 1.7. If the organization's consent to the dual representation is required by Rule 1.7, the consent shall be given by an appropriate official of the organization other than the individual who is to be represented, or by the shareholders.

Comment
The Entity as the Client

[1]   An organizational client is a legal entity, but it cannot act except through its officers, directors, employees, shareholders and other constituents. Officers, directors, employees and shareholders are the constituents of the corporate organizational client. The duties defined in this Comment apply equally to unincorporated associations. "Other constituents" as used in this Comment means the positions equivalent to officers, directors, employees and shareholders held by persons acting for organizational clients that are not corporations.

[2]   When one of the constituents of an organizational client communicates with the organization's lawyer in that person's organizational capacity, the communication is protected by Rule 1.6. Thus, by way of example, if an organizational client requests its lawyer to investigate allegations of wrongdoing, interviews made in the course of that investigation between the lawyer and the client's employees or other constituents are covered by Rule 1.6. This does not mean, however, that constituents of an organizational client are the clients of the lawyer. The lawyer may not disclose to such constituents information relating to the representation except for disclosures explicitly or impliedly authorized by the organizational client in order to carry out the representation or as otherwise permitted by Rule 1.6.

[3]   When constituents of the organization make decisions for it, the decisions ordinarily must be accepted by the lawyer even if their utility or prudence is doubtful. Decisions concerning policy and operations, including ones entailing serious risk, are not as such in the lawyer's province. Paragraph (b) makes clear, however, that when the lawyer knows that the organization is likely to be substantially injured by action of an officer or other constituent that violates a legal obligation to the organization or is in violation of law that might be imputed to the organization, the lawyer must

proceed as is reasonably necessary in the best interest of the organization. As defined in Rule 1.0(f), knowledge can be inferred from circumstances, and a lawyer cannot ignore the obvious.

[4] In determining how to proceed under paragraph (b), the lawyer should give due consideration to the seriousness of the violation and its consequences, the responsibility in the organization and the apparent motivation of the person involved, the policies of the organization concerning such matters, and any other relevant considerations. Ordinarily, referral to a higher authority would be necessary. In some circumstances, however, it may be appropriate for the lawyer to ask the constituent to reconsider the matter; for example, if the circumstances involve a constituent's innocent misunderstanding of law and subsequent acceptance of the lawyer's advice, the lawyer may reasonably conclude that the best interest of the organization does not require that the matter be referred to higher authority. If a constituent persists in conduct contrary to the lawyer's advice, it will be necessary for the lawyer to take steps to have the matter reviewed by a higher authority in the organization. If the matter is of sufficient seriousness and importance or urgency to the organization, referral to higher authority in the organization may be necessary even if the lawyer has not communicated with the constituent. Any measures taken should, to the extent practicable, minimize the risk of revealing information relating to the representation to persons outside the organization. Even in circumstances where a lawyer is not obligated by Rule 1.13 to proceed, a lawyer may bring to the attention of an organizational client, including its highest authority, matters that the lawyer reasonably believes to be of sufficient importance to warrant doing so in the best interest of the organization.

[5] Paragraph (b) also makes clear that when it is reasonably necessary to enable the organization to address the matter in a timely and appropriate manner, the lawyer must refer the matter to higher authority, including, if warranted by the circumstances, the highest authority that can act on behalf of the organization under applicable law. The organization's highest authority to whom a matter may be referred ordinarily will be the board of directors or similar governing body. However, applicable law may prescribe that under certain conditions the highest authority reposes elsewhere, for example, in the independent directors of a corporation.

Relation to Other Rules

[6] The authority and responsibility provided in this Rule are concurrent with the authority and responsibility provided in other Rules. In particular, this Rule does not limit or expand the lawyer's responsibility under Rules 1.8, 1.16, 3.3 or 4.1. Paragraph (c) of this Rule supplements Rule 1.6(b) by providing an additional basis upon which the lawyer may reveal information relating to the representation, but does not modify, restrict, or limit the provisions of Rule 1.6(b)(1)–(6). Under paragraph (c) the lawyer may reveal such information only when the organization's highest authority insists upon or fails to address threatened or ongoing action that is clearly a violation of

law, and then only to the extent the lawyer reasonably believes necessary to prevent reasonably certain substantial injury to the organization. It is not necessary that the lawyer's services be used in furtherance of the violation, but it is required that the matter be related to the lawyer's representation of the organization. If the lawyer's services are being used by an organization to further a crime or fraud by the organization, Rules 1.6(b)(2) and 1.6(b)(3) may permit the lawyer to disclose confidential information. In such circumstances Rule 1.2(d) may also be applicable, in which event, withdrawal from the representation under Rule 1.16(a)(1) may be required.

[7]   Paragraph (d) makes clear that the authority of a lawyer to disclose information relating to a representation in circumstances described in paragraph (c) does not apply with respect to information relating to a lawyer's engagement by an organization to investigate an alleged violation of law or to defend the organization or an officer, employee or other person associated with the organization against a claim arising out of an alleged violation of law. This is necessary in order to enable organizational clients to enjoy the full benefits of legal counsel in conducting an investigation or defending against a claim.

[8]   A lawyer who reasonably believes that he or she has been discharged because of the lawyer's actions taken pursuant to paragraph (b) or (c), or who withdraws in circumstances that require or permit the lawyer to take action under either of these paragraphs, must proceed as the lawyer reasonably believes necessary to assure that the organization's highest authority is informed of the lawyer's discharge or withdrawal.

Government Agency

[9]   The duty defined in this Rule applies to governmental organizations. Defining precisely the identity of the client and prescribing the resulting obligations of such lawyers may be more difficult in the government context and is a matter beyond the scope of these Rules. See Scope [18]. Although in some circumstances the client may be a specific agency, it may also be a branch of government, such as the executive branch, or the government as a whole. For example, if the action or failure to act involves the head of a bureau, either the department of which the bureau is a part or the relevant branch of government may be the client for purposes of this Rule. Moreover, in a matter involving the conduct of government officials, a government lawyer may have authority under applicable law to question such conduct more extensively than that of a lawyer for a private organization in similar circumstances. Thus, when the client is a governmental organization, a different balance may be appropriate between maintaining confidentiality and assuring that the wrongful act is prevented or rectified, for public business is involved. In addition, duties of lawyers employed by the government or lawyers in military service may be defined by statutes and regulation. This Rule does not limit that authority. See Scope.

Clarifying the Lawyer's Role

[10]   There are times when the organization's interest may be or become adverse to those of one or more of its constituents. In such circumstances the lawyer should advise any constituent, whose interest the lawyer finds adverse to that of the organization of the conflict or potential conflict of interest, that the lawyer cannot represent such constituent, and that such person may wish to obtain independent representation. Care must be taken to assure that the individual understands that, when there is such adversity of interest, the lawyer for the organization cannot provide legal representation for that constituent individual, and that discussions between the lawyer for the organization and the individual may not be privileged.

[11]   Whether such a warning should be given by the lawyer for the organization to any constituent individual may turn on the facts of each case.

Dual Representation

[12]   Paragraph (g) recognizes that a lawyer for an organization may also represent a principal officer or major shareholder.

Derivative Actions

[13]   Under generally prevailing law, the shareholders or members of a corporation may bring suit to compel the directors to perform their legal obligations in the supervision of the organization. Members of unincorporated associations have essentially the same right. Such an action may be brought nominally by the organization, but usually is, in fact, a legal controversy over management of the organization.

[14]   The question can arise whether counsel for the organization may defend such an action. The proposition that the organization is the lawyer's client does not alone resolve the issue. Most derivative actions are a normal incident of an organization's affairs, to be defended by the organization's lawyer like any other suit. However, if the claim involves serious charges of wrongdoing by those in control of the organization, a conflict may arise between the lawyer's duty to the organization and the lawyer's relationship with the board. In those circumstances, Rule 1.7 governs who should represent the directors and the organization.

RULE 1.14: CLIENT WITH DIMINISHED CAPACITY

(a) When a client's capacity to make adequately considered decisions in connection with a representation is diminished, whether because of minority, mental impairment or for some other reason, the lawyer shall, as far as reasonably possible, maintain a normal client-lawyer relationship with the client.

(b) When the lawyer reasonably believes that the client has diminished capacity, is at risk of substantial physical, financial or other harm unless action is taken and cannot adequately act in the

client's own interest, the lawyer may take reasonably necessary protective action, including consulting with individuals or entities that have the ability to take action to protect the client and, in appropriate cases, seeking the appointment of a guardian ad litem, conservator or guardian.

(c) Information relating to the representation of a client with diminished capacity is protected by Rule 1.6. When taking protective action pursuant to paragraph (b), the lawyer is impliedly authorized under Rule 1.6(a) to reveal information about the client, but only to the extent reasonably necessary to protect the client's interests.

Comment

[1] The normal client-lawyer relationship is based on the assumption that the client, when properly advised and assisted, is capable of making decisions about important matters. When the client is a minor or suffers from a diminished mental capacity, however, maintaining the ordinary client-lawyer relationship may not be possible in all respects. In particular, a severely incapacitated person may have no power to make legally binding decisions. Nevertheless, a client with diminished capacity often has the ability to understand, deliberate upon, and reach conclusions about matters affecting the client's own well-being. For example, children as young as five or six years of age, and certainly those of ten or twelve, are regarded as having opinions that are entitled to weight in legal proceedings concerning their custody. So also, it is recognized that some persons of advanced age can be quite capable of handling routine financial matters while needing special legal protection concerning major transactions.

[2] The fact that a client suffers a disability does not diminish the lawyer's obligation to treat the client with attention and respect. Even if the person has a legal representative, the lawyer should as far as possible accord the represented person the status of client, particularly in maintaining communication.

[3] The client may wish to have family members or other persons participate in discussions with the lawyer. When necessary to assist in the representation, the presence of such persons generally does not affect the applicability of the attorney-client evidentiary privilege. Nevertheless, the lawyer must keep the client's interests foremost and, except for protective action authorized under paragraph (b), must to look to the client, and not family members, to make decisions on the client's behalf.

[4] If a legal representative has already been appointed for the client, the lawyer should ordinarily look to the representative for decisions on behalf of the client. In matters involving a minor, whether the lawyer should look to the parents as natural guardians may depend on the type of proceeding or matter in which the lawyer is representing the minor. If the lawyer represents the guardian as distinct from the ward, and is aware that the guardian is

acting adversely to the ward's interest, the lawyer may have an obligation to prevent or rectify the guardian's misconduct. See Rule 1.2(d).

Taking Protective Action

[5]   If a lawyer reasonably believes that a client is at risk of substantial physical, financial or other harm unless action is taken, and that a normal client-lawyer relationship cannot be maintained as provided in paragraph (a) because the client lacks sufficient capacity to communicate or to make adequately considered decisions in connection with the representation, then paragraph (b) permits the lawyer to take protective measures deemed necessary. Such measures could include: consulting with family members, using a reconsideration period to permit clarification or improvement of circumstances, using voluntary surrogate decisionmaking tools such as durable powers of attorney or consulting with support groups, professional services, adult-protective agencies or other individuals or entities that have the ability to protect the client. In taking any protective action, the lawyer should be guided by such factors as the wishes and values of the client to the extent known, the client's best interests and the goals of intruding into the client's decisionmaking autonomy to the least extent feasible, maximizing client capacities and respecting the client's family and social connections.

[6]   In determining the extent of the client's diminished capacity, the lawyer should consider and balance such factors as: the client's ability to articulate reasoning leading to a decision, variability of state of mind and ability to appreciate consequences of a decision; the substantive fairness of a decision; and the consistency of a decision with the known long-term commitments and values of the client. In appropriate circumstances, the lawyer may seek guidance from an appropriate diagnostician.

[7]   If a legal representative has not been appointed, the lawyer should consider whether appointment of a guardian ad litem, conservator or guardian is necessary to protect the client's interests. Thus, if a client with diminished capacity has substantial property that should be sold for the client's benefit, effective completion of the transaction may require appointment of a legal representative. In addition, rules of procedure in litigation sometimes provide that minors or persons with diminished capacity must be represented by a guardian or next friend if they do not have a general guardian. In many circumstances, however, appointment of a legal representative may be more expensive or traumatic for the client than circumstances in fact require. Evaluation of such circumstances is a matter entrusted to the professional judgment of the lawyer. In considering alternatives, however, the lawyer should be aware of any law that requires the lawyer to advocate the least restrictive action on behalf of the client.

Disclosure of the Client's Condition

[8]   Disclosure of the client's diminished capacity could adversely affect the client's interests. For example, raising the question of diminished capacity could, in some circumstances, lead to proceedings for involuntary commit-

ment. Information relating to the representation is protected by Rule 1.6. Therefore, unless authorized to do so, the lawyer may not disclose such information. When taking protective action pursuant to paragraph (b), the lawyer is impliedly authorized to make the necessary disclosures, even when the client directs the lawyer to the contrary. Nevertheless, given the risks of disclosure, paragraph (c) limits what the lawyer may disclose in consulting with other individuals or entities or seeking the appointment of a legal representative. At the very least, the lawyer should determine whether it is likely that the person or entity consulted with will act adversely to the client's interests before discussing matters related to the client. The lawyer's position in such cases is an unavoidably difficult one.

Emergency Legal Assistance

[9] In an emergency where the health, safety or a financial interest of a person with seriously diminished capacity is threatened with imminent and irreparable harm, a lawyer may take legal action on behalf of such a person even though the person is unable to establish a client-lawyer relationship or to make or express considered judgments about the matter, when the person or another acting in good faith on that person's behalf has consulted with the lawyer. Even in such an emergency, however, the lawyer should not act unless the lawyer reasonably believes that the person has no other lawyer, agent or other representative available. The lawyer should take legal action on behalf of the person only to the extent reasonably necessary to maintain the status quo or otherwise avoid imminent and irreparable harm. A lawyer who undertakes to represent a person in such an exigent situation has the same duties under these Rules as the lawyer would with respect to a client.

[10] A lawyer who acts on behalf of a person with seriously diminished capacity in an emergency should keep the confidences of the person as if dealing with a client, disclosing them only to the extent necessary to accomplish the intended protective action. The lawyer should disclose to any tribunal involved and to any other counsel involved the nature of his or her relationship with the person. The lawyer should take steps to regularize the relationship or implement other protective solutions as soon as possible. Normally, a lawyer would not seek compensation for such emergency actions taken.

RULE 1.15: SAFEKEEPING PROPERTY

(a) A lawyer shall hold property of clients or third persons that is in a lawyer's possession in connection with a representation separate from the lawyer's own property. Funds shall be kept in a separate account maintained in the state where the lawyer's office is situated, or elsewhere with the consent of the client or third person. Other property shall be identified as such and appropriately safeguarded. Complete records of such account funds and other property shall be kept by the lawyer and shall be preserved for a period of [five years] after termination of the representation.

(b) A lawyer may deposit the lawyer's own funds in a client trust account for the sole purpose of paying bank service charges on that account, but only in an amount necessary for that purpose.

(c) A lawyer shall deposit into a client trust account legal fees and expenses that have been paid in advance, to be withdrawn by the lawyer only as fees are earned or expenses incurred.

(d) Upon receiving funds or other property in which a client or third person has an interest, a lawyer shall promptly notify the client or third person. Except as stated in this rule or otherwise permitted by law or by agreement with the client, a lawyer shall promptly deliver to the client or third person any funds or other property that the client or third person is entitled to receive and, upon request by the client or third person, shall promptly render a full accounting regarding such property.

(e) When in the course of representation a lawyer is in possession of property in which two or more persons (one of whom may be the lawyer) claim interests, the property shall be kept separate by the lawyer the dispute is resolved. The lawyer shall promptly distribute all portions of the property as to which the interests are not in dispute.

Comment

[1] A lawyer should hold property of others with the care required of a professional fiduciary. Securities should be kept in a safe deposit box, except when some other form of safekeeping is warranted by special circumstances. All property that is the property of clients or third persons, including prospective clients, must be kept separate from the lawyer's business and personal property and, if monies, in one or more trust accounts. Separate trust accounts may be warranted when administering estate monies or acting in similar fiduciary capacities. A lawyer should maintain on a current basis books and records in accordance with generally accepted accounting practice and comply with any recordkeeping rules established by law or court order. See, e.g., ABA Model Financial Recordkeeping Rule.

[2] While normally it is impermissible to commingle the lawyer's own funds with client funds, paragraph (b) provides that it is permissible when necessary to pay bank service charges on that account. Accurate records must be kept regarding which part of the funds are the lawyer's.

[3] Lawyers often receive funds from which the lawyer's fee will be paid. The lawyer is not required to remit to the client funds that the lawyer reasonably believes represent fees owed. However, a lawyer may not hold funds to coerce a client into accepting the lawyer's contention. The disputed portion of the funds must be kept in a trust account and the lawyer should suggest means for prompt resolution of the dispute, such as arbitration. The undisputed portion of the funds shall be promptly distributed.

[4] Paragraph (e) also recognizes that third parties may have lawful claims against specific funds or other property in a lawyer's custody, such as a client's creditor who has a lien on funds recovered in a personal injury action. A lawyer may have a duty under applicable law to protect such third-party claims against wrongful interference by the client. In such cases, when the third-party claim is not frivolous under applicable law, the lawyer must refuse to surrender the property to the client until the claims are resolved. A lawyer should not unilaterally assume to arbitrate a dispute between the client and the third party, but, when there are substantial grounds for dispute as to the person entitled to the funds, the lawyer may file an action to have a court resolve the dispute.

[5] The obligations of a lawyer under this Rule are independent of those arising from activity other than rendering legal services. For example, a lawyer who serves only as an escrow agent is governed by the applicable law relating to fiduciaries even though the lawyer does not render legal services in the transaction and is not governed by this Rule.

[6] A lawyers' fund for client protection provides a means through the collective efforts of the bar to reimburse persons who have lost money or property as a result of dishonest conduct of a lawyer. Where such a fund has been established, a lawyer must participate where it is mandatory, and, even when it is voluntary, the lawyer should participate.

RULE 1.16: DECLINING OR TERMINATING REPRESENTATION

(a) **Except as stated in paragraph (c), a lawyer shall not represent a client or, where representation has commenced, shall withdraw from the representation of a client if:**

    (1) the representation will result in violation of the rules of professional conduct or other law;

    (2) the lawyer's physical or mental condition materially impairs the lawyer's ability to represent the client; or

    (3) the lawyer is discharged.

(b) **Except as stated in paragraph (c), a lawyer may withdraw from representing a client if:**

    (1) withdrawal can be accomplished without material adverse effect on the interests of the client;

    (2) the client persists in a course of action involving the lawyer's services that the lawyer reasonably believes is criminal or fraudulent;

    (3) the client has used the lawyer's services to perpetrate a crime or fraud;

    (4) the client insists upon taking action that the lawyer considers repugnant or with which the lawyer has a fundamental disagreement;

(5) the client fails substantially to fulfill an obligation to the lawyer regarding the lawyer's services and has been given reasonable warning that the lawyer will withdraw unless the obligation is fulfilled;

(6) the representation will result in an unreasonable financial burden on the lawyer or has been rendered unreasonably difficult by the client; or

(7) other good cause for withdrawal exists.

(c) A lawyer must comply with applicable law requiring notice to or permission of a tribunal when terminating a representation. When ordered to do so by a tribunal, a lawyer shall continue representation notwithstanding good cause for terminating the representation.

(d) Upon termination of representation, a lawyer shall take steps to the extent reasonably practicable to protect a client's interests, such as giving reasonable notice to the client, allowing time for employment of other counsel, surrendering papers and property to which the client is entitled and refunding any advance payment of fee or expense that has not been earned or incurred. The lawyer may retain papers relating to the client to the extent permitted by other law.

Comment

[1]   A lawyer should not accept representation in a matter unless it can be performed competently, promptly, without improper conflict of interest and to completion. Ordinarily, a representation in a matter is completed when the agreed-upon assistance has been concluded. See Rules 1.2(c) and 6.5. See also Rule 1.3, Comment [4].

Mandatory Withdrawal

[2]   A lawyer ordinarily must decline or withdraw from representation if the client demands that the lawyer engage in conduct that is illegal or violates the Rules of Professional Conduct or other law. The lawyer is not obliged to decline or withdraw simply because the client suggests such a course of conduct; a client may make such a suggestion in the hope that a lawyer will not be constrained by a professional obligation.

[3]   When a lawyer has been appointed to represent a client, withdrawal ordinarily requires approval of the appointing authority. See also Rule 6.2. Similarly, court approval or notice to the court is often required by applicable law before a lawyer withdraws from pending litigation. Difficulty may be encountered if withdrawal is based on the client's demand that the lawyer engage in unprofessional conduct. The court may request an explanation for the withdrawal, while the lawyer may be bound to keep confidential the facts that would constitute such an explanation. The lawyer's statement that professional considerations require termination of the representation ordi-

narily should be accepted as sufficient. Lawyers should be mindful of their obligations to both clients and the court under Rules 1.6 and 3.3.

Discharge

[4] A client has a right to discharge a lawyer at any time, with or without cause, subject to liability for payment for the lawyer's services. Where future dispute about the withdrawal may be anticipated, it may be advisable to prepare a written statement reciting the circumstances.

[5] Whether a client can discharge appointed counsel may depend on applicable law. A client seeking to do so should be given a full explanation of the consequences. These consequences may include a decision by the appointing authority that appointment of successor counsel is unjustified, thus requiring self-representation by the client.

[6] If the client has severely diminished capacity, the client may lack the legal capacity to discharge the lawyer, and in any event the discharge may be seriously adverse to the client's interests. The lawyer should make special effort to help the client consider the consequences and may take reasonably necessary protective action as provided in Rule 1.14.

Optional Withdrawal

[7] A lawyer may withdraw from representation in some circumstances. The lawyer has the option to withdraw if it can be accomplished without material adverse effect on the client's interests. Withdrawal is also justified if the client persists in a course of action that the lawyer reasonably believes is criminal or fraudulent, for a lawyer is not required to be associated with such conduct even if the lawyer does not further it. Withdrawal is also permitted if the lawyer's services were misused in the past even if that would materially prejudice the client. The lawyer may also withdraw where the client insists on taking action that the lawyer considers repugnant or with which the lawyer has a fundamental disagreement.

[8] A lawyer may withdraw if the client refuses to abide by the terms of an agreement relating to the representation, such as an agreement concerning fees or court costs or an agreement limiting the objectives of the representation.

Assisting the Client upon Withdrawal

[9] Even if the lawyer has been unfairly discharged by the client, a lawyer must take all reasonable steps to mitigate the consequences to the client. The lawyer may retain papers as security for a fee only to the extent permitted by law. See Rule 1.15.

RULE 1.17: SALE OF LAW PRACTICE

A lawyer or a law firm may sell or purchase a law practice, or an area of law practice, including good will, if the following conditions are satisfied:

(a) The seller ceases to engage in the private practice of law, or in the area of practice that has been sold, [in the geographic area] [in the jurisdiction] (a jurisdiction nay elect either version) in which the practice has been conducted;

(b) The entire practice, or the entire area of practice, is sold to one or more lawyers or law firms;

(c) The seller gives written notice to each of the seller's clients regarding:

(1) the proposed sale;

(2) the client's right to retain other counsel or to take possession of the file; and

(3) the fact that the client's consent to the transfer of the client's files will be presumed if the client does not take any action or does not otherwise object within ninety (90) days of receipt of the notice.

If a client cannot be given notice, the representation of that client may be transferred to the purchaser only upon entry of an order so authorizing by a court having jurisdiction. The seller may disclose to the court in camera information relating to the representation only to the extent necessary to obtain an order authorizing the transfer of a file.

(d) The fees charged clients shall not be increased by reason of the sale.

Comment

[1]   The practice of law is a profession, not merely a business. Clients are not commodities that can be purchased and sold at will. Pursuant to this Rule, when a lawyer or an entire firm ceases to practice, or ceases to practice in an area of law, and other lawyers or firms take over the representation, the selling lawyer or firm may obtain compensation for the reasonable value of the practice as may withdrawing partners of law firms. See Rules 5.4 and 5.6.

Termination of Practice by the Seller

[2]   The requirement that all of the private practice, or all of an area of practice, be sold is satisfied if the seller in good faith makes the entire practice, or the area of practice, available for sale to the purchasers. The fact that a number of the seller's clients decide not to be represented by the purchasers but take their matters elsewhere, therefore, does not result in a violation. Return to private practice as a result of an unanticipated change in circumstances does not necessarily result in a violation. For example, a lawyer who has sold the practice to accept an appointment to judicial office does not violate the requirement that the sale be attendant to cessation of practice if the lawyer later resumes private practice upon being defeated in a contested or a retention election for the office or resigns from a judiciary position.

[3] The requirement that the seller cease to engage in the private practice of law does not prohibit employment as a lawyer on the staff of a public agency or a legal services entity that provides legal services to the poor, or as in-house counsel to a business.

[4] The Rule permits a sale of an entire practice attendant upon retirement from the private practice of law within the jurisdiction. Its provisions, therefore, accommodate the lawyer who sells the practice on the occasion of moving to another state. Some states are so large that a move from one locale therein to another is tantamount to leaving the jurisdiction in which the lawyer has engaged in the practice of law. To also accommodate lawyers so situated, states may permit the sale of the practice when the lawyer leaves the geographical area rather than the jurisdiction. The alternative desired should be indicated by selecting one of the two provided for in Rule 1.17(a).

[5] This Rule also permits a lawyer or law firm to sell an area of practice. If an area of practice is sold and the lawyer remains in the active practice of law, the lawyer must cease accepting any matters in the area of practice that has been sold, either as counsel or co-counsel or by assuming joint responsibility for a matter in connection with the division of a fee with another lawyer as would otherwise be permitted by Rule 1.5(e). For example, a lawyer with a substantial number of estate planning matters and a substantial number of probate administration cases may sell the estate planning portion of the practice but remain in the practice of law by concentrating on probate administration; however, that practitioner may not thereafter accept any estate planning matters. Although a lawyer who leaves a jurisdiction or geographical area typically would sell the entire practice, this Rule permits the lawyer to limit the sale to one or more areas of the practice, thereby preserving the lawyer's right to continue practice in the areas of the practice that were not sold.

Sale of Entire Practice or Entire Area of Practice

[6] The Rule requires that the seller's entire practice, or an entire area of practice, be sold. The prohibition against sale of less than an entire practice area protects those clients whose matters are less lucrative and who might find it difficult to secure other counsel if a sale could be limited to substantial fee-generating matters. The purchasers are required to undertake all client matters in the practice or practice area, subject to client consent. This requirement is satisfied, however, even if a purchaser is unable to undertake a particular client matter because of a conflict of interest.

Client Confidences, Consent and Notice

[7] Negotiations between seller and prospective purchaser prior to disclosure of information relating to a specific representation of an identifiable client no more violate the confidentiality provisions of Model Rule 1.6 than do preliminary discussions concerning the possible association of another lawyer or mergers between firms, with respect to which client consent is not

required. Providing the purchaser access to client-specific information relating to the representation and to the file, however, requires client consent. The Rule provides that before such information can be disclosed by the seller to the purchaser the client must be given actual written notice of the contemplated sale, including the identity of the purchaser, and must be told that the decision to consent or make other arrangements must be made within 90 days. If nothing is heard from the client within that time, consent to the sale is presumed.

[8] A lawyer or law firm ceasing to practice cannot be required to remain in practice because some clients cannot be given actual notice of the proposed purchase. Since these clients cannot themselves consent to the purchase or direct any other disposition of their files, the Rule requires an order from a court having jurisdiction authorizing their transfer or other disposition. The Court can be expected to determine whether reasonable efforts to locate the client have been exhausted, and whether the absent client's legitimate interests will be served by authorizing the transfer of the file so that the purchaser may continue the representation. Preservation of client confidences requires that the petition for a court order be considered in camera. (A procedure by which such an order can be obtained needs to be established in jurisdictions in which it presently does not exist).

[9] All elements of client autonomy, including the client's absolute right to discharge a lawyer and transfer the representation to another, survive the sale of the practice or area of practice.

Fee Arrangements Between Client and Purchaser

[10] The sale may not be financed by increases in fees charged the clients of the practice. Existing arrangements between the seller and the client as to fees and the scope of the work must be honored by the purchaser.

Other Applicable Ethical Standards

[11] Lawyers participating in the sale of a law practice or a practice area are subject to the ethical standards applicable to involving another lawyer in the representation of a client. These include, for example, the seller's obligation to exercise competence in identifying a purchaser qualified to assume the practice and the purchaser's obligation to undertake the representation competently (see Rule 1.1); the obligation to avoid disqualifying conflicts, and to secure the client's informed consent for those conflicts that can be agreed to (see Rule 1.7 regarding conflicts and Rule 1.0(e) for the definition of informed consent); and the obligation to protect information relating to the representation (see Rules 1.6 and 1.9).

[12] If approval of the substitution of the purchasing lawyer for the selling lawyer is required by the rules of any tribunal in which a matter is pending, such approval must be obtained before the matter can be included in the sale (see Rule 1.16).

Applicability of the Rule

[13]   This Rule applies to the sale of a law practice of a deceased, disabled or disappeared lawyer. Thus, the seller may be represented by a non-lawyer representative not subject to these Rules. Since, however, no lawyer may participate in a sale of a law practice which does not conform to the requirements of this Rule, the representatives of the seller as well as the purchasing lawyer can be expected to see to it that they are met.

[14]   Admission to or retirement from a law partnership or professional association, retirement plans and similar arrangements, and a sale of tangible assets of a law practice, do not constitute a sale or purchase governed by this Rule.

[15]   This Rule does not apply to the transfers of legal representation between lawyers when such transfers are unrelated to the sale of a practice or an area of practice.

RULE 1.18: DUTIES TO PROSPECTIVE CLIENT

(a) A person who discusses with a lawyer the possibility of forming a client-lawyer relationship with respect to a matter is a prospective client.

(b) Even when no client-lawyer relationship ensues, a lawyer who has had discussions with a prospective client shall not use or reveal information learned in the consultation, except as Rule 1.9 would permit with respect to information of a former client.

(c) A lawyer subject to paragraph (b) shall not represent a client with interests materially adverse to those of a prospective client in the same or a substantially related matter if the lawyer received information from the prospective client that could be significantly harmful to that person in the matter, except as provided in paragraph (d). If a lawyer is disqualified from representation under this paragraph, no lawyer in a firm with which that lawyer is associated may knowingly undertake or continue representation in such a matter, except as provided in paragraph (d).

(d) When the lawyer has received disqualifying information as defined in paragraph (c), representation is permissible if:

(1) both the affected client and the prospective client have given informed consent, confirmed in writing, or:

(2) the lawyer who received the information took reasonable measures to avoid exposure to more disqualifying information than was reasonably necessary to determine whether to represent the prospective client; and

(i) the disqualified lawyer is timely screened from any participation in the matter and is apportioned no part of the fee therefrom; and

(ii) written notice is promptly given to the prospective client.

Comment

[1] Prospective clients, like clients, may disclose information to a lawyer, place documents or other property in the lawyer's custody, or rely on the lawyer's advice. A lawyer's discussions with a prospective client usually are limited in time and depth and leave both the prospective client and the lawyer free (and sometimes required) to proceed no further. Hence, prospective clients should receive some but not all of the protection afforded clients.

[2] Not all persons who communicate information to a lawyer are entitled to protection under this Rule. A person who communicates information unilaterally to a lawyer, without any reasonable expectation that the lawyer is willing to discuss the possibility of forming a client-lawyer relationship, is not a "prospective client" within the meaning of paragraph (a).

[3] It is often necessary for a prospective client to reveal information to the lawyer during an initial consultation prior to the decision about formation of a client-lawyer relationship. The lawyer often must learn such information to determine whether there is a conflict of interest with an existing client and whether the matter is one that the lawyer is willing to undertake. Paragraph (b) prohibits the lawyer from using or revealing that information, except as permitted by Rule 1.9, even if the client or lawyer decides not to proceed with the representation. The duty exists regardless of how brief the initial conference may be.

[4] In order to avoid acquiring disqualifying information from a prospective client, a lawyer considering whether or not to undertake a new matter should limit the initial interview to only such information as reasonably appears necessary for that purpose. Where the information indicates that a conflict of interest or other reason for non-representation exists, the lawyer should so inform the prospective client or decline the representation. If the prospective client wishes to retain the lawyer, and if consent is possible under Rule 1.7, then consent from all affected present or former clients must be obtained before accepting the representation.

[5] A lawyer may condition conversations with a prospective client on the person's informed consent that no information disclosed during the consultation will prohibit the lawyer from representing a different client in the matter. See Rule 1.0(e) for the definition of informed consent. If the agreement expressly so provides, the prospective client may also consent to the lawyer's subsequent use of information received from the prospective client.

[6] Even in the absence of an agreement, under paragraph (c), the lawyer is not prohibited from representing a client with interests adverse to those of the prospective client in the same or a substantially related matter unless the lawyer has received from the prospective client information that could be significantly harmful if used in the matter.

[7]   Under paragraph (c), the prohibition in this Rule is imputed to other lawyers as provided in Rule 1.10, but, under paragraph (d)(1), imputation may be avoided if the lawyer obtains the informed consent, confirmed in writing, of both the prospective and affected clients. In the alternative, imputation may be avoided if the conditions of paragraph (d)(2) are met and all disqualified lawyers are timely screened and written notice is promptly given to the prospective client. See Rule 1.0(k) (requirements for screening procedures). Paragraph (d)(2)(i) does not prohibit the screened lawyer from receiving a salary or partnership share established by prior independent agreement, but that lawyer may not receive compensation directly related to the matter in which the lawyer is disqualified.

[8]   Notice, including a general description of the subject matter about which the lawyer was consulted, and of the screening procedures employed, generally should be given as soon as practicable after the need for screening becomes apparent.

[9]   For the duty of competence of a lawyer who gives assistance on the merits of a matter to a prospective client, see Rule 1.1. For a lawyer's duties when a prospective client entrusts valuables or papers to the lawyer's care, see Rule 1.15.

COUNSELOR

RULE 2.1: ADVISOR

In representing a client, a lawyer shall exercise independent professional judgment and render candid advice. In rendering advice, a lawyer may refer not only to law but to other considerations such as moral, economic, social and political factors, that may be relevant to the client's situation.

Comment
Scope of Advice

[1]   A client is entitled to straightforward advice expressing the lawyer's honest assessment. Legal advice often involves unpleasant facts and alternatives that a client may be disinclined to confront. In presenting advice, a lawyer endeavors to sustain the client's morale and may put advice in as acceptable a form as honesty permits. However, a lawyer should not be deterred from giving candid advice by the prospect that the advice will be unpalatable to the client.

[2]   Advice couched in narrow legal terms may be of little value to a client, especially where practical considerations, such as cost or effects on other people, are predominant. Purely technical legal advice, therefore, can sometimes be inadequate. It is proper for a lawyer to refer to relevant moral and ethical considerations in giving advice. Although a lawyer is not a moral advisor as such, moral and ethical considerations impinge upon most legal questions and may decisively influence how the law will be applied.

[3] A client may expressly or impliedly ask the lawyer for purely technical advice. When such a request is made by a client experienced in legal matters, the lawyer may accept it at face value. When such a request is made by a client inexperienced in legal matters, however, the lawyer's responsibility as advisor may include indicating that more may be involved than strictly legal considerations.

[4] Matters that go beyond strictly legal questions may also be in the domain of another profession. Family matters can involve problems within the professional competence of psychiatry, clinical psychology or social work; business matters can involve problems within the competence of the accounting profession or of financial specialists. Where consultation with a professional in another field is itself something a competent lawyer would recommend, the lawyer should make such a recommendation. At the same time, a lawyer's advice at its best often consists of recommending a course of action in the face of conflicting recommendations of experts.

Offering Advice

[5] In general, a lawyer is not expected to give advice until asked by the client. However, when a lawyer knows that a client proposes a course of action that is likely to result in substantial adverse legal consequences to the client, the lawyer's duty to the client under Rule 1.4 may require that the lawyer offer advice if the client's course of action is related to the representation. Similarly, when a matter is likely to involve litigation, it may be necessary under Rule 1.4 to inform the client of forms of dispute resolution that might constitute reasonable alternatives to litigation. A lawyer ordinarily has no duty to initiate investigation of a client's affairs or to give advice that the client has indicated is unwanted, but a lawyer may initiate advice to a client when doing so appears to be in the client's interest.

RULE 2.2 (Deleted)

RULE 2.3: EVALUATION FOR USE BY THIRD PERSONS

(a) A lawyer may provide an evaluation of a matter affecting a client for the use of someone other than the client if the lawyer reasonably believes that making the evaluation is compatible with other aspects of the lawyer's relationship with the client.

(b) When the lawyer knows or reasonably should know that the evaluation is likely to affect the client's interests materially and adversely, the lawyer shall not provide the evaluation unless the client gives informed consent.

(c) Except as disclosure is authorized in connection with a report of an evaluation, information relating to the evaluation is otherwise protected by Rule 1.6.

Comment
Definition

[1]   An evaluation may be performed at the client's direction or when impliedly authorized in order to carry out the representation. See Rule 1.2. Such an evaluation may be for the primary purpose of establishing information for the benefit of third parties; for example, an opinion concerning the title of property rendered at the behest of a vendor for the information of a prospective purchaser, or at the behest of a borrower for the information of a prospective lender. In some situations, the evaluation may be required by a government agency; for example, an opinion concerning the legality of the securities registered for sale under the securities laws. In other instances, the evaluation may be required by a third person, such as a purchaser of a business.

[2]   A legal evaluation should be distinguished from an investigation of a person with whom the lawyer does not have a client-lawyer relationship. For example, a lawyer retained by a purchaser to analyze a vendor's title to property does not have a client-lawyer relationship with the vendor. So also, an investigation into a person's affairs by a government lawyer, or by special counsel by a government lawyer, or by special counsel employed by the government, is not an evaluation as that term is used in this Rule. The question is whether the lawyer is retained by the person whose affairs are being examined. When the lawyer is retained by that person, the general rules concerning loyalty to client and preservation of confidences apply, which is not the case if the lawyer is retained by someone else. For this reason, it is essential to identify the person by whom the lawyer is retained. This should be made clear not only to the person under examination, but also to others to whom the results are to be made available.

Duties Owed to Third Person and Client

[3]   When the evaluation is intended for the information or use of a third person, a legal duty to that person may or may not arise. That legal question is beyond the scope of this Rule. However, since such an evaluation involves a departure from the normal client-lawyer relationship, careful analysis of the situation is required. The lawyer must be satisfied as a matter of professional judgment that making the evaluation is compatible with other functions undertaken in behalf of the client. For example, if the lawyer is acting as advocate in defending the client against charges of fraud, it would normally be incompatible with that responsibility for the lawyer to perform an evaluation for others concerning the same or a related transaction. Assuming no such impediment is apparent, however, the lawyer should advise the client of the implications of the evaluation, particularly the lawyer's responsibilities to third persons and the duty to disseminate the findings.

Access to and Disclosure of Information

[4]   The quality of an evaluation depends on the freedom and extent of the investigation upon which it is based. Ordinarily a lawyer should have

whatever latitude of investigation seems necessary as a matter of professional judgment. Under some circumstances, however, the terms of the evaluation may be limited. For example, certain issues or sources may be categorically excluded, or the scope of search may be limited by time constraints or the noncooperation of persons having relevant information. Any such limitations that are material to the evaluation should be described in the report. If after a lawyer has commenced an evaluation, the client refuses to comply with the terms upon which it was understood the evaluation was to have been made, the lawyer's obligations are determined by law, having reference to the terms of the client's agreement and the surrounding circumstances. In no circumstances is the lawyer permitted to knowingly make a false statement of material fact or law in providing an evaluation under this Rule. See Rule 4.1.

Obtaining Client's Informed Consent

[5] Information relating to an evaluation is protected by Rule 1.6. In many situations, providing an evaluation to a third party poses no significant risk to the client; thus, the lawyer may be impliedly authorized to disclose information to carry out the representation. See Rule 1.6(a). Where, however, it is reasonably likely that providing the evaluation will affect the client's interests materially and adversely, the lawyer must first obtain the client's consent after the client has been adequately informed concerning the important possible effects on the client's interests. See Rules 1.6(a) and 1.0(e).

Financial Auditors' Requests for Information

[6] When a question concerning the legal situation of a client arises at the instance of the client's financial auditor and the question is referred to the lawyer, the lawyer's response may be made in accordance with procedures recognized in the legal profession. Such a procedure is set forth in the American Bar Association Statement of Policy Regarding Lawyers' Responses to Auditors' Requests for Information, adopted in 1975.

RULE 2.4: LAWYER SERVING AS THIRD–PARTY NEUTRAL

(a) A lawyer serves as a third-party neutral when the lawyer assists two or more persons who are not clients of the lawyer to reach a resolution of a dispute or other matter that has arisen between them. Service as a third-party neutral may include service as an arbitrator, a mediator or in such other capacity as will enable the lawyer to assist the parties to resolve the matter.

(b) A lawyer serving as a third-party neutral shall inform unrepresented parties that the lawyer is not representing them. When the lawyer knows or reasonably should know that a party does not understand the lawyer's role in the matter, the lawyer shall explain the difference between the lawyer's role as a third-party neutral and a lawyer's role as one who represents a client.

Comment

[1]   Alternative dispute resolution has become a substantial part of the civil justice system. Aside from representing clients in dispute-resolution processes, lawyers often serve as third-party neutrals. A third-party neutral is a person, such as a mediator, arbitrator, conciliator or evaluator, who assists the parties, represented or unrepresented, in the resolution of a dispute or in the arrangement of a transaction. Whether a third-party neutral serves primarily as a facilitator, evaluator or decisionmaker depends on the particular process that is either selected by the parties or mandated by a court.

[2]   The role of a third-party neutral is not unique to lawyers, although, in some court-connected contexts, only lawyers are allowed to serve in this role or to handle certain types of cases. In performing this role, the lawyer may be subject to court rules or other law that apply either to third-party neutrals generally or to lawyers serving as third-party neutrals. Lawyer-neutrals may also be subject to various codes of ethics, such as the Code of Ethics for Arbitration in Commercial Disputes prepared by a joint committee of the American Bar Association and the American Arbitration Association or the Model Standards of Conduct for Mediators jointly prepared by the American Bar Association, the American Arbitration Association and the Society of Professionals in Dispute Resolution.

[3]   Unlike nonlawyers who serve as third-party neutrals, lawyers serving in this role may experience unique problems as a result of differences between the role of a third-party neutral and a lawyer's service as a client representative. The potential for confusion is significant when the parties are unrepresented in the process. Thus, paragraph (b) requires a lawyer-neutral to inform unrepresented parties that the lawyer is not representing them. For some parties, particularly parties who frequently use dispute-resolution processes, this information will be sufficient. For others, particularly those who are using the process for the first time, more information will be required. Where appropriate, the lawyer should inform unrepresented parties of the important differences between the lawyer's role as third-party neutral and a lawyer's role as a client representative, including the inapplicability of the attorney-client evidentiary privilege. The extent of disclosure required under this paragraph will depend on the particular parties involved and the subject matter of the proceeding, as well as the particular features of the dispute-resolution process selected.

[4]   A lawyer who serves as a third-party neutral subsequently may be asked to serve as a lawyer representing a client in the same matter. The conflicts of interest that arise for both the individual lawyer and the lawyer's law firm are addressed in Rule 1.12.

[5]   Lawyers who represent clients in alternative dispute-resolution processes are governed by the Rules of Professional Conduct. When the dispute-resolution process takes place before a tribunal, as in binding arbitration (see Rule 1.0(m)), the lawyer's duty of candor is governed by Rule 3.3. Otherwise,

the lawyer's duty of candor toward both the third-party neutral and other parties is governed by Rule 4.1.

ADVOCATE

RULE 3.1: MERITORIOUS CLAIMS AND CONTENTIONS

A lawyer shall not bring or defend a proceeding, or assert or controvert an issue therein, unless there is a basis in law and fact for doing so that is not frivolous, which includes a good faith argument for an extension, modification or reversal of existing law. A lawyer for the defendant in a criminal proceeding, or the respondent in a proceeding that could result in incarceration, may nevertheless so defend the proceeding as to require that every element of the case be established.

Comment

[1] The advocate has a duty to use legal procedure for the fullest benefit of the client's cause, but also a duty not to abuse legal procedure. The law, both procedural and substantive, establishes the limits within which an advocate may proceed. However, the law is not always clear and never is static. Accordingly, in determining the proper scope of advocacy, account must be taken of the law's ambiguities and potential for change.

[2] The filing of an action or defense or similar action taken for a client is not frivolous merely because the facts have not first been fully substantiated or because the lawyer expects to develop vital evidence only by discovery. What is required of lawyers, however, is that they inform themselves about the facts of their clients' cases and the applicable law and determine that they can make good faith arguments in support of their clients' positions. Such action is not frivolous even though the lawyer believes that the client's position ultimately will not prevail. The action is frivolous, however, if the lawyer is unable either to make a good faith argument on the merits of the action taken or to support the action taken by a good faith argument for an extension, modification or reversal of existing law.

[3] The lawyer's obligations under this Rule are subordinate to federal or state constitutional law that entitles a defendant in a criminal matter to the assistance of counsel in presenting a claim or contention that otherwise would be prohibited by this Rule.

RULE 3.2: EXPEDITING LITIGATION

A lawyer shall make reasonable efforts to expedite litigation consistent with the interests of the client.

Comment

[1] Dilatory practices bring the administration of justice into disrepute. Although there will be occasions when a lawyer may properly seek a postpone-

ment for personal reasons, it is not proper for a lawyer to routinely fail to expedite litigation solely for the convenience of the advocates. Nor will a failure to expedite be reasonable if done for the purpose of frustrating an opposing party's attempt to obtain rightful redress or repose. It is not a justification that similar conduct is often tolerated by the bench and bar. The question is whether a competent lawyer acting in good faith would regard the course of action as having some substantial purpose other than delay. Realizing financial or other benefit from otherwise improper delay in litigation is not a legitimate interest of the client.

RULE 3.3: CANDOR TOWARD THE TRIBUNAL

(a) A lawyer shall not knowingly:

(1) make a false statement of fact or law to a tribunal or fail to correct a false statement of material fact or law previously made to the tribunal by the lawyer;

(2) fail to disclose to the tribunal legal authority in the controlling jurisdiction known to the lawyer to be directly adverse to the position of the client and not disclosed by opposing counsel; or

(3) offer evidence that the lawyer knows to be false. If a lawyer, the lawyer's client, or a witness called by the lawyer, has offered material evidence and the lawyer comes to know of its falsity, the lawyer shall take reasonable remedial measures, including, if necessary, disclosure to the tribunal. A lawyer may refuse to offer evidence, other than the testimony of a defendant in a criminal matter, that the lawyer reasonably believes is false.

(b) A lawyer who represents a client in an adjudicative proceeding and who knows that a person intends to engage, is engaging or has engaged in criminal or fraudulent conduct related to the proceeding shall take reasonable remedial measures, including, if necessary, disclosure to the tribunal.

(c) The duties stated in paragraphs (a) and (b) continue to the conclusion of the proceeding, and apply even if compliance requires disclosure of information otherwise protected by Rule 1.6.

(d) In an ex parte proceeding, a lawyer shall inform the tribunal of all material facts known to the lawyer that will enable the tribunal to make an informed decision, whether or not the facts are adverse.

Comment

[1] This Rule governs the conduct of a lawyer who is representing a client in the proceedings of a tribunal. See Rule 1.0(m) for the definition of "tribunal." It also applies when the lawyer is representing a client in an ancillary proceeding conducted pursuant to the tribunal's adjudicative author-

ity, such as a deposition. Thus, for example, paragraph (a)(3) requires a lawyer to take reasonable remedial measures if the lawyer comes to know that a client who is testifying in a deposition has offered evidence that is false.

[2] This Rule sets forth the special duties of lawyers as officers of the court to avoid conduct that undermines the integrity of the adjudicative process. A lawyer acting as an advocate in an adjudicative proceeding has an obligation to present the client's case with persuasive force. Performance of that duty while maintaining confidences of the client, however, is qualified by the advocate's duty of candor to the tribunal. Consequently, although a lawyer in an adversary proceeding is not required to present an impartial exposition of the law or to vouch for the evidence submitted in a cause, the lawyer must not allow the tribunal to be misled by false statements of law or fact or evidence that the lawyer knows to be false.

Representations by a Lawyer

[3] An advocate is responsible for pleadings and other documents prepared for litigation, but is usually not required to have personal knowledge of matters asserted therein, for litigation documents ordinarily present assertions by the client, or by someone on the client's behalf, and not assertions by the lawyer. Compare Rule 3.1. However, an assertion purporting to be on the lawyer's own knowledge, as in an affidavit by the lawyer or in a statement in open court, may properly be made only when the lawyer knows the assertion is true or believes it to be true on the basis of a reasonably diligent inquiry. There are circumstances where failure to make a disclosure is the equivalent of an affirmative misrepresentation. The obligation prescribed in Rule 1.2(d) not to counsel a client to commit or assist the client in committing a fraud applies in litigation. Regarding compliance with Rule 1.2(d), see the Comment to that Rule. See also the Comment to Rule 8.4(b).

Legal Argument

[4] Legal argument based on a knowingly false representation of law constitutes dishonesty toward the tribunal. A lawyer is not required to make a disinterested exposition of the law, but must recognize the existence of pertinent legal authorities. Furthermore, as stated in paragraph (a)(2), an advocate has a duty to disclose directly adverse authority in the controlling jurisdiction that has not been disclosed by the opposing party. The underlying concept is that legal argument is a discussion seeking to determine the legal premises properly applicable to the case.

Offering Evidence

[5] Paragraph (a)(3) requires that the lawyer refuse to offer evidence that the lawyer knows to be false, regardless of the client's wishes. This duty is premised on the lawyer's obligation as an officer of the court to prevent the trier of fact from being misled by false evidence. A lawyer does not violate this Rule if the lawyer offers the evidence for the purpose of establishing its falsity.

[6]   If a lawyer knows that the client intends to testify falsely or wants the lawyer to introduce false evidence, the lawyer should seek to persuade the client that the evidence should not be offered. If the persuasion is ineffective and the lawyer continues to represent the client, the lawyer must refuse to offer the false evidence. If only a portion of a witness's testimony will be false, the lawyer may call the witness to testify but may not elicit or otherwise permit the witness to present the testimony that the lawyer knows is false.

[7]   The duties stated in paragraphs (a) and (b) apply to all lawyers, including defense counsel in criminal cases. In some jurisdictions, however, courts have required counsel to present the accused as a witness or to give a narrative statement if the accused so desires, even if counsel knows that the testimony or statement will be false. The obligation of the advocate under the Rules of Professional Conduct is subordinate to such requirements. See also Comment [9].

[8]   The prohibition against offering false evidence only applies if the lawyer knows that the evidence is false. A lawyer's reasonable belief that evidence is false does not preclude its presentation to the trier of fact. A lawyer's knowledge that evidence is false, however, can be inferred from the circumstances. See Rule 1.0(f). Thus, although a lawyer should resolve doubts about the veracity of testimony or other evidence in favor of the client, the lawyer cannot ignore an obvious falsehood.

[9]   Although paragraph (a)(3) only prohibits a lawyer from offering evidence the lawyer knows to be false, it permits the lawyer to refuse to offer testimony or other proof that the lawyer reasonably believes is false. Offering such proof may reflect adversely on the lawyer's ability to discriminate in the quality of evidence and thus impair the lawyer's effectiveness as an advocate. Because of the special protections historically provided criminal defendants, however, this Rule does not permit a lawyer to refuse to offer the testimony of such a client where the lawyer reasonably believes but does not know that the testimony will be false. Unless the lawyer knows the testimony will be false, the lawyer must honor the client's decision to testify. See also Comment [7].

Remedial Measures

[10]   Having offered material evidence in the belief that it was true, a lawyer may subsequently come to know that the evidence is false. Or, a lawyer may be surprised when the lawyer's client, or another witness called by the lawyer, offers testimony the lawyer knows to be false, either during the lawyer's direct examination or in response to cross-examination by the opposing lawyer. In such situations or if the lawyer knows of the falsity of testimony elicited from the client during a deposition, the lawyer must take reasonable remedial measures. In such situations, the advocate's proper course is to remonstrate with the client confidentially, advise the client of the lawyer's duty of candor to the tribunal and seek the client's cooperation with respect to the withdrawal or correction of the false statements or evidence. If that fails, the advocate must take further remedial action. If withdrawal from the representation is not permitted or will not undo the effect of the false

evidence, the advocate must make such disclosure to the tribunal as is reasonably necessary to remedy the situation, even if doing so requires the lawyer to reveal information that otherwise would be protected by Rule 1.6. It is for the tribunal then to determine what should be done—making a statement about the matter to the trier of fact, ordering a mistrial or perhaps nothing.

[11] The disclosure of a client's false testimony can result in grave consequences to the client, including not only a sense of betrayal but also loss of the case and perhaps a prosecution for perjury. But the alternative is that the lawyer cooperate in deceiving the court, thereby subverting the truth-finding process which the adversary system is designed to implement. See Rule 1.2(d). Furthermore, unless it is clearly understood that the lawyer will act upon the duty to disclose the existence of false evidence, the client can simply reject the lawyer's advice to reveal the false evidence and insist that the lawyer keep silent. Thus the client could in effect coerce the lawyer into being a party to fraud on the court.

Preserving Integrity of Adjudicative Process

[12] Lawyers have a special obligation to protect a tribunal against criminal or fraudulent conduct that undermines the integrity of the adjudicative process, such as bribing, intimidating or otherwise unlawfully communicating with a witness, juror, court official or other participant in the proceeding, unlawfully destroying or concealing documents or other evidence or failing to disclose information to the tribunal when required by law to do so. Thus, paragraph (b) requires a lawyer to take reasonable remedial measures, including disclosure if necessary, whenever the lawyer knows that a person, including the lawyer's client, intends to engage, is engaging or has engaged in criminal or fraudulent conduct related to the proceeding.

Duration of Obligation

[13] A practical time limit on the obligation to rectify false evidence or false statements of law and fact has to be established. The conclusion of the proceeding is a reasonably definite point for the termination of the obligation. A proceeding has concluded within the meaning of this Rule when a final judgment in the proceeding has been affirmed on appeal or the time for review has passed.

Ex Parte Proceedings

[14] Ordinarily, an advocate has the limited responsibility of presenting one side of the matters that a tribunal should consider in reaching a decision; the conflicting position is expected to be presented by the opposing party. However, in any ex parte proceeding, such as an application for a temporary restraining order, there is no balance of presentation by opposing advocates. The object of an ex parte proceeding is nevertheless to yield a substantially just result. The judge has an affirmative responsibility to accord the absent party just consideration. The lawyer for the represented party has the

correlative duty to make disclosures of material facts known to the lawyer and that the lawyer reasonably believes are necessary to an informed decision.

Withdrawal

[15] Normally, a lawyer's compliance with the duty of candor imposed by this Rule does not require that the lawyer withdraw from the representation of a client whose interests will be or have been adversely affected by the lawyer's disclosure. The lawyer may, however, be required by Rule 1.16(a) to seek permission of the tribunal to withdraw if the lawyer's compliance with this Rule's duty of candor results in such an extreme deterioration of the client-lawyer relationship that the lawyer can no longer competently represent the client. Also see Rule 1.16(b) for the circumstances in which a lawyer will be permitted to seek a tribunal's permission to withdraw. In connection with a request for permission to withdraw that is premised on a client's misconduct, a lawyer may reveal information relating to the representation only to the extent reasonably necessary to comply with this Rule or as otherwise permitted by Rule 1.6.

RULE 3.4: FAIRNESS TO OPPOSING PARTY AND COUNSEL

A lawyer shall not:

(a) unlawfully obstruct another party's access to evidence or unlawfully alter, destroy or conceal a document or other material having potential evidentiary value. A lawyer shall not counsel or assist another person to do any such act;

(b) falsify evidence, counsel or assist a witness to testify falsely, or offer an inducement to a witness that is prohibited by law;

(c) knowingly disobey an obligation under the rules of a tribunal, except for an open refusal based on an assertion that no valid obligation exists;

(d) in pretrial procedure, make a frivolous discovery request or fail to make reasonably diligent effort to comply with a legally proper discovery request by an opposing party;

(e) in trial, allude to any matter that the lawyer does not reasonably believe is relevant or that will not be supported by admissible evidence, assert personal knowledge of facts in issue except when testifying as a witness, or state a personal opinion as to the justness of a cause, the credibility of a witness, the culpability of a civil litigant or the guilt or innocence of an accused; or

(f) request a person other than a client to refrain from voluntarily giving relevant information to another party unless:

(1) the person is a relative or an employee or other agent of a client; and

(2) the lawyer reasonably believes that the person's interests will not be adversely affected by refraining from giving such information.

Comment

[1] The procedure of the adversary system contemplates that the evidence in a case is to be marshalled competitively by the contending parties. Fair competition in the adversary system is secured by prohibitions against destruction or concealment of evidence, improperly influencing witnesses, obstructive tactics in discovery procedure, and the like.

[2] Documents and other items of evidence are often essential to establish a claim or defense. Subject to evidentiary privileges, the right of an opposing party, including the government, to obtain evidence through discovery or subpoena is an important procedural right. The exercise of that right can be frustrated if relevant material is altered, concealed or destroyed. Applicable law in many jurisdictions makes it an offense to destroy material for purpose of impairing its availability in a pending proceeding or one whose commencement can be foreseen. Falsifying evidence is also generally a criminal offense. Paragraph (a) applies to evidentiary material generally, including computerized information. Applicable law may permit a lawyer to take temporary possession of physical evidence of client crimes for the purpose of conducting a limited examination that will not alter or destroy material characteristics of the evidence. In such a case, applicable law may require the lawyer to turn the evidence over to the police or other prosecuting authority, depending on the circumstances.

[3] With regard to paragraph (b), it is not improper to pay a witness's expenses or to compensate an expert witness on terms permitted by law. The common law rule in most jurisdictions is that it is improper to pay an occurrence witness any fee for testifying and that it is improper to pay an expert witness a contingent fee.

[4] Paragraph (f) permits a lawyer to advise employees of a client to refrain from giving information to another party, for the employees may identify their interests with those of the client. See also Rule 4.2.

RULE 3.5: IMPARTIALITY AND DECORUM OF THE TRIBUNAL

A lawyer shall not:

(a) seek to influence a judge, juror, prospective juror or other official by means prohibited by law;

(b) communicate ex parte with such a person during the proceeding unless authorized to do so by law or court order;

(c) communicate with a juror or prospective juror after discharge of the jury if:

(1) the communication is prohibited by law or court order;

(2) the juror has made known to the lawyer a desire not to communicate; or

(3) the communication involves misrepresentation, coercion, duress or harassment; or

(d) engage in conduct intended to disrupt a tribunal.

Comment

[1] Many forms of improper influence upon a tribunal are proscribed by criminal law. Others are specified in the ABA Model Code of Judicial Conduct, with which an advocate should be familiar. A lawyer is required to avoid contributing to a violation of such provisions.

[2] During a proceeding a lawyer may not communicate ex parte with persons serving in an official capacity in the proceeding, such as judges, masters or jurors, unless authorized to do so by law or court order.

[3] A lawyer may on occasion want to communicate with a juror or prospective juror after the jury has been discharged. The lawyer may do so unless the communication is prohibited by law or a court order but must respect the desire of the juror not to talk with the lawyer. The lawyer may not engage in improper conduct during the communication.

[4] The advocate's function is to present evidence and argument so that the cause may be decided according to law. Refraining from abusive or obstreperous conduct is a corollary of the advocate's right to speak on behalf of litigants. A lawyer may stand firm against abuse by a judge but should avoid reciprocation; the judge's default is no justification for similar dereliction by an advocate. An advocate can present the cause, protect the record for subsequent review and preserve professional integrity by patient firmness no less effectively than by belligerence or theatrics.

[5] The duty to refrain from disruptive conduct applies to any proceeding of a tribunal, including a deposition. See Rule 1.0(m).

RULE 3.6: TRIAL PUBLICITY

(a) A lawyer who is participating or has participated in the investigation or litigation of a matter shall not make an extrajudicial statement that the lawyer knows or reasonably should know will be disseminated by means of public communication and will have a substantial likelihood of materially prejudicing an adjudicative proceeding in the matter.

(b) Notwithstanding paragraph (a), a lawyer may state:

(1) the claim, offense or defense involved and, except when prohibited by law, the identity of the persons involved;

(2) information contained in a public record;

(3) that an investigation of a matter is in progress;

(4) the scheduling or result of any step in litigation;

(5) a request for assistance in obtaining evidence and information necessary thereto;

(6) a warning of danger concerning the behavior of a person involved, when there is reason to believe that there exists the likelihood of substantial harm to an individual or to the public interest; and

(7) in a criminal case, in addition to subparagraphs (1) through (6):

> (i) the identity, residence, occupation and family status of the accused;

> (ii) if the accused has not been apprehended, information necessary to aid in apprehension of that person;

> (iii) the fact, time and place of arrest; and

> (iv) the identity of investigating and arresting officers or agencies and the length of the investigation.

(c) Notwithstanding paragraph (a), a lawyer may make a statement that a reasonable lawyer would believe is required to protect a client from the substantial undue prejudicial effect of recent publicity not initiated by the lawyer or the lawyer's client. A statement made pursuant to this paragraph shall be limited to such information as is necessary to mitigate the recent adverse publicity.

(d) No lawyer associated in a firm or government agency with a lawyer subject to paragraph (a) shall make a statement prohibited by paragraph (a).

Comment

[1] It is difficult to strike a balance between protecting the right to a fair trial and safeguarding the right of free expression. Preserving the right to a fair trial necessarily entails some curtailment of the information that may be disseminated about a party prior to trial, particularly where trial by jury is involved. If there were no such limits, the result would be the practical nullification of the protective effect of the rules of forensic decorum and the exclusionary rules of evidence. On the other hand, there are vital social interests served by the free dissemination of information about events having legal consequences and about legal proceedings themselves. The public has a right to know about threats to its safety and measures aimed at assuring its security. It also has a legitimate interest in the conduct of judicial proceedings, particularly in matters of general public concern. Furthermore, the subject matter of legal proceedings is often of direct significance in debate and deliberation over questions of public policy.

[2]   Special rules of confidentiality may validly govern proceedings in juvenile, domestic relations and mental disability proceedings, and perhaps other types of litigation. Rule 3.4(c) requires compliance with such rules.

[3]   The Rule sets forth a basic general prohibition against a lawyer's making statements that the lawyer knows or should know will have a substantial likelihood of materially prejudicing an adjudicative proceeding. Recognizing that the public value of informed commentary is great and the likelihood of prejudice to a proceeding by the commentary of a lawyer who is not involved in the proceeding is small, the rule applies only to lawyers who are, or who have been involved in the investigation or litigation of a case, and their associates.

[4]   Paragraph (b) identifies specific matters about which a lawyer's statements would not ordinarily be considered to present a substantial likelihood of material prejudice, and should not in any event be considered prohibited by the general prohibition of paragraph (a). Paragraph (b) is not intended to be an exhaustive listing of the subjects upon which a lawyer may make a statement, but statements on other matters may be subject to paragraph (a).

[5]   There are, on the other hand, certain subjects that are more likely than not to have a material prejudicial effect on a proceeding, particularly when they refer to a civil matter triable to a jury, a criminal matter, or any other proceeding that could result in incarceration. These subjects relate to:

(1) the character, credibility, reputation or criminal record of a party, suspect in a criminal investigation or witness, or the identity of a witness, or the expected testimony of a party or witness;

(2) in a criminal case or proceeding that could result in incarceration, the possibility of a plea of guilty to the offense or the existence or contents of any confession, admission, or statement given by a defendant or suspect or that person's refusal or failure to make a statement;

(3) the performance or results of any examination or test or the refusal or failure of a person to submit to an examination or test, or the identity or nature of physical evidence expected to be presented;

(4) any opinion as to the guilt or innocence of a defendant or suspect in a criminal case or proceeding that could result in incarceration;

(5) information that the lawyer knows or reasonably should know is likely to be inadmissible as evidence in a trial and that would, if disclosed, create a substantial risk of prejudicing an impartial trial; or

(6) the fact that a defendant has been charged with a crime, unless there is included therein a statement explaining that the charge is merely an accusation and that the defendant is presumed innocent until and unless proven guilty.

[6]   Another relevant factor in determining prejudice is the nature of the proceeding involved. Criminal jury trials will be most sensitive to extrajudicial speech. Civil trials may be less sensitive. Non-jury hearings and arbitration

proceedings may be even less affected. The Rule will still place limitations on prejudicial comments in these cases, but the likelihood of prejudice may be different depending on the type of proceeding.

[7] Finally, extrajudicial statements that might otherwise raise a question under this Rule may be permissible when they are made in response to statements made publicly by another party, another party's lawyer, or third persons, where a reasonable lawyer would believe a public response is required in order to avoid prejudice to the lawyer's client. When prejudicial statements have been publicly made by others, responsive statements may have the salutary effect of lessening any resulting adverse impact on the adjudicative proceeding. Such responsive statements should be limited to contain only such information as is necessary to mitigate undue prejudice created by the statements made by others.

[8] See Rule 3.8(f) for additional duties of prosecutors in connection with extrajudicial statements about criminal proceedings.

RULE 3.7: LAWYER AS WITNESS

(a) A lawyer shall not act as advocate at a trial in which the lawyer is likely to be a necessary witness unless:

(1) the testimony relates to an uncontested issue;

(2) the testimony relates to the nature and value of legal services rendered in the case; or

(3) disqualification of the lawyer would work substantial hardship on the client.

(b) A lawyer may act as advocate in a trial in which another lawyer in the lawyer's firm is likely to be called as a witness unless precluded from doing so by Rule 1.7 or Rule 1.9.

Comment

[1] Combining the roles of advocate and witness can prejudice the tribunal and the opposing party and can also involve a conflict of interest between the lawyer and client.

Advocate–Witness Rule

[2] The tribunal has proper objection when the trier of fact may be confused or misled by a lawyer serving as both advocate and witness. The opposing party has proper objection where the combination of roles may prejudice that party's rights in the litigation. A witness is required to testify on the basis of personal knowledge, while an advocate is expected to explain and comment on evidence given by others. It may not be clear whether a statement by an advocate-witness should be taken as proof or as an analysis of the proof.

[3]   To protect the tribunal, paragraph (a) prohibits a lawyer from simultaneously serving as advocate and necessary witness except in those circumstances specified in paragraphs (a)(1) through (a)(3). Paragraph (a)(1) recognizes that if the testimony will be uncontested, the ambiguities in the dual role are purely theoretical. Paragraph (a)(2) recognizes that where the testimony concerns the extent and value of legal services rendered in the action in which the testimony is offered, permitting the lawyers to testify avoids the need for a second trial with new counsel to resolve that issue. Moreover, in such a situation the judge has firsthand knowledge of the matter in issue; hence, there is less dependence on the adversary process to test the credibility of the testimony.

[4]   Apart from these two exceptions, paragraph (a)(3) recognizes that a balancing is required between the interests of the client and those of the tribunal and the opposing party. Whether the tribunal is likely to be misled or the opposing party is likely to suffer prejudice depends on the nature of the case, the importance and probable tenor of the lawyer's testimony, and the probability that the lawyer's testimony will conflict with that of other witnesses. Even if there is risk of such prejudice, in determining whether the lawyer should be disqualified, due regard must be given to the effect of disqualification on the lawyer's client. It is relevant that one or both parties could reasonably foresee that the lawyer would probably be a witness. The conflict of interest principles stated in Rules 1.7, 1.9 and 1.10 have no application to this aspect of the problem.

[5]   Because the tribunal is not likely to be misled when a lawyer acts as advocate in a trial in which another lawyer in the lawyer's firm will testify as a necessary witness, paragraph (b) permits the lawyer to do so except in situations involving a conflict of interest.

Conflict of Interest

[6]   In determining if it is permissible to act as advocate in a trial in which the lawyer will be a necessary witness, the lawyer must also consider that the dual role may give rise to a conflict of interest that will require compliance with Rules 1.7 or 1.9. For example, if there is likely to be substantial conflict between the testimony of the client and that of the lawyer the representation involves a conflict of interest that requires compliance with Rule 1.7. This would be true even though the lawyer might not be prohibited by paragraph (a) from simultaneously serving as advocate and witness because the lawyer's disqualification would work a substantial hardship on the client. Similarly, a lawyer who might be permitted to simultaneously serve as an advocate and a witness by paragraph (a)(3) might be precluded from doing so by Rule 1.9. The problem can arise whether the lawyer is called as a witness on behalf of the client or is called by the opposing party. Determining whether or not such a conflict exists is primarily the responsibility of the lawyer involved. If there is a conflict of interest, the lawyer must secure the client's informed consent, confirmed in writing. In some cases, the lawyer will be precluded from seeking the client's consent. See Rule 1.7. See Rule 1.0(b)

for the definition of "confirmed in writing" and Rule 1.0(e) for the definition of "informed consent."

[7]   Paragraph (b) provides that a lawyer is not disqualified from serving as an advocate because a lawyer with whom the lawyer is associated in a firm is precluded from doing so by paragraph (a). If, however, the testifying lawyer would also be disqualified by Rule 1.7 or Rule 1.9 from representing the client in the matter, other lawyers in the firm will be precluded from representing the client by Rule 1.10 unless the client gives informed consent under the conditions stated in Rule 1.7.

RULE 3.8: SPECIAL RESPONSIBILITIES OF A PROSECUTOR

The prosecutor in a criminal case shall:

(a) refrain from prosecuting a charge that the prosecutor knows is not supported by probable cause;

(b) make reasonable efforts to assure that the accused has been advised of the right to, and the procedure for obtaining, counsel and has been given reasonable opportunity to obtain counsel;

(c) not seek to obtain from an unrepresented accused a waiver of important pretrial rights, such as the right to a preliminary hearing;

(d) make timely disclosure to the defense of all evidence or information known to the prosecutor that tends to negate the guilt of the accused or mitigates the offense, and, in connection with sentencing, disclose to the defense and to the tribunal all unprivileged mitigating information known to the prosecutor, except when the prosecutor is relieved of this responsibility by a protective order of the tribunal;

(e) not subpoena a lawyer in a grand jury or other criminal proceeding to present evidence about a past or present client unless the prosecutor reasonably believes:

(1) the information sought is not protected from disclosure by any applicable privilege;

(2) the evidence sought is essential to the successful completion of an ongoing investigation or prosecution; and

(3) there is no other feasible alternative to obtain the information;

(f) except for statements that are necessary to inform the public of the nature and extent of the prosecutor's action and that serve a legitimate law enforcement purpose, refrain from making extrajudicial comments that have a substantial likelihood of heightening public condemnation of the accused and exercise reasonable care to prevent investigators, law enforcement personnel, employees or other persons assisting or associated with the prosecutor in a criminal

case from making an extrajudicial statement that the prosecutor would be prohibited from making under Rule 3.6 or this Rule.

(g) When a prosecutor knows of new, credible and material evidence creating a reasonable likelihood that a convicted defendant did not commit an offense of which the defendant was convicted, the prosecutor shall:

    (1) promptly disclose that evidence to an appropriate court or authority, and

    (2) if the conviction was obtained in the prosecutor's jurisdiction,

        (i) promptly disclose that evidence to the defendant unless a court authorizes delay, and

        (ii) undertake further investigation, or make reasonable efforts to cause an investigation, to determine whether the defendant was convicted of an offense that the defendant did not commit.

(h) When a prosecutor knows of clear and convincing evidence establishing that a defendant in the prosecutor's jurisdiction was convicted of an offense that the defendant did not commit, the prosecutor shall seek to remedy the conviction.

Comment

[1] A prosecutor has the responsibility of a minister of justice and not simply that of an advocate. This responsibility carries with it specific obligations to see that the defendant is accorded procedural justice, that guilt is decided upon the basis of sufficient evidence, and that special precautions are taken to prevent and to rectify the conviction of innocent persons. The extent of mandated remedial action is a matter of debate and varies in different jurisdictions. Many jurisdictions have adopted the ABA Standards of Criminal Justice Relating to the Prosecution Function, which are the product of prolonged and careful deliberation by lawyers experienced in both criminal prosecution and defense. Competent representation of the sovereignty may require a prosecutor to undertake some procedural and remedial measures as a matter of obligation. Applicable law may require other measures by the prosecutor and knowing disregard of those obligations or a systematic abuse of prosecutorial discretion could constitute a violation of Rule 8.4.

[2] In some jurisdictions, a defendant may waive a preliminary hearing and thereby lose a valuable opportunity to challenge probable cause. Accordingly, prosecutors should not seek to obtain waivers of preliminary hearings or other important pretrial rights from unrepresented accused persons. Paragraph (c) does not apply, however, to an accused appearing *pro se* with the approval of the tribunal. Nor does it forbid the lawful questioning of an uncharged suspect who has knowingly waived the rights to counsel and silence.

[3]   The exception in paragraph (d) recognizes that a prosecutor may seek an appropriate protective order from the tribunal if disclosure of information to the defense could result in substantial harm to an individual or to the public interest.

[4]   Paragraph (e) is intended to limit the issuance of lawyer subpoenas in grand jury and other criminal proceedings to those situations in which there is a genuine need to intrude into the client-lawyer relationship.

[5]   Paragraph (f) supplements Rule 3.6, which prohibits extrajudicial statements that have a substantial likelihood of prejudicing an adjudicatory proceeding. In the context of a criminal prosecution, a prosecutor's extrajudicial statement can create the additional problem of increasing public condemnation of the accused. Although the announcement of an indictment, for example, will necessarily have severe consequences for the accused, a prosecutor can, and should, avoid comments which have no legitimate law enforcement purpose and have a substantial likelihood of increasing public opprobrium of the accused. Nothing in this Comment is intended to restrict the statements which a prosecutor may make which comply with Rule 3.6(b) or 3.6(c).

[6]   Like other lawyers, prosecutors are subject to Rules 5.1 and 5.3, which relate to responsibilities regarding lawyers and nonlawyers who work for or are associated with the lawyer's office. Paragraph (f) reminds the prosecutor of the importance of these obligations in connection with the unique dangers of improper extrajudicial statements in a criminal case. In addition, paragraph (f) requires a prosecutor to exercise reasonable care to prevent persons assisting or associated with the prosecutor from making improper extrajudicial statements, even when such persons are not under the direct supervision of the prosecutor. Ordinarily, the reasonable care standard will be satisfied if the prosecutor issues the appropriate cautions to law-enforcement personnel and other relevant individuals.

[7]   When a prosecutor knows of new, credible and material evidence creating a reasonable likelihood that a person outside the prosecutor's jurisdiction was convicted of a crime that the person did not commit, paragraph (g) requires prompt disclosure to the court or other appropriate authority, such as the chief prosecutor of the jurisdiction where the conviction occurred. If the conviction was obtained in the prosecutor's jurisdiction, paragraph (g) requires the prosecutor to examine the evidence and undertake further investigation to determine whether the defendant is in fact innocent or make reasonable efforts to cause another appropriate authority to undertake the necessary investigation, and to promptly disclose the evidence to the court and, absent court-authorized delay, to the defendant. Consistent with the objectives of Rules 4.2 and 4.3, disclosure to a represented defendant must be made through the defendant's counsel, and, in the case of an unrepresented defendant, would ordinarily be accompanied by a request to a court for the appointment of counsel to assist the defendant in taking such legal measures as may be appropriate.

[8] Under paragraph (h), once the prosecutor knows of clear and convincing evidence that the defendant was convicted of an offense that the defendant did not commit, the prosecutor must seek to remedy the conviction. Necessary steps may include disclosure of the evidence to the defendant, requesting that the court appoint counsel for an unrepresented indigent defendant and, where appropriate, notifying the court that the prosecutor has knowledge that the defendant did not commit the offense of which the defendant was convicted.

[9] A prosecutor's independent judgment, made in good faith, that the new evidence is not of such nature as to trigger the obligations of sections (g) and (h), though subsequently determined to have been erroneous, does not constitute a violation of this Rule.

RULE 3.9: ADVOCATE IN NONADJUDICATIVE PROCEEDINGS

A lawyer representing a client before a legislative body or administrative agency in a nonadjudicative proceeding shall disclose that the appearance is in a representative capacity and shall conform to the provisions of Rules 3.3(a) through (c), 3.4(a) through (c), and 3.5.

Comment

[1] In representation before bodies such as legislatures, municipal councils, and executive and administrative agencies acting in a rule-making or policy-making capacity, lawyers present facts, formulate issues and advance argument in the matters under consideration. The decision-making body, like a court, should be able to rely on the integrity of the submissions made to it. A lawyer appearing before such a body must deal with it honestly and in conformity with applicable rules of procedure. See Rules 3.3(a) through (c), 3.4(a) through (c) and 3.5.

[2] Lawyers have no exclusive right to appear before nonadjudicative bodies, as they do before a court. The requirements of this Rule therefore may subject lawyers to regulations inapplicable to advocates who are not lawyers. However, legislatures and administrative agencies have a right to expect lawyers to deal with them as they deal with courts.

[3] This Rule only applies when a lawyer represents a client in connection with an official hearing or meeting of a governmental agency or a legislative body to which the lawyer or the lawyer's client is presenting evidence or argument. It does not apply to representation of a client in a negotiation or other bilateral transaction with a governmental agency or in connection with an application for a license or other privilege or the client's compliance with generally applicable reporting requirements, such as the filing of income-tax returns. Nor does it apply to the representation of a client in connection with an investigation or examination of the client's affairs conducted by government investigators or examiners. Representation in such matters is governed by Rules 4.1 through 4.4.

TRANSACTIONS WITH PERSONS OTHER THAN CLIENTS

RULE 4.1: TRUTHFULNESS IN STATEMENTS TO OTHERS

In the course of representing a client a lawyer shall not knowingly:

(a) make a false statement of material fact or law to a third person; or

(b) fail to disclose a material fact when disclosure is necessary to avoid assisting a criminal or fraudulent act by a client, unless disclosure is prohibited by Rule 1.6.

Comment

Misrepresentation

[1] A lawyer is required to be truthful when dealing with others on a client's behalf, but generally has no affirmative duty to inform an opposing party of relevant facts. A misrepresentation can occur if the lawyer incorporates or affirms a statement of another person that the lawyer knows is false. Misrepresentations can also occur by partially true but misleading statements or omissions that are the equivalent of affirmative false statements. For dishonest conduct that does not amount to a false statement or for misrepresentations by a lawyer other than in the course of representing a client, see Rule 8.4.

Statements of Fact

[2] This Rule refers to statements of fact. Whether a particular statement should be regarded as one of fact can depend on the circumstances. Under generally accepted conventions in negotiation, certain types of statements ordinarily are not taken as statements of material fact. Estimates of price or value placed on the subject of a transaction and a party's intentions as to an acceptable settlement of a claim are ordinarily in this category, and so is the existence of an undisclosed principal except where nondisclosure of the principal would constitute fraud. Lawyers should be mindful of their obligations under applicable law to avoid criminal and tortious misrepresentation.

Crime or Fraud by Client

[3] Under Rule 1.2(d), a lawyer is prohibited from counseling or assisting a client in conduct that the lawyer knows is criminal or fraudulent. Paragraph (b) states a specific application of the principle set forth in Rule 1.2(d) and addresses the situation where a client's crime or fraud takes the form of a lie or misrepresentation. Ordinarily, a lawyer can avoid assisting a client's crime or fraud by withdrawing from the representation. Sometimes it may be necessary for the lawyer to give notice of the fact of withdrawal and to disaffirm an opinion, document, affirmation or the like. In extreme cases,

substantive law may require a lawyer to disclose information relating to the representation to avoid being deemed to have assisted the client's crime or fraud. If the lawyer can avoid assisting a client's crime or fraud only by disclosing this information, then under paragraph (b) the lawyer is required to do so, unless the disclosure is prohibited by Rule 1.6.

RULE 4.2: COMMUNICATION WITH PERSON REPRESENTED BY COUNSEL

In representing a client, a lawyer shall not communicate about the subject of the representation with a person the lawyer knows to be represented by another lawyer in the matter, unless the lawyer has the consent of the other lawyer or is authorized to do so by law or a court order.

Comment

[1]   This Rule contributes to the proper functioning of the legal system by protecting a person who has chosen to be represented by a lawyer in a matter against possible overreaching by other lawyers who are participating in the matter, interference by those lawyers with the client-lawyer relationship and the uncounselled disclosure of information relating to the representation.

[2]   This Rule applies to communications with any person who is represented by counsel concerning the matter to which the communication relates.

[3]   The Rule applies even though the represented person initiates or consents to the communication. A lawyer must immediately terminate communication with a person if, after commencing communication, the lawyer learns that the person is one with whom communication is not permitted by this Rule.

[4]   This Rule does not prohibit communication with a represented person, or an employee or agent of such a person, concerning matters outside the representation. For example, the existence of a controversy between a government agency and a private party, or between two organizations, does not prohibit a lawyer for either from communicating with nonlawyer representatives of the other regarding a separate matter. Nor does this Rule preclude communication with a represented person who is seeking advice from a lawyer who is not otherwise representing a client in the matter. A lawyer may not make a communication prohibited by this Rule through the acts of another. See Rule 8.4(a). Parties to a matter may communicate directly with each other, and a lawyer is not prohibited from advising a client concerning a communication that the client is legally entitled to make. Also, a lawyer having independent justification or legal authorization for communicating with a represented person is permitted to do so.

[5]   Communications authorized by law may include communications by a lawyer on behalf of a client who is exercising a constitutional or other legal

right to communicate with the government. Communications authorized by law may also include investigative activities of lawyers representing governmental entities, directly or through investigative agents, prior to the commencement of criminal or civil enforcement proceedings. When communicating with the accused in a criminal matter, a government lawyer must comply with this Rule in addition to honoring the constitutional rights of the accused. The fact that a communication does not violate a state or federal constitutional right is insufficient to establish that the communication is permissible under this Rule.

[6] A lawyer who is uncertain whether a communication with a represented person is permissible may seek a court order. A lawyer may also seek a court order in exceptional circumstances to authorize a communication that would otherwise be prohibited by this Rule, for example, where communication with a person represented by counsel is necessary to avoid reasonably certain injury.

[7] In the case of a represented organization, this Rule prohibits communications with a constituent of the organization who supervises, directs or regularly consults with the organization's lawyer concerning the matter or has authority to obligate the organization with respect to the matter or whose act or omission in connection with the matter may be imputed to the organization for purposes of civil or criminal liability. Consent of the organization's lawyer is not required for communication with a former constituent. If a constituent of the organization is represented in the matter by his or her own counsel, the consent by that counsel to a communication will be sufficient for purposes of this Rule. Compare Rule 3.4(f). In communicating with a current or former constituent of an organization, a lawyer must not use methods of obtaining evidence that violate the legal rights of the organization. See Rule 4.4.

[8] The prohibition on communications with a represented person only applies in circumstances where the lawyer knows that the person is in fact represented in the matter to be discussed. This means that the lawyer has actual knowledge of the fact of the representation; but such actual knowledge may be inferred from the circumstances. See Rule 1.0(f). Thus, the lawyer cannot evade the requirement of obtaining the consent of counsel by closing eyes to the obvious.

[9] In the event the person with whom the lawyer communicates is not known to be represented by counsel in the matter, the lawyer's communications are subject to Rule 4.3.

RULE 4.3: DEALING WITH UNREPRESENTED PERSON

In dealing on behalf of a client with a person who is not represented by counsel, a lawyer shall not state or imply that the lawyer is disinterested. When the lawyer knows or reasonably should know that the unrepresented person misunderstands the lawyer's role in the matter, the lawyer shall make reasonable efforts to correct the

misunderstanding. The lawyer shall not give legal advice to an un-represented person, other than the advice to secure counsel, if the lawyer knows or reasonably should know that the interests of such a person are or have a reasonable possibility of being in conflict with the interests of the client.

Comment

[1] An unrepresented person, particularly one not experienced in dealing with legal matters, might assume that a lawyer is disinterested in loyalties or is a disinterested authority on the law even when the lawyer represents a client. In order to avoid a misunderstanding, a lawyer will typically need to identify the lawyer's client and, where necessary, explain that the client has interests opposed to those of the unrepresented person. For misunderstandings that sometimes arise when a lawyer for an organization deals with an unrepresented constituent, see Rule 1.13(f).

[2] The Rule distinguishes between situations involving unrepresented persons whose interests may be adverse to those of the lawyer's client and those in which the person's interests are not in conflict with the client's. In the former situation, the possibility that the lawyer will compromise the unrepresented person's interests is so great that the Rule prohibits the giving of any advice, apart from the advice to obtain counsel. Whether a lawyer is giving impermissible advice may depend on the experience and sophistication of the unrepresented person, as well as the setting in which the behavior and comments occur. This Rule does not prohibit a lawyer from negotiating the terms of a transaction or settling a dispute with an unrepresented person. So long as the lawyer has explained that the lawyer represents an adverse party and is not representing the person, the lawyer may inform the person of the terms on which the lawyer's client will enter into an agreement or settle a matter, prepare documents that require the person's signature and explain the lawyer's own view of the meaning of the document or the lawyer's view of the underlying legal obligations.

RULE 4.4: RESPECT FOR RIGHTS OF THIRD PERSONS

(a) In representing a client, a lawyer shall not use means that have no substantial purpose other than to embarrass, delay, or burden a third person, or use methods of obtaining evidence that violate the legal rights of such a person.

(b) A lawyer who receives a document relating to the representation of the lawyer's client and knows or reasonably should know that the document was inadvertently sent shall promptly notify the sender.

Comment

[1] Responsibility to a client requires a lawyer to subordinate the interests of others to those of the client, but that responsibility does not imply

that a lawyer may disregard the rights of third persons. It is impractical to catalogue all such rights, but they include legal restrictions on methods of obtaining evidence from third persons and unwarranted intrusions into privileged relationships, such as the client-lawyer relationship.

[2] Paragraph (b) recognizes that lawyers sometimes receive documents that were mistakenly sent or produced by opposing parties or their lawyers. If a lawyer knows or reasonably should know that such a document was sent inadvertently, then this Rule requires the lawyer to promptly notify the sender in order to permit that person to take protective measures. Whether the lawyer is required to take additional steps, such as returning the original document, is a matter of law beyond the scope of these Rules, as is the question of whether the privileged status of a document has been waived. Similarly, this Rule does not address the legal duties of a lawyer who receives a document that the lawyer knows or reasonably should know may have been wrongfully obtained by the sending person. For purposes of this Rule, "document" includes e-mail or other electronic modes of transmission subject to being read or put into readable form.

[3] Some lawyers may choose to return a document unread, for example, when the lawyer learns before receiving the document that it was inadvertently sent to the wrong address. Where a lawyer is not required by applicable law to do so, the decision to voluntarily return such a document is a matter of professional judgment ordinarily reserved to the lawyer. See Rules 1.2 and 1.4.

LAW FIRMS AND ASSOCIATIONS

RULE 5.1: RESPONSIBILITIES OF PARTNERS, MANAGERS, AND SUPERVISORY LAWYERS

(a) A partner in a law firm, and a lawyer who individually or together with other lawyers possesses comparable managerial authority in a law firm, shall make reasonable efforts to ensure that the firm has in effect measures giving reasonable assurance that all lawyers in the firm conform to the Rules of Professional Conduct.

(b) A lawyer having direct supervisory authority over another lawyer shall make reasonable efforts to ensure that the other lawyer conforms to the Rules of Professional Conduct.

(c) A lawyer shall be responsible for another lawyer's violation of the Rules of Professional Conduct if:

(1) the lawyer orders or, with knowledge of the specific conduct, ratifies the conduct involved; or

(2) the lawyer is a partner or has comparable managerial authority in the law firm in which the other lawyer practices, or has direct supervisory authority over the other lawyer, and

knows of the conduct at a time when its consequences can be avoided or mitigated but fails to take reasonable remedial action.

Comment

[1] Paragraph (a) applies to lawyers who have managerial authority over the professional work of a firm. See Rule 1.0(c). This includes members of a partnership, the shareholders in a law firm organized as a professional corporation, and members of other associations authorized to practice law; lawyers having comparable managerial authority in a legal services organization or a law department of an enterprise or government agency; and lawyers who have intermediate managerial responsibilities in a firm. Paragraph (b) applies to lawyers who have supervisory authority over the work of other lawyers in a firm.

[2] Paragraph (a) requires lawyers with managerial authority within a firm to make reasonable efforts to establish internal policies and procedures designed to provide reasonable assurance that all lawyers in the firm will conform to the Rules of Professional Conduct. Such policies and procedures include those designed to detect and resolve conflicts of interest, identify dates by which actions must be taken in pending matters, account for client funds and property and ensure that inexperienced lawyers are properly supervised.

[3] Other measures that may be required to fulfill the responsibility prescribed in paragraph (a) can depend on the firm's structure and the nature of its practice. In a small firm of experienced lawyers, informal supervision and periodic review of compliance with the required systems ordinarily will suffice. In a large firm, or in practice situations in which difficult ethical problems frequently arise, more elaborate measures may be necessary. Some firms, for example, have a procedure whereby junior lawyers can make confidential referral of ethical problems directly to a designated senior partner or special committee. See Rule 5.2. Firms, whether large or small, may also rely on continuing legal education in professional ethics. In any event, the ethical atmosphere of a firm can influence the conduct of all its members, and the partners may not assume that all lawyers associated with the firm will inevitably conform to the Rules.

[4] Paragraph (c) expresses a general principle of personal responsibility for acts of another. See also Rule 8.4(a).

[5] Paragraph (c)(2) defines the duty of a partner or other lawyer having comparable managerial authority in a law firm, as well as a lawyer who has direct supervisory authority over performance of specific legal work by another lawyer. Whether a lawyer has supervisory authority in particular circumstances is a question of fact. Partners and lawyers with comparable authority have at least indirect responsibility for all work being done by the firm, while a partner or manager in charge of a particular matter ordinarily also has supervisory responsibility for the work of other firm lawyers engaged in the matter. Appropriate remedial action by a partner or managing lawyer would depend on the immediacy of that lawyer's involvement and the seriousness of

the misconduct. A supervisor is required to intervene to prevent avoidable consequences of misconduct if the supervisor knows that the misconduct occurred. Thus, if a supervising lawyer knows that a subordinate misrepresented a matter to an opposing party in negotiation, the supervisor as well as the subordinate has a duty to correct the resulting misapprehension.

[6] Professional misconduct by a lawyer under supervision could reveal a violation of paragraph (b) on the part of the supervisory lawyer even though it does not entail a violation of paragraph (c) because there was no direction, ratification or knowledge of the violation.

[7] Apart from this Rule and Rule 8.4(a), a lawyer does not have disciplinary liability for the conduct of a partner, associate or subordinate. Whether a lawyer may be liable civilly or criminally for another lawyer's conduct is a question of law beyond the scope of these Rules.

[8] The duties imposed by this Rule on managing and supervising lawyers do not alter the personal duty of each lawyer in a firm to abide by the Rules of Professional Conduct. See Rule 5.2(a).

RULE 5.2: RESPONSIBILITIES OF A SUBORDINATE LAWYER

(a) A lawyer is bound by the Rules of Professional Conduct notwithstanding that the lawyer acted at the direction of another person.

(b) A subordinate lawyer does not violate the Rules of Professional Conduct if that lawyer acts in accordance with a supervisory lawyer's reasonable resolution of an arguable question of professional duty.

Comment

[1] Although a lawyer is not relieved of responsibility for a violation by the fact that the lawyer acted at the direction of a supervisor, that fact may be relevant in determining whether a lawyer had the knowledge required to render conduct a violation of the Rules. For example, if a subordinate filed a frivolous pleading at the direction of a supervisor, the subordinate would not be guilty of a professional violation unless the subordinate knew of the document's frivolous character.

[2] When lawyers in a supervisor-subordinate relationship encounter a matter involving professional judgment as to ethical duty, the supervisor may assume responsibility for making the judgment. Otherwise a consistent course of action or position could not be taken. If the question can reasonably be answered only one way, the duty of both lawyers is clear and they are equally responsible for fulfilling it. However, if the question is reasonably arguable, someone has to decide upon the course of action. That authority ordinarily reposes in the supervisor, and a subordinate may be guided accordingly. For example, if a question arises whether the interests of two clients conflict under Rule 1.7, the supervisor's reasonable resolution of the question should

protect the subordinate professionally if the resolution is subsequently challenged.

RULE 5.3: RESPONSIBILITIES REGARDING NONLAWYER ASSISTANTS

With respect to a nonlawyer employed or retained by or associated with a lawyer:

(a) a partner, and a lawyer who individually or together with other lawyers possesses comparable managerial authority in a law firm shall make reasonable efforts to ensure that the firm has in effect measures giving reasonable assurance that the person's conduct is compatible with the professional obligations of the lawyer;

(b) a lawyer having direct supervisory authority over the nonlawyer shall make reasonable efforts to ensure that the person's conduct is compatible with the professional obligations of the lawyer; and

(c) a lawyer shall be responsible for conduct of such a person that would be a violation of the Rules of Professional Conduct if engaged in by a lawyer if:

(1) the lawyer orders or, with the knowledge of the specific conduct, ratifies the conduct involved; or

(2) the lawyer is a partner or has comparable managerial authority in the law firm in which the person is employed, or has direct supervisory authority over the person, and knows of the conduct at a time when its consequences can be avoided or mitigated but fails to take reasonable remedial action.

Comment

[1] Lawyers generally employ assistants in their practice, including secretaries, investigators, law student interns, and paraprofessionals. Such assistants, whether employees or independent contractors, act for the lawyer in rendition of the lawyer's professional services. A lawyer must give such assistants appropriate instruction and supervision concerning the ethical aspects of their employment, particularly regarding the obligation not to disclose information relating to representation of the client, and should be responsible for their work product. The measures employed in supervising nonlawyers should take account of the fact that they do not have legal training and are not subject to professional discipline.

[2] Paragraph (a) requires lawyers with managerial authority within a law firm to make reasonable efforts to establish internal policies and procedures designed to provide reasonable assurance that nonlawyers in the firm will act in a way compatible with the Rules of Professional Conduct. See Comment [1] to Rule 5.1. Paragraph (b) applies to lawyers who have supervisory authority over the work of a nonlawyer. Paragraph (c) specifies the

circumstances in which a lawyer is responsible for conduct of a nonlawyer that would be a violation of the Rules of Professional Conduct if engaged in by a lawyer.

RULE 5.4: PROFESSIONAL INDEPENDENCE OF A LAWYER

(a) A lawyer or law firm shall not share legal fees with a nonlawyer, except that:

(1) an agreement by a lawyer with the lawyer's firm, partner, or associate may provide for the payment of money, over a reasonable period of time after the lawyer's death, to the lawyer's estate or to one or more specified persons;

(2) a lawyer who purchases the practice of a deceased, disabled, or disappeared lawyer may, pursuant to the provisions of Rule 1.17, pay to the estate or other representative of that lawyer the agreed-upon purchase price;

(3) a lawyer or law firm may include nonlawyer employees in a compensation or retirement plan, even though the plan is based in whole or in part on a profit-sharing arrangement; and

(4) a lawyer may share court-awarded legal fees with a nonprofit organization that employed, retained or recommended employment of the lawyer in the matter.

(b) A lawyer shall not form a partnership with a nonlawyer if any of the activities of the partnership consist of the practice of law.

(c) A lawyer shall not permit a person who recommends, employs, or pays the lawyer to render legal services for another to direct or regulate the lawyer's professional judgment in rendering such legal services.

(d) A lawyer shall not practice with or in the form of a professional corporation or association authorized to practice law for a profit, if:

(1) a nonlawyer owns any interest therein, except that a fiduciary representative of the estate of a lawyer may hold the stock or interest of the lawyer for a reasonable time during administration;

(2) a nonlawyer is a corporate director or officer thereof or occupies the position of similar responsibility in any form of association other than a corporation; or

(3) a nonlawyer has the right to direct or control the professional judgment of a lawyer.

Comment

[1] The provisions of this Rule express traditional limitations on sharing fees. These limitations are to protect the lawyer's professional independence

of judgment. Where someone other than the client pays the lawyer's fee or salary, or recommends employment of the lawyer, that arrangement does not modify the lawyer's obligation to the client. As stated in paragraph (c), such arrangements should not interfere with the lawyer's professional judgment.

[2]   This Rule also expresses traditional limitations on permitting a third party to direct or regulate the lawyer's professional judgment in rendering legal services to another. See also Rule 1.8(f) (lawyer may accept compensation from a third party as long as there is no interference with the lawyer's independent professional judgment and the client gives informed consent).

RULE 5.5: UNAUTHORIZED PRACTICE
OF LAW; MULTIJURISDICTIONAL
PRACTICE OF LAW

(a) A lawyer shall not practice law in a jurisdiction in violation of the regulation of the legal profession in that jurisdiction, or assist another in doing so.

(b) A lawyer who is not admitted to practice in this jurisdiction shall not:

(1) except as authorized by these Rules or other law, establish an office or other systematic and continuous presence in this jurisdiction for the practice of law; or

(2) hold out to the public or otherwise represent that the lawyer is admitted to practice law in this jurisdiction.

(c) A lawyer admitted in another United States jurisdiction, and not disbarred or suspended from practice in any jurisdiction, may provide legal services on a temporary basis in this jurisdiction that:

(1) are undertaken in association with a lawyer who is admitted to practice in this jurisdiction and who actively participates in the matter;

(2) are in or reasonably related to a pending or potential proceeding before a tribunal in this or another jurisdiction, if the lawyer, or a person the lawyer is assisting, is authorized by law or order to appear in such proceeding or reasonably expects to be so authorized;

(3) are in or reasonably related to a pending or potential arbitration, mediation, or other alternative dispute resolution proceeding in this or another jurisdiction, if the services arise out of or are reasonably related to the lawyer's practice in a jurisdiction in which the lawyer is admitted to practice and are not services for which the forum requires pro hac vice admission; or

(4) are not within paragraphs (c)(2) or (c)(3) and arise out of or are reasonably related to the lawyer's practice in a jurisdiction in which the lawyer is admitted to practice.

(d) A lawyer admitted in another United States jurisdiction, and not disbarred or suspended from practice in any jurisdiction, may provide legal services in this jurisdiction that:

(1) are provided to the lawyer's employer or its organizational affiliates and are not services for which the forum requires pro hac vice admission; or

(2) are services that the lawyer is authorized by federal or other law to provide in this jurisdiction.

Comment

[1] A lawyer may practice law only in a jurisdiction in which the lawyer is authorized to practice. A lawyer may be admitted to practice law in a jurisdiction on a regular basis or may be authorized by court rule or order or by law to practice for a limited purpose or on a restricted basis. Paragraph (a) applies to unauthorized practice of law by a lawyer, whether through the lawyer's direct action or by the lawyer assisting another person.

[2] The definition of the practice of law is established by law and varies from one jurisdiction to another. Whatever the definition, limiting the practice of law to members of the bar protects the public against rendition of legal services by unqualified persons. This Rule does not prohibit a lawyer from employing the services of paraprofessionals and delegating functions to them, so long as the lawyer supervises the delegated work and retains responsibility for their work. See Rule 5.3.

[3] A lawyer may provide professional advice and instruction to nonlawyers whose employment requires knowledge of the law; for example, claims adjusters, employees of financial or commercial institutions, social workers, accountants and persons employed in government agencies. Lawyers also may assist independent nonlawyers, such as paraprofessionals, who are authorized by the law of a jurisdiction to provide particular law-related services. In addition, a lawyer may counsel nonlawyers who wish to proceed pro se.

[4] Other than as authorized by law or this Rule, a lawyer who is not admitted to practice generally in this jurisdiction violates paragraph (b) if the lawyer establishes an office or other systematic and continuous presence in this jurisdiction for the practice of law. Presence may be systematic and continuous even if the lawyer is not physically present here. Such a lawyer must not hold out to the public or otherwise represent that the lawyer is admitted to practice law in this jurisdiction. See also Rules 7.1(a) and 7.5(b).

[5] There are occasions in which a lawyer admitted to practice in another United States jurisdiction, and not disbarred or suspended from practice in any jurisdiction, may provide legal services on a temporary basis in this jurisdiction under circumstances that do not create an unreasonable risk

to the interests of their clients, the public or the courts. Paragraph (c) identifies four such circumstances. The fact that conduct is not so identified does not imply that the conduct is or is not authorized. With the exception of paragraphs (d)(1) and (d)(2), this Rule does not authorize a lawyer to establish an office or other systematic and continuous presence in this jurisdiction without being admitted to practice generally here.

[6]   There is no single test to determine whether a lawyer's services are provided on a "temporary basis" in this jurisdiction, and may therefore be permissible under paragraph (c). Services may be "temporary" even though the lawyer provides services in this jurisdiction on a recurring basis, or for an extended period of time, as when the lawyer is representing a client in a single lengthy negotiation or litigation.

[7]   Paragraphs (c) and (d) apply to lawyers who are admitted to practice law in any United States jurisdiction, which includes the District of Columbia and any state, territory or commonwealth of the United States. The word "admitted" in paragraph (c) contemplates that the lawyer is authorized to practice in the jurisdiction in which the lawyer is admitted and excludes a lawyer who while technically admitted is not authorized to practice, because, for example, the lawyer is on inactive status.

[8]   Paragraph (c)(1) recognizes that the interests of clients and the public are protected if a lawyer admitted only in another jurisdiction associates with a lawyer licensed to practice in this jurisdiction. For this paragraph to apply, however, the lawyer admitted to practice in this jurisdiction must actively participate in and share responsibility for the representation of the client.

[9]   Lawyers not admitted to practice generally in a jurisdiction may be authorized by law or order of a tribunal or an administrative agency to appear before the tribunal or agency. This authority may be granted pursuant to formal rules governing admission pro hac vice or pursuant to informal practice of the tribunal or agency. Under paragraph (c)(2), a lawyer does not violate this Rule when the lawyer appears before a tribunal or agency pursuant to such authority. To the extent that a court rule or other law of this jurisdiction requires a lawyer who is not admitted to practice in this jurisdiction to obtain admission pro hac vice before appearing before a tribunal or administrative agency, this Rule requires the lawyer to obtain that authority.

[10]   Paragraph (c)(2) also provides that a lawyer rendering services in this jurisdiction on a temporary basis does not violate this Rule when the lawyer engages in conduct in anticipation of a proceeding or hearing in a jurisdiction in which the lawyer is authorized to practice law or in which the lawyer reasonably expects to be admitted pro hac vice. Examples of such conduct include meetings with the client, interviews of potential witnesses, and the review of documents. Similarly, a lawyer admitted only in another jurisdiction may engage in conduct temporarily in this jurisdiction in connection with pending litigation in another jurisdiction in which the lawyer is or

reasonably expects to be authorized to appear, including taking depositions in this jurisdiction.

[11] When a lawyer has been or reasonably expects to be admitted to appear before a court or administrative agency, paragraph (c)(2) also permits conduct by lawyers who are associated with that lawyer in the matter, but who do not expect to appear before the court or administrative agency. For example, subordinate lawyers may conduct research, review documents, and attend meetings with witnesses in support of the lawyer responsible for the litigation.

[12] Paragraph (c)(3) permits a lawyer admitted to practice law in another jurisdiction to perform services on a temporary basis in this jurisdiction if those services are in or reasonably related to a pending or potential arbitration, mediation, or other alternative dispute resolution proceeding in this or another jurisdiction, if the services arise out of or are reasonably related to the lawyer's practice in a jurisdiction in which the lawyer is admitted to practice. The lawyer, however, must obtain admission pro hac vice in the case of a court-annexed arbitration or mediation or otherwise if court rules or law so require.

[13] Paragraph (c)(4) permits a lawyer admitted in another jurisdiction to provide certain legal services on a temporary basis in this jurisdiction that arise out of or are reasonably related to the lawyer's practice in a jurisdiction in which the lawyer is admitted but are not within paragraphs (c)(2) or (c)(3). These services include both legal services and services that nonlawyers may perform but that are considered the practice of law when performed by lawyers.

[14] Paragraphs (c)(3) and (c)(4) require that the services arise out of or be reasonably related to the lawyer's practice in a jurisdiction in which the lawyer is admitted. A variety of factors evidence such a relationship. The lawyer's client may have been previously represented by the lawyer, or may be resident in or have substantial contacts with the jurisdiction in which the lawyer is admitted. The matter, although involving other jurisdictions, may have a significant connection with that jurisdiction. In other cases, significant aspects of the lawyer's work might be conducted in that jurisdiction or a significant aspect of the matter may involve the law of that jurisdiction. The necessary relationship might arise when the client's activities or the legal issues involve multiple jurisdictions, such as when the officers of a multinational corporation survey potential business sites and seek the services of their lawyer in assessing the relative merits of each. In addition, the services may draw on the lawyer's recognized expertise developed through the regular practice of law on behalf of clients in matters involving a particular body of federal, nationally-uniform, foreign, or international law. Lawyers desiring to provide *pro bono* legal services on a temporary basis in a jurisdiction that has been affected by a major disaster, but in which they are not otherwise authorized to practice law, as well as lawyers from the affected jurisdiction who seek to practice law temporarily in another jurisdiction, but in which they are not otherwise authorized to practice law, should consult the [*Model*

Court Rule on Provision of Legal Services Following Determination of Major Disaster].

[15] Paragraph (d) identifies two circumstances in which a lawyer who is admitted to practice in another United States jurisdiction, and is not disbarred or suspended from practice in any jurisdiction, may establish an office or other systematic and continuous presence in this jurisdiction for the practice of law as well as provide legal services on a temporary basis. Except as provided in paragraphs (d)(1) and (d)(2), a lawyer who is admitted to practice law in another jurisdiction and who establishes an office or other systematic or continuous presence in this jurisdiction must become admitted to practice law generally in this jurisdiction.

[16] Paragraph (d)(1) applies to a lawyer who is employed by a client to provide legal services to the client or its organizational affiliates, i.e., entities that control, are controlled by, or are under common control with the employer. This paragraph does not authorize the provision of personal legal services to the employer's officers or employees. The paragraph applies to in-house corporate lawyers, government lawyers and others who are employed to render legal services to the employer. The lawyer's ability to represent the employer outside the jurisdiction in which the lawyer is licensed generally serves the interests of the employer and does not create an unreasonable risk to the client and others because the employer is well situated to assess the lawyer's qualifications and the quality of the lawyer's work.

[17] If an employed lawyer establishes an office or other systematic presence in this jurisdiction for the purpose of rendering legal services to the employer, the lawyer may be subject to registration or other requirements, including assessments for client protection funds and mandatory continuing legal education.

[18] Paragraph (d)(2) recognizes that a lawyer may provide legal services in a jurisdiction in which the lawyer is not licensed when authorized to do so by federal or other law, which includes statute, court rule, executive regulation or judicial precedent.

[19] A lawyer who practices law in this jurisdiction pursuant to paragraphs (c) or (d) or otherwise is subject to the disciplinary authority of this jurisdiction. See Rule 8.5(a).

[20] In some circumstances, a lawyer who practices law in this jurisdiction pursuant to paragraphs (c) or (d) may have to inform the client that the lawyer is not licensed to practice law in this jurisdiction. For example, that may be required when the representation occurs primarily in this jurisdiction and requires knowledge of the law of this jurisdiction. See Rule 1.4(b).

[21] Paragraphs (c) and (d) do not authorize communications advertising legal services to prospective clients in this jurisdiction by lawyers who are admitted to practice in other jurisdictions. Whether and how lawyers may communicate the availability of their services to prospective clients in this jurisdiction is governed by Rules 7.1 to 7.5.

RULE 5.6: RESTRICTIONS ON RIGHT TO PRACTICE

A lawyer shall not participate in offering or making:

(a) a partnership, shareholders, operating, employment, or other similar type of agreement that restricts the right of a lawyer to practice after termination of the relationship, except an agreement concerning benefits upon retirement; or

(b) an agreement in which a restriction on the lawyer's right to practice is part of the settlement of a client controversy.

Comment

[1] An agreement restricting the right of lawyers to practice after leaving a firm not only limits their professional autonomy but also limits the freedom of clients to choose a lawyer. Paragraph (a) prohibits such agreements except for restrictions incident to provisions concerning retirement benefits for service with the firm.

[2] Paragraph (b) prohibits a lawyer from agreeing not to represent other persons in connection with settling a claim on behalf of a client.

[3] This Rule does not apply to prohibit restrictions that may be included in the terms of the sale of a law practice pursuant to Rule 1.17.

RULE 5.7: RESPONSIBILITIES REGARDING LAW–RELATED SERVICES

(a) A lawyer shall be subject to the Rules of Professional Conduct with respect to the provision of law-related services, as defined in paragraph (b), if the law-related services are provided:

(1) by the lawyer in circumstances that are not distinct from the lawyer's provision of legal services to clients; or

(2) in other circumstances by an entity controlled by the lawyer individually or with others if the lawyer fails to take reasonable measures to assure that a person obtaining the law-related services knows that the services are not legal services and that the protections of the client-lawyer relationship do not exist.

(b) The term "law-related services" denotes services that might reasonably be performed in conjunction with and in substance are related to the provision of legal services, and that are not prohibited as unauthorized practice of law when provided by a nonlawyer.

Comment

[1] When a lawyer performs law-related services or controls an organization that does so, there exists the potential for ethical problems. Principal

among these is the possibility that the person for whom the law-related services are performed fails to understand that the services may not carry with them the protections normally afforded as part of the client-lawyer relationship. The recipient of the law-related services may expect, for example, that the protection of client confidences, prohibitions against representation of persons with conflicting interests, and obligations of a lawyer to maintain professional independence apply to the provision of law-related services when that may not be the case.

[2]   Rule 5.7 applies to the provision of law-related services by a lawyer even when the lawyer does not provide any legal services to the person for whom the law-related services are performed and whether the law-related services are performed through a law firm or a separate entity. The Rule identifies the circumstances in which all of the Rules of Professional Conduct apply to the provision of law-related services. Even when those circumstances do not exist, however, the conduct of a lawyer involved in the provision of law-related services is subject to those Rules that apply generally to lawyer conduct, regardless of whether the conduct involves the provision of legal services. See, e.g., Rule 8.4.

[3]   When law-related services are provided by a lawyer under circumstances that are not distinct from the lawyer's provision of legal services to clients, the lawyer in providing the law-related services must adhere to the requirements of the Rules of Professional Conduct as provided in paragraph (a)(1). Even when the law-related and legal services are provided in circumstances that are distinct from each other, for example through separate entities or different support staff within the law firm, the Rules of Professional Conduct apply to the lawyer as provided in paragraph (a)(2) unless the lawyer takes reasonable measures to assure that the recipient of the law-related services knows that the services are not legal services and that the protections of the client-lawyer relationship do not apply.

[4]   Law-related services also may be provided through an entity that is distinct from that through which the lawyer provides legal services. If the lawyer individually or with others has control of such an entity's operations, the Rule requires the lawyer to take reasonable measures to assure that each person using the services of the entity knows that the services provided by the entity are not legal services and that the Rules of Professional Conduct that relate to the client-lawyer relationship do not apply. A lawyer's control of an entity extends to the ability to direct its operation. Whether a lawyer has such control will depend upon the circumstances of the particular case.

[5]   When a client-lawyer relationship exists with a person who is referred by a lawyer to a separate law-related service entity controlled by the lawyer, individually or with others, the lawyer must comply with Rule 1.8(a).

[6]   In taking the reasonable measures referred to in paragraph (a)(2) to assure that a person using law-related services understands the practical effect or significance of the inapplicability of the Rules of Professional Conduct, the lawyer should communicate to the person receiving the law-related

services, in a manner sufficient to assure that the person understands the significance of the fact, that the relationship of the person to the business entity will not be a client-lawyer relationship. The communication should be made before entering into an agreement for provision of or providing law-related services, and preferably should be in writing.

[7] The burden is upon the lawyer to show that the lawyer has taken reasonable measures under the circumstances to communicate the desired understanding. For instance, a sophisticated user of law-related services, such as a publicly held corporation, may require a lesser explanation than someone unaccustomed to making distinctions between legal services and law-related services, such as an individual seeking tax advice from a lawyer-accountant or investigative services in connection with a lawsuit.

[8] Regardless of the sophistication of potential recipients of law-related services, a lawyer should take special care to keep separate the provision of law-related and legal services in order to minimize the risk that the recipient will assume that the law-related services are legal services. The risk of such confusion is especially acute when the lawyer renders both types of services with respect to the same matter. Under some circumstances the legal and law-related services may be so closely entwined that they cannot be distinguished from each other, and the requirement of disclosure and consultation imposed by paragraph (a)(2) of the Rule cannot be met. In such a case a lawyer will be responsible for assuring that both the lawyer's conduct and, to the extent required by Rule 5.3, that of nonlawyer employees in the distinct entity that the lawyer controls complies in all respects with the Rules of Professional Conduct.

[9] A broad range of economic and other interests of clients may be served by lawyers' engaging in the delivery of law-related services. Examples of law-related services include providing title insurance, financial planning, accounting, trust services, real estate counseling, legislative lobbying, economic analysis, social work, psychological counseling, tax preparation, and patent, medical or environmental consulting.

[10] When a lawyer is obliged to accord the recipients of such services the protections of those Rules that apply to the client-lawyer relationship, the lawyer must take special care to heed the proscriptions of the Rules addressing conflict of interest (Rules 1.7 through 1.11, especially Rules 1.7(a)(2) and 1.8(a), (b) and (f)), and to scrupulously adhere to the requirements of Rule 1.6 relating to disclosure of confidential information. The promotion of the law-related services must also in all respects comply with Rules 7.1 through 7.3, dealing with advertising and solicitation. In that regard, lawyers should take special care to identify the obligations that may be imposed as a result of a jurisdiction's decisional law.

[11] When the full protections of all of the Rules of Professional Conduct do not apply to the provision of law-related services, principles of law external to the Rules, for example, the law of principal and agent, govern the legal duties owed to those receiving the services. Those other legal principles

may establish a different degree of protection for the recipient with respect to confidentiality of information, conflicts of interest and permissible business relationships with clients. See also Rule 8.4 (Misconduct).

PUBLIC SERVICE

RULE 6.1: VOLUNTARY PRO BONO PUBLICO SERVICE

Every lawyer has a professional responsibility to provide legal services to those unable to pay. A lawyer should aspire to render at least (50) hours of pro bono publico legal services per year. In fulfilling this responsibility, the lawyer should:

(a) provide a substantial majority of the (50) hours of legal services without fee or expectation of fee to:

(1) persons of limited means or

(2) charitable, religious, civic, community, governmental and educational organizations in matters that are designed primarily to address the needs of persons of limited means; and

(b) provide any additional services through:

(1) delivery of legal services at no fee or substantially reduced fee to individuals, groups or organizations seeking to secure or protect civil rights, civil liberties or public rights, or charitable, religious, civic, community, governmental and educational organizations in matters in furtherance of their organizational purposes, where the payment of standard legal fees would significantly deplete the organization's economic resources or would be otherwise inappropriate;

(2) delivery of legal services at a substantially reduced fee to persons of limited means; or

(3) participation in activities for improving the law, the legal system or the legal profession.

In addition, a lawyer should voluntarily contribute financial support to organizations that provide legal services to persons of limited means.

Comment

[1] Every lawyer, regardless of professional prominence or professional work load, has a responsibility to provide legal services to those unable to pay, and personal involvement in the problems of the disadvantaged can be one of the most rewarding experiences in the life of a lawyer. The American Bar Association urges all lawyers to provide a minimum of 50 hours of pro bono services annually. States, however, may decide to choose a higher or lower number of hours of annual service (which may be expressed as a percentage of a lawyer's professional time) depending upon local needs and local conditions.

It is recognized that in some years a lawyer may render greater or fewer hours than the annual standard specified, but during the course of his or her legal career, each lawyer should render on average per year, the number of hours set forth in this Rule. Services can be performed in civil matters or in criminal or quasi-criminal matters for which there is no government obligation to provide funds for legal representation, such as post-conviction death penalty appeal cases.

[2]   Paragraphs (a)(1) and (2) recognize the critical need for legal services that exists among persons of limited means by providing that a substantial majority of the legal services rendered annually to the disadvantaged be furnished without fee or expectation of fee. Legal services under these paragraphs consist of a full range of activities, including individual and class representation, the provision of legal advice, legislative lobbying, administrative rule making and the provision of free training or mentoring to those who represent persons of limited means. The variety of these activities should facilitate participation by government lawyers, even when restrictions exist on their engaging in the outside practice of law.

[3]   Persons eligible for legal services under paragraphs (a)(1) and (2) are those who qualify for participation in programs funded by the Legal Services Corporation and those whose incomes and financial resources are slightly above the guidelines utilized by such programs but nevertheless, cannot afford counsel. Legal services can be rendered to individuals or to organizations such as homeless shelters, battered women's centers and food pantries that serve those of limited means. The term "governmental organizations" includes, but is not limited to, public protection programs and sections of governmental or public sector agencies.

[4]   Because service must be provided without fee or expectation of fee, the intent of the lawyer to render free legal services is essential for the work performed to fall within the meaning of paragraphs (a)(1) and (2). Accordingly, services rendered cannot be considered pro bono if an anticipated fee is uncollected, but the award of statutory attorneys' fees in a case originally accepted as pro bono would not disqualify such services from inclusion under this section. Lawyers who do receive fees in such cases are encouraged to contribute an appropriate portion of such fees to organizations or projects that benefit persons of limited means.

[5]   While it is possible for a lawyer to fulfill the annual responsibility to perform pro bono services exclusively through activities described in paragraphs (a)(1) and (2), to the extent that any hours of service remained unfulfilled, the remaining commitment can be met in a variety of ways as set forth in paragraph (b). Constitutional, statutory or regulatory restrictions may prohibit or impede government and public sector lawyers and judges from performing the pro bono services outlined in paragraphs (a)(1) and (2). Accordingly, where those restrictions apply, government and public sector lawyers and judges may fulfill their pro bono responsibility by performing services outlined in paragraph (b).

[6] Paragraph (b)(1) includes the provision of certain types of legal services to those whose incomes and financial resources place them above limited means. It also permits the pro bono lawyer to accept a substantially reduced fee for services. Examples of the types of issues that may be addressed under this paragraph include First Amendment claims, Title VII claims and environmental protection claims. Additionally, a wide range of organizations may be represented, including social service, medical research, cultural and religious groups.

[7] Paragraph (b)(2) covers instances in which lawyers agree to and receive a modest fee for furnishing legal services to persons of limited means. Participation in judicare programs and acceptance of court appointments in which the fee is substantially below a lawyer's usual rate are encouraged under this section.

[8] Paragraph (b)(3) recognizes the value of lawyers engaging in activities that improve the law, the legal system or the legal profession. Serving on bar association committees, serving on boards of pro bono or legal services programs, taking part in Law Day activities, acting as a continuing legal education instructor, a mediator or an arbitrator and engaging in legislative lobbying to improve the law, the legal system or the profession are a few examples of the many activities that fall within this paragraph.

[9] Because the provision of pro bono services is a professional responsibility, it is the individual ethical commitment of each lawyer. Nevertheless, there may be times when it is not feasible for a lawyer to engage in pro bono services. At such times a lawyer may discharge the pro bono responsibility by providing financial support to organizations providing free legal services to persons of limited means. Such financial support should be reasonably equivalent to the value of the hours of service that would have otherwise been provided. In addition, at times it may be more feasible to satisfy the pro bono responsibility collectively, as by a firm's aggregate pro bono activities.

[10] Because the efforts of individual lawyers are not enough to meet the need for free legal services that exists among persons of limited means, the government and the profession have instituted additional programs to provide those services. Every lawyer should financially support such programs, in addition to either providing direct pro bono services or making financial contributions when pro bono service is not feasible.

[11] Law firms should act reasonably to enable and encourage all lawyers in the firm to provide the pro bono legal services called for by this Rule.

[12] The responsibility set forth in this Rule is not intended to be enforced through disciplinary process.

RULE 6.2: ACCEPTING APPOINTMENTS

A lawyer shall not seek to avoid appointment by a tribunal to represent a person except for good cause, such as:

(a) representing the client is likely to result in violation of the Rules of Professional Conduct or other law;

(b) representing the client is likely to result in an unreasonable financial burden on the lawyer; or

(c) the client or the cause is so repugnant to the lawyer as to be likely to impair the client-lawyer relationship or the lawyer's ability to represent the client.

Comment

[1] A lawyer ordinarily is not obliged to accept a client whose character or cause the lawyer regards as repugnant. The lawyer's freedom to select clients is, however, qualified. All lawyers have a responsibility to assist in providing pro bono publico service. See Rule 6.1. An individual lawyer fulfills this responsibility by accepting a fair share of unpopular matters or indigent or unpopular clients. A lawyer may also be subject to appointment by a court to serve unpopular clients or persons unable to afford legal services.

Appointed Counsel

[2] For good cause a lawyer may seek to decline an appointment to represent a person who cannot afford to retain counsel or whose cause is unpopular. Good cause exists if the lawyer could not handle the matter competently, see Rule 1.1, or if undertaking the representation would result in an improper conflict of interest, for example, when the client or the cause is so repugnant to the lawyer as to be likely to impair the client-lawyer relationship or the lawyer's ability to represent the client. A lawyer may also seek to decline an appointment if acceptance would be unreasonably burdensome, for example, when it would impose a financial sacrifice so great as to be unjust.

[3] An appointed lawyer has the same obligations to the client as retained counsel, including the obligations of loyalty and confidentiality, and is subject to the same limitations on the client-lawyer relationship, such as the obligation to refrain from assisting the client in violation of the Rules.

RULE 6.3: MEMBERSHIP IN LEGAL SERVICES ORGANIZATION

A lawyer may serve as a director, officer or member of a legal services organization, apart from the law firm in which the lawyer practices, notwithstanding that the organization serves persons having interests adverse to a client of the lawyer. The lawyer shall not knowingly participate in a decision or action of the organization:

(a) if participating in the decision or action would be incompatible with the lawyer's obligations to a client under Rule 1.7; or

(b) where the decision or action could have a material adverse effect on the representation of a client of the organization whose interests are adverse to a client of the lawyer.

Comment

[1] Lawyers should be encouraged to support and participate in legal service organizations. A lawyer who is an officer or a member of such an organization does not thereby have a client-lawyer relationship with persons served by the organization. However, there is potential conflict between the interests of such persons and the interests of the lawyer's clients. If the possibility of such conflict disqualified a lawyer from serving on the board of a legal services organization, the profession's involvement in such organizations would be severely curtailed.

[2] It may be necessary in appropriate cases to reassure a client of the organization that the representation will not be affected by conflicting loyalties of a member of the board. Established, written policies in this respect can enhance the credibility of such assurances.

RULE 6.4: LAW REFORM ACTIVITIES AFFECTING CLIENT INTERESTS

A lawyer may serve as a director, officer or member of an organization involved in reform of the law or its administration notwithstanding that the reform may affect the interests of a client of the lawyer. When the lawyer knows that the interests of a client may be materially benefitted by a decision in which the lawyer participates, the lawyer shall disclose that fact but need not identify the client.

Comment

[1] Lawyers involved in organizations seeking law reform generally do not have a client-lawyer relationship with the organization. Otherwise, it might follow that a lawyer could not be involved in a bar association law reform program that might indirectly affect a client. See also Rule 1.2(b). For example, a lawyer specializing in antitrust litigation might be regarded as disqualified from participating in drafting revisions of rules governing that subject. In determining the nature and scope of participation in such activities, a lawyer should be mindful of obligations to clients under other Rules, particularly Rule 1.7. A lawyer is professionally obligated to protect the integrity of the program by making an appropriate disclosure within the organization when the lawyer knows a private client might be materially benefitted.

RULE 6.5: NONPROFIT AND COURT–ANNEXED LIMITED LEGAL SERVICES PROGRAMS

(a) A lawyer who, under the auspices of a program sponsored by a nonprofit organization or court, provides short-term limited legal services to a client without expectation by either the lawyer or the client that the lawyer will provide continuing representation in the matter:

(1) is subject to Rules 1.7 and 1.9(a) only if the lawyer knows that the representation of the client involves a conflict of interest; and

(2) is subject to Rule 1.10 only if the lawyer knows that another lawyer associated with the lawyer in a law firm is disqualified by Rule 1.7 or 1.9(a) with respect to the matter.

(b) Except as provided in paragraph (a)(2), Rule 1.10 is inapplicable to a representation governed by this Rule.

Comment

[1] Legal services organizations, courts and various nonprofit organizations have established programs through which lawyers provide short-term limited legal services—such as advice or the completion of legal forms—that will assist persons to address their legal problems without further representation by a lawyer. In these programs, such as legal-advice hotlines, advice-only clinics or pro se counseling programs, a client-lawyer relationship is established, but there is no expectation that the lawyer's representation of the client will continue beyond the limited consultation. Such programs are normally operated under circumstances in which it is not feasible for a lawyer to systematically screen for conflicts of interest as is generally required before undertaking a representation. See, e.g., Rules 1.7, 1.9 and 1.10.

[2] A lawyer who provides short-term limited legal services pursuant to this Rule must secure the client's informed consent to the limited scope of the representation. See Rule 1.2(c). If a short-term limited representation would not be reasonable under the circumstances, the lawyer may offer advice to the client but must also advise the client of the need for further assistance of counsel. Except as provided in this Rule, the Rules of Professional Conduct, including Rules 1.6 and 1.9(c), are applicable to the limited representation.

[3] Because a lawyer who is representing a client in the circumstances addressed by this Rule ordinarily is not able to check systematically for conflicts of interest, paragraph (a) requires compliance with Rules 1.7 or 1.9(a) only if the lawyer knows that the representation presents a conflict of interest for the lawyer, and with Rule 1.10 only if the lawyer knows that another lawyer in the lawyer's firm is disqualified by Rules 1.7 or 1.9(a) in the matter.

[4] Because the limited nature of the services significantly reduces the risk of conflicts of interest with other matters being handled by the lawyer's firm, paragraph (b) provides that Rule 1.10 is inapplicable to a representation governed by this Rule except as provided by paragraph (a)(2). Paragraph (a)(2) requires the participating lawyer to comply with Rule 1.10 when the lawyer knows that the lawyer's firm is disqualified by Rules 1.7 or 1.9(a). By virtue of paragraph (b), however, a lawyer's participation in a short-term limited legal services program will not preclude the lawyer's firm from undertaking or continuing the representation of a client with interests adverse to a client being represented under the program's auspices. Nor will the

117

personal disqualification of a lawyer participating in the program be imputed to other lawyers participating in the program.

[5] If, after commencing a short-term limited representation in accordance with this Rule, a lawyer undertakes to represent the client in the matter on an ongoing basis, Rules 1.7, 1.9(a) and 1.10 become applicable.

INFORMATION ABOUT LEGAL SERVICES

RULE 7.1: COMMUNICATIONS CONCERNING A LAWYER'S SERVICES

A lawyer shall not make a false or misleading communication about the lawyer or the lawyer's services. A communication is false or misleading if it contains a material misrepresentation of fact or law, or omits a fact necessary to make the statement considered as a whole not materially misleading.

Comment

[1] This Rule governs all communications about a lawyer's services, including advertising permitted by Rule 7.2. Whatever means are used to make known a lawyer's services, statements about them must be truthful.

[2] Truthful statements that are misleading are also prohibited by this Rule. A truthful statement is misleading if it omits a fact necessary to make the lawyer's communication considered as a whole not materially misleading. A truthful statement is also misleading if there is a substantial likelihood that it will lead a reasonable person to formulate a specific conclusion about the lawyer or the lawyer's services for which there is no reasonable factual foundation.

[3] An advertisement that truthfully reports a lawyer's achievements on behalf of clients or former clients may be misleading if presented so as to lead a reasonable person to form an unjustified expectation that the same results could be obtained for other clients in similar matters without reference to the specific factual and legal circumstances of each client's case. Similarly, an unsubstantiated comparison of the lawyer's services or fees with the services or fees of other lawyers may be misleading if presented with such specificity as would lead a reasonable person to conclude that the comparison can be substantiated. The inclusion of an appropriate disclaimer or qualifying language may preclude a finding that a statement is likely to create unjustified expectations or otherwise mislead a prospective client.

[4] See also Rule 8.4(e) for the prohibition against stating or implying an ability to influence improperly a government agency or official or to achieve results by means that violate the Rules of Professional Conduct or other law.

RULE 7.2: ADVERTISING

(a) Subject to the requirements of Rules 7.1 and 7.3, a lawyer may advertise services through written, recorded or electronic communication, including public media.

(b) A lawyer shall not give anything of value to a person for recommending the lawyer's services except that a lawyer may

(1) pay the reasonable costs of advertisements or communications permitted by this Rule;

(2) pay the usual charges of a legal service plan or a not-for-profit or qualified lawyer referral service. A qualified lawyer referral service is a lawyer referral service that has been approved by an appropriate regulatory authority;

(3) pay for a law practice in accordance with Rule 1.17; and

(4) refer clients to another lawyer or a nonlawyer professional pursuant to an agreement not otherwise prohibited under these Rules that provides for the other person to refer clients or customers to the lawyer, if

(i) the reciprocal referral agreement is not exclusive, and

(ii) the client is informed of the existence and nature of the agreement.

(c) Any communication made pursuant to this rule shall include the name and office address of at least one lawyer or law firm responsible for its content.

Comment

[1] To assist the public in obtaining legal services, lawyers should be allowed to make known their services not only through reputation but also through organized information campaigns in the form of advertising. Advertising involves an active quest for clients, contrary to the tradition that a lawyer should not seek clientele. However, the public's need to know about legal services can be fulfilled in part through advertising. This need is particularly acute in the case of persons of moderate means who have not made extensive use of legal services. The interest in expanding public information about legal services ought to prevail over considerations of tradition. Nevertheless, advertising by lawyers entails the risk of practices that are misleading or overreaching.

[2] This Rule permits public dissemination of information concerning a lawyer's name or firm name, address and telephone number; the kinds of services the lawyer will undertake; the basis on which the lawyer's fees are determined, including prices for specific services and payment and credit arrangements; a lawyer's foreign language ability; names of references and,

with their consent, names of clients regularly represented; and other information that might invite the attention of those seeking legal assistance.

[3] Questions of effectiveness and taste in advertising are matters of speculation and subjective judgment. Some jurisdictions have had extensive prohibitions against television advertising, against advertising going beyond specified facts about a lawyer, or against "undignified" advertising. Television is now one of the most powerful media for getting information to the public, particularly persons of low and moderate income; prohibiting television advertising, therefore, would impede the flow of information about legal services to many sectors of the public. Limiting the information that may be advertised has a similar effect and assumes that the bar can accurately forecast the kind of information that the public would regard as relevant. Similarly, electronic media, such as the Internet, can be an important source of information about legal services, and lawful communication by electronic mail is permitted by this Rule. But see Rule 7.3(a) for the prohibition against the solicitation of a prospective client through a real-time electronic exchange that is not initiated by the prospective client.

[4] Neither this Rule nor Rule 7.3 prohibits communications authorized by law, such as notice to members of a class in class action litigation.

Paying Others to Recommend a Lawyer

[5] Lawyers are not permitted to pay others for channeling professional work. Paragraph (b)(1), however, allows a lawyer to pay for advertising and communications permitted by this Rule, including the costs of print directory listings, on-line directory listings, newspaper ads, television and radio airtime, domain-name registrations, sponsorship fees, banner ads, and group advertising. A lawyer may compensate employees, agents and vendors who are engaged to provide marketing or client-development services, such as publicists, public-relations personnel, business-development staff and website designers. See Rule 5.3 for the duties of lawyers and law firms with respect to the conduct of nonlawyers who prepare marketing materials for them.

[6] A lawyer may pay the usual charges of a legal service plan or a not-for-profit or qualified lawyer referral service. A legal service plan is a prepaid or group legal service plan or a similar delivery system that assists prospective clients to secure legal representation. A lawyer referral service, on the other hand, is any organization that holds itself out to the public as a lawyer referral service. Such referral services are understood by laypersons to be consumer-oriented organizations that provide unbiased referrals to lawyers with appropriate experience in the subject matter of the representation and afford other client protections, such as complaint procedures or malpractice insurance requirements. Consequently, this Rule only permits a lawyer to pay the usual charges of a not-for-profit or qualified lawyer referral service. A qualified lawyer referral service is one that is approved by an appropriate regulatory authority as affording adequate protections for prospective clients. See, e.g., the American Bar Association's Model Supreme Court Rules Governing Lawyer Referral Services and Model Lawyer Referral and Information

Service Quality Assurance Act (requiring that organizations that are identified as lawyer referral services (i) permit the participation of all lawyers who are licensed and eligible to practice in the jurisdiction and who meet reasonable objective eligibility requirements as may be established by the referral service for the protection of prospective clients; (ii) require each participating lawyer to carry reasonably adequate malpractice insurance; (iii) act reasonably to assess client satisfaction and address client complaints; and (iv) do not refer prospective clients to lawyers who own, operate or are employed by the referral service.)

[7]   A lawyer who accepts assignments or referrals from a legal service plan or referrals from a lawyer referral service must act reasonably to assure that the activities of the plan or service are compatible with the lawyer's professional obligations. See Rule 5.3. Legal service plans and lawyer referral services may communicate with prospective clients, but such communication must be in conformity with these Rules. Thus, advertising must not be false or misleading, as would be the case if the communications of a group advertising program or a group legal services plan would mislead prospective clients to think that it was a lawyer referral service sponsored by a state agency or bar association. Nor could the lawyer allow in-person, telephonic, or real-time contacts that would violate Rule 7.3.

[8]   A lawyer also may agree to refer clients to another lawyer or a nonlawyer professional, in return for the undertaking of that person to refer clients or customers to the lawyer. Such reciprocal referral arrangements must not interfere with the lawyer's professional judgment as to making referrals or as to providing substantive legal services. See Rules 2.1 and 5.4(c). Except as provided in Rule 1.5(e), a lawyer who receives referrals from a lawyer or nonlawyer professional must not pay anything solely for the referral, but the lawyer does not violate paragraph (b) of this Rule by agreeing to refer clients to the other lawyer or nonlawyer professional, so long as the reciprocal referral agreement is not exclusive and the client is informed of the referral agreement. Conflicts of interest created by such arrangements are governed by Rule 1.7. Reciprocal referral agreements should not be of indefinite duration and should be reviewed periodically to determine whether they comply with these Rules. This Rule does not restrict referrals or divisions of revenues or net income among lawyers within firms comprised of multiple entities.

RULE 7.3: DIRECT CONTACT WITH PROSPECTIVE CLIENTS

(a) A lawyer shall not by in-person, live telephone or real-time electronic contact solicit professional employment from a prospective client when a significant motive for the lawyer's doing so is the lawyer's pecuniary gain, unless the person contacted:

(1) is a lawyer; or

(2) has a family, close personal, or prior professional relationship with the lawyer.

(b) A lawyer shall not solicit professional employment from a prospective client by written, recorded or electronic communication or by in-person, telephone or real-time electronic contact even when not otherwise prohibited by paragraph (a), if:

> **(1)** the prospective client has made known to the lawyer a desire not to be solicited by the lawyer; or

> **(2)** the solicitation involves coercion, duress or harassment.

(c) Every written, recorded or electronic communication from a lawyer soliciting professional employment from a prospective client known to be in need of legal services in a particular matter shall include the words "Advertising Material" on the outside envelope, if any, and at the beginning and ending of any recorded or electronic communication, unless the recipient of the communication is a person specified in paragraphs (a)(1) or (a)(2).

(d) Notwithstanding the prohibitions in paragraph (a), a lawyer may participate with a prepaid or group legal service plan operated by an organization not owned or directed by the lawyer that uses in-person or telephone contact to solicit memberships or subscriptions for the plan from persons who are not known to need legal services in a particular matter covered by the plan.

Comment

[1] There is a potential for abuse inherent in direct in-person, live telephone or real-time electronic contact by a lawyer with a prospective client known to need legal services. These forms of contact between a lawyer and a prospective client subject the layperson to the private importuning of the trained advocate in a direct interpersonal encounter. The prospective client, who may already feel overwhelmed by the circumstances giving rise to the need for legal services, may find it difficult fully to evaluate all available alternatives with reasoned judgment and appropriate self-interest in the face of the lawyer's presence and insistence upon being retained immediately. The situation is fraught with the possibility of undue influence, intimidation, and over-reaching.

[2] This potential for abuse inherent in direct in-person, live telephone or real-time electronic solicitation of prospective clients justifies its prohibition, particularly since lawyer advertising and written and recorded communication permitted under Rule 7.2 offer alternative means of conveying necessary information to those who may be in need of legal services. Advertising and written and recorded communications which may be mailed or autodialed make it possible for a prospective client to be informed about the need for legal services, and about the qualifications of available lawyers and law firms, without subjecting the prospective client to direct in-person, telephone or real-time electronic persuasion that may overwhelm the client's judgment.

[3] The use of general advertising and written, recorded or electronic communications to transmit information from lawyer to prospective client,

rather than direct in-person, live telephone or real-time electronic contact, will help to assure that the information flows cleanly as well as freely. The contents of advertisements and communications permitted under Rule 7.2 can be permanently recorded so that they cannot be disputed and may be shared with others who know the lawyer. This potential for informal review is itself likely to help guard against statements and claims that might constitute false and misleading communications, in violation of Rule 7.1. The contents of direct in-person, live telephone or real-time electronic conversations between a lawyer and a prospective client can be disputed and may not be subject to third-party scrutiny. Consequently, they are much more likely to approach (and occasionally cross) the dividing line between accurate representations and those that are false and misleading.

[4] There is far less likelihood that a lawyer would engage in abusive practices against an individual who is a former client, or with whom the lawyer has a close personal or family relationship, or in situations in which the lawyer is motivated by considerations other than the lawyer's pecuniary gain. Nor is there a serious potential for abuse when the person contacted is a lawyer. Consequently, the general prohibition in Rule 7.3(a) and the requirements of Rule 7.3(c) are not applicable in those situations. Also, paragraph (a) is not intended to prohibit a lawyer from participating in constitutionally protected activities of public or charitable legal-service organizations or bona fide political, social, civic, fraternal, employee or trade organizations whose purposes include providing or recommending legal services to its members or beneficiaries.

[5] But even permitted forms of solicitation can be abused. Thus, any solicitation which contains information which is false or misleading within the meaning of Rule 7.1, which involves coercion, duress or harassment within the meaning of Rule 7.3(b)(2), or which involves contact with a prospective client who has made known to the lawyer a desire not to be solicited by the lawyer within the meaning of Rule 7.3(b)(1) is prohibited. Moreover, if after sending a letter or other communication to a client as permitted by Rule 7.2 the lawyer receives no response, any further effort to communicate with the prospective client may violate the provisions of Rule 7.3(b).

[6] This Rule is not intended to prohibit a lawyer from contacting representatives of organizations or groups that may be interested in establishing a group or prepaid legal plan for their members, insureds, beneficiaries or other third parties for the purpose of informing such entities of the availability of and details concerning the plan or arrangement which the lawyer or lawyer's firm is willing to offer. This form of communication is not directed to a prospective client. Rather, it is usually addressed to an individual acting in a fiduciary capacity seeking a supplier of legal services for others who may, if they choose, become prospective clients of the lawyer. Under these circumstances, the activity which the lawyer undertakes in communicating with such representatives and the type of information transmitted to the individual are functionally similar to and serve the same purpose as advertising permitted under Rule 7.2.

[7] The requirement in Rule 7.3(c) that certain communications be marked "Advertising Material" does not apply to communications sent in response to requests of potential clients or their spokespersons or sponsors. General announcements by lawyers, including changes in personnel or office location, do not constitute communications soliciting professional employment from a client known to be in need of legal services within the meaning of this Rule.

[8] Paragraph (d) of this Rule permits a lawyer to participate with an organization which uses personal contact to solicit members for its group or prepaid legal service plan, provided that the personal contact is not undertaken by any lawyer who would be a provider of legal services through the plan. The organization must not be owned by or directed (whether as manager or otherwise) by any lawyer or law firm that participates in the plan. For example, paragraph (d) would not permit a lawyer to create an organization controlled directly or indirectly by the lawyer and use the organization for the in-person or telephone solicitation of legal employment of the lawyer through memberships in the plan or otherwise. The communication permitted by these organizations also must not be directed to a person known to need legal services in a particular matter, but is to be designed to inform potential plan members generally of another means of affordable legal services. Lawyers who participate in a legal service plan must reasonably assure that the plan sponsors are in compliance with Rules 7.1, 7.2 and 7.3(b). See 8.4(a).

RULE 7.4: COMMUNICATION OF FIELDS OF PRACTICE AND SPECIALIZATION

(a) A lawyer may communicate the fact that the lawyer does or does not practice in particular fields of law.

(b) A lawyer admitted to engage in patent practice before the United States Patent and Trademark Office may use the designation "Patent Attorney" or a substantially similar designation.

(c) A lawyer engaged in Admiralty practice may use the designation "Admiralty," "Proctor in Admiralty" or a substantially similar designation.

(d) A lawyer shall not state or imply that a lawyer is certified as a specialist in a particular field of law, unless:

(1) the lawyer has been certified as a specialist by an organization that has been approved by an appropriate state authority or that has been accredited by the American Bar Association; and

(2) the name of the certifying organization is clearly identified in the communication.

Comment

[1] Paragraph (a) of this Rule permits a lawyer to indicate areas of practice in communications about the lawyer's services. If a lawyer practices

only in certain fields, or will not accept matters except in a specified field or fields, the lawyer is permitted to so indicate. A lawyer is generally permitted to state that the lawyer is a "specialist," practices a "specialty," or "specializes in" particular fields, but such communications are subject to the "false and misleading" standard applied in Rule 7.1 to communications concerning a lawyer's services.

[2]   Paragraph (b) recognizes the long-established policy of the Patent and Trademark Office for the designation of lawyers practicing before the Office. Paragraph (c) recognizes that designation of Admiralty practice has a long historical tradition associated with maritime commerce and the federal courts.

[3]   Paragraph (d) permits a lawyer to state that the lawyer is certified as a specialist in a field of law if such certification is granted by an organization approved by an appropriate state authority or accredited by the American Bar Association or another organization, such as a state bar association, that has been approved by the state authority to accredit organizations that certify lawyers as specialists. Certification signifies that an objective entity has recognized an advanced degree of knowledge and experience in the specialty area greater than is suggested by general licensure to practice law. Certifying organizations may be expected to apply standards of experience, knowledge and proficiency to insure that a lawyer's recognition as a specialist is meaningful and reliable. In order to insure that consumers can obtain access to useful information about an organization granting certification, the name of the certifying organization must be included in any communication regarding the certification.

RULE 7.5: FIRM NAMES AND LETTERHEADS

(a) A lawyer shall not use a firm name, letterhead or other professional designation that violates Rule 7.1. A trade name may be used by a lawyer in private practice if it does not imply a connection with a government agency or with a public or charitable legal services organization and is not otherwise in violation of Rule 7.1.

(b) A law firm with offices in more than one jurisdiction may use the same name or other professional designation in each jurisdiction, but identification of the lawyers in an office of the firm shall indicate the jurisdictional limitations on those not licensed to practice in the jurisdiction where the office is located.

(c) The name of a lawyer holding a public office shall not be used in the name of a law firm, or in communications on its behalf, during any substantial period in which the lawyer is not actively and regularly practicing with the firm.

(d) Lawyers may state or imply that they practice in a partnership or other organization only when that is the fact.

Comment

[1]   A firm may be designated by the names of all or some of its members, by the names of deceased members where there has been a continuing succession in the firm's identity or by a trade name such as the "ABC Legal Clinic." A lawyer or law firm may also be designated by a distinctive website address or comparable professional designation. Although the United States Supreme Court has held that legislation may prohibit the use of trade names in professional practice, use of such names in law practice is acceptable so long as it is not misleading. If a private firm uses a trade name that includes a geographical name such as "Springfield Legal Clinic," an express disclaimer that it is a public legal aid agency may be required to avoid a misleading implication. It may be observed that any firm name including the name of a deceased partner is, strictly speaking, a trade name. The use of such names to designate law firms has proven a useful means of identification. However, it is misleading to use the name of a lawyer not associated with the firm or a predecessor of the firm, or the name of a nonlawyer.

[2]   With regard to paragraph (d), lawyers sharing office facilities, but who are not in fact associated with each other in a law firm, may not denominate themselves as, for example, "Smith and Jones," for that title suggests that they are practicing law together in a firm.

RULE 7.6: POLITICAL CONTRIBUTIONS TO OBTAIN GOVERNMENT LEGAL ENGAGEMENTS OR APPOINTMENTS BY JUDGES

A lawyer or law firm shall not accept a government legal engagement or an appointment by a judge if the lawyer or law firm makes a political contribution or solicits political contributions for the purpose of obtaining or being considered for that type of legal engagement or appointment.

Comment

[1]   Lawyers have a right to participate fully in the political process, which includes making and soliciting political contributions to candidates for judicial and other public office. Nevertheless, when lawyers make or solicit political contributions in order to obtain an engagement for legal work awarded by a government agency, or to obtain appointment by a judge, the public may legitimately question whether the lawyers engaged to perform the work are selected on the basis of competence and merit. In such a circumstance, the integrity of the profession is undermined.

[2]   The term "political contribution" denotes any gift, subscription, loan, advance or deposit of anything of value made directly or indirectly to a candidate, incumbent, political party or campaign committee to influence or provide financial support for election to or retention in judicial or other government office. Political contributions in initiative and referendum elec-

tions are not included. For purposes of this Rule, the term "political contribution" does not include uncompensated services.

[3] Subject to the exceptions below, (i) the term "government legal engagement" denotes any engagement to provide legal services that a public official has the direct or indirect power to award; and (ii) the term "appointment by a judge" denotes an appointment to a position such as referee, commissioner, special master, receiver, guardian or other similar position that is made by a judge. Those terms do not, however, include (a) substantially uncompensated services; (b) engagements or appointments made on the basis of experience, expertise, professional qualifications and cost following a request for proposal or other process that is free from influence based upon political contributions; and (c) engagements or appointments made on a rotational basis from a list compiled without regard to political contributions.

[4] The term "lawyer or law firm" includes a political action committee or other entity owned or controlled by a lawyer or law firm.

[5] Political contributions are for the purpose of obtaining or being considered for a government legal engagement or appointment by a judge if, but for the desire to be considered for the legal engagement or appointment, the lawyer or law firm would not have made or solicited the contributions. The purpose may be determined by an examination of the circumstances in which the contributions occur. For example, one or more contributions that in the aggregate are substantial in relation to other contributions by lawyers or law firms, made for the benefit of an official in a position to influence award of a government legal engagement, and followed by an award of the legal engagement to the contributing or soliciting lawyer or the lawyer's firm would support an inference that the purpose of the contributions was to obtain the engagement, absent other factors that weigh against existence of the proscribed purpose. Those factors may include among others that the contribution or solicitation was made to further a political, social, or economic interest or because of an existing personal, family, or professional relationship with a candidate.

[6] If a lawyer makes or solicits a political contribution under circumstances that constitute bribery or another crime, Rule 8.4(b) is implicated.

MAINTAINING THE INTEGRITY OF THE PROFESSION

RULE 8.1: BAR ADMISSION AND DISCIPLINARY MATTERS

An applicant for admission to the bar, or a lawyer in connection with a bar admission application or in connection with a disciplinary matter, shall not:

(a) knowingly make a false statement of material fact; or

(b) fail to disclose a fact necessary to correct a misapprehension known by the person to have arisen in the matter, or knowingly fail to respond to a lawful demand for information from an admissions or

disciplinary authority, except that this rule does not require disclosure of information otherwise protected by Rule 1.6.

Comment

[1] The duty imposed by this Rule extends to persons seeking admission to the bar as well as to lawyers. Hence, if a person makes a material false statement in connection with an application for admission, it may be the basis for subsequent disciplinary action if the person is admitted, and in any event may be relevant in a subsequent admission application. The duty imposed by this Rule applies to a lawyer's own admission or discipline as well as that of others. Thus, it is a separate professional offense for a lawyer to knowingly make a misrepresentation or omission in connection with a disciplinary investigation of the lawyer's own conduct. Paragraph (b) of this Rule also requires correction of any prior misstatement in the matter that the applicant or lawyer may have made and affirmative clarification of any misunderstanding on the part of the admissions or disciplinary authority of which the person involved becomes aware.

[2] This Rule is subject to the provisions of the fifth amendment of the United States Constitution and corresponding provisions of state constitutions. A person relying on such a provision in response to a question, however, should do so openly and not use the right of nondisclosure as a justification for failure to comply with this Rule.

[3] A lawyer representing an applicant for admission to the bar, or representing a lawyer who is the subject of a disciplinary inquiry or proceeding, is governed by the rules applicable to the client-lawyer relationship, including Rule 1.6 and, in some cases, Rule 3.3.

RULE 8.2: JUDICIAL AND LEGAL OFFICIALS

(a) A lawyer shall not make a statement that the lawyer knows to be false or with reckless disregard as to its truth or falsity concerning the qualifications or integrity of a judge, adjudicatory officer or public legal officer, or of a candidate for election or appointment to judicial or legal office.

(b) A lawyer who is a candidate for judicial office shall comply with the applicable provisions of the Code of Judicial Conduct.

Comment

[1] Assessments by lawyers are relied on in evaluating the professional or personal fitness of persons being considered for election or appointment to judicial office and to public legal offices, such as attorney general, prosecuting attorney and public defender. Expressing honest and candid opinions on such matters contributes to improving the administration of justice. Conversely, false statements by a lawyer can unfairly undermine public confidence in the administration of justice.

[2]   When a lawyer seeks judicial office, the lawyer should be bound by applicable limitations on political activity.

[3]   To maintain the fair and independent administration of justice, lawyers are encouraged to continue traditional efforts to defend judges and courts unjustly criticized.

RULE 8.3: REPORTING PROFESSIONAL MISCONDUCT

(a) A lawyer who knows that another lawyer has committed a violation of the Rules of Professional Conduct that raises a substantial question as to that lawyer's honesty, trustworthiness or fitness as a lawyer in other respects, shall inform the appropriate professional authority.

(b) A lawyer who knows that a judge has committed a violation of applicable rules of judicial conduct that raises a substantial question as to the judge's fitness for office shall inform the appropriate authority.

(c) This Rule does not require disclosure of information otherwise protected by Rule 1.6 or information gained by a lawyer or judge while participating in an approved lawyers assistance program.

Comment

[1]   Self-regulation of the legal profession requires that members of the profession initiate disciplinary investigation when they know of a violation of the Rules of Professional Conduct. Lawyers have a similar obligation with respect to judicial misconduct. An apparently isolated violation may indicate a pattern of misconduct that only a disciplinary investigation can uncover. Reporting a violation is especially important where the victim is unlikely to discover the offense.

[2]   A report about misconduct is not required where it would involve violation of Rule 1.6. However, a lawyer should encourage a client to consent to disclosure where prosecution would not substantially prejudice the client's interests.

[3]   If a lawyer were obliged to report every violation of the Rules, the failure to report any violation would itself be a professional offense. Such a requirement existed in many jurisdictions but proved to be unenforceable. This Rule limits the reporting obligation to those offenses that a self-regulating profession must vigorously endeavor to prevent. A measure of judgment is, therefore, required in complying with the provisions of this Rule. The term "substantial" refers to the seriousness of the possible offense and not the quantum of evidence of which the lawyer is aware. A report should be made to the bar disciplinary agency unless some other agency, such as a peer review agency, is more appropriate in the circumstances. Similar considerations apply to the reporting of judicial misconduct.

[4] The duty to report professional misconduct does not apply to a lawyer retained to represent a lawyer whose professional conduct is in question. Such a situation is governed by the Rules applicable to the client-lawyer relationship.

[5] Information about a lawyer's or judge's misconduct or fitness may be received by a lawyer in the course of that lawyer's participation in an approved lawyers or judges assistance program. In that circumstance, providing for an exception to the reporting requirements of paragraphs (a) and (b) of this Rule encourages lawyers and judges to seek treatment through such a program. Conversely, without such an exception, lawyers and judges may hesitate to seek assistance from these programs, which may then result in additional harm to their professional careers and additional injury to the welfare of clients and the public. These Rules do not otherwise address the confidentiality of information received by a lawyer or judge participating in an approved lawyers assistance program; such an obligation, however, may be imposed by the rules of the program or other law.

RULE 8.4: MISCONDUCT

It is professional misconduct for a lawyer to:

(a) violate or attempt to violate the Rules of Professional Conduct, knowingly assist or induce another to do so, or do so through the acts of another;

(b) commit a criminal act that reflects adversely on the lawyer's honesty, trustworthiness or fitness as a lawyer in other respects;

(c) engage in conduct involving dishonesty, fraud, deceit or misrepresentation;

(d) engage in conduct that is prejudicial to the administration of justice;

(e) state or imply an ability to influence improperly a government agency or official or to achieve results by means that violate the Rules of Professional Conduct or other law; or

(f) knowingly assist a judge or judicial officer in conduct that is a violation of applicable rules of judicial conduct or other law.

Comment

[1] Lawyers are subject to discipline when they violate or attempt to violate the Rules of Professional Conduct, knowingly assist or induce another to do so or do so through the acts of another, as when they request or instruct an agent to do so on the lawyer's behalf. Paragraph (a), however, does not prohibit a lawyer from advising a client concerning action the client is legally entitled to take.

[2] Many kinds of illegal conduct reflect adversely on fitness to practice law, such as offenses involving fraud and the offense of willful failure to file

an income tax return. However, some kinds of offenses carry no such implication. Traditionally, the distinction was drawn in terms of offenses involving "moral turpitude." That concept can be construed to include offenses concerning some matters of personal morality, such as adultery and comparable offenses, that have no specific connection to fitness for the practice of law. Although a lawyer is personally answerable to the entire criminal law, a lawyer should be professionally answerable only for offenses that indicate lack of those characteristics relevant to law practice. Offenses involving violence, dishonesty, breach of trust, or serious interference with the administration of justice are in that category. A pattern of repeated offenses, even ones of minor significance when considered separately, can indicate indifference to legal obligation.

[3] A lawyer who, in the course of representing a client, knowingly manifests by words or conduct, bias or prejudice based upon race, sex, religion, national origin, disability, age, sexual orientation or socioeconomic status, violates paragraph (d) when such actions are prejudicial to the administration of justice. Legitimate advocacy respecting the foregoing factors does not violate paragraph (d). A trial judge's finding that peremptory challenges were exercised on a discriminatory basis does not alone establish a violation of this rule.

[4] A lawyer may refuse to comply with an obligation imposed by law upon a good faith belief that no valid obligation exists. The provisions of Rule 1.2(d) concerning a good faith challenge to the validity, scope, meaning or application of the law apply to challenges of legal regulation of the practice of law.

[5] Lawyers holding public office assume legal responsibilities going beyond those of other citizens. A lawyer's abuse of public office can suggest an inability to fulfill the professional role of lawyers. The same is true of abuse of positions of private trust such as trustee, executor, administrator, guardian, agent and officer, director or manager of a corporation or other organization.

RULE 8.5: DISCIPLINARY AUTHORITY; CHOICE OF LAW

(a) Disciplinary Authority. A lawyer admitted to practice in this jurisdiction is subject to the disciplinary authority of this jurisdiction, regardless of where the lawyer's conduct occurs. A lawyer not admitted in this jurisdiction is also subject to the disciplinary authority of this jurisdiction if the lawyer provides or offers to provide any legal services in this jurisdiction. A lawyer may be subject to the disciplinary authority of both this jurisdiction and another jurisdiction for the same conduct.

(b) Choice of Law. In any exercise of the disciplinary authority of this jurisdiction, the rules of professional conduct to be applied shall be as follows:

(1) for conduct in connection with a matter pending before a tribunal, the rules of the jurisdiction in which the tribunal sits, unless the rules of the tribunal provide otherwise; and

> **(2) for any other conduct, the rules of the jurisdiction in which the lawyer's conduct occurred, or, if the predominant effect of the conduct is in a different jurisdiction, the rules of that jurisdiction shall be applied to the conduct. A lawyer shall not be subject to discipline if the lawyer's conduct conforms to the rules of a jurisdiction in which the lawyer reasonably believes the predominant effect of the lawyer's conduct will occur.**

Comment
Disciplinary Authority

[1]   It is longstanding law that the conduct of a lawyer admitted to practice in this jurisdiction is subject to the disciplinary authority of this jurisdiction. Extension of the disciplinary authority of this jurisdiction to other lawyers who provide or offer to provide legal services in this jurisdiction is for the protection of the citizens of this jurisdiction. Reciprocal enforcement of a jurisdiction's disciplinary findings and sanctions will further advance the purposes of this Rule. See, Rules 6 and 22, ABA *Model Rules for Lawyer Disciplinary Enforcement*. A lawyer who is subject to the disciplinary authority of this jurisdiction under Rule 8.5(a) appoints an official to be designated by this Court to receive service of process in this jurisdiction. The fact that the lawyer is subject to the disciplinary authority of this jurisdiction may be a factor in determining whether personal jurisdiction may be asserted over the lawyer for civil matters.

Choice of Law

[2]   A lawyer may be potentially subject to more than one set of rules of professional conduct which impose different obligations. The lawyer may be licensed to practice in more than one jurisdiction with differing rules, or may be admitted to practice before a particular court with rules that differ from those of the jurisdiction or jurisdictions in which the lawyer is licensed to practice. Additionally, the lawyer's conduct may involve significant contacts with more than one jurisdiction.

[3]   Paragraph (b) seeks to resolve such potential conflicts. Its premise is that minimizing conflicts between rules, as well as uncertainty about which rules are applicable, is in the best interest of both clients and the profession (as well as the bodies having authority to regulate the profession). Accordingly, it takes the approach of (i) providing that any particular conduct of a lawyer shall be subject to only one set of rules of professional conduct, (ii) making the determination of which set of rules applies to particular conduct as straightforward as possible, consistent with recognition of appropriate regulatory interests of relevant jurisdictions, and (iii) providing protection from discipline for lawyers who act reasonably in the face of uncertainty.

[4]   Paragraph (b)(1) provides that as to a lawyer's conduct relating to a proceeding pending before a tribunal, the lawyer shall be subject only to the rules of professional conduct of that tribunal. As to all other conduct, including conduct in anticipation of a proceeding not yet pending before a

tribunal, paragraph (b)(2) provides that a lawyer shall be subject to the rules of the jurisdiction in which the lawyer's conduct occurred, or, if the predominant effect of the conduct is in another jurisdiction, the rules of that jurisdiction shall be applied to the conduct. In the case of conduct in anticipation of a proceeding that is likely to be before a tribunal, the predominant effect of such conduct could be where the conduct occurred, where the tribunal sits or in another jurisdiction.

[5] When a lawyer's conduct involves significant contacts with more than one jurisdiction, it may not be clear whether the predominant effect of the lawyer's conduct will occur in a jurisdiction other than the one in which the conduct occurred. So long as the lawyer's conduct conforms to the rules of a jurisdiction in which the lawyer reasonably believes the predominant effect will occur, the lawyer shall not be subject to discipline under this Rule.

[6] If two admitting jurisdictions were to proceed against a lawyer for the same conduct, they should, applying this rule, identify the same governing ethics rules. They should take all appropriate steps to see that they do apply the same rule to the same conduct, and in all events should avoid proceeding against a lawyer on the basis of two inconsistent rules.

[7] The choice of law provision applies to lawyers engaged in transnational practice, unless international law, treaties or other agreements between competent regulatory authorities in the affected jurisdictions provide otherwise.

INDEX

A

INDEX

Appointed counsel,
    Accepting appointments, Rule 6.2
    Endorsement of client's views, Rule 1.2(b)
    Requirement of competence, Rule 1.1
    Withdrawal by, Rule 1.16 (Comment)

Arbitrator,
    Disqualification of, Rule 1.12
    Former arbitrator negotiating for private employment, Rule 1.12(b)
    Serving as, Rule 2.4

Attorney-client privilege,
    Distinguished from confidentiality rule, Rule 1.6 (Comment)

Attorney General,
    Authority of, Scope

Authority of lawyer,
    Decisionmaking authority, Rule 1.2(a)
    Government lawyer, Scope

Autonomy of legal profession, Preamble

B

Belief,
    Defined, Rule 1.0(a)

Believes,
    Defined, Rule 1.0(a)

Business affairs of lawyer,
    Duty to conduct in compliance with law, Preamble
    Transaction with client, Rule 1.8(a)

C

Candor toward the tribunal,
    Requirements of, Rule 3.3

Cause of action,
    Violation of Rules as basis for, Scope

Choice of Law, Rule 8.5(b)

Civil disobedience,
    To test validity of statute, Rule 1.2 (Comment)

Civil liability,
    Violation of Rules as basis for, Scope

Class actions,
    Notice to members, Rule 7.2 (Comment)

Client-lawyer relationship,
    Existence of, defined by substantive law, Scope

Client's security fund,
    Participation in, Rule 1.15 (Comment)

Comments,
    Do not expand lawyer's responsibilities, Scope

Communication,
    Duty to maintain with client, Preamble, Rule 1.4 (Comment)
    With represented party, Rule 4.2

INDEX

137

INDEX

INDEX

E

F

INDEX

Former government lawyer,—Continued
    "Matter" defined, Rule 1.11(e)
    Successive government and private employment, Rule 1.11

Former judge, see Judges

Fraud,
    Defined, Rule 1.0(d)
        Confidentiality of information and, 1.6(b), (Comment)

Fraudulent,
    Defined, Rule 1.0(d)

Fraudulent conduct,
    Counseling or assisting client to engage in, Rule 1.2(d)
    Disclosure of client's, Rule 4.1(b)

Frivolous claims and defenses, Rule 3.1

Funds of client,
    Handling of, Rule 1.15(a)
    Lawyer claims interest in, Rule 1.15(c)

G

Gift,
    To lawyer by client, Rule 1.8(c)

Government agency,
    Representation of, Rule 1.13 (Comment)

Government lawyer,
    Authority established by constitution, statutes and common law, Scope
    Conflict of interest, Rule 1.7 (Comment)
    Representing multiple clients, Scope
    Subject to rules, Rule 1.11 (Comment)

H

Harass,
    Law's procedures used to, Preamble

I

Impartiality and decorum of the tribunal, Rule 3.5

Imputed disqualification,
    General rule, Rule 1.10
    Government lawyers, Rule 1.11 (Comment)
    Witness, when member of firm serves as, Rule 3.7(b)

Incompetent client,
    Appointment of guardian for, Rule 1.14(b)
    Representation of, Rule 1.14(a)

Independence of the legal profession, Preamble

Independent professional judgment,
    Duty to exercise, Rule 2.1; Rule 5.4

Indigent client,
    Paying court costs and expenses on behalf of, Rule 1.8(e)(2)

INDEX

Informed Consent,
    Affecting conflict of interest, Rule 1.7 (Comment)
    Defined as, Terminology
    Required for evaluation, Rule 2.3(b)
    Required if former judge, arbitrator, mediator, or third-party neutral, Rule 1.12(a)
    Required to inform client on basis of, Rule 1.42(a)(1)
    That of former clients, Rule 1.9(a)

Insurance representation,
    Conflict of interest, Rule 1.8(f), (Comment 11)

Intermediary,
    Lawyer as, Preamble

Intimidate,
    Law's procedures used to, Preamble

J

Judges,
    Appointments by judges and political contributions, Rule 7.6
    Duty to show respect for, Preamble
    Ex parte communication with, Rule 3.5(b)
    Former judge, disqualification, Rule 1.12
    Improper influence on, Rule 3.5(a)
    Reporting misconduct by, Rule 8.3(b)
    Statements about, Rule 8.2

Juror,
    Improper influence on, Rule 3.5(a)

Jury trial,
    Client's right to waive, Rule 1.2(a)

K

Know, Knows, Knowingly,
    Defined as, Rule 1.0(f)
    Legal knowledge required for competence, Rule 1.1

L

Law clerk,
    Negotiating for private employment, Rule 1.12(b)

Law firm,
    Ancillary services, Rule 5.7
    Defined, Terminology
    Nonlawyer assistants, responsibility for, Rule 5.3
    Responsibility of partner or supervisory lawyer, Rule 5.1
    Subordinate lawyer, responsibility of, Rule 5.2

Law reform activities,
    Affecting clients' interests, Rule 6.4

Lawyer referral service,
    Advertising by way of, Rule 7.2(c)(2)
    Financial support of, Rule 6.1 (Comment)
    Legal aid and, Rule 6.1 (Comment)

INDEX

INDEX

Nonlawyers,
    Division of fees with, Rule 5.4(a)
    Partnership with, Rule 5.4(b)

O

Objectives of the representation,
    Client's right to determine, Rule 1.2(a)
    Lawyer's right to limit, Rule 1.2(c)

Opposing party,
    Communications with represented party, Rule 4.2
    Duty of fairness to, Rule 3.4

Organization, representation of,
    Board of directors, lawyer for serving on, Rule 1.7 (Comment)
    Communication with, Rule 1.4 (Comment)
    Conflict of interest, Rule 1.7 (Comment)
    Conflicting interests among officers and employees, Rule 1.7 (Comment)
    Constituents, representing, Rule 1.13(e)
    Identity of client, Rule 1.13(a); Rule 1.13(d)
    Misconduct, client engaged in, Rule 1.13(b)

P

Partner,
    Defined, Rule 1.0(g)

Patent practice,
    Advertising, Rule 7.4(b)

Perjury,
    Criminal defendant, Rule 3.3 (Comment)
    Disclosure of, Rule 3.3(b)

Personal affairs of lawyer,
    Duty to conduct in compliance with law, Preamble

Plea bargain,
    Client's right to accept or reject, Rule 1.2(a)

Pleadings,
    Verification of, Rule 3.3 (Comment)

Political contributions to secure legal work, Rule 7.6

Positional conflicts, Rule 1.7 (Comment)

Precedent,
    Failure to disclose to court, Rule 3.3(a)(2)

Prepaid legal services,
    Advertising for, Rule 7.2 (Comment)

Pro bono publico service, Rule 6.1

Procedural law,
    Lawyer's professional responsibilities proscribed by, Preamble

Professional corporation,
    Ownership in, Rule 5.4(d)

Prompt,
    Lawyer's duty to be, Preamble

INDEX

144

INDEX

INDEX

Z

APPENDIX A

Ethics Rules on Disclosure of Client Confidences

*Table of Contents**

Section 1. Introduction

One of the most vexing professional liability questions that can confront a lawyer is whether the lawyer may, or must, reveal confidential client information. This Appendix contains three charts that summarize a lawyer's obligations regarding the disclosure of client misconduct, disclosures of confidential client information to comply with other law or a court order, and disclosure of confidential client information outside of an organizational client. These charts are summary in nature, providing only a starting point for the analysis that is required in each situation.

Disclosures that are required or permitted by money-laundering statutes and directives applicable in the United Kingdom, Europe, or elsewhere are beyond the scope of this tab.

1.1 Disclosure of Client Misconduct

The chart in Section 2 below summarizes the provisions of the ABA Model Rules of Professional Conduct, as amended, the ABA Model Code of Professional Responsibility (1969), the various state versions of the Code and the Rules, and related comments, ethics opinions, and case law that are applicable on the controversial "whistle-blowing" issue, the ability of a lawyer to disclose client misconduct.

The chart indicates, with citations, whether a lawyer "May," "Must," or "Must Not" disclose confidential client information, or take some other action, relating to the following:

A. Client's intention to commit any crime.

B. Client's or other's intention to commit a crime or other act likely to result in death or bodily injury.

147

C. Client's intention to commit a criminal fraud.

D. Client's intention to commit a noncriminal fraud. (In some states, criminal statutes may be interpreted broadly, such that virtually any fraud likely to result in injury to the financial interest or property of another would be a crime.)

E. Client's prior commission of a crime or fraud, using the lawyer's services, resulting in injury to the financial interest or property of another party.

F. Client's prior or contemporaneous commission of perjury or other fraud on a tribunal.

G. Client's ongoing criminal or fraudulent act.

It must be emphasized that the chart in Section 2 below is only a summary intended to alert the reader to situations that raise the question whether disclosure of confidential client information is discretionary, mandatory, or prohibited, and to direct the reader to the relevant provision and language in the Code or in the Rules and related authorities. There are many subtle distinctions and refinements that emerge when one compares the ABA Model Code, the ABA Model Rules, the code or rules of any particular state, the local rules of federal district courts, a state's comments and ethics opinions, and case law. For example, the ABA Model Rules permit a lawyer to disclose confidential information to *prevent* a client crime or fraud that threatens substantial financial harm to others, but only when the lawyer's services are used in connection with the threatened conduct. Many states, however, permit such disclosure without requiring any nexus between the lawyer's services and the potential crime or fraud, and many of those states do not require the crime or fraud to threaten substantial financial harm. The notes following the chart identify these and many other distinctions. We recommend review of the applicable notes when using the chart. In all events, there is no substitute for reading the relevant rule and related authorities. Unfortunately, in certain situations (as indicated by the notes following the chart) the applicable rules, relevant ethics opinions, and case law are often ambiguous. In addition, because of the dearth of case law, a court is likely to look to cases decided in other jurisdictions for assistance and persuasive support.

The chart in Section 2 below reflects amendments to the Model Rules, the Model Code, and the relevant state rules or codes of which we are aware as of March 2009. We have not undertaken to determine the existence or effect of amendments effective after that date.

The *Restatement Third, The Law Governing Lawyers* (2000) generally supports disclosures of client wrongdoing in the same range of circumstances as do the Model Rules. Sections 59 through 67 of the *Restatement* deal generally with lawyer-client confidentiality. Section 120 describes "remedial measures" (including revealing confidential client information if necessary) that a lawyer should take upon learning that false evidence has been offered in litigation.

When a lawyer invokes an exception to the general prohibition against disclosing client confidences, the burden of proof to show that exception applies may rest with the lawyer. The New Hampshire Supreme Court, after noting the paucity of authority from other jurisdictions, ruled that the lawyer does bear the burden of proof under Rule 1.6 to establish that disclosure was necessary to prevent his former client from stealing money from his father's estate. *Lane's Case*, 889 A.2d 3 (N.H. 2005). The court reasoned that putting the burden of proof on the lawyer properly balances the public's interest in assuring the integrity of lawyers and the lawyer's right to avoid discipline when there is justification for making an unauthorized disclosure. According to that court, Maryland has by rule put the burden of establishing a defense in a disciplinary proceeding on the lawyer. 889 A.2d at 12 (citing Maryland Rule 16–757(b)). Other jurisdictions have cases reaching the same result. *See Beery v. State Bar of California*, 739 P.2d 1289 (Cal. 1987) (lawyer had the burden to prove an exception to a professional misconduct charge for entering into a prohibited business transaction with the client); *In re Disciplinary Proceeding Against Cohen*, 82 P.3d 224, 230 (Wash. 2004) (*en banc*) (lawyer had the burden to prove the applicability of an exception to a disciplinary rule forbidding prejudicial withdrawals); *Rodgers v. Commission for Lawyer Discipline*, 151 S.W.3d 602, 615 (Tex. App. 2004) (lawyer had burden to prove applicability of exception to disciplinary rule requiring attorneys to officially file their advertisements).

1.2 Disclosure to Comply with Law

The chart in Section 4 below sets forth for each jurisdiction whether a lawyer is permitted to disclose confidential client information to comply with other law. Former Comment [21] to Model Rule 1.6 of the 1983 version of the Model Rules (described in the chart as 1983 Model Rule 1.6) acknowledged that other provisions of law might obligate or permit a lawyer to disclose confidential client information, but cautioned: "Whether another provision of law supersedes Rule 1.6 is a matter of interpretation beyond the scope of these Rules, but a presumption should exist against such a supersession." As shown by the chart, the states are divided on whether their ethics rules permit disclosure to comply with other law, such as the permissive reporting out provisions of the Sarbanes–Oxley Act. *See* Section 1.3 below.

The 2003 version of the Model Rules expressly provides in Rule 1.6(b)(6) that a lawyer may reveal information relating to the representation of a client "to comply with other law or a court order." Comments [12] and [13] to Model Rule 1.6 remind lawyers that they must discuss the matter with the affected client to the extent required by Model Rule 1.4.

1.3 Disclosure Outside the Organization

The chart in Section 5 below sets forth for each jurisdiction whether a lawyer is permitted to disclose confidential information of an organizational client outside the organization even if Rule 1.6 does not permit such disclosure.

Model Rule 1.13 of the 1983 version of the Model Rules (described in the chart as 1983 Model Rule 1.13) provided that a lawyer who "knows" that an officer or other agent of an organizational client is engaged in misconduct that will cause substantial injury to the organization must "proceed as reasonably necessary in the best interest of the organization." That rule required no particular course of action of the lawyer, but identified up-the-line reporting of the misconduct, including reporting to the entity's board of directors, as a potential option.

The version of Model Rule 1.13 adopted in 2002 (described in the chart as Ethics 2000) made only one substantive change to Model Rule 1.13, requiring a lawyer to explain to constituents the identity of the client as the organization when the lawyer "knows or reasonably should know" of a conflict between the organization and its constituents. *See* 2002 version of Model Rule 1.13(d). The 1983 version of Model Rule 1.13(d) required an explanation when the conflict is "apparent."

The 2003 version of Model Rule 1.13 (described in the chart as August 2003) requires a lawyer who knows of corporate misconduct to report such misconduct up the line, to the organization's board of directors if necessary, unless the lawyer reasonably believes it is "not necessary in the best interest of the organization" to do so. As noted above, such up-the-line reporting was formerly just one option that the lawyer could consider.

Paragraph (c) of this new version of Model Rule 1.13 further provides that when a lawyer has reported corporate misconduct to the organization's highest authority, and the organization fails to take timely remedial action, the lawyer *may* reveal client confidences outside the organization to the extent necessary to prevent substantial injury to the organizational client. Paragraph (e) of the current rule also provides that a lawyer who reasonably believes that he or she has been discharged because of reporting up the line, or making an authorized outside report, or who withdraws under circumstances that would permit such reporting, must inform the organization's board of the discharge or withdrawal, and what the lawyer reasonably believes to be the basis for the discharge or withdrawal.

The up-the-line reporting obligations imposed by § 307 of the Sarbanes–Oxley Act, and SEC Rule 205 implementing § 307, are similar to those in Model Rule 1.13. Model Rule 1.13, however, requires up-the-line reporting with respect to *all* organizational clients, not just the public companies covered by Sarbanes–Oxley.

Another important distinction between SEC Rule 205 and the Model Rules is that SEC Rule 205 permits disclosure of confidential information in certain cases of client misconduct even though the rules in the lawyer's home state forbid disclosure. SEC Rule 205(d)(2) permits a lawyer to disclose to the SEC, without the client-issuer's consent, confidential information related to the representation that the lawyer reasonably believes is necessary: (1) to prevent the issuer from committing a material violation that is likely to cause substantial injury to the financial interest or property of the issuer or investors; (2) to prevent the issuer from committing or suborning perjury in a SEC investigation or administrative proceeding or otherwise perpetrating a fraud upon the SEC; or (3) to rectify the consequences of the issuer's material violation in the furtherance of which the lawyer's services were used that caused, or may cause, substantial injury to the financial interest or property of the issuer or investors.

The chart in Section 2 below shows that several states forbid such disclosures. Yet, SEC Rule 205, in theory, provides a safe harbor for lawyers who make disclosures in violation of state ethics rules, stating: "An attorney who complies in good faith with the provisions of this part shall not be subject to discipline or otherwise liable under inconsistent standards imposed by any state or other United States jurisdiction where the attorney is admitted or practices." SEC Rule 205.6(c). The California Bar, however, has cautioned its lawyers not to make any disclosures permitted by the SEC but forbidden by California law unless and until a court of competent jurisdiction decides whether SEC Rule 205 could and properly did preempt state ethics rules. *See* California Bar Association, Corporations Committee of the Business Law Section and Committee on Professional Responsibility and Conduct, Ethics Alert, "The New SEC Attorney Conduct Rules v. California's Duty of Confidentiality" (2003).

For a brief period, Washington lawyers were subject to a similar warning, as set out in interim Washington State Bar Association Formal Opinion 197 (2003). As of January 2007, the bar's Web site reported without explanation that the Board of Governors withdrew this opinion in October 2006.

North Carolina has rejected California's approach and assured lawyers that the SEC safe harbor should protect them. Without citing the California or Washington authorities discussed above, the North Carolina state bar concluded that "unless and until the Fourth Circuit Court of Appeals or the United States Supreme Court determines that [SEC] Rule 205 was not validly promulgated, . . . a North Carolina attorney may, without violating the North Carolina Rules of Professional Conduct, disclose confidential information as permitted by [SEC] Rule 205 although such disclosure would not otherwise be permitted by [North Carolina] Rule [1.6]." North Carolina State Bar Ethics Committee, 2005 Formal Ethics Opinion 9 (January 20, 2006). A 2005 amendment to North Carolina Rule 1.13(c), which permits "reporting out" in specified circumstances, received final approval on March 2, 2006, a few months after the ethics opinion was issued.

Section 2. Chart of Ethics Rules on Disclosure of Client Misconduct

A. Client's intention to commit any crime.

B. Client's or other's intention to commit a crime or other act likely to result in death or substantial bodily harm.

C. Client's intention to commit a criminal fraud.

D. Client's intention to commit a *noncriminal* fraud.

E. Client's prior commission of a financial crime or fraud using the lawyer's services.

F. Client's prior or contemporaneous commission of perjury or other fraud on a tribunal.

G. Client's ongoing criminal or fraudulent act.

	INTENT TO COMMIT/PREVENTION				RECTIFICATION		
	A Any Crime	**B** Death/Injury	**C** Criminal Fraud	**D** Noncriminal Fraud	**E** Prior Crime/ Fraud-Lawyer's Services	**F** Prior Perjury/Fraud on Tribunal	**G** Ongoing Client Crime or Fraud
ABA Model Rule (2003)	Must Not 1.6(a)	May 1.6(b)(1)	May 1.6(b)(2) [1]	May 1.6(b)(2) [1]	May 1.6(b)(3) [2]	Must 3.3(a)(1), (a)(3) and (b) [3]	Must 4.1(b) [4] See also 1.2(d)
Alabama	Must Not 1.6(a)	May 1.6(b)(1)	Must Not 1.6(a)	Must Not 1.6(a)	Must Not 1.6(a)	Must 3.3(b)	Must 4.1(b) [4] See also 1.2(d)
Alaska	Must Not 1.6(a)	May 1.6(b)(1)	May 1.6(b)(2) [1]	May 1.6(b)(2) [1]	May 1.6(b)(3) [2]	Must 3.3(a)(3) and (b) [3]	Must 4.1(b) [4] See also 1.2(d)
Arizona	May 1.6(c)	Must 1.6(b)	May 1.6(d)(1)	May 1.6(d)(1)	May 1.6(d)(2) [2]	Must 3.3(a)(3) and (b) [5]	Must 4.1(b) [4] See also 1.2(d)
Arkansas	May 1.6(b)(1)	May 1.6(b)(1)	May 1.6(b)(1)	May 1.6(b)(2)	May 1.6(b)(3)	Must 3.3(a)(1), (a)(3) and (b) [3]	Must 4.1(b) [4] See also 1.2(d)
California	Must Not 3-100(A) § 6068(e) Business and Professions Code [6]	May 3-100(B) § 6068(e)(2) Business and Professions Code [6]	Must Not 3-100(A) § 6068(e) Business and Professions Code [6]	Must Not 3-100(A) § 6068(e) Business and Professions Code [6]	Must Not 3-100(A) § 6068(e) Business and Professions Code [6]	Must Not 3-100(A) § 6068(e) Business and Professions Code [6]	Must Not 3-100(A) § 6068(e) Business and Professions Code [6]

A. Client's intention to commit any crime.

B. Client's or other's intention to commit a crime or other act likely to result in death or substantial bodily harm.

C. Client's intention to commit a criminal fraud.

D. Client's intention to commit a *noncriminal* fraud.

E. Client's prior commission of a financial crime or fraud using the lawyer's services.

F. Client's prior or contemporaneous commission of perjury or other fraud on a tribunal.

G. Client's ongoing criminal or fraudulent act.

	INTENT TO COMMIT/PREVENTION				RECTIFICATION		
	A Any Crime	**B** Death/Injury	**C** Criminal Fraud	**D** Noncriminal Fraud	**E** Prior Crime/ Fraud-Lawyer's Services	**F** Prior Perjury/Fraud on Tribunal	**G** Ongoing Client Crime or Fraud
Colorado	May 1.6(b)(2)	May 1.6(b)(1)	May 1.6(b)(2)	May 1.6(b)(3)	May 1.6(b)(4)	Must 3.3(a)(3) [3] and (b)	Must 4.1(b) [4] See also 1.2(d)
Connecticut	Must Not 1.6(a)	Must 1.6(b)	May 1.6(c)(1)	May 1.6(c)(1)	May 1.6(c)(2)	Must 3.3(a)(3) and (b)	Must 4.1(2) [4] See also 1.2 (d)
Delaware	Must Not 1.6(a)	May 1.6(b)(1)	May 1.6(b)(2)	May 1.6(b)(2)	May 1.6(b)(3) [2]	Must 3.3(a)(3) and (b)	Must 4.1(b) [4] See also 1.2 (d)
District of Columbia	Must Not 1.6(a)(1) [7]	May 1.6(c)(1)	May 1.6(d)(1)	May 1.6(d)(1)	May 1.6(d)(2)	May 3.3(a)(1) and (d); 1.6(c)(2) and (d) [7]	Must 1.6(d), 4.1(b) [4] See also 1.2 (e)
Florida	Must 4-1.6(b)(1)	Must 4-1.6(b)(2)	Must 4-1.6(b)(1)	Must Not 4-1.6(a)	Must Not 4-1.6(a) [8]	Must 4-3.3(a)(2)	Must 4-4.1(b) [4] See also 4-1.2 (d)
Georgia	May 1.6(b)(1)(i) [9]	May 1.6(b)(1)(ii) [9]	May 1.6(b)(1)(i) [9]	Must Not 1.6(a)	Must Not 1.6(a)	Must 3.3(a)(2)	Must 4.1(b) [4] See also 1.2(d)
Hawaii	Must Not 1.6(a)	May 1.6(c)(1)	May 1.6(c)(1)	May 1.6(c)(1)	Must 1.6(b)	Must 3.3(a)(2)	Must 4.1(b) [10] See also 1.2(d)

A. Client's intention to commit any crime.

B. Client's or other's intention to commit a crime or other act likely to result in death or substantial bodily harm.

C. Client's intention to commit a criminal fraud.

D. Client's intention to commit a *noncriminal* fraud.

E. Client's prior commission of a financial crime or fraud using the lawyer's services.

F. Client's prior or contemporaneous commission of perjury or other fraud on a tribunal.

G. Client's ongoing criminal or fraudulent act.

	INTENT TO COMMIT/PREVENTION				RECTIFICATION		
	A Any Crime	**B** Death/Injury	**C** Criminal Fraud	**D** Noncriminal Fraud	**E** Prior Crime/ Fraud-Lawyer's Services	**F** Prior Perjury/Fraud on Tribunal	**G** Ongoing Client Crime or Fraud
Idaho	May 1.6(b)(1)	May 1.6(b)(2)	May 1.6(b)(1)	Must Not 1.6(a)	May 1.6(b)(3) [2]	Must 3.3(a)(3)	Must 4.1(b) [4] See also 1.2(d)
Illinois	May 1.6(c)(2)	Must 1.6(b)	May 1.6(c)(2)	Must Not 1.6(a)	Must Not 1.6(a) [11] and 1.2(g)	Must 3.3(a)(2) [11]	Must 4.1(b) [4]
Indiana	Must Not 1.6(a)	May 1.6(b)(1)	May 1.6(b)(2)	May 1.6(b)(2)	May 1.6(b)(3) [2]	Must 3.3(a)(3)	Must 4.1(b) [4] See also 1.2(d)
Iowa	Must Not 32:1.6(a)	Must 32:1.6(c)	May 32:1.6(b)(2)	May 32:1.6(b)(2)	May 32:1.6(b)(3) [2]	Must 32:3.3(a)(3) [3]	May 32:4.1(b) [4]
Kansas	May 1.6(b)(1)	Must Not 1.6(a)	May 1.6(b)(1)	Must Not 1.16(a)	Must Not 1.6(a)	Must 3.3(a)(3) [3] and (b)	Must 4.1(b) [4] See also 1.2(d)
Kentucky	Must Not 1.6(a)	May 1.6(b)(1)	Must Not 1.6(a)	Must Not 1.6(a)	Must Not 1.6(a)	Must 3.3(a)(2)	May See note [12]
Louisiana	Must Not 1.6(a)	May 1.6(b)(1)	May 1.6(b)(2)	May 1.6(b)(2)	May 1.6(b)(3) [2]	Must 3.3(a)(3)	Must 4.1(b) [4] See also 1.2(d)
Maine (Effective Aug. 1, 2009)	Must Not 1.6(a)	May 1.6(b)(1)	May 1.6(b)(2)	May 1.6(b)(2)	May 1.6(b)(3) [2]	Must 3.3(a)(3) and (b) [3]	Must 4.1(b) [4] See also 1.2(e)

A.	Client's intention to commit any crime.						
B.	Client's or other's intention to commit a crime or other act likely to result in death or substantial bodily harm.						
C.	Client's intention to commit a criminal fraud.						
D.	Client's intention to commit a *noncriminal* fraud.						
E.	Client's prior commission of a financial crime or fraud using the lawyer's services.						
F.	Client's prior or contemporaneous commission of perjury or other fraud on a tribunal.						
G.	Client's ongoing criminal or fraudulent act.						

	INTENT TO COMMIT/PREVENTION				RECTIFICATION		
	A Any Crime	**B** Death/Injury	**C** Criminal Fraud	**D** Noncriminal Fraud	**E** Prior Crime/ Fraud-Lawyer's Services	**F** Prior Perjury/Fraud on Tribunal	**G** Ongoing Client Crime or Fraud
Maryland	Must Not 1.6(a)	May 1.6(b)(1)	May 1.6(b)(2)	May 1.6(b)(2)	May 1.6(b)(3) [2]	Must 3.3(a)(2) [13]	Must 4.1(a)(2) and (b) [10] See also 1.2(d)
Massachusetts	Must Not 1.6(a)	May 1.6(b)(1) [14]	May 1.6(b)(1)	May 1.6(b)(1)	May 1.6(b)(3)	Must 3.3(a)(2) [15]	Must 4.1(b) [4] See also 1.2(d)
Michigan	May 1.6(c)(4)	Must Not 1.6(b)(1)	May 1.6(c)(4)	Must Not 1.6(b)(1)	May 1.6(c)(3)	Must 3.3(a)(2)	May 1.6(c)(3) See also 1.2(c)
Minnesota	May 1.6(b)(4)	May 1.6(b)(6)	May 1.6(b)(4)	May 1.6(b)(4)	May 1.6(b)(5)	Must 3.3(a)(3) and (b)	May 1.6(b)(4) See also 1.2(d)
Mississippi	Must Not 1.6(a)	May 1.6(b)(1)	May 1.6(b)(2)	May 1.6(b)(2)	May 1.6(b)(3)	Must 3.3(a)(2)	Must 4.1(b) [4] See also 1.2(d)
Missouri	Must Not 1.6(a)	May 1.6(b)(1)	Must Not 1.6(a)	Must Not 1.6(a)	Must Not 1.6(a)	Must 3.3(a)(3) and (b) [3]	Must 4.1(b) [4] See also 1.2(d)
Montana	Must Not 1.6(a)	May 1.6(b)(1)	Must Not 1.6(a)	Must Not 1.6(a)	Must Not 1.6(a)	Must 3.3(a)(3) and (b) [16]	Must 4.1(b) [4] See also 1.2(d)

155

A. Client's intention to commit any crime.
B. Client's or other's intention to commit a crime or other act likely to result in death or substantial bodily harm.
C. Client's intention to commit a criminal fraud.
D. Client's intention to commit a *noncriminal* fraud.
E. Client's prior commission of a financial crime or fraud using the lawyer's services.
F. Client's prior or contemporaneous commission of perjury or other fraud on a tribunal.
G. Client's ongoing criminal or fraudulent act.

	INTENT TO COMMIT/PREVENTION				RECTIFICATION		
	A Any Crime	**B** Death/Injury	**C** Criminal Fraud	**D** Noncriminal Fraud	**E** Prior Crime/ Fraud-Lawyer's Services	**F** Prior Perjury/Fraud on Tribunal	**G** Ongoing Client Crime or Fraud
Nebraska	May 1.6(b)(1)	May 1.6(b)(1)	May 1.6(b)(1)	Must Not 1.6(a)	Must Not 1.6(a)	Must 3.3(a)(3) and (b)	Must 4.1(b) [4] See also 1.2(f)
Nevada	May 1.6(b)(2)	Must 1.6(c)	May 1.6(b)(2)	May 1.6(b)(2)	May 1.6(b)(3)	Must 3.3(a)(3) and (b)	Must Rule 4.1(b) [4] See also 1.2(d)
New Hampshire	Must Not 1.6(a)	May 1.6(b)(1)	May 1.6(b)(1)	Must Not 1.6(a)	Must Not 1.6(a)	Must 3.3(a)(3) and (b) [17]	Must 4.1(b) [4] See also 1.2(d)
New Jersey	Must Not 1.6(a)	Must 1.6(b)(1) [18]	Must 1.6(b)(1) [18]	Must 1.6(b)(1) [18]	May 1.6(d)(1) [18]	Must 3.3(a)(2) [19]	Must 4.1(a) and (b) [10] See also 1.2(d)
New Mexico	Must Not 16-106(A)	May 16-106(B)(1)	May 16-106(B)(2)	May 16-106(B)(2)	May 16-106(B)(3)	Must 16-303(A)(3) and (B)	Must 16-401(B) [4] See also 16-102(D)
New York	May 1.6(b)(2)	May 1.6(b)(1)	May 1.6(b)(2)	Must Not 1.6(a)	May 1.6(b)(3) [20]	Must 3.3(a)(3) and (b)	May 1.6(b)(3) [20] See also 1.2(d)
North Carolina	May 1.6(b)(2)	May 1.6(b)(3)	May 1.6(b)(4) [21]	May 1.6(b)(4) [21]	May 1.6(b)(4) [21]	Must 3.3(a)(3) and (b)	May 1.6(b)(4) [21] See also 1.2(d)

A. Client's intention to commit any crime.

B. Client's or other's intention to commit a crime or other act likely to result in death or substantial bodily harm.

C. Client's intention to commit a criminal fraud.

D. Client's intention to commit a *noncriminal* fraud.

E. Client's prior commission of a financial crime or fraud using the lawyer's services.

F. Client's prior or contemporaneous commission of perjury or other fraud on a tribunal.

G. Client's ongoing criminal or fraudulent act.

	INTENT TO COMMIT/PREVENTION				RECTIFICATION		
	A Any Crime	**B** Death/Injury	**C** Criminal Fraud	**D** Noncriminal Fraud	**E** Prior Crime/ Fraud-Lawyer's Services	**F** Prior Perjury/Fraud on Tribunal	**G** Ongoing Client Crime or Fraud
North Dakota	Must Not 1.6(a)	Must 1.6(b)	May 1.6(c)(1)	May 1.6(c)(1)	May 1.6(c)(2)	Must Not 1.6(a) and 3.3(a)(3)	May 1.6(c)(2) See also 1.2(d)
Ohio	May 1.6(b)(2)	May 1.6(b)(1)	May 1.6(b)(2)	Must Not 1.6(a)	May 1.6(b)(3)	Must 3.3(a)(3) and (b) [22]	Must 4.1(b) [4] See also 1.2(d) and 1.6(c)
Oklahoma	May 1.6(b)(2)(i)	May 1.6(b)(1)	May 1.6(b)(2)(i)	May 1.6(b)(2)(ii)	May 1.6(b)(3)	Must 3.3(a)(3) and (b) [3]	Must 4.1(b) [4] See also 1.2(d)
Oregon	May 1.6(b)(1)	May 1.6(b)(2)	May 1.6(b)(1)	Must Not 1.6(a)	Must Not 1.6(a)	Must 3.3(a)(3) and (b)	Must 4.1(b) [4] See also 1.2(c)
Pennsylvania	May 1.6(c)(3) [23]	May 1.6(c)(1)	May 1.6(c)(2)	May 1.6(c)(3)	May 1.6(c)(3)	Must 3.3(a)(3) [24] and (b) See also 1.6(b)	Must 4.1(b) [4] See also 1.2(d)
Rhode Island	Must Not 1.6(a)	May 1.6(b)(1)	Must Not 1.6(a)	Must Not 1.6(a)	Must Not 1.6(a)	Must 3.3(a)(3) and (b) [3]	Must 4.1(b) [4] See also 1.2(d)
South Carolina	May 1.6(b)(1)	May 1.6(b)(2)	May 1.6(b)(3)	May 1.6(b)(3)	May 1.6(b)(4)	Must 3.3(a)(3) and (b)	Must 4.1(b) [4] See also 1.2(d)

A. Client's intention to commit any crime.

B. Client's or other's intention to commit a crime or other act likely to result in death or substantial bodily harm.

C. Client's intention to commit a criminal fraud.

D. Client's intention to commit a *noncriminal* fraud.

E. Client's prior commission of a financial crime or fraud using the lawyer's services.

F. Client's prior or contemporaneous commission of perjury or other fraud on a tribunal.

G. Client's ongoing criminal or fraudulent act.

	INTENT TO COMMIT/PREVENTION				RECTIFICATION		
	A Any Crime	**B** Death/Injury	**C** Criminal Fraud	**D** Noncriminal Fraud	**E** Prior Crime/ Fraud-Lawyer's Services	**F** Prior Perjury/Fraud on Tribunal	**G** Ongoing Client Crime or Fraud
South Dakota	Must Not 1.6(a)	May 1.6(b)(1)	Must Not 1.6(a)	Must Not 1.6(a)	May 1.6(b)(4)	Must 3.3(a)(3) and (b)	Must 4.1(b) [4] See also 1.2(d) and 1.6(b)(4)
Tennessee	May 1.6(b)(1) [25]	Must 1.6(c)(1)	May 1.6(b)(1) [25]	Must Withdraw 4.1(b) [25]	Must Withdraw 4.1(c) [25]	Must Seek Withdrawal 3.3(f) [25]	Must Withdraw 4.1(b) [25]
Texas	May 1.05(c)(7)	Must 1.05(e)	May 1.05(c)(7)	May 1.05(c)(7)	May 1.05(c)(8)	Must 3.03(b) [26]	Must 4.01(b) See also 1.02(c)
Utah	Must Not 1.6(a)	May 1.6(b)(1)	May 1.6(b)(2)	May 1.6(b)(2)	May 1.6(b)(3)	Must 3.3(a)(3) and (b)	Must 4.1(b) [4] See also 1.2(d)
Vermont	May 1.6(c)(1)	Must 1.6(b)(1)	May 1.6(c)(1)	Must Not 1.6(a)	Must Not See 1.6(a)	Must 3.3(a)(4)	Must 1.6(b)(2) [27]
Virginia	Must 1.6(c)(1) [28]	Must 1.6(c)(1)	Must 1.6(c)(1) [28]	Must Not 1.6(a)	May 1.6(b)(3)	Must 1.6(c)(2) and 3.3(a)(4)	Must 4.1(b) [4] See also 1.2(c)
Washington	May 1.6(b)(2)	Must 1.6(b)(1)	May 1.6(b)(2)	May 1.6(b)(3)	May 1.6(b)(3) and 1.6(b)(7) [29]	Must Not 3.3(a)(2) [30]	Must 4.1(b) [4] See also 1.2(d)

A. Client's intention to commit any crime.
B. Client's or other's intention to commit a crime or other act likely to result in death or substantial bodily harm.
C. Client's intention to commit a criminal fraud.
D. Client's intention to commit a *noncriminal* fraud.
E. Client's prior commission of a financial crime or fraud using the lawyer's services.
F. Client's prior or contemporaneous commission of perjury or other fraud on a tribunal.
G. Client's ongoing criminal or fraudulent act.

	INTENT TO COMMIT/PREVENTION				RECTIFICATION		
	A Any Crime	**B** Death/Injury	**C** Criminal Fraud	**D** Noncriminal Fraud	**E** Prior Crime/ Fraud-Lawyer's Services	**F** Prior Perjury/Fraud on Tribunal	**G** Ongoing Client Crime or Fraud
West Virginia	May 1.6(b)(1)	Must Not 1.6(a) [31]	May 1.6(b)(1)	Must Not 1.6(a)	Must Not 1.6(a)	Must 3.3(a)(4)	Must 4.1(b) [4] See also 1.2(d)
Wisconsin	Must Not 20:1.6(a)	Must 20:1.6(b)	Must 20:1.6(b)	Must 20:1.6(b)	May 20:1.6(c)(2)	Must 20:3.3(a)(3) and (b)	Must 20:4.1(a)(2) [4] See also 20:1.2(d)
Wyoming	May 1.6(b)(1)	May 1.6(a)	May 1.6(b)(1)	Must Not 1.6(a)	Must Not 1.6(a)	Must 3.3(a)(4)	Must 4.1(b) [4] See also 1.2(d)
TOTALS	**Must: 2** **May: 24** **Must Not: 25**	**Must: 14** **May: 33** **Must Not: 4**	**Must: 4** **May: 40** **Must Not: 7**	**Must: 2** **May: 26** **Must Not: 22** **Must Withdraw: 1**	**Must: 1** **May: 33** **Must Not: 16** **Must Withdraw: 1**	**Must: 46** **May: 1** **Must Not: 3** **Must Seek Withdrawal: 1**	**Must: 42** **May: 7** **Must Not: 1** **Must Withdraw: 1**

Section 3.   Explanatory Notes to Chart in Section 2

(1) **Model Rule 1.6 and Disclosures to Prevent Client Crimes or Frauds.** Model Rule 1.6(b)(2) permits a lawyer to disclose confidential information to *prevent* a threatened client crime or fraud that is likely to result in substantial financial harm to others, but only when the lawyer's services are used in connection with the threatened conduct. Some states that have adopted a version of Model Rule 1.6 that permits disclosure of a client's threatened crime or fraud do not require this nexus between the lawyer's services and the threatened conduct.

(2) **Model Rule 1.6 and Disclosures Regarding Prior Client Crimes or Frauds.** Model Rule 1.6(b)(3) permits a lawyer to disclose confidential information to mitigate or rectify the consequences of *prior* client crimes or frauds that threaten

substantial financial harm to others and in which the lawyer's services were used. When "substantial" financial harm is not threatened, however, Model Rule 1.6 prohibits a lawyer from revealing client confidences with respect to a prior crime or fraud. Nevertheless, Comment [16] to the 1983 version of Model Rule 1.6, Comment [10] to Model Rule 1.2, and Comment [3] to Model Rule 4.1, as well as the comments to many state versions of Model Rule 1.6, permit under some circumstances what has been referred to as a "noisy withdrawal" from the representation. The idea is that, although the lawyer is prohibited from disclosing any specifics about the client's conduct, the lawyer's resignation, accompanied by the "withdrawal" or "disaffirmance" of the lawyer's previous "opinion, document, affirmation, or the like," will in most in-

159

stances signal the other parties involved in the transaction that the client may be engaged in wrongdoing. The 2003 version of the ABA Model Rules inexplicably omits "noisy withdrawal" from the comments to Model Rule 1.6, but the inclusion of the "noisy withdrawal" comments to the 2003 versions of Model Rule 1.2, Comment [10], and Model Rule 4.1, Comment [3], indicates the continued vitality of this concept. *See* ABA Formal Opinion 92–366 (Aug. 8, 1992) for an analysis of the "noisy withdrawal" concept. ABA Formal Opinion 92–366 is discussed in "Ethics Update—Analysis of 'Noisy Withdrawal' Comment Under ABA Model Rule of Professional Conduct 1.6," ALAS *Loss Prevention Journal*, Jan. 1993, page 14.

(3) **Disclosing Confidential Client Information to Avoid Perjury or Fraud on a Tribunal under Model Rule 3.3.** The disclosure obligations under Model Rule 3.3 were strengthened in a 2002 amendment to the Rule. Rules 3.3(a) and (b) support the "must disclose" obligation. Model Rule 3.3(c) provides that the duties stated in Model Rule 3.3(a) and (b) apply even if compliance requires disclosure of information otherwise protected by Model Rule 1.6. *See* ABA Formal Opinion 87–353 (Apr. 20, 1987). That opinion was sharply criticized in Goldberg, "Heaven Help the Lawyer for a Civil Liar," 2 Geo. J. Legal Ethics 885 (1989). *See also* ABA Formal Opinion 93–376 (Aug. 6, 1993) discussing the application of Model Rule 3.3(a) to client perjury in a pretrial deposition.

(4) **Disclosing Ongoing Crime or Fraud and the Relationship of Model Rules 4.1(b) and 1.6.** The permissive reporting provisions of Model Rule 1.6 become mandatory if Model Rule 4.1(b) applies, which is why we classify the ongoing crime or fraud situation as one the lawyer "Must" disclose. The starting point of our analysis is Model Rule 4.1(b), which provides that:

In the course of representing a client a lawyer shall not knowingly: . . . (b) fail to disclose a material fact when disclosure is necessary to avoid assisting a criminal or fraudulent act by a client, *unless disclosure is prohibited by Rule 1.6* (emphasis added).

The italicized clause was a last-minute addition during the final drafting process in 1983 to make Model Rule 4.1(b) consistent with the 1983 version of Model Rule 1.6. Some suggested that this effectively negated the entire paragraph (b) of Model Rule 4.1. We think that is incorrect.

The 2003 amendments to Model Rule 1.6 *permit* disclosure of client crimes and frauds involving substantial financial interests. If disclosure of a client's intent to commit a crime or fraud is permitted under the current version of Model Rule 1.6, then such disclosure becomes mandatory under the "shall not knowingly . . . fail to disclose" language of Model Rule 4.1(b) if the situation also meets the requirements of that rule. Even under the 1983 version of Model Rule 1.6, a lawyer prohibited by the final clause of Model Rule 4.1(b) from explicitly disclosing that the client is concealing or misrepresenting material facts was nevertheless *required* by Model Rules 1.2(d) and 1.16(a)(1) to resign immediately as counsel if the client cannot be persuaded to correct the record. Further, under Comment [10] to Model Rule 1.2 and Comment [3] to Model Rule 4.1, discussed in note 2 above, after resigning the lawyer also may noisily "withdraw or disaffirm" *any* fraudulent statement of the client with which the lawyer might be deemed to be associated by reason of the lawyer's prior presence as the client's counsel. *See* G.C. Hazard and W.W. Hodes, *The Law of Lawyering* §§ 9.30–31 (3d ed. 2001). *See also* ABA Formal Opinion 93–375 (Aug. 6, 1993), analyzing a lawyer's disclosure obligations in the context of representing a financial institution in connection with the statutory examination of the institution by the regulators.

For all these reasons, we believe that the ongoing crime or fraud situation is a "Must" disclose case.

(5) **Arizona.** Arizona Opinion 2000–02 (Mar. 2000) concluded that constitutional concerns might call for a different standard in criminal cases. Specifically, in responding to a series of hypothetical situations, the committee concluded that a lawyer is not required to disclose a client's factual misrepresentations to the court in connection with a plea bargain. The committee cautioned, however, that the lawyer cannot, in any way, become a party to or endorse any misrepresentation.

(6) **California.** The obligation to maintain client confidences in California is governed by § 6068(e) of the California Business and Professions Code, as well as by the California Rules of Professional Conduct. Section 6068(e)(2) permits, but does not require, a lawyer to disclose confidential information to prevent a criminal act that the lawyer believes is likely to result in death or substantial bodily harm. Section 6068(e)(2) closely tracks the 1983 version of Model

Rule 1.6(b)(1), except that the potential death or bodily harm does not have to be "imminent" as required by the 1983 version of Rule 1.6.

Rule 3–100 of the California Rules of Professional Conduct also addresses a lawyer's duty of confidentiality. Like § 6068(e)(2), Rule 3–100(B) provides that a lawyer may, but is not required to, disclose confidential client information "to prevent a criminal act that the [lawyer] reasonably believes is likely to result in death of, or substantial bodily harm to, an individual." Although narrower than Model Rule 1.6(b)(1) because it applies only to a future or ongoing "criminal act," the new rule is broader than the 1983 version of Model Rule 1.6 because it does not require that the criminal act be committed by the client, or that the death or injury be "imminent." Also, Rule 3–100(C) requires the lawyer, before revealing confidential information, to attempt, if reasonable under the circumstances, to dissuade the client from the criminal act or to pursue a course of conduct that will prevent any injury or both, and inform the client of the lawyer's ability or decision to reveal the information.

The limited relaxation of the lawyer's duty to maintain client confidentiality does not extend to financial crimes or frauds. California Opinion 1996–146 (undated) reiterated the duty of confidentiality in the context of a case in which a lawyer learns that a client general contractor is using inferior piping in violation of contractual warranties. The opinion discusses steps a lawyer might take when faced with such conduct, but allows no room for disclosure.

Los Angeles County Opinion No. 519 (Feb. 26, 2007) concluded that there is no "self-defense" exception to a lawyer's confidentiality obligations when a third party complains about a lawyer's conduct. The inquiring lawyer was a defendant in two actions, a legal malpractice claim asserted by the former client's bankruptcy trustee, and a class action brought by purchasers of notes issued by the client. After a thorough discussion of California and federal law on this subject, the opinion concluded that even if the lawyer were permitted or compelled to disclose confidential information in the legal malpractice case under California Evidence Code § 958 (permitting disclosure where client accuses lawyer of wrongdoing), she still could not use that information to defend herself in the investors' class action because: (1) § 958 was limited to disputes with clients; and (2) no California authority permitted lawyers to disclose privileged or confidential information to defend attacks from someone other than the client.

(7) **District of Columbia.** A lawyer may reveal client confidences and secrets to prevent the bribery or intimidation of witnesses, jurors, court officials, or other persons involved in proceedings before a tribunal. D.C. Rule 1.6(c)(2). *See also* Maryland Opinion 86–28 (undated), discussed in note 13 below.

(8) **Florida.** In *TransPetrol, Ltd. v. Radulovic*, 764 So. 2d 878 (Fla. Dist. Ct. App. 2000), the court dismissed a claim against lawyers and accountants who allegedly had failed to disclose a client's fraudulent scheme to avoid payment of a debt. The court held that there was no duty of disclosure to a third party, and also rejected claims of aiding and abetting, and of RICO violations. The opinion does not refer to Florida Rule 4–1.6. The May 2006 revisions to the Florida rules did not change the substance of Rule 4–1.6.

(9) **Georgia.** Georgia Rule 1.6(b)(1)(i) also permits disclosure to avoid or prevent harm or substantial financial loss to another as a result of third-party criminal conduct.

(10) **Disclosing Ongoing Client Fraud under Model Rule 4.1.** Some state versions of Model Rule 4.1(b) do not contain the ABA's confusing limiting clause at the end ("unless disclosure is prohibited by Rule 1.6") referred to in note 4 above. Therefore, in the context of an ongoing transaction where the lawyer's client has committed a criminal or fraudulent act by concealing or misrepresenting a material fact, the lawyer *must* disclose the full truth to the affected third parties. As a general proposition, the lawyer should first remonstrate with the client if practicable, then act affirmatively to reveal the client's deceit only if and after the client has refused to rectify the situation. In *Davin, L.L.C. v. Daham*, 746 A.2d 1034 (N.J. Super. App. Div. 2000), the court reversed a summary judgment in favor of a landlord's lawyer on a claim asserted by a tenant against the lawyer based on the lawyer's failure to disclose (or urge his client to disclose) during lease negotiations that the property was in foreclosure. The court cited New Jersey Rule 4.1 in holding that the lawyer might have a duty of disclosure on the facts presented. The court's opinion includes some rather broad language about a lawyer's duty of candor.

(11) **Illinois.** Illinois adopted a modified version of the Model Rules in August 1990, but retained the substance of Model Code DR 7–102(B)(1) as Illinois Rule 1.2(g). At the same time, it adopted the substance of Model Rule 3.3(a)(2), which requires a lawyer to disclose to a tribunal material facts necessary to avoid assisting a client's crime or fraud. *See* Illinois Opinion 94–24 (May 17, 1995), for a discussion of the relationship between Illinois Rule 1.2(g) and Illinois Rule 3.3(a). As a result, Illinois is classified as a "Must Not" disclose state in column E and a "Must" disclose state in column F.

(12) **Kentucky.** A special drafting committee recommended that Kentucky Rule 4.1(b) be deleted, stating that "sufficient guidance is provided by Rules 1.2(d), 1.6, and 1.16." The Kentucky Supreme Court adopted that recommendation. *See* note 4 above regarding Model Rule 4.1(b) generally. Because the Kentucky version of Model Rule 4.1 does not contain a counterpart to Model Rule 4.1(b), and thus places no affirmative obligation on the lawyer to disclose a material fact to avoid assisting a client crime or fraud, we have classified Kentucky as a "May" disclose state in column G.

(13) **Maryland.** In Maryland Opinion No. 86–28 (undated), the inquiring lawyer was a member of the Maryland and District of Columbia bars. The lawyer had introduced evidence in a court proceeding in the District of Columbia and subsequently learned that his client had forged the documents. The Maryland rules required disclosure, while the D.C. rules prohibited it. The Maryland opinion concluded that when a Maryland lawyer acts in accordance with a foreign jurisdiction's ethics rules, the conduct is *per se* ethical.

(14) **Massachusetts.** Massachusetts Rule 1.6(b)(1) also provides that a lawyer may reveal confidential information to prevent the wrongful execution or incarceration of another. Massachusetts Opinion 01–2 (undated) concluded that a lawyer may disclose a client's believable threat of suicide to family members or appropriate authorities.

(15) **Massachusetts.** Massachusetts Rule 3.3(e) provides an exception to Rule 3.3(a) that applies only in criminal cases.

(16) **Montana.** The Montana Supreme Court censured a lawyer for not disclosing, at his client's direction, facts that would have clarified a litigation opponent's misunderstanding regarding the value of a settlement, holding that the lawyer should have withdrawn pursuant to Rule 1.16. *In re Potts*, 158 P.3d 418 (Mont. 2007). The court acknowledged that Rule 1.6 prohibited disclosure, but further stated that Rule 1.6 "does not stand alone," and must be read in conjunction with Rule 1.2(d). Moreover, the court also stated that the obligation of candor to the court under the Montana version of 1983 Model Rule 3.3(a)(2) "trumped any duty of confidentiality that [the lawyer] owed to his clients." 158 P.3d at 424. The court applied Rule 3.3(a)(2) because the settlement resulted in a stipulation that was filed with the court.

(17) **New Hampshire.** In *Feld's Case*, 815 A.2d 383 (N.H. 2002), the New Hampshire Supreme Court suspended a lawyer from the practice of law for one year for failing to advise his client to correct false testimony in a civil deposition.

(18) **New Jersey.** New Jersey Rule 1.6(b)(1) requires disclosure to prevent the client *or another person* from committing a crime, fraud, or "illegal act" that is likely to result in death or substantial bodily harm or substantial financial injury, and Rule 1.6(b)(2) contains the same requirement regarding conduct that is likely to perpetrate a fraud on a tribunal. New Jersey Rule 1.6(d)(1) *permits* disclosure to rectify the consequences of a client's crime, fraud, or "illegal act" in which the lawyer's services were used.

New Jersey Opinion 677 (Oct. 10, 1994) opined that a supervisory and regulatory "department of the state of New Jersey" is a "tribunal" within the meaning of New Jersey Rule 1.6. If the lawyer reveals the information pursuant to New Jersey Rule 1.6, the lawyer may also reveal the information to the person threatened to the extent reasonably necessary to protect that person from substantial bodily harm, substantial financial injury, or substantial property loss.

(19) **New Jersey.** In *In re Forrest*, 730 A.2d 340 (N.J. 1999), the New Jersey Supreme Court held that withholding a material fact from an arbitrator violates the duty of candor to a "tribunal" under New Jersey Rule 3.3(a).

(20) **New York.** New York Rule 1.6(b)(3) permits a lawyer to withdraw a written or oral representation if the lawyer believes it was materially inaccurate or being used to further a crime or fraud. But New York did not adopt Model Rule 4.1(b), so New York is designated "May" disclose in columns E and G.

New York City Opinion 1994–10 (Oct. 21, 1994) held that a lawyer who represents a limited partnership and the general partner on partnership and other matters *must* disclose wrongdoing by the general partner to the limited partners. A discussion of this opinion and related opinions appears in Tab II, Section 2.3.3.

Disclosure may be permissive, not mandatory, if the threatened misconduct remains unexecuted when the representation ends. In Nassau County, New York, Opinion 01–7 (undated), the client advised his lawyer of his intention to omit a half-sibling from the list of potential distributees in a probate proceeding. When the lawyer advised that this would be improper, the client discharged the lawyer before proceeding to do it anyway. The opinion said that the lawyer may disclose the fraud, but was not obligated to do so because the lawyer had not assisted in the fraud.

(21) **North Carolina.** Similar to Model Rule 1.6, North Carolina Rule 1.6(b)(4) permits, but does not require, disclosure "to prevent, mitigate, or rectify the consequences of a client's criminal or fraudulent act in the commission of which the lawyer's services were used." North Carolina is thus listed as a "May" disclose state in columns C, D, and E. North Carolina did not, however, adopt Model Rule 4.1(b), which *requires* disclosure to avoid assisting a client crime or fraud if such disclosure is not prohibited by Rule 1.6. Therefore, North Carolina is designated "May" disclose in column G. *See also* North Carolina Opinion 2005–9 (Jan. 20, 2006) (addressing "safe harbor" in Sarbanes–Oxley's reporting out provision).

(22) **Ohio.** Ohio Rule 3.3(c) defines the duration of the lawyer's duty under Rule 3.3 to rectify false evidence or false statements of law or fact to last. The lawyer's duty lasts only "until the issue to which the duty relates is determined by the highest tribunal that may consider the issue, or the time has expired for such determination." Comment [13] to that rule modifies the rule set forth in *Office of Disciplinary Counsel v. Heffernan*, 569 N.E.2d 1027 (Ohio 1991), to the extent that *Heffernan* could be read to impose a duty to disclose that was not limited in time. In *Heffernan*, the Ohio Supreme Court suspended a lawyer for six months because the lawyer had failed to inform a lower court that the lawyer's client had perpetrated a fraud upon that court, even though the lawyer learned of the client's fraud "a few months" after the fact.

(23) **Pennsylvania.** Disclosure is authorized "to prevent, mitigate or rectify ... a client's criminal or fraudulent act in the commission of which the lawyer's services are being or had been used." Pennsylvania Rule 1.6(c)(3).

(24) **Pennsylvania.** There is no obligation to disclose matters of which the lawyer does not learn until after the matter is closed, according to Philadelphia Opinion 2001–2 (Mar. 2001).

(25) **Tennessee.** Tennessee Rule 1.6(b)(1) permits disclosure to prevent a client *or another person* from committing a crime unless disclosure is prohibited by Rule 3.3. In matters pending before a tribunal, Rule 3.3(f) requires a lawyer who is unable to dissuade a client from perpetrating a fraud on a tribunal or from failing to rectify a prior fraud on a tribunal to seek permission from the tribunal to withdraw. A lawyer seeking permission to withdraw "shall inform the tribunal, without further disclosure of information protected by Rule 1.6, that the lawyer's request to withdraw is required by the Rules of Professional Conduct."

For nonadjudicative matters, Rule 4.1(b) requires a lawyer who learns that a client intends to perpetrate a crime or fraud to consult with the client about the consequences of the client's conduct. If the consultation fails to change the client's intent, the lawyer must withdraw and give notice of the withdrawal to those likely to be injured as well as disaffirm any existing written materials prepared by the lawyer that may be used by the client in furtherance of the crime or fraud. If the client's intended conduct is a crime relating to a nonadjudicative matter, disclosure by the lawyer is permitted by Rule 1.6(b)(1), but not required by Rule 4.1(b). If the client's crime or fraud relating to a nonadjudicative matter has been completed before the lawyer learns of the misconduct, Rule 4.1(c) requires the lawyer to advise the client to rectify the crime or fraud and consult with the client about the consequences of the client's failure to do so. If the client refuses or is unable to rectify the crime or fraud, the lawyer must withdraw, give notice of the withdrawal to those likely to be injured, and disaffirm any written materials prepared by the lawyer that may be used by the client in furtherance of the crime or fraud.

(26) **Texas.** Texas Disciplinary Rule 3.03(b) requires disclosure of "true facts" after offering material evidence the lawyer later knows to be false, but only after at-

tempting to persuade the client to authorize the lawyer to correct or withdraw the false evidence.

(27) **Vermont.** The Reporter's Note to Vermont Rule 4.1 states that the subject of Model Rule 4.1(b) was moved to Vermont Rule 1.6(b)(2) and changed to make the disclosure requirement absolute and not subject to the prohibition of Rule 1.6(a) or the discretion of Rule 1.6(c). However, we have designated columns D and E as "Must Not" because it is not clear that a lawyer must disclose when the crime or fraud is completed but the effects of the crime or fraud are continuing.

(28) **Virginia.** Virginia Rule 1.6(c)(1), in addition to requiring disclosure of a client's intent to commit a crime, also directs the lawyer to "seek to withdraw as counsel" if the crime involves client perjury.

(29) **Washington.** Washington Rule 1.6(b)(7) permits a lawyer to "reveal to the tribunal confidences or secrets which disclose any breach of fiduciary responsibility by a client who is a guardian, personal representative, receiver, or other court appointed fiduciary."

(30) **Washington.** Washington Rule 3.3(a)(2) differs from the Model Rule. The Washington rule provides that a lawyer shall not knowingly fail to disclose a material fact to a tribunal when disclosure is necessary to avoid assisting a criminal or fraudulent act by the client *unless* such disclosure is prohibited by Rule 1.6. The Washington rules do not have a provision equivalent to Model Rule 3.3(b). There-fore, Washington is designated as "Must Not" disclose in column F.

(31) **West Virginia.** In *In re Christina W.*, 639 S.E.2d 770 (W. Va. 2006), the court addressed the issue of whether a guardian *ad litem* appointed in an abuse case owes her child client a duty of confidentiality that prohibits the lawyer from disclosing confidential information regarding abuse to the court. The 14–year–old client initially told officers who responded to a domestic disturbance call that her mother's boyfriend touched her inappropriately. She later recanted. When the lawyer was appointed for the girl, however, she sought assurances that the lawyer would not reveal the client's confidences. Upon receiving those assurances, the girl told the lawyer that the boyfriend had in fact sexually abused her. The lawyer kept that disclosure in confidence, but when the client later told caseworkers, they asked the court to remove the lawyer as guardian. On appeal from the denial of that motion, the court cited West Virginia Rules 1.6 and 1.14 (client under a disability) in disapproving the lawyer's conduct. The court held that a guardian *ad litem*'s duty of confidentiality to the children he or she represents in child abuse and neglect proceedings "is not absolute," and that when honoring that duty of confidentiality would expose the clients to a "high risk of probable harm," then the guardian must make a disclosure to the presiding court in order to safeguard the child's best interests.

Section 4. Chart on Disclosure to Comply with Law

State	Permit Lawyer Disclosure to Comply with Law?
Alabama	No, but has former Comment [21] to 1983 Model Rule 1.6
Alaska	Yes, Alaska RPC 1.6(b)(6)
Arizona	Yes, Arizona RPC 1.6(d)(5)
Arkansas	Yes, Arkansas RPC 1.6(b)(6)
California	No
Colorado	Yes, Colorado RPC 1.6(b)(7)
Connecticut	Yes, Connecticut RPC 1.6(c)(4)
Delaware	Yes, Delaware RPC 1.6(b)(6)
District of Columbia	Yes, DC RPC 1.6(e)(2)(A)
Florida	No, but has former Comment [21] to 1983 Model Rule 1.6
Georgia	No, but has former Comment [21] to 1983 Model Rule 1.6 as Comment [19]
Hawaii	Yes, Hawaii RPC 1.6(c)(6)
Idaho	Yes, Idaho RPC 1.6(b)(6)

State	Permit Lawyer Disclosure to Comply with Law?
Illinois	Yes, Illinois RPC 1.6(c)(1)
Indiana	Yes, Indiana RPC 1.6(b)(6)
Iowa	Yes, Iowa RPC 32:1.6(b)(6)
Kansas	Yes, Kansas RPC 1.6(b)(2)
Kentucky	Yes, Kentucky RPC 3.130 (1.6(b)(3))
Louisiana	Yes, Louisiana RPC 1.6(b)(6)
Maine	Yes, Maine RPC 1.6(b)(6)
Maryland	Yes, Maryland RPC 1.6(b)(6)
Massachusetts	Yes, Massachusetts RPC 1.6(b)(4)
Michigan	Yes, Michigan RPC 1.6(c)(2)
Minnesota	Yes, Minnesota RPC 1.6(b)(9)
Mississippi	Yes, Mississippi RPC 1.6(e)
Missouri	Yes, Missouri RPC 4–1.6(b)(4)
Montana	Yes, Montana RPC 1.6(b)(4)
Nebraska	Yes, Nebraska RPC 1.6(b)(4)
Nevada	Yes, Nevada RPC 1.6(b)(6)
New Hampshire	Yes, New Hampshire RPC 1.6(b)(4)
New Jersey	Yes, New Jersey RPC 1.6(d)(3)
New Mexico	Yes, New Mexico RPC 1.6(b)(6)
New York	Yes, New York RPC 1.6(b)(6)
North Carolina	Yes, North Carolina RPC 1.6(b)(1)
North Dakota	Yes, North Dakota RPC 1.6(c)(5)
Ohio	Yes, Ohio RPC 1.6(b)(6)
Oklahoma	Yes, Oklahoma RPC 1.6(b)(6)
Oregon	Yes, Oregon RPC 1.6(b)(5)
Pennsylvania	No, *but see* Comments [18] and [19] to RPC 1.6
Rhode Island	Yes, Rhode Island RPC 1.6(b)(4)
South Carolina	Yes, South Carolina RPC 1.6(b)(7)
South Dakota	Yes, South Dakota RPC 1.6(b)(5)
Tennessee	Yes, Tennessee RPC 1.6(c)(3)
Texas	Yes, Texas RPC 1.05(c)(4)
Utah	Yes, Utah RPC 1.6(b)(6)
Vermont	Yes, Vermont RPC 1.6(c)
Virginia	Yes, Virginia RPC 1.6(b)(1)
Washington	No, but may reveal to comply with "court order," Washington RPC 1.6(b)(6)
West Virginia	No, but has former Comment [21] to 1983 Model Rule 1.6
Wisconsin	Yes, Wisconsin RPC 1.6(c)(5)
Wyoming	Yes, Wyoming RPC 1.6(b)(4)

Section 5. Chart on Disclosure Outside
an Organization under Rule 1.13

State	Permit Lawyer Disclosure Outside the Organization?
Alabama	No, Alabama RPC 1.13 (1983 Model Rule 1.13)
Alaska	Yes, Alaska RPC 1.13 (modified Aug. 2003)
Arizona	Yes, Arizona ER 1.13(c) (Aug. 2003)
Arkansas	Yes, Arkansas RPC 1.13(c) (Aug. 2003)
California	No, California RPC 3–600 (modified 1983 Model Rule 1.13)
Colorado	Yes, Colorado RPC 1.13(c) (Aug. 2003)
Connecticut	Yes, Connecticut RPC 1.13(c) (Aug. 2003)
Delaware	No, Delaware RPC 1.13 (Ethics 2000)
District of Columbia	No, District of Columbia RPC 1.13 (modified 1983 Model Rule 1.13)
Florida	No, Florida RPC 4–1.13 (Ethics 2000)
Georgia	No, Georgia RPC 1.13 (1983 Model Rule 1.13)
Hawaii	No, Hawaii RPC 1.13 (modified 1983 Model Rule 1.13)
Idaho	Yes, Idaho RPC 1.13(c) (Aug. 2003)
Illinois	No, Illinois RPC 1.13 (1983 Model Rule 1.13)
Indiana	Yes, Indiana RPC 1.13(c) (Aug. 2003)
Iowa	Yes, Iowa RPC 32:1.13(c) (Aug. 2003)
Kansas	No, Kansas RPC 1.13 (1983 Model Rule 1.13)
Kentucky	No, Kentucky SCR 3.130 (1983 Model Rule 1.13)
Louisiana	Yes, Louisiana RPC 1.13(c) (Aug. 2003)
Maine	Yes, Maine RPC 1.13(c) (modified Aug. 2003)
Maryland	Yes, Maryland RPC 1.13(c) (modified Aug. 2003)
Massachusetts	Yes, Massachusetts RPC 1.13(c) (Aug. 2003)
Michigan	Yes, Michigan RPC 1.13(c) (modified 1983 Model Rule 1.13)
Minnesota	Yes, Minnesota RPC 1.13(c) (modified Aug. 2003)
Mississippi	No, Mississippi RPC 1.13 (1983 Model Rule 1.13)
Missouri	No, Missouri RPC 4–1.13 (Ethics 2000)
Montana	No, Montana RPC 1.13 (Ethics 2000)
Nebraska	Yes, Nebraska RPC 1.13(c) (Aug. 2003)
Nevada	Yes, Nevada RPC 1.13(c) (modified Aug. 2003)
New Hampshire	Yes, New Hampshire RPC 1.13(c) (Aug. 2003)
New Jersey	Yes, New Jersey RPC 1.13(c) (modified 1983 Model Rule 1.13)
New Mexico	Yes, New Mexico RPC 16–113 (modified Aug. 2003)
New York	Yes, New York RPC 1.13(c) (but only if permitted by RPC 1.6)
North Carolina	Yes, North Carolina RPC 1.13(c) (modified Aug. 2003)
North Dakota	Yes, North Dakota RPC 1.13(c) (Aug. 2003)
Ohio	Yes, Ohio RPC 1.13(c) (modified Aug. 2003)
Oklahoma	Yes, Oklahoma RPC 1.13(c) (Aug. 2003)
Oregon	Yes, Oregon 1.13(c) (modified Aug. 2003)
Pennsylvania	No, Pennsylvania RPC 1.13 (Ethics 2000)
Rhode Island	Yes, Rhode Island RPC 1.13(c) (Aug. 2003)

State	Permit Lawyer Disclosure Outside the Organization?
South Carolina	Yes, South Carolina RPC 1.13(c) (Aug. 2003)
South Dakota	No, South Dakota RPC 1.13 (Ethics 2000)
Tennessee	No, Tennessee RPC 1.13 (modified 1983 Model Rule 1.13)
Texas	No, Texas RPC 1.12 (modified 1983 Model Rule 1.13)
Utah	Yes, Utah RPC 1.13(c) (August 2003)
Vermont	Yes, Vermont RPC 1.13 (modified 1983 Model Rule 1.13)
Virginia	No, Virginia RPC 1.13 (1983 Model Rule 1.13)
Washington	Yes, Washington RPC 1.13(c) (Aug. 2003)
West Virginia	No, West Virginia RPC 1.13 (1983 Model Rule 1.13)
Wisconsin	Yes, Wisconsin RPC 1.13(c) (Aug. 2003)
Wyoming	No, Wyoming RPC 1.13(c) (modified Ethics 2000)

APPENDIX B

Chart on Lateral Lawyer Screening*

The following chart analyzes in summary form the provisions of the ABA Model Code of Professional Responsibility, the ABA Model Rules of Professional Conduct, the *Restatement*, and the various state versions of the Code and Rules on the issue of imputed disqualification, the subissues relating to screening generally, and the efficacy of an "ethical wall" without client consent.

The chart indicates, with appropriate citations, whether a firm can avoid the general imputed disqualification rule by constructing an "ethical wall" or similar screening device in the case of movement from one law firm to another by a lawyer who is personally disqualified from a matter because of his or her participation in it at a previous firm. A "No" answer to that question on the chart means that the "ethical wall" or screening device is not sufficient by itself, and that, in addition to the ethical wall, the firm to which the lawyer is moving must seek and obtain the consent of the previous firm's client if the second firm is acting as counsel in the matter adverse to the previous firm's client. This must be done before the disqualified lawyer begins work at the new firm. Failure to recognize this rule and obtain consent of the previous firm's client ordinarily will subject the second firm to immediate disqualification. If that happens, a malpractice claim by the second firm's client is likely. The lesson that emerges from the chart is that more than half of the jurisdictions (30 out of 51) do not recognize screening of a tainted lawyer alone as a cure for imputed disqualification. As the notes to the chart demonstrate, federal courts may differ with courts and ethics committees of the states in which they sit.

We emphasize that this chart and the subsequent notes deal only with movement from one private firm to another. In the case of a new lawyer who is a former member of the executive or judicial branch of government, some form of effective screening device is usually acceptable.

Lateral Lawyer Screening

Jurisdiction	Applicable Rules	Screening by Rule?	Rule Provision	Note
	Model Rules of Professional Conduct	Yes	1.10(a)	
	Restatement	Limited	§ 124(2)	
AL	Rules of Professional Conduct	No	1.10(b)	1
AK	Rules of Professional Conduct	No	1.10(a)	2
AZ	Rules of Professional Conduct	Limited	1.10(d)	3
AR	Rules of Professional Conduct	No	1.9(b) and 1.10(a)	4

Jurisdiction	Applicable Rules	Screening by Rule?	Rule Provision	Note
CA	Rules of Professional Conduct	No		5
CO	Rules of Professional Conduct	Limited	1.10(e)	6
CT	Rules of Professional Conduct	No	1.10(a)	7
DE	Lawyers' Rules of Professional Conduct	Yes	1.10(c)	8
DC	Rules of Professional Conduct	No	1.10(b)	9
FL	Rules of Professional Conduct	No	4–1.10(b)	10
GA	Rules of Professional Conduct	No	1.9(b) and 1.10(a)	11
HI	Rules of Professional Conduct	No	1.9(b) and 1.10(a)	12
ID	Rules of Professional Conduct	No	1.10(b)	
IL	Rules of Professional Conduct	Yes	1.10(b)(2) and 1.10(e)	13
IN	Rules of Professional Conduct	Limited	1.10(c)	14
IA	Rules of Professional Conduct	No	32:1.10	15
KS	Rules of Professional Conduct	No	1.10(b)	16
KY	Rules of Professional Conduct	Yes	SCR 3.130(d)(1.10(d))	17
LA	Rules of Professional Conduct	No	1.10(b)	18
ME	Code of Professional Responsibility Effective 8/1/09, Rules of Professional Conduct	No	3.4(d)(1)(ii) 1.10(a)	19
MD	Rules of Professional Conduct	Yes	1.10(c)	20
MA	Rules of Professional Conduct	Limited	1.10(d)(2)	21
MI	Rules of Professional Conduct	Yes	1.10(b)	22
MN	Rules of Professional Conduct	Limited	1.10(b)	23
MS	Rules of Professional Conduct	No	1.10(b)	24
MO	Rules of Professional Conduct	No	4–1.10(a)	25
MT	Rules of Professional Conduct	Yes	1.10(c)(1)	
NE	Rules of Professional Conduct	No	3–501.10(a)	26
NV	Rules of Professional Conduct	Limited	Rule 1.10(e)	27
NH	Rules of Professional Conduct	No	1.10(b)	
NJ	Rules of Professional Conduct	Limited	1.10(c)	28
NM	Rules of Professional Conduct	Limited	16–110(C)(2)	
NY	Rules of Professional Conduct	No	1.10(c)	29
NC	Rules of Professional Conduct	Yes	1.10(c)	
ND	Rules of Professional Conduct	Limited	1.10(b)	30
OH	Rules of Professional Conduct	Limited	1.10(d)	31
OK	Rules of Professional Conduct	No	1.10(b)	
OR	Rules of Professional Conduct	Yes	1.10(c)	32
PA	Rules of Professional Conduct	Yes	1.10(b)(1) and (2)	33
RI	Rules of Professional Conduct	Yes	1.10(c)	
SC	Rules of Professional Conduct	No	1.9(b) and 1.10(a)	34
SD	Rules of Professional Conduct	No	1.9(b) and 1.10(a)	
TN	Rules of Professional Conduct	Limited	1.10(c) and (d)	35
TX	Disciplinary Rules of Professional Conduct	No	1.09(b)	36
UT	Rules of Professional Conduct	Yes	1.10(c)	37
VT	Rules of Professional Conduct	No	1.9(b) and 1.10(a)	38
VA	Rules of Professional Conduct	No	1.9(b)	39
WA	Rules of Professional Conduct	Yes	1.10(e)	
WV	Rules of Professional Conduct	No	1.10(b)	40

Jurisdiction	Applicable Rules	Screening by Rule?	Rule Provision	Note
WI	Rules of Professional Conduct for Attorneys	Limited	20:1.10(a)(2)	41
WY	Rules of Professional Conduct for Attorneys at Law	No	1.10(b)	

Notes for Chart

1. *See also Roberts v. Hutchins*, 572 So. 2d 1231 (Ala. 1990).

2. *See also Richard B. v. Department of Health and Social Services*, 71 P.3d 811 (Alaska 2003) (screen does not prevent disqualification in Alaska).

3. *See also Eberle Design, Inc. v. Reno A & E*, 354 F.Supp.2d 1093 (D. Ariz. 2005).

4. *See also Burnette v. Morgan*, 794 S.W.2d 145 (Ark. 1990).

5. California has no ethics rule on this subject, and the California Supreme Court has not decided the issue. In *Department of Corporations v. SpeeDee Oil Change Systems, Inc.*, 980 P.2d 371 (Cal. 1999), the California Supreme Court opened the door to screening by discussing and not rejecting the idea, but ultimately held it need not decide the issue. Other California decisions (state and federal) on this issue are mixed. In *Panther v. Park*, 101 Cal. App. 4th 69 (2002) (not citable), the Fourth District of the California Court of Appeals soundly rejected the idea of automatic imputed disqualification, finding that a "firm may rebut a presumption of shared confidences and avoid vicarious disqualification by showing that effective screening methods were in place." However, that order was vacated without opinion by the California Supreme Court. *Panther v. Park*, 63 P.3d 215 (Cal. 2003). Some California decisions have been hostile to screening. *See Hitachi, Ltd. v. Tatung Co.*, 419 F.Supp.2d 1158 (N.D. Cal. 2006); *Andric v. State*, 55 F.Supp.2d 1056 (C.D. Cal. 1999); *Employers Ins. of Wausau v. Albert D. Seeno Construction Co.*, 692 F.Supp. 1150 (N.D. Cal. 1988); *In re Mortgage & Realty Trust*, 195 B.R. 740 (Bankr. C.D. Cal. 1996); and *Henriksen v. Great American Savings and Loan*, 11 Cal. App. 4th 109 (1992). *But see City of Santa Barbara v. Superior Court of Santa Barbara County*, 122 Cal. App. 4th 17 (2004), where the court approved screening for government lawyers; *All American Semiconductor, Inc. v. Hynix Semiconductor, Inc.*, 2008 WL 5484552 (N.D. Cal. Dec. 18, 2008) (disapproved screen, but indicated law in California "might well be headed" toward approval in some circumstances); and *Klein v. Superior Court of Santa Clara County*, 198 Cal. App. 3d 894 (1988), where the court implied that California courts *might* approve an "ethical wall" provided the new lawyer had not actually worked on the affected client's matter while at the previous firm. *Cf. City and County of San Francisco v. Cobra Solutions, Inc.*, 135 P.3d 20 (Cal. 2006) (California Supreme Court rejected screening with respect to city government law office) and *In re Charlisse C.*, 194 P.3d 330 (Cal. 2008) (public law firm might be able to cure conflict by erecting screen). The Ninth Circuit approved of screening in *In re County of Los Angeles*, 223 F.3d 990 (9th Cir. 2000), but in the context of a federal magistrate judge moving to private practice.

6. In *Hunter Douglas, Inc. v. Home Fashions, Inc.*, 811 F.Supp. 566 (D. Colo. 1992), a Colorado federal court, applying Illinois ethics rules, found a lateral lawyer had been effectively screened. *See also* Colorado Opinion No. 88 (May 18, 1991), which precedes the new Rule 1.10(e) permitting limited screening.

7. *See* Connecticut Informal Opinion 01–16 (Dec. 28, 2001). *But see Horch v. United of Omaha Life Ins.*, 25 Conn. L. Rptr. 18 (Super. Ct. 1999) (refusal to disqualify a firm that hired a lawyer who had worked on the other side because the lawyer had been effectively screened from the matter) and *Wellner v. Carroll*, 1995 WL 55048 (Jan. 6, 1995), suggesting a screen might have avoided disqualification.

8. *See* Delaware Opinion 1986–1 (undated). The opinion relates specifically to nonlawyers; however, it relies, in part, on a case that extended Rule 1.11(b) screening provisions to private lawyers, *Nemours Foundation v. Gilbane, Aetna, Federal Ins. Co.*, 632 F.Supp. 418 (D. Del. 1986).

9. *See* D.C. Opinion 273 (Sept. 17, 1997). The former client may consent to the representation, however, and require screening as a condition of its consent under Rule 1.10(d). Consent of the former client is not required under Rule 1.10(b) in the case of a new lawyer who was "tainted" solely because of work at a previous firm in the capacity of summer associate, law clerk, paralegal, or any other similar capacity "prior to becoming a lawyer." Of course, the second firm would be expected to take steps to ensure that such persons do not

170

have any involvement with, or make any improper disclosure regarding, any case in which they were previously involved (similar to the traditional requirement applicable to former judicial clerks). *See* D.C. Opinion 279 (Mar. 18, 1998).

10. *See Nissan Motor Corp. in U.S.A. v. Orozco*, 595 So. 2d 240 (Fla. Dist. Ct. App. 1992); *Birdsall v. Crowngap, Ltd.*, 575 So. 2d 231 (Fla. Dist. Ct. App. 1991); and *Edward J. DeBartolo Corp. v. Petrin*, 516 So. 2d 6 (Fla. Dist. Ct. App. 1987).

11. We are not aware of any Georgia court or ethics committee ruling squarely deciding the screening issue. However, in *Georgia Baptist Health Care System, Inc. v. Hanafi*, 559 S.E.2d 746, 749 (Ga. Ct. App. 2002), the court in *dicta* said the conflict was of the type that could be "managed and ameliorated" through screening. Also, a Georgia federal court said in *dicta* it would reject screening measures in *Amoco Chemicals Corp. v. MacArthur*, 568 F.Supp. 42 (N.D. Ga. 1983).

12. *See Otaka, Inc. v. Klein*, 791 P.2d 713 (Haw. 1990).

13. *Amurol Confections Co. v. Morris National, Inc.*, 2003 WL 21321344 (N.D. Ill. June 4, 2003); *Van Jackson v. Check 'N Go of Illinois, Inc.*, 114 F.Supp.2d 731 (N.D. Ill. 2000) (recognized screening but nevertheless disqualified the firm because screen probably ineffective). *See also Cromley v. Board of Education of Lockport High School District 205*, 17 F.3d 1059 (7th Cir. 1994) and *Miller v. Chicago and North Western Transportation Co.*, 938 F.Supp. 503 (N.D. Ill. 1996).

14. An Indiana appellate court approved the concept of screening in *Gerald v. Turnock Plumbing, Heating and Cooling, LLC*, 768 N.E.2d 498 (Ind. Ct. App. 2002), but held the screen at issue was implemented too late. In *Chapman v. Chrysler Corp.*, 54 F.Supp.2d 864 (S.D. Ind. 1999), and *Speedy v. Rexnord Corp.*, 54 F.Supp.2d 867 (S.D. Ind. 1999), Indiana federal district courts found screening measures effective and, following Seventh Circuit precedent, refused to disqualify the law firms with the alleged conflicts.

15. Although Iowa Rules of Professional Conduct generally do not approve of screening for lawyers, Comment [4] to Rule 1.10 states that a lawyer whose conduct before he or she became a lawyer causes a conflict can be screened. In *Doe v. Perry Community School District*, 650 N.W.2d 594 (Iowa 2002), the Iowa Supreme Court rejected lawyer screening.

16. *Lansing–Delaware Water District v. Oak Lane Park, Inc.*, 808 P.2d 1369 (Kan. 1991); *Parker v. Volkswagenwerk Aktiengesellschaft*, 781 P.2d 1099 (Kan. 1989); *Graham by Graham v. Wyeth Laboratories Division of American Home Products Corp.*, 906 F.2d 1419 (10th Cir. 1990); and *Pacific Employers Ins. Co. v. P.B. Hoidale Co. Inc.*, 796 F.Supp. 1428 (D. Kan. 1992).

17. The literal language of the Kentucky screening rule permits screening of any lawyer who has a conflict because of a former client, not just lateral lawyers. It is highly questionable, however, whether any court would interpret the rule this broadly.

18. *But see Petrovich v. Petrovich*, 556 So. 2d 281 (La. Ct. App. 1990) (upholding trial court's finding that lawyers had established "cone of silence" and therefore no disqualification). Federal courts in Louisiana follow Fifth Circuit precedent and refuse to allow the use of a screen to cure an imputed disqualification. *Green v. Administrators of Tulane Educational Fund*, 1998 WL 24424 (E.D. La. Jan. 22, 1998).

19. *See Casco Northern Bank v. JBI Associates, Ltd.*, 667 A.2d 856 (Me. 1995).

20. *See Compass Marketing, Inc. v. Schering–Plough Corp.*, 2006 WL 1892405 (D. Md. July 6, 2006).

21. *See United States Filter Corp. v. Ionics, Inc.*, 68 F.Supp.2d 48 (D. Mass. 1999) (refusing to approve a screen because Massachusetts Rule 1.10(d)(2) requirements for a screen were not satisfied). At least one decision decided prior to the 1998 rule change allowed limited screening. *See Thomalen v. Marriott Corp.*, 1994 WL 524123 (D. Mass. Sept. 19, 1994).

22. *See National Union Fire Ins. Co. of Pittsburgh, Pennsylvania v. Alticor, Inc.*, 472 F.3d 436 (6th Cir. 2007), discussed in "The Wild Card in Analyzing Conflicts or Other Legal Ethics Issues—'Questionable' Judicial Decisions," *Journal*, Winter 2007, page 14, 15. *See also Cobb Publishing Inc. v. Hearst Corp.*, 907 F.Supp. 1038 (E.D. Mich. 1995) and Michigan Opinions RI–115 (Jan. 31, 1992) and R–4 (Jan. 5, 1989).

23. Under Minnesota Rule 1.10(b), a lateral lawyer's conflict will not be imputed to others in the firm if: (1) the lawyer does not have "significant" confidential information; (2) the lawyer is screened; and (3) affected clients receive timely and adequate notice of the screen. In *Lennartson v. Anoka–Hennepin Independent School*

171

District No. 11, 662 N.W.2d 125 (Minn. 2003), the Minnesota Supreme Court held Rule 1.10(b) should be read literally so that a conflict will be imputed unless all of the rule's subparts are satisfied.

24. *But see Aldridge v. State*, 583 So. 2d 203 (Miss. 1991) (in criminal case, when deciding a motion to disqualify counsel, court should consider whether the conflicted attorney was screened).

25. Missouri Informal Opinions 20050030 (undated) and 20030007 (undated) (screening will not avoid disqualification). *But see School District of Kansas City, Missouri v. ACandS, Inc.*, 1989 WL 99138 (W.D. Mo. Aug. 23, 1989); and *Hallmark Cards, Inc. v. Hallmark Dodge, Inc.*, 616 F.Supp. 516 (W.D. Mo. 1985).

26. *Nebraska ex rel. FirsTier Bank, N.A. v. Buckley*, 503 N.W.2d 838 (Neb. 1993).

27. *Ogilvie v. Eighth Judicial District Court*, 999 P.2d 393 (Nev. 1996) (holding that Nevada's screening procedures apply only to lawyers moving from government service to private employment and issuing writ of *mandamus* directing district court to disqualify law firm) was decided before Nevada's 2006 adoption of limited lateral screening.

28. The following opinions were issued before New Jersey Rule 1.10 was amended to allow limited screening: New Jersey Opinion 667 (Nov. 2, 1992), discussed in "Ethics Update—Imputed Disqualification: Opinion 667 of New Jersey Advisory Committee on Professional Ethics," *Journal*, Jan. 1993, page 23 (required consent as a condition precedent to screening), and *Cardona v. General Motors Corp.*, 942 F.Supp. 968 (D.N.J. 1996) (court said that in New Jersey "ethics screens" had not been approved to preclude imputed disqualification).

29. *Kassis v. Teacher's Ins. and Annuity Association*, 717 N.E.2d 674 (N.Y. 1999) (if moving lawyer has information that is either "significant" or "material," screen will not work); *Alicea v. Bencivenga*, 704 N.Y.S.2d 578 (App. Div. 2000); *Cummin v. Cummin*, 695 N.Y.S.2d 346 (App. Div. 1999) (screen around lawyer with preliminary consultation conflict provided adequate safeguard); and *Trustco Bank New York v. Melino*, 625 N.Y.S.2d 803 (Sup. Ct. 1995) (rejected screening). In *Reilly v. Computer Associates Long–Term Disability Plan*, 423 F.Supp.2d 5 (E.D.N.Y. 2006); *Papyrus Technology Corp. v. New York Stock Exchange, Inc.*, 325 F.Supp.2d 270 (S.D.N.Y. 2004); *G.D. Searle & Co. v.*

Nutrapharm, Inc., 1999 WL 249725 (S.D.N.Y. Apr. 26, 1999); *Schwed v. General Electric Co.*, 990 F.Supp. 113 (N.D.N.Y. 1998); and *In re Del–Val Financial Corp. Securities Litigation*, 158 F.R.D. 270 (S.D.N.Y. 1994), New York federal courts approved screening measures. *But see United States v. Salvagno*, 2003 WL 21939629 (N.D.N.Y. Feb. 28, 2003) (screen will not work in two-lawyer office); and *Decora Inc. v. DW Wallcovering, Inc.*, 899 F.Supp. 132 (S.D.N.Y. 1995) (new firm too small and screen erected too late).

30. *But see Ness, Motley, Loadholt, Richardson and Poole, P.A. v. Aetna Casualty & Surety Co.*, No. 88–CV–00157–RSW (D.N.D. 1990).

31. The Ohio Supreme Court generally approved screening in *Kala v. Aluminum Smelting & Refining Co., Inc.*, 688 N.E.2d 258 (Ohio 1998), although on the basis of the particular facts of that case, it disqualified the law firm because of a strong appearance of impropriety. *See also* Ohio Opinion 89–013 (May 30, 1989).

32. Rule 1.10(c) of the Oregon Rules of Professional Conduct approved screening provided the disqualified lawyer and his or her firm take certain steps prescribed by the rule. In *Portland General Electric Co. v. Duncan, Weinberg, Miller & Pembroke, P.C.*, 986 P.2d 35 (Or. Ct. App. 1999), an Oregon appellate court held that a screen could prevent imputation of a conflict, but that the screen would need to be approved either by the lower court or by the ethics experts who testified in the matter.

33. Philadelphia Opinion 91–18 (July 1991) confirms that consent is not required where screening is used. The court applied that rule in *Dworkin v. General Motors Corp.*, 906 F.Supp. 273 (E.D. Pa. 1995). *See also Norfolk Southern Railway Co. v. Reading Blue Mountain & Northern Railroad Co.*, 397 F.Supp.2d 551 (M.D. Pa. 2005) (screen ineffective because, among other reasons, it failed to provide sanctions for violation); and *James v. Teleflex, Inc.*, 1999 WL 98559 (E.D. Pa. Feb. 24, 1999) (screen inadequate).

34. *See* South Carolina Opinion 92–23 (Oct. 1992). However, the South Carolina Rules of Professional Conduct allow screening of lawyers participating in a "program serving indigent clients shall not be disqualified under [Rule 1.10] because of the program's representation of another client in the same or a substantially related matter

. . . ." *See* South Carolina Rule of Professional Conduct 1.10(e).

35. Prior to the new Tennessee Rules of Professional Conduct, the Tennessee Supreme Court held that screening provisions adequately rebutted the presumption of shared confidences, but nevertheless, disqualified the firm involved because of an appearance of impropriety. *Clinard v. Blackwood*, 46 S.W.3d 177 (Tenn. 2001). The Sixth Circuit and Tennessee federal district courts also have approved screening. *See Manning v. Waring, Cox, James, Sklar and Allen*, 849 F.2d 222 (6th Cir. 1988); *Vergos v. Timber Creek, Inc.*, 200 B.R. 624 (W.D. Tenn. 1996) (bankruptcy matter); and *In re Club Income Properties*, No. 92–11434 (E.D. Tenn. Sept 13, 1993) (same). *But see Penn Mutual Life Ins. Co. v. Cleveland Mall Associates*, 841 F.Supp. 815 (E.D. Tenn. 1993), where on facts similar to those in *Club Income Properties*, a district court ruled that the law firm should be disqualified.

36. *Henderson v. Floyd*, 891 S.W.2d 252 (Tex. 1995) and *Phoenix Founders, Inc. v. Marshall*, 887 S.W.2d 831 (Tex. 1994). *But see COC Services, Ltd. v. CompUSA, Inc.*, 2002 WL 1792479 (Aug. 6, 2002) (defendant's firm not disqualified, even though it hired lawyer who had worked on matter for plaintiff, because moving lawyer's work was minimal and equities weighed against disqualification).

37. Rule 1.10(c) of the Utah Rules of Professional Conduct approves screening provided the lawyer is apportioned no part of the fee from the matter and a notice is promptly given to any affected former client.

38. *See* Vermont Opinion 87–07 (undated).

39. Virginia Opinion 1428 (Feb. 22, 1992) specifically disapproves of screening without consent.

40. *Burgess–Lester v. Ford Motor Co.*, 2008 WL 4643362 (N.D. W. Va. Oct. 17, 2008) recognized that screening might be effective in a particular case but said that all doubts should be resolved in favor of disqualification. It found the screen at issue to be ineffective because the tainted lawyer was unsure of its precise parameters. Other federal courts in West Virginia also have rejected screening. *See CSX Transportation, Inc. v. Gilkison*, 2006 WL 3203419 (N.D. W. Va. Nov. 3, 2006); *Healthnet, Inc. v. Health Net, Inc.*, 289 F.Supp.2d 755 (S.D. W. Va. 2003); and *Roberts & Schaefer Co. v. San–Con, Inc.*, 898 F.Supp. 356 (S.D. W. Va. 1995).

41. *But see Nelson v. Green Builders, Inc.*, 823 F.Supp. 1439 (E.D. Wis. 1993), where the court indicated that a timely screen would have prevented disqualification. In *Nelson* the screen was not created until the disqualified firm was challenged by the other side; the court said that was too late to avoid disqualification.

APPENDIX C

When a *Written* Fee Agreement Is Required*

The following chart analyzes in summary form the provisions of the ABA Model Rules of Professional Conduct (2003) and the various state versions of the Rules on whether a lawyer *must* have a *written* fee agreement with a client in contingent fee matters and other circumstances or whether a written agreement is "preferred." The jurisdictions that require written fee agreements for all new clients are Arizona, Colorado, Connecticut, the District of Columbia, New Jersey, Pennsylvania, Rhode Island, and Wisconsin (after July 1, 2007). California requires written fee agreements for all noncorporate clients if fees will exceed $1,000. Alaska and Montana require a written fee agreement if fees will exceed $500. By court rule (not disciplinary rule), New York requires written engagement letters with new clients unless the fee is expected to be less than $3,000.

Several states have no provision relating to the need for written agreements in the *ethics* rules, but deal with the issue elsewhere in court rules or statutes. We have included the appropriate references where we are aware of them.

Generally, but not always, the "Others" column cites a provision that refers to a new client, noncontingent fee situation. The statutes and ethics codes rarely cover the case of a new matter for an existing client where the fee for that matter is not a contingent fee.

Chart on Written Fee Agreements

Jurisdiction	Applicable Rules	Contingent	Others
	Model Rules of Professional Conduct	Must: 1.5(c)	Preferred: 1.5(b)
AL	Rules of Professional Conduct	Must: 1.5(c)	Preferred: 1.5(b)
AK	Rules of Professional Conduct	Must: 1.5(c)	Must: (if over $1000) 1.5(b)
AZ	Rules of Professional Conduct	Must: 1.5(c)	Must: 1.5(b)
AR	Rules of Professional Conduct	Must: 1.5(c)	Preferred: 1.5(b)
CA	Statutory Provisions	Must: § 6147 of Business and Professions Code	Must: (If not a corporation and over $1,000) § 6148 of Business and Professions Code
CO	Rules of Professional Conduct, Rules of Civil Procedure, and Court Rules	Must: Chapt. 23.3 Col. Rules of Civil Procedure, Court Rule 4(b)	Must: 1.5(b)

WHEN A WRITTEN FEE AGREEMENT IS REQUIRED

Jurisdiction	Applicable Rules	Contingent	Others
CT	Rules of Professional Conduct	Must: 1.5(c)	Must: 1.5(b)
DE	Lawyers' Rules of Professional Conduct	Must: 1.5(c)	Preferred: 1.5(b)
DC	Rules of Professional Conduct	Must: 1.5(c)	Must: 1.5(b)
FL	Rules of Professional Conduct	Must: 4–1.5(f)	Preferred: 4–1.5(e)
GA	Rules of Professional Conduct	Must: 1.5(c)	Must: 1.5(b) (if lawyer has not regularly represented client)
HI	Rules of Professional Conduct	Must: 1.5(c)	Preferred: 1.5(b)
ID	Rules of Professional Conduct	Must: 1.5(c)	Preferred: 1.5(b)
IL	Rules of Professional Conduct	Must: 1.5(c)	No provision
IN	Rules of Professional Conduct	Must: 1.5(c)	Preferred: 1.5(b)
IA	Rules of Professional Conduct	Must: 32: 1.5(c)	Preferred: 32: 1.5(b)
KS	Rules of Professional Conduct	Must: 1.5(d)	Preferred: 1.5(b)
KY	Rules of Professional Conduct	Must: 1.5(c)	Preferred: 1.5(b)
LA	Rules of Professional Conduct	Must: 1.5(c)	Preferred: 1.5(b)
ME	Rules of Professional Conduct	Must: 1.5(c)	Preferred: 1.5(b)
MD	Rules of Professional Conduct	Must: 1.5(c)	Preferred: 1.5(b)
MA	Rules of Professional Conduct	Must: 1.5(c)	Preferred: 1.5(b)
MI	Rules of Professional Conduct	Must: 1.5(c)	Preferred: 1.5(b)
MN	Rules of Professional Conduct	Must: 1.5(c)	Preferred: 1.5(b)
MS	Rules of Professional Conduct	Must: 1.5(c)	Preferred: 1.5(b)
MO	Rules of Professional Conduct	Must: 1.5(c)	Preferred: 1.5(b)
MT	Rules of Professional Conduct	Must: 1.5(c)	Must: (if over $500) 1.5(b)
NE	Rules of Professional Conduct	Must: 1.5(c)	Preferred: 1.5(b)
NV	Rules of Professional Conduct	Must: 1.5(c)	Preferred: 1.5(b)
NH	Rules of Professional Conduct	Must: 1.5(c)	Preferred: 1.5(b)
NJ	Rules of Professional Conduct	Must: 1.5(c)	Must: 1.5(b)
NM	Rules of Professional Conduct	Must: 16–105(C)	Preferred: 16–105(B)

Jurisdiction	Applicable Rules	Contingent	Others
NY	Rules of Professional Conduct	Must: 1.5(c)	Must where required by statute or court rule, Rule 1.5(b); Must in domestic relations matters, Rule 1.5(d)(5)(ii)
	Official Compilation of Codes, Rules and Regulations of the State of New York, Title 22 Part 1215.1, 1215.2		Must unless fee is expected to be less than $3,000
NC	Revised Rules of Professional Conduct	Must: 1.5(c)	Preferred: 1.5(b)
ND	Rules of Professional Conduct	Must: 1.5(c)	Preferred: 1.5(b)
OH	Rules of Professional Conduct	Must: 1.5(c)(1)	Preferred: 1.5(b)
OK	Rules of Professional Conduct	Must: 1.5(c)	Preferred: 1.5(b)
OR	Rules of Professional Conduct; Oregon Revised Statutes	Must for personal injury and property damage claims: Oregon Revised Statutes, § 20.340	No Provision
PA	Rules of Professional Conduct	Must: 1.5(c)	Must: 1.5(b) (if lawyer has not regularly represented client)
RI	Rules of Professional Conduct	Must: 1.5(c)	Must: 1.5(b) (unless lawyer regularly represents client on same basis)
SC	Rules of Professional Conduct	Must: 1.5(c)	Preferred: 1.5(b)
SD	Rules of Professional Conduct	Must: 1.5(c)	Preferred: 1.5(b)
TN	Rules of Professional Conduct	Must: 1.5(c)	Preferred: 1.5(b)
TX	Disciplinary Rules of Professional Conduct	Must: 1.04(d)	Preferred: 1.04(c)
UT	Rules of Professional Conduct	Must: 1.5(c)	Preferred: 1.5(b)
VT	Rules of Professional Conduct	Must: 1.5(c)	Preferred: 1.5(b)
VA	Rules of Professional Conduct	Must: 1.5(c)	Preferred: 1.5(b)
WA	Rules of Professional Conduct	Must: 1.5(c)(1)	Preferred: 1.5(b)
WV	Rules of Professional Conduct	Must: 1.5(c)	Preferred: 1.5(b)
WI	Rules of Professional Conduct for Attorneys	Must: 20:1.5(c)	Must (if over $1,000): 20:1.5(b)
WY	Rules of Professional Conduct for Attorneys at Law	Must: 1.5(c)	Preferred: 1.5(b)

AMERICAN BAR ASSOCIATION MODEL CODE OF PROFESSIONAL RESPONSIBILITY

As Amended

PREAMBLE AND PRELIMINARY STATEMENT

Preamble[1]

The continued existence of a free and democratic society depends upon recognition of the concept that justice is based upon the rule of law grounded in respect for the dignity of the individual and his capacity through reason for enlightened self-government.[2] Law so grounded makes justice possible, for only through such law does the dignity of the individual attain respect and protection. Without it, individual rights become subject to unrestrained power, respect for law is destroyed, and rational self-government is impossible.

Lawyers, as guardians of the law, play a vital role in the preservation of society.

The fulfillment of this role requires an understanding by lawyers of their relationship with and function in our legal system.[3] A consequent obligation of lawyers is to maintain the highest standards of ethical conduct.

In fulfilling his professional responsibilities, a lawyer necessarily assumes various roles that require the performance of many difficult tasks. Not every situation which he may encounter can be foreseen,[4] but fundamental ethical principles are always present to guide him. Within the framework of these principles, a lawyer must with courage and foresight be able and ready to shape the body of the law to the ever-changing relationships of society.[5]

---

1. The footnotes are intended merely to enable the reader to relate the provisions of this Code to the ABA Canons of Professional Ethics adopted in 1908, as amended, the Opinions of the ABA Committee on Professional Ethics, and a limited number of other sources; they are not intended to be an annotation of the views taken by the ABA Special Committee on Evaluation of Ethical Standards. Footnotes citing ABA Canons refer to the ABA Canons of Professional Ethics, adopted in 1908, as amended.

2. Cf. ABA Canons, Preamble.

3. "[T]he lawyer stands today in special need of a clear understanding of his obligations and of the vital connection between these obligations and the role his profession plays in society." *Professional Responsibility: Report of the Joint Conference*, 44 A.B.A.J. 1159, 1160 (1958).

4. "No general statement of the responsibilities of the legal profession can encompass all the situations in which the lawyer may be placed. Each position held by him makes its own peculiar demands. These demands the lawyer must clarify for himself in the light of the particular role in which he serves." *Professional Responsibility: Report of the Joint Conference*, 44 A.B.A.J. 1159, 1218 (1958).

5. "The law and its institutions change as social conditions change. They must change if they are to preserve, much less advance, the political and social values from which they derive their purposes and their life. This is true of the most important of legal institutions, the profession of law. The profession, too, must change when conditions change in order to preserve and advance the social values that are its reasons for being." Cheatham, *Availability*

The Code of Professional Responsibility points the way to the aspiring and provides standards by which to judge the transgressor. Each lawyer must find within his own conscience the touchstone against which to test the extent to which his actions should rise above minimum standards. But in the last analysis it is the desire for the respect and confidence of the members of his profession and of the society which he serves that should provide to a lawyer the incentive for the highest possible degree of ethical conduct. The possible loss of that respect and confidence is the ultimate sanction. So long as its practitioners are guided by these principles, the law will continue to be a noble profession. This is its greatness and its strength, which permit of no compromise.

Preliminary Statement

In furtherance of the principles stated in the Preamble, the American Bar Association has promulgated this Model Code of Professional Responsibility, consisting of three separate but interrelated parts: Canons, Ethical Considerations, and Disciplinary Rules.[6] The Code is designed to be adopted by appropriate agencies both as an inspirational guide to the members of the profession and as a basis for disciplinary action when the conduct of a law-

yer falls below the required minimum standards stated in the Disciplinary Rules.

Obviously the Canons, Ethical Considerations, and Disciplinary Rules cannot apply to non-lawyers; however, they do define the type of ethical conduct that the public has a right to expect not only of lawyers but also of their non-professional employees and associates in all matters pertaining to professional employment. A lawyer should ultimately be responsible for the conduct of his employees and associates in the course of the professional representation of the client.

The Canons are statements of axiomatic norms, expressing in general terms the standards of professional conduct expected of lawyers in their relationships with the public, with the legal system, and with the legal profession. They embody the general concepts from which the Ethical Considerations and the Disciplinary Rules are derived.

The Ethical Considerations are aspirational in character and represent the objectives toward which every member of the profession should strive. They constitute a body of principles upon which the lawyer can rely for guidance in many specific situations.[7]

of Legal Services: The Responsibility of the Individual Lawyer and the Organized Bar, 12 U.C.L.A.L.Rev. 438, 440 (1965).

6. The Supreme Court of Wisconsin adopted a Code of Judicial Ethics in 1967. "The code is divided into standards and rules, the standards being statements of what the general desirable level of conduct should be, the rules being particular canons, the violation of which shall subject an individual judge to sanctions." In re Promulgation of a Code of Judicial Ethics, 36 Wis.2d 252, 255, 153 N.W.2d 873, 874 (1967).

The portion of the Wisconsin Code of Judicial Ethics entitled "Standards" states that "[t]he following standards set forth the significant qualities of the ideal judge...." Id., 36 Wis.2d at 256, 153 N.W.2d at 875. The portion entitled "Rules" states that "[t]he court promulgates the following rules because the requirements of judicial conduct embodied

therein are of sufficient gravity to warrant sanctions if they are not obeyed...." Id., 36 Wis.2d at 259, 153 N.W.2d at 876.

7. "Under the conditions of modern practice it is peculiarly necessary that the lawyer should understand, not merely the established standards of professional conduct, but the reasons underlying these standards. Today the lawyer plays a changing and increasingly varied role. In many developing fields the precise contribution of the legal profession is as yet undefined." *Professional Responsibility: Report of the Joint Conference*, 44 A.B.A.J. 1159 (1958).

"A true sense of professional responsibility must derive from an understanding of the reasons that lie back of specific restraints, such as those embodied in the Canons. The grounds for the lawyer's peculiar obligations are to be found in the nature of his calling. The lawyer who seeks a clear understanding of his duties

The Disciplinary Rules, unlike the Ethical Considerations, are mandatory in character. The Disciplinary Rules state the minimum level of conduct below which no lawyer can fall without being subject to disciplinary action. Within the framework of fair trial,[8] the Disciplinary Rules should be uniformly applied to all lawyers,[9] regardless of the nature of their professional activities.[10] The Code makes

no attempt to prescribe either disciplinary procedures or penalties[11] for violation of a Disciplinary Rule,[12] nor does it undertake to define standards for civil liability of lawyers for professional conduct. The severity of judgment against one found guilty of violating a Disciplinary Rule should be determined by the character of the offense and the attendant circumstances.[13] An enforcing agency, in apply-

will be led to reflect on the special services his profession renders to society and the services it might render if its full capacities were realized. When the lawyer fully understands the nature of his office, he will then discern what restraints are necessary to keep that office wholesome and effective." *Id.*

8. "Disbarment, designed to protect the public, is a punishment or penalty imposed on the lawyer. *** He is accordingly entitled to procedural due process, which includes fair notice of the charge." In re Ruffalo, 390 U.S. 544, 550, 20 L.Ed.2d 117, 122, 88 S.Ct. 1222, 1226 (1968), rehearing denied, 391 U.S. 961, 20 L.Ed.2d 874, 88 S.Ct. 1833 (1968).

"A State cannot exclude a person from the practice of law or from any other occupation in a manner or for reasons that contravene the Due Process or Equal Protection Clause of the Fourteenth Amendment.... A State can require high standards of qualification ... but any qualification must have a rational connection with the applicant's fitness or capacity to practice law." Schware v. Bd. of Bar Examiners, 353 U.S. 232, 239, 1 L.Ed.2d 796, 801–02, 77 S.Ct. 752, 756 (1957).

"[A]n accused lawyer may expect that he will not be condemned out of a capricious self-righteousness or denied the essentials of a fair hearing." Kingsland v. Dorsey, 338 U.S. 318, 320, 94 L.Ed. 123, 126, 70 S.Ct. 123, 124–25 (1949).

"The attorney and counsellor being, by the solemn judicial act of the court, clothed with his office, does not hold it as a matter of grace and favor. The right which it confers upon him to appear for suitors, and to argue causes is something more than a mere indulgence, revocable at the pleasure of the court, or at the command of the legislature. It is a right of which he can only be deprived by the judgment of the court, for moral or professional delinquency." Ex parte Garland, 71 U.S. (4 Wall.) 333, 378–79, 18 L.Ed. 366, 370 (1866).

See generally Comment, *Procedural Due Process and Character Hearings for Bar Applicants*, 15 Stan.L.Rev. 500 (1963).

9. "The canons of professional ethics must be enforced by the Courts and must be respected by members of the Bar if we are to maintain public confidence in the integrity and impartiality of the administration of justice." In re Meeker, 76 N.M. 354, 357, 414 P.2d 862, 864 (1966), appeal dismissed, 385 U.S. 449 (1967).

10. See ABA Canon 45.

"The Canons of this Association govern all its members, irrespective of the nature of their practice, and the application of the Canons is not affected by statutes or regulations governing certain activities of lawyers which may prescribe less stringent standards." ABA Comm. on Professional Ethics, Opinions, No. 203 (1940) [hereinafter each Opinion is cited as "ABA Opinion"].

Cf. *ABA Opinion* 152 (1936).

11. "There is generally no prescribed discipline for any particular type of improper conduct. The disciplinary measures taken are discretionary with the courts, which may disbar, suspend, or merely censure the attorney as the nature of the offense and past indicia of character may warrant." Note, 43 Cornell L.Q. 489, 495 (1958).

12. The Code seeks only to specify conduct for which a lawyer should be disciplined. Recommendations as to the procedures to be used in disciplinary actions and the gravity of disciplinary measures appropriate for violations of the Code are within the jurisdiction of the American Bar Association Special Committee on Evaluation of Disciplinary Enforcement.

13. "The severity of the judgment of this court should be in proportion to the gravity of the offenses, the moral turpitude involved, and the extent that the defendant's acts and conduct affect his professional qualifications to practice law." Louisiana State Bar Ass'n v. Steiner, 204 La. 1073, 1092–93, 16 So.2d 843, 850 (1944) (Higgins, J., concurring in decree).

"Certainly an erring lawyer who has been disciplined and who having paid the penalty has given satisfactory evidence of repentance and has been rehabilitated and restored to his ing the Disciplinary Rules, may find interpretive guidance in the basic principles embodied in the Canons and in the objectives reflected in the Ethical Considerations.

CANON 1

A Lawyer Should Assist in Maintaining the Integrity and Competence of the Legal Profession

ETHICAL CONSIDERATIONS

EC 1–1 A basic tenet of the professional responsibility of lawyers is that every person in our society should have ready access to the independent professional services of a lawyer of integrity and competence. Maintaining the integrity and improving the competence of the bar to meet the highest standards is the ethical responsibility of every lawyer.

EC 1–2 The public should be protected from those who are not qualified to be lawyers by reason of a deficiency in education[1] or moral standards[2] or of other relevant factors[3] but who nevertheless seek to practice law. To assure the maintenance of high moral and educational standards of the legal profession, lawyers should affirmatively assist courts and other appropriate bodies in promulgating,

place at the bar by the court which knows him best ought not to have what amounts to an order of permanent disbarment entered against him by a federal court solely on the basis of an earlier criminal record and without regard to his subsequent rehabilitation and present good character.... We think, therefore, that the district court should reconsider the appellant's application for admission and grant it unless the court finds it to be a fact that the appellant is not presently of good moral or professional character." In re Dreier, 258 F.2d 68, 69–70 (3d Cir.1958).

1. "[W]e cannot conclude that all educational restrictions [on bar admission] are unlawful. We assume that few would deny that a grammar school education requirement, before taking the bar examination, was reasonable. Or that an applicant had to be able to read or write. Once we conclude that *some* restriction is proper, then it becomes a matter of degree— the problem of drawing the line.

. . .

"We conclude the fundamental question here is whether Rule IV, Section 6 of the Rules Pertaining to Admission of Applicants to the State Bar of Arizona is 'arbitrary, capricious and unreasonable.' We conclude an educational requirement of graduation from an accredited law school is not." Hackin v. Lockwood, 361 F.2d 499, 503–04 (9th Cir.1966), cert. denied, 385 U.S. 960, 17 L.Ed.2d 305, 87 S.Ct. 396 (1966).

2. "Every state in the United States, as a prerequisite for admission to the practice of law, requires that applicants possess 'good moral character.' Although the requirement is of judicial origin, it is now embodied in legislation in most states." Comment, *Procedural Due Process and Character Hearings for Bar Applicants*, 15 Stan.L.Rev. 500 (1963).

"Good character in the members of the bar is essential to the preservation of the integrity of the courts. The duty and power of the court to guard its portals against intrusion by men and women who are mentally and morally dishonest, unfit because of bad character, evidenced by their course of conduct, to participate in the administrative law, would seem to be unquestioned in the matter of preservation of judicial dignity and integrity." In re Monaghan, 126 Vt. 53, 222 A.2d 665, 670 (1966).

"Fundamentally, the question involved in both situations [i.e. admission and disciplinary proceedings] is the same—is the applicant for admission or the attorney sought to be disciplined a fit and proper person to be permitted to practice law, and that usually turns upon whether he has committed or is likely to continue to commit acts of moral turpitude. At the time of oral argument the attorney for respondent frankly conceded that the test for admission and for discipline is and should be the same. We agree with this concession." Hallinan v. Comm. of Bar Examiners, 65 Cal.2d 447, 453, 421 P.2d 76, 81, 55 Cal.Rptr. 228, 233 (1966).

3. "Proceedings to gain admission to the bar are for the purpose of protecting the public and the courts from the ministrations of persons unfit to practice the profession. Attorneys are officers of the court appointed to assist the court in the administration of justice. Into their hands are committed the property, the liberty and sometimes the lives of their clients. This commitment demands a high degree of intelligence, knowledge of the law, respect for its function in society, sound and faithful judgment and, above all else, integrity of character in private and professional conduct." In re Monaghan, 126 Vt. 53, 222 A.2d 665, 676 (1966) (Holden, C.J., dissenting).

enforcing, and improving requirements for admission to the bar.[4] In like manner, the bar has a positive obligation to aid in the continued improvement of all phases of pre-admission and post-admission legal education.

EC 1-3 Before recommending an applicant for admission, a lawyer should satisfy himself that the applicant is of good moral character. Although a lawyer should not become a self-appointed investigator or judge of applicants for admission, he should report to proper officials all unfavorable information he possesses relating to the character or other qualifications of an applicant.[5]

EC 1-4 The integrity of the profession can be maintained only if conduct of lawyers in violation of the Disciplinary Rules is brought to the attention of the proper officials. A lawyer should reveal voluntarily to those officials all unprivileged knowledge of conduct of lawyers which he believes clearly to be in violation of the Disciplinary Rules.[6] A lawyer should, upon request, serve on and assist commit-

tees and boards having responsibility for the administration of the Disciplinary Rules.[7]

EC 1-5 A lawyer should maintain high standards of professional conduct and should encourage fellow lawyers to do likewise. He should be temperate and dignified, and he should refrain from all illegal and morally reprehensible conduct.[8] Because of his position in society, even minor violations of law by a lawyer may tend to lessen public confidence in the legal profession. Obedience to law exemplifies respect for law. To lawyers especially, respect for the law should be more than a platitude.

EC 1-6 An applicant for admission to the bar or a lawyer may be unqualified, temporarily or permanently, for other than moral and educational reasons, such as mental or emotional instability. Lawyers should be diligent in taking steps to see that during a period of disqualification such person is not granted a license or, if licensed, is not permitted to practice.[9] In like manner, when the disquali-

4. "A bar composed of lawyers of good moral character is a worthy objective but it is unnecessary to sacrifice vital freedoms in order to obtain that goal. It is also important both to society and the bar itself that lawyers be unintimidated—free to think, speak, and act as members of an Independent Bar." Konigsberg v. State Bar, 353 U.S. 252, 273, 1 L.Ed.2d 810, 825, 77 S.Ct. 722, 733 (1957).

5. *See* ABA Canon 29.

6. ABA Canon 28 designates certain conduct as unprofessional and then states that: "A duty to the public and to the profession devolves upon every member of the Bar having knowledge of such practices upon the part of any practitioner immediately to inform thereof, to the end that the offender may be disbarred." ABA Canon 29 states a broader admonition: "Lawyers should expose without fear or favor before the proper tribunals corrupt or dishonest conduct in the profession."

7. "It is the obligation of the organized Bar and the individual lawyer to give unstinted cooperation and assistance to the highest court of the state in discharging its function and duty with respect to discipline and in purging the profession of the unworthy." *Report of the Special Committee on Disciplinary Procedures*, 80 A.B.A.Rep. 463, 470 (1955).

8. Cf. ABA Canon 32.

9. "We decline, on the present record, to disbar Mr. Sherman or to reprimand him—not because we condone his actions, but because, as heretofore indicated, we are concerned with whether he is mentally responsible for what he has done.

"The logic of the situation would seem to dictate the conclusion that, if he was mentally responsible for the conduct we have outlined, he should be disbarred; and, if he was not mentally responsible, he should not be permitted to practice law.

"However, the flaw in the logic is that he may have been mentally irresponsible [at the time of his offensive conduct] ..., and, yet, have sufficiently improved in the almost two and one-half years intervening to be able to capably and competently represent his clients....

. . .

"We would make clear that we are satisfied that a case has been made against Mr. Sherman, warranting a refusal to permit him to further practice law in this state unless he can establish his mental irresponsibility at the time fication has terminated, members of the bar should assist such person in being licensed, or, if licensed, in being restored to his full right to practice.

DISCIPLINARY RULES

DR 1–101 Maintaining Integrity and Competence of the Legal Profession.

(A) A lawyer is subject to discipline if he has made a materially false statement in, or if he has deliberately failed to disclose a material fact requested in connection with, his application for admission to the bar.[10]

of the offenses charged. The burden of proof is upon him.

"If he establishes such mental irresponsibility, the burden is then upon him to establish his present capability to practice law." In re Sherman, 58 Wash.2d 1, 6–7, 354 P.2d 888, 890 (1960), cert. denied, 371 U.S. 951, 9 L.Ed.2d 499, 83 S.Ct. 506 (1963).

10. "This Court has the inherent power to revoke a license to practice law in this State, where such license was issued by this Court, and its issuance was procured by the fraudulent concealment, or by the false and fraudulent representation by the applicant of a fact which was manifestly material to the issuance of the license." North Carolina ex rel. Attorney General v. Gorson, 209 N.C. 320, 326, 183 S.E. 392, 395 (1936), cert. denied, 298 U.S. 662, 80 L.Ed. 1387, 56 S.Ct. 752 (1936).

See also Application of Patterson, 318 P.2d 907, 913 (Or.1957), cert. denied, 356 U.S. 947, 2 L.Ed.2d 822, 78 S.Ct. 795 (1958).

11. See ABA Canon 29.

12. In *ABA Opinion* 95 (1933), which held that a municipal attorney could not permit police officers to interview persons with claims against the municipality when the attorney knew the claimants to be represented by counsel, the Committee on Professional Ethics said:

"The law officer is, of course, responsible for the acts of those in his department who are under his supervision and control." *Opinion 85.* In re Robinson, 136 N.Y.S. 548 (affirmed 209 N.Y. 354–1912) held that it was a matter of disbarment for an attorney to adopt a general course of approving the unethical conduct of employees of his client, even though he did not actively participate therein.

(B) A lawyer shall not further the application for admission to the bar of another person known by him to be unqualified in respect to character, education, or other relevant attribute.[11]

DR 1–102 Misconduct.

(A) A lawyer shall not:

(1) Violate a Disciplinary Rule.

(2) Circumvent a Disciplinary Rule through actions of another.[12]

(3) Engage in illegal conduct involving moral turpitude.[13]

" '. . . The attorney should not advise or sanction acts by his client which he himself should not do.' *Opinion 75.*"

13. "The most obvious non-professional ground for disbarment is conviction for a felony. Most states make conviction for a felony grounds for automatic disbarment. Some of these states, including New York, make disbarment mandatory upon conviction for *any* felony, while others require disbarment only for those felonies which involve moral turpitude. There are strong arguments that some felonies, such as involuntary manslaughter, reflect neither on an attorney's fitness, trustworthiness, nor competence and, therefore, should not be grounds for disbarment, but most states tend to disregard these arguments and, following the common law rule, make disbarment mandatory on conviction for any felony." Note, 43 Cornell L.Q. 489, 490 (1958).

"Some states treat conviction for misdemeanors as grounds for automatic disbarment. . . . However, the vast majority, accepting the common law rule, require that the misdemeanor involve moral turpitude. While the definition of moral turpitude may prove difficult, it seems only proper that those minor offenses which do not affect the attorney's fitness to continue in the profession should not be grounds for disbarment. A good example is an assault and battery conviction which would not involve moral turpitude unless done with malice and deliberation." Id. at 491.

"The term 'moral turpitude' has been used in the law for centuries. It has been the subject of many decisions by the courts but has never been clearly defined because of the nature of the term. Perhaps the best general definition of the term 'moral turpitude' is that it imports

(4) **Engage in conduct involving dishonesty, fraud, deceit, or misrepresentation.**

(5) **Engage in conduct that is prejudicial to the administration of justice.**

(6) **Engage in any other conduct that adversely reflects on his fitness to practice law.**[14]

DR 1-103 Disclosure of Information to Authorities.

(A) **A lawyer possessing unprivileged knowledge of a violation of DR 1-102 shall report such knowledge to a tribunal or other authority empowered to investigate or act upon such violation.**[15]

(B) **A lawyer possessing unprivileged knowledge or evidence concern-** ing another lawyer or a judge shall reveal fully such knowledge or evidence upon proper request of a tribunal or other authority empowered to investigate or act upon the conduct of lawyers or judges.[16]

CANON 2

A Lawyer Should Assist the Legal Profession in Fulfilling Its Duty to Make Legal Counsel Available

ETHICAL CONSIDERATIONS

EC 2-1 The need of members of the public for legal services[1] is met only if they recognize their legal problems, appreciate the importance of seeking assistance,[2] and are able to obtain the services

an act of baseness, vileness or depravity in the duties which one person owes to another or to society in general, which is contrary to the usual, accepted and customary rule of right and duty which a person should follow. 58 C.J.S. at page 1201. Although offenses against revenue laws have been held to be crimes of moral turpitude, it has also been held that the attempt to evade the payment of taxes due to the government or any subdivision thereof, while wrong and unlawful, does not involve moral turpitude. 58 C.J.S. at page 1205." Comm. on Legal Ethics v. Scherr, 149 W.Va. 721, 726–27, 143 S.E.2d 141, 145 (1965).

"The right and power to discipline an attorney, as one of its officers, is inherent in the court.... This power is not limited to those instances of misconduct wherein he has been employed, or has acted, in a professional capacity; but, on the contrary, this power may be exercised where his misconduct outside the scope of his professional relations shows him to be an unfit person to practice law." In re Wilson, 391 S.W.2d 914, 917–18 (Mo.1965).

14. "It is a fair characterization of the lawyer's responsibility in our society that he stands 'as a shield,' to quote Devlin, J., in defense of right and to ward off wrong. From a profession charged with these responsibilities there must be exacted those qualities of truth-speaking, of a high sense of honor, of granite discretion, of the strictest observance of fiduciary responsibility, that have, throughout the centuries, been compendiously described as 'moral character.'" Schware v. Bd. of Bar Ex-

aminers, 353 U.S. 232, 1 L.Ed.2d 796, 806, 77 S.Ct. 752, 761 (1957) (Frankfurter, J., concurring).

"Particularly applicable here is Rule 4.47 providing that 'A lawyer should always maintain his integrity; and shall not willfully commit any act against the interest of the public; nor shall he violate his duty to the courts or his clients; *nor shall he, by any misconduct, commit any offense against the laws of Missouri or the United States of America, which amounts to a crime involving acts done by him contrary to justice, honesty, modesty or good morals*; nor shall he be guilty of any other misconduct whereby, for the protection of the public and those charged with the administration of justice, he should no longer be entrusted with the duties and responsibilities belonging to the office of an attorney.'" In re Wilson, 391 S.W.2d 914, 917 (Mo.1965).

15. See ABA Canon 29; cf. ABA Canon 28.

16. Cf. ABA Canons 28 and 29.

1. "Men have need for more than a system of law; they have need for a system of law which functions, and that means they have need for lawyers." Cheatham, *The Lawyer's Role and Surroundings*, 25 Rocky Mt.L.Rev. 405 (1953).

2. "Law is not self-applying; men must apply and utilize it in concrete cases. But the ordinary man is incapable. He cannot know the principles of law or the rules guiding the machinery of law administration; he does not of acceptable legal counsel.[3] Hence, important functions of the legal profession are to educate laymen to recognize their problems, to facilitate the process of intelligent selection of lawyers, and to assist in making legal services fully available.[4]

Recognition of Legal Problems

EC 2–2 The legal profession should assist lay-persons to recognize legal problems because such problems may not be self-revealing and often are not timely noticed. Therefore, lawyers should encourage and participate in educational and public relations programs concerning our legal system with particular reference to legal problems that frequently arise. Preparation of advertisements and professional articles for lay publications[5] and participation in seminars, lectures, and civic programs should be motivated by a desire to educate the public to an awareness of legal needs and to provide information relevant to the selection of the most appropriate counsel rather than to obtain publicity for particular lawyers. The problems of advertising on television require special consideration, due to the style, cost, and transitory nature of such media. If the interests of laypersons in receiving relevant lawyer advertising are not adequately served by print media and radio advertising, and if adequate safeguards to protect the public can reasonably be formulated, television advertising may serve a public interest.

EC 2–3 Whether a lawyer acts properly in volunteering in-person advice to a layperson to seek legal services depends upon the circumstances.[6] The giving of advice that one should take legal action could well be in fulfillment of the duty of the legal profession to assist laypersons in

know how to formulate his desires with precision and to put them into writing; he is ineffective in the presentation of his claims." Cheatham, *The Lawyer's Role and Surroundings*, 25 Rocky Mt.L.Rev. 405 (1953).

3. "This need [to provide legal services] was recognized by ... Mr. [Lewis F.] Powell [Jr., President, American Bar Association, 1963–64], who said: 'Looking at contemporary America realistically, we must admit that despite all our efforts to date (and these have not been insignificant), far too many persons are not able to obtain equal justice under law. This usually results because their poverty or their ignorance has prevented them from obtaining legal counsel.'" Address by E. Clinton Bamberger, Association of American Law Schools 1965 Annual Meeting, Dec. 28, 1965, in Proceedings, Part II, 1965, 61, 63–64 (1965).

"A wide gap separates the need for legal services and its satisfaction, as numerous studies reveal. Looked at from the side of the layman, one reason for the gap is poverty and the consequent inability to pay legal fees. Another set of reasons is ignorance of the need for and the value of legal services, and ignorance of where to find a dependable lawyer. There is fear of the mysterious processes and delays of the law, and there is fear of overreaching and overcharging by lawyers, a fear stimulated by the occasional exposure of shysters." Cheatham, *Availability of Legal Services: The Responsibility of the Individual Lawyer and of the Organized Bar*, 12 U.C.L.A.L.Rev. 438 (1965).

4. "It is not only the right but the duty of the profession as a whole to utilize such methods as may be developed to bring the services of its members to those who need them, so long as this can be done ethically and with dignity." *ABA Opinion* 320 (1968).

"[T]here is a responsibility on the bar to make legal services available to those who need them. The maxim, 'privilege brings responsibilities,' can be expanded to read, exclusive privilege to render public service brings responsibility to assure that the service is available to those in need of it." Cheatham, *Availability of Legal Services: The Responsibility of the Individual Lawyer and of the Organized Bar*, 12 U.C.L.A.L.Rev. 438, 443 (1965).

"The obligation to provide legal services for those actually caught up in litigation carries with it the obligation to make preventive legal advice accessible to all. It is among those unaccustomed to business affairs and fearful of the ways of the law that such advice is often most needed. If it is not received in time, the most valiant and skillful representation in court may come too late." *Professional Responsibility: Report of the Joint Conference*, 44 A.B.A.J. 1159, 1216 (1958).

5. "A lawyer may with propriety write articles for publications in which he gives information upon the law ...." A.B.A. Canon 40.

6. See ABA Canon 28.

recognizing legal problems.[7] The advice is proper only if motivated by a desire to protect one who does not recognize that he may have legal problems or who is ignorant of his legal rights or obligations. It is improper if motivated by a desire to obtain personal benefit, secure personal publicity, or cause legal action to be taken merely to harass or injure another. A lawyer should not initiate an in-person contact with a non-client, personally or through a representative, for the purpose of being retained to represent him for compensation.

EC 2-4 Since motivation is subjective and often difficult to judge, the motives of a lawyer who volunteers in-person advice likely to produce legal controversy may well be suspect if he receives professional employment or other benefits as a result.[8] A lawyer who volunteers in-person advice

that one should obtain the services of a lawyer generally should not himself accept employment, compensation, or other benefit in connection with that matter. However, it is not improper for a lawyer to volunteer such advice and render resulting legal services to close friends, relatives, former clients (in regard to matters germane to former employment), and regular clients.[9]

EC 2-5 A lawyer who writes or speaks for the purpose of educating members of the public to recognize their legal problems should carefully refrain from giving or appearing to give a general solution applicable to all apparently similar individual problems,[10] since slight changes in fact situations may require a material variance in the applicable advice; otherwise, the public may be mislead and misadvised. Talks and writings by lawyers for laypersons should caution them not to

7. This question can assume constitutional dimensions: "We meet at the outset the contention that 'solicitation' is wholly outside the area of freedoms protected by the First Amendment. To this contention there are two answers. The first is that a State cannot foreclose the exercise of constitutional rights by mere labels. The second is that abstract discussion is not the only species of communication which the Constitution protects; the First Amendment also protects vigorous advocacy, certainly of lawful ends, against governmental intrusion. . . .

. . .

"However valid may be Virginia's interest in regulating the traditionally illegal practice of barratry, maintenance and champerty, that interest does not justify the prohibition of the NAACP activities disclosed by this record. Malicious intent was of the essence of the common-law offenses of fomenting or stirring up litigation. And whatever may be or may have been true of suits against governments in other countries, the exercise in our own, as in this case of First Amendment rights to enforce Constitutional rights through litigation, as a matter of law, cannot be deemed malicious." NAACP v. Button, 371 U.S. 415, 429, 439–40, 9 L.Ed.2d 405, 415–16, 422, 83 S.Ct. 328, 336, 341 (1963).

8. "It is disreputable for an attorney to breed litigation by seeking out those who have

claims for personal injuries or other grounds of action in order to secure them as clients, or to employ agents or runners, or to reward those who bring or influence the bringing of business to his office. . . . Moreover, it tends quite easily to the institution of baseless litigation and the manufacture of perjured testimony. From early times, this danger has been recognized in the law by the condemnation of the crime of common barratry, or the stirring up of suits or quarrels between individuals at law or otherwise." In re Ades, 6 F.Supp. 467, 474–75 (D.Md.1934).

9. "*Rule 2.*

"§ a. . . .

"[A] member of the State Bar shall not solicit professional employment by

"(1) Volunteering counsel or advice except where ties of blood relationship or trust make it appropriate." Cal.Business and Professions Code § 6076 (West 1962).

10. "*Rule 18* . . . A member of the State Bar shall not advise inquirers or render opinions to them through or in connection with a newspaper, radio or other publicity medium of any kind in respect to their specific legal problems, whether or not such attorney shall be compensated for his services." Cal.Business and Professions Code § 6076 (West 1962).

attempt to solve individual problems upon the basis of the information contained therein.[11]

Selection of a Lawyer

EC 2–6 Formerly a potential client usually knew the reputations of local lawyers for competency and integrity and therefore could select a practitioner in whom he had confidence. This traditional selection process worked well because it was initiated by the client and the choice was an informed one.

EC 2–7 Changed conditions, however, have seriously restricted the effectiveness of the traditional selection process. Often the reputations of lawyers are not sufficiently known to enable laypersons to make intelligent choices.[12] The law has become increasingly complex and specialized. Few lawyers are willing and competent to deal with every kind of legal matter, and many laypersons have difficulty in determining the competence of lawyers to render different types of legal services. The selection of legal counsel is particularly difficult for transients, persons moving into new areas, persons of limited education or means, and others who have little or no contact with lawyers.[13] Lack of information about the availability of lawyers, the qualifications of particular lawyers, and the expense of legal representation leads laypersons to avoid seeking legal advice.

EC 2–8 Selection of a lawyer by a layperson should be made on an informed basis. Advice and recommendation of third parties—relatives, friends, acquaintances, business associates, or other lawyers—and disclosure of relevant information about the lawyer and his practice may be helpful. A layperson is best served if the recommendation is disinterested and informed. In order that the recommendation be disinterested, a lawyer should not seek to influence another to recommend his employment. A lawyer should not compensate another person for recommending him, for influencing a prospective client to employ him, or to encourage future recommendations.[14] Advertisements and public communications, whether in law lists, telephone directories, newspapers, other forms of print media, television or radio, should be formulated to convey only information that is necessary to make an appropriate selection. Such information includes: (1) office information, such as, name, including name of law firm and names of professional associates; addresses; telephone numbers; credit card acceptability; fluency in foreign languages; and office hours; (2) relevant biographical information; (3) description of the practice, but only by using designations and definitions authorized by [the agency having jurisdiction of the subject under state law], for example, one or more fields of law in which the lawyer or law firm practices; a statement that practice is limited to one or more fields of law; and/or a statement that the lawyer or law firm specializes in a particular field of law practice, but only by using designations, definitions and standards authorized by [the agency having jurisdiction of the subject under state

---

11. "In any case where a member might well apply the advice given in the opinion to his individual affairs, the lawyer rendering the opinion [concerning problems common to members of an association and distributed to the members through a periodic bulletin] should specifically state that this opinion should not be relied on by any member as a basis for handling his individual affairs, but that in every case he should consult his counsel. In the publication of the opinion the association should make a similar statement." *ABA Opinion* 273 (1946).

12. "A group of recent interrelated changes bears directly on the availability of legal ser-

vices.... [One] change is the constantly accelerating urbanization of the country and the decline of personal and neighborhood knowledge of whom to retain as a professional man." Cheatham, *Availability of Legal Services: The Responsibility of the Individual Lawyer and of the Organized Bar*, 12 U.C.L.A.L.Rev. 438, 440 (1965).

13. Cf. Cheatham, *A Lawyer When Needed: Legal Services for the Middle Classes*, 63 Colum.L.Rev. 973, 974 (1963).

14. See ABA Canon 28.

law]; and (4) permitted fee information. Self-laudation should be avoided.[15]

Selection of a Lawyer: Lawyer Advertising

EC 2–9 The lack of sophistication on the part of many members of the public concerning legal services, the importance of the interests affected by the choice of a lawyer and prior experience with unrestricted lawyer advertising, require that special care be taken by lawyers to avoid misleading the public and to assure that the information set forth in any advertising is relevant to the selection of a lawyer. The lawyer must be mindful that the benefits of lawyer advertising depend upon its reliability and accuracy. Examples of information in lawyer advertising that would be deceptive include misstatements of fact, suggestions that the ingenuity or prior record of a lawyer rather than the justice of the claim are the principal factors likely to determine the result, inclusion of information irrelevant to selecting a lawyer, and representations concerning the quality of service, which cannot be measured or verified. Since lawyer advertising is calculated and not spontaneous, reasonable regulation of lawyer advertising designed to foster compliance with appropriate standards serves the public interest without impeding the flow of useful, meaningful, and relevant information to the public.

EC 2–10 A lawyer should ensure that the information contained in any advertising which the lawyer publishes, broadcasts or causes to be published or broadcast is relevant, is disseminated in an objective and understandable fashion, and would facilitate the prospective client's ability to compare the qualifications of the lawyers available to represent him. A lawyer should strive to communicate such information without undue emphasis upon style and advertising stratagems which serve to hinder rather than to facilitate intelligent selection of counsel. Because technological change is a recurrent

feature of communications forms, and because perceptions of what is relevant in lawyer selection may change, lawyer advertising regulations should not be cast in rigid, unchangeable terms. Machinery is therefore available to advertisers and consumers for prompt consideration of proposals to change the rules governing lawyer advertising. The determination of any request for such change should depend upon whether the proposal is necessary in light of existing Code provisions, whether the proposal accords with standards of accuracy, reliability and truthfulness, and whether the proposal would facilitate informed selection of lawyers by potential consumers of legal services. Representatives of lawyers and consumers should be heard in addition to the applicant concerning any proposed change. Any change which is approved should be promulgated in the form of an amendment to the Code so that all lawyers practicing in the jurisdiction may avail themselves of its provisions.

EC 2–11 The name under which a lawyer conducts his practice may be a factor in the selection process.[16] The use of a trade name or an assumed name could mislead laypersons concerning the identity, responsibility, and status of those practicing thereunder.[17] Accordingly, a lawyer in private practice should practice only under a designation containing his own name, the name of a lawyer employing him, the name of one or more of the lawyers practicing in a partnership, or, if permitted by law, the name of a professional legal corporation, which should be clearly designated as such. For many years some law firms have used a firm name retaining one or more names of deceased or retired partners and such practice is not improper if the firm is a bona fide successor of a firm in which the deceased or retired person was a member, if the use of the name is authorized by law or by contract, and if the public is not

---

15. Amended, August 1978, House Informational Report No. 118.

16. *Cf. ABA Opinion* 303 (1961).

17. *See* ABA Canon 33.

misled thereby.[18]   However, the name of a partner who withdraws from a firm but continues to practice law should be omitted from the firm name in order to avoid misleading the public.

EC 2–12 A lawyer occupying a judicial, legislative, or public executive or administrative position who has the right to practice law concurrently may allow his name to remain in the name of the firm if he actively continues to practice law as a member thereof. Otherwise, his name should be removed from the firm name,[19] and he should not be identified as a past or present member of the firm; and he should not hold himself out as being a practicing lawyer.

EC 2–13 In order to avoid the possibility of misleading persons with whom he deals, a lawyer should be scrupulous in

18. Id.

"The continued use of a firm name by one or more surviving partners after the death of a member of the firm whose name is in the firm title is expressly permitted by the Canons of Ethics. The reason for this is that all of the partners have by their joint and several efforts over a period of years contributed to the good will attached to the firm name. In the case of a firm having widespread connections, this good will is disturbed by a change in firm name every time a name partner dies, and that reflects a loss in some degree of the good will to the building up of which the surviving partners have contributed their time, skill and labor through a period of years. To avoid this loss the firm name is continued, and to meet the requirements of the Canon the individuals constituting the firm from time to time are listed." *ABA Opinion* 267 (1945).

"Accepted local custom in New York recognizes that the name of a law firm does not necessarily identify the individual members of the firm, and hence the continued use of a firm name after the death of one or more partners is not a deception and is permissible.... The continued use of a deceased partner's name in the firm title is not affected by the fact that another partner withdraws from the firm and his name is dropped, or the name of the new partner is added to the firm name." *Opinion* No. 45, Committee on Professional Ethics, New York State Bar Ass'n, 39 N.Y.St.B.J. 455 (1967).

Cf. *ABA Opinion* 258 (1943).

the representation of his professional status.[20] He should not hold himself out as being a partner or associate of a law firm if he is not one in fact,[21] and thus should not hold himself out as partner or associate if he only shares offices with another lawyer.[22]

EC 2–14 In some instances a lawyer confines his practice to a particular field of law.[23] In the absence of state controls to insure the existence of special competence, a lawyer should not be permitted to hold himself out as a specialist or as having official recognition as a specialist, other than in the fields of admiralty, trademark, and patent law where a holding out as a specialist historically has been permitted. A lawyer may, however, indicate in permitted advertising, if it is factual, a limitation of his practice or one

19. Cf. *ABA Canon* 33 and *ABA Opinion* 315 (1965).

20. Cf. *ABA Opinions* 283 (1950) and 81 (1932).

21. See *ABA Opinion* 316 (1967).

22. "The word 'associates' has a variety of meanings. Principally through custom the word when used on the letterheads of law firms has come to be regarded as describing those who are employees of the firm. Because the word has acquired this special significance in connection with the practice of the law the use of the word to describe lawyer relationships other than employer-employee is likely to be misleading." In re Sussman and Tanner, 241 Ore. 246, 248, 405 P.2d 355, 356 (1965).

According to *ABA Opinion* 310 (1963), use of the term "associates" would be misleading in two situations: (1) where two lawyers are partners and they share both responsibility and liability for the partnership; and (2) where two lawyers practice separately, sharing no responsibility or liability, and only share a suite of offices and some costs.

23. "For a long time, many lawyers have, of necessity, limited their practice to certain branches of law. The increasing complexity of the law and the demand of the public for more expertness on the part of the lawyer has, in the past few years—particularly in the last ten years—brought about specialization on an increasing scale." *Report of the Special Committee on Specialization and Specialized Legal Services,* 79 A.B.A.Rep. 582, 584 (1954).

or more particular areas or fields of law in which he practices using designations and definitions authorized for that purpose by [the state agency having jurisdiction]. A lawyer practicing in a jurisdiction which certifies specialists must also be careful not to confuse laypersons as to his status. If a lawyer discloses areas of law in which he practices or to which he limits his practice, but is not certified in [the jurisdiction], he, and the designation authorized in [the jurisdiction], should avoid any implication that he is in fact certified.

EC 2–15 The legal profession has developed lawyer referral systems designed to aid individuals who are able to pay fees but need assistance in locating lawyers competent to handle their particular problems. Use of a lawyer referral system enables a layman to avoid an uninformed selection of a lawyer because such a system makes possible the employment of competent lawyers who have indicated an interest in the subject matter involved. Lawyers should support the principle of lawyer referral systems and should encourage the evolution of other ethical plans which aid in the selection of qualified counsel.

Financial Ability to Employ Counsel: Generally

EC 2–16 The legal profession cannot remain a viable force in fulfilling its role in our society unless its members receive adequate compensation for services rendered, and reasonable fees[24] should be charged in appropriate cases to clients able to pay them. Nevertheless, persons unable to pay all or a portion of a reasonable fee should be able to obtain necessary legal services,[25] and lawyers should support and participate in ethical activities designed to achieve that objective.[26]

Financial Ability to Employ Counsel: Persons Able to Pay Reasonable Fees

EC 2–17 The determination of a proper fee requires consideration of the interests of both client and lawyer.[27] A lawyer should not charge more than a reasonable fee,[28] for excessive cost of legal service would deter laymen from utilizing the legal system in protection of their rights. Furthermore, an excessive charge abuses the professional relationship between lawyer and client. On the other hand, adequate compensation is necessary in order to enable the lawyer to serve his client effectively and to preserve the integrity and independence of the profession.[29]

EC 2–18 The determination of the reasonableness of a fee requires consideration of all relevant circumstances,[30] including those stated in the Disciplinary Rules. The fees of a lawyer will vary according to many factors, including the time required, his experience, ability, and reputation, the nature of the employment, the responsibility involved, and the results obtained. It is a commendable and long-standing tradition of the bar that special consideration is given in the fixing of any fee for services rendered a brother lawyer or a member of his immediate family.

24. See ABA Canon 12.

25. Cf. ABA Canon 12.

26. "If there is any fundamental proposition of government on which all would agree, it is that one of the highest goals of society must be to achieve and maintain equality before the law. Yet this ideal remains an empty form of words unless the legal profession is ready to provide adequate representation for those unable to pay the usual fees." *Professional Representation: Report of the Joint Conference*, 44 A.B.A.J. 1159, 1216 (1958).

27. See ABA Canon 12.

28. Cf. ABA Canon 12.

29. "When members of the Bar are induced to render legal services for inadequate compensation as a consequence the quality of the service rendered may be lowered, the welfare of the profession injured and the administration of justice made less efficient." *ABA Opinion* 302 (1961).

Cf. *ABA Opinion* 307 (1962).

30. See ABA Canon 12.

EC 2–19 As soon as feasible after a lawyer has been employed, it is desirable that he reach a clear agreement with his client as to the basis of the fee charges to be made. Such a course will not only prevent later misunderstanding but will also work for good relations between the lawyer and the client. It is usually beneficial to reduce to writing the understanding of the parties regarding the fee, particularly when it is contingent. A lawyer should be mindful that many persons who desire to employ him may have had little or no experience with fee charges of lawyers, and for this reason he should explain fully to such persons the reasons for the particular fee arrangement he proposes.

EC 2–20 Contingent fee arrangements[31] in civil cases have long been commonly accepted in the United States in proceedings to enforce claims. The historical bases of their acceptance are that (1) they often, and in a variety of circumstances, provide the only practical means by which one having a claim against another can economically afford, finance, and obtain the services of a competent lawyer to prosecute his claim, and (2) a successful prosecution of the claim produces a *res* out of which the fee can be paid.[32] Although a lawyer generally should decline to accept employment on a contingent fee basis by one who is able to pay a reasonable fixed fee, it is not neces-

sarily improper for a lawyer, where justified by the particular circumstances of a case, to enter into a contingent fee contract in a civil case with any client who, after being fully informed of all relevant factors, desires that arrangement. Because of the human relationships involved and the unique character of the proceedings, contingent fee arrangements in domestic relation cases are rarely justified. In administrative agency proceedings contingent fee contracts should be governed by the same consideration as in other civil cases. Public policy properly condemns contingent fee arrangements in criminal cases, largely on the ground that legal services in criminal cases do not produce a *res* with which to pay the fee.

EC 2–21 A lawyer should not accept compensation or any thing of value incident to his employment or services from one other than his client without the knowledge and consent of his client after full disclosure.[33]

EC 2–22 Without the consent of his client, a lawyer should not associate in a particular matter another lawyer outside his firm. A fee may properly be divided between lawyers[34] properly associated if the division is in proportion to the services performed and the responsibility assumed by each lawyer[35] and if the total fee is reasonable.

31. See ABA Canon 13; see also Mac-Kinnon, Contingent Fees for Legal Services (1964) (A report of the American Bar Foundation).

"A contract for a reasonable contingent fee where sanctioned by law is permitted by *Canon 13*, but the client must remain responsible to the lawyer for expenses advanced by the latter. 'There is to be no barter of the privilege of prosecuting a cause for gain in exchange for the promise of the attorney to prosecute at his own expense.' (Cardozo, C.J. In Matter of Gilman, 251 N.Y. 265, 270–271.)" *ABA Opinion* 246 (1942).

32. See Comment, *Providing Legal Services for the Middle Class in Civil Matters: The Problem, the Duty and a Solution*, 26 U.Pitt. L.Rev. 811, 829 (1965).

33. See ABA Canon 38.

"Of course, as ... [Informal Opinion 679] points out, there must be full disclosure of the arrangement [that an entity other than the client pays the attorney's fee] by the attorney to the client...." *ABA Opinion* 320 (1968).

34. "Only lawyers may share in ... a division of fees, but ... it is not necessary that both lawyers be admitted to practice in the same state, so long as the division was based on the division of services or responsibility." *ABA Opinion* 316 (1967).

35. See ABA Canon 34.

"We adhere to our previous rulings that where a lawyer merely brings about the employment of another lawyer *but renders no service and assumes no responsibility in the matter*, a division of the latter's fee is improper. *(Opinions 18 and 153).*

EC 2–23 A lawyer should be zealous in his efforts to avoid controversies over fees with clients[36] and should attempt to resolve amicably any differences on the subject.[37] He should not sue a client for a fee unless necessary to prevent fraud or gross imposition by the client.[38]

Financial Ability to Employ Counsel: Persons Unable to Pay Reasonable Fees

EC 2–24 A layman whose financial ability is not sufficient to permit payment of any fee cannot obtain legal services, other than in cases where a contingent fee is appropriate, unless the services are provided for him. Even a person of moderate means may be unable to pay a reasonable fee which is large because of the complexity, novelty, or difficulty of the problem or similar factors.[39]

"It is assumed that the bar, generally, understands what acts or conduct of a lawyer may constitute 'services' to a client within the intendment of *Canon 12*. Such acts or conduct invariably, if not always, involve 'responsibility' on the part of the lawyer, whether the word 'responsibility' be construed to denote the possible resultant legal or moral liability on the part of the lawyer to the client or to others, or the onus of deciding what should or should not be done in behalf of the client. The word 'services' in *Canon 12* must be construed in this broad sense and may apply to the selection and retainer of associate counsel as well as to others acts or conduct in the client's behalf." *ABA Opinion* 204 (1940).

36. See ABA Canon 14.

37. Cf. *ABA Opinion* 320 (1968).

38. See ABA Canon 14.

"Ours is a learned profession, not a mere money-getting trade.... Suits to collect fees should be avoided. Only where the circumstances imperatively require, should resort be had to a suit to compel payment. And where a lawyer does resort to a suit to enforce payment of fees which involves a disclosure, he should carefully avoid any disclosure not clearly necessary to obtaining or defending his rights." *ABA Opinion* 250 (1943).

But cf. *ABA Opinion* 320 (1968).

39. "As a society increases in size, sophistication and technology, the body of laws which is required to control that society also increases in size, scope and complexity. With this growth, the law directly affects more and more

EC 2–25 Historically, the need for legal services of those unable to pay reasonable fees has been met in part by lawyers who donated their services or accepted court appointments on behalf of such individuals. The basic responsibility for providing legal services for those unable to pay ultimately rests upon the individual lawyer, and personal involvement in the problems of the disadvantaged can be one of the most rewarding experiences in the life of a lawyer. Every lawyer, regardless of professional prominence or professional workload, should find time to participate in serving the disadvantaged. The rendition of free legal services to those unable to pay reasonable fees continues to be an obligation of each lawyer, but the efforts of individual lawyers are often not enough to meet the need.[40] Thus it has

facets of individual behavior, creating an expanding need for legal services on the part of the individual members of the society.... As legal guidance in social and commercial behavior increasingly becomes necessary, there will come a concurrent demand from the layman that such guidance be made available to him. This demand will not come from those who are able to employ the best legal talent, nor from those who can obtain legal assistance at little or no cost. It will come from the large 'forgotten middle income class,' who can neither afford to pay proportionately large fees nor qualify for ultra-low-cost services. The legal profession must recognize this inevitable demand and consider methods whereby it can be satisfied. If the profession fails to provide such methods, the laity will." Comment, *Providing Legal Services for the Middle Class in Civil Matters: The Problem, the Duty and a Solution*, 26 U.Pitt.L.Rev. 811, 811–12 (1965).

"The issue is not whether we shall do something or do nothing. The demand for ordinary everyday legal justice is so great and the moral nature of the demand is so strong that the issue has become whether we devise, maintain, and support suitable agencies able to satisfy the demand or, by our own default, force the government to take over the job, supplant us, and ultimately dominate us." Smith, *Legal Service Offices for Persons of Moderate Means*, 1949 Wis.L.Rev. 416, 418 (1949).

40. "Lawyers have peculiar responsibilities for the just administration of the law, and these responsibilities include providing advice been necessary for the profession to institute additional programs to provide legal services.[41] Accordingly, legal aid offices,[42] lawyer referral services, and other related programs have been developed, and others will be developed, by the profession.[43] Every lawyer should support all proper efforts to meet this need for legal services.[44]

Acceptance and Retention of Employment

EC 2–26 A lawyer is under no obligation to act as advisor or advocate for every person who may wish to become his client; but in furtherance of the objective

of the bar to make legal services fully available, a lawyer should not lightly decline proffered employment. The fulfillment of this objective requires acceptance by a lawyer of his share of tendered employment which may be unattractive both to him and the bar generally.[45]

EC 2–27 History is replete with instances of distinguished and sacrificial services by lawyers who have represented unpopular clients and causes. Regardless of his personal feelings, a lawyer should not decline representation because a client or a cause is unpopular or community reaction is adverse.[46]

and representation for needy persons. To a degree not always appreciated by the public at large, the bar has performed these obligations with zeal and devotion. The Committee is persuaded, however, that a system of justice that attempts, in mid-twentieth century America, to meet the needs of the financially incapacitated accused through primary or exclusive reliance on the uncompensated services of counsel will prove unsuccessful and inadequate. . . . A system of adequate representation, therefore, should be structured and financed in a manner reflecting its public importance. . . . We believe that fees for private appointed counsel should be set by the court within maximum limits established by the statute." Report of the Att'y Gen's Comm. on Poverty and the Administration of Criminal Justice 41–43 (1963).

41. "At present this representation [of those unable to pay usual fees] is being supplied in some measure through the spontaneous generosity of individual lawyers, through legal aid societies, and—increasingly—through the organized efforts of the Bar. If those who stand in need of this service know of its availability and their need is in fact adequately met, the precise mechanism by which this service is provided becomes of secondary importance. It is of great importance, however, that both the impulse to render this service, and the plan for making that impulse effective, should arise within the legal profession itself." *Professional Responsibility: Report of the Joint Conference*, 44 A.B.A.J. 1159, 1216 (1958).

42. "Free legal clinics carried on by the organized bar are not ethically objectionable. On the contrary, they serve a very worthwhile purpose and should be encouraged." *ABA Opinion* 191 (1939).

43. "Whereas the American Bar Association believes that it is a fundamental duty of the bar to see to it that all persons requiring

legal advice be able to attain it, irrespective of their economic status. . . .

"Resolved, that the Association approves and sponsors the setting up by state and local bar associations of lawyer referral plans and low-cost legal service methods for the purpose of dealing with cases of persons who might not otherwise have the benefit of legal advice. . . ." *Proceedings of the House of Delegates of the American Bar Association*, Oct. 30, 1946, 71 A.B.A.Rep. 103, 109–10 (1946).

44. "The defense of indigent citizens, without compensation, is carried on throughout the country by lawyers representing legal aid societies, not only with the approval, but with the commendation of those acquainted with the work. Not infrequently services are rendered out of sympathy or for other philanthropic reasons, by individual lawyers who do not represent legal aid societies. There is nothing whatever in the Canons to prevent a lawyer from performing such an act, nor should there be." *ABA Opinion* 148 (1935).

45. But cf. ABA Canon 31.

46. "One of the highest services the lawyer can render to society is to appear in court on behalf of clients whose causes are in disfavor with the general public." *Professional Responsibility: Report of the Joint Conference*, 44 A.B.A.J. 1159, 1216 (1958).

One author proposes the following proposition to be included in "A Proper Oath for Advocates": "I recognize that it is sometimes difficult for clients with unpopular causes to obtain proper legal representation. I will do all that I can to assure that the client with the unpopular cause is properly represented, and that the lawyer representing such a client receives credit from and support of the bar for handling such a matter." Thode, *The Ethical*

EC 2–28 The personal preference of a lawyer to avoid adversary alignment against judges, other lawyers,[47] public officials, or influential members of the community does not justify his rejection of tendered employment.

EC 2–29 When a lawyer is appointed by a court or requested by a bar association to undertake representation of a person unable to obtain counsel, whether for financial or other reasons, he should not seek to be excused from undertaking the representation except for compelling reasons.[48] Compelling reasons do not include such factors as the repugnance of the subject matter of the proceeding, the identity[49] or position of a person involved in the case, the belief of the lawyer that the defendant in a criminal proceeding is guilty,[50] or the belief of the lawyer regarding the merits of the civil case.[51]

EC 2–30 Employment should not be accepted by a lawyer when he is unable to render competent service[52] or when he knows or it is obvious that the person seeking to employ him desires to institute or maintain an action merely for the purpose of harassing or maliciously injuring another.[53] Likewise, a lawyer should decline employment if the intensity of his personal feeling, as distinguished from a community attitude, may impair his effective representation of a prospective client. If a lawyer knows a client has previously obtained counsel, he should not accept employment in the matter unless the other counsel approves[54] or withdraws, or the client terminates the prior employment.[55]

Standard for the Advocate, 39 Texas L.Rev. 575, 592 (1961).

"§ 6068. ... It is the duty of an attorney:

. . .

"(h) Never to reject, for any consideration personal to himself, the cause of the defenseless or the oppressed." Cal.Business and Professions Code § 6068 (West 1962). Virtually the same language is found in the Oregon statutes at Ore.Rev.Stats. Ch. 9, § 9.460(8).

See Rostow, *The Lawyer and His Client*, 48 A.B.A.J. 25 and 146 (1962).

47. See ABA Canons 7 and 29.

"We are of the opinion that it is not professionally improper for a lawyer to accept employment to compel another lawyer to honor the just claim of a layman. On the contrary, it is highly proper that he do so. Unfortunately, there appears to be a widespread feeling among laymen that it is difficult, if not impossible, to obtain justice when they have claims against members of the Bar because other lawyers will not accept employment to proceed against them. The honor of the profession, whose members proudly style themselves officers of the court, must surely be sullied if its members bind themselves by custom to refrain from enforcing just claims of laymen against lawyers." *ABA Opinion* 144 (1935).

48. ABA Canon 4 uses a slightly different test, saying, "A lawyer assigned as counsel for an indigent prisoner ought not to ask to be excused for any trivial reason...."

49. Cf. ABA Canon 7.

50. See ABA Canon 5.

51. Dr. Johnson's reply to Boswell upon being asked what he thought of "supporting a cause which you know to be bad" was: "Sir, you do not know it to be good or bad till the Judge determines it. I have said that you are to state facts fairly; so that your thinking, or what you call knowing, a cause to be bad, must be from reasoning, must be from supposing your arguments to be weak and inconclusive. But, Sir, that is not enough. An argument which does not convince yourself, may convince the Judge to whom you urge it; and if it does convince him, why, then, Sir, you are wrong, and he is right." 2 Boswell, The Life of Johnson 47–48 (Hill ed. 1887).

52. "The lawyer deciding whether to undertake a case must be able to judge objectively whether he is capable of handling it and whether he can assume its burdens without prejudice to previous commitments....." *Professional Responsibility: Report of the Joint Conference*, 44 A.B.A.J. 1158, 1218 (1958).

53. "The lawyer must decline to conduct a civil cause or to make a defense when convinced that it is intended merely to harass or to injure the opposite party or to work oppression or wrong." ABA Canon 30.

54. See ABA Canon 7.

55. Id.

"From the facts stated we assume that the client has discharged the first attorney and given notice of the discharge. Such being the case, the second attorney may properly accept employment. *Canon 7; Opinions 10, 130, 149.*" *ABA Opinion* 209 (1941).

EC 2-31 Full availability of legal counsel requires both that persons be able to obtain counsel and that lawyers who undertake representation complete the work involved. Trial counsel for a convicted defendant should continue to represent his client by advising whether to take an appeal and, if the appeal is prosecuted, by representing him through the appeal unless new counsel is substituted or withdrawal is permitted by the appropriate court.

EC 2-32 A decision by a lawyer to withdraw should be made only on the basis of compelling circumstances,[56] and in a matter pending before a tribunal he must comply with the rules of the tribunal regarding withdrawal. A lawyer should not withdraw without considering carefully and endeavoring to minimize the possible adverse effect on the rights of his client and the possibility of prejudice to his client[57] as a result of his withdrawal. Even when he justifiably withdraws, a lawyer should protect the welfare of his client by giving due notice of his withdrawal,[58] suggesting employment of other counsel, delivering to the client all papers and property to which the client is entitled, cooperating with counsel subsequently employed, and otherwise endeavoring to minimize the possibility of harm. Further, he should refund to the client any compensation not earned during the employment.[59]

EC 2-33 As a part of the legal profession's commitment to the principle that high quality legal services should be available to all, attorneys are encouraged to cooperate with qualified legal assistance organizations providing prepaid legal services. Such participation should at all times be in accordance with the basic tenets of the profession: independence, integrity, competence and devotion to the interests of individual clients. An attorney so participating should make certain that his relationship with a qualified legal assistance organization in no way interferes with his independent, professional representation of the interests of the individual client. An attorney should avoid situations in which officials of the organization who are not lawyers attempt to direct attorneys concerning the manner in which legal services are performed for individual members, and should also avoid situations in which considerations of economy are given undue weight in determining the attorneys employed by an organization or the legal services to be performed for the member or beneficiary rather than competence and quality of service. An attorney interested in maintaining the historic traditions of the profession and preserving the function of a lawyer as a trusted and independent advisor to individual members of society should carefully assess such factors when accepting employment by, or otherwise participating in, a particular qualified legal assistance organization, and while so participating should adhere to the highest professional standards of effort and competence.

DISCIPLINARY RULES

DR 2-101 Publicity.

(A) A lawyer shall not, on behalf of himself, his partner, associate or any other lawyer affiliated with

---

56. See ABA Canon 44.

"I will carefully consider, before taking a case, whether it appears that I can fully represent the client within the framework of law. If the decision is in the affirmative, then it will take extreme circumstances to cause me to decide later that I cannot so represent him." Thode, *The Ethical Standard for the Advocate,* 39 Texas L.Rev. 575, 592 (1961) (from "A Proper Oath for Advocates").

57. *ABA Opinion* 314 (1965) held that a lawyer should not disassociate himself from a cause when "it is obvious that the very act of disassociation would have the effect of violating *Canon 37.*"

58. ABA Canon 44 enumerates instances in which " ... the lawyer may be warranted in withdrawing on due notice to the client, allowing him time to employ another lawyer."

59. *See* ABA Canon 44.

him or his firm, use or participate in the use of any form of public communication containing a false, fraudulent, misleading, deceptive, self-laudatory or unfair statement or claim.

(B) In order to facilitate the process of informed selection of a lawyer by potential consumers of legal services, a lawyer may publish or broadcast, subject to DR 2–103, the following information in print media distributed or over television or radio broadcast in the geographic area or areas in which the lawyer resides or maintains offices or in which a significant part of the lawyer's clientele resides, provided that the information disclosed by the lawyer in such publication or broadcast complies with DR 2–101(A), and is presented in a dignified manner:

(1) Name, including name of law firm and names of professional associates; addresses and telephone numbers;

(2) One or more fields of law in which the lawyer or law firm practices, a statement that practice is limited to one or more fields of law, or a statement that the lawyer or law firm specializes in a particular field of law practice, to the extent authorized under DR 2–105;

(3) Date and place of birth;

(4) Date and place of admission to the bar of state and federal courts;

(5) Schools attended, with dates of graduation, degrees and other scholastic distinctions;

(6) Public or quasi-public offices;

(7) Military service;

(8) Legal authorships;

(9) Legal teaching positions;

(10) Memberships, offices, and committee assignments, in bar associations;

(11) Membership and offices in legal fraternities and legal societies;

(12) Technical and professional licenses;

(13) Memberships in scientific, technical and professional associations and societies;

(14) Foreign language ability;

(15) Names and addresses of bank references;

(16) With their written consent, names of clients regularly represented;

(17) Prepaid or group legal services programs in which the lawyer participates;

(18) Whether credit cards or other credit arrangements are accepted;

(19) Office and telephone answering service hours;

(20) Fee for an initial consultation;

(21) Availability upon request of a written schedule of fees and/or an estimate of the fee to be charged for specific services;

(22) Contingent fee rates subject to DR 2–106(C), provided that the statement discloses whether percentages are computed before or after deduction of costs;

(23) Range of fees for services, provided that the statement discloses that the specific fee within the range which will be charged will vary depending upon the particular matter to be handled for each client and the client is entitled without obligation to an estimate of the fee within the range likely to be charged, in print size equivalent to the

largest print used in setting forth the fee information;

(24) Hourly rate, provided that the statement discloses that the total fee charged will depend upon the number of hours which must be devoted to the particular matter to be handled for each client and the client is entitled to without obligation an estimate of the fee likely to be charged, in print size at least equivalent to the largest print used in setting forth the fee information;

(25) Fixed fees for specific legal services,* the description of which would not be misunderstood or be deceptive, provided that the statement discloses that the quoted fee will be available only to clients whose matters fall into the services described and that the client is entitled without obligation to a specific estimate of the fee likely to be charged in print size at least equivalent to the largest print used in setting forth the fee information.

(C) Any person desiring to expand the information authorized for disclosure in DR 2–101(B), or to provide for its dissemination through other forums may apply to [the agency having jurisdiction under state law]. Any such application shall be served upon [the agencies having jurisdiction under state law over the regulation of the legal profession and consumer matters] who shall be heard, together with the applicant, on the issue of whether the proposal is necessary in light of the existing provisions of the Code, accords with standards of accuracy, reliability and truth-

fulness, and would facilitate the process of informed selection of lawyers by potential consumers of legal services. The relief granted in response to any such application shall be promulgated as an amendment to DR 2–101(B), universally applicable to all lawyers.**

(D) If the advertisement is communicated to the public over television or radio, it shall be prerecorded, approved for broadcast by the lawyer, and a recording of the actual transmission shall be retained by the lawyer.

(E) If a lawyer advertises a fee for a service, the lawyer must render that service for no more than the fee advertised.

(F) Unless otherwise specified in the advertisement if a lawyer publishes any fee information authorized under DR 2–101(B) in a publication that is published more frequently than one time per month, the lawyer shall be bound by any representation made therein for a period of not less than 30 days after such publication. If a lawyer publishes any fee information authorized under DR 2–101(B) in a publication that is published once a month or less frequently, he shall be bound by any representation made therein until the publication of the succeeding issue. If a lawyer publishes any fee information authorized under DR 2–101(B) in a publication which has no fixed date for publication of a succeeding issue, the lawyer shall be bound by any representation made therein for a reasonable period of time after publication but in no event less than one year.

(G) Unless otherwise specified, if a lawyer broadcasts any fee infor-

---

* The agency having jurisdiction under state law may desire to issue appropriate guidelines defining "specific legal services."

** The agency having jurisdiction under state law should establish orderly and expeditious procedures for ruling on such applications.

mation authorized under DR 2–101(B), the lawyer shall be bound by any representation made therein for a period of not less than 30 days after such broadcast.

(H) This rule does not prohibit limited and dignified identification of a lawyer as a lawyer as well as by name:

(1) In political advertisements when his professional status is germane to the political campaign or to a political issue.

(2) In public notices when the name and profession of a lawyer are required or authorized by law or are reasonably pertinent for a purpose other than the attraction of potential clients.

(3) In routine reports and announcements of a bona fide business, civic, professional, or political organization in which he serves as a director or officer.

(4) In and on legal documents prepared by him.

(5) In and on legal textbooks, treatises, and other legal publications, and in dignified advertisements thereof.

(I) A lawyer shall not compensate or give any thing of value to representatives of the press, radio, television, or other communication medium in anticipation of or in return for professional publicity in a news item.

DR 2–102 Professional Notices, Letterheads and Offices.

(A) A lawyer or law firm shall not use or participate in the use of professional cards, professional announcement cards, office signs, letterheads, or similar professional notices or devices, except that the following may be used if they are in dignified form:

(1) A professional card of a lawyer identifying him by name and as a lawyer, and giving his addresses, telephone numbers, the name of his law firm, and any information permitted under DR 2–105. A professional card of a law firm may also give the names of members and associates. Such cards may be used for identification.

(2) A brief professional announcement card stating new or changed associations or addresses, change of firm name, or similar matters pertaining to the professional offices of a lawyer or law firm, which may be mailed to lawyers, clients, former clients, personal friends, and relatives.[60] It shall not state biographical data except to the extent reasonably necessary to identify the lawyer or to explain the change in his association, but it may state the immediate past position of the lawyer.[61] It may give the names and dates of predecessor firms in a continuing line of succession. It shall not

60. See *ABA Opinion* 301 (1961).

61. "[I]t has become commonplace for many lawyers to participate in government service; to deny them the right, upon their return to private practice, to refer to their prior employment in a brief and dignified manner, would place an undue limitation upon a large element of our profession. It is entirely proper for a member of the profession to explain his

absence from private practice, where such is the primary purpose of the announcement, by a brief and dignified reference to the prior employment.

"... [A]ny such announcement should be limited to the immediate past connection of the lawyer with the government, made upon his leaving that position to enter private practice." *ABA Opinion* 301 (1961).

state the nature of the practice except as permitted under DR 2–105.[62]

(3) A sign on or near the door of the office and in the building directory identifying the law office. The sign shall not state the nature of the practice, except as permitted under DR 2–105.

(4) A letter head of a lawyer identifying him by name and as a lawyer, and giving his addresses, telephone numbers, the name of his law firm, associates and any information permitted under DR 2–105. A letterhead of a law firm may also give the names of members and associates,[63] and names and dates relating to deceased and retired members.[64] A lawyer may be designated "Of Counsel" on a letterhead if he has a continuing relationship with a lawyer or law firm, other than as a partner or associate. A lawyer or law firm may be designated as "General Counsel" or by similar professional reference on stationary of a client if he or the firm devotes a substantial amount of professional time in the representation of that client.[65] The letterhead of a law firm may give the names

and dates of predecessor firms in a continuing line of succession.

(B) A lawyer in private practice shall not practice under a trade name, a name that is misleading as to the identity of the lawyer or lawyers practicing under such name, or a firm name containing names other than those of one or more of the lawyers in the firm, except that the name of a professional corporation or professional association may contain "P.C." or "P.A." or similar symbols indicating the nature of the organization, and if otherwise lawful a firm may use as, or continue to include in, its name the name or names of one or more deceased or retired members of the firm or of a predecessor firm in a continuing line of succession.[66] A lawyer who assumes a judicial, legislative, or public executive or administrative post or office shall not permit his name to remain in the name of a law firm or to be used in professional notices of the firm during any significant period in which he is not actively and regularly practicing law as a member of the firm,[67] and during such period other members of the firm shall not use his name in the firm name or in professional notices of the firm.[68]

---

62. See *ABA Opinion* 251 (1943).

63. "Those lawyers who are working for an individual lawyer or a law firm may be designated on the letterhead and in other appropriate places as 'associates'." *ABA Opinion* 310 (1963).

64. See ABA Canon 33.

65. But see *ABA Opinion* 285 (1951).

66. See ABA Canon 33; cf. *ABA Opinions* 318 (1967), 267 (1945), 219 (1941), 208 (1940), 192 (1939), 97 (1933), and 6 (1925).

67. *ABA Opinion* 318 (1967) held, "anything to the contrary in Formal Opinion 315 or in the other opinions cited notwithstanding," that: "Where a partner whose name appears in the name of a law firm is elected or appointed to high local, state or federal office, which

office he intends to occupy only temporarily, at the end of which time he intends to return to his position with the firm, and provided that he is not precluded by holding such office from engaging in the practice of law and does not in fact sever his relationship with the firm but only takes a leave of absence, and provided that there is no local law, statute or custom to the contrary, his name may be retained in the firm name during his term or terms of office, but only if proper precautions are taken not to mislead the public as to his degree of participation in the firm's affairs."

Cf. *ABA Opinion* 143 (1935). New York County Opinion 67, and New York City Opinions 36 and 798; but cf. *ABA Opinion* 192 (1939) and Michigan Opinion 164.

68. Cf. ABA Canon 33.

(C) A lawyer shall not hold himself out as having a partnership with one or more other lawyers or professional corporations unless they are in fact partners.[69]

(D) A partnership shall not be formed or continued between or among lawyers licensed in different jurisdictions unless all enumerations of the members and associates of the firm on its letterhead and in other permissible listings make clear the jurisdictional limitations on those members and associates of the firm not licensed to practice in all listed jurisdictions;[70] however, the same firm name may be used in each jurisdiction.

(E) Nothing contained herein shall prohibit a lawyer from using or permitting the use of, in connection with his name, an earned degree or title derived therefrom indicating his training in the law.

DR 2–103 Recommendation of Professional Employment.[71]

(A) A lawyer shall not, except as authorized in DR 2–101(B), recommend employment as a private practitioner,[72] of himself, his partner, or associate to a layperson who has not sought his advice regarding employment of a lawyer.[73]

(B) A lawyer shall not compensate or give anything of value to a person or organization to recommend or secure his employment[74] by a client, or as a reward for having made a recommendation resulting in his employment[75] by a client, except that he may pay the usual and reasonable fees or dues charged by any of the organizations listed in DR 2–103(D).

(C) A lawyer shall not request a person or organization to recommend or promote the use of his services or those of his partner or associate, or any other lawyer affiliated with him or his firm, as a private practitioner,[76] except as authorized in DR 2–101, and except that

  (1) He may request referrals from a lawyer referral service operated, sponsored, or approved by a bar association and may pay its fees incident thereto.[77]

---

69. See *ABA Opinion* 277 (1948); cf. ABA Canon 33 and *ABA Opinions* 318 (1967), 126 (1935), 115 (1934), and 106 (1934).

70. See *ABA Opinions* 318 (1967) and 316 (1967); cf. ABA Canon 33.

71. Cf. ABA Canon 28.

72. "We think it clear that a lawyer's seeking employment in an ordinary law office, or appointment to a civil service position, is not prohibited by . . . [Canon 27]." *ABA Opinion* 197 (1939).

73. "[A] lawyer may not seek from persons not his clients the opportunity to perform . . . a [legal] checkup." *ABA Opinion* 307 (1962).

74. Cf. *ABA Opinion* 78 (1932).

75. " 'No financial connection of any kind between the Brotherhood and any lawyer is permissible. No lawyer can properly pay any amount whatsoever to the Brotherhood or any of its departments, officers or members as compensation, reimbursement of expenses or gra-

tuity in connection with the procurement of a case.' " In re Brotherhood of R.R. Trainmen, 13 Ill.2d 391, 398, 150 N.E.2d 163, 167 (1958), quoted in In re Ratner, 194 Kan. 362, 372, 399 P.2d 865, 873 (1956).

See *ABA Opinion* 147 (1935).

76. "This Court has condemned the practice of ambulance chasing through the media of runners and touters. In similar fashion we have with equal emphasis condemned the practice of direct solicitation by a lawyer. We have classified both offenses as serious breaches of the Canons of Ethics demanding severe treatment of the offending lawyer." State v. Dawson, 111 So.2d 427, 431 (Fla.1959).

77. "Registrants [of a lawyer referral plan] may be required to contribute to the expense of operating it by a reasonable registration charge or by a reasonable percentage of fees collected by them." *ABA Opinion* 291 (1956).

Cf. *ABA Opinion* 227 (1941).

(2) He may cooperate with the legal service activities of any of the offices or organizations enumerated in DR 2–103(D)(1) through (4) and may perform legal services for those to whom he was recommended by it to do such work if:

    (a) The person to whom the recommendation is made is a member or beneficiary of such office or organization; and

    (b) The lawyer remains free to exercise his independent professional judgment on behalf of his client.

(D) A lawyer or his partner or associate or any other lawyer affiliated with him or his firm may be recommended, employed or paid by, or may cooperate with, one of the following offices or organizations that promote the use of his services or those of his partner or associate or any other lawyer affiliated with him or his firm if there is no interference with the exercise of independent professional judgment in behalf of his client:

(1) A legal aid office or public defender office:

    (a) Operated or sponsored by a duly accredited law school.

    (b) Operated or sponsored by a bona fide nonprofit community organization.

    (c) Operated or sponsored by a governmental agency.

    (d) Operated, sponsored, or approved by a bar association.[78]

(2) A military legal assistance office.

(3) A lawyer referral service operated, sponsored, or approved by a bar association.

(4) Any bona fide organization that recommends, furnishes or pays for legal services to its members or beneficiaries[79] provided the following conditions are satisfied:

    (a) Such organization, including any affiliate, is so organized and operated that no profit is derived by it from the rendition of legal services by lawyers, and that, if the organization is organized for profit, the legal services are not rendered by lawyers employed, directed, supervised or selected by it except in connection with matters where such organization bears ultimate liability of its member or beneficiary.

    (b) Neither the lawyer, nor his partner, nor associate, nor any other lawyer affiliated with him or his firm, nor any non-lawyer, shall have initiated or promoted such organization for the primary purpose of providing financial or other benefit to such lawyer, partner, associate or affiliated lawyer.

    (c) Such organization is not operated for the purpose of procuring legal work or financial benefit for any

---

78. Cf. *ABA Opinion* 148 (1935).

79. United Mine Workers v. Ill. State Bar Ass'n., 389 U.S. 217, 19 L.Ed.2d 426, 88 S.Ct. 353 (1967); Brotherhood of R.R. Trainmen v. Virginia, 377 U.S. 1, 12 L.Ed.2d 89, 84 S.Ct. 1113 (1964); NAACP v. Button, 371 U.S. 415, 9 L.Ed.2d 405, 83 S.Ct. 328 (1963).

lawyer as a private practitioner outside of the legal services program of the organization.

(d) The member or beneficiary to whom the legal services are furnished, and not such organization, is recognized as the client of the lawyer in the matter.

(e) Any member or beneficiary who is entitled to have legal services furnished or paid for by the organization may, if such member or beneficiary so desires, select counsel other than that furnished, selected or approved by the organization for the particular matter involved; and the legal service plan of such organization provides appropriate relief for any member or beneficiary who asserts a claim that representation by counsel furnished, selected or approved would be unethical, improper or inadequate under the circumstances of the matter involved and the plan provides an appropriate procedure for seeking such relief.

(f) The lawyer does not know or have cause to know that such organization is in violation of applicable laws, rules of court and other legal requirements that govern its legal service operations.

(g) Such organization has filed with the appropriate disciplinary authority at least annually a report with respect to its legal service plan, if any, showing its terms, its schedule of benefits, its subscription charges, agreements with counsel, and financial results of its legal service activities or, if it has failed to do so, the lawyer does not know or have cause to know of such failure.

(E) A lawyer shall not accept employment when he knows or it is obvious that the person who seeks his services does so as a result of conduct prohibited under this Disciplinary Rule.

DR 2-104 Suggestion of Need of Legal Services.[80,81]

(A) A lawyer who has given in-person unsolicited advice to a layperson that he should obtain counsel or take legal action shall not accept employment resulting from that advice,[82] except that:

(1) A lawyer may accept employment by a close friend, relative, former client (if the advice is germane to the former employment), or one whom the lawyer reasonably believes to be a client.[83]

(2) A lawyer may accept employment that results from his

---

80. "If a bar association has embarked on a program of institutional advertising for an annual legal check-up and provides brochures and reprints, it is not improper to have these available in the lawyer's office for persons to read and take." *ABA Opinion* 307 (1962).

Cf. *ABA Opinion* 121 (1934).

81. ABA Canon 28.

82. Cf. *ABA Opinions* 229 (1941) and 173 (1937).

83. "It certainly is not improper for a lawyer to advise his regular clients of new statutes, court decisions, and administrative rulings, which may affect the client's interests, provided the communication is strictly limited to such information...

"When such communications go to concerns or individuals other than regular clients of the lawyer, they are thinly disguised advertise-participation in activities designed to educate laypersons to recognize legal problems, to make intelligent selection of counsel, or to utilize available legal services if such activities are conducted or sponsored by a qualified legal assistance organization.

(3) A lawyer who is recommended, furnished or paid by a qualified legal assistance organization enumerated in DR 2–103(D)(1) through (4) may represent a member or beneficiary thereof, to the extent and under the conditions prescribed therein.

(4) Without affecting his right to accept employment, a lawyer may speak publicly or write for publication on legal topics[84] so long as he does not emphasize his own professional experience or reputation and does not undertake to give individual advice.

(5) If success in asserting rights or defenses of his client in litigation in the nature of a class action is dependent upon the joinder of others, a lawyer may accept, but shall not seek, employment from those contacted for the purpose of obtaining their joinder.[85]

DR 2–105 Limitation of Practice.[86]

(A) A lawyer shall not hold himself out publicly as a specialist, as

practicing in certain areas of law or as limiting his practice permitted under DR 2–101(B), except as follows:

(1) A lawyer admitted to practice before the United States Patent and Trademark Office may use the designation "Patents," "Patent Attorney," "Patent Lawyer," or "Registered Patent Attorney" or any combination of those terms, on his letterhead and office sign.

(2) A lawyer who publicly discloses fields of law in which the lawyer or the law firm practices or states that his practice is limited to one or more fields of law shall do so by using designations and definitions authorized and approved by [the agency having jurisdiction of the subject under state law].

(3) A lawyer who is certified as a specialist in a particular field of law or law practice by [the authority having jurisdiction under state law over the subject of specialization by lawyers] may hold himself out as such, but only in accordance with the rules prescribed by that authority.[87]

DR 2–106 Fees for Legal Services.[88]

(A) A lawyer shall not enter into an agreement for, charge, or collect an illegal or clearly excessive fee.[89]

ments for professional employment, and are obviously improper." *ABA Opinion* 213 (1941).

"It is our opinion that where the lawyer has no reason to believe that he has been supplanted by another lawyer, it is not only his right, but it might even be his duty to advise his client of any change of fact or law which might defeat the client's testamentary purpose as expressed in the will.

"Periodic notices might be sent to the client for whom a lawyer has drawn a will, suggesting that it might be wise for the client to reexamine his will to determine whether or not there has been any change in his situation

requiring a modification of his will." *ABA Opinion* 210 (1941).

Cf. ABA Canon 28.

84. Cf. *ABA Opinion* 168 (1937).

85. But cf. *ABA Opinion* 111 (1934).

86. See ABA Canon 45; cf. ABA Canons 43, and 46.

87. This provision is included to conform to action taken by the ABA House of Delegates at the Mid–Winter Meeting, January, 1969.

88. See ABA Canon 12.

89. The charging of a "clearly excessive fee" is a ground for discipline. State ex rel.

(B) A fee is clearly excessive when, after a review of the facts, a lawyer of ordinary prudence would be left with a definite and firm conviction that the fee is in excess of a reasonable fee. Factors to be considered as guides in determining the reasonableness of a fee include the following:

(1) The time and labor required, the novelty and difficulty of the questions involved, and the skill requisite to perform the legal service properly.

(2) The likelihood, if apparent to the client, that the acceptance of the particular employment will preclude other employment by the lawyer.

(3) The fee customarily charged in the locality for similar legal services.

(4) The amount involved and the results obtained.

(5) The time limitations imposed by the client or by the circumstances.

(6) The nature and length of the professional relationship with the client.

(7) The experience, reputation, and ability of the lawyer or lawyers performing the services.

(8) Whether the fee is fixed or contingent.[90]

(C) A lawyer shall not enter into an arrangement for, charge, or collect a contingent fee for representing a defendant in a criminal case.[91]

DR 2–107 Division of Fees Among Lawyers

(A) A lawyer shall not divide a fee for legal services with another lawyer who is not a partner in or associate of his law firm or law office, unless:

(1) The client consents to employment of the other lawyer after a full disclosure that a division of fees will be made.

(2) The division is made in proportion to the services performed and responsibility assumed by each.[92]

(3) The total fee of the lawyers does not clearly exceed reasonable compensation for all legal services they rendered the client.[93]

Nebraska State Bar Ass'n. v. Richards, 165 Neb. 80, 90, 84 N.W.2d 136, 143 (1957).

"An attorney has the right to contract for any fee he chooses so long as it is not excessive (see Opinion 190), and this Committee is not concerned with the amount of such fees unless so excessive as to constitute a misappropriation of the client's funds (see Opinion 27)." *ABA Opinion* 320 (1968).

Cf. *ABA Opinions* 209 (1940), 190 (1939), and 27 (1930) and State ex rel. Lee v. Buchanan, 191 So.2d 33 (Fla.1966).

90. Cf. ABA Canon 13; see generally MacKinnon, Contingent Fees for Legal Services (1964) (A Report of the American Bar Foundation).

91. "Contingent fees, whether in civil or criminal cases, are a special concern of the law.....

"In criminal cases, the rule is stricter because of the danger of corrupting justice. The second part of Section 542 of the Restatement [of Contracts] reads: 'A bargain to conduct a criminal case ... in consideration of a promise of a fee contingent on success is illegal....' "

Peyton v. Margiotti, 398 Pa. 86, 156 A.2d 865, 967 (1959).

"The third area of practice in which the use of the contingent fee is generally considered to be prohibited is the prosecution and defense of criminal cases. However, there are so few cases, and these are predominantly old, that it is doubtful that there can be said to be any current law on the subject.... In the absence of cases on the validity of contingent fees for defense attorneys, it is necessary to rely on the consensus among commentators that such a fee is void as against public policy. The nature of criminal practice itself makes unlikely the use of contingent fee contracts." MacKinnon, Contingent Fees for Legal Services 52 (1964) (A Report of the American Bar Foundation).

92. See ABA Canon 34 and *ABA Opinions* 316 (1967) and 294 (1958); see generally *ABA Opinions* 265 (1945), 204 (1940), 190 (1939), 171 (1937), 153 (1936), 97 (1933), 63 (1932), 28 (1930), 27 (1930), and 18 (1930).

93. "*Canon 12* contemplates that a lawyer's fee should not exceed *the value of the services* rendered...."

(B) This Disciplinary Rule does not prohibit payment to a former partner or associate pursuant to a separation or retirement agreement.

DR 2–108 Agreements Restricting the Practice of a Lawyer.

(A) A lawyer shall not be a party to or participate in a partnership or employment agreement with another lawyer that restricts the right of a lawyer to practice law after the termination of a relationship created by the agreement, except as a condition to payment of retirement benefits.[94]

(B) In connection with the settlement of a controversy or suit, a lawyer shall not enter into an agreement that restricts his right to practice law.

DR 2–109 Acceptance of Employment.

(A) A lawyer shall not accept employment on behalf of a person if he knows or it is obvious that such person wishes to:

(1) Bring a legal action, conduct a defense, or assert a position in litigation, or otherwise have steps taken for him, merely for the purpose of harassing or maliciously injuring any person.[95]

(2) Present a claim or defense in litigation that is not warranted under existing law, unless it can be supported by good faith argument for an exten-

sion, modification, or reversal of existing law.

DR 2–110 Withdrawal from Employment.[96]

(A) In general.

(1) If permission for withdrawal from employment is required by the rules of a tribunal, a lawyer shall not withdraw from employment in a proceeding before that tribunal without its permission.

(2) In any event, a lawyer shall not withdraw from employment until he has taken reasonable steps to avoid foreseeable prejudice to the rights of his client, including giving due notice to his client, allowing time for employment of other counsel, delivering to the client all papers and property to which the client is entitled, and complying with applicable laws and rules.

(3) A lawyer who withdraws from employment shall refund promptly any part of a fee paid in advance that has not been earned.

(B) Mandatory Withdrawal.

A lawyer representing a client before a tribunal, with its permission if required by its rules, shall withdraw from employment, and a lawyer representing a client in other matters shall withdraw from employment, if:

(1) He knows or it is obvious that his client is bringing the legal action, conducting the de-

"*Canon 12* applies, whether joint or separate fees are charged [by associate attorneys] ...." *ABA Opinion* 204 (1940).

94. "[A] general covenant restricting an employed lawyer, after leaving the employment, from practicing in the community for a stated period, appears to this Committee to be an unwarranted restriction on the right of a lawyer to choose where he will practice and inconsistent with our professional status. Accordingly, the Committee is of the opinion it would be improper for the employing lawyer to

require the covenant and likewise for the employed lawyer to agree to it." *ABA Opinion* 300 (1961).

95. See ABA Canon 30.

"*Rule 13.* ... A member of the State Bar shall not accept employment to prosecute or defend a case solely out of spite, or solely for the purpose of harassing or delaying another...." Cal.Business and Professions Code § 6067 (West 1962).

96. Cf. ABA Canon 44.

fense, or asserting a position in the litigation, or is otherwise having steps taken for him, merely for the purpose of harassing or maliciously injuring any person.

(2) He knows or it is obvious that his continued employment will result in violation of a Disciplinary Rule.[97]

(3) His mental or physical condition renders it unreasonably difficult for him to carry out the employment effectively.

(4) He is discharged by his client.

(C) Permissive withdrawal.[98]

If DR 2–110(B) is not applicable, a lawyer may not request permission to withdraw in matters pending before a tribunal, and may not withdraw in other matters, unless such request or such withdrawal is because:

(1) His client:

    (a) Insists upon presenting a claim or defense that is not warranted under existing law and cannot be supported by good faith argument for an extension, modification, or reversal of existing law.[99]

    (b) Personally seeks to pursue an illegal course of conduct.

    (c) Insists that the lawyer pursue a course of conduct that is illegal or that is prohibited under the Disciplinary Rules.

    (d) By other conduct renders it unreasonably difficult for the lawyer to carry out his employment effectively.

    (e) Insists, in a matter not pending before a tribunal, that the lawyer engage in conduct that is contrary to the judgment and advice of the lawyer but not prohibited under the Disciplinary Rules.

    (f) Deliberately disregards an agreement or obligation to the lawyer as to expenses or fees.

(2) His continued employment is likely to result in a violation of a Disciplinary Rule.

(3) His inability to work with co-counsel indicates that the best interests of the client likely will be served by withdrawal.

(4) His mental or physical condition renders it difficult for him to carry out the employment effectively.

(5) His client knowingly and freely assents to termination of his employment.

(6) He believes in good faith, in a proceeding pending before a tribunal, that the tribunal will find the existence of other good cause for withdrawal.

CANON 3

A Lawyer Should Assist in Preventing the Unauthorized Practice of Law

ETHICAL CONSIDERATIONS

EC 3–1 The prohibition against the practice of law by a layman is grounded in the need of the public for integrity and competence of those who undertake to render legal services. Because of the fiduciary and personal character of the lawyer-client relationship and the inherently complex nature of our legal system, the

97. See also Code of Professional Responsibility, DR 5–102 and DR 5–105.

98. Cf. ABA Canon 4.

99. Cf. Anders v. California, 386 U.S. 738, 18 L.Ed.2d 493, 87 S.Ct. 1396 (1967), rehearing denied, 388 U.S. 924, 18 L.Ed.2d 1377, 87 S.Ct. 2094 (1967).

public can better be assured of the requisite responsibility and competence if the practice of law is confined to those who are subject to the requirements and regulations imposed upon members of the legal profession.

EC 3–2 The sensitive variations in the considerations that bear on legal determinations often make it difficult even for a lawyer to exercise appropriate professional judgment, and it is therefore essential that the personal nature of the relationship of client and lawyer be preserved. Competent professional judgment is the product of a trained familiarity with law and legal processes, a disciplined, analytical approach to legal problems, and a firm ethical commitment.

EC 3–3 A non-lawyer who undertakes to handle legal matters is not governed as to integrity or legal competence by the same rules that govern the conduct of a lawyer. A lawyer is not only subject to that regulation but also is committed to high standards of ethical conduct. The public interest is best served in legal matters by a regulated profession committed to such standards.[1] The Disciplinary Rules protect the public in that they prohibit a lawyer from seeking employment by improper overtures, from acting in cases of divided loyalties, and from submitting to the control of others in the exercise of his judgment. Moreover, a person who entrusts legal matters to a lawyer is protected by the attorney-client privilege and by the duty of the lawyer to hold inviolate the confidences and secrets of his client.

EC 3–4 A layman who seeks legal services often is not in a position to judge whether he will receive proper professional attention. The entrustment of a legal matter may well involve the confidences, the reputation, the property, the freedom, or even the life of the client. Proper protection of members of the public demands that no person be permitted to act in the confidential and demanding capacity of a lawyer unless he is subject to the regulations of the legal profession.

EC 3–5 It is neither necessary nor desirable to attempt the formulation of a single, specific definition of what constitutes the practice of law.[2] Functionally, the practice of law relates to the rendition of services for others that call for the professional judgment of a lawyer. The essence of the professional judgment of the lawyer is his educated ability to relate the general body and philosophy of law to a specific legal problem of a client; and thus, the public interest will be better served if only lawyers are permitted to act in matters involving professional judgment. Where this professional judgment is not involved, non-lawyers, such as court clerks, police officers, abstracters, and many governmental employees, may engage in occupations that require a special knowledge of law in certain areas. But the services of a lawyer are essential in the public interest whenever the exercise of professional legal judgment is required.

EC 3–6 A lawyer often delegates tasks to clerks, secretaries, and other lay persons. Such delegation is proper if the lawyer maintains a direct relationship with

---

1. "The condemnation of the unauthorized practice of law is designed to protect the public from legal services by persons unskilled in the law. The prohibition of lay intermediaries is intended to insure the loyalty of the lawyer to the client unimpaired by intervening and possibly conflicting interests." Cheatham, *Availability of Legal Services: The Responsibility of the Individual Lawyer and of the Organized Bar*, 12 U.C.L.A.L.Rev. 438, 439 (1965).

2. "What constitutes unauthorized practice of the law in a particular jurisdiction is a matter for determination by the courts of that jurisdiction." *ABA Opinion* 198 (1939).

"In the light of the historical development of the lawyer's functions, it is impossible to lay down an exhaustive definition of 'the practice of law' by attempting to enumerate every conceivable act performed by lawyers in the normal course of their work." State Bar of Arizona v. Arizona Land Title & Trust Co., 90 Ariz. 76, 87, 366 P.2d 1, 8–9 (1961), modified, 91 Ariz. 293, 371 P.2d 1020 (1962).

his client, supervises the delegated work, and has complete professional responsibility for the work product.[3] This delegation enables a lawyer to render legal service more economically and efficiently.

EC 3–7 The prohibition against a non-lawyer practicing law does not prevent a layman from representing himself, for then he is ordinarily exposing only himself to possible injury. The purpose of the legal profession is to make educated legal representation available to the public; but anyone who does not wish to avail himself of such representation is not required to do so. Even so, the legal profession should help members of the public to recognize legal problems and to understand why it may be unwise for them to act for themselves in matters having legal consequences.

EC 3–8 Since a lawyer should not aid or encourage a layman to practice law, he should not practice law in association with a layman or otherwise share legal fees with a layman.[4] This does not mean, however, that the pecuniary value of the interest of a deceased lawyer in his firm or practice may not be paid to his estate or specified persons such as his widow or heirs.[5] In like manner, profit-sharing retirement plans of a lawyer or law firm which include non-lawyer office employ-

---

3. "A lawyer can employ lay secretaries, lay investigators, lay detectives, lay researchers, accountants, lay scriveners, nonlawyer draftsmen or nonlawyer researchers. In fact, he may employ nonlawyers to do any task for him except counsel clients about law matters, engage directly in the practice of law, appear in court or appear in formal proceedings a part of the judicial process, so long as it is he who takes the work and vouches for it to the client and becomes responsible to the client." *ABA Opinion* 316 (1967).

ABA Opinion 316 (1967) also stated that if a lawyer practices law as part of a law firm which includes lawyers from several states, he may delegate tasks to firm members in other states so long as he "is the person who, on behalf of the firm, vouched for the work of all of the others and, with the client and in the courts, did the legal acts defined by that state as the practice of law."

"A lawyer cannot delegate his professional responsibility to a law student employed in his office. He may avail himself of the assistance of the student in many of the fields of the lawyer's work, such as examination of case law, finding and interviewing witnesses, making collections of claims, examining court records, delivering papers, conveying important messages, and other similar matters. But the student is not permitted, until he is admitted to the Bar, to perform the professional functions of a lawyer, such as conducting court trials, giving professional advice to clients or drawing legal documents for them. The student in all his work must act as agent for the lawyer employing him, who must supervise his work and be responsible for his good conduct." *ABA Opinion* 85 (1932).

4. "No division of fees for legal services is proper, except with another lawyer...." *ABA*

Canon 34. Otherwise, according to *ABA Opinion* 316 (1967), "[t]he Canons of Ethics do not examine into the method by which such persons are remunerated by the lawyer.... They may be paid a salary, a per diem charge, a flat fee, a contract price, etc."

See ABA Canons 33 and 47.

5. "Many partnership agreements provide that the active partners, on the death of any one of them, are to make payments to the estate or to the nominee of a deceased partner on a pre-determined formula. It is only where the effect of such an arrangement is to make the estate or nominee a member of the partnership along with the surviving partners that it is prohibited by *Canon 34*. Where the payments are made in accordance with a pre-existing agreement entered into by the deceased partner during his lifetime and providing for a fixed method for determining their amount based upon the value of services rendered during the partner's lifetime and providing for a fixed period over which the payments are to be made, this is not the case. Under these circumstances, whether the payments are considered to be delayed payment of compensation earned but withheld during the partner's lifetime, or whether they are considered to be an approximation of his interest in matters pending at the time of his death, is immaterial. In either event, as Henry S. Drinker says in his book, Legal Ethics, at page 189: 'It would seem, however, that a reasonable agreement to pay the estate a proportion of the receipts for a reasonable period is a proper practical settlement for the lawyer's services to his retirement or death.' " *ABA Opinion* 308 (1963).

ees are not improper.[6] These limited exceptions to the rule against sharing legal fees with laymen are permissible since they do not aid or encourage laymen to practice law.

EC 3–9 Regulation of the practice of law is accomplished principally by the respective states.[7] Authority to engage in the practice of law conferred in any jurisdiction is not per se a grant of the right to practice elsewhere, and it is improper for a lawyer to engage in practice where he is not permitted by law or by court order to do so. However, the demands of business and the mobility of our society pose distinct problems in the regulation of the practice of law by the states.[8] In furtherance of the public interest, the legal profession should discourage regulation that unreasonably imposes territorial limitations upon the right of a lawyer to handle the legal affairs of his client or upon the opportunity of a client to obtain the services of a lawyer of his choice in all matters including the presentation of a contested matter in a tribunal before which the lawyer is not permanently admitted to practice.[9]

DISCIPLINARY RULES

DR 3–101 Aiding Unauthorized Practice of Law.[10]

(A) A lawyer shall not aid a non-lawyer in the unauthorized practice of law.[11]

(B) A lawyer shall not practice law in a jurisdiction where to do so would be in violation of regulations of the profession in that jurisdiction.[12]

DR 3–102 Dividing Legal Fees with a Non–Lawyer.

(A) A lawyer or law firm shall not share legal fees with a non-lawyer,[13] **except that:**

(1) An agreement by a lawyer with his firm, partner, or associate may provide for the payment of money, over a

---

6. Cf. ABA Opinion 311 (1964).

7. "That the States have broad power to regulate the practice of law is, of course, beyond question." United Mine Workers v. Ill. State Bar Ass'n, 389 U.S. 217, 222 (1967).

"It is a matter of law, not of ethics, as to where an individual may practice law. Each state has its own rules." *ABA Opinion* 316 (1967).

8. "Much of clients' business crosses state lines. People are mobile, moving from state to state. Many metropolitan areas cross state lines. It is common today to have a single economic and social community involving more than one state. The business of a single client may involve legal problems in several states." *ABA Opinion* 316 (1967).

9. "[W]e reaffirmed the general principle that legal services to New Jersey residents with respect to New Jersey matters may ordinarily be furnished only by New Jersey counsel; but we pointed out that there may be multistate transactions where strict adherence to this thesis would not be in the public interest and that, under the circumstances, it would have been not only more costly to the client but also 'grossly impractical and inefficient' to have had the settlement negotiations conduct-

ed by separate lawyers from different states." In re Estate of Waring, 47 N.J. 367, 376, 221 A.2d 193, 197 (1966).

Cf. *ABA Opinion* 316 (1967).

10. Conduct permitted by the Disciplinary Rules of Canons 2 and 5 does not violate DR 3–101.

11. See ABA Canon 47.

12. It should be noted, however, that a lawyer may engage in conduct, otherwise prohibited by this Disciplinary Rule, where such conduct is authorized by preemptive federal legislation. See Sperry v. Florida, 373 U.S. 379, 10 L.Ed.2d 428, 83 S.Ct. 1322 (1963).

13. See ABA Canon 34 and *ABA Opinions* 316 (1967), 180 (1938), and 48 (1931).

"The receiving attorney shall not under any guise or form share his fee for legal services with a lay agency, personal or corporate, without prejudice, however, to the right of the lay forwarder to charge and collect from the creditor proper compensation for non-legal services rendered by the law [sic] forwarder which are separate and apart from the services performed by the receiving attorney." *ABA Opinion* 294 (1958).

reasonable period of time after his death, to his estate or to one or more specified persons.[14]

(2) A lawyer who undertakes to complete unfinished legal business of a deceased lawyer may pay to the estate of the deceased lawyer that proportion of the total compensation which fairly represents the services rendered by the deceased lawyer.

(3) A lawyer or law firm may include non-lawyer employees in a compensation or retirement plan, even though the plan is based in whole or in part on a profit-sharing arrangement[15] providing such plan does not circumvent another disciplinary rule.[16]

14. See *ABA Opinion* 266 (1945).

15. Cf. *ABA Opinion* 311 (1964).

16. See ABA Informal Opinion 1440 (1979).

17. See ABA Canon 33; cf. *ABA Opinions* 239 (1942) and 201 (1940).

ABA Opinion 316 (1967) states that lawyers licensed in different jurisdictions may, under certain conditions, enter "into an arrangement for the practice of law" and that a lawyer licensed in State A is not, for such purpose a layman in State B.

1. See ABA Canons 6 and 37 and *ABA Opinion* 287 (1953). "The reason underlying the rule with respect to confidential communications between attorney and client is well stated in Mechem on Agency, 2d Ed., Vol. 2, § 2297, as follows: 'The purposes and necessities of the relation between a client and his attorney require, in many cases, on the part of the client, the fullest and freest disclosures to the attorney of the client's objectives, motives and acts. This disclosure is made in the strictest confidence, relying upon the attorney's honor and fidelity. To permit the attorney to reveal to others what is so disclosed, would be not only a gross violation of a sacred trust upon his part, but it would utterly destroy and prevent the usefulness and benefits to be derived from professional assistance. Based upon considerations of public policy, therefore, the law wisely declares that all confidential com-

DR 3–103 Forming a Partnership with a Non–Lawyer.

(A) A lawyer shall not form a partnership with a non-lawyer if any of the activities of the partnership consist of the practice of law.[17]

CANON 4

A Lawyer Should Preserve the Confidences and Secrets of a Client

ETHICAL CONSIDERATIONS

EC 4–1 Both the fiduciary relationship existing between lawyer and client and the proper functioning of the legal system require the preservation by the lawyer of confidences and secrets of one who has employed or sought to employ him.[1] A client must feel free to discuss whatever he wishes with his lawyer and a lawyer must be equally free to obtain information beyond that volunteered by his client.[2] A lawyer should be fully in-

munications and disclosures, made by a client to his legal adviser for the purpose of obtaining his professional aid or advice, shall be strictly privileged:—that the attorney shall not be permitted, without the consent of his client,—and much less will he be compelled—to reveal or disclose communications made to him under such circumstances.'" *ABA Opinion* 250 (1943).

"While it is true that complete revelation of relevant facts should be encouraged for trial purposes, nevertheless an attorney's dealings with his client, if both are sincere, and if the dealings involve more than mere technical matters, should be immune to discovery proceedings. There must be freedom from fear of revealment of matters disclosed to an attorney because of the peculiarly intimate relationship existing." Ellis–Foster Co. v. Union Carbide & Carbon Corp., 159 F.Supp. 917, 919 (D.N.J. 1958).

Cf. *ABA Opinions* 314 (1965), 274 (1946) and 268 (1945).

2. "While it is the great purpose of law to ascertain the truth, there is the countervailing necessity of insuring the right of every person to freely and fully confer and confide in one having knowledge of the law, and skilled in its practice, in order that the former may have adequate advice and a proper defense. This assistance can be made safely and readily available only when the client is free from the

formed of all the facts of the matter he is handling in order for his client to obtain the full advantage of our legal system. It is for the lawyer in the exercise of his independent professional judgment to separate the relevant and important from the irrelevant and unimportant. The observance of the ethical obligation of a lawyer to hold inviolate the confidences and secrets of his client not only facilitates the full development of facts essential to proper representation of the client but also encourages laymen to seek early legal assistance.

EC 4–2 The obligation to protect confidences and secrets obviously does not preclude a lawyer from revealing information when his client consents after full disclosure,[3] when necessary to perform his professional employment, when permitted by a Disciplinary Rule, or when required by law. Unless the client otherwise directs, a lawyer may disclose the affairs of his client to partners or associates of his firm. It is a matter of common knowledge that the normal operation of a law office exposes confidential professional information to non-lawyer employees of the office, particularly secretaries and those having access to the files; and this obligates a lawyer to exercise care in selecting and training his employees so that the sanctity of all confidences and secrets of his clients may be preserved. If the obligation extends to two or more clients as to the same information, a lawyer should obtain the permission of all before revealing the information. A lawyer must always be sensitive to the rights and wishes of his client and act scrupulously in the making of decisions which may involve

the disclosure of information obtained in his professional relationship.[4] Thus, in the absence of consent of his client after full disclosure, a lawyer should not associate another lawyer in the handling of a matter; nor should he, in the absence of consent, seek counsel from another lawyer if there is a reasonable possibility that the identity of the client or his confidences or secrets would be revealed to such lawyer. Both social amenities and professional duty should cause a lawyer to shun indiscreet conversations concerning his clients.

EC 4–3 Unless the client otherwise directs, it is not improper for a lawyer to give limited information from his files to an outside agency necessary for statistical, bookkeeping, accounting, data processing, banking, printing, or other legitimate purposes, provided he exercises due care in the selection of the agency and warns the agency that the information must be kept confidential.

EC 4–4 The attorney-client privilege is more limited than the ethical obligation of a lawyer to guard the confidences and secrets of his client. This ethical precept, unlike the evidentiary privilege, exists without regard to the nature or source of information or the fact that others share the knowledge. A lawyer should endeavor to act in a manner which preserves the evidentiary privilege; for example, he should avoid professional discussions in the presence of persons to whom the privilege does not extend. A lawyer owes an obligation to advise the client of the attorney-client privilege and timely to assert

---

consequences of apprehension of disclosure by reason of the subsequent statements of the skilled lawyer." Baird v. Koerner, 279 F.2d 623, 629–30 (9th Cir.1960).

Cf. *ABA Opinion* 150 (1936).

3. "Where ... [a client] knowingly and after full disclosure participates in a [legal fee] financing plan which requires the furnishing of certain information to the bank, clearly by his conduct he has waived any privilege as to that information." *ABA Opinion* 320 (1968).

4. "The lawyer must decide when he takes a case whether it is a suitable one for him to undertake and after this decision is made, he is not justified in turning against his client by exposing injurious evidence entrusted to him. . . . [D]oing something intrinsically regrettable, because the only alternative involves worse consequences, is a necessity in every profession." Williston, Life and Law 271 (1940).

Cf. *ABA Opinions* 177 (1938) and 83 (1932).

the privilege unless it is waived by the client.

EC 4–5 A lawyer should not use information acquired in the course of the representation of a client to the disadvantage of the client and a lawyer should not use, except with the consent of his client after full disclosure, such information for his own purposes.[5] Likewise, a lawyer should be diligent in his efforts to prevent the misuse of such information by his employees and associates.[6] Care should be exercised by a lawyer to prevent the disclosure of the confidences and secrets of one client to another,[7] and no employment should be accepted that might require such disclosure.

EC 4–6 The obligation of a lawyer to preserve the confidences and secrets of his client continues after the termination of his employment.[8] Thus a lawyer should not attempt to sell a law practice as a going business because, among other reasons, to do so would involve the disclosure of confidences and secrets.[9] A lawyer should also provide for the protection of the confidences and secrets of his client following the termination of the practice of the lawyer, whether termination is due to death, disability, or retirement. For

5. See ABA Canon 11.

6. See ABA Canon 37.

7. See ABA Canons 6 and 37.

"[A]n attorney must not accept professional employment against a client or a former client which will, or even *may* require him to use confidential information obtained by the attorney in the course of his professional relations with such client regarding the subject matter of the employment...." *ABA Opinion* 165 (1936).

8. See ABA Canon 37.

"Confidential communications between an attorney and his client, made because of the relationship and concerning the subject-matter of the attorney's employment, are generally privileged from disclosure without the consent of the client, and this privilege outlasts the attorney's employment. *Canon* 37." *ABA Opinion* 154 (1936).

9. Cf. *ABA Opinion* 266 (1945).

10. See ABA Canon 37; cf. ABA Canon 6.

example, a lawyer might provide for the personal papers of the client to be returned to him and for the papers of the lawyer to be delivered to another lawyer or to be destroyed. In determining the method of disposition, the instructions and wishes of the client should be a dominant consideration.

DISCIPLINARY RULES

DR 4–101 Preservation of Confidences and Secrets of a Client.[10]

(A) "Confidence" refers to information protected by the attorney-client privilege under applicable law, and "secret" refers to other information gained in the professional relationship that the client has requested be held inviolate or the disclosure of which would be embarrassing or would be likely to be detrimental to the client.

(B) Except when permitted under DR 4–101(C), a lawyer shall not knowingly:

(1) Reveal a confidence or secret of his client.[11]

11. "§ 6068 ... It is the duty of an attorney: ...."

"(e) To maintain inviolate the confidence, and at every peril to himself to preserve the secrets, of his client." Cal. Business and Professions Code § 6068 (West 1962). Virtually the same provision is found in the Oregon statutes. Ore.Rev.Stat. ch. 9, § 9.460(5).

"Communications between lawyer and client are privileged (Wigmore on Evidence, 3d Ed., Vol. 8, §§ 2290–2329). The modern theory underlying the privilege is subjective and is to give the client freedom of apprehension in consulting his legal advisor (ibid., § 2290, p. 548). The privilege applies to communications made in seeking legal advice for any purpose (ibid., § 2294, p. 563). The mere circumstance that the advice is given without charge therefore does not nullify the privilege (ibid., § 2303)." *ABA Opinion* 216 (1941).

"It is the duty of an attorney to maintain the confidence and preserve inviolate the secrets of his client...." *ABA Opinion* 155 (1936).

(2) Use a confidence or secret of his client to the disadvantage of the client.

(3) Use a confidence or secret of his client for the advantage of himself[12] or of a third person,[13] unless the client consents after full disclosure.

(C) A lawyer may reveal:

(1) Confidences or secrets with the consent of the client or

clients affected, but only after a full disclosure to them.[14]

(2) Confidences or secrets when permitted under Disciplinary Rules or required by law or court order.[15]

(3) The intention of his client to commit a crime[16] and the information necessary to prevent the crime.[17]

(4) Confidences or secrets necessary to establish or collect his fee[18] or to defend himself or

12. See ABA Canon 11.

"The provision respecting employment is in accord with the general rule announced in the adjudicated cases that a lawyer may not make use of knowledge or information acquired by him through his professional relations with his client, or in the conduct of his client's business, to his own advantage or profit (7 C.J.S., § 125, p. 958; Healy v. Gray, 184 Iowa 111, 168 N.W. 222; Baumgardner v. Hudson, D.C.App., 277 F. 552; Goodrum v. Clement, D.C.App., 277 F. 586)." *ABA Opinion* 250 (1943).

13. See *ABA Opinion* 177 (1938).

14. "[A lawyer] may not divulge confidential communications, information, and secrets imparted to him by the client or acquired during their professional relations, unless he is authorized to do so by the client (People v. Gerold, 265 Ill. 448, 107 N.E. 165, 178; Murphy v. Riggs, 238 Mich. 151, 213 N.W. 110, 112; Opinion of this Committee, No. 91)." *ABA Opinion* 202 (1940).

Cf. *ABA Opinion* 91 (1933).

15. "A defendant in a criminal case when admitted to bail is not only regarded as in the custody of his bail, but he is also in the custody of the law, and admission to bail does not deprive the court of its inherent power to deal with the person of the prisoner. Being in lawful custody, the defendant is guilty of an escape when he gains his liberty before he is delivered in due process of law, and is guilty of a separate offense for which he may be punished. In failing to disclose his client's whereabouts as a fugitive under these circumstances the attorney would not only be aiding his client to escape trial on the charge for which he was indicted, but would likewise be aiding him in evading prosecution for the additional offense of escape.

"It is the opinion of the committee that under such circumstances the attorney's knowledge of his client's whereabouts is not privileged, and that he may be disciplined for

failing to disclose that information to the proper authorities...." *ABA Opinion* 155 (1936).

"We held in *Opinion* 155 that a communication by a client to his attorney in respect to the future commission of an unlawful act or to a continuing wrong is not privileged from disclosure. Public policy forbids that the relation of attorney and client should be used to conceal wrongdoing on the part of the client.

. . .

"When an attorney representing a defendant in a criminal case applies on his behalf for probation or suspension of sentence, he represents to the court, by implication at least, that his client will abide by the terms and conditions of the court's order. When that attorney is later advised of a violation of that order, it is his duty to advise his client of the consequences of his act, and endeavor to prevent a continuance of the wrongdoing. If his client thereafter persists in violating the terms and conditions of his probation, it is the duty of the attorney as an officer of the court to advise the proper authorities concerning his client's conduct. Such information, even though coming to the attorney from the client in the course of his professional relations with respect to other matters in which he represents the defendant, is not privileged from disclosure...." *ABA Opinion* 156 (1936).

See *ABA Opinion* 155 (1936).

16. *ABA Opinion* 314 (1965) indicates that a lawyer must disclose even the confidences of his clients if "the facts in the attorney's possession indicate beyond reasonable doubt that a crime will be committed."

See *ABA Opinion* 155 (1936).

17. See ABA Canon 37 and *ABA Opinion* 202 (1940).

18. Cf. *ABA Opinion* 250 (1943).

his employees or associates against an accusation of wrongful conduct.[19]

(D) A lawyer shall exercise reasonable care to prevent his employees, associates, and others whose services are utilized by him from disclosing or using confidences or secrets of a client, except that a lawyer may reveal the information allowed by DR 4–101(C) through an employee.

19. See ABA Canon 37 and *ABA Opinions* 202 (1940) and 19 (1930).

"[T]he adjudicated cases recognize an exception to the rule [that a lawyer shall not reveal the confidences of his client], where disclosure is necessary to protect the attorney's interests arising out of the relation of attorney and client in which disclosure was made.

"The exception is stated in Mechem on Agency, 2d Ed., Vol. 2, § 2313, as follows: 'But the attorney may disclose information received from the client when it becomes necessary for his own protection, as if the client should bring an action against the attorney for negligence or misconduct, and it became necessary for the attorney to show what his instructions were, or what was the nature of the duty which the client expected him to perform. So if it became necessary for the attorney to bring an action against the client, the client's privilege could not prevent the attorney from disclosing what was essential as a means of obtaining or defending his own rights.'

"Mr. Jones, in his Commentaries on Evidence, 2d Ed., Vol. 5, § 2165, states the exception thus: 'It has frequently been held that the rule as to privileged communications does not apply when litigation arises between attorney and client to the extent that their communications are relevant to the issue. In such cases, if the disclosure of privileged communications becomes necessary to protect the attorney's rights, he is released from those obligations of secrecy which the law places upon him. He should not, however, disclose more than is necessary for his own protection. It would be a manifest injustice to allow the client to take advantage of the rule of exclusion as to professional confidence to the prejudice of his attorney, or that it should be carried to the extent of depriving the attorney of the means of obtaining or defending his own rights. In such cases the attorney is exempted from the obligations of secrecy.' " *ABA Opinion* 250 (1943).

1. Cf. ABA Canon 35.

CANON 5

A Lawyer Should Exercise Independent Professional Judgment on Behalf of a Client

ETHICAL CONSIDERATIONS

EC 5–1 The professional judgment of a lawyer should be exercised, within the bounds of the law, solely for the benefit of his client and free of compromising influences and loyalties.[1] Neither his person-

"[A lawyer's] fiduciary duty is of the highest order and he must not represent interests adverse to those of the client. It is true that because of his professional responsibility and the confidence and trust which his client may legitimately repose in him, he must adhere to a high standard of honesty, integrity and good faith in dealing with his client. He is not permitted to take advantage of his position or superior knowledge to impose upon the client; nor to conceal facts or law, nor in any way deceive him without being held responsible therefor." Smoot v. Lund, 13 Utah 2d 168, 172, 369 P.2d 933, 936 (1962).

"When a client engages the services of a lawyer in a given piece of business he is entitled to feel that, until that business is finally disposed of in some manner, he has the undivided loyalty of the one upon whom he looks as his advocate and champion. If, as in this case, he is sued and his home attached by his own attorney, who is representing him in another matter, all feeling of loyalty is necessarily destroyed, and the profession is exposed to the charge that it is interested only in money." Grievance Comm. v. Rottner, 152 Conn. 59, 65, 203 A.2d 82, 84 (1964).

"One of the cardinal principles confronting every attorney in the representation of a client is the requirement of complete loyalty and service in good faith to the best of his ability. In a criminal case the client is entitled to a fair trial, but not a perfect one. These are fundamental requirements of due process under the Fourteenth Amendment.... The same principles are applicable in Sixth Amendment cases (not pertinent herein) and suggest that an attorney should have no conflict of interest and that he must devote his full and faithful efforts toward the defense of his client." Johns v. Smyth, 176 F.Supp. 949, 952 (E.D.Va.1959), modified, United States ex rel. Wilkins v. Banmiller, 205 F.Supp. 123, 128 n. 5 (E.D.Pa. 1962), aff'd 325 F.2d 514 (3d Cir.1963), cert. denied, 379 U.S. 847, 13 L.Ed.2d 51, 85 S.Ct. 87 (1964).

al interests, the interests of other clients, nor the desires of third persons should be permitted to dilute his loyalty to his client.

Interests of a Lawyer That May Affect His Judgment

EC 5–2 A lawyer should not accept proffered employment if his personal interests or desires will, or there is a reasonable probability that they will, affect adversely the advice to be given or services to be rendered the prospective client.[2] After accepting employment, a lawyer carefully should refrain from acquiring a property right or assuming a position that would tend to make his judgment less protective of the interests of his client.

EC 5–3 The self-interest of a lawyer resulting from his ownership of property in which his client also has an interest or which may affect property of his client may interfere with the exercise of free judgment on behalf of his client. If such interference would occur with respect to a prospective client, a lawyer should decline employment proffered by him. After accepting employment, a lawyer should not acquire property rights that would adversely affect his professional judgment in the representation of his client. Even if the property interests of a lawyer do not presently interfere with the exercise of his independent judgment, but the likelihood of interference can reasonably be foreseen by him, a lawyer should explain the situation to his client and should decline employment or withdraw unless the

client consents to the continuance of the relationship after full disclosure. A lawyer should not seek to persuade his client to permit him to invest in an undertaking of his client nor make improper use of his professional relationship to influence his client to invest in an enterprise in which the lawyer is interested.

EC 5–4 If, in the course of his representation of a client, a lawyer is permitted to receive from his client a beneficial ownership in publication rights relating to the subject matter of the employment, he may be tempted to subordinate the interests of his client to his own anticipated pecuniary gain. For example, a lawyer in a criminal case who obtains from his client television, radio, motion picture, newspaper, magazine, book, or other publication rights with respect to the case may be influenced, consciously or unconsciously, to a course of conduct that will enhance the value of his publication rights to the prejudice of his client. To prevent these potentially differing interests, such arrangements should be scrupulously avoided prior to the termination of all aspects of the matter giving rise to the employment, even though his employment has previously ended.

EC 5–5 A lawyer should not suggest to his client that a gift be made to himself or for his benefit. If a lawyer accepts a gift from his client, he is peculiarly susceptible to the charge that he unduly influenced or over-reached the client. If a client voluntarily offers to make a gift to his lawyer, the lawyer may accept the

---

2. "Attorneys must not allow their private interests to conflict with those of their clients. . . . They owe their entire devotion to the interests of their clients." United States v. Anonymous, 215 F.Supp. 111, 113 (E.D.Tenn. 1963).

"[T]he court [below] concluded that a firm may not accept any action against a person whom they are presently representing even though there is no relationship between the two cases. In arriving at this conclusion, the court cites an opinion of the Committee on Professional Ethics of the New York County

Lawyers' Association which stated in part: 'While under the circumstances . . . there may be no actual conflict of interest . . . "maintenance of public confidence in the Bar requires an attorney who has accepted representation of a client to decline, while representing such client, any employment from an adverse party in any matter even though wholly unrelated to the original retainer." See Question and Answer No. 350, N.Y. County L. Ass'n, Question and Answer No. 450 (June 21, 1956).' " Grievance Comm. v. Rottner, 152 Conn. 59, 65, 203 A.2d 82, 84 (1964).

gift, but before doing so, he should urge that his client secure disinterested advice from an independent, competent person who is cognizant of all the circumstances.[3] Other than in exceptional circumstances, a lawyer should insist that an instrument in which his client desires to name him beneficially be prepared by another lawyer selected by the client.[4]

EC 5–6 A lawyer should not consciously influence a client to name him as executor, trustee, or lawyer in an instrument. In those cases where a client wishes to name his lawyer as such, care should be taken by the lawyer to avoid even the appearance of impropriety.[5]

EC 5–7 The possibility of an adverse effect upon the exercise of free judgment by a lawyer on behalf of his client during litigation generally makes it undesirable for the lawyer to acquire a proprietary interest in the cause of his client or otherwise to become financially interested in the outcome of the litigation.[6] However, it is not improper for a lawyer to protect his right to collect a fee for his services by the assertion of legally permissible liens, even though by doing so he may acquire an interest in the outcome of litigation. Although a contingent fee arrangement[7] gives a lawyer a financial interest in the outcome of litigation, a reasonable contingent fee is permissible in civil cases because it may be the only means by which a layman can obtain the services of a lawyer of his choice. But a lawyer, because he is in a better position to evaluate a cause of action, should enter into a contingent fee arrangement only in those instances where the arrangement will be beneficial to the client.

EC 5–8 A financial interest in the outcome of litigation also results if monetary advances are made by the lawyer to his client.[8] Although this assistance generally is not encouraged, there are instances when it is not improper to make loans to a client. For example, the advancing or guaranteeing of payment of the costs and expenses of litigation by a lawyer may be the only way a client can enforce his cause of action,[9] but the ultimate liability

---

3. "Courts of equity will scrutinize with jealous vigilance transactions between parties occupying fiduciary relations toward each other. . . . A deed will not be held invalid, however, if made by the grantor with full knowledge of its nature and effect, and because of the deliberate, voluntary and intelligent desire of the grantor. . . . Where a fiduciary relation exists, the burden of proof is on the grantee or beneficiary of an instrument executed during the existence of such relationship to show the fairness of the transaction, that it was equitable and just and that it did not proceed from undue influence. . . . The same rule has application where an attorney engages in a transaction with a client during the existence of the relation and is benefited thereby. . . . Conversely, an attorney is not prohibited from dealing with his client or buying his property, and such contracts, if open, fair and honest, when deliberately made, are as valid as contracts between other parties. . . . [I]mportant factors in determining whether a transaction is fair include a showing by the fiduciary (1) that he made a full and frank disclosure of all the relevant information that he had; (2) that the consideration was adequate; and (3) that the principal had independent advice before completing the transaction." McFail v. Braden, 19 Ill.2d 108, 117–18, 166 N.E.2d 46, 52 (1960).

4. See State ex rel. Nebraska State Bar Ass'n v. Richards, 165 Neb. 80, 94–95, 84 N.W.2d 136, 146 (1957).

5. See ABA Canon 9.

6. See ABA Canon 10.

7. See Code of Professional Responsibility, EC 2–20.

8. See ABA Canon 42.

9. "*Rule 3a. . . .* A member of the State Bar shall not directly or indirectly pay or agree to pay, or represent or sanction the representation that he will pay, medical, hospital or nursing bills or other personal expenses incurred by or for a client, prospective or existing; provided this rule shall not prohibit a member:

"(1) with the consent of the client, from paying or agreeing to pay to third persons such expenses from funds collected or to be collected for the client; or

"(2) after he has been employed, from lending money to his client upon the client's promise in writing to repay such loan; or

"(3) from advancing the costs of prosecuting or defending a claim or action. Such costs within the meaning of this subparagraph (3)

for such costs and expenses must be that of the client.

EC 5–9 Occasionally a lawyer is called upon to decide in a particular case whether he will be a witness or an advocate. If a lawyer is both counsel and witness, he becomes more easily impeachable for interest and thus may be a less effective witness. Conversely, the opposing counsel may be handicapped in challenging the credibility of the lawyer when the lawyer also appears as an advocate in the case. An advocate who becomes a witness is in the unseemly and ineffective position of arguing his own credibility. The roles of an advocate and of a witness are inconsistent; the function of an advocate is to advance or argue the cause of another, while that of a witness is to state facts objectively.

EC 5–10 Problems incident to the lawyer-witness relationship arise at different stages; they relate either to whether a lawyer should accept employment or should withdraw from employment.[10] Regardless of when the problem arises, his decision is to be governed by the same

basic considerations. It is not objectionable for a lawyer who is a potential witness to be an advocate if it is unlikely that he will be called as a witness because his testimony would be merely cumulative or if his testimony will relate only to an uncontested issue.[11] In the exceptional situation where it will be manifestly unfair to the client for the lawyer to refuse employment or to withdraw when he will likely be a witness on a contested issue, he may serve as advocate even though he may be a witness.[12] In making such decision, he should determine the personal or financial sacrifice of the client that may result from his refusal of employment or withdrawal therefrom, the materiality of his testimony, and the effectiveness of his representation in view of his personal involvement. In weighing these factors, it should be clear that refusal or withdrawal will impose an unreasonable hardship upon the client before the lawyer accepts or continues the employment.[13] Where the question arises, doubts should be resolved in favor of the lawyer testifying and against his becoming or continuing as an advocate.[14]

include all taxable costs or disbursements, costs of investigation and costs of obtaining and presenting evidence." Cal. Business and Professions Code § 6076 (West Supp.1967).

10. "When a lawyer knows, prior to trial, that he will be a necessary witness, except as to merely formal matters such as identification or custody of a document or the like, neither he nor his firm or associates should conduct the trial. If, during the trial, he discovers that the ends of justice require his testimony, he should, from that point on, if feasible and not prejudicial to his client's case, leave further conduct of the trial to other counsel. If circumstances do not permit withdrawal from the conduct of the trial, the lawyer should not argue the credibility of his own testimony." *A Code of Trial Conduct: Promulgated by the American College of Trial Lawyers*, 43 A.B.A.J. 223, 224–25 (1957).

11. Cf. Canon 19: "When a lawyer is a witness for his client, except as to merely formal matters, such as the attestation or custody of an instrument and the like, he should leave the trial of the case to other counsel."

12. "It is the general rule that a lawyer may not testify in litigation in which he is an

advocate unless circumstances arise which could not be anticipated and it is necessary to prevent a miscarriage of justice. In those rare cases where the testimony of an attorney is needed to protect his client's interests, it is not only proper but mandatory that it be forthcoming." Schwartz v. Wenger, 267 Minn. 40, 43–44, 124 N.W.2d 489, 492 (1963).

13. "The great weight of authority in this country holds that the attorney who acts as counsel and witness, in behalf of his client, in the same cause on a material matter, not of a merely formal character, and not in an emergency, but having knowledge that he would be required to be a witness in ample time to have secured other counsel and given up his service in the case, violates a highly important provision of the Code of Ethics and a rule of professional conduct, but does not commit a legal error in so testifying, as a result of which a new trial will be granted." Erwin M. Jennings Co. v. DiGenova, 107 Conn. 491, 499, 141 A. 866, 869 (1928).

14. "[C]ases may arise, and in practice often do arise, in which there would be a failure of justice should the attorney withhold his

EC 5-11 A lawyer should not permit his personal interests to influence his advice relative to a suggestion by his client that additional counsel be employed.[15] In like manner, his personal interests should not deter him from suggesting that additional counsel be employed; on the contrary, he should be alert to the desirability of recommending additional counsel when, in his judgment, the proper representation of his client requires it. However, a lawyer should advise his client not to employ additional counsel suggested by the client if the lawyer believes that such employment would be a disservice to the client, and he should disclose the reasons for his belief.

EC 5-12 Inability of co-counsel to agree on a matter vital to the representation of their client requires that their disagreement be submitted by them jointly to their client for his resolution, and the decision of the client shall control the action to be taken.[16]

EC 5-13 A lawyer should not maintain membership in or be influenced by any organization of employees that undertakes to prescribe, direct, or suggest when or how he should fulfill his professional obligations to a person or organization that employs him as a lawyer. Although it is not necessarily improper for a lawyer employed by a corporation or similar entity to be a member of an organization of employees, he should be vigilant to safeguard his fidelity as a lawyer to his employer, free from outside influences.

Interests of Multiple Clients

EC 5-14 Maintaining the independence of professional judgment required of a lawyer precludes his acceptance or continuation of employment that will adversely affect his judgment on behalf of or dilute his loyalty to a client.[17] This problem arises whenever a lawyer is asked to represent two or more clients who may have differing interests, whether such interests be conflicting, inconsistent, diverse, or otherwise discordant.[18]

EC 5-15 If a lawyer is requested to undertake or to continue representation of multiple clients having potentially differing interests, he must weigh carefully the possibility that his judgment may be impaired or his loyalty divided if he accepts or continues the employment. He should resolve all doubts against the propriety of the representation. A lawyer should never represent in litigation multiple clients with differing interests;[19] and there are

---

testimony. In such a case it would be a vicious professional sentiment which would deprive the client of the benefit of his attorney's testimony." Connolly v. Straw, 53 Wis. 645, 649, 11 N.W. 17, 19 (1881).

But see canon 19: "Except when essential to the ends of justice, a lawyer should avoid testifying in court in behalf of his client."

15. Cf. ABA Canon 7.

16. See ABA Canon 7.

17. See ABA Canon 6; cf. *ABA Opinions* 261 (1944), 242 (1942), 142 (1935), and 30 (1931).

18. The ABA Canons speak of "conflicting interests" rather than "differing interests" but make no attempt to define such other than the statement in Canon 6: "Within the meaning of this canon, a lawyer represents conflicting interests when, in behalf of one client, it is his duty to contend for that which duty to another client requires him to oppose."

19. "Canon 6 of the Canons of Professional Ethics, adopted by the American Bar Association on September 30, 1937, and by the Pennsylvania Bar Association on January 7, 1938, provides in part that 'It is unprofessional to represent conflicting interests, except by express consent of all concerned given after a full disclosure of the facts. Within the meaning of this Canon, a lawyer represents conflicting interests when, in behalf of one client, it is his duty to contend for that which duty to another client requires him to oppose.' The full disclosure required by this canon contemplates that the possibly adverse effect of the conflict be fully explained by the attorney to the client to be affected and by him thoroughly understood. . . .

"The foregoing canon applies to cases where the circumstances are such that possibly conflicting interests may permissibly be represented by the same attorney. But manifestly, there are instances where the conflicts of interest are so critically adverse as not to admit of one

217

few situations in which he would be justified in representing in litigation multiple clients with potentially differing interests. If a lawyer accepted such employment and the interests did become actually differing, he would have to withdraw from employment with likelihood of resulting hardship on the clients; and for this reason it is preferable that he refuse the employment initially. On the other hand, there are many instances in which a lawyer may properly serve multiple clients having potentially differing interests in matters not involving litigation. If the interests vary only slightly, it is generally likely that the lawyer will not be subjected to an adverse influence and that he can retain his independent judgment on behalf of each client; and if the interests become differing, withdrawal is less likely to have a disruptive effect upon the causes of his clients.

EC 5–16 In those instances in which a lawyer is justified in representing two or

more clients having differing interests, it is nevertheless essential that each client be given the opportunity to evaluate his need for representation free of any potential conflict and to obtain other counsel if he so desires.[20] Thus before a lawyer may represent multiple clients, he should explain fully to each client the implications of the common representation and should accept or continue employment only if the clients consent.[21] If there are present other circumstances that might cause any of the multiple clients to question the undivided loyalty of the lawyer, he should also advise all of the clients of those circumstances.[22]

EC 5–17 Typically recurring situations involving potentially differing interests are those in which a lawyer is asked to represent co-defendants in a criminal case, co-plaintiffs in a personal injury case, an insured and his insurer,[23] and

attorney's representing both sides. Such is the situation which this record presents. No one could conscionably contend that the same attorney may represent both the plaintiff and defendant in an adversary action. Yet, that is what is being done in this case." Jedwabny v. Philadelphia Transportation Co., 390 Pa. 231, 235, 135 A.2d 252, 254 (1957), cert. denied, 355 U.S. 966, 2 L.Ed.2d 541, 78 S.Ct. 557 (1958).

20. "Glasser wished the benefit of the undivided assistance of counsel of his own choice. We think that such a desire on the part of an accused should be respected. Irrespective of any conflict of interest, the additional burden of representing another party may conceivably impair counsel's effectiveness.

"To determine the precise degree of prejudice sustained by Glasser as a result of the court's appointment of Stewart as counsel for Kretske is at once difficult and unnecessary. The right to have the assistance of counsel is too fundamental and absolute to allow courts to indulge in nice calculations as to the amount of prejudice arising from its denial." Glasser v. United States, 315 U.S. 60, 75–76, 86 L.Ed. 680, 62 S.Ct. 457, 467 (1942).

21. See ABA Canon 6.

22. Id.

23. Cf. *ABA Opinion* 282 (1950).

"When counsel, although paid by the casualty company, undertakes to represent the poli-

cyholder and files his notice of appearance, he owes to his client, the assured, an undeviating and single allegiance. His fealty embraces the requirement to produce in court all witnesses, fact and expert, who are available and necessary for the proper protection of the rights of his client. . . .

" . . . The Canons of Professional Ethics make it pellucid that there are not two standards, one applying to counsel privately retained by a client, and the other to counsel paid by an insurance carrier." American Employers Ins. Co. v. Goble Aircraft Specialties, 205 Misc. 1066, 1075, 131 N.Y.S.2d 393, 401 (1954), motion to withdraw appeal granted, 1 App.Div.2d 1008, 154 N.Y.S.2d 835 (1956).

"[C]ounsel, selected by State Farm to defend Dorothy Walker's suit for $50,000 damages, was apprised by Walker that his earlier version of the accident was untrue and that actually the accident occurred because he lost control of his car in passing a Cadillac just ahead. At that point, Walker's counsel should have refused to participate further in view of the conflict of interest between Walker and State Farm. . . . Instead he participated in the ensuing deposition of the Walkers, even took an *ex parte* sworn statement from Mr. Walker in order to advise State Farm what action it should take, and later used the statement against Walker in the District Court. This action appears to con-beneficiaries of the estate of a decedent. Whether a lawyer can fairly and adequately protect the interests of multiple clients in these and similar situations depends upon an analysis of each case. In certain circumstances, there may exist little chance of the judgment of the lawyer being adversely affected by the slight possibility that the interests will become actually differing; in other circumstances, the chance of adverse effect upon his judgment is not unlikely.

EC 5–18 A lawyer employed or retained by a corporation or similar entity owes his allegiance to the entity and not to a stockholder, director, officer, employee, representative, or other person connected with the entity. In advising the entity, a lawyer should keep paramount its interests and his professional judgment should not be influenced by the personal desires of any person or organization. Occasionally a lawyer for an entity is requested by a stockholder, director, officer, employee, representative, or other person connected with the entity to represent him in an individual capacity; in such case the lawyer may serve the individual only if the lawyer is convinced that differing interests are not present.

EC 5–19 A lawyer may represent several clients whose interests are not actually or potentially differing. Nevertheless, he should explain any circumstances that might cause a client to question his undivided loyalty.[24] Regardless of the belief of a lawyer that he may properly repre-

sent multiple clients, he must defer to a client who holds the contrary belief and withdraw from representation of that client.

EC 5–20 A lawyer is often asked to serve as an impartial arbitrator or mediator in matters which involve present or former clients. He may serve in either capacity if he first discloses such present or former relationships. After a lawyer has undertaken to act as an impartial arbitrator or mediator, he should not thereafter represent in the dispute any of the parties involved.

Desires of Third Persons

EC 5–21 The obligation of a lawyer to exercise professional judgment solely on behalf of his client requires that he disregard the desires of others that might impair his free judgment.[25] The desires of a third person will seldom adversely affect a lawyer unless that person is in a position to exert strong economic, political, or social pressures upon the lawyer. These influences are often subtle, and a lawyer must be alert to their existence. A lawyer subjected to outside pressures should make full disclosure of them to his client;[26] and if he or his client believes that the effectiveness of his representation has been or will be impaired thereby, the lawyer should take proper steps to withdraw from representation of his client.

travene an Indiana attorney's duty 'at every peril to himself, to preserve the secrets of his client'...." State Farm Mut. Auto Ins. Co. v. Walker, 382 F.2d 548, 552 (1967), cert. denied, 389 U.S. 1045, 19 L.Ed.2d 837, 88 S.Ct. 789 (1968).

24. See ABA Canon 6.

25. See ABA Canon 35.

"Objection to the intervention of a lay intermediary, who may control litigation or otherwise interfere with the rendering of legal services in a confidential relationship, ... derives from the element of pecuniary gain. Fearful of dangers thought to arise from that element,

the courts of several States have sustained regulations aimed at these activities. We intimate no view one way or the other as to the merits of those decisions with respect to the particular arrangements against which they are directed. It is enough that the superficial resemblance in form between those arrangements and that at bar cannot obscure the vital fact that here the entire arrangement employs constitutionally privileged means of expression to secure constitutionally guaranteed civil rights." NAACP v. Button, 371 U.S. 415, 441–42, 9 L.Ed.2d 405, 423–24, 83 S.Ct. 328, 342–43 (1963).

26. Cf. ABA Canon 38.

EC 5–22 Economic, political, or social pressures by third persons are less likely to impinge upon the independent judgment of a lawyer in a matter in which he is compensated directly by his client and his professional work is exclusively with his client. On the other hand, if a lawyer is compensated from a source other than his client, he may feel a sense of responsibility to someone other than his client.

EC 5–23 A person or organization that pays or furnishes lawyers to represent others possesses a potential power to exert strong pressures against the independent judgment of those lawyers. Some employers may be interested in furthering their own economic, political, or social goals without regard to the professional responsibility of the lawyer to his individual client. Others may be far more concerned with establishment or extension of legal principles than in the immediate protection of the rights of the lawyer's individual client. On some occasions, decisions on priority of work may be made by the employer rather than the lawyer with the result that prosecution of work already undertaken for clients is postponed to their detriment. Similarly, an employer may seek, consciously or unconsciously, to further its own economic interests through the action of the lawyers employed by it. Since a lawyer must always be free to exercise his professional judgment without regard to the interests or motives of a third person, the lawyer who is employed by one to represent another must constantly guard against erosion of his professional freedom.[27]

EC 5–24 To assist a lawyer in preserving his professional independence, a number of courses are available to him. For example, a lawyer should not practice with or in the form of a professional legal corporation, even though the corporate form is permitted by law,[28] if any director, officer, or stockholder of it is a non-lawyer. Although a lawyer may be employed by a business corporation with non-lawyers serving as directors or officers, and they necessarily have the right to make decisions of business policy, a lawyer must decline to accept direction of his professional judgment from any layman. Various types of legal aid offices are administered by boards of directors composed of lawyers and laymen. A lawyer should not accept employment from such an organization unless the board sets only broad policies and there is no interference in the relationship of the lawyer and the individual client he serves. Where a lawyer is employed by an organization, a written agreement that defines the relationship between him and the organization and provides for his independence is desirable since it may serve to prevent misunderstanding as to their respective roles. Although other innovations in the means of supplying legal counsel may develop, the responsibility of the lawyer to maintain his professional independence remains constant, and the legal profession must insure that changing circum-

27. "Certainly it is true that 'the professional relationship between an attorney and his client is highly personal, involving an intimate appreciation of each individual client's particular problem.' And this Committee does not condone practices which interfere with that relationship. However, the mere fact the lawyer is actually paid by some entity other than the client does not affect that relationship, so long as the lawyer is selected by and is directly responsible to the client. See Informal Opinions 469 and 679. Of course, as the latter decision points out, there must be full disclosure of the arrangement by the attorney to the client. . . ." *ABA Opinion* 320 (1968).

"[A] third party may pay the cost of legal services as long as control remains in the client and the responsibility of the lawyer is solely to the client. Informal Opinions 469 ad [*sic*] 679. See also *Opinion* 237." Id.

28. *ABA Opinion* 303 (1961) recognized that "[s]tatutory provisions now exist in several states which are designed to make [the practice of law in a form that will be classified as a corporation for federal income tax purposes] legally possible, either as a result of lawyers incorporating or forming associations with various corporate characteristics."

stances do not result in loss of the professional independence of the lawyer.

DISCIPLINARY RULES

DR 5-101 Refusing Employment When the Interests of the Lawyer May Impair His Independent Professional Judgment.

(A) Except with the consent of his client after full disclosure, a lawyer shall not accept employment if the exercise of his professional judgment on behalf of his client will be or reasonably may be affected by his own financial, business, property, or personal interests.[29]

(B) A lawyer shall not accept employment in contemplated or pending litigation if he knows or it is obvious that he or a lawyer in his firm ought to be called as a witness, except that he may undertake the employment and he or a lawyer in his firm may testify:

(1) If the testimony will relate solely to an uncontested matter.

(2) If the testimony will relate solely to a matter of formality and there is no reason to believe that substantial evidence will be offered in opposition to the testimony.

(3) If the testimony will relate solely to the nature and value of legal services rendered in the case by the lawyer or his firm to the client.

(4) As to any matter, if refusal would work a substantial hardship on the client because of the distinctive value of the lawyer or his firm as counsel in the particular case.

DR 5-102 Withdrawal as Counsel When the Lawyer Becomes a Witness.[30]

(A) If, after undertaking employment in contemplated or pending litigation, a lawyer learns or it is obvious that he or a lawyer in his firm ought to be called as a witness on behalf of his client, he shall withdraw from the conduct of the trial and his firm, if any, shall not continue representation in the trial, except that he may continue the representation and he or a lawyer in his firm may testify in the circumstances enumerated in DR 5-101(B)(1) through (4).

(B) If, after undertaking employment in contemplated or pending litigation, a lawyer learns or it is obvious that he or a lawyer in his firm may be called as a witness other than on behalf of his client, he may continue the representation until it is appar-

---

29. Cf. ABA Canon 6 and *ABA Opinions* 181 (1938), 104 (1934), 103 (1933), 72 (1932), 50 (1931), 49 (1931), and 33 (1931).

"New York County [Opinion] 203.... [A lawyer] should not advise a client to employ an investment company in which he is interested, without informing him of this." Drinker, *Legal Ethics* 956 (1953).

"In *Opinions* 72 and 49 this Committee held: The relations of partners in a law firm are such that neither the firm nor any member or associate thereof, may accept any professional employment which any member of the firm cannot properly accept.

"In *Opinion* 16 this Committee held that a member of a law firm could not represent a defendant in a criminal case which was being prosecuted by another member of the firm who was public prosecuting attorney. The Opinion stated that it was clearly unethical for one member of the firm to oppose the interest of the state while another member represented those interests.... Since the prosecutor himself could not represent both the public and the defendant, no member of his law firm could either." *ABA Opinion* 296 (1959).

30. Cf. ABA Canon 19 and *ABA Opinions* 220 (1941), 185 (1938), 50 (1931), and 33 (1931); but cf. Erwin M. Jennings Co. v. DiGenova, 107 Conn. 491, 498–99, 141 A. 866, 868 (1928).

ent that his testimony is or may be prejudicial to his client.[31]

DR 5-103 Avoiding Acquisition of Interest in Litigation.

(A) A lawyer shall not acquire a proprietary interest in the cause of action or subject matter of litigation he is conducting for a client,[32] except that he may:

   (1) Acquire a lien granted by law to secure his fee or expenses.

   (2) Contract with a client for a reasonable contingent fee in a civil case.[33]

(B) While representing a client in connection with contemplated or pending litigation, a lawyer shall not advance or guarantee financial assistance to his client,[34] except that a lawyer may advance or guarantee the expenses of litigation, including court costs, expenses of investigation, expenses of medical examination, and costs of obtaining and presenting evidence, provided the client remains ultimately liable for such expenses.

DR 5-104 Limiting Business Relations With a Client.

(A) A lawyer shall not enter into a business transaction with a

client if they have differing interests therein and if the client expects the lawyer to exercise his professional judgment therein for the protection of the client, unless the client has consented after full disclosure.

(B) Prior to conclusion of all aspects of the matter giving rise to his employment, a lawyer shall not enter into any arrangement or understanding with a client or a prospective client by which he acquires an interest in publication rights with respect to the subject matter of his employment or proposed employment.

DR 5-105 Refusing to Accept or Continue Employment if the Interests of Another Client May Impair the Independent Professional Judgment of the Lawyer.

(A) A lawyer shall decline proffered employment if the exercise of his independent professional judgment in behalf of a client will be or is likely to be adversely affected by the acceptance of the proffered employment,[35] or if it would be likely to involve him in representing differing interests, except to the extent permitted under DR 5-105(C).[36]

31. "This *Canon* [19] *of Ethics* needs no elaboration to be applied to the facts here. Apparently, the object of this precept is to avoid putting a lawyer in the obviously embarrassing predicament of testifying and then having to argue the credibility and effect of his own testimony. It was not designed to permit a lawyer to call opposing counsel as a witness and thereby disqualify him as counsel." Galarowicz v. Ward, 119 Utah 611, 620, 230 P.2d 576, 580 (1951).

32. ABA Canon 10 and *ABA Opinions* 279 (1949), 246 (1942) and 176 (1938).

33. See Code of Professional Responsibility, DR 2-106(C).

34. See ABA Canon 42; cf. *ABA Opinion* 288 (1954).

35. See ABA Canon 6; cf. *ABA Opinions* 167 (1937), 60 (1931), and 40 (1931).

36. *ABA Opinion* 247 (1942) held that an attorney could not investigate a night club shooting on behalf of one of the owner's liability insurers, obtaining the cooperation of the owner, and later represent the injured patron in an action against the owner and a different insurance company unless the attorney obtain the "express consent of all concerned given after a full disclosure of the facts," since to do so would be to represent conflicting interests.

See *ABA Opinions* 247 (1942), 224 (1941), 222 (1941), 218 (1941), 112 (1934), 83 (1932), and 86 (1932).

(B) A lawyer shall not continue multiple employment if the exercise of his independent professional judgment in behalf of a client will be or is likely to be adversely affected by his representation of another client, or if it would be likely to involve him in representing differing interests, except to the extent permitted under DR 5–105(C).[37]

(C) In the situations covered by DR 5–105(A) and (B), a lawyer may represent multiple clients if it is obvious that he can adequately represent the interest of each and if each consents to the representation after full disclosure of the possible effect of such representation on the exercise of his independent professional judgment on behalf of each.

(D) If a lawyer is required to decline employment or to withdraw from employment under a Disciplinary Rule, no partner or associate, or any other lawyer affiliated with him or his firm may accept or continue such employment.

DR 5–106 Settling Similar Claims of Clients.[38]

(A) A lawyer who represents two or more clients shall not make or participate in the making of an aggregate settlement of the claims of or against his clients, unless each client has consented to the settlement after being advised of the existence and nature of all the claims involved in the proposed settlement, of the total amount of the settlement, and of the participation of each person in the settlement.

DR 5–107 Avoiding Influence by Others Than the Client.

(A) Except with the consent of his client after full disclosure, a lawyer shall not:

(1) Accept compensation for his legal services from one other than his client.

(2) Accept from one other than his client any thing of value related to his representation of or his employment by his client.[39]

(B) A lawyer shall not permit a person who recommends, employs, or pays him to render legal services for another to direct or regulate his professional judgment in rendering such legal services.[40]

(C) A lawyer shall not practice with or in the form of a professional corporation or association authorized to practice law for a profit, if:

(1) A non-lawyer owns any interest therein,[41] except that a fi-

---

37. Cf. *ABA Opinions* 231 (1941) and 160 (1936).

38. Cf. *ABA Opinions* 243 (1942) and 235 (1941).

39. See ABA Canon 38.

"A lawyer who receives a commission (whether delayed or not) from a title insurance company or guaranty fund for recommending or selling the insurance to his client, or for work done for the client or the company, without either fully disclosing to the client his financial interest in the transaction, or crediting the client's bill with the amount thus received, is guilty of unethical conduct." *ABA Opinion* 304 (1962).

40. See ABA Canon 35; cf. *ABA Opinion* 237 (1941).

"When the lay forwarder, as agent for the creditor, forwards a claim to an attorney, the direct relationship of attorney and client shall then exist between the attorney and the creditor, and the forwarder shall not interpose itself as an intermediary to control the activities of the attorney." *ABA Opinion* 294 (1958).

41. "Permanent beneficial and voting rights in the organization set up to practice law, whatever its form, must be restricted to lawyers while the organization is engaged in the practice of law." *ABA Opinion* 303 (1961).

duciary representative of the estate of a lawyer may hold the stock or interest of the lawyer for a reasonable time during administration;

(2) **A non-lawyer is a corporate director or officer thereof;**[42] **or**

(3) **A non-lawyer has the right to direct or control the professional judgment of a lawyer.**[43]

CANON 6
A Lawyer Should Represent a Client Competently

ETHICAL CONSIDERATIONS

EC 6–1 Because of his vital role in the legal process, a lawyer should act with competence and proper care in representing clients. He should strive to become and remain proficient in his practice[1] and should accept employment only in matters which he is or intends to become competent to handle.

EC 6–2 A lawyer is aided in attaining and maintaining his competence by keeping abreast of current legal literature and developments, participating in continuing legal education programs,[2] concentrating in particular areas of the law, and by utilizing other available means. He has the additional ethical obligation to assist in improving the legal profession, and he may do so by participating in bar activities intended to advance the quality and standards of members of the profession.

42. "*Canon 33* ... promulgates underlying principles that must be observed no matter in what form of organization lawyers practice law. Its requirement that no person shall be admitted or held out as a practitioner or member who is not a member of the legal profession duly authorized to practice, and amendable to professional discipline, makes it clear that any centralized management must be in lawyers to avoid a violation of this Canon." *ABA Opinion* 303 (1961).

43. "There is no intervention of any lay agency between lawyer and client when centralized management provided only by lawyers may give guidance or direction to the services being rendered by a lawyer-member of the organization to a client. The language in *Canon 35* that a lawyer should avoid all relations which direct the performance of his duties by or in the interest of an intermediary refers to lay intermediaries and not lawyer intermediaries with whom he is associated in the practice of law." *ABA Opinion* 303 (1961).

1. "[W]hen a citizen is faced with the need for a lawyer, he wants, and is entitled to, the best informed counsel he can obtain. Changing times produce changes in our laws and legal procedures. The natural complexities of law require continuing intensive study by a lawyer if he is to render his clients a maximum of efficient service. And, in so doing, he maintains the high standards of the legal profession; and he also increases respect and confidence by the general public." Rochelle & Payne, *The Struggle for Public Understanding*, 25 Texas B.J. 109, 160 (1962).

"We have undergone enormous changes in the last fifty years within the lives of most of the adults living today who may be seeking advice. Most of these changes have been accompanied by changes and developments in the law.... Every practicing lawyer encounters these problems and is often perplexed with his own inability to keep up, not only with changes in the law, but also with changes in the lives of his clients and their legal problems.

"To be sure, no client has a right to expect that his lawyer will have all of the answers at the end of his tongue or even in the back of his head at all times. But the client does have the right to expect that the lawyer will have devoted his time and energies to maintaining and improving his competence to know where to look for the answers, to know how to deal with the problems, and to know how to advise to the best of his legal talents and abilities." Levy & Sprague, *Accounting and Law: Is Dual Practice in the Public Interest?*, 52 A.B.A.J. 1110, 1112 (1966).

2. "The whole purpose of continuing legal education, so enthusiastically supported by the ABA, is to make it possible for lawyers to make themselves better lawyers. But there are no nostrums for proficiency in the law; it must come through the hard work of the lawyer himself. To the extent that that work, whether it be in attending institutes or lecture courses, in studying after hours or in the actual day in and day out practice of his profession, can be concentrated within a limited field, the greater the proficiency and expertness that can be developed." *Report of the Special Committee on Specialization and Specialized Legal Education*, 79 A.B.A.Rep. 582, 588 (1954).

Of particular importance is the careful training of his younger associates and the giving of sound guidance to all lawyers who consult him. In short, a lawyer should strive at all levels to aid the legal profession in advancing the highest possible standards of integrity and competence and to meet those standards himself.

EC 6–3 While the licensing of a lawyer is evidence that he has met the standards then prevailing for admission to the bar, a lawyer generally should not accept employment in any area of the law in which he is not qualified.[3] However, he may accept such employment if in good faith he expects to become qualified through study and investigation, as long as such preparation would not result in unreasonable delay or expense to his client. Proper preparation and representation may require the association by the lawyer of professionals in other disciplines. A lawyer offered employment in a matter in which he is not and does not expect to become so qualified should either decline the employment or, with the consent of his client, accept the employment and associate a lawyer who is competent in the matter.

EC 6–4 Having undertaken representation, a lawyer should use proper care to safeguard the interests of his client. If a lawyer has accepted employment in a matter beyond his competence but in which he expected to become competent, he should diligently undertake the work and study necessary to qualify himself. In addition to being qualified to handle a particular matter, his obligation to his client requires him to prepare adequately for and give appropriate attention to his legal work.

EC 6–5 A lawyer should have pride in his professional endeavors. His obligation to act competently calls for higher motivation than that arising from fear of civil liability or disciplinary penalty.

EC 6–6 A lawyer should not seek, by contract or other means, to limit his individual liability to his client for his malpractice. A lawyer who handles the affairs of his client properly has no need to attempt to limit his liability for his professional activities and one who does not handle the affairs of his client properly should not be permitted to do so. A lawyer who is a stockholder in or is associated with a professional legal corporation may, however, limit his liability for malpractice of his associates in the corporation, but only to the extent permitted by law.[4]

DISCIPLINARY RULES

DR 6–101 Failing to Act Competently.

(A) A lawyer shall not:

  (1) Handle a legal matter which he knows or should know that he is not competent to handle, without associating with him a lawyer who is competent to handle it.

  (2) Handle a legal matter without preparation adequate in the circumstances.

  (3) Neglect a legal matter entrusted to him.[5]

3. "If the attorney is not competent to skillfully and properly perform the work, he should not undertake the service." Degen v. Steinbrink, 202 App.Div. 477, 481, 195 N.Y.S. 810, 814 (1922), aff'd mem., 236 N.Y. 669, 142 N.E. 328 (1923).

4. See *ABA Opinion* 303 (1961); cf. Code of Professional Responsibility EC 2–11.

5. The annual report for 1967–1968 of the Committee on Grievances of the Association of the Bar of the City of New York showed a receipt of 2,232 complaints; of the 828 offenses against clients, 76 involved conversion, 49 involved "overreaching," and 452, or more than half of all such offenses, involved neglect. *Annual Report of the Committee on Grievances of the Association of the Bar of the City of New York*, N.Y.L.J., Sept. 12, 1968, at 4, col. 5.

DR 6–102 Limiting Liability to Client.

(A) A lawyer shall not attempt to exonerate himself from or limit his liability to his client for his personal malpractice.

1. "The right to be heard would be, in many cases, of little avail if it did not comprehend the right to be heard by counsel. Even the intelligent and educated layman has small and sometimes no skill in the science of law." Powell v. Alabama, 287 U.S. 45, 68–69, 77 L.Ed. 158, 170, 53 S.Ct. 55, 64 (1932).

2. Cf. ABA Canon 4.

"At times . . . [the tax lawyer] will be wise to discard some arguments and he should exercise discretion to emphasize the arguments which in his judgment are most likely to be persuasive. But this process involves legal judgment rather than moral attitudes. The tax lawyer should put aside private disagreements with Congressional and Treasury policies. His own notions of policy, and his personal view of what the law should be, are irrelevant. The job entrusted to him by his client is to use all his learning and ability to protect his client's rights, not to help in the process of promoting a better tax system. The tax lawyer need not accept his client's economic and social opinions, but the client is paying for technical attention and undivided concentration upon his affairs. He is equally entitled to performance unfettered by his attorney's economic and social predilections." Paul, *The Lawyer as a Tax Advisor*, 25 Rocky Mt.L.Rev. 412, 418 (1953).

3. See ABA Canons 15 and 32.

ABA Canon 5, although only speaking of one accused of crime, imposes a similar obligation on the lawyer: "[T]he lawyer is bound, by all fair and honorable means, to present every defense that the law of the land permits, to the end that no person may be deprived of life or liberty, but by due process of law."

"Any persuasion or pressure on the advocate which deters him from planning and carrying out the litigation on the basis of 'what, within the framework of the law, is best for my client's interest?' interferes with the obligation to represent the client fully within the law.

"This obligation, in its fullest sense, is the heart of the adversary process. Each attorney, as an advocate, acts for and seeks that which in his judgment is best for his client, within the bounds authoritatively established. The advocate does not *decide* what is just in this case—he would be usurping the function of the

judge and jury—he acts for and seeks for his client that which he is entitled to under the law. He can do no less and properly represent the client." Thode, *The Ethical Standard for the Advocate*, 39 Texas L.Rev. 575, 584 (1961).

"The [Texas public opinion] survey indicates that distrust of the lawyer can be traced directly to certain factors. Foremost of these is a basic misunderstanding of the function of the lawyer as an advocate in an adversary system.

"Lawyers are accused of taking advantage of 'loopholes' and 'technicalities' to win. Persons who make this charge are unaware, or do not understand, that the lawyer is hired to win, and if he does not exercise every legitimate effort in his client's behalf, then he is betraying a sacred trust." Rochelle & Payne, *The Struggle for Public Understanding*, 25 Texas B.J. 109, 159 (1962).

"The importance of the attorney's undivided allegiance and faithful service to one accused of crime, irrespective of the attorney's personal opinion as to the guilt of his client, lies in Canon 5 of the American Bar Association Canon of Ethics.

"The difficulty lies, of course, in ascertaining whether the attorney has been guilty of an error of judgment, such as an election with respect to trial tactics, or has otherwise been actuated by his conscience or belief that his client should be convicted in any event. All too frequently courts are called upon to review actions of defense counsel which are, at the most, errors of judgment, not properly reviewable on habeas corpus unless the trial is a farce and a mockery of justice which requires the court to intervene. . . . But when defense counsel, in a truly adverse proceeding, admits that his conscience would not permit him to adopt certain customary trial procedures, this extends beyond the realm of judgment and strongly suggests an invasion of constitutional rights." Johns v. Smyth, 176 F.Supp. 949, 952 (E.D.Va.1959), modified, United States ex rel. Wilkins v. Banmiller, 205 F.Supp. 123, 128, n. 5 (E.D. Pa.1962), aff'd 325 F.2d 514 (3d Cir. 1963), cert. denied, 379 U.S. 847, 13 L.Ed.2d 51, 85 S.Ct. 87 (1964).

CANON 7
A Lawyer Should Represent a Client Zealously Within the Bounds of the Law

ETHICAL CONSIDERATIONS

EC 7–1 The duty of a lawyer, both to his client[1] and to the legal system, is to represent his client zealously[2] within the bounds of the law,[3] which includes Disciplinary Rules and enforceable professional regulations.[4] The professional responsibility of a lawyer derives from his membership in a profession which has the duty of assisting members of the public to secure and protect available legal rights and benefits. In our government of laws and not of men, each member of our society is entitled to have his conduct judged and regulated in accordance with the law;[5] to seek any lawful objective[6] through legally permissible means;[7] and to present for adjudication any lawful claim, issue, or defense.

EC 7–2 The bounds of the law in a given case are often difficult to ascertain.[8] The language of legislative enactments and judicial opinions may be uncertain as applied to varying factual situations. The limits and specific meaning of apparently relevant law may be made doubtful by changing or developing constitutional interpretations, inadequately expressed statutes or judicial opinions, and changing public and judicial attitudes. Certainty of law ranges from well-settled rules through areas of conflicting authority to areas without precedent.

EC 7–3 Where the bounds of law are uncertain, the action of a lawyer may depend on whether he is serving as advocate or adviser. A lawyer may serve simultaneously as both advocate and adviser, but the two roles are essentially

"The adversary system in law administration bears a striking resemblance to the competitive economic system. In each we assume that the individual through partisanship or through self-interest will strive mightily for his side, and that kind of striving we must have. But neither system would be tolerable without restraints and modifications, and at times without outright departures from the system itself. Since the legal profession is entrusted with the system of law administration, a part of its task is to develop in its members appropriate restraints without impairing the values of partisan striving. An accompanying task is to aid in the modification of the adversary system or departure from it in areas to which the system is unsuited." Cheatham, *The Lawyer's Role and Surroundings*, 25 Rocky Mt. L.Rev. 405, 410 (1953).

4. "Rule 4.15 prohibits, in the pursuit of a client's cause, 'any manner of fraud or chicane'; Rule 4.22 requires 'candor and fairness' in the conduct of the lawyer, and forbids the making of knowing misquotations; Rule 4.47 provides that a lawyer 'should always maintain his integrity,' and generally forbids all misconduct injurious to the interests of the public, the courts, or his clients, and acts contrary to 'justice, honesty, modesty or good morals.' Our Commissioner has accurately paraphrased these rules as follows: 'An attorney does not have the duty to do all and whatever he can that may enable him to win his client's cause or to further his client's interest. His duty and efforts in these respects, although they should be prompted by his "entire devotion" to the interest of his client, must be within and not without the bounds of the law.' " In re Wines, 370 S.W.2d 328, 333 (Mo.1963).

See Note, 38 Texas L.Rev. 107, 110 (1959).

5. "Under our system of government the process of adjudication is surrounded by safeguards evolved from centuries of experience. These safeguards are not designed merely to lend formality and decorum to the trial of causes. They are predicated on the assumption that to secure for any controversy a truly informed and dispassionate decision is a difficult thing, requiring for its achievement a special summoning and organization of human effort and the adoption of measures to exclude the biases and prejudgments that have free play outside the courtroom. All of this goes for naught if the man with an unpopular cause is unable to find a competent lawyer courageous enough to represent him. His chance to have his day in court loses much of its meaning if his case is handicapped from the outset by the very kind of prejudgment our rules of evidence and procedure are intended to prevent." *Professional Responsibility: Report of the Joint Conference*, 44 A.B.A.J. 1159, 1216 (1958).

6. "[I]t is ... [the tax lawyer's] positive duty to show the client how to avail himself to the full of what the law permits. He is not the keeper of the Congressional conscience." Paul, *The Lawyer as a Tax Adviser*, 25 Rocky Mt. L.Rev. 412, 418 (1953).

7. See ABA Canons 15 and 30.

8. "The fact that it desired to evade the law, as it is called, is immaterial, because the very meaning of a line in the law is that you intentionally may go as close to it as you can if you do not pass it .... It is a matter of proximity and degree as to which minds will differ...." Justice Holmes, in Superior Oil Co. v. Mississippi, 280 U.S. 390, 395–96, 74 L.Ed. 504, 508, 50 S.Ct. 169, 170 (1930).

different.[9] In asserting a position on behalf of his client, an advocate for the most part deals with past conduct and must take the facts as he finds them. By contrast, a lawyer serving as adviser primarily assists his client in determining the course of future conduct and relationships. While serving as advocate, a lawyer should resolve in favor of his client doubts as to the bounds of the law.[10] In serving a client as adviser, a lawyer in appropriate circumstances should give his professional opinion as to what the ultimate decisions of the courts would likely be as to the applicable law.

9. "Today's lawyers perform two distinct types of functions, and our ethical standards should, but in the main do not, recognize these two functions. Judge Philbrick McCoy recently reported to the American Bar Association the need for a reappraisal of the Canons in light of the new and distinct function of counselor, as distinguished from advocate, which today predominates in the legal profession. . . .

" . . . In the first place, any revision of the canons must take into account and speak to this new and now predominant function of the lawyer. . . . It is beyond the scope of this paper to discuss the ethical standards to be applied to the counselor except to state that in my opinion such standards should require a greater recognition and protection for the interest of the public generally than is presently expressed in the canons. Also, the counselor's obligation should extend to requiring him to inform and to impress upon the client a just solution of the problem, considering all interests involved." Thode, *The Ethical Standard for the Advocate*, 39 Texas L.Rev. 575, 578–79 (1961).

"The man who has been called into court to answer for his own actions is entitled to fair hearing. Partisan advocacy plays its essential part in such a hearing, and the lawyer pleading his client's case may properly present it in the most favorable light. A similar resolution of doubts in one direction becomes inappropriate when the lawyer acts as counselor. The reasons that justify and even require partisan advocacy in the trial of a cause do not grant any license to the lawyer to participate as legal advisor in a line of conduct that is immoral, unfair, or of doubtful legality. In saving himself from this unworthy involvement, the lawyer cannot be guided solely by an unreflective inner sense of good faith; he must be at pains to preserve a sufficient detachment from his client's interests so that he remains capable of a sound and

Duty of the Lawyer to a Client

EC 7–4 The advocate may urge any permissible construction of the law favorable to his client, without regard to his professional opinion as to the likelihood that the construction will ultimately prevail.[11] His conduct is within the bounds of the law, and therefore permissible, if the position taken is supported by the law or is supportable by a good faith argument for an extension, modification, or reversal of the law. However, a lawyer is not justified in asserting a position in litigation that is frivolous.[12]

objective appraisal of the propriety of what his client proposes to do." *Professional Responsibility: Report of the Joint Conference*, 44 A.B.J. 1159, 1161 (1958).

10. "[A] lawyer who is asked to advise his client . . . may freely urge the statement of positions most favorable to the client just as long as there is reasonable basis for those positions." *ABA Opinion* 314 (1965).

11. "The lawyer . . . is not an umpire, but an advocate. He is under no duty to refrain from making every proper argument in support of any legal point because he is not convinced of its inherent soundness. . . . His personal belief in the soundness of his cause or of the authorities supporting it, is irrelevant." *ABA Opinion* 280 (1949).

"Counsel apparently misconceived his role. It was his duty to honorably present his client's contentions in the light most favorable to his client. Instead he presumed to advise the court as to the validity and sufficiency of prisoner's motion, by letter. We therefore conclude that the prisoner had no effective assistance of counsel and remand this case to the District Court with instructions to set aside the Judgment, appoint new counsel to represent the prisoner if he makes no objection thereto, and proceed anew." McCartney v. United States, 343 F.2d 471, 472 (9th Cir.1965).

12. "Here the court-appointed counsel had the transcript but refused to proceed with the appeal because he found no merit in it. . . . We cannot say that there was a finding of frivolity by either of the California courts or that counsel acted in any greater capacity than merely as *amicus curiae* which was condemned in *Ellis*, supra. Hence California's procedure did not furnish petitioner with counsel acting in the role of an advocate nor did it provide

EC 7–5 A lawyer as adviser furthers the interest of his client by giving his professional opinion as to what he believes would likely be the ultimate decision of the courts on the matter at hand and by informing his client of the practical effect of such decision.[13] He may continue in the representation of his client even though his client has elected to pursue a course of conduct contrary to the advice of the lawyer so long as he does not thereby knowingly assist the client to engage in illegal conduct or to take a frivolous legal position. A lawyer should never encourage or aid his client to commit criminal acts or counsel his client on how to violate the law and avoid punishment therefor.[14]

EC 7–6 Whether the proposed action of a lawyer is within the bounds of the law may be a perplexing question when his client is contemplating a course of conduct having legal consequences that vary according to the client's intent, motive, or

desires at the time of the action. Often a lawyer is asked to assist his client in developing evidence relevant to the state of mind of the client at a particular time. He may properly assist his client in the development and preservation of evidence of existing motive, intent, or desire; obviously, he may not do anything furthering the creation or preservation of false evidence. In many cases a lawyer may not be certain as to the state of mind of his client, and in those situations he should resolve reasonable doubts in favor of his client.

EC 7–7 In certain areas of legal representation not affecting the merits of the cause or substantially prejudicing the rights of a client, a lawyer is entitled to make decisions on his own. But otherwise the authority to make decisions is exclusively that of the client and, if made within the framework of the law, such decisions are binding on his lawyer. As typical examples in civil cases, it is for the client

that full consideration and resolution of the matter as is obtained when counsel is acting in that capacity. . . .

"The constitutional requirement of substantial equality and fair process can only be attained where counsel acts in the role of an active advocate in behalf of his client, as opposed to that of *amicus curiae*. The no-merit letter and the procedure it triggers do not reach that dignity. Counsel should, and can with honor and without conflict, be of more assistance to his client and to the court. His role as advocate requires that he support his client's appeal to the best of his ability. Of course, if counsel finds his case to be wholly frivolous, after a conscientious examination of it, he should so advise the court and request permission to withdraw. That request must, however, be accompanied by a brief referring to anything in the record that might arguably support the appeal. A copy of counsel's brief should be furnished the indigent and time allowed him to raise any points that he chooses; the court—not counsel—then proceeds, after a full examination of all the proceedings, to decide whether the case is wholly frivolous. If it so finds it may grant counsel's request to withdraw and dismiss the appeal insofar as federal requirements are concerned, or proceed to a decision on the merits, if state law so requires. On the other hand, if it finds any of the legal points arguable on their merits (and therefore

not frivolous) it must, prior to decision, afford the indigent the assistance of counsel to argue the appeal." *Anders v. California*, 386 U.S. 738, 744, 18 L.Ed.2d 493, 498, 87 S.Ct. 1396, 1399–1400 (1967), rehearing denied, 388 U.S. 924, 18 L.Ed.2d 1377, 87 S.Ct. 2094 (1967).

See Paul, *The Lawyer As a Tax Adviser*, 25 Rocky Mt.L.Rev. 412, 432 (1953).

13. See ABA Canon 32.

14. "For a lawyer to represent a syndicate notoriously engaged in the violation of the law for the purpose of advising the members how to break the law and at the same time escape it, is manifestly improper. While a lawyer may see to it that anyone accused of crime, no matter how serious and flagrant, has a fair trial, and present all available defenses, he may not co-operate in planning violations of the law. There is a sharp distinction, of course, between advising what can lawfully be done and advising how unlawful acts can be done in a way to avoid conviction. Where a lawyer accepts a retainer from an organization, known to be unlawful, and agrees in advance to defend its members when from time to time they are accused of crime arising out of its unlawful activities, this is equally improper."

"See also *Opinion* 155." *ABA Opinion* 281 (1952).

to decide whether he will accept a settlement offer or whether he will waive his right to plead an affirmative defense. A defense lawyer in a criminal case has the duty to advise his client fully on whether a particular plea to a charge appears to be desirable and as to the prospects of success on appeal, but it is for the client to decide what plea should be entered and whether an appeal should be taken.[15]

EC 7–8 A lawyer should exert his best efforts to insure that decisions of his client are made only after the client has been informed of relevant considerations. A lawyer ought to initiate this decision-making process if the client does not do so. Advice of a lawyer to his client need not be confined to purely legal considerations.[16] A lawyer should advise his client of the possible effect of each legal alternative.[17] A lawyer should bring to bear upon this decision-making process the fullness of his experience as well as his objective viewpoint.[18] In assisting his client to reach a proper decision, it is often desirable for a lawyer to point out those factors which may lead to a decision that is morally just as well as legally permissible.[19] He may emphasize the possibility of harsh consequences that might result from assertion of legally permissible positions. In the final analysis, however, the lawyer should always remember that the decision whether to forego legally available objectives or methods because of non-legal factors is ultimately for the client and not for himself. In the event that the client in a non-adjudicatory matter insists upon a course of conduct that is contrary to the judgment and advice of the lawyer but not prohibited by Disciplinary Rules, the lawyer may withdraw from the employment.[20]

15. See ABA Special Committee on Minimum Standards for the Administration of Criminal Justice, *Standards Relating to Pleas of Guilty*, pp. 69–70 (1968).

16. "First of all, a truly great lawyer is a wise counselor to all manner of men in the varied crises of their lives when they most need disinterested advice. Effective counseling necessarily involves a thoroughgoing knowledge of the principles of the law not merely as they appear in the books but as they actually operate in action." Vanderbilt, *The Five Functions of the Lawyer: Service to Clients and the Public*, 40 A.B.A.J. 31 (1954).

17. "A lawyer should endeavor to obtain full knowledge of his client's cause before advising thereon. . . ." ABA Canon 8.

18. "[I]n devising charters of collaborative effort the lawyer often acts where all of the affected parties are present as participants. But the lawyer also performs a similar function in situations where this is not so, as, for example, in planning estates and drafting wills. Here the instrument defining the terms of collaboration may affect persons not present and often not born. Yet here, too, the good lawyer does not serve merely as a legal conduit for his client's desires, but as a wise counselor, experienced in the art of devising arrangements that will put in workable order the entangled affairs and interests of human beings." *Professional Responsibility: Report of the Joint Conference*, 44 A.B.A.J. 1159, 1162 (1958).

19. See ABA Canon 8.

"Vital as is the lawyer's role in adjudication, it should not be thought that it is only as an advocate pleading in open court that he contributes to the administration of the law. The most effective realization of the law's aims often takes place in the attorney's office, where litigation is forestalled by anticipating its outcome, where the lawyer's quiet counsel takes the place of public force. Contrary to popular belief, the compliance with the law thus brought about is not generally lip-serving and narrow, for by reminding him of its long-run costs the lawyer often deters his client from a course of conduct technically permissible under existing law, though inconsistent with its underlying spirit and purpose." *Professional Responsibility: Report of the Joint Conference*, 44 A.B.A.J. 1159, 1161 (1958).

20. "My summation of Judge Sharswood's view of the advocate's duty to the client is that he owes to the client the duty to use all legal means in support of the client's case. However, at the same time Judge Sharswood recognized that many advocates would find this obligation unbearable if applicable without exception. Therefore, the individual lawyer is given the choice of representing his client fully within the bounds set by the law *or of telling his client that he cannot do so*, so that the client may obtain another attorney if he wishes." Thode, *The Ethical Standard for the Advocate*, 39 Texas L.Rev. 575, 582 (1961).

EC 7–9 In the exercise of his professional judgment on those decisions which are for his determination in the handling of a legal matter,[21] a lawyer should always act in a manner consistent with the best interests of his client.[22] However, when an action in the best interest of his client seems to him to be unjust, he may ask his client for permission to forego such action.[23]

EC 7–10 The duty of a lawyer to represent his client with zeal does not militate against his concurrent obligation to treat with consideration all persons involved in the legal process and to avoid the infliction of needless harm.

EC 7–11 The responsibilities of a lawyer may vary according to the intelligence, experience, mental condition or age of a client, the obligation of a public officer, or the nature of a particular proceeding. Examples include the representation of an illiterate or an incompetent, service as a public prosecutor or other government lawyer, and appearances before administrative and legislative bodies.

EC 7–12 Any mental or physical condition of a client that renders him incapable of making a considered judgment on his own behalf casts additional responsibilities upon his lawyer. Where an incompetent is acting through a guardian or other legal representative, a lawyer must look to such representative for those decisions which are normally the prerogative of the client to make. If a client under disability has no legal representative, his lawyer may be compelled in court proceedings to make decisions on behalf of the client. If the client is capable of understanding the matter in question or of contributing to the advancement of his interests, regardless of whether he is legally disqualified from performing certain acts, the lawyer should obtain from him all possible aid. If the disability of a client and the lack of a legal representative compel the lawyer to make decisions for his client, the lawyer should consider all circumstances then prevailing and act with care to safeguard and advance the interests of his client. But obviously a lawyer cannot perform any act or make any decision which the law requires his client to perform or make, either acting for himself if competent, or by a duly constituted representative if legally incompetent.

EC 7–13 The responsibility of a public prosecutor differs from that of the usual advocate; his duty is to seek justice, not merely to convict.[24] This special duty exists because: (1) the prosecutor represents the sovereign and therefore should use restraint in the discretionary exercise of governmental powers, such as in the selection of cases to prosecute; (2) during trial the prosecutor is not only an advocate but he also may make decisions normally made by an individual client, and

Cf. Code of Professional Responsibility, DR 2–110(C).

21. See ABA Canon 24.

22. Thode, *The Ethical Standard for the Advocate*, 39 Texas L.Rev. 575, 592 (1961).

23. Cf. *ABA Opinions* 253 (1946) and 178 (1938).

24. See ABA Canon 5 and Berger v. United States, 295 U.S. 78, 79 L.Ed. 1314, 55 S.Ct. 629 (1935).

"The public prosecutor cannot take as a guide for the conduct of his office the standards of an attorney appearing on behalf of an individual client. The freedom elsewhere wisely granted to a partisan advocate must be severely curtailed if the prosecutor's duties are to be properly discharged. The public prosecutor must recall that he occupies a dual role, being obligated, on the one hand, to furnish that adversary element essential to the informed decision of any controversy, but being possessed, on the other, of important governmental powers that are pledged to the accomplishment of one objective only, that of impartial justice. Where the prosecutor is recreant to the trust implicit in his office, he undermines confidence, not only in his profession, but in government and the very ideal of justice itself." *Professional Responsibility: Report of the Joint Conference*, 44 A.B.A.J. 1159, 1218 (1958).

"The prosecuting attorney is the attorney for the state, and it is his primary duty not to convict but to see that justice is done." *ABA Opinion* 150 (1936).

those affecting the public interest should be fair to all; and (3) in our system of criminal justice the accused is to be given the benefit of all reasonable doubts. With respect to evidence and witnesses, the prosecutor has responsibilities different from those of a lawyer in private practice; the prosecutor should make timely disclosure to the defense of available evidence, known to him, that tends to negate the guilt of the accused, mitigate the degree of the offense, or reduce the punishment. Further, a prosecutor should not intentionally avoid pursuit of evidence merely because he believes it will damage the prosecutor's case or aid the accused.

EC 7–14 A government lawyer who has discretionary power relative to litigation should refrain from instituting or continuing litigation that is obviously unfair. A government lawyer not having such discretionary power who believes there is lack of merit in a controversy submitted to him should so advise his superiors and recommend the avoidance of unfair litigation. A government lawyer in a civil action or administrative proceeding has the responsibility to seek justice and to develop a full and fair record, and he should not use his position or the economic power of the government to harass parties or to bring about unjust settlements or results.

EC 7–15 The nature and purpose of proceedings before administrative agencies vary widely. The proceedings may be legislative or quasi-judicial, or a combination of both. They may be *ex parte* in character, in which event they may originate either at the instance of the agency or upon motion of an interested party. The scope of an inquiry may be purely

investigative or it may be truly adversary looking toward the adjudication of specific rights of a party or of classes of parties. The foregoing are but examples of some of the types of proceedings conducted by administrative agencies. A lawyer appearing before an administrative agency,[25] regardless of the nature of the proceeding it is conducting, has the continuing duty to advance the cause of his client within the bounds of the law.[26] Where the applicable rules of the agency impose specific obligations upon a lawyer, it is his duty to comply therewith, unless the lawyer has a legitimate basis for challenging the validity thereof. In all appearances before administrative agencies, a lawyer should identify himself, his client if identity of his client is not privileged,[27] and the representative nature of his appearance. It is not improper, however, for a lawyer to seek from an agency information available to the public without identifying his client.

EC 7–16 The primary business of a legislative body is to enact laws rather than to adjudicate controversies, although on occasion the activities of a legislative body may take on the characteristics of an adversary proceeding, particularly in investigative and impeachment matters. The role of a lawyer supporting or opposing proposed legislation normally is quite different from his role in representing a person under investigation or on trial by a legislative body. When a lawyer appears in connection with proposed legislation, he seeks to affect the lawmaking process, but when he appears on behalf of a client in investigatory or impeachment proceedings, he is concerned with the protection

25. As to appearances before a department of government, Canon 26 provides: "A lawyer openly ... may render professional services ... in advocacy of claims before departments of government, upon the same principles of ethics which justify his appearance before the Courts...."

26. "But as an advocate before a service which itself represents the adversary point of view, where his client's case is fairly arguable,

a lawyer is under no duty to disclose its weaknesses, any more than he would be to make such a disclosure to a brother lawyer. The limitations within which he must operate are best expressed in Canon 22...." *ABA Opinion* 314 (1965).

27. See Baird v. Koerner, 279 F.2d 623 (9th Cir.1960).

of the rights of his client. In either event, he should identify himself and his client, if identity of his client is not privileged, and should comply with applicable laws and legislative rules.[28]

EC 7–17 The obligation of loyalty to his client applies only to a lawyer in the discharge of his professional duties and implies no obligation to adopt a personal viewpoint favorable to the interests or desires of his client.[29] While a lawyer must act always with circumspection in order that his conduct will not adversely affect the rights of a client in a matter he is then handling, he may take positions on public issues and espouse legal reforms he favors without regard to the individual views of any client.

EC 7–18 The legal system in its broadest sense functions best when persons in need of legal advice or assistance are represented by their own counsel. For this reason a lawyer should not communicate on the subject matter of the representation of his client with a person he knows to be represented in the matter by a lawyer, unless pursuant to law or rule of court or unless he has the consent of the lawyer for that person.[30] If one is not represented by counsel, a lawyer representing another may have to deal directly with the unrepresented person; in such an instance, a lawyer should not undertake to give advice to the person who is attempting to represent himself,[31] except that he may advise him to obtain a lawyer.

Duty of the Lawyer to the Adversary System of Justice

EC 7–19 Our legal system provides for the adjudication of disputes governed by the rules of substantive, evidentiary, and procedural law. An adversary presentation counters the natural human tendency to judge too swiftly in terms of the familiar that which is not yet fully known;[32] the advocate, by his zealous preparation and presentation of facts and law, enables the tribunal to come to the hearing with an open and neutral mind and to render impartial judgments.[33]

---

28. See ABA Canon 26.

29. "Law should be so practiced that the lawyer remains free to make up his own mind how he will vote, what causes he will support, what economic and political philosophy he will espouse. It is one of the glories of the profession that it admits of this freedom. Distinguished examples can be cited of lawyers whose views were at variance with those of their clients, lawyers whose skill and wisdom make them valued advisers to those who had little sympathy with their views as citizens." *Professional Responsibility: Report of the Joint Conference*, 44 A.B.A.J. 1159, 1217 (1958).

"No doubt some tax lawyers feel constrained to abstain from activities on behalf of a better tax system because they think that their clients may object. Clients have no right to object if the tax adviser handles their affairs competently and faithfully and independently of his private views as to tax policy. They buy his expert services, not his private opinions or his silence on issues that gravely affect the public interest." Paul, *The Lawyer as a Tax Adviser*, 25 Rocky Mt.L.Rev. 412, 434 (1953).

30. See ABA Canon 9.

31. Id.

32. See *Professional Responsibility: Report of the Joint Conference*, 44 A.B.A.J. 1159, 1160 (1958).

33. "Without the participation of someone who can act responsibly for each of the parties, this essential narrowing of the issues [by exchange of written pleadings or stipulations of counsel] becomes impossible. But here again the true significance of partisan advocacy lies deeper, touching once more the integrity of the adjudicative process itself. It is only through the advocate's participation that the hearing may remain in fact what it purports to be in theory: a public trial of the facts and issues. Each advocate comes to the hearing prepared to present his proofs and arguments, knowing at the same time that his arguments may fail to persuade and that his proof may be rejected as inadequate. . . . The deciding tribunal, on the other hand, comes to the hearing uncommitted. It has not represented to the public that any fact can be proved, that any argument is sound, or that any particular way of stating a litigant's case is the most effective expression of its merits." *Professional Responsibility: Report of the Joint Conference*, 44 A.B.A.J. 1159, 1160–61 (1958).

The duty of a lawyer to his client and his duty to the legal system are the same: to represent his client zealously within the bounds of the law.[34]

EC 7–20 In order to function properly, our adjudicative process requires an informed, impartial tribunal capable of administering justice promptly and efficiently[35] according to procedures that command public confidence and respect.[36] Not only must there be competent, adverse presentation of evidence and issues, but a tribunal must be aided by rules appropriate to an effective and dignified process. The procedures under which tribunals operate in our adversary system have been prescribed largely by legislative enactments, court rules and decisions, and administrative rules. Through the years certain concepts of proper professional conduct have become rules of law applicable to the adversary adjudicative process. Many of these concepts are the bases for standards of professional conduct set forth in the Disciplinary Rules.

EC 7–21 The civil adjudicative process is primarily designed for the settlement of disputes between parties, while the criminal process is designed for the protection of society as a whole. Threatening to use, or using, the criminal process to coerce adjustment of private civil claims or controversies is a subversion of that process;[37] further, the person against whom the criminal process is so misused may be deterred from asserting his legal rights and thus the usefulness of the civil process in settling private disputes is impaired. As in all cases of abuse of judicial process, the improper use of criminal process tends to diminish public confidence in our legal system.

EC 7–22 Respect for judicial rulings is essential to the proper administration of justice; however, a litigant or his lawyer may, in good faith and within the framework of the law, take steps to test the correctness of a ruling of a tribunal.[38]

EC 7–23 The complexity of law often makes it difficult for a tribunal to be fully informed unless the pertinent law is presented by the lawyers in the cause. A tribunal that is fully informed on the applicable law is better able to make a fair and accurate determination of the matter before it. The adversary system contemplates that each lawyer will present and argue the existing law in the light most favorable to his client.[39] Where a lawyer knows of legal authority in the controlling jurisdiction directly adverse to the position of his client, he should inform the tribunal of its existence unless his adversary has done so; but, having

---

34. Cf. ABA Canons 15 and 32.

35. Cf. ABA Canon 21.

36. See *Professional Responsibility: Report of the Joint Conference*, 44 A.B.A.J. 1159, 1216 (1958).

37. "We are of the opinion that the letter in question was improper, and that in writing and sending it respondent was guilty of unprofessional conduct. This court has heretofore expressed its disapproval of using threats of criminal prosecution as a means of forcing settlement of civil claims. . . .

"Respondent has been guilty of a violation of a principle which condemns any confusion of threats of criminal prosecution with the enforcement of civil claims. For this misconduct he should be severely censured." Matter of Gelman, 230 App.Div. 524, 527, 245 N.Y.S. 416, 419 (1930).

38. "An attorney has the duty to protect the interests of his client. He has a right to press legitimate argument and to protest an erroneous ruling." Gallagher v. Municipal Court, 31 Cal.2d 784, 796, 192 P.2d 905, 913 (1948).

"There must be protection, however, in the far more frequent case of the attorney who stands on his rights and combats the order in good faith and without disrespect believing with good cause that it is void, for it is here that the independence of the bar becomes valuable." Note, 39 Colum.L.Rev. 433, 438 (1939).

39. "Too many do not understand that accomplishment of the layman's abstract ideas of justice is the function of the judge and jury, and that it is the lawyer's sworn duty to portray his client's case in its most favorable light." Rochelle & Payne, *The Struggle for Public Understanding*, 25 Texas B.J. 109, 159 (1962).

made such disclosure, he may challenge its soundness in whole or in part.[40]

EC 7–24   In order to bring about just and informed decisions, evidentiary and procedural rules have been established by tribunals to permit the inclusion of relevant evidence and argument and the exclusion of all other considerations. The expression by a lawyer of his personal opinion as to the justness of a cause, as to the credibility of a witness, as to the culpability of a civil litigant, or as to the guilt or innocence of an accused is not a proper subject for argument to the trier of fact.[41] It is improper as to factual matters because admissible evidence possessed by a lawyer should be presented only as sworn testimony. It is improper as to all other matters because, were the rule otherwise, the silence of a lawyer on a given occasion could be construed unfavorably to his client. However, a lawyer may argue, on his analysis of the evidence, for any position or conclusion with respect to any of the foregoing matters.

EC 7–25   Rules of evidence and procedure are designed to lead to just decisions and are part of the framework of the law. Thus while a lawyer may take steps in good faith and within the framework of the law to test the validity of rules, he is not justified in consciously violating such rules and he should be diligent in his

efforts to guard against his unintentional violation of them.[42] As examples, a lawyer should subscribe to or verify only those pleadings that he believes are in compliance with applicable law and rules; a lawyer should not make any prefatory statement before a tribunal in regard to the purported facts of the case on trial unless he believes that his statement will be supported by admissible evidence; a lawyer should not ask a witness a question solely for the purpose of harassing or embarrassing him; and a lawyer should not by subterfuge put before a jury matters which it cannot properly consider.

EC 7–26   The law and Disciplinary Rules prohibit the use of fraudulent, false, or perjured testimony or evidence.[43] A lawyer who knowingly[44] participates in introduction of such testimony or evidence is subject to discipline. A lawyer should, however, present any admissible evidence his client desires to have presented unless he knows, or from facts within his knowledge should know, that such testimony or evidence is false, fraudulent, or perjured.[45]

EC 7–27   Because it interferes with the proper administration of justice, a lawyer should not suppress evidence that he or his client has a legal obligation to reveal or produce. In like manner, a lawyer

---

40. "We are of the opinion that this Canon requires the lawyer to disclose such decisions [that are adverse to his client's contentions] to the court. He may, of course, after doing so, challenge the soundness of the decisions or present reasons which he believes would warrant the court in not following them in the pending case." *ABA Opinion* 146 (1935).

Cf. *ABA Opinion* 280 (1949) and Thode, *The Ethical Standard for the Advocate*, 39 Texas L.Rev. 575, 585–86 (1961).

41. See ABA Canon 15.

"The traditional duty of an advocate is that he honorably uphold the contentions of his client. He should not voluntarily undermine them." Harders v. State of California, 373 F.2d 839, 842 (9th Cir.1967).

42. See ABA Canon 22.

43. Id. Cf. ABA Canon 41.

44. See generally *ABA Opinion* 287 (1953) as to a lawyer's duty when he unknowingly participates in introducing perjured testimony.

45. "Under any standard of proper ethical conduct an attorney should not sit by silently and permit his client to commit what may have been perjury, and which certainly would mislead the court and the opposing party on a matter vital to the issue under consideration. . . .

. . .

"Respondent next urges that it was his duty to observe the utmost good faith toward his client, and therefore he could not divulge any confidential information. This duty to the client of course does not extend to the point of authorizing collaboration with him in the commission of fraud." In re Carroll, 244 S.W.2d 474, 474–75 (Ky.1951).

should not advise or cause a person to secrete himself or to leave the jurisdiction of a tribunal for the purpose of making him unavailable as a witness therein.[46]

EC 7–28 Witnesses should always testify truthfully[47] and should be free from any financial inducements that might tempt them to do otherwise.[48] A lawyer should not pay or agree to pay a non-expert witness an amount in excess of reimbursement for expenses and financial loss incident to his being a witness; however, a lawyer may pay or agree to pay an expert witness a reasonable fee for his services as an expert. But in no event should a lawyer pay or agree to pay a contingent fee to any witness. A lawyer should exercise reasonable diligence to see that his client and lay associates conform to these standards.[49]

EC 7–29 To safeguard the impartiality that is essential to the judicial process, veniremen and jurors should be protected against extraneous influences.[50] When

impartiality is present, public confidence in the judicial system is enhanced. There should be no extrajudicial communication with veniremen prior to trial or with jurors during trial by or on behalf of a lawyer connected with the case. Furthermore, a lawyer who is not connected with the case should not communicate with or cause another to communicate with a venireman or a juror about the case. After the trial, communication by a lawyer with jurors is permitted so long as he refrains from asking questions or making comments that tend to harass or embarrass the juror[51] or to influence actions of the juror in future cases. Were a lawyer to be prohibited from communicating after a trial with a juror, he could not ascertain if the verdict might be subject to legal challenge, in which event the invalidity of a verdict might go undetected.[52] When an extrajudicial communication by a lawyer with a juror is permitted by law, it should

---

46. See ABA Canon 5; cf. *ABA Opinion* 131 (1935).

47. Cf. ABA Canon 39.

48. "The prevalence of perjury is a serious menace to the administration of justice, to prevent which no means have as yet been satisfactorily devised. But there certainly can be no greater incentive to perjury than to allow a party to make payments to its opponents witnesses under any guise or on any excuse, and at least attorneys who are officers of the court to aid it in the administration of justice, must keep themselves clear of any connection which in the slightest degree tends to induce witnesses to testify in favor of their clients." In re Robinson, 151 App.Div. 589, 600, 136 N.Y.S. 548, 556–57 (1912), aff'd, 209 N.Y. 354, 103 N.E. 160 (1913).

49. "It will not do for an attorney who seeks to justify himself against charges of this kind to show that he has escaped criminal responsibility under the Penal Law, nor can he blindly shut his eyes to a system which tends to suborn witnesses, to produce perjured testimony, and to suppress the truth. He has an active affirmative duty to protect the administration of justice from perjury and fraud, and that duty is not performed by allowing his subordinates and assistants to attempt to subvert justice and procure results for his clients based upon false testimony and perjured wit-

nesses." Id., 151 App.Div. at 592, 136 N.Y.S. at 551.

50. See ABA Canon 23.

51. "[I]t is unfair to jurors to permit a disappointed litigant to pick over their private associations in search of something to discredit them and their verdict. And it would be unfair to the public too if jurors should understand that they cannot convict a man of means without risking an inquiry of that kind by paid investigators, with, to boot, the distortions an inquiry of that kind can produce." State v. LaFera, 42 N.J. 97, 107, 199 A.2d 630, 636 (1964).

52. *ABA Opinion* 319 (1968) points out that "[m]any courts today, and the trend is in this direction, allow the testimony of jurors as to all irregularities in and out of the courtroom except those irregularities whose existence can be determined only by exploring the consciousness of a single particular juror, New Jersey v. Kociolek, 20 N.J. 92, 118 A.2d 812 (1955). Model Code of Evidence Rule 301. Certainly as to states in which the testimony and affidavits of jurors may be received in support of or against a motion for new trial, a lawyer, in his obligation to protect his client, must have the tools for ascertaining whether or not grounds for a new trial exist and it is not unethical for him to talk to and question jurors."

be made considerately and with deference to the personal feelings of the juror.

EC 7–30 Vexatious or harassing investigations of veniremen or jurors seriously impair the effectiveness of our jury system. For this reason, a lawyer or anyone on his behalf who conducts an investigation of veniremen or jurors should act with circumspection and restraint.

EC 7–31 Communications with or investigations of members of families of veniremen or jurors by a lawyer or by anyone on his behalf are subject to the restrictions imposed upon the lawyer with respect to his communications with or investigations of veniremen and jurors.

EC 7–32 Because of his duty to aid in preserving the integrity of the jury system, a lawyer who learns of improper conduct by or towards a venireman, a juror, or a member of the family of either should make a prompt report to the court regarding such conduct.

EC 7–33 A goal of our legal system is that each party shall have his case, criminal or civil, adjudicated by an impartial tribunal. The attainment of this goal may be defeated by dissemination of news or comments which tend to influence judge or jury.[53] Such news or comments may prevent prospective jurors from being impartial at the outset of the trial[54] and may also interfere with the obligation of jurors to base their verdict solely upon the evidence admitted in the trial.[55] The

53. Generally see ABA Advisory Committee on Fair Trial and Free Press, Standards Relating to Fair Trial and Free Press (1966).

"[T]he trial court might well have proscribed extrajudicial statements by any lawyer, party, witness, or court official which divulged prejudicial matters.... See State v. Van Dwyne, 43 N.J. 369, 389, 204 A.2d 841, 852 (1964), in which the court interpreted Canon 20 of the American Bar Association's Canons of Professional Ethics to prohibit such statements. Being advised of the great public interest in the case, the mass coverage of the press, and the potential prejudicial impact of publicity, the court could also have requested the appropriate city and county officials to promulgate a regulation with respect to dissemination of information about the case by their employees. In addition, reporters who wrote or broadcast prejudicial stories, could have been warned as to the impropriety of publishing material not introduced in the proceedings.... In this manner, Sheppard's right to a trial free from outside interference would have been given added protection without corresponding curtailment of the news media. Had the judge, the other officers of the court, and the police placed the interest of justice first, the news media would have soon learned to be content with the task of reporting the case as it unfolded in the courtroom—not pieced together from extrajudicial statements." Sheppard v. Maxwell, 384 U.S. 333, 361–62, 16 L.Ed.2d 600, 619–20, 86 S.Ct. 1507, 1521–22 (1966).

"Court proceedings are held for the solemn purpose of endeavoring to ascertain the truth which is the *sine qua non* of a fair trial. Over the centuries Anglo–American courts have de-

vised careful safeguards by rule and otherwise to protect and facilitate the performance of this high function. As a result, at this time those safeguards do not permit the televising and photographing of a criminal trial, save in two States and there only under restrictions. The federal courts prohibit it by specific rule. This is weighty evidence that our concepts of a fair trial do not tolerate such an indulgence. We have always held that the atmosphere essential to the preservation of a fair trial—the most fundamental of all freedoms—must be maintained at all costs." Estes v. State of Texas, 381 U.S. 532, 540, 14 L.Ed.2d 543, 549, 85 S.Ct. 1628, 1631–32 (1965), rehearing denied, 382 U.S. 875, 15 L.Ed.2d 118, 86 S.Ct. 18 (1965).

54. "Pretrial can create a major problem for the defendant in a criminal case. Indeed, it may be more harmful than publicity during the trial for it may well set the community opinion as to guilt or innocence.... The trial witnesses present at the hearing, as well as the original jury panel, were undoubtedly made aware of the peculiar public importance of the case by the press and television coverage being provided, and by the fact that they themselves were televised live and their pictures rebroadcast on the evening show." Id., 381 U.S. at 536–37, 14 L.Ed.2d at 546–47, 85 S.Ct. at 1629–30.

55. "The undeviating rule of this Court was expressed by Mr. Justice Holmes over half a century ago in Patterson v. Colorado, 205 U.S. 454, 462 (1907):

"The theory of our system is that the conclusions to be reached in a case will be induced release by a lawyer of out-of-court statements regarding an anticipated or pending trial may improperly affect the impartiality of the tribunal.[56] For these reasons, standards for permissible and prohibited conduct of a lawyer with respect to trial publicity have been established.

EC 7–34 The impartiality of a public servant in our legal system may be impaired by the receipt of gifts or loans. A lawyer,[57] therefore, is never justified in making a gift or a loan to a judge, a hearing officer, or an official or employee of a tribunal, except as permitted by Section C(4) of Canon 5 of the Code of Judicial Conduct, but a lawyer may make a contribution to the campaign fund of a candidate for judicial office in conformity with Section B(2) under Canon 7 of the Code of Judicial Conduct.[58]

EC 7–35 All litigants and lawyers should have access to tribunals on an equal basis. Generally, in adversary proceedings a lawyer should not communicate with a judge relative to a matter pending before, or which is to be brought before, a tribunal over which he presides in circumstances which might have the

only by evidence and argument in open court, and not by any outside influence, whether of private talk or public print." Sheppard v. Maxwell, 384 U.S. 333, 351, 16 L.Ed.2d 600, 614, 86 S.Ct. 1507, 1516 (1966).

"The trial judge has a large discretion in ruling on the issue of prejudice resulting from the reading by jurors of news articles concerning the trial.... Generalizations beyond that statement are not profitable, because each case must turn on its special facts. We have here the exposure of jurors to information of a character which the trial judge ruled was so prejudicial it could not be directly offered as evidence. The prejudice to the defendant is almost certain to be as great when that evidence reaches the jury through news accounts as when it is a part of the prosecution's evidence.... It may indeed be greater for it is then not tempered by protective procedures." Marshall v. United States, 360 U.S. 310, 312–13, 3 L.Ed.2d 1250, 1252, 79 S.Ct. 1171, 1173 (1959).

"The experienced trial lawyer knows that an adverse public opinion is a tremendous disadvantage to the defense of his client. Although grand jurors conduct their deliberations in secret, they are selected from the body of the public. They are likely to know what the general public knows and to reflect the public attitude. Trials are open to the public, and aroused public opinion respecting the merits of a legal controversy creates a court room atmosphere which, without any vocal expression in the presence of the petit jury, makes itself felt and has its effect upon the action of the petit jury. Our fundamental concepts of justice and our American sense of fair play requires that the petit jury shall be composed of persons with fair and impartial minds and without preconceived views as to the merits of the controversy, and that it shall determine the issues presented to it solely upon the evidence adduced

at the trial and according to the law given in the instructions of the trial judge.

"While we may doubt that the effect of public opinion would sway or bias the judgment of the trial judge in an equity proceeding, the defendant should not be called upon to run that risk and the trial court should not have his work made more difficult by any dissemination of statements to the public that would be calculated to create a public demand for a particular judgment in a prospective or pending case." *ABA Opinion* 199 (1940).

Cf. Estes v. State of Texas, 381 U.S. 532, 544–45, 14 L.Ed.2d 543, 551, 85 S.Ct. 1628, 1634 (1965), rehearing denied, 382 U.S. 875, 15 L.Ed.2d 118, 86 S.Ct. 18 (1965).

56. See ABA Canon 20.

57. Canon 3 observes that a lawyer "deserves rebuke and denunciation for any device or attempt to gain from a Judge special personal consideration or favor."

See ABA Canon 32.

58. "*Judicial Canon 32* provides:

" 'A judge should not accept any presents or favors from litigants, or from lawyers practicing before him or from others whose interests are likely to be submitted to him for judgment.'

"The language of this Canon is perhaps broad enough to prohibit campaign contributions by lawyers, practicing before the court upon which the candidate hopes to sit. However, we do not think it was intended to prohibit such contributions when the candidate is obligated, by force of circumstances over which he has no control, to conduct a campaign, the expense of which exceeds that which he should reasonably be expected to personally bear!" *ABA Opinion* 226 (1941).

effect or give the appearance of granting undue advantage to one party.[59] For example, a lawyer should not communicate with a tribunal by a writing unless a copy thereof is promptly delivered to opposing counsel or to the adverse party if he is not represented by a lawyer. Ordinarily an oral communication by a lawyer with a judge or hearing officer should be made only upon adequate notice to opposing counsel, or, if there is none, to the opposing party. A lawyer should not condone or lend himself to private importunities by another with a judge or hearing officer on behalf of himself or his client.

EC 7–36 Judicial hearings ought to be conducted through dignified and orderly procedures designed to protect the rights of all parties. Although a lawyer has the duty to represent his client zealously, he should not engage in any conduct that offends the dignity and decorum of proceedings.[60] While maintaining his independence, a lawyer should be respectful, courteous, and above-board in his relations with a judge or hearing officer before whom he appears.[61] He should avoid undue solicitude for the comfort or convenience of judge or jury and should avoid any other conduct calculated to gain special consideration.

EC 7–37 In adversary proceedings, clients are litigants and though ill feeling may exist between clients, such ill feeling should not influence a lawyer in his conduct, attitude, and demeanor towards opposing lawyers.[62] A lawyer should not make unfair or derogatory personal reference to opposing counsel. Haranguing and offensive tactics by lawyers interfere with the orderly administration of justice and have no proper place in our legal system.

EC 7–38 A lawyer should be courteous to opposing counsel and should accede to reasonable requests regarding court proceedings, settings, continuances, waiver of procedural formalities, and similar matters which do not prejudice the rights of his client.[63] He should follow local customs of courtesy or practice, unless he gives timely notice to opposing counsel of his intention not to do so.[64] A lawyer should be punctual in fulfilling all professional commitments.[65]

EC 7–39 In the final analysis, proper functioning of the adversary system depends upon cooperation between lawyers and tribunals in utilizing procedures which will preserve the impartiality of tribunals and make their decisional processes prompt and just, without impinging upon the obligation of lawyers to represent their clients zealously within the framework of the law.

DISCIPLINARY RULES

DR 7–101 Representing a Client Zealously.

(A) A lawyer shall not intentionally:[66]

(1) Fail to seek the lawful objectives of his client through reasonably available means[67] permitted by law and the Disciplinary Rules, except as provided by DR 7–101(B). A lawyer does not violate this Disciplinary Rule, however, by acceding to reasonable requests of opposing counsel which do not prejudice the rights of his client, by being punctual in fulfilling all professional commitments, by avoiding offensive tactics, or by treating with courtesy and consideration all persons involved in the legal process.

(2) Fail to carry out a contract of employment entered into

59. See ABA Canons 3 and 32.
60. Cf. ABA Canon 18.
61. See ABA Canons 1 and 3.
62. See ABA Canon 17.
63. See ABA Canon 24.

64. See ABA Canon 25.
65. See ABA Canon 21.
66. See ABA Canon 15.
67. See ABA Canons 5 and 15; cf. ABA Canons 4 and 32.

239

with a client for professional services, but he may withdraw as permitted under DR 2–110, DR 5–102, and DR 5–105.

(3) Prejudice or damage his client during the course of the professional relationship[68] except as required under DR 7–102(B).

(B) In his representation of a client, a lawyer may:

(1) Where permissible, exercise his professional judgment to waive or fail to assert a right or position of his client.

(2) Refuse to aid or participate in conduct that he believes to be unlawful, even though there is some support for an argument that the conduct is legal.

DR 7–102 Representing a Client Within the Bounds of the Law.

(A) In his representation of a client, a lawyer shall not:

(1) File a suit, assert a position, conduct a defense, delay a trial, or take other action on behalf of his client when he knows or when it is obvious that such action would serve merely to harass or maliciously injure another.[69]

(2) Knowingly advance a claim or defense that is unwarranted under existing law, except that he may advance such claim or defense if it can be supported by good faith argument for an extension, modification, or reversal of existing law.

(3) Conceal or knowingly fail to disclose that which he is required by law to reveal.

(4) Knowingly use perjured testimony or false evidence.[70]

(5) Knowingly make a false statement of law or fact.

(6) Participate in the creation or preservation of evidence when he knows or it is obvious that the evidence is false.

(7) Counsel or assist his client in conduct that the lawyer knows to be illegal or fraudulent.

(8) Knowingly engage in other illegal conduct or conduct contrary to a Disciplinary Rule.

(B) A lawyer who receives information clearly establishing that:

(1) His client has, in the course of the representation, perpetrated a fraud upon a person or tribunal shall promptly call upon his client to rectify the same, and if his client refuses or is unable to do so, he shall reveal the fraud to the affected person or tribunal, except when the information is protected as a privileged communication.[71]

(2) A person other than his client has perpetrated a fraud upon a tribunal shall promptly reveal the fraud to the tribunal.[72]

DR 7–103 Performing the Duty of Public Prosecutor or Other Government Lawyer.[73]

(A) A public prosecutor or other government lawyer shall not institute or cause to be instituted criminal charges when he knows or it is obvious that the charges are not supported by probable cause.

---

68. Cf. ABA Canon 24.
69. See ABA Canon 30.
70. Cf. ABA Canons 22 and 29.
71. See ABA Canon 41; cf. Hinds v. State Bar, 19 Cal.2d 87, 92–93, 119 P.2d 134, 137 (1941); but see *ABA Opinion* 287 (1953) and

Texas Canon 38. Also see Code of Professional Responsibility. DR 4–101(C)(2).

72. See Precision Inst. Mfg. Co. v. Automotive M.M. Co., 324 U.S. 806, 89 L.Ed. 1381, 65 S.Ct. 993 (1945).

73. Cf. ABA Canon 5.

(B) A public prosecutor or other government lawyer in criminal litigation shall make timely disclosure to counsel for the defendant, or to the defendant if he has no counsel, of the existence of evidence, known to the prosecutor or other government lawyer, that tends to negate the guilt of the accused, mitigate the degree of the offense, or reduce the punishment.

DR 7-104 Communicating With One of Adverse Interest.[74]

(A) During the course of his representation of a client a lawyer shall not:

(1) Communicate or cause another to communicate on the subject of the representation with a party he knows to be represented by a lawyer in that matter unless he has the prior consent of the lawyer representing such other party[75] or is authorized by law to do so.

(2) Give advice to a person who is not represented by a lawyer, other than the advice to

secure counsel,[76] if the interests of such person are or have a reasonable possibility of being in conflict with the interests of his client.[77]

DR 7-105 Threatening Criminal Prosecution.

(A) A lawyer shall not present, participate in presenting, or threaten to present criminal charges solely to obtain an advantage in a civil matter.

DR 7-106 Trial Conduct.

(A) A lawyer shall not disregard or advise his client to disregard a standing rule of a tribunal or a ruling of a tribunal made in the course of a proceeding, but he may take appropriate steps in good faith to test the validity of such rule or ruling.

(B) In presenting a matter to a tribunal, a lawyer shall disclose:[78]

(1) Legal authority in the controlling jurisdiction known to him to be directly adverse to the position of his client and which is not disclosed by opposing counsel.[79]

---

74. "*Rule 12. . . .* A member of the State Bar shall not communicate with a party represented by counsel upon a subject of controversy, in the absence and without the consent of such counsel. This rule shall not apply to communications with a public officer, board, committee or body." Cal. Business and Professions Code § 6076 (West 1962).

75. See ABA Canon 9; cf. *ABA Opinions* 124 (1934), 108 (1934), 95 (1933), and 75 (1932); also see In re Schwabe, 242 Or. 169, 174–75, 408 P.2d 922, 924 (1965).

"It is clear from the earlier opinions of this committee that *Canon 9* is to be construed literally and does not allow a communication with an opposing party, without the consent of his counsel, though the purpose merely be to investigate the facts. *Opinions 117, 55, 66,*" ABA Opinion 187 (1938).

76. Cf. *ABA Opinion* 102 (1933).

77. Cf. ABA Canon 9 and *ABA Opinion* 58 (1931).

78. Cf. Note, 38 Texas L.Rev. 107, 108–09 (1959).

79. "In the brief summary in the 1947 edition of the Committee's decisions (p. 17), *Opinion 146* was thus summarized: *Opinion 146*—A lawyer should disclose to the court a decision directly adverse to his client's case that is unknown to his adversary.

. . .

"We would not confine the Opinion to 'controlling authorities'—i.e., those decisive of the pending case—but, in accordance with the tests hereafter suggested, would apply it to a decision directly adverse to any proposition of law on which the lawyer expressly relies, which would reasonably be considered important by the judge sitting on the case.

. . .

"... The test in every case should be: Is the decision which opposing counsel has overlooked one which the court should clearly consider in deciding the case? Would a reasonable judge properly feel that a lawyer who advanced, as the law, a proposition adverse to the

(2) **Unless privileged or irrelevant, the identities of the clients he represents and of the persons who employed him.[80]**

(C) **In appearing in his professional capacity before a tribunal, a lawyer shall not:**

(1) **State or allude to any matter that he has no reasonable basis to believe is relevant to the case or that will not be supported by admissible evidence.[81]**

(2) **Ask any question that he has no reasonable basis to believe is relevant to the case and that is intended to degrade a witness or other person.[82]**

(3) **Assert his personal knowledge of the facts in issue, except when testifying as a witness.**

(4) **Assert his personal opinion as to the justness of a cause, as to the credibility of a witness, as to the culpability of a civil litigant, or as to the guilt or innocence of an accused;[83] but he may argue, on his analysis of the evidence, for any position or conclusion with respect to the matters stated herein.**

(5) **Fail to comply with known local customs of courtesy or practice of the bar or a particular tribunal without giving to opposing counsel timely notice of his intent not to comply.[84]**

(6) **Engage in undignified or discourteous conduct which is degrading to a tribunal.**

(7) **Intentionally or habitually violate any established rule of procedure or of evidence.**

undisclosed decision, was lacking in candor and fairness to him? Might the judge consider himself misled by an implied representation that the lawyer knew of no adverse authority?" *ABA Opinion* 280 (1949).

80. "The authorities are substantially uniform against any privilege as applied to the fact of retainer or identity of the client. The privilege is limited to confidential communications, and a retainer is not a confidential communication, although it cannot come into existence without some communication between the attorney and the—at that stage prospective—client." United States v. Pape, 144 F.2d 778, 782 (2d Cir. 1944), cert. denied, 323 U.S. 752, 89 L.Ed.2d 602, 65 S.Ct. 86 (1944).

"To be sure, there may be circumstances under which the identification of a client may amount to the prejudicial disclosure of a confidential communication, as where the substance of a disclosure has already been revealed but not its source." Colton v. United States, 306 F.2d 633, 637 (2d Cir. 1962).

81. See ABA Canon 22; cf. ABA Canon 17.

"The rule allowing counsel when addressing the jury the widest latitude in discussing the evidence and presenting the client's theories falls far short of authorizing the statement by counsel of matter not in evidence, or indulging in argument founded on no proof, or demanding verdicts for purposes other than the just settlement of the matters at issue between the litigants, or appealing to prejudice or passion. The rule confining counsel to legitimate argument is not based on etiquette, but on justice.

Its violation is not merely an overstepping of the bounds of propriety, but a violation of a party's rights. The jurors must determine the issues upon the evidence. Counsel's address should help them do this, not tend to lead them astray." Cherry Creek Nat. Bank v. Fidelity & Cas. Co., 207 App.Div. 787, 790–91, 202 N.Y.S. 611, 614 (1924).

82. Cf. ABA Canon 18.

§ 6068.... It is the duty of an attorney:

. . .

"(f) To abstain from all offensive personality, and to advance no fact prejudicial to the honor or reputation of a party or witness, unless required by the justice of the cause with which he is charged." Cal.Business and Professions Code § 6068 (West 1962).

83. "The record in the case at bar was silent concerning the qualities and character of the deceased. It is especially improper, in addressing the jury in a murder case, for the prosecuting attorney to make reference to his knowledge of the good qualities of the deceased where there is no evidence in the record bearing upon his character.... A prosecutor should never inject into his argument evidence not introduced at the trial." People v. Dukes, 12 Ill.2d 334, 341, 146 N.E.2d 14, 17–18 (1957).

84. "A lawyer should not ignore known customs or practice of the Bar or of a particular Court, even when the law permits, without giving timely notice to the opposing counsel." ABA Canon 25.

DR 7-107 Trial Publicity.[85]

(A) A lawyer participating in or associated with the investigation of a criminal matter shall not make or participate in making an extrajudicial statement that a reasonable person would expect to be disseminated by means of public communication and that does more than state without elaboration:

(1) Information contained in a public record.

(2) That the investigation is in progress.

(3) The general scope of the investigation including a description of the offense and, if permitted by law, the identity of the victim.

(4) A request for assistance in apprehending a suspect or assistance in other matters and the information necessary thereto.

(5) A warning to the public of any dangers.

(B) A lawyer or law firm associated with the prosecution or defense of a criminal matter shall not, from the time of the filing of a complaint, information, or indictment, the issuance of an arrest warrant, or arrest until the commencement of the trial or disposition without trial, make or participate in making an extrajudicial statement that a reasonable person would expect to be disseminated by means of public communication and that relates to:

(1) The character, reputation, or prior criminal record (including arrests, indictments, or other charges of crime) of the accused.

(2) The possibility of a plea of guilty to the offense charged or to a lesser offense.

(3) The existence or contents of any confession, admission, or statement given by the accused or his refusal or failure to make a statement.

(4) The performance or results of any examinations or tests or the refusal or failure of the

---

85. The provisions of Sections (A), (B), (C), and (D) of this Disciplinary Rule incorporate the fair trial-free press standards which apply to lawyers as adopted by the ABA House of Delegates, Feb. 19, 1968, upon the recommendation of the Fair Trial and Free Press Advisory Committee of the ABA Special Committee on Minimum Standards for the Administration of Criminal Justice.

Cf. ABA Canon 20; see generally ABA Advisory Committee on Fair Trial and Free Press, Standards Relating to Fair Trial and Free Press (1966).

"From the cases coming here we note that unfair and prejudicial news comment on pending trials has become increasingly prevalent. Due process requires that the accused receive a trial by an impartial jury free from outside influences. Given the pervasiveness of modern communications and the difficulty of effacing prejudicial publicity from the minds of the jurors, the trial courts must take strong measures to ensure that the balance is never weighed against the accused. And appellate tribunals have the duty to make an independent evaluation of the circumstances. Of course, there is nothing that prescribes the press from reporting events that transpire in the courtroom. But where there is a reasonable likelihood that prejudicial news prior to trial will prevent a fair trial, the judge should continue the case until the threat abates, or transfer it to another county not so permeated with publicity.... The courts must take such steps by rule and regulation that will protect their processes from prejudicial outside interferences. Neither prosecutors, counsel for defense, the accused, witnesses, court staff nor enforcement officers coming under the jurisdiction of the court should be permitted to frustrate its function. Collaboration between counsel and the press as to information affecting the fairness of a criminal trial is not only subject to regulation, but is highly censurable and worthy of disciplinary measures." Sheppard v. Maxwell, 384 U.S. 333, 362-63, 16 L.Ed.2d 600, 620, 86 S.Ct. 1507, 1522 (1966).

accused to submit to examinations or tests.

(5) The identity, testimony, or credibility of a prospective witness.

(6) Any opinion as to the guilt or innocence of the accused, the evidence, or the merits of the case.

(C) DR 7–107(B) does not preclude a lawyer during such period from announcing:

(1) The name, age, residence, occupation, and family status of the accused.

(2) If the accused has not been apprehended, any information necessary to aid in his apprehension or to warn the public of any dangers he may present.

(3) A request for assistance in obtaining evidence.

(4) The identity of the victim of the crime.

(5) The fact, time, and place of arrest, resistance, pursuit, and use of weapons.

(6) The identity of investigating and arresting officers or agencies and the length of the investigation.

(7) At the time of seizure, a description of the physical evidence seized, other than a confession, admission, or statement.

(8) The nature, substance, or text of the charge.

(9) Quotations from or references to public records of the court in the case.

(10) The scheduling or result of any step in the judicial proceedings.

(11) That the accused denies the charges made against him.

(D) During the selection of a jury or the trial of a criminal matter, a lawyer or law firm associated with the prosecution or defense

of a criminal matter shall not make or participate in making an extra-judicial statement that a reasonable person would expect to be disseminated by means of public communication and that relates to the trial, parties, or issues in the trial or other matters that are reasonably likely to interfere with a fair trial, except that he may quote from or refer without comment to public records of the court in the case.

(E) After the completion of a trial or disposition without trial of a criminal matter and prior to the imposition of sentence, a lawyer or law firm associated with the prosecution or defense shall not make or participate in making an extra-judicial statement that a reasonable person would expect to be disseminated by public communication and that is reasonably likely to affect the imposition of sentence.

(F) The foregoing provisions of DR 7–107 also apply to professional disciplinary proceedings and juvenile disciplinary proceedings when pertinent and consistent with other law applicable to such proceedings.

(G) A lawyer or law firm associated with a civil action shall not during its investigation or litigation make or participate in making an extra-judicial statement, other than a quotation from or reference to public records, that a reasonable person would expect to be disseminated by means of public communication and that relates to:

(1) Evidence regarding the occurrence or transaction involved.

(2) The character, credibility, or criminal record of a party, witness, or prospective witness.

(3) The performance or results of any examinations or tests

or the refusal or failure of a party to submit to such.

(4) His opinion as to the merits of the claims or defenses of a party, except as required by law or administrative rule.

(5) Any other matter reasonably likely to interfere with a fair trial of the action.

(H) During the pendency of an administrative proceeding, a lawyer or law firm associated therewith shall not make or participate in making a statement, other than a quotation from or reference to public records, that a reasonable person would expect to be disseminated by means of public communication if it is made outside the official course of the proceeding and relates to:

(1) Evidence regarding the occurrence or transaction involved.

(2) The character, credibility, or criminal record of a party, witness, or prospective witness.

(3) Physical evidence or the performance or results of any examinations or tests or the refusal or failure of a party to submit to such.

(4) His opinion as to the merits of the claims, defenses, or positions of an interested person.

(5) Any other matter reasonably likely to interfere with a fair hearing.

(I) The foregoing provisions of DR 7–107 do not preclude a lawyer from replying to charges of misconduct publicly made against him or from participating in the proceedings of legislative, administrative, or other investigative bodies.

(J) A lawyer shall exercise reasonable care to prevent his employees and associates from making an extra-judicial statement that he would be prohibited from making under DR 7–107.

DR 7–108 Communication with or Investigation of Jurors.

(A) Before the trial of a case a lawyer connected therewith shall not communicate with or cause another to communicate with anyone he knows to be a member of the venire from which the jury will be selected for the trial of the case.

(B) During the trial of a case:

(1) A lawyer connected therewith shall not communicate with or cause another to communicate with any member of the jury.[86]

(2) A lawyer who is not connected therewith shall not communicate with or cause another to communicate with a juror concerning the case.

(C) DR 7–108(A) and (B) do not prohibit a lawyer from communicating with veniremen or jurors in the course of official proceedings.

(D) After discharge of the jury from further consideration of a case with which the lawyer was connected, the lawyer shall not ask questions of or make comments to a member of that jury that are calculated merely to harass or embarrass the juror or to influence his actions in future jury service.[87]

(E) A lawyer shall not conduct or cause, by financial support or

---

86. See ABA Canon 23.

87. "[I]t would be unethical for a lawyer to harass, entice, induce or exert influence on a juror to obtain his testimony." *ABA Opinion* 319 (1968).

otherwise, another to conduct a vexatious or harassing investigation of either a venireman or a juror.

(F) All restrictions imposed by DR 7–108 upon a lawyer also apply to communications with or investigations of members of a family of a venireman or a juror.

(G) A lawyer shall reveal promptly to the court improper conduct by a venireman or a juror, or by another toward a venireman or a juror or a member of his family, of which the lawyer has knowledge.

DR 7–109 Contact With Witnesses.

(A) A lawyer shall not suppress any evidence that he or his client has a legal obligation to reveal or produce.[88]

(B) A lawyer shall not advise or cause a person to secrete himself or to leave the jurisdiction of a tribunal for the purpose of making him unavailable as a witness therein.[89]

(C) A lawyer shall not pay, offer to pay, or acquiesce in the payment of compensation to a witness contingent upon the content of his testimony or the outcome of the case.[90] But a lawyer may advance, guarantee, or acquiesce in the payment of:

(1) Expenses reasonably incurred by a witness in attending or testifying.

(2) Reasonable compensation to a witness for his loss of time in attending or testifying.

(3) A reasonable fee for the professional services of an expert witness.

DR 7–110 Contact With Officials.[91]

(A) A lawyer shall not give or lend any thing of value to a judge, official, or employee of a tribunal, except as permitted by Section C(4) of Canon 5 of the Code of Judicial Conduct, but a lawyer may make a contribution to the campaign fund of a candidate for judicial office in conformity with Section B(2) under Canon 7 of the Code of Judicial Conduct.

(B) In an adversary proceeding, a lawyer shall not communicate, or cause another to communicate, as to the merits of the cause with a judge or an official before whom the proceeding is pending, except:

(1) In the course of official proceedings in the cause.

(2) In writing if he promptly delivers a copy of the writing to opposing counsel or to the adverse party if he is not represented by a lawyer.

(3) Orally upon adequate notice to opposing counsel or to the adverse party if he is not represented by a lawyer.

(4) As otherwise authorized by law, or by Section A(4) under Canon 3 of the Code of Judicial Conduct.[92]

---

88. See ABA Canon 5.

89. Cf. ABA Canon 5.

"*Rule 15*.... A member of the State Bar shall not advise a person, whose testimony could establish or tend to establish a material fact, to avoid service of process, or secrete himself, or otherwise to make his testimony unavailable." Cal.Business and Professions Code § 6076 (West 1962).

90. See In re O'Keefe, 49 Mont. 369, 142 P. 638 (1914).

91. Cf. ABA Canon 3.

92. "*Rule 16*.... A member of the State Bar shall not, in the absence of opposing counsel, communicate with or argue to a judge or judicial officer except in open court upon the merits of a contested matter pending before such judge or judicial officer; nor shall he, without furnishing opposing counsel with a copy thereof, address a written communication to a judge or judicial officer concerning the merits of a contested matter pending before such judge or judicial officer. This rule shall

CANON 8

A Lawyer Should Assist in Improving the Legal System

ETHICAL CONSIDERATIONS

EC 8–1 Changes in human affairs and imperfections in human institutions make necessary constant efforts to maintain and improve our legal system.[1] This system should function in a manner that commands public respect and fosters the use of legal remedies to achieve redress of grievances. By reason of education and experience, lawyers are especially qualified to recognize deficiencies in the legal system and to initiate corrective measures therein. Thus they should participate in proposing and supporting legislation and programs to improve the system,[2] without regard to the general interests or desires of clients or former clients.[3]

EC 8–2 Rules of law are deficient if they are not just, understandable, and responsive to the needs of society. If a lawyer believes that the existence or absence of a rule of law, substantive or procedural, causes or contributes to an unjust result, he should endeavor by lawful means to obtain appropriate changes in the law. He should encourage the simplification of laws and the repeal or amendment of laws that are outmoded.[4] Likewise, legal procedures should be improved whenever experience indicates a change is needed.

EC 8–3 The fair administration of justice requires the availability of competent lawyers. Members of the public should be educated to recognize the existence of legal problems and the resultant need for legal services, and should be provided methods for intelligent selection of counsel. Those persons unable to pay for legal services should be provided needed services. Clients and lawyers should not be penalized by undue geographical restraints upon representation in legal mat-

not apply to ex parte matters." Cal.Business and Professions Code § 6076 (West 1962).

1. "... [Another] task of the great lawyer is to do his part individually and as a member of the organized bar to improve his profession, the courts, and the law. As President Theodore Roosevelt aptly put it, 'Every man owes some of his time to the upbuilding of the profession to which he belongs.' Indeed, this obligation is one of the great things which distinguishes a profession from a business. The soundness and the necessity of President Roosevelt's admonition insofar as it relates to the legal profession cannot be doubted. The advances in natural science and technology are so startling and the velocity of change in business and in social life is so great that the law along with the other social sciences, and even human life itself, is in grave danger of being extinguished by new gods of its own invention if it does not awake from its lethargy. Vanderbilt, *The Five Functions of the Lawyer: Service to Clients and the Public*, 40 A.B.A.J. 31, 31–32 (1954).

2. See ABA Cannon 29; Cf. Cheatham, *The Lawyer's Role and Surroundings*, 25 Rocky Mt.L.Rev. 405, 406–07 (1953).

"The lawyer tempted by repose should recall the heavy costs paid by his profession when needed legal reform has to be accomplished through the initiative of public-spirited lay-

men. Where change must be thrust from without upon an unwilling Bar, the public's least flattering picture of the lawyer seems confirmed. The lawyer concerned for the standing of his profession will, therefore, interest himself actively in the improvement of the law. In doing so he will not only help to maintain confidence in the Bar, but will have the satisfaction of meeting a responsibility inhering in the nature of his calling." *Professional Responsibility: Report of the Joint Conference*, 44 A.B.A.J. 1159, 1217 (1958).

3. See Stayton, *Cum Honore Officium*, 19 Tex.B.J. 765, 766 (1956); *Professional Responsibility: Report of the Joint Conference*, 44 A.B.A.J. 1159, 1162 (1958); and Paul, *The Lawyer as a Tax Adviser*, 25 Rocky Mt.L.Rev. 412, 433–34 (1953).

4. "There are few great figures in the history of the Bar who have not concerned themselves with the reform and improvement of the law. The special obligation of the profession with respect to legal reform rests on considerations too obvious to require enumeration. Certainly it is the lawyer who has both the best chance to know when the law is working badly and the special competence to put it in order." *Professional Responsibility: Report of the Joint Conference*, 44 A.B.A.J. 1159, 1217 (1958).

ters, and the bar should address itself to improvements in licensing, reciprocity, and admission procedures consistent with the needs of modern commerce.

EC 8–4 Whenever a lawyer seeks legislative or administrative changes, he should identify the capacity in which he appears, whether on behalf of himself, a client, or the public.[5] A lawyer may advocate such changes on behalf of a client even though he does not agree with them. But when a lawyer purports to act on behalf of the public, he should espouse only those changes which he conscientiously believes to be in the public interest.

EC 8–5 Fraudulent, deceptive, or otherwise illegal conduct by a participant in a proceeding before a tribunal or legislative body is inconsistent with fair administration of justice, and it should never be participated in or condoned by lawyers. Unless constrained by his obligation to preserve the confidences and secrets of his client, a lawyer should reveal to appropriate authorities any knowledge he may have of such improper conduct.

EC 8–6 Judges and administrative officials having adjudicatory powers ought to be persons of integrity, competence, and suitable temperament. Generally, lawyers are qualified, by personal observation or investigation, to evaluate the qualifications of persons seeking or being considered for such public offices, and for this reason they have a special responsibility to aid in the selection of only those who are qualified.[6] It is the duty of lawyers to endeavor to prevent political considerations from outweighing judicial fitness in the selection of judges. Lawyers should protest earnestly against the appointment or election of those who are unsuited for the bench and should strive to have elected[7] or appointed thereto only those who are willing to forego pursuits, whether of a business, political, or other nature, that may interfere with the free and fair consideration of questions presented for adjudication. Adjudicatory officials, not being wholly free to defend themselves, are entitled to receive the support of the bar against unjust criticism.[8] While a lawyer as a citizen has a right to criticize such officials publicly,[9] he should be certain of the merit of his complaint, use appropriate language, and avoid petty criticisms, for unrestrained and intemperate statements tend to lessen public confidence in

5. *"Rule 14. . . .* A member of the State Bar shall not communicate with, or appear before, a public officer, board, committee or body, in his professional capacity, without first disclosing that he is an attorney representing interests that may be affected by action of such officer, board, committee or body." Cal.Business and Professions Code § 6076 (West 1962).

6. See ABA Canon 2.

"Lawyers are better able than laymen to appraise accurately the qualifications of candidates for judicial office. It is proper that they should make that appraisal known to the voters in a proper and dignified manner. A lawyer may with propriety endorse a candidate for judicial office and seek like endorsement from other lawyers. But the lawyer who endorses a judicial candidate or seeks that endorsement from other lawyers should be actuated by a sincere belief in the superior qualifications of the candidate for judicial service and not by personal or selfish motives; and a lawyer should not use or attempt to use the power or prestige of the judicial office to secure such endorsement. On the other hand, the lawyer whose endorsement is sought, if he believes the candidate lacks the essential qualifications for the office or believes the opposing candidate is better qualified, should have the courage and moral stamina to refuse the request for endorsement." *ABA Opinion* 189 (1938).

7. "[W]e are of the opinion that, whenever a candidate for judicial office merits the endorsement and support of lawyers, the lawyers may make financial contributions toward the campaign if its cost, when reasonably conducted, exceeds that which the candidate would be expected to bear personally." *ABA Opinion* 226 (1941).

8. See ABA Canon 1.

9. "Citizens have a right under our constitutional system to criticize governmental officials and agencies. Courts are not, and should not be, immune to such criticism." Konigsberg v. State Bar of California, 353 U.S. 252, 269 (1957).

our legal system.[10] Criticisms motivated by reasons other than a desire to improve the legal system are not justified.

EC 8–7   Since lawyers are a vital part of the legal system, they should be persons of integrity, of professional skill, and of dedication to the improvement of the system. Thus a lawyer should aid in establishing, as well as enforcing, standards of conduct adequate to protect the public by insuring that those who practice law are qualified to do so.

EC 8–8   Lawyers often serve as legislators or as holders of other public offices. This is highly desirable, as lawyers are uniquely qualified to make significant contributions to the improvement of the legal system. A lawyer who is a public officer, whether full or part-time, should not engage in activities in which his personal or professional interests are or foreseeably may be in conflict with his official duties.[11]

EC 8–9   The advancement of our legal system is of vital importance in maintaining the rule of law and in facilitating orderly changes; therefore, lawyers should encourage, and should aid in making, needed changes and improvements.

DISCIPLINARY RULES

DR 8–101   Action as a Public Official.

(A)   A lawyer who holds public office shall not:

> **(1)   Use his public position to obtain, or attempt to obtain, a special advantage in legislative matters for himself or for a client under circumstances where he knows or it is obvi-**

10.   "[E]very lawyer, worthy of respect, realizes that public confidence in our courts is the cornerstone of our governmental structure, and will refrain from unjustified attack on the character of the judges, while recognizing the duty to denounce and expose a corrupt or dishonest judge." Kentucky State Bar Ass'n v. Lewis, 282 S.W.2d 321, 326 (Ky.1955).

"We should be the last to deny that Mr. Meeker has the right to uphold the honor of the profession and to expose without fear or favor corrupt or dishonest conduct in the profession, whether the conduct be that of a judge or not.... However, this Canon [29] does not permit one to make charges which are false and untrue and unfounded in fact. When one's fancy leads him to make false charges, attacking the character and integrity of others, he does so at his peril. He should not do so without adequate proof of his charges and he is certainly not authorized to make careless, untruthful and vile charges against his professional brethren." In re Meeker, 76 N.M. 354, 364–65, 414 P.2d 862, 869 (1966), appeal dismissed, 385 U.S. 449, 17 L.Ed.2d 510, 87 S.Ct. 613 (1967).

11.   "*Opinions 16, 30, 34, 77, 118* and *134* relate to *Canon 6*, and pass on questions concerning the propriety of the conduct of an attorney who is a public officer, in representing private interests adverse to those of the public body which he represents. The principle applied in those opinions is that an attorney holding public office should avoid all conduct which might lead the layman to conclude that the attorney is utilizing his public position to further his professional success or personal interests." *ABA Opinion 192* (1939).

"The next question is whether a lawyer-member of a legislative body may appear as counsel or co-counsel at hearings before a zoning board of appeals, or similar tribunal, created by the legislative group of which he is a member. We are of the opinion that he may practice before fact-finding officers, hearing bodies and commissioners, since under our views he may appear as counsel in the courts where his municipality is a party. Decisions made at such hearings are usually subject to administrative review by the courts upon the record there made. It would be inconsistent to say that a lawyer-member of a legislative body could not participate in a hearing at which the record is made, but could appear thereafter when the cause is heard by the courts on administrative review. This is subject to an important exception. He should not appear as counsel where the matter is subject to review by the legislative body of which he is a member.... We are of the opinion that where a lawyer does so appear there would be conflict of interests between his duty as an advocate for his client on the one hand and the obligation to his governmental unit on the other." In re Becker, 16 Ill.2d 488, 494–95, 158 N.E.2d 753, 756–57 (1959).

Cf. *ABA Opinions* 186 (1938), 136 (1935), 118 (1934), and 77 (1932).

ous that such action is not in the public interest.

(2) Use his public position to influence, or attempt to influence, a tribunal to act in favor of himself or of a client.

(3) Accept any thing of value from any person when the lawyer knows or it is obvious that the offer is for the purpose of influencing his action as a public official.

DR 8–102 Statements Concerning Judges and Other Adjudicatory Officers.[12]

(A) A lawyer shall not knowingly make false statements of fact concerning the qualifications of a candidate for election or appointment to a judicial office.

(B) A lawyer shall not knowingly make false accusations against a judge or other adjudicatory officer.

DR 8–103 Lawyer Candidate for Judicial Office.

(A) A lawyer who is a candidate for judicial office shall comply with the applicable provisions of Canon 7 of the Code of Judicial Conduct.

CANON 9

A Lawyer Should Avoid Even the Appearance of Professional Impropriety

ETHICAL CONSIDERATIONS

EC 9–1 Continuation of the American concept that we are to be governed by rules of law requires that the people have faith that justice can be obtained through our legal system.[1] A lawyer should promote public confidence in our system and in the legal profession.[2]

EC 9–2 Public confidence in law and lawyers may be eroded by irresponsible or improper conduct of a lawyer. On occasion, ethical conduct of a lawyer may appear to laymen to be unethical. In order to avoid misunderstandings and hence to maintain confidence, a lawyer should fully and promptly inform his client of material developments in the matters being handled for the client. While a lawyer should guard against otherwise proper conduct that has a tendency to diminish public confidence in the legal system or in the legal profession, his duty to clients or to the public should never be subordinate merely because the full discharge of his obligation may be misunderstood or may tend to subject him or the legal profession to criticism. When explicit ethical guidance does not exist, a lawyer should determine his conduct by acting in a manner that promotes public confidence in the integrity and efficiency of the legal system and the legal profession.[3]

EC 9–3 After a lawyer leaves judicial office or other public employment, he should not accept employment in connection with any matter in which he had substantial responsibility prior to his leaving, since to accept employment would give the appearance of impropriety even if none exists.[4]

EC 9–4 Because the very essence of the legal system is to provide procedures by which matters can be presented in an impartial manner so that they may be decided solely upon the merits, any state-

12. Cf. ABA Canons 1 and 2.

1. "Integrity is the very breath of justice. Confidence in our law, our courts, and in the administration of justice is our supreme interest. No practice must be permitted to prevail which invites towards the administration of justice a doubt or distrust of its integrity." Erwin M. Jennings Co. v. DiGenova, 107 Conn. 491, 499, 141 A. 866, 868 (1928).

2. "A lawyer should never be reluctant or too proud to answer unjustified criticism of his profession, of himself, or of his brother lawyer. He should guard the reputation of his profession and of his brothers as zealously as he guards his own." Rochelle & Payne, *The Struggle for Public Understanding*, 25 Texas B.J. 109, 162 (1962).

3. See ABA Canon 29.
4. See ABA Canon 36.

ment or suggestion by a lawyer that he can or would attempt to circumvent those procedures is detrimental to the legal system and tends to undermine public confidence in it.

EC 9-5 Separation of the funds of a client from those of his lawyer not only serves to protect the client but also avoids even the appearance of impropriety, and therefore commingling of such funds should be avoided.

EC 9-6 Every lawyer owes a solemn duty to uphold the integrity and honor of his profession; to encourage respect for the law and for the courts and the judges thereof; to observe the Code of Professional Responsibility; to act as a member of a learned profession, one dedicated to public service; to cooperate with his brother lawyers in supporting the organized bar through the devoting of his time, efforts, and financial support as his professional standing and ability reasonably permit; to conduct himself so as to

reflect credit on the legal profession and to inspire the confidence, respect, and trust of his clients and of the public; and to strive to avoid not only professional impropriety but also the appearance of impropriety.[5]

EC 9-7 A lawyer has an obligation to the public to participate in collective efforts of the bar to reimburse persons who have lost money or property as a result of the misappropriation or defalcation of another lawyer, and contribution to a clients' security fund is an acceptable method of meeting this obligation.

DISCIPLINARY RULES

DR 9-101 Avoiding Even the Appearance of Impropriety.[6]

(A) A lawyer shall not accept private employment in a matter upon the merits of which he has acted in a judicial capacity.[7]

---

5. "As said in Opinion 49 of the Committee on Professional Ethics and Grievances of the American Bar Association, page 134: 'An attorney should not only avoid impropriety but should avoid the appearance of impropriety.'" State ex rel. Nebraska State Bar Ass'n v. Richards, 165 Neb. 80, 93, 84 N.W.2d 136, 145 (1957).

"It would also be preferable that such contribution [to the campaign of a candidate for judicial office] be made to a campaign committee rather than to the candidate personally. In so doing, possible appearances of impropriety would be reduced to a minimum." *ABA Opinion* 226 (1941).

"The lawyer assumes high duties, and has imposed upon him grave responsibilities. He may be the means of much good or much mischief. Interests of vast magnitude are entrusted to him; confidence is reposed in him; life, liberty, character and property should be protected by him. He should guard, with jealous watchfulness, his own reputation, as well as that of his profession." People ex rel. Cutler v. Ford, 54 Ill. 520, 522 (1870), and also quoted in State Board of Law Examiners v. Sheldon, 43 Wyo. 522, 526, 7 P.2d 226, 227 (1932).

See *ABA Opinion* 150 (1936).

6. Cf. Code of Professional Responsibility, EC 5-6.

7. See *ABA* Canon 36.

"It is the duty of the judge to rule on questions of law and evidence in misdemeanor cases and examinations in felony cases. That duty calls for impartial and uninfluenced judgment, regardless of the effect on those immediately involved or others who may, directly or indirectly, be affected. Discharge of that duty might be greatly interfered with if the judge, in another capacity, were permitted to hold himself out to employment by those who are to be, or who may be, brought to trial in felony cases, even though he did not conduct the examination. His private interests as a lawyer in building up his clientele, his duty as such zealously to espouse the cause of his private clients and to defend against charges of crime brought by law-enforcement agencies of which he is a part, might prevent, or even destroy, that unbiased judicial judgment which is so essential in the administration of justice.

"In our opinion, acceptance of a judgeship with the duties of conducting misdemeanor trials, and examinations in felony cases to determine whether those accused should be bound over for trial in a higher court, ethically bars the judge from acting as attorney for the defendants upon such trial, whether they were examined by him or by some other judge. Such a practice would not only diminish public confidence in the administration of justice in both courts, but would produce serious conflict be-

(B) A lawyer shall not accept private employment in a matter in which he had substantial responsibility while he was a public employee.[8]

(C) A lawyer shall not state or imply that he is able to influence improperly or upon irrelevant grounds any tribunal, legislative body,[9] or public official.

DR 9–102 Preserving Identity of Funds and Property of a Client.[10]

(A) All funds of clients paid to a lawyer or law firm, other than advances for costs and expenses, shall be deposited in one or more identifiable bank accounts maintained in the state in which the law office is situated and no funds belonging to the lawyer or law firm shall be deposited therein except as follows:

(1) Funds reasonably sufficient to pay bank charges may be deposited therein.

(2) Funds belonging in part to a client and in part presently or potentially to the lawyer or law firm must be deposited therein, but the portion belonging to the lawyer or law firm may be withdrawn when due unless the right of the lawyer or law firm to receive it is disputed by the client, in which event the disputed portion shall not be withdrawn until the dispute is finally resolved.

(B) A lawyer shall:

(1) Promptly notify a client of the receipt of his funds, securities, or other properties.

tween the private interests of the judge as a lawyer, and of his clients, and his duties as a judge in adjudicating important phases of criminal processes in other cases. The public and private duties would be incompatible. The prestige of the judicial office would be diverted to private benefit, and the judicial office would be demeaned thereby." *ABA Opinion* 242 (1942).

"A lawyer, who has previously occupied a judicial position or acted in a judicial capacity, should refrain from accepting employment in any matter involving the same facts as were involved in any specific question which he acted upon in a judicial capacity and, for the same reasons, should also refrain from accepting any employment which might reasonably appear to involve the same facts." *ABA Opinion* 49 (1931).

See *ABA Opinion* 110 (1934).

8. See *ABA Opinions* 135 (1935) and 134 (1935); cf. ABA Canon 36 and *ABA Opinions* 39 (1931) and 26 (1930). But see *ABA Opinion* 37 (1931).

9. "[A statement by a governmental department or agency with regard to a lawyer resigning from its staff that includes a laudation of his legal ability] carries implications, probably not founded in fact, that the lawyer's acquaintance and previous relations with the personnel of the administrative agencies of the government place him in an advantageous position in practicing before such agencies. So to imply would not only represent what probably

is untrue, but would be highly reprehensible." *ABA Opinion* 184 (1938).

10. See ABA Canon 11.

"*Rule 9*.... A member of the State Bar shall not commingle the money or other property of a client with his own; and he shall promptly report to the client the receipt by him of all money and other property belonging to such client. Unless the client otherwise directs in writing, he shall promptly deposit his client's funds in a bank or trust company ... in a bank account separate from his own account and clearly designated as 'Clients' Funds Account' or 'Trust Funds Account' or words of similar import. Unless the client otherwise directs in writing, securities of a client in bearer form shall be kept by the attorney in a safe deposit box at a bank or trust company, ... which safe deposit box shall be clearly designated as 'Clients' Account' or 'Trust Account' or words of similar import, and be separate from the attorney's own safe deposit box." Cal.Business and Professions Code § 6076 (West 1962).

"[C]ommingling is committed when a client's money is intermingled with that of his attorney and its separate identity lost so that it may be used for the attorney's personal expenses or subjected to claims of his creditors.... The rule against commingling was adopted to provide against the probability in some cases, the possibility in many cases, and the danger in all cases that such commingling will result in the loss of clients' money." Black v. State Bar, 57 Cal.2d 219, 225–26, 368 P.2d 118, 122, 18 Cal.Rptr. 518, 522 (1962).

(2) Identify and label securities and properties of a client promptly upon receipt and place them in a safe deposit box or other place of safekeeping as soon as practicable.

(3) Maintain complete records of all funds, securities, and other properties of a client coming into the possession of the lawyer and render appropriate accounts to his client regarding them.

(4) Promptly pay or deliver to the client as requested by a client the funds, securities, or other properties in the possession of the lawyer which the client is entitled to receive.

DEFINITIONS*

As used in the Disciplinary Rules of the Code of Professional Responsibility:

(1) "Differing interests" include every interest that will adversely affect either the judgment or the loyalty of a lawyer to a client, whether it be a conflicting, inconsistent, diverse, or other interest.

(2) "Law firm" includes a professional legal corporation.

(3) "Person" includes a corporation, an association, a trust, a partnership, and any other organization or legal entity.

(4) "Professional legal corporation" means a corporation, or an association treated as a corporation, authorized by law to practice law for profit.

(5) "State" includes the District of Columbia, Puerto Rico, and other federal territories and possessions.

(6) "Tribunal" includes all courts and all other adjudicatory bodies.

(7) "A Bar association" includes a bar association of specialists as referred to in DR 2–105(A)(1) or (3).

(8) "Qualified legal assistance organization" means an office or organization of one of the four types listed in DR 2–103(D)(1)–(4), inclusive that meets all the requirements thereof.

* "Confidence" and "secret" are defined in DR 4–101(A).

INDEX TO MODEL CODE

A

ABA CODE

Advertising,   EC 2–2, 2–6 to 2–15, DR 2–101, 2–102(A)—Continued
  Clients, regular, DR 2–101(B)(16)
  Commercial publicity, EC 2–8 to 2–10, DR 2–101, 2–102(A)
  Compensation for, EC 2–8, DR 2–101(B), (I), 2–103(B)
  Credit arrangements, EC 2–8, DR 2–101(B)(18)
  Deceptive, EC 2–9, DR 2–101(A)
  Display, DR 2–101(B)
  Fees, EC 2–8, DR 2–101(B)(18), (20), (25), (E), (F), (G)
      Consultation, DR 2–101(B)(20)
      Contingent, rates, DR 2–101(B)(22)
      Credit arrangements, DR 2–101(B)(18)
      Estimate, DR 2–101(B)(21), (23), (24), (25)
      Fixed, for specific services, DR 2–101(B)(25)
      Hourly rate, DR 2–101(B)(24)
      Schedule, DR 2–101(B)(23)
  Foreign language, fluency in, EC 2–8, DR 2–101(B)(14)
  Jurisdictional limitations of members of firm, required notice of, DR 2–102(D)
  Justification for, EC 2–2, 2–7, 2–8
  Law lists, EC 2–8
  Law office establishment, DR 2–102(A)(2)
  Law office, identification of, DR 2–102(A)(3)
  Legal directories, EC 2–8
  Legal documents, DR 2–101(H)(4)
  Legal notices, DR 2–101(B)(2)
  Legal publications, DR 2–101(B)(8), (H)(5)
  Letterheads,
      Of clients, DR 2–102(A)(4)
      Of law firm, DR 2–102(A)(4)
      Of lawyer, DR 2–102(A)(4), 2–102(B)
  Limited practice, EC 2–7, 2–8, 2–14, DR 2–101(B)(2), 2–105(A)(2)
  Magazine, EC 2–8, DR 2–101
  Memberships,
      Bar association, DR 2–101(B)(10)
      Legal fraternities and societies, DR 2–101(B)(11)
      Scientific, professional and technical associations, DR 2–101(B)(11)
  Military service, DR 2–101(B)(7)
  Name. *See* Name, use of
  Newspaper, EC 2–8, DR 2–101
  Office,
      Establishment, DR 2–102(A)(2)
      Identification of, DR 2–101(B)(1), 2–102(A)(3)
  Office address change, DR 2–102(A)(2)
  Office building directory, DR 2–102(A)(3)
  Office hours, EC 2–8, DR 2–101(B)(19)
  Office sign, DR 2–102(A)(3)
  Political, DR 2–101(H)(1)
  Prepaid or group service programs, participation in, DR 2–101(17)
  Public notices, DR 2–101(H)(2)
  Public office, DR 2–101(B)(6)
  Quality of service, representation concerning, EC 2–9
  Radio, EC 2–8, DR 2–101(B), (D), (I)
  References, bank, DR 2–101(B)(15)
  Regulation, reasons for, EC 2–2, 2–6 to 2–13
  Rules, change in, EC 2–10, DR 2–101(C)
  Schools and degrees, DR 2–101(B)(5)
  Self-laudation, EC 2–8, 2–101(A)
  Sign, DR 2–102(A)(3)
  Specialization, EC 2–8, 2–14, DR 2–101(B)(2), 2–105
  Teaching positions, DR 2–101(B)(9)
  Technical and professional licenses, DR 2–101(B)(12)
  Telephone directory, EC 2–8
  Television, EC 2–8, DR 2–101(B), (D), (I)

PROFESSIONAL RESPONSIBILITY

Advertising, EC 2–2, 2–6 to 2–15, DR 2–101, 2–102(A)—Continued
   Textbook, DR 2–101(H)(5)
   Trade names, EC 2–11, DR 2–102(A)(4)
   Treatises, DR 2–101(H)(5)

Advice by lawyer to secure legal services, EC 2–3 to 2–5, 7–18, DR 2–104, 7–104(A)(2)
   Client, former or regular, EC 2–4, DR 2–104(A)(1)
   Close friend, EC 2–4, DR 2–104(A)(1)
   Employment resulting from, EC 2–4, 2–104
   Motivation, effect of, EC 2–4
   One with adverse interest, EC 7–18, DR 7–104(A)(2)
   Other laymen parties to class action, DR 2–104(A)(5)
   Relative, EC 2–4, DR 2–104(A)(1)
   Volunteered, EC 2–3, 2–4, DR 2–104
   Within permissible legal service programs, DR 2–103(D), 2–104(A)(3)

Advocacy, professional, Canon 7

Aiding unauthorized practice of law, EC 3–8, DR 3–101

Ambulance chasing. See Recommendation of professional employment

Announcement card. See Advertising, cards

Appeal, duty to handle, EC 2–31

Appearance of impropriety, avoiding, EC 5–6, 9–2, 9–3, 9–5, 9–6, DR 9–101.

Appearance of lawyer. See Administrative agencies and tribunals, representation of client before; Courts, representation of client before; Legislature, representation of client before; Witness, lawyer acting as

Application for bar admission. See Admission to practice

Arbitrator, lawyer as, EC 5–20

Argument,
   Before administrative agency, EC 7–15
   Before jury, EC 7–24, 7–25, 7–37, DR 7–102(A), 7–106(C)
   Before legislature, EC 7–16, 7–17
   Before tribunal, EC 7–19 to 7–25, DR 7–102(A), 7–106

Associates of lawyer, duty to control, EC 1–4, 3–8, 3–9, 4–2, 4–5, 6–2, DR 2–103, 4–101(D), 7–107(J)

Association of counsel,
   See also Co-counsel; Division of legal fees
   Client's consent, requirement of, EC 2–22
   Client's suggestion of, EC 5–10, 5–11
   Lawyer's suggestion of, EC 5–10, 5–11, 6–3, DR 6–101(A)(1)

Assumed name. See Name, use of, assumed name

Attempts to exert personal influence on tribunal, EC 7–24, 7–29, 7–34 to 7–36, DR 7–110, 8–101(A)(2)

Attorney-client privilege. DR 1–103, EC 3–3, Canon 4, DR 7–101(B)(1), 7–102(B)(1)
   See also Confidences of client; Secrets of client

Attorney's lien. See Fee for legal services, collection of

Availability of counsel, EC 2–1, 2–7, 2–24 to 2–33

B

Bank accounts for clients' funds, EC 9–5, DR 9–102(A)

Bank charges on clients' accounts, EC 9–5, DR 9–102(A)(1)

257

Bar applicant,
> *See also* Admission to practice
> Bar examiners, assisting, EC 1–2, 1–3, DR 1–101(B)

Bar associations,
> Advertising, DR 2–101(B)(10)
> Definitions, (7)
> Disciplinary authorities, assisting, EC 1–4, DR 1–103
> Educational activities, EC 6–2
> Lawyer referral service, DR 2–103(C)(1), (D)(3)
> Legal service programs, DR 2–103(D)(1)(d)
> Requesting lawyer's representation of individual, EC 2–29

Barratry. See Advice by lawyer to secure legal services; Recommendation of professional employment

Bequest by client to lawyer,   EC 5–5

Best efforts. See Zeal

Bounds of law,
> Difficulty of ascertaining, EC 7–2 to 7–6
> Duty to observe, EC 7–1, DR 7–102

Bribes. See Gifts to tribunal officer or employee by lawyer

Building directory. See Advertising, building directory

Business card. See Advertising, cards, professional

Business relations with clients,   EC 5–3 to 5–7, DR 5–104

C

Calling card. See Advertising, cards, professional

Candidate. See Political activity

Canons, purpose of, preliminary statement

Card. See Advertising, cards

Change of association. See Advertising, announcement of change of association

Change of firm name. See Advertising, announcement of change of firm name

Change of office address. See Advertising, announcement of change of office

Character requirements,   Canon 1, EC 1–3

Circumvention of disciplinary rule,   DR 1–102(A)(2)

Class action. See Advice by lawyer to secure legal services

Clients,
> *See also* Employment; Adverse effect on professional judgment; Fee for legal services; Indigents, representation of; Mental competence of client; Unpopular party, representation of
> Appearance as witness for, EC 5–9, 5–10, DR 5–101(B), 5–102
> Attorney-client privilege, EC 3–3, Canon 4
> Commingling of funds of, EC 9–5, DR 9–102
>> Confidences of, Canon 4
>> Counseling, EC 7–3, 7–5 to 7–9, 7–12, DR 7–102(A)(7), (B)(1), 7–106(A), 7–109(B)
>> Decisions of, EC 5–12, 7–7, 7–8, 7–12
>> Property, protection of, DR 9–102
>> Secrets of, EC 3–3, Canon 4

PROFESSIONAL RESPONSIBILITY

Co-counsel,
> *See also* Association of counsel
> Disagreements with, EC 5–12
> Division of fee with, DR 2–107(A)
> Inability to work with, DR 2–110(C)(3)

Commercial publicity. See Advertising, commercial publicity

Commingling of funds,   EC 9–5, DR 9–102

Communications with,
> Judicial officers, EC 7–34, 7–35, 7–36, DR 7–110(B)
> Jurors, EC 7–29 to 7–32, DR 7–108
> One of adverse interests, EC 7–18, DR 7–104
> Opposing party, EC 7–21, DR 7–104
> Veniremen, EC 7–29 to 7–32, DR 7–108
> Witnesses, EC 7–27, 7–28, DR 7–109

Compensation for recommendation of employment, prohibition against,   EC 2–8, DR 2–103(B)

Competence, mental. See Mental competence of bar applicant; Mental competence of client, effect on representation; Mental competence of lawyer

Competence, professional,   EC 2–30, Canon 6

Confidences of client,   EC 3–3, 3–4, Canon 4

Conflicting interests. See Adverse effect on professional judgment

Consent of client, requirement of,
> Acceptance of employment though interests conflict, EC 5–3, 5–14 to 5–20, DR 5–101(A), 5–104(A), 5–105(C)
> Acceptance of value from third person, EC 2–21, 5–22, 5–23, DR 5–107(A), (B)
> Advice requested from another lawyer, EC 4–2
> Aggregate settlement of claims, DR 5–106
> Association of lawyer, EC 2–22, DR 2–107(A)(1)
> Division of legal fees, DR 2–107(A)(1)
> Foregoing legal action, EC 7–7, 7–8, 7–9
> Multiple representation, EC 5–16, DR 5–105(C)
> Revelation of client's confidences and secrets, EC 4–2, 4–4, 4–5, DR 4–101(B)(3), (C)
> Use of client's confidences and secrets, EC 4–2, 4–5, DR 4–101(B)(3), (C)
> Withdrawal from employment, EC 2–32, DR 2–110(A)(2), (C)(5)

Consent of tribunal to lawyer's withdrawal, requirement of,   EC 2–32, DR 2–110(A)(1), (C)

Contingent fee, propriety of,
> In administrative actions, EC 2–20
> In civil actions, EC 2–20, 5–7, DR 5–103(A)(2)
> In criminal actions, EC 2–20, DR 2–106(C)
> In domestic relation actions, EC 2–20

Continuing legal education programs,   EC 1–2, 6–2

Contract of employment,
> Fee provisions, desirability of writing, EC 2–19
> Restrictive covenant in, DR 2–108

Controversy over fee, avoiding,   EC 2–19, 2–23

Corporation,
> Lawyer employed by, EC 5–18, 5–24, DR 5–107(C)
> Professional legal, EC 2–11, 5–24, DR 5–107(C), definitions (4)

Counsel, designation as,
> "General Counsel" designation, DR 2–102(A)(4)
> "Of Counsel" designation, DR 2–102(A)(4)

259

Counseling, client,   EC 7–3, 7–5 to 7–8, DR 7–102(A)(7), (B)(1), 7–106(A)

Courts,
>   *See also* Consent of tribunal to lawyer's withdrawal, requirement of; Evidence, conduct
>   regarding; Trial tactics
>   Appointment of lawyer as counsel, EC 2–29
>   Courtesy, known customs of, EC 7–36, 7–38, DR 7–106(C)(5), (6)
>   Personal influence, prohibitions against exerting, EC 7–34 to 7–36, DR 7–110
>   Representation of client before, Canon 7

Criminal conduct,
>   As basis for discipline of lawyer, EC 1–5, DR 1–102(A)(3), 7–102(A)

Criticism of judges and administrative officials,   EC 8–6, DR 8–102

Cross-examination of witness. See Witnesses, questioning of
>   Duty to reveal information as to,   EC 1–4, DR 1–103
>   Providing counsel for those accused of,   EC 2–26 to 2–31

D

De facto specialization,   EC 2–8, 2–14, DR 2–101(B)(2), 2–105(A)(2)

Deceased lawyer,
>   Payment to estate of, EC 3–8, DR 3–102(A)(1), (2)
>   Use of name by law firm, EC 2–11, DR 2–102(A)(4), (B)

Defender, public, working with. See Public defender office, working with

Defense against accusation by client, privilege to disclose confidences and secrets, DR 4–101(C)(4)

Defense of those accused of crime, EC 2–26 to 2–31

Definitions, following,   Canon 9
>   A bar association, definitions (7)
>   Differing interests, definitions (1), EC 5–14
>   Law firm, definitions (2)
>   Person, definitions (3)
>   Professional legal corporation, definitions (4)
>   Qualified legal assistance organization, definitions (8)
>   State, definitions (5)
>   Tribunal, definitions (6)

Delegation of tasks to lay employees,   EC 3–6

Desires of third parties, duty to avoid influence of,   EC 5–21 to 5–24, DR 5–107

Differing interests, definitions (1),   EC 5–14
>   *See also* Adverse effect on professional judgment

Disciplinary procedures, preliminary statement

Disciplinary rules, preliminary statement,
>   Application of, preliminary statement
>   Fair trial, requirement of, preliminary statement
>   Penalties imposed, preliminary statement
>   Purpose and function of, preliminary statement

Disciplinary sanction, preliminary statement

Discipline of lawyer, grounds for,
>   Advertising, improper, DR 1–102, 2–101(A), 2–102
>   Associates, failure to exercise reasonable care toward, DR 4–101(D)
>   Bribery of legal officials, DR 7–110(A)
>   Circumvention of disciplinary rule, DR 1–102(A)(2)
>   Clients' funds, mismanagement of, DR 9–102
>   Communication with adverse party, improper, DR 7–104

PROFESSIONAL RESPONSIBILITY

E

PROFESSIONAL RESPONSIBILITY

Fee for legal services,—Continued
Establishment of fee, use of client's confidences and secrets, DR 4–101(C)(4)
Excessive fee, EC 2–17, DR 2–106(A), (B)
Explanation of, EC 2–17, 2–18, 2–19
Illegal fee, prohibition against, DR 2–106(A)
Persons able to pay reasonable fee, EC 2–17 to 2–23
Persons only able to pay a partial fee, EC 2–16
Persons without means to pay a fee, EC 2–24, 2–25
Reasonable fee, EC 2–17, 2–18, DR 2–106(B)
Rebate, propriety of accepting, EC 2–21, 22, DR 2–107, 5–107(A)
Refund of unearned portion to client, EC 2–32, DR 2–110(A)(3)

Fee of lawyer referral service, propriety of paying,   DR 2–103(C)(1)

Felony.   See Criminal conduct; Discipline of lawyer, grounds for, illegal conduct

Firm name.   See Name, use of, firm name

Framework of law.   See Bounds of law

Fraud, duty to reveal, EC 8–5, DR 7–102(B)

Frivolous position avoiding, EC 7–4, DR 7–102(A)(1), (2), 7–106(C)(1)

Funds of client, protection of, EC 9–5, DR 9–102

Future conduct of client, counseling as to.   See Clients, counseling

G

"General counsel" designation,   DR 2–102(A)(4)

Gift to lawyer by client,   EC 5–5

Gifts to tribunal officer or employee by lawyer,   EC 7–34, 7–110(A)

Government, employment in,
Civil cases, EC 7–14
Criminal cases, EC 7–11, 7–13, 7–14, DR 7–103
Name in partnership name, EC 2–12, DR 2–102(B)
Retirement from government service, EC 9–3, DR 9–101(B)

Government legal assistance agencies, working with,   DR 2–103(C)(2), (D)(1)(c)

Grievance committee.   See Bar applicant, disciplinary authority, assisting

Guaranteeing payment of client's costs and expenses,   EC 5–8, DR 5–103(B)

H

Harassment, duty to avoid litigation involving,   EC 2–30, DR 2–109(A)(1), 2–110(B)(1), 7–102(A)(1)

Holding out,
As being engaged in both law and another field, DR 2–102(E)
As limiting practice, EC 2–8, 2–14, DR 2–101(B)(2), 2–105
As partnership, EC 2–13, DR 2–102(C)
As specialist, EC 2–8, 2–14, DR 2–101(B)(2), 2–105

I

Identity of client, duty to reveal,   EC 7–15, 7–16, 8–4, 8–5, DR 7–106(B)(2)

Illegal conduct, as cause for discipline,   EC 1–5, 7–26, DR 1–102(A)(3), 7–102(A)

Impartiality of tribunal, aiding in the,   EC 7–34, 7–35, DR 7–110

Improper influences,
Gift or loan to judicial officer, EC 7–34, DR 7–110(A)
On judgment of lawyer. *See* Adverse effect on professional judgment

J

Jury,—Continued
    Misconduct toward, EC 7–30, 7–31, DR 7–108(E), (G)
    Questioning members of after their dismissal, EC 7–29, DR 7–108(D)

K

Knowledge of intended crime, revealing,   DR 4–101(C)(3)

L

Law firm, definitions (2)

Law lists. See Advertising law lists

Law office. See Partnership

Law school, working with legal aid office or public defender office sponsored by, DR 2–103(D)(1)(a)

Lawyer-client privilege. See Attorney-client privilege

Lawyer referral services,   EC 2–15
    Fee for listing, propriety of paying, DR 2–103(C)(1)
    Listing of type referrals accepted, propriety of, DR 2–105(A)(2)
    Request for referrals, propriety of, DR 2–103(C)(1), (D)
    Working with, DR 2–103(C), (D)

Laypersons,
    See also Unauthorized practice of law,
    Need to legal services, EC 2–1 to 2–3, 2–6 to 2–8, 3–3, DR 2–104
    Recognition of legal problems, need to improve, EC 2–1 to 2–3, 8–3
    Selection of lawyer, need to facilitate, EC 2–7 to 2–10, 8–3

Legal aid offices, working with,   EC 2–25, DR 2–103(D)(1)

Legal corporation. See Professional legal corporation

Legal directory. See Advertising, law lists

Legal documents of clients, duty to safeguard,   EC 4–2, 4–3

Legal education programs. See Continuing legal education programs

Legal problems, recognition of by laymen,   EC 2–1 to 2–3, 8–3, DR 2–104

Legal system, duty to improve,   Canon 8

Legislature,
    Improper influence upon, EC 9–2, 9–3, 9–4, DR 8–101(A)(1), 9–101(B), (C)
    Representation of client before, EC 7–16, 7–17, 8–4, 8–5
    Serving as member of, EC 8–8, DR 8–101

Letterhead. See Advertising, letterheads

Liability to client, limiting,   EC 6–6, DR 6–102

Licensing of lawyers,
    As evidence of competence, EC 6–3
    Control of, EC 3–1, 3–3 to 3–6, 3–9, DR 3–101
    Modernization of, EC 3–5, 3–9, 8–3

Liens, attorneys',   EC 5–7, DR 5–103(A)(1)

Limited practice, holding out as having,   EC 2–8, 2–14, DR 2–101(B)(2), 2–105(A)(2)

Litigation,
    Acquiring an interest in, EC 5–7, 5–8, DR 5–103
    Expenses of, advancing or guaranteeing payment of, EC 5–7, 5–8, DR 5–103(B)

M

N

Name, use of,—Continued
  Proper for law firm, EC 2–11, DR 2–102(B)
  Proper for lawyer in law practice, EC 2–11, DR 2–102(B)
  Retired partner, EC 2–11, DR 2–102(A)(4), (B)
  Trade name, EC 2–11, DR 2–102(B)
  Withdrawn partner's, EC 2–11, 2–12, DR 2–102(B)

Need for legal services, suggestion of. See Advice by lawyer to secure legal services

Negligence of lawyer, Canon 6

Negotiations with opposite party, EC 7–18, 7–20, DR 7–104, 7–105

Neighborhood law offices, working with, EC 2–6, 2–7, 2–25, DR 2–103(D)(1)(b)

Newspapers,
  Advertising in, EC 2–8 to 2–10, DR 2–101(A) to (C), (E), (F), (I)
  News releases in, during or pending trial, EC 7–33, DR 7–107
  News stories in, DR 2–101(I)

Non-meritorious position, duty to avoid, EC 7–4, 7–5, 7–14, DR 2–109, 2–110(B)(1), 7–102(A)(1), (2), 7–103(A), 7–106(C)(1)

Non-profit organization, legal aid services of, EC 2–24, 2–25, DR 2–103(D)(1), (4)(a), 2–104(A)(2), (3)

Notices. See Advertising

O

Objectives of client, duty to seek, EC 7–1, 7–10, DR 7–101(A)(1), 7–102

"Of Counsel" designation, DR 2–102(A)(4)

Offensive tactics by lawyer, EC 7–4, 7–5, 7–10, DR 7–101, 7–102, 7–104, 7–105

Office building directory. See Advertising, building directory

Office sign, DR 2–102(A)(3)

Opposing counsel, EC 5–9, 7–20, 7–23, 7–35, 7–37, 7–38, DR 7–101(A)(1), 7–104(A)(1), 7–106(C)(5), 7–110(B)(2), (3)

Opposing party, communications with, EC 7–18, DR 7–104

P

Partnership,
  Advertising. *See* Advertising
  Conflicts of interest, DR 5–105(D)
  Deceased member,
    Payments to estate of, EC 3–8, DR 3–102(A)(1), (2)
    Use of name, EC 2–11, DR 2–102(A)(4), (B)
  Dissolved, use of name of, EC 2–11 to 2–13, DR 2–102(A)(4), (B), (C)
  Holding out as, falsely, EC 2–13, DR 2–102(B), (C)
  Imputed disability of partner and associates, DR 5–105(D)
  Layperson, partnership with, EC 3–8, DR 3–103
  Members licensed in different jurisdictions, DR 2–102(D)
  Name, EC 2–11, 2–12, 2–13, DR 2–102(B)
  Nonexistent, holding out falsely, EC 2–13, DR 2–102(B), (C)

PROFESSIONAL RESPONSIBILITY

Patent practitioner,   EC 2–14, DR 2–105(A)(1)

Payment to obtain recommendation of employment, prohibition against,   EC 2–8, DR 2–103(B), (D)

Pending litigation, discussion of in media,   EC 7–33, DR 7–107

Perjury,   EC 7–5, 7–6, 7–26, 7–28, DR 7–102(A)(4), (6), (7), 7–102(B)

Person, definitions (3)

Personal interests of lawyer. See Adverse effect on professional judgment, interests of lawyer

Personal opinion of client's cause,   EC 2–27 to 2–30, 7–24, DR 7–106(C)(4)

Phone directory, listing in. See Advertising, telephone directory

Political activity,   EC 8–6, 8–8, DR 2–101(H)(1), 8–101, 8–102, 8–103

Political considerations in selection of judges,   EC 8–6, DR 8–103

Potentially differing interest. See Adverse effect on professional judgment

Prejudice to right of client, duty to avoid,   EC 2–32, DR 2–110(A)(2), (C)(3), (C)(4), 7–101(A)(3)

Prepaid legal services,   EC 2–33, 5–23, DR 2–101(B)(17), 2–103(D)(4)

Preservation of confidences and secrets of client,   EC 3–3, Canon 4

Pressure on lawyer by third person. See Adverse effect on professional judgment of lawyer

Privilege, attorney-client. See Attorney-client privilege

Procedures, duty to help improve,   EC 8–1, 8–2, 8–9

Professional card of lawyer. See Advertising cards, professional

Professional impropriety, avoiding appearance of,   EC 5–1, 5–6, Canon 9

Professional judgment, duty to protect independence of,   EC 2–33, Canon 5

Professional legal corporations,   EC 2–11, 5–24, DR 2–102(B)(C), 5–107(C), definitions (4)
    Partnership with, DR 2–102(C)

Professional notices. See Advertising

Professional status, responsibility not to mislead concerning,   EC 2–11 to 2–14, DR 2–102(B) to (D)

Profit-sharing with lay employees, authorization of,   EC 3–8, DR 3–102(A)(3)

Property of client, handling,   EC 9–5, DR 9–102

Prosecuting attorney, duty of,   EC 7–13, 7–14, DR 7–103

Public defender office, working with,   DR 2–103(C)(2), (D)(1)

Public employment, retirement from,   EC 9–3, DR 9–101(A), (B)

Public office, duty of holder,   EC 8–8, DR 8–101

Public opinion, irrelevant to acceptance of employment,   EC 2–26 to 2–29

Public prosecutor. See Prosecuting attorney, duty of

Publication of articles for lay press,   EC 2–2, 2–5, DR 2–104(A)(4)
    Publication rights of lawyer, relating to subject matter of employment, EC 5–4, DR 5–104(B)
    Publicity,
        Commercial. *See* Advertising, commercial publicity
        Trial. *See* Trial publicity

Q

Qualified legal assistance organization,   EC 2–33, DR 2–103(C)(2), (D), 2–104(A)(2), (3), definitions (8)

Quasi-judicial proceedings,   EC 7–15, 7–16, 8–4, DR 7–107(H)

R

Radio, broadcasting. See Advertising, radio

Reasonable fee. See Fee for legal services, amount of

Rebate, propriety of accepting,   EC 2–21, 2–22, 5–22, DR 2–107, 5–107

Recognition of legal problems, aiding laymen in,   EC 2–1 to 2–5, 8–3, DR 2–104

Recommendation of bar applicant, duty of lawyer to satisfy himself that applicant is qualified,   EC 1–3, DR 1–101(B)

Recommendation of professional employment,   EC 2–8, 2–15, DR 2–103

Records of funds, securities, and properties of clients,   EC 9–5, DR 9–102(B)(3)

Referral service. See Lawyer referral services

Refund of unearned fee when withdrawing, duty to give to client,   EC 2–32, DR 2–110(A)(3)

Regulation of legal profession,   EC 3–1, 3–3, 3–9, 8–3, 8–7, DR 3–101(B)

Rehabilitation of bar applicant or lawyer, recognition of,   EC 1–6

Representation of multiple clients. See Adverse effect on professional judgment, interests of other clients

Reputation of lawyer,   EC 2–6, 2–7

Requests for recommendation for employment,   EC 2–8, DR 2–103(C)

Requirements for bar admission,   EC 1–2, 1–6, DR 1–101(B)

Respect for law,   EC 1–5, 9–6

Restrictive covenant,   DR 2–108

Retention of employment. See Employment

Retirement,
        See also Name, use of, retired partner
    From judicial office, EC 9–3, DR 9–101(A)
    From public employment, EC 9–3, DR 9–101(B)
    Plan for laymen employees', EC 3–8, DR 3–102(A)(3)

Revealing of confidences, Canon 4

Revealing of secrets, Canon 4

Revealing to tribunal,
    Jury misconduct, EC 7–32, DR 7–108(G)
    Representative capacity in which appearing, EC 7–15, 7–16, DR 7–106(B)(2)

Runner, prohibition against use of. See Recommendation of professional employment

PROFESSIONAL RESPONSIBILITY

S

Sanction for violating disciplinary rules, preliminary statement

Secrets of client, Canon 4

Selection of lawyer.   EC 2–6 to 2–15, DR 2–101 to 2–105

Selection of judges, duty of lawyers,   EC 8–6, DR 8–102

Self-interest of lawyer.   See Adverse effect on professional judgment, interests of lawyer

Self-representation, privilege of,   EC 3–7

Settlement agreement.   EC 7–7, DR 5–106

Solicitation of business.   See Advertising; Advice by lawyer to secure legal services; Recommendation of professional employment

Specialist, holding out as,   EC 2–8, 2–14, DR 2–101(B)(2), 2–105

Specialization,   EC 2–8, 2–14, DR 2–101(B)(2), 2–105
   Admiralty, EC 2–14
   Holding out as having, EC 2–8, 2–14, DR 2–101(B)(2), 2–105
   Patents, EC 2–14, DR 2–105(A)(1)
   Trademark, EC 2–14, DR 2–105(A)(1)

Speeches to lay groups,   EC 2–2, 2–5, DR 2–104(A)(4)

State, definitions (5)

State of mind of client, effect of in advising him,   EC 7–6, 7–11, 7–12

State's attorney.   See Prosecuting attorney

"Stirring up litigation."   See Advertising; Advice by lawyer to secure legal services; Recommendation of; professional employment

Stockholders of corporation, corporate counsel's allegiance to,   EC 5–18

Suggestion of need for legal services.   See Advice by lawyer to secure legal services

Suit to harass or maliciously harm another, duty to avoid,   EC 2–30, 7–10, 7–14, DR 2–109, 2–110(B)(1), 7–102(A)(1)

Suppression of evidence,   EC 7–27, DR 7–102(A)(3), 7–103(B), 7–106(C)(7), 7–109(A)

T

Technical and professional licenses.   See Advertising, technical and professional licenses

Telephone directory.   See Advertising, telephone directory

Television.   See Advertising, television

Termination of employment.   See Confidences of client; Employment, withdrawal from

Third persons, desires of.   See Adverse effect on professional judgment, desires of third persons

Threatening criminal process,   EC 7–21, DR 7–105

Trade name,   EC 2–11, DR 2–102(B)

Trademark practitioner,   EC 2–14, DR 2–105(A)(1)

Trial publicity,   EC 7–33, DR 7–107

Trial tactics,   EC 7–19 to 7–39, DR 7–101(A)(1), 7–102, 7–103(B), 7–105 to 7–110

Tribunal,
   Definitions (6)
   Representation of client before, Canon 7

Trustee, client naming lawyer as,   EC 5–6

U

Unauthorized practice of law,   Canon 3
> *See also* Division of legal fees, with laymen; Partnership, laypersons with
> Aiding a layman in the prohibited, EC 3–8, DR 3–101
> Distinguished from delegation of tasks to subprofessionals, EC 3–5, 3–6, DR 3–102(A)(3)
> Functional meaning of, EC 3–5, 3–9
> Self-representation by layman not included in, EC 3–7

Undignified conduct, duty to avoid,   EC 7–36 to 7–38, DR 7–106(C)(6)

Unions, lawyers as members of,   EC 5–13

Unlawful conduct, aiding client in,   EC 7–5, 7–6, DR 7–102(A)(6), (7), (B)(1)

Unpopular party, representation of,   EC 2–27, 2–29 to 2–31

Unreasonable fees. See Fee for legal services, amount of, excessive

Unsolicited advice. See Advice by lawyer to secure legal services

V

Varying interests of clients. See Adverse effect on professional judgment, interests of other clients

Veniremen. See Communications with, venireman; Jury

Violation of disciplinary rule as cause for discipline,   DR 1–102(A)(1), (2)

Violation of law as cause for discipline,   EC 1–5, 7–6, DR 1–102(A)(3), (A)(4), 7–102(A)(3) to (A)(8)

Voluntary gifts by client to lawyer,   EC 5–5

Volunteered advice to secure legal services. See Advice by lawyer to secure legal services

W

Waiver of position of client,   DR 7–101(B)(1)

Will of client, gift to lawyer in,   EC 5–5

Withdrawal. See Employment, withdrawal from

Witness,
> Communications with. *See* Communications with, witnesses
> Expert, EC 7–28, DR 7–109(C)(3)
> False testimony by, EC 7–26, 7–28, DR 7–102(A)(4), (B)(2)
> Lawyer acting as, EC 5–9, 5–10, DR 5–101(B), 5–102
> Member of lawyer's firm acting as, DR 5–101(B), 5–102
> Payment to, EC 7–28, DR 7–109(C)
> Questioning of, EC 7–25, DR 7–106(C)(2)
> Secreting of, EC 7–27, DR 7–109(B)

Writing for lay publication, avoiding appearance of giving general solution,   EC 2–2, 2–5, DR 2–104(4)

Z

RESTATEMENT OF LAW GOVERNING LAWYERS

In 1986 the American Law Institute ("ALI"), a prestigious group of practicing lawyers, judges, and academics, began drafting a *Restatement of the Law Governing Lawyers*. Unlike the ABA's Model Rules, the ALI has not proposed a code of regulations that it expects state courts to adopt as rules of court. Instead, it has drafted a series of principles, also called "black letter rules," followed by commentary and examples. Because the Restatement analyses and systematizes the law governing the practice of law, it goes beyond the ethics rules to cover other areas that affect the practice of law, such as tort doctrines relating to malpractice, vicarious liability, the work-product doctrine, the attorney-client evidentiary privilege, the agent-principal relationship, and related areas. The Restatement of the Law Governing Lawyers follows in the tradition of the other Restatements that the ALI has drafted over many years.

In 1998, the ALI completed this project and approved the Restatement, which it labeled "Restatement of the Law, Third," to signify that the American Law Institute is now working on a third major series of Restatements. The ALI published the final version of its Restatement in late 2000, which included various stylistic changes and a renumbering of most section numbers.

Following the Table of Contents is a *Conversion Table* of section numbers. This table lists the final and former section number for each section.

Table of Contents

Restatement of the Law (Third): The Law Governing Lawyers

CONVERSION TABLE – Tentative Drafts to Final Version
Numbers Shown are Section Numbers

Chapter I		Chapter III		Chapter V		Chapter VII	
Final	Former	Final	Former	Final	Former	Final	Former
1	1	34	46	68	118	105	165
2	2	35	47	69	119	106	166
3	3	36	48	70	120	107	167
4	4	37	49	71	121	108	168
5	5	38	50	72	122	109	169
6	6	39	51	73	123	110	170
7	7	40	52	74	124	111	171
8	8	41	53	75	125	112	172
9	10	42	54	76	126	113	173
10	11	43	55	77	127	114	174
11	12	44	56	78	128	115	175
12	13	45	57	79	129	116	176
13	14	46	58	80	130	117	177
		47	59	81	131	118	178
				82	132	119	179
Chapter II				83	133	120	180
Final	Former	**Chapter IV**		84	134A		
14	26	Final	Former	85	134B	**Chapter VIII**	
15	27	48	71	86	135	Final	Former
16	28	49	—	87	136	121	201
17	29	50	72	88	137	122	202
18	29A	51	73	89	138	123	203
19	30	52	74	90	139	124	204
20	31	53	75	91	140	125	206
21	32	54	76	92	141	126	207
22	33	55	76A	93	142	127	208
23	34	56	77			128	209
24	35	57	78	**Chapter VI**		129	210
25	37	58	79	Final	Former	130	211
26	38			94	151	131	212
27	39	**Chapter V**		95	152	132	213
28	40	Final	Former	96	155	133	214
29	41	59	111	97	156	134	215
30	42	60	112	98	157	135	216
31	43	61	113	99	158		
32	44	62	114	100	159		
33	45	63	115	101	161		
		64	116	102	162		
		65	117	103	163		
		66	117A	104	164		
		67	117B				

§ 1. Regulation of Lawyers—In General

Upon admission to the bar of any jurisdiction, a person becomes a lawyer and is subject to applicable law governing such matters as professional discipline, procedure and evidence, civil remedies, and criminal sanctions.

§ 2. Admission to Practice Law

In order to become a lawyer and qualify to practice law in a jurisdiction of admission, a prospective lawyer must comply with requirements of the jurisdiction relating to such matters as education, other demonstration of competence such as success in a bar examination, and character.

§ 3. Jurisdictional Scope of the Practice of Law by a Lawyer

A lawyer currently admitted to practice in a jurisdiction may provide legal services to a client:

> (1) at any place within the admitting jurisdiction;

> (2) before a tribunal or administrative agency of another jurisdiction or the federal government in compliance with requirements for temporary or regular admission to practice before that tribunal or agency; and

> (3) at a place within a jurisdiction in which the lawyer is not admitted to the extent that the lawyer's activities arise out of or are otherwise reasonably related to the lawyer's practice under Subsection (1) or (2).

§ 4. Unauthorized Practice by a Nonlawyer

A person not admitted to practice as a lawyer (see § 2) may not engage in the unauthorized practice of law, and a lawyer may not assist a person to do so.

§ 5. Professional Discipline

> (1) A lawyer is subject to professional discipline for violating any provision of an applicable lawyer code.

> (2) A lawyer is also subject to professional discipline under Subsection (1) for attempting to commit a violation, knowingly assisting or inducing another to do so, or knowingly doing so through the acts of another.

> (3) A lawyer who knows of another lawyer's violation of applicable rules of professional conduct raising a substantial question of the lawyer's honesty or trustworthiness or the lawyer's fitness as a lawyer in some other respect must report that information to appropriate disciplinary authorities.

§ 6. Judicial Remedies Available to a Client or Nonclient for Lawyer Wrongs

For a lawyer's breach of a duty owed to the lawyer's client or to a nonclient, judicial remedies may be available through judgment or order entered in accordance with the standards applicable to the remedy awarded, including standards concerning limitation of remedies. Judicial remedies include the following:

> (1) awarding a sum of money as damages;

279

(2) providing injunctive relief, including requiring specific performance of a contract or enjoining its nonperformance;

(3) requiring restoration of a specific thing or awarding a sum of money to prevent unjust enrichment;

(4) ordering cancellation or reformation of a contract, deed, or similar instrument;

(5) declaring the rights of the parties, such as determining that an obligation claimed by the lawyer to be owed to the lawyer is not enforceable;

(6) punishing the lawyer for contempt;

(7) enforcing an arbitration award;

(8) disqualifying a lawyer from a representation;

(9) forfeiting a lawyer's fee (see § 37);

(10) denying the admission of evidence wrongfully obtained;

(11) dismissing the claim or defense of a litigant represented by the lawyer;

(12) granting a new trial; and

(13) entering a procedural or other sanction.

§ 7. Judicial Remedies Available to a Lawyer for Client Wrongs

A lawyer may obtain a remedy based on a present or former client's breach of a duty to the lawyer if the remedy:

(1) is appropriate under applicable law governing the remedy; and

(2) does not put the lawyer in a position prohibited by an applicable lawyer code.

§ 8. Lawyer Criminal Offenses

The traditional and appropriate activities of a lawyer in representing a client in accordance with the requirements of the applicable lawyer code are relevant factors for the tribunal in assessing the propriety of the lawyer's conduct under the criminal law. In other respects, a lawyer is guilty of an offense for an act committed in the course of representing a client to the same extent and on the same basis as would a nonlawyer acting similarly.

§ 9. Law–Practice Organizations—In General

(1) A lawyer may practice as a solo practitioner, as an employee of another lawyer or law firm, or as a member of a law firm constituted as a partnership, professional corporation, or similar entity.

(2) A lawyer employed by an entity described in Subsection (1) is subject to applicable law governing the creation, operation, management, and dissolution of the entity.

(3) Absent an agreement with the firm providing a more permissive rule, a lawyer leaving a law firm may solicit firm clients:

    (a) prior to leaving the firm:

        (i) only with respect to firm clients on whose matters the lawyer is actively and substantially working; and

        (ii) only after the lawyer has adequately and timely informed the firm of the lawyer's intent to contact firm clients for that purpose; and

    (b) after ceasing employment in the firm, to the same extent as any other nonfirm lawyer.

§ 10. Limitations on Nonlawyer Involvement in a Law Firm

(1) A nonlawyer may not own any interest in a law firm, and a nonlawyer may not be empowered to or actually direct or control the professional activities of a lawyer in the firm.

(2) A lawyer may not form a partnership or other business enterprise with a nonlawyer if any of the activities of the enterprise consist of the practice of law.

(3) A lawyer or law firm may not share legal fees with a person not admitted to practice as a lawyer, except that:

    (a) an agreement by a lawyer with the lawyer's firm or another lawyer in the firm may provide for payment, over a reasonable period of time after the lawyer's death, to the lawyer's estate or to one or more specified persons;

    (b) a lawyer who undertakes to complete unfinished legal business of a deceased lawyer may pay to the estate of the deceased lawyer a portion of the total compensation that fairly represents services rendered by the deceased lawyer; and

    (c) a lawyer or law firm may include nonlawyer employees in a compensation or retirement plan, even though the plan is based in whole or in part on a profit-sharing arrangement.

§ 11. A Lawyer's Duty of Supervision

(1) A lawyer who is a partner in a law-firm partnership or a principal in a law firm organized as a corporation or similar entity is subject to professional discipline for failing to make reasonable efforts to ensure that the firm has in effect measures giving reasonable assurance that all lawyers in the firm conform to applicable lawyer-code requirements.

(2) A lawyer who has direct supervisory authority over another lawyer is subject to professional discipline for failing to make reasonable efforts to ensure that the other lawyer conforms to applicable lawyer-code requirements.

(3) A lawyer is subject to professional discipline for another lawyer's violation of the rules of professional conduct if:

(a) the lawyer orders or, with knowledge of the specific conduct, ratifies the conduct involved; or

(b) the lawyer is a partner or principal in the law firm, or has direct supervisory authority over the other lawyer, and knows of the conduct at a time when its consequences can be avoided or mitigated but fails to take reasonable remedial measures.

(4) With respect to a nonlawyer employee of a law firm, the lawyer is subject to professional discipline if either:

(a) the lawyer fails to make reasonable efforts to ensure:

(i) that the firm in which the lawyer practices has in effect measures giving reasonable assurance that the nonlawyer's conduct is compatible with the professional obligations of the lawyer; and

(ii) that conduct of a nonlawyer over whom the lawyer has direct supervisory authority is compatible with the professional obligations of the lawyer; or

(b) the nonlawyer's conduct would be a violation of the applicable lawyer code if engaged in by a lawyer, and

(i) the lawyer orders or, with knowledge of the specific conduct, ratifies the conduct; or

(ii) the lawyer is a partner or principal in the law firm, or has direct supervisory authority over the nonlawyer, and knows of the conduct at a time when its consequences can be avoided or mitigated but fails to take reasonable remedial measures.

§ 12.   Duty of a Lawyer Subject to Supervision

(1) For purposes of professional discipline, a lawyer must conform to the requirements of an applicable lawyer code even if the lawyer acted at the direction of another lawyer or other person.

(2) For purposes of professional discipline, a lawyer under the direct supervisory authority of another lawyer does not violate an applicable lawyer code by acting in accordance with the supervisory lawyer's direction based on a reasonable resolution of an arguable question of professional duty.

§ 13.   Restrictions on the Right to Practice Law

(1) A lawyer may not offer or enter into a law-firm agreement that restricts the right of the lawyer to practice law after terminating the relationship, except for a restriction incident to the lawyer's retirement from the practice of law.

(2) In settling a client claim, a lawyer may not offer or enter into an agreement that restricts the right of the lawyer to practice law, including the right to represent or take particular action on behalf of other clients.

§ 14. Formation of a Client–Lawyer Relationship

A relationship of client and lawyer arises when:

(1) a person manifests to a lawyer the person's intent that the lawyer provide legal services for the person; and either

(a) the lawyer manifests to the person consent to do so; or

(b) the lawyer fails to manifest lack of consent to do so, and the lawyer knows or reasonably should know that the person reasonably relies on the lawyer to provide the services; or

(2) a tribunal with power to do so appoints the lawyer to provide the services.

§ 15. A Lawyer's Duties to a Prospective Client

(1) When a person discusses with a lawyer the possibility of their forming a client-lawyer relationship for a matter and no such relationship ensues, the lawyer must:

(a) not subsequently use or disclose confidential information learned in the consultation, except to the extent permitted with respect to confidential information of a client or former client as stated in §§ 61–67;

(b) protect the person's property in the lawyer's custody as stated in §§ 44–46; and

(c) use reasonable care to the extent the lawyer provides the person legal services.

(2) A lawyer subject to Subsection (1) may not represent a client whose interests are materially adverse to those of a former prospective client in the same or a substantially related matter when the lawyer or another lawyer whose disqualification is imputed to the lawyer under §§ 123 and 124 has received from the prospective client confidential information that could be significantly harmful to the prospective client in the matter, except that such a representation is permissible if:

(a) (i) any personally prohibited lawyer takes reasonable steps to avoid exposure to confidential information other than information appropriate to determine whether to represent the prospective client, and (ii) such lawyer is screened as stated in § 124(2)(b) and (c); or

(b) both the affected client and the prospective client give informed consent to the representation under the limitations and conditions provided in § 122.

§ 16. A Lawyer's Duties to a Client—In General

To the extent consistent with the lawyer's other legal duties and subject to the other provisions of this Restatement, a lawyer must, in matters within the scope of the representation:

(1) proceed in a manner reasonably calculated to advance a client's lawful objectives, as defined by the client after consultation;

(2) act with reasonable competence and diligence;

(3) comply with obligations concerning the client's confidences and property, avoid impermissible conflicting interests, deal honestly with the client, and not employ advantages arising from the client-lawyer relationship in a manner adverse to the client; and

(4) fulfill valid contractual obligations to the client.

§ 17. A Client's Duties to a Lawyer

Subject to the other provisions of this Restatement, in matters covered by the representation a client must:

(1) compensate a lawyer for services and expenses as stated in Chapter 3;

(2) indemnify the lawyer for liability to which the client has exposed the lawyer without the lawyer's fault; and

(3) fulfill any valid contractual obligations to the lawyer.

§ 18. Client–Lawyer Contracts

(1) A contract between a lawyer and client concerning the client-lawyer relationship, including a contract modifying an existing contract, may be enforced by either party if the contract meets other applicable requirements, except that:

(a) if the contract or modification is made beyond a reasonable time after the lawyer has begun to represent the client in the matter (see § 38(1)), the client may avoid it unless the lawyer shows that the contract and the circumstances of its formation were fair and reasonable to the client; and

(b) if the contract is made after the lawyer has finished providing services, the client may avoid it if the client was not informed of facts needed to evaluate the appropriateness of the lawyer's compensation or other benefits conferred on the lawyer by the contract.

(2) A tribunal should construe a contract between client and lawyer as a reasonable person in the circumstances of the client would have construed it.

§ 19. Agreements Limiting Client or Lawyer Duties

(1) Subject to other requirements stated in this Restatement, a client and lawyer may agree to limit a duty that a lawyer would otherwise owe to the client if:

(a) the client is adequately informed and consents; and

(b) the terms of the limitation are reasonable in the circumstances.

(2) A lawyer may agree to waive a client's duty to pay or other duty owed to the lawyer.

§ 20. A Lawyer's Duty to Inform and Consult with a Client

(1) A lawyer must keep a client reasonably informed about the matter and must consult with a client to a reasonable extent concerning decisions to be made by the lawyer under §§ 21–23.

(2) A lawyer must promptly comply with a client's reasonable requests for information.

(3) A lawyer must notify a client of decisions to be made by the client under §§ 21–23 and must explain a matter to the extent reasonably necessary to permit the client to make informed decisions regarding the representation.

§ 21. Allocating the Authority to Decide Between a Client and a Lawyer

As between client and lawyer:

(1) A client and lawyer may agree which of them will make specified decisions, subject to the requirements stated in §§ 18, 19, 22, 23, and other provisions of this Restatement. The agreement may be superseded by another valid agreement.

(2) A client may instruct a lawyer during the representation, subject to the requirements stated in §§ 22, 23, and other provisions of this Restatement.

(3) Subject to Subsections (1) and (2) a lawyer may take any lawful measure within the scope of representation that is reasonably calculated to advance a client's objectives as defined by the client, consulting with the client as required by § 20.

(4) A client may ratify an act of a lawyer that was not previously authorized.

§ 22. Authority Reserved to a Client

(1) As between client and lawyer, subject to Subsection (2) and § 23, the following and comparable decisions are reserved to the client except when the client has validly authorized the lawyer to make the particular decision: whether and on what terms to settle a claim; how a criminal defendant should plead; whether a criminal defendant should waive jury trial; whether a criminal defendant should testify; and whether to appeal in a civil proceeding or criminal prosecution.

(2) A client may not validly authorize a lawyer to make the decisions described in Subsection (1) when other law (such as criminal-procedure rules governing pleas, jury-trial waiver, and defendant testimony) requires the client's personal participation or approval.

(3) Regardless of any contrary contract with a lawyer, a client may revoke a lawyer's authority to make the decisions described in Subsection (1).

§ 23. Authority Reserved to a Lawyer

As between client and lawyer, a lawyer retains authority that may not be overridden by a contract with or an instruction from the client:

(1) to refuse to perform, counsel, or assist future or ongoing acts in the representation that the lawyer reasonably believes to be unlawful;

(2) to make decisions or take actions in the representation that the lawyer reasonably believes to be required by law or an order of a tribunal.

§ 24. A Client with Diminished Capacity

(1) When a client's capacity to make adequately considered decisions in connection with the representation is diminished, whether because of minority, physical illness, mental disability, or other cause, the lawyer must, as far as reasonably possible, maintain a normal client-lawyer relationship with the client and act in the best interests of the client as stated in Subsection (2).

(2) A lawyer representing a client with diminished capacity as described in Subsection (1) and for whom no guardian or other representative is available to act, must, with respect to a matter within the scope of the representation, pursue the lawyer's reasonable view of the client's objectives or interests as the client would define them if able to make adequately considered decisions on the matter, even if the client expresses no wishes or gives contrary instructions.

(3) If a client with diminished capacity as described in Subsection (1) has a guardian or other person legally entitled to act for the client, the client's lawyer must treat that person as entitled to act with respect to the client's interests in the matter, unless:

(a) the lawyer represents the client in a matter against the interests of that person; or

(b) that person instructs the lawyer to act in a manner that the lawyer knows will violate the person's legal duties toward the client.

(4) A lawyer representing a client with diminished capacity as described in Subsection (1) may seek the appointment of a guardian or take other protective action within the scope of the representation when doing so is practical and will advance the client's objectives or interests, determined as stated in Subsection (2).

§ 25. Appearance Before a Tribunal

A lawyer who enters an appearance before a tribunal on behalf of a person is presumed to represent that person as a client. The presumption may be rebutted.

§ 26. A Lawyer's Actual Authority

A lawyer's act is considered to be that of a client in proceedings before a tribunal or in dealings with third persons when:

(1) the client has expressly or impliedly authorized the act;

(2) authority concerning the act is reserved to the lawyer as stated in § 23; or

(3) the client ratifies the act.

§ 27. A Lawyer's Apparent Authority

A lawyer's act is considered to be that of the client in proceedings before a tribunal or in dealings with a third person if the tribunal or third person reasonably assumes that the lawyer is authorized to do the act on the basis of the client's (and not the lawyer's) manifestations of such authorization.

§ 28. A Lawyer's Knowledge; Notification to a Lawyer; and Statements of a Lawyer

(1) Information imparted to a lawyer during and relating to the representation of a client is attributed to the client for the purpose of determining the client's rights and liabilities in matters in which the lawyer represents the client, unless those rights or liabilities require proof of the client's personal knowledge or intentions or the lawyer's legal duties preclude disclosure of the information to the client.

(2) Unless applicable law otherwise provides, a third person may give notification to a client, in a matter in which the client is represented by a lawyer, by giving notification to the client's lawyer, unless the third person knows of circumstances reasonably indicating that the lawyer's authority to receive notification has been abrogated.

(3) A lawyer's unprivileged statement is admissible in evidence against a client as if it were the client's statement if either:

(a) the client authorized the lawyer to make a statement concerning the subject; or

(b) the statement concerns a matter within the scope of the representation and was made by the lawyer during it.

§ 29. A Lawyer's Act or Advice as Mitigating or Avoiding a Client's Responsibility

(1) When a client's intent or mental state is in issue, a tribunal may consider otherwise admissible evidence of a lawyer's advice to the client.

(2) In deciding whether to impose a sanction on a person or to relieve a person from a criminal or civil ruling, default, or judgment, a tribunal may consider otherwise admissible evidence to prove or disprove that the lawyer who represented the person did so inadequately or contrary to the client's instructions.

§ 30. A Lawyer's Liability to a Third Person for Conduct on Behalf of a Client

(1) For improper conduct while representing a client, a lawyer is subject to professional discipline as stated in § 5, to civil liability as stated in Chapter 4, and to prosecution as provided in the criminal law (see § 7).

(2) Unless at the time of contracting the lawyer or third person disclaimed such liability, a lawyer is subject to liability to third persons on contracts the lawyer entered into on behalf of a client if:

>   (a) the client's existence or identity was not disclosed to the third person; or

>   (b) the contract is between the lawyer and a third person who provides goods or services used by lawyers and who, as the lawyer knows or reasonably should know, relies on the lawyer's credit.

(3) A lawyer is subject to liability to a third person for damages for loss proximately caused by the lawyer's acting without authority from a client under § 26 if:

>   (a) the lawyer tortiously misrepresents to the third person that the lawyer has authority to make a contract, conveyance, or affirmation on behalf of the client and the third person reasonably relies on the misrepresentation; or

>   (b) the lawyer purports to make a contract, conveyance, or affirmation on behalf of the client, unless the lawyer manifests that the lawyer does not warrant that the lawyer is authorized to act or the other party knows that the lawyer is not authorized to act.

§ 31. Termination of a Lawyer's Authority

(1) A lawyer must comply with applicable law requiring notice to or permission of a tribunal when terminating a representation and with an order of a tribunal requiring the representation to continue.

(2) Subject to Subsection (1) and § 33, a lawyer's actual authority to represent a client ends when:

>   (a) the client discharges the lawyer;

>   (b) the client dies or, in the case of a corporation or similar organization, loses its capacity to function as such;

>   (c) the lawyer withdraws;

>   (d) the lawyer dies or becomes physically or mentally incapable of providing representation, is disbarred or suspended from practicing law, or is ordered by a tribunal to cease representing a client; or

>   (e) the representation ends as provided by contract or because the lawyer has completed the contemplated services.

(3) A lawyer's apparent authority to act for a client with respect to another person ends when the other person knows or should know of facts

from which it can be reasonably inferred that the lawyer lacks actual authority, including knowledge of any event described in Subsection (2).

§ 32. Discharge by a Client and Withdrawal by a Lawyer

(1) Subject to Subsection (5), a client may discharge a lawyer at any time.

(2) Subject to Subsection (5), a lawyer may not represent a client or, where representation has commenced, must withdraw from the representation of a client if:

> (a) the representation will result in the lawyer's violating rules of professional conduct or other law;

> (b) the lawyer's physical or mental condition materially impairs the lawyer's ability to represent the client; or

> (c) the client discharges the lawyer.

(3) Subject to Subsections (4) and (5), a lawyer may withdraw from representing a client if:

> (a) withdrawal can be accomplished without material adverse effect on the interests of the client;

> (b) the lawyer reasonably believes withdrawal is required in circumstances stated in Subsection (2);

> (c) the client gives informed consent;

> (d) the client persists in a course of action involving the lawyer's services that the lawyer reasonably believes is criminal, fraudulent, or in breach of the client's fiduciary duty;

> (e) the lawyer reasonably believes the client has used or threatens to use the lawyer's services to perpetrate a crime or fraud;

> (f) the client insists on taking action that the lawyer considers repugnant or imprudent;

> (g) the client fails to fulfill a substantial financial or other obligation to the lawyer regarding the lawyer's services and the lawyer has given the client reasonable warning that the lawyer will withdraw unless the client fulfills the obligation;

> (h) the representation has been rendered unreasonably difficult by the client or by the irreparable breakdown of the client-lawyer relationship; or

> (i) other good cause for withdrawal exists.

(4) In the case of permissive withdrawal under Subsections (3)(f)–(i), a lawyer may not withdraw if the harm that withdrawal would cause significantly exceeds the harm to the lawyer or others in not withdrawing.

(5) Notwithstanding Subsections (1)–(4), a lawyer must comply with applicable law requiring notice to or permission of a tribunal when terminat-

ing a representation and with a valid order of a tribunal requiring the representation to continue.

§ 33. A Lawyer's Duties When a Representation Terminates

(1) In terminating a representation, a lawyer must take steps to the extent reasonably practicable to protect the client's interests, such as giving notice to the client of the termination, allowing time for employment of other counsel, surrendering papers and property to which the client is entitled, and refunding any advance payment of fee the lawyer has not earned.

(2) Following termination of a representation, a lawyer must:

(a) observe obligations to a former client such as those dealing with client confidences (see Chapter 5), conflicts of interest (see Chapter 8), client property and documents (see §§ 44–46), and fee collection (see § 41);

(b) take no action on behalf of a former client without new authorization and give reasonable notice, to those who might otherwise be misled, that the lawyer lacks authority to act for the client;

(c) take reasonable steps to convey to the former client any material communication the lawyer receives relating to the matter involved in the representation; and

(d) take no unfair advantage of a former client by abusing knowledge or trust acquired by means of the representation.

§ 34. Reasonable and Lawful Fees

A lawyer may not charge a fee larger than is reasonable in the circumstances or that is prohibited by law.

§ 35. Contingent–Fee Arrangements

(1) A lawyer may contract with a client for a fee the size or payment of which is contingent on the outcome of a matter, unless the contract violates § 34 or another provision of this Restatement or the size or payment of the fee is:

(a) contingent on success in prosecuting or defending a criminal proceeding; or

(b) contingent on a specified result in a divorce proceeding or a proceeding concerning custody of a child.

(2) Unless the contract construed in the circumstances indicates otherwise, when a lawyer has contracted for a contingent fee, the lawyer is entitled to receive the specified fee only when and to the extent the client receives payment.

§ 36. Forbidden Client–Lawyer Financial Arrangements

(1) A lawyer may not acquire a proprietary interest in the cause of action or subject matter of litigation that the lawyer is conducting for a client, except that the lawyer may:

> (a) acquire a lien as provided by § 43 to secure the lawyer's fee or expenses; and

> (b) contract with a client for a contingent fee in a civil case except when prohibited as stated in § 35.

(2) A lawyer may not make or guarantee a loan to a client in connection with pending or contemplated litigation that the lawyer is conducting for the client, except that the lawyer may make or guarantee a loan covering court costs and expenses of litigation, the repayment of which to the lawyer may be contingent on the outcome of the matter.

(3) A lawyer may not, before the lawyer ceases to represent a client, make an agreement giving the lawyer literary or media rights to a portrayal or account based in substantial part on information relating to the representation.

§ 37. Partial or Complete Forfeiture of a Lawyer's Compensation

A lawyer engaging in clear and serious violation of duty to a client may be required to forfeit some or all of the lawyer's compensation for the matter. Considerations relevant to the question of forfeiture include the gravity and timing of the violation, its willfulness, its effect on the value of the lawyer's work for the client, any other threatened or actual harm to the client, and the adequacy of other remedies.

§ 38. Client–Lawyer Fee Contracts

(1) Before or within a reasonable time after beginning to represent a client in a matter, a lawyer must communicate to the client, in writing when applicable rules so provide, the basis or rate of the fee, unless the communication is unnecessary for the client because the lawyer has previously represented that client on the same basis or at the same rate.

(2) The validity and construction of a contract between a client and a lawyer concerning the lawyer's fees are governed by § 18.

(3) Unless a contract construed in the circumstances indicates otherwise:

> (a) a lawyer may not charge separately for the lawyer's general office and overhead expenses;

> (b) payments that the law requires an opposing party or that party's lawyer to pay as attorney-fee awards or sanctions are credited to the client, not the client's lawyer, absent a contrary statute or court order; and

(c) when a lawyer requests and receives a fee payment that is not for services already rendered, that payment is to be credited against whatever fee the lawyer is entitled to collect.

§ 39.   A Lawyer's Fee in the Absence of a Contract

If a client and lawyer have not made a valid contract providing for another measure of compensation, a client owes a lawyer who has performed legal services for the client the fair value of the lawyer's services.

§ 40.   Fees on Termination

If a client-lawyer relationship ends before the lawyer has completed the services due for a matter and the lawyer's fee has not been forfeited under § 37:

(1) a lawyer who has been discharged or withdraws may recover the lesser of the fair value of the lawyer's services as determined under § 39 and the ratable proportion of the compensation provided by any otherwise enforceable contract between lawyer and client for the services performed; except that

(2) the tribunal may allow such a lawyer to recover the ratable proportion of the compensation provided by such a contract if:

(a) the discharge or withdrawal is not attributable to misconduct of the lawyer;

(b) the lawyer has performed severable services; and

(c) allowing contractual compensation would not burden the client's choice of counsel or the client's ability to replace counsel.

§ 41.   Fee–Collection Methods

In seeking compensation claimed from a client or former client, a lawyer may not employ collection methods forbidden by law, use confidential information (as defined in Chapter 5) when not permitted under § 65, or harass the client.

§ 42.   Remedies and the Burden of Persuasion

(1) A fee dispute between a lawyer and a client may be adjudicated in any appropriate proceeding, including a suit by the lawyer to recover an unpaid fee, a suit for a refund by a client, an arbitration to which both parties consent unless applicable law renders the lawyer's consent unnecessary, or in the court's discretion a proceeding ancillary to a pending suit in which the lawyer performed the services in question.

(2) In any such proceeding the lawyer has the burden of persuading the trier of fact, when relevant, of the existence and terms of any fee contract, the making of any disclosures to the client required to render a contract enforceable, and the extent and value of the lawyer's services.

§ 43. Lawyer Liens

(1) Except as provided in Subsection (2) or by statute or rule, a lawyer does not acquire a lien entitling the lawyer to retain the client's property in the lawyer's possession in order to secure payment of the lawyer's fees and disbursements. A lawyer may decline to deliver to a client or former client an original or copy of any document prepared by the lawyer or at the lawyer's expense if the client or former client has not paid all fees and disbursements due for the lawyer's work in preparing the document and nondelivery would not unreasonably harm the client or former client.

(2) Unless otherwise provided by statute or rule, client and lawyer may agree that the lawyer shall have a security interest in property of the client recovered for the client through the lawyer's efforts, as follows:

(a) the lawyer may contract in writing with the client for a lien on the proceeds of the representation to secure payment for the lawyer's services and disbursements in that matter;

(b) the lien becomes binding on a third party when the party has notice of the lien;

(c) the lien applies only to the amount of fees and disbursements claimed reasonably and in good faith for the lawyer's services performed in the representation; and

(d) the lawyer may not unreasonably impede the speedy and inexpensive resolution of any dispute concerning those fees and disbursements or the lien.

(3) A tribunal where an action is pending may in its discretion adjudicate any fee or other dispute concerning a lien asserted by a lawyer on property of a party to the action, provide for custody of the property, release all or part of the property to the client or lawyer, and grant such other relief as justice may require.

(4) With respect to property neither in the lawyer's possession nor recovered by the client through the lawyer's efforts, the lawyer may obtain a security interest on property of a client only as provided by other law and consistent with §§ 18 and 126. Acquisition of such a security interest is a business or financial transaction with a client within the meaning of § 126.

§ 44. Safeguarding and Segregating Property

(1) A lawyer holding funds or other property of a client in connection with a representation, or such funds or other property in which a client claims an interest, must take reasonable steps to safeguard the funds or property. A similar obligation may be imposed by law on funds or other property so held and owned or claimed by a third person. In particular, the lawyer must hold such property separate from the lawyer's property, keep records of it, deposit funds in an account separate from the lawyer's own funds, identify tangible objects, and comply with related requirements imposed by regulatory authorities.

(2) Upon receiving funds or other property in a professional capacity and in which a client or third person owns or claims an interest, a lawyer must promptly notify the client or third person. The lawyer must promptly render a full accounting regarding such property upon request by the client or third person.

§ 45. Surrendering Possession of Property

(1) Except as provided in Subsection (2), a lawyer must promptly deliver, to the client or nonclient so entitled, funds or other property in the lawyer's possession belonging to a client or nonclient.

(2) A lawyer may retain possession of funds or other property of a client or nonclient if:

(a) the client or nonclient consents;

(b) the lawyer's client is entitled to the property, the lawyer appropriately possesses the property for purposes of the representation, and the client has not asked for delivery of the property;

(c) the lawyer has a valid lien on the property (see § 43);

(d) there are substantial grounds for dispute as to the person entitled to the property; or

(e) delivering the property to the client or nonclient would violate a court order or other legal obligation of the lawyer.

§ 46. Documents Relating to a Representation

(1) A lawyer must take reasonable steps to safeguard documents in the lawyer's possession relating to the representation of a client or former client.

(2) On request, a lawyer must allow a client or former client to inspect and copy any document possessed by the lawyer relating to the representation, unless substantial grounds exist to refuse.

(3) Unless a client or former client consents to nondelivery or substantial grounds exist for refusing to make delivery, a lawyer must deliver to the client or former client, at an appropriate time and in any event promptly after the representation ends, such originals and copies of other documents possessed by the lawyer relating to the representation as the client or former client reasonably needs.

(4) Notwithstanding Subsections (2) and (3), a lawyer may decline to deliver to a client or former client an original or copy of any document under circumstances permitted by § 43(1).

§ 47. Fee–Splitting Between Lawyers Not in the Same Firm

A division of fees between lawyers who are not in the same firm may be made only if:

(1) (a) the division is in proportion to the services performed by each lawyer or (b) by agreement with the client, the lawyers assume joint responsibility for the representation;

(2) the client is informed of and does not object to the fact of division, the terms of the division, and the participation of the lawyers involved; and

(3) the total fee is reasonable (see § 34).

§ 48. Professional Negligence—Elements and Defenses Generally

In addition to the other possible bases of civil liability described in §§ 49, 55, and 56, a lawyer is civilly liable for professional negligence to a person to whom the lawyer owes a duty of care within the meaning of § 50 or § 51, if the lawyer fails to exercise care within the meaning of § 52 and if that failure is a legal cause of injury within the meaning of § 53, unless the lawyer has a defense within the meaning of § 54.

§ 49. Breach of Fiduciary Duty—Generally

In addition to the other possible bases of civil liability described in §§ 48, 55, and 56, a lawyer is civilly liable to a client if the lawyer breaches a fiduciary duty to the client set forth in § 16(3) and if that failure is a legal cause of injury within the meaning of § 53, unless the lawyer has a defense within the meaning of § 54.

§ 50. Duty of Care to a Client

For purposes of liability under § 48, a lawyer owes a client the duty to exercise care within the meaning of § 52 in pursuing the client's lawful objectives in matters covered by the representation.

§ 51. Duty of Care to Certain Nonclients

For purposes of liability under § 48, a lawyer owes a duty to use care within the meaning of § 52 in each of the following circumstances:

(1) to a prospective client, as stated in § 15;

(2) to a nonclient when and to the extent that:

(a) the lawyer or (with the lawyer's acquiescence) the lawyer's client invites the nonclient to rely on the lawyer's opinion or provision of other legal services, and the nonclient so relies; and

(b) the nonclient is not, under applicable tort law, too remote from the lawyer to be entitled to protection;

(3) to a nonclient when and to the extent that:

(a) the lawyer knows that a client intends as one of the primary objectives of the representation that the lawyer's services benefit the nonclient;

(b) such a duty would not significantly impair the lawyer's performance of obligations to the client; and

(c) the absence of such a duty would make enforcement of those obligations to the client unlikely; and

(4) to a nonclient when and to the extent that:

(a) the lawyer's client is a trustee, guardian, executor, or fiduciary acting primarily to perform similar functions for the nonclient;

(b) the lawyer knows that appropriate action by the lawyer is necessary with respect to a matter within the scope of the representation to prevent or rectify the breach of a fiduciary duty owed by the client to the nonclient, where (i) the breach is a crime or fraud or (ii) the lawyer has assisted or is assisting the breach;

(c) the nonclient is not reasonably able to protect its rights; and

(d) such a duty would not significantly impair the performance of the lawyer's obligations to the client.

§ 52. The Standard of Care

(1) For purposes of liability under §§ 48 and 49, a lawyer who owes a duty of care must exercise the competence and diligence normally exercised by lawyers in similar circumstances.

(2) Proof of a violation of a rule or statute regulating the conduct of lawyers:

(a) does not give rise to an implied cause of action for professional negligence or breach of fiduciary duty;

(b) does not preclude other proof concerning the duty of care in Subsection (1) or the fiduciary duty; and

(c) may be considered by a trier of fact as an aid in understanding and applying the standard of Subsection (1) or § 49 to the extent that (i) the rule or statute was designed for the protection of persons in the position of the claimant and (ii) proof of the content and construction of such a rule or statute is relevant to the claimant's claim.

§ 53. Causation and Damages

A lawyer is liable under § 48 or § 49 only if the lawyer's breach of a duty of care or breach of fiduciary duty was a legal cause of injury, as determined under generally applicable principles of causation and damages.

§ 54. Defenses; Prospective Liability Waiver; Settlement with a Client

(1) Except as otherwise provided in this Section, liability under §§ 48 and 49 is subject to the defenses available under generally applicable principles of law governing respectively actions for professional negligence and breach of fiduciary duty. A lawyer is not liable under § 48 or § 49 for any action or

inaction the lawyer reasonably believed to be required by law, including a professional rule.

(2) An agreement prospectively limiting a lawyer's liability to a client for malpractice is unenforceable.

(3) The client or former client may rescind an agreement settling a claim by the client or former client against the person's lawyer if:

(a) the client or former client was subjected to improper pressure by the lawyer in reaching the settlement; or

(b) (i) the client or former client was not independently represented in negotiating the settlement, and (ii) the settlement was not fair and reasonable to the client or former client.

(4) For purposes of professional discipline, a lawyer may not:

(a) make an agreement prospectively limiting the lawyer's liability to a client for malpractice; or

(b) settle a claim for such liability with an unrepresented client or former client without first advising that person in writing that independent representation is appropriate in connection therewith.

§ 55. Civil Remedies of a Client Other Than for Malpractice

(1) A lawyer is subject to liability to a client for injury caused by breach of contract in the circumstances and to the extent provided by contract law.

(2) A client is entitled to restitutionary, injunctive, or declaratory remedies against a lawyer in the circumstances and to the extent provided by generally applicable law governing such remedies.

§ 56. Liability to a Client or Nonclient Under General Law

Except as provided in § 57 and in addition to liability under §§ 48–55, a lawyer is subject to liability to a client or nonclient when a nonlawyer would be in similar circumstances.

§ 57. Nonclient Claims—Certain Defenses and Exceptions to Liability

(1) In addition to other absolute or conditional privileges, a lawyer is absolutely privileged to publish matter concerning a nonclient if:

(a) the publication occurs in communications preliminary to a reasonably anticipated proceeding before a tribunal or in the institution or during the course and as a part of such a proceeding;

(b) the lawyer participates as counsel in that proceeding; and

(c) the matter is published to a person who may be involved in the proceeding, and the publication has some relation to the proceeding.

(2) A lawyer representing a client in a civil proceeding or procuring the institution of criminal proceedings by a client is not liable to a nonclient for

wrongful use of civil proceedings or for malicious prosecution if the lawyer has probable cause for acting, or if the lawyer acts primarily to help the client obtain a proper adjudication of the client's claim in that proceeding.

(3) A lawyer who advises or assists a client to make or break a contract, to enter or dissolve a legal relationship, or to enter or not enter a contractual relation, is not liable to a nonclient for interference with contract or with prospective contractual relations or with a legal relationship, if the lawyer acts to advance the client's objectives without using wrongful means.

§ 58. Vicarious Liability

(1) A law firm is subject to civil liability for injury legally caused to a person by any wrongful act or omission of any principal or employee of the firm who was acting in the ordinary course of the firm's business or with actual or apparent authority.

(2) Each of the principals of a law firm organized as a general partnership without limited liability is liable jointly and severally with the firm.

(3) A principal of a law firm organized other than as a general partnership without limited liability as authorized by law is vicariously liable for the acts of another principal or employee of the firm to the extent provided by law.

§ 59. Definition of "Confidential Client Information"

Confidential client information consists of information relating to representation of a client, other than information that is generally known.

§ 60. A Lawyer's Duty to Safeguard Confidential Client Information

(1) Except as provided in §§ 61–67, during and after representation of a client:

(a) the lawyer may not use or disclose confidential client information as defined in § 59 if there is a reasonable prospect that doing so will adversely affect a material interest of the client or if the client has instructed the lawyer not to use or disclose such information;

(b) the lawyer must take steps reasonable in the circumstances to protect confidential client information against impermissible use or disclosure by the lawyer's associates or agents that may adversely affect a material interest of the client or otherwise than as instructed by the client.

(2) Except as stated in § 62, a lawyer who uses confidential information of a client for the lawyer's pecuniary gain other than in the practice of law must account to the client for any profits made.

§ 61. Using or Disclosing Information to Advance Client Interests

A lawyer may use or disclose confidential client information when the lawyer reasonably believes that doing so will advance the interests of the client in the representation.

§ 62. Using or Disclosing Information with Client Consent

A lawyer may use or disclose confidential client information when the client consents after being adequately informed concerning the use or disclosure.

§ 63. Using or Disclosing Information When Required by Law

A lawyer may use or disclose confidential client information when required by law, after the lawyer takes reasonably appropriate steps to assert that the information is privileged or otherwise protected against disclosure.

§ 64. Using or Disclosing Information in a Lawyer's Self–Defense

A lawyer may use or disclose confidential client information when and to the extent that the lawyer reasonably believes necessary to defend the lawyer or the lawyer's associate or agent against a charge or threatened charge by any person that the lawyer or such associate or agent acted wrongfully in the course of representing a client.

§ 65. Using or Disclosing Information in a Compensation Dispute

A lawyer may use or disclose confidential client information when and to the extent that the lawyer reasonably believes necessary to permit the lawyer to resolve a dispute with the client concerning compensation or reimbursement that the lawyer reasonably claims the client owes the lawyer.

§ 66. Using or Disclosing Information to Prevent Death or Serious Bodily Harm

(1) A lawyer may use or disclose confidential client information when the lawyer reasonably believes that its use or disclosure is necessary to prevent reasonably certain death or serious bodily harm to a person.

(2) Before using or disclosing information under this Section, the lawyer must, if feasible, make a good-faith effort to persuade the client not to act. If the client or another person has already acted, the lawyer must, if feasible, advise the client to warn the victim or to take other action to prevent the harm and advise the client of the lawyer's ability to use or disclose information as provided in this Section and the consequences thereof.

(3) A lawyer who takes action or decides not to take action permitted under this Section is not, solely by reason of such action or inaction, subject to professional discipline, liable for damages to the lawyer's client or any third person, or barred from recovery against a client or third person.

§ 67. Using or Disclosing Information to Prevent, Rectify, or Mitigate Substantial Financial Loss

(1) A lawyer may use or disclose confidential client information when the lawyer reasonably believes that its use or disclosure is necessary to prevent a crime or fraud, and:

(a) the crime or fraud threatens substantial financial loss;

(b) the loss has not yet occurred;

(c) the lawyer's client intends to commit the crime or fraud either personally or through a third person; and

(d) the client has employed or is employing the lawyer's services in the matter in which the crime or fraud is committed.

(2) If a crime or fraud described in Subsection (1) has already occurred, a lawyer may use or disclose confidential client information when the lawyer reasonably believes its use or disclosure is necessary to prevent, rectify, or mitigate the loss.

(3) Before using or disclosing information under this Section, the lawyer must, if feasible, make a good-faith effort to persuade the client not to act. If the client or another person has already acted, the lawyer must, if feasible, advise the client to warn the victim or to take other action to prevent, rectify, or mitigate the loss. The lawyer must, if feasible, also advise the client of the lawyer's ability to use or disclose information as provided in this Section and the consequences thereof.

(4) A lawyer who takes action or decides not to take action permitted under this Section is not, solely by reason of such action or inaction, subject to professional discipline, liable for damages to the lawyer's client or any third person, or barred from recovery against a client or third person.

§ 68. Attorney–Client Privilege

Except as otherwise provided in this Restatement, the attorney-client privilege may be invoked as provided in § 86 with respect to:

(1) a communication

(2) made between privileged persons

(3) in confidence

(4) for the purpose of obtaining or providing legal assistance for the client.

§ 69. Attorney–Client Privilege—"Communication"

A communication within the meaning of § 68 is any expression through which a privileged person, as defined in § 70, undertakes to convey information to another privileged person and any document or other record revealing such an expression.

§ 70. Attorney–Client Privilege—"Privileged Persons"

Privileged persons within the meaning of § 68 are the client (including a prospective client), the client's lawyer, agents of either who facilitate communications between them, and agents of the lawyer who facilitate the representation.

§ 71. Attorney–Client Privilege—"In Confidence"

A communication is in confidence within the meaning of § 68 if, at the time and in the circumstances of the communication, the communicating person reasonably believes that no one will learn the contents of the communication except a privileged person as defined in § 70 or another person with whom communications are protected under a similar privilege.

§ 72. Attorney–Client Privilege—Legal Assistance as the Object of a Privileged Communication

A communication is made for the purpose of obtaining or providing legal assistance within the meaning of § 68 if it is made to or to assist a person:

(1) who is a lawyer or who the client or prospective client reasonably believes to be a lawyer; and

(2) whom the client or prospective client consults for the purpose of obtaining legal assistance.

§ 73. The Privilege for an Organizational Client

When a client is a corporation, unincorporated association, partnership, trust, estate, sole proprietorship, or other for-profit or not-for-profit organization, the attorney-client privilege extends to a communication that:

(1) otherwise qualifies as privileged under §§ 68–72;

(2) is between an agent of the organization and a privileged person as defined in § 70;

(3) concerns a legal matter of interest to the organization; and

(4) is disclosed only to:

(a) privileged persons as defined in § 70; and

(b) other agents of the organization who reasonably need to know of the communication in order to act for the organization.

§ 74. The Privilege for a Governmental Client

Unless applicable law otherwise provides, the attorney-client privilege extends to a communication of a governmental organization as stated in § 73 and of an individual employee or other agent of a governmental organization as a client with respect to his or her personal interest as stated in §§ 68–72.

301

§ 75. The Privilege of Co–Clients

(1) If two or more persons are jointly represented by the same lawyer in a matter, a communication of either co-client that otherwise qualifies as privileged under §§ 68–72 and relates to matters of common interest is privileged as against third persons, and any co-client may invoke the privilege, unless it has been waived by the client who made the communication.

(2) Unless the co-clients have agreed otherwise, a communication described in Subsection (1) is not privileged as between the co-clients in a subsequent adverse proceeding between them.

§ 76. The Privilege in Common–Interest Arrangements

(1) If two or more clients with a common interest in a litigated or nonlitigated matter are represented by separate lawyers and they agree to exchange information concerning the matter, a communication of any such client that otherwise qualifies as privileged under §§ 68–72 that relates to the matter is privileged as against third persons. Any such client may invoke the privilege, unless it has been waived by the client who made the communication.

(2) Unless the clients have agreed otherwise, a communication described in Subsection (1) is not privileged as between clients described in Subsection (1) in a subsequent adverse proceeding between them.

§ 77. Duration of the Privilege

Unless waived (see §§ 78–80) or subject to exception (see §§ 81–85), the attorney-client privilege may be invoked as provided in § 86 at any time during or after termination of the relationship between client or prospective client and lawyer.

§ 78. Agreement, Disclaimer, or Failure to Object

The attorney-client privilege is waived if the client, the client's lawyer, or another authorized agent of the client:

(1) agrees to waive the privilege;

(2) disclaims protection of the privilege and

(a) another person reasonably relies on the disclaimer to that person's detriment; or

(b) reasons of judicial administration require that the client not be permitted to revoke the disclaimer; or

(3) in a proceeding before a tribunal, fails to object properly to an attempt by another person to give or exact testimony or other evidence of a privileged communication.

§ 79. Subsequent Disclosure

The attorney-client privilege is waived if the client, the client's lawyer, or another authorized agent of the client voluntarily discloses the communication in a nonprivileged communication.

§ 80. Putting Assistance or a Communication in Issue

(1) The attorney-client privilege is waived for any relevant communication if the client asserts as to a material issue in a proceeding that:

(a) the client acted upon the advice of a lawyer or that the advice was otherwise relevant to the legal significance of the client's conduct; or

(b) a lawyer's assistance was ineffective, negligent, or otherwise wrongful.

(2) The attorney-client privilege is waived for a recorded communication if a witness:

(a) employs the communication to aid the witness while testifying; or

(b) employed the communication in preparing to testify, and the tribunal finds that disclosure is required in the interests of justice.

§ 81. A Dispute Concerning a Decedent's Disposition of Property

The attorney-client privilege does not apply to a communication from or to a decedent relevant to an issue between parties who claim an interest through the same deceased client, either by testate or intestate succession or by an inter vivos transaction.

§ 82. Client Crime or Fraud

The attorney-client privilege does not apply to a communication occurring when a client:

(a) consults a lawyer for the purpose, later accomplished, of obtaining assistance to engage in a crime or fraud or aiding a third person to do so, or

(b) regardless of the client's purpose at the time of consultation, uses the lawyer's advice or other services to engage in or assist a crime or fraud.

§ 83. Lawyer Self–Protection

The attorney-client privilege does not apply to a communication that is relevant and reasonably necessary for a lawyer to employ in a proceeding:

(1) to resolve a dispute with a client concerning compensation or reimbursement that the lawyer reasonably claims the client owes the lawyer; or

(2) to defend the lawyer or the lawyer's associate or agent against a charge by any person that the lawyer, associate, or agent acted wrongfully during the course of representing a client.

§ 84. Fiduciary–Lawyer Communications

In a proceeding in which a trustee of an express trust or similar fiduciary is charged with breach of fiduciary duties by a beneficiary, a communication otherwise within § 68 is nonetheless not privileged if the communication:

(a) is relevant to the claimed breach; and

(b) was between the trustee and a lawyer (or other privileged person within the meaning of § 70) who was retained to advise the trustee concerning the administration of the trust.

§ 85. Communications Involving a Fiduciary Within an Organization

In a proceeding involving a dispute between an organizational client and shareholders, members, or other constituents of the organization toward whom the directors, officers, or similar persons managing the organization bear fiduciary responsibilities, the attorney-client privilege of the organization may be withheld from a communication otherwise within § 68 if the tribunal finds that:

(a) those managing the organization are charged with breach of their obligations toward the shareholders, members, or other constituents or toward the organization itself;

(b) the communication occurred prior to the assertion of the charges and relates directly to those charges; and

(c) the need of the requesting party to discover or introduce the communication is sufficiently compelling and the threat to confidentiality sufficiently confined to justify setting the privilege aside.

§ 86. Invoking the Privilege and Its Exceptions

(1) When an attempt is made to introduce in evidence or obtain discovery of a communication privileged under § 68:

(a) A client, a personal representative of an incompetent or deceased client, or a person succeeding to the interest of a client may invoke or waive the privilege, either personally or through counsel or another authorized agent.

(b) A lawyer, an agent of the lawyer, or an agent of a client from whom a privileged communication is sought must invoke the privilege when doing so appears reasonably appropriate, unless the client:

(i) has waived the privilege; or

(ii) has authorized the lawyer or agent to waive it.

(c) Notwithstanding failure to invoke the privilege as specified in Subsections (1)(a) and (1)(b), the tribunal has discretion to invoke the privilege.

(2) A person invoking the privilege must ordinarily object contemporaneously to an attempt to disclose the communication and, if the objection is contested, demonstrate each element of the privilege under § 68.

(3) A person invoking a waiver of or exception to the privilege (§§ 78–85) must assert it and, if the assertion is contested, demonstrate each element of the waiver or exception.

§ 87. Lawyer Work–Product Immunity

(1) Work product consists of tangible material or its intangible equivalent in unwritten or oral form, other than underlying facts, prepared by a lawyer for litigation then in progress or in reasonable anticipation of future litigation.

(2) Opinion work product consists of the opinions or mental impressions of a lawyer; all other work product is ordinary work product.

(3) Except for material which by applicable law is not so protected, work product is immune from discovery or other compelled disclosure to the extent stated in §§ 88 (ordinary work product) and 89 (opinion work product) when the immunity is invoked as described in § 90.

§ 88. Ordinary Work Product

When work product protection is invoked as described in § 90, ordinary work product (§ 87(2)) is immune from discovery or other compelled disclosure unless either an exception recognized in §§ 91–93 applies or the inquiring party:

(1) has a substantial need for the material in order to prepare for trial; and

(2) is unable without undue hardship to obtain the substantial equivalent of the material by other means.

§ 89. Opinion Work Product

When work product protection is invoked as described in § 90, opinion work product (§ 87(2)) is immune from discovery or other compelled disclosure unless either the immunity is waived or an exception applies (§§ 91–93) or extraordinary circumstances justify disclosure.

§ 90. Invoking the Lawyer Work–Product Immunity and Its Exceptions

(1) Work-product immunity may be invoked by or for a person on whose behalf the work product was prepared.

305

(2) The person invoking work-product immunity must object and, if the objection is contested, demonstrate each element of the immunity.

(3) Once a claim of work product has been adequately supported, a person entitled to invoke a waiver or exception must assert it and, if the assertion is contested, demonstrate each element of the waiver or exception.

§ 91. Voluntary Acts

Work-product immunity is waived if the client, the client's lawyer, or another authorized agent of the client:

(1) agrees to waive the immunity;

(2) disclaims protection of the immunity and:

(a) another person reasonably relies on the disclaimer to that person's detriment; or

(b) reasons of judicial administration require that the client not be permitted to revoke the disclaimer; or

(3) in a proceeding before a tribunal, fails to object properly to an attempt by another person to give or exact testimony or other evidence of work product; or

(4) discloses the material to third persons in circumstances in which there is a significant likelihood that an adversary or potential adversary in anticipated litigation will obtain it.

§ 92. Use of Lawyer Work Product in Litigation

(1) Work-product immunity is waived for any relevant material if the client asserts as to a material issue in a proceeding that:

(a) the client acted upon the advice of a lawyer or that the advice was otherwise relevant to the legal significance of the client's conduct; or

(b) a lawyer's assistance was ineffective, negligent, or otherwise wrongful.

(2) The work-product immunity is waived for recorded material if a witness

(a) employs the material to aid the witness while testifying, or

(b) employed the material in preparing to testify, and the tribunal finds that disclosure is required in the interests of justice.

§ 93. Client Crime or Fraud

Work-product immunity does not apply to materials prepared when a client consults a lawyer for the purpose, later accomplished, of obtaining assistance to engage in a crime or fraud or to aid a third person to do so or uses the materials for such a purpose.

§ 94. Advising and Assisting a Client—In General

(1) A lawyer who counsels or assists a client to engage in conduct that violates the rights of a third person is subject to liability:

(a) to the third person to the extent stated in §§ 51 and 56–57; and

(b) to the client to the extent stated in §§ 50, 55, and 56.

(2) For purposes of professional discipline, a lawyer may not counsel or assist a client in conduct that the lawyer knows to be criminal or fraudulent or in violation of a court order with the intent of facilitating or encouraging the conduct, but the lawyer may counsel or assist a client in conduct when the lawyer reasonably believes:

(a) that the client's conduct constitutes a good-faith effort to determine the validity, scope, meaning, or application of a law or court order; or

(b) that the client can assert a nonfrivolous argument that the client's conduct will not constitute a crime or fraud or violate a court order.

(3) In counseling a client, a lawyer may address nonlegal aspects of a proposed course of conduct, including moral, reputational, economic, social, political, and business aspects.

§ 95. An Evaluation Undertaken for a Third Person

(1) In furtherance of the objectives of a client in a representation, a lawyer may provide to a nonclient the results of the lawyer's investigation and analysis of facts or the lawyer's professional evaluation or opinion on the matter.

(2) When providing the information, evaluation, or opinion under Subsection (1) is reasonably likely to affect the client's interests materially and adversely, the lawyer must first obtain the client's consent after the client is adequately informed concerning important possible effects on the client's interests.

(3) In providing the information, evaluation, or opinion under Subsection (1), the lawyer must exercise care with respect to the nonclient to the extent stated in § 51(2) and not make false statements prohibited under § 98.

§ 96. Representing an Organization as Client

(1) When a lawyer is employed or retained to represent an organization:

(a) the lawyer represents the interests of the organization as defined by its responsible agents acting pursuant to the organization's decision-making procedures; and

(b) subject to Subsection (2), the lawyer must follow instructions in the representation, as stated in § 21(2), given by persons authorized so to act on behalf of the organization.

307

(2) If a lawyer representing an organization knows of circumstances indicating that a constituent of the organization has engaged in action or intends to act in a way that violates a legal obligation to the organization that will likely cause substantial injury to it, or that reasonably can be foreseen to be imputable to the organization and likely to result in substantial injury to it, the lawyer must proceed in what the lawyer reasonably believes to be the best interests of the organization.

(3) In the circumstances described in Subsection (2), the lawyer may, in circumstances warranting such steps, ask the constituent to reconsider the matter, recommend that a second legal opinion be sought, and seek review by appropriate supervisory authority within the organization, including referring the matter to the highest authority that can act in behalf of the organization.

§ 97. Representing a Governmental Client

A lawyer representing a governmental client must proceed in the representation as stated in § 96, except that the lawyer:

(1) possesses such rights and responsibilities as may be defined by law to make decisions on behalf of the governmental client that are within the authority of a client under §§ 22 and 21(2);

(2) except as otherwise provided by law, must proceed as stated in §§ 96(2) and 96(3) with respect to an act of a constituent of the governmental client that violates a legal obligation that will likely cause substantial public or private injury or that reasonably can be foreseen to be imputable to and thus likely result in substantial injury to the client;

(3) if a prosecutor or similar lawyer determining whether to file criminal proceedings or take other steps in such proceedings, must do so only when based on probable cause and the lawyer's belief, formed after due investigation, that there are good factual and legal grounds to support the step taken; and

(4) must observe other applicable restrictions imposed by law on those similarly functioning for the governmental client.

§ 98. Statements to a Nonclient

A lawyer communicating on behalf of a client with a nonclient may not:

(1) knowingly make a false statement of material fact or law to the nonclient,

(2) make other statements prohibited by law; or

(3) fail to make a disclosure of information required by law.

§ 99. A Represented Nonclient—The General Anti–Contact Rule

(1) A lawyer representing a client in a matter may not communicate about the subject of the representation with a nonclient whom the lawyer knows to be represented in the matter by another lawyer or with a represen-

tative of an organizational nonclient so represented as defined in § 100, unless:

> (a) the communication is with a public officer or agency to the extent stated in § 101;

> (b) the lawyer is a party and represents no other client in the matter;

> (c) the communication is authorized by law;

> (d) the communication reasonably responds to an emergency; or

> (e) the other lawyer consents.

(2) Subsection (1) does not prohibit the lawyer from assisting the client in otherwise proper communication by the lawyer's client with a represented nonclient.

§ 100. Definition of a Represented Nonclient

Within the meaning of § 99, a represented nonclient includes:

> (1) a natural person represented by a lawyer; and:

> (2) a current employee or other agent of an organization represented by a lawyer:

>> (a) if the employee or other agent supervises, directs, or regularly consults with the lawyer concerning the matter or if the agent has power to compromise or settle the matter;

>> (b) if the acts or omissions of the employee or other agent may be imputed to the organization for purposes of civil or criminal liability in the matter; or

>> (c) if a statement of the employee or other agent, under applicable rules of evidence, would have the effect of binding the organization with respect to proof of the matter.

§ 101. A Represented Governmental Agency or Officer

(1) Unless otherwise provided by law (see § 99(1)(c)) and except as provided in Subsection (2), the prohibition stated in § 99 against contact with a represented nonclient does not apply to communications with employees of a represented governmental agency or with a governmental officer being represented in the officer's official capacity.

(2) In negotiation or litigation by a lawyer of a specific claim of a client against a governmental agency or against a governmental officer in the officer's official capacity, the prohibition stated in § 99 applies, except that the lawyer may contact any officer of the government if permitted by the agency or with respect to an issue of general policy.

§ 102. Information of a Nonclient Known to be Legally Protected

A lawyer communicating with a nonclient in a situation permitted under § 99 may not seek to obtain information that the lawyer reasonably should know the nonclient may not reveal without violating a duty of confidentiality to another imposed by law.

§ 103. Dealings with an Unrepresented Nonclient

In the course of representing a client and dealing with a nonclient who is not represented by a lawyer:

>(1) the lawyer may not mislead the nonclient, to the prejudice of the nonclient, concerning the identity and interests of the person the lawyer represents; and

>(2) when the lawyer knows or reasonably should know that the unrepresented nonclient misunderstands the lawyer's role in the matter, the lawyer must make reasonable efforts to correct the misunderstanding when failure to do so would materially prejudice the nonclient.

§ 104. Representing a Client in Legislative and Administrative Matters

A lawyer representing a client before a legislature or administrative agency:

>(1) must disclose that the appearance is in a representative capacity and not misrepresent the capacity in which the lawyer appears;

>(2) must comply with applicable law and regulations governing such representations; and

>(3) except as applicable law otherwise provides:

>>(a) in an adjudicative proceeding before a government agency or involving such an agency as a participant, has the legal rights and responsibilities of an advocate in a proceeding before a judicial tribunal; and

>>(b) in other types of proceedings and matters, has the legal rights and responsibilities applicable in the lawyer's dealings with a private person.

§ 105. Complying with Law and Tribunal Rulings

In representing a client in a matter before a tribunal, a lawyer must comply with applicable law, including rules of procedure and evidence and specific tribunal rulings.

§ 106. Dealing with Other Participants in Proceedings

In representing a client in a matter before a tribunal, a lawyer may not use means that have no substantial purpose other than to embarrass, delay, or burden a third person or use methods of obtaining evidence that are prohibited by law.

§ 107. Prohibited Forensic Tactics

In representing a client in a matter before a tribunal, a lawyer may not, in the presence of the trier of fact:

(1) state a personal opinion about the justness of a cause, the credibility of a witness, the culpability of a civil litigant, or the guilt or innocence of an accused, but the lawyer may argue any position or conclusion adequately supported by the lawyer's analysis of the evidence; or

(2) allude to any matter that the lawyer does not reasonably believe is relevant or that will not be supported by admissible evidence.

§ 108. An Advocate as a Witness

(1) Except as provided in Subsection (2), a lawyer may not represent a client in a contested hearing or trial of a matter in which:

(a) the lawyer is expected to testify for the lawyer's client; or

(b) the lawyer does not intend to testify but (i) the lawyer's testimony would be material to establishing a claim or defense of the client, and (ii) the client has not consented as stated in § 122 to the lawyer's intention not to testify.

(2) A lawyer may represent a client when the lawyer will testify as stated in Subsection (1)(a) if:

(a) the lawyer's testimony relates to an issue that the lawyer reasonably believes will not be contested or to the nature and value of legal services rendered in the proceeding;

(b) deprivation of the lawyer's services as advocate would work a substantial hardship on the client; or

(c) consent has been given by (i) opposing parties who would be adversely affected by the lawyer's testimony and, (ii) if relevant, the lawyer's client, as stated in § 122 with respect to any conflict of interest between lawyer and client (see § 125) that the lawyer's testimony would create.

(3) A lawyer may not represent a client in a litigated matter pending before a tribunal when the lawyer or a lawyer in the lawyer's firm will give testimony materially adverse to the position of the lawyer's client or materially adverse to a former client of any such lawyer with respect to a matter substantially related to the earlier representation, unless the affected client has consented as stated in § 122 with respect to any conflict of interest between lawyer and client (see § 125) that the testimony would create.

(4) A tribunal should not permit a lawyer to call opposing trial counsel as a witness unless there is a compelling need for the lawyer's testimony.

§ 109. An Advocate's Public Comment on Pending Litigation

(1) In representing a client in a matter before a tribunal, a lawyer may not make a statement outside the proceeding that a reasonable person would expect to be disseminated by means of public communication when the lawyer knows or reasonably should know that the statement will have a substantial likelihood of materially prejudicing a juror or influencing or intimidating a prospective witness in the proceeding. However, a lawyer may in any event make a statement that is reasonably necessary to mitigate the impact on the lawyer's client of substantial, undue, and prejudicial publicity recently initiated by one other than the lawyer or the lawyer's client.

(2) A prosecutor must, except for statements necessary to inform the public of the nature and extent of the prosecutor's action and that serve a legitimate law-enforcement purpose, refrain from making extrajudicial comments that have a substantial likelihood of heightening public condemnation of the accused.

§ 110. Frivolous Advocacy

(1) A lawyer may not bring or defend a proceeding or assert or controvert an issue therein, unless there is a basis for doing so that is not frivolous, which includes a good-faith argument for an extension, modification, or reversal of existing law.

(2) Notwithstanding Subsection (1), a lawyer for the defendant in a criminal proceeding or the respondent in a proceeding that could result in incarceration may so defend the proceeding as to require that the prosecutor establish every necessary element.

(3) A lawyer may not make a frivolous discovery request, fail to make a reasonably diligent effort to comply with a proper discovery request of another party, or intentionally fail otherwise to comply with applicable procedural requirements concerning discovery.

§ 111. Disclosure of Legal Authority

In representing a client in a matter before a tribunal, a lawyer may not knowingly:

(1) make a false statement of a material proposition of law to the tribunal; or

(2) fail to disclose to the tribunal legal authority in the controlling jurisdiction known to the lawyer to be directly adverse to the position asserted by the client and not disclosed by opposing counsel.

§ 112. Advocacy in Ex Parte and Other Proceedings

In representing a client in a matter before a tribunal, a lawyer applying for ex parte relief or appearing in another proceeding in which similar special requirements of candor apply must comply with the requirements of § 110 and §§ 118–120 and further:

(1) must not present evidence the lawyer reasonably believes is false;

(2) must disclose all material and relevant facts known to the lawyer that will enable the tribunal to reach an informed decision; and

(3) must comply with any other applicable special requirements of candor imposed by law.

§ 113. Improperly Influencing a Judicial Officer

(1) A lawyer may not knowingly communicate ex parte with a judicial officer before whom a proceeding is pending concerning the matter, except as authorized by law.

(2) A lawyer may not make a gift or loan prohibited by law to a judicial officer, attempt to influence the officer otherwise than by legally proper procedures, or state or imply an ability so to influence a judicial officer.

§ 114. A Lawyer's Statements Concerning a Judicial Officer

A lawyer may not knowingly or recklessly make publicly a false statement of fact concerning the qualifications or integrity of an incumbent of a judicial office or a candidate for election to such an office.

§ 115. Lawyer Contact with a Juror

A lawyer may not:

(1) except as allowed by law, communicate with or seek to influence a person known by the lawyer to be a member of a jury pool from which the jury will be drawn;

(2) except as allowed by law, communicate with or seek to influence a member of a jury; or

(3) communicate with a juror who has been excused from further service:

(a) when that would harass the juror or constitute an attempt to influence the juror's actions as a juror in future cases; or

(b) when otherwise prohibited by law.

§ 116. Interviewing and Preparing a Prospective Witness

(1) A lawyer may interview a witness for the purpose of preparing the witness to testify.

(2) A lawyer may not unlawfully obstruct another party's access to a witness.

(3) A lawyer may not unlawfully induce or assist a prospective witness to evade or ignore process obliging the witness to appear to testify.

(4) A lawyer may not request a person to refrain from voluntarily giving relevant testimony or information to another party, unless:

(a) the person is the lawyer's client in the matter; or

(b) (i) the person is not the lawyer's client but is a relative or employee or other agent of the lawyer or the lawyer's client, and (ii) the lawyer reasonably believes compliance will not materially and adversely affect the person's interests.

§ 117. Compensating a Witness

A lawyer may not offer or pay to a witness any consideration:

(1) in excess of the reasonable expenses of the witness incurred and the reasonable value of the witness's time spent in providing evidence, except that an expert witness may be offered and paid a noncontingent fee;

(2) contingent on the content of the witness's testimony or the outcome of the litigation; or

(3) otherwise prohibited by law.

§ 118. Falsifying or Destroying Evidence

(1) A lawyer may not falsify documentary or other evidence.

(2) A lawyer may not destroy or obstruct another party's access to documentary or other evidence when doing so would violate a court order or other legal requirements, or counsel or assist a client to do so.

§ 119. Physical Evidence of a Client Crime

With respect to physical evidence of a client crime, a lawyer:

(1) may, when reasonably necessary for purposes of the representation, take possession of the evidence and retain it for the time reasonably necessary to examine it and subject it to tests that do not alter or destroy material characteristics of the evidence; but

(2) following possession under Subsection (1), the lawyer must notify prosecuting authorities of the lawyer's possession of the evidence or turn the evidence over to them.

§ 120. False Testimony or Evidence

(1) A lawyer may not:

(a) knowingly counsel or assist a witness to testify falsely or otherwise to offer false evidence;

(b) knowingly make a false statement of fact to the tribunal;

(c) offer testimony or other evidence as to an issue of fact known by the lawyer to be false.

(2) If a lawyer has offered testimony or other evidence as to a material issue of fact and comes to know of its falsity, the lawyer must take reasonable remedial measures and may disclose confidential client information when necessary to take such a measure.

(3) A lawyer may refuse to offer testimony or other evidence that the lawyer reasonably believes is false, even if the lawyer does not know it to be false.

§ 121. The Basic Prohibition of Conflicts of Interest

Unless all affected clients and other necessary persons consent to the representation under the limitations and conditions provided in § 122, a lawyer may not represent a client if the representation would involve a conflict of interest. A conflict of interest is involved if there is a substantial risk that the lawyer's representation of the client would be materially and adversely affected by the lawyer's own interests or by the lawyer's duties to another current client, a former client, or a third person.

§ 122. Client Consent to a Conflict of Interest

(1) A lawyer may represent a client notwithstanding a conflict of interest prohibited by § 121 if each affected client or former client gives informed consent to the lawyer's representation. Informed consent requires that the client or former client have reasonably adequate information about the material risks of such representation to that client or former client.

(2) Notwithstanding the informed consent of each affected client or former client, a lawyer may not represent a client if:

(a) the representation is prohibited by law;

(b) one client will assert a claim against the other in the same litigation; or

(c) in the circumstances, it is not reasonably likely that the lawyer will be able to provide adequate representation to one or more of the clients.

§ 123. Imputation of a Conflict of Interest to an Affiliated Lawyer

Unless all affected clients consent to the representation under the limitations and conditions provided in § 122 or unless imputation hereunder is removed as provided in § 124, the restrictions upon a lawyer imposed by §§ 125–135 also restrict other affiliated lawyers who:

(1) are associated with that lawyer in rendering legal services to others through a law partnership, professional corporation, sole proprietorship, or similar association;

(2) are employed with that lawyer by an organization to render legal services either to that organization or to others to advance the interests or objectives of the organization; or

(3) share office facilities without reasonably adequate measures to protect confidential client information so that it will not be available to other lawyers in the shared office.

315

§ 124. Removing Imputation

(1) Imputation specified in § 123 does not restrict an affiliated lawyer when the affiliation between the affiliated lawyer and the personally prohibited lawyer that required the imputation has been terminated, and no material confidential information of the client, relevant to the matter, has been communicated by the personally prohibited lawyer to the affiliated lawyer or that lawyer's firm.

(2) Imputation specified in § 123 does not restrict an affiliated lawyer with respect to a former-client conflict under § 132, when there is no substantial risk that confidential information of the former client will be used with material adverse effect on the former client because:

   (a) any confidential client information communicated to the personally prohibited lawyer is unlikely to be significant in the subsequent matter;

   (b) the personally prohibited lawyer is subject to screening measures adequate to eliminate participation by that lawyer in the representation; and

   (c) timely and adequate notice of the screening has been provided to all affected clients.

(3) Imputation specified in § 123 does not restrict a lawyer affiliated with a former government lawyer with respect to a conflict under § 133 if:

   (a) the personally prohibited lawyer is subject to screening measures adequate to eliminate involvement by that lawyer in the representation; and

   (b) timely and adequate notice of the screening has been provided to the appropriate government agency and to affected clients.

§ 125. A Lawyer's Personal Interest Affecting the Representation of a Client

Unless the affected client consents to the representation under the limitations and conditions provided in § 122, a lawyer may not represent a client if there is a substantial risk that the lawyer's representation of the client would be materially and adversely affected by the lawyer's financial or other personal interests.

§ 126. Business Transactions Between a Lawyer and a Client

A lawyer may not participate in a business or financial transaction with a client, except a standard commercial transaction in which the lawyer does not render legal services, unless:

   (1) the client has adequate information about the terms of the transaction and the risks presented by the lawyer's involvement in it;

   (2) the terms and circumstances of the transaction are fair and reasonable to the client; and

(3) the client consents to the lawyer's role in the transaction under the limitations and conditions provided in § 122 after being encouraged, and given a reasonable opportunity, to seek independent legal advice concerning the transaction.

§ 127. A Client Gift to a Lawyer

(1) A lawyer may not prepare any instrument effecting any gift from a client to the lawyer, including a testamentary gift, unless the lawyer is a relative or other natural object of the client's generosity and the gift is not significantly disproportionate to those given other donees similarly related to the donor.

(2) A lawyer may not accept a gift from a client, including a testamentary gift, unless:

(a) the lawyer is a relative or other natural object of the client's generosity;

(b) the value conferred by the client and the benefit to the lawyer are insubstantial in amount; or

(c) the client, before making the gift, has received independent advice or has been encouraged, and given a reasonable opportunity, to seek such advice.

§ 128. Representing Clients with Conflicting Interests in Civil Litigation

Unless all affected clients consent to the representation under the limitations and conditions provided in § 122, a lawyer in civil litigation may not:

(1) represent two or more clients in a matter if there is a substantial risk that the lawyer's representation of one client would be materially and adversely affected by the lawyer's duties to another client in the matter; or

(2) represent one client to assert or defend a claim against or brought by another client currently represented by the lawyer, even if the matters are not related.

§ 129. Conflicts of Interest in Criminal Litigation

Unless all affected clients consent to the representation under the limitations and conditions provided in § 122, a lawyer in a criminal matter may not represent:

(1) two or more defendants or potential defendants in the same matter; or

(2) a single defendant, if the representation would involve a conflict of interest as defined in § 121.

§ 130. Multiple Representation in a Nonlitigated Matter

Unless all affected clients consent to the representation under the limitations and conditions provided in § 122, a lawyer may not represent two or more clients in a matter not involving litigation if there is a substantial risk that the lawyer's representation of one or more of the clients would be materially and adversely affected by the lawyer's duties to one or more of the other clients.

§ 131. Conflicts of Interest in Representing an Organization

Unless all affected clients consent to the representation under the limitations and conditions provided in § 122, a lawyer may not represent both an organization and a director, officer, employee, shareholder, owner, partner, member, or other individual or organization associated with the organization if there is a substantial risk that the lawyer's representation of either would be materially and adversely affected by the lawyer's duties to the other.

§ 132. A Representation Adverse to the Interests of a Former Client

Unless both the affected present and former clients consent to the representation under the limitations and conditions provided in § 122, a lawyer who has represented a client in a matter may not thereafter represent another client in the same or a substantially related matter in which the interests of the former client are materially adverse. The current matter is substantially related to the earlier matter if:

(1) the current matter involves the work the lawyer performed for the former client; or

(2) there is a substantial risk that representation of the present client will involve the use of information acquired in the course of representing the former client, unless that information has become generally known.

§ 133. A Former Government Lawyer or Officer

(1) A lawyer may not act on behalf of a client with respect to a matter in which the lawyer participated personally and substantially while acting as a government lawyer or officer unless both the government and the client consent to the representation under the limitations and conditions provided in § 122.

(2) A lawyer who acquires confidential information while acting as a government lawyer or officer may not:

(a) if the information concerns a person, represent a client whose interests are materially adverse to that person in a matter in which the information could be used to the material disadvantage of that person; or

(b) if the information concerns the governmental client or employer, represent another public or private client in circumstances described in § 132(2).

318

§ 134. Compensation or Direction of a Lawyer by a Third Person

(1) A lawyer may not represent a client if someone other than the client will wholly or partly compensate the lawyer for the representation, unless the client consents under the limitations and conditions provided in § 122 and knows of the circumstances and conditions of the payment.

(2) A lawyer's professional conduct on behalf of a client may be directed by someone other than the client if:

(a) the direction does not interfere with the lawyer's independence of professional judgment;

(b) the direction is reasonable in scope and character, such as by reflecting obligations borne by the person directing the lawyer; and

(c) the client consents to the direction under the limitations and conditions provided in § 122.

§ 135. A Lawyer with a Fiduciary or Other Legal Obligation to a Nonclient

Unless the affected client consents to the representation under the limitations and conditions provided in § 122, a lawyer may not represent a client in any matter with respect to which the lawyer has a fiduciary or other legal obligation to another if there is a substantial risk that the lawyer's representation of the client would be materially and adversely affected by the lawyer's obligation.

RULES OF PROFESSIONAL CONDUCT OF THE STATE BAR OF CALIFORNIA

(Adopted by the Board of Governors, Effective May 27, 1989.
Including Amendments Through Sept. 1, 2009)

Table of Rules

CHAPTER 1. PROFESSIONAL INTEGRITY IN GENERAL

RULE 1–100. Rules of Professional Conduct, in General

(A) Purpose and Function. The following rules are intended to regulate professional conduct of members of the State Bar through discipline. They have been adopted by the Board of Governors of the State Bar of California and approved by the Supreme Court of California pursuant to Business and Professions Code sections 6076 and 6077 to protect the public and to promote respect and confidence in the legal profession. These rules together with any standards adopted by the Board of Governors pursuant to these rules shall be binding upon all members of the State Bar.

For a willful breach of any of these rules, the Board of Governors has the power to discipline members as provided by law.

The prohibition of certain conduct in these rules is not exclusive. Members are also bound by applicable law including the State Bar Act (Bus. & Prof. Code, § 6000 et seq.) and opinions of California courts. Although not binding, opinions of ethics committees in California should be consulted by members for guidance on proper professional conduct. Ethics opinions and rules and standards promulgated by other jurisdictions and bar associations may also be considered.

These rules are not intended to create new civil causes of action. Nothing in these rules shall be deemed to create, augment, diminish, or eliminate any substantive legal duty of lawyers or the non-disciplinary consequences of violating such a duty.

(B) Definitions.

(1) "Law Firm" means:

(a) two or more lawyers whose activities constitute the practice of law, and who share its profits, expenses, and liabilities; or

(b) a law corporation which employs more than one lawyer; or

(c) a division, department, office, or group within a business entity, which includes more than one lawyer who performs legal services for the business entity; or

(d) a publicly funded entity which employs more than one lawyer to perform legal services.

(2) "Member" means a member of the State Bar of California.

(3) "Lawyer" means a member of the State Bar of California or a person who is admitted in good standing of and eligible to practice before the bar of any United States court or the highest court of the District of Columbia or any state, territory, or insular possession of the United States, or is licensed to practice law in, or is admitted in good standing and eligible to practice before the bar of the highest court of, a foreign country or any political subdivision thereof.

(4) "Associate" means an employee or fellow employee who is employed as a lawyer.

(5) "Shareholder" means a shareholder in a professional corporation pursuant to Business and Professions Code section 6160 et seq.

(C) Purpose of Discussions. Because it is a practical impossibility to convey in black letter form all of the nuances of these disciplinary rules, the comments contained in the Discussions of the rules, while they do not add independent basis for imposing discipline, are intended to provide guidance for interpreting the rules and practicing in compliance with them.

(D) Geographic Scope of Rules.

(1) *As to members:* These rules shall govern the activities of members in and outside this state, except as members lawfully practicing outside this state may be specifically required by a jurisdiction in which they are practicing to follow rules of professional conduct different from these rules.

(2) *As to lawyers from other jurisdictions who are not members:* These rules shall also govern the activities of lawyers while engaged in the performance of lawyer functions in this state; but nothing contained in these rules shall be deemed to authorize the performance of such functions by such persons in this state except as otherwise permitted by law.

(E) These rules may be cited and referred to as "Rules of Professional Conduct of the State Bar of California."

Discussion

The Rules of Professional Conduct are intended to establish the standards for members for purposes of discipline. (See *Ames v. State Bar* (1973) 8 Cal.3d 910

[106 Cal.Rptr. 489].) The fact that a member has engaged in conduct that may be contrary to these rules does not automatically give rise to a civil cause of action. (See *Noble v. Sears, Roebuck & Co.* (1973) 33 Cal.App.3d 654 [109 Cal.Rptr. 269]; *Wilhelm v. Pray, Price, Williams & Russell* (1986) 186 Cal.App.3d 1324 [231 Cal.Rptr. 355].) These rules are not intended to supercede existing law relating to members in non-disciplinary contexts. (See, e.g., *Klemm v. Superior Court* (1977) 75 Cal.App.3d 893 [142 Cal.Rptr. 509] (motion for disqualification of counsel due to a conflict of interest); *Academy of California Optometrists, Inc. v. Superior Court* (1975) 51 Cal.App.3d 999 [124 Cal.Rptr. 668] (duty to return client files); *Chronometrics, Inc. v. Sysgen, Inc.* (1980) 110 Cal.App.3d 597 [168 Cal.Rptr. 196] (disqualification of member appropriate remedy for improper communication with adverse party).)

Law firm, as defined by subparagraph (B)(1), is not intended to include an association of lawyers who do not share profits, expenses, and liabilities. The subparagraph is not intended to imply that a law firm may include a person who is not a member in violation of the law governing the unauthorized practice of law.

RULE 1–110. Disciplinary Authority of the State Bar

A member shall comply with conditions attached to public or private reprovals or other discipline administered by the State Bar pursuant to Business and Professions Code sections 6077 and 6078 and rule 9.19, California Rules of Court.

RULE 1–120. Assisting, Soliciting, or Inducing Violations

A member shall not knowingly assist in, solicit, or induce any violation of these rules or the State Bar Act.

RULE 1–200. False Statement Regarding Admission to the State Bar

(A) A member shall not knowingly make a false statement regarding a material fact or knowingly fail to disclose a material fact in connection with an application for admission to the State Bar.

(B) A member shall not further an application for admission to the State Bar of a person whom the member knows to be unqualified in respect to character, education, or other relevant attributes.

(C) This rule shall not prevent a member from serving as counsel of record for an applicant for admission to practice in proceedings related to such admission.

Discussion

For purposes of rule 1–200 "admission" includes readmission.

RULE 1–300. Unauthorized Practice of Law

(A) A member shall not aid any person or entity in the unauthorized practice of law.

(B) A member shall not practice law in a jurisdiction where to do so would be in violation of regulations of the profession in that jurisdiction.

RULE 1–310. Forming a Partnership With a Non-lawyer

A member shall not form a partnership with a person who is not a lawyer if any of the activities of that partnership consist of the practice of law.

Discussion

Rule 1–310 is not intended to govern members' activities which cannot be considered to constitute the practice of law. It is intended solely to preclude a member from being involved in the practice of law with a person who is not a lawyer.

RULE 1–311. Employment of Disbarred, Suspended, Resigned, or Involuntarily Inactive Member

(A) For purposes of this rule:

(1) "Employ" means to engage the services of another, including employees, agents, independent contractors and consultants, regardless of whether any compensation is paid;

(2) "Involuntarily inactive member" means a member who is ineligible to practice law as a result of action taken pursuant to Business and Professions Code sections 6007, 6203(c), or California Rule of Court 9.31; and

(3) "Resigned member" means a member who has resigned from the State Bar while disciplinary charges are pending.

(B) A member shall not employ, associate professionally with, or aid a person the member knows or reasonably should know is a disbarred, suspended, resigned, or involuntarily inactive member to perform the following on behalf of the member's client:

(1) Render legal consultation or advice to the client;

(2) Appear on behalf of a client in any hearing or proceeding or before any judicial officer, arbitrator, mediator, court, public agency, referee, magistrate, commissioner, or hearing officer;

(3) Appear as a representative of the client at a deposition or other discovery matter;

(4) Negotiate or transact any matter for or on behalf of the client with third parties;

(5) Receive, disburse or otherwise handle the client's funds; or

(6) Engage in activities which constitute the practice of law.

(C) A member may employ, associate professionally with, or aid a disbarred, suspended, resigned, or involuntarily inactive member to perform research, drafting or clerical activities, including but not limited to:

(1) Legal work of a preparatory nature, such as legal research, the assemblage of data and other necessary information, drafting of pleadings, briefs, and other similar documents;

(2) Direct communication with the client or third parties regarding matters such as scheduling, billing, updates, confirmation of receipt or sending of correspondence and messages; or

(3) Accompanying an active member in attending a deposition or other discovery matter for the limited purpose of providing clerical assistance to the active member who will appear as the representative of the client.

(D) Prior to or at the time of employing a person the member knows or reasonably should know is a disbarred, suspended, resigned, or involuntarily inactive member, the member shall serve upon the State Bar written notice of the employment, including a full description of such person's current bar status. The written notice shall also list the activities prohibited in paragraph (B) and state that the disbarred, suspended, resigned, or involuntarily inactive member will not perform such activities. The member shall serve similar written notice upon each client on whose specific matter such person will work, prior to or at the time of employing such person to work on the client's specific matter. The member shall obtain proof of service of the client's written notice and shall retain such proof and a true and correct copy of the client's written notice for two years following termination of the member's employment with the client.

(E) A member may, without client or State Bar notification, employ a disbarred, suspended, resigned or involuntarily inactive member whose sole function is to perform office physical plant or equipment maintenance, courier or delivery services, catering, reception, typing or transcription, or other similar support activities.

(F) Upon termination of the disbarred, suspended, resigned, or involuntarily inactive member, the member shall promptly serve upon the State Bar written notice of the termination.

Discussion

For discussion of the activities that constitute the practice of law, see *Farnham v. State Bar* (1976) 17 Cal.3d 605 [131 Cal.Rptr. 611]; *Bluestein v. State Bar* (1974) 13 Cal.3d 162 [118 Cal.Rptr. 175]; *Baron v. City of Los Angeles* (1970) 2 Cal.3d 535 [86 Cal.Rptr. 673]; *Crawford v. State Bar* (1960) 54 Cal.2d 659 [7 Cal.Rptr. 746]; *People v. Merchants Protective Corporation* (1922) 189 Cal. 531 [209 P. 363]; *People v. Landlords Professional Services* (1989) 215 Cal.App.3d 1599 [264 Cal.Rptr. 548]; and *People v. Sipper* (1943) 61 Cal.App.2d Supp. 844 [142 P.2d 960].

Paragraph (D) is not intended to prevent or discourage a member from fully discussing with the client the activities that will be performed by the disbarred, suspended, resigned, or involuntarily inactive member on the client's matter. If a member's client is an organization, then the written notice required by paragraph (D) shall be served upon the highest authorized officer, employee, or constituent overseeing the particular engagement. (See rule 3–600.)

Nothing in rule 1–311 shall be deemed to limit or preclude any activity engaged in pursuant to rules 9.40, 9.41, 9.42, and 9.44 of the California Rules of

Court, or any local rule of a federal district court concerning admission pro hac vice.

RULE 1–320. Financial Arrangements With Non–Lawyers

(A) Neither a member nor a law firm shall directly or indirectly share legal fees with a person who is not a lawyer, except that:

(1) An agreement between a member and a law firm, partner, or associate may provide for the payment of money after the member's death to the member's estate or to one or more specified persons over a reasonable period of time; or

(2) A member or law firm undertaking to complete unfinished legal business of a deceased member may pay to the estate of the deceased member or other person legally entitled thereto that proportion of the total compensation which fairly represents the services rendered by the deceased member; or

(3) A member or law firm may include non-member employees in a compensation, profit-sharing, or retirement plan even though the plan is based in whole or in part on a profit-sharing arrangement, if such plan does not circumvent these rules or Business and Professions Code section 6000 et seq.; or

(4) A member may pay a prescribed registration, referral, or participation fee to a lawyer referral service established, sponsored, and operated in accordance with the State Bar of California's Minimum Standards for a Lawyer Referral Service in California.

(B) A member shall not compensate, give, or promise anything of value to any person or entity for the purpose of recommending or securing employment of the member or the member's law firm by a client, or as a reward for having made a recommendation resulting in employment of the member or the member's law firm by a client. A member's offering of or giving a gift or gratuity to any person or entity having made a recommendation resulting in the employment of the member or the member's law firm shall not of itself violate this rule, provided that the gift or gratuity was not offered or given in consideration of any promise, agreement, or understanding that such a gift or gratuity would be forthcoming or that referrals would be made or encouraged in the future.

(C) A member shall not compensate, give, or promise anything of value to any representative of the press, radio, television, or other communication medium in anticipation of or in return for publicity of the member, the law firm, or any other member as such in a news item, but the incidental provision of food or beverage shall not of itself violate this rule.

Discussion

Rule 1–320(C) is not intended to preclude compensation to the communications media in exchange for advertising the member's or law firm's availability for professional employment.

RULE 1–400. Advertising and Solicitation

(A) For purposes of this rule, "communication" means any message or offer made by or on behalf of a member concerning the availability for professional employment of a member or a law firm directed to any former, present, or prospective client, including but not limited to the following:

(1) Any use of firm name, trade name, fictitious name, or other professional designation of such member or law firm; or

(2) Any stationery, letterhead, business card, sign, brochure, or other comparable written material describing such member, law firm, or lawyers; or

(3) Any advertisement (regardless of medium) of such member or law firm directed to the general public or any substantial portion thereof; or

(4) Any unsolicited correspondence from a member or law firm directed to any person or entity.

(B) For purposes of this rule, a "solicitation" means any communication:

(1) Concerning the availability for professional employment of a member or a law firm in which a significant motive is pecuniary gain; and

(2) Which is;

(a) delivered in person or by telephone, or

(b) directed by any means to a person known to the sender to be represented by counsel in a matter which is a subject of the communication.

(C) A solicitation shall not be made by or on behalf of a member or law firm to a prospective client with whom the member or law firm has no family or prior professional relationship, unless the solicitation is protected from abridgment by the Constitution of the United States or by the Constitution of the State of California. A solicitation to a former or present client in the discharge of a member's or law firm's professional duties is not prohibited.

(D) A communication or a solicitation (as defined herein) shall not:

(1) Contain any untrue statement; or

(2) Contain any matter, or present or arrange any matter in a manner or format which is false, deceptive, or which tends to confuse, deceive, or mislead the public; or

(3) Omit to state any fact necessary to make the statements made, in the light of circumstances under which they are made, not misleading to the public; or

(4) Fail to indicate clearly, expressly, or by context, that it is a communication or solicitation, as the case may be; or

(5) Be transmitted in any manner which involves intrusion, coercion, duress, compulsion, intimidation, threats, or vexatious or harassing conduct.

(6) State that a member is a "certified specialist" unless the member holds a current certificate as a specialist issued by the Board of Legal Specialization, or any other entity accredited by the State Bar to designate specialists pursuant to standards adopted by the Board of Governors, and states the complete name of the entity which granted certification.

(E) The Board of Governors of the State Bar shall formulate and adopt standards as to communications which will be presumed to violate this rule 1–400. The standards shall only be used as presumptions affecting the burden of proof in disciplinary proceedings involving alleged violations of these rules. "Presumption affecting the burden of proof" means that presumption defined in Evidence Code sections 605 and 606. Such standards formulated and adopted by the Board, as from time to time amended, shall be effective and binding on all members.

(F) A member shall retain for two years a true and correct copy or recording of any communication made by written or electronic media. Upon written request, the member shall make any such copy or recording available to the State Bar, and, if requested, shall provide to the State Bar evidence to support any factual or objective claim contained in the communication.

Standards:

Pursuant to rule 1–400(E) the Board of Governors of the State Bar has adopted the following standards, effective May 27, 1989, unless noted otherwise, as forms of "communication" defined in rule 1–400(A) which are presumed to be in violation of rule 1–400:

(1) A "communication" which contains guarantees, warranties, or predictions regarding the result of the representation.

(2) A "communication" which contains testimonials about or endorsements of a member unless such communication also contains an express disclaimer such as "this testimonial or endorsement does not constitute a guarantee, warranty, or prediction regarding the outcome of your legal matter."

(3) A "communication" which is delivered to a potential client whom the member knows or should reasonably know is in such a physical, emotional, or mental state that he or she would not be expected to exercise reasonable judgment as to the retention of counsel.

(4) A "communication" which is transmitted at the scene of an accident or at or en route to a hospital, emergency care center, or other health care facility.

(5) A "communication," except professional announcements, seeking professional employment for pecuniary gain, which is transmitted by mail or equivalent means which does not bear the word "Advertisement," "Newsletter" or words of similar import in 12 point print on the first page. If such communication, including firm brochures, newsletters, recent legal developments advisories, and similar materials, is transmit-

ted in an envelope, the envelope shall bear the word "Advertisement," "Newsletter" or words of similar import on the outside thereof.

(6) A "communication" in the form of a firm name, trade name, fictitious name, or other professional designation which states or implies a relationship between any member in private practice and a government agency or instrumentality or a public or non-profit legal services organization.

(7) A "communication" in the form of a firm name, trade name, fictitious name, or other professional designation which states or implies that a member has a relationship to any other member or a law firm as a partner or associate, or officer or shareholder pursuant to Business and Professions Code sections 6160–6172 unless such relationship in fact exists.

(8) A "communication" which states or implies that a member or law firm is "of counsel" to another lawyer or a law firm unless the former has a relationship with the latter (other than as a partner or associate, or officer or shareholder pursuant to Business and Professions Code sections 6160–6172) which is close, personal, continuous, and regular.

(9) A "communication" in the form of a firm name, trade name, fictitious name, or other professional designation used by a member or law firm in private practice which differs materially from any other such designation used by such member or law firm at the same time in the same community.

(10) A "communication" which implies that the member or law firm is participating in a lawyer referral service which has been certified by the State Bar of California or as having satisfied the Minimum Standards for Lawyer Referral Services in California, when that is not the case.

(11) [Repealed, effective June 1, 1997. See rule 1–400(D)(6)]

(12) A "communication," except professional announcements, in the form of an advertisement primarily directed to seeking professional employment primarily for pecuniary gain transmitted to the general public or any substantial portion thereof by mail or equivalent means or by means of television, radio, newspaper, magazine or other form of commercial mass media which does not state the name of the member responsible for the communication. When the communication is made on behalf of a law firm, the communication shall state the name of at least one member responsible for it.

(13) A "communication" which contains a dramatization unless such communication contains a disclaimer which states "this is a dramatization" or words of similar import.

(14) A "communication" which states or implies "no fee without recovery" unless such communication also expressly discloses whether or not the client will be liable for costs.

329

(15) A "communication" which states or implies that a member is able to provide legal services in a language other than English unless the member can actually provide legal services in such language or the communication also states in the language of the communication (a) the employment title of the person who speaks such language and (b) that the person is not a member of the State Bar of California, if that is the case.

(16) An unsolicited "communication" transmitted to the general public or any substantial portion thereof primarily directed to seeking professional employment primarily for pecuniary gain which sets forth a specific fee or range of fees for a particular service where, in fact, the member charges a greater fee than advertised in such communication within a period of 90 days following dissemination of such communication, unless such communication expressly specifies a shorter period of time regarding the advertised fee. Where the communication is published in the classified or "yellow pages" section of telephone, business or legal directories or in other media not published more frequently than once a year, the member shall conform to the advertised fee for a period of one year from initial publication, unless such communication expressly specifies a shorter period of time regarding the advertised fee.

RULE 1–500. Agreements Restricting a Member's Practice

(A) A member shall not be a party to or participate in offering or making an agreement, whether in connection with the settlement of a lawsuit or otherwise, if the agreement restricts the right of a member to practice law, except that this rule shall not prohibit such an agreement which:

(1) Is a part of an employment, shareholders', or partnership agreement among members provided the restrictive agreement does not survive the termination of the employment, shareholder, or partnership relationship; or

(2) Requires payments to a member upon the member's retirement from the practice of law; or

(3) Is authorized by Business and Professions Code sections 6092.5, subdivision (i) or 6093.

(B) A member shall not be a party to or participate in offering or making an agreement which precludes the reporting of a violation of these rules.

Discussion

Paragraph (A) makes it clear that the practice, in connection with settlement agreements, of proposing that a member refrain from representing other clients in similar litigation, is prohibited. Neither counsel may demand or suggest such provisions nor may opposing counsel accede or agree to such provisions.

Paragraph (A) permits a restrictive covenant in a law corporation, partnership, or employment agreement. The law corporation shareholder, partner, or associate may agree not to have a separate practice during the existence of the relationship; however, upon termination of the relationship (whether voluntary or involuntary), the member is free to practice law without any contractual restriction except in the case of retirement from the active practice of law.

RULE 1–600. Legal Service Programs

(A) A member shall not participate in a nongovernmental program, activity, or organization furnishing, recommending, or paying for legal services, which allows any third person or organization to interfere with the member's independence of professional judgment, or with the client-lawyer relationship, or allows unlicensed persons to practice law, or allows any third person or organization to receive directly or indirectly any part of the consideration paid to the member except as permitted by these rules, or otherwise violates the State Bar Act or these rules.

(B) The Board of Governors of the State Bar shall formulate and adopt Minimum Standards for Lawyer Referral Services, which, as from time to time amended, shall be binding on members.

Discussion

The participation of a member in a lawyer referral service established, sponsored, supervised, and operated in conformity with the Minimum Standards for a Lawyer Referral Service in California is encouraged and is not, of itself, a violation of these rules.

Rule 1–600 is not intended to override any contractual agreement or relationship between insurers and insureds regarding the provision of legal services.

Rule 1–600 is not intended to apply to the activities of a public agency responsible for providing legal services to a government or to the public.

For purposes of paragraph (A), "a nongovernmental program, activity, or organization" includes, but is not limited to group, prepaid, and voluntary legal service programs, activities, or organizations.

RULE 1–650. Limited Legal Services Programs

(A) A member who, under the auspices of a program sponsored by a court, government agency, bar association, law school, or nonprofit organization, provides short-term limited legal services to a client without expectation by either the member or the client that the member will provide continuing representation in the matter:

(1) is subject to rule 3–310 only if the member knows that the representation of the client involves a conflict of interest; and

(2) has an imputed conflict of interest only if the member knows that another lawyer associated with the member in a law firm would have a conflict of interest under rule 3–310 with respect to the matter.

(B) Except as provided in paragraph (A)(2), a conflict of interest that arises from a member's participation in a program under paragraph (A) will not be imputed to the member's law firm.

(C) The personal disqualification of a lawyer participating in the program will not be imputed to other lawyers participating in the program.

Discussion

Courts, government agencies, bar associations, law schools and various non-profit organizations have established programs through which lawyers provide short-term limited legal services—such as advice or the completion of legal forms—that will assist persons in addressing their legal problems without further representation by a lawyer. In these programs, such as legal-advice hotlines, advice-only clinics or pro se counseling programs, whenever a lawyer-client relationship is established, there is no expectation that the lawyer's representation of the client will continue beyond that limited consultation. Such programs are normally operated under circumstances in which it is not feasible for a lawyer to systematically screen for conflicts of interest as is generally required before undertaking a representation.

A member who provides short-term limited legal services pursuant to rule 1-650 must secure the client's informed consent to the limited scope of the representation. If a short-term limited representation would not be reasonable under the circumstances, the member may offer advice to the client but must also advise the client of the need for further assistance of counsel. See rule 3-110. Except as provided in this rule 1-650, the Rules of Professional Conduct and the State Bar Act, including the member's duty of confidentiality under Business and Professions Code § 6068(e)(1), are applicable to the limited representation.

A member who is representing a client in the circumstances addressed by rule 1-650 ordinarily is not able to check systematically for conflicts of interest. Therefore, paragraph (A)(1) requires compliance with rule 3-310 only if the member knows that the representation presents a conflict of interest for the member. In addition, paragraph (A)(2) imputes conflicts of interest to the member only if the member knows that another lawyer in the member's law firm would be disqualified under rule 3-310.

Because the limited nature of the services significantly reduces the risk of conflicts of interest with other matters being handled by the member's law firm, paragraph (B) provides that imputed conflicts of interest are inapplicable to a representation governed by this rule except as provided by paragraph (A)(2). Paragraph (A)(2) imputes conflicts of interest to the participating member when the member knows that any lawyer in the member's firm would be disqualified under rule 3-310. By virtue of paragraph (B), moreover, a member's participation in a short-term limited legal services program will not be imputed to the member's law firm or preclude the member's law firm from undertaking or continuing the representation of a client with interests adverse to a client being represented under the program's auspices. Nor will the personal disqualification of a lawyer participating in the program be imputed to other lawyers participating in the program.

If, after commencing a short-term limited representation in accordance with rule 1-650, a member undertakes to represent the client in the matter on an ongoing basis, rule 3-310 and all other rules become applicable.

RULE 1-700. Member as Candidate for Judicial Office

(A) A member who is a candidate for judicial office in California shall comply with Canon 5 of the Code of Judicial Ethics.

(B) For purposes of this rule, "candidate for judicial office" means a member seeking judicial office by election. The determination of when a member is a candidate for judicial office is defined in the terminology section of the California Code of Judicial Ethics. A member's duty to comply with paragraph (A) shall end when the member announces withdrawal of the member's candidacy or when the results of the election are final, whichever occurs first.

Discussion

Nothing in rule 1–700 shall be deemed to limit the applicability of any other rule or law.

RULE 1–710. Member as Temporary Judge, Referee, or Court-Appointed Arbitrator

A member who is serving as a temporary judge, referee, or court-appointed arbitrator, and is subject under the Code of Judicial Ethics to Canon 6D, shall comply with the terms of that canon.

Discussion

This rule is intended to permit the State Bar to discipline members who violate applicable portions of the Code of Judicial Ethics while acting in a judicial capacity pursuant to an order or appointment by a court.

Nothing in rule 1–710 shall be deemed to limit the applicability of any other rule or law.

CHAPTER 2. RELATIONSHIP AMONG MEMBERS

RULE 2–100. Communication With a Represented Party

(A) While representing a client, a member shall not communicate directly or indirectly about the subject of the representation with a party the member knows to be represented by another lawyer in the matter, unless the member has the consent of the other lawyer.

(B) For purposes of this rule, a "party" includes:

(1) An officer, director, or managing agent of a corporation or association, and a partner or managing agent of a partnership; or

(2) An association member or an employee of an association, corporation, or partnership, if the subject of the communication is any act or omission of such person in connection with the matter which may be binding upon or imputed to the organization for purposes of civil or criminal liability or whose statement may constitute an admission on the part of the organization.

(C) This rule shall not prohibit:

(1) Communications with a public officer, board, committee, or body;

(2) Communications initiated by a party seeking advice or representation from an independent lawyer of the party's choice; or

(3) Communications otherwise authorized by law.

Discussion

Rule 2-100 is intended to control communications between a member and persons the member knows to be represented by counsel unless a statutory scheme or case law will override the rule. There are a number of express statutory schemes which authorize communications between a member and person who would otherwise be subject to this rule. These statutes protect a variety of other rights such as the right of employees to organize and to engage in collective bargaining, employee health and safety, or equal employment opportunity. Other applicable law also includes the authority of government prosecutors and investigators to conduct criminal investigations, as limited by the relevant decisional law.

Rule 2-100 is not intended to prevent the parties themselves from communicating with respect to the subject matter of the representation, and nothing in the rule prevents a member from advising the client that such communication can be made. Moreover, the rule does not prohibit a member who is also a party to a legal matter from directly or indirectly communicating on his or her own behalf with a represented party. Such a member has independent rights as a party which should not be abrogated because of his or her professional status. To prevent any possible abuse in such situations, the counsel for the opposing party may advise that party (1) about the risks and benefits of communications with a lawyer-party, and (2) not to accept or engage in communications with the lawyer-party.

Rule 2-100 also addresses the situation in which member A is contacted by an opposing party who is represented and, because of dissatisfaction with that party's counsel, seeks A's independent advice. Since A is employed by the opposition, the member cannot give independent advice.

As used in paragraph (A), "the subject of the representation," "matter," and "party" are not limited to a litigation context.

Paragraph (B) is intended to apply only to persons employed at the time of the communication. (See *Triple A Machine Shop, Inc. v. State of California* (1989) 213 Cal.App.3d 131 [261 Cal.Rptr. 493].)

Subparagraph (C)(2) is intended to permit a member to communicate with a party seeking to hire new counsel or to obtain a second opinion. A member contacted by such a party continues to be bound by other Rules of Professional Conduct. (See, e.g., rules 1-400 and 3-310.)

RULE 2-200.   Financial Arrangements Among Lawyers

(A) A member shall not divide a fee for legal services with a lawyer who is not a partner of, associate of, or shareholder with the member unless:

(1) The client has consented in writing thereto after a full disclosure has been made in writing that a division of fees will be made and the terms of such division; and

(2) The total fee charged by all lawyers is not increased solely by reason of the provision for division of fees and is not unconscionable as that term is defined in rule 4-200.

(B) Except as permitted in paragraph (A) of this rule or rule 2–300, a member shall not compensate, give, or promise anything of value to any lawyer for the purpose of recommending or securing employment of the member or the member's law firm by a client, or as a reward for having made a recommendation resulting in employment of the member or the member's law firm by a client. A member's offering of or giving a gift or gratuity to any lawyer who has made a recommendation resulting in the employment of the member or the member's law firm shall not of itself violate this rule, provided that the gift or gratuity was not offered in consideration of any promise, agreement, or understanding that such a gift or gratuity would be forthcoming or that referrals would be made or encouraged in the future.

RULE 2–300. Sale or Purchase of a Law Practice of a Member, Living or Deceased

All or substantially all of the law practice of a member, living or deceased, including goodwill, may be sold to another member or law firm subject to all the following conditions:

(A) Fees charged to clients shall not be increased solely by reason of such sale.

(B) If the sale contemplates the transfer of responsibility for work not yet completed or responsibility for client files or information protected by Business and Professions Code section 6068, subdivision (e), then:

(1) if the seller is deceased or has a conservator or other person acting in a representative capacity, and no member has been appointed to act for the seller pursuant to Business and Professions Code section 6180.5, then prior to the transfer;

(a) the purchaser shall cause a written notice to be given to the client stating that the interest in the law practice is being transferred to the purchaser; that the client has the right to retain other counsel; that the client may take possession of any client papers and property, as required by rule 3–700(D); and that if no response is received to the notification within 90 days of the sending of such notice, or in the event the client's rights would be prejudiced by a failure to act during that time, the purchaser may act on behalf of the client until otherwise notified by the client. Such notice shall comply with the requirements as set forth in rule 1–400(D) and any provisions relating to attorney-client fee arrangements, and

(b) the purchaser shall obtain the written consent of the client provided that such consent shall be presumed until otherwise notified by the client if no response is received to the notification specified in subparagraph (a) within 90 days of the date of the sending of such notification to the client's last address as shown on the records of the seller, or the client's rights would be prejudiced by a failure to act during such 90-day period.

(2) in all other circumstances, not less than 90 days prior to the transfer;

(a) the seller, or the member appointed to act for the seller pursuant to Business and Professions Code Section 6180.5, shall cause a written notice to be given to the client stating that the interest in the law practice is being transferred to the purchaser; that the client has the right to retain other counsel; that the client may take possession of any client papers and property, as required by rule 3–700(D); and that if no response is received to the notification within 90 days of the sending of such notice, the purchaser may act on behalf of the client until otherwise notified by the client. Such notice shall comply with the requirements as set forth in rule 1–400(D) and any provisions relating to attorney-client fee arrangements, and

(b) the seller, or the member appointed to act for the seller pursuant to Business and Professions Code section 6180.5, shall obtain the written consent of the client prior to the transfer provided that such consent shall be presumed until otherwise notified by the client if no response is received to the notification specified in subparagraph (a) within 90 days of the date of the sending of such notification to the client's last address as shown on the records of the seller.

(C) If substitution is required by the rules of a tribunal in which a matter is pending, all steps necessary to substitute a member shall be taken.

(D) All activity of a purchaser or potential purchaser under this rule shall be subject to compliance with rules 3–300 and 3–310 where applicable.

(E) Confidential information shall not be disclosed to a non-member in connection with a sale under this rule.

(F) Admission to or retirement from a law partnership or law corporation, retirement plans and similar arrangements, or sale of tangible assets of a law practice shall not be deemed a sale or purchase under this rule.

Discussion

Paragraph (A) is intended to prohibit the purchaser from charging the former clients of the seller a higher fee than the purchaser is charging his or her existing clients.

"All or substantially all of the law practice of a member" means, for purposes of rule 2–300 that, for example, a member may retain one or two clients who have such a longstanding personal and professional relationship with the member that transfer of those clients' files is not feasible. Conversely, rule 2–300 is not intended to authorize the sale of a law practice in a piecemeal fashion except as may be required by subparagraph (B)(1)(a) or paragraph (D).

Transfer of individual client matters, where permitted, is governed by rule 2–200. Payment of a fee to a non-lawyer broker for arranging the sale or purchase of a law practice is governed by rule 1–320.

RULE 2–400. Prohibited Discriminatory Conduct in a Law Practice

(A) For purposes of this rule:

(1) "law practice" includes sole practices, law partnerships, law corporations, corporate and governmental legal departments, and other entities which employ members to practice law;

(2) "knowingly permit" means a failure to advocate corrective action where the member knows of a discriminatory policy or practice which results in the unlawful discrimination prohibited in paragraph (B); and

(3) "unlawfully" and "unlawful" shall be determined by reference to applicable state or federal statutes or decisions making unlawful discrimination in employment and in offering goods and services to the public.

(B) In the management or operation of a law practice, a member shall not unlawfully discriminate or knowingly permit unlawful discrimination on the basis of race, national origin, sex, sexual orientation, religion, age or disability in:

(1) hiring, promoting, discharging or otherwise determining the conditions of employment of any person; or

(2) accepting or terminating representation of any client.

(C) No disciplinary investigation or proceeding may be initiated by the State Bar against a member under this rule unless and until a tribunal of competent jurisdiction, other than a disciplinary tribunal, shall have first adjudicated a complaint of alleged discrimination and found that unlawful conduct occurred. Upon such adjudication, the tribunal finding or verdict shall then be admissible evidence of the occurrence or non-occurrence of the alleged discrimination in any disciplinary proceeding initiated under this rule. In order for discipline to be imposed under this rule, however, the finding of unlawfulness must be upheld and final after appeal, the time for filing an appeal must have expired, or the appeal must have been dismissed.

Discussion

In order for discriminatory conduct to be actionable under this rule, it must first be found to be unlawful by an appropriate civil administrative or judicial tribunal under applicable state or federal law. Until there is a finding of civil unlawfulness, there is no basis for disciplinary action under this rule.

A complaint of misconduct based on this rule may be filed with the State Bar following a finding of unlawfulness in the first instance even though that finding is thereafter appealed.

A disciplinary investigation or proceeding for conduct coming within this rule may be initiated and maintained, however, if such conduct warrants discipline under California Business and Professions Code sections 6106 and 6068, the California Supreme Court's inherent authority to impose discipline, or other disciplinary standard.

CHAPTER 3. PROFESSIONAL RELATIONSHIP WITH CLIENTS

RULE 3–100. Confidential Information of a Client

(A) A member shall not reveal information protected from disclosure by Business and Professions Code section 6068, subdivision (e)(1) without the informed consent of the client, or as provided in paragraph (B) of this rule.

(B) A member may, but is not required to, reveal confidential information relating to the representation of a client to the extent that the member reasonably believes the disclosure is necessary to prevent a criminal act that the member reasonably believes is likely to result in death of, or substantial bodily harm to, an individual.

(C) Before revealing confidential information to prevent a criminal act as provided in paragraph (B), a member shall, if reasonable under the circumstances:

(1) make a good faith effort to persuade the client: (i) not to commit or to continue the criminal act or (ii) to pursue a course of conduct that will prevent the threatened death or substantial bodily harm; or do both (i) and (ii); and

(2) inform the client, at an appropriate time, of the member's ability or decision to reveal information as provided in paragraph (B).

(D) In revealing confidential information as provided in paragraph (B), the member's disclosure must be no more than is necessary to prevent the criminal act, given the information known to the member at the time of the disclosure.

(E) A member who does not reveal information permitted by paragraph (B) does not violate this rule.

Discussion

[1] *Duty of confidentiality.* Paragraph (A) relates to a member's obligations under Business and Professions Code section 6068, subdivision (e)(1), which provides it is a duty of a member: "To maintain inviolate the confidence, and at every peril to himself or herself to preserve the secrets, of his or her client." A member's duty to preserve the confidentiality of client information involves public policies of paramount importance. (*In Re Jordan* (1974) 12 Cal.3d 575, 580 [116 Cal.Rptr. 371].) Preserving the confidentiality of client information contributes to the trust that is the hallmark of the client-lawyer relationship. The client is thereby encouraged to seek legal assistance and to communicate fully and frankly with the lawyer even as to embarrassing or legally damaging subject matter. The lawyer needs this information to represent the client effectively and, if necessary, to advise the client to refrain from wrongful conduct. Almost without exception, clients come to lawyers in order to determine their rights and what is, in the complex of laws and regulations, deemed to be legal and correct. Based upon experience, lawyers know that almost all clients follow the advice given, and the law is upheld. Paragraph (A) thus recognizes a fundamental principle in the client-lawyer relationship, that, in the absence of the client's informed consent, a

member must not reveal information relating to the representation. (See, e.g., *Commercial Standard Title Co. v. Superior Court* (1979) 92 Cal.App.3d 934, 945 [155 Cal.Rptr.393].)

[2] *Client-lawyer confidentiality encompasses the attorney-client privilege, the work-product doctrine and ethical standards of confidentiality.* The principle of client-lawyer confidentiality applies to information relating to the representation, whatever its source, and encompasses matters communicated in confidence by the client, and therefore protected by the attorney-client privilege, matters protected by the work product doctrine, and matters protected under ethical standards of confidentiality, all as established in law, rule and policy. (See *In the Matter of Johnson* (Rev. Dept. 2000) 4 Cal. State Bar Ct. Rptr. 179; *Goldstein v. Lees* (1975) 46 Cal.3d 614, 621 [120 Cal. Rptr. 253].) The attorney-client privilege and work-product doctrine apply in judicial and other proceedings in which a member may be called as a witness or be otherwise compelled to produce evidence concerning a client. A member's ethical duty of confidentiality is not so limited in its scope of protection for the client-lawyer relationship of trust and prevents a member from revealing the client's confidential information even when not confronted with such compulsion. Thus, a member may not reveal such information except with the consent of the client or as authorized or required by the State Bar Act, these rules, or other law.

[3] *Narrow exception to duty of confidentiality under this Rule.* Notwithstanding the important public policies promoted by lawyers adhering to the core duty of confidentiality, the overriding value of life permits disclosures otherwise prohibited under Business & Professions Code section 6068(e), subdivision (1). Paragraph (B), which restates Business and Professions Code section 6068, subdivision (e)(2), identifies a narrow confidentiality exception, absent the client's informed consent, when a member reasonably believes that disclosure is necessary to prevent a criminal act that the member reasonably believes is likely to result in the death of, or substantial bodily harm to an individual. Evidence Code section 956.5, which relates to the evidentiary attorney-client privilege, sets forth a similar express exception. Although a member is not permitted to reveal confidential information concerning a client's past, completed criminal acts, the policy favoring the preservation of human life that underlies this exception to the duty of confidentiality and the evidentiary privilege permits disclosure to prevent a future or ongoing criminal act.

[4] *Member not subject to discipline for revealing confidential information as permitted under this Rule.* Rule 3–100, which restates Business and Professions Code section 6068, subdivision (e)(2), reflects a balancing between the interests of preserving client confidentiality and of preventing a criminal act that a member reasonably believes is likely to result in death or substantial bodily harm to an individual. A member who reveals information as permitted under this rule is not subject to discipline.

[5] *No duty to reveal confidential information.* Neither Business and Professions Code section 6068, subdivision (e)(2) nor this rule imposes an affirmative obligation on a member to reveal information in order to prevent harm. (See rule 1–100(A).) A member may decide not to reveal confidential information. Whether a member chooses to reveal confidential information as permitted under this rule is a matter for the individual member to decide, based on all the facts and circumstances, such as those discussed in paragraph [6] of this discussion.

[6]   *Deciding to reveal confidential information as permitted under paragraph (B).* Disclosure permitted under paragraph (B) is ordinarily a last resort, when no other available action is reasonably likely to prevent the criminal act. Prior to revealing information as permitted under paragraph (B), the member must, if reasonable under the circumstances, make a good faith effort to persuade the client to take steps to avoid the criminal act or threatened harm. Among the factors to be considered in determining whether to disclose confidential information are the following:

(1) the amount of time that the member has to make a decision about disclosure;

(2) whether the client or a third party has made similar threats before and whether they have ever acted or attempted to act upon them;

(3) whether the member believes the member's efforts to persuade the client or a third person not to engage in the criminal conduct have or have not been successful;

(4) the extent of adverse effect to the client's rights under the Fifth, Sixth and Fourteenth Amendments of the United States Constitution and analogous rights and privacy rights under Article 1 of the Constitution of the State of California that may result from disclosure contemplated by the member;

(5) the extent of other adverse effects to the client that may result from disclosure contemplated by the member; and

(6) the nature and extent of information that must be disclosed to prevent the criminal act or threatened harm.

A member may also consider whether the prospective harm to the victim or victims is imminent in deciding whether to disclose the confidential information. However, the imminence of the harm is not a prerequisite to disclosure and a member may disclose the information without waiting until immediately before the harm is likely to occur.

[7]   *Counseling client or third person not to commit a criminal act reasonably likely to result in death or substantial bodily harm.* Subparagraph (C)(1) provides that before a member may reveal confidential information, the member must, if reasonable under the circumstances, make a good faith effort to persuade the client not to commit or to continue the criminal act, or to persuade the client to otherwise pursue a course of conduct that will prevent the threatened death or substantial bodily harm, or if necessary, do both. The interests protected by such counseling is the client's interest in limiting disclosure of confidential information and in taking responsible action to deal with situations attributable to the client. If a client, whether in response to the member's counseling or otherwise, takes corrective action—such as by ceasing the criminal act before harm is caused—the option for permissive disclosure by the member would cease as the threat posed by the criminal act would no longer be present. When the actor is a nonclient or when the act is deliberate or malicious, the member who contemplates making adverse disclosure of confidential information may reasonably conclude that the compelling interests of the member or others in their own personal safety preclude personal contact with the actor. Before counseling an actor who is a nonclient, the member should, if reasonable under the circumstances, first advise the client of the member's intended course of action. If a client or another person has already acted but the intended harm has not yet occurred, the member should consider, if

reasonable under the circumstances, efforts to persuade the client or third person to warn the victim or consider other appropriate action to prevent the harm. Even when the member has concluded that paragraph (B) does not permit the member to reveal confidential information, the member nevertheless is permitted to counsel the client as to why it may be in the client's best interest to consent to the attorney's disclosure of that information.

[8] *Disclosure of confidential information must be no more than is reasonably necessary to prevent the criminal act.* Under paragraph (D), disclosure of confidential information, when made, must be no more extensive than the member reasonably believes necessary to prevent the criminal act. Disclosure should allow access to the confidential information to only those persons who the member reasonably believes can act to prevent the harm. Under some circumstances, a member may determine that the best course to pursue is to make an anonymous disclosure to the potential victim or relevant law-enforcement authorities. What particular measures are reasonable depends on the circumstances known to the member. Relevant circumstances include the time available, whether the victim might be unaware of the threat, the member's prior course of dealings with the client, and the extent of the adverse effect on the client that may result from the disclosure contemplated by the member.

[9] *Informing client of member's ability or decision to reveal confidential information under subparagraph (C)(2).* A member is required to keep a client reasonably informed about significant developments regarding the employment or representation. Rule 3–500; Business and Professions Code, section 6068, subdivision (m). Paragraph (C)(2), however, recognizes that under certain circumstances, informing a client of the member's ability or decision to reveal confidential information under paragraph (B) would likely increase the risk of death or substantial bodily harm, not only to the originally-intended victims of the criminal act, but also to the client or members of the client's family, or to the member or the member's family or associates. Therefore, paragraph (C)(2) requires a member to inform the client of the member's ability or decision to reveal confidential information as provided in paragraph (B) only if it is reasonable to do so under the circumstances. Paragraph (C)(2) further recognizes that the appropriate time for the member to inform the client may vary depending upon the circumstances. (See paragraph [10] of this discussion.) Among the factors to be considered in determining an appropriate time, if any, to inform a client are:

(1) whether the client is an experienced user of legal services;

(2) the frequency of the member's contact with the client;

(3) the nature and length of the professional relationship with the client;

(4) whether the member and client have discussed the member's duty of confidentiality or any exceptions to that duty;

(5) the likelihood that the client's matter will involve information within paragraph (B);

(6) the member's belief, if applicable, that so informing the client is likely to increase the likelihood that a criminal act likely to result in the death of, or substantial bodily harm to, an individual; and

(7) the member's belief, if applicable, that good faith efforts to persuade a client not to act on a threat have failed.

[10] *Avoiding a chilling effect on the lawyer-client relationship.* The foregoing flexible approach to the member's informing a client of his or her ability or decision to reveal confidential information recognizes the concern that informing a client about limits on confidentiality may have a chilling effect on client communication. (See Discussion paragraph [1].) To avoid that chilling effect, one member may choose to inform the client of the member's ability to reveal information as early as the outset of the representation, while another member may choose to inform a client only at a point when that client has imparted information that may fall under paragraph (B), or even choose not to inform a client until such time as the member attempts to counsel the client as contemplated in Discussion paragraph [7]. In each situation, the member will have discharged properly the requirement under subparagraph (C)(2), and will not be subject to discipline.

[11] *Informing client that disclosure has been made; termination of the lawyer-client relationship.* When a member has revealed confidential information under paragraph (B), in all but extraordinary cases the relationship between member and client will have deteriorated so as to make the member's representation of the client impossible. Therefore, the member is required to seek to withdraw from the representation (see rule 3-700(B)), unless the member is able to obtain the client's informed consent to the member's continued representation. The member must inform the client of the fact of the member's disclosure unless the member has a compelling interest in not informing the client, such as to protect the member, the member's family or a third person from the risk of death or substantial bodily harm.

[12] *Other consequences of the member's disclosure.* Depending upon the circumstances of a member's disclosure of confidential information, there may be other important issues that a member must address. For example, if a member will be called as a witness in the client's matter, then rule 5-210 should be considered. Similarly, the member should consider his or her duties of loyalty and competency (rule 3-110).

[13] *Other exceptions to confidentiality under California law.* Rule 3-100 is not intended to augment, diminish, or preclude reliance upon, any other exceptions to the duty to preserve the confidentiality of client information recognized under California law.

RULE 3-110. Failing to Act Competently

(A) A member shall not intentionally, recklessly, or repeatedly fail to perform legal services with competence.

(B) For purposes of this rule, "competence" in any legal service shall mean to apply the 1) diligence, 2) learning and skill, and 3) mental, emotional, and physical ability reasonably necessary for the performance of such service.

(C) If a member does not have sufficient learning and skill when the legal service is undertaken the member may nonetheless perform such services competently by 1) associating with or where appropriate, professionally consulting another lawyer reasonably believed to be competent, or 2) by acquiring sufficient learning and skill before performance is required.

Discussion

The duties set forth in rule 3–110 include the duty to supervise the work of subordinate attorney and non-attorney employees or agents. (See, e.g., *Waysman v. State Bar* (1986) 41 Cal.3d 452; *Trousil v. State Bar* (1985) 38 Cal.3d 337, 342 [211 Cal.Rptr. 525]; *Palomo v. State Bar* (1984) 36 Cal.3d 785 [205 Cal.Rptr. 834]; *Crane v. State Bar* (1981) 30 Cal.3d 117, 122; *Black v. State Bar* (1972) 7 Cal.3d 676, 692 [103 Cal.Rptr. 288; 499 P.2d 968]; *Vaughn v. State Bar* (1972) 6 Cal.3d 847, 857–858 [100 Cal.Rptr. 713; 494 P.2d 1257]; *Moore v. State Bar* (1964) 62 Cal.2d 74, 81 [41 Cal.Rptr. 161; 396 P.2d 577].)

In an emergency a lawyer may give advice or assistance in a matter in which the lawyer does not have the skill ordinarily required where referral to or consultation with another lawyer would be impractical. Even in an emergency, however, assistance should be limited to that reasonably necessary in the circumstances.

RULE 3–120.   Sexual Relations With Client

(A) For purposes of this rule, "sexual relations" means sexual intercourse or the touching of an intimate part of another person for the purpose of sexual arousal, gratification, or abuse.

(B) A member shall not:

(1) Require or demand sexual relations with a client incident to or as a condition of any professional representation; or

(2) Employ coercion, intimidation, or undue influence in entering into sexual relations with a client; or

(3) Continue representation of a client with whom the member has sexual relations if such sexual relations cause the member to perform legal services incompetently in violation of rule 3–110.

(C) Paragraph (B) shall not apply to sexual relations between members and their spouses or to ongoing consensual sexual relationships which predate the initiation of the lawyer-client relationship.

(D) Where a lawyer in a firm has sexual relations with a client but does not participate in the representation of that client, the lawyers in the firm shall not be subject to discipline under this rule solely because of the occurrence of such sexual relations.

Discussion

Rule 3–120 is intended to prohibit sexual exploitation by a lawyer in the course of a professional representation. Often, based upon the nature of the underlying representation, a client exhibits great emotional vulnerability and dependence upon the advice and guidance of counsel. Attorneys owe the utmost duty of good faith and fidelity to clients. (See, e.g., *Greenbaum v. State Bar* (1976) 15 Cal.3d 893, 903 [126 Cal.Rptr. 785]; *Alkow v. State Bar* (1971) 3 Cal.3d 924, 935 [92 Cal.Rptr. 278]; *Cutler v. State Bar* (1969) 71 Cal.2d 241, 251 [78 Cal.Rptr. 172]; *Clancy v. State Bar* (1969) 71 Cal.2d 140, 146 [77 Cal.Rptr. 657].) The relationship between an attorney and client is a fiduciary relationship of the very highest character and all dealings between an attorney and client that are beneficial to the attorney will be closely scrutinized with the utmost strictness for unfairness. (See, e.g., *Giovanazzi v. State Bar* (1980) 28 Cal.3d 465, 472 [169 Cal.Rptr. 581]; *Benson v. State Bar* (1975) 13 Cal.3d 581, 586 [119 Cal.Rptr. 297]; *Lee v. State Bar* (1970) 2 Cal.3d 927, 939 [88 Cal.Rptr. 361]; *Clancy v. State Bar* (1969) 71 Cal.2d 140, 146 [77 Cal.Rptr. 657].) Where attorneys exercise undue influence over clients or take unfair advantage of clients, discipline is appropriate. (See, e.g., *Magee v. State Bar* (1962) 58 Cal.2d 423 [24 Cal.Rptr. 839]; *Lantz v. State Bar* (1931) 212 Cal. 213 [298 P. 497].) In all client matters, a member is advised to keep clients' interests paramount in the course of the member's representation.

For purposes of this rule, if the client is an organization, any individual overseeing the representation shall be deemed to be the client. (See rule 3–600.)

Although paragraph (C) excludes representation of certain clients from the scope of rule 3–120, such exclusion is not intended to preclude the applicability of other Rules of Professional Conduct, including rule 3–110.

RULE 3–200. Prohibited Objectives of Employment

A member shall not seek, accept, or continue employment if the member knows or should know that the objective of such employment is:

(A) To bring an action, conduct a defense, assert a position in litigation, or take an appeal, without probable cause and for the purpose of harassing or maliciously injuring any person; or

(B) To present a claim or defense in litigation that is not warranted under existing law, unless it can be supported by a good faith argument for an extension, modification, or reversal of such existing law.

RULE 3–210. Advising the Violation of Law

A member shall not advise the violation of any law, rule, or ruling of a tribunal unless the member believes in good faith that such law, rule, or ruling is invalid. A member may take appropriate steps in good faith to test the validity of any law, rule, or ruling of a tribunal.

Discussion

Rule 3–210 is intended to apply not only to the prospective conduct of a client but also to the interaction between the member and client and to the specific legal service sought by the client from the member. An example of the former is the handling of physical evidence of a crime in the possession of the client and offered to the member. (See *People v. Meredith* (1981) 29 Cal.3d 682 [175 Cal.Rptr. 612].) An example of the latter is a request that the member negotiate the return of stolen property in exchange for the owner's agreement not to report the theft to the police or prosecutorial authorities. (See *People v. Pic'l* (1982) 31 Cal.3d 731 [183 Cal.Rptr. 685].)

RULE 3–300. Avoiding Interests Adverse to a Client

A member shall not enter into a business transaction with a client; or knowingly acquire an ownership, possessory, security, or other pecuniary interest adverse to a client, unless each of the following requirements has been satisfied:

(A) The transaction or acquisition and its terms are fair and reasonable to the client and are fully disclosed and transmitted in writing to the client in a manner which should reasonably have been understood by the client; and

(B) The client is advised in writing that the client may seek the advice of an independent lawyer of the client's choice and is given a reasonable opportunity to seek that advice; and

(C) The client thereafter consents in writing to the terms of the transaction or the terms of the acquisition.

Discussion

Rule 3–300 is not intended to apply to the agreement by which the member is retained by the client, unless the agreement confers on the member an ownership, possessory, security, or other pecuniary interest adverse to the client. Such an agreement is governed, in part, by rule 4–200.

Rule 3–300 is not intended to apply where the member and client each make an investment on terms offered to the general public or a significant portion thereof. For example, rule 3–300 is not intended to apply where A, a member, invests in a limited partnership syndicated by a third party. B, A's client, makes the same investment. Although A and B are each investing in the same business, A did not enter into the transaction "with" B for the purposes of the rule.

Rule 3–300 is intended to apply where the member wishes to obtain an interest in client's property in order to secure the amount of the member's past due or future fees.

RULE 3–310. Avoiding the Representation of Adverse Interests

(A) For purposes of this rule:

(1) "Disclosure" means informing the client or former client of the relevant circumstances and of the actual and reasonably foreseeable adverse consequences to the client or former client;

(2) "Informed written consent" means the client's or former client's written agreement to the representation following written disclosure;

(3) "Written" means any writing as defined in Evidence Code section 250.

(B) A member shall not accept or continue representation of a client without providing written disclosure to the client where:

(1) The member has a legal, business, financial, professional, or personal relationship with a party or witness in the same matter; or

(2) The member knows or reasonably should know that:

(a) the member previously had a legal, business, financial, professional, or personal relationship with a party or witness in the same matter; and

345

(b) the previous relationship would substantially affect the member's representation; or

(3) The member has or had a legal, business, financial, professional, or personal relationship with another person or entity the member knows or reasonably should know would be affected substantially by resolution of the matter; or

(4) The member has or had a legal, business, financial, or professional interest in the subject matter of the representation.

(C) A member shall not, without the informed written consent of each client:

(1) Accept representation of more than one client in a matter in which the interests of the clients potentially conflict; or

(2) Accept or continue representation of more than one client in a matter in which the interests of the clients actually conflict; or

(3) Represent a client in a matter and at the same time in a separate matter accept as a client a person or entity whose interest in the first matter is adverse to the client in the first matter.

(D) A member who represents two or more clients shall not enter into an aggregate settlement of the claims of or against the clients without the informed written consent of each client.

(E) A member shall not, without the informed written consent of the client or former client, accept employment adverse to the client or former client where, by reason of the representation of the client or former client, the member has obtained confidential information material to the employment.

(F) A member shall not accept compensation for representing a client from one other than the client unless:

(1) There is no interference with the member's independence of professional judgment or with the client-lawyer relationship; and

(2) Information relating to representation of the client is protected as required by Business and Professions Code section 6068, subdivision (e); and

(3) The member obtains the client's informed written consent, provided that no disclosure or consent is required if;

(a) such nondisclosure is otherwise authorized by law; or

(b) the member is rendering legal services on behalf of any public agency which provides legal services to other public agencies or the public.

Discussion

Rule 3–310 is not intended to prohibit a member from representing parties having antagonistic positions on the same legal question that has arisen in different cases, unless representation of either client would be adversely affected.

Other rules and laws may preclude making adequate disclosure under this rule. If such disclosure is precluded, informed written consent is likewise precluded. (See, e.g., Business and Professions Code section 6068, subsection (e).)

Paragraph (B) is not intended to apply to the relationship of a member to another party's lawyer. Such relationships are governed by rule 3–320.

Paragraph (B) is not intended to require either the disclosure of the new engagement to a former client or the consent of the former client to the new engagement. However, such disclosure or consent is required if paragraph (E) applies.

While paragraph (B) deals with the issues of adequate disclosure to the present client or clients of the member's present or past relationships to other parties or witnesses or present interest in the subject matter of the representation, paragraph (E) is intended to protect the confidences of another present or former client. These two paragraphs are to apply as complementary provisions.

Paragraph (B) is intended to apply only to a member's own relationships or interests, unless the member knows that a partner or associate in the same firm as the member has or had a relationship with another party or witness or has or had an interest in the subject matter of the representation.

Subparagraphs (C)(1) and (C)(2) are intended to apply to all types of legal employment, including the concurrent representation of multiple parties in litigation or in a single transaction or in some other common enterprise or legal relationship. Examples of the latter include the formation of a partnership for several partners or a corporation for several shareholders, the preparation of an ante-nuptial agreement, or joint or reciprocal wills for a husband and wife, or the resolution of an "uncontested" marital dissolution. In such situations, for the sake of convenience or economy, the parties may well prefer to employ a single counsel, but a member must disclose the potential adverse aspects of such multiple representation (e.g., Evid. Code, § 962) and must obtain the informed written consent of the clients thereto pursuant to subparagraph (C)(1). Moreover, if the potential adversity should become actual, the member must obtain the further informed written consent of the clients pursuant to paragraph (C)(2).

Subparagraph (C)(3) is intended to apply to representations of clients in both litigation and transactional matters.

In *State Farm Mutual Automobile Insurance Company v. Federal Insurance Company* (1999) 72 Cal.App.4th 1422 [86 Cal.Rptr.2d 20], the court held that subparagraph (C)(3) was violated when a member, retained by an insurer to defend one suit, and while that suit was still pending, filed a direct action against the same insurer in an unrelated action without securing the insurer's consent. Notwithstanding *State Farm*, subparagraph (C)(3) is not intended to apply with respect to the relationship between an insurer and a member when, in each matter, the insurer's interest is only as an indemnity provider and not as a direct party to the action.

There are some matters in which the conflicts are such that written consent may not suffice for non-disciplinary purposes. (See *Woods v. Superior Court* (1983) 149 Cal.App.3d 931 [197 Cal.Rptr. 185]; *Klemm v. Superior Court* (1977) 75 Cal.App.3d 893 [142 Cal.Rptr. 509]; *Ishmael v. Millington* (1966) 241 Cal.App.2d 520 [50 Cal.Rptr. 592].)

Paragraph (D) is not intended to apply to class action settlements subject to court approval.

Paragraph (F) is not intended to abrogate existing relationships between insurers and insureds whereby the insurer has the contractual right to unilaterally select counsel for the insured, where there is no conflict of interest. (See *San Diego Navy Federal Credit Union v. Cumis Insurance Society* (1984) 162 Cal. App.3d 358 [208 Cal.Rptr. 494].)

RULE 3–320.   Relationship With Other Party's Lawyer

A member shall not represent a client in a matter in which another party's lawyer is a spouse, parent, child, or sibling of the member, lives with the member, is a client of the member, or has an intimate personal relationship with the member, unless the member informs the client in writing of the relationship.

Discussion

Rule 3–320 is not intended to apply to circumstances in which a member fails to advise the client of a relationship with another lawyer who is merely a partner or associate in the same law firm as the adverse party's counsel, and who has no direct involvement in the matter.

RULE 3–400.   Limiting Liability to Client

A member shall not:

(A) Contract with a client prospectively limiting the member's liability to the client for the member's professional malpractice; or

(B) Settle a claim or potential claim for the member's liability to the client for the member's professional malpractice, unless the client is informed in writing that the client may seek the advice of an independent lawyer of the client's choice regarding the settlement and is given a reasonable opportunity to seek that advice.

Discussion

Rule 3–400 is not intended to apply to customary qualifications and limitations in legal opinions and memoranda, nor is it intended to prevent a member from reasonably limiting the scope of the member's employment or representation.

RULE 3–410.   Disclosure of Professional Liability Insurance

(A) A member who knows or should know that he or she does not have professional liability insurance shall inform a client in writing, at the time of the client's engagement of the member, that the member does not have professional liability insurance whenever it is reasonably foreseeable that the total amount of the member's legal representation of the client in the matter will exceed four hours.

(B) If a member does not provide the notice required under paragraph (A) at the time of a client's engagement of the member, and the member subsequently knows or should know that he or she no longer has professional liability insurance during the representation of the client, the member shall inform the client in writing within thirty days of the date that the member knows or should know that he or she no longer has professional liability insurance.

(C) This rule does not apply to a member who is employed as a government lawyer or in-house counsel when that member is representing or providing legal advice to a client in that capacity.

(D) This rule does not apply to legal services rendered in an emergency to avoid foreseeable prejudice to the rights or interests of the client.

(E) This rule does not apply where the member has previously advised the client under Paragraph (A) or (B) that the member does not have professional liability insurance.

Discussion

The disclosure obligation imposed by Paragraph (A) of this rule applies with respect to new clients and new engagements with returning clients.

A member may use the following language in making the disclosure required by Rule 3–410(A), and may include that language in a written fee agreement with the client or in a separate writing:

"Pursuant to California Rule of Professional Conduct 3–410, I am informing you in writing that I do not have professional liability insurance."

A member may use the following language in making the disclosure required by Rule 3–410(B):

"Pursuant to California Rule of Professional Conduct 3–410, I am informing you in writing that I no longer have professional liability insurance."

Rule 3–410(C) provides an exemption for a "government lawyer or in-house counsel when that member is representing or providing legal advice to a client in that capacity." The basis of both exemptions is essentially the same. The purpose of this rule is to provide information directly to a client if a member is not covered by professional liability insurance. If a member is employed directly by and provides legal services directly for a private entity or a federal, state or local governmental entity, that entity presumably knows whether the member is or is not covered by professional liability insurance. The exemptions under this rule are limited to situations involving direct employment and representation, and do not, for example, apply to outside counsel for a private or governmental entity, or to counsel retained by an insurer to represent an insured.

RULE 3–500. Communication

A member shall keep a client reasonably informed about significant developments relating to the employment or representation, including promptly complying with reasonable requests for information and copies of significant documents when necessary to keep the client so informed.

Comment

Rule 3–500 is not intended to change a member's duties to his or her clients. It is intended to make clear that, while a client must be informed of significant developments in the matter, a member will not be disciplined for failing to communicate insignificant or irrelevant information. (See Bus. & Prof. Code, § 6068, subd. (m).)

A member may contract with the client in their employment agreement that the client assumes responsibility for the cost of copying significant documents. This rule is not intended to prohibit a claim for the recovery of the member's expense in any subsequent legal proceeding.

Rule 3–500 is not intended to create, augment, diminish, or eliminate any application of the work product rule. The obligation of the member to provide work product to the client shall be governed by relevant statutory and decisional law. Additionally, this rule is not intended to apply to any document or correspondence that is subject to a protective order or non-disclosure agreement, or to override applicable statutory or decisional law requiring that certain information not be provided to criminal defendants who are clients of the member.

RULE 3–510. Communication of Settlement Offer

(A) A member shall promptly communicate to the member's client:

(1) All terms and conditions of any offer made to the client in a criminal matter; and

(2) All amounts, terms, and conditions of any written offer of settlement made to the client in all other matters.

(B) As used in this rule, "client" includes a person who possesses the authority to accept an offer of settlement or plea, or, in a class action, all the named representatives of the class.

Discussion

Rule 3–510 is intended to require that counsel in a criminal matter convey all offers, whether written or oral, to the client, as give and take negotiations are less common in criminal matters, and, even were they to occur, such negotiations should require the participation of the accused.

Any oral offers of settlement made to the client in a civil matter should also be communicated if they are "significant" for the purposes of rule 3–500.

RULE 3–600. Organization as Client

(A) In representing an organization, a member shall conform his or her representation to the concept that the client is the organization itself, acting through its highest authorized officer, employee, body, or constituent overseeing the particular engagement.

(B) If a member acting on behalf of an organization knows that an actual or apparent agent of the organization acts or intends or refuses to act in a manner that is or may be a violation of law reasonably imputable to the organization, or in a manner which is likely to result in substantial injury to the organization, the member shall not violate his or her duty of protecting all confidential information as provided in Business and Professions Code section 6068, subdivision (e). Subject to Business and Professions Code section 6068, subdivision (e), the member may take such actions as appear to the member to be in the best lawful interest of the organization. Such actions may include among others:

(1) Urging reconsideration of the matter while explaining its likely consequences to the organization; or

(2) Referring the matter to the next higher authority in the organization, including, if warranted by the seriousness of the matter, referral to the highest internal authority that can act on behalf of the organization.

(C) If, despite the member's actions in accordance with paragraph (B), the highest authority that can act on behalf of the organization insists upon action or a refusal to act that is a violation of law and is likely to result in substantial injury to the organization, the member's response is limited to the member's right, and, where appropriate, duty to resign in accordance with rule 3–700.

(D) In dealing with an organization's directors, officers, employees, members, shareholders, or other constituents, a member shall explain the identity of the client for whom the member acts, whenever it is or becomes apparent that the organization's interests are or may become adverse to those of the constituent(s) with whom the member is dealing. The member shall not mislead such a constituent into believing that the constituent may communicate confidential information to the member in a way that will not be used in the organization's interest if that is or becomes adverse to the constituent.

(E) A member representing an organization may also represent any of its directors, officers, employees, members, shareholders, or other constituents, subject to the provisions of rule 3–310. If the organization's consent to the dual representation is required by rule 3–310, the consent shall be given by an appropriate constituent of the organization other than the individual or constituent who is to be represented, or by the shareholder(s) or organization members.

Discussion

Rule 3–600 is not intended to enmesh members in the intricacies of the entity and aggregate theories of partnership.

Rule 3–600 is not intended to prohibit members from representing both an organization and other parties connected with it, as for instance (as simply one example) in establishing employee benefit packages for closely held corporations or professional partnerships.

Rule 3–600 is not intended to create or to validate artificial distinctions between entities and their officers, employees, or members, nor is it the purpose of the rule to deny the existence or importance of such formal distinctions. In dealing with a close corporation or small association, members commonly perform professional engagements for both the organization and its major constituents. When a change in control occurs or is threatened, members are faced with complex decisions involving personal and institutional relationships and loyalties and have frequently had difficulty in perceiving their correct duty. (See *People ex rel. Deukmejian v. Brown* (1981) 29 Cal.3d 150 [172 Cal.Rptr. 478]; *Goldstein v. Lees*

(1975) 46 Cal.App.3d 614 [120 Cal.Rptr. 253]; *Woods v. Superior Court* (1983) 149 Cal.App.3d 931 [197 Cal.Rptr. 185]; *In re Banks* (1978) 283 Or. 459 [584 P.2d 284]; 1 A.L.R. 4th 1105.)   In resolving such multiple relationships, members must rely on case law.

RULE 3–700. Termination of Employment

(A) In General.

(1) If permission for termination of employment is required by the rules of a tribunal, a member shall not withdraw from employment in a proceeding before that tribunal without its permission.

(2) A member shall not withdraw from employment until the member has taken reasonable steps to avoid reasonably foreseeable prejudice to the rights of the client, including giving due notice to the client, allowing time for employment of other counsel, complying with rule 3–700(D), and complying with applicable laws and rules.

(B) Mandatory Withdrawal. A member representing a client before a tribunal shall withdraw from employment with the permission of the tribunal, if required by its rules, and a member representing a client in other matters shall withdraw from employment, if:

(1) The member knows or should know that the client is bringing an action, conducting a defense, asserting a position in litigation, or taking an appeal, without probable cause and for the purpose of harassing or maliciously injuring any person; or

(2) The member knows or should know that continued employment will result in violation of these rules or of the State Bar Act; or

(3) The member's mental or physical condition renders it unreasonably difficult to carry out the employment effectively.

(C) Permissive Withdrawal. If rule 3–700(B) is not applicable, a member may not request permission to withdraw in matters pending before a tribunal, and may not withdraw in other matters, unless such request or such withdrawal is because:

(1) The client

(a) insists upon presenting a claim or defense that is not warranted under existing law and cannot be supported by good faith argument for an extension, modification, or reversal of existing law, or

(b) seeks to pursue an illegal course of conduct, or

(c) insists that the member pursue a course of conduct that is illegal or that is prohibited under these rules or the State Bar Act, or

(d) by other conduct renders it unreasonably difficult for the member to carry out the employment effectively, or

(e) insists, in a matter not pending before a tribunal, that the member engage in conduct that is contrary to the judgment and advice of the member but not prohibited under these rules or the State Bar Act, or

(f) breaches an agreement or obligation to the member as to expenses or fees.

(2) The continued employment is likely to result in a violation of these rules or of the State Bar Act; or

(3) The inability to work with co-counsel indicates that the best interests of the client likely will be served by withdrawal; or

(4) The member's mental or physical condition renders it difficult for the member to carry out the employment effectively; or

(5) The client knowingly and freely assents to termination of the employment; or

(6) The member believes in good faith, in a proceeding pending before a tribunal, that the tribunal will find the existence of other good cause for withdrawal.

(D) Papers, Property, and Fees. A member whose employment has terminated shall:

(1) Subject to any protective order or non-disclosure agreement, promptly release to the client, at the request of the client, all the client papers and property. "Client papers and property" includes correspondence, pleadings, deposition transcripts, exhibits, physical evidence, expert's reports, and other items reasonably necessary to the client's representation, whether the client has paid for them or not; and

(2) Promptly refund any part of a fee paid in advance that has not been earned. This provision is not applicable to a true retainer fee which is paid solely for the purpose of ensuring the availability of the member for the matter.

Discussion

Subparagraph (A)(2) provides that "a member shall not withdraw from employment until the member has taken reasonable steps to avoid reasonably foreseeable prejudice to the rights of the clients." What such steps would include, of course, will vary according to the circumstances. Absent special circumstances, "reasonable steps" do not include providing additional services to the client once the successor counsel has been employed and rule 3–700(D) has been satisfied.

Paragraph (D) makes clear the member's duties in the recurring situation in which new counsel seeks to obtain client files from a member discharged by the client. It codifies existing case law. (See *Academy of California Optometrists v. Superior Court* (1975) 51 Cal.App.3d 999 [124 Cal.Rptr. 668]; *Weiss v. Marcus* (1975) 51 Cal.App.3d 590 [124 Cal.Rptr. 297].) Paragraph (D) also requires that the member "promptly" return unearned fees paid in advance. If a client disputes the amount to be returned, the member shall comply with rule 4–100(A)(2).

Paragraph (D) is not intended to prohibit a member from making, at the member's own expense, and retaining copies of papers released to the client, nor to prohibit a claim for the recovery of the member's expense in any subsequent legal proceeding.

CHAPTER 4. FINANCIAL RELATIONSHIP WITH CLIENTS

RULE 4–100. Preserving Identity of Funds and Property of a Client

(A) All funds received or held for the benefit of clients by a member or law firm, including advances for costs and expenses, shall be deposited in one or more identifiable bank accounts labelled "Trust Account," "Client's Funds Account" or words of similar import, maintained in the State of California, or, with written consent of the client, in any other jurisdiction where there is a substantial relationship between the client or the client's business and the other jurisdiction. No funds belonging to the member or the law firm shall be deposited therein or otherwise commingled therewith except as follows:

(1) Funds reasonably sufficient to pay bank charges.

(2) In the case of funds belonging in part to a client and in part presently or potentially to the member or the law firm, the portion belonging to the member or law firm must be withdrawn at the earliest reasonable time after the member's interest in that portion becomes fixed. However, when the right of the member or law firm to receive a portion of trust funds is disputed by the client, the disputed portion shall not be withdrawn until the dispute is finally resolved.

(B) A member shall:

(1) Promptly notify a client of the receipt of the client's funds, securities, or other properties.

(2) Identify and label securities and properties of a client promptly upon receipt and place them in a safe deposit box or other place of safekeeping as soon as practicable.

(3) Maintain complete records of all funds, securities, and other properties of a client coming into the possession of the member or law firm and render appropriate accounts to the client regarding them; preserve such records for a period of no less than five years after final appropriate distribution of such funds or properties; and comply with any order for an audit of such records issued pursuant to the Rules of Procedure of the State Bar.

(4) Promptly pay or deliver, as requested by the client, any funds, securities, or other properties in the possession of the member which the client is entitled to receive.

(C) The Board of Governors of the State Bar shall have the authority to formulate and adopt standards as to what "records" shall be maintained by members and law firms in accordance with subparagraph (B)(3). The standards formulated and adopted by the Board, as from time to time amended, shall be effective and binding on all members.

Standards:

Pursuant to rule 4–100(C) the Board of Governors of the State Bar adopted the following standards, effective January 1, 1993, as to what "records" shall be maintained by members and law firms in accordance with subparagraph (B)(3).

(1) A member shall, from the date of receipt of client funds through the period ending five years from the date of appropriate disbursement of such funds, maintain:

(a) a written ledger for each client on whose behalf funds are held that sets forth:

(i) the name of such client,

(ii) the date, amount and source of all funds received on behalf of such client,

(iii) the date, amount, payee and purpose of each disbursement made on behalf of such client, and

(iv) the current balance for such client;

(b) a written journal for each bank account that sets forth:

(i) the name of such account,

(ii) the date, amount and client affected by each debit and credit, and

(iii) the current balance in such account;

(c) all bank statements and cancelled checks for each bank account; and

(d) each monthly reconciliation (balancing) of (a), (b), and (c).

(2) A member shall, from the date of receipt of all securities and other properties held for the benefit of client through the period ending five years from the date of appropriate disbursement of such securities and other properties, maintain a written journal that specifies:

(a) each item of security and property held;

(b) the person on whose behalf the security or property is held;

(c) the date of receipt of the security or property;

(d) the date of distribution of the security or property; and

(e) person to whom the security or property was distributed.

RULE 4–200. Fees for Legal Services

(A) A member shall not enter into an agreement for, charge, or collect an illegal or unconscionable fee.

(B) Unconscionability of a fee shall be determined on the basis of all the facts and circumstances existing at the time the agreement is entered into except where the parties contemplate that the fee will be affected by later events. Among the factors to be considered, where appropriate, in determining the conscionability of a fee are the following:

(1) The amount of the fee in proportion to the value of the services performed.

(2) The relative sophistication of the member and the client.

(3) The novelty and difficulty of the questions involved and the skill requisite to perform the legal service properly.

(4) The likelihood, if apparent to the client, that the acceptance of the particular employment will preclude other employment by the member.

(5) The amount involved and the results obtained.

(6) The time limitations imposed by the client or by the circumstances.

(7) The nature and length of the professional relationship with the client.

(8) The experience, reputation, and ability of the member or members performing the services.

(9) Whether the fee is fixed or contingent.

(10) The time and labor required.

(11) The informed consent of the client to the fee.

RULE 4–210. Payment of Personal or Business Expenses Incurred by or for a Client

(A) A member shall not directly or indirectly pay or agree to pay, guarantee, represent, or sanction a representation that the member or member's law firm will pay the personal or business expenses of a prospective or existing client, except that this rule shall not prohibit a member:

(1) With the consent of the client, from paying or agreeing to pay such expenses to third persons from funds collected or to be collected for the client as a result of the representation; or

(2) After employment, from lending money to the client upon the client's promise in writing to repay such loan; or

(3) From advancing the costs of prosecuting or defending a claim or action or otherwise protecting or promoting the client's interests, the repayment of which may be contingent on the outcome of the matter. Such costs within the meaning of this subparagraph (3) shall be limited to all reasonable expenses of litigation or reasonable expenses in preparation for litigation or in providing any legal services to the client.

(B) Nothing in rule 4–210 shall be deemed to limit rules 3–300, 3–310, and 4–300.

RULE 4–300. Purchasing Property at a Foreclosure or a Sale Subject to Judicial Review

(A) A member shall not directly or indirectly purchase property at a probate, foreclosure, receiver's, trustee's, or judicial sale in an action or proceeding in which such member or any lawyer affiliated by reason of personal, business, or professional relationship with that member or with that member's law firm is acting as a lawyer for a party or as executor, receiver, trustee, administrator, guardian, or conservator.

(B) A member shall not represent the seller at a probate, foreclosure, receiver, trustee, or judicial sale in an action or proceeding in which the purchaser is a spouse or relative of the member or of another lawyer in the member's law firm or is an employee of the member or the member's law firm.

RULE 4–400. Gifts From Client

A member shall not induce a client to make a substantial gift, including a testamentary gift, to the member or to the member's parent, child, sibling, or spouse, except where the client is related to the member.

Discussion

A member may accept a gift from a member's client, subject to general standards of fairness and absence of undue influence. The member who participates in the preparation of an instrument memorializing a gift which is otherwise permissible ought not to be subject to professional discipline. On the other hand, where impermissible influence occurred, discipline is appropriate. (See *Magee v. State Bar* (1962) 58 Cal.2d 423 [24 Cal.Rptr. 839].)

CHAPTER 5. ADVOCACY AND REPRESENTATION

RULE 5–100. Threatening Criminal, Administrative, or Disciplinary Charges

(A) A member shall not threaten to present criminal, administrative, or disciplinary charges to obtain an advantage in a civil dispute.

(B) As used in paragraph (A) of this rule, the term "administrative charges" means the filing or lodging of a complaint with a federal, state, or local governmental entity which may order or recommend the loss or suspension of a license, or may impose or recommend the imposition of a fine, pecuniary sanction, or other sanction of a quasi-criminal nature but does not include filing charges with an administrative entity required by law as a condition precedent to maintaining a civil action.

(C) As used in paragraph (A) of this rule, the term "civil dispute" means a controversy or potential controversy over the rights and duties of two or more parties under civil law, whether or not an action has been commenced, and includes an administrative proceeding of a quasi-civil nature pending before a federal, state, or local governmental entity.

Discussion

Rule 5–100 is not intended to apply to a member's threatening to initiate contempt proceedings against a party for a failure to comply with a court order.

Paragraph (B) is intended to exempt the threat of filing an administrative charge which is a prerequisite to filing a civil complaint on the same transaction or occurrence.

For purposes of paragraph (C), the definition of "civil dispute" makes clear that the rule is applicable prior to the formal filing of a civil action.

RULE 5–110. Performing the Duty of Member in Government Service

A member in government service shall not institute or cause to be instituted criminal charges when the member knows or should know that the charges are not supported by probable cause. If, after the institution of criminal charges, the member in government service having responsibility for prosecuting the charges becomes aware that those charges are not supported by probable cause, the member shall promptly so advise the court in which the criminal matter is pending.

RULE 5–120. Trial Publicity

(A) A member who is participating or has participated in the investigation or litigation of a matter shall not make an extrajudicial statement that a reasonable person would expect to be disseminated by means of public communication if the member knows or reasonably should know that it will have a substantial likelihood of materially prejudicing an adjudicative proceeding in the matter.

(B) Notwithstanding paragraph (A), a member may state:

(1) the claim, offense or defense involved and, except when prohibited by law, the identity of the persons involved;

(2) the information contained in a public record;

(3) that an investigation of the matter is in progress;

(4) the scheduling or result of any step in litigation;

(5) a request for assistance in obtaining evidence and information necessary thereto;

(6) a warning of danger concerning the behavior of a person involved, when there is reason to believe that there exists the likelihood of substantial harm to an individual or the public interest; and

(7) in a criminal case, in addition to subparagraphs (1) through (6):

(a) the identity, residence, occupation, and family status of the accused;

(b) if the accused has not been apprehended, information necessary to aid in apprehension of that person;

(c) the fact, time, and place of arrest; and

(d) the identity of investigating and arresting officers or agencies and the length of the investigation.

(C) Notwithstanding paragraph (A), a member may make a statement that a reasonable member would believe is required to protect a client from the substantial undue prejudicial effect of recent publicity not initiated by the member or the member's client. A statement made pursuant to this paragraph shall be limited to such information as is necessary to mitigate the recent adverse publicity.

Discussion

Rule 5-120 is intended to apply equally to prosecutors and criminal defense counsel. Whether an extrajudicial statement violates rule 5-120 depends on many factors, including:

(1) whether the extrajudicial statement presents information clearly inadmissible as evidence in the matter for the purpose of proving or disproving a material fact in issue;

(2) whether the extrajudicial statement presents information the member knows is false, deceptive, or the use of which would violate Business and Professions Code section 6068(d);

(3) whether the extrajudicial statement violates a lawful "gag" order, or protective order, statute, rule of court, or special rule of confidentiality (for example, in juvenile, domestic, mental disability, and certain criminal proceedings); and

(4) the timing of the statement.

Paragraph (A) is intended to apply to statements made by or on behalf of the member. Subparagraph (B)(6) is not intended to create, augment, diminish, or eliminate any application of the lawyer-client privilege or of Business and Professions Code section 6068(e) regarding the member's duty to maintain client confidence and secrets.

RULE 5-200.   Trial Conduct

In presenting a matter to a tribunal, a member:

(A) Shall employ, for the purpose of maintaining the causes confided to the member such means only as are consistent with truth;

(B) Shall not seek to mislead the judge, judicial officer, or jury by an artifice or false statement of fact or law;

(C) Shall not intentionally misquote to a tribunal the language of a book, statute, or decision;

(D) Shall not, knowing its invalidity, cite as authority a decision that has been overruled or a statute that has been repealed or declared unconstitutional; and

(E) Shall not assert personal knowledge of the facts at issue, except when testifying as a witness.

RULE 5–210. Member as Witness

A member shall not act as an advocate before a jury which will hear testimony from the member unless:

(A) The testimony relates to an uncontested matter; or

(B) The testimony relates to the nature and value of legal services rendered in the case; or

(C) The member has the informed, written consent of the client. If the member represents the People or a governmental entity, the consent shall be obtained from the head of the office or a designee of the head of the office by which the member is employed and shall be consistent with principles of recusal.

Discussion

Rule 5–210 is intended to apply to situations in which the member knows or should know that he or she ought to be called as a witness in litigation in which there is a jury. This rule is not intended to encompass situations in which the member is representing the client in an adversarial proceeding and is testifying before a judge. In non-adversarial proceedings, as where the member testifies on behalf of the client in a hearing before a legislative body, rule 5–210 is not applicable.

Rule 5–210 is not intended to apply to circumstances in which a lawyer in an advocate's firm will be a witness.

RULE 5–220. Suppression of Evidence

A member shall not suppress any evidence that the member or the member's client has a legal obligation to reveal or to produce.

RULE 5–300. Contact With Officials

(A) A member shall not directly or indirectly give or lend anything of value to a judge, official, or employee of a tribunal unless the personal or family relationship between the member and the judge, official, or employee is such that gifts are customarily given and exchanged. Nothing contained in this rule shall prohibit a member from contributing to the campaign fund of a judge running for election or confirmation pursuant to applicable law pertaining to such contributions.

(B) A member shall not directly or indirectly communicate with or argue to a judge or judicial officer upon the merits of a contested matter pending before such judge or judicial officer, except:

(1) In open court; or

(2) With the consent of all other counsel in such matter; or

(3) In the presence of all other counsel in such matter; or

(4) In writing with a copy thereof furnished to such other counsel; or

(5) In ex parte matters.

(C) As used in this rule, "judge" and "judicial officer" shall include law clerks, research attorneys, or other court personnel who participate in the decision-making process.

RULE 5–310. Prohibited Contact With Witnesses

A member shall not:

(A) Advise or directly or indirectly cause a person to secrete himself or herself or to leave the jurisdiction of a tribunal for the purpose of making that person unavailable as a witness therein.

(B) Directly or indirectly pay, offer to pay, or acquiesce in the payment of compensation to a witness contingent upon the content of the witness's testimony or the outcome of the case. Except where prohibited by law, a member may advance, guarantee, or acquiesce in the payment of:

(1) Expenses reasonably incurred by a witness in attending or testifying.

(2) Reasonable compensation to a witness for loss of time in attending or testifying.

(3) A reasonable fee for the professional services of an expert witness.

RULE 5–320. Contact With Jurors

(A) A member connected with a case shall not communicate directly or indirectly with anyone the member knows to be a member of the venire from which the jury will be selected for trial of that case.

(B) During trial a member connected with the case shall not communicate directly or indirectly with any juror.

(C) During trial a member who is not connected with the case shall not communicate directly or indirectly concerning the case with anyone the member knows is a juror in the case.

(D) After discharge of the jury from further consideration of a case a member shall not ask questions of or make comments to a member of that jury that are intended to harass or embarrass the juror or to influence the juror's actions in future jury service.

(E) A member shall not directly or indirectly conduct an out of court investigation of a person who is either a member of the venire or a juror in a manner likely to influence the state of mind of such person in connection with present or future jury service.

(F) All restrictions imposed by this rule also apply to communications with, or investigations of, members of the family of a person who is either a member of the venire or a juror.

(G) A member shall reveal promptly to the court improper conduct by a person who is either a member of a venire or a juror, or by another toward a person who is either a member of a venire or a juror or a member of his or her family, of which the member has knowledge.

(H) This Rule does not prohibit a member from communicating with persons who are members of a venire or jurors as a part of the official proceedings.

(I) For purpose of this rule "juror" means any empaneled, discharged, or excused juror.

SELECTED PROVISIONS FROM THE CALIFORNIA BUSINESS AND PROFESSIONS CODE

As of September, 2009

Table of Sections

363

ARTICLE 4. ADMISSION TO THE PRACTICE OF LAW

§ 6067. Oath

Every person on his admission shall take an oath to support the Constitution of the United States and the Constitution of the State of California, and faithfully to discharge the duties of any attorney at law to the best of his knowledge and ability. A certificate of the oath shall be indorsed upon his license.

§ 6068. Duties of Attorney

It is the duty of an attorney to do all of the following:

(a) To support the Constitution and laws of the United States and of this state.

(b) To maintain the respect due to the courts of justice and judicial officers.

(c) To counsel or maintain those actions, proceedings, or defenses only as appear to him or her legal or just, except the defense of a person charged with a public offense.

(d) To employ, for the purpose of maintaining the causes confided to him or her those means only as are consistent with truth, and never to seek to mislead the judge or any judicial officer by an artifice or false statement of fact or law.

(e)(1) To maintain inviolate the confidence, and at every peril to himself or herself to preserve the secrets, of his or her client.

(2) Notwithstanding paragraph (1), an attorney may, but is not required to, reveal confidential information relating to the representation of a client to the extent that the attorney reasonably believes the disclosure is necessary to prevent a criminal act that the attorney reasonably believes is likely to result in death of, or substantial bodily harm to, an individual.

(f) To advance no fact prejudicial to the honor or reputation of a party or witness, unless required by the justice of the cause with which he or she is charged.

(g) Not to encourage either the commencement or the continuance of an action or proceeding from any corrupt motive of passion or interest.

(h) Never to reject, for any consideration personal to himself or herself, the cause of the defenseless or the oppressed.

(i) To cooperate and participate in any disciplinary investigation or other regulatory or disciplinary proceeding pending against himself or herself. However, this subdivision shall not be construed to deprive an attorney of any privilege guaranteed by the Fifth Amendment to the Constitution of the United States or any other constitutional or statutory privileges. This subdivision shall not be construed to require an attorney to cooperate with a request that requires him or her to waive any constitutional or statutory privilege or to comply with a request for information or other matters within an unreasonable period of time in light of the time constraints of the attorney's practice. Any exercise by an attorney of any constitutional or statutory privilege shall not be used against the attorney in a regulatory or disciplinary proceeding against him or her.

(j) To comply with the requirements of Section 6002.1.

(k) To comply with all conditions attached to any disciplinary probation, including a probation imposed with the concurrence of the attorney.

(*l*) To keep all agreements made in lieu of disciplinary prosecution with the agency charged with attorney discipline.

(m) To respond promptly to reasonable status inquiries of clients and to keep clients reasonably informed of significant developments in matters with regard to which the attorney has agreed to provide legal services.

(n) To provide copies to the client of certain documents under time limits and as prescribed in a rule of professional conduct which the board shall adopt.

(o) To report to the agency charged with attorney discipline, in writing, within 30 days of the time the attorney has knowledge of any of the following:

(1) The filing of three or more lawsuits in a 12–month period against the attorney for malpractice or other wrongful conduct committed in a professional capacity.

(2) The entry of judgment against the attorney in any civil action for fraud, misrepresentation, breach of fiduciary duty, or gross negligence committed in a professional capacity.

(3) The imposition of any judicial sanctions against the attorney, except for sanctions for failure to make discovery or monetary sanctions of less than one thousand dollars ($1,000).

(4) The bringing of an indictment or information charging a felony against the attorney.

(5) The conviction of the attorney, including any verdict of guilty, or plea of guilty or no contest, of any felony, or any misdemeanor committed in the course of the practice of law, or in any manner such that a client of the attorney was the victim, or a necessary element of which, as determined by the statutory or common law definition of the misdemeanor, involves improper conduct of an attorney, including dishonesty or other moral turpitude, or an attempt or a conspiracy or solicitation of another to commit a felony or any misdemeanor of that type.

(6) The imposition of discipline against the attorney by any professional or occupational disciplinary agency or licensing board, whether in California or elsewhere.

(7) Reversal of judgment in a proceeding based in whole or in part upon misconduct, grossly incompetent representation, or willful misrepresentation by an attorney.

(8) As used in this subdivision, "against the attorney" includes claims and proceedings against any firm of attorneys for the practice of law in which the attorney was a partner at the time of the conduct complained of and any law corporation in which the attorney was a shareholder at the time of the conduct complained of unless the matter has to the attorney's knowledge already been reported by the law firm or corporation.

(9) The State Bar may develop a prescribed form for the making of reports required by this section, usage of which it may require by rule or regulation.

(10) This subdivision is only intended to provide that the failure to report as required herein may serve as a basis of discipline.

ARTICLE 6.   DISCIPLINARY AUTHORITY OF THE COURTS

§ 6100.   Disbarment or Suspension

For any of the causes provided in this article, arising after an attorney's admission to practice, he or she may be disbarred or suspended by the Supreme Court. Nothing in this article limits the inherent power of the Supreme Court to discipline, including to summarily disbar, any attorney.

§ 6101.   Conviction of Crime; Notice of Pendency of Action; Record of Conviction; Proceedings

(a) Conviction of a felony or misdemeanor, involving moral turpitude, constitutes a cause for disbarment or suspension.

In any proceeding, whether under this article or otherwise, to disbar or suspend an attorney on account of that conviction, the record of conviction shall be conclusive evidence of guilt of the crime of which he or she has been convicted.

(b) The district attorney, city attorney, or other prosecuting agency shall notify the Office of the State Bar of California of the pendency of an action against an attorney charging a felony or misdemeanor immediately upon obtaining information that the defendant is an attorney. The notice shall identify the attorney and describe the crimes charged and the alleged facts. The prosecuting agency shall also notify the clerk of the court in which the action is pending that the defendant is an attorney, and the clerk shall record prominently in the file that the defendant is an attorney.

(c) The clerk of the court in which an attorney is convicted of a crime shall, within 48 hours after the conviction, transmit a certified copy of the record of conviction to the Office of the State Bar. Within five days of receipt, the Office of the State Bar shall transmit the record of any conviction which involves or may involve moral turpitude to the Supreme Court with such other records and information as may be appropriate to establish the Supreme Court's jurisdiction. The State Bar of California may procure and transmit the record of conviction to the Supreme Court when the clerk has not done so or when the conviction was had in a court other than a court of this state.

(d) The proceedings to disbar or suspend an attorney on account of such a conviction shall be undertaken by the Supreme Court pursuant to the procedure provided in this section and Section 6102, upon the receipt of the certified copy of the record of conviction.

(e) A plea or verdict of guilty, an acceptance of a nolo contendre plea, or a conviction after a plea of nolo contendere is deemed to be a conviction within the meaning of those sections.

§ 6102. Immediate Suspension and Subsequent Disbarment Upon Conviction of Crime; Crimes Involving Moral Turpitude or Felonies; Procedure

(a) Upon the receipt of the certified copy of the record of conviction, if it appears therefrom that the crime of which the attorney was convicted involved or that there is probable cause to believe that it involved moral turpitude or is a felony under the laws of California, the United States, or any state or territory thereof, the Supreme Court shall suspend the attorney until the time for appeal has elapsed, if no appeal has been taken, or until the judgment of conviction has been affirmed on appeal, or has otherwise become final, and until the further order of the court. Upon its own motion or upon good cause shown, the court may decline to impose, or may set aside, the suspension when it appears to be in the interest of justice to do so, with due regard being given to maintaining the integrity of, and confidence in, the profession.

(b) For the purposes of this section, a crime is a felony under the law of California if it is declared to be so specifically or by subdivision (a) of Section 17 of the Penal Code, unless it is charged as a misdemeanor pursuant to paragraph (4) or (5) of subdivision (b) of Section 17 of the Penal Code, irrespective of whether in a particular case the crime may be considered a misdemeanor as a result of postconviction proceedings, including proceedings resulting in punishment or probation set forth in paragraph (1) or (3) of subdivision (b) of Section 17 of the Penal Code.

(c) After the judgment of conviction of an offense specified in subdivision (a) has become final or, irrespective of any subsequent order under Section 1203.4 of the Penal Code or similar statutory provision, an order granting probation has been made suspending the imposition of sentence, the Supreme Court shall summarily disbar the attorney if the offense is a felony under the laws of California, the United States, or any state or territory thereof, and an element of the offense is the specific intent to deceive, defraud, steal, or make or suborn a false statement, or involved moral turpitude.

(d) For purposes of this section, a conviction under the laws of another state or territory of the United States shall be deemed a felony if:

(1) The judgment or conviction was entered as a felony irrespective of any subsequent order suspending sentence or granting probation and irrespective of whether the crime may be considered a misdemeanor as a result of postconviction proceedings.

(2) The elements of the offense for which the member was convicted would constitute a felony under the laws of the State of California at the time the offense was committed.

(e) Except as provided in subdivision (c), if after adequate notice and opportunity to be heard (which hearing shall not be had until the judgment of conviction has become final or, irrespective of any subsequent order under Section 1203.4 of the Penal Code, an order granting probation has been made suspending the imposition of sentence), the court finds that the crime of which the attorney was convicted, or the circumstances of its commission, involved moral turpitude, it shall enter an order disbarring the attorney or suspending him or her from practice for a limited time, according to the gravity of the crime and the circumstances of the case; otherwise it shall dismiss the proceedings. In determining the extent of the discipline to be imposed in a proceeding pursuant to this article, any prior discipline imposed upon the attorney may be considered.

(f) The court may refer the proceedings or any part thereof or issue therein, including the nature or extent of discipline, to the State Bar for hearing, report, and recommendation.

(g) The record of the proceedings resulting in the conviction, including a transcript of the testimony therein, may be received in evidence.

(h) The Supreme Court shall prescribe rules for the practice and procedure in proceedings conducted pursuant to this section and Section 6101.

(i) The other provisions of this article providing a procedure for the disbarment or suspension of an attorney do not apply to proceedings pursuant to this section and Section 6101, unless expressly made applicable.

§ 6103. Disobedience of Court Order; Violation of Oath or Attorney's Duties

A wilful disobedience or violation of an order of the court requiring him to do or forbear an act connected with or in the course of his profession, which he ought in good faith to do or forbear, and any violation of the oath taken by him, or of his duties as such attorney, constitute causes for disbarment or suspension.

§ 6103.5 Written Offers of Settlement; Required Communication to Client; Discovery

(a) A member of the State Bar shall promptly communicate to the member's client all amounts, terms, and conditions of any written offer of settlement made by or on behalf of an opposing party. As used in this section, "client" includes any person employing the member of the State Bar who possesses the authority to accept an offer of settlement, or in a class action, who is a representative of the class.

(b) Any written offer of settlement or any required communication of a settlement offer, as described in subdivision (a), shall be discoverable by either party in any action in which the existence or communication of the offer of settlement is an issue before the trier of fact.

§ 6103.6 Compensation for Trustee Services; Donative Transfers; Violations Constituting Grounds for Discipline

Violation of Section 15687 of the Probate Code, or of Part 3.5 (commencing with Section 21350) of Division 11 of the Probate Code, shall be grounds for discipline, if the attorney knew or should have known of the facts leading to the violation. This section shall only apply to violations that occur on or after January 1, 1994.

§ 6104. Unauthorized Appearance

Corruptly or wilfully and without authority appearing as attorney for a party to an action or proceeding constitutes a cause for disbarment or suspension.

§ 6105. Permitting Misuse of Name

Lending his name to be used as attorney by another person who is not an attorney constitutes a cause for disbarment or suspension.

§ 6106. Moral Turpitude, Dishonesty or Corruption Irrespective of Criminal Conviction

The commission of any act involving moral turpitude, dishonesty or corruption, whether the act is committed in the course of his relations as an attorney or otherwise, and whether the act is a felony or misdemeanor or not, constitutes a cause for disbarment or suspension.

If the act constitutes a felony or misdemeanor, conviction thereof in a criminal proceeding is not a condition precedent to disbarment or suspension from practice therefor.

§ 6106.1 Advocacy of Overthrow of Government

Advocating the overthrow of the Government of the United States or of this State by force, violence, or other unconstitutional means, constitutes a cause for disbarment or suspension.

§ 6106.5 Insurance Claims; Fraud

It shall constitute cause for disbarment or suspension for an attorney to engage in any conduct prohibited under Section 1871.4 of the Insurance Code or Section 550 of the Penal Code.

§ 6106.7 Miller–Ayala Athlete Agents Act; Violation of Requirements

It shall constitute cause for the imposition of discipline of an attorney within the meaning of this chapter for an attorney to violate any provision of the Miller–Ayala Athlete Agents Act (Chapter 2.5 (commencing with Section 18895) of Division 8), or to violate any provision of Chapter 1 (commencing with Section 1500) of Part 6 of Division 2 of the Labor Code, prior to January 1, 1997, or to violate any provision of the law of any other state regulating athlete agents.

§ 6106.8 Sexual Involvement Between Lawyers and Clients; Rule of Professional Conduct

(a) The Legislature hereby finds and declares that there is no rule that governs propriety of sexual relationships between lawyers and clients. The Legislature further finds and declares that it is difficult to separate sound judgment from emotion or bias which may result from sexual involvement between a lawyer and his or her client during the period that an attorney-client relationship exists, and that emotional detachment is essential to the lawyer's ability to render competent legal services. Therefore, in order to ensure that a lawyer acts in the best interest of his or her client, a rule of professional conduct governing sexual relations between attorneys and their clients shall be adopted.

(b) With the approval of the Supreme Court, the State Bar shall adopt a rule of professional conduct governing sexual relations between attorneys and their clients in cases involving, but not limited to, probate matters and domestic relations, including dissolution proceedings, child custody cases, and settlement proceedings.

(c) The State Bar shall submit the proposed rule to the Supreme Court for approval no later than January 1, 1991.

(d) Intentional violation of this rule shall constitute a cause for suspension or disbarment.

[Editors' Note: See California Rules of Professional Conduct, Rule 3–120, reprinted supra.]

§ 6106.9 Sexual Relations Between Attorney and Client; Cause for Discipline; Complaints to State Bar

(a) It shall constitute cause for the imposition of discipline of an attorney within the meaning of this chapter for an attorney to do any of the following:

(1) Expressly or impliedly condition the performance of legal services for a current or prospective client upon the client's willingness to engage in sexual relations with the attorney.

(2) Employ coercion, intimidation, or undue influence in entering into sexual relations with a client.

(3) Continue representation of a client with whom the attorney has sexual relations if the sexual relations cause the attorney to perform legal

services incompetently in violation of Rule 3–110 of the Rules of Professional Conduct of the State Bar of California, or if the sexual relations would, or would be likely to, damage or prejudice the client's case.

(b) Subdivision (a) shall not apply to sexual relations between attorneys and their spouses or persons in an equivalent domestic relationship or to ongoing consensual sexual relationships that predate the initiation of the attorney-client relationship.

(c) Where an attorney in a firm has sexual relations with a client but does not participate in the representation of that client, the attorneys in the firm shall not be subject to discipline under this section solely because of the occurrence of those sexual relations.

(d) For the purposes of this section, "sexual relations" means sexual intercourse or the touching of an intimate part of another person for the purpose of sexual arousal, gratification, or abuse.

(e) Any complaint made to the State Bar alleging a violation of subdivision (a) shall be verified under oath by the person making the complaint.

[Editors' Note: The Governor of California signed the bill that enacted § 6106.9 on September 16th, 1992. The second section of that bill also provided that—

"SEC. 2. Commencing January 1, 1993, the State Bar shall maintain statistical data regarding the number of complaints presented and the disposition or discipline imposed pursuant to Section 6106.9 of the Business and Professions Code. The State Bar shall submit a report to the Legislature regarding the statistical compilation on or before January 1, 1996.

"The State Bar shall also develop and implement uniform standards for the implementation of Section 6106.9 of the Business and Professions Code and policies and procedures to ensure that complaints will be handled in a responsive and sensitive manner. The State Bar shall also provide appropriate training to staff on the standards, policies, and practices."]

ARTICLE 7. UNLAWFUL PRACTICE OF LAW

§ 6125. Necessity of active membership in state bar

No person shall practice law in California unless the person is an active member of the State Bar.

§ 6126. Unauthorized Practice or Attempted Practice; Advertising or Holding Out; Penalties

(a) Any person advertising or holding himself or herself out as practicing or entitled to practice law or otherwise practicing law who is not an active member of the State Bar, or otherwise authorized pursuant to statute or court rule to practice law in this state at the time of doing so, is guilty of a misdemeanor punishable by up to one year in a county jail or by a fine of up to one thousand dollars ($1,000), or by both that fine and imprisonment. Upon a second or subsequent conviction, the person shall be confined in a county jail for not less than 90 days, except in an unusual case where the interests of justice would be served by imposition of a lesser sentence or a fine. If the court imposes only a fine or a sentence of less than 90 days for a second or subsequent conviction under this subdivision, the court shall state the reasons for its sentencing choice on the record.

(b) Any person who has been involuntarily enrolled as an inactive member of the State Bar, or has been suspended from membership from the State Bar, or has been disbarred, or has resigned from the State Bar with charges pending, and thereafter practices or attempts to practice law, advertises or holds himself or herself out as practicing or otherwise entitled to practice law, is guilty of a crime punishable by imprisonment in the state prison or county jail. However, any person who has been involuntarily enrolled as an inactive member of the State Bar pursuant to paragraph (1) of subdivision (e) of Section 6007 and who knowingly thereafter practices or attempts to practice law, or advertises or holds himself or herself out as practicing or otherwise entitled to practice law, is guilty of a crime punishable by imprisonment in the state prison or county jail.

(c) The willful failure of a member of the State Bar, or one who has resigned or been disbarred, to comply with an order of the Supreme Court to comply with Rule 9.20 of California Rules of Court, constitutes a crime punishable by imprisonment in the state prison or county jail.

(d) The penalties provided in this section are cumulative to each other and to any other remedies or penalties provided by law.

§ 6128. Deceit, Collusion, Delay of Suit and Improper Receipt of Money as Misdemeanor

Every attorney is guilty of a misdemeanor who either:

(a) Is guilty of any deceit or collusion, or consents to any deceit or collusion, with intent to deceive the court or any party.

(b) Willfully delays his client's suit with a view to his own gain.

(c) Willfully receives any money or allowance for or on account of any money which he has not laid out or become answerable for.

Any violation of the provisions of this section is punishable by imprisonment in the county jail not exceeding six months, or by a fine not exceeding two thousand five hundred dollars ($2,500), or by both.

§ 6129. Buying Claim as Misdemeanor

Every attorney who, either directly or indirectly, buys or is interested in buying any evidence of debt or thing in action, with intent to bring suit thereon, is guilty of a misdemeanor.

Any violation of the provisions of this section is punishable by imprisonment in the county jail not exceeding six months, or by a fine not exceeding two thousand five hundred dollars ($2,500), or by both.

§ 6130. Disbarred or Suspended Attorney Suing as Assignee

No person, who has been an attorney, shall while a judgment of disbarment or suspension is in force appear on his own behalf as plaintiff in the prosecution of any action where the subject of the action has been assigned to him subsequent to the entry of the judgment of disbarment or suspension and solely for purpose of collection.

§ 6131. Aiding Defense Where Partner or Self Has Acted as Public Prosecutor; Misdemeanor and Disbarment

Every attorney is guilty of a misdemeanor and, in addition to the punishment prescribed therefor, shall be disbarred:

(a) Who directly or indirectly advises in relation to, or aids, or promotes the defense of any action or proceeding in any court the prosecution of which is carried on, aided or promoted by any person as district attorney or other public prosecutor with whom such person is directly or indirectly connected as a partner.

(b) Who, having himself prosecuted or in any manner aided or promoted any action or proceeding in any court as district attorney or other public prosecutor, afterwards, directly or indirectly, advises in relation to or takes any part in the defense thereof, as attorney or otherwise, or who takes or receives any valuable consideration from or on behalf of any defendant in any such action upon any understanding or agreement whatever having relation to the defense thereof.

This section does not prohibit an attorney from defending himself in person, as attorney or counsel, when prosecuted, either civilly or criminally.

ARTICLE 8.5   FEE AGREEMENTS

§ 6146. Limitations; Periodic Payments

(a) An attorney shall not contract for or collect a contingency fee for representing any person seeking damages in connection with an action for injury or damage against a health care provider based upon such person's alleged professional negligence in excess of the following limits:

(1) Forty percent of the first fifty thousand dollars ($50,000) recovered.

(2) Thirty-three and one-third percent of the next fifty thousand dollars ($50,000) recovered.

(3) Twenty-five percent of the next five hundred thousand dollars ($500,-000) recovered.

(4) Fifteen percent of any amount on which the recovery exceeds six hundred thousand dollars ($600,000).

The limitations shall apply regardless of whether the recovery is by settlement, arbitration, or judgment, or whether the person for whom the recovery is made is a responsible adult, an infant, or a person of unsound mind.

(b) If periodic payments are awarded to the plaintiff pursuant to Section 667.7 of the Code of Civil Procedure, the court shall place a total value on these payments based upon the projected life expectancy of the plaintiff and include this amount in computing the total award from which attorney's fees are calculated under this section.

(c) For purposes of this section:

(1) "Recovered" means the net sum recovered after deducting any disbursements or costs incurred in connection with prosecution or settlement of the claim. Costs of medical care incurred by the plaintiff and the attorney's office-overhead costs or charges are not deductible disbursements or costs for such purpose.

(2) "Health care provider" means any person licensed or certified pursuant to Division 2 (commencing with Section 500), or licensed pursuant to the Osteopathic Initiative Act, or the Chiropractic Initiative Act, or licensed pursuant to Chapter 2.5 (commencing with Section 1440) of Division 2 of the Health and Safety Code; and any clinic, health dispensary, or health facility, licensed pursuant to Division 2 (commencing with Section 1200) of the Health and Safety Code. "Health care provider" includes the legal representatives of a health care provider.

(3) "Professional negligence" is a negligent act or omission to act by a health care provider in the rendering of professional services, which act or omission is the proximate cause of a personal injury or wrongful death, provided that the services are within the scope of services for which the provider is licensed and which are not within any restriction imposed by the licensing agency or licensed hospital.

§ 6147. Contingency Fee Contracts; Duplicate Copy; Contents; Effect of Noncompliance; Recovery of Workers' Compensation Benefits

(a) An attorney who contracts to represent a client on a contingency fee basis shall, at the time the contract is entered into, provide a duplicate copy of the contract, signed by both the attorney and the client, or the client's guardian or representative, to the plaintiff, or to the plaintiff's guardian or representative. The contract shall be in writing and shall include, but is not limited to, all of the following:

(1) A statement of the contingency fee rate which the client and attorney have agreed upon.

(2) A statement as to how disbursements and costs incurred in connection with the prosecution or settlement of the claim will affect the contingency fee and the client's recovery.

(3) A statement as to what extent, if any, the client could be required to pay any compensation to the attorney for related matters that arise out

of their relationship not covered by their contingency fee contract. This may include any amounts collected for the plaintiff by the attorney.

(4) Unless the claim is subject to the provisions of Section 6146, a statement that the fee is not set by law but is negotiable between attorney and client.

(5) If the claim is subject to the provisions of Section 6146, a statement that the rates set forth in that section are the maximum limits for the contingency fee agreement, and that the attorney and client may negotiate a lower rate.

(b) Failure to comply with any provision of this section renders the agreement voidable at the option of the plaintiff, and the attorney shall thereupon be entitled to collect a reasonable fee.

(c) This section shall not apply to contingency fee contracts for the recovery of workers' compensation benefits.

(d) This section shall become operative on January 1, 2000.

§ 6147.5 Contingency Fee Contracts; Recovery of Claims Between Merchants

(a) Sections 6147 and 6148 shall not apply to contingency fee contracts for the recovery of claims between merchants as defined in Section 2104 of the Commercial Code, arising from the sale or lease of goods or services rendered, or money loaned for use, in the conduct of a business or profession if the merchant contracting for legal services employs 10 or more individuals.

(b)(1) In the instances in which no written contract for legal services exists as permitted by subdivision (a), an attorney shall not contract for or collect a contingency fee in excess of the following limits:

(A) Twenty percent of the first three hundred dollars ($300) collected.

(B) Eighteen percent of the next one thousand seven hundred dollars ($1,700) collected.

(C) Thirteen percent of sums collected in excess of two thousand dollars ($2,000).

(2) However, the following minimum charges may be charged and collected:

(A) Twenty-five dollars ($25) in collections of seventy-five dollars ($75) to one hundred twenty-five dollars ($125).

(B) Thirty-three and one-third percent of collections less than seventy-five dollars ($75).

§ 6148. Contracts for Services in Cases Not Coming Within § 6147; Bills Rendered by Attorney; Contents; Failure to Comply

(a) In any case not coming within Section 6147 in which it is reasonably foreseeable that total expense to a client, including attorney fees will exceed one thousand dollars ($1,000), the contract for services in the case shall be in writing. At the time the contract is entered into, the attorney shall provide a duplicate copy of the contract signed by both the attorney and the client or the client's guardian or representative, to the client or to the client's guardian or representative. The written contract shall contain all of the following:

(1) Any basis of compensation including, but not limited to, hourly rates, statutory fees or flat fees, and other standard rates, fees, and charges applicable to the case.

(2) The general nature of the legal services to be provided to the client.

(3) The respective responsibilities of the attorney and the client as to the performance of the contract.

(b) All bills rendered by an attorney to a client shall clearly state the basis thereof. Bills for the fee portion of the bill shall include the amount, rate, basis for calculation, or other method of determination of the attorney's fees and costs. Bills for the cost and expense portion of the bill shall clearly identify the costs and expenses incurred and the amount of the costs and expenses. Upon request by the client, the attorney shall provide a bill to the client no later than 10 days following the request unless the attorney has provided a bill to the client within 31 days prior to the request, in which case the attorney may provide a bill to the client no later than 31 days following the date the most recent bill was provided. The client is entitled to make similar requests at intervals of no less than 30 days following the initial request. In providing responses to client requests for billing information, the attorney may use billing data that is currently effective on the date of the request, or, if any fees or costs to that date cannot be accurately determined, they shall be described and estimated.

(c) Failure to comply with any provision of this section renders the agreement voidable at the option of the client, and the attorney shall, upon the agreement being voided, be entitled to collect a reasonable fee.

(d) This section shall not apply to any of the following:

(1) Services rendered in an emergency to avoid foreseeable prejudice to the rights or interests of the client or where a writing is otherwise impractical.

(2) An arrangement as to the fee implied by the fact that the attorney's services are of the same general kind as previously rendered to and paid for by the client.

(3) If the client knowingly states in writing, after full disclosure of this section, that a writing concerning fees is not required.

(4) If the client is a corporation.

(e) This section applies prospectively only to fee agreements following its operative date.

(f) This section shall become operative on January 1, 2000.

§ 6149. Written Fee Contract: Confidential Communication

A written fee contract shall be deemed to be a confidential communication within the meaning of subdivision (e) of Section 6068 and of Section 952 of the Evidence Code.

§ 6149.5 Third–Party Liability Claim; Settlement by Insurer; Notice to Claimant; Effect on Action or Defense

(a) Upon the payment of one hundred dollars ($100) or more in settlement of any third-party liability claim the insurer shall provide written notice to the claimant if both of the following apply:

(1) The claimant is a natural person.

(2) The payment is delivered to the claimant's lawyer or other representative by draft, check, or otherwise.

(b) For purposes of this section, "written notice" includes providing to the claimant a copy of the cover letter sent to the claimant's attorney or other representative that accompanied the settlement payment.

(c) This section shall not create any cause of action for any person against the insurer based upon the insurer's failure to provide the notice to a claimant required by this section. This section shall not create a defense for any party to any cause of action based upon the insurer's failure to provide this notice.

ARTICLE 9.   UNLAWFUL SOLICITATION

§ 6151. Definitions

As used in this article:

(a) A runner or capper is any person, firm, association or corporation acting for consideration in any manner or in any capacity as an agent for an attorney at law or law firm, whether the attorney or any member of the law firm is admitted in California or any other jurisdiction, in the solicitation or procurement of business for the attorney at law or law firm as provided in this article.

(b) An agent is one who represents another in dealings with one or more third persons.

§ 6152. Prohibition of Solicitation

(a) It is unlawful for:

(1) Any person, in an individual capacity or in a capacity as a public or private employee, or for any firm, corporation, partnership or association to act as a runner or capper for any attorneys or to solicit any business for any attorneys in and about the state prisons, county jails, city jails, city prisons, or other places of detention of persons, city receiving hospitals, city and county receiving hospitals, county hospitals, superior courts, or in any public institu-

tion or in any public place or upon any public street or highway or in and about private hospitals, sanitariums or in and about any private institution or upon private property of any character whatsoever.

(2) Any person to solicit another person to commit or join in the commission of a violation of subdivision (a).

(b) A general release from a liability claim obtained from any person during the period of the first physical confinement, whether as an inpatient or outpatient, in a clinic or health facility as defined in Sections 1203 and 1250 of the Health and Safety Code, as a result of the injury alleged to have given rise to the claim and primarily for treatment of the injury, is presumed fraudulent if the release is executed within 15 days after the commencement of confinement or prior to release from confinement, whichever occurs first.

(c) Nothing in this section shall be construed to prevent the recommendation of professional employment where that recommendation is not prohibited by the Rules of Professional Conduct of the State Bar of California.

(d) Nothing in this section shall be construed to mean that a public defender or assigned counsel may not make known his or her services as a criminal defense attorney to persons unable to afford legal counsel whether such persons are in custody or otherwise.

§ 6153. Violations; Penalty

Any person, firm, partnership, association, or corporation violating subdivision (a) of Section 6152 is punishable, upon a first conviction, by imprisonment in a county jail for not more than one year or by a fine not exceeding fifteen thousand dollars ($15,000), or by both that imprisonment and fine. Upon a second or subsequent conviction, a person, firm, partnership, association, or corporation is punishable by imprisonment in a county jail for not more than one year, or by imprisonment in the state prison for two, three, or four years, or by a fine not exceeding fifteen thousand dollars ($15,000), or by both that imprisonment and fine.

Any person employed either as an officer, director, trustee, clerk, servant or agent of this state or of any county or other municipal corporation or subdivision thereof, who is found guilty of violating any of the provisions of this article, shall forfeit the right to his office and employment in addition to any other penalty provided in this article.

§ 6154. Runner or Capper Used to Procure Business; Void Contract; Divesting of Fees and Other Compensation; Fees Recovered From Workers' Compensation Actions

(a) Any contract for professional services secured by any attorney at law or law firm in this state through the services of a runner or capper is void. In any action against any attorney or law firm under the Unfair Practices Act, Chapter 4 (commencing with Section 17000) of Division 7, or Chapter 5 (commencing with Section 17200) of Division 7, any judgment shall include an order divesting the attorney or law firm of any fees and other compensation received pursuant to any such void contract. Those fees and compensation shall be recoverable as additional civil penalties under Chapter 4 (commencing with Section 17000) or Chapter 5 (commencing with Section 17200) of Division 7.

(b) Notwithstanding section 17206 or any other provision of law, any fees recovered pursuant to subdivision (a) in an action involving professional services related to the provision of workers' compensation shall be allocated as follows: if the action is brought by the Attorney General, one-half of the penalty collected shall be paid to the State General Fund, and one-half of the penalty collected shall be paid to the Workers' Compensation Fraud Account in the Insurance Fund; if the action is brought by a district attorney, one-half of the penalty collected shall be paid to the treasurer of the county in which the judgment was entered, and one-half of the penalty collected shall be paid to the Workers' Compensation Fraud Account in the Insurance Fund; if the action is brought by a city attorney or city prosecutor, one-half of the penalty collected shall be paid to the treasurer of the city in which the judgment was entered, and one-half of the penalty collected shall be paid to the Workers' Compensation Fraud Account in the Insurance Fund. Moneys deposited into the Workers' Compensation Fraud Account pursuant to this subdivision shall be used in the investigation and prosecution of workers' compensation fraud, as appropriated by the Legislature.

ARTICLE 13.   ARBITRATION OF ATTORNEYS' FEES

§ 6200.   Establishment of System and Procedure; Arbitration and Mediation; Application of Article; Voluntary or Mandatory Nature; Rules; Immunity of Arbitrator and Mediator; Powers of Arbitrator; Confidentiality of Mediation

(a) The board of governors shall, by rule, establish, maintain, and administer a system and procedure for the arbitration, and may establish, maintain, and administer a system and procedure for mediation of disputes concerning fees, costs, or both, charged for professional services by members of the State Bar or by members of the bar of other jurisdictions. The rules may include provision for a filing fee in such amount as the board may, from time to time, determine.

(b) This article shall not apply to any of the following:

(1) Disputes where a member of the State Bar of California is also admitted to practice in another jurisdiction or where an attorney is only admitted to practice in another jurisdiction, and he or she maintains no office in the State of California, and no material portion of the services were rendered in the State of California.

(2) Claims for affirmative relief against the attorney for damages or otherwise based upon alleged malpractice or professional misconduct, except as provided in subdivision (a) of Section 6203.

(3) Disputes where the fee or cost to be paid by the client or on his or her behalf has been determined pursuant to statute or court order.

(c) Unless the client has agreed in writing to arbitration under this article of all disputes concerning fees, costs, or both, arbitration under this article shall be voluntary for a client and shall be mandatory for an attorney if commenced by a client. Mediation under this article shall be voluntary for an attorney and a client.

(d) The board of governors shall adopt rules to allow arbitration and mediation of attorney fee and cost disputes under this article to proceed under arbitration and mediation systems sponsored by local bar associations in this state. Rules of procedure promulgated by local bar associations are subject to review by the board to insure that they provide for a fair, impartial, and speedy hearing and award.

(e) In adopting or reviewing rules of arbitration under this section the board shall provide that the panel shall include one attorney member whose area of practice is either, at the option of the client, civil law, if the attorney's representation involved civil law, or criminal law, if the attorney's representation involved criminal law, as follows:

(1) If the panel is composed of three members the panel shall include one attorney member whose area of practice is either, at the option of the client, civil or criminal law, and shall include one lay member.

(2) If the panel is composed of one member, that member shall be an attorney whose area of practice is either, at the option of the client, civil or criminal law.

(f) In any arbitration or mediation conducted pursuant to this article by the State Bar or by a local bar association, pursuant to rules of procedure approved by the board of governors, an arbitrator or mediator, as well as the arbitrating association and its directors, officers, and employees, shall have the same immunity which attaches in judicial proceedings.

(g) In the conduct of arbitrations under this article the arbitrator or arbitrators may do all of the following:

(1) Take and hear evidence pertaining to the proceeding.

(2) Administer oaths and affirmations.

(3) Compel, by subpoena, the attendance of witnesses and the production of books, papers, and documents pertaining to the proceeding.

(h) Participation in mediation is a voluntary consensual process, based on direct negotiations between the attorney and his or her client, and is an extension of the negotiated settlement process. All discussions and offers of settlement are confidential and may not be disclosed in any subsequent arbitration or other proceedings.

ARTICLE 14.   FUNDS FOR THE PROVISION OF
LEGAL SERVICES TO INDIGENT PERSONS

§ 6210.   Legislative Findings; Purpose

The Legislature finds that, due to insufficient funding, existing programs providing free legal services in civil matters to indigent persons, especially underserved client groups, such as the elderly, the disabled, juveniles, and non-English-speaking persons, do not adequately meet the needs of these persons. It is the purpose of this article to expand the availability and improve the quality of existing free legal services in civil matters to indigent persons, and to initiate new programs that will provide services to them. The Legislature finds that the use of funds collected by the State Bar pursuant to this article for these purposes is in the public interest, is a proper use of the funds, and is consistent with essential public and governmental purposes in the judicial branch of government. The Legislature further finds that the expansion, improvement, and initiation of legal services to indigent persons will aid in the advancement of the science of jurisprudence and the improvement of the administration of justice.

§ 6211.   Establishment by Attorney of Demand Trust Account; Interest Earned to Be Paid to State Bar; Other Accounts Not Prohibited; Rules of Professional Conduct, Authority of Supreme Court or State Bar Not Affected

(a) An attorney or law firm that, in the course of the practice of law, receives or disburses trust funds shall establish and maintain an IOLTA account in which the attorney or law firm shall deposit or invest all client deposits or funds that are nominal in amount or are on deposit or invested for a short period of time. All such client funds may be deposited or invested in a single unsegregated account. The interest and dividends earned on all those accounts shall be paid to the State Bar of California to be used for the purposes set forth in this article.

(b) Nothing in this article shall be construed to prohibit an attorney or law firm from establishing one or more interest bearing bank trust deposit accounts or dividend-paying trust investment accounts as may be permitted by the Supreme Court, with the interest or dividends earned on the accounts payable to clients for trust funds not deposited or invested in accordance with subdivision (a).

(c) With the approval of the Supreme Court, the State Bar may formulate and enforce rules of professional conduct pertaining to the use by attorneys or law firms of an IOLTA account for unsegregated client funds pursuant to this article.

(d) Nothing in this article shall be construed as affecting or impairing the disciplinary powers and authority of the Supreme Court or of the State Bar or as modifying the statutes and rules governing the conduct of members of the State Bar.

§ 6212. Establishment by Attorney of Demand Trust Account; Amount of Interest; Remittance to State Bar; Statements and Reports

An attorney who, or a law firm that, establishes an IOLTA account pursuant to subdivision (a) of Section 6211 shall comply with all of the following provisions:

(a) The IOLTA account shall be established and maintained with an eligible institution offering or making available an IOLTA account that meets the requirements of this article. The IOLTA account shall be established and maintained consistent with the attorney's or law firm's duties of professional responsibility. An eligible financial institution shall have no responsibility for selecting the deposit or investment product chosen for the IOLTA account.

(b) Except as provided in subdivision (e), the rate of interest or dividends payable on any IOLTA account shall not be less than the interest rate or dividends generally paid by the eligible institution to nonattorney customers on accounts of the same type meeting the same minimum balance and other eligibility requirements as the IOLTA account. In determining the interest rate or dividend payable on any IOLTA account, an eligible institution may consider, in addition to the balance in the IOLTA account, risk or other factors customarily considered by the eligible institution when setting the interest rate or dividends for its non-IOLTA accounts, provided that the factors do not discriminate between IOLTA customers and non-IOLTA customers and that these factors do not include the fact that the account is an IOLTA account. The eligible institution shall calculate interest and dividends in accordance with its standard practice for non-IOLTA customers. Nothing in this article shall preclude an eligible institution from paying a higher interest rate or dividend on an IOLTA account or from electing to waive any fees and service charges on an IOLTA account.

(c) Reasonable fees may be deducted from the interest or dividends remitted on an IOLTA account only at the rates and in accordance with the customary practices of the eligible institution for non-IOLTA customers. No other fees or service charges may be deducted from the interest or dividends earned on an IOLTA account. Unless and until the State Bar enacts regulations exempting from compliance with subdivision (a) of Section 6211 those accounts for which maintenance fees exceed the interest or dividends paid, an eligible institution may deduct the fees and service charges in excess of the interest or dividends paid on an IOLTA account from the aggregate interest and dividends remitted to the State Bar. Fees and service charges other than reasonable fees shall be the sole responsibility of, and may only be charged to, the attorney or law firm maintaining the IOLTA account. Fees and charges shall not be assessed against or deducted from the principal of any IOLTA account. It is the intent of the Legislature that the State Bar develop policies so that eligible institutions do not incur uncompensated administrative costs in adapting their systems to comply with the provisions of Chapter 422 of the Statutes of 2007 or in making investment products available to IOLTA members.

(d) The eligible institution shall be directed to do all of the following:

(1) To remit interest or dividends on the IOLTA account, less reasonable fees, to the State Bar, at least quarterly.

(2) To transmit to the State Bar with each remittance a statement showing the name of the attorney or law firm for which the remittance is sent, for each account the rate of interest applied or dividend paid, the amount and type of fees deducted, if any, and the average balance for each account for each month of the period for which the report is made.

(3) To transmit to the attorney or law firm customer at the same time a report showing the amount paid to the State Bar for that period, the rate of interest or dividend applied, the amount of fees and service charges deducted, if any, and the average daily account balance for each month of the period for which the report is made.

(e) An eligible institution has no affirmative duty to offer or make investment products available to IOLTA customers. However, if an eligible institution offers or makes investment products available to non-IOLTA customers, in order to remain an IOLTA-eligible institution, it shall make those products available to IOLTA customers or pay an interest rate on the IOLTA deposit account that is comparable to the rate of return or the dividends generally paid on that investment product for similar customers meeting the same minimum balance and other requirements applicable to the investment product. If the eligible institution elects to pay that higher interest rate, the eligible institution may subject the IOLTA deposit account to equivalent fees and charges assessable against the investment product.

§ 6213. Definitions

As used in this article:

(a) "Qualified legal services project" means either of the following:

(1) A nonprofit project incorporated and operated exclusively in California which provides as its primary purpose and function legal services without charge to indigent persons and which has quality control procedures approved by the State Bar of California.

(2) A program operated exclusively in California by a nonprofit law school accredited by the State Bar of California which meets the requirements of subparagraphs (A) and (B).

(A) The program shall have operated for at least two years at a cost of at least twenty thousand dollars ($20,000) per year as an identifiable law school unit with a primary purpose and function of providing legal services without charge to indigent persons.

(B) The program shall have quality control procedures approved by the State Bar of California.

(b) "Qualified support center" means an incorporated nonprofit legal services center that has as its primary purpose and function the provision of legal training, legal technical assistance, or advocacy support without charge and which actually provides through an office in California a significant level of legal training, legal technical assistance, or advocacy support without charge to qualified legal services projects on a statewide basis in California.

(c) "Recipient" means a qualified legal services project or support center receiving financial assistance under this article.

(d) "Indigent person" means a person whose income is (1) 125 percent or less of the current poverty threshold established by the United States Office of Management and Budget, or (2) who is eligible for Supplemental Security Income or free services under the Older Americans Act or Developmentally Disabled Assistance Act. With regard to a project that provides free services of attorneys in private practice without compensation, "indigent person" also means a person whose income is 75 percent or less of the maximum levels of income for lower income households as defined in Section 50079.5 of the Health and Safety Code. For the purpose of this subdivision, the income of a person who is disabled shall be determined after deducting the costs of medical and other disability-related special expenses.

(e) "Fee generating case" means a case or matter that, if undertaken on behalf of an indigent person by an attorney in private practice, reasonably may be expected to result in payment of a fee for legal services from an award to a client, from public funds, or from the opposing party. A case shall not be considered fee generating if adequate representation is unavailable and any of the following circumstances exist:

(1) The recipient has determined that free referral is not possible because of any of the following reasons:

(A) The case has been rejected by the local lawyer referral service, or if there is no such service, by two attorneys in private practice who have experience in the subject matter of the case.

(B) Neither the referral service nor any attorney will consider the case without payment of a consultation fee.

(C) The case is of the type that attorneys in private practice in the area ordinarily do not accept, or do not accept without prepayment of a fee.

(D) Emergency circumstances compel immediate action before referral can be made, but the client is advised that, if appropriate and consistent with professional responsibility, referral will be attempted at a later time.

(2) Recovery of damages is not the principal object of the case and a request for damages is merely ancillary to an action for equitable or other nonpecuniary relief, or inclusion of a counterclaim requesting damages is

necessary for effective defense or because of applicable rules governing joinder of counterclaims.

(3) A court has appointed a recipient or an employee of a recipient pursuant to a statute or a court rule or practice of equal applicability to all attorneys in the jurisdiction.

(4) The case involves the rights of a claimant under a publicly supported benefit program for which entitlement to benefit is based on need.

(f) "Legal Services Corporation" means the Legal Services Corporation established under the Legal Services Corporation Act of 1974 (Public Law 93–355; 42 U.S.C. Sec. 2996 et seq.).

(g) "Older Americans Act" means the Older Americans Act of 1965, as amended (Public Law 89–73; 42 U.S.C. Sec. 3001 et seq.).

(h) "Developmentally Disabled Assistance Act" means the Developmentally Disabled Assistance and Bill of Rights Act, as amended (P.L. 94–103; 42 U.S.C. Sec. 6001 et seq.).

(i) "Supplemental security income recipient" means an individual receiving or eligible to receive payments under Title XVI of the federal Social Security Act, or payments under Chapter 3 (commencing with Section 12000) of Part 3 of Division 9 of the Welfare and Institutions Code.

(j) "IOLTA account" means an account or investment product established and maintained pursuant to subdivision (a) of Section 6211 that is any of the following:

(1) An interest-bearing checking account.

(2) An investment sweep product that is a daily (overnight) financial institution repurchase agreement or an open-end money-market fund.

(3) An investment product authorized by California Supreme Court rule or order.

A daily financial institution repurchase agreement shall be fully collateralized by United States Government Securities or other comparably conservative debt securities, and may be established only with any eligible institution that is "well-capitalized" or "adequately capitalized" as those terms are defined by applicable federal statutes and regulations. An open-end money-market fund shall be invested solely in United States Government Securities or repurchase agreements fully collateralized by United States Government Securities or other comparably conservative debt securities, shall hold itself out as a "money-market fund" as that term is defined by federal statutes and regulations under the Investment Company Act of 1940 (15 U.S.C. § 80a–1 et seq.), and, at the time of the investment, shall have total assets of at least two hundred fifty million dollars ($250,000,000).

(k) "Eligible institution" means a bank or any other type of financial institution authorized by the Supreme Court.

§ 6214. Qualified Legal Service Projects

(a) Projects meeting the requirements of subdivision (a) of Section 6213 which are funded either in whole or part by the Legal Services Corporation or with Older American Act funds shall be presumed qualified legal services projects for the purpose of this article.

(b) Projects meeting the requirements of subdivision (a) of Section 6213 but not qualifying under the presumption specified in subdivision (a) shall qualify for funds under this article if they meet all of the following additional criteria:

(1) They receive cash funds from other sources in the amount of at least twenty thousand dollars ($20,000) per year to support free legal representation to indigent persons.

(2) They have demonstrated community support for the operation of a viable ongoing program.

(3) They provide one or both of the following special services:

(A) The coordination of the recruitment of substantial numbers of attorneys in private practice to provide free legal representation to indigent persons or to qualified legal services projects in California.

(B) The provision of legal representation, training, or technical assistance on matters concerning special client groups, including the elderly, the disabled, juveniles, and non-English-speaking groups, or on matters of specialized substantive law important to the special client groups.

§ 6214.5 Qualified Legal Services Projects; Eligibility for Distributions of Funds

A law school program that meets the definition of a "qualified legal services project" as defined in paragraph (2) of subdivision (a) of Section 6213, and that applied to the State Bar for funding under this article not later than February 17, 1984, shall be deemed eligible for all distributions of funds made under Section 6216.

§ 6215. Qualified Support Centers

(a) Support centers satisfying the qualifications specified in subdivision (b) of Section 6213 which were operating an office and providing services in California on December 31, 1980, shall be presumed to be qualified support centers for the purposes of this article.

(b) Support centers not qualifying under the presumption specified in subdivision (a) may qualify as a support center by meeting both of the following additional criteria:

(1) Meeting quality control standards established by the State Bar.

(2) Being deemed to be of special need by a majority of the qualified legal services projects.

§ 6216. Distribution of Funds

The State Bar shall distribute all moneys received under the program established by this article for the provision of civil legal services to indigent persons. The funds first shall be distributed 18 months from the effective date of this article, or upon such a date, as shall be determined by the State Bar, that adequate funds are available to initiate the program. Thereafter, the funds shall be distributed on an annual basis. All distributions of funds shall be made in the following order and in the following manner:

(a) To pay the actual administrative costs of the program, including any costs incurred after the adoption of this article and a reasonable reserve therefor.

(b) Eighty-five percent of the funds remaining after payment of administrative costs allocated pursuant to this article shall be distributed to qualified legal services projects. Distribution shall be by a pro rata county-by-county formula based upon the number of persons whose income is 125 percent or less of the current poverty threshold per county. For the purposes of this section, the source of data identifying the number of persons per county shall be the latest available figures from the United States Department of Commerce, Bureau of the Census. Projects from more than one county may pool their funds to operate a joint, multicounty legal services project serving each of their respective counties.

(1)(A) In any county which is served by more than one qualified legal services project, the State Bar shall distribute funds for the county to those projects which apply on a pro rata basis, based upon the amount of their total budget expended in the prior year for legal services in that county as compared to the total expended in the prior year for legal services by all qualified legal services projects applying therefor in the county. In determining the amount of funds to be allocated to a qualified legal services project specified in paragraph (2) of subdivision (a) of Section 6213, the State Bar shall recognize only expenditures attributable to the representation of indigent persons as constituting the budget of the program.

(B) The State Bar shall reserve 10 percent of the funds allocated to the county for distribution to programs meeting the standards of subparagraph (A) of paragraph (3) and paragraphs (1) and (2) of subdivision (b) of Section 6214 and which perform the services described in subparagraph (A) of paragraph (3) of Section 6214 as their principal means of delivering legal services. The State Bar shall distribute the funds for that county to those programs which apply on a pro rata basis, based upon the amount of their total budget expended for free legal services in that county as compared to the total expended for free legal services by all programs meeting the standards of subparagraph (A) of paragraph (3) and paragraphs (1) and (2) of subdivision (b) of Section 6214 in that county. The State Bar shall distribute any funds for which no program has qualified pursuant hereto, in accordance with the provisions of subparagraph (A) of paragraph (1) of this subdivision.

(2) In any county in which there is no qualified legal services project providing services, the State Bar shall reserve for the remainder of the fiscal year for distribution the pro rata share of funds as provided for by this article. Upon application of a qualified legal services project proposing to provide legal services to the indigent of the county, the State Bar shall distribute the funds to the project. Any funds not so distributed shall be added to the funds to be distributed the following year.

(c) Fifteen percent of the funds remaining after payment of administrative costs allocated for the purposes of this article shall be distributed equally by the State Bar to qualified support centers which apply for the funds. The funds provided to support centers shall be used only for the provision of legal services within California. Qualified support centers that receive funds to provide services to qualified legal services projects from sources other than this article, shall submit and shall have approved by the State Bar a plan assuring that the services funded under this article are in addition to those already funded for qualified legal services projects by other sources.

§ 6217. Maintenance of Quality Services, Professional Standards, Attorney–Client Privilege; Funds to Be Expended in Accordance With Article; Interference With Attorney Prohibited

With respect to the provision of legal assistance under this article, each recipient shall ensure all of the following:

(a) The maintenance of quality service and professional standards.

(b) The expenditure of funds received in accordance with the provisions of this article.

(c) The preservation of the attorney-client privilege in any case, and the protection of the integrity of the adversary process from any impairment in furnishing legal assistance to indigent persons.

(d) That no one shall interfere with any attorney funded in whole or in part by this article in carrying out his or her professional responsibility to his or her client as established by the rules of professional responsibility and this chapter.

§ 6218. Eligibility for Services; Establishment of Guidelines; Funds to Be Expended in Accordance With Article

All legal services projects and support centers receiving funds pursuant to this article shall adopt financial eligibility guidelines for indigent persons.

(a) Qualified legal services programs shall ensure that funds appropriated pursuant to this article shall be used solely to defray the costs of providing legal services to indigent persons or for such other purposes as set forth in this article.

(b) Funds received pursuant to this article by support centers shall only be used to provide services to qualified legal services projects as defined in subdivision (a) of Section 6213 which are used pursuant to a plan as required by subdivision (c) of Section 6216, or as permitted by Section 6219.

§ 6219. Provision of Work Opportunities and Scholarships for Disadvantaged Law Students

Qualified legal services projects and support centers may use funds provided under this article to provide work opportunities with pay, and where feasible, scholarships for disadvantaged law students to help defray their law school expenses.

§ 6220. Private Attorneys Providing Legal Services Without Charge; Support Center Services

Attorneys in private practice who are providing legal services without charge to indigent persons shall not be disqualified from receiving the services of the qualified support centers.

§ 6221. Services for Indigent Members of Disadvantaged and Underserved Groups

Qualified legal services projects shall make significant efforts to utilize 20 percent of the funds allocated under this article for increasing the availability of services to the elderly, the disabled, juveniles, or other indigent persons who are members of disadvantaged and underserved groups within their service area.

§ 6222. Financial Statements; Submission to State Bar; State Bar Report

A recipient of funds allocated pursuant to this article annually shall submit a financial statement to the State Bar, including an audit of the funds by a certified public accountant or a fiscal review approved by the State Bar, a report demonstrating the programs on which they were expended, a report on the recipient's compliance with the requirements of Section 6217, and progress in meeting the service expansion requirements of Section 6221.

The Board of Governors of the State Bar shall include a report of receipts of funds under this article, expenditures for administrative costs, and disbursements of the funds, on a county-by-county basis, in the annual report of State Bar receipts and expenditures required pursuant to Section 6145.

§ 6223. Expenditure of Funds; Prohibitions

No funds allocated by the State Bar pursuant to this article shall be used for any of the following purposes:

(a) The provision of legal assistance with respect to any fee generating case, except in accordance with guidelines which shall be promulgated by the State Bar.

(b) The provision of legal assistance with respect to any criminal proceeding.

(c) The provision of legal assistance, except to indigent persons or except to provide support services to qualified legal services projects as defined by this article.

§ 6224. State Bar; Powers; Determination of Qualifications to Receive Funds; Denial of Funds; Termination; Procedures

The State Bar shall have the power to determine that an applicant for funding is not qualified to receive funding, to deny future funding, or to terminate existing funding because the recipient is not operating in compliance with the requirements or restrictions of this article.

A denial of an application for funding or for future funding or an action by the State Bar to terminate an existing grant of funds under this article shall not become final until the applicant or recipient has been afforded reasonable notice and an opportunity for a timely and fair hearing. Pending final determination of any hearing held with reference to termination of funding, financial assistance shall be continued at its existing level on a month-to-month basis. Hearings for denial shall be conducted by an impartial hearing officer whose decision shall be final. The hearing officer shall render a decision no later than 30 days after the conclusion of the hearing. Specific procedures governing the conduct of the hearings of this section shall be determined by the State Bar pursuant to Section 6225.

§ 6225. Implementation of Article; Adoption of Rules and Regulations; Procedures

The Board of Governors of the State Bar shall adopt the regulations and procedures necessary to implement this article and to ensure that the funds allocated herein are utilized to provide civil legal services to indigent persons, especially underserved client groups such as but not limited to the elderly, the disabled, juveniles, and non-English-speaking persons.

In adopting the regulations the Board of Governors shall comply with the following procedures:

(a) The board shall publish a preliminary draft of the regulations and procedures, which shall be distributed, together with notice of the hearings required by subdivision (b), to commercial banking institutions, to members of the State Bar, and to potential recipients of funds.

(b) The board shall hold at least two public hearings, one in southern California and one in northern California where affected and interested parties shall be afforded an opportunity to present oral and written testimony regarding the proposed regulations and procedures.

§ 6226. Implementation of Article; Resolution

The program authorized by this article shall become operative only upon the adoption of a resolution by the Board of Governors of the State Bar stating that regulations have been adopted pursuant to Section 6225 which conform the program to all applicable tax and banking statutes, regulations, and rulings.

§ 6227. Credit of State Not Pledged

Nothing in this article shall create an obligation or pledge of the credit of the State of California or of the State Bar of California. Claims arising by reason of acts done pursuant to this article shall be limited to the moneys generated hereunder.

§ 6228. Severability

If any provision of this article or the application thereof to any group or circumstances is held invalid, such invalidity shall not affect the other provisions or applications of this article which can be given effect without the invalid provision or application, and to this end the provisions of this article are severable.

———

NOTE, SOME IMPORTANT STATUTES FOR LAWYERS IN CALIFORNIA GOVERNMENT

The State has a large number of statutes dealing with professional responsibilities of governmental officials, particularly if they are lawyers. West's California Government Code, provides in part:

§ 8920. Prohibited Acts

(a) No Member of the Legislature, state elective or appointive officer, or judge or justice shall, while serving as such, have any interest, financial or otherwise, direct or indirect, or engage in any business or transaction or professional activity, or incur any obligation of any nature, which is in substantial conflict with the proper discharge of his duties in the public interest and of his responsibilities as prescribed in the laws of this state.

(b) No Member of the Legislature shall do any of the following:

(1) Accept other employment which he has reason to believe will either impair his independence of judgment as to his official duties or require him, or induce him, to disclose confidential information acquired by him in the course of and by reason of his official duties.

(2) Willfully and knowingly disclose, for pecuniary gain, to any other person, confidential information acquired by him in the course of and by reason of his official duties or use any such information for the purpose of pecuniary gain.

(3) Accept or agree to accept, or be in partnership with any person who accepts or agrees to accept, any employment, fee, or other thing of monetary value, or portion thereof, in consideration of his appearing, agreeing to

appear, or taking any other action on behalf of another person before any state board or agency.

This subdivision shall not be construed to prohibit a member who is an attorney at law from practicing in that capacity before any court or before the Workers' Compensation Appeals Board and receiving compensation therefor. This subdivision shall not act to prohibit a member from acting as an advocate without compensation or making inquiry for information on behalf of a constituent before a state board or agency, or from engaging in activities on behalf of another which require purely ministerial acts by the board or agency and which in no way require the board or agency to exercise any discretion, or from engaging in activities involving a board or agency which are strictly on his or her own behalf. The prohibition contained in this subdivision shall not apply to a partnership or firm of which the Member of the Legislature is a member if the Member of the Legislature does not share directly or indirectly in the fee, less any expenses attributable to that fee, resulting from the transaction. The prohibition contained in this subdivision as it read immediately prior to January 1, 1983, shall not apply in connection with any matter pending before any state board or agency on or before January 2, 1967, if the affected member of the Legislature was an attorney of record or representative in the matter prior to January 2, 1967. The prohibition contained in this subdivision, as amended and operative on January 1, 1983, shall not apply to any activity of any Member in connection with a matter pending before any state board or agency on January 1, 1983, which was not prohibited by this section prior to that date, if the affected Member of the Legislature was an attorney of record or representative in the matter prior to January 1, 1983.

(4) Receive or agree to receive, directly or indirectly, any compensation, reward, or gift from any source except the State of California for any service, advice, assistance or other matter related to the legislative process, except fees for speeches or published works on legislative subjects and except, in connection therewith, reimbursement of expenses for actual expenditures for travel and reasonable subsistence for which no payment or reimbursement is made by the State of California;

(5) Participate, by voting or any other action, on the floor of either house, in committee, or elsewhere, in the passage or defeat of legislation in which he has a personal interest, except as follows:

(i) If, on the vote for final passage by the house of which he is a member, of the legislation in which he has a personal interest, he first files a statement (which shall be entered verbatim on the journal) stating in substance that he has a personal interest in the legislation to be voted on and, notwithstanding that interest, he is able to cast a fair and objective vote on that legislation, he may cast his vote without violating any provision of this article;

(ii) If the member believes that, because of his personal interest, he should abstain from participating in the vote on the legislation, he shall so advise the presiding officer prior to the commencement of the vote and shall be excused from voting on the legislation without any entry on the journal of the fact of his personal interest. In the event a rule of the house requiring that each member who is present vote aye or nay is invoked, the presiding officer shall order the member excused from compliance and shall order entered on the journal a simple statement that the member was excused from voting on the legislation pursuant to law.

The provisions of this section do not apply to persons who are members of the state civil service as defined in Article VII of the California Constitution.

§ 8921. Interest in Substantial Conflict With Proper Discharge of Duties

A person subject to this article has an interest which is in substantial conflict with the proper discharge of his duties in the public interest and of his responsibilities as prescribed in the laws of this state or a personal interest, arising from any situation, within the scope of this article, if he has reason to believe or expect that he will derive a direct monetary gain or suffer a direct monetary loss, as the case may be, by reason of his official activity. He does not have an interest which is in substantial conflict with the proper discharge of his duties in the public interest and of his responsibilities as prescribed in the laws of this state or a personal interest, arising from any situation, within the scope of this article, if any benefit or detriment accrues to him as a member of a business, profession, occupation, or group to no greater extent than any other member of that business, profession, occupation, or group.

––––––

See also: West California Government Code, Section 24004—restrictions on practice of law by sheriff, clerk, constable, or any of their deputies.

Id. Section 31000.6—employment of legal counsel by board of supervisors to assist county assessor where county counsel or district attorney have a conflict of interest; in the event of a dispute as to whether a conflict exists, the presiding judge of superior court decides.

Id. Section 41805—representation of defendants in criminal matters by city attorney (or his partner or associate) if the defendant is not accused of violation of such city's ordinances, the city expressly relieves the city attorney of all prosecutorial functions on his behalf, and the defendant is "informed of and expressly waives any rights created as a result of any potential conflict *** ."

NEW YORK RULES OF PROFESSIONAL CONDUCT

(Effective April 1, 2009)

PREAMBLE: A LAWYER'S RESPONSIBILITIES

[1] A lawyer, as a member of the legal profession, is a representative of clients and an officer of the legal system with special responsibility for the quality of justice. As a representative of clients, a lawyer assumes many roles, including advisor, advocate, negotiator, and evaluator. As an officer of the legal system, each lawyer has a duty to uphold the legal process; to demonstrate respect for the legal system; to seek improvement of the law; and to promote access to the legal system and the administration of justice. In addition, a lawyer should further the public's understanding of and confidence in the rule of law and the justice system because, in a constitutional democracy, legal institutions depend on popular participation and support to maintain their authority.

[2] The touchstone of the client-lawyer relationship is the lawyer's obligation to assert the client's position under the rules of the adversary system, to maintain the client's confidential information except in limited circumstances, and to act with loyalty during the period of the representation.

[3] A lawyer's responsibilities in fulfilling these many roles and obligations are usually harmonious. In the course of law practice, however, conflicts may arise among the lawyer's responsibilities to clients, to the legal system and to the lawyer's own interests. The Rules of Professional Conduct often prescribe terms for resolving such conflicts. Nevertheless, within the framework of the Rules, many difficult issues of professional discretion can arise. The lawyer must resolve such issues through the exercise of sensitive professional and moral judgment, guided by the basic principles underlying the Rules.

[4] The legal profession is largely self-governing. An independent legal profession is an important force in preserving government under law, because abuse of legal authority is more readily challenged by a profession whose members are not dependent on government for the right to practice law. To the extent that lawyers meet these professional obligations, the occasion for government regulation is obviated.

[5] The relative autonomy of the legal profession carries with it special responsibilities of self-governance. Every lawyer is responsible for observance of the Rules of Professional Conduct and also should aid in securing their observance by other lawyers. Neglect of these responsibilities compromises the independence of the profession and the public interest that it serves. Compliance with the Rules depends primarily upon the lawyer's understanding of the Rules and desire to comply with the professional norms they

embody for the benefit of clients and the legal system, and, secondarily, upon reinforcement by peer and public opinion. So long as its practitioners are guided by these principles, the law will continue to be a noble profession.

SCOPE

[6] The Rules of Professional Conduct are rules of reason. They should be interpreted with reference to the purposes of legal representation and of the law itself. Some of the Rules are imperatives, cast in the terms "shall" or "shall not." These Rules define proper conduct for purposes of professional discipline. Others, generally cast in the term "may," are permissive and define areas under the Rules in which the lawyer has discretion to exercise professional judgment. No disciplinary action should be taken when the lawyer chooses not to act or acts within the bounds of such discretion. Other Rules define the nature of relationships between the lawyer and others. The Rules are thus partly obligatory and disciplinary and partly constitutive and descriptive in that they define a lawyer's professional role. Many of the Comments use the term "should." Comments do not add obligations to the Rules but provide guidance for practicing in compliance with the Rules. The Rules state the minimum level of conduct below which no lawyer can fall without being subject to disciplinary action.

[7] The Rules presuppose a larger legal context shaping the lawyer's role. That context includes court rules and statutes relating to matters of licensure, laws defining specific obligations of lawyers, and substantive and procedural law in general. The Comments are sometimes used to alert lawyers to their responsibilities under such other law.

[8] The Rules provide a framework for the ethical practice of law. Compliance with the Rules, as with all law in an open society, depends primarily upon understanding and voluntary compliance, secondarily upon reinforcement by peer and public opinion and finally, when necessary, upon enforcement through disciplinary proceedings. The Rules do not, however, exhaust the moral and ethical considerations that should inform a lawyer, for no worthwhile human activity can be completely defined by legal rules.

[9] Furthermore, for purposes of determining the lawyer's authority and responsibility, principles of substantive law external to these Rules determine whether a client-lawyer relationship exists. Most of the duties flowing from the client-lawyer relationship attach only after the client has requested the lawyer to render legal services and the lawyer has agreed to do so. But there are some duties, such as that of confidentiality under Rule 1.6, that attach when the lawyer agrees to consider whether a client-lawyer relationship shall be established. *See* Rule 1.18. Whether a client-lawyer relationship exists for any specific purpose can depend on the circumstances and may be a question of fact.

[10] Under various legal provisions, including constitutional, statutory and common law, the responsibilities of government lawyers may include authority concerning legal matters that ordinarily reposes in the client in

private client-lawyer relationships. For example, a lawyer for a government agency may have authority on behalf of the government to decide whether to agree to a settlement or to appeal from an adverse judgment. Such authority in various respects is generally vested in the attorney general and the state's attorney in state government, and in their federal counterparts, and the same may be true of other government law officers. Also, lawyers under the supervision of these officers may be authorized to represent several government agencies in intragovernmental legal controversies in circumstances where a private lawyer could not represent multiple private clients. These Rules do not abrogate any such authority.

[11]   Failure to comply with an obligation or prohibition imposed by a Rule is a basis for invoking the disciplinary process. The Rules presuppose that disciplinary assessment of a lawyer's conduct will be made on the basis of the facts and circumstances as they existed at the time of the conduct in question and in recognition of the fact that a lawyer often has to act upon uncertain or incomplete evidence of the situation. Moreover, the Rules presuppose that whether discipline should be imposed for a violation, and the severity of a sanction, depend on all the circumstances, such as the willfulness and seriousness of the violation, extenuating factors and whether there have been previous violations.

[12]   Violation of a Rule should not itself give rise to a cause of action against a lawyer nor should it create any presumption in such a case that a legal duty has been breached. In addition, violation of a Rule does not necessarily warrant any other nondisciplinary remedy, such as disqualification of a lawyer in pending litigation. The Rules are designed to provide guidance to lawyers and to provide a structure for regulating conduct through disciplinary agencies. They are not designed to be a basis for civil liability. Furthermore, the purpose of the Rules can be subverted when they are invoked by opposing parties as procedural weapons. The fact that a Rule is a just basis for a lawyer's self-assessment, or for sanctioning a lawyer under the administration of a disciplinary authority, does not imply that an antagonist in a collateral proceeding or transaction has standing to seek enforcement of the Rule. Nevertheless, because the Rules do establish standards of conduct by lawyers, a lawyer's violation of a Rule may be evidence of breach of the applicable standard of conduct.

[13]   The Comment accompanying each Rule explains and illustrates the meaning and purpose of the Rule. The Preamble and this note on Scope provide general orientation. The Comments are intended as guides to interpretation, but the text of each Rule is authoritative.

RULE 1.0: TERMINOLOGY

(a) **"Advertisement" means any public or private communication made by or on behalf of a lawyer or law firm about that lawyer or law firm's services, the primary purpose of which is for the retention of the lawyer or law firm. It does not include communications to existing clients or other lawyers.**

(b) "Belief" or "believes" denotes that the person involved actually believes the fact in question to be true. A person's belief may be inferred from circumstances.

(c) "Computer-accessed communication" means any communication made by or on behalf of a lawyer or law firm that is disseminated through the use of a computer or related electronic device, including, but not limited to, web sites, weblogs, search engines, electronic mail, banner advertisements, pop-up and pop-under advertisements, chat rooms, list servers, instant messaging, or other internet presences, and any attachments or links related thereto.

(d) "Confidential information" is defined in Rule 1.6.

(e) "Confirmed in writing" denotes (i) a writing from the person to the lawyer confirming that the person has given consent, (ii) a writing that the lawyer promptly transmits to the person confirming the person's oral consent, or (iii) a statement by the person made on the record of any proceeding before a tribunal. If it is not feasible to obtain or transmit the writing at the time the person gives oral consent, then the lawyer must obtain or transmit it within a reasonable time thereafter.

(f) "Differing interests" include every interest that will adversely affect either the judgment or the loyalty of a lawyer to a client, whether it be a conflicting, inconsistent, diverse, or other interest.

(g) "Domestic relations matter" denotes representation of a client in a claim, action or proceeding, or preliminary to the filing of a claim, action or proceeding, in either Supreme Court or Family Court, or in any court of appellate jurisdiction, for divorce, separation, annulment, custody, visitation, maintenance, child support or alimony, or to enforce or modify a judgment or order in connection with any such claim, action or proceeding.

(h) "Firm" or "law firm" includes, but is not limited to, a lawyer or lawyers in a law partnership, professional corporation, sole proprietorship or other association authorized to practice law; or lawyers employed in a qualified legal assistance organization, a government law office, or the legal department of a corporation or other organization.

(i) "Fraud" or "fraudulent" denotes conduct that is fraudulent under the substantive or procedural law of the applicable jurisdiction or has a purpose to deceive, provided that it does not include conduct that, although characterized as fraudulent by statute or administrative rule, lacks an element of scienter, deceit, intent to mislead, or knowing failure to correct misrepresentations that can be reasonably expected to induce detrimental reliance by another.

(j) "Informed consent" denotes the agreement by a person to a proposed course of conduct after the lawyer has communicated information adequate for the person to make an informed decision, and after the lawyer has adequately explained to the person the material risks of the proposed course of conduct and reasonably available alternatives.

(k) "Knowingly," "known," "know," or "knows" denotes actual knowledge of the fact in question. A person's knowledge may be inferred from circumstances.

(*l*) "Matter" includes any litigation, judicial or administrative proceeding, case, claim, application, request for a ruling or other determination, contract, controversy, investigation, charge, accusation, arrest, negotiation, arbitration, mediation or any other representation involving a specific party or parties.

(m) "Partner" denotes a member of a partnership, a shareholder in a law firm organized as a professional legal corporation or a member of an association authorized to practice law.

(n) "Person" includes an individual, a corporation, an association, a trust, a partnership, and any other organization or entity.

(*o*) "Professional legal corporation" means a corporation, or an association treated as a corporation, authorized by law to practice law for profit.

(p) "Qualified legal assistance organization" means an office or organization of one of the four types listed in Rule 7.2(b)(1)–(4) that meets all of the requirements thereof.

(q) "Reasonable" or "reasonably," when used in relation to conduct by a lawyer, denotes the conduct of a reasonably prudent and competent lawyer. When used in the context of conflict of interest determinations, "reasonable lawyer" denotes a lawyer acting from the perspective of a reasonably prudent and competent lawyer who is personally disinterested in commencing or continuing the representation.

(r) "Reasonable belief" or "reasonably believes," when used in reference to a lawyer, denotes that the lawyer believes the matter in question and that the circumstances are such that the belief is reasonable.

(s) "Reasonably should know," when used in reference to a lawyer, denotes that a lawyer of reasonable prudence and competence would ascertain the matter in question.

(t) "Screened" or "screening" denotes the isolation of a lawyer from any participation in a matter through the timely imposition of procedures within a firm that are reasonably adequate under the circumstances to protect information that the isolated lawyer or the firm is obligated to protect under these Rules or other law.

(u) **"Sexual relations" denotes sexual intercourse or the touching of an intimate part of the lawyer or another person for the purpose of sexual arousal, sexual gratification or sexual abuse.**

(v) **"State" includes the District of Columbia, Puerto Rico, and other federal territories and possessions.**

(w) **"Tribunal" denotes a court, an arbitrator in an arbitration proceeding or a legislative body, administrative agency or other body acting in an adjudicative capacity. A legislative body, administrative agency or other body acts in an adjudicative capacity when a neutral official, after the presentation of evidence or legal argument by a party or parties, will render a legal judgment directly affecting a party's interests in a particular matter.**

(x) **"Writing" or "written" denotes a tangible or electronic record of a communication or representation, including handwriting, typewriting, printing, photocopying, photography, audio or video recording and email. A "signed" writing includes an electronic sound, symbol or process attached to or logically associated with a writing and executed or adopted by a person with the intent to sign the writing.**

Comment

Confirmed in Writing

[1]   Some Rules require that a person's oral consent be "confirmed in writing." *E.g.*, Rules 1.5(g)(2) (client's consent to division of fees with lawyer in another firm must be confirmed in writing), 1.7(b)(4) (client's informed consent to conflict of interest must be confirmed in writing) and 1.9(a) (former client's informed consent to conflict of interest must be confirmed in writing). The definition of "confirmed in writing" provides three distinct methods of confirming a person's consent: (i) a writing from the person to the lawyer, (ii) a writing from the lawyer to the person, or (iii) consent by the person on the record in any proceeding before a tribunal. The confirming writing need not recite the information that the lawyer communicated to the person in order to obtain the person's consent. For the definition of "informed consent" *see* Rule 1.0(j). If it is not feasible for the lawyer to obtain or transmit a written confirmation at the time the client gives oral consent, then the lawyer must obtain or transmit the confirming writing within a reasonable time thereafter. If a lawyer has obtained a client's informed oral consent, the lawyer may act in reliance on that consent so long as it is confirmed in writing within a reasonable time thereafter.

Firm

[2]   Whether two or more lawyers constitute a firm within paragraph (h) will depend on the specific facts. For example, two practitioners who share office space and occasionally consult or assist each other ordinarily would not be regarded as constituting a firm. However, if they present themselves to the

public in a way that suggests that they are a firm or conduct themselves as a firm, they should be regarded as a firm for purposes of the Rules. The terms of any formal agreement between associated lawyers are relevant in determining whether they are a firm, as is the fact that they have mutual access to information concerning the clients they serve. Furthermore, it is relevant in doubtful cases to consider the underlying purpose of the Rule that is involved. For example, a group of lawyers could be regarded as a firm for purposes of determining whether a conflict of interest exists but not for application of the advertising rules.

[3]   With respect to the law department of an organization, there is ordinarily no question that the members of the department constitute a firm within the meaning of the Rules of Professional Conduct. There can be uncertainty, however, as to the identity of the client. For example, it may not be clear whether the law department of a corporation represents a subsidiary or an affiliated corporation, as well as the corporation by which the members of the department are directly employed. A similar question can arise concerning an unincorporated association and its local affiliates. Whether lawyers in a government agency or department constitute a firm may depend upon the issue involved or be governed by other law.

[4]   Similar questions can also arise with respect to lawyers in legal aid and legal services organizations. Depending upon the structure of the organization, the entire organization or components of it may constitute a firm or firms for purposes of these Rules.

Fraud

[5]   When used in these Rules, the terms "fraud" and "fraudulent" refer to conduct that is characterized as such under the substantive or procedural law of the applicable jurisdiction and has a purpose to deceive. This does not include merely negligent misrepresentation or negligent failure to apprise another of relevant information. For purposes of these Rules, it is not necessary that anyone has suffered damages or relied on the misrepresentation or failure to inform, so long as the necessary scienter is present and the conduct in question could be reasonably expected to induce detrimental reliance.

Informed Consent

[6]   Many of the Rules of Professional Conduct require the lawyer to obtain the informed consent of a client or other person (*e.g.*, a former client or, under certain circumstances, a prospective client) before accepting or continuing representation or pursuing a course of conduct. *E.g.*, Rules 1.2(c), 1.6(a) and 1.7(b). The communication necessary to obtain such consent will vary according to the Rule involved and the circumstances giving rise to the need to obtain informed consent. The lawyer must make reasonable efforts to ensure that the client or other person possesses information reasonably adequate to make an informed decision. Ordinarily, this will require communication that includes a disclosure of the facts and circumstances giving rise

to the situation, any explanation reasonably necessary to inform the client or other person of the material advantages and disadvantages of the proposed course of conduct, and a discussion of the client's or other person's options and alternatives. In some circumstances it may be appropriate for a lawyer to advise a client or other person to seek the advice of other counsel. A lawyer need not inform a client or other person of facts or implications already known to the client or other person; nevertheless, a lawyer who does not personally inform the client or other person assumes the risk that the client or other person is inadequately informed and the consent is invalid. In determining whether the information and explanation provided are reasonably adequate, relevant factors include whether the client or other person is experienced in legal matters generally and in making decisions of the type involved, and whether the client or other person is independently represented by other counsel in giving the consent. Normally, such persons need less information and explanation than others, and generally a client or other person who is independently represented by other counsel in giving the consent should be assumed to have given informed consent. Other considerations may apply in representing impaired clients. *See* Rule 1.14.

[7] Obtaining informed consent will usually require an affirmative response by the client or other person. In general, a lawyer may not assume consent from a client's or other person's silence. Consent may be inferred, however, from the conduct of a client or other person who has reasonably adequate information about the matter. A number of Rules require that a person's consent be confirmed in writing. *E.g.*, Rules 1.7(b) and 1.9(a). For definitions of "writing" and "confirmed in writing" *see* paragraphs (x) and (e), respectively. Other Rules require that a client's consent be obtained in a writing signed by the client. *E.g.*, Rules 1.8(a) and (g). For the meaning of "signed," *see* paragraph (x).

Screened or Screening

[8] The definition of "screened" or "screening" applies to situations where screening of a personally disqualified lawyer is permitted to remove imputation of a conflict of interest under Rule 1.11, 1.12 or 1.18. *See* those Rules for the particular requirements of establishing effective screening.

[9] The purpose of screening is to ensure that confidential information known by the personally disqualified lawyer remains protected. The personally disqualified lawyer should acknowledge the obligation not to communicate with any of the other lawyers in the firm with respect to the matter. Similarly, other lawyers in the firm who are working on the matter should promptly be informed that the screening is in place and that they may not communicate with the personally disqualified lawyer with respect to the matter. Additional screening measures that are appropriate for the particular matter will depend on the circumstances. In any event, procedures should be adequate to protect confidential information.

[10]   In order to be effective, screening measures must be implemented as soon as practicable after a lawyer or law firm knows or reasonably should know that there is a need for screening.

RULE 1.1: COMPETENCE

(a) **A lawyer should provide competent representation to a client. Competent representation requires the legal knowledge, skill, thoroughness and preparation reasonably necessary for the representation.**

(b) **A lawyer shall not handle a legal matter that the lawyer knows or should know that the lawyer is not competent to handle, without associating with a lawyer who is competent to handle it.**

(c) **A lawyer shall not intentionally:**

(1) **fail to seek the objectives of the client through reasonably available means permitted by law and these Rules; or**

(2) **prejudice or damage the client during the course of the representation except as permitted or required by these Rules.**

Comment
Legal Knowledge and Skill

[1]   In determining whether a lawyer employs the requisite knowledge and skill in a particular matter, relevant factors include the relative complexity and specialized nature of the matter, the lawyer's general experience, the lawyer's training and experience in the field in question, the preparation and study the lawyer is able to give the matter, and whether it is feasible to associate with a lawyer of established competence in the field in question. In many instances, the required proficiency is that of a general practitioner. Expertise in a particular field of law may be required in some circumstances. One such circumstance would be where the lawyer, by representations made to the client, has led the client reasonably to expect a special level of expertise in the matter undertaken by the lawyer.

[2]   A lawyer need not necessarily have special training or prior experience to handle legal problems of a type with which the lawyer is unfamiliar. A newly admitted lawyer can be as competent as a practitioner with long experience. Some important legal skills, such as the analysis of precedent, the evaluation of evidence and legal drafting, are required in all legal problems. Perhaps the most fundamental legal skill consists of determining what kinds of legal problems a situation may involve, a skill that necessarily transcends any particular specialized knowledge. A lawyer can provide adequate representation in a wholly novel field through necessary study. Competent representation can also be provided through the association of a lawyer of established competence in the field in question.

[3]   [Omitted.]

[4]   A lawyer may accept representation where the requisite level of competence can be achieved by adequate preparation before handling the legal matter. This applies as well to a lawyer who is appointed as counsel for an unrepresented person.

Thoroughness and Preparation

[5]   Competent handling of a particular matter includes inquiry into and analysis of the factual and legal elements of the problem, and use of methods and procedures meeting the standards of competent practitioners. It also includes adequate preparation. The required attention and preparation are determined in part by what is at stake; major litigation and complex transactions ordinarily require more extensive treatment than matters of lesser complexity and consequence. An agreement between the lawyer and the client may limit the scope of the representation if the agreement complies with Rule 1.2(c).

Maintaining Competence

[6]   To maintain the requisite knowledge and skill, a lawyer should keep abreast of changes in the law and its practice, engage in continuing study and education, and comply with all continuing legal education requirements to which the lawyer is subject. *See* 22 N.Y.C.R.R. Part 1500.

RULE 1.2: SCOPE OF REPRESENTATION AND ALLOCATION OF AUTHORITY BETWEEN CLIENT AND LAWYER

(a) Subject to the provisions herein, a lawyer shall abide by a client's decisions concerning the objectives of representation and, as required by Rule 1.4, shall consult with the client as to the means by which they are to be pursued. A lawyer shall abide by a client's decision whether to settle a matter. In a criminal case, the lawyer shall abide by the client's decision, after consultation with the lawyer, as to a plea to be entered, whether to waive jury trial and whether the client will testify.

(b) A lawyer's representation of a client, including representation by appointment, does not constitute an endorsement of the client's political, economic, social or moral views or activities.

(c) A lawyer may limit the scope of the representation if the limitation is reasonable under the circumstances, the client gives informed consent and where necessary notice is provided to the tribunal and/or opposing counsel.

(d) A lawyer shall not counsel a client to engage, or assist a client, in conduct that the lawyer knows is illegal or fraudulent, except that the lawyer may discuss the legal consequences of any proposed course of conduct with a client.

(e) A lawyer may exercise professional judgment to waive or fail to assert a right or position of the client, or accede to reasonable requests of opposing counsel, when doing so does not prejudice the rights of the client.

(f) A lawyer may refuse to aid or participate in conduct that the lawyer believes to be unlawful, even though there is some support for an argument that the conduct is legal.

(g) A lawyer does not violate this Rule by being punctual in fulfilling all professional commitments, by avoiding offensive tactics, and by treating with courtesy and consideration all persons involved in the legal process.

Comment

Allocation of Authority Between Client and Lawyer

[1] Paragraph (a) confers upon the client the ultimate authority to determine the purposes to be served by legal representation, within the limits imposed by law and the lawyer's professional obligations. The decisions specified in paragraph (a), such as whether to settle a civil matter, must also be made by the client. *See* Rule 1.4(a)(1) for the lawyer's duty to communicate with the client about such decisions. The lawyer shall consult with the client with respect to the means by which the client's objectives are to be pursued. *See* Rule 1.4(a)(2).

[2] Clients normally defer to the special knowledge and skill of their lawyer with respect to the means to be used to accomplish their objectives, particularly with respect to technical, legal and tactical matters. On the other hand, lawyers usually defer to their clients regarding such questions as the expense to be incurred and concern for third persons who might be adversely affected. On occasion, however, a lawyer and a client may disagree about the means to be used to accomplish the client's objectives. Because of the varied nature of the matters about which a lawyer and client might disagree, and because the actions in question may implicate the interests of a tribunal or other persons, this Rule does not prescribe how such disagreements are to be resolved. Other law, however, may be applicable and should be consulted by the lawyer. The lawyer should also consult with the client and seek a mutually acceptable resolution of the disagreement. If such efforts are unavailing and the lawyer has a fundamental disagreement with the client, the lawyer may withdraw from the representation. *See* Rule 1.16(c)(4). Likewise, the client may resolve the disagreement by discharging the lawyer, in which case the lawyer must withdraw from the representation. *See* Rule 1.16(b)(3).

[3] At the outset of a representation, the client may authorize the lawyer to take specific action on the client's behalf without further consultation. Absent a material change in circumstances and subject to Rule 1.4, a lawyer may rely on such an advance authorization. The client, however, may revoke such authority at any time.

[4] In a case in which the client appears to be suffering diminished capacity, the lawyer's duty to abide by the client's decisions is to be guided by reference to Rule 1.14.

Independence from Client's Views or Activities

[5] Legal representation should not be denied to any person who is unable to afford legal services, or whose cause is controversial or the subject of popular disapproval. By the same token, representing a client does not constitute approval of the client's views or activities.

Agreements Limiting Scope of Representation

[6] The scope of services to be provided by a lawyer may be limited by agreement with the client or by the terms under which the lawyer's services are made available to the client. When a lawyer has been retained by an insurer to represent an insured, for example, the representation may be limited to issues related to the insurance coverage. A limited representation may be appropriate because the client has limited objectives for the representation. In addition, the terms upon which representation is undertaken may exclude specific means that might otherwise be used to accomplish the client's objectives. Such limitations may exclude actions that the client thinks are too costly or that the lawyer regards as repugnant or imprudent.

[6A] In obtaining consent from the client, the lawyer must adequately disclose the limitations on the scope of the engagement and the matters that will be excluded. In addition, the lawyer must disclose the reasonably foreseeable consequences of the limitation. In making such disclosure, the lawyer should explain that if the lawyer or the client determines during the representation that additional services outside the limited scope specified in the engagement are necessary or advisable to represent the client adequately, then the client may need to retain separate counsel, which could result in delay, additional expense, and complications.

[7] Although this Rule affords the lawyer and client substantial latitude to limit the representation, the limitation must be reasonable under the circumstances. If, for example, a client's objective is limited to securing general information about the law the client needs in order to handle a common and typically uncomplicated legal problem, the lawyer and client may agree that the lawyer's services will be limited to a brief telephone consultation. Such a limitation, however, would not be reasonable if the time allotted were not sufficient to yield advice upon which the client could rely. Although an agreement for a limited representation does not exempt a lawyer from the duty to provide competent representation, the limitation is a factor to be considered when determining the legal knowledge, skill, thoroughness and preparation reasonably necessary for the representation. *See* Rule 1.1.

[8] All agreements concerning a lawyer's representation of a client must accord with the Rules of Professional Conduct and other law. *See* Rules 1.1, 1.8 and 5.6.

Illegal and Fraudulent Transactions

[9] Paragraph (d) prohibits a lawyer from counseling or assisting a client in conduct that the lawyer knows is illegal or fraudulent. This prohibition, however, does not preclude the lawyer from giving an honest opinion about the consequences that appear likely to result from a client's conduct. Nor does the fact that a client uses advice in a course of action that is illegal or fraudulent of itself make a lawyer a party to the course of action. There is a critical distinction between presenting an analysis of legal aspects of questionable conduct and recommending the means by which a crime or fraud might be committed with impunity.

[10] When the client's course of action has already begun and is continuing, the lawyer's responsibility is especially delicate. The lawyer is required to avoid assisting the client, for example, by drafting or delivering documents that the lawyer knows are fraudulent or by suggesting how the wrongdoing might be concealed. When the representation will result in violation of the Rules of Professional Conduct or other law, the lawyer must advise the client of any relevant limitation on the lawyer's conduct and remonstrate with the client. *See* Rules 1.4(a)(5) and 1.16(b)(1). Persuading a client to take necessary preventive or corrective action that will bring the client's conduct within the bounds of the law is a challenging but appropriate endeavor. If the client fails to take necessary corrective action and the lawyer's continued representation would assist client conduct that is illegal or fraudulent, the lawyer is required to withdraw. *See* Rule 1.16(b)(1). In some circumstances, withdrawal alone might be insufficient. In those cases the lawyer may be required to give notice of the fact of withdrawal and to disaffirm any opinion, document, affirmation or the like. *See* Rule 1.6(b)(3); Rule 4.1, Comment [3].

[11] Where the client is a fiduciary, the lawyer may be charged with special obligations in dealings with a beneficiary.

[12] Paragraph (d) prohibits a lawyer from assisting a client's illegal or fraudulent activity against a third person, whether or not the defrauded party is a party to the transaction. Paragraph (d) does not preclude undertaking a criminal defense incident to a general retainer for legal services to a lawful enterprise, but does preclude such a retainer for an enterprise known to be engaged in illegal or fraudulent activity.

[13] If a lawyer comes to know or reasonably should know that a client expects assistance not permitted by the Rules of Professional Conduct or other law, or if the lawyer intends to act contrary to the client's instructions, the lawyer must consult with the client regarding the limitations on the lawyer's conduct. *See* Rule 1.4(a)(5).

RULE 1.3: DILIGENCE

(a) A lawyer shall act with reasonable diligence and promptness in representing a client.

(b) A lawyer shall not neglect a legal matter entrusted to the lawyer.

(c) A lawyer shall not intentionally fail to carry out a contract of employment entered into with a client for professional services, but the lawyer may withdraw as permitted under these Rules.

Comment

[1] A lawyer should pursue a matter on behalf of a client despite opposition, obstruction or personal inconvenience to the lawyer, and take whatever lawful and ethical measures are required to vindicate a client's cause or endeavor. A lawyer must also act with commitment and dedication to the interests of the client and in advocacy upon the client's behalf. A lawyer is not bound, however, to press for every advantage that might be realized for a client. For example, a lawyer may have authority to exercise professional discretion in determining the means by which a matter should be pursued. *See* Rule 1.2. Notwithstanding the foregoing, the lawyer should not use offensive tactics or fail to treat all persons involved in the legal process with courtesy and respect.

[2] A lawyer's work load must be controlled so that each matter can be handled diligently and promptly. Lawyers are encouraged to adopt and follow effective office procedures and systems; neglect may occur when such arrangements are not in place or are ineffective.

[3] Perhaps no professional shortcoming is more widely resented than procrastination. A client's interests often can be adversely affected by the passage of time or the change of conditions; in extreme instances, as when a lawyer overlooks a statute of limitations, the client's legal position may be destroyed. Even when the client's interests are not affected in substance, unreasonable delay can cause a client needless anxiety and undermine confidence in the lawyer's trustworthiness. A lawyer's duty to act with reasonable promptness, however, does not preclude the lawyer from agreeing to a reasonable request for a postponement that will not prejudice the lawyer's client.

[4] Unless the relationship is terminated, as provided in Rule 1.16, a lawyer should carry through to conclusion all matters undertaken for a client. If a lawyer's employment is limited to a specific matter, the relationship terminates when the matter has been resolved. If a lawyer has served a client over a substantial period in a variety of matters, the client sometimes may assume that the lawyer will continue to serve on a continuing basis unless the lawyer gives notice of withdrawal. Doubt about whether a client-lawyer relationship still exists should be clarified by the lawyer, preferably in writing, so that the client will not mistakenly suppose the lawyer is looking after the client's affairs when the lawyer has ceased to do so. If a lawyer has handled a judicial or administrative proceeding that produced a result adverse to the client and the lawyer and the client have not agreed that the lawyer will handle the matter on appeal, Rule 1.16(e) may require the lawyer to consult

with the client about the possibility of appeal before relinquishing responsibility for the matter. Whether the lawyer is obligated to prosecute the appeal for the client depends on the scope of the representation the lawyer has agreed to provide to the client. *See* Rule 1.2.

[5]   To avoid possible prejudice to client interests, a sole practitioner is well advised to prepare a plan that designates another competent lawyer to review client files, notify each client of the lawyer's death or disability, and determine whether there is a need for immediate protective action.

RULE 1.4: COMMUNICATION

(a) A lawyer shall:

(1) promptly inform the client of:

(i) any decision or circumstance with respect to which the client's informed consent, as defined in Rule 1.0(j), is required by these Rules;

(ii) any information required by court rule or other law to be communicated to a client; and

(iii) material developments in the matter including settlement or plea offers.

(2) reasonably consult with the client about the means by which the client's objectives are to be accomplished;

(3) keep the client reasonably informed about the status of the matter;

(4) promptly comply with a client's reasonable requests for information; and

(5) consult with the client about any relevant limitation on the lawyer's conduct when the lawyer knows that the client expects assistance not permitted by these Rules or other law.

(b) A lawyer shall explain a matter to the extent reasonably necessary to permit the client to make informed decisions regarding the representation.

Comment

[1]   Reasonable communication between the lawyer and the client is necessary for the client to participate effectively in the representation.

Communicating with Client

[2]   In instances where these Rules require that a particular decision about the representation be made by the client, paragraph (a)(1) requires that the lawyer promptly consult with the client and secure the client's consent prior to taking action, unless prior discussions with the client have resolved what action the client wants the lawyer to take. For example, paragraph

(a)(1)(iii) requires that a lawyer who receives from opposing counsel an offer of settlement in a civil controversy or a proffered plea bargain in a criminal case must promptly inform the client of its substance unless the client has previously made clear that the proposal will be acceptable or unacceptable or has authorized the lawyer to accept or to reject the offer. *See* Rule 1.2(a).

[3]   Paragraph (a)(2) requires that the lawyer reasonably consult with the client about the means to be used to accomplish the client's objectives. In some situations—depending on both the importance of the action under consideration and the feasibility of consulting with the client—this duty will require consultation prior to taking action. In other circumstances, such as during a trial when an immediate decision must be made, the exigency of the situation may require the lawyer to act without prior consultation. In such cases, the lawyer must nonetheless act reasonably to inform the client of actions the lawyer has taken on the client's behalf. Likewise, for routine matters such as scheduling decisions not materially affecting the interests of the client, the lawyer need not consult in advance, but should keep the client reasonably informed thereafter. Additionally, paragraph (a)(3) requires that the lawyer keep the client reasonably informed about the status of the matter, such as significant developments affecting the timing or the substance of the representation.

[4]   A lawyer's regular communication with clients will minimize the occasions on which a client will need to request information concerning the representation. When a client makes a reasonable request for information, however, paragraph (a)(4) requires prompt compliance with the request, or if a prompt response is not feasible, that the lawyer or a member of the lawyer's staff acknowledge receipt of the request and advise the client when a response may be expected. Client telephone calls should be promptly returned or acknowledged.

Explaining Matters

[5]   The client should have sufficient information to participate intelligently in decisions concerning the objectives of the representation and the means by which they are to be pursued, to the extent the client is willing and able to do so. Adequacy of communication depends in part on the kind of advice or assistance that is involved. For example, when there is time to explain a proposal made in a negotiation, the lawyer should review all important provisions with the client before proceeding to an agreement. In litigation a lawyer should explain the general strategy and prospects of success and ordinarily should consult the client on tactics that are likely to result in significant expense or to injure or coerce others. On the other hand, a lawyer ordinarily will not be expected to describe trial or negotiation strategy in detail. The guiding principle is that the lawyer should fulfill reasonable client expectations for information consistent with the duty to act in the client's best interest and the client's overall requirements as to the character of representation. In certain circumstances, such as when a lawyer

asks a client to consent to a representation affected by a conflict of interest, the client must give informed consent, as defined in Rule 1.0(j).

[6] Ordinarily, the information to be provided is that appropriate for a client who is a comprehending and responsible adult. However, fully informing the client according to this standard may be impracticable, for example, where the client is a child or suffers from diminished capacity. *See* Rule 1.14. When the client is an organization or group, it is often impossible or inappropriate to inform every one of its members about its legal affairs; ordinarily, the lawyer should address communications to those who the lawyer reasonably believes to be appropriate persons within the organization. *See* Rule 1.13. Where many routine matters are involved, a system of limited or occasional reporting may be arranged with the client.

Withholding Information

[7] In some circumstances, a lawyer may be justified in delaying transmission of information when the client would be likely to react imprudently to an immediate communication. Thus, a lawyer might withhold a psychiatric diagnosis of a client when the examining psychiatrist indicates that disclosure would harm the client. A lawyer may not withhold information to serve the lawyer's own interest or convenience or the interests or convenience of another person. Rules or court orders governing litigation may provide that information supplied to a lawyer may not be disclosed to the client. Rule 3.4(c) directs compliance with such rules or orders.

RULE 1.5: FEES AND DIVISION OF FEES

(a) A lawyer shall not make an agreement for, charge, or collect an excessive or illegal fee or expense. A fee is excessive when, after a review of the facts, a reasonable lawyer would be left with a definite and firm conviction that the fee is excessive. The factors to be considered in determining whether a fee is excessive may include the following:

(1) the time and labor required, the novelty and difficulty of the questions involved, and the skill requisite to perform the legal service properly;

(2) the likelihood, if apparent or made known to the client, that the acceptance of the particular employment will preclude other employment by the lawyer;

(3) the fee customarily charged in the locality for similar legal services;

(4) the amount involved and the results obtained;

(5) the time limitations imposed by the client or by circumstances;

(6) the nature and length of the professional relationship with the client;

(7) the experience, reputation and ability of the lawyer or lawyers performing the services; and

(8) whether the fee is fixed or contingent.

(b) A lawyer shall communicate to a client the scope of the representation and the basis or rate of the fee and expenses for which the client will be responsible. This information shall be communicated to the client before or within a reasonable time after commencement of the representation and shall be in writing where required by statute or court rule. This provision shall not apply when the lawyer will charge a regularly represented client on the same basis or rate and perform services that are of the same general kind as previously rendered to and paid for by the client. Any changes in the scope of the representation or the basis or rate of the fee or expenses shall also be communicated to the client.

(c) A fee may be contingent on the outcome of the matter for which the service is rendered, except in a matter in which a contingent fee is prohibited by paragraph (d) or other law. Promptly after a lawyer has been employed in a contingent fee matter, the lawyer shall provide the client with a writing stating the method by which the fee is to be determined, including the percentage or percentages that shall accrue to the lawyer in the event of settlement, trial or appeal; litigation and other expenses to be deducted from the recovery; and whether such expenses are to be deducted before or, if not prohibited by statute or court rule, after the contingent fee is calculated. The writing must clearly notify the client of any expenses for which the client will be liable regardless of whether the client is the prevailing party. Upon conclusion of a contingent fee matter, the lawyer shall provide the client with a writing stating the outcome of the matter and, if there is a recovery, showing the remittance to the client and the method of its determination.

(d) A lawyer shall not enter into an arrangement for, charge or collect:

(1) a contingent fee for representing a defendant in a criminal matter;

(2) a fee prohibited by law or rule of court;

(3) a fee based on fraudulent billing;

(4) a nonrefundable retainer fee; provided that a lawyer may enter into a retainer agreement with a client containing a reasonable minimum fee clause if it defines in plain language and sets forth the circumstances under which such fee may be incurred and how it will be calculated; or

(5) any fee in a domestic relations matter if:

(i) the payment or amount of the fee is contingent upon the securing of a divorce or of obtaining child custody or visitation or is in any way determined by reference to the amount of maintenance, support, equitable distribution, or property settlement;

(ii) a written retainer agreement has not been signed by the lawyer and client setting forth in plain language the nature of the relationship and the details of the fee arrangement; or

(iii) the written retainer agreement includes a security interest, confession of judgment or other lien without prior notice being provided to the client in a signed retainer agreement and approval from a tribunal after notice to the adversary. A lawyer shall not foreclose on a mortgage placed on the marital residence while the spouse who consents to the mortgage remains the titleholder and the residence remains the spouse's primary residence.

(e) In domestic relations matters, a lawyer shall provide a prospective client with a Statement of Client's Rights and Responsibilities at the initial conference and prior to the signing of a written retainer agreement.

(f) Where applicable, a lawyer shall resolve fee disputes by arbitration at the election of the client pursuant to a fee arbitration program established by the Chief Administrator of the Courts and approved by the Administrative Board of the Courts.

(g) A lawyer shall not divide a fee for legal services with another lawyer who is not associated in the same law firm unless:

(1) the division is in proportion to the services performed by each lawyer or, by a writing given to the client, each lawyer assumes joint responsibility for the representation;

(2) the client agrees to employment of the other lawyer after a full disclosure that a division of fees will be made, including the share each lawyer will receive, and the client's agreement is confirmed in writing; and

(3) the total fee is not excessive.

(h) Rule 1.5(g) does not prohibit payment to a lawyer formerly associated in a law firm pursuant to a separation or retirement agreement.

Comment

[1]   Paragraph (a) requires that lawyers not charge fees that are excessive or illegal under the circumstances. The factors specified in paragraphs (a)(1) through (a)(8) are not exclusive, nor will each factor be relevant in each instance. The time and labor required for a matter may be affected by the

actions of the lawyer's own client or by those of the opposing party and counsel. Paragraph (a) also requires that expenses for which the client will be charged must not be excessive or illegal. A lawyer may seek payment for services performed in-house, such as copying, or for other expenses incurred in-house, such as telephone charges, either by charging an amount to which the client has agreed in advance or by charging an amount that reflects the cost incurred by the lawyer, provided in either case that the amount charged is not excessive.

[1A]   A billing is fraudulent if it is knowingly and intentionally based on false or inaccurate information. Thus, under an hourly billing arrangement, it would be fraudulent to knowingly and intentionally charge a client for more than the actual number of hours spent by the lawyer on the client's matter; similarly, where the client has agreed to pay the lawyer's cost of in-house services, such as for photocopying or telephone calls, it would be fraudulent knowingly and intentionally to charge a client more than the actual costs incurred. Fraudulent billing requires an element of scienter and does not include inaccurate billing due to an innocent mistake.

[1B]   A supervising lawyer who submits a fraudulent bill for fees or expenses to a client based on submissions by a subordinate lawyer has not automatically violated this Rule. Whether the lawyer is responsible for a violation must be determined by reference to Rule 5.1, 5.2 and 5.3.

Basis or Rate of Fee

[2]   When the lawyer has regularly represented a client, they ordinarily will have evolved an understanding concerning the basis or rate of the fee and the expenses for which the client will be responsible. In a new client-lawyer relationship, however, an understanding as to fees and expenses must be promptly established. Court rules regarding engagement letters require that such an understanding be memorialized in writing in certain cases. *See* 22 N.Y.C.R.R. Part 1215. Even where not required, it is desirable to furnish the client with at least a simple memorandum or copy of the lawyer's customary fee arrangements that states the general nature of the legal services to be provided, the basis, rate or total amount of the fee, and whether and to what extent the client will be responsible for any costs, expenses or disbursements in the course of the representation. A written statement concerning the terms of the engagement reduces the possibility of misunderstanding.

[3]   Contingent fees, like any other fees, are subject to the excessiveness standard of paragraph (a). In determining whether a particular contingent fee is excessive, or whether it is excessive to charge any form of contingent fee, a lawyer must consider the factors that are relevant under the circumstances. Applicable law may impose limitations on contingent fees, such as a ceiling on the percentage allowable, or may regulate the type or amount of the fee that may be charged.

Terms of Payment

[4]   A lawyer may require advance payment of a fee, but is obliged to return any unearned portion. *See* Rule 1.16(e). A lawyer may charge a minimum fee, if that fee is not excessive, and if the wording of the minimum fee clause of the retainer agreement meets the requirements of paragraph (d)(4). A lawyer may accept property in payment for services, such as an ownership interest in an enterprise, providing this does not involve acquisition of a proprietary interest in the cause of action or subject matter of the litigation contrary to Rule 1.8(i). A fee paid in property instead of money may, however, be subject to the requirements of Rule 1.8(a), because such fees often have the essential qualities of a business transaction with the client.

[5]   An agreement may not be made if its terms might induce the lawyer improperly to curtail services for the client or perform them in a way contrary to the client's interest. For example, a lawyer should not enter into an agreement whereby services are to be provided only up to a stated amount when it is foreseeable that more extensive services probably will be required, unless the situation is adequately explained to the client. Otherwise, the client might have to bargain for further assistance in the midst of a proceeding or transaction. In matters in litigation, the court's approval for the lawyer's withdrawal may be required. *See* Rule 1.16(d). It is proper, however, to define the extent of services in light of the client's ability to pay. A lawyer should not exploit a fee arrangement based primarily on hourly charges by using wasteful procedures.

[5A]   The New York Court Rules require every lawyer with an office located in New York to post in that office, in a manner visible to clients of the lawyer, a "Statement of Client's Rights." *See* 22 N.Y.C.R.R. § 1210.1. Paragraph (e) requires a lawyer in a domestic relations matter, as defined in Rule 1.0(g), to provide a prospective client with the "Statement of Client's Rights and Responsibilities," as further set forth in 22 N.Y.C.R.R. § 1400.2, at the initial conference and, in any event, prior to the signing of a written retainer agreement.

Prohibited Contingent Fees

[6]   Paragraph (d) prohibits a lawyer from charging a contingent fee in a domestic relations matter when payment is contingent upon the securing of a divorce or upon the amount of alimony or support or property settlement to be obtained or upon obtaining child custody or visitation. This provision does not preclude a contract for a contingent fee for legal representation in connection with the recovery of post-judgment balances due under support, alimony or other financial orders because such contracts do not implicate the same policy concerns.

Division of Fee

[7]   A division of fee is a single billing to a client covering the fee of two or more lawyers who are not affiliated in the same firm. A division of fee facilitates association of more than one lawyer in a matter in which neither

alone could serve the client as well. Paragraph (g) permits the lawyers to divide a fee either on the basis of the proportion of services they render or if each lawyer assumes responsibility for the representation as a whole in a writing given to the client. In addition, the client must agree to the arrangement, including the share that each lawyer is to receive, and the client's agreement must be confirmed in writing. Contingent fee arrangements must comply with paragraph (c). Joint responsibility for the representation entails financial and ethical responsibility for the representation as if the lawyers were associated in a partnership. *See* Rule 5.1. A lawyer should refer a matter only to a lawyer who the referring lawyer reasonably believes is competent to handle the matter. *See* Rule 1.1.

[8]   Paragraph (g) does not prohibit or regulate division of fees to be received in the future for work done when lawyers were previously associated in a law firm. Paragraph (h) recognizes that this Rule does not prohibit payment to a previously associated lawyer pursuant to a separation or retirement agreement.

Disputes over Fees

[9]   A lawyer should seek to avoid controversies over fees with clients and should attempt to resolve amicably any differences on the subject. The New York courts have established a procedure for resolution of fee disputes through arbitration and the lawyer must comply with the procedure when it is mandatory. Even when it is voluntary, the lawyer should conscientiously consider submitting to it.

RULE 1.6: CONFIDENTIALITY OF INFORMATION

(a) A lawyer shall not knowingly reveal confidential information, as defined in this Rule, or use such information to the disadvantage of a client or for the advantage of the lawyer or a third person, unless:

(1) the client gives informed consent, as defined in Rule 1.0(j);

(2) the disclosure is impliedly authorized to advance the best interests of the client and is either reasonable under the circumstances or customary in the professional community; or

(3) the disclosure is permitted by paragraph (b). "Confidential information" consists of information gained during or relating to the representation of a client, whatever its source, that is (a) protected by the attorney-client privilege, (b) likely to be embarrassing or detrimental to the client if disclosed, or (c) information that the client has requested be kept confidential. "Confidential information" does not ordinarily include (i) a lawyer's legal knowledge or legal research or (ii) information that is

generally known in the local community or in the trade, field or profession to which the information relates.

(b) A lawyer may reveal or use confidential information to the extent that the lawyer reasonably believes necessary:

(1) to prevent reasonably certain death or substantial bodily harm;

(2) to prevent the client from committing a crime;

(3) to withdraw a written or oral opinion or representation previously given by the lawyer and reasonably believed by the lawyer still to be relied upon by a third person, where the lawyer has discovered that the opinion or representation was based on materially inaccurate information or is being used to further a crime or fraud;

(4) to secure legal advice about compliance with these Rules or other law by the lawyer, another lawyer associated with the lawyer's firm or the law firm;

(5) (i) to defend the lawyer or the lawyer's employees and associates against an accusation of wrongful conduct; or

(ii) to establish or collect a fee; or

(6) when permitted or required under these Rules or to comply with other law or court order.

(c) A lawyer shall exercise reasonable care to prevent the lawyer's employees, associates, and others whose services are utilized by the lawyer from disclosing or using confidential information of a client, except that a lawyer may reveal the information permitted to be disclosed by paragraph (b) through an employee.

Comment

Scope of the Professional Duty of Confidentiality

[1]   This Rule governs the disclosure of information protected by the professional duty of confidentiality. Such information is described in these Rules as "confidential information" as defined in this Rule. Other rules also deal with confidential information. *See* Rule 1.9(c)(1) for the lawyer's duties with respect to the use of such information to the disadvantage of clients and former clients; Rule 1.9(c)(2) for the lawyer's duty not to reveal information relating to the lawyer's prior representation of a former client; Rule 1.14(c) for information relating to representation of a client with diminished capacity; Rule 1.18(b) for the lawyer's duties with respect to information provided to the lawyer by a prospective client; Rule 3.3 for the lawyer's duty of candor to a tribunal; and Rule 8.3(c) for information gained by a lawyer or judge while participating in an approved lawyer assistance program.

[2]   A fundamental principle in the client-lawyer relationship is that, in the absence of the client's informed consent, or except as permitted or

required by these Rules, the lawyer must not knowingly reveal information gained during and related to the representation, whatever its source. *See* Rule 1.0(j) for the definition of informed consent. The lawyer's duty of confidentiality contributes to the trust that is the hallmark of the client-lawyer relationship. The client is thereby encouraged to seek legal assistance and to communicate fully and frankly with the lawyer, even as to embarrassing or legally damaging subject matter. The lawyer needs this information to represent the client effectively and, if necessary, to advise the client to refrain from wrongful conduct. Typically, clients come to lawyers to determine their rights and what is, in the complex of laws and regulations, deemed to be legal and correct. Based upon experience, lawyers know that almost all clients follow the advice given, and the law is thereby upheld.

[3] The principle of client-lawyer confidentiality is given effect in three related bodies of law: the attorney-client privilege of evidence law, the work-product doctrine of civil procedure and the professional duty of confidentiality established in legal ethics codes. The attorney-client privilege and the work-product doctrine apply when compulsory process by a judicial or other governmental body seeks to compel a lawyer to testify or produce information or evidence concerning a client. The professional duty of client-lawyer confidentiality, in contrast, applies to a lawyer in all settings and at all times, prohibiting the lawyer from disclosing confidential information unless permitted or required by these Rules or to comply with other law or court order. The confidentiality duty applies not only to matters communicated in confidence by the client, which are protected by the attorney-client privilege, but also to all information gained during and relating to the representation, whatever its source. The confidentiality duty, for example, prohibits a lawyer from volunteering confidential information to a friend or to any other person except in compliance with the provisions of this Rule, including the Rule's reference to other law that may compel disclosure. *See* Comments [12]-[13]; *see also* Scope.

[4] Paragraph (a) prohibits a lawyer from knowingly revealing confidential information as defined by this Rule. This prohibition also applies to disclosures by a lawyer that do not in themselves reveal confidential information but could reasonably lead to the discovery of such information by a third person. A lawyer's use of a hypothetical to discuss issues relating to the representation with persons not connected to the representation is permissible so long as there is no reasonable likelihood that the listener will be able to ascertain the identity of the client.

[4A] Paragraph (a) protects all factual information "gained during or relating to the representation of a client," but not information obtained before a representation begins or after it ends. *See* Rule 1.18, dealing with duties to prospective clients. Information relates to the representation if it has any possible relevance to the representation or is received because of the representation. The accumulation of legal knowledge or legal research that a lawyer acquires through practice ordinarily is not client information protected by this Rule. However, in some circumstances, including where the client and the lawyer have so agreed, a client may have a proprietary interest in a particular product of the lawyer's research. Information that is generally known in the local community or in the trade, field or profession to which the information relates is also not protected, unless the client and the lawyer have otherwise agreed. Information that is in the public domain is not protected unless the information is difficult or expensive to discover. For example, a public record is confidential information when it may be obtained only through great effort or by means of a Freedom of Information request or other process.

Use of Information Related to Representation

[4B]   The duty of confidentiality also prohibits a lawyer from using confidential information to the advantage of the lawyer or a third person or to the disadvantage of a client or former client unless the client or former client has given informed consent. *See* Rule 1.0(j) for the definition of "informed consent." This part of paragraph (a) applies when information is used to benefit either the lawyer or a third person, such as another client, a former client or a business associate of the lawyer. For example, if a lawyer learns that a client intends to purchase and develop several parcels of land, the lawyer may not (absent the client's informed consent) use that information to buy a nearby parcel that is expected to appreciate in value due to the client's purchase, or to recommend that another client buy the nearby land, even if the lawyer does not reveal any confidential information. The duty also prohibits disadvantageous use of confidential information unless the client gives informed consent, except as permitted or required by these Rules. For example, a lawyer assisting a client in purchasing a parcel of land may not make a competing bid on the same land. However, the fact that a lawyer has once served a client does not preclude the lawyer from using generally known information about that client, even to the disadvantage of the former client, after the client-lawyer relationship has terminated. *See* Rule 1.9(c)(1).

Authorized Disclosure

[5]   Except to the extent that the client's instructions or special circumstances limit that authority, a lawyer is impliedly authorized to make disclosures about a client when appropriate in carrying out the representation. In some situations, for example, a lawyer may be impliedly authorized to admit a fact that cannot properly be disputed or to make a disclosure that facilitates a satisfactory conclusion to a matter. Implied disclosures are permissible when they (i) advance the best interest of the client and (ii) are either reasonable under the circumstances or customary in the professional community. In addition, lawyers in a firm may, in the course of the firm's practice, disclose to each other information relating to a client of the firm, unless the client has instructed that particular information be confined to specified lawyers. Lawyers are also impliedly authorized to reveal information about a client with diminished capacity when necessary to take protective action to safeguard the client's interests. *See* Rules 1.14(b) and (c).

Disclosure Adverse to Client

[6]   Although the public interest is usually best served by a strict rule requiring lawyers to preserve the confidentiality of information relating to the representation of their clients, the confidentiality rule is subject to limited exceptions that prevent substantial harm to important interests, deter wrongdoing by clients, prevent violations of the law, and maintain the impartiality and integrity of judicial proceedings. Paragraph (b) permits, but does not require, a lawyer to disclose information relating to the representation to accomplish these specified purposes.

[6A]   The lawyer's exercise of discretion conferred by paragraphs (b)(1) through (b)(3) requires consideration of a wide range of factors and should therefore be given great weight. In exercising such discretion under these paragraphs, the lawyer should consider such factors as: (i) the seriousness of the potential injury to others if the prospective harm or crime occurs, (ii) the likelihood that it will occur and its imminence, (iii) the apparent absence of any other feasible way to prevent the potential injury, (iv) the extent to which the client may be using the lawyer's services in bringing about the harm or crime, (v) the circumstances under which the lawyer acquired the information of the client's intent or prospective course of action, and (vi) any other aggravating or extenuating circumstances. In any case, disclosure adverse to the client's interest should be no greater than the lawyer reasonably believes necessary to prevent the threatened harm or crime. When a lawyer learns that a client intends to pursue or is pursuing a course of conduct that would permit disclosure under paragraphs (b)(1), (b)(2) or (b)(3), the lawyer's initial duty, where practicable, is to remonstrate with the client. In the rare situation in which the client is reluctant to accept the lawyer's advice, the lawyer's threat of disclosure is a measure of last resort that may persuade the client. When the lawyer reasonably believes that the client will carry out the threatened harm or crime, the lawyer may disclose confidential information when permitted by paragraphs (b)(1), (b)(2) or (b)(3). A lawyer's permissible disclosure under paragraph (b) does not waive the client's attorney-client privilege; neither the lawyer nor the client may be forced to testify about communications protected by the privilege, unless a tribunal or body with authority to compel testimony makes a determination that the crime-fraud exception to the privilege, or some other exception, has been satisfied by a party to the proceeding. For a lawyer's duties when representing an organizational client engaged in wrongdoing, *see* Rule 1.13(b).

[6B]   Paragraph (b)(1) recognizes the overriding value of life and physical integrity and permits disclosure reasonably necessary to prevent reasonably certain death or substantial bodily harm. Such harm is reasonably certain to occur if it will be suffered imminently or if there is a present and substantial risk that a person will suffer such harm at a later date if the lawyer fails to take action necessary to eliminate the threat. Thus, a lawyer who knows that a client has accidentally discharged toxic waste into a town's water supply may reveal this information to the authorities if there is a present and substantial risk that a person who drinks the water will contract a life-threatening or debilitating disease and the lawyer's disclosure is necessary to eliminate the threat or reduce the number of victims. Wrongful execution of a person is a life-threatening and imminent harm under paragraph (b)(1) once the person has been convicted and sentenced to death. On the other hand, an event that will cause property damage but is unlikely to cause substantial bodily harm is not a present and substantial risk under paragraph (b)(1); similarly, a statistical likelihood that a mass-distributed product is expected to cause some injuries to unspecified persons over a period of years is not a present and substantial risk under this paragraph.

[6C] Paragraph (b)(2) recognizes that society has important interests in preventing a client's crime. Disclosure of the client's intention is permitted to the extent reasonably necessary to prevent the crime. In exercising discretion under this paragraph, the lawyer should consider such factors as those stated in Comment [6A].

[6D] Some crimes, such as criminal fraud, may be ongoing in the sense that the client's past material false representations are still deceiving new victims. The law treats such crimes as continuing crimes in which new violations are constantly occurring. The lawyer whose services were involved in the criminal acts that constitute a continuing crime may reveal the client's refusal to bring an end to a continuing crime, even though that disclosure may also reveal the client's past wrongful acts, because refusal to end a continuing crime is equivalent to an intention to commit a new crime. Disclosure is not permitted under paragraph (b)(2), however, when a person who may have committed a crime employs a new lawyer for investigation or defense. Such a lawyer does not have discretion under paragraph (b)(2) to use or disclose the client's past acts that may have continuing criminal consequences. Disclosure is permitted, however, if the client uses the new lawyer's services to commit a further crime, such as obstruction of justice or perjury.

[6E] Paragraph (b)(3) permits a lawyer to withdraw a legal opinion or to disaffirm a prior representation made to third parties when the lawyer reasonably believes that third persons are still relying on the lawyer's work and the work was based on "materially inaccurate information or is being used to further a crime or fraud." *See* Rule 1.16(b)(1), requiring the lawyer to withdraw when the lawyer knows or reasonably should know that the representation will result in a violation of law. Paragraph (b)(3) permits the lawyer to give only the limited notice that is implicit in withdrawing an opinion or representation, which may have the collateral effect of inferentially revealing confidential information. The lawyer's withdrawal of the tainted opinion or representation allows the lawyer to prevent further harm to third persons and to protect the lawyer's own interest when the client has abused the professional relationship, but paragraph (b)(3) does not permit explicit disclosure of the client's past acts unless such disclosure is permitted under paragraph (b)(2).

[7] [Omitted.]

[8] [Omitted.]

[9]   A lawyer's confidentiality obligations do not preclude a lawyer from securing confidential legal advice about compliance with these Rules and other law by the lawyer, another lawyer in the lawyer's firm, or the law firm. In many situations, disclosing information to secure such advice will be impliedly authorized for the lawyer to carry out the representation. Even when the disclosure is not impliedly authorized, paragraph (b)(4) permits such disclosure because of the importance of a lawyer's compliance with these Rules, court orders and other law.

[10]   Where a claim or charge of any kind alleges misconduct of the lawyer related to the representation of a current or former client, the lawyer may respond to the extent the lawyer reasonably believes necessary to establish a defense. Such a claim can arise in a civil, criminal, disciplinary or other proceeding and can be based on a wrong allegedly committed by the lawyer against the client or on a wrong alleged by a third person, such as a person claiming to have been defrauded by the lawyer and client acting together or by the lawyer acting alone. However, the lawyer's right to respond under paragraph (b)(5) does not arise until a client, former client or third person makes an accusation of such wrongdoing and the lawyer reasonably believes that an action or proceeding making such a claim will be brought. Paragraph (b)(5) does not permit a lawyer to disclose confidential information to counter adverse public criticism of the lawyer when a proceeding is unlikely to be brought. The lawyer may respond directly to the person who has made an accusation that permits disclosure, provided that (i) the lawyer reasonably believes an action or proceeding will be brought and (ii) the lawyer's response complies with Rule 4.2 and Rule 4.3, and other Rules or applicable law. A lawyer may make the disclosures authorized by paragraph (b)(5) through counsel. The right to respond also applies to accusations of wrongful conduct concerning the lawyer's law firm, employees or associates.

[11]   A lawyer entitled to a fee is permitted by paragraph (b)(5) to prove the services rendered in an action to collect it. This aspect of the rule expresses the principle that the beneficiary of a fiduciary relationship may not exploit it to the detriment of the fiduciary.

[12]   Paragraph (b) does not mandate any disclosures. However, other law may require that a lawyer disclose confidential information. Whether such a law supersedes Rule 1.6 is a question of law beyond the scope of these Rules. When disclosure of confidential information appears to be required by other law, the lawyer must consult with the client to the extent required by Rule 1.4 before making the disclosure, unless such consultation would be prohibited by other law. If the lawyer concludes that other law supersedes this Rule and requires disclosure, paragraph (b)(6) permits the lawyer to make such disclosures as are necessary to comply with the law.

[13]   A tribunal or governmental entity claiming authority pursuant to other law to compel disclosure may order a lawyer to reveal confidential information. Absent informed consent of the client to comply with the order, the lawyer should assert on behalf of the client nonfrivolous arguments that the order is not authorized by law, the information sought is protected against

disclosure by an applicable privilege or other law, or the order is invalid or defective for some other reason. In the event of an adverse ruling, the lawyer must consult with the client to the extent required by Rule 1.4 about the possibility of an appeal or further challenge, unless such consultation would be prohibited by other law. If such review is not sought or is unsuccessful, paragraph (b)(6) permits the lawyer to comply with the order.

[14] Paragraph (b) permits disclosure only to the extent the lawyer reasonably believes the disclosure is necessary to accomplish one of the purposes specified in paragraphs (b)(1) through (b)(6). Before making a disclosure, the lawyer should, where practicable, first seek to persuade the client to take suitable action to obviate the need for disclosure. In any case, a disclosure adverse to the client's interest should be no greater than the lawyer reasonably believes necessary to accomplish the purpose, particularly when accusations of wrongdoing in the representation of a client have been made by a third party rather than by the client. If the disclosure will be made in connection with an adjudicative proceeding, the disclosure should be made in a manner that limits access to the information to the tribunal or other persons having a need to know the information, and appropriate protective orders or other arrangements should be sought by the lawyer to the fullest extent practicable.

[15] Paragraph (b) permits but does not require the disclosure of information relating to a client's representation to accomplish the purposes specified in paragraphs (b)(1) through (b)(6). A lawyer's decision not to disclose as permitted by paragraph (b) does not violate this Rule. Disclosure may, however, be required by other Rules or by other law. *See* Comments [12]-[13]. Some Rules require disclosure only if such disclosure would be permitted by paragraph (b). *E.g.*, Rule 8.3(c)(1). Rule 3.3(c), on the other hand, requires disclosure in some circumstances whether or not disclosure is permitted or prohibited by this Rule.

Withdrawal

[15A] If the lawyer's services will be used by the client in materially furthering a course of criminal or fraudulent conduct, the lawyer must withdraw pursuant to Rule 1.16(b)(1). Withdrawal may also be required or permitted for other reasons under Rule 1.16. After withdrawal, the lawyer is required to refrain from disclosing or using information protected by Rule 1.6, except as this Rule permits such disclosure. Neither this Rule, nor Rule 1.9(c), nor Rule 1.16(e) prevents the lawyer from giving notice of the fact of withdrawal. For withdrawal or disaffirmance of an opinion or representation, *see* paragraph (b)(3) and Comment [6E]. Where the client is an organization, the lawyer may be in doubt whether the organization will actually carry out the contemplated conduct. Where necessary to guide conduct in connection with this Rule, the lawyer may, and sometimes must, make inquiry within the organization. *See* Rules 1.13(b) and (c).

Duty to Preserve Confidentiality

[16]   Paragraph (c) requires a lawyer to exercise reasonable care to prevent disclosure of information related to the representation by employees, associates and others whose services are utilized in connection with the representation. *See also* Rules 1.1, 5.1 and 5.3. However, a lawyer may reveal the information permitted to be disclosed by this Rule through an employee.

[17]   When transmitting a communication that includes information relating to the representation of a client, the lawyer must take reasonable precautions to prevent the information from coming into the hands of unintended recipients. This duty does not require that the lawyer use special security measures if the method of communication affords a reasonable expectation of privacy. Special circumstances, however, may warrant special precautions. Factors to be considered in determining the reasonableness of the lawyer's expectation of confidentiality include the sensitivity of the information and the extent to which the privacy of the communication is protected by law or by a confidentiality agreement. A client may require the lawyer to use a means of communication or security measures not required by this Rule, or may give informed consent (as in an engagement letter or similar document) to the use of means or measures that would otherwise be prohibited by this Rule.

[18]   [Omitted.]

RULE 1.7: CONFLICT OF INTEREST: CURRENT CLIENTS

(a) **Except as provided in paragraph (b), a lawyer shall not represent a client if a reasonable lawyer would conclude that either:**

(1) **the representation will involve the lawyer in representing differing interests; or**

(2) **there is a significant risk that the lawyer's professional judgment on behalf of a client will be adversely affected by the lawyer's own financial, business, property or other personal interests.**

(b) **Notwithstanding the existence of a concurrent conflict of interest under paragraph (a), a lawyer may represent a client if:**

(1) **the lawyer reasonably believes that the lawyer will be able to provide competent and diligent representation to each affected client;**

(2) **the representation is not prohibited by law;**

(3) **the representation does not involve the assertion of a claim by one client against another client represented by the lawyer in the same litigation or other proceeding before a tribunal; and**

(4) **each affected client gives informed consent, confirmed in writing.**

Comment

General Principles

[1]   Loyalty and independent judgment are essential aspects of a lawyer's relationship with a client. The professional judgment of a lawyer should be exercised, within the bounds of the law, solely for the benefit of the client and free of compromising influences and loyalties. Concurrent conflicts of interest, which can impair a lawyer's professional judgment, can arise from the lawyer's responsibilities to another client, a former client or a third person, or from the lawyer's own interests. A lawyer should not permit these competing responsibilities or interests to impair the lawyer's ability to exercise professional judgment on behalf of each client. For specific Rules regarding certain concurrent conflicts of interest, *see* Rule 1.8. For former client conflicts of interest, *see* Rule 1.9. For conflicts of interest involving prospective clients, *see* Rule 1.18. For definitions of "differing interests," "informed consent" and "confirmed in writing," *see* Rules 1.0(f), (j) and (e), respectively.

[2]   Resolution of a conflict of interest problem under this Rule requires the lawyer, acting reasonably, to: (i) identify clearly the client or clients, (ii) determine whether a conflict of interest exists, *i.e.*, whether the lawyer's judgment may be impaired or the lawyer's loyalty may be divided if the lawyer accepts or continues the representation, (iii) decide whether the representation may be undertaken despite the existence of a conflict, *i.e.*, whether the conflict is consentable under paragraph (b); and if so (iv) consult with the clients affected under paragraph (a) and obtain their informed consent, confirmed in writing. The clients affected under paragraph (a) include all of the clients who may have differing interests under paragraph (a)(1) and any clients whose representation might be adversely affected under paragraph (a)(2).

[3]   A conflict of interest may exist before representation is undertaken, in which event the representation must be declined, unless the lawyer obtains the informed consent of each client under the conditions of paragraph (b). *See* Rule 1.10(e), which requires every law firm to create, implement and maintain a conflict-checking system.

[4]   If a conflict arises after representation has been undertaken, the lawyer ordinarily must withdraw from the representation unless the lawyer has obtained the informed consent of the client under the conditions of paragraph (b). *See* Rule 1.16(b)(1). Where more than one client is involved, whether the lawyer may continue to represent any of the clients is determined both by the lawyer's ability to comply with duties owed to the former client and by the lawyer's ability to represent adequately the remaining client or clients, given the lawyer's duties to the former client. *See* Rule 1.9; *see also* Comments [5], [29A].

[5]   Unforeseeable developments, such as changes in corporate and other organizational affiliations or the addition or realignment of parties in litigation, might create conflicts in the midst of a representation, as when a company sued by the lawyer on behalf of one client is acquired by another

client represented by the lawyer in an unrelated matter. Depending on the circumstances, the lawyer may have the option to withdraw from one of the representations in order to avoid the conflict. The lawyer must seek court approval where necessary and take steps to minimize harm to the clients. *See* Rules 1.16(d) and (e). The lawyer must continue to protect the confidences of the client from whose representation the lawyer has withdrawn. *See* Rule 1.9(c).

Identifying Conflicts of Interest

[6]   The duty to avoid the representation of differing interest prohibits, among other things, undertaking representation directly adverse to a current client without that client's informed consent. For example, absent consent, a lawyer may not advocate in one matter against another client that the lawyer represents in some other matter, even when the matters are wholly unrelated. The client as to whom the representation is directly adverse is likely to feel betrayed and the resulting damage to the client-lawyer relationship is likely to impair the lawyer's ability to represent the client effectively. In addition, the client on whose behalf the adverse representation is undertaken may reasonably fear that the lawyer will pursue that client's case less effectively out of deference to the other client, that is, that the lawyer's exercise of professional judgment on behalf of that client will be adversely affected by the lawyer's interest in retaining the current client. Similarly, a directly adverse conflict may arise when a lawyer is required to cross-examine a client appearing as a witness in a lawsuit involving another client, as when the testimony will be damaging to the client represented in the lawsuit. On the other hand, simultaneous representation in unrelated matters of clients whose interests are only economically adverse, such as representation of competing economic enterprises in unrelated litigation, does not ordinarily constitute a conflict of interest and thus may not require consent of the respective clients.

[7]   Differing interests can also arise in transactional matters. For example, if a lawyer is asked to represent the seller of a business in negotiations with a buyer represented by the lawyer, not in the same transaction but in another, unrelated matter, the lawyer could not undertake the representation without the informed consent of each client.

[8]   Differing interests exist if there is a significant risk that a lawyer's exercise of professional judgment in considering, recommending or carrying out an appropriate course of action for the client will be adversely affected or the representation would otherwise be materially limited by the lawyer's other responsibilities or interests. For example, the professional judgment of a lawyer asked to represent several individuals operating a joint venture is likely to be adversely affected to the extent that the lawyer is unable to recommend or advocate all possible positions that each client might take because of the lawyer's duty of loyalty to the others. The conflict in effect forecloses alternatives that would otherwise be available to the client. The mere possibility of subsequent harm does not itself require disclosure and consent. The critical questions are the likelihood that a difference in interests

will eventuate and, if it does, whether it will adversely affect the lawyer's professional judgment in considering alternatives or foreclose courses of action that reasonably should be pursued on behalf of the client.

Lawyer's Responsibilities to Former Clients and Other Third Persons

[9]   In addition to conflicts with other current clients, a lawyer's duties of loyalty and independence may be adversely affected by responsibilities to former clients under Rule 1.9, or by the lawyer's responsibilities to other persons, such as fiduciary duties arising from a lawyer's service as a trustee, executor or corporate director.

Personal-Interest Conflicts

[10]   The lawyer's own financial, property, business or other personal interests should not be permitted to have an adverse effect on representation of a client. For example, if the probity of a lawyer's own conduct in a transaction is in serious question, it may be difficult or impossible for the lawyer to give a client detached advice. Similarly, when a lawyer has discussions concerning possible employment with an opponent of the lawyer's client or with a law firm representing the opponent, such discussions could materially limit the lawyer's representation of the client. In addition, a lawyer may not allow related business interests to affect representation, for example, by referring clients to an enterprise in which the lawyer has an undisclosed financial interest. *See* Rule 5.7 on responsibilities regarding nonlegal services and Rule 1.8 pertaining to a number of personal-interest conflicts, including business transactions with clients.

[11]   When lawyers representing different clients in the same matter or in substantially related matters are closely related, there may be a significant risk that client confidences will be revealed and that the lawyer's family relationship will interfere with both loyalty and professional judgment. As a result, each client is entitled to know of the existence and implications of the relationship between the lawyers, before the lawyer agrees to undertake the representation. Thus, a lawyer who has a significant intimate or close family relationship with another lawyer ordinarily may not represent a client in a matter where that other lawyer is representing another party, unless each client gives informed consent, as defined in Rule 1.0(j).

[12]   A lawyer is prohibited from engaging in sexual relations with a client in domestic relations matters. In all other matters a lawyer's sexual relations with a client are circumscribed by the provisions of Rule 1.8(j).

Interest of Person Paying for Lawyer's Services

[13]   A lawyer may be paid from a source other than the client, including a co-client, if the client is informed of that fact and consents and the arrangement does not compromise the lawyer's duty of loyalty or independent judgment to the client. *See* Rule 1.8(f). If acceptance of the payment from any other source presents a significant risk that the lawyer's exercise of professional judgment on behalf of a client will be adversely affected by the lawyer's

own interest in accommodating the person paying the lawyer's fee or by the lawyer's responsibilities to a payer who is also a co-client, then the lawyer must comply with the requirements of paragraph (b) before accepting the representation, including determining whether the conflict is consentable and, if so, that the client has adequate information about the material risks of the representation.

Prohibited Representations

[14]   Ordinarily, clients may consent to representation notwithstanding a conflict. As paragraph (b) indicates, however, some conflicts are nonconsentable. If a lawyer does not reasonably believe that the conditions set forth in paragraph (b) can be met, the lawyer should neither ask for the client's consent nor provide representation on the basis of the client's consent. A client's consent to a nonconsentable conflict is ineffective. When the lawyer is representing more than one client, the question of consentability must be resolved as to each client.

[15]   Consentability is typically determined by considering whether the interests of the clients will be adequately protected if the clients consent to representation burdened by a conflict of interest. Thus, under paragraph (b)(1), notwithstanding client consent, a representation is prohibited if, in the circumstances, the lawyer cannot reasonably conclude that the lawyer will be able to provide competent and diligent representation. *See* Rule 1.1 regarding competence and Rule 1.3 regarding diligence.

[16]   Paragraph (b)(2) describes conflicts that are nonconsentable because the representation is prohibited by applicable law. For example, federal criminal statutes prohibit certain representations by a former government lawyer despite the informed consent of the former governmental client. In addition, there are some instances where conflicts are nonconsentable under decisional law.

[17]   Paragraph (b)(3) describes conflicts that are nonconsentable because of the institutional interest in vigorous development of each client's position when the clients are aligned directly against each other in the same litigation or other proceeding before a tribunal. Whether clients are aligned directly against each other within the meaning of this paragraph requires examination of the context of the proceeding. Although this paragraph does not preclude a lawyer's multiple representation of adverse parties to mediation (because mediation is not a proceeding before a "tribunal" as defined in Rule 1.0(w)), such representation may be precluded by paragraph (b)(1).

Informed Consent

[18]   Informed consent requires that each affected client be aware of the relevant circumstances, including the material and reasonably foreseeable ways that the conflict could adversely affect the interests of that client. Informed consent also requires that the client be given the opportunity to obtain other counsel if the client so desires. *See* Rule 1.0(j). The information that a lawyer is required to communicate to a client depends on the nature of

the conflict and the nature of the risks involved, and a lawyer should take into account the sophistication of the client in explaining the potential adverse consequences of the conflict. There are circumstances in which it is appropriate for a lawyer to advise a client to seek the advice of a disinterested lawyer in reaching a decision as to whether to consent to the conflict. When representation of multiple clients in a single matter is undertaken, the information must include the implications of the common representation, including possible effects on loyalty, confidentiality and the attorney-client privilege, and the advantages and risks involved. *See* Comments [30] and [31] concerning the effect of common representation on confidentiality.

[19] Under some circumstances it may be impossible to make the disclosure necessary to obtain consent. For example, when the lawyer represents different clients in related matters and one client refuses to consent to the disclosure necessary to permit the other client to make an informed decision, the lawyer cannot properly ask the latter to consent. In some cases the alternative to common representation is that each party obtains separate representation with the possibility of incurring additional costs. These costs, along with the benefits of securing separate representation, are factors that may be considered by the affected client in determining whether common representation is in the client's interests. Where the fact, validity or propriety of client consent is called into question, the lawyer has the burden of establishing that the client's consent was properly obtained in accordance with the Rule.

Client Consent Confirmed in Writing

[20] Paragraph (b) requires the lawyer to obtain the informed consent of the client, confirmed in writing. Such a writing may consist of (i) a document from the client, (ii) a document that the lawyer promptly transmits to the client confirming an oral informed consent, or (iii) a statement by the client made on the record of any proceeding before a tribunal, whether before, during or after a trial or hearing. *See* Rule 1.0(e) for the definition of "confirmed in writing." *See also* Rule 1.0(x) ("writing" includes electronic transmission). If it is not feasible to obtain or transmit the writing at the time the client gives informed consent, then the lawyer must obtain or transmit it within a reasonable time thereafter. The Rule does not require that the information communicated to the client by the lawyer necessary to make the consent "informed" be in writing or in any particular form in all cases. *See* Rules 1.0(e) and (j). The requirement of a writing does not supplant the need in most cases for the lawyer to talk with the client to explain the risks and advantages, if any, of representation burdened with a conflict of interest, as well as reasonably available alternatives, and to afford the client a reasonable opportunity to consider the risks and alternatives and to raise questions and concerns. Rather, the writing is required in order to impress upon clients the seriousness of the decision the client is being asked to make and to avoid disputes or ambiguities that might later occur in the absence of a writing. *See* Comment [18].

Revoking Consent

[21]   A client who has given consent to a conflict may revoke the consent and, like any other client, may terminate the lawyer's representation at any time. Whether revoking consent to the client's own representation precludes the lawyer from continuing to represent other clients depends on the circumstances, including the nature of the conflict, whether the client revoked consent because of a material change in circumstances, the reasonable expectations of the other clients, and whether material detriment to the other clients or the lawyer would result.

Consent to Future Conflict

[22]   Whether a lawyer may properly request a client to waive conflicts that might arise in the future is subject to the conditions set forth in paragraph (b). The effectiveness of advance waivers is generally determined by the extent to which the client reasonably understands the material risks that the waiver entails. At a minimum, the client should be advised generally of the types of possible future adverse representations that the lawyer envisions, as well as the types of clients and matters that may present such conflicts. The more comprehensive the explanation and disclosure of the types of future representations that might arise and the actual and reasonably foreseeable adverse consequences of those representations, the greater the likelihood that the client will have the understanding necessary to make the consent "informed" and the waiver effective. *See* Rule 1.0(j). The lawyer should also disclose the measures that will be taken to protect the client should a conflict arise, including procedures such as screening that would be put in place. *See* Rule 1.0(t) for the definition of "screening." The adequacy of the disclosure necessary to obtain valid advance consent to conflicts may also depend on the sophistication and experience of the client. For example, if the client is unsophisticated about legal matters generally or about the particular type of matter at hand, the lawyer should provide more detailed information about both the nature of the anticipated conflict and the adverse consequences to the client that may ensue should the potential conflict become an actual one. In other instances, such as where the client is a child or an incapacitated or impaired person, it may be impossible to inform the client sufficiently, and the lawyer should not seek an advance waiver. On the other hand, if the client is an experienced user of the legal services involved and is reasonably informed regarding the risk that a conflict may arise, an advance waiver is more likely to be effective, particularly if, for example, the client is independently represented or advised by in-house or other counsel in giving consent. Thus, in some circumstances, even general and open-ended waivers by experienced users of legal services may be effective.

[22A]   Even if a client has validly consented to waive future conflicts, however, the lawyer must reassess the propriety of the adverse concurrent representation under paragraph (b) when an actual conflict arises. If the actual conflict is materially different from the conflict that has been waived, the lawyer may not rely on the advance consent previously obtained. Even if the actual conflict is not materially different from the conflict the client has previously waived, the client's advance consent cannot be effective if the particular circumstances that have created an actual conflict during the course of the representation would make the conflict nonconsentable under paragraph (b). *See* Comments [14]-[17] and [28] addressing nonconsentable conflicts.

Conflicts in Litigation

[23]   Paragraph (b)(3) prohibits representation of opposing parties in the same litigation, regardless of the clients' consent. On the other hand, simultaneous representation of parties whose interests in litigation may conflict, such as co-plaintiffs or codefendants, is governed by paragraph (a)(1). A conflict may exist by reason of substantial discrepancy in the parties' testimony, incompatibility in positions in relation to an opposing party or the fact that there are substantially different possibilities of settlement of the claims or liabilities in question. Such conflicts can arise in criminal as well as civil cases. Some examples are those in which a lawyer is asked to represent codefendants in a criminal case, co-plaintiffs or codefendants in a personal injury case, an insured and insurer, or beneficiaries of the estate of a decedent. In a criminal case, the potential for conflict of interest in representing multiple defendants is so grave that ordinarily a lawyer should decline to represent more than one codefendant. On the other hand, multiple representation of persons having similar interests in civil litigation is proper if the requirements of paragraph (b) are met.

[24]   Ordinarily a lawyer may take inconsistent legal positions in different tribunals at different times on behalf of different clients. The mere fact that advocating a legal position on behalf of one client might create precedent adverse to the interests of a client represented by the lawyer in an unrelated matter does not create a conflict of interest. A conflict of interest exists, however, if there is a significant risk that a lawyer's action on behalf of one client will materially limit the lawyer's representation of another client in a different case; for example, when a decision favoring one client will create a precedent likely to weaken seriously the position taken on behalf of the other client. Factors relevant in determining whether the clients need to be advised of this risk include: (i) where the cases are pending, (ii) whether the issue is substantive or procedural, (iii) the temporal relationship between the matters, (iv) the significance of the issue to the immediate and long-term interests of the clients involved, and (v) the clients' reasonable expectations in retaining the lawyer. Similar concerns may be present when lawyers advocate on behalf of clients before other entities, such as regulatory authorities whose regulations or rulings may significantly implicate clients' interests. If there is significant risk of an adverse effect on the lawyer's professional judgment, then absent informed consent of the affected clients, the lawyer must decline the representation.

[25]   When a lawyer represents or seeks to represent a class of plaintiffs or defendants in a class-action lawsuit, unnamed members of the class are

ordinarily not considered to be clients of the lawyer for purposes of applying paragraph (a)(1). Thus, the lawyer does not typically need to get the consent of such a person before representing a client suing the person in an unrelated matter. Similarly, a lawyer seeking to represent an opponent in a class action does not typically need the consent of an unnamed member of the class whom the lawyer represents in an unrelated matter.

Nonlitigation Conflicts

[26]   Conflicts of interest under paragraph (a)(1) arise in contexts other than litigation. For a discussion of directly adverse conflicts in transactional matters, *see* Comment [7]. Relevant factors in determining whether there is a significant risk that the lawyer's professional judgment will be adversely affected include: (i) the importance of the matter to each client, (ii) the duration and intimacy of the lawyer's relationship with the client or clients involved, (iii) the functions being performed by the lawyer, (iv) the likelihood that significant disagreements will arise, (v) the likelihood that negotiations will be contentious, (vi) the likelihood that the matter will result in litigation, and (vii) the likelihood that the client will suffer prejudice from the conflict. The issue is often one of proximity (how close the situation is to open conflict) and degree (how serious the conflict will be if it does erupt). *See* Comments [8], [29] and [29A].

[27]   For example, conflict questions may arise in estate planning and estate administration. A lawyer may be called upon to prepare wills for several family members, such as husband and wife, and, depending upon the circumstances, a conflict of interest may be present at the outset or may arise during the representation. In order to avoid the development of a disqualifying conflict, the lawyer should, at the outset of the common representation and as part of the process of obtaining each client's informed consent, advise each client that information will be shared (and regardless of whether it is shared, may not be privileged in a subsequent dispute between the parties) and that the lawyer will have to withdraw from one or both representations if one client decides that some matter material to the representation should be kept secret from the other. *See* Comment [31].

[28]   Whether a conflict is consentable depends on the circumstances. For example, a lawyer may not represent multiple parties to a negotiation if their interests are fundamentally antagonistic to one another, but common representation is permissible where the clients are generally aligned in interest, even though there is some difference in interest among them. Thus, a lawyer may seek to establish or adjust a relationship between clients on an amicable and mutually advantageous basis. Examples include helping to organize a business in which two or more clients are entrepreneurs, working out the financial reorganization of an enterprise in which two or more clients have an interest, and arranging a property distribution in settlement of an estate. The lawyer seeks to resolve potentially adverse interests by developing the parties' mutual interests. Otherwise, each party might have to obtain separate representation, with the possibility of incurring additional cost,

complication or even litigation. Given these and other relevant factors, the clients may prefer that the lawyer act for all of them.

Special Considerations in Common Representation

[29]   In civil matters, two or more clients may wish to be represented by a single lawyer in seeking to establish or adjust a relationship between them on an amicable and mutually advantageous basis. For example, clients may wish to be represented by a single lawyer in helping to organize a business, working out a financial reorganization of an enterprise in which two or more clients have an interest, arranging a property distribution of an estate or resolving a dispute between clients. The alternative to common representation can be that each party may have to obtain separate representation, with the possibility of incurring additional cost, complication or even litigation that might otherwise be avoided, or that some parties will have no lawyer at all. Given these and other relevant factors, clients may prefer common representation to separate representation or no representation. A lawyer should consult with each client concerning the implications of the common representation, including the advantages and the risks involved, and the effect on the attorney-client privilege, and obtain each client's informed consent, confirmed in writing, to the common representation.

[29A]   Factors may be present that militate against a common representation. In considering whether to represent multiple clients in the same matter, a lawyer should be mindful that if the common representation fails because the potentially adverse interests cannot be reconciled, the result can be additional cost, embarrassment and recrimination. Ordinarily, absent the informed consent of all clients, the lawyer will be forced to withdraw from representing all of the clients if the common representation fails. *See* Rule 1.9(a). In some situations, the risk of failure is so great that multiple representation is plainly impossible. For example, a lawyer cannot undertake common representation of clients where contentious litigation or negotiations between them are imminent or contemplated. Moreover, because the lawyer is required to be impartial between or among commonly represented clients, representation of multiple clients is improper when it is unlikely that impartiality can be maintained. Generally, if the relationship between the parties has already assumed antagonism, it is unlikely that the clients' interests can be adequately served by common representation. For example, a lawyer who has represented one of the clients for a long period or in multiple matters might have difficulty being impartial between that client and one to whom the lawyer has only recently been introduced.

[30]   A particularly important factor in determining the appropriateness of common representation is the effect on client-lawyer confidentiality and the attorney-client privilege. With regard to the attorney-client privilege, the prevailing rule is that, as between commonly represented clients, the privilege does not attach. It must therefore be assumed that if litigation eventuates between the clients, the privilege will not protect any such communications, and the clients should be so advised.

[31]   As to the duty of confidentiality, continued common representation will almost certainly be inadequate if one client asks the lawyer not to disclose to the other client information relevant to the common representation. This is so because the lawyer has an equal duty of loyalty to each client, and each client has the right to be informed of anything bearing on the representation that might affect that client's interests and the right to expect that the lawyer will use that information to that client's benefit. *See* Rule 1.4. At the outset of the common representation and as part of the process of obtaining each client's informed consent, the lawyer should advise each client that information will be shared and that the lawyer will have to withdraw if one client decides that some matter material to the representation should be kept from the other. In limited circumstances, it may be appropriate for the lawyer to proceed with the representation when the clients have agreed, after being properly informed, that the lawyer will keep certain information confidential even as among the commonly represented clients. For example, the lawyer may reasonably conclude that failure to disclose one client's trade secrets to another client will not adversely affect representation involving a joint venture between the two clients and agree to keep that information confidential with the informed consent of both clients.

[32]   When seeking to establish or adjust a relationship between clients, the lawyer should make clear that the lawyer's role is not that of partisanship normally expected in other circumstances and, thus, that the clients may be required to assume greater responsibility for decisions than when each client is separately represented. Any limitation on the scope of the representation made necessary as a result of the common representation should be fully explained to the clients at the outset of the representation. *See* Rule 1.2(c).

[33]   Subject to the above limitations, each client in the common representation has the right to loyal and diligent representation and the protection of Rule 1.9 concerning the obligations to a former client. The client also has the right to discharge the lawyer as stated in Rule 1.16.

Organizational Clients

[34]   A lawyer who represents a corporation or other organization does not, simply by virtue of that representation, necessarily represent any constituent or affiliated organization, such as a parent or subsidiary. *See* Rule 1.13(a). Although a desire to preserve good relationships with clients may strongly suggest that the lawyer should always seek informed consent of the client organization before undertaking any representation that is adverse to its affiliates, Rule 1.7 does not require the lawyer to obtain such consent unless: (i) the lawyer has an understanding with the organizational client that the lawyer will avoid representation adverse to the client's affiliates, (ii) the lawyer's obligations to either the organizational client or the new client are likely to adversely affect the lawyer's exercise of professional judgment on behalf of the other client, or (iii) the circumstances are such that the affiliate should also be considered a client of the lawyer. Whether the affiliate should be considered a client will depend on the nature of the lawyer's relationship

with the affiliate or on the nature of the relationship between the client and its affiliate. For example, the lawyer's work for the client organization may be intended to benefit its affiliates. The overlap or identity of the officers and boards of directors, and the client's overall mode of doing business, may be so extensive that the entities would be viewed as "alter egos." Under such circumstances, the lawyer may conclude that the affiliate is the lawyer's client despite the lack of any formal agreement to represent the affiliate.

[34A]   Whether the affiliate should be considered a client of the lawyer may also depend on: (i) whether the affiliate has imparted confidential information to the lawyer in furtherance of the representation, (ii) whether the affiliated entities share a legal department and general counsel, and (iii) other factors relating to the legitimate expectations of the client as to whether the lawyer also represents the affiliate. Where the entities are related only through stock ownership, the ownership is less than a controlling interest, and the lawyer has had no significant dealings with the affiliate or access to its confidences, the lawyer may reasonably conclude that the affiliate is not the lawyer's client.

[34B]   Finally, before accepting a representation adverse to an affiliate of a corporate client, a lawyer should consider whether the extent of the possible adverse economic impact of the representation on the entire corporate family might be of such a magnitude that it would materially limit the lawyer's ability to represent the client opposing the affiliate. In those circumstances, Rule 1.7 will ordinarily require the lawyer to decline representation adverse to a member of the same corporate family, absent the informed consent of the client opposing the affiliate of the lawyer's corporate client.

Lawyer as Corporate Director

[35]   A lawyer for a corporation or other organization who is also a member of its board of directors should determine whether the responsibilities of the two roles may conflict. The lawyer may be called on to advise the corporation in matters involving actions of the directors. Consideration should be given to the frequency with which such situations may arise, the potential intensity of the conflict, the effect of the lawyer's resignation from the board, and the possibility of the corporation's obtaining legal advice from another lawyer in such situations. If there is material risk that the dual role will compromise the lawyer's professional judgment, the lawyer should not serve as a director or should cease to act as the corporation's lawyer when conflicts of interest arise. The lawyer should advise the other members of the board that, in some circumstances, matters discussed at board meetings while the lawyer is present in the capacity of director might not be protected by the attorney-client privilege and that conflict of interest considerations might require the lawyer's recusal as a director or might require the lawyer and the lawyer's firm to decline representation of the corporation in a matter.

RULE 1.8: CURRENT CLIENTS: SPECIFIC CONFLICT OF INTEREST RULES

(a) A lawyer shall not enter into a business transaction with a client if they have differing interests therein and if the client expects the lawyer to exercise professional judgment therein for the protection of the client, unless:

(1) the transaction is fair and reasonable to the client and the terms of the transaction are fully disclosed and transmitted in writing in a manner that can be reasonably understood by the client;

(2) the client is advised in writing of the desirability of seeking, and is given a reasonable opportunity to seek, the advice of independent legal counsel on the transaction; and

(3) the client gives informed consent, in a writing signed by the client, to the essential terms of the transaction and the lawyer's role in the transaction, including whether the lawyer is representing the client in the transaction.

(b) A lawyer shall not use information relating to representation of a client to the disadvantage of the client unless the client gives informed consent, except as permitted or required by these Rules.

(c) A lawyer shall not:

(1) solicit any gift from a client, including a testamentary gift, for the benefit of the lawyer or a person related to the lawyer; or

(2) prepare on behalf of a client an instrument giving the lawyer or a person related to the lawyer any gift, unless the lawyer or other recipient of the gift is related to the client and a reasonable lawyer would conclude that the transaction is fair and reasonable.

For purposes of this paragraph, related persons include a spouse, child, grandchild, parent, grandparent or other relative, or an individual with whom the lawyer or the client maintains a close, familial relationship.

(d) Prior to conclusion of all aspects of the matter giving rise to the representation or proposed representation of the client or prospective client, a lawyer shall not negotiate or enter into any arrangement or understanding with:

(1) a client or a prospective client by which the lawyer acquires an interest in literary or media rights with respect to the subject matter of the representation or proposed representation; or

(2) any person by which the lawyer transfers or assigns any interest in literary or media rights with respect to the subject matter of the representation of a client or prospective client.

(e) While representing a client in connection with contemplated or pending litigation, a lawyer shall not advance or guarantee financial assistance to the client, except that:

(1) a lawyer may advance court costs and expenses of litigation, the repayment of which may be contingent on the outcome of the matter;

(2) a lawyer representing an indigent or pro bono client may pay court costs and expenses of litigation on behalf of the client; and

(3) a lawyer, in an action in which an attorney's fee is payable in whole or in part as a percentage of the recovery in the action, may pay on the lawyer's own account court costs and expenses of litigation. In such case, the fee paid to the lawyer from the proceeds of the action may include an amount equal to such costs and expenses incurred.

(f) A lawyer shall not accept compensation for representing a client, or anything of value related to the lawyer's representation of the client, from one other than the client unless:

(1) the client gives informed consent;

(2) there is no interference with the lawyer's independent professional judgment or with the client-lawyer relationship; and

(3) the client's confidential information is protected as required by Rule 1.6.

(g) A lawyer who represents two or more clients shall not participate in making an aggregate settlement of the claims of or against the clients, absent court approval, unless each client gives informed consent in a writing signed by the client. The lawyer's disclosure shall include the existence and nature of all the claims involved and of the participation of each person in the settlement.

(h) A lawyer shall not:

(1) make an agreement prospectively limiting the lawyer's liability to a client for malpractice; or

(2) settle a claim or potential claim for such liability with an unrepresented client or former client unless that person is advised in writing of the desirability of seeking, and is given a reasonable opportunity to seek, the advice of independent legal counsel in connection therewith.

(i) A lawyer shall not acquire a proprietary interest in the cause of action or subject matter of litigation the lawyer is conducting for a client, except that the lawyer may:

(1) acquire a lien authorized by law to secure the lawyer's fee or expenses; and

(2) contract with a client for a reasonable contingent fee in a civil matter subject to Rule 1.5(d) or other law or court rule.

(j) (1) A lawyer shall not:

(i) as a condition of entering into or continuing any professional representation by the lawyer or the lawyer's firm, require or demand sexual relations with any person;

(ii) employ coercion, intimidation or undue influence in entering into sexual relations incident to any professional representation by the lawyer or the lawyer's firm; or

(iii) in domestic relations matters, enter into sexual relations with a client during the course of the lawyer's representation of the client.

(2) Rule 1.8(j)(1) shall not apply to sexual relations between lawyers and their spouses or to ongoing consensual sexual relationships that predate the initiation of the client-lawyer relationship.

(k) Where a lawyer in a firm has sexual relations with a client but does not participate in the representation of that client, the lawyers in the firm shall not be subject to discipline under this Rule solely because of the occurrence of such sexual relations.

Comment

Business Transactions Between Client and Lawyer

[1] A lawyer's legal skill and training, together with the relationship of trust and confidence between lawyer and client, create the possibility of overreaching when the lawyer participates in a business, property or financial transaction with a client, for example, a loan or sales transaction or a lawyer's investment on behalf of a client. For these reasons business transactions between a lawyer and client are not advisable. If a lawyer nevertheless elects to enter into a business transaction with a current client, the requirements of paragraph (a) must be met if the client and lawyer have differing interests in the transaction and the client expects the lawyer to exercise professional judgment therein for the benefit of the client. This will ordinarily be the case even when the transaction is not related to the subject matter of the representation, as when a lawyer drafting a will for a client learns that the client needs money for unrelated expenses and offers to make a loan to the client. The Rule applies to lawyers engaged in the sale of goods or services related to the practice of law, such as the sale of title insurance or investment services to existing clients of the lawyer's legal practice. *See* Rule 5.7. It also applies to lawyers purchasing property from estates they represent.

[2] Paragraphs (a)(1), (a)(2) and (a)(3) set out the conditions that a lawyer must satisfy under this Rule. Paragraph (a)(1) requires that the

transaction itself be fair to the client and that its essential terms be communicated in writing to the client in a manner that can be reasonably understood. Paragraph (a)(2) requires that the client also be advised in writing of the desirability of seeking the advice of independent legal counsel. It also requires that the client be given a reasonable opportunity to obtain such advice. Paragraph (a)(3) requires that the lawyer obtain the client's informed consent, in a writing signed by the client, both to the essential terms of the transaction and to the lawyer's role. When necessary, the lawyer should discuss both the material risks of the proposed transaction, including any risk presented by the lawyer's involvement and the existence of reasonably available alternatives, and should explain why the advice of independent legal counsel is desirable. *See* Rule 1.0(j) for the definition of "informed consent."

[3]   The risk to a client is greatest when the client expects the lawyer to represent the client in the transaction itself or when the lawyer's financial interest otherwise poses a significant risk that the lawyer's representation of the client will be materially adversely affected by the lawyer's financial interest in the transaction. Here the lawyer's role requires that the lawyer must comply, not only with the requirements of paragraph (a), but also with the requirements of Rule 1.7. Under that Rule, the lawyer must disclose the risks associated with the lawyer's dual role as both legal adviser and participant in the transaction, such as the risk that the lawyer will structure the transaction or give legal advice in a way that favors the lawyer's interests at the client's expense. Moreover, the lawyer must obtain the client's informed consent. In some cases, the lawyer's interest may be such that Rule 1.7 will preclude the lawyer from seeking the client's consent to the transaction. A lawyer has a continuing duty to monitor the inherent conflicts of interest that arise out of the lawyer's business transaction with a client or because the lawyer has an ownership interest in property in which the client also has an interest. A lawyer is also required to make such additional disclosures to the client as are necessary to obtain the client's informed consent to the continuation of the representation.

[3A]   The self-interest of a lawyer resulting from a business transaction with a client may interfere with the lawyer's exercise of independent judgment on behalf of the client. If such interference will occur should a lawyer agree to represent a prospective client, the lawyer should decline the proffered employment. After accepting employment, a lawyer should not acquire property rights that would adversely affect the lawyer's professional judgment in representing the client. Even if the property interests of a lawyer do not presently interfere with the exercise of independent judgment, but the likelihood of interference can be reasonably foreseen by the lawyer, the lawyer should explain the situation to the client and should decline employment or withdraw unless the client gives informed consent to the continued representation, confirmed in writing. A lawyer should not seek to persuade a client to permit the lawyer to invest in an undertaking of the client nor make improper use of a professional relationship to influence the client to invest in an enterprise in which the lawyer is interested.

[4]   If the client is independently represented in the transaction, paragraph (a)(2) is inapplicable, and the requirement of full disclosure in paragraph (a)(1) is satisfied by a written disclosure by either the lawyer involved in the transaction or the client's independent counsel. The fact that the client was independently represented in the transaction is relevant in determining whether the agreement was fair and reasonable to the client, as paragraph (a)(1) further requires.

[4A]   Rule 1.8(a) does not apply to business transactions with former clients, but the line between current and former clients is not always clear. A lawyer entering into a business transaction with a former client may not use information relating to the representation to the disadvantage of the former client unless the information has become generally known. *See* Rule 1.9(c).

[4B]   The Rule does not apply to standard commercial transactions between the lawyer and the client for products or services that the client generally markets to others, for example, banking or brokerage services, medical services, products manufactured or distributed by the client, and utilities services. In such transactions, the lawyer has no advantage in dealing with the client, and the restrictions in paragraph (a) are unnecessary and impracticable.

[4C]   This Rule also does not apply to ordinary fee arrangements between client and lawyer reached at the inception of the client-lawyer relationship, which are governed by Rule 1.5. The requirements of the Rule ordinarily must be met, however, when the lawyer accepts an interest in the client's business or other nonmonetary property as payment of all or part of the lawyer's fee. For example, the requirements of paragraph (a) must ordinarily be met if a lawyer agrees to take stock (or stock options) in the client in lieu of cash fees. Such an exchange creates a risk that the lawyer's judgment will be skewed in favor of closing a transaction to such an extent that the lawyer may fail to exercise professional judgment as to whether it is in the client's best interest for the transaction to close. This may occur where the client expects the lawyer to provide professional advice in structuring a securities-for-services exchange. If the lawyer is expected to play any role in advising the client regarding the securities-for-services exchange, especially if the client lacks sophistication, the requirements of fairness, full disclosure and written consent set forth in paragraph (a) must be met. When a lawyer represents a client in a transaction concerning literary property, Rule 1.8(d) does not prohibit the lawyer from agreeing that the lawyer's fee shall consist of a share of the ownership of the literary property or a share of the royalties or license fees from the property, but the lawyer must ordinarily comply with Rule 1.8(a).

[4D]   An exchange of securities for legal services will also trigger the requirements of Rule 1.7 if the lawyer's ownership interest in the client would, or reasonably may, affect the lawyer's exercise of professional judgment on behalf of the client. For example, where a lawyer has agreed to accept securities in a client corporation as a fee for negotiating and documenting an equity investment, or for representing a client in connection with an initial public offering, there is a risk that the lawyer's judgment will be skewed in favor of closing the transaction to such an extent that that the lawyer may fail to exercise professional judgment. (The lawyer's judgment may be skewed because unless the transaction closes, the securities will be worthless.) Unless a lawyer reasonably concludes that he or she will be able to provide competent, diligent and loyal representation to the client, the lawyer may not undertake or continue the representation, even with the client's consent. To determine whether a reasonable possibility of such an adverse effect on the representation exists, the lawyer should analyze the nature and relationship of the particular interest and the specific legal services to be rendered. Some salient factors may be (i) the size of the lawyer's investment in proportion to the holdings of other investors, (ii) the potential value of the investment in relation to the lawyer's or law firm's earnings or other assets, and (iii) whether the investment is active or passive.

[4E]   If the lawyer reasonably concludes that the lawyer's representation of the client will not be adversely affected by the agreement to accept client securities as a legal fee, the Rules permit the representation, but only if full disclosure is made to the client and the client's informed consent is obtained and confirmed in writing. *See* Rules 1.0(e) (defining "confirmed in writing"), 1.0(j) (defining "informed consent"), and 1.7.

[4F]   A lawyer must also consider whether accepting securities in a client as payment for legal services constitutes charging or collecting an unreasonable or excessive fee in violation of Rule 1.5. Determining whether a fee accepted in the form of securities is unreasonable or excessive requires a determination of the value of the securities at the time the agreement is reached and may require the lawyer to engage the services of an investment professional to appraise the value of the securities to be given. The lawyer and client can then make their own advised decisions as to whether the securities-for-fees exchange results in a reasonable fee.

[5]   [Omitted.]

Gifts to Lawyers

[6]   A lawyer may accept a gift from a client if the transaction meets general standards of fairness. If a client offers the lawyer a gift, paragraph (c) does not prohibit the lawyer from accepting it, although such a gift may be voidable by the client. Before accepting a gift offered by a client, a lawyer should urge the client to secure disinterested advice from an independent, competent person who is cognizant of all of the circumstances. In any event, due to concerns about overreaching and imposition on clients, a lawyer may not suggest that a gift be made to the lawyer or for the lawyer's benefit.

[6A]   This Rule does not apply to success fees, bonuses and the like from clients for legal services. These are governed by Rule 1.5.

[7]   If effectuation of a gift requires preparing a legal instrument such as a will or conveyance, the client should have the detached advice that another lawyer can provide. The sole exception to this Rule is where the client is

related to the done and a reasonable lawyer would conclude that the transaction is fair and reasonable, as set forth in paragraph (c).

[8] This Rule does not prohibit a lawyer from seeking to have the lawyer or a partner or associate of the lawyer named as executor of the client's estate or named to another fiduciary position. Nevertheless, such appointments will be subject to the general conflict of interest provision in Rule 1.7 when there is a significant risk that the lawyer's interest in obtaining the appointment will adversely affect the lawyer's professional judgment in advising the client concerning the choice of an executor or other fiduciary. In obtaining the client's informed consent to the conflict, the lawyer should advise the client concerning the nature and extent of the lawyer's financial interest in the appointment, as well as the availability of alternative candidates for the position.

Literary or Media Rights

[9] An agreement by which a lawyer acquires literary or media rights concerning the subject matter of the representation creates a conflict between the interest of the client and the personal interests of the lawyer. The lawyer may be tempted to subordinate the interests of the client to the lawyer's own anticipated pecuniary gain. For example, a lawyer in a criminal case who obtains from the client television, radio, motion picture, newspaper, magazine, book, or other literary or media rights with respect to the case may be influenced, consciously or unconsciously, to a course of conduct that will enhance the value of the literary or media rights to the prejudice of the client. To prevent this adverse impact on the representation, such arrangements should be scrupulously avoided prior to the termination of all aspects of the matter giving rise to the representation, even though the representation has previously ended. Likewise, arrangements with third parties, such as book, newspaper or magazine publishers or television, radio or motion picture producers, pursuant to which the lawyer conveys whatever literary or media rights the lawyer may have, should not be entered into prior to the conclusion of all aspects of the matter giving rise to the representation.

[9A] Rule 1.8(d) does not prohibit a lawyer representing a client in a transaction concerning intellectual property from agreeing that the lawyer's fee shall consist of an ownership share in the property, if the arrangement conforms to paragraph (a) and Rule 1.5.

Financial Assistance

[9B] Paragraph (e) eliminates the former requirement that the client remain "ultimately liable" to repay any costs and expenses of litigation that were advanced by the lawyer regardless of whether the client obtained a recovery. Accordingly, a lawyer may make repayment from the client contingent on the outcome of the litigation, and may forgo repayment if the client obtains no recovery or a recovery less than the amount of the advanced costs and expenses. A lawyer may also, in an action in which the lawyer's fee is payable in whole or in part as a percentage of the recovery, pay court costs and litigation expenses on the lawyer's own account. However, like the former New York rule, paragraph (e) limits permitted financial assistance to court costs directly related to litigation. Examples of permitted expenses include filing fees, expenses of investigation, medical diagnostic work connected with the matter under litigation and treatment necessary for the diagnosis, and the costs of obtaining and presenting evidence. Permitted expenses do not include living or medical expenses other than those listed above.

[10]   Lawyers may not subsidize lawsuits or administrative proceedings brought on behalf of their clients, including making or guaranteeing loans to their clients for living expenses, because to do so would encourage clients to pursue lawsuits that might not otherwise be brought and because such assistance gives lawyers too great a financial stake in the litigation. These dangers do not warrant a prohibition against a lawyer lending a client money for court costs and litigation expenses, including the expenses of medical examination and testing and the costs of obtaining and presenting evidence, because these advances are virtually indistinguishable from contingent fee agreements and help ensure access to the courts. Similarly, an exception is warranted permitting lawyers representing indigent or pro bono clients to pay court costs and litigation expenses whether or not these funds will be repaid.

Person Paying for a Lawyer's Services

[11]   Lawyers are frequently asked to represent clients under circumstances in which a third person will compensate them, in whole or in part. The third person might be a relative or friend, an indemnitor (such as a liability insurance company) or a co-client (such as a corporation sued along with one or more of its employees). Third-party payers frequently have interests that may differ from those of the client. A lawyer is therefore prohibited from accepting or continuing such a representation unless the lawyer determines that there will be no interference with the lawyer's professional judgment and there is informed consent from the client. *See also* Rule 5.4(c), prohibiting interference with a lawyer's professional judgment by one who recommends, employs or pays the lawyer to render legal services for another.

[12]   Sometimes it will be sufficient for the lawyer to obtain the client's informed consent regarding the fact of the payment and the identity of the third-party payer. If, however, the fee arrangement creates a conflict of interest for the lawyer, then the lawyer must comply with Rule 1.7. The lawyer must also conform to the requirements of Rule 1.6 concerning confidentiality. Under Rule 1.7(a), a conflict of interest may exist if the lawyer will be involved in representing differing interests or if there is a significant risk that the lawyer's professional judgment on behalf of the client will be adversely affected by the lawyer's own interest in the fee arrangement or by the lawyer's responsibilities to the third-party payer (for example, when the third-party payer is a co-client). Under Rule 1.7(b), the lawyer may accept or continue the representation with the informed consent of each affected client, unless the conflict is nonconsentable under that paragraph. Under Rule

1.7(b), the informed consent must be confirmed in writing. *See* Rules 1.0(e) (definition of "confirmed in writing"), 1.0(j) (definition of "informed consent"), and 1.0(x) (definition of "writing" or "written").

Aggregate Settlements

[13] Differences in willingness to make or accept an offer of settlement are among the risks of common representation of multiple clients by a single lawyer. Under Rule 1.7, this is one of the risks that should be discussed before undertaking the representation, as part of the process of obtaining the clients' informed consents. In addition, Rule 1.2(a) protects each client's right to have the final say in deciding whether to accept or reject an offer of settlement. Paragraph (g) is a corollary of both these Rules and provides that, before any settlement offer is made or accepted on behalf of multiple clients, the lawyer must inform each of them about all the material terms of the settlement, including what the other clients will receive or pay if the settlement is accepted. *See also* Rule 1.0(j) (definition of "informed consent"). Lawyers representing a class of plaintiffs or defendants, or those proceeding derivatively, may not have a full client-lawyer relationship with each member of the class; nevertheless, such lawyers must comply with applicable rules regulating notification of class members and other procedural requirements designed to ensure adequate protection of the entire class.

Limiting Liability and Settling Malpractice Claims

[14] Agreements prospectively limiting a lawyer's liability for malpractice are prohibited because they are likely to undermine competent and diligent representation. Also, many clients are unable to evaluate the desirability of making such an agreement before a dispute has arisen, particularly if they are currently represented by the lawyer seeking the agreement. This paragraph does not, however, prohibit a lawyer from entering into an agreement with the client to arbitrate legal malpractice claims, provided such agreements are enforceable and the client is fully informed of the scope and effect of the agreement. Nor does this paragraph limit the ability of lawyers to practice in the form of a limited-liability entity, where permitted by law, provided that each lawyer remains personally liable to the client for the lawyer's own conduct and the firm complies with any conditions required by law, such as provisions requiring client notification or maintenance of adequate liability insurance. Nor does it prohibit an agreement in accordance with Rule 1.2 that defines the scope of the representation, although a definition of scope that makes the obligations of representation illusory will amount to an attempt to limit liability.

[15] Agreements settling a claim or a potential claim for malpractice are not prohibited by this Rule. Nevertheless, in view of the danger that a lawyer will take unfair advantage of an unrepresented client or former client, the lawyer must first advise such a person in writing of the appropriateness of independent representation in connection with such a settlement. In addition,

the lawyer must give the client or former client a reasonable opportunity to find and consult independent counsel.

Acquiring Proprietary Interest in Litigation

[16]   Paragraph (i) states the traditional general rule that lawyers are prohibited from acquiring a proprietary interest in litigation. Like paragraph (e), the general rule has its basis in common law champerty and maintenance and is designed to avoid giving the lawyer too great an interest in the representation. In addition, when the lawyer acquires an ownership interest in the subject of the representation, it will be more difficult for a client to discharge the lawyer if the client so desires. The rule is subject to specific exceptions developed in decisional law and continued in these Rules. The exception for certain advances of the costs of litigation is set forth in paragraph (e). In addition, paragraph (i) sets forth exceptions for liens authorized by law to secure the lawyer's fees or expenses and contracts for reasonable contingent fees. These may include liens granted by statute, liens originating in common law and liens acquired by contract with the client. When a lawyer acquires by contract a security interest in property other than that recovered through the lawyer's efforts in the litigation, such an acquisition is a business or financial transaction with a client and is governed by the requirements of paragraph (a). Contracts for contingent fees in civil matters are governed by Rule 1.5.

Client-Lawyer Sexual Relationships

[17]   The relationship between lawyer and client is a fiduciary one in which the lawyer occupies the highest position of trust and confidence. The relationship is often unequal; thus, a sexual relationship between lawyer and client can involve unfair exploitation of the lawyer's fiduciary role, in violation of the lawyer's basic ethical obligation not to use the trust of the client to the client's disadvantage. In addition, such a relationship presents a significant danger that if the sexual relationship leads to the lawyer's emotional involvement, the lawyer will be unable to represent the client without impairing the lawyer's exercise of professional judgment. Moreover, a blurred line between the professional and personal relationships may make it difficult to predict the extent to which client confidences will be protected by the attorney-client evidentiary privilege. A client's sexual involvement with the client's lawyer, especially if the sexual relations create emotional involvement, will often render it unlikely that the client could rationally determine whether to consent to the conflict created by the sexual relations. If a client were to consent to the conflict created by the sexual relations without fully appreciating the nature and implications of that conflict, there is a significant risk of harm to client interests. Therefore, sexual relations between lawyers and their clients are dangerous and inadvisable. Out of respect for the desires of consenting adults, however, paragraph (j) does not flatly prohibit client-lawyer sexual relations in matters other than domestic relations matters. Even when sexual relations between a lawyer and client are permitted under paragraph (j), however, they may lead to incompetent representation in violation of Rule

1.1. Because domestic relations clients are often emotionally vulnerable, domestic relations matters entail a heightened risk of exploitation of the client. Accordingly, lawyers are flatly prohibited from entering into sexual relations with domestic relations clients during the course of the representation even if the sexual relationship is consensual and even if prejudice to the client is not immediately apparent. For a definition of "sexual relations" for the purposes of this Rule, *see* Rule 1.0(u).

[17A]   The prohibitions in paragraph (j)(1) apply to all lawyers in a firm who know of the representation, whether or not they are personally representing the client. The Rule prohibits any lawyer in the firm from exploiting the client-lawyer relationship by directly or indirectly requiring or demanding sexual relations as a condition of representation by the lawyer or the lawyer's firm. Paragraph (j)(1)(i) thus seeks to prevent a situation where a client may fear that a willingness or unwillingness to have sexual relations with a lawyer in the firm may have an impact on the representation, or even on the firm's willingness to represent or continue representing the client. The Rule also prohibits the use of coercion, undue influence or intimidation to obtain sexual relations with a person known to that lawyer to be a client or a prospective client of the firm. Paragraph (j)(1)(ii) thus seeks to prevent a lawyer from exploiting the professional relationship between the client and the lawyer's firm. Even if a lawyer does not know that the firm represents a person, the lawyer's use of coercion or intimidation to obtain sexual relations with that person might well violate other Rules or substantive law. Where the representation of the client involves a domestic relations matter, the restrictions stated in paragraphs (j)(1)(i) and (j)(1)(ii), and not the per se prohibition imposed by paragraph (j)(1)(iii), apply to lawyers in a firm who know of the representation but who are not personally representing the client. Nevertheless, because domestic relations matters may be volatile and may entail a heightened risk of exploitation of the client, the risk that a sexual relationship with a client of the firm may result in a violation of other Rules is likewise heightened, even if the sexual relations are not per se prohibited by paragraph (j).

[17B]   A law firm's failure to educate lawyers about the restrictions on sexual relations–or a firm's failure to enforce those restrictions against lawyers who violate them–may constitute a violation of Rule 5.1, which obligates a law firm to make reasonable efforts to ensure that all lawyers in the firm conform to these Rules.

[18]   Sexual relationships between spouses or those that predate the client-lawyer relationship are not prohibited. Issues relating to the exploitation of the fiduciary relationship and client dependency are diminished when the sexual relationship existed prior to the commencement of the client-lawyer relationship. However, before proceeding with the representation in these circumstances, the lawyer should consider whether the lawyer's ability to represent the client will be materially limited by the sexual relationship and therefore constitute an impermissible conflict of interest. *See* Rule 1.7(a)(2).

446

[19]   When the client is an organization, paragraph (j) applies to sexual relations between a lawyer for the organization (whether inside counsel or outside counsel) and a constituent of the organization who supervises, directs or regularly consults with that lawyer or a lawyer in that lawyer's firm concerning the organization's legal matters.

Imputation of Prohibitions

[20]   Where a lawyer who is not personally representing a client has sexual relations with a client of the firm in violation of paragraph (j), the other lawyers in the firm are not subject to discipline solely because those improper sexual relations occurred. There may be circumstances, however, where a violation of paragraph (j) by one lawyer in a firm gives rise to violations of other Rules by the other lawyers in the firm through imputation. For example, sexual relations between a lawyer and a client may give rise to a violation of Rule 1.7(a), and such a conflict under Rule 1.7 may be imputed to all other lawyers in the firm under Rule 1.10(a).

RULE 1.9: DUTIES TO FORMER CLIENTS

(a) A lawyer who has formerly represented a client in a matter shall not thereafter represent another person in the same or a substantially related matter in which that person's interests are materially adverse to the interests of the former client unless the former client gives informed consent, confirmed in writing.

(b) Unless the former client gives informed consent, confirmed in writing, a lawyer shall not knowingly represent a person in the same or a substantially related matter in which a firm with which the lawyer formerly was associated had previously represented a client:

> **(1) whose interests are materially adverse to that person; and**

> **(2) about whom the lawyer had acquired information protected by Rules 1.6 or paragraph (c) of this Rule that is material to the matter.**

(c) A lawyer who has formerly represented a client in a matter or whose present or former firm has formerly represented a client in a matter shall not thereafter:

> **(1) use confidential information of the former client protected by Rule 1.6 to the disadvantage of the former client, except as these Rules would permit or require with respect to a current client or when the information has become generally known; or**

> **(2) reveal confidential information of the former client protected by Rule 1.6 except as these Rules would permit or require with respect to a current client.**

Comment

[1]   After termination of a client-lawyer relationship, a lawyer has certain continuing duties with respect to confidentiality and conflicts of interest and thus may not represent another client except in conformity with these Rules. Under this Rule, for example, a lawyer could not properly seek to rescind on behalf of a new client a contract drafted on behalf of a former client. So also, a lawyer who has prosecuted an accused person could not properly represent that person in a subsequent civil action against the government concerning the same transaction. Nor could a lawyer who has represented multiple clients in a matter represent one of the clients against the others in the same or a substantially related matter after a dispute arose among the clients in that matter, unless all affected clients give informed consent. *See* Comment [9]. Current and former government lawyers must comply with this Rule to the extent required by Rule 1.11.

[2]   The scope of a "matter" for purposes of this Rule depends on the facts of a particular situation or transaction. The lawyer's involvement in a matter can also be a question of degree. When a lawyer has been directly involved in a specific transaction, subsequent representation of other clients with materially adverse interests in that transaction clearly is prohibited. On the other hand, a lawyer who recurrently handled a type of problem for a former client is not precluded from later representing another client in a factually distinct problem of that type, even though the subsequent representation involves a position adverse to the prior client. Similar considerations can apply to the reassignment of military lawyers between defense and prosecution functions within the same military jurisdictions. The underlying question is whether the lawyer was so involved in the matter that the subsequent representation can be justly regarded as a changing of sides in the matter in question.

[3]   Matters are "substantially related" for purposes of this Rule if they involve the same transaction or legal dispute or if, under the circumstances, a reasonable lawyer would conclude that there is otherwise a substantial risk that confidential factual information that would normally have been obtained in the prior representation would materially advance the client's position in the subsequent matter. For example, a lawyer who has represented a businessperson and learned extensive private financial information about that person may not then represent that person's spouse in seeking a divorce. Similarly, a lawyer who has previously represented a client in securing environmental permits to build a shopping center would be precluded from representing neighbors seeking to oppose rezoning of the property on the basis of environmental considerations; however, the lawyer would not be precluded, on the grounds of substantial relationship, from defending a tenant of the completed shopping center in resisting eviction for nonpayment of rent. Information that has been disclosed to the public or to other parties adverse to the former client ordinarily will not be disqualifying. Information acquired in a prior representation may have been rendered obsolete by the passage of time, a circumstance that may be relevant in determining whether two

representations are substantially related. In the case of an organizational client, general knowledge of the client's policies and practices ordinarily will not preclude a subsequent representation. On the other hand, knowledge of specific facts gained in a prior representation that are relevant to the matter in question ordinarily will preclude such a representation. A former client is not required to reveal the confidential information learned by the lawyer in order to establish a substantial risk that the lawyer has confidential information to use in the subsequent matter. A conclusion about the possession of such information may be based on the nature of the services the lawyer provided the former client and information that would in ordinary practice be learned by a lawyer providing such services.

[4]   [Moved to Comment to Rule 1.10.]

[5]   [Moved to Comment to Rule 1.10.]

[6]   [Moved to Comment to Rule 1.10.]

[7]   Independent of the prohibition against subsequent representation, a lawyer changing professional association has a continuing duty to preserve confidentiality of information about a client formerly represented. *See* Rules 1.6, 1.9(c).

[8]   Paragraph (c) generally extends the confidentiality protections of Rule 1.6 to a lawyer's former clients. Paragraph (c)(1) provides that information acquired by the lawyer in the course of representing a client may not subsequently be used by the lawyer to the disadvantage of the client. However, the fact that a lawyer has once served a client does not preclude the lawyer from using generally known information about that client when later representing another client. Paragraph (c)(2) provides that a lawyer may not reveal information acquired in the course of representing a client except as these Rules would permit or require with respect to a current client. *See* Rules 1.6, 3.3.

[9]   The provisions of this Rule are for the protection of former clients and can be waived if the client gives informed consent, which consent must be confirmed in writing under paragraph (a). *See also* Rule 1.0(j) for the definition of "informed consent." With regard to the effectiveness of an advance waiver, *see* Rule 1.7, Comments [22]-[22A]. With regard to disqualification of a firm with which a lawyer is or was formerly associated, *see* Rule 1.10.

RULE 1.10: IMPUTATION OF CONFLICTS OF INTEREST

(a) While lawyers are associated in a firm, none of them shall knowingly represent a client when any one of them practicing alone would be prohibited from doing so by Rule 1.7, 1.8 or 1.9, except as otherwise provided therein.

(b) When a lawyer has terminated an association with a firm, the firm is prohibited from thereafter representing a person with inter-

ests that the firm knows or reasonably should know are materially adverse to those of a client represented by the formerly associated lawyer and not currently represented by the firm if the firm or any lawyer remaining in the firm has information protected by Rule 1.6 or Rule 1.9(c) that is material to the matter.

(c) When a lawyer becomes associated with a firm, the firm may not knowingly represent a client in a matter that is the same as or substantially related to a matter in which the newly associated lawyer, or a firm with which that lawyer was associated, formerly represented a client whose interests are materially adverse to the prospective or current client unless the newly associated lawyer did not acquire any information protected by Rule 1.6 or Rule 1.9(c) that is material to the current matter.

(d) A disqualification prescribed by this Rule may be waived by the affected client or former client under the conditions stated in Rule 1.7.

(e) A law firm shall make a written record of its engagements, at or near the time of each new engagement, and shall implement and maintain a system by which proposed engagements are checked against current and previous engagements when:

   (1) the firm agrees to represent a new client;

   (2) the firm agrees to represent an existing client in a new matter;

   (3) the firm hires or associates with another lawyer; or

   (4) an additional party is named or appears in a pending matter.

(f) Substantial failure to keep records or to implement or maintain a conflict-checking system that complies with paragraph (e) shall be a violation thereof regardless of whether there is another violation of these Rules.

(g) Where a violation of paragraph (e) by a law firm is a substantial factor in causing a violation of paragraph (a) by a lawyer, the law firm, as well as the individual lawyer, shall be responsible for the violation of paragraph (a).

(h) A lawyer related to another lawyer as parent, child, sibling or spouse shall not represent in any matter a client whose interests differ from those of another party to the matter who the lawyer knows is represented by the other lawyer unless the client consents to the representation after full disclosure and the lawyer concludes that the lawyer can adequately represent the interests of the client.

Comment

Definition of "Firm"

[1] For purposes of these Rules, the term "firm" includes, but is not limited to, (i) a lawyer or lawyers in a law partnership, professional corporation, sole proprietorship or other association authorized to practice law, and (ii) lawyers employed in a legal services organization, a government law office or the legal department of a corporation or other organization. *See* Rule 1.0(h). Whether two or more lawyers constitute a "firm" within this definition will depend on the specific facts. *See* Rule 1.0, Comments [2]-[4].

Principles of Imputed Disqualification

[2] The rule of imputed disqualification stated in paragraph (a) gives effect to the principle of loyalty to the client as it applies to lawyers who practice in a law firm. Such situations can be considered from the premise that a firm of lawyers is essentially one lawyer for purposes of the rules governing loyalty to the client, or from the premise that each lawyer is vicariously bound by the obligation of loyalty owed by each lawyer with whom the lawyer is associated. Paragraph (a) operates only among the lawyers currently associated in a firm. When a lawyer moves from one firm to another, the situation is governed by paragraphs (b) and (c).

[3] Paragraph (a) does not prohibit representation where neither questions of client loyalty nor questions of protection of confidential information are presented. Where one lawyer in a firm could not effectively represent a given client because of strong political beliefs, for example, but that lawyer will do no work on the case and the personal beliefs of the lawyer will not materially limit the representation by others in the firm or adversely affect the ability of the others in the firm to exercise professional judgment on behalf of the client, the firm should not be disqualified. On the other hand, if an opposing party in a case is owned by a lawyer in the law firm, and others in the firm would be materially limited in pursuing the matter because of loyalty to that lawyer, the personal disqualification of the lawyer would be imputed to all others in the firm.

[4] The rule in paragraph (a) also does not prohibit representation by others in the law firm where the person prohibited from involvement in a matter is a nonlawyer, such as a paralegal or legal secretary. Nor does paragraph (a) prohibit representation if the lawyer is prohibited from acting because of events that took place before admission to the bar, such as work that the person did while a law student. Such persons, however, ordinarily must be screened from any personal participation in the matter to avoid communication to others in the firm of confidential information that both the nonlawyers and the firm have a legal duty to protect. *See* Rules 1.0(t), 5.3.

Lawyers Moving Between Firms

[4A] The principles of imputed disqualification are modified when lawyers have been associated in a firm and then end their association. The nature of contemporary law practice and the organization of law firms have made the fiction that the law firm is the same as a single lawyer unrealistic in certain situations. In crafting a rule to govern imputed conflicts, there are several competing considerations. First, the former client must be reasonably assured that the client's confidentiality interests are not compromised. Second, the principles of imputed disqualification should not be so broadly cast as to preclude others from having reasonable choice of counsel. Third, the principles of imputed disqualification should not unreasonably hamper lawyers from forming new associations and taking on new clients after leaving a firm. In this connection, it should be recognized that today most lawyers practice in firms, that many limit their practice to, or otherwise concentrate in, one area of law, and that many move from one association to another multiple times in their careers. If the principles of imputed disqualification were defined too strictly, the result would be undue curtailment of the opportunity of lawyers to move from one practice setting to another, of the opportunity of clients to choose counsel, and of the opportunity of firms to retain qualified lawyers. For these reasons, a functional analysis that focuses on preserving the former client's reasonable confidentiality interests is appropriate in balancing the competing interests.

[5]   Paragraph (b) permits a law firm, under certain circumstances, to represent a client with interests directly adverse to those of a client represented by a lawyer who formerly was associated with the firm. The Rule applies regardless of when the formerly associated lawyer represented the client. However, under Rule 1.7 the law firm may not represent a client with interests adverse to those of a current client of the firm. Moreover, the firm may not represent the client where the matter is the same or substantially related to a matter in which (i) the formerly associated lawyer represented the client, and (ii) the firm or any lawyer currently in the firm has material information protected by Rule 1.6 and Rule 1.9(c) that is likely to be significant to the matter.

[5A]   In addition to information that may be in the possession of one or more of the lawyers remaining in the firm, information in documents or files retained by the firm itself may preclude the firm from opposing the former client in the same or substantially related matter if (i) the information is protected by Rule 1.6 and Rule 1.9(c) and likely to be significant and material to the current matter, and (ii) the documents or files containing confidential client information are retained in a place or in a form that is accessible to lawyers participating in the current adverse matter. A law firm seeking to avoid disqualification under this Rule should therefore take reasonable steps to ensure that any confidential information relating to the prior representation that is maintained in the firm's hard copy or electronic files is not accessible to any lawyer who is participating in the current adverse representation.

[5B]   Rule 1.10(c) permits a law firm to represent a client in a matter that is the same as or substantially related to a matter in which the newly associated lawyer, or the firm with which the lawyer was previously associated, represented a client whose interests are materially adverse to that client, provided the newly associated lawyer did not acquire any confidential information of the previously represented client that is material to the current matter.

[5C] The bookkeeping and accounting problems that may arise from prohibiting a personally disqualified lawyer from being apportioned a share of the fees from a matter make it inadvisable to impose an unqualified rule prohibiting this practice. Although this Rule does not prohibit a personally disqualified lawyer from being apportioned a share of the fees in the matter, if the disqualified lawyer's share of the fee would represent a significant increase in that lawyer's compensation over what the lawyer would otherwise earn, permitting the lawyer to be apportioned a share in the fee may create incentives that would call into question the effectiveness of the screening procedures. In such situations, a firm seeking to avoid imputed disqualification under this Rule would be well-advised to prohibit the personally disqualified lawyer from sharing in the fees in the matter.

Client Consent

[6] Rule 1.10(d) removes imputation with the informed consent of the affected client or former client under the conditions stated in Rule 1.7. The conditions stated in Rule 1.7 require the lawyer to determine that the representation is not prohibited by Rule 1.7(b) and that each affected client or former client has given informed consent to the representation, confirmed in writing. In some cases, the risk may be so severe that the conflict cannot be cured by client consent. For a discussion of the effectiveness of client waivers of conflicts that might arise in the future, *see* Rule 1.7, Comments [22]-[22A]. For a definition of "informed consent," *see* Rule 1.0(j).

Former and Current Government Lawyers

[7] Where a lawyer has joined a private firm after having represented the government, imputation is governed by Rule 1.11(b), not this Rule. The imputation of conflicts among current government lawyers employed by the same office, agency or department is governed by Rule 1.11(b), not this Rule.

Relationship Between this Rule and Rule 1.8(k)

[8] Subject to paragraph (a), where a lawyer is prohibited from engaging in certain transactions under Rule 1.8(a) through (i), that Rule determines whether that prohibition also applies to other lawyers associated in a firm with the personally prohibited lawyer.

Conflict-Checking Procedures

[9] Under paragraph (f), every law firm, no matter how large or small (including sole practitioners), is responsible for creating, implementing and maintaining a system to check proposed engagements against current and previous engagements and against new parties in pending matters. The system must be adequate to detect conflicts that will or reasonably may arise

if: (i) the firm agrees to represent a new client, (ii) the firm agrees to represent an existing client in a new matter, (iii) the firm hires or associates with another lawyer, or (iv) an additional party is named or appears in a pending matter. The system will thus render effective assistance to lawyers in the firm in avoiding conflicts of interest. *See also* Rule 5.1.

[9A]   Failure to create, implement and maintain a conflict-checking system adequate for this purpose is a violation of this Rule by the firm. In cases in which a lawyer, despite reasonably diligent efforts to do so, could not acquire the information that would have revealed a conflict because of the firm's failure to maintain an adequate conflict-checking system, the firm shall be responsible for the violation. However, a lawyer who knows or should know of a conflict in a matter that the lawyer is handling remains individually responsible for the violation of these Rules, whether or not the firm's conflict-checking system has identified the conflict. In cases in which a violation of paragraph (f) by the firm is a substantial factor in causing a violation of these Rules by a lawyer, the firm, as well as the individual lawyer, is responsible for the violation. As to whether a client-lawyer relationship exists or is continuing, *see* Scope [9]-[10]; Rule 1.3, Comment [4].

[9B]   The records required to be maintained under paragraph (f) must be in written form. *See* Rule 1.0(x) for the definition of "written," which includes tangible or electronic records. To be effective, a conflict-checking system may also need to supplement written information with recourse to the memory of the firm's lawyers through in-person, telephonic, or electronic communications. An effective conflict-checking system as required by this Rule may not, however, depend solely on recourse to lawyers' memories or other such informal sources of information.

[9C]   The nature of the records needed to render effective assistance to lawyers will vary depending on the size, structure, history, and nature of the firm's practice. At a minimum, however, a firm must record information that will enable the firm to identify (i) each client that the firm represents, (ii) each party in a litigated, transactional or other matter whose interests are materially adverse to the firm's clients, and (iii) the general nature of each matter.

[9D]   To the extent that the records made and maintained for the purpose of complying with this Rule contain confidential information, a firm must exercise reasonable care to protect the confidentiality of these records. *See* Rule 1.6(c).

[9E]   The nature of a firm's conflict-checking system may vary depending on a number of factors, including the size and structure of the firm, the nature of the firm's practice, the number and location of the firm offices, and the relationship among the firm's separate offices. In all cases, however, an effective conflict-checking system should record and maintain information in a way that permits the information to be checked systematically and accurately when the firm is considering a proposed engagement. A small firm or a firm with a small number of engagements may be able to create and maintain an effective conflict-checking system through the use of hard-copy rather than electronic records. But larger firms, or firms with a large number of engagements, may need to create and maintain records in electronic form so that the information can be accessed quickly and efficiently.

Organizational Clients

[9F] Representation of corporate or other organizational clients makes it prudent for a firm to maintain additional information in its conflict-checking system. For example, absent an agreement with the client to the contrary, a conflict may arise when a firm desires to oppose an entity that is part of a current or former client's corporate family (*e.g.*, an affiliate, subsidiary, parent or sister organization). *See* Rule 1.7, Comments [34]-[34A]. Although a law firm is not required to maintain records showing every corporate affiliate of every corporate client, if a law firm frequently represents corporations that belong to large corporate families, the law firm should make reasonable efforts to institute and maintain a system for alerting the firm to potential conflicts with the members of the corporate client's family.

[9G] Under certain circumstances, a law firm may also need to include information about the constituents of a corporate client. Although Rule 1.13 provides that a firm is the lawyer for the entity and not for any of its constituents, confusion may arise when a law firm represents small or closely held corporations with few shareholders, or when a firm represents both the corporation and individual officers or employees but bills the corporate client for the legal services. In other situations, a client-lawyer relationship may develop unintentionally between the law firm and one or more individual constituents of the entity. Accordingly, a firm that represents corporate clients may need a system for determining whether or not the law firm has a client-lawyer relationship with individual constituents of an organizational client. If so, the law firm should add the names of those constituents to the data base of its conflict-checking system.

RULE 1.11: SPECIFIC CONFLICTS OF INTEREST FOR FORMER AND CURRENT GOVERNMENT OFFICERS AND EMPLOYEES

(a) **Except as law may otherwise expressly provide, a lawyer who has formerly served as a public officer or employee of the government:**

(1) **shall comply with Rule 1.9(c); and**

(2) **shall not represent a client in connection with a matter in which the lawyer participated personally and substantially as a public officer or employee, unless the appropriate government agency gives its informed consent, confirmed in writing, to the representation. This provision shall not apply to matters governed by Rule 1.12(a).**

(b) When a lawyer is disqualified from representation under paragraph (a), no lawyer in a firm with which that lawyer is associated may knowingly undertake or continue representation in such a matter unless:

    (1) the firm acts promptly and reasonably to:

        (i) notify, as appropriate, lawyers and nonlawyer personnel within the firm that the personally disqualified lawyer is prohibited from participating in the representation of the current client;

        (ii) implement effective screening procedures to prevent the flow of information about the matter between the personally disqualified lawyer and the others in the firm;

        (iii) ensure that the disqualified lawyer is apportioned no part of the fee therefrom; and

        (iv) give written notice to the appropriate government agency to enable it to ascertain compliance with the provisions of this Rule; and

    (2) there are no other circumstances in the particular representation that create an appearance of impropriety.

(c) Except as law may otherwise expressly provide, a lawyer having information that the lawyer knows is confidential government information about a person, acquired when the lawyer was a public officer or employee, may not represent a private client whose interests are adverse to that person in a matter in which the information could be used to the material disadvantage of that person. As used in this Rule, the term "confidential government information" means information that has been obtained under governmental authority and that, at the time this Rule is applied, the government is prohibited by law from disclosing to the public or has a legal privilege not to disclose, and that is not otherwise available to the public. A firm with which that lawyer is associated may undertake or continue representation in the matter only if the disqualified lawyer is timely and effectively screened from any participation in the matter in accordance with the provisions of paragraph (b).

(d) Except as law may otherwise expressly provide, a lawyer currently serving as a public officer or employee shall not:

    (1) participate in a matter in which the lawyer participated personally and substantially while in private practice or nongovernmental employment, unless under applicable law no one is, or by lawful delegation may be, authorized to act in the lawyer's stead in the matter; or

    (2) negotiate for private employment with any person who is involved as a party or as lawyer for a party in a matter in which the lawyer is participating personally and substantially.

(e) As used in this Rule, the term "matter" as defined in Rule 1.0(*l*) does not include or apply to agency rulemaking functions.

(f) A lawyer who holds public office shall not:

(1) use the public position to obtain, or attempt to obtain, a special advantage in legislative matters for the lawyer or for a client under circumstances where the lawyer knows or it is obvious that such action is not in the public interest;

(2) use the public position to influence, or attempt to influence, a tribunal to act in favor of the lawyer or of a client; or

(3) accept anything of value from any person when the lawyer knows or it is obvious that the offer is for the purpose of influencing the lawyer's action as a public official.

Comment

[1]   A lawyer who has served or is currently serving as a public officer or employee is personally subject to the Rules of Professional Conduct, including the prohibition against concurrent conflicts of interest stated in Rule 1.7. In addition, such a lawyer may be subject to statutes and government regulations regarding conflicts of interest. Such statutes and regulations may circumscribe the extent to which the government agency may give consent under this Rule. *See* Rule 1.0(j) for the definition of "informed consent."

[2]   Paragraphs (a)(1), (a)(2), (d) and (f) restate the obligations of an individual lawyer who has served or is currently serving as an officer or employee of the government toward a former government or private client. Rule 1.10 is not applicable to the conflicts of interest addressed by this Rule. Rather, paragraph (b) sets forth special imputation rules for former government lawyers, with screening and notice provisions. *See* Comments [6]-[7B] concerning imputation of the conflicts of former government lawyers; *see* Comments [9A]-[9B] concerning imputation of the conflicts of current government lawyers.

[3]   Paragraphs (a)(2), (d) and (f) apply regardless of whether a lawyer is adverse to a former client and are thus designed not only to protect the former client, but also to prevent a lawyer from exploiting public office for the advantage of another client. For example, a lawyer who has pursued a claim on behalf of the government may not pursue the same claim on behalf of a private client after the lawyer has left government service, except when authorized to do so by the government agency under paragraph (a). Similarly, a lawyer who has pursued a claim on behalf of a private client may not pursue the claim on behalf of the government, except when authorized to do so. As with paragraph (a)(1), Rule 1.10 is not applicable to the conflicts of interest addressed by paragraphs (a)(2), (d)(1), (d)(2) and (f).

[4]   This Rule represents a balancing of interests. On the one hand, where the successive clients are a government agency and another client, public or private, the risk exists that power or discretion vested in that agency

might be used for the special benefit of the other client. A lawyer should not be in a position where benefit to the other client might affect performance of the lawyer's professional functions on behalf of the government. Also, unfair advantage could accrue to the other client by reason of access to confidential government information about the client's adversary obtainable only through the lawyer's government service. On the other hand, the rules governing lawyers presently or formerly employed by a government agency should not be so restrictive as to inhibit transfer of employment to and from the government. The government has a legitimate need to attract qualified lawyers as well as to maintain high ethical standards. A former government lawyer is therefore disqualified only from particular matters in which the lawyer participated personally and substantially. The provisions for screening and waiver in paragraph (b) are necessary to prevent the disqualification rule from imposing too severe a deterrent to entering public service. The limitation on disqualification in paragraphs (a)(2), (d)(1) and (d)(2) to matters involving a specific party or specific parties, rather than extending disqualification to all substantive issues on which the lawyer worked, serves a similar function.

[4A] By requiring a former government lawyer to comply with Rule 1.9(c), Rule 1.11(a)(1) protects information obtained while working for the government to the same extent as information learned while representing a private client. Accordingly, unless the information acquired during government service is "generally known" or these Rules would otherwise permit or require its use or disclosure, the information may not be used or revealed to the government's disadvantage. This provision applies regardless of whether the lawyer was working in a "legal" capacity. Thus, information learned by the lawyer while in public service in an administrative, policy or advisory position also is covered by Rule 1.11(a)(1). Paragraph (c) of Rule 1.11 adds further protections against exploitation of confidential information. Paragraph (c) prohibits a lawyer who has information about a person acquired when the lawyer was a public officer or employee, that the lawyer knows is confidential government information, from representing a private client whose interests are adverse to that person in a matter in which the information could be used to that person's material disadvantage. A firm with which the lawyer is associated may undertake or continue representation in the matter only if the lawyer who possesses the confidential government information is timely and effectively screened. Thus, the purpose and effect of the prohibitions contained in Rule 1.11(c) are to prevent the lawyer's subsequent private client from obtaining an unfair advantage because the lawyer has confidential government information about the client's adversary.

[5] When a lawyer has been employed by one government agency and then moves to a second government agency, it may be appropriate to treat that second agency as another client for purposes of this Rule, as when a lawyer is employed by a municipality and subsequently is employed by a federal agency. The question whether two government agencies should be regarded as the same or different clients for conflict of interest purposes is beyond the scope of these Rules. *See* Rule 1.13, Comment [9].

Former Government Lawyers: Using Screening to Avoid Imputed Disqualification

[6] Paragraphs (b) and (c) contemplate the use of screening procedures that permit the law firm of a personally disqualified former government lawyer to avoid imputed disqualification. There may be circumstances where representation by the personally disqualified lawyer's firm may undermine the public's confidence in the integrity of the legal system. Such a circumstance may arise, for example, where the personally disqualified lawyer occupied a highly visible government position prior to entering private practice, or where the facts and circumstances of the representation itself create a risk that the representation will appear to be improper. Where the particular circumstances create such a risk, a law firm may find it prudent to decline the representation, but Rule 1.11 does not require it to do so. *See* Rule 1.0(t) for the definition of "screened" and "screening."

[6A] The bookkeeping and accounting problems that may arise from prohibiting a personally disqualified lawyer from being apportioned a share of the fees from a matter make it inadvisable to impose an unqualified rule prohibiting this practice. Although this Rule does not prohibit a personally disqualified lawyer from being apportioned a share of the fees in the matter, if the disqualified lawyer's share of the fee would represent a significant increase in that lawyer's compensation over what the lawyer would otherwise earn, permitting the lawyer to be apportioned a share in the fee may create incentives that would call into question the effectiveness of the screening procedures. In such situations, a firm seeking to avoid imputed disqualification under this Rule would be well-advised to prohibit the personally disqualified lawyer from sharing in the fees in the matter.

[7] A firm seeking to avoid disqualification under this Rule should also consider its ability to implement, maintain, and monitor the screening procedures permitted by paragraphs (b) and (c) before undertaking or continuing the representation. In deciding whether the screening procedures permitted by this Rule will be effective to avoid imputed disqualification, a firm should consider a number of factors, including how the size, practices and organization of the firm will affect the likelihood that any confidential information acquired about the matter by the personally disqualified lawyer can be protected. If the firm is large and is organized into separate departments, or maintains offices in multiple locations, or for any reason the structure of the firm facilitates preventing the sharing of information with lawyers not participating in the particular matter, it is more likely that the requirements of this Rule can be met and imputed disqualification avoided. Although a large firm will find it easier to maintain effective screening, lack of timeliness in instituting, or lack of vigilance in maintaining, the procedures required by this Rule may make those procedures ineffective in avoiding imputed disqualification. If a personally disqualified lawyer is working on other matters with lawyers who are participating in a matter requiring screening, it may be impossible to maintain effective screening procedures. The size of the firm may be considered as one of the factors affecting the firm's ability to institute

and maintain effective screening procedures, it is not a dispositive factor. A small firm may need to exercise special care and vigilance to maintain effective screening but, if appropriate precautions are taken, small firms can satisfy the requirements of paragraphs (b) and (c).

[7A]   In order to prevent any lawyer in the firm from acquiring confidential information about the matter from the newly associated lawyer, it is essential that notification be given and screening procedures implemented promptly. If the matter requiring screening is already pending before the personally disqualified lawyer joins the firm, the procedures required by this Rule should be implemented before the lawyer joins the firm. If a newly associated lawyer joins a firm before a conflict requiring screening arises, the requirements of this Rule should be satisfied as soon as practicable after the conflict arises. If any lawyer in the firm acquires confidential information about the matter from the personally disqualified lawyer, the requirements of this Rule cannot be met, and any subsequent efforts to institute or maintain screening will not be effective in avoiding the firm's disqualification. Other factors may affect the likelihood that screening procedures will be effective in preventing the flow of confidential information between the personally disqualified lawyer and other lawyers in the firm in a given matter.

[7B]   Notice to the appropriate government agency, including a description of the screened lawyer's prior representation and of the screening procedures employed, generally should be given as soon as practicable after the need for screening becomes apparent.

[8]   Paragraph (c) operates only when the lawyer in question has actual knowledge of the information. It does not operate with respect to information that merely could be imputed to the lawyer.

[9]   Paragraph (a) does not prohibit a lawyer from representing a private party and a government agency jointly when doing so is permitted by Rule 1.7 and is not otherwise prohibited by law.

Current Government Lawyers: Using Screening to Avoid Imputed Disqualification

[9A]   Where the conflict arises from the government lawyer's prior representation of a client, the office, agency or department is required to notify the former client of the circumstances warranting the use of screening and the actions that have been taken to comply with the requirements of this Rule, unless providing notice would be in violation of law or Rule 1.6. The requirement that the government lawyer's former client be notified is suspended under circumstances where notice would make information public that the agency is required to keep secret. For example, a prosecutor's office would not be required to notify a personally disqualified lawyer's former client if that former client is now the subject of a pending grand jury investigation.

[9B]   Whether a lawyer's belief that the lawyer can provide competent and diligent representation is reasonable may depend on various factors including, for example, the nature of the conflict or the role of the personally disqualified lawyer in the office, agency or department in which the lawyer also serves. Thus, all other things being equal, it may be reasonable for a lawyer to conclude that the lawyer can act competently and diligently in the matter where the personally disqualified lawyer does not occupy a supervisory position; it may be unreasonable for a lawyer to reach this conclusion where the personally disqualified lawyer is the head of the office, agency or department.

[10]   For purposes of paragraph (e), a "matter" may continue in another form. In determining whether two particular matters are the same, the lawyer should consider the extent to which (i) the matters involve the same basic facts, (ii) the matters involve the same or related parties, and (iii) time has elapsed between the matters.

RULE 1.12: SPECIFIC CONFLICTS OF INTEREST FOR FORMER JUDGES, ARBITRATORS, MEDIATORS OR OTHER THIRD–PARTY NEUTRALS

(a) A lawyer shall not accept private employment in a matter upon the merits of which the lawyer has acted in a judicial capacity.

(b) Except as stated in paragraph (e), and unless all parties to the proceeding give informed consent, confirmed in writing, a lawyer shall not represent anyone in connection with a matter in which the lawyer participated personally and substantially as:

(1) an arbitrator, mediator or other third-party neutral; or

(2) a law clerk to a judge or other adjudicative officer or an arbitrator, mediator or other third-party neutral.

(c) A lawyer shall not negotiate for employment with any person who is involved as a party or as lawyer for a party in a matter in which the lawyer is participating personally and substantially as a judge or other adjudicative officer or as an arbitrator, mediator or other third-party neutral.

(d) When a lawyer is disqualified from representation under this Rule, no lawyer in a firm with which that lawyer is associated may knowingly undertake or continue representation in such a matter unless:

(1) the firm acts promptly and reasonably to:

(i) notify, as appropriate, lawyers and nonlawyer personnel within the firm that the personally disqualified lawyer is prohibited from participating in the representation of the current client;

(ii) implement effective screening procedures to prevent the flow of information about the matter between the personally disqualified lawyer and the others in the firm;

(iii) ensure that the disqualified lawyer is apportioned no part of the fee therefrom; and

(iv) give written notice to the parties and any appropriate tribunal to enable it to ascertain compliance with the provisions of this Rule; and

(2) there are no other circumstances in the particular representation that create an appearance of impropriety.

(e) An arbitrator selected as a partisan of a party in a multimember arbitration panel is not prohibited from subsequently representing that party.

Comment

[1]   This Rule generally parallels Rule 1.11. The term "personally and substantially" signifies that a judge who was a member of a multimember court, and thereafter left judicial office to practice law, is not prohibited from representing a client in a matter pending in the court, but in which the former judge did not participate. So also, the fact that a former judge exercised administrative responsibility in a court does not prevent the former judge from acting as a lawyer in a matter where the judge had previously exercised remote or incidental administrative responsibility that did not affect the merits. *See* Rule 1.11, Comment [4]. The term "adjudicative officer" includes such officials as judges pro tempore, referees, special masters, hearing officers and other parajudicial officers, and also lawyers who serve as part-time judges. Compliance Canons A(2), B(2) and C of the Model Code of Judicial Conduct provide that a part-time judge, judge pro tempore or retired judge recalled to active service may not "act as a lawyer in any proceeding in which he served as a judge or in any other proceeding related thereto." Although phrased differently from this Rule, those Canons have the same meaning.

[2]   Like a former judge, a lawyer who has served as an arbitrator, mediator or other third-party neutral may be asked to represent a client in a matter in which the lawyer participated personally and substantially. This Rule forbids such representation unless all of the parties to the proceedings give their informed consents, confirmed in writing. *See* Rules 1.0(j), (e). Other law or codes of ethics governing third-party neutrals may impose more stringent standards of personal or imputed disqualification. *See* Rule 2.4.

[3]   Although lawyers who serve as third-party neutrals do not obtain information concerning the parties that is protected under Rule 1.6, they typically owe the parties an obligation of confidentiality under law or codes of ethics governing third-party neutrals. Paragraph (d) therefore provides that conflicts of the personally disqualified lawyer will be imputed to other lawyers in a law firm unless the conditions of this paragraph are met.

[4]   Requirements for screening procedures are stated in paragraph (d). "Screened" and "screening" are defined in Rule 1.0(t).

[4A] The bookkeeping and accounting problems that may arise from prohibiting a personally disqualified lawyer from being apportioned a share of the fees from a matter make it inadvisable to impose an unqualified rule prohibiting this practice. Although this Rule does not prohibit a personally disqualified lawyer from being apportioned a share of the fees in the matter, if the disqualified lawyer's share of the fee would represent a significant increase in that lawyer's compensation over what the lawyer would otherwise earn, permitting the lawyer to be apportioned a share in the fee may create incentives that would call into question the effectiveness of the screening procedures. In such situations, a firm seeking to avoid imputed disqualification under this Rule would be well-advised to prohibit the personally disqualified lawyer from sharing in the fees in the matter.

[4B] A firm seeking to avoid disqualification under this Rule should also consider its ability to implement, maintain, and monitor the screening procedures permitted by paragraph (d) before undertaking or continuing the representation. In deciding whether the screening procedures permitted by this Rule will be effective to avoid imputed disqualification, a firm should consider a number of factors, including how the size, practices and organization of the firm will affect the likelihood that any confidential information acquired about the matter by the personally disqualified lawyer can be protected. If the firm is large and is organized into separate departments, or maintains offices in multiple locations, or for any reason the structure of the firm facilitates preventing the sharing of information with lawyers not participating in the particular matter, it is more likely that the requirements of this Rule can be met and imputed disqualification avoided. Although a large firm will find it easier to maintain effective screening, lack of timeliness in instituting, or lack of vigilance in maintaining, the procedures required by this Rule may make those procedures ineffective in avoiding imputed disqualification. If a personally disqualified lawyer is working on other matters with lawyers who are participating in a matter requiring screening, it may be impossible to maintain effective screening procedures. The size of the firm may be considered as one of the factors affecting the firm's ability to institute and maintain effective screening procedures, it is not a dispositive factor. A small firm may need to exercise special care and vigilance to maintain effective screening but, if appropriate precautions are taken, small firms can satisfy the requirements of paragraph (d).

[4C] In order to prevent any lawyer in the firm from acquiring confidential information about the matter from the newly associated lawyer, it is essential that notification be given and screening procedures implemented promptly. If the matter requiring screening is already pending before the personally disqualified lawyer joins the firm, the procedures required by this Rule should be implemented before the lawyer joins the firm. If a newly associated lawyer joins a firm before a conflict requiring screening arises, the requirements of this Rule should be satisfied as soon as practicable after the conflict arises. If any lawyer in the firm acquires confidential information about the matter from the personally disqualified lawyer, the requirements of this Rule cannot be met, and any subsequent efforts to institute or maintain screening will not be effective in avoiding the firm's disqualification. Other factors may affect the likelihood that screening procedures will be effective in preventing the flow of confidential information between the personally disqualified lawyer and others in the firm in a given matter.

[5] Notice to the parties and any appropriate tribunal, including a description of the screened lawyer's prior representation and of the screening procedures employed, generally should be given as soon as practicable after the need for screening becomes apparent.

RULE 1.13: ORGANIZATION AS CLIENT

(a) **When a lawyer employed or retained by an organization is dealing with the organization's directors, officers, employees, members, shareholders or other constituents, and it appears that the organization's interests may differ from those of the constituents with whom the lawyer is dealing, the lawyer shall explain that the lawyer is the lawyer for the organization and not for any of the constituents.**

(b) **If a lawyer for an organization knows that an officer, employee or other person associated with the organization is engaged in action or intends to act or refuses to act in a matter related to the representation that (i) is a violation of a legal obligation to the organization or a violation of law that reasonably might be imputed to the organization, and (ii) is likely to result in substantial injury to the organization, then the lawyer shall proceed as is reasonably necessary in the best interest of the organization. In determining how to proceed, the lawyer shall give due consideration to the seriousness of the violation and its consequences, the scope and nature of the lawyer's representation, the responsibility in the organization and the apparent motivation of the person involved, the policies of the organization concerning such matters and any other relevant considerations. Any measures taken shall be designed to minimize disruption of the organization and the risk of revealing information relating to the representation to persons outside the organization. Such measures may include, among others:**

(1) **asking reconsideration of the matter;**

(2) **advising that a separate legal opinion on the matter be sought for presentation to an appropriate authority in the organization; and**

(3) **referring the matter to higher authority in the organization, including, if warranted by the seriousness of the matter, referral to the highest authority that can act in behalf of the organization as determined by applicable law.**

(c) If, despite the lawyer's efforts in accordance with paragraph **(b)**, the highest authority that can act on behalf of the organization insists upon action, or a refusal to act, that is clearly in violation of law and is likely to result in a substantial injury to the organization, the lawyer may reveal confidential information only if permitted by Rule 1.6, and may resign in accordance with Rule 1.16.

(d) A lawyer representing an organization may also represent any of its directors, officers, employees, members, shareholders or other constituents, subject to the provisions of Rule 1.7. If the organization's consent to the concurrent representation is required by Rule 1.7, the consent shall be given by an appropriate official of the organization other than the individual who is to be represented, or by the shareholders.

Comment

The Entity as the Client

[1] An organizational client is a legal entity, but it cannot act except through its officers, directors, employees, members, shareholders and other constituents. Officers, directors, employees and shareholders are the constituents of the corporate organizational client. The duties defined in this Rule apply equally to unincorporated associations. "Other constituents" as used in this Rule means the positions equivalent to officers, directors, employees, and shareholders held by persons acting for organizational clients that are not corporations.

[2] When one of the constituents of an organizational client communicates with the organization's lawyer in that person's organizational capacity, the communication is protected by Rule 1.6. Thus, for example, if an organizational client requests its lawyer to investigate allegations of wrongdoing, interviews between the lawyer and the client's employees or other constituents made in the course of that investigation are covered by Rule 1.6. This does not mean, however, that constituents of an organizational client are the clients of the lawyer. The lawyer may not disclose to such constituents information relating to the representation except for disclosures explicitly or impliedly authorized by the organizational client in order to carry out the representation or as otherwise permitted by Rule 1.6.

[2A] There are times when the organization's interests may differ from those of one or more of its constituents. In such circumstances, the lawyer should advise any constituent whose interest differs from that of the organization: (i) that a conflict or potential conflict of interest exists, (ii) that the lawyer does not represent the constituent in connection with the matter, unless the representation has been approved in accordance with Rule 1.13(d), (iii) that the constituent may wish to obtain independent representation, and (iv) that any attorney-client privilege that applies to discussions between the lawyer and the constituent belongs to the organization and may be waived by the organization. Care must be taken to ensure that the constituent understands that, when there is such adversity of interest, the lawyer for the organization cannot provide legal representation for that constituent, and that discussions between the lawyer for the organization and the constituent may not be privileged.

[2B]   Whether such a warning should be given by the lawyer for the organization to any constituent may turn on the facts of each case.

Acting in the Best Interest of the Organization

[3]   When constituents of the organization make decisions for it, the decisions ordinarily must be accepted by the lawyer, even if their utility or prudence is doubtful. Decisions concerning policy and operations, including ones entailing serious risk, are not as such in the lawyer's province. Paragraph (b) makes clear, however, that when the lawyer knows that the organization is likely to be substantially injured by action of an officer or other constituent that violates a legal obligation to the organization or is in violation of law that might be imputed to the organization, the lawyer must proceed as is reasonably necessary in the best interest of the organization. Under Rule 1.0(k), a lawyer's knowledge can be inferred from circumstances, and a lawyer cannot ignore the obvious. The terms "reasonable" and "reasonably" connote a range of conduct that will satisfy the requirements of Rule 1.13. In determining what is reasonable in the best interest of the organization, the circumstances at the time of determination are relevant. Such circumstances may include, among others, the lawyer's area of expertise, the time constraints under which the lawyer is acting, and the lawyer's previous experience and familiarity with the client.

[4]   In determining how to proceed under paragraph (b), the lawyer should give due consideration to the seriousness of the violation and its consequences, the scope and nature of the lawyer's representation, the responsibility within the organization and the apparent motivation of the person involved, the policies of the organization concerning such matters, and any other relevant considerations. Measures to be taken may include, among others, asking the constituent to reconsider the matter. For example, if the circumstances involve a constituent's innocent misunderstanding of law and subsequent acceptance of the lawyer's advice, the lawyer may reasonably conclude that the best interest of the organization does not require that the matter be referred to higher authority. If a constituent persists in conduct contrary to the lawyer's advice, it may be necessary for the lawyer to take steps to have the matter reviewed by a higher authority in the organization. If the matter is of sufficient seriousness and importance or urgency to the organization, referral to higher authority in the organization may be necessary even if the lawyer has not communicated with the constituent. Any measures taken should, to the extent practicable, minimize the risk of revealing information relating to the representation to persons outside the organization. Even in circumstances where a lawyer is not obligated by Rule 1.13 to proceed, a lawyer may bring to the attention of an organizational client, including its highest authority, matters that the lawyer reasonably

believes to be of sufficient importance to warrant doing so in the best interest of the organization. *See* Rule 1.4.

[5] The organization's highest authority to which a matter may be referred ordinarily will be the board of directors or similar governing body. However, applicable law may prescribe that under certain conditions the highest authority reposes elsewhere, for example, in the independent directors of a corporation.

Relation to Other Rules

[6] The authority and responsibility provided in this Rule are concurrent with the authority and responsibility provided in other Rules. In particular, this Rule does not limit or expand the lawyer's responsibility under Rule 1.6, Rule 1.8, Rule 1.16, Rule 3.3 or Rule 4.1. Rules 1.6(b)(2) and (b)(3) may permit the lawyer in some circumstances to disclose confidential information. In such circumstances Rule 1.2(d) may also be applicable, in which event withdrawal from the representation under Rule 1.16(b)(1) may be required.

[7] The authority of a lawyer to disclose information relating to a representation under Rule 1.6 does not apply with respect to information relating to a lawyer's engagement by an organization to investigate an alleged violation of law or to defend the organization or an officer, employee or other person associated with the organization against a claim arising out of an alleged past violation of law. Having a lawyer who cannot disclose confidential information concerning past acts relevant to the representation for which the lawyer was retained enables an organizational client to enjoy the full benefits of legal counsel in conducting an investigation or defending against a claim.

[8] A lawyer for an organization who reasonably believes that the lawyer's discharge was because of actions taken pursuant to paragraph (b), or who withdraws in circumstances that require or permit the lawyer to take action under paragraph (b), must proceed as "reasonably necessary in the best interest of the organization." Under some circumstances, the duty of communication under Rule 1.4 and the duty under Rule 1.16(e) to protect a client's interest upon termination of the representation, in conjunction with this Rule, may require the lawyer to inform the organization's highest authority of the lawyer's discharge or withdrawal, and of what the lawyer reasonably believes to be the basis for the discharge or withdrawal.

Government Agency

[9] The duties defined in this Rule apply to governmental organizations. Defining precisely the identity of the client and prescribing the resulting obligations of such lawyers may be more difficult in the government context. Although in some circumstances the client may be a specific agency, it may also be a branch of government, such as the executive branch, or the government as a whole. For example, if the action or failure to act involves the head of a bureau, either the department of which the bureau is a part or the relevant branch of government may be the client for purposes of this Rule. Defining or identifying the client of a lawyer representing a government

entity depends on applicable federal, state and local law and is a matter beyond the scope of these Rules. *See* Scope [9]. Moreover, in a matter involving the conduct of government officials, a government lawyer may have greater authority under applicable law to question such conduct than would a lawyer for a private organization in similar circumstances. Thus, when the client is a governmental organization, a different balance may be appropriate between maintaining confidentiality and assuring that the wrongful act is prevented or rectified. In addition, duties of lawyers employed by the government or lawyers in military service may be defined by statutes and regulation. This Rule does not limit that authority. *See* Scope [10].

[10]   *See* Comment [2A].

[11]   *See* Comment [2B].

Concurrent Representation

[12]   Paragraph (d) recognizes that a lawyer for an organization may also represent a principal officer or major shareholder, subject to the provisions of Rule 1.7. If the corporation's informed consent to such a concurrent representation is needed, the lawyer should advise the principal officer or major shareholder that any consent given on behalf of the corporation by the conflicted officer or shareholder may not be valid, and the lawyer should explain the potential consequences of an invalid consent.

Derivative Actions

[13]   Under generally prevailing law, the shareholders or members of a corporation may bring suit to compel the directors to perform their legal obligations in the supervision of the organization. Members of unincorporated associations have essentially the same right. Such an action may be brought nominally by the organization, but usually is, in fact, a legal controversy over management of the organization.

[14]   The question can arise whether counsel for the organization may defend such an action. The proposition that the organization is the lawyer's client does not alone resolve the issue. Most derivative actions are normal incidents of an organization's affairs, to be defended by the organization's lawyer like any other suits. However, if the claim involves serious charges of wrongdoing by those in control of the organization, a conflict may arise between the lawyer's duty to the organization and the lawyer's relationship with the board. In those circumstances, Rule 1.7 governs who should represent the directors and the organization.

RULE 1.14: CLIENT WITH DIMINISHED CAPACITY

(a) When a client's capacity to make adequately considered decisions in connection with a representation is diminished, whether because of minority, mental impairment or for some other reason, the lawyer shall, as far as reasonably possible, maintain a conventional relationship with the client.

(b) When the lawyer reasonably believes that the client has diminished capacity, is at risk of substantial physical, financial or other harm unless action is taken and cannot adequately act in the client's own interest, the lawyer may take reasonably necessary protective action, including consulting with individuals or entities that have the ability to take action to protect the client and, in appropriate cases, seeking the appointment of a guardian ad litem, conservator or guardian.

(c) Information relating to the representation of a client with diminished capacity is protected by Rule 1.6. When taking protective action pursuant to paragraph (b), the lawyer is impliedly authorized under Rule 1.6(a) to reveal information about the client, but only to the extent reasonably necessary to protect the client's interests.

Comment

[1] The responsibilities of a lawyer may vary according to the intelligence, experience, mental condition or age of a client, the obligation of a public officer, or the nature of a particular proceeding. The conventional client-lawyer relationship is based on the assumption that the client, when properly advised and assisted, is capable of making decisions about important matters. Any condition that renders a client incapable of communicating or making a considered judgment on the client's own behalf casts additional responsibilities upon the lawyer. When the client is a minor or suffers from a diminished mental capacity, maintaining the conventional client-lawyer relationship may not be possible in all respects. In particular, a severely incapacitated person may have no power to make legally binding decisions. Nevertheless, a client with diminished capacity often has the ability to understand, deliberate upon and reach conclusions about matters affecting the client's own well-being.

[2] The fact that a client suffers a disability does not diminish the lawyer's obligation to treat the client attentively and with respect.

[3] The client may wish to have family members or other persons participate in discussions with the lawyer. The lawyer should consider whether the presence of such persons will affect the attorney-client privilege. Nevertheless, the lawyer must keep the client's interests foremost and, except for protective action authorized under paragraph (b), must look to the client, and not family members, to make decisions on the client's behalf.

[4] If a legal representative has already been appointed for the client, the lawyer should ordinarily look to the representative for decisions on behalf of the client. In matters involving a minor, with or without a disability, the question whether the lawyer should look to the parents as natural guardians may depend on the type of proceeding or matter in which the lawyer is representing the minor. If the lawyer represents the guardian as distinct from the ward, and reasonably believes that the guardian is acting adversely to the

ward's interest, the lawyer may have an obligation to prevent or rectify the guardian's misconduct. *See* Rule 1.2(d).

Taking Protective Action

[5]   If a lawyer reasonably believes that a client is at risk of substantial physical, financial or other harm unless action is taken, and that a conventional client-lawyer relationship cannot be maintained as provided in paragraph (a) because the client lacks sufficient capacity to communicate or to make adequately considered decisions in connection with the representation, then paragraph (b) permits the lawyer to take reasonably necessary protective measures. Such measures could include: consulting with family members, using a reconsideration period to permit clarification or improvement of circumstances, using voluntary surrogate decision-making tools such as durable powers of attorney, or consulting with support groups, professional services, adult-protective agencies or other individuals or entities that have the ability to protect the client. In taking any protective action, the lawyer should be guided by such factors as the wishes and values of the client to the extent known, the client's best interest, and the goals of minimizing intrusion into the client's decision-making autonomy and maximizing respect for the client's family and social connections.

[6]   In determining the extent of the client's diminished capacity, the lawyer should consider and balance such factors as: (i) the client's ability to articulate reasoning leading to a decision, (ii) variability of state of mind and ability to appreciate consequences of a decision; the substantive fairness of a decision, and (iii) the consistency of a decision with the known long-term commitments and values of the client. In appropriate circumstances, the lawyer may seek guidance from an appropriate diagnostician.

[7]   If a legal representative has not been appointed, the lawyer should consider whether appointment of a guardian ad litem, conservator or guardian is necessary to protect the client's interests. Thus, if a client with diminished capacity has substantial property that should be sold for the client's benefit, effective completion of the transaction may require appointment of a legal representative. In addition, rules of procedure in litigation sometimes provide that a minor or a person with diminished capacity must be represented by a guardian or next friend if they do not have a general guardian. In many circumstances, however, appointment of a legal representative may be unnecessarily expensive or traumatic for the client. Seeking a guardian or conservator without the client's consent (including doing so over the client's objection) is appropriate only in the limited circumstances where a client's diminished capacity is such that the lawyer reasonably believes that no other practical method of protecting the client's interests is readily available. The lawyer should always consider less restrictive protective actions before seeking the appointment of a guardian or conservator. The lawyer should act as petitioner in such a proceeding only when no other person is available to do so.

[7A] Prior to withdrawing from the representation of a client whose capacity is in question, the lawyer should consider taking reasonable protective action. *See* Rule 1.16(e).

Disclosure of the Client's Condition

[8] Disclosure of the client's diminished capacity could adversely affect the client's interests. For example, raising the question of diminished capacity could, in some circumstances, lead to proceedings for involuntary commitment. Information relating to the representation is protected by Rule 1.6. Therefore, unless authorized to do so, the lawyer may not disclose such information. When taking protective action pursuant to paragraph (b), the lawyer is impliedly authorized to make the necessary disclosures, even when the client directs the lawyer to the contrary. Nevertheless, given the risks of disclosure, paragraph (c) limits what the lawyer may disclose in consulting with other individuals or entities or in seeking the appointment of a legal representative. At the very least, the lawyer should determine whether it is likely that the person or entity consulted will act adversely to the client's interests before discussing matters related to the client.

RULE 1.15: PRESERVING IDENTITY OF FUNDS AND PROPERTY OF OTHERS; FIDUCIARY RESPONSIBILITY; COMMINGLING AND MISAPPROPRIATION OF CLIENT FUNDS OR PROPERTY; MAINTENANCE OF BANK ACCOUNTS; RECORD KEEPING; EXAMINATION OF RECORDS

(a) Prohibition Against Commingling and Misappropriation of Client Funds or Property. A lawyer in possession of any funds or other property belonging to another person, where such possession is incident to his or her practice of law, is a fiduciary, and must not misappropriate such funds or property or commingle such funds or property with his or her own.

(b) Separate Accounts.

(1) A lawyer who is in possession of funds belonging to another person incident to the lawyer's practice of law shall maintain such funds in a banking institution within New York State that agrees to provide dishonored check reports in accordance with the provisions of 22 N.Y.C.R.R. Part 1300. "Banking institution" means a state or national bank, trust company, savings bank, savings and loan association or credit union. Such funds shall be maintained, in the lawyer's own name, or in the name of a firm of lawyers of which the lawyer is a member, or in the name of the lawyer or firm of lawyers by whom the lawyer is employed, in a special account or accounts, separate from any business or personal accounts of the lawyer or lawyer's firm, and separate from any accounts that the lawyer may maintain as executor, guardian, trustee or receiver, or in any other fiduciary

capacity; into such special account or accounts all funds held in escrow or otherwise entrusted to the lawyer or firm shall be deposited; provided, however, that such funds may be maintained in a banking institution located outside New York State if such banking institution complies with 22 N.Y.C.R.R. Part 1300 and the lawyer has obtained the prior written approval of the person to whom such funds belong specifying the name and address of the office or branch of the banking institution where such funds are to be maintained.

(2) A lawyer or the lawyer's firm shall identify the special bank account or accounts required by Rule 1.15(b)(1) as an "Attorney Special Account," or "Attorney Trust Account," or "Attorney Escrow Account," and shall obtain checks and deposit slips that bear such title. Such title may be accompanied by such other descriptive language as the lawyer may deem appropriate, provided that such additional language distinguishes such special account or accounts from other bank accounts that are maintained by the lawyer or the lawyer's firm.

(3) Funds reasonably sufficient to maintain the account or to pay account charges may be deposited therein.

(4) Funds belonging in part to a client or third person and in part currently or potentially to the lawyer or law firm shall be kept in such special account or accounts, but the portion belonging to the lawyer or law firm may be withdrawn when due unless the right of the lawyer or law firm to receive it is disputed by the client or third person, in which event the disputed portion shall not be withdrawn until the dispute is finally resolved.

(c) Notification of Receipt of Property; Safekeeping; Rendering Accounts; Payment or Delivery of Property. A lawyer shall:

(1) promptly notify a client or third person of the receipt of funds, securities, or other properties in which the client or third person has an interest;

(2) identify and label securities and properties of a client or third person promptly upon receipt and place them in a safe deposit box or other place of safekeeping as soon as practicable;

(3) maintain complete records of all funds, securities, and other properties of a client or third person coming into the possession of the lawyer and render appropriate accounts to the client or third person regarding them; and

(4) promptly pay or deliver to the client or third person as requested by the client or third person the funds, securities, or other properties in the possession of the lawyer that the client or third person is entitled to receive.

(d) Required Bookkeeping Records.

(1) A lawyer shall maintain for seven years after the events that they record:

(i) the records of all deposits in and withdrawals from the accounts specified in Rule 1.15(b) and of any other bank account that concerns or affects the lawyer's practice of law; these records shall specifically identify the date, source and description of each item deposited, as well as the date, payee and purpose of each withdrawal or disbursement;

(ii) a record for special accounts, showing the source of all funds deposited in such accounts, the names of all persons for whom the funds are or were held, the amount of such funds, the description and amounts, and the names of all persons to whom such funds were disbursed;

(iii) copies of all retainer and compensation agreements with clients;

(iv) copies of all statements to clients or other persons showing the disbursement of funds to them or on their behalf;

(v) copies of all bills rendered to clients;

(vi) copies of all records showing payments to lawyers, investigators or other persons, not in the lawyer's regular employ, for services rendered or performed;

(vii) copies of all retainer and closing statements filed with the Office of Court Administration; and

(viii) all checkbooks and check stubs, bank statements, prenumbered canceled checks and duplicate deposit slips.

(2) Lawyers shall make accurate entries of all financial transactions in their records of receipts and disbursements, in their special accounts, in their ledger books or similar records, and in any other books of account kept by them in the regular course of their practice, which entries shall be made at or near the time of the act, condition or event recorded.

(3) For purposes of Rule 1.15(d), a lawyer may satisfy the requirements of maintaining "copies" by maintaining any of the following items: original records, photocopies, microfilm, optical imaging, and any other medium that preserves an image of the document that cannot be altered without detection.

(e) Authorized Signatories. All special account withdrawals shall be made only to a named payee and not to cash. Such withdrawals shall be made by check or, with the prior written approval of the party entitled to the proceeds, by bank transfer. Only a lawyer admitted to practice law in New York State shall be an authorized signatory of a special account.

(f) Missing Clients. Whenever any sum of money is payable to a client and the lawyer is unable to locate the client, the lawyer shall apply to the court in which the action was brought if in the unified court system, or, if no action was commenced in the unified court system, to the Supreme Court in the county in which the lawyer maintains an office for the practice of law, for an order directing payment to the lawyer of any fees and disbursements that are owed by the client and the balance, if any, to the Lawyers' Fund for Client Protection for safeguarding and disbursement to persons who are entitled thereto.

(g) Designation of Successor Signatories.

(1) Upon the death of a lawyer who was the sole signatory on an attorney trust, escrow or special account, an application may be made to the Supreme Court for an order designating a successor signatory for such trust, escrow or special account, who shall be a member of the bar in good standing and admitted to the practice of law in New York State.

(2) An application to designate a successor signatory shall be made to the Supreme Court in the judicial district in which the deceased lawyer maintained an office for the practice of law. The application may be made by the legal representative of the deceased lawyer's estate; a lawyer who was affiliated with the deceased lawyer in the practice of law; any person who has a beneficial interest in such trust, escrow or special account; an officer of a city or county bar association; or counsel for an attorney disciplinary committee. No lawyer may charge a legal fee for assisting with an application to designate a successor signatory pursuant to this Rule.

(3) The Supreme Court may designate a successor signatory and may direct the safeguarding of funds from such trust, escrow or special account, and the disbursement of such funds to persons who are entitled thereto, and may order that funds in such account be deposited with the Lawyers' Fund for Client Protection for safeguarding and disbursement to persons who are entitled thereto.

(h) Dissolution of a Firm. Upon the dissolution of any firm of lawyers, the former partners or members shall make appropriate arrangements for the maintenance, by one of them or by a successor firm, of the records specified in Rule 1.15(d).

(i) Availability of Bookkeeping Records: Records Subject to Production in Disciplinary Investigations and Proceedings. The financial records required by this Rule shall be located, or made available, at the principal New York State office of the lawyers subject hereto, and any such records shall be produced in response to a notice or subpoena duces tecum issued in connection with a complaint before or any investigation by the appropriate grievance or departmental disciplinary committee, or shall be produced at the direction of the appropriate Appellate Division before any person designated by it. All books and records produced pursuant to this Rule shall be kept confidential, except for the purpose of the particular proceeding, and their contents shall not be disclosed by anyone in violation of the attorney-client privilege.

(j) Disciplinary Action. A lawyer who does not maintain and keep the accounts and records as specified and required by this Rule, or who does not produce any such records pursuant to this Rule, shall be deemed in violation of these Rules and shall be subject to disciplinary proceedings.

Comment

[1]   A lawyer should hold the funds and property of others using the care required of a professional fiduciary. Securities and other property should be kept in a safe deposit box, except when some other form of safekeeping is warranted by special circumstances. All property that is the property of clients or third persons, including prospective clients, must be kept separate from the lawyer's business and personal property and, if monies, in one or more trust accounts, including an account established pursuant to the "Interest on Lawyer Accounts" law where appropriate. *See* State Finance Law § 97–v(4)(a); Judiciary Law § 497(2); 21 N.Y.C.R.R. § 7000.10. Separate trust accounts may be warranted or required when administering estate monies or acting in similar fiduciary capacities.

[2]   While normally it is impermissible to commingle the lawyer's own funds with client funds, paragraph (b)(3) provides that it is permissible when necessary to pay bank service charges on that account. Accurate records must be kept regarding which portion of the funds belongs to the lawyer.

[3]   Lawyers often receive funds from which the lawyer's fee will be paid. The lawyer is not required to remit to the client funds that the lawyer reasonably believes represent fees owed. However, a lawyer may not hold undisputed funds to coerce a client into accepting the lawyer's contention. Furthermore, the disputed portion of the funds must be kept in or transferred into a trust account, and the lawyer should suggest means for prompt resolution of the dispute, such as arbitration. Notice to the client of the right to arbitrate fee disputes is required in some circumstances. The undisputed portion of the funds is to be distributed promptly.

[4]   When in the course of representation a lawyer is in possession of funds in which two or more persons (other than the lawyer) claim interests, the funds should be kept separate by the lawyer until the dispute is resolved, by agreement of the parties or court order or commencement by the lawyer of an interpleader action and deposit of the property into court. The lawyer should distribute promptly all portions of the funds as to which the interests are not in dispute.

[5]   The obligations of a lawyer under this Rule are independent of those arising from activity other than rendering legal services. For example, a lawyer who serves only as an escrow agent is governed by the applicable law relating to fiduciaries even though the lawyer does not render legal services in the transaction and is not governed by this Rule.

RULE 1.16: DECLINING OR TERMINATING REPRESENTATION

(a) A lawyer shall not accept employment on behalf of a person if the lawyer knows or reasonably should know that such person wishes to:

(1) bring a legal action, conduct a defense, or assert a position in a matter, or otherwise have steps taken for such person, merely for the purpose of harassing or maliciously injuring any person; or

(2) present a claim or defense in a matter that is not warranted under existing law, unless it can be supported by a good faith argument for an extension, modification, or reversal of existing law.

(b) Except as stated in paragraph (d), a lawyer shall withdraw from the representation of a client when:

(1) the lawyer knows or reasonably should know that the representation will result in a violation of these Rules or of law;

(2) the lawyer's physical or mental condition materially impairs the lawyer's ability to represent the client;

(3) the lawyer is discharged; or

(4) the lawyer knows or reasonably should know that the client is bringing the legal action, conducting the defense, or asserting a position in the matter, or is otherwise having steps taken, merely for the purpose of harassing or maliciously injuring any person.

(c) Except as stated in paragraph (d), a lawyer may withdraw from representing a client when:

(1) withdrawal can be accomplished without material adverse effect on the interests of the client;

(2) the client persists in a course of action involving the lawyer's services that the lawyer reasonably believes is criminal or fraudulent;

(3) the client has used the lawyer's services to perpetrate a crime or fraud;

(4) the client insists upon taking action with which the lawyer has a fundamental disagreement;

(5) the client deliberately disregards an agreement or obligation to the lawyer as to expenses or fees;

(6) the client insists upon presenting a claim or defense that is not warranted under existing law and cannot be supported by good faith argument for an extension, modification, or reversal of existing law;

(7) the client fails to cooperate in the representation or otherwise renders the representation unreasonably difficult for the lawyer to carry out employment effectively;

(8) the lawyer's inability to work with co-counsel indicates that the best interest of the client likely will be served by withdrawal;

(9) the lawyer's mental or physical condition renders it difficult for the lawyer to carry out the representation effectively;

(10) the client knowingly and freely assents to termination of the employment;

(11) withdrawal is permitted under Rule 1.13(c) or other law;

(12) the lawyer believes in good faith, in a matter pending before a tribunal, that the tribunal will find the existence of other good cause for withdrawal; or

(13) the client insists that the lawyer pursue a course of conduct which is illegal or prohibited under these Rules.

(d) If permission for withdrawal from employment is required by the rules of a tribunal, a lawyer shall not withdraw from employment in a matter before that tribunal without its permission. When ordered to do so by a tribunal, a lawyer shall continue representation notwithstanding good cause for terminating the representation.

(e) Even when withdrawal is otherwise permitted or required, upon termination of representation, a lawyer shall take steps, to the extent reasonably practicable, to avoid foreseeable prejudice to the rights of the client, including giving reasonable notice to the client, allowing time for employment of other counsel, delivering to the client all papers and property to which the client is entitled, promptly refunding any part of a fee paid in advance that has not been earned and complying with applicable laws and rules.

Comment

[1] A lawyer should not accept representation in a matter unless it can be performed competently, promptly, without improper conflict of interest and to completion. Ordinarily, a representation in a matter is completed when the agreed-upon assistance has been concluded. *See* Rules 1.2(c), 6.5; *see also* Rule 1.3, Comment [4].

Mandatory Withdrawal

[2]   A lawyer ordinarily must decline or withdraw from representation under paragraph (a), (b)(1) or (b)(4), as the case may be, if the client demands that the lawyer engage in conduct that is illegal or that violates these Rules or other law. The lawyer is not obliged to decline or withdraw simply because the client suggests such a course of conduct; a client may make such a suggestion in the hope that a lawyer will not be constrained by a professional obligation.

[3]   Court approval or notice to the court is often required by applicable law, and when so required by applicable law is also required by paragraph (d), before a lawyer withdraws from pending litigation. Difficulty may be encountered if withdrawal is based on the client's demand that the lawyer engage in unprofessional conduct. The court may request an explanation for the withdrawal, while the lawyer may be bound to keep confidential the facts that would constitute such an explanation. The lawyer's statement that professional considerations require termination of the representation ordinarily should be accepted as sufficient. Lawyers should be mindful of their obligations to both clients and the court under Rule 1.6 and Rule 3.3.

Discharge

[4]   As provided in paragraph (b)(3), a client has a right to discharge a lawyer at any time, with or without cause, subject to liability for payment for the lawyer's services. Where future dispute about the withdrawal may be anticipated, it may be advisable to prepare a written statement reciting the circumstances.

[5]   Whether a client can discharge appointed counsel may depend on applicable law. A client seeking to do so should be given a full explanation of the consequences. These consequences may include a decision by the appointing authority that appointment of successor counsel is unjustified, thus requiring self-representation by the client.

[6]   If the client has severely diminished capacity, the client may lack the legal capacity to discharge the lawyer, and in any event the discharge may be seriously adverse to the client's interests. The lawyer should make special effort to help the client consider the consequences and may take reasonably necessary protective action as provided in Rule 1.14(b).

Optional Withdrawal

[7]   Under paragraph (c), a lawyer may withdraw from representation in some circumstances. The lawyer has the option to withdraw if withdrawal can be accomplished without material adverse effect on the client's interests. Withdrawal is also justified if the client persists in a course of action that the lawyer reasonably believes is criminal or fraudulent, for a lawyer is not required to be associated with such conduct even if the lawyer does not further it. Withdrawal is also permitted if the lawyer's services were misused in the past, even if withdrawal would materially prejudice the client. The

lawyer may also withdraw where the client insists on taking action with which the lawyer has a fundamental disagreement.

[7A] In accordance with paragraph (c)(4), a lawyer should use reasonable foresight in determining whether a proposed representation will involve client objectives or instructions with which the lawyer has a fundamental disagreement. A client's intended action does not create a fundamental disagreement simply because the lawyer disagrees with it. *See* Rule 1.2 regarding the allocation of responsibility between client and lawyer. The client has the right, for example, to accept or reject a settlement proposal; a client's decision on settlement involves a fundamental disagreement only when no reasonable person in the client's position, having regard for the hazards of litigation, would have declined the settlement. In addition, the client should be given notice of intent to withdraw and an opportunity to reconsider.

[8] Under paragraph (c)(5), a lawyer may withdraw if the client refuses to abide by the terms of an agreement concerning fees or court costs (or other expenses or disbursements).

[8A] Continuing to represent a client may impose an unreasonable burden unexpected by the client and lawyer at the outset of the representation. However, lawyers are ordinarily better suited than clients to foresee and provide for the burdens of representation. The burdens of uncertainty should therefore ordinarily fall on lawyers rather than clients unless they are attributable to client misconduct. That a representation will require more work or significantly larger advances of expenses than the lawyer contemplated when the fee was fixed is not grounds for withdrawal under paragraph (c)(5).

Assisting the Client upon Withdrawal

[9] Even if the lawyer has been unfairly discharged by the client, under paragraph (c) a lawyer must take all reasonable steps to mitigate the consequences to the client. The lawyer may retain papers as security for a fee only to the extent permitted by law. *See* Rule 1.15.

RULE 1.17: SALE OF LAW PRACTICE

(a) A lawyer retiring from a private practice of law; a law firm, one or more members of which are retiring from the private practice of law with the firm; or the personal representative of a deceased, disabled or missing lawyer, may sell a law practice, including goodwill, to one or more lawyers or law firms, who may purchase the practice. The seller and the buyer may agree on reasonable restrictions on the seller's private practice of law, notwithstanding any other provision of these Rules. Retirement shall include the cessation of the private practice of law in the geographic area, that is, the county and city and any county or city contiguous thereto, in which the practice to be sold has been conducted.

(b) Confidential information.

(1) With respect to each matter subject to the contemplated sale, the seller may provide prospective buyers with any information not protected as confidential information under Rule 1.6.

(2) Notwithstanding Rule 1.6, the seller may provide the prospective buyer with information as to individual clients:

(i) concerning the identity of the client, except as provided in paragraph (b)(6);

(ii) concerning the status and general nature of the matter;

(iii) available in public court files; and

(iv) concerning the financial terms of the client-lawyer relationship and the payment status of the client's account.

(3) Prior to making any disclosure of confidential information that may be permitted under paragraph (b)(2), the seller shall provide the prospective buyer with information regarding the matters involved in the proposed sale sufficient to enable the prospective buyer to determine whether any conflicts of interest exist. Where sufficient information cannot be disclosed without revealing client confidential information, the seller may make the disclosures necessary for the prospective buyer to determine whether any conflict of interest exists, subject to paragraph (b)(6). If the prospective buyer determines that conflicts of interest exist prior to reviewing the information, or determines during the course of review that a conflict of interest exists, the prospective buyer shall not review or continue to review the information unless the seller shall have obtained the consent of the client in accordance with Rule 1.6(a)(1).

(4) Prospective buyers shall maintain the confidentiality of and shall not use any client information received in connection with the proposed sale in the same manner and to the same extent as if the prospective buyers represented the client.

(5) Absent the consent of the client after full disclosure, a seller shall not provide a prospective buyer with information if doing so would cause a violation of the attorney-client privilege.

(6) If the seller has reason to believe that the identity of the client or the fact of the representation itself constitutes confidential information in the circumstances, the seller may not provide such information to a prospective buyer without first advising the client of the identity of the prospective buyer and obtaining the client's consent to the proposed disclosure.

(c) Written notice of the sale shall be given jointly by the seller and the buyer to each of the seller's clients and shall include information regarding:

(1) the client's right to retain other counsel or to take possession of the file;

(2) the fact that the client's consent to the transfer of the client's file or matter to the buyer will be presumed if the client does not take any action or otherwise object within 90 days of the sending of the notice, subject to any court rule or statute requiring express approval by the client or a court;

(3) the fact that agreements between the seller and the seller's clients as to fees will be honored by the buyer;

(4) proposed fee increases, if any, permitted under paragraph (e); and

(5) the identity and background of the buyer or buyers, including principal office address, bar admissions, number of years in practice in New York State, whether the buyer has ever been disciplined for professional misconduct or convicted of a crime, and whether the buyer currently intends to resell the practice.

(d) When the buyer's representation of a client of the seller would give rise to a waivable conflict of interest, the buyer shall not undertake such representation unless the necessary waiver or waivers have been obtained in writing.

(e) The fee charged a client by the buyer shall not be increased by reason of the sale, unless permitted by a retainer agreement with the client or otherwise specifically agreed to by the client.

Comment

[1]   The practice of law is a profession, not merely a business. Clients are not commodities that can be purchased and sold at will. Pursuant to this Rule, when a lawyer or an entire firm ceases to practice, and other lawyers or firms take over the representation, the selling lawyer or firm may obtain compensation for the reasonable value of the practice, as may withdrawing partners of law firms.

Termination of Practice by Seller

[2]   The requirement that all of the private practice be sold is satisfied if the seller in good faith makes the entire practice available for sale to the buyers. The fact that a number of the seller's clients decide not to be represented by the buyers but take their matters elsewhere, therefore, does not result in a violation. Return to private practice as a result of an unanticipated change in circumstances does not necessarily result in a violation. For example, a lawyer who has sold the practice to accept an appointment to judicial office does not violate the requirement that the sale be

attendant to cessation of practice if the lawyer later resumes private practice upon being defeated in a contested or a retention election for the office or resigns from a judiciary position. Although the requirements of this Rule may not be violated in these situations, contractual provisions in the agreement governing the sale of the practice may contain reasonable restrictions on a lawyer's resuming private practice. *See* Rule 5.6, Comment [1], regarding restrictions on right to practice.

[3]   The private practice of law refers to a private law firm or lawyer, not to a public agency, legal services entity, or in-house counsel to a business. The requirement that the seller cease to engage in the private practice of law therefore does not prohibit employment as a lawyer on the staff of a public agency or a legal services entity that provides legal services to the poor, or as in-house counsel to a business.

[4]   The Rule permits a sale of an entire practice attendant upon retirement from the private practice of law within a geographic area, defined as the county and city and any county or city contiguous thereto, in which the practice to be sold has been conducted. Its provisions therefore accommodate the lawyer who sells the practice on the occasion of moving to another city and county that does not border on the city or county within New York State.

[5]   [Omitted.]

Sale of Entire Practice

[6]   The Rule requires that the seller's entire practice be sold. The prohibition against sale of less than an entire practice protects those clients whose matters are less lucrative and who might find it difficult to secure other counsel if a sale could be limited to substantial fee-generating matters. The buyers are required to undertake all client matters in the practice, subject to client consent. This requirement is not violated even if a buyer is unable to undertake a particular client matter because of a conflict of interest and the seller therefore remains as attorney of record for the matter in question.

Client Confidences, Consent and Notice

[7]   Giving the buyer access to client-specific information relating to the representation and to the file requires client consent. Rule 1.17 provides that before such information can be disclosed by the seller to the buyer, the client must be given actual written notice of the contemplated sale, including the identity of the buyer, and must be told that the decision to consent or make other arrangements must be made within 90 days. If nothing is heard from the client within that time, consent to the sale is presumed under paragraph (c)(2).

[8]   A lawyer or law firm ceasing to practice cannot be required to remain in practice because some clients cannot be given actual notice of the proposed purchase. The selling lawyer must make a good-faith effort to notify all of the lawyer's current clients. Where clients cannot be given actual notice

and therefore cannot themselves consent to the purchase or direct any other disposition of their files, they are nevertheless protected by the fact that the buyer has the duty to maintain their confidences under paragraph (b)(4).

[9]   All elements of client autonomy, including the client's absolute right to discharge a lawyer and transfer the representation to another, survive the sale of the practice.

Fee Arrangements Between Client and Buyer

[10]   The sale may not be financed by increases in fees charged to the clients of the purchased practice except to the extent permitted by subparagraph (e) of this Rule. Under subparagraph (e), the buyer must honor existing arrangements between the seller and the client as to fees unless the seller's retainer agreement with the client permits a fee increase or the buyer obtains a client's specific agreement to a fee increase in compliance with the strict standards of Rule 1.8(a) (governing business transactions between lawyers and clients).

Other Applicable Ethical Standards

[11]   Lawyers participating in the sale or purchase of a law practice are subject to the ethical standards applicable to involving another lawyer in the representation of a client. Examples include (i) the seller's obligation to exercise competence in identifying a buyer qualified to assume the practice and the buyer's obligation to undertake the representation competently under Rule 1.1, (ii) the obligation of the seller and the buyer to avoid disqualifying conflicts, and to secure the client's informed consent for those conflicts that can be agreed to under Rule 1.7, and (iii) the obligation of the seller and the buyer to protect information relating to the representation under Rule 1.6 and Rule 1.9. *See also* Rule 1.0(j) for the definition of "informed consent."

[12]   If approval of the substitution of the purchasing lawyer for the selling lawyer is required by the rules of any tribunal in which a matter is pending, such approval must be obtained before the matter can be included in the sale. *See* Rule 1.16. If a tribunal refuses to give its permission for the substitution and the seller therefore must continue in the matter, the seller does not thereby violate the portion of this Rule requiring the seller to cease practice in the described geographic area.

Applicability of the Rule

[13]   [Omitted.]

[14]   This Rule does not apply to: (i) admission to or retirement from a law partnership or professional association, (ii) retirement plans and similar arrangements, (iii) a sale of tangible assets of a law practice, or (iv) the transfers of legal representation between lawyers when such transfers are unrelated to the sale of a practice. This Rule governs the sale of an entire law practice upon retirement, which is defined in paragraph (a) as the cessation of the private practice of law in a given geographic area. Rule 5.4(a)(2) provides

for the compensation of a lawyer who undertakes to complete one or more unfinished pieces of legal business of a deceased lawyer.

RULE 1.18: DUTIES TO PROSPECTIVE CLIENTS

(a) A person who discusses with a lawyer the possibility of forming a client-lawyer relationship with respect to a matter is a "prospective client."

(b) Even when no client-lawyer relationship ensues, a lawyer who has had discussions with a prospective client shall not use or reveal information learned in the consultation, except as Rule 1.9 would permit with respect to information of a former client.

(c) A lawyer subject to paragraph (b) shall not represent a client with interests materially adverse to those of a prospective client in the same or a substantially related matter if the lawyer received information from the prospective client that could be significantly harmful to that person in the matter, except as provided in paragraph (d). If a lawyer is disqualified from representation under this paragraph, no lawyer in a firm with which that lawyer is associated may knowingly undertake or continue representation in such a matter, except as provided in paragraph (d).

(d) When the lawyer has received disqualifying information as defined in paragraph (c), representation is permissible if:

(1) both the affected client and the prospective client have given informed consent, confirmed in writing; or

(2) the lawyer who received the information took reasonable measures to avoid exposure to more disqualifying information than was reasonably necessary to determine whether to represent the prospective client; and

(i) the firm acts promptly and reasonably to notify, as appropriate, lawyers and nonlawyer personnel within the firm that the personally disqualified lawyer is prohibited from participating in the representation of the current client;

(ii) the firm implements effective screening procedures to prevent the flow of information about the matter between the disqualified lawyer and the others in the firm;

(iii) the disqualified lawyer is apportioned no part of the fee therefrom; and

(iv) written notice is promptly given to the prospective client; and

(3) a reasonable lawyer would conclude that the law firm will be able to provide competent and diligent representation in the matter.

(e) A person who:

(1) communicates information unilaterally to a lawyer, without any reasonable expectation that the lawyer is willing to discuss the possibility of forming a client-lawyer relationship; or

(2) communicates with a lawyer for the purpose of disqualifying the lawyer from handling a materially adverse representation on the same or a substantially related matter, is not a prospective client with the meaning of paragraph (a).

Comment

[1] Prospective clients, like current clients, may disclose information to a lawyer, place documents or other property in the lawyer's custody, or rely on the lawyer's advice. A lawyer's discussions with a prospective client usually are limited in time and depth and leave both the prospective client and the lawyer free (and sometimes required) to proceed no further. Prospective clients should therefore receive some, but not all, of the protection afforded clients.

[2] Not all persons who communicate information to a lawyer are entitled to protection under this Rule. As provided in paragraph (e), a person who communicates information unilaterally to a lawyer, without any reasonable expectation that the lawyer is willing to discuss the possibility of forming a client-lawyer relationship, is not a "prospective client" within the meaning of paragraph (a). Similarly, a person who communicates with a lawyer for the purpose of disqualifying the lawyer from handling a materially adverse representation on the same or a substantially related matter is not entitled to the protection of this Rule. A lawyer may not encourage or induce a person to communicate with a lawyer or lawyers for that improper purpose. *See* Rules 3.1(b)(2), 4.4, 8.4(a).

[3] It is often necessary for a prospective client to reveal information to the lawyer during an initial consultation prior to the decision about formation of a client-lawyer relationship. The lawyer often must learn such information to determine whether there is a conflict of interest with an existing client and whether the matter is one that the lawyer is willing to undertake. Paragraph (b) prohibits the lawyer from using or revealing that information, except as permitted by Rule 1.9, even if the client or lawyer decides not to proceed with the representation. The duty exists regardless of how brief the initial conference may be.

[4] In order to avoid acquiring disqualifying information from a prospective client, a lawyer considering whether to undertake a new matter should limit the initial interview to only such information as reasonably appears necessary for that purpose. Where the information indicates that a conflict of interest or other reason for nonrepresentation exists, the lawyer should so inform the prospective client or decline the representation. If the prospective client wishes to retain the lawyer, and if consent is possible under Rule 1.7 or Rule 1.9, then consent from all affected current or former clients must be

obtained before accepting the representation. The representation must be declined if the lawyer will be unable to provide competent, diligent and adequate representation to the affected current and former clients and the prospective client.

[5]   A lawyer may condition conversations with a prospective client on the person's informed consent that no information disclosed during the consultation will prohibit the lawyer from representing a different client in the matter. *See* Rule 1.0(j) for the definition of "informed consent." If the agreement expressly so provides, the prospective client may also consent to the lawyer's subsequent use of information received from the prospective client.

[6]   Under paragraph (c), even in the absence of an agreement the lawyer is not prohibited from representing a client with interests adverse to those of the prospective client in the same or a substantially related matter unless the lawyer has received from the prospective client information that could be significantly harmful if used in that matter.

[7]   Under paragraph (c), the prohibition in this Rule is imputed to other lawyers as provided in Rule 1.10, but, under paragraph (d)(1), imputation may be avoided if the lawyer obtains the informed consent, confirmed in writing, of both the prospective and affected clients. In the alternative, imputation may be avoided if the conditions of paragraph (d)(2) are met and all disqualified lawyers are timely screened, and written notice is promptly given to the prospective client. *See* Rule 1.10. Paragraph (d)(2)(i) does not prohibit the screened lawyer from receiving a salary or partnership share established by prior independent agreement, but that lawyer may not receive compensation directly related to the matter in which the lawyer is disqualified.

[7A]   Paragraph (d)(2) sets out the basic procedural requirements that a law firm must satisfy to ensure that a personally disqualified lawyer is effectively screened from participation in the matter. This Rule requires that the firm promptly: (i) notify, as appropriate, lawyers and relevant nonlawyer personnel within the firm that the personally disqualified lawyer is prohibited from participating in the representation of the current client, and (ii) implement effective screening procedures to prevent the flow of information about the matter between the personally disqualified lawyer and others in the firm.

[7B]   A firm seeking to avoid disqualification under this Rule should also consider its ability to implement, maintain, and monitor the screening procedures permitted by paragraph (d)(2) before undertaking or continuing the representation. In deciding whether the screening procedures permitted by this Rule will be effective to avoid imputed disqualification, a firm should consider a number of factors, including how the size, practices and organization of the firm will affect the likelihood that any confidential information acquired about the matter by the personally disqualified lawyer can be protected. If the firm is large and is organized into separate departments, or maintains offices in multiple locations, or for any reason the structure of the firm facilitates preventing the sharing of information with lawyers not participating in the particular matter, it is more likely that the requirements of this Rule can be met and imputed disqualification avoided. Although a large firm will find it easier to maintain effective screening, lack of timeliness in instituting, or lack of vigilance in maintaining, the procedures required by this Rule may make those procedures ineffective in avoiding imputed disqualification. If a personally disqualified lawyer is working on other matters with lawyers who are participating in a matter requiring screening, it may be impossible to maintain effective screening procedures. The size of the firm may be considered as one of the factors affecting the firm's ability to institute and maintain effective screening procedures, but it is not a dispositive factor. A small firm may need to exercise special care and vigilance to maintain effective screening but, if appropriate precautions are taken, small firms can satisfy the requirements of paragraph (d)(2).

[7C]   In order to prevent any other lawyer in the firm from acquiring confidential information about the matter from the disqualified lawyer, it is essential that notification be given and screening procedures implemented promptly. If any lawyer in the firm acquires confidential information about the matter from the disqualified lawyer, the requirements of this Rule cannot be met, and any subsequent efforts to institute or maintain screening will not be effective in avoiding the firm's disqualification. Other factors may affect the likelihood that screening procedures will be effective in preventing the flow of confidential information between the disqualified lawyer and other lawyers in the firm in a given matter.

[8]   Notice under paragraph (d)(2), including a general description of the subject matter about which the lawyer was consulted and of the screening procedures employed, generally should be given as soon as practicable after the need for screening becomes apparent.

[9]   For the duty of competence of a lawyer who gives assistance on the merits of a matter to a prospective client, *see* Rule 1.1. For a lawyer's duties when a prospective client entrusts valuables or papers to the lawyer's care, *see* Rule 1.15.

RULE 2.1: ADVISOR

In representing a client, a lawyer shall exercise professional judgment and render candid advice. In rendering advice, a lawyer may refer not only to law but to other considerations such as moral, economic, social, psychological, and political factors that may be relevant to the client's situation.

Comment

Scope of Advice

[1]   When acting as an advisor, a lawyer must be mindful that a client is entitled to straightforward advice expressing the lawyer's honest assessment. Legal advice often involves unpleasant facts and alternatives that a client may

be disinclined to confront. In presenting advice, a lawyer endeavors to sustain the client's morale and may put advice in as acceptable a form as honesty permits. Nevertheless, a lawyer should not be deterred from giving candid advice by the prospect that the advice will be unpalatable to the client.

[2]   Advice couched in narrow legal terms may be of little value to a client, especially where practical considerations, such as cost or effects on other people, are predominant. Purely technical legal advice, therefore, can sometimes be inadequate. It is proper for a lawyer to refer to relevant moral and ethical considerations in giving advice. Although a lawyer is not a moral advisor as such, moral and ethical considerations impinge upon most legal questions and may decisively influence how the law will be applied.

[3]   A client may expressly or impliedly ask the lawyer for purely technical advice. When such a request is made by a client experienced in legal matters, the lawyer may accept it at face value. When such a request is made by a client inexperienced in legal matters, however, the lawyer's responsibilities as advisor may include the responsibility to indicate that more may be involved than strictly legal considerations. For the allocation of responsibility in decision making between lawyer and client, *see* Rule 1.2.

[4]   Matters that go beyond strictly legal questions may also be in the domain of another profession. Family matters can involve problems within the professional competence of psychiatry, clinical psychology or social work; business matters can involve problems within the competence of the accounting profession or of financial or public relations specialists. Where consultation with a professional in another field is itself something a competent lawyer would recommend, the lawyer shall make such a recommendation. At the same time, a lawyer's advice at its best often consists of recommending a course of action in the face of conflicting recommendations of experts.

Offering Advice

[5]   In general, a lawyer is not expected to give advice until asked by the client. However, when a lawyer knows that a client proposes a course of action that is likely to result in substantial adverse legal consequences to the client, the lawyer's duty to the client under Rule 1.4 may require that the lawyer offer advice if the client's course of action is related to the representation. Similarly, when a matter is likely to involve litigation, it may be advisable under Rule 1.4 to inform the client of forms of dispute resolution that might constitute reasonable alternatives to litigation. A lawyer ordinarily has no duty to initiate investigation of a client's affairs or to give advice that the client has indicated is unwanted, but a lawyer may initiate advice to a client when doing so appears to be in the client's interest.

RULE 2.2: [RESERVED]

RULE 2.3: EVALUATION FOR USE BY THIRD PERSONS

   (a) A lawyer may provide an evaluation of a matter affecting a client for the use of someone other than the client if the lawyer

reasonably believes that making the evaluation is compatible with other aspects of the lawyer's relationship with the client.

(b) When the lawyer knows or reasonably should know that the evaluation is likely to affect the client's interests materially and adversely, the lawyer shall not provide the evaluation unless the client gives informed consent.

(c) Unless disclosure is authorized in connection with a report of an evaluation, information relating to the evaluation is protected by Rule 1.6.

Comment

Definition

[1] An evaluation may be performed at the client's direction or when impliedly authorized in order to carry out the representation. *See* Rule 1.2. Such an evaluation may be for the primary purpose of establishing information for the benefit of third parties: for example, an opinion concerning the title of property rendered at the behest of a vendor for the information of a prospective purchaser, or at the behest of a borrower for the information of a prospective lender. In some situations, the evaluation may be required by a government agency: for example, an opinion concerning the legality of securities registered for sale under the securities laws. In other instances, the evaluation may be required by a third person, such as a purchaser of a business, or of intellectual property or a similar asset.

[2] A legal evaluation should be distinguished from an investigation of a person with whom the lawyer does not have a client-lawyer relationship. For example, a lawyer retained by a purchaser to analyze a vendor's title to property does not have a client-lawyer relationship with the vendor. So also, an investigation into a person's affairs by a government lawyer or by special counsel employed by the government is not an "evaluation" as that term is used in this Rule. The question is whether the lawyer is retained by the person whose affairs are being examined. When the lawyer is retained by that person, the general rules concerning loyalty to a client and preservation of confidences apply, which is not the case if the lawyer is retained by someone else. For this reason, it is essential to identify the person by whom the lawyer is retained. This should be made clear not only to the person under examination, but also to others to whom the results are to be made available.

Duties Owed to Third Person and Client

[3] When the evaluation is intended for the information or use of a third person, a legal duty to that person may or may not arise. That legal question is beyond the scope of this Rule. However, because such an evaluation involves a departure from the normal client-lawyer relationship, careful analysis of the situation is required. The lawyer must be satisfied as a matter of professional judgment that making the evaluation is compatible with other functions undertaken on behalf of the client. For example, if the lawyer is

acting as advocate in defending the client against charges of fraud, it would normally be incompatible with that responsibility for the lawyer to perform an evaluation for others concerning the same or a related transaction. Assuming no such impediment is apparent, however, the lawyer should advise the client of the implications of the evaluation, particularly the lawyer's responsibilities to third persons and the duty to disseminate the findings.

Access to and Disclosure of Information

[4]   The quality of an evaluation depends on the freedom and extent of the investigation upon which it is based. Ordinarily a lawyer should have whatever latitude of investigation seems necessary as a matter of professional judgment. Under some circumstances, however, the terms of the evaluation may be limited. For example, certain issues or sources may be categorically excluded, or the scope of the search may be limited by time constraints or the non-cooperation of persons having relevant information. Any such limitations that are material to the evaluation should be described in the report. If, after a lawyer has commenced an evaluation, the client refuses to comply with the terms upon which it was understood the evaluation was to have been made, the lawyer's obligations are determined by law having reference to the terms of the client's agreement and the surrounding circumstances. In no circumstances is the lawyer permitted knowingly to make a false statement of material fact or law in providing an evaluation under this Rule. *See* Rule 4.1. A knowing omission of material information that must be disclosed to make material statements in the evaluation not false or misleading may violate this Rule.

Obtaining Client's Informed Consent

[5]   Information relating to an evaluation is protected by Rule 1.6. In many situations, providing an evaluation to a third party poses no significant risk to the client; thus, the lawyer may be impliedly authorized to disclose information to carry out the representation. *See* Rule 1.6(a)(2). Where, however, it is reasonably likely that providing the evaluation will affect the client's interests materially and adversely, the lawyer must first obtain the client's consent after the lawyer has consulted with the client and the client has been adequately informed concerning the conditions of the evaluation, the nature of the information to be disclosed and important possible effects on the client's interests. *See* Rules 1.0(j), 1.6(a).

Financial Auditors' Requests for Information

[6]   When a question is raised by the client's financial auditor concerning the legal situation of a client, and the question is referred to the lawyer, the lawyer's response may be made in accordance with procedures recognized in the legal profession. Such a procedure is set forth in the American Bar Association Statement of Policy Regarding Lawyers' Responses to Auditors' Requests for Information, adopted in 1975.

RULE 2.4: LAWYER SERVING AS THIRD–PARTY NEUTRAL

(a) A lawyer serves as a "third-party neutral" when the lawyer assists two or more persons who are not clients of the lawyer to reach a resolution of a dispute or other matter that has arisen between them. Service as a third-party neutral may include service as an arbitrator, a mediator or in such other capacity as will enable the lawyer to assist the parties to resolve the matter.

(b) A lawyer serving as a third-party neutral shall inform unrepresented parties that the lawyer is not representing them. When the lawyer knows or reasonably should know that a party does not understand the lawyer's role in the matter, the lawyer shall explain the difference between the lawyer's role as a third-party neutral and a lawyer's role as one who represents a client.

Comment

[1] Alternative dispute resolution has become a substantial part of the civil justice system. In addition to representing clients in dispute-resolution processes, lawyers often serve as third-party neutrals. A "third-party neutral" is a person such as a mediator, arbitrator, conciliator or evaluator or a person serving in another capacity that assists the parties, represented or unrepresented, in the resolution of a dispute or in the arrangement of a transaction. Whether a third-party neutral serves primarily as a facilitator, evaluator or decision maker depends on the particular process that is either selected by the parties or mandated by a court.

[2] The role of a third-party neutral is not unique to lawyers although, in some court-connected contexts, only lawyers are permitted to serve in this role or to handle certain types of cases. In performing this role, the lawyer may be subject to court rules or other law that applies either to third-party neutrals generally or to lawyers serving as third-party neutrals. Lawyer-neutrals may also be subject to various codes of ethics, such as the Code of Ethics for Arbitration in Commercial Disputes prepared by a joint committee of the American Bar Association and the American Arbitration Association or the Model Standards of Conduct for Mediators jointly prepared by the American Bar Association, the American Arbitration Association and the Society of Professionals in Dispute Resolution.

[3] Unlike nonlawyers who serve as third-party neutrals, lawyers serving in this role may experience unique problems as a result of differences between the role of a third-party neutral and a lawyer's service as a client representative. The potential for confusion is significant when the parties are unrepresented in the process. Thus, paragraph (b) requires a lawyer-neutral to inform unrepresented parties that the lawyer is not representing them. For some parties, particularly parties who frequently use dispute-resolution processes, this information will be sufficient. For others, particularly those who are using the process for the first time, more information will be required.

Where appropriate, the lawyer should inform unrepresented parties of the important differences between the lawyer's role as a third-party neutral and as a client representative, including the inapplicability of the attorney-client evidentiary privilege. The extent of disclosure required under this paragraph will depend on the particular parties involved and the subject matter of the proceeding, as well as the particular features of the dispute-resolution process selected.

[4]   A lawyer who serves as a third-party neutral may be asked subsequently to serve as a lawyer representing a client in the same matter. The conflicts of interest that arise for both the lawyer and the lawyer's law firm are addressed in Rule 1.12.

[5]   Lawyers who represent clients in alternative dispute-resolution processes are governed by the Rules of Professional Conduct. When the dispute-resolution process takes place before a tribunal, as in binding arbitration (*see* Rule 1.0(w)), the lawyer's duty of candor is governed by Rule 3.3. Otherwise, the lawyer's duty of candor toward both the third-party neutral and other parties is governed by Rule 4.1.

RULE 3.1: NON–MERITORIOUS CLAIMS AND CONTENTIONS

(a) **A lawyer shall not bring or defend a proceeding, or assert or controvert an issue therein, unless there is a basis in law and fact for doing so that is not frivolous. A lawyer for the defendant in a criminal proceeding or for the respondent in a proceeding that could result in incarceration may nevertheless so defend the proceeding as to require that every element of the case be established.**

(b) **A lawyer's conduct is "frivolous" for purposes of this Rule if:**

(1) **the lawyer knowingly advances a claim or defense that is unwarranted under existing law, except that the lawyer may advance such claim or defense if it can be supported by good faith argument for an extension, modification, or reversal of existing law;**

(2) **the conduct has no reasonable purpose other than to delay or prolong the resolution of litigation, in violation of Rule 3.2, or serves merely to harass or maliciously injure another; or**

(3) **the lawyer knowingly asserts material factual statements that are false.**

Comment

[1]   The advocate has a duty to use legal procedure for the fullest benefit of the client's cause, but also a duty not to abuse legal procedure. The law, both procedural and substantive, establishes the limits within which an advocate may proceed. However, the law is not always clear and is never static. Accordingly, in determining the proper scope of advocacy, account must be taken of the law's ambiguities and potential for change.

[2]   The filing of a claim or defense or similar action taken for a client is not frivolous merely because the facts have not first been fully substantiated or because the lawyer expects to develop vital evidence only by discovery. Lawyers are required, however, to inform themselves about the facts of their clients' cases and the applicable law, and determine that they can make good-faith arguments in support of their clients' positions. Such action is not frivolous even though the lawyer believes that the client's position ultimately will not prevail. The action is frivolous, however, if the action has no substantial purpose other than to harass or maliciously injure a person, or if the lawyer is unable either to make a good-faith argument on the merits of the action taken or to support the action taken by a good-faith argument for an extension, modification or reversal of existing law (which includes the establishment of new judge-made law).

[3]   The lawyer's obligations under this Rule are subordinate to federal or state constitutional law that entitles a defendant in a criminal matter to the assistance of counsel in presenting a claim or contention that otherwise would be prohibited by this Rule.

RULE 3.2: DELAY OF LITIGATION

In representing a client, a lawyer shall not use means that have no substantial purpose other than to delay or prolong the proceeding or to cause needless expense.

Comment

[1]   Dilatory practices bring the administration of justice into disrepute. Such tactics are prohibited if their only substantial purpose is to frustrate an opposing party's attempt to obtain rightful redress or repose. It is not a justification that such tactics are often tolerated by the bench and bar. The question is whether a competent lawyer acting in good faith would regard the course of action as having some substantial purpose other than delay or needless expense. Seeking or realizing financial or other benefit from otherwise improper delay in litigation is not a legitimate interest of the client.

RULE 3.3: CONDUCT BEFORE A TRIBUNAL

(a) A lawyer shall not knowingly:

(1) make a false statement of fact or law to a tribunal or fail to correct a false statement of material fact or law previously made to the tribunal by the lawyer;

(2) fail to disclose to the tribunal controlling legal authority known to the lawyer to be directly adverse to the position of the client and not disclosed by opposing counsel; or

(3) offer or use evidence that the lawyer knows to be false. If a lawyer, the lawyer's client, or a witness called by the lawyer

has offered material evidence and the lawyer comes to know of its falsity, the lawyer shall take reasonable remedial measures, including, if necessary, disclosure to the tribunal. A lawyer may refuse to offer evidence, other than the testimony of a defendant in a criminal matter, that the lawyer reasonably believes is false.

(b) A lawyer who represents a client before a tribunal and who knows that a person intends to engage, is engaging or has engaged in criminal or fraudulent conduct related to the proceeding shall take reasonable remedial measures, including, if necessary, disclosure to the tribunal.

(c) The duties stated in paragraphs (a) and (b) apply even if compliance requires disclosure of information otherwise protected by Rule 1.6.

(d) In an ex parte proceeding, a lawyer shall inform the tribunal of all material facts known to the lawyer that will enable the tribunal to make an informed decision, whether or not the facts are adverse.

(e) In presenting a matter to a tribunal, a lawyer shall disclose, unless privileged or irrelevant, the identities of the clients the lawyer represents and of the persons who employed the lawyer.

(f) In appearing as a lawyer before a tribunal, a lawyer shall not:

(1) fail to comply with known local customs of courtesy or practice of the bar or a particular tribunal without giving to opposing counsel timely notice of the intent not to comply;

(2) engage in undignified or discourteous conduct;

(3) intentionally or habitually violate any established rule of procedure or of evidence; or

(4) engage in conduct intended to disrupt the tribunal.

Comment

[1] This Rule governs the conduct of a lawyer who is representing a client in the proceedings of a tribunal. *See* Rule 1.0(w) for the definition of "tribunal." It also applies when the lawyer is representing a client in an ancillary proceeding conducted pursuant to the tribunal's adjudicative authority, such as a deposition. Thus, for example, paragraph (a)(3) requires a lawyer to take reasonable remedial measures if the lawyer comes to know that a client has offered false evidence in a deposition.

[2] This Rule sets forth the special duties of lawyers as officers of the court to avoid conduct that undermines the integrity of the adjudicative process. A lawyer acting as an advocate in an adjudicative proceeding has an obligation to present the client's case with persuasive force. Performance of that duty while maintaining confidences of the client, however, is qualified by the advocate's duty of candor to the tribunal. Consequently, although a

lawyer in an adversary proceeding is not required to present an impartial exposition of the law and may not vouch for the evidence submitted in a cause, the lawyer must not allow the tribunal to be misled by false statements of law or fact or by evidence that the lawyer knows to be false.

Representations by a Lawyer

[3]   An advocate is responsible for pleadings and other documents prepared for litigation, but is usually not required to have personal knowledge of matters asserted therein because litigation documents ordinarily present assertions by the client or by someone on the client's behalf and not assertions by the lawyer. Compare Rule 3.1. However, an assertion purporting to be based on the lawyer's own knowledge, as in an affidavit or declaration by the lawyer or in a statement in open court, may properly be made only when the lawyer knows the assertion is true or believes it to be true on the basis of a reasonably diligent inquiry. There are circumstances where failure to make a disclosure is the equivalent of an affirmative misrepresentation. The obligation prescribed in Rule 1.2(d) not to counsel a client to commit or assist the client in committing a fraud applies in litigation. *See also* Rule 8.4(b), Comments [2]-[3].

Legal Argument

[4]   Although a lawyer is not required to make a disinterested exposition of the law, legal argument based on a knowingly false representation of law constitutes dishonesty toward the tribunal. Paragraph (a)(2) requires an advocate to disclose directly adverse and controlling legal authority that is known to the lawyer and that has not been disclosed by the opposing party. A tribunal that is fully informed on the applicable law is better able to make a fair and accurate determination of the matter before it.

Offering or Using False Evidence

[5]   Paragraph (a)(3) requires that the lawyer refuse to offer or use evidence that the lawyer knows to be false, regardless of the client's wishes. This duty is premised on the lawyer's obligation as an officer of the court to prevent the trier of fact from being misled by false evidence. A lawyer does not violate this Rule if the lawyer offers the evidence for the purpose of establishing its falsity.

[6]   If a lawyer knows that the client intends to testify falsely or wants the lawyer to introduce or use false evidence, the lawyer should seek to persuade the client that the evidence should not be offered. If the persuasion is ineffective and the lawyer continues to represent the client, the lawyer must refuse to offer the false evidence. If only a portion of a witness's testimony will be false, the lawyer may call the witness to testify but may not (i) elicit or otherwise permit the witness to present testimony that the lawyer knows is false or (ii) base arguments to the trier of fact on evidence known to be false.

[6A]   The prohibition against offering and using false evidence ordinarily requires a prosecutor to correct any false evidence that has been offered by the government, inform the tribunal when the prosecutor reasonably believes that a prosecution witness has testified falsely, and correct any material errors in a presentence report that are detrimental to a defendant.

[7]   The duties stated in paragraphs (a) and (b) apply to all lawyers, including defense counsel in criminal cases. If the criminal defendant insists on testifying and the lawyer knows that the testimony will be false, the lawyer may offer the testimony in a narrative form. The lawyer's ethical duty may be qualified by judicial decisions interpreting the constitutional rights to due process and to counsel in criminal cases. The obligation of the advocate under the Rules of Professional Conduct is subordinate to such requirements.

[8]   The prohibition against offering or using false evidence applies only if the lawyer knows that the evidence is false. A lawyer's reasonable belief that evidence is false does not preclude its presentation to the trier of fact. A lawyer's actual knowledge that evidence is false, however, can be inferred from the circumstances. *See* Rule 1.0(k) for the definition of "knowledge." Thus, although a lawyer should resolve doubts about the veracity of testimony or other evidence in favor of the client, the lawyer cannot ignore an obvious falsehood.

[9]   Although paragraph (a)(3) prohibits a lawyer from offering or using evidence the lawyer knows to be false, it permits the lawyer to refuse to offer testimony or other proof that the lawyer reasonably believes to be false. Offering such proof may impair the integrity of an adjudicatory proceeding. Because of the special protections historically provided criminal defendants, however, this Rule does not permit a lawyer to refuse to offer the testimony of a criminal defense client where the lawyer reasonably believes, but does not know, that the testimony will be false. Unless the lawyer knows the testimony will be false, the lawyer must honor the criminal defendant's decision to testify.

Remedial Measures

[10]   A lawyer who has offered or used material evidence in the belief that it was true may subsequently come to know that the evidence is false. Or, a lawyer may be surprised when the lawyer's client or another witness called by the lawyer offers testimony the lawyer knows to be false, either during the lawyer's direct examination or in response to cross-examination by the opposing lawyer. In such situations, or if the lawyer knows of the falsity of testimony elicited from the client during a deposition, the lawyer must take reasonable remedial measures. The advocate's proper course is to remonstrate with the client confidentially, advise the client of the lawyer's duty of candor to the tribunal, and seek the client's cooperation with respect to the withdrawal or correction of the false statements or evidence. If that fails, the advocate must take further remedial action. If withdrawal from the representation is not permitted or will not undo the effect of the false evidence, the advocate must make such disclosure to the tribunal as is reasonably necessary

to remedy the situation, even if doing so requires the lawyer to reveal confidential information that otherwise would be protected by Rule 1.6. It is for the tribunal then to determine what should be done, such as making a statement about the matter to the trier of fact, ordering a mistrial, taking other appropriate steps or doing nothing.

[11] The disclosure of a client's false testimony can result in grave consequences to the client, including not only a sense of betrayal but also loss of the case and perhaps a prosecution for perjury. But the alternative is for the lawyer to cooperate in deceiving the court, thereby subverting the truth-finding process, which the adversary system is designed to implement. *See* Rule 1.2(d). Furthermore, unless it is clearly understood that the lawyer will act upon the duty to disclose the existence of false evidence, the client can simply reject the lawyer's advice to reveal the false evidence and insist that the lawyer keep silent. The client could therefore in effect coerce the lawyer into being a party to a fraud on the court.

Preserving Integrity of the Adjudicative Process

[12] Lawyers have a special obligation as officers of the court to protect a tribunal against criminal or fraudulent conduct that undermines the integrity of the adjudicative process. Accordingly, paragraph (b) requires a lawyer who represents a client in an adjudicative proceeding to take reasonable remedial measures, including disclosure if necessary, whenever the lawyer knows that a person, including the lawyer's client, intends to engage, is engaging or has engaged in criminal or fraudulent conduct related to the proceeding. Such conduct includes, among other things, bribing, intimidating or otherwise unlawfully communicating with a witness, juror, court official or other participant in the proceeding; unlawfully destroying or concealing documents or other evidence related to the proceeding; and failing to disclose information to the tribunal when required by law to do so. For example, under some circumstances a person's omission of a material fact may constitute a crime or fraud on the tribunal.

[12A] A lawyer's duty to take reasonable remedial measures under paragraph (a)(3) is limited to the proceeding in which the lawyer has offered or used the evidence in question. A lawyer's duty to take reasonable remedial measures under paragraph (b) does not apply to another lawyer who is retained to represent a person in an investigation or proceeding concerning that person's conduct in the prior proceeding.

[13] [Omitted.]

Ex Parte Proceedings

[14] Ordinarily, an advocate has the limited responsibility of presenting one side of the matters that a tribunal should consider in reaching a decision; the opposing position is expected to be presented by the adverse party. However, in any ex parte proceeding, such as an application for a temporary restraining order, there may be no presentation by opposing advocates. The object of an ex parte proceeding is nevertheless to yield a substantially just

result. The judge has an affirmative responsibility to accord the opposing party, if absent, just consideration. The lawyer for the represented party has the correlative duty to make disclosures of material facts known to the lawyer that the lawyer reasonably believes are necessary to an informed decision.

Withdrawal

[15]   A lawyer's compliance with the duty of candor imposed by this Rule does not automatically require that the lawyer withdraw from the representation of a client whose interests will be or have been adversely affected by the lawyer's disclosure. The lawyer, however, may be required by Rule 1.16(d) to seek permission of the tribunal to withdraw if the lawyer's compliance with this Rule's duty of candor results in such an extreme deterioration of the client-lawyer relationship that the lawyer can no longer competently represent the client. *See also* Rule 1.16(c) for the circumstances in which a lawyer will be permitted to seek a tribunal's permission to withdraw. In connection with a request for permission to withdraw that is premised on a client's misconduct, a lawyer may reveal information relating to the representation only to the extent reasonably necessary to comply with this Rule or as otherwise permitted by Rule 1.6.

RULE 3.4: FAIRNESS TO OPPOSING PARTY AND COUNSEL

A lawyer shall not:

(a) (1) suppress any evidence that the lawyer or the client has a legal obligation to reveal or produce;

(2) advise or cause a person to hide or leave the jurisdiction of a tribunal for the purpose of making the person unavailable as a witness therein;

(3) conceal or knowingly fail to disclose that which the lawyer is required by law to reveal;

(4) knowingly use perjured testimony or false evidence;

(5) participate in the creation or preservation of evidence when the lawyer knows or it is obvious that the evidence is false; or

(6) knowingly engage in other illegal conduct or conduct contrary to these Rules;

(b) offer an inducement to a witness that is prohibited by law or pay, offer to pay or acquiesce in the payment of compensation to a witness contingent upon the content of the witness's testimony or the outcome of the matter. A lawyer may advance, guarantee or acquiesce in the payment of:

(1) reasonable compensation to a witness for the loss of time in attending, testifying, preparing to testify or otherwise assisting counsel, and reasonable related expenses; or

(2) a reasonable fee for the professional services of an expert witness and reasonable related expenses;

(c) disregard or advise the client to disregard a standing rule of a tribunal or a ruling of a tribunal made in the course of a proceeding, but the lawyer may take appropriate steps in good faith to test the validity of such rule or ruling;

(d) in appearing before a tribunal on behalf of a client:

(1) state or allude to any matter that the lawyer does not reasonably believe is relevant or that will not be supported by admissible evidence;

(2) assert personal knowledge of facts in issue except when testifying as a witness;

(3) assert a personal opinion as to the justness of a cause, the credibility of a witness, the culpability of a civil litigant or the guilt or innocence of an accused but the lawyer may argue, upon analysis of the evidence, for any position or conclusion with respect to the matters stated herein; or

(4) ask any question that the lawyer has no reasonable basis to believe is relevant to the case and that is intended to degrade a witness or other person; or

(e) present, participate in presenting, or threaten to present criminal charges solely to obtain an advantage in a civil matter.

Comment

[1] The procedure of the adversary system contemplates that the evidence in a case is to be marshaled competitively by the contending parties. Fair competition in the adversary system is secured by prohibitions against destruction or concealment of evidence, improperly influencing witnesses, obstructionist tactics in discovery procedure, and the like. The Rule applies to any conduct that falls within its general terms (for example, "obstruct another party's access to evidence") that is a crime, an intentional tort or prohibited by rules or a ruling of a tribunal. An example is "advis[ing] or caus[ing] a person to hide or leave the jurisdiction of a tribunal for the purpose of making the person unavailable as a witness therein."

[2] Documents and other evidence are often essential to establish a claim or defense. Subject to evidentiary privileges, the right of an opposing party, including the government, to obtain evidence through discovery or subpoena is an important procedural right. The exercise of that right can be frustrated if relevant material is altered, concealed or destroyed. Paragraph (a) protects that right. Evidence that has been properly requested must be produced unless there is a good-faith basis for not doing so. Applicable state and federal law may make it an offense to destroy material for the purpose of impairing its availability in a pending or reasonably foreseeable proceeding, even though no specific request to reveal or produce evidence has been made.

Paragraph (a) applies to evidentiary material generally, including computerized information.

[2A]   Falsifying evidence, dealt with in paragraph (a), is also generally a criminal offense. Of additional relevance is Rule 3.3(a)(3), dealing with use of false evidence in a proceeding before a tribunal. Applicable law may permit a lawyer to take temporary possession of physical evidence of client crimes for the purpose of conducting a limited examination that will not alter or destroy material characteristics of the evidence. In such a case, applicable law may require the lawyer to turn the evidence over to the police or other prosecuting authority, depending on the circumstances.

[3]   Paragraph (b) applies generally to any inducement to a witness that is prohibited by law. It is not improper to pay a witness's reasonable expenses or to compensate an expert witness on terms permitted by law. However, any fee contingent upon the content of a witness' testimony or the outcome of the case is prohibited.

[3A]   Paragraph (d) deals with improper statements relating to the merits of a case when representing a client before a tribunal: alluding to irrelevant matters, asserting personal knowledge of facts in issue, and asserting a personal opinion on issues to be decided by the trier of fact. *See also* Rule 4.4, prohibiting the use of any means that have no substantial purpose other than to embarrass or harm a third person. However, a lawyer may argue, upon analysis of the evidence, for any position or conclusion supported by the record. The term "admissible evidence" refers to evidence considered admissible in the particular context. For example, admission of evidence in an administrative adjudication or an arbitration proceeding may be governed by different standards than those applied in a jury trial.

[4]   In general, a lawyer is prohibited from giving legal advice to an unrepresented person, other than the advice to secure counsel, when the interests of that person are or may have a reasonable possibility of being in conflict with the interests of the lawyer's client. *See* Rule 4.3.

[5]   The use of threats in negotiation may constitute the crime of extortion. However, not all threats are improper. For example, if a lawyer represents a client who has been criminally harmed by a third person (for example, a theft of property), the lawyer's threat to report the crime does not constitute extortion when honestly claimed in an effort to obtain restitution or indemnification for the harm done. But extortion is committed if the threat involves conduct of the third person unrelated to the criminal harm (for example, a threat to report tax evasion by the third person that is unrelated to the civil dispute).

RULE 3.5: MAINTAINING AND PRESERVING THE IMPARTIALITY OF TRIBUNALS AND JURORS

(a) A lawyer shall not:

(1) seek to or cause another person to influence a judge, official or employee of a tribunal by means prohibited by law or

give or lend anything of value to such judge, official, or employee of a tribunal when the recipient is prohibited from accepting the gift or loan but a lawyer may make a contribution to the campaign fund of a candidate for judicial office in conformity with Part 100 of the Rules of the Chief Administrator of the Courts;

(2) in an adversarial proceeding communicate or cause another person to do so on the lawyer's behalf, as to the merits of the matter with a judge or official of a tribunal or an employee thereof before whom the matter is pending, except:

(i) in the course of official proceedings in the matter;

(ii) in writing, if the lawyer promptly delivers a copy of the writing to counsel for other parties and to a party who is not represented by a lawyer;

(iii) orally, upon adequate notice to counsel for the other parties and to any party who is not represented by a lawyer; or

(iv) as otherwise authorized by law, or by Part 100 of the Rules of the Chief Administrator of the Courts;

(3) seek to or cause another person to influence a juror or prospective juror by means prohibited by law;

(4) communicate or cause another to communicate with a member of the jury venire from which the jury will be selected for the trial of a case or, during the trial of a case, with any member of the jury unless authorized to do so by law or court order;

(5) communicate with a juror or prospective juror after discharge of the jury if:

(i) the communication is prohibited by law or court order;

(ii) the juror has made known to the lawyer a desire not to communicate;

(iii) the communication involves misrepresentation, coercion, duress or harassment; or

(iv) the communication is an attempt to influence the juror's actions in future jury service; or

(6) conduct a vexatious or harassing investigation of either a member of the venire or a juror or, by financial support or otherwise, cause another to do so.

(b) During the trial of a case a lawyer who is not connected therewith shall not communicate with or cause another to communicate with a juror concerning the case.

(c) **All restrictions imposed by this Rule also apply to communications with or investigations of members of a family of a member of the venire or a juror.**

(d) **A lawyer shall reveal promptly to the court improper conduct by a member of the venire or a juror, or by another toward a member of the venire or a juror or a member of his or her family of which the lawyer has knowledge.**

Comment

[1] Many forms of improper influence upon a tribunal are proscribed by criminal law. In addition, gifts and loans to judges and judicial employees, as well as contributions to candidates for judicial election, are regulated by the New York Code of Judicial Conduct, with which an advocate should be familiar. *See* New York Code of Judicial Conduct, Canon 4(D)(5), 22 N.Y.C.R.R. § 100.4(D)(5) (prohibition of a judge's receipt of a gift, loan, etc., and exceptions) and Canon 5(A)(5), 22 N.Y.C.R.R. § 100.5(A)(5) (concerning lawyer contributions to the campaign committee of a candidate for judicial office). A lawyer is prohibited from aiding a violation of such provisions. Limitations on contributions in the Election Law may also be relevant.

[2] Unless authorized to do so by law or court order, a lawyer is prohibited from communicating ex parte with persons serving in a judicial capacity in an adjudicative proceeding, such as judges, masters or jurors, or to employees who assist them, such as law clerks. *See* New York Code of Judicial Conduct, Canon 3(B)(6), 22 N.Y.C.R.R. § 100.3(B)(6).

[3] A lawyer may on occasion want to communicate with a juror or prospective juror after the jury has been discharged. Paragraph (a)(5) permits a lawyer to do so unless the communication is prohibited by law or a court order, but the lawyer must respect the desire of a juror not to talk with the lawyer. The lawyer may not engage in improper conduct during the communication.

[4] The advocate's function is to present evidence and argument so that the cause may be decided according to law. Refraining from abusive or obstreperous conduct is a corollary of the advocate's right to speak on behalf of litigants. A lawyer may stand firm against abuse by a judge but should avoid reciprocation; the judge's misbehavior is no justification for similar dereliction by an advocate. An advocate can present the cause, protect the record for subsequent review and preserve professional integrity by patient firmness no less effectively than by belligerence or theatrics.

RULE 3.6: TRIAL PUBLICITY

(a) **A lawyer who is participating in or has participated in a criminal or civil matter shall not make an extrajudicial statement that the lawyer knows or reasonably should know will be disseminated by means of public communication and will have a substantial** likelihood of materially prejudicing an adjudicative proceeding in the matter.

(b) A statement ordinarily is likely to prejudice materially an adjudicative proceeding when it refers to a civil matter triable to a jury, a criminal matter or any other proceeding that could result in incarceration, and the statement relates to:

(1) the character, credibility, reputation or criminal record of a party, suspect in a criminal investigation or witness, or the identity of a witness or the expected testimony of a party or witness;

(2) in a criminal matter that could result in incarceration, the possibility of a plea of guilty to the offense or the existence or contents of any confession, admission or statement given by a defendant or suspect, or that person's refusal or failure to make a statement;

(3) the performance or results of any examination or test, or the refusal or failure of a person to submit to an examination or test, or the identity or nature of physical evidence expected to be presented;

(4) any opinion as to the guilt or innocence of a defendant or suspect in a criminal matter that could result in incarceration;

(5) information the lawyer knows or reasonably should know is likely to be inadmissible as evidence in a trial and would, if disclosed, create a substantial risk of prejudicing an impartial trial; or

(6) the fact that a defendant has been charged with a crime, unless there is included therein a statement explaining that the charge is merely an accusation and that the defendant is presumed innocent until and unless proven guilty.

(c) Provided that the statement complies with paragraph (a), a lawyer may state the following without elaboration:

(1) the claim, offense or defense and, except when prohibited by law, the identity of the persons involved;

(2) information contained in a public record;

(3) that an investigation of a matter is in progress;

(4) the scheduling or result of any step in litigation;

(5) a request for assistance in obtaining evidence and information necessary thereto;

(6) a warning of danger concerning the behavior of a person involved, when there is reason to believe that there exists the likelihood of substantial harm to an individual or to the public interest; and

(7) in a criminal matter:

(i) the identity, age, residence, occupation and family status of the accused;

(ii) if the accused has not been apprehended, information necessary to aid in apprehension of that person;

(iii) the identity of investigating and arresting officers or agencies and the length of the investigation; and

(iv) the fact, time and place of arrest, resistance, pursuit and use of weapons, and a description of physical evidence seized, other than as contained only in a confession, admission or statement.

(d) Notwithstanding paragraph (a), a lawyer may make a statement that a reasonable lawyer would believe is required to protect a client from the substantial prejudicial effect of recent publicity not initiated by the lawyer or the lawyer's client. A statement made pursuant to this paragraph shall be limited to such information as is necessary to mitigate the recent adverse publicity.

(e) No lawyer associated in a firm or government agency with a lawyer subject to paragraph (a) shall make a statement prohibited by paragraph (a).

Comment

[1]   It is difficult to strike a balance between protecting the right to a fair trial and safeguarding the right of free expression. Preserving the right to a fair trial necessarily entails some curtailment of the information that may be disseminated about a party prior to trial, particularly where trial by jury is involved. If there were no such limits, the result would be the practical nullification of the protective effect of the rules of forensic decorum and the exclusionary rules of evidence. On the other hand, there are vital social interests served by the free dissemination of information about events having legal consequences and about legal proceedings themselves. The public has a right to know about threats to its safety and measures aimed at assuring its security. It also has a legitimate interest in the conduct of judicial proceedings, particularly in matters of general public concern. Furthermore, the subject matter of legal proceedings is often of direct significance in debate and deliberation over questions of public policy.

[2]   Special rules of confidentiality may validly govern proceedings in juvenile, domestic relations and mental disability proceedings and perhaps other types of litigation. Rule 3.4(c) requires compliance with such rules.

[3]   The Rule sets forth a basic general prohibition against a lawyer making statements that the lawyer knows or reasonably should know will have a substantial likelihood of materially prejudicing an adjudicative proceeding. It recognizes that the public value of informed commentary is great and that the likelihood of prejudice to a proceeding because of the commen-

tary of a lawyer who is not involved in the proceeding is small. Thus, the Rule applies only to lawyers who are participating or have participated in the investigation or litigation of a matter and their associates.

[4]   There are certain subjects that are more likely than not to have a material prejudicial effect on a proceeding, particularly when they refer to a civil matter triable to a jury, a criminal matter or any other proceeding that could result in incarceration. Paragraph (b) specifies certain statements that ordinarily will have prejudicial effect.

[5]   Paragraph (c) identifies specific matters about which a lawyer's statements would not ordinarily be considered to present a substantial likelihood of material prejudice. Nevertheless, some statements in criminal cases are also required to meet the fundamental requirements of paragraph (a), for example, those identified in paragraph (c)(7)(iv). Paragraph (c) is not intended to be an exhaustive listing of the subjects upon which a lawyer may make a statement; statements on other matters may be permissible under paragraph (a).

[6]   Another relevant factor in determining prejudice is the nature of the proceeding involved. Criminal jury trials will be most sensitive to extrajudicial speech. Civil trials may be less sensitive. Non-jury hearings and arbitration proceedings may be even less affected. The Rule will still place limitations on prejudicial comments in these cases, but the likelihood of prejudice may be different depending on the type of proceeding.

[7]   Extrajudicial statements that might otherwise raise a question under this Rule may be permissible when they are made in response to statements made publicly by another party, another party's lawyer or third persons, where a reasonable lawyer would believe a public response is required in order to avoid prejudice to the lawyer's client. When prejudicial statements have been publicly made by others, responsive statements may have the salutary effect of lessening any resulting adverse impact on the adjudicative proceeding. Paragraph (d) permits such responsive statements, provided they contain only such information as is necessary to mitigate undue prejudice created by the statements made by others.

[8]   *See* Rule 3.8 Comment [5] for additional duties of prosecutors in connection with extrajudicial statements about criminal proceedings.

RULE 3.7: LAWYER AS WITNESS

(a) A lawyer shall not act as advocate at a trial in which the lawyer is likely to be a necessary witness on a significant issue of fact unless:

> **(1) the testimony relates solely to an uncontested issue;**

> **(2) the testimony relates solely to the nature and value of legal services rendered in the matter;**

> **(3) disqualification of the lawyer would work substantial hardship on the client;**

(4) the testimony will relate solely to a matter of formality, and there is no reason to believe that substantial evidence will be offered in opposition to the testimony; or

(5) the testimony is authorized by the tribunal.

(b) A lawyer may not act as advocate before a tribunal in a matter if:

(1) another lawyer in the lawyer's firm is likely to be called as a witness on a significant issue other than on behalf of the client, and it is apparent that the testimony may be prejudicial to the client; or

(2) the lawyer is precluded from doing so by Rule 1.7 or Rule 1.9.

Comment

[1] Combining the roles of advocate and witness can prejudice the tribunal and the opposing party and also can create a conflict of interest between the lawyer and client.

Advocate-Witness Rule

[2] The tribunal may properly object when the trier of fact may be confused or misled by a lawyer's serving as both advocate and witness. The opposing party may properly object where the combination of roles may prejudice that party's rights in the litigation. A witness is required to testify on the basis of personal knowledge, while an advocate is expected to explain and comment on evidence given by others. It may not be clear whether a statement by an advocate-witness should be taken as proof or as an analysis of the proof. The requirement that the testimony of the advocate-witness be on a significant issue of fact provides a materiality limitation.

[3] To protect the tribunal, the Rule prohibits a lawyer from simultaneously serving as advocate and necessary witness except in those circumstances specified in paragraph (a). Paragraph (a)(1) recognizes that if the testimony will be uncontested, the ambiguities in the dual role are purely theoretical. Testimony relating solely to a formality is uncontested when the lawyer reasonably believes that no substantial evidence will be offered in opposition to the testimony. Paragraph (a)(2) recognizes that where the testimony concerns the extent and value of legal services rendered in the action in which the testimony is offered, permitting the lawyer to testify avoids the need for a second trial with new counsel to resolve that issue. Moreover, in such a situation the judge has firsthand knowledge of the matter in issue; hence, there is less dependence on the adversary process to test the credibility of the testimony.

[4] Apart from these two exceptions, paragraph (a)(3) recognizes that a balancing is required among the interests of the client, of the tribunal, and of the opposing party. Whether the tribunal is likely to be misled or the opposing party is likely to suffer prejudice depends on the nature of the case, the

importance and probable tenor of the lawyer's testimony and the probability that the lawyer's testimony will conflict with that of other witnesses. Even if there is risk of such prejudice, in determining whether the lawyer should be disqualified, due regard must be given to the effect of disqualification on the lawyer's client. It is relevant that one or both parties could reasonably foresee that the lawyer would probably be a witness. The conflict of interest principles stated in Rule 1.7, 1.9 and 1.10, which may separately require disqualification of the lawyer-advocate, have no application to the tribunal's determination of the balancing of judicial and party interests required by paragraph (a)(3).

[5] Because the tribunal is may be misled when a lawyer acts as advocate in a trial in which another lawyer in the lawyer's firm will testify as a necessary witness on a significant issue other than on behalf of the client where it is apparent that the testimony may be prejudicial to the client, paragraph (b) prohibits the non-testifying lawyer to act as advocate.

Conflict of Interest

[6] In determining whether it is permissible to act as advocate in a trial in which the lawyer will be a necessary witness, the lawyer must also consider that the dual role may give rise to a conflict of interest that will require compliance with Rule 1.7 or Rule 1.9. For example, if there is likely to be substantial conflict between the testimony of the client and that of the lawyer, the representation involves a conflict of interest that requires compliance with Rule 1.7. This would be true even though the lawyer might not be prohibited by paragraph (a) from simultaneously serving as advocate and witness because the lawyer's disqualification would work a substantial hardship on the client. Similarly, a lawyer who might be permitted to serve simultaneously as an advocate and a witness by paragraph (a)(3) might be precluded from doing so by Rule 1.9. The problem can arise whether the lawyer is called as a witness on behalf of the client or is called by the opposing party. Determining whether such a conflict exists is primarily the responsibility of the lawyer involved. If there is a conflict of interest, the lawyer must secure the client's informed consent, confirmed in writing. In some cases, the lawyer will be precluded from seeking the client's consent. *See* Rule 1.7. *See* Rule 1.0(e) for the definition of "confirmed in writing" and Rule 1.0(j) for the definition of "informed consent."

RULE 3.8: SPECIAL RESPONSIBILITIES OF PROSECUTORS AND OTHER GOVERNMENT LAWYERS

(a) A prosecutor or other government lawyer shall not institute, cause to be instituted or maintain a criminal charge when the prosecutor or other government lawyer knows or it is obvious that the charge is not supported by probable cause.

(b) A prosecutor or other government lawyer in criminal litigation shall make timely disclosure to counsel for the defendant or to a

defendant who has no counsel of the existence of evidence or information known to the prosecutor or other government lawyer that tends to negate the guilt of the accused, mitigate the degree of the offense, or reduce the sentence, except when relieved of this responsibility by a protective order of a tribunal.

Comment

[1]   A prosecutor has the responsibility of a minister of justice and not simply that of an advocate. This responsibility carries with it specific obligations to see that the defendant is accorded procedural justice and that guilt is decided upon the basis of sufficient evidence. Applicable state or federal law may require other measures by the prosecutor, and knowing disregard of those obligations or a systematic abuse of prosecutorial discretion could constitute a violation of Rule 8.4. A government lawyer in a criminal case is considered a "prosecutor" for purposes of this Rule.

[2]   A defendant who has no counsel may waive a preliminary hearing or other important pretrial rights and thereby lose a valuable opportunity to challenge probable cause. Accordingly, prosecutors should not seek to obtain waivers of preliminary hearings or other important pretrial rights from unrepresented accused persons. This would not be applicable, however, to an accused appearing pro se with the approval of the tribunal, or to the lawful questioning of an uncharged suspect who has knowingly waived the rights to counsel and silence.

[3]   The exception in paragraph (b) recognizes that a prosecutor may seek an appropriate protective order from the tribunal if disclosure of information to the defense could result in substantial harm to an individual or to the public interest.

[4]   [Omitted.]

[5]   Rule 3.6 prohibits extrajudicial statements that have a substantial likelihood of prejudicing an adjudicatory proceeding. In the context of a criminal prosecution, a prosecutor's extrajudicial statement can create the additional problem of increasing public condemnation of the accused. Although the announcement of an indictment, for example, will necessarily have severe consequences for the accused, a prosecutor can, and should, avoid comments that have no legitimate law enforcement purpose and have a substantial likelihood of increasing public opprobrium against the accused. A prosecutor in a criminal case should make reasonable efforts to prevent persons under the prosecutor's supervisory authority, which may include investigators, law enforcement personnel, employees and other persons assisting or associated with the prosecutor, from making extrajudicial statements that the prosecutor would be prohibited from making under Rule 3.6. *See* Rule 5.3. Nothing in this Comment is intended to restrict the statements that a prosecutor may make that comply with Rule 3.6(c) or Rule 3.6(d).

[6]   Like other lawyers, prosecutors are subject to Rule 5.1 and Rule 5.3, which relate to responsibilities regarding lawyers and nonlawyers who work

for or are associated with the lawyer's office. Prosecutors should bear in mind the importance of these obligations in connection with the unique dangers of improper extrajudicial statements in a criminal case, and should exercise reasonable care to prevent persons assisting or associated with the prosecutor from making improper extrajudicial statements. Ordinarily, the reasonable care standard will be satisfied if the prosecutor issues the appropriate cautions to law enforcement personnel and other relevant individuals.

[6A] Reference to a "prosecutor" in this Rule includes the office of the prosecutor and all lawyers affiliated with the prosecutor's office who are responsible for the prosecution function. Like other lawyers, prosecutors are subject to Rule 3.3, which requires a lawyer to take reasonable remedial measures to correct material evidence that the lawyer has offered when the lawyer comes to know of its falsity. *See* Rule 3.3, Comment [6A].

[6B] The prosecutor's duty to seek justice has traditionally been understood not only to require the prosecutor to take precautions to avoid convicting innocent individuals, but also to require the prosecutor to take reasonable remedial measures when it appears likely that an innocent person was wrongly convicted. Accordingly, when a prosecutor comes to know of new and material evidence creating a reasonable likelihood that a person was wrongly convicted, the prosecutor should examine the evidence and undertake such further inquiry or investigation as may be necessary to determine whether the conviction was wrongful. The scope of the inquiry will depend on the circumstances. In some cases, the prosecutor may recognize the need to reinvestigate the underlying case; in others, it may be appropriate to await development of the record in collateral proceedings initiated by the defendant. The nature of the inquiry or investigation should be such as to provide a "reasonable belief," as defined in Rule 1.0(r), that the conviction should or should not be set aside.

[6C] When a prosecutor comes to know of clear and convincing evidence establishing that a conviction was wrongful, the prosecutor should disclose the new evidence to the defendant so that defense counsel may conduct any necessary investigation and make any appropriate motions directed at setting aside the verdict, and should disclose the new evidence to the court or other appropriate authority so that the court can determine whether to initiate its own inquiry. The evidence should be disclosed in a timely manner, depending on the particular circumstances. For example, disclosure of the evidence might be deferred where it could prejudice the prosecutor's investigation into the matter. If the convicted defendant is unrepresented and cannot afford to retain counsel, the prosecutor should request that the court appoint counsel for purposes of these post-conviction proceedings. The post-conviction disclosure duty raised by this Comment applies to new and material evidence of innocence, regardless of whether it could previously have been discovered by the defense.

[6D] If the prosecutor comes to know of clear and convincing evidence that the defendant was convicted of an offense that the defendant did not commit, the prosecutor should seek to remedy the injustice by taking appropriate steps to remedy the wrongful conviction. These steps may include, depending on the particular circumstances, disclosure of the evidence to the defendant, requesting that the court appoint counsel for an unrepresented indigent defendant and, where appropriate, notifying the court that the prosecutor believes that the defendant was wrongfully convicted.

[6E]   The duties in Comments [6B], [6C] and [6D] apply whether the new evidence comes to the attention of the prosecutor who obtained the defendant's conviction or to a different prosecutor. If the evidence comes to the attention of a prosecutor in a different prosecutor's office, the prosecutor should notify the office of the prosecutor who obtained the conviction.

RULE 3.9: ADVOCATE IN NON–ADJUDICATIVE MATTERS

A lawyer communicating in a representative capacity with a legislative body or administrative agency in connection with a pending non-adjudicative matter or proceeding shall disclose that the appearance is in a representative capacity, except when the lawyer seeks information from an agency that is available to the public.

Comment

[1]   In representation before bodies such as legislatures, municipal councils and executive and administrative agencies acting in a rule-making or policy-making capacity, lawyers present facts, formulate issues and advance argument regarding the matters under consideration. The legislative body or administrative agency is entitled to know that the lawyer is appearing in a representative capacity. Ordinarily the client will consent to being identified, but if not, such as when the lawyer is appearing on behalf of an undisclosed principal, the governmental body at least knows that the lawyer is acting in a representative capacity as opposed to advancing the lawyer's personal opinion as a citizen. Representation in such matters is governed by Rule 4.1 through 4.4, and 8.4.

[1A]   Rule 3.9 does not apply to adjudicative proceedings before a tribunal. Court rules and other law require a lawyer, in making an appearance before a tribunal in a representative capacity, to identify the client or clients and provide other information required for communication with the tribunal or other parties.

[2]   [Omitted.]

[3]   [Omitted.]

RULE 4.1: TRUTHFULNESS IN STATEMENTS TO OTHERS

In the course of representing a client, a lawyer shall not knowingly make a false statement of fact or law to a third person.

Comment

Misrepresentation

[1]   A lawyer is required to be truthful when dealing with others on a client's behalf, but generally has no affirmative duty to inform an opposing party of relevant facts. A misrepresentation can occur if the lawyer incorporates or affirms a statement of another person that the lawyer knows is false. Misrepresentations can also occur by partially true but misleading statements or omissions that are the equivalent of affirmative false statements. As to dishonest conduct that does not amount to a false statement or for misrepresentations by a lawyer other than in the course of representing a client, *see* Rule 8.4.

Statements of Fact

[2]   This Rule refers to statements of fact. Whether a particular statement should be regarded as one of fact can depend on the circumstances. Under generally accepted conventions in negotiation, certain types of statements ordinarily are not taken as statements of material fact. Estimates of price or value placed on the subject of a transaction and a party's intentions as to an acceptable settlement of a claim are ordinarily in this category; so is the existence of an undisclosed principal, except where nondisclosure of the principal would constitute fraud. Lawyers should be mindful of their obligations under applicable law to avoid criminal and tortious misrepresentation.

Illegal or Fraudulent Conduct by Client

[3]   Under Rule 1.2(d), a lawyer is prohibited from counseling or assisting a client as to conduct that the lawyer knows is illegal or fraudulent. Ordinarily, a lawyer can avoid assisting a client's illegality or fraud by withdrawing from the representation. *See* Rule 1.16(c)(2). Sometimes it may be necessary for the lawyer to give notice of the fact of withdrawal and to disaffirm an opinion, document, affirmation or the like. *See* Rules 1.2(d), 1.6(b)(3).

RULE 4.2: COMMUNICATION WITH PERSON REPRESENTED BY COUNSEL

(a) **In representing a client, a lawyer shall not communicate or cause another to communicate about the subject of the representation with a party the lawyer knows to be represented by another lawyer in the matter, unless the lawyer has the prior consent of the other lawyer or is authorized to do so by law.**

(b) **Notwithstanding the prohibitions of paragraph (a), and unless otherwise prohibited by law, a lawyer may cause a client to communicate with a represented person unless the represented person is not legally competent, and may counsel the client with respect to those communications, provided the lawyer gives reasonable ad-**

vance notice to the represented person's counsel that such communications will be taking place.

Comment

[1]   This Rule contributes to the proper functioning of the legal system by protecting a person who has chosen to be represented by a lawyer in a matter against possible overreaching by other lawyers who are participating in the matter, interference by those lawyers with the client-lawyer relationship, and un-counseled disclosure of information relating to the representation.

[2]   This Rule applies to communications with any person who is represented by counsel concerning the matter to which the communication relates.

[3]   Paragraph (a) applies even though the represented party initiates or consents to the communication. A lawyer must immediately terminate communication with a party if after commencing communication, the lawyer learns that the party is one with whom communication is not permitted by this Rule.

[4]   This Rule does not prohibit communication with a represented party or person or an employee or agent of such a party or person concerning matters outside the representation. For example, the existence of a controversy between a government agency and a private party or person or between two organizations does not prohibit a lawyer for either from communicating with nonlawyer representatives of the other regarding a separate matter. Nor does this Rule preclude communication with a represented party or person who is seeking advice from a lawyer who is not otherwise representing a client in the matter. A lawyer having independent justification or legal authorization for communicating with a represented party or person is permitted to do so.

[5]   Communications authorized by law may include communications by a lawyer on behalf of a client who is exercising a constitutional or other legal right to communicate with the government. Communications authorized by law may also include investigative activities of lawyers representing governmental entities, directly or through investigative agents, prior to the commencement (as defined by law) of criminal or civil enforcement proceedings. When communicating with the accused in a criminal matter, a government lawyer must comply with this Rule in addition to honoring the state or federal rights of the accused. The fact that a communication does not violate a state or federal right is insufficient to establish that the communication is permissible under this Rule. This Rule is not intended to effect any change in the scope of the anti-contact rule in criminal cases.

[6]   [Omitted.]

[7]   In the case of a represented organization, paragraph (a) ordinarily prohibits communications with a constituent of the organization who: (i) supervises, directs or regularly consults with the organization's lawyer concerning the matter, (ii) has authority to obligate the organization with respect

to the matter, or (iii) whose act or omission in connection with the matter may be imputed to the organization for purposes of civil or criminal liability. Consent of the organization's lawyer is not required for communication with a former unrepresented constituent. If an individual constituent of the organization is represented in the matter by the person's own counsel, the consent by that counsel to a communication will be sufficient for purposes of this Rule. In communicating with a current or former constituent of an organization, a lawyer must not use methods of obtaining evidence that violate the legal rights of the organization. *See* Rules 1.13, 4.4.

[8]   The prohibition on communications with a represented person applies only in circumstances where the lawyer knows that the person is in fact represented in the matter to be discussed. This means that the lawyer has actual knowledge of the fact of the representation; but such actual knowledge may be inferred from the circumstances. *See* Rule 1.0(k) for the definition of "knowledge." Thus, the lawyer cannot evade the requirement of obtaining the consent of counsel by ignoring the obvious.

[9]   In the event the party with whom the lawyer communicates is not known to be represented by counsel in the matter, the lawyer's communications are subject to Rule 4.3.

[10]   A lawyer may not make a communication prohibited by paragraph (a) through the acts of another. *See* Rule 8.4(a).

Client-to-Client Communications

[11]   Persons represented in a matter may communicate directly with each other. A lawyer may properly advise a client to communicate directly with a represented person, and may counsel the client with respect to those communications, provided the lawyer complies with paragraph (b). Agents for lawyers, such as investigators, are not considered clients within the meaning of this Rule even where the represented entity is an agency, department or other organization of the government, and therefore a lawyer may not cause such an agent to communicate with a represented person, unless the lawyer would be authorized by law or a court order to do so. A lawyer may also counsel a client with respect to communications with a represented person, including by drafting papers for the client to present to the represented person. In advising a client in connection with such communications, a lawyer may not advise the client to seek privileged information or other information that the represented person is not personally authorized to disclose or is prohibited from disclosing, such as a trade secret or other information protected by law, or to encourage or invite the represented person to take actions without the advice of counsel.

[12]   A lawyer who advises a client with respect to communications with a represented person should be mindful of the obligation to avoid abusive, harassing, or unfair conduct with regard to the represented person. The lawyer should advise the client against such conduct. A lawyer shall not

advise a client to communicate with a represented person if the lawyer knows that the represented person is legally incompetent. *See* Rule 4.4.

RULE 4.3: COMMUNICATING WITH UNREPRESENTED PERSONS

In communicating on behalf of a client with a person who is not represented by counsel, a lawyer shall not state or imply that the lawyer is disinterested. When the lawyer knows or reasonably should know that the unrepresented person misunderstands the lawyer's role in the matter, the lawyer shall make reasonable efforts to correct the misunderstanding. The lawyer shall not give legal advice to an unrepresented person other than the advice to secure counsel if the lawyer knows or reasonably should know that the interests of such a person are or have a reasonable possibility of being in conflict with the interests of the client.

Comment

[1] An unrepresented person, particularly one not experienced in dealing with legal matters, might assume that a lawyer is disinterested in loyalties or is a disinterested authority on the law even when the lawyer represents a client. In order to avoid a misunderstanding, a lawyer will typically need to identify the lawyer's client and, where necessary, explain that the client has interests opposed to those of the unrepresented person. As to misunderstandings that sometimes arise when a lawyer for an organization deals with an unrepresented constituent, *see* Rule 1.13(a), Comment [2A].

[2] The Rule distinguishes between situations involving unrepresented parties whose interests may be adverse to those of the lawyer's client and those in which the person's interests are not in conflict with the client's. In the former situation, the possibility that the lawyer will compromise the unrepresented person's interests is so great that the Rule prohibits the giving of any advice apart from the advice to obtain counsel. Whether a lawyer is giving impermissible advice may depend on the experience and sophistication of the unrepresented party, as well as the setting in which the behavior and comments occur. This Rule does not prohibit a lawyer from negotiating the terms of a transaction or settling a dispute with an unrepresented person. So long as the lawyer has explained that the lawyer represents an adverse party and is not representing the person, the lawyer may inform the person of the terms on which the lawyer's client will enter into an agreement or settle a matter, prepare documents that require the person's signature, and explain the lawyer's own view of the meaning of the document or the lawyer's view of the underlying legal obligations.

RULE 4.4: RESPECT FOR RIGHTS OF THIRD PERSONS

(a) In representing a client, a lawyer shall not use means that have no substantial purpose other than to embarrass or harm a third

person or use methods of obtaining evidence that violate the legal rights of such a person.

(b) A lawyer who receives a document relating to the representation of the lawyer's client and knows or reasonably should know that the document was inadvertently sent shall promptly notify the sender.

Comment

[1] Responsibility to a client requires a lawyer to subordinate the interests of others to those of the client, but that responsibility does not imply that a lawyer may disregard the rights of third persons. It is impractical to catalogue all such rights, but they include legal restrictions on methods of obtaining evidence from third persons and unwarranted intrusions into privileged relationships, such as the client-lawyer relationship.

[2] Paragraph (b) recognizes that lawyers sometimes receive documents that were mistakenly sent, produced, or otherwise inadvertently made available by opposing parties or their lawyers. One way to resolve this situation is for lawyers to enter into agreements containing explicit provisions as to how the parties will deal with inadvertently sent documents. In the absence of such an agreement, however, if a lawyer knows or reasonably should know that such a document was sent inadvertently, this Rule requires only that the lawyer promptly notify the sender in order to permit that person to take protective measures. Although this Rule does not require that the lawyer refrain from reading or continuing to read the document, a lawyer who reads or continues to read a document that contains privileged or confidential information may be subject to court-imposed sanctions, including disqualification and evidence-preclusion. Whether the lawyer is required to take additional steps, such as returning the original document, is a matter of law beyond the scope of these Rules, as is the question whether the privileged status of a document has been waived. Similarly, this Rule does not address the legal duties of a lawyer who receives a document that the lawyer knows or reasonably should know may have been wrongfully obtained by the sending person. For purposes of this Rule, "document" includes email and other electronically stored information subject to being read or put into readable form.

[3] Refraining from reading or continuing to read a document once a lawyer realizes that it was inadvertently sent to the wrong address and returning the document to the sender honors the policy of these Rules to protect the principles of client confidentiality. Because there are circumstances where a lawyer's ethical obligations should not bar use of the information obtained from an inadvertently sent document, however, this Rule does not subject a lawyer to professional discipline for reading and using that information. Nevertheless, substantive law or procedural rules may require a lawyer to refrain from reading an inadvertently sent document, or to return the document to the sender, or both. Accordingly, in deciding whether to retain or use an inadvertently received document, some lawyers

may take into account whether the attorney-client privilege would attach. But if applicable law or rules do not address the situation, decisions to refrain from reading such documents or to return them, or both, are matters of professional judgment reserved to the lawyer. *See* Rules 1.2, 1.4.

RULE 4.5: COMMUNICATION AFTER INCIDENTS INVOLVING PERSONAL INJURY OR WRONGFUL DEATH

(a) In the event of a specific incident involving potential claims for personal injury or wrongful death, no unsolicited communication shall be made to an individual injured in the incident or to a family member or legal representative of such an individual, by a lawyer or law firm, or by any associate, agent, employee or other representative of a lawyer or law firm representing actual or potential defendants or entities that may defend and/or indemnify said defendants, before the 30th day after the date of the incident, unless a filing must be made within 30 days of the incident as a legal prerequisite to the particular claim, in which case no unsolicited communication shall be made before the 15th day after the date of the incident.

(b) An unsolicited communication by a lawyer or law firm, seeking to represent an injured individual or the legal representative thereof under the circumstance described in paragraph (a) shall comply with Rule 7.3(e).

Comment

[1]   Paragraph (a) imposes a 30–day (or 15–day) restriction on solicitations directed to potential claimants relating to a specific incident involving potential claims for personal injury or wrongful death, by lawyers or law firms who represent actual or potential defendants or entities that may defend or indemnify those defendants. However, if potential claimants are represented by counsel, it is proper for defense counsel to communicate with potential plaintiffs' counsel even during the 30–day (or 15–day) period. *See also* Rule 7.3(e).

RULE 5.1: RESPONSIBILITIES OF LAW FIRMS, PARTNERS, MANAGERS AND SUPERVISORY LAWYERS

(a) A law firm shall make reasonable efforts to ensure that all lawyers in the firm conform to these Rules.

(b) (1) A lawyer with management responsibility in a law firm shall make reasonable efforts to ensure that other lawyers in the law firm conform to these Rules.

(2) A lawyer with direct supervisory authority over another lawyer shall make reasonable efforts to ensure that the supervised lawyer conforms to these Rules.

(c) A law firm shall ensure that the work of partners and associates is adequately supervised, as appropriate. A lawyer with direct supervisory authority over another lawyer shall adequately supervise the work of the other lawyer, as appropriate. In either case, the degree of supervision required is that which is reasonable under the circumstances, taking into account factors such as the experience of the person whose work is being supervised, the amount of work involved in a particular matter, and the likelihood that ethical problems might arise in the course of working on the matter.

(d) A lawyer shall be responsible for a violation of these Rules by another lawyer if:

(1) the lawyer orders or directs the specific conduct or, with knowledge of the specific conduct, ratifies it; or

(2) the lawyer is a partner in a law firm or is a lawyer who individually or together with other lawyers possesses comparable managerial responsibility in a law firm in which the other lawyer practices or is a lawyer who has supervisory authority over the other lawyer; and

(i) knows of such conduct at a time when it could be prevented or its consequences avoided or mitigated but fails to take reasonable remedial action; or

(ii) in the exercise of reasonable management or supervisory authority should have known of the conduct so that reasonable remedial action could have been taken at a time when the consequences of the conduct could have been avoided or mitigated.

Comment

[1] Paragraph (a) applies to law firms; paragraph (b) applies to lawyers with management responsibility in a law firm or a lawyer with direct supervisory authority over another lawyer.

[2] Paragraph (b) requires lawyers with management authority within a firm or those having direct supervisory authority over other lawyers to make reasonable efforts to establish internal policies and procedures designed to provide reasonable assurance that all lawyers in the firm will conform to these Rules. Such policies and procedures include those designed (i) to detect and resolve conflicts of interest (*see* Rule 1.10(f)), (ii) to identify dates by which actions must be taken in pending matters, (iii) to account for client funds and property, and (iv) to ensure that inexperienced lawyers are appropriately supervised.

[3] Other measures that may be required to fulfill the responsibility prescribed in paragraph (b) can depend on the firm's structure and the nature of its practice. In a small firm of experienced lawyers, informal supervision and periodic review of compliance with the required systems ordinarily will

suffice. In a large firm, or in practice situations in which difficult ethical problems frequently arise, more elaborate measures may be necessary. Some firms, for example, have a procedure whereby junior lawyers can make confidential referral of ethical problems directly to a designated senior partner or special committee. *See* Rule 5.2. Firms, whether large or small, may also rely on continuing legal education in professional ethics. In any event, the ethical atmosphere of a firm can influence the conduct of all its members and lawyers with management authority may not assume that all lawyers associated with the firm will inevitably conform to the Rules.

[4]   Paragraph (d) expresses a general principle of personal responsibility for acts of other lawyers in the law firm. *See also* Rule 8.4(a).

[5]   Paragraph (d) imposes such responsibility on a lawyer who orders, directs or ratifies wrongful conduct and on lawyers who are partners or who have comparable managerial authority in a law firm who know or reasonably should know of the conduct. Whether a lawyer has supervisory authority in particular circumstances is a question of fact. Partners and lawyers with comparable authority have at least indirect responsibility for all work being done by the firm, while a partner or manager in charge of a particular matter ordinarily also has supervisory responsibility for the work of other firm lawyers engaged in the matter. Partners and lawyers with comparable authority, as well as those who supervise other lawyers, are indirectly responsible for improper conduct of which they know or should have known in the exercise of reasonable managerial or supervisory authority. Appropriate remedial action by a partner or managing lawyer would depend on the immediacy of that lawyer's involvement and the seriousness of the misconduct. A supervisor is required to intervene to prevent misconduct or to prevent or mitigate avoidable consequences of misconduct if the supervisor knows that the misconduct occurred.

[6]   Professional misconduct by a lawyer under supervision could reveal a violation of paragraph (a), (b) or (c) on the part of a law firm, partner or supervisory lawyer even though it does not entail a violation of paragraph (d) because there was no direction, ratification or knowledge of the violation or no violation occurred.

[7]   Apart from this Rule and Rule 8.4(a), a lawyer does not have disciplinary liability for the conduct of another lawyer. Whether a lawyer may be liable civilly or criminally for another lawyer's conduct is a question of law beyond the scope of these Rules.

[8]   The duties imposed by this Rule on managing and supervising lawyers do not alter the personal duty of each lawyer in a firm to abide by these Rules. *See* Rule 5.2(a).

RULE 5.2: RESPONSIBILITIES OF A SUBORDINATE LAWYER

(a) A lawyer is bound by these Rules notwithstanding that the lawyer acted at the direction of another person.

(b) A subordinate lawyer does not violate these Rules if that lawyer acts in accordance with a supervisory lawyer's reasonable resolution of an arguable question of professional duty.

Comment

[1]   Although a lawyer is not relieved of responsibility for a violation by the fact that the lawyer acted at the direction of a supervisor, that fact may be relevant in determining whether a lawyer had the knowledge required to render conduct a violation of these Rules. For example, if a subordinate filed a frivolous pleading at the direction of a supervisor, the subordinate would not be guilty of a professional violation unless the subordinate knew of the document's frivolous character.

[2]   When lawyers in a supervisor-subordinate relationship encounter a matter involving professional judgment as to ethical duty, the supervisor may assume responsibility for making the judgment. Otherwise, a consistent course of action or position could not be taken. If the question can reasonably be answered only one way, the duty of both lawyers is clear, and they are equally responsible for fulfilling it. However, if the question is reasonably arguable, someone has to decide upon the course of action. That authority ordinarily reposes in the supervisor, and a subordinate may be guided accordingly. To evaluate the supervisor's conclusion that the question is arguable and the supervisor's resolution of it is reasonable in light of applicable law, it is advisable that the subordinate lawyer undertake research, consult with a designated senior partner or special committee, if any (*see* Rule 5.1, Comment [3]), or use other appropriate means. For example, if a question arises whether the interests of two clients conflict under Rule 1.7, the supervisor's reasonable resolution of the question should protect the subordinate professionally if the resolution is subsequently challenged.

RULE 5.3: LAWYER'S RESPONSIBILITY FOR CONDUCT OF NONLAWYERS

(a) A law firm shall ensure that the work of nonlawyers who work for the firm is adequately supervised, as appropriate. A lawyer with direct supervisory authority over a nonlawyer shall adequately supervise the work of the nonlawyer, as appropriate. In either case, the degree of supervision required is that which is reasonable under the circumstances, taking into account factors such as the experience of the person whose work is being supervised, the amount of work involved in a particular matter and the likelihood that ethical problems might arise in the course of working on the matter.

(b) A lawyer shall be responsible for conduct of a nonlawyer employed or retained by or associated with the lawyer that would be a violation of these Rules if engaged in by a lawyer, if:

(1) the lawyer orders or directs the specific conduct or, with knowledge of the specific conduct, ratifies it; or

(2) the lawyer is a partner in a law firm or is a lawyer who individually or together with other lawyers possesses comparable managerial responsibility in a law firm in which the nonlawyer is employed or is a lawyer who has supervisory authority over the nonlawyer; and

(i) knows of such conduct at a time when it could be prevented or its consequences avoided or mitigated but fails to take reasonable remedial action; or

(ii) in the exercise of reasonable management or supervisory authority should have known of the conduct so that reasonable remedial action could have been taken at a time when the consequences of the conduct could have been avoided or mitigated.

Comment

[1]   This Rule requires a law firm to ensure that work of nonlawyers is appropriately supervised. In addition, a lawyer with direct supervisory authority over the work of nonlawyers must adequately supervise those nonlawyers. Comments [2] and [3] to Rule 5.1, which concern supervision of lawyers, provide guidance by analogy for the methods and extent of supervising nonlawyers.

[2]   With regard to nonlawyers, who are not themselves subject to these Rules, the purpose of the supervision is to give reasonable assurance that the conduct of all nonlawyers employed by or retained by or associated with the law firm is compatible with the professional obligations of the lawyers and firm. Lawyers generally employ assistants in their practice, including secretaries, investigators, law student interns and paraprofessionals. Such assistants, whether they are employees or independent contractors, act for the lawyer in rendition of the lawyer's professional services. A law firm must ensure that such assistants are given appropriate instruction and supervision concerning the ethical aspects of their employment, particularly regarding the obligation not to disclose information relating to representation of the client, and should be responsible for their work product. The measures employed in supervising nonlawyers should take account of the fact that they do not have legal training and are not subject to professional discipline. A law firm should make reasonable efforts to establish internal policies and procedures designed to provide reasonable assurance that nonlawyers in the firm will act in a way compatible with these Rules. A lawyer with direct supervisory authority over a nonlawyer has a parallel duty to provide appropriate supervision of the supervised nonlawyer.

[3]   Paragraph (b) specifies the circumstances in which a lawyer is responsible for conduct of a nonlawyer that would be a violation of these Rules if engaged in by a lawyer. For guidance by analogy, *see* Rule 5.1, Comments [5]-[8].

RULE 5.4: PROFESSIONAL INDEPENDENCE OF A LAWYER

(a) A lawyer or law firm shall not share legal fees with a nonlawyer, except that:

(1) an agreement by a lawyer with the lawyer's firm or another lawyer associated in the firm may provide for the payment of money, over a reasonable period of time after the lawyer's death, to the lawyer's estate or to one or more specified persons;

(2) a lawyer who undertakes to complete unfinished legal business of a deceased lawyer may pay to the estate of the deceased lawyer that portion of the total compensation that fairly represents the services rendered by the deceased lawyer; and

(3) a lawyer or law firm may compensate a nonlawyer employee or include a nonlawyer employee in a retirement plan based in whole or in part on a profit-sharing arrangement.

(b) A lawyer shall not form a partnership with a nonlawyer if any of the activities of the partnership consist of the practice of law.

(c) Unless authorized by law, a lawyer shall not permit a person who recommends, employs or pays the lawyer to render legal service for another to direct or regulate the lawyer's professional judgment in rendering such legal services or to cause the lawyer to compromise the lawyer's duty to maintain the confidential information of the client under Rule 1.6.

(d) A lawyer shall not practice with or in the form of an entity authorized to practice law for profit, if:

(1) a nonlawyer owns any interest therein, except that a fiduciary representative of the estate of a lawyer may hold the stock or interest of the lawyer for a reasonable time during administration;

(2) a nonlawyer is a member, corporate director or officer thereof or occupies a position of similar responsibility in any form of association other than a corporation; or

(3) a nonlawyer has the right to direct or control the professional judgment of a lawyer.

Comment

[1] The provisions of this Rule express traditional limitations on sharing fees. These limitations are to protect the lawyer's professional independence of judgment. Where someone other than the client pays the lawyer's fee or salary, or recommends employment of the lawyer, that arrangement does not modify the lawyer's obligation to the client. As stated in paragraph (c), such arrangements should not interfere with the lawyer's professional judgment.

[1A]   Paragraph (a)(2) governs the compensation of a lawyer who undertakes to complete one or more unfinished pieces of legal business of a deceased lawyer. Rule 1.17 governs the sale of an entire law practice upon retirement, which is defined as the cessation of the private practice of law in a given geographic area.

[1B]   Paragraph (a)(3) permits limited fee sharing with a nonlawyer employee, where the employee's compensation or retirement plan is based in whole or in part on a profit-sharing arrangement. Such sharing of profits with a nonlawyer employee must be based on the total profitability of the law firm or a department within a law firm and may not be based on the fee resulting from a single case.

[2]   This Rule also expresses traditional limitations on permitting a third party to direct or regulate the lawyer's professional judgment in rendering legal services to another. *See also* Rule 1.8(f), providing that a lawyer may accept compensation from a third party as long as there is no interference with the lawyer's professional judgment and the client gives informed consent.

RULE 5.5: UNAUTHORIZED PRACTICE OF LAW

(a) A lawyer shall not practice law in a jurisdiction in violation of the regulation of the legal profession in that jurisdiction.

(b) A lawyer shall not aid a nonlawyer in the unauthorized practice of law.

Comment

[1]   A lawyer may practice law only in a jurisdiction in which the lawyer is authorized to practice. A lawyer may be admitted to practice law in a jurisdiction on a regular basis or may be authorized by court rule or order or by law to practice for a limited purpose or on a restricted basis. Paragraph (a) applies to unauthorized practice of law in another jurisdiction by a lawyer through the lawyer's direct action, and paragraph (b) prohibits a lawyer from aiding a nonlawyer in the unauthorized practice of law.

[2]   The definition of the "practice of law" is established by law and varies from one jurisdiction to another. Whatever the definition, limiting the practice of law to members of the bar protects the public against rendition of legal services by unqualified persons. This Rule does not prohibit a lawyer from employing the services of paraprofessionals and delegating functions to them, so long as the lawyer supervises the delegated work and retains responsibility for their work. *See* Rule 5.3.

RULE 5.6: RESTRICTIONS ON RIGHT TO PRACTICE

(a) A lawyer shall not participate in offering or making:

(1) a partnership, shareholder, operating, employment, or other similar type of agreement that restricts the right of a

lawyer to practice after termination of the relationship, except an agreement concerning benefits upon retirement; or

(2) an agreement in which a restriction on a lawyer's right to practice is part of the settlement of a client controversy.

(b) This Rule does not prohibit restrictions that may be included in the terms of the sale of a law practice pursuant to Rule 1.17.

Comment

[1] An agreement restricting the right of lawyers to practice after leaving a firm not only limits their professional autonomy but also limits the freedom of clients to choose a lawyer. Paragraph (a) prohibits such agreements except for restrictions incident to provisions concerning retirement benefits for service with the firm.

[2] Paragraph (a)(2) prohibits a lawyer from agreeing not to represent other persons in connection with settling a claim on behalf of a client.

[3] This Rule does not apply to prohibit restrictions that may be included in the terms of the sale of a law practice pursuant to Rule 1.17.

RULE 5.7: RESPONSIBILITIES REGARDING NONLEGAL SERVICES

(a) With respect to lawyers or law firms providing nonlegal services to clients or other persons:

(1) A lawyer or law firm that provides nonlegal services to a person that are not distinct from legal services being provided to that person by the lawyer or law firm is subject to these Rules with respect to the provision of both legal and nonlegal services.

(2) A lawyer or law firm that provides nonlegal services to a person that are distinct from legal services being provided to that person by the lawyer or law firm is subject to these Rules with respect to the nonlegal services if the person receiving the services could reasonably believe that the nonlegal services are the subject of a client-lawyer relationship.

(3) A lawyer or law firm that is an owner, controlling party or agent of, or that is otherwise affiliated with, an entity that the lawyer or law firm knows to be providing nonlegal services to a person is subject to these Rules with respect to the nonlegal services if the person receiving the services could reasonably believe that the nonlegal services are the subject of a client-lawyer relationship.

(4) For purposes of paragraphs (a)(2) and (a)(3), it will be presumed that the person receiving nonlegal services believes the services to be the subject of a client-lawyer relationship unless the lawyer or law firm has advised the person receiving

the services in writing that the services are not legal services and that the protection of a client-lawyer relationship does not exist with respect to the nonlegal services, or if the interest of the lawyer or law firm in the entity providing nonlegal services is *de minimis.*

(b) Notwithstanding the provisions of paragraph (a), a lawyer or law firm that is an owner, controlling party, agent, or is otherwise affiliated with an entity that the lawyer or law firm knows is providing nonlegal services to a person shall not permit any nonlawyer providing such services or affiliated with that entity to direct or regulate the professional judgment of the lawyer or law firm in rendering legal services to any person, or to cause the lawyer or law firm to compromise its duty under Rule 1.6(a) and Rule 1.6(c) with respect to the confidential information of a client receiving legal services.

(c) For purposes of this Rule, "nonlegal services" shall mean those services that lawyers may lawfully provide and that are not prohibited as an unauthorized practice of law when provided by a nonlawyer.

Comment

[1] For many years, lawyers have provided nonlegal services to their clients. By participating in the delivery of these services, lawyers can serve a broad range of economic and other interests of clients. Whenever a lawyer directly provides nonlegal services, the lawyer must avoid confusion on the part of the client as to the nature of the lawyer's role, so that the person for whom the nonlegal services are performed understands that the services may not carry with them the legal and ethical protections that ordinarily accompany a client-lawyer relationship. The recipient of the nonlegal services may expect, for example, that the protection of client confidences and secrets, prohibitions against representation of persons with conflicting interests, and obligations of a lawyer to maintain professional independence apply to the provision of nonlegal services when that may not be the case. The risk of confusion is especially acute when the lawyer renders both legal and nonlegal services with respect to the same matter. Under some circumstances, the legal and nonlegal services may be so closely entwined that they cannot be distinguished from each other. In this situation, the recipient is likely to be confused as to whether and when the relationship is protected as a client-lawyer relationship. Therefore, where the legal and nonlegal services are not distinct, paragraph (a)(1) requires that the lawyer providing nonlegal services adhere to all of the requirements of these Rules with respect to the nonlegal services. Paragraph (a)(1) applies to the provision of nonlegal services by a law firm if the person for whom the nonlegal services are being performed is also receiving legal services from the firm that are not distinct from the nonlegal services.

[2]   Even when the lawyer believes that the provision of nonlegal services is distinct from any legal services being provided, there is still a risk that the recipient of the nonlegal services might reasonably believe that the recipient is receiving the protection of a client-lawyer relationship. Therefore, paragraph (a)(2) requires that the lawyer providing the nonlegal services adhere to these Rules, unless the person understands that the nonlegal services are not the subject of a client-lawyer relationship. Nonlegal services also may be provided through an entity with which a lawyer is affiliated, for example, as owner, controlling party or agent. In this situation, there is still a risk that the recipient of the nonlegal services might reasonably believe that the recipient is receiving the protection of a client-lawyer relationship. Therefore, paragraph (a)(3) requires that the lawyer involved with the entity providing nonlegal services adhere to all of these Rules with respect to the nonlegal services, unless the person understands that the nonlegal services are not the subject of a client-lawyer relationship.

[3]   These Rules will be presumed to apply to a lawyer who directly provides or is otherwise involved in the provision of nonlegal services unless the lawyer complies with paragraph (a)(4) by communicating in writing to the person receiving the nonlegal services that the services are not legal services and that the protection of a client-lawyer relationship does not exist with respect to the nonlegal services. Such a communication should be made before entering into an agreement for the provision of nonlegal services in a manner sufficient to ensure that the person understands the significance of the communication. In certain circumstances, however, additional steps may be required to ensure that the person understands the distinction. For example, while the written disclaimer set forth in paragraph (a)(4) will be adequate for a sophisticated user of legal and nonlegal services, a more detailed explanation may be required for someone unaccustomed to making distinctions between legal services and nonlegal services. Where appropriate and especially where legal services are provided in the same transaction as nonlegal services, the lawyer should counsel the client about the possible effect of the proposed provision of services on the availability of the attorney-client privilege. The lawyer or law firm will not be required to comply with these requirements if its interest in the entity providing the nonlegal services is so small as to be de minimis.

[4]   Although a lawyer may be exempt from the application of these Rules with respect to nonlegal services on the face of paragraph (a), the scope of the exemption is not absolute. A lawyer who provides or who is involved in the provision of nonlegal services may be excused from compliance with only those Rules that are dependent upon the existence of a representation or client-lawyer relationship. Other Rules, such as those prohibiting lawyers from misusing the confidences or secrets of a former client (*see* Rule 1.9), requiring lawyers to report certain lawyer misconduct (*see* Rule 8.3), and prohibiting lawyers from engaging in illegal, dishonest, fraudulent or deceptive conduct (*see* Rule 8.4), apply to a lawyer irrespective of the existence of a

representation, and thus govern a lawyer not covered by paragraph (a). A lawyer or law firm rendering legal services is always subject to these Rules.

Provision of Legal and Nonlegal Services in the Same Transaction

[5]　In some situations it may be beneficial to a client to purchase both legal and nonlegal services from a lawyer, law firm or affiliated entity in the same matter or in two or more substantially related matters. Examples include: (i) a law firm that represents corporations and also provides public lobbying, public relations, investment banking and business relocation services, (ii) a law firm that represents clients in environmental matters and also provides engineering consulting services to those clients, and (iii) a law firm that represents clients in litigation and also provides consulting services relating to electronic document discovery. In these situations, the lawyer may have a financial interest in the nonlegal services that would constitute a conflict of interest under Rule 1.7(a)(2), which governs conflicts between a client and a lawyer's personal interests.

[5A]　Under Rule 1.7(a)(2), a concurrent conflict of interest exists when a reasonable lawyer would perceive a significant risk that the representation will be materially limited or that the lawyer's professional judgment on behalf of a client will be adversely affected by the lawyer's responsibilities to another client, a former client or a third person or by the lawyer's own financial, business, property or personal interests. When a lawyer or law firm provides both legal and nonlegal services in the same matter (or in substantially related matters), a conflict with the lawyer's own interests will nearly always arise. For example, if the legal representation involves exercising judgment about whether to recommend nonlegal services and which provider to recommend, or if it involves overseeing the provision of the nonlegal services, then a conflict with the lawyer's own interests under Rule 1.7(a)(2) is likely to arise. However, when seeking the consent of a client to such a conflict, the lawyer should comply with both Rule 1.7(b) regarding the conflict affecting the legal representation of the client and Rule 1.8(a) regarding the business transaction with the client.

[5B]　Thus, the client may consent if: (i) the lawyer complies with Rule 1.8(a) with respect to the transaction in which the lawyer agrees to provide the nonlegal services, including obtaining the client's informed consent in a writing signed by the client, (ii) the lawyer reasonably believes that the lawyer can provide competent and diligent legal representation despite the conflict within the meaning of Rule 1.7(b), and (iii) the client gives informed consent pursuant to Rule 1.7(b), confirmed in writing. In certain cases, it will not be possible to provide both legal and nonlegal services because the lawyer could not reasonably believe that he or she can represent the client competently and diligently while providing both legal and nonlegal services in the same or substantially related matters. Whether providing dual services gives rise to an impermissible conflict must be determined on a case-by-case basis, taking into account all of the facts and circumstances, including factors such as: (i) the experience and sophistication of the client in obtaining legal and nonlegal services of the kind being provided in the matter, (ii) the relative size of the anticipated fees for the legal and nonlegal services, (iii) the closeness of the relationship between the legal and nonlegal services, and (iv) the degree of discretion the lawyer has in providing the legal and nonlegal services.

[6] In the context of providing legal and nonlegal services in the same transaction, Rule 1.8(a) first requires that: (i) the nonlegal services be provided on terms that are fair and reasonable to the client, (ii) full disclosure of the terms on which the nonlegal services will be provided be made in writing to the client in a manner understandable by the client, (iii) the client is advised to seek the advice of independent counsel about the provision of the nonlegal services by the lawyer, and (iv) the client gives informed consent, as set forth in Rule 1.8(a)(3), in a writing signed by the client, to the terms of the transaction in which the nonlegal services are provided and to the lawyer's inherent conflict of interest.

[7] In addition, in the context providing legal and nonlegal services in the same transaction, Rule 1.8(a) requires a full disclosure of the nature and extent of the lawyer's financial interest or stake in the provision of the nonlegal services. By its terms, Rule 1.8(a) requires that the nonlegal services be provided on terms that are fair and reasonable to the client. (Where the nonlegal services are provided on terms generally available to the public in the marketplace, that requirement is ordinarily met.) Consequently, as a further safeguard against conflicts that may arise when the same lawyer provides both legal and nonlegal services in the same or substantially related matters, a lawyer may do so only if the lawyer not only complies with Rule 1.8(a) with respect to the nonlegal services, but also obtains the client's informed consent, pursuant to Rule 1.7(b), confirmed in writing, after fully disclosing the advantages and risks of obtaining legal and nonlegal services from the same or affiliated providers in a single matter (or in substantially related matters), including the lawyer's conflict of interest arising from the lawyer's financial interest in the provision of the nonlegal services.

[8] [Omitted.]

[9] [Omitted.]

[10] [Omitted.]

[11] [Omitted.]

RULE 5.8: CONTRACTUAL RELATIONSHIPS BETWEEN LAWYERS AND NONLEGAL PROFESSIONALS

(a) The practice of law has an essential tradition of complete independence and uncompromised loyalty to those it serves. Recognizing this tradition, clients of lawyers practicing in New York State are guaranteed "independent professional judgment and undivided loyalty uncompromised by conflicts of interest." Indeed, these guarantees represent the very foundation of the profession and allow and foster its continued role as a protector of the system of law. There-

fore, a lawyer must remain completely responsible for his or her own independent professional judgment, maintain the confidences and secrets of clients, preserve funds of clients and third parties in his or her control, and otherwise comply with the legal and ethical principles governing lawyers in New York State.

Multi-disciplinary practice between lawyers and nonlawyers is incompatible with the core values of the legal profession and therefore, a strict division between services provided by lawyers and those provided by nonlawyers is essential to protect those values. However, a lawyer or law firm may enter into and maintain a contractual relationship with a nonlegal professional or nonlegal professional service firm for the purpose of offering to the public, on a systematic and continuing basis, legal services performed by the lawyer or law firm as well as other nonlegal professional services, notwithstanding the provisions of Rule 1.7(a), provided that:

(1) the profession of the nonlegal professional or nonlegal professional service firm is included in a list jointly established and maintained by the Appellate Divisions pursuant to Section 1205.3 of the Joint Appellate Division Rules;

(2) the lawyer or law firm neither grants to the nonlegal professional or nonlegal professional service firm, nor permits such person or firm to obtain, hold or exercise, directly or indirectly, any ownership or investment interest in, or managerial or supervisory right, power or position in connection with the practice of law by the lawyer or law firm, nor, as provided in Rule 7.2(a)(1), shares legal fees with a nonlawyer or receives or gives any monetary or other tangible benefit for giving or receiving a referral; and

(3) the fact that the contractual relationship exists is disclosed by the lawyer or law firm to any client of the lawyer or law firm before the client is referred to the nonlegal professional service firm, or to any client of the nonlegal professional service firm before that client receives legal services from the lawyer or law firm; and the client has given informed written consent and has been provided with a copy of the "Statement of Client's Rights In Cooperative Business Arrangements" pursuant to section 1205.4 of the Joint Appellate Divisions Rules.

(b) For purposes of paragraph (a):

(1) each profession on the list maintained pursuant to a Joint Rule of the Appellate Divisions shall have been designated sua sponte, or approved by the Appellate Divisions upon application of a member of a nonlegal profession or nonlegal professional service firm, upon a determination that the profession is composed of individuals who, with respect to their profession:

(i) have been awarded a bachelor's degree or its equivalent from an accredited college or university, or have attained an equivalent combination of educational credit from such a college or university and work experience;

(ii) are licensed to practice the profession by an agency of the State of New York or the United States Government; and

(iii) are required under penalty of suspension or revocation of license to adhere to a code of ethical conduct that is reasonably comparable to that of the legal profession;

(2) the term "ownership or investment interest" shall mean any such interest in any form of debt or equity, and shall include any interest commonly considered to be an interest accruing to or enjoyed by an owner or investor.

(c) This Rule shall not apply to relationships consisting solely of non-exclusive reciprocal referral agreements or understandings between a lawyer or law firm and a nonlegal professional or nonlegal professional service firm.

Comment

Contractual Relationships Between Lawyers and Nonlegal Professionals

[1] Lawyers may enter into interprofessional contractual relationships for the systematic and continuing provision of legal and nonlegal professional services, provided the nonlegal professional or nonlegal professional service firm with which the lawyer or law firm is affiliated does not own, control, supervise or manage, directly or indirectly, in whole or in part, the lawyer's or law firm's practice of law. The nonlegal professional or nonlegal professional service firm may not play a role in, for example, (i) deciding whether to accept or terminate an engagement to provide legal services in a particular matter or to a particular client, (ii) determining the manner in which lawyers are hired or trained, (iii) assigning lawyers to handle particular matters or to provide legal services to particular clients, (iv) deciding whether to undertake pro bono and other public-interest legal work, (v) making financial and budgetary decisions relating to the legal practice, and (vi) determining the compensation and advancement of lawyers and of persons assisting lawyers on legal matters.

[2] The contractual relationship permitted by this Rule may include the sharing of premises, general overhead or administrative costs and services on an arm's length basis. Such financial arrangements, in the context of an agreement between lawyers and other professionals to provide legal and other professional services on a systematic and continuing basis, are permitted subject to the requirements of paragraph (a) and Rule 7.2(a). Similarly, lawyers participating in such arrangements remain subject to general ethical principles in addition to those set forth in this Rule including, at a minimum, Rule 1.7, Rule 1.8(f), Rule 1.9, Rule 5.7(b) and Rule 7.5(a). Thus, the lawyer or

law firm may not, for example, include in its firm name the name of the nonlegal professional service firm or any individual nonlegal professional, enter into formal partnerships with nonlawyers, or practice in an organization authorized to practice law for a profit in which nonlawyers own any interest. Moreover, a lawyer or law firm may not enter into an agreement or arrangement for the use of a name in respect of which a nonlegal professional or nonlegal professional service firm has or exercises a proprietary interest if, under or pursuant to the agreement or arrangement, that nonlegal professional or firm acts or is entitled to act in a manner inconsistent with paragraph (a)(2) or Comment [1]. More generally, the existence of a contractual relationship permitted by this Rule does not by itself create a conflict of interest in violation of Rule 1.8(a). Whenever a law firm represents a client in a matter in which the nonlegal professional service firm's client is also involved, the law firm's interest in maintaining an advantageous relationship with a nonlegal professional service firm might, in certain circumstances, adversely affect the professional judgment of the law firm.

[3]   Each lawyer and law firm having a contractual relationship under paragraph (a) has an ethical duty to observe these Rules with respect to the lawyer's or law firm's own conduct in the context of that relationship. For example, the lawyer or law firm cannot permit the obligation to maintain client confidences, as required by Rule 1.6, to be compromised by the contractual relationship or by its implementation by or on behalf of nonlawyers involved in the relationship. In addition, the prohibition in Rule 8.4(a) against circumventing a Rule through actions of another applies generally to the lawyer or law firm in the contractual relationship.

[4]   The contractual relationship permitted by paragraph (a) may provide for the reciprocal referral of clients by and between the lawyer or law firm and the nonlegal professional or nonlegal professional service firm. When in the context of such a contractual relationship a lawyer or law firm refers a client to the nonlegal professional or nonlegal professional service firm, the lawyer or law firm shall observe the ethical standards of the legal profession in verifying the competence of the nonlegal professional or nonlegal professional services firm to handle the relevant affairs and interests of the client. Referrals should be made only when requested by the client or deemed to be reasonably necessary to serve the client. Thus, even if otherwise permitted by paragraph (a), a contractual relationship may not require referrals on an exclusive basis. *See* Rule 7.2(a).

[5]   To ensure that only appropriate professional services are involved, a contractual relationship for the provision of services is permitted under paragraph (a) only if the nonlegal party thereto is a professional or professional service firm meeting appropriate standards regarding ethics, education, training and licensing. The Appellate Divisions maintain a public list of eligible professions at 22 N.Y.C.R.R. § 1205.5. A member of the nonlegal profession or a professional service firm may apply for the inclusion of particular professions on the list or professions may be added to the list by the Appellate Divisions sua sponte. A lawyer or law firm not wishing to affiliate

with a nonlawyer on a systematic and continuing basis, but only to engage a nonlawyer on an ad hoc basis to assist in a specific matter, is not governed by this Rule when so dealing with the nonlawyer. Thus, a lawyer advising a client in connection with a discharge of chemical wastes may engage the services of and consult with an environmental engineer on that matter without the need to comply with this Rule. Likewise, the requirements of this Rule need not be met when a lawyer retains an expert witness in a particular litigation.

[6] Depending upon the extent and nature of the relationship between the lawyer or law firm, on the one hand, and the nonlegal professional or nonlegal professional service firm, on the other hand, it may be appropriate to treat the parties to a contractual relationship permitted by paragraph (a) as a single law firm for purposes of these Rules, as would be the case if the nonlegal professional or nonlegal professional service firm were in an "of counsel" relationship with the lawyer or law firm. If the parties to the relationship are treated as a single law firm, the principal effects would be that conflicts of interest are imputed as between them pursuant to Rule 1.10(a) and that the law firm would be required to maintain systems for determining whether such conflicts exist pursuant to Rule 1.10(f). To the extent that the rules of ethics of the nonlegal profession conflict with these Rules, the rules of the legal profession will still govern the conduct of the lawyers and the law firm participants in the relationship. A lawyer or law firm may also be subject to legal obligations arising from a relationship with nonlawyer professionals, who are themselves subject to regulation.

RULE 6.1: VOLUNTARY PRO BONO SERVICE

Lawyers are strongly encouraged to provide pro bono legal services to benefit poor persons.

(a) Every lawyer should aspire to:

(1) provide at least 20 hours of pro bono legal services each year to poor persons; and

(2) contribute financially to organizations that provide legal services to poor persons.

(b) Pro bono legal services that meet this goal are:

(1) professional services rendered in civil matters, and in those criminal matters for which the government is not obliged to provide funds for legal representation, to persons who are financially unable to compensate counsel;

(2) activities related to improving the administration of justice by simplifying the legal process for, or increasing the availability and quality of legal services to, poor persons; and

(3) professional services to charitable, religious, civic and educational organizations in matters designed predominantly to address the needs of poor persons.

(c) Appropriate organizations for financial contributions are:

(1) organizations primarily engaged in the provision of legal services to the poor; and

(2) organizations substantially engaged in the provision of legal services to the poor, provided that the donated funds are to be used for the provision of such legal services.

(d) This Rule is not intended to be enforced through the disciplinary process, and the failure to fulfill the aspirational goals contained herein should be without legal consequence.

Comment

[1]   Legal services organizations, courts, government agencies, bar associations and various non-profit organizations have established programs through which lawyers provide free short-term limited legal services, such as advice or the completion of legal forms, to assist persons to address their legal problems without further representation by a lawyer. In these programs, such as legal-advice hotlines, advice-only clinics or pro se counseling programs, a client-lawyer relationship is established, but there is no expectation that the lawyer's representation of the client will continue beyond the limited consultation. Such programs are normally operated under circumstances in which it is not feasible for a lawyer to utilize the conflict-checking system required by Rule 1.10(f) before providing the short-term limited legal services contemplated by this Rule. *See also* Rules 1.7, 1,8, 1.9, 1.10.

[2]   To meet this professional obligation, paragraph (a) urges all lawyers to provide a minimum of 20 hours of pro bono legal service annually without fee or expectation of fee, either directly to poor persons or to organizations that serve the legal or other basic needs of persons of limited financial means. It is recognized that in some years a lawyer may render greater or fewer hours than the annual standard specified, but during the course of the lawyer's career, the lawyer should render on average per year, the number of hours set forth in this Rule. Services can be performed in civil matters or in criminal or quasi-criminal matters for which there is no government obligation to provide funds for legal representation, such as post-conviction death penalty appeal cases.

[2A]   Paragraph (a)(2) provides that, in addition to providing the services described in paragraph (a), lawyers should provide financial support to organizations that provide legal services to the poor. This goal is separate from and not a substitute for the provision of legal services described in paragraph (a). To assist the funding of civil legal services for low income people, when selecting a bank for deposit of funds into an "IOLA" account pursuant to Judiciary Law § 497, a lawyer should take into consideration the interest rate offered by the bank on such funds.

[2B]   Paragraphs (a)(1) and (a)(2) recognize the critical need for legal services that exists among poor persons. Legal services under these paragraphs consist of a full range of activities, including individual and class representation, the provision of legal advice, legislative lobbying, administrative rulemaking and the provision of free training or mentoring to those who represent persons of limited means. The variety of these activities should facilitate participation by government lawyers, even when restrictions exist on their engaging in the outside practice of law.

[3] Because a lawyer who is representing a client in the circumstances addressed by this Rule ordinarily is not able to check systematically for conflicts of interest, paragraph (a) requires compliance with Rules 1.7, 1.8 and 1.9 only if the lawyer knows that the representation presents a conflict of interest for the lawyer, and with Rule 1.10 only if the lawyer knows that another lawyer in the lawyer's firm is disqualified by Rule 1.7, 1.8 or 1.9 in the matter.

[4] To qualify as pro bono service within the meaning of paragraph (a)(1) the service must be provided without fee or expectation of fee, so the intent of the lawyer to render free legal services is essential. Accordingly, services rendered cannot be considered pro bono if an anticipated fee is uncollected, but the award of statutory attorneys' fees in a case originally accepted as pro bono would not disqualify such services from inclusion under this Rule. Lawyers who do receive fees in such cases are encouraged to contribute an appropriate portion of such fees to organizations or projects that benefit persons of limited means.

[5] While a lawyer may fulfill the annual goal to perform pro bono service exclusively through activities described in paragraphs (a)(1) and (a)(2), all lawyers are urged to render public-interest and pro bono service in addition to assistance to the poor. This responsibility can be met in a variety of ways as set forth in paragraph (b). Constitutional, statutory or regulatory restrictions may prohibit or impede government and public sector lawyers and judges from performing the pro bono service outlined in paragraph (a)(1). Accordingly, where those restrictions apply, government and public sector lawyers and judges may fulfill their pro bono responsibility by making financial contributions to organizations that help meet the legal and other basic needs of the poor, as described in paragraphs (a)(2), (c)(1) and (c)(2) or by performing some of the services outlined in paragraph (b)(2) or (b)(3).

[6] Paragraph (b)(1) includes the provision of legal services to those whose incomes and financial resources place them above limited means but are yet unable to meet the financial burdens of a given civil or criminal matter.

[7] Paragraphs (b)(2) and (b)(3) recognize the value of lawyers' engaging in activities that improve the law, the legal system or the legal profession. Examples of the many activities that fall within this paragraph include: (i) serving on bar association committees, (ii) serving on boards of pro bono or legal services programs, (iii) taking part in Law Day activities, (iv) acting as a continuing legal education instructor, a mediator or an arbitrator, and (v) engaging in legislative lobbying to improve the law, the legal system or the profession. In addition to rendering pro bono services directly to the poor and

making financial contributions, lawyers may fulfill the goal of rendering pro bono services by serving on the boards or giving legal advice to organizations whose mission is helping the poor.

[8]   Paragraphs (b)(1) and (b)(2) essentially reiterate the goal as set forth in (a)(2) with the further provision that the lawyer should seek to insure that the donated money be directed to providing legal assistance to the poor rather than the general charitable objectives of such organizations.

[9]   Law firms should act reasonably to enable and encourage all lawyers in the firm to provide the pro bono legal service called for by this Rule.

RULE 6.2: [RESERVED]

RULE 6.3: MEMBERSHIP IN A LEGAL SERVICES ORGANIZATION

A lawyer may serve as a director, officer or member of a not-for-profit legal services organization, apart from the law firm in which the lawyer practices, notwithstanding that the organization serves persons having interests that differ from those of a client of the lawyer or the lawyer's firm. The lawyer shall not knowingly participate in a decision or action of the organization:

(a) if participating in the decision or action would be incompatible with the lawyer's obligations to a client under Rules 1.7 through 1.13; or

(b) where the decision or action could have a material adverse effect on the representation of a client of the organization whose interests differ from those of a client of the lawyer or the lawyer's firm.

Comment

[1]   Lawyers should be encouraged to support and participate in legal services organizations. A lawyer who is an officer or a member of such an organization does not thereby have a client-lawyer relationship with persons served by the organization. However, there is potential conflict between the interests of such persons and the interests of the lawyer's clients. If the possibility of such conflict disqualified a lawyer from serving on the board of a legal services organization, the profession's involvement in such organizations would be severely curtailed.

[1A]   This Rule applies to legal services organizations organized and operating on a not-for-profit basis.

[2]   It may be necessary in appropriate cases to reassure a client of the organization that the representation will not be affected by conflicting loyalties of a member of the board. Established, written policies in this respect can enhance the credibility of such assurances.

RULE 6.4: LAW REFORM ACTIVITIES
AFFECTING CLIENT INTERESTS

A lawyer may serve as a director, officer or member of an organization involved in reform of the law or its administration, notwithstanding that the reform may affect the interests of a client of the lawyer. When the lawyer knows that the interests of a client may be materially benefitted by a decision in which the lawyer actively participates, the lawyer shall disclose that fact to the organization, but need not identify the client. When the lawyer knows that the interests of a client may be adversely affected by a decision in which the lawyer actively participates, the lawyer shall disclose that fact to the client.

Comment

[1]   Lawyers involved in organizations seeking law reform generally do not have a client-lawyer relationship with the organization. Otherwise, it might follow that a lawyer could not be involved in a bar association law reform program that might indirectly affect a client. For example, a lawyer concentrating in antitrust litigation might be regarded as disqualified from participating in drafting revisions of rules governing that subject. In determining the nature and scope of participation in such activities, a lawyer should be mindful of obligations to clients. A lawyer's identification with the organization's aims and purposes, under some circumstances, may give rise to a personal-interest conflict with client interests implicating the lawyer's obligations under other Rules, particularly Rule 1.7. A lawyer is also professionally obligated to protect the integrity of the law reform program by making an appropriate disclosure within the organization when the lawyer knows a private client might be materially affected.

RULE 6.5: PARTICIPATION IN LIMITED PRO
BONO LEGAL SERVICES PROGRAMS

(a) A lawyer who, under the auspices of a program sponsored by a court, government agency, bar association or not-for-profit legal services organization, provides short-term limited legal services to a client without expectation by either the lawyer or the client that the lawyer will provide continuing representation in the matter:

(1) shall comply with Rules 1.7, 1.8 and 1.9, concerning restrictions on representations where there are or may be conflicts of interest as that term is defined in these Rules, only if the lawyer has actual knowledge at the time of commencement of representation that the representation of the client involves a conflict of interest; and

(2) shall comply with Rule 1.10 only if the lawyer has actual knowledge at the time of commencement of representation that

another lawyer associated with the lawyer in a law firm is affected by Rules 1.7, 1.8 and 1.9.

(b) Except as provided in paragraph (a)(2), Rule 1.7 and Rule 1.9 are inapplicable to a representation governed by this Rule.

(c) Short-term limited legal services are services providing legal advice or representation free of charge as part of a program described in paragraph (a) with no expectation that the assistance will continue beyond what is necessary to complete an initial consultation, representation or court appearance.

(d) The lawyer providing short-term limited legal services must secure the client's informed consent to the limited scope of the representation, and such representation shall be subject to the provisions of Rule 1.6.

(e) This Rule shall not apply where the court before which the matter is pending determines that a conflict of interest exists or, if during the course of the representation, the lawyer providing the services becomes aware of the existence of a conflict of interest precluding continued representation.

Comment

[1]   [Omitted.]

[2]   A lawyer who provides short-term limited legal services pursuant to this Rule must secure the client's informed consent to the limited scope of the representation. *See* Rule 1.2(c). If a short-term limited representation would not be reasonable under the circumstances, the lawyer may offer advice to the client, but must also advise the client of the need for further assistance of counsel. Except as provided in this Rule, these Rules, including Rules 1.6 and Rule 1.9(c), are applicable to the limited representation.

[3]   Because a lawyer who is representing a client in the circumstances addressed by this Rule ordinarily is not able to check systematically for conflicts of interest, paragraph (a) requires compliance with Rules 1.7, 1.8 and 1.9 only if the lawyer knows that the representation presents a conflict of interest for the lawyer, and with Rule 1.10 only if the lawyer knows that another lawyer in the lawyer's firm is disqualified in the matter.

[4]   Because the limited nature of the services significantly reduces the risk of conflicts of interest with other matters being handled by the lawyer's firm, paragraph (b) provides that Rules 1.7 and 1.9 are inapplicable to a representation governed by this Rule, except as provided by paragraph (a)(2). Paragraph (a)(2) requires the participating lawyer to comply with Rule 1.10 only when the lawyer knows that the lawyer's firm is affected by Rules 1.7, 1.8 or 1.9. By virtue of paragraph (b), however, a lawyer's participation in a short-term limited legal services program will not preclude the lawyer from undertaking or continuing the representation of a client with interests adverse to a client being represented under the program's auspices. Because the

lawyer is not precluded pursuant to this rule Rule 1.10 becomes inapplicable. Nor will the personal disqualification of a lawyer participating in the program be imputed to other lawyers participating in the program.

[5]   If, after commencing a short-term limited representation in accordance with this Rule, a lawyer undertakes to represent the client in the matter on an ongoing basis, Rules 1.7, 1.9(a) and 1.10 become applicable.

RULE 7.1: ADVERTISING

(a) A lawyer or law firm shall not use or disseminate or participate in the use or dissemination of any advertisement that:

(1) contains statements or claims that are false, deceptive or misleading; or

(2) violates a Rule.

(b) Subject to the provisions of paragraph (a), an advertisement may include information as to:

(1) legal and nonlegal education; degrees and other scholastic distinctions; dates of admission to any bar; areas of the law in which the lawyer or law firm practices, as authorized by these Rules; public offices and teaching positions held; publications of law-related matters authored by the lawyer; memberships in bar associations or other professional societies or organizations, including offices and committee assignments therein; foreign language fluency; and bona fide professional ratings;

(2) names of clients regularly represented, provided that the client has given prior written;

(3) bank references; credit arrangements accepted; prepaid or group legal services programs in which the lawyer or law firm participates; nonlegal services provided by the lawyer or law firm or by an entity owned and controlled by the lawyer or law firm; the existence of contractual relationships between the lawyer or law firm and a nonlegal professional or nonlegal professional service firm, to the extent permitted by Rule 5.8, and the nature and extent of services available through those contractual relationships; and

(4) legal fees for initial consultation; contingent fee rates in civil matters, when accompanied by a statement disclosing the information required by paragraph (p); range of fees for legal and nonlegal services, provided that there be available to the public free of charge a written statement clearly describing the scope of each advertised service, hourly rates, and fixed fees for specified legal and nonlegal services.

(c) An advertisement shall not:

(1) include an endorsement of, or testimonial about, a lawyer or law firm from a client with respect to a matter that is still pending;

(2) include a paid endorsement of, or testimonial about, a lawyer or law firm without disclosing that the person is being compensated therefor;

(3) include the portrayal of a judge, the portrayal of a fictitious law firm, the use of a fictitious name to refer to lawyers not associated together in a law firm, or otherwise imply that lawyers are associated in a law firm if that is not the case;

(4) use actors to portray the lawyer, members of the law firm, or clients, or utilize depictions of fictionalized events or scenes, without disclosure of same;

(5) rely on techniques to obtain attention that demonstrate a clear and intentional lack of relevance to the selection of counsel, including the portrayal of lawyers exhibiting characteristics clearly unrelated to legal competence;

(6) be made to resemble legal documents; or

(7) utilize a nickname, moniker, motto or trade name that implies an ability to obtain results in a matter.

(d) An advertisement that complies with paragraph (e) may contain the following:

(1) statements that are reasonably likely to create an expectation about results the lawyer can achieve;

(2) statements that compare the lawyer's services with the services of other lawyers;

(3) testimonials or endorsements of clients, where not prohibited by paragraph (c)(1), and of former clients; or

(4) statements describing or characterizing the quality of the lawyer's or law firm's services.

(e) It is permissible to provide the information set forth in paragraph (d) provided:

(1) its dissemination does not violate paragraph (a);

(2) it can be factually supported by the lawyer or law firm as of the date on which the advertisement is published or disseminated; and

(3) it is accompanied by the following disclaimer: "Prior results do not guarantee a similar outcome."

(f) Every advertisement other than those appearing in a radio, television or billboard advertisement, in a directory, newspaper, magazine or other periodical (and any web sites related thereto), or made in person pursuant to Rule 7.3(a)(1), shall be labeled "Attorney

Advertising" on the first page, or on the home page in the case of a web site. If the communication is in the form of a self-mailing brochure or postcard, the words "Attorney Advertising" shall appear therein. In the case of electronic mail, the subject line shall contain the notation "ATTORNEY ADVERTISING."

(g) A lawyer or law firm shall not utilize:

(1) a pop-up or pop-under advertisement in connection with computer-accessed communications, other than on the lawyer's or law firm's own web site or other Internet presence; or

(2) meta-tags or other hidden computer codes that, if displayed, would violate these Rules.

(h) All advertisements shall include the name, principal law office address and telephone number of the lawyer or law firm whose services are being offered.

(i) Any words or statements required by this Rule to appear in an advertisement must be clearly legible and capable of being read by the average person, if written, and intelligible if spoken aloud. In the case of a web site, the required words or statements shall appear on the home page.

(j) A lawyer or law firm advertising any fixed fee for specified legal services shall, at the time of fee publication, have available to the public a written statement clearly describing the scope of each advertised service, which statement shall be available to the client at the time of retainer for any such service. Such legal services shall include all those services that are recognized as reasonable and necessary under local custom in the area of practice in the community where the services are performed.

(k) All advertisements shall be pre-approved by the lawyer or law firm, and a copy shall be retained for a period of not less than three years following its initial dissemination. Any advertisement contained in a computer-accessed communication shall be retained by the lawyer for a period of not less than one year. A copy of the contents of any web site covered by this Rule shall be preserved upon the initial publication of the web site, any major web site redesign, or a meaningful and extensive content change, but in no event less frequently than once every 90 days.

(l) If a lawyer or law firm advertises a range of fees or an hourly rate for services, the lawyer or law firm shall not charge more than the fee advertised for such services. If a lawyer or law firm advertises a fixed fee for specified legal services, or performs services described in a fee schedule, the lawyer or law firm shall not charge more than the fixed fee for such stated legal service as set forth in the advertisement or fee schedule, unless the client agrees in writing that the services performed or to be performed were not legal services referred to or implied in the advertisement or in the fee schedule and, further, that a different fee arrangement shall apply to the transaction.

(m) Unless otherwise specified in the advertisement, if a lawyer publishes any fee information authorized under this Rule in a publication that is published more frequently than once per month, the lawyer shall be bound by any representation made therein for a period of not less than 30 days after such publication. If a lawyer publishes any fee information authorized under this Rule in a publication that is published once per month or less frequently, the lawyer shall be bound by any representation made therein until the publication of the succeeding issue. If a lawyer publishes any fee information authorized under this Rule in a publication that has no fixed date for publication of a succeeding issue, the lawyer shall be bound by any representation made therein for a reasonable period of time after publication, but in no event less than 90 days.

(n) Unless otherwise specified, if a lawyer broadcasts any fee information authorized under this Rule, the lawyer shall be bound by any representation made therein for a period of not less than 30 days after such broadcast.

(o) A lawyer shall not compensate or give anything of value to representatives of the press, radio, television or other communication medium in anticipation of or in return for professional publicity in a news item.

(p) All advertisements that contain information about the fees charged by the lawyer or law firm, including those indicating that in the absence of a recovery no fee will be charged, shall comply with the provisions of Judiciary Law § 488(3).

(q) A lawyer may accept employment that results from participation in activities designed to educate the public to recognize legal problems, to make intelligent selection of counsel or to utilize available legal services.

(r) Without affecting the right to accept employment, a lawyer may speak publicly or write for publication on legal topics so long as the lawyer does not undertake to give individual advice.

Comment

Advertising

[1]   The need of members of the public for legal services is met only if they recognize their legal problems, appreciate the importance of seeking assistance, and are able to obtain the services of competent legal counsel. Hence, important functions of the legal profession are to educate people to recognize their problems, to facilitate the process of intelligent selection of lawyers, and to assist in making legal services fully available.

[2] The public's need to know about legal services can be fulfilled in part through advertising. People of limited means who have not made extensive use of legal services in many instances rely on advertising to find appropriate counsel. While a lawyer's reputation may attract some clients, lawyers may also make the public aware of their services by advertising to obtain work.

[3] Advertising by lawyers serves two principal purposes: first, it educates potential clients regarding their need for legal advice and assists them in obtaining a lawyer appropriate for those needs. Second, it enables lawyers to attract clients. To carry out these two purposes and because of the critical importance of legal services, it is of the utmost importance that lawyer advertising not be false, deceptive or misleading. Truthful statements that are misleading are prohibited by this Rule. A truthful statement is misleading if it omits a fact necessary to make the lawyer's communication, considered as a whole, not materially misleading. A truthful statement is also misleading if there is a substantial likelihood that it will lead a reasonable person to formulate a specific conclusion about the lawyer or the lawyer's services, or about the results a lawyer can achieve, for which there is no reasonable factual foundation. For example, a lawyer might truthfully state, "I have never lost a case," but that statement would be misleading if the lawyer settled virtually all cases that the lawyer handled. A communication to anyone that states or implies that the lawyer has the ability to influence improperly a court, court officer, governmental agency or government official is improper under Rule 8.4(e).

[4] To be effective, advertising must attract the attention of viewers, readers or recipients and convey its content in ways that will be understandable and helpful to them. Lawyers may therefore use advertising techniques intended to attract attention, such as music, sound effects, graphics and the like, so long as those techniques do not render the advertisement false, deceptive or misleading. Lawyer advertising may use actors or fictionalized events or scenes for this purpose, provided appropriate disclosure of their use is made. Some images or techniques, however, are highly likely to be misleading. So, for instance, legal advertising should not be made to resemble legal documents.

[5] The "Attorney Advertising" label serves to dispel any confusion or concern that might be created when nonlawyers receive letters or emails from lawyers. The label is not necessary for advertising in newspapers or on television, or similar communications that are self-evidently advertisements, such as billboards or press releases transmitted to news outlets, and as to which there is no risk of such confusion or concern. An advertisement in a newspaper may nevertheless require the label if it is a paid article about a law firm adjacent to other articles written by the newspaper, where there is a reasonable risk that readers will confuse the two. The ultimate purpose of the label is to inform readers where they might otherwise be confused.

[6] Not all communications made by lawyers about the lawyer or the law firm's services are advertising. Advertising by lawyers consists of communications made in any form about the lawyer or the law firm's services, the

primary purpose of which is retention of the lawyer or law firm for pecuniary gain as a result of the communication. However, non-commercial communications motivated by a not-for-profit organization's interest in political expression and association are generally not considered advertising. Of course, all communications by lawyers, whether subject to the special rules governing lawyer advertising or not, are governed by the general rule that lawyers may not engage in conduct involving dishonesty, fraud, deceit or misrepresentation, or knowingly make a material false statement of fact or law. By definition, communications to existing clients are excluded from the Rules governing advertising. A client who is a current client in any matter is an existing client for all purposes of these Rules. (Whether a client is a current client for purposes of conflicts of interest and other issues may depend on other considerations. Generally, the term "current client" for purposes of the advertising exemption should be interpreted more broadly than it is for determining whether a client is a "current client" for purposes of a conflict of interest analysis.)

[7]   Communications to former clients that are germane to the earlier representation are not considered to be advertising. Likewise, communications to other lawyers, including those made in bar association publications and other publications targeted primarily at lawyers, are excluded from the special rules governing lawyer advertising even if their purpose is the retention of the lawyer or law firm. Topical newsletters, client alerts, or blogs intended to educate recipients about new developments in the law are generally not considered advertising. However, a newsletter, client alert, or blog that provides information or news primarily about the lawyer or law firm (for example, the lawyer or law firm's cases, personnel, clients or achievements) generally would be considered advertising. Communications, such as proposed retainer agreements or ordinary correspondence with a prospective client who has expressed interest in, and requested information about, a lawyer's services, are not advertising. Accordingly, the special restrictions on advertising and solicitation would not apply to a lawyer's response to a prospective client who has asked the lawyer to outline the lawyer's qualifications to undertake a proposed retention or the terms of a potential retention.

[8]   The circulation or distribution to prospective clients by a lawyer of an article or report published about the lawyer by a third party is advertising if the lawyer's primary purpose is to obtain retentions. In circulating or distributing such materials the lawyer should include information or disclaimers as necessary to dispel any misconceptions to which the article may give rise. For example, if a lawyer circulates an article discussing the lawyer's successes that is reasonably likely to create an expectation about the results the lawyer will achieve in future cases, a disclaimer is required by paragraph (e)(3). If the article contains misinformation about the lawyer's qualifications, any circulation of the article by the lawyer should make any necessary corrections or qualifications. This may be necessary even when the article included misinformation through no fault of the lawyer or because the article is out of date, so that material information that was true at the time is no

longer true. Some communications by a law firm that may constitute marketing or branding are not necessarily advertisements. For example, pencils, legal pads, greeting cards, coffee mugs, T-shirts or the like with the law firm name, logo, and contact information printed on them do not constitute "advertisements" within the definition of this Rule if their primary purpose is general awareness and branding, rather than the retention of the law firm for a particular matter.

Recognition of Legal Problems

[9] The legal professional should help the public to recognize legal problems because such problems may not be self-revealing and might not be timely noticed. Therefore, lawyers should encourage and participate in educational and public-relations programs concerning the legal system, with particular reference to legal problems that frequently arise. A lawyer's participation in an educational program is ordinarily not considered to be advertising because its primary purpose is to educate and inform rather than to attract clients. Such a program might be considered to be advertising if, in addition to its educational component, participants or recipients are expressly encouraged to hire the lawyer or law firm. A lawyer who writes or speaks for the purpose of educating members of the public to recognize their legal problems should carefully refrain from giving or appearing to give a general solution applicable to all apparently similar individual problems, because slight changes in fact situations may require a material variance in the applicable advice; otherwise, the public may be misled and misadvised. Talks and writings by lawyers for nonlawyers should caution them not to attempt to solve individual problems on the basis of the information contained therein.

[10] As members of their communities, lawyers may choose to sponsor or contribute to cultural, sporting, charitable or other events organized by not-for-profit organizations. If information about the lawyer or law firm disseminated in connection with such an event is limited to the identification of the lawyer or law firm, the lawyer's or law firm's contact information, a brief description of areas of practice, and the fact of sponsorship or contribution, the communication is not considered advertising.

Statements Creating Expectations, Characterizations of Quality, and Comparisons

[11] Lawyer advertising may include statements that are reasonably likely to create an expectation about results the lawyer can achieve, statements that compare the lawyer's services with the services of other lawyers, or statements describing or characterizing the quality of the lawyer's or law firm's services, only if they can be factually supported by the lawyer or law firm as of the date on which the advertisement is published or disseminated and are accompanied by the following disclaimer: "Prior results do not guarantee a similar outcome." Accordingly, if true and accompanied by the disclaimer, a lawyer or law firm could advertise "Our firm won 10 jury verdicts over $1,000,000 in the last five years," "We have more Patent

Lawyers than any other firm in X County," or "I have been practicing in the area of divorce law for more than 10 years." Even true factual statements may be misleading if presented out of the context of additional information needed to properly understand and evaluate the statements. For example, a truthful statement by a lawyer that the lawyer's average jury verdict for a given year was $100,000 may be misleading if that average was based on a large number of very small verdicts and one $10,000,000 verdict. Likewise, advertising that truthfully recites judgment amounts would be misleading if the lawyer failed to disclose that the judgments described were overturned on appeal or were obtained by default.

[12] Descriptions of characteristics of the lawyer or law firm that are not comparative and do not involve results obtained are permissible even though they cannot be factually supported. Such statements are understood to be general descriptions and not claims about quality, and would not be likely to mislead potential clients. Accordingly, a law firm could advertise that it is "Hard–Working," "Dedicated," or "Compassionate" without the necessity to provide factual support for such subjective claims. On the other hand, descriptions of characteristics of the law firm that compare its services with those of other law firms and that are not susceptible of being factually supported could be misleading to potential clients. Accordingly, a lawyer may not advertise that the lawyer is the "Best," "Most Experienced," or "Hardest Working." Similarly, some claims that involve results obtained are not susceptible of being factually supported and could be misleading to potential clients. Accordingly, a law firm may not advertise that it will obtain "Big $$$," "Most Money," or "We Win Big."

Bona Fide Professional Ratings

[13] An advertisement may include information regarding bona fide professional ratings by referring to the rating service and how it has rated the lawyer, provided that the advertisement contains the "past results" disclaimer as required under paragraphs (d) and (e). However, a rating is not "bona fide" unless it is unbiased and nondiscriminatory. Thus, it must evaluate lawyers based on objective criteria or legitimate peer review in a manner unbiased by the rating service's economic interests (such as payment to the rating service by the rated lawyer) and not subject to improper influence by lawyers who are being evaluated. Further, the rating service must fairly consider all lawyers within the pool of those who are purported to be covered. For example, a rating service that purports to evaluate all lawyers practicing in a particular geographic area or in a particular area of practice or of a particular age must apply its criteria to all lawyers within that geographic area, practice area, or age group.

Meta-Tags

[14] Meta-tags are hidden computer software codes that direct certain Internet search engines to the web site of a lawyer or law firm. For example, if a lawyer places the meta-tag "NY personal injury specialist" on the lawyer's

web site, then a person who enters the search term "personal injury specialist" into a search engine will be directed to that lawyer's web page. That particular meta-tag is prohibited because Rule 7.4(a) generally prohibits the use of the word "specialist." However, a lawyer may use an advertisement employing meta-tags or other hidden computer codes that, if displayed, would not violate a Rule.

Advertisements Referring to Fees and Advances

[15] All advertisements that contain information about the fees or expenses charged by the lawyer or law firm, including advertisements indicating that in the absence of a recovery no fee will be charged, must comply with the provisions of section 488(3) of the Judiciary Law. However, a lawyer or law firm that offers any of the fee and expense arrangements permitted by section 488(3) must not, either directly or in any advertisement, state or imply that the lawyer's or law firm's ability to advance or pay costs and expenses of litigation is unique or extraordinary when that is not the case. For example, if an advertisement promises that the lawyer or law firm will advance the costs and expenses of litigation contingent on the outcome of the matter, or promises that the lawyer or law firm will pay the costs and expenses of litigation for indigent clients, then the advertisement must not say that such arrangements are "unique in the area," "unlike other firms," available "only at our firm," "extraordinary," or words to that effect, unless that is actually the case. However, if the lawyer or law firm can objectively demonstrate that this arrangement is unique or extraordinary, then the lawyer or law firm may make such a claim in the advertisement.

Retention of Copies; Filing of Copies; Designation of Principal Office

[16] Where these Rules require that a lawyer retain a copy of an advertisement or file a copy of a solicitation or other information, that obligation may be satisfied by any of the following: original records, photocopies, microfilm, optical imaging, and any other medium that preserves an image of the document that cannot be altered without detection.

[17] A law firm that has no office it considers its principal office may comply with paragraph (h) by listing one or more offices where a substantial amount of the law firm's work is performed.

RULE 7.2: PAYMENT FOR REFERRALS

(a) A lawyer shall not compensate or give anything of value to a person or organization to recommend or obtain employment by a client, or as a reward for having made a recommendation resulting in employment by a client, except that:

(1) a lawyer or law firm may refer clients to a nonlegal professional or nonlegal professional service firm pursuant to a contractual relationship with such nonlegal professional or nonlegal professional service firm to provide legal and other profes-

sional services on a systematic and continuing basis as permitted by Rule 5.8, provided however that such referral shall not otherwise include any monetary or other tangible consideration or reward for such, or the sharing of legal fees; and

(2) a lawyer may pay the usual and reasonable fees or dues charged by a qualified legal assistance organization or referral fees to another lawyer as permitted by Rule 1.5(g).

(b) A lawyer or the lawyer's partner or associate or any other affiliated lawyer may be recommended, employed or paid by, or may cooperate with one of the following offices or organizations that promote the use of the lawyer's services or those of a partner or associate or any other affiliated lawyer, or request one of the following offices or organizations to recommend or promote the use of the lawyer's services or those of the lawyer's partner or associate, or any other affiliated lawyer as a private practitioner, if there is no interference with the exercise of independent professional judgment on behalf of the client:

(1) a legal aid office or public defender office:

(i) operated or sponsored by a duly accredited law school;

(ii) operated or sponsored by a bona fide, non-profit community organization;

(iii) operated or sponsored by a governmental agency; or

(iv) operated, sponsored, or approved by a bar association;

(2) a military legal assistance office;

(3) a lawyer referral service operated, sponsored or approved by a bar association or authorized by law or court rule; or

(4) any bona fide organization that recommends, furnishes or pays for legal services to its members or beneficiaries provided the following conditions are satisfied:

(i) Neither the lawyer, nor the lawyer's partner, nor associate, nor any other affiliated lawyer nor any nonlawyer, shall have initiated or promoted such organization for the primary purpose of providing financial or other benefit to such lawyer, partner, associate or affiliated lawyer;

(ii) Such organization is not operated for the purpose of procuring legal work or financial benefit for any lawyer as a private practitioner outside of the legal services program of the organization;

(iii) The member or beneficiary to whom the legal services are furnished, and not such organization, is recognized as the client of the lawyer in the matter;

(iv) The legal service plan of such organization provides appropriate relief for any member or beneficiary who asserts a claim that representation by counsel furnished, selected or approved by the organization for the particular matter involved would be unethical, improper or inadequate under the circumstances of the matter involved; and the plan provides an appropriate procedure for seeking such relief;

(v) The lawyer does not know or have cause to know that such organization is in violation of applicable laws, rules of court or other legal requirements that govern its legal service operations; and

(vi) Such organization has filed with the appropriate disciplinary authority, to the extent required by such authority, at least annually a report with respect to its legal service plan, if any, showing its terms, its schedule of benefits, its subscription charges, agreements with counsel and financial results of its legal service activities or, if it has failed to do so, the lawyer does not know or have cause to know of such failure.

Comment

Paying Others to Recommend a Lawyer

[1] Lawyers are not permitted to pay others for channeling professional work. Paragraph (a)(3), however, allows a lawyer to pay for advertising and communications permitted by these Rules, including the costs of print directory listings, online directory listings, newspaper ads, television and radio airtime, domain name registrations, sponsorship fees, banner ads and group advertising. A lawyer may compensate employees, agents and vendors who are engaged to provide marketing or client development services, such as publicists, public-relations personnel, marketing personnel and web site designers. *See* Rule 5.3 for the duties of lawyers and law firms with respect to the conduct of nonlawyers who prepare marketing materials for them.

[2] A lawyer may pay the usual charges of a qualified legal assistance organization. A lawyer so participating should make certain that the relationship with a qualified legal assistance organization in no way interferes with independent professional representation of the interests of the individual client. A lawyer should avoid situations in which officials of the organization who are not lawyers attempt to direct lawyers concerning the manner in which legal services are performed for individual members and should also avoid situations in which considerations of economy are given undue weight in determining the lawyers employed by an organization or the legal services to be performed for the member or beneficiary, rather than competence and quality of service.

[3] A lawyer who accepts assignments or referrals from a qualified legal assistance organization must act reasonably to ensure that the activities of

the plan or service are compatible with the lawyer's professional obligations. *See* Rule 5.3. The lawyer must ensure that the organization's communications with prospective clients are in conformity with these Rules. Thus, advertising must not be false or misleading, as would be the case if the communications of a qualified legal assistance organization would mislead prospective clients to think that it was a lawyer referral service sponsored by a state agency or bar association. Nor could the lawyer allow in-person, telephonic or real-time interactive electronic contacts that would violate Rule 7.3.

[4] A lawyer also may agree to refer clients to another lawyer or a nonlawyer in return for the undertaking of that person to refer clients or customers to the lawyer. Such reciprocal referral arrangements must not interfere with the lawyer's professional judgment as to making referrals or as to providing substantive legal services. *See* Rules 2.1, 5.4(c). Except as provided in Rule 1.5(e), a lawyer who receives referrals from a lawyer or nonlawyer must not pay anything solely for the referral, but the lawyer does not violate paragraph (a) by agreeing to refer clients to the other lawyer or nonlawyer so long as the reciprocal referral agreement is not exclusive and the client is informed of the referral agreement. A lawyer may enter into such an arrangement only if it is nonexclusive on both sides, so that both the lawyer and the nonlawyer are free to refer clients to others if that is in the best interest of those clients. Conflicts of interest created by such arrangements are governed by Rule 1.7. A lawyer's interest in receiving a steady stream of referrals from a particular source must not undermine the lawyer's professional judgment on behalf of clients. Reciprocal referral agreements should not be of indefinite duration and should be reviewed periodically to determine whether they comply with these Rules. This Rule does not restrict referrals or divisions of revenues or net income among lawyers within firms comprising multiple entities.

[5] Campaign contributions by lawyers to government officials or candidates for public office who are, or may be, in a position to influence the award of a legal engagement may threaten governmental integrity by subjecting the recipient to a conflict of interest. Correspondingly, when a lawyer makes a significant contribution to a public official or an election campaign for a candidate for public office and is later engaged by the official to perform legal services for the official's agency, it may appear that the official has been improperly influenced in selecting the lawyer, whether or not this is so. This appearance of influence reflects poorly on the integrity of the legal profession and government as a whole. For these reasons, just as the Code prohibits a lawyer from compensating or giving anything of value to a person or organization to recommend or obtain employment by a client, the Code prohibits a lawyer from making or soliciting a political contribution to any candidate for government office, government official, political campaign committee or political party, if a disinterested person would conclude that the contribution is being made or solicited for the purpose of obtaining or being considered eligible to obtain a government legal engagement. This would be true even in the absence of an understanding between the lawyer and any government

official or candidate that special consideration will be given in return for the political contribution or solicitation.

[6]   In determining whether a disinterested person would conclude that a contribution to a candidate for government office, government official, political campaign committee or political party is or has been made for the purpose of obtaining or being considered eligible to obtain a government legal engagement, the factors to be considered include

(a) whether legal work awarded to the contributor or solicitor, if any, was awarded pursuant to a process that was insulated from political influence, such as a "Request for Proposal" process,

(b) the amount of the contribution or the contributions resulting from a solicitation,

(c) whether the contributor or any law firm with which the lawyer is associated has sought or plans to seek government legal work from the official or candidate,

(d) whether the contribution or solicitation was made because of an existing personal, family or non-client professional relationship with the government official or candidate,

(e) whether prior to the contribution or solicitation in question, the contributor or solicitor had made comparable contributions or had engaged in comparable solicitations on behalf of governmental officials or candidates for public office for which the lawyer or any law firm with which the lawyer is associated did not perform or seek to perform legal work,

(f) whether the contributor has made a contribution to the government official's or candidate's opponent(s) during the same campaign period and, if so, the amounts thereof, and

(g) whether the contributor is eligible to vote in the jurisdiction of the governmental official or candidate, and if not, whether other factors indicate that the contribution or solicitation was nonetheless made to further a genuinely held political, social or economic belief or interest rather than to obtain a legal engagement.

RULE 7.3: SOLICITATION AND RECOMMENDATION OF PROFESSIONAL EMPLOYMENT

(a) A lawyer shall not engage in solicitation:

(1) by in-person or telephone contact, or by real-time or interactive computer-accessed communication unless the recipient is a close friend, relative, former client or existing client; or

(2) by any form of communication if:

(i) the communication or contact violates Rule 4.5, Rule 7.1(a), or paragraph (e) of this Rule;

(ii) the recipient has made known to the lawyer a desire not to be solicited by the lawyer;

(iii) the solicitation involves coercion, duress or harassment;

(iv) the lawyer knows or reasonably should know that the age or the physical, emotional or mental state of the recipient makes it unlikely that the recipient will be able to exercise reasonable judgment in retaining a lawyer; or

(v) the lawyer intends or expects, but does not disclose, that the legal services necessary to handle the matter competently will be performed primarily by another lawyer who is not affiliated with the soliciting lawyer as a partner, associate or of counsel.

(b) For purposes of this Rule, "solicitation" means any advertisement initiated by or on behalf of a lawyer or law firm that is directed to, or targeted at, a specific recipient or group of recipients, or their family members or legal representatives, the primary purpose of which is the retention of the lawyer or law firm, and a significant motive for which is pecuniary gain. It does not include a proposal or other writing prepared and delivered in response to a specific request of a prospective client.

(c) A solicitation directed to a recipient in this State shall be subject to the following provisions:

(1) A copy of the solicitation shall at the time of its dissemination be filed with the attorney disciplinary committee of the judicial district or judicial department wherein the lawyer or law firm maintains its principal office. Where no such office is maintained, the filing shall be made in the judicial department where the solicitation is targeted. A filing shall consist of:

(i) a copy of the solicitation;

(ii) a transcript of the audio portion of any radio or television solicitation; and

(iii) if the solicitation is in a language other than English, an accurate English-language translation.

(2) Such solicitation shall contain no reference to the fact of filing.

(3) If a solicitation is directed to a predetermined recipient, a list containing the names and addresses of all recipients shall be retained by the lawyer or law firm for a period of not less than three years following the last date of its dissemination.

(4) Solicitations filed pursuant to this subdivision shall be open to public inspection.

(5) The provisions of this paragraph shall not apply to:

(i) a solicitation directed or disseminated to a close friend, relative, or former or existing client;

(ii) a web site maintained by the lawyer or law firm, unless the web site is designed for and directed to or targeted at a prospective client affected by an identifiable actual event or occurrence or by an identifiable prospective defendant; or

(iii) professional cards or other announcements the distribution of which is authorized by Rule 7.5(a).

(d) A written solicitation shall not be sent by a method that requires the recipient to travel to a location other than that at which the recipient ordinarily receives business or personal mail or that requires a signature on the part of the recipient.

(e) No solicitation relating to a specific incident involving potential claims for personal injury or wrongful death shall be disseminated before the 30th day after the date of the incident, unless a filing must be made within 30 days of the incident as a legal prerequisite to the particular claim, in which case no unsolicited communication shall be made before the 15th day after the date of the incident.

(f) Any solicitation made in writing or by computer-accessed communication and directed to a pre-determined recipient, if prompted by a specific occurrence involving or affecting a recipient, shall disclose how the lawyer obtained the identity of the recipient and learned of the recipient's potential legal need.

(g) If a retainer agreement is provided with any solicitation, the top of each page shall be marked "SAMPLE" in red ink in a type size equal to the largest type size used in the agreement and the words "DO NOT SIGN" shall appear on the client signature line.

(h) Any solicitation covered by this section shall include the name, principal law office address and telephone number of the lawyer or law firm whose services are being offered.

(i) The provisions of this Rule shall apply to a lawyer or members of a law firm not admitted to practice in this State who shall solicit retention by residents of this State.

Comment

Solicitation

[1] In addition to seeking clients through general advertising (either by public communications in the media or by private communications to potential clients who are neither current clients nor other lawyers), many lawyers attempt to attract clients through a specialized category of advertising called "solicitation." Not all advertisements are solicitations within the meaning of this Rule. All solicitations, however, are advertisements with certain additional characteristics. By definition, a communication that is not an advertisement is not a solicitation. Solicitations are subject to all of the Rules governing advertising and are also subject to additional Rules, including filing

a copy of the solicitation with the appropriate attorney disciplinary authority (including a transcript of the audio portion of any radio or television solicitation and, if the solicitation is in a language other than English, an accurate English language translation). These and other additional requirements will facilitate oversight by disciplinary authorities.

[2]   A "solicitation" means any advertisement: (i) that is initiated by a lawyer or law firm (as opposed to a communication made in response to an inquiry initiated by a potential client), (ii) with a primary purpose of persuading recipients to retain the lawyer or law firm (as opposed to providing educational information about the law, *see* Rule 7.1, Comment [7]), (iii) that has as a significant motive for the lawyer to make money (as opposed to a public-interest lawyer offering pro bono services), and (iv) that is directed to or targeted at a specific recipient or group of recipients, or their family members or legal representatives. Any advertisement that meets all four of these criteria is a solicitation, and is governed not only by the Rules that govern all advertisements but also by special Rules governing solicitation.

Directed or Targeted

[3]   An advertisement may be considered to be directed to or targeted at a specific recipient or recipients in two different ways. First, an advertisement is considered "directed to or targeted at" a specific recipient or recipients if it is made by in-person or telephone contact or by real-time or interactive computer-accessed communication or if it is addressed so that it will be delivered to the specific recipient or recipients or their families or agents (as with letters, emails, express packages). Advertisements made by in-person or telephone contact or by real-time or interactive computer-accessed communication are prohibited unless the recipient is a close friend, relative, former client or current client. Advertisements addressed so that they will be delivered to the specific recipient or recipients or their families or agents (as with letters, emails, express packages) are subject to various additional rules governing solicitation (including filing and public inspection) because otherwise they would not be readily subject to disciplinary oversight and review. Second, an advertisement in public media such as newspapers, television, billboards, web sites or the like is a solicitation if it makes reference to a specific person or group of people whose legal needs arise out of a specific incident to which the advertisement explicitly refers. The term "specific incident" is explained in Comment [5].

[4]   Unless it falls within Comment [3], an advertisement in public media such as newspapers, television, billboards, web sites or the like is presumed not to be directed to or targeted at a specific recipient or recipients. For example, an advertisement in a public medium is not directed to or targeted at "a specific recipient or group of recipients" simply because it is intended to attract potential clients with needs in a specified area of law. Thus, a lawyer could advertise in the local newspaper that the lawyer is available to assist homeowners in reducing property tax assessments. Likewise, an advertisement by a patent lawyer is not directed or targeted within the meaning of the

definition solely because the magazine is geared toward inventors. Similarly, a lawyer could advertise on television or in a newspaper or web site to the general public that the lawyer practices in the area of personal injury or Workers' Compensation law. The fact that some recipients of such advertisements might actually be in need of specific legal services at the time of the communication does not transform such advertisements into solicitations.

Solicitations Relating To a Specific Incident Involving Potential Claims for Personal Injury or Wrongful Death

[5]   Solicitations relating to a specific incident involving potential claims for personal injury or wrongful death are subject to a further restriction, in that they may not be disseminated until 30 days (or in some cases 15 days) after the date of the incident. This restriction applies even where the recipient is a close friend, relative, or former client, but not where the recipient is an current client. A "specific incident" is a particular identifiable event (or a sequence of related events occurring at approximately the same time and place) that causes harm to one or more people. Specific incidents include such events as traffic accidents, plane or train crashes, explosions, building collapses, and the like.

[6]   A solicitation that is intended to attract potential claims for personal injury or wrongful death arising from a common cause but at disparate times and places, does not relate to a specific incident and is not subject to the special 30–day (or 15–day) rule, even though it is addressed so that it will be delivered to specific recipients or their families or agents (as with letters, emails, express packages), or is made in a public medium such as newspapers, television, billboards, web sites or the like and makes reference to a specific person or group of people, *see* Comments [3]-[4]. For example, solicitations intended to be of interest only to potential claimants injured over a period of years by a defective medical device or medication do not relate to a specific incident and are not subject to the special 30–day (or 15–day) rule.

[7]   An advertisement in the public media that makes no express reference to a specific incident does not become a solicitation subject to the 30–day (or 15–day) rule solely because a specific incident has occurred within the last 30 (or 15) days. Thus, a law firm that advertises on television or in newspapers that it can "help injured people explore their legal rights" is not violating the 30–day (or 15–day) rule by running or continuing to run its advertisements even though a mass disaster injured many people within hours or days before the advertisement appeared. Unless an advertisement in the public media explicitly refers to a specific incident, it is not a solicitation subject to the 30–day (or 15–day) blackout period. However, if a lawyer causes an advertisement to be delivered (whether by mail, email, express service, courier, or any other form of direct delivery) to a specific recipient (i) with knowledge that the addressee is either a person killed or injured in a specific incident or that person's family member or agent, and (ii) with the intent to communicate with that person because of that knowledge, then the advertise-

ment is a solicitation subject to the 30–day (or 15–day) rule even if it makes no reference to a specific incident and even if it is part of a mass mailing.

Extraterritorial Application of Solicitation Rules

[8]   All of the special solicitation rules, including the special 30–day (or 15–day) rule, apply to solicitations directed to recipients in New York State, whether made by a lawyer admitted in New York State or a lawyer admitted in any another jurisdiction. Solicitations by a lawyer admitted in New York State directed to or targeted at a recipient or recipients outside of New York State are not subject to the filing and related requirements set out in Rule 7.3(c). Whether such solicitations are subject to the special 30–day (or 15–day) rule depends on the application of Rule 8.5.

In-Person, Telephone and Real–Time or Interactive Computer–Accessed Communication

[9]   Paragraph (a) generally prohibits in-person solicitation, which has historically been disfavored by the bar because it poses serious dangers to potential clients. For example, in-person solicitation poses the risk that a lawyer, who is trained in the arts of advocacy and persuasion, may pressure a potential client to hire the lawyer without adequate consideration. These same risks are present in telephone contact or by real-time or interactive computer-accessed communication and are regulated in the same manner. The prohibitions on in-person or telephone contact and by real-time or interactive computer-accessed communication do not apply if the recipient is a close friend, relative, former or current client. Communications with these individuals do not pose the same dangers as solicitations to others. However, when the special 30–day (or 15–day) rule applies, it does so even where the recipient is a close friend, relative, or former client. Ordinary email and web sites are not considered to be real-time or interactive communication. Similarly, automated pop-up advertisements on a web site that are not a live response are not considered to be real-time or interactive communication. Instant messaging, chat rooms, and other similar types of conversational computer-accessed communication are considered to be real-time or interactive communication.

RULE 7.4: IDENTIFICATION OF PRACTICE AND SPECIALTY

(a) **A lawyer or law firm may publicly identify one or more areas of law in which the lawyer or the law firm practices, or may state that the practice of the lawyer or law firm is limited to one or more areas of law, provided that the lawyer or law firm shall not state that the lawyer or law firm is a specialist or specializes in a particular field of law, except as provided in Rule 7.4(c).**

(b) **A lawyer admitted to engage in patent practice before the United States Patent and Trademark Office may use the designation "Patent Attorney" or a substantially similar designation.**

(c) A lawyer may state that the lawyer has been recognized or certified as a specialist only as follows:

(1) A lawyer who is certified as a specialist in a particular area of law or law practice by a private organization approved for that purpose by the American Bar Association may state the fact of certification if, in conjunction therewith, the certifying organization is identified and the following statement is prominently made: "The [name of the private certifying organization] is not affiliated with any governmental authority. Certification is not a requirement for the practice of law in the State of New York and does not necessarily indicate greater competence than other attorneys experienced in this field of law;"

(2) A lawyer who is certified as a specialist in a particular area of law or law practice by the authority having jurisdiction over specialization under the laws of another state or territory may state the fact of certification if, in conjunction therewith, the certifying state or territory is identified and the following statement is prominently made: "Certification granted by the [identify state or territory] is not recognized by any governmental authority within the State of New York. Certification is not a requirement for the practice of law in the State of New York and does not necessarily indicate greater competence than other attorneys experienced in this field of law."

Comment

[1]   Paragraph (a) permits a lawyer to indicate areas of practice in which the lawyer practices, or that his or her practice is limited to those areas.

[2]   Paragraph (b) recognizes the long-established policy of the Patent and Trademark Office for the designation of lawyers practicing before the Office.

[3]   Paragraph (c) permits a lawyer to state that the lawyer specializes or is certified as a specialist in a field of law if such certification is granted by an organization approved or accredited by the American Bar Association or by the authority having jurisdiction over specialization under the laws of another jurisdiction provided that the name of the certifying organization or authority must be included in any communication regarding the certification together with the disclaimer required by paragraph (c).

RULE 7.5: PROFESSIONAL NOTICES, LETTERHEADS AND SIGNS

(a) A lawyer or law firm may use internet web sites, professional cards, professional announcement cards, office signs, letterheads or similar professional notices or devices, provided the same do not violate any statute or court rule and are in accordance with Rule 7.1, including the following:

(1) a professional card of a lawyer identifying the lawyer by name and as a lawyer, and giving addresses, telephone numbers, the name of the law firm, and any information permitted under Rule 7.1(b) or Rule 7.4. A professional card of a law firm may also give the names of members and associates;

(2) a professional announcement card stating new or changed associations or addresses, change of firm name, or similar matters pertaining to the professional offices of a lawyer or law firm or any nonlegal business conducted by the lawyer or law firm pursuant to Rule 5.7. It may state biographical data, the names of members of the firm and associates, and the names and dates of predecessor firms in a continuing line of succession. It may state the nature of the legal practice if permitted under Rule 7.4;

(3) a sign in or near the office and in the building directory identifying the law office and any nonlegal business conducted by the lawyer or law firm pursuant to Rule 5.7. The sign may state the nature of the legal practice if permitted under Rule 7.4; or

(4) a letterhead identifying the lawyer by name and as a lawyer, and giving addresses, telephone numbers, the name of the law firm, associates and any information permitted under Rule 7.1(b) or Rule 7.4. A letterhead of a law firm may also give the names of members and associates, and names and dates relating to deceased and retired members. A lawyer or law firm may be designated "Of Counsel" on a letterhead if there is a continuing relationship with a lawyer or law firm, other than as a partner or associate. A lawyer or law firm may be designated as "General Counsel" or by similar professional reference on stationery of a client if the lawyer or the firm devotes a substantial amount of professional time in the representation of that client. The letterhead of a law firm may give the names and dates of predecessor firms in a continuing line of succession.

(b) A lawyer in private practice shall not practice under a trade name, a name that is misleading as to the identity of the lawyer or lawyers practicing under such name, or a firm name containing names other than those of one or more of the lawyers in the firm, except that the name of a professional corporation shall contain "PC" or such symbols permitted by law, the name of a limited liability company or partnership shall contain "LLC," "LLP" or such symbols permitted by law and, if otherwise lawful, a firm may use as, or continue to include in its name the name or names of one or more deceased or retired members of the firm or of a predecessor firm in a continuing line of succession. Such terms as "legal clinic," "legal aid," "legal service office," "legal assistance office," "defender office" and the like may be used only by qualified legal assistance organizations, except that the term "legal clinic" may be used by any lawyer or law firm provided the name of a participating lawyer or firm is incorporated therein. A lawyer or law firm may not include the name of a nonlawyer in its firm name, nor may a lawyer or law firm that has a contractual relationship with a nonlegal professional or nonlegal professional service firm pursuant to Rule 5.8 to provide legal and other professional services on a systematic and continuing basis include in its firm name the name of the nonlegal professional service firm or any individual nonlegal professional affiliated therewith. A lawyer who assumes a judicial, legislative or public executive or administrative post or office shall not permit the lawyer's name to remain in the name of a law firm or to be used in professional notices of the firm during any significant period in which the lawyer is not actively and regularly practicing law as a member of the firm and, during such period, other members of the firm shall not use the lawyer's name in the firm name or in professional notices of the firm.

(c) Lawyers shall not hold themselves out as having a partnership with one or more other lawyers unless they are in fact partners.

(d) A partnership shall not be formed or continued between or among lawyers licensed in different jurisdictions unless all enumerations of the members and associates of the firm on its letterhead and in other permissible listings make clear the jurisdictional limitations on those members and associates of the firm not licensed to practice in all listed jurisdictions; however, the same firm name may be used in each jurisdiction.

(e) A lawyer or law firm may utilize a domain name for an internet web site that does not include the name of the lawyer or law firm provided:

(1) all pages of the web site clearly and conspicuously include the actual name of the lawyer or law firm;

(2) the lawyer or law firm in no way attempts to engage in the practice of law using the domain name;

(3) the domain name does not imply an ability to obtain results in a matter; and

(4) the domain name does not otherwise violate these Rules.

(f) A lawyer or law firm may utilize a telephone number which contains a domain name, nickname, moniker or motto that does not otherwise violate these Rules.

Comment

Professional Status

[1]   In order to avoid the possibility of misleading persons with whom a lawyer deals, a lawyer should be scrupulous in the representation of professional status. Lawyers should not hold themselves out as being partners or

associates of a law firm if that is not the fact, and thus lawyers should not hold themselves out as being a partners or associates if they only share offices.

Trade Names and Domain Names

[2]   A lawyer may not practice under a trade name. Many law firms have created Internet web sites to provide information about their firms. A web site is reached through an Internet address, commonly called a "domain name." As long as a law firm's name complies with other Rules, it is always proper for a law firm to use its own name or its initials or some abbreviation or variation of its own name as its domain name. For example, the law firm of Able and Baker may use the domain name www.ableandbaker.com, or www.ab.com, or www.able.com, or www.ablelaw.com. However, to make domain names easier for clients and potential clients to remember and to locate, some law firms may prefer to use terms other than the law firm's name. If Able and Baker practices real estate law, for instance, it may prefer a descriptive domain name such as www.realestatelaw.com or www.ablerealestatelaw.com or a colloquial domain name such as www.dirtlawyers.com. Accordingly, a law firm may utilize a domain name for an Internet web site that does not include the name of the law firm, provided the domain name meets four conditions: First, all pages of the web site created by the law firm must clearly and conspicuously include the actual name of the law firm. Second, the law firm must in no way attempt to engage in the practice of law using the domain name. This restriction is parallel to the general prohibition against the use of trade names. For example, if Able and Baker uses the domain name www.realestate law.com, the firm may not advertise that people buying or selling homes should "contact www.realestatelaw.com" unless the firm also clearly and conspicuously includes the name of the law firm in the advertisement. Third, the domain name must not imply an ability to obtain results in a matter. For example, a personal injury firm could not use the domain name www.win-your-case.com or www.settle-for-more.com because such names imply that the law firm can obtain favorable results in every matter regardless of the particular facts and circumstances. Fourth, the domain name must not otherwise violate a Rule. If a domain name meets the three criteria listed here but violates another Rule, then the domain name is improper under this Rule as well. For example, if Able and Baker are each solo practitioners who are not partners, they may not jointly establish a web site with the domain name www.ableandbaker.com because the lawyers would be holding themselves out as having a partnership when they are in fact not partners.

Telephone Numbers

[3]   Many lawyers and law firms use telephone numbers that spell words, because such telephone numbers are generally easier to remember than strings of numbers. As with domain names, lawyers and law firms may always properly use their own names, initials, or combinations of names, initials, numbers, and legal words as telephone numbers. For example, the law firm of

Red & Blue may properly use phone numbers such as RED–BLUE, 4–RED-LAW, or RB–LEGAL.

[4]   Some lawyers and firms may instead (or in addition) wish to use telephone numbers that contain a domain name, nickname, moniker, or motto. A lawyer or law firm may use such telephone numbers as long as they do not violate any Rules, including those governing domain names. For example, a personal injury law firm may use the numbers 1–800–ACCIDENT, 1–800–HURT-BAD, or 1–800–INJURY-LAW, but may not use the numbers 1–800–WINNERS, 1–800–2WIN–BIG, or 1–800–GET-CASH. (Phone numbers with more letters than the number of digits in a phone number are acceptable as long as the words do not violate a Rule.) *See* Rule 7.1, Comment [12].

RULE 8.1: CANDOR IN THE BAR ADMISSION PROCESS

(a) A lawyer shall be subject to discipline if, in connection with the lawyer's own application for admission to the bar previously filed in this state or in any other jurisdiction, or in connection with the application of another person for admission to the bar, the lawyer knowingly:

(1) has made or failed to correct a false statement of material fact; or

(2) has failed to disclose a material fact requested in connection with a lawful demand for information from an admissions authority.

Comment

[1]   If a person makes a material false statement in connection with an application for admission, it may be the basis for subsequent disciplinary action if the person is admitted and in any event may be relevant in a subsequent admission application. The duty imposed by this Rule applies to a lawyer's own admission as well as that of another.

[2]   This Rule is subject to the provisions of the Fifth Amendment to the United States Constitution and corresponding provisions of state constitutions. A person relying on such a provision in response to a question, however, should do so openly and not use the right of nondisclosure as a justification for failure to comply with this Rule.

RULE 8.2: JUDICIAL OFFICERS AND CANDIDATES

(a) A lawyer shall not knowingly make a false statement of fact concerning the qualifications, conduct or integrity of a judge or other adjudicatory officer or of a candidate for election or appointment to judicial office.

(b) A lawyer who is a candidate for judicial office shall comply with the applicable provisions of Part 100 of the Rules of the Chief Administrator of the Courts.

Comment

[1]   Assessments by lawyers are relied on in evaluating the professional or personal fitness of persons being considered for election or appointment to judicial office. Expressing honest and candid opinions on such matters contributes to improving the administration of justice. False statements of fact by a lawyer can unfairly undermine public confidence in the administration of justice.

[2]   When a lawyer seeks judicial office, the lawyer may engage in constitutionally protected speech, but is bound by valid limitations on speech and political activity.

[3]   To maintain the fair and independent administration of justice, lawyers are encouraged to continue traditional efforts to defend judges and courts unjustly criticized.

RULE 8.3: REPORTING PROFESSIONAL MISCONDUCT

(a) A lawyer who knows that another lawyer has committed a violation of the Rules of Professional Conduct that raises a substantial question as to that lawyer's honesty, trustworthiness or fitness as a lawyer shall report such knowledge to a tribunal or other authority empowered to investigate or act upon such violation.

(b) A lawyer who possesses knowledge or evidence concerning another lawyer or a judge shall not fail to respond to a lawful demand for information from a tribunal or other authority empowered to investigate or act upon such conduct.

(c) This Rule does not require disclosure of:

(1) information otherwise protected by Rule 1.6; or

(2) information gained by a lawyer or judge while participating in a bona fide lawyer assistance program.

Comment

[1]   Self-regulation of the legal profession requires that members of the profession initiate disciplinary investigation when they know of a violation of the Rules of Professional Conduct. Lawyers have a similar obligation to cooperate with authorities empowered to investigate judicial misconduct. An apparently isolated violation may indicate a pattern of misconduct that only a disciplinary investigation can uncover. Reporting a violation is especially important where the victim is unlikely to discover the offense.

[2]   A report about misconduct is not required where it would result in violation of Rule 1.6. However, a lawyer should encourage a client to consent to disclosure where prosecution would not substantially prejudice the client's interests.

[3]   If a lawyer were obliged to report every violation of the Rules, the failure to report any violation would itself be a professional offense. Such a

requirement existed in many jurisdictions, but proved to be unenforceable. This Rule limits the reporting obligation to those offenses that a self-regulating profession must vigorously endeavor to prevent. A measure of judgment is therefore required in complying with the provisions of this Rule. The term "substantial" refers to the seriousness of the possible offense and not the quantum of evidence of which the lawyer is aware. A report should be made to a tribunal or other authority empowered to investigate or act upon the violation.

[3A]   Paragraph (b) requires a lawyer in certain situations to respond to a lawful demand for information concerning another lawyer or a judge. This Rule is subject to the provisions of the Fifth Amendment to the United States Constitution and corresponding provisions of state law. A person relying on such a provision in response to a question, however, should do so openly and not use the right of nondisclosure as a justification for failure to comply with this Rule.

[4]   The duty to report professional misconduct does not apply to a lawyer retained to represent a lawyer whose professional conduct is in question. Such a situation is governed by the Rules applicable to the client-lawyer relationship.

[5]   Information about a lawyer's or judge's misconduct or fitness may be received by a lawyer in the course of that lawyer's participation in a bona fide assistance program for lawyers or judges. In that circumstance, providing for an exception to the reporting requirements of paragraphs (a) and (b) encourages lawyers and judges to seek assistance and treatment through such a program. Without such an exception, lawyers and judges may hesitate to seek assistance and treatment from these programs, and this may result in additional harm to their professional careers and additional injury to the welfare of clients and the public.

RULE 8.4: MISCONDUCT

A lawyer or law firm shall not:

(a) violate or attempt to violate the Rules of Professional Conduct, knowingly assist or induce another to do so, or do so through the acts of another;

(b) engage in illegal conduct that adversely reflects on the lawyer's honesty, trustworthiness or fitness as a lawyer;

(c) engage in conduct involving dishonesty, fraud, deceit or misrepresentation;

(d) engage in conduct that is prejudicial to the administration of justice;

(e) state or imply an ability:

(1) to influence improperly or upon irrelevant grounds any tribunal, legislative body or public official; or

(2) to achieve results using means that violate these Rules or other law;

(f) knowingly assist a judge or judicial officer in conduct that is a violation of applicable rules of judicial conduct or other law;

(g) unlawfully discriminate in the practice of law, including in hiring, promoting or otherwise determining conditions of employment on the basis of age, race, creed, color, national origin, sex, disability, marital status or sexual orientation. Where there is a tribunal with jurisdiction to hear a complaint, if timely brought, other than a Departmental Disciplinary Committee, a complaint based on unlawful discrimination shall be brought before such tribunal in the first instance. A certified copy of a determination by such a tribunal, which has become final and enforceable and as to which the right to judicial or appellate review has been exhausted, finding that the lawyer has engaged in an unlawful discriminatory practice shall constitute prima facie evidence of professional misconduct in a disciplinary proceeding; or

(h) engage in any other conduct that adversely reflects on the lawyer's fitness as a lawyer.

Comment

[1] Lawyers are subject to discipline when they violate or attempt to violate the Rules of Professional Conduct, knowingly assist or induce another to do so, or do so through the acts of another, as when they request or instruct an agent to do so on their behalf. Paragraph (a), however, does not prohibit a lawyer from advising a client concerning action the client is legally entitled to take.

[2] Many kinds of illegal conduct reflect adversely on fitness to practice law. Although a lawyer is personally answerable to the entire criminal law, a lawyer should be professionally answerable only for illegal conduct that indicates lack of those characteristics relevant to law practice. Violations involving violence, dishonesty, fraud, breach of trust, or serious interference with the administration of justice are illustrative of illegal conduct that reflects adversely on fitness to practice law. Other types of illegal conduct may or may not fall into that category, depending upon the particular circumstances. A pattern of repeated offenses, even ones of minor significance when considered separately, can indicate indifference to legal obligation.

[3] The prohibition on conduct prejudicial to the administration of justice is generally invoked to punish conduct, whether or not it violates another ethics rule, that results in substantial harm to the justice system comparable to those caused by obstruction of justice, such as advising a client to testify falsely, paying a witness to be unavailable, altering documents, repeatedly disrupting a proceeding, or failing to cooperate in an attorney disciplinary investigation or proceeding. The assertion of the lawyer's constitutional rights consistent with Rule 8.1, Comment [2] does not constitute

failure to cooperate. The conduct must be seriously inconsistent with a lawyer's responsibility as an officer of the court.

[4] A lawyer may refuse to comply with an obligation imposed by law upon a good-faith belief that no valid obligation exists.

[4A] A lawyer harms the integrity of the law and the legal profession when the lawyer states or implies an ability to influence improperly any officer or agency of the executive, legislative or judicial branches of government.

[5] Lawyers holding public office assume legal responsibilities going beyond those of other citizens. A lawyer's abuse of public office can suggest an inability to fulfill the professional role of lawyers. The same is true of abuse of positions of private trust such as trustee, executor, administrator, guardian, agent and officer, director or manager of a corporation or other organization.

[5A] Unlawful discrimination in the practice of law on the basis of age, race, creed, color, national origin, sex, disability, marital status, or sexual orientation is governed by paragraph (g).

RULE 8.5: DISCIPLINARY AUTHORITY AND CHOICE OF LAW

(a) A lawyer admitted to practice in this state is subject to the disciplinary authority of this state, regardless of where the lawyer's conduct occurs. A lawyer may be subject to the disciplinary authority of both this state and another jurisdiction where the lawyer is admitted for the same conduct.

(b) In any exercise of the disciplinary authority of this state, the Rules of Professional Conduct to be applied shall be as follows:

(1) For conduct in connection with a proceeding in a court before which a lawyer has been admitted to practice (either generally or for purposes of that proceeding), the rules to be applied shall be the rules of the jurisdiction in which the court sits, unless the rules of the court provide otherwise; and

(2) For any other conduct:

(i) If the lawyer is licensed to practice only in this state, the rules to be applied shall be the rules of this state, and

(ii) If the lawyer is licensed to practice in this state and another jurisdiction, the rules to be applied shall be the rules of the admitting jurisdiction in which the lawyer principally practices; provided, however, that if particular conduct clearly has its predominant effect in another jurisdiction in which the lawyer is licensed to practice, the rules of that jurisdiction shall be applied to that conduct.

Comment

Disciplinary Authority

[1]   It is longstanding law that the conduct of a lawyer admitted to practice in this state is subject to the disciplinary authority of this state. Extension of the disciplinary authority of this state to other lawyers who provide or offer to provide legal services in this state is for the protection of the citizens of this state. Reciprocal enforcement of a jurisdiction's disciplinary findings and sanctions will further advance the purposes of this Rule. *See* ABA Model Rules for Lawyer Disciplinary Enforcement, Rules 6 and 22. A lawyer who is subject to the disciplinary authority of this state under Rule 8.5(a) appoints an official to be designated by the Appellate Division to receive service of process in New York State. The fact that the lawyer is subject to the disciplinary authority of this state may be a factor in determining whether personal jurisdiction may be asserted over the lawyer for civil matters.

Choice of Law

[2]   A lawyer may be potentially subject to more than one set of rules of professional conduct, imposing different obligations. The lawyer may be licensed to practice in more than one jurisdiction with differing rules, or may be admitted to practice before a particular court with rules that differ from those of the jurisdiction or jurisdictions in which the lawyer is licensed to practice. Additionally, the lawyer's conduct may involve significant contacts with more than one jurisdiction.

[3]   Paragraph (b) seeks to resolve such potential conflicts. Its premise is that minimizing conflicts between rules, as well as uncertainty about which rules are applicable, is in the best interest of clients and the profession (as well as the bodies having authority to regulate the profession). Accordingly, it takes the approach of (i) providing that any particular conduct of a lawyer shall be subject to only one set of rules of professional conduct, (ii) making the determination of which set of rules applies to particular conduct as straightforwardly as possible, consistent with recognition of appropriate regulatory interests of relevant jurisdictions, and (iii) providing protection from discipline for lawyers who act reasonably in the face of uncertainty.

[4]   Paragraph (b)(1) provides that as to a lawyer's conduct relating to a proceeding pending before a tribunal, the lawyer shall be subject only to the rules of the jurisdiction in which the tribunal sits unless the rules of the tribunal, including its choice-of-law rules, provide otherwise. As to all other conduct, including conduct in anticipation of a proceeding not yet pending before a tribunal, paragraph (b)(2) provides that a lawyer shall be subject to the rules of the jurisdiction in which the lawyer's conduct occurred, or, if the predominant effect of the conduct is in another jurisdiction, the rules of that jurisdiction shall be applied to the conduct. In the case of conduct in anticipation of a proceeding that is likely to be before a tribunal, the predominant effect of such conduct could be where the conduct occurred, where the tribunal sits or in another jurisdiction.

[5] When a lawyer's conduct involves significant contacts with more than one jurisdiction, it may not be clear whether the predominant effect of the lawyer's conduct will occur in a jurisdiction other than the one in which the conduct occurred. So long as the lawyer's conduct conforms to the rules of a jurisdiction in which the lawyer reasonably believes the predominant effect will occur, the lawyer shall not be subject to discipline under this Rule.

[6] If two admitting jurisdictions were to proceed against a lawyer for the same conduct, they should, applying this Rule, identify the same governing ethics rules. They should take all appropriate steps to see that they do apply the same rule to the same conduct, and in all events should avoid proceeding against a lawyer on the basis of two inconsistent rules.

[7] The choice-of-law provision applies to lawyers engaged in transnational practice, unless international law, treaties or other agreements between or among competent regulatory authorities in the affected jurisdictions provide otherwise.

AMERICAN BAR ASSOCIATION STANDARDS RELATING TO THE ADMINISTRATION OF CRIMINAL JUSTICE

THIRD EDITION*

Approved February 3, 1992

CHAPTER 3. THE PROSECUTION FUNCTION

Table of Contents

* A.B.A. Standards for Criminal Justice (3d ed. 1992). Copyright © 1993, American Bar Association. Reprinted with permission. On February 3, 1992, the A.B.A. House of Delegates approved new black letter standards concerning the Prosecution Function.

PART I.   GENERAL STANDARDS

Standard 3–1.1   The Function of the Standards

These standards are intended to be used as a guide to professional conduct and performance. They are not intended to be used as criteria for the judicial evaluation of alleged misconduct of the prosecutor to determine the validity of a conviction. They may or may not be relevant in such judicial evaluation, depending upon all the circumstances.

Standard 3–1.2   The Function of the Prosecutor

(a) The office of prosecutor is charged with responsibility for prosecutions in its jurisdiction.

(b) The prosecutor is an administrator of justice, an advocate, and an officer of the court; the prosecutor must exercise sound discretion in the performance of his or her functions.

(c) The duty of the prosecutor is to seek justice, not merely to convict.

(d) It is an important function of the prosecutor to seek to reform and improve the administration of criminal justice. When inadequacies or injustices in the substantive or procedural law come to the prosecutor's attention, he or she should stimulate efforts for remedial action.

(e) It is the duty of the prosecutor to know and be guided by the standards of professional conduct as defined by applicable professional traditions, ethical codes, and law in the prosecutor's jurisdiction. The prosecutor

567

should make use of the guidance afforded by an advisory council of the kind described in standard 4–1.5.

Standard 3-1.3   Conflicts of Interest

(a) A prosecutor should avoid a conflict of interest with respect to his or her official duties.

(b) A prosecutor should not represent a defendant in criminal proceedings in a jurisdiction where he or she is also employed as a prosecutor.

(c) A prosecutor should not, except as law may otherwise expressly permit, participate in a matter in which he or she participated personally and substantially while in private practice or nongovernmental employment unless under applicable law no one is, or by lawful delegation may be, authorized to act in the prosecutor's stead in the matter.

(d) A prosecutor who has formerly represented a client in a matter in private practice should not thereafter use information obtained from that representation to the disadvantage of the former client unless the rules of attorney-client confidentiality do not apply or the information has become generally known.

(e) A prosecutor should not, except as law may otherwise expressly permit, negotiate for private employment with any person who is involved as an accused or as an attorney or agent for an accused in a matter in which the prosecutor is participating personally and substantially.

(f) A prosecutor should not permit his or her professional judgment or obligations to be affected by his or her own political, financial, business, property, or personal interests.

(g) A prosecutor who is related to another lawyer as parent, child, sibling or spouse should not participate in the prosecution of a person who the prosecutor knows is represented by the other lawyer. Nor should a prosecutor who has a significant personal or financial relationship with another lawyer participate in the prosecution of a person who the prosecutor knows is represented by the other lawyer, unless the prosecutor's supervisor, if any, is informed and approves or unless there is no other prosecutor authorized to act in the prosecutor's stead.

(h) A prosecutor should not recommend the services of particular defense counsel to accused persons or witnesses unless requested by the accused person or witness to make such a recommendation, and should not make a referral that is likely to create a conflict of interest. Nor should a prosecutor comment upon the reputation or abilities of defense counsel to an accused person or witness who is seeking or may seek such counsel's services unless requested by such person.

Standard 3-1.4   Public Statements

(a) A prosecutor should not make or authorize the making of an extrajudicial statement that a reasonable person would expect to be disseminated by means of public communication if the prosecutor knows or reasonably should know that it will have a substantial likelihood of prejudicing a criminal proceeding.

(b) A prosecutor should exercise reasonable care to prevent investigators, law enforcement personnel, employees, or other persons assisting or associated with the prosecutor from making an extrajudicial statement that the prosecutor would be prohibited from making under this standard.

Standard 3–1.5 Duty to Respond to Misconduct

(a) Where a prosecutor knows that another person associated with the prosecutor's office is engaged in action, intends to act or refuses to act in a manner that is a violation of a legal obligation to the prosecutor's office or a violation of law, the prosecutor should follow the policies of the prosecutor's office concerning such matters. If such policies are unavailing or do not exist, the prosecutor should ask the person to reconsider the action or inaction which is at issue if such a request is aptly timed to prevent such misconduct and is otherwise feasible. If such a request for reconsideration is unavailing, inapt or otherwise not feasible or if the seriousness of the matter so requires, the prosecutor should refer the matter to higher authority in the prosecutor's office, including, if warranted by the seriousness of the matter, referral to the chief prosecutor.

(b) If, despite the prosecutor's efforts in accordance with section (a), the chief prosecutor insists upon action, or a refusal to act, that is clearly a violation of law, the prosecutor may take further remedial action, including revealing the information necessary to remedy this violation to other appropriate governmental officials not in the prosecutor's office.

PART II.   ORGANIZATION OF THE PROSECUTION FUNCTION

Standard 3–2.1 Prosecution Authority to Be Vested in a Public Official

The prosecution function should be performed by a public prosecutor who is a lawyer subject to the standards of professional conduct and discipline.

Standard 3–2.2 Interrelationship of Prosecution Offices Within a State

(a) Local authority and responsibility for prosecution is properly vested in a district, county, or city attorney. Wherever possible, a unit of prosecution should be designed on the basis of population, caseload, and other relevant factors sufficient to warrant at least one full-time prosecutor and the supporting staff necessary to effective prosecution.

(b) In some states, conditions such as geographical area and population may make it appropriate to create a statewide system of prosecution in which the state attorney general is the chief prosecutor and the local prosecutors are deputies.

(c) In all states, there should be coordination of the prosecution policies of local prosecution offices to improve the administration of justice and assure the maximum practicable uniformity in the enforcement of the criminal law throughout the state. A state association of prosecutors should be established in each state.

(d) To the extent needed, a central pool of supporting resources and personnel, including laboratories, investigators, accountants, special counsel, and other experts, should be maintained by the state government and should be available to assist all local prosecutors.

Standard 3–2.3   Assuring High Standards of Professional Skill

(a) The function of public prosecution requires highly developed professional skills. This objective can best be achieved by promoting continuity of service and broad experience in all phases of the prosecution function.

(b) Wherever feasible, the offices of chief prosecutor and staff should be full-time occupations.

(c) Professional competence should be the basis for selection for prosecutorial office. Prosecutors should select their personnel without regard to partisan political influence.

(d) Special efforts should be made to recruit qualified women and members of minority groups for prosecutorial office.

(e) In order to achieve the objective of professionalism and to encourage competent lawyers to accept such offices, compensation for prosecutors and their staffs should be commensurate with the high responsibilities of the office and comparable to the compensation of their peers in the private sector.

Standard 3–2.4   Special Assistants, Investigative Resources, Experts

(a) Funds should be provided to enable a prosecutor to appoint special assistants from among the trial bar experienced in criminal cases, as needed for the prosecution of a particular case or to assist generally.

(b) Funds should be provided to the prosecutor for the employment of a regular staff of professional investigative personnel and other necessary supporting personnel, under the prosecutor's direct control, to the extent warranted by the responsibilities and scope of the office; the prosecutor should also be provided with funds for the employment of qualified experts as needed for particular cases.

Standard 3–2.5   Prosecutor's Handbook; Policy Guidelines and Procedures

(a) Each prosecutor's office should develop a statement of (i) general policies to guide the exercise of prosecutorial discretion and (ii) procedures of the office. The objectives of these policies as to discretion and procedures should be to achieve a fair, efficient, and effective enforcement of the criminal law.

(b) In the interest of continuity and clarity, such statement of policies and procedures should be maintained in an office handbook. This handbook should be available to the public, except for subject matters declared "confidential," when it is reasonably believed that public access to their contents would adversely affect the prosecution function.

Standard 3–2.6   Training Programs

Training programs should be established within the prosecutor's office for new personnel and for continuing education of the staff. Continuing education programs for prosecutors should be substantially expanded and public funds should be provided to enable prosecutors to attend such programs.

Standard 3–2.7   Relations With Police

(a) The prosecutor should provide legal advice to the police concerning police functions and duties in criminal matters.

(b) The prosecutor should cooperate with police in providing the services of the prosecutor's staff to aid in training police in the performance of their function in accordance with law.

Standard 3–2.8   Relations With the Courts and Bar

(a) A prosecutor should not intentionally misrepresent matters of fact or law to the court.

(b) A prosecutor's duties necessarily involve frequent and regular official contacts with the judge or judges of the prosecutor's jurisdiction. In such contacts the prosecutor should carefully strive to preserve the appearance as well as the reality of the correct relationship which professional traditions, ethical codes, and applicable law require between advocates and judges.

(c) A prosecutor should not engage in unauthorized ex parte discussions with or submission of material to a judge relating to a particular case which is or may come before the judge.

(d) A prosecutor should not fail to disclose to the tribunal legal authority in the controlling jurisdiction known to the prosecutor to be directly adverse to the prosecutor's position and not disclosed by defense counsel.

(e) A prosecutor should strive to develop good working relationships with defense counsel in order to facilitate the resolution of ethical problems. In particular, a prosecutor should assure defense counsel that if counsel finds it necessary to deliver physical items which may be relevant to a pending case or investigation to the prosecutor, the prosecutor will not offer the fact of such delivery by defense counsel as evidence before a jury for purposes of establishing defense counsel's client's culpability. However, nothing in this Standard shall prevent a prosecutor from offering evidence of the fact of such delivery in a subsequent proceeding for the purpose of proving a crime or fraud in the delivery of the evidence.

Standard 3–2.9   Prompt Disposition of Criminal Charges

(a) A prosecutor should avoid unnecessary delay in the disposition of cases. A prosecutor should not fail to act with reasonable diligence and promptness in prosecuting an accused.

(b) A prosecutor should not intentionally use procedural devices for delay for which there is no legitimate basis.

(c) The prosecution function should be so organized and supported with staff and facilities as to enable it to dispose of all criminal charges promptly. The prosecutor should be punctual in attendance in court and in the submission of all motions, briefs, and other papers. The prosecutor should emphasize to all witnesses the importance of punctuality in attendance in court.

(d) A prosecutor should not intentionally misrepresent facts or otherwise mislead the court in order to obtain a continuance.

(e) A prosecutor, without attempting to get more funding for additional staff, should not carry a workload that, by reason of its excessive size, interferes with the rendering of quality representation, endangers the interests of justice in the speedy disposition of charges, or may lead to the breach of professional obligations.

Standard 3–2.10   Supercession and Substitution of Prosecutor

(a) Procedures should be established by appropriate legislation to the end that the governor or other elected state official is empowered by law to suspend and supersede a local prosecutor upon making a public finding, after reasonable notice and hearing, that the prosecutor is incapable of fulfilling the duties of office.

(b) The governor or other elected official should be empowered by law to substitute special counsel in the place of the local prosecutor in a particular case, or category of cases, upon making a public finding that this is required for the protection of the public interest.

Standard 3–2.11   Literary or Media Agreements

A prosecutor, prior to conclusion of all aspects of a matter, should not enter into any agreement or understanding by which the prosecutor acquires an interest in literary or media rights to a portrayal or account based in substantial part on information relating to that matter.

PART III.   INVESTIGATION FOR PROSECUTION DECISION

Standard 3–3.1   Investigative Function of Prosecutor

(a) A prosecutor ordinarily relies on police and other investigative agencies for investigation of alleged criminal acts, but the prosecutor has an affirmative responsibility to investigate suspected illegal activity when it is not adequately dealt with by other agencies.

(b) A prosecutor should not invidiously discriminate against or in favor of any person on the basis of race, religion, sex, sexual preference, or ethnicity in exercising discretion to investigate or to prosecute. A prosecutor should not use other improper considerations in exercising such discretion.

(c) A prosecutor should not knowingly use illegal means to obtain evidence or to employ or instruct or encourage others to use such means.

(d) A prosecutor should not discourage or obstruct communication between prospective witnesses and defense counsel. A prosecutor should not advise any person or cause any person to be advised to decline to give to the defense information which such person has the right to give.

(e) A prosecutor should not secure the attendance of persons for interviews by use of any communication which has the appearance or color of a subpoena or similar judicial process unless the prosecutor is authorized by law to do so.

(f) A prosecutor should not promise not to prosecute for prospective criminal activity, except where such activity is part of an officially supervised investigative and enforcement program.

(g) Unless a prosecutor is prepared to forgo impeachment of a witness by the prosecutor's own testimony as to what the witness stated in an interview or to seek leave to withdraw from the case in order to present the impeaching testimony, a prosecutor should avoid interviewing a prospective witness except in the presence of a third person.

Standard 3–3.2 Relations With Victims and Prospective Witnesses

(a) A prosecutor should not compensate a witness, other than an expert, for giving testimony, but it is not improper to reimburse an ordinary witness for the reasonable expenses of attendance upon court, attendance for depositions pursuant to statute or court rule, or attendance for pretrial interviews. Payments to a witness may be for transportation and loss of income, provided there is no attempt to conceal the fact of reimbursement.

(b) A prosecutor should advise a witness who is to be interviewed of his or her rights against self-incrimination and the right to counsel whenever the law so requires. It is also proper for a prosecutor to so advise a witness whenever the prosecutor knows or has reason to believe that the witness may be the subject of a criminal prosecution. However, a prosecutor should not so advise a witness for the purpose of influencing the witness in favor of or against testifying.

(c) The prosecutor should readily provide victims and witnesses who request it information about the status of cases in which they are interested.

(d) The prosecutor should seek to insure that victims and witnesses who may need protections against intimidation are advised of and afforded such protections where feasible.

(e) The prosecutor should insure that victims and witnesses are given notice as soon as practicable of scheduling changes which will affect the victims' or witnesses' required attendance at judicial proceedings.

(f) The prosecutor should not require victims and witnesses to attend judicial proceedings unless their testimony is essential to the prosecution or is required by law. When their attendance is required, the prosecutor should seek to reduce to a minimum the time they must spend at the proceedings.

(g) The prosecutor should seek to insure that victims of serious crimes or their representatives are given timely notice of: (i) judicial proceedings relating to the victims' case; (ii) disposition of the case, including plea bargains, trial and sentencing; and (iii) any decision or action in the case which results in the accused's provisional or final release from custody.

(h) Where practical, the prosecutor should seek to insure that victims of serious crimes or their representatives are given an opportunity to consult with and to provide information to the prosecutor prior to the decision whether or not to prosecute, to pursue a disposition by plea, or to dismiss the charges.

Standard 3–3.3   Relations With Expert Witnesses

(a) A prosecutor who engages an expert for an opinion should respect the independence of the expert and should not seek to dictate the formation of the expert's opinion on the subject. To the extent necessary, the prosecutor should explain to the expert his or her role in the trial as an impartial expert called to aid the fact finders and the manner in which the examination of witnesses is conducted.

(b) A prosecutor should not pay an excessive fee for the purpose of influencing the expert's testimony or to fix the amount of the fee contingent upon the testimony the expert will give or the result in the case.

Standard 3–3.4   Decision to Charge

(a) The decision to institute criminal proceedings should be initially and primarily the responsibility of the prosecutor.

(b) Prosecutors should take reasonable care to ensure that investigators working at their direction or under their authority are adequately trained in the standards governing the issuance of arrest and search warrants and should inform investigators that they should seek the approval of a prosecutor in close or difficult cases.

(c) The prosecutor should establish standards and procedures for evaluating complaints to determine whether criminal proceedings should be instituted.

(d) Where the law permits a citizen to complain directly to a judicial officer or the grand jury, the citizen complainant should be required to present the complaint for prior approval to the prosecutor, and the prosecutor's action or recommendation thereon should be communicated to the judicial officer or grand jury.

Standard 3–3.5 Relations With Grand Jury

(a) Where the prosecutor is authorized to act as legal adviser to the grand jury, the prosecutor may appropriately explain the law and express an opinion on the legal significance of the evidence but should give due deference to its status as an independent legal body.

(b) The prosecutor should not make statements or arguments in an effort to influence grand jury action in a manner which would be impermissible at trial before a petit jury.

(c) The prosecutor's communications and presentations to the grand jury should be on the record.

Standard 3–3.6 Quality and Scope of Evidence Before Grand Jury

(a) A prosecutor should only make statements or arguments to the grand jury and only present evidence to the grand jury which the prosecutor believes is appropriate or authorized under law for presentation to the grand jury. In appropriate cases, the prosecutor may present witnesses to summarize admissible evidence available to the prosecutor which the prosecutor believes he or she will be able to present at trial. The prosecutor should also inform the grand jurors that they have the right to hear any available witnesses, including eyewitnesses.

(b) No prosecutor should knowingly fail to disclose to the grand jury evidence which tends to negate guilt or mitigate the offense.

(c) A prosecutor should recommend that the grand jury not indict if he or she believes the evidence presented does not warrant an indictment under governing law.

(d) If the prosecutor believes that a witness is a potential defendant, the prosecutor should not seek to compel the witness's testimony before the grand jury without informing the witness that he or she may be charged and that the witness should seek independent legal advice concerning his or her rights.

(e) The prosecutor should not compel the appearance of a witness before the grand jury whose activities are the subject of the inquiry if the witness states in advance that if called he or she will exercise the constitutional privilege not to testify, unless the prosecutor intends to judicially challenge the exercise of the privilege or to seek a grant of immunity according to the law.

(f) A prosecutor in presenting a case to a grand jury should not intentionally interfere with the independence of the grand jury, preempt a function of the grand jury, or abuse the processes of the grand jury.

(g) Unless the law of the jurisdiction so permits, a prosecutor should not use the grand jury in order to obtain tangible, documentary or testimonial evidence to assist the prosecutor in preparation for trial of a defendant who has already been charged by indictment or information.

(h) Unless the law of the jurisdiction so permits, a prosecutor should not use the grand jury for the purpose of aiding or assisting in any administrative inquiry.

Standard 3–3.7   Quality and Scope of Evidence for Information

Where the prosecutor is empowered to charge by information, the prosecutor's decisions should be governed by the principles embodied in standards 3–3.6 and 3–3.9, where applicable.

Standard 3–3.8   Discretion as to Noncriminal Disposition

(a) The prosecutor should consider in appropriate cases the availability of noncriminal disposition, formal or informal, in deciding whether to press criminal charges which would otherwise be supported by probable cause; especially in the case of a first offender, the nature of the offense may warrant noncriminal disposition.

(b) Prosecutors should be familiar with the resources of social agencies which can assist in the evaluation of cases for diversion from the criminal process.

Standard 3–3.9   Discretion in the Charging Decision

(a) A prosecutor should not institute, or cause to be instituted, or permit the continued pendency of criminal charges when the prosecutor knows that the charges are not supported by probable cause. A prosecutor should not institute, cause to be instituted, or permit the continued pendency of criminal charges in the absence of sufficient admissible evidence to support a conviction.

(b) The prosecutor is not obliged to present all charges which the evidence might support. The prosecutor may in some circumstances and for good cause consistent with the public interest decline to prosecute, notwithstanding that sufficient evidence may exist which would support a conviction. Illustrative of the factors which the prosecutor may properly consider in exercising his or her discretion are:

    (i) the prosecutor's reasonable doubt that the accused is in fact guilty;

    (ii) the extent of the harm caused by the offense;

    (iii) the disproportion of the authorized punishment in relation to the particular offense or the offender;

    (iv) possible improper motives of a complainant;

    (v) reluctance of the victim to testify;

    (vi) cooperation of the accused in the apprehension or conviction of others; and

    (vii) availability and likelihood of prosecution by another jurisdiction.

(c) A prosecutor should not be compelled by his or her supervisor to prosecute a case in which he or she has a reasonable doubt about the guilt of the accused.

(d) In making the decision to prosecute, the prosecutor should give no weight to the personal or political advantages or disadvantages which might be involved or to a desire to enhance his or her record of convictions.

(e) In cases which involve a serious threat to the community, the prosecutor should not be deterred from prosecution by the fact that in the jurisdiction juries have tended to acquit persons accused of the particular kind of criminal act in question.

(f) The prosecutor should not bring or seek charges greater in number or degree than can reasonably be supported with evidence at trial or than are necessary to fairly reflect the gravity of the offense.

(g) The prosecutor should not condition a dismissal of charges, nolle prosequi, or similar action on the accused's relinquishment of the right to seek civil redress unless the accused has agreed to the action knowingly and intelligently, freely and voluntarily, and where such waiver is approved by the court.

Standard 3–3.10   Role in First Appearance and Preliminary Hearing

(a) A prosecutor who is present at the first appearance (however denominated) of the accused before a judicial officer should not communicate with the accused unless a waiver of counsel has been entered, except for the purpose of aiding in obtaining counsel or in arranging for the pretrial release of the accused. A prosecutor should not fail to make reasonable efforts to assure that the accused has been advised of the right to, and the procedure for obtaining, counsel and has been given reasonable opportunity to obtain counsel.

(b) The prosecutor should cooperate in good faith in arrangements for release under the prevailing system for pretrial release.

(c) The prosecutor should not seek to obtain from an unrepresented accused a waiver of important pretrial rights, such as the right to a preliminary hearing.

(d) The prosecutor should not seek a continuance solely for the purpose of mooting the preliminary hearing by securing an indictment.

(e) Except for good cause, the prosecutor should not seek delay in the preliminary hearing after an arrest has been made if the accused is in custody.

(f) The prosecutor should ordinarily be present at a preliminary hearing where such hearing is required by law.

Standard 3–3.11   Disclosure of Evidence by the Prosecutor

(a) A prosecutor should not intentionally fail to make timely disclosure to the defense, at the earliest feasible opportunity, of the existence of all evidence or information which tends to negate the guilt of the accused or mitigate the offense charged or which would tend to reduce the punishment of the accused.

(b) A prosecutor should not fail to make a reasonably diligent effort to comply with a legally proper discovery request.

(c) A prosecutor should not intentionally avoid pursuit of evidence because he or she believes it will damage the prosecution's case or aid the accused.

PART IV.   PLEA DISCUSSIONS

Standard 3–4.1   Availability for Plea Discussions

(a) The prosecutor should have and make known a general policy or willingness to consult with defense counsel concerning disposition of charges by plea.

(b) A prosecutor should not engage in plea discussions directly with an accused who is represented by defense counsel, except with defense counsel's approval. Where the defendant has properly waived counsel, the prosecuting attorney may engage in plea discussions with the defendant, although, where feasible, a record of such discussions should be made and preserved.

(c) A prosecutor should not knowingly make false statements or representations as to fact or law in the course of plea discussions with defense counsel or the accused.

Standard 3–4.2   Fulfillment of Plea Discussions

(a) A prosecutor should not make any promise or commitment assuring a defendant or defense counsel that a court will imposed a specific sentence or a suspension of sentence; a prosecutor may properly advise the defense what position will be taken concerning disposition.

(b) A prosecutor should not imply a greater power to influence the disposition of a case than is actually possessed.

(c) A prosecutor should not fail to comply with a plea agreement, unless a defendant fails to comply with a plea agreement or other extenuating circumstances are present.

Standard 3–4.3   Record of Reasons for Nolle Prosequi Disposition

Whenever felony criminal charges are dismissed by way of nolle prosequi (or its equivalent), the prosecutor should make a record of the reasons for the action.

PART V.   THE TRIAL

Standard 3–5.1   Calendar Control

Control over the trial calendar should be vested in the court. The prosecuting attorney should advise the court of facts relevant in determining the order of the cases on the court's calendar.

Standard 3–5.2   Courtroom Professionalism

(a) As an officer of the court, the prosecutor should support the authority of the court and the dignity of the trial courtroom by strict adherence to codes of professionalism and by manifesting a professional attitude toward the judge, opposing counsel, witnesses, defendants, jurors, and others in the courtroom.

(b) When court is in session, the prosecutor should address the court, not opposing counsel, on all matters relating to the case.

(c) A prosecutor should comply promptly with all orders and directives of the court, but the prosecutor has a duty to have the record reflect adverse rulings or judicial conduct which the prosecutor considers prejudicial. The prosecutor has a right to make respectful requests for reconsideration of adverse rulings.

(d) Prosecutors should cooperate with courts and the organized bar in developing codes of professionalism for each jurisdiction.

Standard 3–5.3   Selection of Jurors

(a) The prosecutor should prepare himself or herself prior to trial to discharge effectively the prosecution function in the selection of the jury and the exercise of challenges for cause and peremptory challenges.

(b) In those cases where it appears necessary to conduct a pretrial investigation of the background of jurors, investigatory methods of the prosecutor should neither harass nor unduly embarrass potential jurors or invade their privacy and, whenever possible, should be restricted to an investigation of records and sources of information already in existence.

(c) The opportunity to question jurors personally should be used solely to obtain information for the intelligent exercise of challenges. A prosecutor should not intentionally use the voir dire to present factual matter which the prosecutor knows will not be admissible at trial or to argue the prosecution's case to the jury.

Standard 3–5.4   Relations With Jury

(a) A prosecutor should not intentionally communicate privately with persons summoned for jury duty or impaneled as jurors prior to or during trial. The prosecutor should avoid the reality or appearance of any such communications.

(b) The prosecutor should treat jurors with deference and respect, avoiding the reality or appearance of currying favor by a show of undue solicitude for their comfort or convenience.

(c) After discharge of the jury from further consideration of a case, a prosecutor should not intentionally make comments to or ask questions of a juror for the purpose of harassing or embarrassing the juror in any way which will tend to influence judgment in future jury service. If the prosecutor believes that the verdict may be subject to legal challenge, he or she may properly, if no statute or rule prohibits such course, communicate with jurors to determine whether such challenge may be available.

Standard 3–5.5 Opening Statement

The prosecutor's opening statement should be confined to a statement of the issues in the case and the evidence the prosecutor intends to offer which the prosecutor believes in good faith will be available and admissible. A prosecutor should not allude to any evidence unless there is a good faith and reasonable basis for believing that such evidence will be tendered and admitted in evidence.

Standard 3–5.6 Presentation of Evidence

(a) A prosecutor should not knowingly offer false evidence, whether by documents, tangible evidence, or the testimony of witnesses, or fail to seek withdrawal thereof upon discovery of its falsity.

(b) A prosecutor should not knowingly and for the purpose of bringing inadmissible matter to the attention of the judge or jury offer inadmissible evidence, ask legally objectionable questions, or make other impermissible comments or arguments in the presence of the judge or jury.

(c) A prosecutor should not permit any tangible evidence to be displayed in the view of the judge or jury which would tend to prejudice fair consideration by the judge or jury until such time as a good faith tender of such evidence is made.

(d) A prosecutor should not tender tangible evidence in the view of the judge or jury if it would tend to prejudice fair consideration by the judge or jury unless there is a reasonable basis for its admission in evidence. When there is any substantial doubt about the admissibility of such evidence, it should be tendered by an offer of proof and a ruling obtained.

Standard 3–5.7 Examination of Witnesses

(a) The interrogation of all witnesses should be conducted fairly, objectively, and with due regard for the dignity and legitimate privacy of the witness, and without seeking to intimidate or humiliate the witness unnecessarily.

(b) The prosecutor's belief that the witness is telling the truth does not preclude cross-examination, but may affect the method and scope of cross-examination. A prosecutor should not use the power of cross-examination to discredit or undermine a witness if the prosecutor knows the witness is testifying truthfully.

(c) A prosecutor should not call a witness in the presence of the jury who the prosecutor knows will claim a valid privilege not to testify.

(d) A prosecutor should not ask a question which implies the existence of a factual predicate for which a good faith belief is lacking.

Standard 3–5.8 Argument to the Jury

(a) In closing argument to the jury, the prosecutor may argue all reasonable inferences from evidence in the record. The prosecutor should not intentionally misstate the evidence or mislead the jury as to the inferences it may draw.

(b) The prosecutor should not express his or her personal belief or opinion as to the truth or falsity of any testimony or evidence or the guilt of the defendant.

(c) The prosecutor should not make arguments calculated to appeal to the prejudices of the jury.

(d) The prosecutor should refrain from argument which would divert the jury from its duty to decide the case on the evidence.

Standard 3–5.9 Facts Outside the Record

The prosecutor should not intentionally refer to or argue on the basis of facts outside the record whether at trial or on appeal, unless such facts are matters of common public knowledge based on ordinary human experience or matters of which the court may take judicial notice.

Standard 3–5.10 Comments by Prosecutor After Verdict

The prosecutor should not make public comments critical of a verdict, whether rendered by judge or jury.

PART VI. SENTENCING

Standard 3–6.1 Role in Sentencing

(a) The prosecutor should not make the severity of sentences the index of his or her effectiveness. To the extent that the prosecutor becomes involved in the sentencing process, he or she should seek to assure that a fair and informed judgment is made on the sentence and to avoid unfair sentence disparities.

(b) Where sentence is fixed by the court without jury participation, the prosecutor should be afforded the opportunity to address the court at sentencing and to offer a sentencing recommendation.

(c) Where sentence is fixed by the jury, the prosecutor should present evidence on the issue within the limits permitted in the jurisdiction, but the prosecutor should avoid introducing evidence bearing on sentence which will prejudice the jury's determination of the issue of guilt.

Standard 3–6.2   Information Relevant to Sentencing

(a) The prosecutor should assist the court in basing its sentence on complete and accurate information for use in the presentence report. The prosecutor should disclose to the court any information in the prosecutor's files relevant to the sentence. If incompleteness or inaccurateness in the presentence report comes to the prosecutor's attention, the prosecutor should take steps to present the complete and correct information to the court and to defense counsel.

(b) The prosecutor should disclose to the defense and to the court at or prior to the sentencing proceeding all unprivileged mitigating information known to the prosecutor, except when the prosecutor is relieved of this responsibility by a protective order of the tribunal.

CHAPTER 4.   THE DEFENSE FUNCTION*

Table of Contents

* A.B.A. Standards for Criminal Justice (3d ed. 1991). Copyright © 1993, American Bar Association. Reprinted with permission. On February 11, 1991, the A.B.A. House of Delegates approved new black letter standards concerning the Defense Function.

PART I.   GENERAL STANDARDS

Standard 4–1.1   The Function of the Standards

These standards are intended to be used as a guide to professional conduct and performance. They are not intended to be used as criteria for the judicial evaluation of alleged misconduct of defense counsel to determine the validity of a conviction. They may or may not be relevant in such judicial evaluation, depending upon all the circumstances.

Standard 4–1.2   The Function of Defense Counsel

(a) Counsel for the accused is an essential component of the administration of criminal justice. A court properly constituted to hear a criminal case must be viewed as a tripartite entity consisting of the judge (and jury, where appropriate), counsel for the prosecution, and counsel for the accused.

(b) The basic duty defense counsel owes to the administration of justice and as an officer of the court is to serve as the accused's counselor and advocate with courage and devotion and to render effective, quality representation.

(c) Since the death penalty differs from other criminal penalties in its finality, defense counsel in a capital case should respond to this difference by making extraordinary efforts on behalf of the accused. Defense counsel should comply with the ABA Guidelines for the Appointment and Performance of Counsel in Death Penalty Cases.

(d) Defense counsel should seek to reform and improve the administration of criminal justice. When inadequacies or injustices in the substantive or procedural law come to defense counsel's attention, he or she should stimulate efforts for remedial action.

(e) Defense counsel, in common with all members of the bar, is subject to standards of conduct stated in statutes, rules, decisions of courts, and codes, canons, or other standards of professional conduct. Defense counsel has no duty to execute any directive of the accused which does not comport with law or such standards. Defense counsel is the professional representative of the accused, not the accused's alter ego.

(f) Defense counsel should not intentionally misrepresent matters of fact or law to the court.

(g) Defense counsel should disclose to the tribunal legal authority in the controlling jurisdiction known to defense counsel to be directly adverse to the position of the accused and not disclosed by the prosecutor.

(h) It is the duty of defense counsel to know and be guided by the standards of professional conduct as defined in codes and canons of the legal profession applicable in defense counsel's jurisdiction. Once representation has been undertaken, the functions and duties of defense counsel are the same whether defense counsel is assigned, privately retained, or serving in a legal aid or defender program.

Standard 4–1.3 Delays; Punctuality; Workload

(a) Defense counsel should act with reasonable diligence and promptness in representing a client.

(b) Defense counsel should avoid unnecessary delay in the disposition of cases. Defense counsel should be punctual in attendance upon court and in the submission of all motions, briefs, and other papers. Defense counsel should emphasize to the client and all witnesses the importance of punctuality in attendance in court.

(c) Defense counsel should not intentionally misrepresent facts or otherwise mislead the court in order to obtain a continuance.

(d) Defense counsel should not intentionally use procedural devices for delay for which there is no legitimate basis.

(e) Defense counsel should not carry a workload that, by reason of its excessive size, interferes with the rendering of quality representation, endangers the client's interest in the speedy disposition of charges, or may lead to the breach of professional obligations. Defense counsel should not accept employment for the purpose of delaying trial.

Standard 4–1.4   Public Statements

Defense counsel should not make or authorize the making of an extrajudicial statement that a reasonable person would expect to be disseminated by means of public communication if defense counsel knows or reasonably should know that it will have a substantial likelihood of prejudicing a criminal proceeding.

Standard 4–1.5   Advisory Councils on Professional Conduct

(a) In every jurisdiction, an advisory body of lawyers selected for their experience, integrity, and standing at the trial bar should be established as an advisory council on problems of professional conduct in criminal cases. This council should provide prompt and confidential guidance and advice to lawyers seeking assistance in the application of standards of professional conduct in criminal cases.

(b) Communications between an inquiring lawyer and an advisory council member have the same attorney-client privilege for protection of the client's confidences as ordinarily exists between any other lawyer and client. The council member should be bound by statute or rule of court in the same manner as a lawyer is ordinarily bound in that jurisdiction not to reveal any disclosure of the client. Confidences may also be revealed, however, to the extent necessary:

(i) if the inquiring lawyer's client challenges the effectiveness of the lawyer's conduct of the case and the lawyer relies on the guidance received from the council member, or

(ii) if the inquiring lawyer's conduct is called into question in an authoritative disciplinary inquiry or proceeding.

Standard 4–1.6   Trial Lawyer's Duty to Administration of Justice

(a) The bar should encourage through every available means the widest possible participation in the defense of criminal cases by lawyers. Lawyers should be encouraged to qualify themselves for participation in criminal cases both by formal training and through experience as associate counsel.

(b) All such qualified lawyers should stand ready to undertake the defense of an accused regardless of public hostility toward the accused or personal distaste for the offense charged or the person of the defendant.

(c) Such qualified lawyers should not assert or announce a general unwillingness to appear in criminal cases. Law firms should encourage partners and associates to become qualified and to appear in criminal cases.

(d) Such qualified lawyers should not seek to avoid appointment by a tribunal to represent an accused except for good cause, such as: representing the accused is likely to result in violation of applicable ethical codes or other law, representing the accused is likely to result in an unreasonable financial burden on the lawyer, or the client or crime is so repugnant to the lawyer as to be likely to impair the client-lawyer relationship or the lawyer's ability to represent the client.

PART II. ACCESS TO COUNSEL

Standard 4–2.1 Communication

Every jurisdiction should guarantee by statute or rule of court the right of an accused person to prompt and effective communication with a lawyer and should require that reasonable access to a telephone or other facilities be provided for that purpose.

Standard 4–2.2 Referral Service for Criminal Cases

(a) To assist persons who wish to retain defense counsel privately and who do not know a lawyer or how to engage one, every jurisdiction should have a referral service for criminal cases. The referral service should maintain a list of defense counsel willing and qualified to undertake the defense of a criminal case; it should be so organized that it can provide prompt service at all times.

(b) The availability of the referral service should be publicized. In addition, notices containing the essential information about the referral service and how to contact it should be posted conspicuously in police stations, jails, and wherever else it is likely to give effective notice.

Standard 4–2.3 Prohibited Referrals

(a) Defense counsel should not give anything of value to a person for recommending the lawyer's services.

(b) Defense counsel should not accept a referral from any source, including prosecutors, law enforcement personnel, victims, bondsmen, or court personnel where the acceptance of such a referral is likely to create a conflict of interest.

PART III. LAWYER–CLIENT RELATIONSHIP

Standard 4–3.1 Establishment of Relationship

(a) Defense counsel should seek to establish a relationship of trust and confidence with the accused and should discuss the objectives of the representation and whether defense counsel will continue to represent the accused if there is an appeal. Defense counsel should explain the necessity of full disclosure of all facts known to the client for an effective defense, and defense counsel should explain the extent to which counsel's obligation of confidentiality makes privileged the accused's disclosures.

(b) To ensure the privacy essential for confidential communication between defense counsel and client, adequate facilities should be available for private discussions between counsel and accused in jails, prisons, courthouses, and other places where accused persons must confer with counsel.

(c) Personnel of jails, prisons, and custodial institutions should be prohibited by law or administrative regulations from examining or otherwise interfering with any communication or correspondence between client and defense counsel relating to legal action arising out of charges or incarceration.

Standard 4–3.2   Interviewing the Client

(a) As soon as practicable, defense counsel should seek to determine all relevant facts known to the accused. In so doing, defense counsel should probe for all legally relevant information without seeking to influence the direction of the client's responses.

(b) Defense counsel should not instruct the client or intimate to the client in any way that the client should not be candid in revealing facts so as to afford defense counsel free rein to take action which would be precluded by counsel's knowing of such facts.

Standard 4–3.3   Fees

(a) Defense counsel should not enter into an agreement for, charge, or collect an illegal or unreasonable fee.

(b) In determining the amount of the fee in a criminal case, it is proper to consider the time and effort required, the responsibility assumed by counsel, the novelty and difficulty of the questions involved, the skill requisite to proper representation, the likelihood that other employment will be precluded, the fee customarily charged in the locality for similar services, the gravity of the charge, the experience, reputation, and ability of defense counsel, and the capacity of the client to pay the fee.

(c) Defense counsel should not imply that his or her compensation is for anything other than professional services rendered by defense counsel or by others for defense counsel.

(d) Defense counsel should not divide a fee with a nonlawyer, except as permitted by applicable ethical codes of conduct.

(e) Defense counsel not in the same firm should not divide fees unless the division is in proportion to the services performed by each counsel or, by written agreement with the client, each counsel assumes joint responsibility for the representation, the client is advised of and does not object to the participation of all counsel involved, and the total fee is reasonable.

(f) Defense counsel should not enter into an arrangement for, charge, or collect a contingent fee for representing a defendant in a criminal case.

(g) When defense counsel has not regularly represented the client, defense counsel should communicate the basis or rate of the fee to the client, preferably in writing, before or within a reasonable time after commencing the representation.

Standard 4–3.4   Obtaining Literary or Media Rights From the Accused

Defense counsel, prior to conclusion of all aspects of the matter giving rise to his or her employment, should not enter into any agreement or understanding with a client or a prospective client by which defense counsel acquires an interest in literary or media rights to a portrayal or account based in substantial part on information relating to the employment or proposed employment.

Standard 4–3.5   Conflicts of Interest

(a) Defense counsel should not permit his or her professional judgment or obligations to be affected by his or her own political, financial, business, property, or personal interests.

(b) Defense counsel should disclose to the defendant at the earliest feasible opportunity any interest in or connection with the case or any other matter that might be relevant to the defendant's selection of counsel to represent him or her or counsel's continuing representation. Such disclosure should include communication of information reasonably sufficient to permit the client to appreciate the significance of any conflict or potential conflict of interest.

(c) Except for preliminary matters such as initial hearings or applications for bail, defense counsel who are associated in practice should not undertake to defend more than one defendant in the same criminal case if the duty to one of the defendants may conflict with the duty to another. The potential for conflict of interest in representing multiple defendants is so grave that ordinarily defense counsel should decline to act for more than one of several codefendants except in unusual situations when, after careful investigation, it is clear either that no conflict is likely to develop at trial, sentencing, or at any other time in the proceeding or that common representation will be advantageous to each of the codefendants represented and, in either case, that:

(i) the several defendants give an informed consent to such multiple representation; and

(ii) the consent of the defendants is made a matter of judicial record. In determining the presence of consent by the defendants, the trial judge should make appropriate inquiries respecting actual or potential conflicts of interest of counsel and whether the defendants fully comprehend the difficulties that defense counsel sometimes encounters in defending multiple clients.

(d) Defense counsel who has formerly represented a defendant should not thereafter use information related to the former representation to the disadvantage of the former client unless the information has become generally known or the ethical obligation of confidentiality otherwise does not apply.

(e) In accepting payment of fees by one person for the defense of another, defense counsel should be careful to determine that he or she will not be confronted with a conflict of loyalty since defense counsel's entire loyalty is due the accused. Defense counsel should not accept such compensation unless:

   (i) the accused consents after disclosure;

   (ii) there is no interference with defense counsel's independence of professional judgment or with the client-lawyer relationship; and

   (iii) information relating to the representation of the accused is protected from disclosure as required by defense counsel's ethical obligation of confidentiality.

Defense counsel should not permit a person who recommends, employs, or pays defense counsel to render legal services for another to direct or regulate counsel's professional judgment in rendering such legal services.

   (f) Defense counsel should not defend a criminal case in which counsel's partner or other professional associate is or has been the prosecutor in the same case.

   (g) Defense counsel should not represent a criminal defendant in a jurisdiction in which he or she is also a prosecutor.

   (h) Defense counsel who formerly participated personally and substantially in the prosecution of a defendant should not thereafter represent any person in the same or a substantially related matter. Defense counsel who was formerly a prosecutor should not use confidential information about a person acquired when defense counsel was a prosecutor in the representation of a client whose interests are adverse to that person in a matter.

   (i) Defense counsel who is related to a prosecutor as parent, child, sibling or spouse should not represent a client in a criminal matter where defense counsel knows the government is represented in the matter by such prosecutor. Nor should defense counsel who has a significant personal or financial relationship with a prosecutor represent a client in a criminal matter where defense counsel knows the government is represented in the matter by such prosecutor, except upon consent by the client after consultation regarding the relationship.

   (j) Defense counsel should not act as surety on a bond either for the accused represented by counsel or for any other accused in the same or a related case.

   (k) Except as law may otherwise expressly permit, defense counsel should not negotiate to employ any person who is significantly involved as an attorney or employee of the government in a matter in which defense counsel is participating personally and substantially.

Standard 4–3.6   Prompt Action to Protect the Accused

   Many important rights of the accused can be protected and preserved only by prompt legal action. Defense counsel should inform the accused of his or her rights at the earliest opportunity and take all necessary action to vindicate such rights. Defense counsel should consider all procedural steps which in good faith may be taken, including, for example, motions seeking pretrial release of the accused, obtaining psychiatric examination of the accused when a need appears, moving for change of venue or continuance, moving to suppress illegally obtained evidence, moving for severance from jointly charged defendants, and seeking dismissal of the charges.

Standard 4–3.7 Advice and Service on Anticipated Unlawful Conduct

(a) It is defense counsel's duty to advise a client to comply with the law, but counsel may advise concerning the meaning, scope, and validity of a law.

(b) Defense counsel should not counsel a client in or knowingly assist a client to engage in conduct which defense counsel knows to be illegal or fraudulent but defense counsel may discuss the legal consequences of any proposed course of conduct with a client.

(c) Defense counsel should not agree in advance of the commission of a crime that he or she will serve as counsel for the defendant, except as part of a bona fide effort to determine the validity, scope, meaning, or application of the law, or where the defense is incident to a general retainer for legal services to a person or enterprise engaged in legitimate activity.

(d) Defense counsel should not reveal information relating to representation of a client unless the client consents after consultation, except for disclosures that are impliedly authorized in order to carry out the representation and except that defense counsel may reveal such information to the extent he or she reasonably believes necessary to prevent the client from committing a criminal act that defense counsel believes is likely to result in imminent death or substantial bodily harm.

Standard 4–3.8 Duty to Keep Client Informed

(a) Defense counsel should keep the client informed of the developments in the case and the progress of preparing the defense and should promptly comply with reasonable requests for information.

(b) Defense counsel should explain developments in the case to the extent reasonably necessary to permit the client to make informed decisions regarding the representation.

Standard 4–3.9 Obligations of Hybrid and Standby Counsel

(a) Defense counsel whose duty is to actively assist a pro se accused should permit the accused to make the final decisions on all matters, including strategic and tactical matters relating to the conduct of the case.

(b) Defense counsel whose duty is to assist a pro se accused only when the accused requests assistance may bring to the attention of the accused matters beneficial to him or her, but should not actively participate in the conduct of the defense unless requested by the accused or insofar as directed to do so by the court.

PART IV. INVESTIGATION AND PREPARATION

Standard 4–4.1   Duty to Investigate

(a) Defense counsel should conduct a prompt investigation of the circumstances of the case and to explore all avenues leading to facts relevant to the merits of the case and the penalty in the event of conviction. The investigation should include efforts to secure information in the possession of the prosecution and law enforcement authorities. The duty to investigate exists regardless of the accused's admissions or statements to defense counsel of facts constituting guilt or the accused's stated desire to plead guilty.

(b) Defense counsel should not seek to acquire possession of physical evidence personally or through use of an investigator where defense counsel's sole purpose is to obstruct access to such evidence.

Standard 4–4.2   Illegal Investigation

Defense counsel should not knowingly use illegal means to obtain evidence or information or to employ, instruct, or encourage others to do so.

Standard 4–4.3   Relations With Prospective Witnesses

(a) Defense counsel, in representing an accused, should not use means that have no substantial purpose other than to embarrass, delay, or burden a third person, or use methods of obtaining evidence that violate the legal rights of such a person.

(b) Defense counsel should not compensate a witness, other than an expert, for giving testimony, but it is not improper to reimburse a witness for the reasonable expenses of attendance upon court, including transportation and loss of income, attendance for depositions pursuant to statute or court rule, or attendance for pretrial interviews, provided there is no attempt to conceal the fact of reimbursement.

(c) It is not necessary for defense counsel or defense counsel's investigator, in interviewing a prospective witness, to caution the witness concerning possible self-incrimination and the need for counsel.

(d) Defense counsel should not discourage or obstruct communication between prospective witnesses and the prosecutor. It is unprofessional conduct to advise any person other than a client, or cause such person to be advised, to decline to give to the prosecutor or defense counsel for codefendants information which such person has a right to give.

(e) Unless defense counsel is prepared to forgo impeachment of a witness by counsel's own testimony as to what the witness stated in an interview or to seek leave to withdraw from the case in order to present such impeaching testimony, defense counsel should avoid interviewing a prospective witness except in the presence of a third person.

Standard 4–4.4   Relations With Expert Witnesses

(a) Defense counsel who engages an expert for an opinion should respect the independence of the expert and should not seek to dictate the formation of the expert's opinion on the subject. To the extent necessary, defense counsel should explain to the expert his or her role in the trial as an impartial witness called to aid the fact finders and the manner in which the examination of witnesses is conducted.

(b) Defense counsel should not pay an excessive fee for the purpose of influencing an expert's testimony or fix the amount of the fee contingent upon the testimony an expert will give or the result in the case.

Standard 4–4.5   Compliance With Discovery Procedure

Defense counsel should make a reasonably diligent effort to comply with a legally proper discovery request.

Standard 4–4.6   Physical Evidence

(a) Defense counsel who receives a physical item under circumstances implicating a client in criminal conduct should disclose the location of or should deliver that item to law enforcement authorities only: (1) if required by law or court order, or (2) as provided in paragraph (d).

(b) Unless required to disclose, defense counsel should return the item to the source from whom defense counsel received it, except as provided in paragraphs (c) and (d). In returning the item to the source, defense counsel should advise the source of the legal consequences pertaining to possession or destruction of the item. Defense counsel should also prepare a written record of these events for his or her file, but should not give the source a copy of such record.

(c) Defense counsel may receive the item for a reasonable period of time during which defense counsel: (1) intends to return it to the owner; (2) reasonably fears that return of the item to the source will result in destruction of the item; (3) reasonably fears that return of the item to the source will result in physical harm to anyone; (4) intends to test, examine, inspect, or use the item in any way as part of defense counsel's representation of the client; or (5) cannot return it to the source. If defense counsel tests or examines the item, he or she should thereafter return it to the source unless there is reason to believe that the evidence might be altered or destroyed or used to harm another or return is otherwise impossible. If defense counsel retains the item, he or she should retain it in his or her law office in a manner that does not impede the lawful ability of law enforcement authorities to obtain the item.

(d) If the item received is contraband, i.e. an item, possession of which is in and of itself a crime such as narcotics, defense counsel may suggest that the client destroy it where there is no pending case or investigation relating to this evidence and where such destruction is clearly not in violation of any criminal statute. If such destruction is not permitted by law or if in defense counsel's judgment he or she cannot retain the item, whether or not it is contraband, in a way that does not pose an unreasonable risk of physical harm to anyone, defense counsel should disclose the location of or should deliver the item to law enforcement authorities.

(e) If defense counsel discloses the location of or delivers the item to law enforcement authorities under paragraphs (a) or (d), or to a third party under paragraph (c)(1), he or she should do so in the way best designed to protect the client's interests.

PART V.   CONTROL AND DIRECTION OF LITIGATION

Standard 4–5.1   Advising the Accused

(a) After informing himself or herself fully on the facts and the law, defense counsel should advise the accused with complete candor concerning all aspects of the case, including a candid estimate of the probable outcome.

(b) Defense counsel should not intentionally understate or overstate the risks, hazards, or prospects of the case to exert undue influence on the accused's decision as to his or her plea.

(c) Defense counsel should caution the client to avoid communication about the case with witnesses, except with the approval of counsel, to avoid any contact with jurors or prospective jurors, and to avoid either the reality or the appearance of any other improper activity.

Standard 4–5.2   Control and Direction of the Case

(a) Certain decisions relating to the conduct of the case are ultimately for the accused and others are ultimately for defense counsel. The decisions which are to be made by the accused after full consultation with counsel include:

    (i)   what pleas to enter;

    (ii)   whether to accept a plea agreement;

    (iii)   whether to waive jury trial;

    (iv)   whether to testify in his or her own behalf; and

    (v)   whether to appeal.

(b) Strategic and tactical decisions should be made by defense counsel after consultation with the client where feasible and appropriate. Such decisions include what witnesses to call, whether and how to conduct cross-examination, what jurors to accept or strike, what trial motions should be made, and what evidence should be introduced.

(c) If a disagreement on significant matters of tactics or strategy arises between defense counsel and the client, defense counsel should make a record of the circumstances, counsel's advice and reasons, and the conclusion reached. The record should be made in a manner which protects the confidentiality of the lawyer-client relationship.

PART VI.   DISPOSITION WITHOUT TRIAL

Standard 4–6.1   Duty to Explore Disposition Without Trial

(a) Whenever the law, nature, and circumstances of the case permit, defense counsel should explore the possibility of an early diversion of the case from the criminal process through the use of other community agencies.

(b) Defense counsel may engage in plea discussions with the prosecutor. Under no circumstances should defense counsel recommend to a defendant acceptance of a plea unless appropriate investigation and study of the case has been completed, including an analysis of controlling law and the evidence likely to be introduced at trial.

Standard 4–6.2   Plea Discussions

(a) Defense counsel should keep the accused advised of developments arising out of plea discussions conducted with the prosecutor.

(b) Defense counsel should promptly communicate and explain to the accused all significant plea proposals made by the prosecutor.

(c) Defense counsel should not knowingly make false statements concerning the evidence in the course of plea discussions with the prosecutor.

(d) Defense counsel should not seek concessions favorable to one client by any agreement which is detrimental to the legitimate interests of a client in another case.

(e) Defense counsel representing two or more clients in the same or related cases should not participate in making an aggregated agreement as to guilty or nolo contendere pleas, unless each client consents after consultation, including disclosure of the existence and nature of all the claims or pleas involved.

PART VII.   TRIAL

Standard 4–7.1   Courtroom Professionalism

(a) As an officer of the court, defense counsel should support the authority of the court and the dignity of the trial courtroom by strict adherence to codes of professionalism and by manifesting a professional attitude toward the judge, opposing counsel, witnesses, jurors, and others in the courtroom.

(b) Defense counsel should not engage in unauthorized ex parte discussions with or submission of material to a judge relating to a particular case which is or may come before the judge.

(c) When court is in session, defense counsel should address the court and should not address the prosecutor directly on all matters relating to the case.

(d) Defense counsel should comply promptly with all orders and directives of the court, but defense counsel has a duty to have the record reflect adverse rulings or judicial conduct which counsel considers prejudicial to his or her client's legitimate interests. Defense counsel has a right to make respectful requests for reconsiderations of adverse rulings.

(e) Defense counsel should cooperate with courts and the organized bar in developing codes of professionalism for each jurisdiction.

Standard 4–7.2 Selection of Jurors

(a) Defense counsel should prepare himself or herself prior to trial to discharge effectively his or her function in the selection of the jury, including the raising of any appropriate issues concerning the method by which the jury panel was selected and the exercise of both challenges for cause and peremptory challenges.

(b) In those cases where it appears necessary to conduct a pretrial investigation of the background of jurors, investigatory methods of defense counsel should neither harass nor unduly embarrass potential jurors or invade their privacy and, whenever possible, should be restricted to an investigation of records and sources of information already in existence.

(c) The opportunity to question jurors personally should be used solely to obtain information for the intelligent exercise of challenges. Defense counsel should not intentionally use the voir dire to present factual matter which defense counsel knows will not be admissible at trial or to argue counsel's case to the jury.

Standard 4–7.3 Relations With Jury

(a) Defense counsel should not intentionally communicate privately with persons summoned for jury duty or impaneled as jurors prior to or during the trial. Defense counsel should avoid the reality or appearance of any such communications.

(b) Defense counsel should treat jurors with deference and respect, avoiding the reality or appearance of currying favor by a show of undue solicitude for their comfort or convenience.

(c) After discharge of the jury from further consideration of a case, defense counsel should not intentionally make comments to or ask questions of a juror for the purpose of harassing or embarrassing the juror in any way which will tend to influence judgment in future jury service. If defense counsel believes that the verdict may be subject to legal challenge, he or she may properly, if no statute or rule prohibits such course, communicate with jurors to determine whether such challenge may be available.

Standard 4–7.4 Opening Statement

Defense counsel's opening statement should be confined to a statement of the issues in the case and the evidence defense counsel believes in good faith will be available and admissible. Defense counsel should not allude to any evidence unless there is a good faith and reasonable basis for believing such evidence will be tendered and admitted in evidence.

Standard 4–7.5 Presentation of Evidence

(a) Defense counsel should not knowingly offer false evidence, whether by documents, tangible evidence, or the testimony of witnesses, or fail to take reasonable remedial measures upon discovery of its falsity.

(b) Defense counsel should not knowingly and for the purpose of bringing inadmissible matter to the attention of the judge or jury offer inadmissible evidence, ask legally objectionable questions, or make other impermissible comments or arguments in the presence of the judge or jury.

(c) Defense counsel should not permit any tangible evidence to be displayed in the view of the judge or jury which would tend to prejudice fair consideration of the case by the judge or jury until such time as a good faith tender of such evidence is made.

(d) Defense counsel should not tender tangible evidence in the presence of the judge or jury if it would tend to prejudice fair consideration of the case, unless there is a reasonable basis for its admission in evidence. When there is any substantial doubt about the admissibility of such evidence, it should be tendered by an offer of proof and a ruling obtained.*

Standard 4–7.6 Examination of Witnesses

(a) The interrogation of all witnesses should be conducted fairly, objectively, and with due regard for the dignity and legitimate privacy of the witness, and without seeking to intimidate or humiliate the witness unnecessarily.

* EDITORS' NOTE. The Commentary to this Standard reads, in part, as follows:

Use of False Evidence

When evidence that a lawyer knows to be false is provided by a person who is not the client, the lawyer must refuse to offer it regardless of the client's wishes. When false evidence is offered by the client, however, a conflict may arise between the lawyer's duty to keep the client's revelations confidential and the duty of candor to the court. Upon ascertaining that material evidence is false, the lawyer should seek to persuade the client that the evidence should not be offered or, if it has been offered, that its false character should immediately be disclosed. If the persuasion is ineffective, the lawyer must take reasonable remedial measures. The advocate's proper course with respect to reasonable remedial measures, ordinarily, is to remonstrate with the client confidentially. If that fails, the advocate should seek to withdraw if that will remedy the situation. If withdrawal will not remedy the situation or is impossible, the advocate should make disclosure to the court. It is for the court then to determine what should be done—making a statement about the matter to the trier of fact, ordering a mistrial, or perhaps nothing.[1] Counsel's duty to rectify the presentation of false evidence continues only until the conclusion of the proceeding at which the evidence was offered.[2]

1. A separate standard relating to defense counsel's obligations when his or her client proposes to testify or testifies perjuriously was considered for inclusion in these Standards but was not adopted for lack of consensus as to the appropriate approach. Counsel should pay close attention to the ethics code rules adopted on this subject in his or her jurisdiction. See also ABA Model Rule of Professional Conduct 3.3; ABA Model Code of Professional Responsibility DR 7–102(A)(4); Nix v. Whiteside, 475 U.S. 157 (1986); ABA Standing Committee on Ethics and Professional Responsibility, Formal Opinion 87–353 (1987).

2. See ABA Model Rule of Professional Conduct 3.3(b).

(b) Defense counsel's belief or knowledge that the witness is telling the truth does not preclude cross-examination.

(c) Defense counsel should not call a witness in the presence of the jury who the lawyer knows will claim a valid privilege not to testify.

(d) Defense counsel should not ask a question which implies the existence of a factual predicate for which a good faith belief is lacking.

Standard 4–7.7   Argument to the Jury

(a) In closing argument to the jury, defense counsel may argue all reasonable inferences from the evidence in the record. Defense counsel should not intentionally misstate the evidence or mislead the jury as to the inferences it may draw.

(b) Defense counsel should not express a personal belief or opinion in his or her client's innocence or personal belief or opinion in the truth or falsity of any testimony or evidence.

(c) Defense counsel should not make arguments calculated to appeal to the prejudices of the jury.

(d) Defense counsel should refrain from argument which would divert the jury from its duty to decide the case on the evidence.

Standard 4–7.8   Facts Outside the Record

Defense counsel should not intentionally refer to or argue on the basis of facts outside the record whether at trial or on appeal, unless such facts are matters of common public knowledge based on ordinary human experience or matters of which the court can take judicial notice.

Standard 4–7.9   Posttrial Motions

Defense counsel's responsibility includes presenting appropriate posttrial motions to protect the defendant's rights.

PART VIII.   AFTER CONVICTION

Standard 4–8.1   Sentencing

(a) Defense counsel should, at the earliest possible time, be or become familiar with all of the sentencing alternatives available to the court and with community and other facilities which may be of assistance in a plan for meeting the accused's needs. Defense counsel's preparation should also include familiarization with the court's practices in exercising sentencing discretion, the practical consequences of different sentences, and the normal pattern of sentences for the offense involved, including any guidelines applicable at either the sentencing or parole stages. The consequences of the various dispositions available should be explained fully by defense counsel to the accused.

(b) Defense counsel should present to the court any ground which will assist in reaching a proper disposition favorable to the accused. If a presentence report or summary is made available to defense counsel, he or she should seek to verify the information contained in it and should be prepared to supplement or challenge it if necessary. If there is no presentence report or if it is not disclosed, defense counsel should submit to the court and the prosecutor all favorable information relevant to sentencing and in an appropriate case, with the consent of the accused, be prepared to suggest a program of rehabilitation based on defense counsel's exploration of employment, educational, and other opportunities made available by community services.

(c) Defense counsel should also insure that the accused understands the nature of the presentence investigation process, and in particular the significance of statements made by the accused to probation officers and related personnel. Where appropriate, defense counsel should attend the probation officer's interview with the accused.

(d) Defense counsel should alert the accused to the right of allocution, if any, and to the possible dangers of making a statement that might tend to prejudice an appeal.

Standard 4–8.2 Appeal

(a) After conviction, defense counsel should explain to the defendant the meaning and consequences of the court's judgment and defendant's right of appeal. Defense counsel should give the defendant his or her professional judgment as to whether there are meritorious grounds for appeal and as to the probable results of an appeal. Defense counsel should also explain to the defendant the advantages and disadvantages of an appeal. The decision whether to appeal must be the defendant's own choice.

(b) Defense counsel should take whatever steps are necessary to protect the defendant's rights of appeal.

Standard 4–8.3 Counsel on Appeal

(a) Appellate counsel should not seek to withdraw from a case solely on the basis of his or her own determination that the appeal lacks merit.

(b) Appellate counsel should give a client his or her best professional evaluation of the questions that might be presented on appeal. Counsel, when inquiring into the case, should consider all issues that might affect the validity of the judgment of conviction and sentence, including any that might require initial presentation in a postconviction proceeding. Counsel should advise on the probable outcome of a challenge to the conviction or sentence. Counsel should endeavor to persuade the client to abandon a wholly frivolous appeal or to eliminate contentions lacking in substance.

(c) If the client chooses to proceed with an appeal against the advice of counsel, counsel should present the case, so long as such advocacy does not involve deception of the court. When counsel cannot continue without misleading the court, counsel may request permission to withdraw.

(d) Appellate counsel has the ultimate authority to decide which arguments to make on appeal. When appellate counsel decides not to argue all of the issues that his or her client desires to be argued, appellate counsel should inform the client of his or her pro se briefing rights.

(e) In a jurisdiction with an intermediate appellate court, counsel for a defendant-appellant or a defendant-appellee should continue to represent the client if the prosecution seeks review in the highest court, unless new counsel is substituted or unless the court permits counsel to withdraw. Similarly, in any jurisdiction, such appellate counsel should continue to represent the client if the prosecution seeks review in the Supreme Court of the United States.

Standard 4–8.4   Conduct of Appeal

(a) Appellate counsel should be diligent in perfecting appeals and expediting their prompt submission to appellate courts.

(b) Appellate counsel should be accurate in referring to the record and the authorities upon which counsel relies in the presentation to the court of briefs and oral argument.

(c) Appellate counsel should not intentionally refer to or argue on the basis of facts outside the record on appeal, unless such facts are matters of common public knowledge based on ordinary human experience or matters of which the court may take judicial notice.

Standard 4–8.5   Post-conviction Remedies

After a conviction is affirmed on appeal, appellate counsel should determine whether there is any ground for relief under other post-conviction remedies. If there is a reasonable prospect of a favorable result, counsel should explain to the defendant the advantages and disadvantages of taking such action. Appellate counsel is not obligated to represent the defendant in a post-conviction proceeding unless counsel has agreed to do so. In other respects, the responsibility of a lawyer in a post-conviction proceeding should be guided generally by the standards governing the conduct of lawyers in criminal cases.

Standard 4–8.6   Challenges to the Effectiveness of Counsel

(a) If defense counsel, after investigation, is satisfied that another defense counsel who served in an earlier phase of the case did not provide effective assistance, he or she should not hesitate to seek relief for the defendant on that ground.

(b) If defense counsel, after investigation, is satisfied that another defense counsel who served in an earlier phase of the case provided effective assistance, he or she should so advise the client and may decline to proceed further.

(c) If defense counsel concludes that he or she did not provide effective assistance in an earlier phase of the case, defense counsel should explain this conclusion to the defendant and seek to withdraw from representation with an explanation to the court of the reason therefor.

(d) Defense counsel whose conduct of a criminal case is drawn into question is entitled to testify concerning the matters charged and is not precluded from disclosing the truth concerning the accusation to the extent defense counsel reasonably believes necessary, even though this involves revealing matters which were given in confidence.

SELECTED FEDERAL STATUTES
AND RULES APPLICABLE
TO LAWYERS

1. 15 U.S.C.A. § 7245 (Sarbanes–Oxley Act of 2002, § 307)

§ 7245. Rules of professional responsibility for attorneys

Not later than 180 days after July 30, 2002, the [Securities and Exchange] Commission shall issue rules, in the public interest and for the protection of investors, setting forth minimum standards of professional conduct for attorneys appearing and practicing before the Commission in any way in the representation of issuers, including a rule—

(1) requiring an attorney to report evidence of a material violation of securities law or breach of fiduciary duty or similar violation by the company or any agent thereof, to the chief legal counsel or the chief executive officer of the company (or the equivalent thereof); and

(2) if the counsel or officer does not appropriately respond to the evidence (adopting, as necessary, appropriate remedial measures or sanctions with respect to the violation), requiring the attorney to report the evidence to the audit committee of the board of directors of the issuer or to another committee of the board of directors comprised solely of directors not employed directly or indirectly by the issuer, or to the board of directors.

Sarbanes–Oxley Act of 2002, Pub.L. 107–204, Title III, § 307, July 30, 2002, 116 Stat. 784.

2. Regulations Implementing the Sarbanes–Oxley Act, § 307

17 Code of Federal Regulations, Part 205

STANDARDS OF PROFESSIONAL CONDUCT FOR ATTORNEYS APPEARING AND PRACTICING BEFORE THE COMMISSION IN THE REPRESENTATION OF AN ISSUER
Current through September 24, 2003; 68 Federal Register 55280

§ 205.1 Purpose and scope.
§ 205.2 Definitions.
§ 205.3 Issuer as client.
§ 205.4 Responsibilities of supervisory attorneys.
§ 205.5 Responsibilities of a subordinate attorney.
§ 205.6 Sanctions and discipline.
§ 205.7 No private right of action.

Authority: 15 U.S.C. 77s, 78d–3, 78w, 80a–37, 80a–38, 80b–11, 7202, 7245, and 7262.

§ 205.1   Purpose and scope.

This part sets forth minimum standards of professional conduct for attorneys appearing and practicing before the Commission in the representation of an issuer. These standards supplement applicable standards of any jurisdiction where an attorney is admitted or practices and are not intended to limit the ability of any jurisdiction to impose additional obligations on an attorney not inconsistent with the application of this part. Where the standards of a state or other United States jurisdiction where an attorney is admitted or practices conflict with this part, this part shall govern.

§ 205.2   Definitions.

For purposes of this part, the following definitions apply:

(a) <u>Appearing and practicing before the Commission</u>:

    (1) Means:

        (i) Transacting any business with the Commission, including communications in any form;

        (ii) Representing an issuer in a Commission administrative proceeding or in connection with any Commission investigation, inquiry, information request, or subpoena;

        (iii) Providing advice in respect of the United States securities laws or the Commission's rules or regulations thereunder regarding any document that the attorney has notice will be filed with or submitted to, or incorporated into any document that will be filed with or submitted to, the Commission, including the provision of such advice in the context of preparing, or participating in the preparation of, any such document; or

        (iv) Advising an issuer as to whether information or a statement, opinion, or other writing is required under the United States securities laws or the Commission's rules or regulations thereunder to be filed with or submitted to, or incorporated into any document that will be filed with or submitted to, the Commission; but

    (2) Does not include an attorney who:

        (i) Conducts the activities in paragraphs (a)(1)(i) through (a)(1)(iv) of this section other than in the context of providing legal services to an issuer with whom the attorney has an attorney-client relationship; or

        (ii) Is a non-appearing foreign attorney.

(b) <u>Appropriate response</u> means a response to an attorney regarding reported evidence of a material violation as a result of which the attorney reasonably believes:

(1) That no material violation, as defined in paragraph (i) of this section, has occurred, is ongoing, or is about to occur;

(2) That the issuer has, as necessary, adopted appropriate remedial measures, including appropriate steps or sanctions to stop any material violations that are ongoing, to prevent any material violation that has yet to occur, and to remedy or otherwise appropriately address any material violation that has already occurred and to minimize the likelihood of its recurrence; or

(3) That the issuer, with the consent of the issuer's board of directors, a committee thereof to whom a report could be made pursuant to § 205.3(b)(3), or a qualified legal compliance committee, has retained or directed an attorney to review the reported evidence of a material violation and either:

> (i) Has substantially implemented any remedial recommendations made by such attorney after a reasonable investigation and evaluation of the reported evidence; or

> (ii) Has been advised that such attorney may, consistent with his or her professional obligations, assert a colorable defense on behalf of the issuer (or the issuer's officer, director, employee, or agent, as the case may be) in any investigation or judicial or administrative proceeding relating to the reported evidence of a material violation.

(c) Attorney means any person who is admitted, licensed, or otherwise qualified to practice law in any jurisdiction, domestic or foreign, or who holds himself or herself out as admitted, licensed, or otherwise qualified to practice law.

(d) Breach of fiduciary duty refers to any breach of fiduciary or similar duty to the issuer recognized under an applicable Federal or State statute or at common law, including but not limited to misfeasance, nonfeasance, abdication of duty, abuse of trust, and approval of unlawful transactions.

(e) Evidence of a material violation means credible evidence, based upon which it would be unreasonable, under the circumstances, for a prudent and competent attorney not to conclude that it is reasonably likely that a material violation has occurred, is ongoing, or is about to occur.

(f) Foreign government issuer means a foreign issuer as defined in 17 CFR 230.405 eligible to register securities on Schedule B of the Securities Act of 1933 (15 U.S.C. 77a et seq., Schedule B).

(g) In the representation of an issuer means providing legal services as an attorney for an issuer, regardless of whether the attorney is employed or retained by the issuer.

(h) Issuer means an issuer (as defined in section 3 of the Securities Exchange Act of 1934 (15 U.S.C. 78c)), the securities of which are registered under section 12 of that Act (15 U.S.C. 78l), or that is required to file reports under section 15(d) of that Act (15 U.S.C. 78o(d)), or that files or has filed a registration statement that has not yet become effective under the Securities

Act of 1933 (15 U.S.C. 77a et seq.), and that it has not withdrawn, but does not include a foreign government issuer. For purposes of paragraphs (a) and (g) of this section, the term "issuer" includes any person controlled by an issuer, where an attorney provides legal services to such person on behalf of, or at the behest, or for the benefit of the issuer, regardless of whether the attorney is employed or retained by the issuer.

(i) Material violation means a material violation of an applicable United States federal or state securities law, a material breach of fiduciary duty arising under United States federal or state law, or a similar material violation of any United States federal or state law.

(j) Non-appearing foreign attorney means an attorney:

   (1) Who is admitted to practice law in a jurisdiction outside the United States;

   (2) Who does not hold himself or herself out as practicing, and does not give legal advice regarding, United States federal or state securities or other laws (except as provided in paragraph (j)(3)(ii) of this section); and

   (3) Who:

      (i) Conducts activities that would constitute appearing and practicing before the Commission only incidentally to, and in the ordinary course of, the practice of law in a jurisdiction outside the United States; or

      (ii) Is appearing and practicing before the Commission only in consultation with counsel, other than a non-appearing foreign attorney, admitted or licensed to practice in a state or other United States jurisdiction.

(k) Qualified legal compliance committee means a committee of an issuer (which also may be an audit or other committee of the issuer) that:

   (1) Consists of at least one member of the issuer's audit committee (or, if the issuer has no audit committee, one member from an equivalent committee of independent directors) and two or more members of the issuer's board of directors who are not employed, directly or indirectly, by the issuer and who are not, in the case of a registered investment company, "interested persons" as defined in section 2(a)(19) of the Investment Company Act of 1940 (15 U.S.C. 80a–2(a)(19));

   (2) Has adopted written procedures for the confidential receipt, retention, and consideration of any report of evidence of a material violation under § 205.3;

   (3) Has been duly established by the issuer's board of directors, with the authority and responsibility:

      (i) To inform the issuer's chief legal officer and chief executive officer (or the equivalents thereof) of any report of evidence of a material violation (except in the circumstances described in § 205.3(b) (4));

(ii) To determine whether an investigation is necessary regarding any report of evidence of a material violation by the issuer, its officers, directors, employees or agents and, if it determines an investigation is necessary or appropriate, to:

(A) Notify the audit committee or the full board of directors;

(B) Initiate an investigation, which may be conducted either by the chief legal officer (or the equivalent thereof) or by outside attorneys; and

(C) Retain such additional expert personnel as the committee deems necessary; and

(iii) At the conclusion of any such investigation, to:

(A) Recommend, by majority vote, that the issuer implement an appropriate response to evidence of a material violation; and

(B) Inform the chief legal officer and the chief executive officer (or the equivalents thereof) and the board of directors of the results of any such investigation under this section and the appropriate remedial measures to be adopted; and

(4) Has the authority and responsibility, acting by majority vote, to take all other appropriate action, including the authority to notify the Commission in the event that the issuer fails in any material respect to implement an appropriate response that the qualified legal compliance committee has recommended the issuer to take.

(*l*) Reasonable or reasonably denotes, with respect to the actions of an attorney, conduct that would not be unreasonable for a prudent and competent attorney.

(m) Reasonably believes means that an attorney believes the matter in question and that the circumstances are such that the belief is not unreasonable.

(n) Report means to make known to directly, either in person, by telephone, by e-mail, electronically, or in writing.

§ 205.3   Issuer as client.

(a) Representing an issuer. An attorney appearing and practicing before the Commission in the representation of an issuer owes his or her professional and ethical duties to the issuer as an organization. That the attorney may work with and advise the issuer's officers, directors, or employees in the course of representing the issuer does not make such individuals the attorney's clients.

(b) Duty to report evidence of a material violation.

(1) If an attorney, appearing and practicing before the Commission in the representation of an issuer, becomes aware of evidence of a material violation by the issuer or by any officer, director, employee, or agent of the issuer, the attorney shall report such evidence to the issuer's chief

legal officer (or the equivalent thereof) or to both the issuer's chief legal officer and its chief executive officer (or the equivalents thereof) forthwith. By communicating such information to the issuer's officers or directors, an attorney does not reveal client confidences or secrets or privileged or otherwise protected information related to the attorney's representation of an issuer.

(2) The chief legal officer (or the equivalent thereof) shall cause such inquiry into the evidence of a material violation as he or she reasonably believes is appropriate to determine whether the material violation described in the report has occurred, is ongoing, or is about to occur. If the chief legal officer (or the equivalent thereof) determines no material violation has occurred, is ongoing, or is about to occur, he or she shall notify the reporting attorney and advise the reporting attorney of the basis for such determination. Unless the chief legal officer (or the equivalent thereof) reasonably believes that no material violation has occurred, is ongoing, or is about to occur, he or she shall take all reasonable steps to cause the issuer to adopt an appropriate response, and shall advise the reporting attorney thereof. In lieu of causing an inquiry under this paragraph (b), a chief legal officer (or the equivalent thereof) may refer a report of evidence of a material violation to a qualified legal compliance committee under paragraph (c)(2) of this section if the issuer has duly established a qualified legal compliance committee prior to the report of evidence of a material violation.

(3) Unless an attorney who has made a report under paragraph (b)(1) of this section reasonably believes that the chief legal officer or the chief executive officer of the issuer (or the equivalent thereof) has provided an appropriate response within a reasonable time, the attorney shall report the evidence of a material violation to:

(i) The audit committee of the issuer's board of directors;

(ii) Another committee of the issuer's board of directors consisting solely of directors who are not employed, directly or indirectly, by the issuer and are not, in the case of a registered investment company, "interested persons" as defined in section 2(a)(19) of the Investment Company Act of 1940 (15 U.S.C. 80a–2(a)(19)) (if the issuer's board of directors has no audit committee); or

(iii) The issuer's board of directors (if the issuer's board of directors has no committee consisting solely of directors who are not employed, directly or indirectly, by the issuer and are not, in the case of a registered investment company, "interested persons" as defined in section 2(a)(19) of the Investment Company Act of 1940 (15 U.S.C. 80a–2(a)(19))).

(4) If an attorney reasonably believes that it would be futile to report evidence of a material violation to the issuer's chief legal officer and chief executive officer (or the equivalents thereof) under paragraph (b)(1) of

this section, the attorney may report such evidence as provided under paragraph (b)(3) of this section.

(5) An attorney retained or directed by an issuer to investigate evidence of a material violation reported under paragraph (b)(1), (b)(3), or (b)(4) of this section shall be deemed to be appearing and practicing before the Commission. Directing or retaining an attorney to investigate reported evidence of a material violation does not relieve an officer or director of the issuer to whom such evidence has been reported under paragraph (b)(1), (b)(3), or (b)(4) of this section from a duty to respond to the reporting attorney.

(6) An attorney shall not have any obligation to report evidence of a material violation under this paragraph (b) if:

(i) The attorney was retained or directed by the issuer's chief legal officer (or the equivalent thereof) to investigate such evidence of a material violation and:

(A) The attorney reports the results of such investigation to the chief legal officer (or the equivalent thereof); and

(B) Except where the attorney and the chief legal officer (or the equivalent thereof) each reasonably believes that no material violation has occurred, is ongoing, or is about to occur, the chief legal officer (or the equivalent thereof) reports the results of the investigation to the issuer's board of directors, a committee thereof to whom a report could be made pursuant to paragraph (b)(3) of this section, or a qualified legal compliance committee; or

(ii) The attorney was retained or directed by the chief legal officer (or the equivalent thereof) to assert, consistent with his or her professional obligations, a colorable defense on behalf of the issuer (or the issuer's officer, director, employee, or agent, as the case may be) in any investigation or judicial or administrative proceeding relating to such evidence of a material violation, and the chief legal officer (or the equivalent thereof) provides reasonable and timely reports on the progress and outcome of such proceeding to the issuer's board of directors, a committee thereof to whom a report could be made pursuant to paragraph (b)(3) of this section, or a qualified legal compliance committee.

(7) An attorney shall not have any obligation to report evidence of a material violation under this paragraph (b) if such attorney was retained or directed by a qualified legal compliance committee:

(i) To investigate such evidence of a material violation; or

(ii) To assert, consistent with his or her professional obligations, a colorable defense on behalf of the issuer (or the issuer's officer, director, employee, or agent, as the case may be) in any investigation or judicial or administrative proceeding relating to such evidence of a material violation.

(8) An attorney who receives what he or she reasonably believes is an appropriate and timely response to a report he or she has made pursuant to paragraph (b)(1), (b)(3), or (b)(4) of this section need do nothing more under this section with respect to his or her report.

(9) An attorney who does not reasonably believe that the issuer has made an appropriate response within a reasonable time to the report or reports made pursuant to paragraph (b)(1), (b)(3), or (b)(4) of this section shall explain his or her reasons therefor to the chief legal officer (or the equivalent thereof), the chief executive officer (or the equivalent thereof), and directors to whom the attorney reported the evidence of a material violation pursuant to paragraph (b)(1), (b)(3), or (b)(4) of this section.

(10) An attorney formerly employed or retained by an issuer who has reported evidence of a material violation under this part and reasonably believes that he or she has been discharged for so doing may notify the issuer's board of directors or any committee thereof that he or she believes that he or she has been discharged for reporting evidence of a material violation under this section.

(c) Alternative reporting procedures for attorneys retained or employed by an issuer that has established a qualified legal compliance committee.

(1) If an attorney, appearing and practicing before the Commission in the representation of an issuer, becomes aware of evidence of a material violation by the issuer or by any officer, director, employee, or agent of the issuer, the attorney may, as an alternative to the reporting requirements of paragraph (b) of this section, report such evidence to a qualified legal compliance committee, if the issuer has previously formed such a committee. An attorney who reports evidence of a material violation to such a qualified legal compliance committee has satisfied his or her obligation to report such evidence and is not required to assess the issuer's response to the reported evidence of a material violation.

(2) A chief legal officer (or the equivalent thereof) may refer a report of evidence of a material violation to a previously established qualified legal compliance committee in lieu of causing an inquiry to be conducted under paragraph (b)(2) of this section. The chief legal officer (or the equivalent thereof) shall inform the reporting attorney that the report has been referred to a qualified legal compliance committee. Thereafter, pursuant to the requirements under § 205.2(k), the qualified legal compliance committee shall be responsible for responding to the evidence of a material violation reported to it under this paragraph (c).

(d) Issuer confidences.

(1) Any report under this section (or the contemporaneous record thereof) or any response thereto (or the contemporaneous record thereof) may

be used by an attorney in connection with any investigation, proceeding, or litigation in which the attorney's compliance with this part is in issue.

(2) An attorney appearing and practicing before the Commission in the representation of an issuer may reveal to the Commission, without the issuer's consent, confidential information related to the representation to the extent the attorney reasonably believes necessary:

(i) To prevent the issuer from committing a material violation that is likely to cause substantial injury to the financial interest or property of the issuer or investors;

(ii) To prevent the issuer, in a Commission investigation or administrative proceeding from committing perjury, proscribed in 18 U.S.C. 1621; suborning perjury, proscribed in 18 U.S.C. 1622; or committing any act proscribed in 18 U.S.C. 1001 that is likely to perpetrate a fraud upon the Commission; or

(iii) To rectify the consequences of a material violation by the issuer that caused, or may cause, substantial injury to the financial interest or property of the issuer or investors in the furtherance of which the attorney's services were used.

§ 205.4 Responsibilities of supervisory attorneys.

(a) An attorney supervising or directing another attorney who is appearing and practicing before the Commission in the representation of an issuer is a supervisory attorney. An issuer's chief legal officer (or the equivalent thereof) is a supervisory attorney under this section.

(b) A supervisory attorney shall make reasonable efforts to ensure that a subordinate attorney, as defined in § 205.5(a), that he or she supervises or directs conforms to this part. To the extent a subordinate attorney appears and practices before the Commission in the representation of an issuer, that subordinate attorney's supervisory attorneys also appear and practice before the Commission.

(c) A supervisory attorney is responsible for complying with the reporting requirements in § 205.3 when a subordinate attorney has reported to the supervisory attorney evidence of a material violation.

(d) A supervisory attorney who has received a report of evidence of a material violation from a subordinate attorney under § 205.3 may report such evidence to the issuer's qualified legal compliance committee if the issuer has duly formed such a committee.

§ 205.5 Responsibilities of a subordinate attorney.

(a) An attorney who appears and practices before the Commission in the representation of an issuer on a matter under the supervision or direction of another attorney (other than under the direct supervision or direction of the issuer's chief legal officer (or the equivalent thereof)) is a subordinate attorney.

(b) A subordinate attorney shall comply with this part notwithstanding that the subordinate attorney acted at the direction of or under the supervision of another person.

(c) A subordinate attorney complies with § 205.3 if the subordinate attorney reports to his or her supervising attorney under § 205.3(b) evidence of a material violation of which the subordinate attorney has become aware in appearing and practicing before the Commission.

(d) A subordinate attorney may take the steps permitted or required by § 205.3(b) or (c) if the subordinate attorney reasonably believes that a supervisory attorney to whom he or she has reported evidence of a material violation under § 205.3(b) has failed to comply with § 205.3.

§ 205.6　Sanctions and discipline.

(a) A violation of this part by any attorney appearing and practicing before the Commission in the representation of an issuer shall subject such attorney to the civil penalties and remedies for a violation of the federal securities laws available to the Commission in an action brought by the Commission thereunder.

(b) An attorney appearing and practicing before the Commission who violates any provision of this part is subject to the disciplinary authority of the Commission, regardless of whether the attorney may also be subject to discipline for the same conduct in a jurisdiction where the attorney is admitted or practices. An administrative disciplinary proceeding initiated by the Commission for violation of this part may result in an attorney being censured, or being temporarily or permanently denied the privilege of appearing or practicing before the Commission.

(c) An attorney who complies in good faith with the provisions of this part shall not be subject to discipline or otherwise liable under inconsistent standards imposed by any state or other United States jurisdiction where the attorney is admitted or practices.

(d) An attorney practicing outside the United States shall not be required to comply with the requirements of this part to the extent that such compliance is prohibited by applicable foreign law.

§ 205.7　No private right of action.

(a) Nothing in this part is intended to, or does, create a private right of action against any attorney, law firm, or issuer based upon compliance or noncompliance with its provisions.

(b) Authority to enforce compliance with this part is vested exclusively in the Commission.

3. Bribery, Graft, and Conflicts of Interest, 18 U.S.C.A. §§ 201–216—Excerpts

§ 201. Bribery of public officials and witnesses

(a) For the purpose of this section—

(1) the term "public official" means Member of Congress, Delegate, or Resident Commissioner, either before or after such official has qualified, or an officer or employee or person acting for or on behalf of the United States, or any department, agency or branch of Government thereof, including the District of Columbia, in any official function, under or by authority of any such department, agency, or branch of Government, or a juror;

(2) the term "person who has been selected to be a public official" means any person who has been nominated or appointed to be a public official, or has been officially informed that such person will be so nominated or appointed; and

(3) the term "official act" means any decision or action on any question, matter, cause, suit, proceeding or controversy, which may at any time be pending, or which may by law be brought before any public official, in such official's official capacity, or in such official's place of trust or profit.

(b) Whoever—

(1) directly or indirectly, corruptly gives, offers or promises anything of value to any public official or person who has been selected to be a public official, or offers or promises any public official or any person who has been selected to be a public official to give anything of value to any other person or entity, with intent—

(A) to influence any official act; or

(B) to influence such public official or person who has been selected to be a public official to commit or aid in committing, or collude in, or allow, any fraud, or make opportunity for the commission of any fraud, on the United States; or

(C) to induce such public official or such person who has been selected to be a public official to do or omit to do any act in violation of the lawful duty of such official or person;

(2) being a public official or person selected to be a public official, directly or indirectly, corruptly demands, seeks, receives, accepts, or agrees to receive or accept anything of value personally or for any other person or entity, in return for:

(A) being influenced in the performance of any official act;

(B) being influenced to commit or aid in committing, or to collude in, or allow, any fraud, or make opportunity for the commission of any fraud, on the United States; or

(C) being induced to do or omit to do any act in violation of the official duty of such official or person;

(3) directly or indirectly, corruptly gives, offers, or promises anything of value to any person, or offers or promises such person to give anything of value to any other person or entity, with intent to influence the testimony under oath or affirmation of such first-mentioned person as a witness upon a trial, hearing, or other proceeding, before any court, any committee of either House or both Houses of Congress, or any agency, commission, or officer authorized by the laws of the United States to hear evidence or take testimony, or with intent to influence such person to absent himself therefrom;

(4) directly or indirectly, corruptly demands, seeks, receives, accepts, or agrees to receive or accept anything of value personally or for any other person or entity in return for being influenced in testimony under oath or affirmation as a witness upon any such trial, hearing, or other proceeding, or in return for absenting himself therefrom;

shall be fined under this title or not more than three times the monetary equivalent of the thing of value, whichever is greater, or imprisoned for not more than fifteen years, or both, and may be disqualified from holding any office of honor, trust, or profit under the United States.

(c) Whoever—

(1) otherwise than as provided by law for the proper discharge of official duty—

(A) directly or indirectly gives, offers, or promises anything of value to any public official, former public official, or person selected to be a public official, for or because of any official act performed or to be performed by such public official, former public official, or person selected to be a public official; or

(B) being a public official, former public official, or person selected to be a public official, otherwise than as provided by law for the proper discharge of official duty, directly or indirectly demands, seeks, receives, accepts, or agrees to receive or accept anything of value personally for or because of any official act performed or to be performed by such official or person;

(2) directly or indirectly, gives, offers, or promises anything of value to any person, for or because of the testimony under oath or affirmation given or to be given by such person as a witness upon a trial, hearing, or other proceeding, before any court, any committee of either House or both Houses of Congress, or any agency, commission, or officer authorized by the laws of the United States to hear evidence or take testimony, or for or because of such person's absence therefrom;

(3) directly or indirectly, demands, seeks, receives, accepts, or agrees to receive or accept anything of value personally for or because of the testimony under oath or affirmation given or to be given by such person as a witness upon any such trial, hearing, or other proceeding, or for or because of such person's absence therefrom;

shall be fined under this title or imprisoned for not more than two years, or both.

(d) Paragraphs (3) and (4) of subsection (b) and paragraphs (2) and (3) of subsection (c) shall not be construed to prohibit the payment or receipt of witness fees provided by law, or the payment, by the party upon whose behalf a witness is called and receipt by a witness, of the reasonable cost of travel and subsistence incurred and the reasonable value of time lost in attendance at any such trial, hearing, or proceeding, or in the case of expert witnesses, a reasonable fee for time spent in the preparation of such opinion, and in appearing and testifying.

(e) The offenses and penalties prescribed in this section are separate from and in addition to those prescribed in sections 1503, 1504, and 1505 of this title.

§ 202. Definitions

(a) For the purpose of sections 203, 205, 207, 208, and 209 of this title the term "special Government employee" shall mean an officer or employee of the executive or legislative branch of the United States Government, of any independent agency of the United States or of the District of Columbia, who is retained, designated, appointed, or employed to perform, with or without compensation, for not to exceed one hundred and thirty days during any period of three hundred and sixty-five consecutive days, temporary duties either on a full-time or intermittent basis, a part-time United States commissioner, or a part-time United States magistrate judge, or, regardless of the number of days of appointment, an independent counsel appointed under chapter 40 of title 28 and any person appointed by that independent counsel under section 594(c) of title 28. Notwithstanding the next preceding sentence, every person serving as a part-time local representative of a Member of Congress in the Member's home district or State shall be classified as a special Government employee. Notwithstanding section 29(c) and (d) of the Act of August 10, 1956 (70A Stat. 632; 5 U.S.C. 30r(c) and (d)), a Reserve officer of the Armed Forces, or an officer of the National Guard of the United States, unless otherwise an officer or employee of the United States, shall be classified as a special Government employee while on active duty solely for training. A Reserve officer of the Armed Forces or an officer of the National Guard of the United States who is voluntarily serving a period of extended active duty in excess of one hundred and thirty days shall be classified as an officer of the United States within the meaning of section 203 and sections 205 through 209 and 218. A Reserve officer of the Armed Forces or an officer of the National Guard of the United States who is serving involuntarily shall be classified as a special Government employee. The terms "officer or employee" and "special Government employee" as used in sections 203, 205, 207 through 209, and 218, shall not include enlisted members of the Armed Forces.

(b) For the purposes of sections 205 and 207 of this title, the term "official responsibility" means the direct administrative or operating authority, whether intermediate or final, and either exercisable alone or with others, and either personally or through subordinates, to approve, disapprove, or otherwise direct Government action.

(c) Except as otherwise provided in such sections, the terms "officer" and "employee" in sections 203, 205, 207 through 209, and 218 of this title shall not include the President, the Vice President, a Member of Congress, or a Federal judge.

(d) The term "Member of Congress" in sections 204 and 207 means—

(1) a United States Senator; and

(2) a Representative in, or a Delegate or Resident Commissioner to, the House of Representatives.

(e) As used in this chapter [18 U.S.C.A. §§ 201 et seq.], the term—

(1) "executive branch" includes each executive agency as defined in title 5, and any other entity or administrative unit in the executive branch;

(2) "judicial branch" means the Supreme Court of the United States; the United States courts of appeals; the United States district courts; the Court of International Trade; the United States bankruptcy courts; any court created pursuant to article I of the United States Constitution, including the Court of Appeals for the Armed Forces, the United States Court of Federal Claims, and the United States Tax Court, but not including a court of a territory or possession of the United States; the Federal Judicial Center; and any other agency, office, or entity in the judicial branch; and

(3) "legislative branch" means—

(A) the Congress; and

(B) the Office of the Architect of the Capitol, the United States Botanic Garden, the Government Accountability Office, the Government Printing Office, the Library of Congress, the Office of Technology Assessment, the Congressional Budget Office, the United States Capitol Police, and any other agency, entity, office, or commission established in the legislative branch.

§ 203. Compensation to Members of Congress, officers, and others in matters affecting the Government

(a) Whoever, otherwise than as provided by law for the proper discharge of official duties, directly or indirectly—

(1) demands, seeks, receives, accepts, or agrees to receive or accept any compensation for any representational services, as agent or attorney or otherwise, rendered or to be rendered either personally or by another—

(A) at a time when such person is a Member of Congress, Member of Congress Elect, Delegate, Delegate Elect, Resident Commissioner, or Resident Commissioner Elect; or

(B) at a time when such person is an officer or employee or Federal judge of the United States in the executive, legislative, or judicial branch of the Government, or in any agency of the United States,

in relation to any proceeding, application, request for a ruling or other determination, contract, claim, controversy, charge, accusation, arrest, or other particular matter in which the United States is a party or has a direct and substantial interest, before any department, agency, court, court-martial, officer, or any civil, military, or naval commission; or

(2) knowingly gives, promises, or offers any compensation for any such representational services rendered or to be rendered at a time when the person to whom the compensation is given, promised, or offered, is or was such a Member, Member Elect, Delegate, Delegate Elect, Commissioner, Commissioner Elect, Federal judge, officer, or employee;

shall be subject to the penalties set forth in section 216 of this title.

(b) Whoever, otherwise than as provided by law for the proper discharge of official duties, directly or indirectly—

(1) demands, seeks, receives, accepts, or agrees to receive or accept any compensation for any representational services, as agent or attorney or otherwise, rendered or to be rendered either personally or by another, at a time when such person is an officer or employee of the District of Columbia, in relation to any proceeding, application, request for a ruling or other determination, contract, claim, controversy, charge, accusation, arrest, or other particular matter in which the District of Columbia is a party or has a direct and substantial interest, before any department, agency, court, officer, or commission; or

(2) knowingly gives, promises, or offers any compensation for any such representational services rendered or to be rendered at a time when the person to whom the compensation is given, promised, or offered, is or was an officer or employee of the District of Columbia;

shall be subject to the penalties set forth in section 216 of this title.

(c) A special Government employee shall be subject to subsections (a) and (b) only in relation to a particular matter involving a specific party or parties—

(1) in which such employee has at any time participated personally and substantially as a Government employee or as a special Government

employee through decision, approval, disapproval, recommendation, the rendering of advice, investigation or otherwise; or

(2) which is pending in the department or agency of the Government in which such employee is serving except that paragraph (2) of this subsection shall not apply in the case of a special Government employee who has served in such department or agency no more than sixty days during the immediately preceding period of three hundred and sixty-five consecutive days.

(d) Nothing in this section prevents an officer or employee, including a special Government employee, from acting, with or without compensation, as agent or attorney for or otherwise representing his parents, spouse, child, or any person for whom, or for any estate for which, he is serving as guardian, executor, administrator, trustee, or other personal fiduciary except—

(1) in those matters in which he has participated personally and substantially as a Government employee or as a special Government employee through decision, approval, disapproval, recommendation, the rendering of advice, investigation, or otherwise; or

(2) in those matters that are the subject of his official responsibility,

subject to approval by the Government official responsible for appointment to his position.

(e) Nothing in this section prevents a special Government employee from acting as agent or attorney for another person in the performance of work under a grant by, or a contract with or for the benefit of, the United States if the head of the department or agency concerned with the grant or contract certifies in writing that the national interest so requires and publishes such certification in the Federal Register.

(f) Nothing in this section prevents an individual from giving testimony under oath or from making statements required to be made under penalty of perjury.

§ 204. Practice in United States Court of Federal Claims or the United States Court of Appeals for the Federal Circuit by Members of Congress

Whoever, being a Member of Congress or Member of Congress Elect, practices in the United States Court of Federal Claims or the United States Court of Appeals for the Federal Circuit shall be subject to the penalties set forth in section 216 of this title.

§ 205. Activities of officers and employees in claims against and other matters affecting the Government

(a) Whoever, being an officer or employee of the United States in the executive, legislative, or judicial branch of the Government or in any agency of the United States, other than in the proper discharge of his official duties—

(1) acts as agent or attorney for prosecuting any claim against the United States, or receives any gratuity, or any share of or interest in any such claim, in consideration of assistance in the prosecution of such claim; or

(2) acts as agent or attorney for anyone before any department, agency, court, court-martial, officer, or civil, military, or naval commission in connection with any covered matter in which the United States is a party or has a direct and substantial interest;

shall be subject to the penalties set forth in section 216 of this title.

(b) Whoever, being an officer or employee of the District of Columbia or an officer or employee of the Office of the United States Attorney for the District of Columbia, otherwise than in the proper discharge of official duties—

(1) acts as agent or attorney for prosecuting any claim against the District of Columbia, or receives any gratuity, or any share of or interest in any such claim in consideration of assistance in the prosecution of such claim; or

(2) acts as agent or attorney for anyone before any department, agency, court, officer, or commission in connection with any covered matter in which the District of Columbia is a party or has a direct and substantial interest;

shall be subject to the penalties set forth in section 216 of this title.

(c) A special Government employee shall be subject to subsections (a) and (b) only in relation to a covered matter involving a specific party or parties—

(1) in which he has at any time participated personally and substantially as a Government employee or special Government employee through decision, approval, disapproval, recommendation, the rendering of advice, investigation, or otherwise; or

(2) which is pending in the department or agency of the Government in which he is serving.

Paragraph (2) shall not apply in the case of a special Government employee who has served in such department or agency no more than sixty days during the immediately preceding period of three hundred and sixty-five consecutive days.

(d)(1) Nothing in subsection (a) or (b) prevents an officer or employee, if not inconsistent with the faithful performance of that officer's or employee's duties, from acting without compensation as agent or attorney for, or otherwise representing—

(A) any person who is the subject of disciplinary, loyalty, or other personnel administration proceedings in connection with those proceedings; or

(B) except as provided in paragraph (2), any cooperative, voluntary, professional, recreational, or similar organization or group not established or operated for profit, if a majority of the organization's or group's members are current officers or employees of the United States or of the District of Columbia, or their spouses or dependent children.

(2) Paragraph (1)(B) does not apply with respect to a covered matter that—

(A) is a claim under subsection (a)(1) or (b)(1);

(B) is a judicial or administrative proceeding where the organization or group is a party; or

(C) involves a grant, contract, or other agreement (including a request for any such grant, contract, or agreement) providing for the disbursement of Federal funds to the organization or group.

(e) Nothing in subsection (a) or (b) prevents an officer or employee, including a special Government employee, from acting, with or without compensation, as agent or attorney for, or otherwise representing, his parents, spouse, child, or any person for whom, or for any estate for which, he is serving as guardian, executor, administrator, trustee, or other personal fiduciary except—

(1) in those matters in which he has participated personally and substantially as a Government employee or special Government employee through decision, approval, disapproval, recommendation, the rendering of advice, investigation, or otherwise, or

(2) in those matters which are the subject of his official responsibility,

subject to approval by the Government official responsible for appointment to his position.

(f) Nothing in subsection (a) or (b) prevents a special Government employee from acting as agent or attorney for another person in the performance of work under a grant by, or a contract with or for the benefit of, the United States if the head of the department or agency concerned with the grant or contract certifies in writing that the national interest so requires and publishes such certification in the Federal Register.

(g) Nothing in this section prevents an officer or employee from giving testimony under oath or from making statements required to be made under penalty for perjury or contempt.

(h) For the purpose of this section, the term "covered matter" means any judicial or other proceeding, application, request for a ruling or other determination, contract, claim, controversy, investigation, charge, accusation, arrest, or other particular matter.

(i) Nothing in this section prevents an employee from acting pursuant to—

(1) chapter 71 of title 5;

(2) section 1004 or chapter 12 of title 39;

(3) section 3 of the Tennessee Valley Authority Act of 1933 (16 U.S.C. 831b);

(4) chapter 10 of title I of the Foreign Service Act of 1980 (22 U.S.C. 4104 et seq.); or

(5) any provision of any other Federal or District of Columbia law that authorizes labor-management relations between an agency or instrumentality of the United States or the District of Columbia and any labor organization that represents its employees.

§ 207. Restrictions on former officers, employees, and elected officials of the executive and legislative branches

(a) Restrictions on all officers and employees of the executive branch and certain other agencies.—

(1) Permanent restrictions on representation on particular matters.—Any person who is an officer or employee (including any special Government employee) of the executive branch of the United States (including any independent agency of the United States), or of the District of Columbia, and who, after the termination of his or her service or employment with the United States or the District of Columbia, knowingly makes, with the intent to influence, any communication to or appearance before any officer or employee of any department, agency, court, or court-martial of the United States or the District of Columbia, on behalf of any other person (except the United States or the District of Columbia) in connection with a particular matter—

(A) in which the United States or the District of Columbia is a party or has a direct and substantial interest,

(B) in which the person participated personally and substantially as such officer or employee, and

(C) which involved a specific party or specific parties at the time of such participation,

shall be punished as provided in section 216 of this title.

(2) Two-year restrictions concerning particular matters under official responsibility.—Any person subject to the restrictions contained in paragraph (1) who, within 2 years after the termination of his or her service or employment with the United States or the District of Columbia, knowingly makes, with the intent to influence, any communication to or appearance before any officer or employee of any department, agency, court, or court-martial of the United States or the District of Columbia, on behalf of any other person (except the United States or the District of Columbia), in connection with a particular matter—

(A) in which the United States or the District of Columbia is a party or has a direct and substantial interest,

(B) which such person knows or reasonably should know was actually pending under his or her official responsibility as such officer or employee within a period of 1 year before the termination of his or her service or employment with the United States or the District of Columbia, and

(C) which involved a specific party or specific parties at the time it was so pending,

shall be punished as provided in section 216 of this title.

(3) Clarification of restrictions.—The restrictions contained in paragraphs (1) and (2) shall apply—

(A) in the case of an officer or employee of the executive branch of the United States (including any independent agency), only with respect to communications to or appearances before any officer or employee of any department, agency, court, or court-martial of the United States on behalf of any other person (except the United States), and only with respect to a matter in which the United States is a party or has a direct and substantial interest; and

(B) in the case of an officer or employee of the District of Columbia, only with respect to communications to or appearances before any officer or employee of any department, agency, or court of the District of Columbia on behalf of any other person (except the District of Columbia), and only with respect to a matter in which the District of Columbia is a party or has a direct and substantial interest.

(b) One-year restrictions on aiding or advising.—

(1) In general.—Any person who is a former officer or employee of the executive branch of the United States (including any independent agency) and is subject to the restrictions contained in subsection (a)(1), or any person who is a former officer or employee of the legislative branch or a former Member of Congress, who personally and substantially participated in any ongoing trade or treaty negotiation on behalf of the United States within the 1–year period preceding the date on which his or her service or employment with the United States terminated, and who had access to information concerning such trade or treaty negotiation which is exempt from disclosure under section 552 of title 5, which is so designated by the appropriate department or agency, and which the person knew or should have known was so designated, shall not, on the basis of that information, knowingly represent, aid, or advise any other person (except the United States) concerning such ongoing trade or treaty negotiation for a period of 1 year after his or her service or employment with the United States terminates. Any person who violates this subsection shall be punished as provided in section 216 of this title.

(2) Definition.—For purposes of this paragraph—

(A) the term "trade negotiation" means negotiations which the President determines to undertake to enter into a trade agreement pursuant to section 1102 of the Omnibus Trade and Competitiveness Act of 1988, and does not include any action taken before that determination is made; and

(B) the term "treaty" means an international agreement made by the President that requires the advice and consent of the Senate.

(c) One-year restrictions on certain senior personnel of the executive branch and independent agencies.—

(1) Restrictions.—In addition to the restrictions set forth in subsections (a) and (b), any person who is an officer or employee (including any special Government employee) of the executive branch of the United States (including an independent agency), who is referred to in paragraph (2), and who, within 1 year after the termination of his or her service or employment as such officer or employee, knowingly makes, with the intent to influence, any communication to or appearance before any officer or employee of the department or agency in which such person served within 1 year before such termination, on behalf of any other person (except the United States), in connection with any matter on which such person seeks official action by any officer or employee of such department or agency, shall be punished as provided in section 216 of this title.

(2) Persons to whom restrictions apply.—**(A)** Paragraph (1) shall apply to a person (other than a person subject to the restrictions of subsection (d))—

(i) employed at a rate of pay specified in or fixed according to subchapter II of chapter 53 of title 5,

(ii) employed in a position which is not referred to in clause (i) and for which that person is paid at a rate of basic pay which is equal to or greater than 86.5 percent of the rate of basic pay for level II of the Executive Schedule, or, for a period of 2 years following the enactment of the National Defense Authorization Act for Fiscal Year 2004, a person who, on the day prior to the enactment of that Act, was employed in a position which is not referred to in clause (i) and for which the rate of basic pay, exclusive of any locality-based pay adjustment under section 5304 or section 5304a of title 5, was equal to or greater than the rate of basic pay payable for level 5 of the Senior Executive Service on the day prior to the enactment of that Act,

(iii) appointed by the President to a position under section 105(a)(2)(B) of title 3 or by the Vice President to a position under section 106(a)(1)(B) of title 3,

(iv) employed in a position which is held by an active duty commissioned officer of the uniformed services who is serving in a grade or rank for which the pay grade (as specified in section 201 of title 37) is pay grade O–7 or above; or

(v) assigned from a private sector organization to an agency under chapter 37 of title 5.

(B) Paragraph (1) shall not apply to a special Government employee who serves less than 60 days in the 1–year period before his or her service or employment as such employee terminates.

(C) At the request of a department or agency, the Director of the Office of Government Ethics may waive the restrictions contained in paragraph (1) with respect to any position, or category of positions, referred to in clause (ii) or (iv) of subparagraph (A), in such department or agency if the Director determines that—

(i) the imposition of the restrictions with respect to such position or positions would create an undue hardship on the department or agency in obtaining qualified personnel to fill such position or positions, and

(ii) granting the waiver would not create the potential for use of undue influence or unfair advantage.

(d) Restrictions on very senior personnel of the executive branch and independent agencies.—

(1) Restrictions.—In addition to the restrictions set forth in subsections (a) and (b), any person who—

(A) serves in the position of Vice President of the United States,

(B) is employed in a position in the executive branch of the United States (including any independent agency) at a rate of pay payable for level I of the Executive Schedule or employed in a position in the Executive Office of the President at a rate of pay payable for level II of the Executive Schedule, or

(C) is appointed by the President to a position under section 105(a)(2)(A) of title 3 or by the Vice President to a position under section 106(a)(1)(A) of title 3,

and who, within 2 years after the termination of that person's service in that position, knowingly makes, with the intent to influence, any communication to or appearance before any person described in paragraph (2), on behalf of any other person (except the United States), in connection with any matter on which such person seeks official action by any officer or employee of the executive branch of the United States, shall be punished as provided in section 216 of this title.

(2) Persons who may not be contacted.—The persons referred to in paragraph (1) with respect to appearances or communications by a person in a position described in subparagraph (A), (B), or (C) of paragraph (1) are—

(A) any officer or employee of any department or agency in which such person served in such position within a period of 1 year before such person's service or employment with the United States Government terminated, and

(B) any person appointed to a position in the executive branch which is listed in sections 5312, 5313, 5314, 5315, or 5316 of title 5.

(e) Restrictions on Members of Congress and officers and employees of the legislative branch.—

(1) Members of Congress and elected officers of the house.—

(A) Senators.—Any person who is a Senator and who, within 2 years after that person leaves office, knowingly makes, with the intent to influence, any communication to or appearance before any Member, officer, or employee of either House of Congress or any employee of any other legislative office of the Congress, on behalf of any other person (except the United States) in connection with any matter on which such former Senator seeks action by a Member, officer, or employee of either House of Congress, in his or her official capacity, shall be punished as provided in section 216 of this title.

(B) Members and officers of the House of Representatives.—(i) Any person who is a Member of the House of Representatives or an elected officer of the House of Representatives and who, within 1 year after that person leaves office, knowingly makes, with the intent to influence, any communication to or appearance before any of the persons described in clause (ii) or (iii), on behalf of any other person (except the United States) in connection with any matter on which such former Member of Congress or elected officer seeks action by a Member, officer, or employee of either House of Congress, in his or her official capacity, shall be punished as provided in section 216 of this title.

(ii) The persons referred to in clause (i) with respect to appearances or communications by a former Member of the House of Representatives are any Member, officer, or employee of either House of Congress and any employee of any other legislative office of the Congress.

(iii) The persons referred to in clause (i) with respect to appearances or communications by a former elected officer are any Member, officer, or employee of the House of Representatives.

(2) Officers and staff of the Senate.—Any person who is an elected officer of the Senate, or an employee of the Senate to whom paragraph (7)(A) applies, and who, within 1 year after that person leaves office or employment, knowingly makes, with the intent to influence, any communication to or appearance before any Senator or any officer or employee of the Senate, on behalf of any other person (except the United

States) in connection with any matter on which such former elected officer or former employee seeks action by a Senator or an officer or employee of the Senate, in his or her official capacity, shall be punished as provided in section 216 of this title.

(3) Personal staff.—(A) Any person who is an employee of a Member of the House of Representatives to whom paragraph (7)(A) applies and who, within 1 year after the termination of that employment, knowingly makes, with the intent to influence, any communication to or appearance before any of the persons described in subparagraph (B), on behalf of any other person (except the United States) in connection with any matter on which such former employee seeks action by a Member, officer, or employee of either House of Congress, in his or her official capacity, shall be punished as provided in section 216 of this title.

(B) The persons referred to in subparagraph (A) with respect to appearances or communications by a person who is a former employee are the following:

(i) the Member of the House of Representatives for whom that person was an employee; and

(ii) any employee of that Member of the House of Representatives.

(4) Committee staff.—Any person who is an employee of a committee of the House of Representatives, or an employee of a joint committee of the Congress whose pay is disbursed by the Clerk of the House of Representatives, to whom paragraph (7)(A) applies and who, within 1 year after the termination of that person's employment on such committee or joint committee (as the case may be), knowingly makes, with the intent to influence, any communication to or appearance before any person who is a Member or an employee of that committee or joint committee (as the case may be) or who was a Member of the committee or joint committee (as the case may be) in the year immediately prior to the termination of such person's employment by the committee or joint committee (as the case may be), on behalf of any other person (except the United States) in connection with any matter on which such former employee seeks action by a Member, officer, or employee of either House of Congress, in his or her official capacity, shall be punished as provided in section 216 of this title.

(5) Leadership staff.—(A) Any person who is an employee on the leadership staff of the House of Representatives to whom paragraph (7)(A) applies and who, within 1 year after the termination of that person's employment on such staff, knowingly makes, with the intent to influence, any communication to or appearance before any of the persons described in subparagraph (B), on behalf of any other person (except the United States) in connection with any matter on which such former employee seeks action by a Member, officer, or employee of either House of Congress, in his or her official capacity, shall be punished as provided in section 216 of this title.

(B) The persons referred to in subparagraph (A) with respect to appearances or communications by a former employee are any Member of the leadership of the House of Representatives and any employee on the leadership staff of the House of Representatives.

(6) Other legislative offices.—(A) Any person who is an employee of any other legislative office of the Congress to whom paragraph (7)(B) applies and who, within 1 year after the termination of that person's employment in such office, knowingly makes, with the intent to influence, any communication to or appearance before any of the persons described in subparagraph (B), on behalf of any other person (except the United States) in connection with any matter on which such former employee seeks action by any officer or employee of such office, in his or her official capacity, shall be punished as provided in section 216 of this title.

(B) The persons referred to in subparagraph (A) with respect to appearances or communications by a former employee are the employees and officers of the former legislative office of the Congress of the former employee.

(7) Limitation on restrictions.—(A) The restrictions contained in paragraphs (2), (3), (4), and (5) apply only to acts by a former employee who, for at least 60 days, in the aggregate, during the 1–year period before that former employee's service as such employee terminated, was paid a rate of basic pay equal to or greater than an amount which is 75 percent of the basic rate of pay payable for a Member of the House of Congress in which such employee was employed.

(B) The restrictions contained in paragraph (6) apply only to acts by a former employee who, for at least 60 days, in the aggregate, during the 1–year period before that former employee's service as such employee terminated, was employed in a position for which the rate of basic pay, exclusive of any locality-based pay adjustment under section 5302 of title 5, is equal to or greater than the basic rate of pay payable for level IV of the Executive Schedule.

(8) Exception.—This subsection shall not apply to contacts with the staff of the Secretary of the Senate or the Clerk of the House of Representatives regarding compliance with lobbying disclosure requirements under the Lobbying Disclosure Act of 1995.

(9) Definitions.—As used in this subsection—

(A) the term "committee of Congress" includes standing committees, joint committees, and select committees;

(B) a person is an employee of a House of Congress if that person is an employee of the Senate or an employee of the House of Representatives;

(C) the term "employee of the House of Representatives" means an employee of a Member of the House of Representatives, an employee of a committee of the House of Representatives, an employee of a joint committee of the Congress whose pay is disbursed by the Clerk of the House of Representatives, and an employee on the leadership staff of the House of Representatives;

(D) the term "employee of the Senate" means an employee of a Senator, an employee of a committee of the Senate, an employee of a joint committee of the Congress whose pay is disbursed by the Secretary of the Senate, and an employee on the leadership staff of the Senate;

(E) a person is an employee of a Member of the House of Representatives if that person is an employee of a Member of the House of Representatives under the clerk hire allowance;

(F) a person is an employee of a Senator if that person is an employee in a position in the office of a Senator;

(G) the term "employee of any other legislative office of the Congress" means an officer or employee of the Architect of the Capitol, the United States Botanic Garden, the Government Accountability Office, the Government Printing Office, the Library of Congress, the Office of Technology Assessment, the Congressional Budget Office, the United States Capitol Police, and any other agency, entity, or office in the legislative branch not covered by paragraph (1), (2), (3), (4), or (5) of this subsection;

(H) the term "employee on the leadership staff of the House of Representatives" means an employee of the office of a Member of the leadership of the House of Representatives described in subparagraph (L), and any elected minority employee of the House of Representatives;

(I) the term "employee on the leadership staff of the Senate" means an employee of the office of a Member of the leadership of the Senate described in subparagraph (M);

(J) the term "Member of Congress" means a Senator or a Member of the House of Representatives;

(K) the term "Member of the House of Representatives" means a Representative in, or a Delegate or Resident Commissioner to, the Congress;

(L) the term "Member of the leadership of the House of Representatives" means the Speaker, majority leader, minority leader, majority whip, minority whip, chief deputy majority whip, chief deputy minority whip, chairman of the Democratic Steering Committee, chairman and vice chairman of the Democratic Caucus, chairman, vice chairman, and secretary of the Republican Conference, chairman of the Republican Research Committee, and chairman of the Republican Policy Committee, of the House of Representatives (or any similar position created on or after the effective date set forth in section 102(a) of the Ethics Reform Act of 1989);

(M) the term "Member of the leadership of the Senate" means the Vice President, and the President pro tempore, Deputy President pro tempore, majority leader, minority leader, majority whip, minority whip, chairman and secretary of the Conference of the Majority, chairman and secretary of the Conference of the Minority, chairman and co-chairman of the Majority Policy Committee, and chairman of the Minority Policy Committee, of the Senate (or any similar position created on or after the effective date set forth in section 102(a) of the Ethics Reform Act of 1989).

(f) Restrictions relating to foreign entities.—

(1) Restrictions.—Any person who is subject to the restrictions contained in subsection (c), (d), or (e) and who knowingly, within 1 year after leaving the position, office, or employment referred to in such subsection—

(A) represents a foreign entity before any officer or employee of any department or agency of the United States with the intent to influence a decision of such officer or employee in carrying out his or her official duties, or

(B) aids or advises a foreign entity with the intent to influence a decision of any officer or employee of any department or agency of the United States, in carrying out his or her official duties,

shall be punished as provided in section 216 of this title.

(2) Special rule for Trade Representative.—With respect to a person who is the United States Trade Representative or Deputy United States Trade Representative, the restrictions described in paragraph (1) shall apply to representing, aiding, or advising foreign entities at any time after the termination of that person's service as the United States Trade Representative.

(3) Definition.—For purposes of this subsection, the term "foreign entity" means the government of a foreign country as defined in section 1(e) of the Foreign Agents Registration Act of 1938, as amended, or a foreign political party as defined in section 1(f) of that Act.

(g) Special rules for detailees.—For purposes of this section, a person who is detailed from one department, agency, or other entity to another department, agency, or other entity shall, during the period such person is detailed, be deemed to be an officer or employee of both departments, agencies, or such entities.

(h) Designations of separate statutory agencies and bureaus.—

(1) Designations.—For purposes of subsection (c) and except as provided in paragraph (2), whenever the Director of the Office of Government Ethics determines that an agency or bureau within a department or agency in the executive branch exercises functions which are distinct and separate from the remaining functions of the department or agency and that there exists no potential for use of undue influence or unfair advantage based on past Government service, the Director shall by rule designate such agency or bureau as a separate department or agency. On an annual basis the Director of the Office of Government Ethics shall review the designations and determinations made under this subparagraph and, in consultation with the department or agency concerned, make such additions and deletions as are necessary. Departments and agencies shall cooperate to the fullest extent with the Director of the Office of Government Ethics in the exercise of his or her responsibilities under this paragraph.

(2) Inapplicability of designations.—No agency or bureau within the Executive Office of the President may be designated under paragraph (1) as a separate department or agency. No designation under paragraph (1) shall apply to persons referred to in subsection (c)(2)(A)(i) or (iii).

(i) Definitions.—For purposes of this section—

(1) the term "officer or employee", when used to describe the person to whom a communication is made or before whom an appearance is made, with the intent to influence, shall include—

> **(A)** in subsections (a), (c), and (d), the President and the Vice President; and

> **(B)** in subsection (f), the President, the Vice President, and Members of Congress;

(2) the term "participated" means an action taken as an officer or employee through decision, approval, disapproval, recommendation, the rendering of advice, investigation, or other such action; and

(3) the term "particular matter" includes any investigation, application, request for a ruling or determination, rulemaking, contract, controversy, claim, charge, accusation, arrest, or judicial or other proceeding.

(j) Exceptions.—

(1) Official government duties.—

> **(A) In general.**—The restrictions contained in this section shall not apply to acts done in carrying out official duties on behalf of the United States or the District of Columbia or as an elected official of a State or local government.

> **(B) Tribal organizations and inter-tribal consortiums.**— The restrictions contained in this section shall not apply to acts authorized by section 104(j) of the Indian Self–Determination and Education Assistance Act (25 U.S.C. 450i(j)).

(2) State and local governments and institutions, hospitals, and organizations.—The restrictions contained in subsections (c), (d), and (e) shall not apply to acts done in carrying out official duties as an employee of—

(A) an agency or instrumentality of a State or local government if the appearance, communication, or representation is on behalf of such government, or

(B) an accredited, degree-granting institution of higher education, as defined in section 101 of the Higher Education Act of 1965, or a hospital or medical research organization, exempted and defined under section 501(c)(3) of the Internal Revenue Code of 1986, if the appearance, communication, or representation is on behalf of such institution, hospital, or organization.

(3) **International organizations.**—The restrictions contained in this section shall not apply to an appearance or communication on behalf of, or advice or aid to, an international organization in which the United States participates, if the Secretary of State certifies in advance that such activity is in the interests of the United States.

(4) **Special knowledge.**—The restrictions contained in subsections (c), (d), and (e) shall not prevent an individual from making or providing a statement, which is based on the individual's own special knowledge in the particular area that is the subject of the statement, if no compensation is thereby received.

(5) **Exception for scientific or technological information.**—The restrictions contained in subsections (a), (c), and (d) shall not apply with respect to the making of communications solely for the purpose of furnishing scientific or technological information, if such communications are made under procedures acceptable to the department or agency concerned or if the head of the department or agency concerned with the particular matter, in consultation with the Director of the Office of Government Ethics, makes a certification, published in the Federal Register, that the former officer or employee has outstanding qualifications in a scientific, technological, or other technical discipline, and is acting with respect to a particular matter which requires such qualifications, and that the national interest would be served by the participation of the former officer or employee. For purposes of this paragraph, the term "officer or employee" includes the Vice President.

(6) **Exception for testimony.**—Nothing in this section shall prevent an individual from giving testimony under oath, or from making statements required to be made under penalty of perjury. Notwithstanding the preceding sentence—

(A) a former officer or employee of the executive branch of the United States (including any independent agency) who is subject to the restrictions contained in subsection (a)(1) with respect to a particular matter may not, except pursuant to court order, serve as an expert witness for any other person (except the United States) in that matter; and

(B) a former officer or employee of the District of Columbia who is subject to the restrictions contained in subsection (a)(1) with respect to a particular matter may not, except pursuant to court order, serve as an expert witness for any other person (except the District of Columbia) in that matter.

(7) Political parties and campaign committees.—(A) Except as provided in subparagraph (B), the restrictions contained in subsections (c), (d), and (e) shall not apply to a communication or appearance made solely on behalf of a candidate in his or her capacity as a candidate, an authorized committee, a national committee, a national Federal campaign committee, a State committee, or a political party.

(B) Subparagraph (A) shall not apply to—

(i) any communication to, or appearance before, the Federal Election Commission by a former officer or employee of the Federal Election Commission; or

(ii) a communication or appearance made by a person who is subject to the restrictions contained in subsections (c), (d), or (e) if, at the time of the communication or appearance, the person is employed by a person or entity other than—

(I) a candidate, an authorized committee, a national committee, a national Federal campaign committee, a State committee, or a political party; or

(II) a person or entity who represents, aids, or advises only persons or entities described in subclause (I).

(C) For purposes of this paragraph—

(i) the term "candidate" means any person who seeks nomination for election, or election, to Federal or State office or who has authorized others to explore on his or her behalf the possibility of seeking nomination for election, or election, to Federal or State office;

(ii) the term "authorized committee" means any political committee designated in writing by a candidate as authorized to receive contributions or make expenditures to promote the nomination for election, or the election, of such candidate, or to explore the possibility of seeking nomination for election, or the election, of such candidate, except that a political committee that receives contributions or makes expenditures to promote more than 1 candidate may not be designated as an authorized committee for purposes of subparagraph (A);

(iii) the term "national committee" means the organization which, by virtue of the bylaws of a political party, is responsible for the day-to-day operation of such political party at the national level;

(iv) the term "national Federal campaign committee" means an organization that, by virtue of the bylaws of a political party, is established primarily for the purpose of providing assistance, at the national level, to candidates nominated by that party for election to the office of Senator or Representative in, or Delegate or Resident Commissioner to, the Congress;

(v) the term "State committee" means the organization which, by virtue of the bylaws of a political party, is responsible for the day-to-day operation of such political party at the State level;

(vi) the term "political party" means an association, committee, or organization that nominates a candidate for election to any Federal or State elected office whose name appears on the election ballot as the candidate of such association, committee, or organization; and

(vii) the term "State" means a State of the United States, the District of Columbia, the Commonwealth of Puerto Rico, and any territory or possession of the United States.

(k)(1)(A) The President may grant a waiver of a restriction imposed by this section to any officer or employee described in paragraph (2) if the President determines and certifies in writing that it is in the public interest to grant the waiver and that the services of the officer or employee are critically needed for the benefit of the Federal Government. Not more than 25 officers and employees currently employed by the Federal Government at any one time may have been granted waivers under this paragraph.

(B)(i) A waiver granted under this paragraph to any person shall apply only with respect to activities engaged in by that person after that person's Federal Government employment is terminated and only to that person's employment at a Government-owned, contractor operated entity with which the person served as an officer or employee immediately before the person's Federal Government employment began.

(ii) Notwithstanding clause (i), a waiver granted under this paragraph to any person who was an officer or employee of Lawrence Livermore National Laboratory, Los Alamos National Laboratory, or Sandia National Laboratory immediately before the person's Federal Government employment began shall apply to that person's employment by any such national laboratory after the person's employment by the Federal Government is terminated.

(2) Waivers under paragraph (1) may be granted only to civilian officers and employees of the executive branch, other than officers and employees in the Executive Office of the President.

(3) A certification under paragraph (1) shall take effect upon its publication in the Federal Register and shall identify—

(A) the officer or employee covered by the waiver by name and by position, and

(B) the reasons for granting the waiver.

A copy of the certification shall also be provided to the Director of the Office of Government Ethics.

(4) The President may not delegate the authority provided by this subsection.

(5)(A) Each person granted a waiver under this subsection shall prepare reports, in accordance with subparagraph (B), stating whether the person has engaged in activities otherwise prohibited by this section for each six-month period described in subparagraph (B), and if so, what those activities were.

(B) A report under subparagraph (A) shall cover each six-month period beginning on the date of the termination of the person's Federal Government employment (with respect to which the waiver under this subsection was granted) and ending two years after that date. Such report shall be filed with the President and the Director of the Office of Government Ethics not later than 60 days after the end of the six-month period covered by the report. All reports filed with the Director under this paragraph shall be made available for public inspection and copying.

(C) If a person fails to file any report in accordance with subparagraphs (A) and (B), the President shall revoke the waiver and shall notify the person of the revocation. The revocation shall take effect upon the person's receipt of the notification and shall remain in effect until the report is filed.

(D) Any person who is granted a waiver under this subsection shall be ineligible for appointment in the civil service unless all reports required of such person by subparagraphs (A) and (B) have been filed.

(E) As used in this subsection, the term "civil service" has the meaning given that term in section 2101 of title 5.

(*l*) Contract advice by former details.—Whoever, being an employee of a private sector organization assigned to an agency under chapter 37 of title 5, within one year after the end of that assignment, knowingly represents or aids, counsels, or assists in representing any other person (except the United States) in connection with any contract with that agency shall be punished as provided in section 216 of this title.

§ 208. Acts affecting a personal financial interest

(a) Except as permitted by subsection (b) hereof, whoever, being an officer or employee of the executive branch of the United States Government, or of any independent agency of the United States, a Federal Reserve bank director, officer, or employee, or an officer or employee of the District of Columbia, including a special Government employee, participates personally and substantially as a Government officer or employee, through decision, approval, disapproval, recommendation, the rendering of advice, investigation, or otherwise, in a judicial or other proceeding, application, request for a ruling or other determination, contract, claim, controversy, charge, accusation, arrest, or other particular matter in which, to his knowledge, he, his spouse, minor child, general partner, organization in which he is serving as officer, director, trustee, general partner or employee, or any person or organization with whom he is negotiating or has any arrangement concerning prospective employment, has a financial interest—

Shall be subject to the penalties set forth in section 216 of this title.

(b) Subsection (a) shall not apply—

(1) if the officer or employee first advises the Government official responsible for appointment to his or her position of the nature and circumstances of the judicial or other proceeding, application, request for a ruling or other determination, contract, claim, controversy, charge, accusation, arrest, or other particular matter and makes full disclosure of the financial interest and receives in advance a written determination made by such official that the interest is not so substantial as to be deemed likely to affect the integrity of the services which the Government may expect from such officer or employee;

(2) if, by regulation issued by the Director of the Office of Government Ethics, applicable to all or a portion of all officers and employees covered by this section, and published in the Federal Register, the financial interest has been exempted from the requirements of subsection (a) as being too remote or too inconsequential to affect the integrity of the services of the Government officers or employees to which such regulation applies;

(3) in the case of a special Government employee serving on an advisory committee within the meaning of the Federal Advisory Committee Act (including an individual being considered for an appointment to such a position), the official responsible for the employee's appointment, after review of the financial disclosure report filed by the individual pursuant to the Ethics in Government Act of 1978, certifies in writing that the need for the individual's services outweighs the potential for a conflict of interest created by the financial interest involved; or

(4) if the financial interest that would be affected by the particular matter involved is that resulting solely from the interest of the officer or employee, or his or her spouse or minor child, in birthrights—

(A) in an Indian tribe, band, nation, or other organized group or community, including any Alaska Native village corporation as defined in or established pursuant to the Alaska Native Claims Settlement Act, which is recognized as eligible for the special programs and services provided by the United States to Indians because of their status as Indians,

(B) in an Indian allotment the title to which is held in trust by the United States or which is inalienable by the allottee without the consent of the United States, or

(C) in an Indian claims fund held in trust or administered by the United States, if the particular matter does not involve the Indian allotment or claims fund or the Indian tribe, band, nation, organized group or community, or Alaska Native village corporation as a specific party or parties.

(c)(1) For the purpose of paragraph (1) of subsection (b), in the case of class A and B directors of Federal Reserve banks, the Board of Governors of the Federal Reserve System shall be deemed to be the Government official responsible for appointment.

(2) The potential availability of an exemption under any particular paragraph of subsection (b) does not preclude an exemption being granted pursuant to another paragraph of subsection (b).

(d)(1) Upon request, a copy of any determination granting an exemption under subsection (b)(1) or (b)(3) shall be made available to the public by the agency granting the exemption pursuant to the procedures set forth in section 105 of the Ethics in Government Act of 1978. In making such determination available, the agency may withhold from disclosure any information contained in the determination that would be exempt from disclosure under section 552 of title 5. For purposes of determinations under subsection (b)(3), the information describing each financial interest shall be no more extensive than that required of the individual in his or her financial disclosure report under the Ethics in Government Act of 1978.

(2) The Office of Government Ethics, after consultation with the Attorney General, shall issue uniform regulations for the issuance of waivers and exemptions under subsection (b) which shall—

(A) list and describe exemptions; and

(B) provide guidance with respect to the types of interests that are not so substantial as to be deemed likely to affect the integrity of the services the Government may expect from the employee.

§ 209. Salary of Government officials and employees payable only by United States

(a) Whoever receives any salary, or any contribution to or supplementation of salary, as compensation for his services as an officer or employee of the executive branch of the United States Government, of any independent agency of the United States, or of the District of Columbia, from any source other than the Government of the United States, except as may be contributed out of the treasury of any State, county, or municipality; or

Whoever, whether an individual, partnership, association, corporation, or other organization pays, makes any contribution to, or in any way supplements, the salary of any such officer or employee under circumstances which would make its receipt a violation of this subsection—

Shall be subject to the penalties set forth in section 216 of this title.

(b) Nothing herein prevents an officer or employee of the executive branch of the United States Government, or of any independent agency of the United States, or of the District of Columbia, from continuing to participate in a bona fide pension, retirement, group life, health or accident insurance, profit-sharing, stock bonus, or other employee welfare or benefit plan maintained by a former employer.

(c) This section does not apply to a special Government employee or to an officer or employee of the Government serving without compensation, whether or not he is a special Government employee, or to any person paying, contributing to, or supplementing his salary as such.

(d) This section does not prohibit payment or acceptance of contributions, awards, or other expenses under the terms of Chapter 41 of title 5.

(e) This section does not prohibit the payment of actual relocation expenses incident to participation, or the acceptance of same by a participant in an executive exchange or fellowship program in an executive agency: *Provided*, That such program has been established by statute or Executive order of the President, offers appointments not to exceed three hundred and sixty-five days, and permits no extensions in excess of ninety additional days or, in the case of participants in overseas assignments, in excess of three hundred and sixty-five days.

(f) This section does not prohibit acceptance or receipt, by any officer or employee injured during the commission of an offense described in section 351 or 1751 of this title, of contributions or payments from an organization which is described in section 501(c)(3) of the Internal Revenue Code of 1986 and which is exempt from taxation under section 501(a) of such Code.

(g)(1) This section does not prohibit an employee of a private sector organization, while assigned to an agency under chapter 37 of title 5, from continuing to receive pay and benefits from such organization in accordance with such chapter.

(2) For purposes of this subsection, the term "agency" means an agency (as defined by section 3701 of title 5) and the Office of the Chief Technology Officer of the District of Columbia.

(h) This section does not prohibit a member of the reserve components of the armed forces on active duty pursuant to a call or order to active duty under a provision of law referred to in section 101(a)(13) of title 10 from receiving from any person that employed such member before the call or order to active duty any payment of any part of the salary or wages that such person would have paid the member if the member's employment had not been interrupted by such call or order to active duty.

§ 216. Penalties and injunctions

(a) The punishment for an offense under section 203, 204, 205, 207, 208, or 209 of this title is the following:

(1) Whoever engages in the conduct constituting the offense shall be imprisoned for not more than one year or fined in the amount set forth in this title, or both.

(2) Whoever willfully engages in the conduct constituting the offense shall be imprisoned for not more than five years or fined in the amount set forth in this title, or both.

(b) The Attorney General may bring a civil action in the appropriate United States district court against any person who engages in conduct constituting an offense under section 203, 204, 205, 207, 208, or 209 of this title and, upon proof of such conduct by a preponderance of the evidence, such person shall be subject to a civil penalty of not more than $50,000 for each violation or the amount of compensation which the person received or offered for the prohibited conduct, whichever amount is greater. The imposition of a civil penalty under this subsection does not preclude any other criminal or civil statutory, common law, or administrative remedy, which is available by law to the United States or any other person.

(c) If the Attorney General has reason to believe that a person is engaging in conduct constituting an offense under section 203, 204, 205, 207, 208, or 209 of this title, the Attorney General may petition an appropriate United States district court for an order prohibiting that person from engaging in such conduct. The court may issue an order prohibiting that person from engaging in such conduct if the court finds that the conduct constitutes such an offense. The filing of a petition under this section does not preclude any other remedy which is available by law to the United States or any other person.

4.   18 U.S.C.A. § 1519

§ 1519.   Destruction, alteration, or falsification of records in Federal investigations and bankruptcy

Whoever knowingly alters, destroys, mutilates, conceals, covers up, falsifies, or makes a false entry in any record, document, or tangible object with the intent to impede, obstruct, or influence the investigation or proper administration of any matter within the jurisdiction of any department or agency of the United States or any case filed under title 11, or in relation to or contemplation of any such matter or case, shall be fined under this title, imprisoned not more than 20 years, or both.

5.   18 U.S.C.A. § 1905

§ 1905.   Disclosure of confidential information generally

Whoever, being an officer or employee of the United States or of any department or agency thereof, any person acting on behalf of the Office of Federal Housing Enterprise Oversight, or agent of the Department of Justice as defined in the Antitrust Civil Process Act (15 U.S.C. 1311–1314), or being an employee of a private sector organization who is or was assigned to an agency under chapter 37 of title 5, publishes, divulges, discloses, or makes known in any manner or to any extent not authorized by law any information coming to him in the course of his employment or official duties or by reason of any examination or investigation made by, or return, report or record made to or filled with, such department or agency or officer or employee thereof, which information concerns or relates to the trade secrets, processes, operations, style of work, or apparatus, or to the identity, confidential statistical data, amount or source of any income, profits, losses, or expenditures of any person, firm, partnership, corporation, or association; or permits any income return or copy thereof or any book containing any abstract or particulars thereof to be seen or examined by any person except as provided by law; shall be fined under this title, or imprisoned not more than one year, or both; and shall be removed from office or employment.

6. Citizens Protection Act of 1998 (the McDade Act)

28 U.S.C.A. § 530B

§ 530B. Ethical standards for attorneys for the Government

(a) An attorney for the Government shall be subject to State laws and rules, and local Federal court rules, governing attorneys in each State where such attorney engages in that attorney's duties, to the same extent and in the same manner as other attorneys in that State.

(b) The Attorney General shall make and amend rules of the Department of Justice to assure compliance with this section.

(c) As used in this section, the term "attorney for the Government" includes any attorney described in section 77.2(a) of part 77 of title 28 of the Code of Federal Regulations and also includes any independent counsel, or employee of such a counsel, appointed under chapter 40.

7. Requirements for covered [tax avoidance] opinions

31 CFR § 10.35

§ 10.35 Requirements for covered opinions

(a) A practitioner who provides a covered opinion shall comply with the standards of practice in this section.

(b) Definitions. For purposes of this subpart—

(1) A practitioner includes any individual described in § 10.2(a)(5).

(2) Covered opinion—

(i) In general. A covered opinion is written advice (including electronic communications) by a practitioner concerning one or more Federal tax issues arising from—

(A) A transaction that is the same as or substantially similar to a transaction that, at the time the advice is rendered, the Internal Revenue Service has determined to be a tax avoidance transaction and identified by published guidance as a listed transaction under 26 CFR 1.6011–4(b)(2);

(B) Any partnership or other entity, any investment plan or arrangement, or any other plan or arrangement, the principal purpose of which is the avoidance or evasion of any tax imposed by the Internal Revenue Code; or

(C) Any partnership or other entity, any investment plan or arrangement, or any other plan or arrangement, a significant purpose of which is the avoidance or evasion of any tax imposed by the Internal Revenue Code if the written advice—

(1) Is a reliance opinion;

(2) Is a marketed opinion;

(3) Is subject to conditions of confidentiality; or

(4) Is subject to contractual protection.

(ii) Excluded advice. A covered opinion does not include—

(A) Written advice provided to a client during the course of an engagement if a practitioner is reasonably expected to provide subsequent written advice to the client that satisfies the requirements of this section;

(B) Written advice, other than advice described in paragraph (b)(2)(i)(A) of this section (concerning listed transactions) or paragraph (b)(2)(ii)(B) of this section (concerning the principal purpose of avoidance or evasion) that—

(1) Concerns the qualification of a qualified plan;

(2) Is a State or local bond opinion; or

(3) Is included in documents required to be filed with the Securities and Exchange Commission;

(C) Written advice prepared for and provided to a taxpayer, solely for use by that taxpayer, after the taxpayer has filed a tax return with the Internal Revenue Service reflecting the tax benefits of the transaction. The preceding sentence does not apply if the practitioner knows or has reason to know that the written advice will be relied upon by the taxpayer to take a position on a tax return (including for these purposes an amended return that claims tax benefits not reported on a previously filed return) filed after the date on which the advice is provided to the taxpayer;

(D) Written advice provided to an employer by a practitioner in that practitioner's capacity as an employee of that employer solely for purposes of determining the tax liability of the employer; or

(E) Written advice that does not resolve a Federal tax issue in the taxpayer's favor, unless the advice reaches a conclusion favorable to the taxpayer at any confidence level (e.g., not frivolous, realistic possibility of success, reasonable basis or substantial authority) with respect to that issue. If written advice concerns more than one Federal tax issue, the advice must comply with the requirements of paragraph (c) of this section with respect to any Federal tax issue not described in the preceding sentence.

(3) A Federal tax issue is a question concerning the Federal tax treatment of an item of income, gain, loss, deduction, or credit, the existence or absence of a taxable transfer of property, or the value of property for Federal tax purposes. For purposes of this subpart, a Federal tax issue is significant if the Internal Revenue Service has a reasonable basis for a successful challenge and its resolution could have a significant impact, whether beneficial or adverse and under any reasonably foreseeable circumstance, on the overall Federal tax treatment of the transaction(s) or matter(s) addressed in the opinion.

(4) Reliance opinion—

(i) Written advice is a reliance opinion if the advice concludes at a confidence level of at least more likely than not (a greater than 50 percent likelihood) that one or more significant Federal tax issues would be resolved in the taxpayer's favor.

(ii) For purposes of this section, written advice, other than advice described in paragraph (b)(2)(i)(A) of this section (concerning listed transactions) or paragraph (b)(2)(i)(B) of this section (concerning the principal purpose of avoidance or evasion), is not treated as a reliance opinion if the practitioner prominently discloses in the written advice that it was not intended or written by the practitioner to be used, and that it cannot be used by the taxpayer, for the purpose of avoiding penalties that may be imposed on the taxpayer.

(5) Marketed opinion—(i) Written advice is a marketed opinion if the practitioner knows or has reason to know that the written advice will be used or referred to by a person other than the practitioner (or a person who is a member of, associated with, or employed by the practitioner's firm) in promoting, marketing or recommending a partnership or other entity, investment plan or arrangement to one or more taxpayer(s).

(i) For purposes of this section, written advice, other than advice described in paragraph (b)(2)(i)(A) of this section (concerning listed transactions) or paragraph (b)(2)(i)(B) of this section (concerning the principal purpose of avoidance or evasion), is not treated as a marketed opinion if the practitioner prominently discloses in the written advice that—

(A) The advice was not intended or written by the practitioner to be used, and that it cannot be used by any taxpayer, for the purpose of avoiding penalties that may be imposed on the taxpayer;

(B) The advice was written to support the promotion or marketing of the transaction(s) or matter(s) addressed by the written advice; and

(C) The taxpayer should seek advice based on the taxpayer's particular circumstances from an independent tax advisor.

(6) Conditions of confidentiality. Written advice is subject to conditions of confidentiality if the practitioner imposes on one or more recipients of the written advice a limitation on disclosure of the tax treatment or tax structure of the transaction and the limitation on disclosure protects the confidentiality of that practitioner's tax strategies, regardless of whether the limitation on disclosure is legally binding. A claim that a transaction is proprietary or exclusive is not a limitation on disclosure if the practitioner confirms to all recipients of the written advice that there is no limitation on disclosure of the tax treatment or tax structure of the transaction that is the subject of the written advice.

(7) Contractual protection. Written advice is subject to contractual protection if the taxpayer has the right to a full or partial refund of fees paid to the practitioner (or a person who is a member of, associated with, or employed by the practitioner's firm) if all or a part of the intended tax consequences from the matters addressed in the written advice are not sustained, or if the fees paid to the practitioner (or a person who is a member of, associated with, or employed by the practitioner's firm) are contingent on the taxpayer's realization of tax benefits from the transaction. All the facts and circumstances relating to the matters addressed in the written advice will be considered when determining whether a fee is refundable or contingent, including the right to reimbursements of amounts that the parties to a transaction have not designated as fees or any agreement to provide services without reasonable compensation.

(8) Prominently disclosed. An item is prominently disclosed if it is readily apparent to a reader of the written advice. Whether an item is readily apparent will depend on the facts and circumstances surrounding the written advice including, but not limited to, the sophistication of the taxpayer and the length of the written advice. At a minimum, to be prominently disclosed an item must be set forth in a separate section (and not in a footnote) in a typeface that is the same size or larger than the typeface of any discussion of the facts or law in the written advice.

(9) State or local bond opinion. A State or local bond opinion is written advice with respect to a Federal tax issue included in any materials delivered to a purchaser of a State or local bond in connection with the issuance of the bond in a public or private offering, including an official statement (if one is prepared), that concerns only the excludability of interest on a State or local bond from gross income under section 103 of the Internal Revenue Code, the application of section 55 of the Internal

Revenue Code to a State or local bond, the status of a State or local bond as a qualified tax-exempt obligation under section 265(b)(3) of the Internal Revenue Code, the status of a State or local bond as a qualified zone academy bond under section 1397E of the Internal Revenue Code, or any combination of the above.

(10) *The principal purpose.* For purposes of this section, the principal purpose of a partnership or other entity, investment plan or arrangement, or other plan or arrangement is the avoidance or evasion of any tax imposed by the Internal Revenue Code if that purpose exceeds any other purpose. The principal purpose of a partnership or other entity, investment plan or arrangement, or other plan or arrangement is not to avoid or evade Federal tax if that partnership, entity, plan or arrangement has as its purpose the claiming of tax benefits in a manner consistent with the statute and Congressional purpose. A partnership, entity, plan or arrangement may have a significant purpose of avoidance or evasion even though it does not have the principal purpose of avoidance or evasion under this paragraph (b)(10).

(c) *Requirements for covered opinions.* A practitioner providing a covered opinion must comply with each of the following requirements.

(1) *Factual matters.*

(i) The practitioner must use reasonable efforts to identify and ascertain the facts, which may relate to future events if a transaction is prospective or proposed, and to determine which facts are relevant. The opinion must identify and consider all facts that the practitioner determines to be relevant.

(ii) The practitioner must not base the opinion on any unreasonable factual assumptions (including assumptions as to future events). An unreasonable factual assumption includes a factual assumption that the practitioner knows or should know is incorrect or incomplete. For example, it is unreasonable to assume that a transaction has a business purpose or that a transaction is potentially profitable apart from tax benefits. A factual assumption includes reliance on a projection, financial forecast or appraisal. It is unreasonable for a practitioner to rely on a projection, financial forecast or appraisal if the practitioner knows or should know that the projection, financial forecast or appraisal is incorrect or incomplete or was prepared by a person lacking the skills or qualifications necessary to prepare such projection, financial forecast or appraisal. The opinion must identify in a separate section all factual assumptions relied upon by the practitioner.

(iii) The practitioner must not base the opinion on any unreasonable factual representations, statements or findings of the taxpayer or any other person. An unreasonable factual representation includes a factual representation that the practitioner knows or should know is incorrect or incomplete. For example, a practitioner may not rely on a factual representation that a transaction has a business purpose if the representation does not include a specific description of the business purpose or the practitioner knows or should know that the representation is incorrect or incomplete. The opinion must identify in a separate section all factual representations, statements or findings of the taxpayer relied upon by the practitioner.

(2) Relate law to facts.

(i) The opinion must relate the applicable law (including potentially applicable judicial doctrines) to the relevant facts.

(ii) The practitioner must not assume the favorable resolution of any significant Federal tax issue except as provided in paragraphs (c)(3)(v) and (d) of this section, or otherwise base an opinion on any unreasonable legal assumptions, representations, or conclusions.

(iii) The opinion must not contain internally inconsistent legal analyses or conclusions.

(3) Evaluation of significant Federal tax issues—

(i) In general. The opinion must consider all significant Federal tax issues except as provided in paragraphs (c)(3)(v) and (d) of this section.

(ii) Conclusion as to each significant Federal tax issue. The opinion must provide the practitioner's conclusion as to the likelihood that the taxpayer will prevail on the merits with respect to each significant Federal tax issue considered in the opinion. If the practitioner is unable to reach a conclusion with respect to one or more of those issues, the opinion must state that the practitioner is unable to reach a conclusion with respect to those issues. The opinion must describe the reasons for the conclusions, including the facts and analysis supporting the conclusions, or describe the reasons that the practitioner is unable to reach a conclusion as to one or more issues. If the practitioner fails to reach a conclusion at a confidence level of at least more likely than not with respect to one or more significant Federal tax issues considered, the opinion must include the appropriate disclosure(s) required under paragraph (e) of this section.

(iii) Evaluation based on chances of success on the merits. In evaluating the significant Federal tax issues addressed in the opinion, the practitioner must not take into account the possibility that a tax return will not be audited, that an issue will not be raised on audit, or that an issue will be resolved through settlement if raised.

(iv) Marketed opinions. In the case of a marketed opinion, the opinion must provide the practitioner's conclusion that the taxpayer will prevail on the merits at a confidence level of at least more likely than not with respect to each significant Federal tax issue. If the practitioner is unable to reach a more likely than not conclusion with respect to each significant Federal tax issue, the practitioner must not provide the marketed opinion, but may provide written advice that satisfies the requirements in paragraph (b)(5)(ii) of this section.

(v) Limited scope opinions.

(A) The practitioner may provide an opinion that considers less than all of the significant Federal tax issues if—

(1) The practitioner and the taxpayer agree that the scope of the opinion and the taxpayer's potential reliance on the opinion for purposes of avoiding penalties that may be imposed on the taxpayer are limited to the Federal tax issue(s) addressed in the opinion;

(2) The opinion is not advice described in paragraph (b)(2)(i)(A) of this section (concerning listed transactions), paragraph (b)(2)(i)(B) of this section (concerning the principal purpose of avoidance or evasion) or paragraph (b)(5) of this section (a marketed opinion); and

(3) The opinion includes the appropriate disclosure(s) required under paragraph (e) of this section.

(B) A practitioner may make reasonable assumptions regarding the favorable resolution of a Federal tax issue (an assumed issue) for purposes of providing an opinion on less than all of the significant Federal tax issues as provided in this paragraph (c)(3)(v). The opinion must identify in a separate section all issues for which the practitioner assumed a favorable resolution.

(4) Overall conclusion.

(i) The opinion must provide the practitioner's overall conclusion as to the likelihood that the Federal tax treatment of the transaction or matter that is the subject of the opinion is the proper treatment and the reasons for that conclusion. If the practitioner is unable to reach an overall conclusion, the opinion must state that the practitioner is unable to reach an overall conclusion and describe the reasons for the practitioner's inability to reach a conclusion.

(ii) In the case of a marketed opinion, the opinion must provide the practitioner's overall conclusion that the Federal tax treatment of the transaction or matter that is the subject of the opinion is the proper treatment at a confidence level of at least more likely than not.

(d) Competence to provide opinion; reliance on opinions of others.

(1) The practitioner must be knowledgeable in all of the aspects of Federal tax law relevant to the opinion being rendered, except that the practitioner may rely on the opinion of another practitioner with respect to one or more significant Federal tax issues, unless the practitioner

knows or should know that the opinion of the other practitioner should not be relied on. If a practitioner relies on the opinion of another practitioner, the relying practitioner's opinion must identify the other opinion and set forth the conclusions reached in the other opinion.

(2) The practitioner must be satisfied that the combined analysis of the opinions, taken as a whole, and the overall conclusion, if any, satisfy the requirements of this section.

(e) Required disclosures. A covered opinion must contain all of the following disclosures that apply—

(1) Relationship between promoter and practitioner. An opinion must prominently disclose the existence of—

(i) Any compensation arrangement, such as a referral fee or a fee-sharing arrangement, between the practitioner (or the practitioner's firm or any person who is a member of, associated with, or employed by the practitioner's firm) and any person (other than the client for whom the opinion is prepared) with respect to promoting, marketing or recommending the entity, plan, or arrangement (or a substantially similar arrangement) that is the subject of the opinion; or

(ii) Any referral agreement between the practitioner (or the practitioner's firm or any person who is a member of, associated with, or employed by the practitioner's firm) and a person (other than the client for whom the opinion is prepared) engaged in promoting, marketing or recommending the entity, plan, or arrangement (or a substantially similar arrangement) that is the subject of the opinion.

(2) Marketed opinions. A marketed opinion must prominently disclose that—

(i) The opinion was written to support the promotion or marketing of the transaction(s) or matter(s) addressed in the opinion; and

(ii) The taxpayer should seek advice based on the taxpayer's particular circumstances from an independent tax advisor.

(3) Limited scope opinions. A limited scope opinion must prominently disclose that—

(i) The opinion is limited to the one or more Federal tax issues addressed in the opinion;

(ii) Additional issues may exist that could affect the Federal tax treatment of the transaction or matter that is the subject of the opinion and the opinion does not consider or provide a conclusion with respect to any additional issues; and

(iii) With respect to any significant Federal tax issues outside the limited scope of the opinion, the opinion was not written, and cannot be used by the taxpayer, for the purpose of avoiding penalties that may be imposed on the taxpayer.

(4) *Opinions that fail to reach a more likely than not conclusion.* An opinion that does not reach a conclusion at a confidence level of at least more likely than not with respect to a significant Federal tax issue must prominently disclose that—

(i) The opinion does not reach a conclusion at a confidence level of at least more likely than not with respect to one or more significant Federal tax issues addressed by the opinion; and

(ii) With respect to those significant Federal tax issues, the opinion was not written, and cannot be used by the taxpayer, for the purpose of avoiding penalties that may be imposed on the taxpayer.

(5) *Advice regarding required disclosures.* In the case of any disclosure required under this section, the practitioner may not provide advice to any person that is contrary to or inconsistent with the required disclosure.

(f) *Effect of opinion that meets these standards—*

(1) *In general.* An opinion that meets the requirements of this section satisfies the practitioner's responsibilities under this section, but the persuasiveness of the opinion with regard to the tax issues in question and the taxpayer's good faith reliance on the opinion will be determined separately under applicable provisions of the law and regulations.

(2) *Standards for other written advice.* A practitioner who provides written advice that is not a covered opinion for purposes of this section is subject to the requirements of § 10.37.

(g) *Effective date.* This section applies to written advice that is rendered after June 20, 2005.

8.   Sample Federal District Court Rules

UNITED STATES DISTRICT COURTS FOR THE SOUTHERN AND EASTERN DISTRICTS OF NEW YORK

Local Civil Rule 1.3. Admission to the Bar

(a) A member in good standing of the bar of the state of New York, or a member in good standing of the bar of the United States District Court in Connecticut or Vermont and of the bar of the State in which such district court is located, provided such district court by its rule extends a corresponding privilege to members of the bar of this court, may be admitted to practice in this court on compliance with the following provisions:

In the first instance, each applicant for admission is required to file an application for admission in electronic form on the Court's Website (www. nysd.uscourts.gov). This one application will be utilized both to admit and then to provide the applicant to the bar of this Court with a password and login for use on the court's Electronic Case Filing (ECF) system. The applicant shall adhere to all applicable rules of admission.

The applicant shall (a) complete the application on-line, (b) submit the application electronically, (c) print and sign a copy of the application, and (d) file the printed application and fee with the clerk, together with a certificate(s) of good standing and supporting affidavit(s).

After submitting the application in electronic form, each applicant for admission shall file with the clerk, at least ten (10) days prior to hearing (unless, for good cause shown, the judge shall shorten the time), a verified written petition for admission on a form supplied by the clerk stating: (1) applicant's residence and office address; (2) the time when, and courts where, admitted; (3) applicant's legal training and experience; (4) whether applicant has ever been held in contempt of court, and, if so, the nature of the contempt and the final disposition thereof; (5) whether applicant has ever been censured, suspended or disbarred by any court, and, if so, the facts and circumstances connected therewith; (6) that applicant has read and is familiar with (a) the provisions of the Judicial Code (Title 28, U.S.C.) which pertain to the jurisdiction of, and practice in, the United States District Courts; (b) the Federal Rules of Civil Procedure; (c) the Federal Rules of Criminal Procedure; (d) the Federal Rules of Evidence; (e) the Local Rules of the United States District Court for the Southern and Eastern Districts of New York; and (f) the New York State Lawyer's Code of Professional Responsibility as adopted from time to time by the Appellate Divisions of the State of New York; and (7) that applicant will faithfully adhere to all rules applicable to applicant's conduct in connection with any activities in this court.

The petition shall be accompanied by a certificate of the clerk of the court for each of the states in which the applicant is a member of the bar, which has been issued within thirty (30) days and states that the applicant is a member in good standing of the bar of that state court. The petition shall also be accompanied by an affidavit of an attorney of this court who has known the applicant for at least one year, stating when the affiant was admitted to practice in this court, how long and under what circumstances the attorney has known the applicant, and what the attorney knows of the applicant's character and experience at the bar. Such petition shall be placed at the head of the calendar and, on the call thereof, the attorney whose affidavit accompanied the petition shall personally move the admission of the applicant. If the petition is granted, the applicant shall take the oath of office and sign the roll of attorneys.

A member of the bar of the state of New York, Connecticut, or Vermont who has been admitted to the bar of this court pursuant to this subsection and who thereafter voluntarily resigns from membership in the bar of the state pursuant to which he was admitted to the bar of this court, and who does not within 30 days of that voluntary resignation file an affidavit with the clerk of this court indicating that such person remains eligible to be admitted to the bar of this court pursuant to other provisions of this subsection (as because he is still a member of the bar of another eligible state and, where applicable, a corresponding district court), shall be deemed to have voluntarily resigned from the bar of this court as of the same date the member resigned from the bar of the underlying state, provided that such resignation shall not be deemed to deprive this court of jurisdiction to impose discipline on this person, pursuant to Rule 1.5 infra, for conduct preceding the date of such resignation.

(b) A member in good standing of the bar of either the Southern or Eastern District of New York may be admitted to the bar of the other district without formal application (1) upon filing in that district a certificate of the Clerk of the United States District Court for the district in which the applicant is a member of the bar, which has been issued within thirty (30) days and states that the applicant is a member in good standing of the bar of that court and (2) upon taking the oath of office, signing the roll of attorneys of that district, and paying the fee required in that district.

(c) A member in good standing of the bar of any state or of any United States District Court may be permitted to argue or try a particular case in whole or in part as counsel or advocate, upon motion and upon filing with the Clerk of the District Court a certificate of the court for each of the states in which the applicant is a member of the bar, which has been issued within thirty (30) days and states that the applicant is a member in good standing of the bar of that state court. Only an attorney who has been so admitted or who is a member of the bar of this court may enter appearances for parties, sign stipulations or receive payments upon judgments, decrees or orders.

(d) If an attorney who is a member of the bar of this court, or who has been authorized to appear in a case in this court, changes his or her residence or office address, the attorney shall immediately notify the clerk of the court, in addition to serving and filing a notice of change of address in each pending case in which the attorney has appeared.

9. Federal Rules of Appellate Procedure

RULE 45. Clerk's Duties

(a) General Provisions. *** Neither the clerk nor any deputy clerk may practice as an attorney or counselor in any court while in office. ***

RULE 46. Attorneys

(a) Admission to the Bar.

(1) Eligibility. An attorney is eligible for admission to the bar of a court of appeals if that attorney is of good moral and professional character and is admitted to practice before the Supreme Court of the United States, the highest court of a state, another United States court of appeals, or a United States district court (including the district courts for Guam, the Northern Mariana Islands, and the Virgin Islands).

(2) Application. An applicant must file an application for admission, on a form approved by the court that contains the applicant's personal statement showing eligibility for membership. The applicant must subscribe to the following oath or affirmation:

"I, _____, do solemnly swear [or affirm] that I will conduct myself as an attorney and counselor of this court, uprightly and according to law; and that I will support the Constitution of the United States."

(3) Admission Procedures. On written or oral motion of a member of the court's bar, the court will act on the application. An applicant may be admitted by oral motion in open court. But, unless the court orders otherwise, an applicant need not appear before the court to be admitted. Upon admission, an applicant must pay the clerk the fee prescribed by local rule or court order.

(b) Suspension or Disbarment.

(1) Standard. A member of the court's bar is subject to suspension or disbarment by the court if the member:

(A) has been suspended or disbarred from practice in any other court; or

(B) is guilty of conduct unbecoming a member of the court's bar.

(2) Procedure. The member must be given an opportunity to show good cause, within the time prescribed by the court, why the member should not be suspended or disbarred.

(3) Order. The court must enter an appropriate order after the member responds and a hearing is held, if requested, or after the time prescribed for a response expires, if no response is made.

(c) Discipline. A court of appeals may discipline an attorney who practices before it for conduct unbecoming a member of the bar or for failure to comply with any court rule. First, however, the court must afford the attorney reasonable notice, an opportunity to show cause to the contrary, and, if requested, a hearing.

10.   U.S. Supreme Court Rules

RULE 7.   Prohibition Against Practice

No employee of this Court shall practice as an attorney or counselor in any court or before any agency of government while employed by the Court; nor shall any person after leaving such employment participate in any professional capacity in any case pending before this Court or in any case being considered for filing in this Court, until two years have elapsed after separation; nor shall a former employee ever participate in any professional capacity in any case that was pending in this Court during the employee's tenure.

RULE 8.   Disbarment and Disciplinary Action

1.   Whenever a member of the Bar of this Court has been disbarred or suspended from practice in any court of record, or has engaged in conduct

unbecoming a member of the Bar of this Court, the Court will enter an order suspending that member from practice before this Court and affording the member an opportunity to show cause, within 40 days, why a disbarment order should not be entered. Upon response, or if no response is timely filed, the Court will enter an appropriate order.

2.   After reasonable notice and an opportunity to show cause why disciplinary action should not be taken, and after a hearing if material facts are in dispute, the Court may take any appropriate disciplinary action against any attorney who is admitted to practice before it for conduct unbecoming a member of the Bar or for failure to comply with these Rules or any Rule or order of the Court.

11.   Federal Rules of Civil Procedure, Rules 11 & 23

Rule 11.   Signing of Pleadings, Motions, and Other Papers; Representations to Court; Sanctions

(a) Signature. Every pleading, written motion, and other paper shall be signed by at least one attorney of record in the attorney's individual name, or, if the party is not represented by an attorney, shall be signed by the party. Each paper shall state the signer's address and telephone number, if any. Except when otherwise specifically provided by rule or statute, pleadings need not be verified or accompanied by affidavit. An unsigned paper shall be stricken unless omission of the signature is corrected promptly after being called to the attention of the attorney or party.

(b) Representations to Court. By presenting to the court (whether by signing, filing, submitting, or later advocating) a pleading, written motion, or other paper, an attorney or unrepresented party is certifying that to the best of the person's knowledge, information, and belief, formed after an inquiry reasonable under the circumstances,—

(1) it is not being presented for any improper purpose, such as to harass or to cause unnecessary delay or needless increase in the cost of litigation;

(2) the claims, defenses, and other legal contentions therein are warranted by existing law or by a nonfrivolous argument for the extension, modification, or reversal of existing law or the establishment of new law;

(3) the allegations and other factual contentions have evidentiary support or, if specifically so identified, are likely to have evidentiary support after a reasonable opportunity for further investigation or discovery; and

(4) the denials of factual contentions are warranted on the evidence or, if specifically so identified, are reasonably based on a lack of information or belief.

(c) Sanctions. If, after notice and a reasonable opportunity to respond, the court determines that subdivision (b) has been violated, the court may, subject to the conditions stated below, impose an appropriate sanction upon the attorneys, law firms, or parties that have violated subdivision (b) or are responsible for the violation.

(1) How Initiated.

(A) By Motion. A motion for sanctions under this rule shall be made separately from other motions or requests and shall describe the specific conduct alleged to violate subdivision (b). It shall be served as provided in Rule 5, but shall not be filed with or presented to the court unless, within 21 days after service of the motion (or such other period as the court may prescribe), the challenged paper, claim, defense, contention, allegation, or denial is not withdrawn or appropriately corrected. If warranted, the court may award to the party prevailing on the motion the reasonable expenses and attorney's fees incurred in presenting or opposing the motion. Absent exceptional circumstances, a law firm shall be held jointly responsible for violations committed by its partners, associates, and employees.

(B) On Court's Initiative. On its own initiative, the court may enter an order describing the specific conduct that appears to violate subdivision (b) and directing an attorney, law firm, or party to show cause why it has not violated subdivision (b) with respect thereto.

(2) Nature of Sanction; Limitations. A sanction imposed for violation of this rule shall be limited to what is sufficient to deter repetition of such conduct or comparable conduct by others similarly situated. Subject to the limitations in subparagraphs (A) and (B), the sanction may consist of, or include, directives of a nonmonetary nature, an order to pay a penalty into court, or, if imposed on motion and warranted for effective deterrence, an order directing payment to the movant of some or all of the reasonable attorneys' fees and other expenses incurred as a direct result of the violation.

(A) Monetary sanctions may not be awarded against a represented party for a violation of subdivision (b)(2).

(B) Monetary sanctions may not be awarded on the court's initiative unless the court issues its order to show cause before a voluntary dismissal or settlement of the claims made by or against the party which is, or whose attorneys are, to be sanctioned.

(3) Order. When imposing sanctions, the court shall describe the conduct determined to constitute a violation of this rule and explain the basis for the sanction imposed.

(d) Inapplicability to Discovery. Subdivisions (a) through (c) of this rule do not apply to disclosures and discovery requests, responses, objections, and motions that are subject to the provisions of Rules 26 through 37.

Rule 23. Class Actions

(a) **Prerequisites to a Class Action.** One or more members of a class may sue or be sued as representative parties on behalf of all only if (1) the class is so numerous that joinder of all members is impracticable, (2) there are questions of law or fact common to the class, (3) the claims or defenses of the representative parties are typical of the claims or defenses of the class, and (4) the representative parties will fairly and adequately protect the interests of the class.

(b) **Class Actions Maintainable.** An action may be maintained as a class action if the prerequisites of subdivision (a) are satisfied, and in addition:

(1) the prosecution of separate actions by or against individual members of the class would create a risk of

(A) inconsistent or varying adjudications with respect to individual members of the class which would establish incompatible standards of conduct for the party opposing the class, or

(B) adjudications with respect to individual members of the class which would as a practical matter be dispositive of the interests of the other members not parties to the adjudications or substantially impair or impede their ability to protect their interests; or

(2) the party opposing the class has acted or refused to act on grounds generally applicable to the class, thereby making appropriate final injunctive relief or corresponding declaratory relief with respect to the class as a whole; or

(3) the court finds that the questions of law or fact common to the members of the class predominate over any questions affecting only individual members, and that a class action is superior to other available methods for the fair and efficient adjudication of the controversy. The matters pertinent to the findings include: (A) the interest of members of the class in individually controlling the prosecution or defense of separate actions; (B) the extent and nature of any litigation concerning the controversy already commenced by or against members of the class; (C) the desirability or undesirability of concentrating the litigation of the claims in the particular forum; (D) the difficulties likely to be encountered in the management of a class action.

(c) **Determining by Order Whether to Certify a Class Action; Appointing Class Counsel; Notice and Membership in Class; Judgment; Multiple Classes and Subclasses.**

(1)(A) When a person sues or is sued as a representative of a class, the court must—at an early practicable time—determine by order whether to certify the action as a class action.

(B) An order certifying a class action must define the class and the class claims, issues, or defenses, and must appoint class counsel under Rule 23(g).

(C) An order under Rule 23(c)(1) may be altered or amended before final judgment.

(2)(A) For any class certified under Rule 23(b)(1) or (2), the court may direct appropriate notice to the class.

(B) For any class certified under Rule 23(b)(3), the court must direct to class members the best notice practicable under the circumstances, including individual notice to all members who can be identified through reasonable effort. The notice must concisely and clearly state in plain, easily understood language:

- the nature of the action,
- the definition of the class certified,
- the class claims, issues, or defenses,
- that a class member may enter an appearance through counsel if the member so desires,
- that the court will exclude from the class any member who requests exclusion, stating when and how members may elect to be excluded, and
- the binding effect of a class judgment on class members under Rule 23(c)(3).

(3) The judgment in an action maintained as a class action under subdivision (b)(1) or (b)(2), whether or not favorable to the class, shall include and describe those whom the court finds to be members of the class. The judgment in an action maintained as a class action under subdivision (b)(3), whether or not favorable to the class, shall include and specify or describe those to whom the notice provided in subdivision (c)(2) was directed, and who have not requested exclusion, and whom the court finds to be members of the class.

(4) When appropriate (A) an action may be brought or maintained as a class action with respect to particular issues, or (B) a class may be divided into subclasses and each subclass treated as a class, and the provisions of this rule shall then be construed and applied accordingly.

(d) Orders in Conduct of Actions. In the conduct of actions to which this rule applies, the court may make appropriate orders: (1) determining the course of proceedings or prescribing measures to prevent undue repetition or complication in the presentation of evidence or argument; (2) requiring, for the protection of the members of the class or otherwise for the fair conduct of the action, that notice be given in such manner as the court may direct to some or all of the members of any step in the action, or of the proposed extent of the judgment, or of the opportunity of members to signify whether they consider the representation fair and adequate, to intervene and present claims or defenses, or otherwise to come into the action; (3) imposing conditions on the representative parties or on intervenors; (4) requiring that the pleadings be amended to eliminate therefrom allegations as to representation of absent persons, and that the action proceed accordingly; (5) dealing with similar procedural matters. The orders may be combined with an order under Rule 16, and may be altered or amended as may be desirable from time to time.

(e) Settlement, Voluntary Dismissal, or Compromise.

(1)(A) The court must approve any settlement, voluntary dismissal, or compromise of the claims, issues, or defenses of a certified class.

(B) The court must direct notice in a reasonable manner to all class members who would be bound by a proposed settlement, voluntary dismissal, or compromise.

(C) The court may approve a settlement, voluntary dismissal, or compromise that would bind class members only after a hearing and on finding that the settlement, voluntary dismissal, or compromise is fair, reasonable, and adequate.

(2) The parties seeking approval of a settlement, voluntary dismissal, or compromise under Rule 23(e)(1) must file a statement identifying any agreement made in connection with the proposed settlement, voluntary dismissal, or compromise.

(3) In an action previously certified as a class action under Rule 23(b)(3), the court may refuse to approve a settlement unless it affords a new opportunity to request exclusion to individual class members who had an earlier opportunity to request exclusion but did not do so.

(4)(A) Any class member may object to a proposed settlement, voluntary dismissal, or compromise that requires court approval under Rule 23(e)(1)(A).

(B) An objection made under Rule 23(e)(4)(A) may be withdrawn only with the court's approval.

(f) Appeals. A court of appeals may in its discretion permit an appeal from an order of a district court granting or denying class action certification under this rule if application is made to it within ten days after entry of the order. An appeal does not stay proceedings in the district court unless the district judge or the court of appeals so orders.

(g) Class Counsel.

(1) Appointing Class Counsel.

(A) Unless a statute provides otherwise, a court that certifies a class must appoint class counsel.

(B) An attorney appointed to serve as class counsel must fairly and adequately represent the interests of the class.

(C) In appointing class counsel, the court

(i) must consider:

• the work counsel has done in identifying or investigating potential claims in the action,

• counsel's experience in handling class actions, other complex litigation, and claims of the type asserted in the action,

• counsel's knowledge of the applicable law, and

• the resources counsel will commit to representing the class;

(ii) may consider any other matter pertinent to counsel's ability to fairly and adequately represent the interests of the class;

(iii) may direct potential class counsel to provide information on any subject pertinent to the appointment and to propose terms for attorney fees and nontaxable costs; and

(iv) may make further orders in connection with the appointment.

(2) Appointment Procedure.

(A) The court may designate interim counsel to act on behalf of the putative class before determining whether to certify the action as a class action.

(B) When there is one applicant for appointment as class counsel, the court may appoint that applicant only if the applicant is adequate under Rule 23(g)(1)(B) and (C). If more than one adequate applicant seeks appointment as class counsel, the court must appoint the applicant best able to represent the interests of the class.

(C) The order appointing class counsel may include provisions about the award of attorney fees or nontaxable costs under Rule 23(h).

(h) Attorney Fees Award. In an action certified as a class action, the court may award reasonable attorney fees and nontaxable costs authorized by law or by agreement of the parties as follows:

(1) Motion for Award of Attorney Fees. A claim for an award of attorney fees and nontaxable costs must be made by motion under Rule 54(d)(2), subject to the provisions of this subdivision, at a time set by the court. Notice of the motion must be served on all parties and, for motions by class counsel, directed to class members in a reasonable manner.

(2) Objections to Motion. A class member, or a party from whom payment is sought, may object to the motion.

(3) Hearing and Findings. The court may hold a hearing and must find the facts and state its conclusions of law on the motion under Rule 52(a).

(4) Reference to Special Master or Magistrate Judge. The court may refer issues related to the amount of the award to a special master or to a magistrate judge as provided in Rule 54(d)(2)(D).

ABA MODEL CODE OF JUDICIAL CONDUCT
February 2007

Editors' Note: The ABA Joint Commission to Evaluate the Model Code of Judicial Conduct began its work in 2003. On 12 February 2007, the ABA House of Delegates approved a new version of the Model Rules of Professional Conduct, reprinted here.

Table of Contents

CANON 1

A JUDGE SHALL UPHOLD AND PROMOTE THE INDEPENDENCE, INTEGRITY, AND IMPARTIALITY OF THE JUDICIARY, AND SHALL AVOID IMPROPRIETY AND THE APPEARANCE OF IMPROPRIETY.

CANON 2

A JUDGE SHALL PERFORM THE DUTIES OF JUDICIAL OFFICE IMPARTIALLY, COMPETENTLY, AND DILIGENTLY.

CANON 3

***A** JUDGE SHALL CONDUCT THE JUDGE'S PERSONAL AND EXTRAJUDICIAL ACTIVITIES TO MINIMIZE THE RISK OF CONFLICT WITH THE OBLIGATIONS OF JUDICIAL OFFICE.*

CANON 4

***A** JUDGE OR CANDIDATE FOR JUDICIAL OFFICE SHALL NOT ENGAGE IN POLITICAL OR CAMPAIGN ACTIVITY THAT IS INCONSISTENT WITH THE INDEPENDENCE, INTEGRITY, OR IMPARTIALITY OF THE JUDICIARY.*

PREAMBLE

[1]   An independent, fair and impartial judiciary is indispensable to our system of justice. The United States legal system is based upon the principle that an independent, impartial, and competent judiciary, composed of men and women of integrity, will interpret and apply the law that governs our society. Thus, the judiciary plays a central role in preserving the principles of justice and the rule of law. Inherent in all the Rules contained in this Code are the precepts that judges, individually and collectively, must respect and honor the judicial office as a public trust and strive to maintain and enhance confidence in the legal system.

[2]   Judges should maintain the dignity of judicial office at all times, and avoid both impropriety and the appearance of impropriety in their professional and personal lives. They should aspire at all times to conduct that ensures the greatest possible public confidence in their independence, impartiality, integrity, and competence.

[3]   The Model Code of Judicial Conduct establishes standards for the ethical conduct of judges and judicial candidates. It is not intended as an exhaustive guide for the conduct of judges and judicial candidates, who are governed in their judicial and personal conduct by general ethical standards as well as by the Code. The Code is intended, however, to provide guidance and assist judges in maintaining the highest standards of judicial and personal conduct, and to provide a basis for regulating their conduct through disciplinary agencies.

SCOPE

[1]   The Model Code of Judicial Conduct consists of four Canons, numbered Rules under each Canon, and Comments that generally follow and explain each Rule. Scope and Terminology sections provide additional guidance in interpreting and applying the Code. An Application section establishes when the various Rules apply to a judge or judicial candidate.

[2]   The Canons state overarching principles of judicial ethics that all judges must observe. Although a judge may be disciplined only for violating a Rule, the Canons provide important guidance in interpreting the Rules. Where a Rule contains a permissive term, such as "may" or "should," the conduct being addressed is committed to the personal and professional discretion of the judge or candidate in question, and no disciplinary action should be taken for action or inaction within the bounds of such discretion.

[3]   The Comments that accompany the Rules serve two functions. First, they provide guidance regarding the purpose, meaning, and proper application of the Rules. They contain explanatory material and, in some instances, provide examples of permitted or prohibited conduct. Comments neither add to nor subtract from the binding obligations set forth in the Rules. Therefore, when a Comment contains the term "must," it does not mean that the Comment itself is binding or enforceable; it signifies that the Rule in question, properly understood, is obligatory as to the conduct at issue.

[4]   Second, the Comments identify aspirational goals for judges. To implement fully the principles of this Code as articulated in the Canons, judges should strive to exceed the standards of conduct established by the Rules, holding themselves to the

highest ethical standards and seeking to achieve those aspirational goals, thereby enhancing the dignity of the judicial office.

[5]   The Rules of the Model Code of Judicial Conduct are rules of reason that should be applied consistent with constitutional requirements, statutes, other court rules, and decisional law, and with due regard for all relevant circumstances. The Rules should not be interpreted to impinge upon the essential independence of judges in making judicial decisions.

[6]   Although the black letter of the Rules is binding and enforceable, it is not contemplated that every transgression will result in the imposition of discipline. Whether discipline should be imposed should be determined through a reasonable and reasoned application of the Rules, and should depend upon factors such as the seriousness of the transgression, the facts and circumstances that existed at the time of the transgression, the extent of any pattern of improper activity, whether there have been previous violations, and the effect of the improper activity upon the judicial system or others.

[7]   The Code is not designed or intended as a basis for civil or criminal liability. Neither is it intended to be the basis for litigants to seek collateral remedies against each other or to obtain tactical advantages in proceedings before a court.

TERMINOLOGY

The first time any term listed below is used in a Rule in its defined sense, it is followed by an asterisk (*).

"Aggregate," in relation to contributions for a candidate, means not only contributions in cash or in kind made directly to a candidate's campaign committee, but also all contributions made indirectly with the understanding that they will be used to support the election of a candidate or to oppose the election of the candidate's opponent. See Rules 2.11 and 4.4.

"Appropriate authority" means the authority having responsibility for initiation of disciplinary process in connection with the violation to be reported. See Rules 2.14 and 2.15.

"Contribution" means both financial and in-kind contributions, such as goods, professional or volunteer services, advertising, and other types of assistance, which, if obtained by the recipient otherwise, would require a financial expenditure. See Rules 2.11, 2.13, 3.7, 4.1, and 4.4.

"De minimis," in the context of interests pertaining to disqualification of a judge, means an insignificant interest that could not raise a reasonable question regarding the judge's impartiality. See Rule 2.11.

"Domestic partner" means a person with whom another person maintains a household and an intimate relationship, other than a person to whom he or she is legally married. See Rules 2.11, 2.13, 3.13, and 3.14.

"Economic interest" means ownership of more than a de minimis legal or equitable interest. Except for situations in which the judge participates in the management of such a legal or equitable interest, or the interest could be substantially affected by the outcome of a proceeding before a judge, it does not include:

> (1) an interest in the individual holdings within a mutual or common investment fund;

(2) an interest in securities held by an educational, religious, charitable, fraternal, or civic organization in which the judge or the judge's spouse, domestic partner, parent, or child serves as a director, an officer, an advisor, or other participant;

(3) a deposit in a financial institution or deposits or proprietary interests the judge may maintain as a member of a mutual savings association or credit union, or similar proprietary interests; or

(4) an interest in the issuer of government securities held by the judge.

See Rules 1.3 and 2.11.

"Fiduciary" includes relationships such as executor, administrator, trustee, or guardian. See Rules 2.11, 3.2, and 3.8.

"Impartial," "impartiality," and **"impartially"** mean absence of bias or prejudice in favor of, or against, particular parties or classes of parties, as well as maintenance of an open mind in considering issues that may come before a judge. See Canons 1, 2, and 4, and Rules 1.2, 2.2, 2.10, 2.11, 2.13, 3.1, 3.12, 3.13, 4.1, and 4.2.

"Impending matter" is a matter that is imminent or expected to occur in the near future. See Rules 2.9, 2.10, 3.13, and 4.1.

"Impropriety" includes conduct that violates the law, court rules, or provisions of this Code, and conduct that undermines a judge's independence, integrity, or impartiality. See Canon 1 and Rule 1.2.

"Independence" means a judge's freedom from influence or controls other than those established by law. See Canons 1 and 4, and Rules 1.2, 3.1, 3.12, 3.13, and 4.2.

"Integrity" means probity, fairness, honesty, uprightness, and soundness of character. See Canon 1 and Rule 1.2.

"Judicial candidate" means any person, including a sitting judge, who is seeking selection for or retention in judicial office by election or appointment. A person becomes a candidate for judicial office as soon as he or she makes a public announcement of candidacy, declares or files as a candidate with the election or appointment authority, authorizes or, where permitted, engages in solicitation or acceptance of contributions or support, or is nominated for election or appointment to office. See Rules 2.11, 4.1, 4.2, and 4.4.

"Knowingly," "knowledge," "known," and **"knows"** mean actual knowledge of the fact in question. A person's knowledge may be inferred from circumstances. See Rules 2.11, 2.13, 2.15, 2.16, 3.6, and 4.1.

"Law" encompasses court rules as well as statutes, constitutional provisions, and decisional law. See Rules 1.1, 2.1, 2.2, 2.6, 2.7, 2.9, 3.1, 3.4, 3.9, 3.12, 3.13, 3.14, 3.15, 4.1, 4.2, 4.4, and 4.5.

"Member of the candidate's family" means a spouse, domestic partner, child, grandchild, parent, grandparent, or other relative or person with whom the candidate maintains a close familial relationship.

"Member of the judge's family" means a spouse, domestic partner, child, grandchild, parent, grandparent, or other relative or person with whom the judge maintains a close familial relationship. See Rules 3.7, 3.8, 3.10, and 3.11.

"Member of a judge's family residing in the judge's household" means any relative of a judge by blood or marriage, or a person treated by a judge as a member of the judge's family, who resides in the judge's household. See Rules 2.11 and 3.13.

"Nonpublic information" means information that is not available to the public. Nonpublic information may include, but is not limited to, information that is sealed by statute or court order or impounded or communicated in camera, and information offered in grand jury proceedings, presentencing reports, dependency cases, or psychiatric reports. See Rule 3.5.

"Pending matter" is a matter that has commenced. A matter continues to be pending through any appellate process until final disposition. See Rules 2.9, 2.10, 3.13, and 4.1.

"Personally solicit" means a direct request made by a judge or a judicial candidate for financial support or in-kind services, whether made by letter, telephone, or any other means of communication. See Rule 4.1.

"Political organization" means a political party or other group sponsored by or affiliated with a political party or candidate, the principal purpose of which is to further the election or appointment of candidates for political office. For purposes of this Code, the term does not include a judicial candidate's campaign committee created as authorized by Rule 4.4. See Rules 4.1 and 4.2.

"Public election" includes primary and general elections, partisan elections, nonpartisan elections, and retention elections. See Rules 4.2 and 4.4.

"Third degree of relationship" includes the following persons: great-grandparent, grandparent, parent, uncle, aunt, brother, sister, child, grandchild, great-grandchild, nephew, and niece. See Rule 2.11.

APPLICATION

The Application section establishes when the various Rules apply to a judge or judicial candidate.

I. APPLICABILITY OF THIS CODE

(A) The provisions of the Code apply to all full-time judges. Parts II through V of this section identify those provisions that apply to four distinct categories of part-time judges. The four categories of judicial service in other than a full-time capacity are necessarily defined in general terms because of the widely varying forms of judicial service. Canon 4 applies to judicial candidates.

(B) A judge, within the meaning of this Code, is anyone who is authorized to perform judicial functions, including an officer such as a justice of the peace, magistrate, court commissioner, special master, referee, or member of the administrative law judiciary.[1]

Comment

[1] The Rules in this Code have been formulated to address the ethical obligations of any person who serves a judicial function, and are premised upon the supposition that a uniform system of ethical principles should apply to all those authorized to perform judicial functions.

---

1. Each jurisdiction should consider the characteristics of particular positions within the administrative law judiciary in adopting, adapting, applying, and enforcing the Code for the administrative law judiciary. *See, e.g.,* Model Code of Judicial Conduct for Federal Administrative Law Judges (1989) and Model Code of Judicial Conduct for State Administrative Law Judges (1995). Both Model Codes are endorsed by the ABA National Conference of Administrative Law Judiciary.

[2] The determination of which category and, accordingly, which specific Rules apply to an individual judicial officer, depends upon the facts of the particular judicial service.

[3] In recent years many jurisdictions have created what are often called "problem solving" courts, in which judges are authorized by court rules to act in nontraditional ways. For example, judges presiding in drug courts and monitoring the progress of participants in those courts' programs may be authorized and even encouraged to communicate directly with social workers, probation officers, and others outside the context of their usual judicial role as independent decision makers on issues of fact and law. When local rules specifically authorize conduct not otherwise permitted under these Rules, they take precedence over the provisions set forth in the Code. Nevertheless, judges serving on "problem solving" courts shall comply with this Code except to the extent local rules provide and permit otherwise.

II. RETIRED JUDGE SUBJECT TO RECALL

A retired judge subject to recall for service, who by law is not permitted to practice law, is not required to comply:

(A) with Rule 3.9 (Service as Arbitrator or Mediator), except while serving as a judge; or

(B) at any time with Rule 3.8 (Appointments to Fiduciary Positions).

Comment

[1] For the purposes of this section, as long as a retired judge is subject to being recalled for service, the judge is considered to "perform judicial functions."

III. CONTINUING PART-TIME JUDGE

A judge who serves repeatedly on a part-time basis by election or under a continuing appointment, including a retired judge subject to recall who is permitted to practice law ("continuing part-time judge"),

(A) is not required to comply:

(1) with Rules 2.10(A) and 2.10(B) (Judicial Statements on Pending and Impending Cases), except while serving as a judge; or

(2) at any time with Rules 3.4 (Appointments to Governmental Positions), 3.8 (Appointments to Fiduciary Positions), 3.9 (Service as Arbitrator or Mediator), 3.10 (Practice of Law), 3.11 (Financial, Business, or Remunerative Activities), 3.14 (Reimbursement of Expenses and Waivers of Fees or Charges), 3.15 (Reporting Requirements), 4.1 (Political and Campaign Activities of Judges and Judicial Candidates in General), 4.2 (Political and Campaign Activities of Judicial Candidates in Public Elections), 4.3 (Activities of Candidates for Appointive Judicial Office), 4.4 (Campaign Committees), and 4.5 (Activities of Judges Who Become Candidates for Nonjudicial Office); and

(B) shall not practice law in the court on which the judge serves or in any court subject to the appellate jurisdiction of the court on which the judge serves, and shall not act as a lawyer in a proceeding in which the judge has served as a judge or in any other proceeding related thereto.

Comment

[1]   When a person who has been a continuing part-time judge is no longer a continuing part-time judge, including a retired judge no longer subject to recall, that person may act as a lawyer in a proceeding in which he or she has served as a judge or in any other proceeding related thereto only with the informed consent of all parties, and pursuant to any applicable Model Rules of Professional Conduct. An adopting jurisdiction should substitute a reference to its applicable rule.

IV.   PERIODIC PART-TIME JUDGE

A periodic part-time judge who serves or expects to serve repeatedly on a part-time basis, but under a separate appointment for each limited period of service or for each matter,

> **(A) is not required to comply:**

> > **(1) with Rule 2.10 (Judicial Statements on Pending and Impending Cases), except while serving as a judge; or**

> > **(2) at any time with Rules 3.4 (Appointments to Governmental Positions), 3.7 (Participation in Educational, Religious, Charitable, Fraternal, or Civic Organizations and Activities), 3.8 (Appointments to Fiduciary Positions), 3.9 (Service as Arbitrator or Mediator), 3.10 (Practice of Law), 3.11 (Financial, Business, or Remunerative Activities), 3.13 (Acceptance and Reporting of Gifts, Loans, Bequests, Benefits, or Other Things of Value), 3.15 (Reporting Requirements), 4.1 (Political and Campaign Activities of Judges and Judicial Candidates in General), and 4.5 (Activities of Judges Who Become Candidates for Nonjudicial Office); and**

> **(B) shall not practice law in the court on which the judge serves or in any court subject to the appellate jurisdiction of the court on which the judge serves, and shall not act as a lawyer in a proceeding in which the judge has served as a judge or in any other proceeding related thereto.**

V.   PRO TEMPORE PART-TIME JUDGE

A pro tempore part-time judge who serves or expects to serve once or only sporadically on a part-time basis under a separate appointment for each period of service or for each case heard is not required to comply:

> **(A) except while serving as a judge, with Rules 1.2 (Promoting Confidence in the Judiciary), 2.4 (External Influences on Judicial Conduct), 2.10 (Judicial Statements on Pending and Impending Cases), or 3.2 (Appearances before Governmental Bodies and Consultation with Government Officials); or**

> **(B) at any time with Rules 3.4 (Appointments to Governmental Positions), 3.6 (Affiliation with Discriminatory Organizations), 3.7 (Participation in Educational, Religious, Charitable, Fraternal, or Civic Organizations and Activities), 3.8 (Appointments to Fiduciary Positions), 3.9 (Service as Arbitrator or Mediator), 3.10 (Practice of Law), 3.11 (Financial, Business, or Remunerative Activities), 3.13 (Acceptance and Reporting of Gifts, Loans, Bequests, Benefits, or Other Things of Value), 3.15 (Reporting Requirements), 4.1 (Political and Campaign Activities of**

Judges and Judicial Candidates in General), and 4.5 (Activities of Judges Who Become Candidates for Nonjudicial Office).

VI. Time for Compliance

A person to whom this Code becomes applicable shall comply immediately with its provisions, except that those judges to whom Rules 3.8 (Appointments to Fiduciary Positions) and 3.11 (Financial, Business, or Remunerative Activities) apply shall comply with those Rules as soon as reasonably possible, but in no event later than one year after the Code becomes applicable to the judge.

Comment

[1] If serving as a fiduciary when selected as judge, a new judge may, notwithstanding the prohibitions in Rule 3.8, continue to serve as fiduciary, but only for that period of time necessary to avoid serious adverse consequences to the beneficiaries of the fiduciary relationship and in no event longer than one year. Similarly, if engaged at the time of judicial selection in a business activity, a new judge may, notwithstanding the prohibitions in Rule 3.11, continue in that activity for a reasonable period but in no event longer than one year.

CANON 1

A judge shall uphold and promote the independence, integrity, and impartiality of the judiciary, and shall avoid impropriety and the appearance of impropriety.

RULE 1.1: Compliance with the Law

A judge shall comply with the law,* including the Code of Judicial Conduct.

RULE 1.2: Promoting Confidence in the Judiciary

A judge shall act at all times in a manner that promotes public confidence in the independence,* integrity,* and impartiality* of the judiciary, and shall avoid impropriety and the appearance of impropriety.

Comment

[1] Public confidence in the judiciary is eroded by improper conduct and conduct that creates the appearance of impropriety. This principle applies to both the professional and personal conduct of a judge.

[2] A judge should expect to be the subject of public scrutiny that might be viewed as burdensome if applied to other citizens, and must accept the restrictions imposed by the Code.

[3] Conduct that compromises or appears to compromise the independence, integrity, and impartiality of a judge undermines public confidence in the judiciary. Because it is not practicable to list all such conduct, the Rule is necessarily cast in general terms.

* See, Terminology.

[4]   Judges should participate in activities that promote ethical conduct among judges and lawyers, support professionalism within the judiciary and the legal profession, and promote access to justice for all.

[5]   Actual improprieties include violations of law, court rules or provisions of this Code. The test for appearance of impropriety is whether the conduct would create in reasonable minds a perception that the judge violated this Code or engaged in other conduct that reflects adversely on the judge's honesty, impartiality, temperament, or fitness to serve as a judge.

[6]   A judge should initiate and participate in community outreach activities for the purpose of promoting public understanding of and confidence in the administration of justice. In conducting such activities, the judge must act in a manner consistent with this Code.

RULE 1.3: Avoiding Abuse of the Prestige of Judicial Office

A judge shall not abuse the prestige of judicial office to advance the personal or economic interests* of the judge or others, or allow others to do so.

Comment

[1]   It is improper for a judge to use or attempt to use his or her position to gain personal advantage or deferential treatment of any kind. For example, it would be improper for a judge to allude to his or her judicial status to gain favorable treatment in encounters with traffic officials. Similarly, a judge must not use judicial letterhead to gain an advantage in conducting his or her personal business.

[2]   A judge may provide a reference or recommendation for an individual based upon the judge's personal knowledge. The judge may use official letterhead if the judge indicates that the reference is personal and if there is no likelihood that the use of the letterhead would reasonably be perceived as an attempt to exert pressure by reason of the judicial office.

[3]   Judges may participate in the process of judicial selection by cooperating with appointing authorities and screening committees, and by responding to inquiries from such entities concerning the professional qualifications of a person being considered for judicial office.

[4]   Special considerations arise when judges write or contribute to publications of for-profit entities, whether related or unrelated to the law. A judge should not permit anyone associated with the publication of such materials to exploit the judge's office in a manner that violates this Rule or other applicable law. In contracts for publication of a judge's writing, the judge should retain sufficient control over the advertising to avoid such exploitation.

Canon 2

A judge shall perform the duties of judicial office impartially, competently, and diligently.

RULE 2.1: Giving Precedence to the Duties of Judicial Office

The duties of judicial office, as prescribed by law,* shall take precedence over all of a judge's personal and extrajudicial activities.

* See, Terminology.

Comment

[1]   To ensure that judges are available to fulfill their judicial duties, judges must conduct their personal and extrajudicial activities to minimize the risk of conflicts that would result in frequent disqualification. See Canon 3.

[2]   Although it is not a duty of judicial office unless prescribed by law, judges are encouraged to participate in activities that promote public understanding of and confidence in the justice system.

RULE 2.2: Impartiality and Fairness

A judge shall uphold and apply the law,* and shall perform all duties of judicial office fairly and impartially.*

Comment

[1]   To ensure impartiality and fairness to all parties, a judge must be objective and open-minded.

[2]   Although each judge comes to the bench with a unique background and personal philosophy, a judge must interpret and apply the law without regard to whether the judge approves or disapproves of the law in question.

[3]   When applying and interpreting the law, a judge sometimes may make good-faith errors of fact or law. Errors of this kind do not violate this Rule.

[4]   It is not a violation of this Rule for a judge to make reasonable accommodations to ensure pro se litigants the opportunity to have their matters fairly heard.

RULE 2.3: Bias, Prejudice, and Harassment

(A) A judge shall perform the duties of judicial office, including administrative duties, without bias or prejudice.

(B) A judge shall not, in the performance of judicial duties, by words or conduct manifest bias or prejudice, or engage in harassment, including but not limited to bias, prejudice, or harassment based upon race, sex, gender, religion, national origin, ethnicity, disability, age, sexual orientation, marital status, socioeconomic status, or political affiliation, and shall not permit court staff, court officials, or others subject to the judge's direction and control to do so.

(C) A judge shall require lawyers in proceedings before the court to refrain from manifesting bias or prejudice, or engaging in harassment, based upon attributes including but not limited to race, sex, gender, religion, national origin, ethnicity, disability, age, sexual orientation, marital status, socioeconomic status, or political affiliation, against parties, witnesses, lawyers, or others.

(D) The restrictions of paragraphs (B) and (C) do not preclude judges or lawyers from making legitimate reference to the listed factors, or similar factors, when they are relevant to an issue in a proceeding.

Comment

[1]   A judge who manifests bias or prejudice in a proceeding impairs the fairness of the proceeding and brings the judiciary into disrepute.

* See, Terminology.

[2]   Examples of manifestations of bias or prejudice include but are not limited to epithets; slurs; demeaning nicknames; negative stereotyping; attempted humor based upon stereotypes; threatening, intimidating, or hostile acts; suggestions of connections between race, ethnicity, or nationality and crime; and irrelevant references to personal characteristics. Even facial expressions and body language can convey to parties and lawyers in the proceeding, jurors, the media, and others an appearance of bias or prejudice. A judge must avoid conduct that may reasonably be perceived as prejudiced or biased.

[3]   Harassment, as referred to in paragraphs (B) and (C), is verbal or physical conduct that denigrates or shows hostility or aversion toward a person on bases such as race, sex, gender, religion, national origin, ethnicity, disability, age, sexual orientation, marital status, socioeconomic status, or political affiliation.

[4]   Sexual harassment includes but is not limited to sexual advances, requests for sexual favors, and other verbal or physical conduct of a sexual nature that is unwelcome.

RULE 2.4: External Influences on Judicial Conduct

(A) A judge shall not be swayed by public clamor or fear of criticism.

(B) A judge shall not permit family, social, political, financial, or other interests or relationships to influence the judge's judicial conduct or judgment.

(C) A judge shall not convey or permit others to convey the impression that any person or organization is in a position to influence the judge.

Comment

[1]   An independent judiciary requires that judges decide cases according to the law and facts, without regard to whether particular laws or litigants are popular or unpopular with the public, the media, government officials, or the judge's friends or family. Confidence in the judiciary is eroded if judicial decision making is perceived to be subject to inappropriate outside influences.

RULE 2.5: Competence, Diligence, and Cooperation

(A) A judge shall perform judicial and administrative duties, competently and diligently.

(B) A judge shall cooperate with other judges and court officials in the administration of court business.

Comment

[1]   Competence in the performance of judicial duties requires the legal knowledge, skill, thoroughness, and preparation reasonably necessary to perform a judge's responsibilities of judicial office.

[2]   A judge should seek the necessary docket time, court staff, expertise, and resources to discharge all adjudicative and administrative responsibilities.

[3]   Prompt disposition of the court's business requires a judge to devote adequate time to judicial duties, to be punctual in attending court and expeditious in determining matters under submission, and to take reasonable measures to ensure that court officials, litigants, and their lawyers cooperate with the judge to that end.

[4]   In disposing of matters promptly and efficiently, a judge must demonstrate due regard for the rights of parties to be heard and to have issues resolved without unnecessary cost or delay. A judge should monitor and supervise cases in ways that reduce or eliminate dilatory practices, avoidable delays, and unnecessary costs.

RULE 2.6: Ensuring the Right to Be Heard

(A) A judge shall accord to every person who has a legal interest in a proceeding, or that person's lawyer, the right to be heard according to law.*

(B) A judge may encourage parties to a proceeding and their lawyers to settle matters in dispute but shall not act in a manner that coerces any party into settlement.

Comment

[1]   The right to be heard is an essential component of a fair and impartial system of justice. Substantive rights of litigants can be protected only if procedures protecting the right to be heard are observed.

[2]   The judge plays an important role in overseeing the settlement of disputes, but should be careful that efforts to further settlement do not undermine any party's right to be heard according to law. The judge should keep in mind the effect that the judge's participation in settlement discussions may have, not only on the judge's own views of the case, but also on the perceptions of the lawyers and the parties if the case remains with the judge after settlement efforts are unsuccessful. Among the factors that a judge should consider when deciding upon an appropriate settlement practice for a case are (1) whether the parties have requested or voluntarily consented to a certain level of participation by the judge in settlement discussions, (2) whether the parties and their counsel are relatively sophisticated in legal matters, (3) whether the case will be tried by the judge or a jury, (4) whether the parties participate with their counsel in settlement discussions, (5) whether any parties are unrepresented by counsel, and (6) whether the matter is civil or criminal.

[3]   Judges must be mindful of the effect settlement discussions can have, not only on their objectivity and impartiality, but also on the appearance of their objectivity and impartiality. Despite a judge's best efforts, there may be instances when information obtained during settlement discussions could influence a judge's decision making during trial, and, in such instances, the judge should consider whether disqualification may be appropriate. See Rule 2.11(A)(1).

RULE 2.7: Responsibility to Decide

A judge shall hear and decide matters assigned to the judge, except when disqualification is required by Rule 2.11 or other law.*

Comment

[1]   Judges must be available to decide the matters that come before the court. Although there are times when disqualification is necessary to protect the rights of litigants and preserve public confidence in the independence, integrity, and impartiality of the judiciary, judges must be available to decide matters that come before the courts. Unwarranted disqualification may bring public disfavor to the court and to the judge personally. The dignity of the court, the judge's respect for fulfillment of judicial duties, and a proper concern for the burdens that may be imposed upon the judge's

* See, Terminology.

colleagues require that a judge not use disqualification to avoid cases that present difficult, controversial, or unpopular issues.

RULE 2.8: Decorum, Demeanor, and Communication with Jurors

(A) A judge shall require order and decorum in proceedings before the court.

(B) A judge shall be patient, dignified, and courteous to litigants, jurors, witnesses, lawyers, court staff, court officials, and others with whom the judge deals in an official capacity, and shall require similar conduct of lawyers, court staff, court officials, and others subject to the judge's direction and control.

(C) A judge shall not commend or criticize jurors for their verdict other than in a court order or opinion in a proceeding.

Comment

[1] The duty to hear all proceedings with patience and courtesy is not inconsistent with the duty imposed in Rule 2.5 to dispose promptly of the business of the court. Judges can be efficient and businesslike while being patient and deliberate.

[2] Commending or criticizing jurors for their verdict may imply a judicial expectation in future cases and may impair a juror's ability to be fair and impartial in a subsequent case.

[3] A judge who is not otherwise prohibited by law from doing so may meet with jurors who choose to remain after trial but should be careful not to discuss the merits of the case.

RULE 2.9: Ex Parte Communications

(A) A judge shall not initiate, permit, or consider ex parte communications, or consider other communications made to the judge outside the presence of the parties or their lawyers, concerning a pending* or impending matter,* except as follows:

> **(1) When circumstances require it, ex parte communication for scheduling, administrative, or emergency purposes, which does not address substantive matters, is permitted, provided:**

>> **(a) the judge reasonably believes that no party will gain a procedural, substantive, or tactical advantage as a result of the ex parte communication; and**

>> **(b) the judge makes provision promptly to notify all other parties of the substance of the ex parte communication, and gives the parties an opportunity to respond.**

> **(2) A judge may obtain the written advice of a disinterested expert on the law applicable to a proceeding before the judge, if the judge gives advance notice to the parties of the person to be consulted and the subject matter of the advice to be solicited, and affords the parties a reasonable opportunity to object and respond to the notice and to the advice received.**

* See, Terminology.

(3) A judge may consult with court staff and court officials whose functions are to aid the judge in carrying out the judge's adjudicative responsibilities, or with other judges, provided the judge makes reasonable efforts to avoid receiving factual information that is not part of the record, and does not abrogate the responsibility personally to decide the matter.

(4) A judge may, with the consent of the parties, confer separately with the parties and their lawyers in an effort to settle matters pending before the judge.

(5) A judge may initiate, permit, or consider any ex parte communication when expressly authorized by law* to do so.

(B) If a judge inadvertently receives an unauthorized ex parte communication bearing upon the substance of a matter, the judge shall make provision promptly to notify the parties of the substance of the communication and provide the parties with an opportunity to respond.

(C) A judge shall not investigate facts in a matter independently, and shall consider only the evidence presented and any facts that may properly be judicially noticed.

(D) A judge shall make reasonable efforts, including providing appropriate supervision, to ensure that this Rule is not violated by court staff, court officials, and others subject to the judge's direction and control.

Comment

[1] To the extent reasonably possible, all parties or their lawyers shall be included in communications with a judge.

[2] Whenever the presence of a party or notice to a party is required by this Rule, it is the party's lawyer, or if the party is unrepresented, the party, who is to be present or to whom notice is to be given.

[3] The proscription against communications concerning a proceeding includes communications with lawyers, law teachers, and other persons who are not participants in the proceeding, except to the limited extent permitted by this Rule.

[4] A judge may initiate, permit, or consider ex parte communications expressly authorized by law, such as when serving on therapeutic or problem-solving courts, mental health courts, or drug courts. In this capacity, judges may assume a more interactive role with parties, treatment providers, probation officers, social workers, and others.

[5] A judge may consult with other judges on pending matters, but must avoid ex parte discussions of a case with judges who have previously been disqualified from hearing the matter, and with judges who have appellate jurisdiction over the matter.

[6] The prohibition against a judge investigating the facts in a matter extends to information available in all mediums, including electronic.

[7] A judge may consult ethics advisory committees, outside counsel, or legal experts concerning the judge's compliance with this Code. Such consultations are not subject to the restrictions of paragraph (A)(2).

RULE 2.10: Judicial Statements on Pending and Impending Cases

(A) A judge shall not make any public statement that might reasonably be expected to affect the outcome or impair the fairness of a matter pending* or impending* in any court, or make any nonpublic statement that might substantially interfere with a fair trial or hearing.

(B) A judge shall not, in connection with cases, controversies, or issues that are likely to come before the court, make pledges, promises, or commitments that are inconsistent with the impartial* performance of the adjudicative duties of judicial office.

(C) A judge shall require court staff, court officials, and others subject to the judge's direction and control to refrain from making statements that the judge would be prohibited from making by paragraphs (A) and (B).

(D) Notwithstanding the restrictions in paragraph (A), a judge may make public statements in the course of official duties, may explain court procedures, and may comment on any proceeding in which the judge is a litigant in a personal capacity.

(E) Subject to the requirements of paragraph (A), a judge may respond directly or through a third party to allegations in the media or elsewhere concerning the judge's conduct in a matter.

Comment

[1] This Rule's restrictions on judicial speech are essential to the maintenance of the independence, integrity, and impartiality of the judiciary.

[2] This Rule does not prohibit a judge from commenting on proceedings in which the judge is a litigant in a personal capacity. In cases in which the judge is a litigant in an official capacity, such as a writ of mandamus, the judge must not comment publicly.

[3] Depending upon the circumstances, the judge should consider whether it may be preferable for a third party, rather than the judge, to respond or issue statements in connection with allegations concerning the judge's conduct in a matter.

RULE 2.11: Disqualification

(A) A judge shall disqualify himself or herself in any proceeding in which the judge's impartiality* might reasonably be questioned, including but not limited to the following circumstances:

(1) The judge has a personal bias or prejudice concerning a party or a party's lawyer, or personal knowledge* of facts that are in dispute in the proceeding.

(2) The judge knows* that the judge, the judge's spouse or domestic partner,* or a person within the third degree of relationship* to either of them, or the spouse or domestic partner of such a person is:

(a) a party to the proceeding, or an officer, director, general partner, managing member, or trustee of a party;

(b) acting as a lawyer in the proceeding;

* See, Terminology.

    (c) a person who has more than a de minimis* interest that could be substantially affected by the proceeding; or

    (d) likely to be a material witness in the proceeding.

    (3) The judge knows that he or she, individually or as a fiduciary,* or the judge's spouse, domestic partner, parent, or child, or any other member of the judge's family residing in the judge's household,* has an economic interest* in the subject matter in controversy or is a party to the proceeding.

    (4) The judge knows or learns by means of a timely motion that a party, a party's lawyer, or the law firm of a party's lawyer has within the previous [insert number] year[s] made aggregate* contributions* to the judge's campaign in an amount that [is greater than $[insert amount] for an individual or $[insert amount] for an entity] [is reasonable and appropriate for an individual or an entity].

    (5) The judge, while a judge or a judicial candidate,* has made a public statement, other than in a court proceeding, judicial decision, or opinion, that commits or appears to commit the judge to reach a particular result or rule in a particular way in the proceeding or controversy.

    (6) The judge:

    (a) served as a lawyer in the matter in controversy, or was associated with a lawyer who participated substantially as a lawyer in the matter during such association;

    (b) served in governmental employment, and in such capacity participated personally and substantially as a lawyer or public official concerning the proceeding, or has publicly expressed in such capacity an opinion concerning the merits of the particular matter in controversy;

    (c) was a material witness concerning the matter; or

    (d) previously presided as a judge over the matter in another court.

(B) A judge shall keep informed about the judge's personal and fiduciary economic interests, and make a reasonable effort to keep informed about the personal economic interests of the judge's spouse or domestic partner and minor children residing in the judge's household.

(C) A judge subject to disqualification under this Rule, other than for bias or prejudice under paragraph (A)(1), may disclose on the record the basis of the judge's disqualification and may ask the parties and their lawyers to consider, outside the presence of the judge and court personnel, whether to waive disqualification. If, following the disclosure, the parties and lawyers agree, without participation by the judge or court personnel, that the judge should not be disqualified, the judge may participate in the proceeding. The agreement shall be incorporated into the record of the proceeding.

* See, Terminology.

Comment

[1]   Under this Rule, a judge is disqualified whenever the judge's impartiality might reasonably be questioned, regardless of whether any of the specific provisions of paragraphs (A)(1) through (6) apply. In many jurisdictions, the term "recusal" is used interchangeably with the term "disqualification."

[2]   A judge's obligation not to hear or decide matters in which disqualification is required applies regardless of whether a motion to disqualify is filed.

[3]   The rule of necessity may override the rule of disqualification. For example, a judge might be required to participate in judicial review of a judicial salary statute, or might be the only judge available in a matter requiring immediate judicial action, such as a hearing on probable cause or a temporary restraining order. In matters that require immediate action, the judge must disclose on the record the basis for possible disqualification and make reasonable efforts to transfer the matter to another judge as soon as practicable.

[4]   The fact that a lawyer in a proceeding is affiliated with a law firm with which a relative of the judge is affiliated does not itself disqualify the judge. If, however, the judge's impartiality might reasonably be questioned under paragraph (A), or the relative is known by the judge to have an interest in the law firm that could be substantially affected by the proceeding under paragraph (A)(2)(c), the judge's disqualification is required.

[5]   A judge should disclose on the record information that the judge believes the parties or their lawyers might reasonably consider relevant to a possible motion for disqualification, even if the judge believes there is no basis for disqualification.

[6]   "Economic interest," as set forth in the Terminology section, means ownership of more than a de minimis legal or equitable interest. Except for situations in which a judge participates in the management of such a legal or equitable interest, or the interest could be substantially affected by the outcome of a proceeding before a judge, it does not include:

(1) an interest in the individual holdings within a mutual or common investment fund;

(2) an interest in securities held by an educational, religious, charitable, fraternal, or civic organization in which the judge or the judge's spouse, domestic partner, parent, or child serves as a director, officer, advisor, or other participant;

(3) a deposit in a financial institution or deposits or proprietary interests the judge may maintain as a member of a mutual savings association or credit union, or similar proprietary interests; or

(4) an interest in the issuer of government securities held by the judge.

RULE 2.12: Supervisory Duties

(A) A judge shall require court staff, court officials, and others subject to the judge's direction and control to act in a manner consistent with the judge's obligations under this Code.

(B) A judge with supervisory authority for the performance of other judges shall take reasonable measures to ensure that those judges properly discharge their judicial responsibilities, including the prompt disposition of matters before them.

Comment

[1] A judge is responsible for his or her own conduct and for the conduct of others, such as staff, when those persons are acting at the judge's direction or control. A judge may not direct court personnel to engage in conduct on the judge's behalf or as the judge's representative when such conduct would violate the Code if undertaken by the judge.

[2] Public confidence in the judicial system depends upon timely justice. To promote the efficient administration of justice, a judge with supervisory authority must take the steps needed to ensure that judges under his or her supervision administer their workloads promptly.

RULE 2.13: Administrative Appointments

(A) In making administrative appointments, a judge:

(1) shall exercise the power of appointment impartially* and on the basis of merit; and

(2) shall avoid nepotism, favoritism, and unnecessary appointments.

(B) A judge shall not appoint a lawyer to a position if the judge either knows* that the lawyer, or the lawyer's spouse or domestic partner,* has contributed more than $[insert amount] within the prior [insert number] year[s] to the judge's election campaign, or learns of such a contribution* by means of a timely motion by a party or other person properly interested in the matter, unless:

(1) the position is substantially uncompensated;

(2) the lawyer has been selected in rotation from a list of qualified and available lawyers compiled without regard to their having made political contributions; or

(3) the judge or another presiding or administrative judge affirmatively finds that no other lawyer is willing, competent, and able to accept the position.

(C) A judge shall not approve compensation of appointees beyond the fair value of services rendered.

Comment

[1] Appointees of a judge include assigned counsel, officials such as referees, commissioners, special masters, receivers, and guardians, and personnel such as clerks, secretaries, and bailiffs. Consent by the parties to an appointment or an award of compensation does not relieve the judge of the obligation prescribed by paragraph (A).

[2] Unless otherwise defined by law, nepotism is the appointment or hiring of any relative within the third degree of relationship of either the judge or the judge's spouse or domestic partner, or the spouse or domestic partner of such relative.

[3] The rule against making administrative appointments of lawyers who have contributed in excess of a specified dollar amount to a judge's election campaign includes an exception for positions that are substantially uncompensated, such as those for which the lawyer's compensation is limited to reimbursement for out-of-pocket expenses.

* See, Terminology.

RULE 2.14: Disability and Impairment

A judge having a reasonable belief that the performance of a lawyer or another judge is impaired by drugs or alcohol, or by a mental, emotional, or physical condition, shall take appropriate action, which may include a confidential referral to a lawyer or judicial assistance program.

Comment

[1]   "Appropriate action" means action intended and reasonably likely to help the judge or lawyer in question address the problem and prevent harm to the justice system. Depending upon the circumstances, appropriate action may include but is not limited to speaking directly to the impaired person, notifying an individual with supervisory responsibility over the impaired person, or making a referral to an assistance program.

[2]   Taking or initiating corrective action by way of referral to an assistance program may satisfy a judge's responsibility under this Rule. Assistance programs have many approaches for offering help to impaired judges and lawyers, such as intervention, counseling, or referral to appropriate health care professionals. Depending upon the gravity of the conduct that has come to the judge's attention, however, the judge may be required to take other action, such as reporting the impaired judge or lawyer to the appropriate authority, agency, or body. See Rule 2.15.

RULE 2.15: Responding to Judicial and Lawyer Misconduct

(A) A judge having knowledge* that another judge has committed a violation of this Code that raises a substantial question regarding the judge's honesty, trustworthiness, or fitness as a judge in other respects shall inform the appropriate authority.*

(B) A judge having knowledge that a lawyer has committed a violation of the Rules of Professional Conduct that raises a substantial question regarding the lawyer's honesty, trustworthiness, or fitness as a lawyer in other respects shall inform the appropriate authority.

(C) A judge who receives information indicating a substantial likelihood that another judge has committed a violation of this Code shall take appropriate action.

(D) A judge who receives information indicating a substantial likelihood that a lawyer has committed a violation of the Rules of Professional Conduct shall take appropriate action.

Comment

[1]   Taking action to address known misconduct is a judge's obligation. Paragraphs (A) and (B) impose an obligation on the judge to report to the appropriate disciplinary authority the known misconduct of another judge or a lawyer that raises a substantial question regarding the honesty, trustworthiness, or fitness of that judge or lawyer. Ignoring or denying known misconduct among one's judicial colleagues or members of the legal profession undermines a judge's responsibility to participate in efforts to ensure public respect for the justice system. This Rule limits the reporting obligation to those offenses that an independent judiciary must vigorously endeavor to prevent.

* See, Terminology.

[2]   A judge who does not have actual knowledge that another judge or a lawyer may have committed misconduct, but receives information indicating a substantial likelihood of such misconduct, is required to take appropriate action under paragraphs (C) and (D). Appropriate action may include, but is not limited to, communicating directly with the judge who may have violated this Code, communicating with a supervising judge, or reporting the suspected violation to the appropriate authority or other agency or body. Similarly, actions to be taken in response to information indicating that a lawyer has committed a violation of the Rules of Professional Conduct may include but are not limited to communicating directly with the lawyer who may have committed the violation, or reporting the suspected violation to the appropriate authority or other agency or body.

RULE 2.16: Cooperation with Disciplinary Authorities

(A) A judge shall cooperate and be candid and honest with judicial and lawyer disciplinary agencies.

(B) A judge shall not retaliate, directly or indirectly, against a person known* or suspected to have assisted or cooperated with an investigation of a judge or a lawyer.

Comment

[1]   Cooperation with investigations and proceedings of judicial and lawyer discipline agencies, as required in paragraph (A), instills confidence in judges' commitment to the integrity of the judicial system and the protection of the public.

Canon 3

A judge shall conduct the judge's personal and extrajudicial activities to minimize the risk of conflict with the obligations of judicial office.

RULE 3.1: Extrajudicial Activities in General

A judge may engage in extrajudicial activities, except as prohibited by law* or this Code. However, when engaging in extrajudicial activities, a judge shall not:

(A) participate in activities that will interfere with the proper performance of the judge's judicial duties;

(B) participate in activities that will lead to frequent disqualification of the judge;

(C) participate in activities that would appear to a reasonable person to undermine the judge's independence,* integrity,* or impartiality;*

(D) engage in conduct that would appear to a reasonable person to be coercive; or

(E) make use of court premises, staff, stationery, equipment, or other resources, except for incidental use for activities that concern the law, the legal system, or the administration of justice, or unless such additional use is permitted by law.

* See, Terminology.

Comment

[1]   To the extent that time permits, and judicial independence and impartiality are not compromised, judges are encouraged to engage in appropriate extrajudicial activities. Judges are uniquely qualified to engage in extrajudicial activities that concern the law, the legal system, and the administration of justice, such as by speaking, writing, teaching, or participating in scholarly research projects. In addition, judges are permitted and encouraged to engage in educational, religious, charitable, fraternal or civic extrajudicial activities not conducted for profit, even when the activities do not involve the law. See Rule 3.7.

[2]   Participation in both law-related and other extrajudicial activities helps integrate judges into their communities, and furthers public understanding of and respect for courts and the judicial system.

[3]   Discriminatory actions and expressions of bias or prejudice by a judge, even outside the judge's official or judicial actions, are likely to appear to a reasonable person to call into question the judge's integrity and impartiality. Examples include jokes or other remarks that demean individuals based upon their race, sex, gender, religion, national origin, ethnicity, disability, age, sexual orientation, or socioeconomic status. For the same reason, a judge's extrajudicial activities must not be conducted in connection or affiliation with an organization that practices invidious discrimination. See Rule 3.6.

[4]   While engaged in permitted extrajudicial activities, judges must not coerce others or take action that would reasonably be perceived as coercive. For example, depending upon the circumstances, a judge's solicitation of contributions or memberships for an organization, even as permitted by Rule 3.7(A), might create the risk that the person solicited would feel obligated to respond favorably, or would do so to curry favor with the judge.

RULE 3.2: Appearances before Governmental Bodies and Consultation with Government Officials

A judge shall not appear voluntarily at a public hearing before, or otherwise consult with, an executive or a legislative body or official, except:

(A) in connection with matters concerning the law, the legal system, or the administration of justice;

(B) in connection with matters about which the judge acquired knowledge or expertise in the course of the judge's judicial duties; or

(C) when the judge is acting pro se in a matter involving the judge's legal or economic interests, or when the judge is acting in a fiduciary* capacity.

Comment

[1]   Judges possess special expertise in matters of law, the legal system, and the administration of justice, and may properly share that expertise with governmental bodies and executive or legislative branch officials.

[2]   In appearing before governmental bodies or consulting with government officials, judges must be mindful that they remain subject to other provisions of this Code, such as Rule 1.3, prohibiting judges from using the prestige of office to advance

---

* See, Terminology.

their own or others' interests, Rule 2.10, governing public comment on pending and impending matters, and Rule 3.1(C), prohibiting judges from engaging in extrajudicial activities that would appear to a reasonable person to undermine the judge's independence, integrity, or impartiality.

[3] In general, it would be an unnecessary and unfair burden to prohibit judges from appearing before governmental bodies or consulting with government officials on matters that are likely to affect them as private citizens, such as zoning proposals affecting their real property. In engaging in such activities, however, judges must not refer to their judicial positions, and must otherwise exercise caution to avoid using the prestige of judicial office.

RULE 3.3: Testifying as a Character Witness

A judge shall not testify as a character witness in a judicial, administrative, or other adjudicatory proceeding or otherwise vouch for the character of a person in a legal proceeding, except when duly summoned.

Comment

[1] A judge who, without being subpoenaed, testifies as a character witness abuses the prestige of judicial office to advance the interests of another. See Rule 1.3. Except in unusual circumstances where the demands of justice require, a judge should discourage a party from requiring the judge to testify as a character witness.

RULE 3.4: Appointments to Governmental Positions

A judge shall not accept appointment to a governmental committee, board, commission, or other governmental position, unless it is one that concerns the law, the legal system, or the administration of justice.

Comment

[1] Rule 3.4 implicitly acknowledges the value of judges accepting appointments to entities that concern the law, the legal system, or the administration of justice. Even in such instances, however, a judge should assess the appropriateness of accepting an appointment, paying particular attention to the subject matter of the appointment and the availability and allocation of judicial resources, including the judge's time commitments, and giving due regard to the requirements of the independence and impartiality of the judiciary.

[2] A judge may represent his or her country, state, or locality on ceremonial occasions or in connection with historical, educational, or cultural activities. Such representation does not constitute acceptance of a government position.

RULE 3.5: Use of Nonpublic Information

A judge shall not intentionally disclose or use nonpublic information* acquired in a judicial capacity for any purpose unrelated to the judge's judicial duties.

Comment

[1] In the course of performing judicial duties, a judge may acquire information of commercial or other value that is unavailable to the public. The judge must not reveal or use such information for personal gain or for any purpose unrelated to his or her judicial duties.

[2] This rule is not intended, however, to affect a judge's ability to act on information as necessary to protect the health or safety of the judge or a member of a judge's family, court personnel, or other judicial officers if consistent with other provisions of this Code.

RULE 3.6: Affiliation with Discriminatory Organizations

(A) A judge shall not hold membership in any organization that practices invidious discrimination on the basis of race, sex, gender, religion, national origin, ethnicity, or sexual orientation.

(B) A judge shall not use the benefits or facilities of an organization if the judge knows* or should know that the organization practices invidious discrimination on one or more of the bases identified in paragraph (A). A judge's attendance at an event in a facility of an organization that the judge is not permitted to join is not a violation of this Rule when the judge's attendance is an isolated event that could not reasonably be perceived as an endorsement of the organization's practices.

Comment

[1] A judge's public manifestation of approval of invidious discrimination on any basis gives rise to the appearance of impropriety and diminishes public confidence in the integrity and impartiality of the judiciary. A judge's membership in an organization that practices invidious discrimination creates the perception that the judge's impartiality is impaired.

[2] An organization is generally said to discriminate invidiously if it arbitrarily excludes from membership on the basis of race, sex, gender, religion, national origin, ethnicity, or sexual orientation persons who would otherwise be eligible for admission. Whether an organization practices invidious discrimination is a complex question to which judges should be attentive. The answer cannot be determined from a mere examination of an organization's current membership rolls, but rather, depends upon how the organization selects members, as well as other relevant factors, such as whether the organization is dedicated to the preservation of religious, ethnic, or cultural values of legitimate common interest to its members, or whether it is an intimate, purely private organization whose membership limitations could not constitutionally be prohibited.

[3] When a judge learns that an organization to which the judge belongs engages in invidious discrimination, the judge must resign immediately from the organization.

[4] A judge's membership in a religious organization as a lawful exercise of the freedom of religion is not a violation of this Rule.

[5] This Rule does not apply to national or state military service.

RULE 3.7: Participation in Educational, Religious, Charitable, Fraternal, or Civic Organizations and Activities

(A) Subject to the requirements of Rule 3.1, a judge may participate in activities sponsored by organizations or governmental entities concerned with the law, the legal system, or the administration of justice, and those sponsored by or on behalf of educational, religious, charitable, fraternal, or

---

* See, Terminology.

civic organizations not conducted for profit, including but not limited to the following activities:

(1) assisting such an organization or entity in planning related to fund-raising, and participating in the management and investment of the organization's or entity's funds;

(2) soliciting* contributions* for such an organization or entity, but only from members of the judge's family,* or from judges over whom the judge does not exercise supervisory or appellate authority;

(3) soliciting membership for such an organization or entity, even though the membership dues or fees generated may be used to support the objectives of the organization or entity, but only if the organization or entity is concerned with the law, the legal system, or the administration of justice;

(4) appearing or speaking at, receiving an award or other recognition at, being featured on the program of, and permitting his or her title to be used in connection with an event of such an organization or entity, but if the event serves a fund-raising purpose, the judge may participate only if the event concerns the law, the legal system, or the administration of justice;

(5) making recommendations to such a public or private fund-granting organization or entity in connection with its programs and activities, but only if the organization or entity is concerned with the law, the legal system, or the administration of justice; and

(6) serving as an officer, director, trustee, or nonlegal advisor of such an organization or entity, unless it is likely that the organization or entity:

(a) will be engaged in proceedings that would ordinarily come before the judge; or

(b) will frequently be engaged in adversary proceedings in the court of which the judge is a member, or in any court subject to the appellate jurisdiction of the court of which the judge is a member.

(B) A judge may encourage lawyers to provide pro bono publico legal services.

Comment

[1]   The activities permitted by paragraph (A) generally include those sponsored by or undertaken on behalf of public or private not-for-profit educational institutions, and other not-for-profit organizations, including law-related, charitable, and other organizations.

[2]   Even for law-related organizations, a judge should consider whether the membership and purposes of the organization, or the nature of the judge's participation in or association with the organization, would conflict with the judge's obligation to refrain from activities that reflect adversely upon a judge's independence, integrity, and impartiality.

* See, Terminology.

[3]   Mere attendance at an event, whether or not the event serves a fund-raising purpose, does not constitute a violation of paragraph 4(A). It is also generally permissible for a judge to serve as an usher or a food server or preparer, or to perform similar functions, at fund-raising events sponsored by educational, religious, charitable, fraternal, or civic organizations. Such activities are not solicitation and do not present an element of coercion or abuse the prestige of judicial office.

[4]   Identification of a judge's position in educational, religious, charitable, fraternal, or civic organizations on letterhead used for fund-raising or membership solicitation does not violate this Rule. The letterhead may list the judge's title or judicial office if comparable designations are used for other persons.

[5]   In addition to appointing lawyers to serve as counsel for indigent parties in individual cases, a judge may promote broader access to justice by encouraging lawyers to participate in pro bono publico legal services, if in doing so the judge does not employ coercion, or abuse the prestige of judicial office. Such encouragement may take many forms, including providing lists of available programs, training lawyers to do pro bono publico legal work, and participating in events recognizing lawyers who have done pro bono publico work.

RULE 3.8: Appointments to Fiduciary Positions

(A) A judge shall not accept appointment to serve in a fiduciary* position, such as executor, administrator, trustee, guardian, attorney in fact, or other personal representative, except for the estate, trust, or person of a member of the judge's family,* and then only if such service will not interfere with the proper performance of judicial duties.

(B) A judge shall not serve in a fiduciary position if the judge as fiduciary will likely be engaged in proceedings that would ordinarily come before the judge, or if the estate, trust, or ward becomes involved in adversary proceedings in the court on which the judge serves, or one under its appellate jurisdiction.

(C) A judge acting in a fiduciary capacity shall be subject to the same restrictions on engaging in financial activities that apply to a judge personally.

(D) If a person who is serving in a fiduciary position becomes a judge, he or she must comply with this Rule as soon as reasonably practicable, but in no event later than [one year] after becoming a judge.

Comment

[1]   A judge should recognize that other restrictions imposed by this Code may conflict with a judge's obligations as a fiduciary; in such circumstances, a judge should resign as fiduciary. For example, serving as a fiduciary might require frequent disqualification of a judge under Rule 2.11 because a judge is deemed to have an economic interest in shares of stock held by a trust if the amount of stock held is more than de minimis.

RULE 3.9: Service as Arbitrator or Mediator

A judge shall not act as an arbitrator or a mediator or perform other judicial functions apart from the judge's official duties unless expressly authorized by law.*

* See, Terminology.

Comment

[1]   This Rule does not prohibit a judge from participating in arbitration, mediation, or settlement conferences performed as part of assigned judicial duties. Rendering dispute resolution services apart from those duties, whether or not for economic gain, is prohibited unless it is expressly authorized by law.

RULE 3.10: Practice of Law

A judge shall not practice law. A judge may act pro se and may, without compensation, give legal advice to and draft or review documents for a member of the judge's family,* but is prohibited from serving as the family member's lawyer in any forum.

Comment

[1]   A judge may act pro se in all legal matters, including matters involving litigation and matters involving appearances before or other dealings with governmental bodies. A judge must not use the prestige of office to advance the judge's personal or family interests. See Rule 1.3.

RULE 3.11: Financial, Business, or Remunerative Activities

(A) A judge may hold and manage investments of the judge and members of the judge's family.*

(B) A judge shall not serve as an officer, director, manager, general partner, advisor, or employee of any business entity except that a judge may manage or participate in:

(1) a business closely held by the judge or members of the judge's family; or

(2) a business entity primarily engaged in investment of the financial resources of the judge or members of the judge's family.

(C) A judge shall not engage in financial activities permitted under paragraphs (A) and (B) if they will:

(1) interfere with the proper performance of judicial duties;

(2) lead to frequent disqualification of the judge;

(3) involve the judge in frequent transactions or continuing business relationships with lawyers or other persons likely to come before the court on which the judge serves; or

(4) result in violation of other provisions of this Code.

Comment

[1]   Judges are generally permitted to engage in financial activities, including managing real estate and other investments for themselves or for members of their families. Participation in these activities, like participation in other extrajudicial activities, is subject to the requirements of this Code. For example, it would be improper for a judge to spend so much time on business activities that it interferes with the performance of judicial duties. See Rule 2.1. Similarly, it would be improper for a judge to use his or her official title or appear in judicial robes in business advertising, or to conduct his or her business or financial affairs in such a way that disqualification is frequently required. See Rules 1.3 and 2.11.

[2] As soon as practicable without serious financial detriment, the judge must divest himself or herself of investments and other financial interests that might require frequent disqualification or otherwise violate this Rule.

RULE 3.12: Compensation for Extrajudicial Activities

A judge may accept reasonable compensation for extrajudicial activities permitted by this Code or other law* unless such acceptance would appear to a reasonable person to undermine the judge's independence,* integrity,* or impartiality.*

Comment

[1] A judge is permitted to accept honoraria, stipends, fees, wages, salaries, royalties, or other compensation for speaking, teaching, writing, and other extrajudicial activities, provided the compensation is reasonable and commensurate with the task performed. The judge should be mindful, however, that judicial duties must take precedence over other activities. See Rule 2.1.

[2] Compensation derived from extrajudicial activities may be subject to public reporting. See Rule 3.15.

RULE 3.13: Acceptance and Reporting of Gifts, Loans, Bequests, Benefits, or Other Things of Value

(A) A judge shall not accept any gifts, loans, bequests, benefits, or other things of value, if acceptance is prohibited by law* or would appear to a reasonable person to undermine the judge's independence,* integrity,* or impartiality.*

(B) Unless otherwise prohibited by law, or by paragraph (A), a judge may accept the following without publicly reporting such acceptance:

(1) items with little intrinsic value, such as plaques, certificates, trophies, and greeting cards;

(2) gifts, loans, bequests, benefits, or other things of value from friends, relatives, or other persons, including lawyers, whose appearance or interest in a proceeding pending* or impending* before the judge would in any event require disqualification of the judge under Rule 2.11;

(3) ordinary social hospitality;

(4) commercial or financial opportunities and benefits, including special pricing and discounts, and loans from lending institutions in their regular course of business, if the same opportunities and benefits or loans are made available on the same terms to similarly situated persons who are not judges;

(5) rewards and prizes given to competitors or participants in random drawings, contests, or other events that are open to persons who are not judges;

(6) scholarships, fellowships, and similar benefits or awards, if they are available to similarly situated persons who are not judges, based upon the same terms and criteria;

* See, Terminology.

(7) books, magazines, journals, audiovisual materials, and other resource materials supplied by publishers on a complimentary basis for official use; or

(8) gifts, awards, or benefits associated with the business, profession, or other separate activity of a spouse, a domestic partner,* or other family member of a judge residing in the judge's household,* but that incidentally benefit the judge.

(C) Unless otherwise prohibited by law or by paragraph (A), a judge may accept the following items, and must report such acceptance to the extent required by Rule 3.15:

(1) gifts incident to a public testimonial;

(2) invitations to the judge and the judge's spouse, domestic partner, or guest to attend without charge:

(a) an event associated with a bar-related function or other activity relating to the law, the legal system, or the administration of justice; or

(b) an event associated with any of the judge's educational, religious, charitable, fraternal or civic activities permitted by this Code, if the same invitation is offered to nonjudges who are engaged in similar ways in the activity as is the judge; and

(3) gifts, loans, bequests, benefits, or other things of value, if the source is a party or other person, including a lawyer, who has come or is likely to come before the judge, or whose interests have come or are likely to come before the judge.

Comment

[1] Whenever a judge accepts a gift or other thing of value without paying fair market value, there is a risk that the benefit might be viewed as intended to influence the judge's decision in a case. Rule 3.13 imposes restrictions upon the acceptance of such benefits, according to the magnitude of the risk. Paragraph (B) identifies circumstances in which the risk that the acceptance would appear to undermine the judge's independence, integrity, or impartiality is low, and explicitly provides that such items need not be publicly reported. As the value of the benefit or the likelihood that the source of the benefit will appear before the judge increases, the judge is either prohibited under paragraph (A) from accepting the gift, or required under paragraph (C) to publicly report it.

[2] Gift-giving between friends and relatives is a common occurrence, and ordinarily does not create an appearance of impropriety or cause reasonable persons to believe that the judge's independence, integrity, or impartiality has been compromised. In addition, when the appearance of friends or relatives in a case would require the judge's disqualification under Rule 2.11, there would be no opportunity for a gift to influence the judge's decision making. Paragraph (B)(2) places no restrictions upon the ability of a judge to accept gifts or other things of value from friends or relatives under these circumstances, and does not require public reporting.

[3] Businesses and financial institutions frequently make available special pricing, discounts, and other benefits, either in connection with a temporary promotion or

* See, Terminology.

for preferred customers, based upon longevity of the relationship, volume of business transacted, and other factors. A judge may freely accept such benefits if they are available to the general public, or if the judge qualifies for the special price or discount according to the same criteria as are applied to persons who are not judges. As an example, loans provided at generally prevailing interest rates are not gifts, but a judge could not accept a loan from a financial institution at below-market interest rates unless the same rate was being made available to the general public for a certain period of time or only to borrowers with specified qualifications that the judge also possesses.

[4]   Rule 3.13 applies only to acceptance of gifts or other things of value by a judge. Nonetheless, if a gift or other benefit is given to the judge's spouse, domestic partner, or member of the judge's family residing in the judge's household, it may be viewed as an attempt to evade Rule 3.13 and influence the judge indirectly. Where the gift or benefit is being made primarily to such other persons, and the judge is merely an incidental beneficiary, this concern is reduced. A judge should, however, remind family and household members of the restrictions imposed upon judges, and urge them to take these restrictions into account when making decisions about accepting such gifts or benefits.

[5]   Rule 3.13 does not apply to contributions to a judge's campaign for judicial office. Such contributions are governed by other Rules of this Code, including Rules 4.3 and 4.4.

RULE 3.14: Reimbursement of Expenses and Waivers of Fees or Charges

(A) Unless otherwise prohibited by Rules 3.1 and 3.13(A) or other law,* a judge may accept reimbursement of necessary and reasonable expenses for travel, food, lodging, or other incidental expenses, or a waiver or partial waiver of fees or charges for registration, tuition, and similar items, from sources other than the judge's employing entity, if the expenses or charges are associated with the judge's participation in extrajudicial activities permitted by this Code.

(B) Reimbursement of expenses for necessary travel, food, lodging, or other incidental expenses shall be limited to the actual costs reasonably incurred by the judge and, when appropriate to the occasion, by the judge's spouse, domestic partner,* or guest.

(C) A judge who accepts reimbursement of expenses or waivers or partial waivers of fees or charges on behalf of the judge or the judge's spouse, domestic partner, or guest shall publicly report such acceptance as required by Rule 3.15.

Comment

[1]   Educational, civic, religious, fraternal, and charitable organizations often sponsor meetings, seminars, symposia, dinners, awards ceremonies, and similar events. Judges are encouraged to attend educational programs, as both teachers and participants, in law-related and academic disciplines, in furtherance of their duty to remain competent in the law. Participation in a variety of other extrajudicial activity is also permitted and encouraged by this Code.

* See, Terminology.

[2] Not infrequently, sponsoring organizations invite certain judges to attend seminars or other events on a fee-waived or partial-fee-waived basis, and sometimes include reimbursement for necessary travel, food, lodging, or other incidental expenses. A judge's decision whether to accept reimbursement of expenses or a waiver or partial waiver of fees or charges in connection with these or other extrajudicial activities must be based upon an assessment of all the circumstances. The judge must undertake a reasonable inquiry to obtain the information necessary to make an informed judgment about whether acceptance would be consistent with the requirements of this Code.

[3] A judge must assure himself or herself that acceptance of reimbursement or fee waivers would not appear to a reasonable person to undermine the judge's independence, integrity, or impartiality. The factors that a judge should consider when deciding whether to accept reimbursement or a fee waiver for attendance at a particular activity include:

(a) whether the sponsor is an accredited educational institution or bar association rather than a trade association or a for-profit entity;

(b) whether the funding comes largely from numerous contributors rather than from a single entity and is earmarked for programs with specific content;

(c) whether the content is related or unrelated to the subject matter of litigation pending or impending before the judge, or to matters that are likely to come before the judge;

(d) whether the activity is primarily educational rather than recreational, and whether the costs of the event are reasonable and comparable to those associated with similar events sponsored by the judiciary, bar associations, or similar groups;

(e) whether information concerning the activity and its funding sources is available upon inquiry;

(f) whether the sponsor or source of funding is generally associated with particular parties or interests currently appearing or likely to appear in the judge's court, thus possibly requiring disqualification of the judge under Rule 2.11;

(g) whether differing viewpoints are presented; and

(h) whether a broad range of judicial and nonjudicial participants are invited, whether a large number of participants are invited, and whether the program is designed specifically for judges.

RULE 3.15: Reporting Requirements

(A) A judge shall publicly report the amount or value of:

(1) compensation received for extrajudicial activities as permitted by Rule 3.12;

(2) gifts and other things of value as permitted by Rule 3.13(C), unless the value of such items, alone or in the aggregate with other items received from the same source in the same calendar year, does not exceed $[insert amount]; and

(3) reimbursement of expenses and waiver of fees or charges permitted by Rule 3.14(A), unless the amount of reimbursement or waiver, alone or in the aggregate with other reimbursements or waivers received from the same source in the same calendar year, does not exceed $[insert amount].

(B) When public reporting is required by paragraph (A), a judge shall report the date, place, and nature of the activity for which the judge received any compensation; the description of any gift, loan, bequest, benefit, or other thing of value accepted; and the source of reimbursement of expenses or waiver or partial waiver of fees or charges.

(C) The public report required by paragraph (A) shall be made at least annually, except that for reimbursement of expenses and waiver or partial waiver of fees or charges, the report shall be made within thirty days following the conclusion of the event or program.

(D) Reports made in compliance with this Rule shall be filed as public documents in the office of the clerk of the court on which the judge serves or other office designated by law,* and, when technically feasible, posted by the court or office personnel on the court's website.

CANON 4

A judge or candidate for judicial office shall not engage in political or campaign activity that is inconsistent with the independence, integrity, or impartiality of the judiciary.

RULE 4.1: Political and Campaign Activities of Judges and Judicial Candidates in General

(A) Except as permitted by law,* or by Rules 4.2, 4.3, and 4.4, a judge or a judicial candidate* shall not:

(1) act as a leader in, or hold an office in, a political organization;*

(2) make speeches on behalf of a political organization;

(3) publicly endorse or oppose a candidate for any public office;

(4) solicit funds for, pay an assessment to, or make a contribution* to a political organization or a candidate for public office;

(5) attend or purchase tickets for dinners or other events sponsored by a political organization or a candidate for public office;

(6) publicly identify himself or herself as a candidate of a political organization;

(7) seek, accept, or use endorsements from a political organization;

(8) personally solicit* or accept campaign contributions other than through a campaign committee authorized by Rule 4.4;

(9) use or permit the use of campaign contributions for the private benefit of the judge, the candidate, or others;

(10) use court staff, facilities, or other court resources in a campaign for judicial office;

(11) knowingly,* or with reckless disregard for the truth, make any false or misleading statement;

* See, Terminology.

(12) make any statement that would reasonably be expected to affect the outcome or impair the fairness of a matter pending* or impending* in any court; or

(13) in connection with cases, controversies, or issues that are likely to come before the court, make pledges, promises, or commitments that are inconsistent with the impartial* performance of the adjudicative duties of judicial office.

(B) A judge or judicial candidate shall take reasonable measures to ensure that other persons do not undertake, on behalf of the judge or judicial candidate, any activities prohibited under paragraph (A).

Comment

GENERAL CONSIDERATIONS

[1]   Even when subject to public election, a judge plays a role different from that of a legislator or executive branch official. Rather than making decisions based upon the expressed views or preferences of the electorate, a judge makes decisions based upon the law and the facts of every case. Therefore, in furtherance of this interest, judges and judicial candidates must, to the greatest extent possible, be free and appear to be free from political influence and political pressure. This Canon imposes narrowly tailored restrictions upon the political and campaign activities of all judges and judicial candidates, taking into account the various methods of selecting judges.

[2]   When a person becomes a judicial candidate, this Canon becomes applicable to his or her conduct.

PARTICIPATION IN POLITICAL ACTIVITIES

[3]   Public confidence in the independence and impartiality of the judiciary is eroded if judges or judicial candidates are perceived to be subject to political influence. Although judges and judicial candidates may register to vote as members of a political party, they are prohibited by paragraph (A)(1) from assuming leadership roles in political organizations.

[4]   Paragraphs (A)(2) and (A)(3) prohibit judges and judicial candidates from making speeches on behalf of political organizations or publicly endorsing or opposing candidates for public office, respectively, to prevent them from abusing the prestige of judicial office to advance the interests of others. See Rule 1.3. These Rules do not prohibit candidates from campaigning on their own behalf, or from endorsing or opposing candidates for the same judicial office for which they are running. See Rules 4.2(B)(2) and 4.2(B)(3).

[5]   Although members of the families of judges and judicial candidates are free to engage in their own political activity, including running for public office, there is no "family exception" to the prohibition in paragraph (A)(3) against a judge or candidate publicly endorsing candidates for public office. A judge or judicial candidate must not become involved in, or publicly associated with, a family member's political activity or campaign for public office. To avoid public misunderstanding, judges and judicial candidates should take, and should urge members of their families to take, reasonable steps to avoid any implication that they endorse any family member's candidacy or other political activity.

[6]   Judges and judicial candidates retain the right to participate in the political process as voters in both primary and general elections. For purposes of this Canon, participation in a caucus-type election procedure does not constitute public support for

* See, Terminology.

or endorsement of a political organization or candidate, and is not prohibited by paragraphs (A)(2) or (A)(3).

STATEMENTS AND COMMENTS MADE DURING A CAMPAIGN FOR JUDICIAL OFFICE

[7]   Judicial candidates must be scrupulously fair and accurate in all statements made by them and by their campaign committees. Paragraph (A)(11) obligates candidates and their committees to refrain from making statements that are false or misleading, or that omit facts necessary to make the communication considered as a whole not materially misleading.

[8]   Judicial candidates are sometimes the subject of false, misleading, or unfair allegations made by opposing candidates, third parties, or the media. For example, false or misleading statements might be made regarding the identity, present position, experience, qualifications, or judicial rulings of a candidate. In other situations, false or misleading allegations may be made that bear upon a candidate's integrity or fitness for judicial office. As long as the candidate does not violate paragraphs (A)(11), (A)(12), or (A)(13), the candidate may make a factually accurate public response. In addition, when an independent third party has made unwarranted attacks on a candidate's opponent, the candidate may disavow the attacks, and request the third party to cease and desist.

[9]   Subject to paragraph (A)(12), a judicial candidate is permitted to respond directly to false, misleading, or unfair allegations made against him or her during a campaign, although it is preferable for someone else to respond if the allegations relate to a pending case.

[10]   Paragraph (A)(12) prohibits judicial candidates from making comments that might impair the fairness of pending or impending judicial proceedings. This provision does not restrict arguments or statements to the court or jury by a lawyer who is a judicial candidate, or rulings, statements, or instructions by a judge that may appropriately affect the outcome of a matter.

PLEDGES, PROMISES, OR COMMITMENTS INCONSISTENT WITH IMPARTIAL PERFORMANCE OF THE ADJUDICATIVE DUTIES OF JUDICIAL OFFICE

[11]   The role of a judge is different from that of a legislator or executive branch official, even when the judge is subject to public election. Campaigns for judicial office must be conducted differently from campaigns for other offices. The narrowly drafted restrictions upon political and campaign activities of judicial candidates provided in Canon 4 allow candidates to conduct campaigns that provide voters with sufficient information to permit them to distinguish between candidates and make informed electoral choices.

[12]   Paragraph (A)(13) makes applicable to both judges and judicial candidates the prohibition that applies to judges in Rule 2.10(B), relating to pledges, promises, or commitments that are inconsistent with the impartial performance of the adjudicative duties of judicial office.

[13]   The making of a pledge, promise, or commitment is not dependent upon, or limited to, the use of any specific words or phrases; instead, the totality of the statement must be examined to determine if a reasonable person would believe that the candidate for judicial office has specifically undertaken to reach a particular result. Pledges, promises, or commitments must be contrasted with statements or announcements of personal views on legal, political, or other issues, which are not prohibited. When making such statements, a judge should acknowledge the overarching judicial obligation to apply and uphold the law, without regard to his or her personal views.

[14] A judicial candidate may make campaign promises related to judicial organization, administration, and court management, such as a promise to dispose of a backlog of cases, start court sessions on time, or avoid favoritism in appointments and hiring. A candidate may also pledge to take action outside the courtroom, such as working toward an improved jury selection system, or advocating for more funds to improve the physical plant and amenities of the courthouse.

[15] Judicial candidates may receive questionnaires or requests for interviews from the media and from issue advocacy or other community organizations that seek to learn their views on disputed or controversial legal or political issues. Paragraph (A)(13) does not specifically address judicial responses to such inquiries. Depending upon the wording and format of such questionnaires, candidates' responses might be viewed as pledges, promises, or commitments to perform the adjudicative duties of office other than in an impartial way. To avoid violating paragraph (A)(13), therefore, candidates who respond to media and other inquiries should also give assurances that they will keep an open mind and will carry out their adjudicative duties faithfully and impartially if elected. Candidates who do not respond may state their reasons for not responding, such as the danger that answering might be perceived by a reasonable person as undermining a successful candidate's independence or impartiality, or that it might lead to frequent disqualification. See Rule 2.11.

RULE 4.2: Political and Campaign Activities of Judicial Candidates in Public Elections

(A) A judicial candidate* in a partisan, nonpartisan, or retention public election* shall:

(1) act at all times in a manner consistent with the independence,* integrity,* and impartiality* of the judiciary;

(2) comply with all applicable election, election campaign, and election campaign fund-raising laws and regulations of this jurisdiction;

(3) review and approve the content of all campaign statements and materials produced by the candidate or his or her campaign committee, as authorized by Rule 4.4, before their dissemination; and

(4) take reasonable measures to ensure that other persons do not undertake on behalf of the candidate activities, other than those described in Rule 4.4, that the candidate is prohibited from doing by Rule 4.1.

(B) A candidate for elective judicial office may, unless prohibited by law,* and not earlier than [insert amount of time] before the first applicable primary election, caucus, or general or retention election:

(1) establish a campaign committee pursuant to the provisions of Rule 4.4;

(2) speak on behalf of his or her candidacy through any medium, including but not limited to advertisements, websites, or other campaign literature;

(3) publicly endorse or oppose candidates for the same judicial office for which he or she is running;

* See, Terminology.

   (4) attend or purchase tickets for dinners or other events sponsored by a political organization* or a candidate for public office;

   (5) seek, accept, or use endorsements from any person or organization other than a partisan political organization; and

   (6) contribute to a political organization or candidate for public office, but not more than $[insert amount] to any one organization or candidate.

(C) A judicial candidate in a partisan public election may, unless prohibited by law, and not earlier than [insert amount of time] before the first applicable primary election, caucus, or general election:

   (1) identify himself or herself as a candidate of a political organization; and

   (2) seek, accept, and use endorsements of a political organization.

Comment

[1] Paragraphs (B) and (C) permit judicial candidates in public elections to engage in some political and campaign activities otherwise prohibited by Rule 4.1. Candidates may not engage in these activities earlier than [insert amount of time] before the first applicable electoral event, such as a caucus or a primary election.

[2] Despite paragraphs (B) and (C), judicial candidates for public election remain subject to many of the provisions of Rule 4.1. For example, a candidate continues to be prohibited from soliciting funds for a political organization, knowingly making false or misleading statements during a campaign, or making certain promises, pledges, or commitments related to future adjudicative duties. See Rule 4.1(A), paragraphs (4), (11), and (13).

[3] In partisan public elections for judicial office, a candidate may be nominated by, affiliated with, or otherwise publicly identified or associated with a political organization, including a political party. This relationship may be maintained throughout the period of the public campaign, and may include use of political party or similar designations on campaign literature and on the ballot.

[4] In nonpartisan public elections or retention elections, paragraph (B)(5) prohibits a candidate from seeking, accepting, or using nominations or endorsements from a partisan political organization.

[5] Judicial candidates are permitted to attend or purchase tickets for dinners and other events sponsored by political organizations.

[6] For purposes of paragraph (B)(3), candidates are considered to be running for the same judicial office if they are competing for a single judgeship or if several judgeships on the same court are to be filled as a result of the election. In endorsing or opposing another candidate for a position on the same court, a judicial candidate must abide by the same rules governing campaign conduct and speech as apply to the candidate's own campaign.

[7] Although judicial candidates in nonpartisan public elections are prohibited from running on a ticket or slate associated with a political organization, they may group themselves into slates or other alliances to conduct their campaigns more effectively. Candidates who have grouped themselves together are considered to be running for the same judicial office if they satisfy the conditions described in Comment [6].

* See, Terminology.

RULE 4.3: Activities of Candidates for Appointive Judicial Office

A candidate for appointment to judicial office may:

(A) communicate with the appointing or confirming authority, including any selection, screening, or nominating commission or similar agency; and

(B) seek endorsements for the appointment from any person or organization other than a partisan political organization.

Comment

[1]   When seeking support or endorsement, or when communicating directly with an appointing or confirming authority, a candidate for appointive judicial office must not make any pledges, promises, or commitments that are inconsistent with the impartial performance of the adjudicative duties of the office. See Rule 4.1(A)(13).

RULE 4.4: Campaign Committees

(A) A judicial candidate* subject to public election* may establish a campaign committee to manage and conduct a campaign for the candidate, subject to the provisions of this Code. The candidate is responsible for ensuring that his or her campaign committee complies with applicable provisions of this Code and other applicable law.*

(B) A judicial candidate subject to public election shall direct his or her campaign committee:

(1) to solicit and accept only such campaign contributions* as are reasonable, in any event not to exceed, in the aggregate,* $[insert amount] from any individual or $[insert amount] from any entity or organization;

(2) not to solicit or accept contributions for a candidate's current campaign more than [insert amount of time] before the applicable primary election, caucus, or general or retention election, nor more than [insert number] days after the last election in which the candidate participated; and

(3) to comply with all applicable statutory requirements for disclosure and divestiture of campaign contributions, and to file with [name of appropriate regulatory authority] a report stating the name, address, occupation, and employer of each person who has made campaign contributions to the committee in an aggregate value exceeding $[insert amount]. The report must be filed within [insert number] days following an election, or within such other period as is provided by law.

Comment

[1]   Judicial candidates are prohibited from personally soliciting campaign contributions or personally accepting campaign contributions. See Rule 4.1(A)(8). This Rule recognizes that in many jurisdictions, judicial candidates must raise campaign funds to support their candidacies, and permits candidates, other than candidates for appointive judicial office, to establish campaign committees to solicit and accept reasonable financial contributions or in-kind contributions.

* See, Terminology.

[2] Campaign committees may solicit and accept campaign contributions, manage the expenditure of campaign funds, and generally conduct campaigns. Candidates are responsible for compliance with the requirements of election law and other applicable law, and for the activities of their campaign committees.

[3] At the start of a campaign, the candidate must instruct the campaign committee to solicit or accept only such contributions as are reasonable in amount, appropriate under the circumstances, and in conformity with applicable law. Although lawyers and others who might appear before a successful candidate for judicial office are permitted to make campaign contributions, the candidate should instruct his or her campaign committee to be especially cautious in connection with such contributions, so they do not create grounds for disqualification if the candidate is elected to judicial office. See Rule 2.11.

RULE 4.5: Activities of Judges Who Become Candidates for Nonjudicial Office

(A) Upon becoming a candidate for a nonjudicial elective office, a judge shall resign from judicial office, unless permitted by law* to continue to hold judicial office.

(B) Upon becoming a candidate for a nonjudicial appointive office, a judge is not required to resign from judicial office, provided that the judge complies with the other provisions of this Code.

Comment

[1] In campaigns for nonjudicial elective public office, candidates may make pledges, promises, or commitments related to positions they would take and ways they would act if elected to office. Although appropriate in nonjudicial campaigns, this manner of campaigning is inconsistent with the role of a judge, who must remain fair and impartial to all who come before him or her. The potential for misuse of the judicial office, and the political promises that the judge would be compelled to make in the course of campaigning for nonjudicial elective office, together dictate that a judge who wishes to run for such an office must resign upon becoming a candidate.

[2] The "resign to run" rule set forth in paragraph (A) ensures that a judge cannot use the judicial office to promote his or her candidacy, and prevents post-campaign retaliation from the judge in the event the judge is defeated in the election. When a judge is seeking appointive nonjudicial office, however, the dangers are not sufficient to warrant imposing the "resign to run" rule.

* See, Terminology.

CALIFORNIA CODE OF JUDICIAL ETHICS

**Amended by the Supreme Court of California effective
January 1, 2008; previously amended March 4, 1999,
December 13, 2000, December 30, 2002
and June 18 and December 22, 2003,
January 1 and June 1, 2005, July 1, 2006 and January 1, 2007**

Preface
Preamble
Terminology

Canon 1. A Judge Shall Uphold the Integrity and Independence of the Judiciary.
Canon 2. A Judge Shall Avoid Impropriety and the Appearance of Impropriety in All of the Judge's Activities.
Canon 3. A Judge Shall Perform the Duties of Judicial Office Impartially and Diligently.
Canon 4. A Judge Shall So Conduct the Judge's Quasi–Judicial and Extrajudicial Activities so as to Minimize the Risk of Conflict With Judicial Obligations.
Canon 5. A Judge or Judicial Candidate Shall Refrain From Inappropriate Political Activity.
Canon 6. Compliance With the Code of Judicial Ethics.

PREFACE

Formal standards of judicial conduct have existed for more than 50 years. The original Canons of Judicial Ethics promulgated by the American Bar Association were modified and adopted in 1949 for application in California by the Conference of California Judges (now the California Judges Association).

In 1969, the American Bar Association determined that current needs and problems warranted revision of the Canons. In the revision process, a special American Bar Association committee, headed by former California Chief Justice Roger Traynor, sought and considered the views of the bench and bar and other interested persons. The American Bar Association Code of Judicial Conduct was adopted by the House of Delegates of the American Bar Association August 16, 1972.

Effective January 5, 1975, the California Judges Association adopted a new California Code of Judicial Conduct adapted from the American Bar Association 1972 Model Code. The California code was recast in gender-neutral form in 1986.

In 1990, the American Bar Association Model Code was further revised after a lengthy study. The California Judges Association again reviewed the model code and adopted a revised California Code of Judicial Conduct on October 5, 1992.

Proposition 190 (amending Cal. Const., art. VI, § 18(m), effective March 1, 1995) created a new constitutional provision that states, "The Supreme Court shall make rules for the conduct of judges, both on and off the bench, and for judicial candidates* in the conduct of their campaigns. These rules shall be referred to as the Code of Judicial Ethics."

The Supreme Court formally adopted the 1992 Code of Judicial Conduct in March 1995, as a transitional measure pending further review.

The Supreme Court formally adopted the Code of Judicial Ethics effective January 15, 1996.

The Supreme Court formally adopted amendments to the Code of Judicial Ethics effective April 15, 1996. The *Advisory Committee Commentary* is published by the Supreme Court Advisory Committee on Judicial Ethics.

PREAMBLE

Our legal system is based on the principle that an independent, fair, and competent judiciary will interpret and apply the laws that govern us. The role of the judiciary is central to American concepts of justice and the rule of law. Intrinsic to this code are the precepts that judges, individually and collectively, must respect and honor the judicial office as a public trust and strive to enhance and maintain confidence in our legal system. The judge is an arbiter of facts and law for the resolution of disputes and a highly visible member of government under the rule of law.

The Code of Judicial Ethics ("Code") establishes standards for ethical conduct of judges on and off the bench and for candidates for judicial office. The Code consists of broad declarations called Canons, with subparts, and a Terminology section. Following each Canon is a Commentary section prepared by the Supreme Court Advisory Committee on Judicial Ethics. The Commentary, by explanation and example, provides guidance as to the purpose and meaning of the Canons. The Commentary does not constitute additional rules and should not be so construed. All members of the judiciary must comply with the Code. Compliance is required to preserve the integrity of the bench and to ensure the confidence of the public.

The Canons should be read together as a whole, and each provision should be construed in context and consistent with every other provision. They are to be applied in conformance with constitutional requirements, statutes, other court rules, and decisional law. Nothing in the Code shall either impair the essential independence of judges in making judicial decisions or provide a separate basis for civil liability or criminal prosecution.

The Code governs the conduct of judges and judicial candidates* and is binding upon them. Whether disciplinary action is appropriate, and the degree of discipline to be imposed, requires a reasoned application of the text and consideration of such factors as the seriousness of the transgression, whether there is a pattern of improper activity, and the effect of the improper activity on others or on the judicial system.

TERMINOLOGY

Terms explained below are noted with an asterisk (*) in the Canons where they appear. In addition, the Canons in which terms appear are cited after the explanation of each term below.

"*Appropriate authority*" denotes the authority with responsibility for initiation of the disciplinary process with respect to a violation to be reported. See Commentary to Canon 3D.

"*Candidate.*" A candidate is a person seeking election for or retention of judicial office by election. A person becomes a candidate for judicial office as soon as he or she makes a public announcement of candidacy, declares or files as a candidate with the election authority, or authorizes solicitation or acceptance of contributions or support. The term "candidate" has the same meaning when applied to a judge seeking election to nonjudicial office, unless on leave of absence. See Preamble and Canons 2B(3), the preliminary paragraph of 5, 5A, 5B, 5C, and 6E.

"*Court personnel*" does not include the lawyers in a proceeding before a judge. See Canons 3B(4), 3B(7)(b), 3B(9), and 3C(2).

"*Fiduciary*" includes such relationships as executor, administrator, trustee, and guardian. See Canons 4E, 6B, and 6F (*Commentary*).

"*Law*" denotes court rules as well as statutes, constitutional provisions, and decisional law. See Canons 1 (*Commentary*), 2A, 2C (*Commentary*), 3A, 3B(2), 3B(7), 3E, 4B (*Commentary*), 4C, 4D(6)(a)–(b), 4F, 4H, and 5D.

"*Member of the judge's family*" denotes a spouse, registered domestic partner, child, grandchild, parent, grandparent, or other relative or person with whom the judge maintains a close familial relationship. See Canons 2B(2), 4D(1) (*Commentary*), 4D(2), 4E, 4G (*Commentary*), and 5A.

"*Member of the judge's family residing in the judge's household*" denotes a spouse or registered domestic partner and those persons who reside in the judge's household who are relatives of the judge including relatives by marriage, or persons with whom the judge maintains a close familial relationship. See Canons 4D(5) and 4D(6).

"*Nonprofit youth organization*" is any nonprofit corporation or association, not organized for the private gain of any person, whose purposes are irrevocably dedicated to benefiting and serving the interests of minors and which maintains its nonprofit status in accordance with applicable state and federal tax laws. See Canon 2C.

"*Nonpublic information*" denotes information that, by law, is not available to the public. Nonpublic information may include but is not limited to information that is sealed by statute or court order, impounded, or communicated in camera; and information offered in grand jury proceedings, presentencing reports, dependency cases, or psychiatric reports. See Canon 3B(11).

"*Political organization*" denotes a political party, political action committee, or other group, the principal purpose of which is to further the election or appointment of candidates to nonjudicial office. See Canon 5A.

"*Registered domestic partner*" denotes a person who has registered for domestic partnership pursuant to state law or who is recognized as a domestic partner pursuant to Family Code section 299.2.

"*Temporary Judge.*" A temporary judge is an active or inactive member of the bar who pursuant to article VI, section 21 of the California Constitution, serves or expects to serve as a judge once, sporadically, or regularly on a part-time basis under a separate court appointment for each period of service or for each case heard. See Canons 4C(3)(d)(i), 6A, and 6D.

"*Require.*" Any Canon prescribing that a judge "require" certain conduct of others means that a judge is to exercise reasonable direction and control over the conduct of those persons subject to the judge's direction and control. See Canons 3B(3), 3B(4), 3B(6), 3B(8) (*Commentary*), 3B(9), and 3C(2).

"Subordinate judicial officer." A subordinate judicial officer is, for the purposes of this Code, a person appointed pursuant to article VI, section 22 of the California Constitution, including, but not limited to, a commissioner, referee, and hearing officer. See Canon 6A.

* Terms with an asterisk (*) are defined in the Terminology section.

CANON 1

A Judge Shall Uphold the Integrity and Independence of the Judiciary

An independent and honorable judiciary is indispensable to justice in our society. A judge should participate in establishing, maintaining, and enforcing high standards of conduct, and shall personally observe those standards so that the integrity and independence of the judiciary will be preserved. The provisions of this Code are to be construed and applied to further that objective. A judicial decision or administrative act later determined to be incorrect legally is not itself a violation of this Code.

Advisory Committee Commentary

Deference to the judgments and rulings of courts depends upon public confidence in the integrity and independence of judges. The integrity and independence of judges depend in turn upon their acting without fear or favor. Although judges should be independent, they must comply with the law* and the provisions of this Code. Public confidence in the impartiality of the judiciary is maintained by the adherence of each judge to this responsibility. Conversely, violations of this Code diminish public confidence in the judiciary and thereby do injury to the system of government under law.

The basic function of an independent and honorable judiciary is to maintain the utmost integrity in decision making, and this Code should be read and interpreted with that function in mind.

CANON 2

A Judge Shall Avoid Impropriety and the Appearance of Impropriety in All of the Judge's Activities

A. Promoting Public Confidence. A judge shall respect and comply with the law* and shall act at all times in a manner that promotes public confidence in the integrity and impartiality of the judiciary.

Advisory Committee Commentary

Public confidence in the judiciary is eroded by irresponsible or improper conduct by judges. A judge must avoid all impropriety and appearance of impropriety. A judge must expect to be the subject of constant public scrutiny. A judge must therefore accept restrictions on the judge's conduct that might be viewed as burdensome by other members of the community and should do so freely and willingly.

The prohibition against behaving with impropriety or the appearance of impropriety applies to both the professional and personal conduct of a judge.

* See, Terminology.

The test for the appearance of impropriety is whether a person aware of the facts might reasonably entertain a doubt that the judge would be able to act with integrity, impartiality, and competence.

See also Commentary under Canon 2C.

B. Use of the Prestige of Judicial Office

(1) A judge shall not allow family, social, political, or other relationships to influence the judge's judicial conduct or judgment, nor shall a judge convey or permit others to convey the impression that any individual is in a special position to influence the judge.

(2) A judge shall not lend the prestige of judicial office or use the judicial title in any manner, including any oral or written communication, to advance the pecuniary or personal interests of the judge or others. This Canon does not prohibit the following:

(a) A judge may testify as a character witness, provided the judge does so only when subpoenaed

(b) A judge may, without a subpoena, provide the Commission on Judicial Performance with a written communication containing

(i) factual information regarding a matter pending before the commission, or

(ii) information related to the character of a judge who has a matter pending before the commission, provided that any such factual or character information is based on personal knowledge. In commission proceedings, a judge shall provide information responsive to a subpoena or when officially requested to do so by the commission.

(c) A judge may provide factual information in State Bar disciplinary proceedings and shall provide information responsive to a subpoena or when officially requested to do so by the State Bar.

(d) A judge may respond to judicial selection inquiries, provide recommendations (including a general character reference, relating to the evaluation of persons being considered for a judgeship), and otherwise participate in the process of judicial selection.

(e) A judge may serve as a reference or provide a letter of recommendation only if based on the judge's personal knowledge of the individual. These written communications may include the judge's title and be written on stationery that uses the judicial title.

(3) A judge shall not initiate communications with a sentencing judge or a probation or corrections officer, but may provide them with information for the record in response to an official request. A judge may initiate communications with a probation or corrections officer concerning a member of the judge's family,* provided the judge is not identified as a judge in the communication.

* See, Terminology.

A strong judicial branch, based on the prestige which comes from effective and ethical performance, is essential to a system of government in which the judiciary functions independently of the executive and legislative branches. Judges should distinguish between proper and improper use of the prestige of office in all of their activities.

A judge must avoid lending the prestige of judicial office for the advancement of the private interests of the judge or others. For example, a judge must not use the judicial position to gain advantage in a civil suit involving a member of the judge's family;* or use his or her position to gain deferential treatment when stopped by a police officer for a traffic offense.

As to the use of a judge's title to identify a judge's role in the presentation and creation of legal education programs and materials, see Commentary to Canon 4B. In contracts for publication of a judge's writings, a judge should retain control over the advertising, to the extent feasible, to avoid exploitation of the judge's office. As to the acceptance of awards, see Canon 4D(6)(c) and Commentary.

This Canon does not afford judges a privilege against testifying in response to any official summons.

See also Canons 3D(1) and 3D(2) concerning a judge's obligation to take appropriate corrective action regarding other judges who violate any provision of the Code of Judicial Ethics and attorneys who violate any provision of the Rules of Professional Conduct.

This Canon does not preclude internal discussions among judges regarding the application of substantive or procedural provisions of law to any pending criminal or civil case.

(4) A judge may respond to judicial selection inquiries, provide recommendations (including a general character reference, relating to the evaluation of persons being considered for a judgeship) and otherwise participate in the process of judicial selection.

(5) A judge shall not use the judicial title in any written communication intended to advance the personal or pecuniary interest of the judge. A judge may serve as a reference or provide a letter of recommendation only if based on the judge's personal knowledge of the individual. These written communications may include the judge's title and be written on stationery that uses the judicial title.

C. Membership in Organizations. A judge shall not hold membership in any organization that practices invidious discrimination on the basis of race, sex, religion, national origin, or sexual orientation.

This Canon does not apply to membership in a religious organization or an official military organization of the United States. So long as membership does not violate Canon 4A, this Canon does not bar membership in a nonprofit youth organization.*

Membership of a judge in an organization that practices invidious discrimination gives rise to a perception that the judge's impartiality is impaired. This Canon exempts membership in religious and military organizations and, subject to Canon 4A, does not bar membership in nonprofit youth organizations.* These exemptions are necessary because membership in United States military organizations is subject to current valid military regulations, and religious beliefs are constitutionally protected. Membership in nonprofit youth organizations* is not barred to accommodate individual rights of intimate

* See, Terminology.

association and free expression. See also Canon 3E and its Commentary concerning disqualification and disclosure.

Canon 2C refers to the current practices of the organization. Whether an organization practices invidious discrimination is often a complex question to which judges should be sensitive. The answer cannot be determined from a mere examination of an organization's current membership rolls but rather depends on how the organization selects members and other relevant factors, such as whether the organization is dedicated to the preservation of religious, ethnic, or cultural values of legitimate common interest to its members, or whether it is in fact and effect an intimate, purely private organization whose membership limitations could not be constitutionally prohibited. Absent such factors, an organization is generally said to discriminate invidiously if it arbitrarily excludes from membership on the basis of race, religion, sex, national origin, or sexual orientation persons who would otherwise be admitted to membership.

Although Canon 2C relates only to membership in organizations that invidiously discriminate on the basis of race, sex, religion, national origin, or sexual orientation, a judge's membership in an organization that engages in any discriminatory membership practices prohibited by law* also violates Canon 2 and Canon 2A and gives the appearance of impropriety. In addition, it would be a violation of Canon 2 and Canon 2A for a judge to arrange a meeting at a club that the judge knows practices such invidious discrimination or for the judge to use such a club regularly. Moreover, public manifestation by a judge of the judge's knowing approval of invidious discrimination on any basis gives the appearance of impropriety under Canon 2 and diminishes public confidence in the integrity and impartiality of the judiciary in violation of Canon 2A.

CANON 3

A Judge Shall Perform the Duties of Judicial Office Impartially and Diligently

A. Judicial Duties in General. All of the judicial duties prescribed by law* shall take precedence over all other activities of every judge. In the performance of these duties, the following standards apply.

B. Adjudicative Responsibilities

(1) A judge shall hear and decide all matters assigned to the judge except those in which he or she is disqualified.

Advisory Committee Commentary

Canon 3B(1) is based upon the affirmative obligation contained in the Code of Civil Procedure.

(2) A judge shall be faithful to the law* regardless of partisan interests, public clamor, or fear of criticism, and shall maintain professional competence in the law.*

(3) A judge shall require* order and decorum in proceedings before the judge.

(4) A judge shall be patient, dignified, and courteous to litigants, jurors, witnesses, lawyers, and others with whom the judge deals in an official capacity, and shall require* similar conduct of lawyers and of all court staff and personnel* under the judge's direction and control.

(5) A judge shall perform judicial duties without bias or prejudice. A judge shall not, in the performance of judicial duties, engage in speech, gestures, or other conduct that would reasonably be perceived as (1) bias or

* See, Terminology.

prejudice, including but not limited to bias or prejudice based upon race, sex, religion, national origin, disability, age, sexual orientation, or socioeconomic status, or (2) sexual harassment.

(6) A judge shall require* lawyers in proceedings before the judge to refrain from manifesting, by words or conduct, bias or prejudice based upon race, sex, religion, national origin, disability, age, sexual orientation, or socioeconomic status against parties, witnesses, counsel, or others. This Canon does not preclude legitimate advocacy when race, sex, religion, national origin, disability, age, sexual orientation, socioeconomic status or other similar factors are issues in the proceeding.

(7) A judge shall accord to every person who has a legal interest in a proceeding, or that person's lawyer, full right to be heard according to law.* A judge shall not initiate, permit, or consider ex parte communications, or consider other communications made to the judge outside the presence of the parties concerning a pending or impending proceeding, except as follows:

(a) A judge may obtain the advice of a disinterested expert on the law* applicable to a proceeding before the judge if the judge gives notice to the parties of the person consulted and the substance of the advice, and affords the parties reasonable opportunity to respond.

(b) A judge may consult with court personnel* whose function is to aid the judge in carrying out the judge's adjudicative responsibilities or with other judges.

(c) A judge may, with the consent of the parties, confer separately with the parties and their lawyers in an effort to mediate or settle matters pending before the judge.

(d) A judge may initiate ex parte communications, where circumstances require, for scheduling, administrative purposes, or emergencies that do not deal with substantive matters provided:

(i) the judge reasonably believes that no party will gain a procedural or tactical advantage as a result of the ex parte communication, and

(ii) the judge makes provision promptly to notify all other parties of the substance of the ex parte communication and allows an opportunity to respond.

(e) A judge may initiate or consider any ex parte communication when expressly authorized by law* to do so.

Advisory Committee Commentary

The proscription against communications concerning a proceeding includes communications from lawyers, law professors, and other persons who are not participants in the proceeding, except to the limited extent permitted by the exceptions noted in Canon 3B(7).

This Canon does not prohibit a judge from initiating or considering an ex parte communication when authorized to do so by stipulation of the parties.

* See, Terminology.

This Canon does not prohibit court staff from communicating scheduling information or carrying out similar administrative functions.

An appropriate and often desirable procedure for a court to obtain the advice of a disinterested expert on legal issues is to invite the expert to file an amicus curiae brief.

A judge must not independently investigate facts in a case and must consider only the evidence presented, unless otherwise authorized by law.* For example, a judge is statutorily authorized to investigate and consult witnesses informally in small claims cases.

(8) A judge shall dispose of all judicial matters fairly, promptly, and efficiently. A judge shall manage the courtroom in a manner that provides all litigants the opportunity to have their matters fairly adjudicated in accordance with the law.

Advisory Committee Commentary

The obligation of a judge to dispose of matters promptly and efficiently must not take precedence over the judge's obligation to dispose of the matters fairly and with patience. A judge should monitor and supervise cases so as to reduce or eliminate dilatory practices, avoidable delays, and unnecessary costs. A judge should encourage and seek to facilitate settlement, but parties should not feel coerced into surrendering the right to have their controversy resolved by the courts.

Prompt disposition of the court's business requires a judge to devote adequate time to judicial duties, to be punctual in attending court and expeditious in determining matters under submission, and to require* that court officials, litigants, and their lawyers cooperate with the judge to that end.

(9) A judge shall not make any public comment about a pending or impending proceeding in any court, and shall not make any nonpublic comment that might substantially interfere with a fair trial or hearing. The judge shall require* similar abstention on the part of court personnel* subject to the judge's direction and control. This Canon does not prohibit judges from making statements in the course of their official duties or from explaining for public information the procedures of the court, and does not apply to proceedings in which the judge is a litigant in a personal capacity. Other than cases in which the judge has personally participated, this Canon does not prohibit judges from discussing in legal education programs and materials, cases and issues pending in appellate courts. This education exemption does not apply to cases over which the judge has presided or to comments or discussions that might interfere with a fair hearing of the case.

Advisory Committee Commentary

The requirement that judges abstain from public comment regarding a pending or impending proceeding continues during any appellate process and until final disposition. This Canon does not prohibit a judge from commenting on proceedings in which the judge is a litigant in a personal capacity, but in cases such as a writ of mandamus where the judge is a litigant in an official capacity, the judge must not comment publicly.

(10) A judge shall not commend or criticize jurors for their verdict other than in a court order or opinion in a proceeding, but may express appreciation to jurors for their service to the judicial system and the community.

* See, Terminology.

(11) A judge shall not disclose or use, for any purpose unrelated to judicial duties, nonpublic information* acquired in a judicial capacity.

C. Administrative Responsibilities

(1) A judge shall diligently discharge the judge's administrative responsibilities without bias or prejudice and maintain professional competence in judicial administration, and shall cooperate with other judges and court officials in the administration of court business.

(2) A judge shall require* staff and court personnel* under the judge's direction and control to observe appropriate standards of conduct and to refrain from manifesting bias or prejudice based upon race, sex, religion, national origin, disability, age, sexual orientation, or socioeconomic status in the performance of their official duties.

(3) A judge with supervisory authority for the judicial performance of other judges shall take reasonable measures to ensure the prompt disposition of matters before them and the proper performance of their other judicial responsibilities.

(4) A judge shall not make unnecessary court appointments. A judge shall exercise the power of appointment impartially and on the basis of merit. A judge shall avoid nepotism and favoritism. A judge shall not approve compensation of appointees above the reasonable value of services rendered.

(5) A judge shall perform administrative duties without bias or prejudice. A judge shall not, in the performance of administrative duties, engage in speech, gestures, or other conduct that would reasonably be perceived as (1) bias or prejudice, including but not limited to bias or prejudice based upon race, sex, religion, national origin, disability, age, sexual orientation, or socioeconomic status, or (2) sexual harassment.

D. Disciplinary Responsibilities.

(1) Whenever a judge has reliable information that another judge has violated any provision of the Code of Judicial Ethics, the judge shall take or

* See, Terminology.

initiate appropriate corrective action, which may include reporting the violation to the appropriate authority.*

(2) Whenever a judge has personal knowledge that a lawyer has violated any provision of the Rules of Professional Conduct, the judge shall take appropriate corrective action.

(3) A judge shall promptly report in writing to the Commission on Judicial Performance when he or she is charged in court by misdemeanor citation, prosecutorial complaint, information, or indictment, with any crime in the United States as specified below. Crimes that must be reported are: (1) all crimes, other than those that would be considered misdemeanors not involving moral turpitude or infractions under California law; and (2) all misdemeanors involving violence (including assaults), the use or possession of controlled substances, the misuse of prescriptions, or the personal use or furnishing of alcohol. A judge also shall promptly report in writing upon conviction of such crimes.

If the judge is a retired judge serving in the Assigned Judges Program, he or she shall promptly report such information in writing to the Chief Justice rather than to the Commission on Judicial Performance. If the judge is a subordinate judicial officer, he or she shall promptly report such information in writing to both the presiding judge of the court in which the subordinate judicial officer sits and the Commission on Judicial Performance.

Advisory Committee Commentary

Appropriate corrective action could include direct communication with the judge or lawyer who has committed the violation, other direct action if available, or a report of the violation to the presiding judge, appropriate authority,* or other agency or body. Judges should note that in addition to the action required by Canon 3D(2), California law imposes additional reporting requirements regarding lawyers.

E. Disqualification.

(1) A judge shall disqualify himself or herself in any proceeding in which disqualification is required by law.

(2) In all trial court proceedings, a judge shall disclose on the record information that is reasonably relevant to the question of disqualification under Code of Civil Procedure section 170.1, even if the judge believes there is no actual basis for disqualification.

(3) Ownership of a corporate bond issued by a party to a proceeding and having a fair market value exceeding one thousand five hundred dollars is disqualifying. Ownership of government bonds issued by a party to a proceeding is disqualifying only if the outcome of the proceeding could substantially affect the value of the judge's bond. Ownership in a mutual or common investment fund that holds bonds is not a disqualifying financial interest.

Advisory Committee Commentary

The distinction between corporate and government bonds is consistent with the Political Reform Act (see Gov. Code § 82034), which requires disclosure of corporate

* See, Terminology.

bonds, but not government bonds. Canon 3E(3) is intended to assist judges in complying with Code of Civil Procedure section 170.1(a)(3) and Canon 3E(5)(d).

(4) An appellate justice shall disqualify himself or herself in any proceeding if for any reason:

(a) the justice believes his or her recusal would further the interest of justice; or

(b) the justice substantially doubts his or her capacity to be impartial; or

(c) the circumstances are such that a reasonable person aware of the facts would doubt the justice's ability to be impartial.

(5) Disqualification of an appellate justice is also required in the following instances:

(a) The appellate justice has appeared or otherwise served as a lawyer in the pending matter, or has appeared or served as lawyer in any other matter involving any of the same parties if that other matter related to the same contested issues of fact and law as the present matter.

(b) Within the last two years, (i) a party to the proceeding, or an officer, director or trustee thereof, either was a client of the justice when the justice was engaged in the private practice of law or was a client of a lawyer with whom the justice was associated in the private practice of law; or (ii) a lawyer in the proceeding was associated with the justice in the private practice of law.

(c) The appellate justice represented a public officer or entity and personally advised or in any way represented such officer or entity concerning the factual or legal issues in the present proceeding in which the public officer or entity now appears.

(d) The appellate justice, or his or her spouse or registered domestic partner, or a minor child residing in the household, has a financial interest or is a fiduciary who has a financial interest in the proceeding, or is a director, advisor, or other active participant in the affairs of a party. A financial interest is defined as ownership of more than a 1 percent legal or equitable interest in a party, or a legal or equitable interest in a party of a fair market value exceeding one thousand five hundred dollars. Ownership in a mutual or common investment fund that holds securities does not itself constitute a financial interest; holding office in an educational, religious, charitable, fraternal or civic organization does not confer a financial interest in the organization's securities; and a proprietary interest of a policyholder in a mutual insurance company or mutual savings association or similar interest is not a financial interest unless the outcome of the proceeding could substantially affect the value of the interest. A justice shall make reasonable efforts to keep informed about his or her personal and fiduciary interests and those of his or her spouse or registered domestic partner and of minor children living in the household.

(e) The justice or his or her spouse or registered domestic partner, or a person within the third degree of relationship to either of them, or the spouse or registered domestic partner thereof, is a party or an officer, director or trustee of a party to the proceeding, or a lawyer or spouse or registered domestic partner of a lawyer in the proceeding is the spouse, registered domestic partner, former spouse, former registered domestic partner, child, sibling, or parent of the justice or of the justice's spouse or registered domestic partner, or such person is associated in the private practice of law with a lawyer in the proceeding.

(f) The justice (i) served as the judge before whom the proceeding was tried or heard in the lower court, (ii) has a personal knowledge of disputed evidentiary facts concerning the proceeding, or (iii) has a personal bias or prejudice concerning a party or a party's lawyer. The justice's spouse or registered domestic partner or a person within the third degree of relationship to the justice or his or her spouse or registered domestic partner, or the person's spouse or registered domestic partner, was a witness in the proceeding.

(g) A temporary or permanent physical impairment renders the judge unable properly to perceive the evidence or conduct the proceedings.

(h) The justice has a current arrangement concerning prospective employment or other compensated service as a dispute resolution neutral or is participating in, or, within the last two years has participated in, discussions regarding prospective employment or service as a dispute resolution neutral, or has been engaged in such employment or service, and any of the following applies:

(i) The arrangement is, or the prior employment or discussion was, with a party to the proceeding;

(ii) The matter before the justice includes issues relating to the enforcement of either an agreement to submit a dispute to an alternative dispute resolution process or an award or other final decision by a dispute resolution neutral.

(iii) The justice directs the parties to participate in an alternative dispute resolution process in which the dispute resolution neutral will be an individual or entity with whom the justice has the arrangement, has previously been employed or served, or is discussing or has discussed the employment or service; or

(iv) The justice will select a dispute resolution neutral or entity to conduct an alternative dispute resolution process in the matter before the justice, and among those available for selection is an individual or entity with whom the justice has the arrangement, with whom the justice has previously been employed or served, or with whom the justice is discussing or has discussed the employment or service.

For purposes of this canon, "participating in discussions" or "has participated in discussions" means that the justice solicited or otherwise indicated an interest in accepting or negotiating possible employment or service as an alternative dispute resolution neutral or responded to an unsolicited statement regarding, or an offer of, such employment or service by expressing an interest in that employment or service, making any inquiry regarding the employment or service, or encouraging the person making the statement or offer to provide additional information about that possible employment or service. If a justice's response to an unsolicited statement regarding, a question about, or offer of, prospective employment or other compensated service as a dispute resolution neutral is limited to responding negatively, declining the offer, or declining to discuss such employment or service, that response does not constitute participating in discussions.

For purposes of this canon, "party" includes the parent, subsidiary, or other legal affiliate of any entity that is a party and is involved in the transaction, contract, or facts that gave rise to the issues subject to the proceeding.

For purposes of this canon, "dispute resolution neutral" means an arbitrator, a mediator, a temporary judge appointed under section 21 of article VI of the California Constitution, a referee appointed under Code of Civil Procedure section 638 or 639, a special master, a neutral evaluator, a settlement officer, or a settlement facilitator.

(i) The justice's spouse or registered domestic partner or a person within the third degree of relationship to the justice or his or her spouse or registered domestic partner, or the person's spouse or registered domestic partner, was a witness in the proceeding.

Advisory Committee Commentary

Canon 3(E)(1) sets forth the general duty to disqualify applicable to a judge of any court. Sources for determining when recusal or disqualification is appropriate may include the applicable provisions of the Code of Civil Procedure, other provisions of the Code of Judicial Ethics, the Code of Conduct for United States Judges, the American Bar Association's Model Code of Judicial Conduct, and related case law.

Canon 3E(4) sets forth the general standards for recusal of an appellate justice. The term "appellate justice" includes justices of both the Courts of Appeal and the Supreme Court. Generally, the provisions concerning disqualification of an appellate justice are intended to assist justices in determining whether recusal is appropriate and to inform the public why recusal may occur.

However, the rule of necessity may override the rule of disqualification. For example, a judge might be required to participate in judicial review of a judicial salary statute, or might be the only judge available in a matter requiring judicial action, such as a hearing on probable cause or a temporary restraining order. In the latter case, the judge must promptly disclose on the record the basis for possible disqualification and use reasonable efforts to transfer the matter to another judge as soon as practicable.

In some instances, membership in certain organizations may have the potential to give an appearance of partiality, although membership in the organization generally may not be barred by Canon 2C, Canon 4, or any other specific canon. A judge holding membership in an organization should disqualify himself or herself whenever doing so would be appropriate in accordance with Canon 3E(1), 3E(4), or 3E(5) or statutory requirements. *In addition, in some circumstances, the parties or their lawyers may consider a judge's membership in an organization relevant to the question of disqualification, even if the judge believes there is no actual basis for disqualification. In accordance with this Canon, a judge should disclose to the parties his or her membership in an organization, in any proceeding in which the judge believes the parties or their lawyers might consider this information relevant to the question of disqualification, even if the judge concludes there is no actual basis for disqualification.*

CANON 4

A Judge Shall so Conduct the Judge's Quasi–Judicial and Extrajudicial Activities so as to Minimize the Risk of Conflict with Judicial Obligations

A.   Extrajudicial Activities in General. A judge shall conduct all of the judge's extrajudicial activities so that they do not

(1) cast reasonable doubt on the judge's capacity to act impartially;

(2) demean the judicial office; or

(3) interfere with the proper performance of judicial duties.

Advisory Committee Commentary

Complete separation of a judge from extrajudicial activities is neither possible nor wise; a judge should not become isolated from the community in which the judge lives.

Expressions of bias or prejudice by a judge, even outside the judge's judicial activities, may cast reasonable doubt on the judge's capacity to act impartially as a judge. Expressions which may do so include jokes or other remarks demeaning individuals on the basis of a classification such as their race, sex, religion, sexual orientation, or national origin. See Canon 2C and accompanying Commentary.

B.   Quasi–Judicial and Avocational Activities. A judge may speak, write, lecture, teach, and participate in activities concerning legal and nonlegal subject matters, subject to the requirements of this Code.

Advisory Committee Commentary

As a judicial officer and person specially learned in the law,* a judge is in a unique position to contribute to the improvement of the law,* the legal system, and the administration of justice, including revision of substantive and procedural law* and improvement of criminal and juvenile justice. To the extent that time permits, a judge may do so, either independently or through a bar or judicial association or other group dedicated to the improvement of the law.*

It may be necessary to promote legal education programs and materials by identifying authors and speakers by judicial title. This is permissible, provided such use of the judicial title does not contravene Canons 2A and 2B.

Judges are not precluded by their office from engaging in other social, community, and intellectual endeavors so long as they do not interfere with the obligations under Canons 2C and 4A.

C.   Governmental, Civic, or Charitable Activities

(1) A judge shall not appear at a public hearing or officially consult with an executive or legislative body or public official except on matters concerning the law,* the legal system, or the administration of justice or in matters involving the judge's private economic or personal interests.

* See, Terminology.

See Canon 2B regarding the obligation to avoid improper influence.

(2) A judge shall not accept appointment to a governmental committee or commission or other governmental position that is concerned with issues of fact or policy on matters other than the improvement of the law,* the legal system, or the administration of justice. A judge may, however, serve in the military reserve or represent a national, state, or local government on ceremonial occasions or in connection with historical, educational, or cultural activities.

Advisory Committee Commentary

Canon 4C(2) prohibits a judge from accepting any governmental position except one relating to the law, legal system, or administration of justice as authorized by Canon 4C(3). The appropriateness of accepting extrajudicial assignments must be assessed in light of the demands on judicial resources and the need to protect the courts from involvement in extrajudicial matters that may prove to be controversial. Judges shall not accept governmental appointments that are likely to interfere with the effectiveness and independence of the judiciary, or which constitute a public office within the meaning of the California Constitution, article VI, section 17.*

Canon 4C(2) does not govern a judge's service in a nongovernmental position. See Canon 4C(3) permitting service by a judge with organizations devoted to the improvement of the law, the legal system, or the administration of justice and with educational, religious, charitable, fraternal, or civic organizations not conducted for profit. For example, service on the board of a public educational institution, other than a law school, would be prohibited under Canon 4C(2), but service on the board of a public law school or any private educational institution would generally be permitted under Canon 4C(3).*

(3) Subject to the following limitations and the other requirements of this Code,

    (a) a judge may serve as an officer, director, trustee, or nonlegal advisor of an organization or governmental agency devoted to the improvement of the law,* the legal system, or the administration of justice provided that such position does not constitute a public office within the meaning of the California Constitution, article VI, section 17;

    (b) a judge may serve as an officer, director, trustee, or nonlegal advisor of an educational, religious, charitable, fraternal, or civic organization not conducted for profit;

Advisory Committee Commentary

Canon 4C(3) does not apply to a judge's service in a governmental position unconnected with the improvement of the law, the legal system, or the administration of justice. See Canon 4C(2).*

Canon 4C(3) uses the phrase, "Subject to the following limitations and the other requirements of this Code." As an example of the meaning of the phrase, a judge permitted by Canon 4C(3) to serve on the board of a fraternal institution may be prohibited from such service by Canon 2C or 4A if the institution practices invidious discrimination or if service on the board otherwise casts reasonable doubt on the judge's capacity to act impartially as a judge.

Service by a judge on behalf of a civic or charitable organization may be governed by other provisions of Canon 4 in addition to Canon 4C. For example, a judge is prohibited by Canon 4G from serving as a legal advisor to a civic or charitable organization.

* See, Terminology.

Service on the board of a homeowners' association or a neighborhood protective group is proper if it is related to the protection of the judge's own economic interests. See Canons 4D(2) and 4D(4). See Canon 2B regarding the obligation to avoid improper use of the prestige of a judge's office.

(c) a judge shall not serve as an officer, director, trustee, or nonlegal advisor if it is likely that the organization

(i) will be engaged in judicial proceedings that would ordinarily come before the judge, or

(ii) will be engaged frequently in adversary proceedings in the court of which the judge is a member or in any court subject to the appellate jurisdiction of the court of which the judge is a member;

Advisory Committee Commentary

The changing nature of some organizations and of their relationship to the law* makes it necessary for the judge regularly to reexamine the activities of each organization with which the judge is affiliated to determine if it is proper for the judge to continue the affiliation. Some organizations regularly engage in litigation to achieve their goals or fulfill their purposes. Judges should avoid a leadership role in such organizations as it could compromise the appearance of impartiality.

(d) a judge as an officer, director, trustee, or nonlegal advisor, or as a member or otherwise

(i) may assist such an organization in planning fund raising and may participate in the management and investment of the organization's funds, but shall not personally participate in the solicitation of funds or other fund-raising activities, except that a judge may privately solicit funds for such an organization from other judges (excluding court commissioners, referees, retired judges, and temporary judges*);

(ii) may make recommendations to public and private fund-granting organizations on projects and programs concerning the law,* the legal system, or the administration of justice;

(iii) shall not personally participate in membership solicitation if the solicitation might reasonably be perceived as coercive or if the membership solicitation is essentially a fund-raising mechanism, except as permitted in Canon 4C(3)(d)(i);

(iv) shall not permit the use of the prestige of his or her judicial office for fund raising or membership solicitation but may be a speaker, guest of honor, or recipient of an award for public or charitable service provided the judge does not personally solicit funds and complies with Canon 4A(1), (2), and (3).

Advisory Committee Commentary

A judge may solicit membership or endorse or encourage membership efforts for an organization devoted to the improvement of the law,* the legal system, or the administration of justice, or a nonprofit educational, religious, charitable, fraternal, or civic organization as long as the solicitation cannot reasonably be perceived as coercive and is not essentially a fund-raising mechanism. Solicitation of funds for an organization and

* See, Terminology.

solicitation of memberships similarly involve the danger that the person solicited will feel obligated to respond favorably to the solicitor if the solicitor is in a position of influence or control. A judge must not engage in direct, individual solicitation of funds or memberships in person, in writing, or by telephone except in the following cases: (1) a judge may solicit other judges (excluding court commissioners, referees, retired judges, court-appointed arbitrators, and temporary judges*) for funds or memberships; (2) a judge may solicit other persons for membership in the organizations described above if neither those persons nor persons with whom they are affiliated are likely ever to appear before the court on which the judge serves; and (3) a judge who is an officer of such an organization may send a general membership solicitation mailing over the judge's signature.

Use of an organization letterhead for fund raising or membership solicitation does not violate Canon 4C(3)(d), provided the letterhead lists only the judge's name and office or other position in the organization, and designates the judge's judicial title only if other persons whose names appear on the letterhead have comparable designations. In addition, a judge must also make reasonable efforts to ensure that the judge's staff, court officials, and others subject to the judge's direction and control do not solicit funds on the judge's behalf for any purpose, charitable or otherwise.

D. Financial Activities

(1) A judge shall not engage in financial and business dealings that

(a) may reasonably be perceived to exploit the judge's judicial position, or

(b) involve the judge in frequent transactions or continuing business relationships with lawyers or other persons likely to appear before the court on which the judge serves.

Advisory Committee Commentary

The Time for Compliance provision of this Code (Canon 6F) postpones the time for compliance with certain provisions of this Canon in some cases.

A judge must avoid financial and business dealings that involve the judge in frequent transactions or continuing business relationships with persons likely to appear either before the judge personally or before other judges on the judge's court. A judge shall discourage members of the judge's family* from engaging in dealings that would reasonably appear to exploit the judge's judicial position or that involve family members in frequent transactions or continuing business relationships with persons likely to appear before the judge. This rule is necessary to avoid creating an appearance of exploitation of office or favoritism and to minimize the potential for disqualification.

Participation by a judge in financial and business dealings is subject to the general prohibitions in Canon 4A against activities that tend to reflect adversely on impartiality, demean the judicial office, or interfere with the proper performance of judicial duties. Such participation is also subject to the general prohibition in Canon 2 against activities involving impropriety or the appearance of impropriety and the prohibition in Canon 2B against the misuse of the prestige of judicial office.

In addition, a judge must maintain high standards of conduct in all of the judge's activities, as set forth in Canon 1.

(2) A judge may, subject to the requirements of this Code, hold and manage investments of the judge and members of the judge's family,* including real estate, and engage in other remunerative activities. A judge shall not participate in, nor permit the judge's name to be used in connection with, any business venture or commercial advertising that indicates the judge's title or affiliation with the judiciary or otherwise lend the power or prestige of his or her office to promote a business or any commercial venture.

* See, Terminology.

710

(3) A judge shall not serve as an officer, director, manager, or employee of a business affected with a public interest, including, without limitation, a financial institution, insurance company, or public utility.

Advisory Committee Commentary

Although participation by a judge in business activities might otherwise be permitted by Canon 4D, a judge may be prohibited from participation by other provisions of this Code when, for example, the business entity frequently appears before the judge's court or the participation requires significant time away from judicial duties. Similarly, a judge must avoid participating in any business activity if the judge's participation would involve misuse of the prestige of judicial office. See Canon 2B.

(4) A judge shall manage personal investments and financial activities so as to minimize the necessity for disqualification. As soon as reasonably possible, a judge shall divest himself or herself of investments and other financial interests that would require frequent disqualification.

(5) Under no circumstance shall a judge accept a gift, bequest, or favor if the donor is a party whose interests have come or are reasonably likely to come before the judge. A judge shall discourage members of the judge's family residing in the judge's household* from accepting similar benefits from parties who have come or are reasonably likely to come before the judge.

Advisory Committee Commentary

In addition to the prohibitions set forth in Canon 4D(5) regarding gifts, other laws may be applicable to judges, including, for example, Code of Civil Procedure section 170.9 and the Political Reform Act of 1974 (Gov. Code, § 81000 et seq.).

Canon 4D(5) does not apply to contributions to a judge's campaign for judicial office, a matter governed by Canon 5.

Because a gift, bequest, or favor to a member of the judge's family residing in the judge's household might be viewed as intended to influence the judge, a judge must inform those family members of the relevant ethical constraints upon the judge in this regard and discourage those family members from violating them. A judge cannot, however, reasonably be expected to know or control all of the financial or business activities of all family members residing in the judge's household.**

The application of Canon 4D(5) requires recognition that a judge cannot reasonably be expected to anticipate all persons or interests that may come before the court.

(6) A judge shall not accept and shall discourage members of the judge's family residing in the judge's household* from accepting a gift, bequest, favor, or loan from anyone except as hereinafter provided:

(a) any gift incidental to a public testimonial, books, tapes, and other resource materials supplied by publishers on a complimentary basis for official use, or an invitation to the judge and the judge's spouse or registered domestic partner or guest to attend a bar-related function or an activity devoted to the improvement of the law,* the legal system, or the administration of justice;

(b) advances or reimbursement for the reasonable cost of travel, transportation, lodging, and subsistence which is directly related to participation in any judicial, educational, civic, or governmental program,

* See, Terminology.

or bar-related function or activity, devoted to the improvement of the law,* the legal system, or the administration of justice;

Advisory Committee Commentary

Acceptance of an invitation to a law-related function is governed by Canon 4D(6)(a); acceptance of an invitation paid for by an individual lawyer or group of lawyers is governed by Canon 4D(6)(d).

(c) a gift, award, or benefit incident to the business, profession, or other separate activity of a spouse or registered domestic partner or other member of the judge's family residing in the judge's household,* including gifts, awards, and benefits for the use of both the spouse or registered domestic partner or other family member and the judge, provided the gift, award, or benefit could not reasonably be perceived as intended to influence the judge in the performance of judicial duties;

(d) ordinary social hospitality;

Advisory Committee Commentary

Although Canon 4D(6)(d) does not preclude ordinary social hospitality between members of the bench and bar, a judge should carefully weigh acceptance of such hospitality to avoid any appearance of bias. See Canon 2B.

(e) a gift for a special occasion from a relative or friend, if the gift is fairly commensurate with the occasion and the relationship;

Advisory Committee Commentary

A gift to a judge, or to a member of the judge's family residing in the judge's household, that is excessive in value raises questions about the judge's impartiality and the integrity of the judicial office and might require disqualification of the judge where disqualification would not otherwise be required. See, however, Canon 4D(6)(f).*

(f) a gift, bequest, favor, or loan from a relative or close personal friend whose appearance or interest in a case would in any event require disqualification under Canon 3E;

(g) a loan in the regular course of business on the same terms generally available to persons who are not judges;

(h) a scholarship or fellowship awarded on the same terms and based on the same criteria applied to other applicants.

E. Fiduciary Activities

(1) A judge shall not serve as executor, administrator, or other personal representative, trustee, guardian, attorney in fact, or other fiduciary,* except for the estate, trust, or person of a member of the judge's family,* and then only if such service will not interfere with the proper performance of judicial duties.

(2) A judge shall not serve as a fiduciary* if it is likely that the judge as a fiduciary* will be engaged in proceedings that would ordinarily come before the judge, or if the estate, trust, or minor or conservatee becomes engaged in

* See, Terminology.

contested proceedings in the court on which the judge serves or one under its appellate jurisdiction.

(3) The same restrictions on financial activities that apply to a judge personally also apply to the judge while acting in a fiduciary* capacity.

Advisory Committee Commentary

The Time for Compliance provision of this Code (Canon 6F) postpones the time for compliance with certain provisions of this Canon in some cases.

The restrictions imposed by this Canon may conflict with the judge's obligation as a fiduciary.* For example, a judge shall resign as trustee if detriment to the trust would result from divestiture of trust holdings the retention of which would place the judge in violation of Canon 4D(4).

F. Service as Arbitrator or Mediator. A judge shall not act as an arbitrator or mediator or otherwise perform judicial functions in a private capacity unless expressly authorized by law.*

Advisory Committee Commentary

Canon 4F does not prohibit a judge from participating in arbitration, mediation, or settlement conferences performed as part of his or her judicial duties.

G. Practice of Law. A judge shall not practice law.

Advisory Committee Commentary

This prohibition refers to the practice of law in a representative capacity and not in a pro se capacity. A judge may act for himself or herself in all legal matters, including matters involving litigation and matters involving appearances before or other dealings with legislative and other governmental bodies. However, in so doing, a judge must not abuse the prestige of office to advance the interests of the judge or member of the judge's family.* See Canon 2B.

This prohibition applies to subordinate judicial officers, magistrates, special masters, and judges of the State Bar Court.

H. Compensation and Reimbursement. A judge may receive compensation and reimbursement of expenses as provided by law* for the extrajudicial activities permitted by this Code, if the source of such payments does not give the appearance of influencing the judge's performance of judicial duties or otherwise give the appearance of impropriety.

(1) Compensation shall not exceed a reasonable amount nor shall it exceed what a person who is not a judge would receive for the same activity.

(2) Expense reimbursement shall be limited to the actual cost of travel, food, lodging, and other costs reasonably incurred by the judge and, where appropriate to the occasion, by the judge's spouse or registered domestic partner or guest. Any payment in excess of such an amount is compensation.

Advisory Committee Commentary

Judges should be aware of the statutory limitations on accepting gifts, including honoraria.

CANON 5

A Judge or Judicial Candidate* Shall Refrain
from Inappropriate Political Activity

Judges are entitled to entertain their personal views on political questions. They are not required to surrender their rights or opinions as citizens.

* See, Terminology.

713

They shall, however, avoid political activity that may create the appearance of political bias or impropriety. Judicial independence and impartiality should dictate the conduct of judges and candidates* for judicial office.

    A. Political Organizations. Judges and candidates* for judicial office shall not

    (1) act as leaders or hold any office in a political organization;*

    (2) make speeches for a political organization* or candidate* for nonjudicial office or publicly endorse or publicly oppose a candidate for nonjudicial office; or

    (3) personally solicit funds for a political organization* or nonjudicial candidate;* or make contributions to a political party or political organization* or to a nonjudicial candidate in excess of five hundred dollars in any calendar year per political party or political organization* or candidate,* or in excess of an aggregate of one thousand dollars in any calendar year for all political parties or political organizations* or nonjudicial candidates.*

Advisory Committee Commentary

The term "political activity" should not be construed so narrowly as to prevent private comment.

This provision does not prohibit a judge from signing a petition to qualify a measure for the ballot without the use of the judge's official title.

In judicial elections, judges are neither required to shield themselves from campaign contributions nor are they prohibited from soliciting contributions from anyone including attorneys. Nevertheless, there are necessary limits on judges facing election if the appearance of impropriety is to be avoided. Although it is improper for a judge to receive a gift from an attorney subject to exceptions noted in Canon 4D(6), a judge's campaign may receive attorney contributions.

Although attendance at political gatherings is not prohibited, any such attendance should be restricted so that it would not constitute an express public endorsement of a nonjudicial candidate* or a measure not directly affecting the administration of justice otherwise prohibited by this Canon.

Subject to the monetary limitation herein to political contributions, a judge may purchase tickets for political dinners or other similar dinner functions. Any admission price to such a political dinner or function in excess of the actual cost of the meal shall be considered a political contribution. The prohibition in Canon 5A(3) does not preclude judges from contributing to a campaign fund for distribution among judges who are candidates for reelection or retention, nor does it apply to contributions to any judge or candidate* for judicial office.

Under this Canon, a judge may publicly endorse another judicial candidate.* Such endorsements are permitted because judicial officers have a special obligation to uphold the integrity and impartiality of the judiciary and are in a unique position to know the qualifications necessary to serve as a competent judicial officer.

Although members of the judge's family* are not subject to the provisions of this Code, a judge shall not avoid compliance with this Code by making contributions through a spouse or registered domestic partner or other family member.

* See, Terminology.

B. Conduct During Judicial Campaigns. A candidate* for election or appointment to judicial office shall not (1) make statements to the electorate or the appointing authority that commit the candidate with respect to cases, controversies, or issues that could come before the courts, or (2) knowingly, or with reckless disregard for the truth, misrepresent the identity, qualifications, present position, or any other fact concerning the candidate or his or her opponent.

Advisory Committee Commentary

This code does not contain the "announce clause" that was the subject of the United States Supreme Court's decision in Republican Party of Minnesota v. White (2002) 536 U.S. 765. That opinion did not address the "commit clause," which is contained in Canon 5B(1). The phrase "appear to commit" has been deleted because, although judicial candidates cannot promise to take a particular position on cases, controversies, or issues prior to taking the bench and presiding over individual cases, the phrase may have been overinclusive.

Canon 5B(2) prohibits making knowing misrepresentations, including false or misleading statements, during an election campaign because doing so would violate Canons 1 and 2A, and may violate other canons.

C. Speaking at Political Gatherings. Candidates* for judicial office may speak to political gatherings only on their own behalf or on behalf of another candidate for judicial office.

D. Measures to Improve the Law. Except as otherwise permitted in this Code, judges shall not engage in any political activity, other than in relation to measures concerning the improvement of the law,* the legal system, or the administration of justice.

CANON 6

Compliance With The Code of Judicial Ethics

A. Judges. Anyone who is an officer of the state judicial system and who performs judicial functions, including, but not limited to, a subordinate judicial officer, magistrate, court-appointed arbitrator, judge of the State Bar Court, temporary judge, and special master, is a judge within the meaning of this Code. All judges shall comply with this Code except as provided below.

Advisory Committee Commentary

For the purposes of this Canon, if a retired judge is serving in the assigned judges program, the judge is considered to "perform judicial functions." Because retired judges who are privately retained may perform judicial functions, their conduct while performing those functions should be guided by this Code.

B. Retired Judge Serving in the Assigned Judges Program. A retired judge who has filed an application to serve on assignment, meets the eligibility requirements set by the Chief Justice for service, and has received an acknowledgment of participation in the assigned judges program shall comply with all provisions of this Code, except for the following:

4C(2)—Appointment to governmental positions

4E—Fiduciary* activities

* See, Terminology.

C. Retired Judge as Arbitrator or Mediator. A retired judge serving in the assigned judges program is not required to comply with Canon 4F of this Code relating to serving as an arbitrator or mediator, or performing judicial functions in a private capacity, except as otherwise provided in the *Standards and Guidelines for Judges Serving on Assignment* promulgated by the Chief Justice.

Advisory Committee Commentary

In California, article VI, section 6 of the California Constitution provides that a "retired judge who consents may be assigned to any court" by the Chief Justice. Retired judges who are serving in the assigned judges program pursuant to the above provision are bound by Canon 6B, including the requirement of Canon 4G barring the practice of law. Other provisions of California law, and standards and guidelines for eligibility and service set by the Chief Justice, further define the limitations on who may serve on assignment.

D. Temporary Judge*, Referee, or Court-appointed Arbitrator.[1]

A temporary judge, a person serving as a referee pursuant to Code of Civil Procedure section 638 or 639, or a court-appointed arbitrator shall comply only with the following Code provisions:

(1) A temporary judge, referee or court-appointed arbitrator shall comply with Canons 1 [integrity and independence of the judiciary], 2A [promoting public confidence], 3B(3) [order and decorum] and (4) [patient, dignified, and courteous treatment], 3B(6) [require lawyers to refrain from manifestations of any form of bias or prejudice], 3D(1) [action regarding misconduct by another judge] and (2) [action regarding misconduct by a lawyer], when the temporary judge, referee or court-appointed arbitrator is actually presiding in a proceeding or communicating with the parties, counsel, or court personnel while serving in the capacity of a temporary judge, referee, or court-appointed arbitrator in the case.

(2) A temporary judge, referee, or court-appointed arbitrator shall, from the time of notice and acceptance of appointment until termination of the appointment:

    (a) Comply with Canons 2B(1) [not allow family or other relationships to influence judicial conduct], 3B(1) [hear and decide all matters unless disqualified] and (2) [be faithful to and maintain competence in the law], 3B(5) [perform judicial duties without bias or prejudice], 3B(7) [accord full right to be heard to those entitled; avoid ex parte communications, except as specified] and (8) [dispose of matters fairly and promptly], 3C(1)[discharge administrative responsibilities without bias and with competence and cooperatively], (2) [require staff and personnel to observe standards of conduct and refrain from bias and prejudice] and (4) [make only fair, necessary, and appropriate appointments];

    (b) Not lend the prestige of judicial office to advance his, her, or another person's pecuniary or personal interests and not use his or her judicial title in any written communication intended to advance his, her,

---

* See, Terminology.

1. Reference should be made to relevant commentary to analogous or individual Canons cited or described in this Canon and appearing elsewhere in this Code.

or another person's pecuniary or personal interests, except to show his, her, or another person's qualifications;

(c) Not personally solicit memberships or donations for religious, fraternal, educational, civic, or charitable organizations from the parties and lawyers appearing before the temporary judge, referee, or court-appointed arbitrator;

(d) Under no circumstance accept a gift, bequest, or favor if the donor is a party, person, or entity whose interests are reasonably likely to come before the temporary judge, referee, or court-appointed arbitrator. A temporary judge, referee, or court-appointed arbitrator shall discourage members of the judge's family residing in the judge's household from accepting benefits from parties who are reasonably likely to come before the temporary judge, referee, or court-appointed arbitrator.

(3) A temporary judge shall, from the time of notice and acceptance of appointment until termination of the appointment, disqualify himself or herself in any proceeding as follows:

(a) A temporary judge—other than a temporary judge solely conducting settlement conferences—is disqualified to serve in a proceeding if any one or more of the following is true:

(i) the temporary judge has personal knowledge (as defined in Code of Civil Procedure section 170.1(a)(1)) of disputed evidentiary facts concerning the proceeding;

(ii) the temporary judge has served as a lawyer (as defined in Code of Civil Procedure section 170.1(a)(2)) in the proceeding;

(iii) the temporary judge, within the past five years, has given legal advice to, or served as a lawyer (as defined in Code of Civil Procedure section 170.1(a)(2), except that this provision requires disqualification if the temporary judge represented a party in the past five years rather than the two-year period specified in section 170.1(a)(2)) for a party in the present proceeding;

(iv) the temporary judge has a financial interest (as defined in Code of Civil Procedure sections 170.1(a)(3) and 170.5) in the subject matter in the proceeding or in a party to the proceeding;

(v) the temporary judge, or the spouse or registered domestic partner of the temporary judge, or a person within the third degree of relationship to either of them, or the spouse or registered domestic partner of such a person is a party to the proceeding or is an officer, director, or trustee of a party;

(vi) a lawyer or a spouse or registered domestic partner of a lawyer in the proceeding is the spouse, former spouse, registered domestic partner, former registered domestic partner, child, sibling, or parent of the temporary judge or the temporary judge's spouse or registered domestic partner, or if such a person is associated in the private practice of law with a lawyer in the proceeding; or

(vii) for any reason:

(A) the temporary judge believes his or her recusal would further the interests of justice;

(B) the temporary judge believes there is a substantial doubt as to his or her capacity to be impartial; or

(C) a person aware of the facts might reasonably entertain a doubt that the temporary judge would be able to be impartial. Bias or prejudice toward an attorney in the proceeding may be grounds for disqualification;

ADVISORY COMMITTEE COMMENTARY

The application of Canon 6D(3)(a)(iii), providing that a temporary judge is disqualified if he or she has given legal advice or served as a lawyer for a party to the proceeding in the past five years, may depend on the type of assignment and the amount of time available to investigate whether the temporary judge has previously represented a party. If time permits, the temporary judge must conduct such an investigation. Thus, if a temporary judge is privately compensated by the parties or is presiding over a particular matter known in advance of the hearing, the temporary judge is presumed to have adequate time to investigate. If, however, a temporary judge is assigned to a high volume calendar, such as traffic or small claims, and has not been provided with the names of the parties prior to the assignment, the temporary judge may rely on his or her memory to determine whether he or she has previously represented a party.

(b) A temporary judge before whom a proceeding was tried or heard is disqualified from participating in any appellate review of that proceeding.

(c) If the temporary judge has a current arrangement concerning prospective employment or other compensated service as a dispute resolution neutral or is participating in, or, within the last two years has participated in, discussions regarding prospective employment or service as a dispute resolution neutral, or has been engaged in such employment or service, and any of the following applies:

(i) The arrangement or current employment is, or the prior employment or discussion was, with a party to the proceeding.

(ii) The temporary judge directs the parties to participate in an alternative dispute resolution process in which the dispute resolution neutral will be an individual or entity with whom the temporary judge has the arrangement, is currently employed or serves, has previously been employed or served, or is discussing or has discussed the employment or service.

(iii) The temporary judge will select a dispute resolution neutral or entity to conduct an alternative dispute resolution process in the matter before the temporary judge, and among those available for selection is an individual or entity with whom the temporary judge has the arrangement, is currently employed or serves, has previously been employed or served, or is discussing or has discussed the employment or service.

For the purposes of canon 6D(3)(c), the definitions of "participating in discussions," "has participated in discussions," "party," and "dispute resolution neutral" are set forth in Code of Civil Procedure section 170.1(a)(8), except that the words "temporary judge" shall be substituted for the word "judge" in such definitions.

(d) A lawyer is disqualified from serving as a temporary judge in a family law or unlawful detainer proceeding if in the same type of proceeding:

(i) the lawyer holds himself or herself out to the public as representing exclusively one side; or

(ii) the lawyer represents one side in 90 percent or more of the cases in which he or she appears.

ADVISORY COMMITTEE COMMENTARY

Under Canon 6D(3)(d), "one side" means a category of persons such as landlords, tenants, or litigants exclusively of one gender.

(4) After a temporary judge who has determined himself or herself to be disqualified from serving under Canon 6D(3)(a)–(d) has disclosed the basis for his or her disqualification on the record, the parties and their lawyers may agree to waive the disqualification and the temporary judge may accept the waiver. The temporary judge shall not seek to induce a waiver and shall avoid any effort to discover which lawyers or parties favored or opposed a waiver.

ADVISORY COMMITTEE COMMENTARY

Provisions addressing waiver of mandatory disqualifications or limitations, late discovery of grounds for disqualification or limitation, notification of the court when a disqualification or limitation applies, and requests for disqualification by the parties are located in rule 2.818 of the California Rules of Court. Rule 2.818 states that the waiver must be in writing, must recite the basis for the disqualification or limitation, and must state that it was knowingly made. It also states that the waiver is effective only when signed by all parties and their attorneys and filed in the record.

(5) A temporary judge, referee, or court-appointed arbitrator shall, from the time of notice and acceptance of appointment until termination of the appointment:

(a) In all proceedings, disclose in writing or on the record information as required by law, or information that the parties or their lawyers might reasonably consider relevant to the question of disqualification under Canon 6D(3), including personal or professional relationships known to the temporary judge, referee, or court-appointed arbitrator that he or she or his or her law firm has had with a party, lawyer, or law firm in the current proceeding, even though the temporary judge concludes that there is no actual basis for disqualification; and

(b) In all proceedings, disclose in writing or on the record membership of the temporary judge, referee, or court-appointed arbitrator, in any organization that practices invidious discrimination on the basis of race, sex, religion, national origin, or sexual orientation, except for membership in a religious or an official military organization of the United States and membership in a nonprofit youth organization* so long as membership does not violate Canon 4A [conduct of extrajudicial activities].

(6) A temporary judge, referee, or court-appointed arbitrator, from the time of notice and acceptance of appointment until the case is no longer pending in any court, shall not make any public comment about a pending or impending proceeding in which the temporary judge, referee, or court-appointed arbitrator has been engaged, and shall not make any nonpublic comment that might substantially interfere with such proceeding. The temporary judge, referee, or court-appointed arbitrator shall require similar abstention on the part of court personnel subject to his or her control. This Canon does not prohibit the following:

(a) Statements made in the course of the official duties of the temporary judge, referee, or court-appointed arbitrator; and

(b) Explanations for public information about the procedures of the court.

(7) From the time of appointment and continuing for two years after the case is no longer pending in any court, a temporary judge, referee, or court-appointed arbitrator shall under no circumstances accept a gift, bequest, or favor from a party, person, or entity whose interests have come before the temporary judge, referee, or court-appointed arbitrator in the matter. The temporary judge, referee, or court-appointed arbitrator shall discourage family members residing in the household of the temporary judge, referee, or court-appointed arbitrator from accepting any benefits from such parties, persons or entities during the time period stated in this subdivision. The demand for or receipt by a temporary judge, referee, or court-appointed arbitrator of a fee for his or her services rendered or to be rendered shall not be a violation of this Canon.

(8) A temporary judge, referee, or court-appointed arbitrator shall, from time of notice and acceptance of appointment and continuing indefinitely after the termination of the appointment:

(a) Comply with Canons 3(B)(11) [no disclosure of nonpublic information acquired in a judicial capacity] (except as required by law); and

(b) Not commend or criticize jurors sitting in a proceeding before the temporary judge, referee, or court-appointed arbitrator for their verdict other than in a court order or opinion in such proceeding, but may express appreciation to jurors for their service to the judicial system and the community.

(9)(a) A temporary judge appointed under rule 2.810 of the California Rules of Court, from the time of appointment and continuing indefinitely after the termination of the appointment, shall not use his or her title or service as a temporary judge as a description of the lawyer's current or former principal profession, vocation, or occupation on a ballot designation for judicial or other elected office, in an advertisement about

* See, Terminology.

the lawyer's law firm or business, or on a letterhead, business card, or other document that is distributed to the public identifying the lawyer or the lawyer's law firm.

(b) This Canon does not prohibit a temporary judge appointed under rule 2.810 of the California Rules of Court from using his or her title or service as a temporary judge on an application to serve as a temporary judge, including an application in other courts, on an application for employment or for an appointment to a judicial position, on an individual resume or a descriptive statement submitted in connection with an application for employment or for appointment or election to a judicial position, or in response to a request for information about the public service in which the lawyer has engaged.

(10) A temporary judge, referee, or court-appointed arbitrator shall comply with Canon 6D(2) until the appointment has been terminated formally or until there is no reasonable probability that the temporary judge, referee, or court-appointed arbitrator will further participate in the matter. A rebuttable presumption that the appointment has been formally terminated shall arise if, within one year from the appointment or from the date of the last hearing scheduled in the matter, whichever is later, neither the appointing court nor counsel for any party in the matter has informed the temporary judge, referee, or court-appointed arbitrator that the appointment remains in effect.

(11) A lawyer who has been a temporary judge, referee, or court-appointed arbitrator in a matter shall not accept any representation relating to the matter without the informed written consent of all parties.

(12) When by reason of serving as a temporary judge, referee, or court-appointed arbitrator in a matter, he or she has received confidential information from a party, the person shall not, without the informed written consent of the party, accept employment in another matter in which the confidential information is material.

Advisory Committee Commentary

Any exceptions to the Canons do not excuse a judicial officer's separate statutory duty to disclose information that may result in the judicial officer's recusal or disqualification.

E. Judicial Candidate. A candidate* for judicial office shall comply with the provisions of Canon 5.

F. Time for Compliance A person to whom this Code becomes applicable shall comply immediately with all provisions of this Code except Canons 4D(2) and 4F and shall comply with these Canons as soon as reasonably possible and shall do so in any event within a period of one year.

Advisory Committee Commentary

If serving as a fiduciary* when selected as a judge, a new judge may, notwithstanding the prohibitions in Canon 4F, continue to serve as fiduciary* but only for that period of time necessary to avoid adverse consequences to the beneficiary of the fiduciary relationship and in no event longer than one year. Similarly, if engaged at the time of

* See, Terminology.

judicial selection in a business activity, a new judge may, notwithstanding the prohibitions in Canon 4D(2), continue in that activity for a reasonable period but in no event longer than one year.

G. [Repealed].

H. Judges on Leave Running for Other Public Office.

A judge who is on leave while running for other public office pursuant to article VI, section 17 of the California Constitution shall comply with all provisions of this Code, except for the following, insofar as the conduct relates to the campaign for public office for which the judge is on leave:

2B(2)—Leading the prestige of judicial office to advance the judge's personal interest

2B(4)—Using the judicial title in written communications intended to advance the judge's personal interest

4C(1)—Appearing at public hearings

5—Engaging in political activity (including soliciting and accepting campaign contributions for the other public office).

Advisory Committee Commentary

These exceptions are applicable only during the time the judge is on leave while running for other public office. All of the provisions of this Code will become applicable at the time a judge resumes his or her position as a judge.

Conduct during elections for judicial office is governed by Canon 5.

CALIFORNIA RULE ON CONFIDENTIALITY OF PROCEEDINGS BEFORE THE COMMISSION ON JUDICIAL PERFORMANCE

(as amended effective 5/22/07)

RULE 102. Confidentiality and Disclosure

(a) (Scope of rule) Except as provided in this rule, all papers filed with and proceedings before the commission shall be confidential. Nothing in this rule prohibits the respondent judge or anyone other than a commission member or member of commission staff from making statements regarding the judge's conduct underlying a complaint or proceeding.

(b) (Disclosure after institution of formal proceedings) When the commission institutes formal proceedings, the following shall not be confidential:

(1) The notice of formal proceedings and all subsequent papers filed with the commission and the special masters, all stipulations entered, all findings of fact and conclusions of law made by the special masters and by the commission, and all determinations of removal, censure and public admonishment made by the commission;

(2) The formal hearing before the special masters and the appearance before the commission.

(c) (Explanatory statements) The commission may issue explanatory statements under article VI, section 18(k) of the California Constitution.

(d) (Submission of proposed statement of clarification and correction regarding commission proceedings by judge) Notwithstanding rule 102(a), if public reports concerning a commission proceeding result in substantial unfairness to the judge involved in the proceeding, including unfairness resulting from reports which are false or materially misleading or inaccurate, the involved judge may submit a proposed statement of clarification and correction to the commission and request its issuance. The commission shall either issue the requested statement, advise the judge in writing that it declines to issue the requested statement, or issue a modified statement.

(e) (Disclosure to complainant) Upon completion of an investigation or proceeding, the commission shall disclose to the person complaining against the judge that the commission (1) has found no basis for action against the judge or determined not to proceed further in this matter, (2) has taken an appropriate corrective action, the nature of which shall not be disclosed, or (3) has publicly admonished, censured, removed, or retired the judge, or has found the person unfit to serve as a subordinate judicial officer. Where a matter is referred to the commission by a presiding judge or other public official in his or her official capacity, disclosure under this subdivision concerning that matter shall be made to the individual serving in that office at the time the matter is concluded. The name of the judge shall not be used in any written communication to the complainant, unless formal proceedings have been instituted or unless the complainant is a presiding judge or other public official in his or her official capacity. Written communications in which the judge's name is not used shall include the date of the complaint as a cross-reference.

(f) (Public safety) When the commission receives information concerning a threat to the safety of any person or persons, information concerning such a threat may be provided to the person threatened, to persons or organizations responsible for the safety of the person threatened, and to law enforcement and/or any appropriate prosecutorial agency.

(g) (Disclosure of information to prosecuting authorities) The commission may release to prosecuting authorities at any time information which reveals possible criminal conduct by the judge or former judge or by any other individual or entity.

(h) (Disclosure of records of disciplinary action to public entity upon request or consent of judge) If a judge or former judge requests or consents to release of commission records to a public entity, the commission may release that judge's records.

(i) (Disclosure of records of disciplinary action to appointing authorities) The commission shall, upon request, provide to the Governor of any State of the Union, the President of the United States, or the Commission on Judicial Appointments the text of any private admonishment or advisory letter issued after March 1, 1995 or any other disciplinary action together with any information that the commission deems necessary to a full understanding of the commission's action, with respect to any applicant under consideration for any judicial appointment, provided that:

(1) The request is in writing; and

(2) Any information released to the appointing authority is simultaneously provided to the applicant.

All information disclosed to appointing authorities under this subdivision remains privileged and confidential. Private admonishments and advisory letters issued before March 1, 1995 shall only be disclosed under this section with the judge's written consent.

(j) (Disclosure of information regarding pending proceedings to appointing authorities) The commission may, upon request, in the interest of justice or to maintain public confidence in the administration of justice, provide to the Governor of any State of the Union, the President of the United States, the Commission on Judicial Appointments, or any other state or federal authorities responsible for judicial appointments information concerning any pending investigation or proceeding with respect to any applicant under consideration for any judicial appointment, provided that:

(1) The request is in writing; and

(2) Any information released to the appointing authority is simultaneously provided to the applicant.

If a disclosure about a pending matter is made and that matter subsequently is closed by the commission without discipline being imposed, disclosure of the latter fact shall be made promptly to the appointing authority and the judge.

All information disclosed to appointing authorities under this subdivision remains privileged and confidential.

(k) (Disclosure of information to regulatory agencies upon retirement or resignation) If a judge retires or resigns from office or if a subordinate judicial officer retires, resigns or is terminated from employment after a complaint is filed with the commission, or if a complaint is filed after the retirement, resignation or termination, the commission may, in the interest of justice or to maintain public confidence in the administration of justice, release information concerning the complaint, investigation and proceedings to the State Bar or to other regulatory agencies, provided that the commission has commenced a preliminary investigation or other proceeding and the judge or subordinate judicial officer has had an opportunity to respond to the commission's inquiry or preliminary investigation letter.

(*l*) (Disclosure of information about subordinate judicial officers to presiding judges) The commission may release to a presiding judge or his or her designee information concerning a complaint, investigation or disposition involving a subordinate judicial officer, consistent with the commission's jurisdiction under article VI, section 18.1 of the California Constitution.

(m) (Disclosure of information regarding disciplinary action and pending proceedings to the Chief Justice) With respect to any judge who is under consideration for judicial assignment following retirement or resignation, or is sitting on assignment, the commission may, upon the request of the Chief Justice of California and with the consent of that judge, in the interest of justice or to maintain public confidence in the administration of justice, provide the Chief Justice information concerning any record of disciplinary action or any pending investigation or proceeding with respect to that judge, provided that:

(1) The request and consent are in writing;

(2) If the disclosure involves a pending investigation or proceeding, the judge has had an opportunity to respond to the pending investigation or proceeding; and

(3) Any information released to the Chief Justice is simultaneously provided to the judge seeking assignment.

If the disclosure involves disciplinary action, the commission may include any information the commission deems necessary to a full understanding of its action.

If a disclosure about a pending matter is made and that matter subsequently is closed by the commission without discipline being imposed, disclosure of the latter fact shall be made promptly to the Chief Justice and the judge.

All information disclosed to the Chief Justice under this subdivision remains privileged and confidential.

(n) (Disclosure of information to presiding judges about possible lack of capacity or other inability to perform) The commission may release to a presiding judge or his or her designee information concerning an investigation involving possible lack of capacity or other inability to perform judicial duties on the part of a judge of that court, except that no confidential medical information concerning the judge may be released.

SELECTED FEDERAL STATUTES
APPLICABLE TO FEDERAL JUDGES

1. 28 U.S.C.A. § 47

§ 47. Disqualification of trial judge to hear appeal

No judge shall hear or determine an appeal from the decision of a case or issue tried by him.

2. 28 U.S.C.A. § 144

§ 144. Bias or prejudice of judge

Whenever a party to any proceeding in a district court makes and files a timely and sufficient affidavit that the judge before whom the matter is pending has a personal bias or prejudice either against him or in favor of any adverse party, such judge shall proceed no further therein, but another judge shall be assigned to hear such proceeding.

The affidavit shall state the facts and the reasons for the belief that bias or prejudice exists, and shall be filed not less than ten days before the beginning of the term at which the proceeding is to be heard, or good cause shall be shown for failure to file it within such time. A party may file only one such affidavit in any case. It shall be accompanied by a certificate of counsel of record stating that it is made in good faith.

3. 28 U.S.C.A. § 454

§ 454. Practice of law by justices and judges

Any justice or judge appointed under the authority of the United States who engages in the practice of law is guilty of a high misdemeanor.

4. 28 U.S.C.A. § 455

§ 455. Disqualification of justice, judge, or magistrate judge

(a) Any justice, judge, or magistrate judge of the United States shall disqualify himself in any proceeding in which his impartiality might reasonably be questioned.

(b) He shall also disqualify himself in the following circumstances:

(1) Where he has a personal bias or prejudice concerning a party, or personal knowledge of disputed evidentiary facts concerning the proceeding;

(2) Where in private practice he served as lawyer in the matter in controversy, or a lawyer with whom he previously practiced law served

during such association as a lawyer concerning the matter, or the judge or such lawyer has been a material witness concerning it;

(3) Where he has served in governmental employment and in such capacity participated as counsel, adviser or material witness concerning the proceeding or expressed an opinion concerning the merits of the particular case in controversy;

(4) He knows that he, individually or as a fiduciary, or his spouse or minor child residing in his household, has a financial interest in the subject matter in controversy or in a party to the proceeding, or any other interest that could be substantially affected by the outcome of the proceeding;

(5) He or his spouse, or a person within the third degree of relationship to either of them, or the spouse of such a person:

   (i) Is a party to the proceeding, or an officer, director, or trustee of a party;

   (ii) Is acting as a lawyer in the proceeding;

   (iii) Is known by the judge to have an interest that could be substantially affected by the outcome of the proceeding;

   (iv) Is to the judge's knowledge likely to be a material witness in the proceeding.

(c) A judge should inform himself about his personal and fiduciary financial interests, and make a reasonable effort to inform himself about the personal financial interests of his spouse and minor children residing in his household.

(d) For the purposes of this section the following words or phrases shall have the meaning indicated:

   (1) "proceeding" includes pretrial, trial, appellate review, or other stages of litigation;

   (2) the degree of relationship is calculated according to the civil law system;

   (3) "fiduciary" includes such relationships as executor, administrator, trustee, and guardian;

   (4) "financial interest" means ownership of a legal or equitable interest, however small, or a relationship as director, adviser, or other active participant in the affairs of a party, except that:

      (i) Ownership in a mutual or common investment fund that holds securities is not a "financial interest" in such securities unless the judge participates in the management of the fund;

      (ii) An office in an educational, religious, charitable, fraternal, or civic organization is not a "financial interest" in securities held by the organization;

(iii) The proprietary interest of a policyholder in a mutual insurance company, of a depositor in a mutual savings association, or a similar proprietary interest, is a "financial interest" in the organization only if the outcome of the proceeding could substantially affect the value of the interest;

(iv) Ownership of government securities is a "financial interest" in the issuer only if the outcome of the proceeding could substantially affect the value of the securities.

(e) No justice, judge, or magistrate judge shall accept from the parties to the proceeding a waiver of any ground for disqualification enumerated in subsection (b). Where the ground for disqualification arises only under subsection (a), waiver may be accepted provided it is preceded by a full disclosure on the record of the basis for disqualification.

(f) Notwithstanding the preceding provisions of this section, if any justice, judge, magistrate judge, or bankruptcy judge to whom a matter has been assigned would be disqualified, after substantial judicial time has been devoted to the matter, because of the appearance or discovery, after the matter was assigned to him or her, that he or she individually or as a fiduciary, or his or her spouse or minor child residing in his or her household, has a financial interest in a party (other than an interest that could be substantially affected by the outcome), disqualification is not required if the justice, judge, magistrate judge, bankruptcy judge, spouse or minor child, as the case may be, divests himself or herself of the interest that provides the grounds for the disqualification.

5. 5 U.S.C.A. APPENDIX 4, §§ 101–111 (Excerpts)

FINANCIAL DISCLOSURE REQUIREMENTS OF FEDERAL PERSONNEL

§ 101. Persons required to file

(a) Within thirty days of assuming the position of an officer or employee described in subsection (f), an individual shall file a report containing the information described in section 102(b) unless the individual has left another position described in subsection (f) within thirty days prior to assuming such new position or has already filed a report under this title with respect to nomination for the new position or as a candidate for the position.

(b)(1) Within five days of the transmittal by the President to the Senate of the nomination of an individual (other than an individual nominated for appointment to a position as a Foreign Service Officer or a grade or rank in the uniformed services for which the pay grade prescribed by section 201 of title 37, United States Code, is O–6 or below) to a position, appointment to which requires the advice and consent of the Senate, such individual shall file a report containing the information described in section 102(b). Such individual shall, not later than the date of the first hearing to consider the nomination of such individual, make current the report filed pursuant to this paragraph by filing the information required by section 102(a)(1)(A) with respect to income and honoraria received as of the date which occurs five days before the date of such hearing. Nothing in this Act shall prevent any Congressional committee from requesting, as a condition of confirmation, any additional financial information from any Presidential nominee whose nomination has been referred to that committee.

(**2**) An individual whom the President or the President-elect has publicly announced he intends to nominate to a position may file the report required by paragraph (1) at any time after that public announcement, but not later than is required under the first sentence of such paragraph.

(**c**) Within thirty days of becoming a candidate as defined in section 301 of the Federal Campaign Act of 1971, in a calendar year for nomination or election to the office of President, Vice President, or Member of Congress, or on or before May 15 of that calendar year, whichever is later, but in no event later than 30 days before the election, and on or before May 15 of each successive year an individual continues to be a candidate, an individual other than an incumbent President, Vice President, or Member of Congress shall file a report containing the information described in section 102(b). Notwithstanding the preceding sentence, in any calendar year in which an individual continues to be a candidate for any office but all elections for such office relating to such candidacy were held in prior calendar years, such individual need not file a report unless he becomes a candidate for another vacancy in that office or another office during that year.

(**d**) Any individual who is an officer or employee described in subsection (f) during any calendar year and performs the duties of his position or office for a period in excess of sixty days in that calendar year shall file on or before May 15 of the succeeding year a report containing the information described in section 102(a).

(**e**) Any individual who occupies a position described in subsection (f) shall, on or before the thirtieth day after termination of employment in such position, file a report containing the information described in section 102(a) covering the preceding calendar year if the report required by subsection (d) has not been filed and covering the portion of the calendar year in which such termination occurs up to the date the individual left such office or position, unless such individual has accepted employment in another position described in subsection (f).

(**f**) The officers and employees referred to in subsections (a), (d), and (e) are—

(**1**) the President;

(**2**) the Vice President;

(**3**) each officer or employee in the executive branch, including a special Government employee as defined in section 202 of title 18, United States Code, who occupies a position classified above GS–15 of the

General Schedule or, in the case of positions not under the General Schedule, for which the rate of basic pay is equal to or greater than 120 percent of the minimum rate of basic pay payable for GS–15 of the General Schedule; each member of a uniformed service whose pay grade is at or in excess of O–7 under section 201 of title 37, United States Code; and each officer or employee in any other position determined by the Director of the Office of Government Ethics to be of equal classification;

(**4**) each employee appointed pursuant to section 3105 of title 5, United States Code;

(**5**) any employee not described in paragraph (3) who is in a position in the executive branch which is excepted from the competitive service by reason of being of a confidential or policymaking character, except that the Director of the Office of Government Ethics may, by regulation, exclude from the application of this paragraph any individual, or group of individuals, who are in such positions, but only in cases in which the Director determines such exclusion would not affect adversely the integrity of the Government or the public's confidence in the integrity of the Government;

(**6**) the Postmaster General, the Deputy Postmaster General, each Governor of the Board of Governors of the United States Postal Service and each officer or employee of the United States Postal Service or Postal Regulatory Commission who occupies a position for which the rate of basic pay is equal to or greater than 120 percent of the minimum rate of basic pay payable for GS–15 of the General Schedule;

(**7**) the Director of the Office of Government Ethics and each designated agency ethics official;

(**8**) any civilian employee not described in paragraph (3), employed in the Executive Office of the President (other than a special government employee) who holds a commission of appointment from the President;

(**9**) a Member of Congress as defined under section 109(12);

(**10**) an officer or employee of the Congress as defined under section 109(13);

(**11**) a judicial officer as defined under section 109(10); and

(**12**) a judicial employee as defined under section 109(8).

(**g**)(**1**) Reasonable extensions of time for filing any report may be granted under procedures prescribed by the supervising ethics office for each branch, but the total of such extensions shall not exceed ninety days.

* * *

(**i**) The supervising ethics office for each branch may grant a publicly available request for a waiver of any reporting requirement under this section for an individual who is expected to perform or has performed the duties of his office or position less than one hundred and thirty days in a calendar year, but only if the supervising ethics office determines that—

(**1**) such individual is not a full-time employee of the Government,

(**2**) such individual is able to provide services specially needed by the Government,

(**3**) it is unlikely that the individual's outside employment or financial interests will create a conflict of interest, and

(**4**) public financial disclosure by such individual is not necessary in the circumstances.

§ 102.   Contents of reports

(**a**) Each report filed pursuant to section 101(d) and (e) shall include a full and complete statement with respect to the following:

(**1**)(**A**) The source, type, and amount or value of income (other than income referred to in subparagraph (B)) from any source (other than from current employment by the United States Government), and the source, date, and amount of honoraria from any source, received during the preceding calendar year, aggregating $200 or more in value and, effective January 1, 1991, the source, date, and amount of payments made to charitable organizations in lieu of honoraria, and the reporting individual shall simultaneously file with the applicable supervising ethics office, on a confidential basis, a corresponding list of recipients of all such payments, together with the dates and amounts of such payments.

(**B**) The source and type of income which consists of dividends, rents, interest, and capital gains, received during the preceding calendar year which exceeds $200 in amount or value, and an indication of which of the following categories the amount or value of such item of income is within:

(**i**) not more than $1,000,

(**ii**) greater than $1,000 but not more than $2,500,

(**iii**) greater than $2,500 but not more than $5,000,

(**iv**) greater than $5,000 but not more than $15,000,

(**v**) greater than $15,000 but not more than $50,000,

(**vi**) greater than $50,000 but not more than $100,000,

(**vii**) greater than $100,000 but not more than $1,000,000,

(**viii**) greater than $1,000,000 but not more than $5,000,000, or

(**ix**) greater than $5,000,000.

(**2**)(**A**) The identity of the source, a brief description, and the value of all gifts aggregating more than the minimal value as established by section 7342(a)(5) of title 5, United States Code, or $250, whichever is greater, received from any source other than a relative of the reporting individual during the preceding calendar year, except that any food, lodging, or entertainment received as personal hospitality of an individual need not be reported, and any gift with a fair market value of $100 or less, as adjusted at the same time and by the same percentage as the minimal value is adjusted, need not be aggregated for purposes of this subparagraph.

(B) The identity of the source and a brief description (including a travel itinerary, dates, and nature of expenses provided) of reimbursements received from any source aggregating more than the minimal value as established by section 7342(a)(5) of title 5, United States Code, or $250, whichever is greater and received during the preceding calendar year.

(C) In an unusual case, a gift need not be aggregated under subparagraph (A) if a publicly available request for a waiver is granted.

(3) The identity and category of value of any interest in property held during the preceding calendar year in a trade or business, or for investment or the production of income, which has a fair market value which exceeds $1,000 as of the close of the preceding calendar year, excluding any personal liability owned to the reporting individual by a spouse, or by a parent, brother, sister, or child of the reporting individual or of the reporting individual's spouse, or any deposits aggregating $5,000 or less in a personal savings account. For purposes of this paragraph, a personal savings account shall include any certificate of deposit or any other form of deposit in a bank, savings and loan association, credit union, or similar financial institution.

(4) The identity and category of value of the total liabilities owed to any creditor other than a spouse, or a parent, brother, sister, or child of the reporting individual or of the reporting individual's spouse which exceed $10,000 at any time during the preceding calendar year, excluding—

(A) any mortgage secured by real property which is a personal residence of the reporting individual or his spouse; and

(B) any loan secured by a personal motor vehicle, household furniture, or appliances, which loan does not exceed the purchase price of the item which secures it.

With respect to revolving charge accounts, only those with an outstanding liability which exceeds $10,000 as of the close of the preceding calendar year need be reported under this paragraph.

(5) Except as provided in this paragraph, a brief description, the date, and category of value of any purchase, sale or exchange during the preceding calendar year which exceeds $1,000—

(A) in real property, other than property used solely as a personal residence of the reporting individual or his spouse; or

(B) in stocks, bonds, commodities futures, and other forms of securities.

Reporting is not required under this paragraph of any transaction solely by and between the reporting individual, his spouse, or dependent children.

(6)(A) The identity of all positions held on or before the date of filing during the current calendar year (and, for the first report filed by an individual, during the two-year period preceding such calendar year) as an officer, director, trustee, partner, proprietor, representative, employee, or consultant of any corporation, company, firm, partnership, or other business enterprise, any nonprofit organization, any labor organization, or any educational or other institution other than the United States. This subparagraph shall not require the reporting of positions held in any religious, social, fraternal, or political entity and positions solely of an honorary nature.

(B) If any person, other than the United States Government, paid a nonelected reporting individual compensation in excess of $5,000 in any of the two calendar years prior to the calendar year during which the individual files his first report under this title, the individual shall include in the report—

    (i) the identity of each source of such compensation; and

    (ii) a brief description of the nature of the duties performed or services rendered by the reporting individual for each such source.

The preceding sentence shall not require any individual to include in such report any information which is considered confidential as a result of a privileged relationship, established by law, between such individual and any person nor shall it require an individual to report any information with respect to any person for whom services were provided by any firm or association of which such individual was a member, partner, or employee unless such individual was directly involved in the provision of such services.

(7) A description of the date, parties to, and terms of any agreement or arrangement with respect to (A) future employment; (B) a leave of absence during the period of the reporting individual's Government service; (C) continuation of payments by a former employer other than the United States Government; and (D) continuing participation in an employee welfare or benefit plan maintained by a former employer.

(8) The category of the total cash value of any interest of the reporting individual in a qualified blind trust, unless the trust instrument was executed prior to July 24, 1995 and precludes the beneficiary from receiving information on the total cash value of any interest in the qualified blind trust.

(b)(1) Each report filed pursuant to subsections (a), (b), and (c) of section 101 shall include a full and complete statement with respect to the information required by—

(A) paragraph (1) of subsection (a) for the year of filing and the preceding calendar year,

(B) paragraphs (3) and (4) of subsection (a) as of the date specified in the report but which is less than thirty-one days before the filing date, and

(C) paragraphs (6) and (7) of subsection (a) as of the filing date but for periods described in such paragraphs.

(2)(A) In lieu of filling out one or more schedules of a financial disclosure form, an individual may supply the required information in an alternative format, pursuant to either rules adopted by the supervising ethics office for the branch in which such individual serves or pursuant to a specific written determination by such office for a reporting individual.

(B) In lieu of indicating the category of amount or value of any item contained in any report filed under this title, a reporting individual may indicate the exact dollar amount of such item.

(c) In the case of any individual described in section 101(e), any reference to the preceding calendar year shall be considered also to include that part of the calendar year of filing up to the date of the termination of employment.

(d)(1) The categories for reporting the amount or value of the items covered in paragraphs (3), (4), (5), and (8) of subsection (a) are as follows:

(A) not more than $15,000;

(B) greater than $15,000 but not more than $50,000;

(C) greater than $50,000 but not more than $100,000;

(D) greater than $100,000 but not more than $250,000;

(E) greater than $250,000 but not more than $500,000;

(F) greater than $500,000 but not more than $1,000,000;

(G) greater than $1,000,000 but not more than $5,000,000;

(H) greater than $5,000,000 but not more than $25,000,000;

(I) greater than $25,000,000 but not more than $50,000,000; and

(J) greater than $50,000,000.

(2) For the purposes of paragraph (3) of subsection (a) if the current value of an interest in real property (or an interest in a real estate partnership) is not ascertainable without an appraisal, an individual may list (A) the date of purchase and the purchase price of the interest in the real property, or (B) the assessed value of the real property for tax purposes, adjusted to reflect the market value of the property used for the assessment if the assessed value is computed at less than 100 percent of such market value, but such individual shall include in his report a full and complete description of the method used to determine such assessed value, instead of specifying a category of value pursuant to paragraph (1) of this subsection. If the current value of any other item required to be reported under paragraph (3) of subsection (a) is not ascertainable without an appraisal, such individual may list the book value of a corporation whose stock is not publicly traded, the net worth of a business partnership, the equity value of an individually owned business, or with respect to other holdings, any recognized indication of value, but such individual shall include in his report a full and complete description of the method used in determining such value. In lieu of any value referred to in the preceding sentence, an individual may list the assessed value of the item for tax purposes, adjusted to reflect the market value of the item used for the assessment if the assessed value is computed at less than 100 percent of such market value, but a full and complete description of the method used in determining such assessed value shall be included in the report.

(e)(1) Except as provided in the last sentence of this paragraph, each report required by section 101 shall also contain information listed in paragraphs (1) through (5) of subsection (a) of this section respecting the spouse or dependent child of the reporting individual as follows:

(A) The source of items of earned income earned by a spouse from any person which exceed $1,000 and the source and amount of any honoraria received by a spouse, except that, with respect to earned income (other than honoraria), if the spouse is self-employed in business or a profession, only the nature of such business or profession need be reported.

(B) All information required to be reported in subsection (a)(1)(B) with respect to income derived by a spouse or dependent child from any asset held by the spouse or dependent child and reported pursuant to subsection (a)(3).

(C) In the case of any gifts received by a spouse or dependent child which are not received totally independent of the relationship of the spouse or dependent child to the reporting individual, the identity of the source and a brief description of gifts of transportation, lodging, food, or entertainment and a brief description and the value of other gifts.

(D) In the case of any reimbursements received by a spouse or dependent child which are not received totally independent of the relationship of the spouse or dependent child to the reporting individual, the identity of the source and a brief description of each such reimbursement.

(E) In the case of items described in paragraphs (3) through (5) of subsection (a), all information required to be reported under these paragraphs other than items (i) which the reporting individual certifies represent the spouse's or dependent child's sole financial interest or responsibility and which the reporting individual has no knowledge of, (ii) which are not in any way, past or present, derived from the income, assets, or activities of the reporting individual, and (iii) from which the reporting individual neither derives, nor expects to derive, any financial or economic benefit.

(F) For purposes of this section, categories with amounts or values greater than $1,000,000 set forth in sections 102(a)(1)(B) and 102(d)(1) shall apply to the income, assets, or liabilities of spouses and dependent children only if the income, assets, or liabilities are held jointly with the reporting individual. All other income, assets, or liabilities of the spouse or dependent children required to be reported under this section in an amount or value greater than $1,000,000 shall be categorized only as an amount or value greater than $1,000,000.

Reports required by subsections (a), (b), and (c) of section 101 shall, with respect to the spouse and dependent child of the reporting individual, only contain information listed in paragraphs (1), (3), and (4) of subsection (a), as specified in this paragraph.

(2) No report shall be required with respect to a spouse living separate and apart from the reporting individual with the intention of terminating the marriage or providing for permanent separation; or with respect to any income or obligations of an individual arising from the dissolution of his marriage or the permanent separation from his spouse.

(f)(1) Except as provided in paragraph (2), each reporting individual shall report the information required to be reported pursuant to subsections (a), (b), and (c) of this section with respect to the holdings of and the income from a trust or other financial arrangement from which income is received by, or with respect to which a beneficial interest in principal or income is held by, such individual, his spouse, or any dependent child.

(2) A reporting individual need not report the holdings of or the source of income from any of the holdings of—

(A) any qualified blind trust (as defined in paragraph (3));

(B) a trust—

(i) which was not created directly by such individual, his spouse, or any dependent child, and

(ii) the holdings or sources of income of which such individual, his spouse, and any dependent child have no knowledge of; or

(C) an entity described under the provisions of paragraph (8),

but such individual shall report the category of the amount of income received by him, his spouse, or any dependent child from the trust or other entity under subsection (a)(1)(B) of this section.

(3) For purposes of this subsection, the term "qualified blind trust" includes any trust in which a reporting individual, his spouse, or any minor or dependent child has a beneficial interest in the principal or income, and which meets the following requirements:

(A)(i) The trustee of the trust and any other entity designated in the trust instrument to perform fiduciary duties is a financial institution, an attorney, a certified public accountant, a broker, or an investment advisor who—

(I) is independent of and not associated with any interested party so that the trustee or other person cannot be controlled or influenced in the administration of the trust by any interested party; and

(II) is not and has not been an employee of or affiliated with any interested party and is not a partner of, or involved in any joint venture or other investment with, any interested party; and

(III) is not a relative of any interested party.

(ii) Any officer or employee of a trustee or other entity who is involved in the management or control of the trust—

(I) is independent of and not associated with any interested party so that such officer or employee cannot be controlled or influenced in the administration of the trust by any interested party;

(II) is not a partner of, or involved in any joint venture or other investment with, any interested party; and

(III) is not a relative of any interested party.

(B) Any asset transferred to the trust by an interested party is free of any restriction with respect to its transfer or sale unless such restriction is expressly approved by the supervising ethics office of the reporting individual.

(C) The trust instrument which establishes the trust provides that—

(i) except to the extent provided in subparagraph (B) of this paragraph, the trustee in the exercise of his authority and discretion to manage and control the assets of the trust shall not consult or notify any interested party;

(ii) the trust shall not contain any asset the holding of which by an interested party is prohibited by any law or regulation;

(iii) the trustee shall promptly notify the reporting individual and his supervising ethics office when the holdings of any particular asset transferred to the trust by any interested party are disposed of or when the value of such holding is less than $1,000;

(iv) the trust tax return shall be prepared by the trustee or his designee, and such return and any information relating thereto (other than the trust income summarized in appropriate categories necessary to complete an interested party's tax return), shall not be disclosed to any interested party;

(v) an interested party shall not receive any report on the holdings and sources of income of the trust, except a report at the end of each calendar quarter with respect to the total cash value of the interest of the interested party in the trust or the net income or loss of the trust or any reports necessary to enable the interested party to complete an individual tax return required by law or to provide the information required by subsection (a)(1) of this section, but such report shall not identify any asset or holding;

(vi) except for communications which solely consist of requests for distributions of cash or other unspecified assets of the trust, there shall be no direct or indirect communication between the trustee and an interested party with respect to the trust unless such communication is in writing and unless it relates only (I) to the general financial interest and needs of the interested party (including, but not limited to, an interest in maximizing income or long-term capital gain), (II) to the notification of the trustee of a law or regulation subsequently applicable to the reporting individual which prohibits the interested party from holding an asset, which notification directs that the asset not be held by the trust, or (III) to directions to the trustee to sell all of an asset initially placed in the trust by an interested party which in the determination of the reporting individual creates a conflict of interest or the appearance thereof due to the subsequent assumption of duties by the reporting individual (but nothing herein shall require any such direction); and

(vii) the interested parties shall make no effort to obtain information with respect to the holdings of the trust, including obtaining a copy of any trust tax return filed or any information relating thereto except as otherwise provided in this subsection.

(D) The proposed trust instrument and the proposed trustee is approved by the reporting individual's supervising ethics office.

(E) For purposes of this subsection, "interested party" means a reporting individual, his spouse, and any minor or dependent child; "broker" has the meaning set forth in section 3(a)(4) of the Securities and Exchange Act of 1934 (15 U.S.C. 78c(a)(4)); and "investment adviser" includes any investment adviser who, as determined under regulations prescribed by the supervising ethics office, is generally involved in his role as such an adviser in the management or control of trusts.

(F) Any trust qualified by a supervising ethics office before the effective date of title II of the Ethics Reform Act of 1989 shall continue to be governed by the law and regulations in effect immediately before such effective date.

(4)(A) An asset placed in a trust by an interested party shall be considered a financial interest of the reporting individual, for the purposes of any applicable conflict of interest statutes, regulations, or rules of the Federal Government (including section 208 of title 18, United States Code), until such time as the reporting individual is notified by the trustee that such asset has been disposed of, or has a value of less than $1,000.

(B)(i) The provisions of subparagraph (A) shall not apply with respect to a trust created for the benefit of a reporting individual, or the spouse, dependent child, or minor child of such a person, if the supervising ethics office for such reporting individual finds that—

(I) the assets placed in the trust consist of a well-diversified portfolio of readily marketable securities;

(II) none of the assets consist of securities of entities having substantial activities in the area of the reporting individual's primary area of responsibility;

(III) the trust instrument prohibits the trustee, notwithstanding the provisions of paragraphs (3)(C)(iii) and (iv) of this subsection, from making public or informing any interested party of the sale of any securities;

(IV) the trustee is given power of attorney, notwithstanding the provisions of paragraph (3)(C)(v) of this subsection, to prepare on behalf of any interested party the personal income tax returns and similar returns which may contain information relating to the trust; and

(V) except as otherwise provided in this paragraph, the trust instrument provides (or in the case of a trust established prior to the effective date of this Act which by its terms does not permit amendment, the trustee, the reporting individual, and any other interested party agree in writing) that the trust shall be administered in accordance with the requirements of this subsection and the trustee of such trust meets the requirements of paragraph (3)(A).

(ii) In any instance covered by subparagraph (B) in which the reporting individual is an individual whose nomination is being considered by a congressional committee, the reporting individual shall inform the congressional committee considering his nomination before or during the period of such individual's confirmation hearing of his intention to comply with this paragraph.

(5)(A) The reporting individual shall, within thirty days after a qualified blind trust is approved by his supervising ethics office, file with such office a copy of—

(i) the executed trust instrument of such trust (other than those provisions which relate to the testamentary disposition of the trust assets), and

(ii) a list of the assets which were transferred to such trust, including the category of value of each asset as determined under subsection (d) of this section.

This subparagraph shall not apply with respect to a trust meeting the requirements for being considered a qualified blind trust under paragraph (7) of this subsection.

(B) The reporting individual shall, within thirty days of transferring an asset (other than cash) to a previously established qualified blind trust, notify his supervising ethics office of the identity of each such asset and the category of value of each asset as determined under subsection (d) of this section.

(C) Within thirty days of the dissolution of a qualified blind trust, a reporting individual shall—

(i) notify his supervising ethics office of such dissolution, and

(ii) file with such office a copy of a list of the assets of the trust at the time of such dissolution and the category of value under subsection (d) of this section of each such asset.

(D) Documents filed under subparagraphs (A), (B), and (C) of this paragraph and the lists provided by the trustee of assets placed in the trust by an interested party which have been sold shall be made available to the public in the same manner as a report is made available under section 105 and the provisions of that section shall apply with respect to such documents and lists.

(E) A copy of each written communication with respect to the trust under paragraph (3)(C)(vi) shall be filed by the person initiating the communication with the reporting individual's supervising ethics office within five days of the date of the communication.

(6)(A) A trustee of a qualified blind trust shall not knowingly and willfully, or negligently, (i) disclose any information to an interested party with respect to such trust that may not be disclosed under paragraph (3) of this subsection; (ii) acquire any holding the ownership of which is prohibited by the trust instrument; (iii) solicit advice from any interested party with respect to such trust, which solicitation is prohibited by paragraph (3) of this subsection or the trust agreement; or (iv) fail to file any document required by this subsection.

(B) A reporting individual shall not knowingly and willfully, or negligently, (i) solicit or receive any information with respect to a qualified blind trust of which he is an interested party that may not be disclosed under paragraph (3)(C) of this subsection or (ii) fail to file any document required by this subsection.

(C)(i) The Attorney General may bring a civil action in any appropriate United States district court against any individual who knowingly and willfully violates the provisions of subparagraph (A) or (B) of this paragraph. The court in which such action is brought may assess against such individual a civil penalty in any amount not to exceed $10,000.

(ii) The Attorney General may bring a civil action in any appropriate United States district court against any individual who negligently violates the provisions of subparagraph (A) or (B) of this paragraph. The court in which such action is brought may assess against such individual a civil penalty in any amount not to exceed $5,000.

(7) Any trust may be considered to be a qualified blind trust if—

(A) the trust instrument is amended to comply with the requirements of paragraph (3) or, in the case of a trust instrument which does not by its terms permit amendment, the trustee, the reporting individual, and any other interested party agree in writing that the trust shall be administered in accordance with the requirements of this subsection and

741

the trustee of such trust meets the requirements of paragraph (3)(A); except that in the case of any interested party who is a dependent child, a parent or guardian of such child may execute the agreement referred to in this subparagraph;

(B) a copy of the trust instrument (except testamentary provisions) and a copy of the agreement referred to in subparagraph (A), and a list of the assets held by the trust at the time of approval by the supervising ethics office, including the category of value of each asset as determined under subsection (d) of this section, are filed with such office and made available to the public as provided under paragraph (5)(D) of this subsection; and

(C) the supervising ethics office determines that approval of the trust arrangement as a qualified blind trust is in the particular case appropriate to assure compliance with applicable laws and regulations.

(8) A reporting individual shall not be required to report the financial interests held by a widely held investment fund (whether such fund is a mutual fund, regulated investment company, pension or deferred compensation plan, or other investment fund), if—

(A)(i) the fund is publicly traded; or

(ii) the assets of the fund are widely diversified; and

(B) the reporting individual neither exercises control over nor has the ability to exercise control over the financial interests held by the fund.

(g) Political campaign funds, including campaign receipts and expenditures, need not be included in any report filed pursuant to this title.

(h) A report filed pursuant to subsection (a), (d), or (e) of section 101 need not contain the information described in subparagraphs (A), (B), and (C) of subsection (a)(2) with respect to gifts and reimbursements received in a period when the reporting individual was not an officer or employee of the Federal Government.

(i) A reporting individual shall not be required under this title to report—

(1) financial interests in or income derived from—

(A) any retirement system under title 5, United States Code (including the Thrift Savings Plan under subchapter III of chapter 84 of such title); or

(B) any other retirement system maintained by the United States for officers or employees of the United States, including the President, or for members of the uniformed services; or

(2) benefits received under the Social Security Act [42 U.S.C.A. § 301 et seq.].

742

§ 103. Filing of reports

(a) Except as otherwise provided in this section, the reports required under this title shall be filed by the reporting individual with the designated agency ethics official at the agency by which he is employed (or in the case of an individual described in section 101(e), was employed) or in which he will serve. The date any report is received (and the date of receipt of any supplemental report) shall be noted on such report by such official.

* * *

§ 104. Failure to file or filing false reports

(a)(1) The Attorney General may bring a civil action in any appropriate United States district court against any individual who knowingly and willfully falsifies or who knowingly and willfully fails to file or report any information that such individual is required to report pursuant to section 102. The court in which such action is brought may assess against such individual a civil penalty in any amount, not to exceed $50,000.

(2)(A) It shall be unlawful for any person to knowingly and willfully–

(i) falsify any information that such person is required to report under section 102; and

(ii) fail to file or report any information that such person is required to report under section 102.

(B) Any person who–

(i) violates subparagraph (A)(i) shall be fined under title 18, United States Code, imprisoned for not more than 1 year, or both; and

(ii) violates subparagraph (A)(ii) shall be fined under title 18, United States Code.

(b) The head of each agency, each Secretary concerned, the Director of the Office of Government Ethics, each congressional ethics committee, or the Judicial Conference, as the case may be, shall refer to the Attorney General the name of any individual which such official or committee has reasonable cause to believe has willfully failed to file a report or has willfully falsified or willfully failed to file information required to be reported. Whenever the Judicial Conference refers a name to the Attorney General under this subsection, the Judicial Conference also shall notify the judicial council of the circuit in which the named individual serves of the referral.

(c) The President, the Vice President, the Secretary concerned, the head of each agency, the Office of Personnel Management, a congressional ethics committee, and the Judicial Conference, may take any appropriate personnel or other action in accordance with applicable law or regulation against any individual failing to file a report or falsifying or failing to report information required to be reported.

(d)(1) Any individual who files a report required to be filed under this title more than 30 days after the later of—

(A) the date such report is required to be filed pursuant to the provisions of this title and the rules and regulations promulgated thereunder; or

(B) if a filing extension is granted to such individual under section 101(g), the last day of the filing extension period,

shall *** pay a filing fee of $200. All such fees shall be deposited in the miscellaneous receipts of the Treasury. The authority under this paragraph to direct the payment of a filing fee may be delegated by the supervising ethics office in the executive branch to other agencies in the executive branch.

(2) The supervising ethics office may waive the filing fee under this subsection in extraordinary circumstances.

§ 105. Custody of and public access to reports

(a) Each agency, each supervising ethics office in the executive or judicial branch, the Clerk of the House of Representatives, and the Secretary of the Senate shall make available to the public, in accordance with subsection (b), each report filed under this title with such agency or office * * *

(b)(1) Except as provided in the second sentence of this subsection, each agency, each supervising ethics office in the executive or judicial branch, the Clerk of the House of Representatives, and the Secretary of the Senate shall, within thirty days after any report is received under this title by such agency or office or by the Clerk or the Secretary of the Senate, as the case may be, permit inspection of such report by or furnish a copy of such report to any person requesting such inspection or copy. * * * The agency, office, Clerk, or Secretary of the Senate, as the case may be may require a reasonable fee to be paid in any amount which is found necessary to recover the cost of reproduction or mailing of such report excluding any salary of any employee involved in such reproduction or mailing. A copy of such report may be furnished without charge or at a reduced charge if it is determined that waiver or reduction of the fee is in the public interest.

(2) Notwithstanding paragraph (1), a report may not be made available under this section to any person nor may any copy thereof be provided under this section to any person except upon a written application by such person stating—

(A) that person's name, occupation and address;

(B) the name and address of any other person or organization on whose behalf the inspection or copy is requested; and

(C) that such person is aware of the prohibitions on the obtaining or use of the report.

Any such application shall be made available to the public throughout the period during which the report is made available to the public.

(3)(A) This section does not require the immediate and unconditional availability of reports filed by an individual described in section 109(8) or 109(10) of this Act [sections 109(8) or 109(10) or Appendix 4 of this title] if a finding is made by the Judicial Conference, in consultation with United States Marshall Service, that revealing personal and sensitive information could endanger that individual or a family member of that individual.

(B) A report may be redacted pursuant to this paragraph only—

(i) to the extent necessary to protect the individual who filed the report or a family member of that individual; and

(ii) for as long as the danger to such individual exists.

(C) The Administrative Office of the United States Courts shall submit to the Committees on the Judiciary of the House of Representatives and of the Senate an annual report with respect to the operation of this paragraph including—

(i) the total number of reports redacted pursuant to this paragraph;

(ii) the total number of individuals whose reports have been redacted pursuant to this paragraph;

(iii) the types of threats against individuals whose reports are redacted, if appropriate;

(iv) the nature or type of information redacted;

(v) what steps or procedures are in place to ensure that sufficient information is available to litigants to determine if there is a conflict of interest;

(vi) principles used to guide implementation of redaction authority; and

(vii) any public complaints received relating to redaction.

(D) The Judicial Conference, in consultation with the Department of Justice, shall issue regulations setting forth the circumstances under which redaction is appropriate under this paragraph and the procedures for redaction.

(E) This paragraph shall expire on December 31, 2009, and apply to filings through calendar year 2009.

(c)(1) It shall be unlawful for any person to obtain or use a report—

(A) for any unlawful purpose;

(B) for any commercial purpose, other than by news and communications media for dissemination to the general public;

(C) for determining or establishing the credit rating of any individual; or

(D) for use, directly or indirectly, in the solicitation of money for any political, charitable, or other purpose.

(2) The Attorney General may bring a civil action against any person who obtains or uses a report for any purpose prohibited in paragraph (1) of this subsection. The court in which such action is brought may assess against such person a penalty in any amount not to exceed $10,000. Such remedy shall be in addition to any other remedy available under statutory or common law.

(d) Any report filed with or transmitted to an agency or supervising ethics office or to the Clerk of the House of Representatives or the Secretary of the Senate pursuant to this title shall be retained by such agency or office or by the Clerk or the Secretary of the Senate, as the case may be. Such report shall be made available to the public for a period of six years after receipt of the report. After such six-year period the report shall be destroyed unless needed in an ongoing investigation, except that in the case of an individual who filed the report pursuant to section 101(b) and was not subsequently confirmed by the Senate, or who filed the report pursuant to section 101(c) and was not subsequently elected, such reports shall be destroyed one year after the individual either is no longer under consideration by the Senate or is no longer a candidate for nomination or election to the Office of President, Vice President, or as a Member of Congress, unless needed in an ongoing investigation.

§ 106. Review of reports

(a)(1) Each designated agency ethics official or Secretary concerned shall make provisions to ensure that each report filed with him under this title is reviewed within sixty days after the date of such filing, except that the Director of the Office of Government Ethics shall review only those reports required to be transmitted to him under this title within sixty days after the date of transmittal.

(2) Each congressional ethics committee and the Judicial Conference shall make provisions to ensure that each report filed under this title is reviewed within sixty days after the date of such filing.

(b)(1) If after reviewing any report under subsection (a), the Director of the Office of Government Ethics, the Secretary concerned, the designated agency ethics official, a person designated by the congressional ethics committee, or a person designated by the Judicial Conference, as the case may be, is of the opinion that on the basis of information contained in such report the individual submitting such report is in compliance with applicable laws and regulations, he shall state such opinion on the report, and shall sign such report.

(2) If the Director of the Office of Government Ethics, the Secretary concerned, the designated agency ethics official, a person designated by the congressional ethics committee, or a person designated by the Judicial Conference, after reviewing any report under subsection (a)—

(A) believes additional information is required to be submitted, he shall notify the individual submitting such report what additional information is required and the time by which it must be submitted, or

(B) is of the opinion, on the basis of information submitted, that the individual is not in compliance with applicable laws and regulations, he shall notify the individual, afford a reasonable opportunity for a written or oral response, and after consideration of such response, reach an opinion as to whether or not, on the basis of information submitted, the individual is in compliance with such laws and regulations.

(3) If the Director of the Office of Government Ethics, the Secretary concerned, the designated agency ethics official, a person designated by a congressional ethics committee, or a person designated by the Judicial Conference, reaches an opinion under paragraph (2)(B) that an individual is not in compliance with applicable laws and regulations, the official or committee shall notify the individual of that opinion and, after an opportunity for personal consultation (if practicable), determine and notify the individual of which steps, if any, would in the opinion of such official or committee be appropriate for assuring compliance with such laws and regulations and the date by which such steps should be taken. Such steps may include, as appropriate—

(A) divestiture,

(B) restitution,

(C) the establishment of a blind trust,

(D) request for an exemption under section 208(b) of title 18, United States Code, or

(E) voluntary request for transfer, reassignment, limitation of duties, or resignation.

The use of any such steps shall be in accordance with such rules or regulations as the supervising ethics office may prescribe.

(4) If steps for assuring compliance with applicable laws and regulations are not taken by the date set under paragraph (3) by an individual in a position in the executive branch (other than in the Foreign Service or the uniformed services), appointment to which requires the advice and consent of the Senate, the matter shall be referred to the President for appropriate action.

(5) If steps for assuring compliance with applicable laws and regulations are not taken by the date set under paragraph (3) by a member of the Foreign Service or the uniformed services, the Secretary concerned shall take appropriate action.

(6) If steps for assuring compliance with applicable laws and regulations are not taken by the date set under paragraph (3) by any other officer or employee, the matter shall be referred to the head of the appropriate agency, the congressional ethics committee, or the Judicial Conference, for appropriate action; except that in the case of the Postmaster General or Deputy Postmaster General, the Director of the Office of Government Ethics shall recommend to the Governors of the Board of Governors of the United States Postal Service the action to be taken.

(7) Each supervising ethics office may render advisory opinions interpreting this title within its respective jurisdiction. Notwithstanding any other provision of law, the individual to whom a public advisory opinion is rendered in accordance with this paragraph, and any other individual covered by this title who is involved in a fact situation which is indistinguishable in all material aspects, and who acts in good faith in accordance with the provisions and findings of such advisory opinion shall not, as a result of such act, be subject to any penalty or sanction provided by this title.

§ 107. Confidential reports and other additional requirements

(a)(1) Each supervising ethics office may require officers and employees under its jurisdiction (including special Government employees as defined in section 202 of title 18, United States Code) to file confidential financial disclosure reports, in such form as the supervising ethics office may prescribe. The information required to be reported under this subsection by the officers and employees of any department or agency shall be set forth in rules or regulations prescribed by the supervising ethics office, and may be less extensive than otherwise required by this title, or more extensive when determined by the supervising ethics office to be necessary and appropriate in light of sections 202 through 209 of title 18, United States Code, regulations promulgated thereunder, or the authorized activities of such officers or employees. Any individual required to file a report pursuant to section 101 shall not be required to file a confidential report pursuant to this subsection, except with respect to information which is more extensive than information otherwise required by this title. Subsections (a), (b), and (d) of section 105 shall not apply with respect to any such report.

(2) Any information required to be provided by an individual under this subsection shall be confidential and shall not be disclosed to the public.

(3) Nothing in this subsection exempts any individual otherwise covered by the requirement to file a public financial disclosure report under this title from such requirement.

(b) The provisions of this title requiring the reporting of information shall supersede any general requirement under any other provision of law or regulation with respect to the reporting of information required for purposes of preventing conflicts of interest or apparent conflicts of interest. Such provisions of this title shall not supersede the requirements of section 7342 of title 5, United States Code.

(c) Nothing in this Act requiring reporting of information shall be deemed to authorize the receipt of income, gifts, or reimbursements; the holding of assets, liabilities, or positions; or the participation in transactions that are prohibited by law, Executive order, rule, or regulation.

§ 108. Authority of Comptroller General

(**a**) The Comptroller General shall have access to financial disclosure reports filed under this title for the purposes of carrying out his statutory responsibilities.

(**b**) No later than December 31, 1992, and regularly thereafter, the Comptroller General shall conduct a study to determine whether the provisions of this title are being carried out effectively.

§ 109. Definitions

For the purposes of this title, the term—

(**1**) "congressional ethics committees" means the Select Committee on Ethics of the Senate and the Committee on Standards of Official Conduct of the House of Representatives;

(**2**) "dependent child" means, when used with respect to any reporting individual, any individual who is a son, daughter, stepson, or stepdaughter and who—

(**A**) is unmarried and under age 21 and is living in the household of such reporting individual; or

(**B**) is a dependent of such reporting individual within the meaning of section 152 of the Internal Revenue Code of 1986 [26 U.S.C.A. § 152];

(**3**) "designated agency ethics official" means an officer or employee who is designated to administer the provisions of this title within an agency;

(**4**) "executive branch" includes each Executive agency (as defined in section 105 of title 5, United States Code), other than the Government Accountability Office, and any other entity or administrative unit in the executive branch;

(**5**) "gift" means a payment, advance, forbearance, rendering, or deposit of money, or any thing of value, unless consideration of equal or greater value is received by the donor, but does not include—

(**A**) bequest and other forms of inheritance;

(**B**) suitable mementos of a function honoring the reporting individual;

(**C**) food, lodging, transportation, and entertainment provided by a foreign government within a foreign country or by the United States Government, the District of Columbia, or a State or local government or political subdivision thereof;

(**D**) food and beverages which are not consumed in connection with a gift of overnight lodging;

(**E**) communications to the offices of a reporting individual, including subscriptions to newspapers and periodicals; or

(F) consumable products provided by home-State businesses to the offices of a reporting individual who is an elected official, if those products are intended for consumption by persons other than such reporting individual;

(6) "honoraria" has the meaning given such term in section 505 of this Act;

(7) "income" means all income from whatever source derived, including but not limited to the following items: compensation for services, including fees, commissions, and similar items; gross income derived from business (and net income if the individual elects to include it); gains derived from dealings in property; interest; rents; royalties; dividends; annuities; income from life insurance and endowment contracts; pensions; income from discharge of indebtedness; distributive share of partnership income; and income from an interest in an estate or trust;

(8) "judicial employee" means any employee of the judicial branch of the Government, of the United States Sentencing Commission, of the Tax Court, of the Court of Federal Claims, of the Court of Appeals for Veterans Claims, or of the United States Court of Appeals for the Armed Forces, who is not a judicial officer and who is authorized to perform adjudicatory functions with respect to proceedings in the judicial branch, or who occupies a position for which the rate of basic pay is equal to or greater than 120 percent of the minimum rate of basic pay payable for GS–15 of the General Schedule;

(9) "Judicial Conference" means the Judicial Conference of the United States;

(10) "judicial officer" means the Chief Justice of the United States, the Associate Justices of the Supreme Court, and the judges of the United States courts of appeals, United States district courts, including the district courts in Guam, the Northern Mariana Islands, and the Virgin Islands, Court of Appeals for the Federal Circuit, Court of International Trade, Tax Court, Court of Federal Claims, Court of Appeals for Veterans Claims, United States Court of Appeals for the Armed Forces, and any court created by Act of Congress, the judges of which are entitled to hold office during good behavior;

* * *

(14) "personal hospitality of any individual" means hospitality extended for a nonbusiness purpose by an individual, not a corporation or organization, at the personal residence of that individual or his family or on property or facilities owned by that individual or his family;

(15) "reimbursement" means any payment or other thing of value received by the reporting individual, other than gifts, to cover travel-related expenses of such individual other than those which are—

(A) provided by the United States Government, the District of Columbia, or a State or local government or political subdivision thereof;

(B) required to be reported by the reporting individual under section 7342 of title 5, United States Code; or

(C) required to be reported under section 304 of the Federal Election Campaign Act of 1971 (2 U.S.C. 434);

(16) "relative" means an individual who is related to the reporting individual, as father, mother, son, daughter, brother, sister, uncle, aunt, great aunt, great uncle, first cousin, nephew, niece, husband, wife, grandfather, grandmother, grandson, granddaughter, father-in-law, mother-in-law, son-in-law, daughter-in-law, brother-in-law, sister-in-law, stepfather, stepmother, stepson, stepdaughter, stepbrother, stepsister, half brother, half sister, or who is the grandfather or grandmother of the spouse of the reporting individual, and shall be deemed to include the fiance or fiancee of the reporting individual;

* * *

(18) "supervising ethics office" means—

(A) the Select Committee on Ethics of the Senate, for Senators, officers and employees of the Senate, and other officers or employees of the legislative branch required to file financial disclosure reports with the Secretary of the Senate pursuant to section 103(h) of this title;

(B) the Committee on Standards of Official Conduct of the House of Representatives, for Members, officers and employees of the House of Representatives and other officers or employees of the legislative branch required to file financial disclosure reports with the Clerk of the House of Representatives pursuant to section 103(h) of this title;

(C) the Judicial Conference for judicial officers and judicial employees; and

(D) the Office of Government Ethics for all executive branch officers and employees; and

(19) "value" means a good faith estimate of the dollar value if the exact value is neither known nor easily obtainable by the reporting individual.

§ 110. Notice of actions taken to comply with ethics agreements

(a) In any case in which an individual agrees with that individual's designated agency ethics official, the Office of Government Ethics, a Senate confirmation committee, a congressional ethics committee, or the Judicial Conference, to take any action to comply with this Act or any other law or regulation governing conflicts of interest of, or establishing standards of conduct applicable with respect to, officers or employees of the Government, that individual shall notify in writing the designated agency ethics official, the Office of Government Ethics, the appropriate committee of the Senate, the congressional ethics committee, or the Judicial Conference, as the case may be, of any action taken by the individual pursuant to that agreement. Such notification shall be made not later than the date specified in the agreement by which action by the individual must be taken, or not later than three months after the date of the agreement, if no date for action is so specified.

(**b**) If an agreement described in subsection (a) requires that the individual recuse himself or herself from particular categories of agency or other official action, the individual shall reduce to writing those subjects regarding which the recusal agreement will apply and the process by which it will be determined whether the individual must recuse himself or herself in a specific instance. An individual shall be considered to have complied with the requirements of subsection (a) with respect to such recusal agreement if such individual files a copy of the document setting forth the information described in the preceding sentence with such individual's designated agency ethics official or the appropriate supervising ethics office within the time prescribed in the last sentence of subsection (a).

§ 111. Administration of provisions

The provisions of this title shall be administered by—

(**1**) the Director of the Office of Government Ethics, the designated agency ethics official, or the Secretary concerned, as appropriate, with regard to officers and employees described in paragraphs (1) through (8) of section 101(f);

(**2**) the Select Committee on Ethics of the Senate and the Committee on Standards of Official Conduct of the House of Representatives, as appropriate, with regard to officers and employees described in paragraphs (9) and (10) of section 101(f); and

(**3**) the Judicial Conference in the case of an officer or employee described in paragraphs (11) and (12) of section 101(f).

The Judicial Conference may delegate any authority it has under this title to an ethics committee established by the Judicial Conference.

AMERICAN BAR ASSOCIATION CANONS OF PROFESSIONAL ETHICS*

Preamble

In America, where the stability of Courts and of all departments of government rests upon the approval of the people, it is peculiarly essential that the system for establishing and dispensing Justice be developed to a high point of efficiency and so maintained that the public shall have absolute confidence in the integrity and impartiality of its administration. The future of the Republic, to a great extent, depends upon our maintenance of Justice pure and unsullied. It cannot be so maintained unless the conduct and the motives of the members of our profession are such as to merit the approval of all just men.

No code or set of rules can be framed, which will particularize all the duties of the lawyer in the varying phases of litigation or in all the relations of professional life. The following canons of ethics are adopted by the American Bar Association as a general guide, yet the enumeration of particular duties should not be construed as a denial of the existence of others equally imperative, though not specifically mentioned.

1. The Duty of the Lawyer to the Courts

It is the duty of the lawyer to maintain towards the Courts a respectful attitude, not for the sake of the temporary incumbent of the judicial office, but for the maintenance of its supreme importance. Judges, not being wholly free to defend themselves, are peculiarly entitled to receive the support of the Bar against unjust criticism and clamor. Whenever there is proper ground for serious complaint of a judicial officer, it is the right and duty of the lawyer to submit his grievances to the proper authorities. In such cases, but not otherwise, such charges should be encouraged and the person making them should be protected.

2. The Selection of Judges

It is the duty of the Bar to endeavor to prevent political considerations from outweighing judicial fitness in the selections of Judges. It should protest earnestly and actively against the appointment or election of those who are unsuitable for the Bench; and it should strive to have elevated thereto only those willing to forego other employments, whether of a business, political or other character, which may embarrass their free and fair consideration of

* These Canons, to and including Canon 32 and the recommended oath, were adopted by the American Bar Association at Its Thirty–First Annual Meeting at Seattle, Washington, on August 27, 1908. The Canons were applied, as amended, until the adoption of the Code in 1970. Reprinted with permission. Copyright © American Bar Association.

questions before them for decision. The aspiration of lawyers for judicial position should be governed by an impartial estimate of their ability to add honor to the office and not by a desire for the distinction the position may bring to themselves.

3. Attempts to Exert Personal Influence on the Court

Marked attention and unusual hospitality on the part of a lawyer to a Judge, uncalled for by the personal relations of the parties, subject both the Judge and the lawyer to misconstructions of motive and should be avoided. A lawyer should not communicate or argue privately with the Judge as to the merits of a pending cause, and he deserves rebuke and denunciation for any device or attempt to gain from a Judge special personal consideration or favor. A self-respecting independence in the discharge of professional duty, without denial or diminution of the courtesy and respect due the Judge's station, is the only proper foundation for cordial personal and official relations between Bench and Bar.

4. When Counsel for an Indigent Prisoner

A lawyer assigned as counsel for an indigent prisoner ought not to ask to be excused for any trivial reason, and should always exert his best efforts in his behalf.

5. The Defense or Prosecution of Those Accused of Crime

It is the right of the lawyer to undertake the defense of a person accused of crime, regardless of his personal opinion as to the guilt of the accused; otherwise innocent persons, victims only of suspicious circumstances, might be denied proper defense. Having undertaken such defense, the lawyer is bound, by all fair and honorable means, to present every defense that the law of the land permits, to the end that no person may be deprived of life or liberty, but by due process of law.

The primary duty of a lawyer engaged in public prosecution is not to convict, but to see that justice is done. The suppression of facts or the secreting of witnesses capable of establishing the innocence of the accused is highly reprehensible.

6. Adverse Influences and Conflicting Interests

It is the duty of a lawyer at the time of retainer to disclose to the client all the circumstances of his relations to the parties, and any interest in or connection with the controversy, which might influence the client in the selection of counsel.

It is unprofessional to represent conflicting interests, except by express consent of all concerned given after a full disclosure of the facts. Within the meaning of this canon, a lawyer represents conflicting interests when, in behalf of one client, it is his duty to contend for that which duty to another client requires him to oppose.

The obligation to represent the client with undivided fidelity and not to divulge his secrets or confidences forbids also the subsequent acceptance of retainers or employment from others in matters adversely affecting any interest of the client with respect to which confidence has been reposed.

7. Professional Colleagues and Conflicts of Opinion

A client's proffer of assistance of additional counsel should not be regarded as evidence of want of confidence, but the matter should be left to the determination of the client. A lawyer should decline association as colleague if it is objectionable to the original counsel, but if the lawyer first retained is relieved, another may come into the case.

When lawyers jointly associated in a cause cannot agree as to any matter vital to the interest of the client, the conflict of opinion should be frankly stated to him for his final determination. His decision should be accepted unless the nature of the difference makes it impracticable for the lawyer whose judgment has been overruled to co-operate effectively. In this event it is his duty to ask the client to relieve him.

Efforts, direct or indirect, in any way to encroach upon the professional employment of another lawyer, are unworthy of those who should be brethren at the Bar; but, nevertheless, it is the right of any lawyer, without fear or favor, to give proper advice to those seeking relief against unfaithful or neglectful counsel, generally after communication with the lawyer of whom the complaint is made.

8. Advising Upon the Merits of a Client's Cause

A lawyer should endeavor to obtain full knowledge of his client's cause before advising thereon, and he is bound to give a candid opinion of the merits and probable result of pending or contemplated litigation. The miscarriages to which justice is subject, by reason of surprises and disappointments in evidence and witnesses, and through mistakes of juries and errors of Courts, even though only occasional, admonish lawyers to beware of bold and confident assurances to clients, especially where the employment may depend upon such assurance. Whenever the controversy will admit of fair adjustment, the client should be advised to avoid or to end the litigation.

9. Negotiations With Opposite Party

A lawyer should not in any way communicate upon the subject of controversy with a party represented by counsel; much less should he undertake to negotiate or compromise the matter with him, but should deal only with his counsel. It is incumbent upon the lawyer most particularly to avoid everything that may tend to mislead a party not represented by counsel, and he should not undertake to advise him as to the law.

10. Acquiring Interest in Litigation

The lawyer should not purchase any interest in the subject matter of the litigation which he is conducting.

11. Dealing With Trust Property

The lawyer should refrain from any action whereby for his personal benefit or gain he abuses or takes advantage of the confidence reposed in him by his client.

Money of the client or collected for the client or other trust property coming into the possession of the lawyer should be reported and accounted for promptly, and should not under any circumstances be commingled with his own or be used by him.

12. Fixing the Amount of the Fee

In fixing fees, lawyers should avoid charges which overestimate their advice and services, as well as those which undervalue them. A client's ability to pay cannot justify a charge in excess of the value of the service, though his poverty may require a less charge, or even none at all. The reasonable requests of brother lawyers, and of their widows and orphans without ample means, should receive special and kindly consideration.

In determining the amount of the fee, it is proper to consider: (1) the time and labor required, the novelty and difficulty of the questions involved and the skill requisite properly to conduct the cause; (2) whether the acceptance of employment in the particular case will preclude the lawyer's appearance for others in cases likely to arise out of the transaction, and in which there is a reasonable expectation that otherwise he would be employed, or will involve the loss of other employment while employed in the particular case or antagonisms with other clients; (3) the customary charges of the Bar for similar services; (4) the amount involved in the controversy and the benefits resulting to the client from the services; (5) the contingency or the certainty of the compensation; and (6) the character of the employment, whether casual or for an established and constant client. No one of these considerations in itself is controlling. They are mere guides in ascertaining the real value of the service.

In determining the customary charges of the Bar for similar services, it is proper for a lawyer to consider a schedule of minimum fees adopted by a Bar Association, but no lawyer should permit himself to be controlled thereby or to follow it as his sole guide in determining the amount of his fee.

In fixing fees it should never be forgotten that the profession is a branch of the administration of justice and not a mere money-getting trade.

13. Contingent Fees

A contract for a contingent fee, where sanctioned by law, should be reasonable under all the circumstances of the case, including the risk and uncertainty of the compensation, but should always be subject to the supervision of a court, as to its reasonableness.

14. Suing a Client for a Fee

Controversies with clients concerning compensation are to be avoided by the lawyer so far as shall be compatible with his self-respect and with his right to receive reasonable recompense for his services; and lawsuits with clients should be resorted to only to prevent injustice, imposition or fraud.

15. How Far a Lawyer May Go in Supporting a Client's Cause

Nothing operates more certainly to create or to foster popular prejudice against lawyers as a class, and to deprive the profession of that full measure of public esteem and confidence which belongs to the proper discharge of its duties than does the false claim, often set up by the unscrupulous in defense of questionable transactions, that it is the duty of the lawyer to do whatever may enable him to succeed in winning his client's cause.

It is improper for a lawyer to assert in argument his personal belief in his client's innocence or in the justice of his cause.

The lawyer owes "entire devotion to the interest of the client, warm zeal in the maintenance and defense of his rights and the exertion of his utmost learning and ability," to the end that nothing be taken or be withheld from him, save by the rules of law, legally applied. No fear of judicial disfavor or public unpopularity should restrain him from the full discharge of his duty. In the judicial forum the client is entitled to the benefit of any and every remedy and defense that is authorized by the law of the land, and he may expect his lawyer to assert every such remedy or defense. But it is steadfastly to be borne in mind that the great trust of the lawyer is to be performed within and not without the bounds of the law. The office of attorney does not permit, much less does it demand of him for any client, violation of law or any manner of fraud or chicane. He must obey his own conscience and not that of his client.

16. Restraining Clients from Improprieties

A lawyer should use his best efforts to restrain and to prevent his clients from doing those things which the lawyer himself ought not to do, particularly with reference to their conduct towards Courts, judicial officers, jurors, witnesses and suitors. If a client persists in such wrongdoing the lawyer should terminate their relation.

17. Ill–Feeling and Personalities Between Advocates

Clients, not lawyers, are the litigants. Whatever may be the ill-feeling existing between clients, it should not be allowed to influence counsel in their conduct and demeanor toward each other or toward suitors in the case. All personalities between counsel should be scrupulously avoided. In the trial of a cause it is indecent to allude to the personal history or the personal peculiarities and idiosyncrasies of counsel on the other side. Personal colloquies between counsel which cause delay and promote unseemly wrangling should also be carefully avoided.

18. Treatment of Witnesses and Litigants

A lawyer should always treat adverse witnesses and suitors with fairness and due consideration, and he should never minister to the malevolence or prejudices of a client in the trial or conduct of a cause. The client cannot be made the keeper of the lawyer's conscience in professional matters. He has no right to demand that his counsel shall abuse the opposite party or indulge in offensive personalities. Improper speech is not excusable on the ground that it is what the client would say if speaking in his own behalf.

19. Appearance of Lawyer as Witness for His Client

When a lawyer is a witness for his client, except as to merely formal matters, such as the attestation or custody of an instrument and the like, he should leave the trial of the case to other counsel. Except when essential to the ends of justice, a lawyer should avoid testifying in court in behalf of his client.

20. Newspaper Discussion of Pending Litigation

Newspaper publications by a lawyer as to pending or anticipated litigation may interfere with a fair trial in the Courts and otherwise prejudice the due administration of justice. Generally they are to be condemned. If the extreme circumstances of a particular case justify a statement to the public, it is unprofessional to make it anonymously. An *ex parte* reference to the facts should not go beyond quotation from the records and papers on file in the court; but even in extreme cases it is better to avoid any *ex parte* statement.

21. Punctuality and Expedition

It is the duty of the lawyer not only to his client, but also to the Courts and to the public to be punctual in attendance, and to be concise and direct in the trial and disposition of causes.

22. Candor and Fairness

The conduct of the lawyer before the Court and with other lawyers should be characterized by candor and fairness.

It is not candid or fair for the lawyer knowingly to misquote the contents of a paper, the testimony of a witness, the language or the argument of opposing counsel, or the language of a decision or a textbook; or with knowledge of its invalidity, to cite as authority a decision that has been overruled, or a statute that has been repealed; or in argument to assert as a fact that which has not been proved, or in those jurisdictions where a side has the opening and closing arguments to mislead his opponent by concealing or withholding positions in his opening argument upon which his side then intends to rely.

It is unprofessional and dishonorable to deal other than candidly with the facts in taking the statements of witnesses, in drawing affidavits and other documents, and in the presentation of causes.

A lawyer should not offer evidence which he knows the Court should reject, in order to get the same before the jury by argument for its admissibility, nor should he address to the Judge arguments upon any point not properly calling for determination by him. Neither should he introduce into an argument, addressed to the court, remarks or statements intended to influence the jury or bystanders.

These and all kindred practices are unprofessional and unworthy of an officer of the law charged, as is the lawyer, with the duty of aiding in the administration of justice.

23. Attitude Toward Jury

All attempts to curry favor with juries by fawning, flattery or pretended solicitude for their personal comfort are unprofessional. Suggestions of counsel, looking to the comfort or convenience of jurors, and propositions to dispense with argument, should be made to the Court out of the jury's hearing. A lawyer must never converse privately with jurors about the case; and both before and during the trial he should avoid communicating with them, even as to matters foreign to the cause.

24. Right of Lawyer to Control the Incidents of the Trial

As to incidental matters pending the trial, not affecting the merits of the cause, or working substantial prejudice to the rights of the client, such as forcing the opposite lawyer to trial when he is under affliction or bereavement; forcing the trial on a particular day to the injury of the opposite lawyer when no harm will result from a trial at a different time; agreeing to an extension of time for signing a bill of exceptions, cross interrogatories and the like, the lawyer must be allowed to judge. In such matters no client has a right to demand that his counsel shall be illiberal, or that he do anything therein repugnant to his own sense of honor and propriety.

25. Taking Technical Advantage of Opposite Counsel; Agreements With Him

A lawyer should not ignore known customs or practice of the Bar or of a particular Court, even when the law permits, without giving timely notice to the opposing counsel. As far as possible, important agreements, affecting the rights of clients, should be reduced to writing; but it is dishonorable to avoid performance of an agreement fairly made because it is not reduced to writing, as required by rules of Court.

26. Professional Advocacy Other Than Before Courts

A lawyer openly, and in his true character may render professional services before legislative or other bodies, regarding proposed legislation and in advocacy of claims before departments of government, upon the same principles of ethics which justify his appearance before the Courts; but it is unprofessional for a lawyer so engaged to conceal his attorneyship, or to

759

employ secret personal solicitations, or to use means other than those addressed to the reason and understanding, to influence action.

27. Advertising, Direct or Indirect

It is unprofessional to solicit professional employment by circulars, advertisements, through touters or by personal communications or interviews not warranted by personal relations. Indirect advertisements for professional employment such as furnishing or inspiring newspaper comments, or procuring his photograph to be published in connection with causes in which the lawyer has been or is engaged or concerning the manner of their conduct, the magnitude of the interest involved, the importance of the lawyer's position, and all other like self-laudation, offend the traditions and lower the tone of our profession and are reprehensible; but the customary use of simple professional cards is not improper.

Publication in reputable law lists in a manner consistent with the standards of conduct imposed by these canons of brief biographical and informative data is permissible. Such data must not be misleading and may include only a statement of the lawyer's name and the names of his professional associates; addresses, telephone numbers, cable addresses; branches of the profession practiced; date and place of birth and admission to the bar; schools attended; with dates of graduation, degrees and other educational distinctions; public or quasi-public offices; posts of honor; legal authorships; legal teaching positions; memberships and offices in bar associations and committees thereof, in legal and scientific societies and legal fraternities; foreign language ability; the fact of listings in other reputable law lists; the names and addresses of references; and, with their written consent, the names of clients regularly represented. A certificate of compliance with the Rules and Standards issued by the Standing Committee on Law Lists may be treated as evidence that such list is reputable.

It is not improper for a lawyer who is admitted to practice as a proctor in admiralty to use that designation on his letterhead or shingle or for a lawyer who has complied with the statutory requirements of admission to practice before the patent office, to so use the designation "patent attorney" or "patent lawyer" or "trademark attorney" or "trademark lawyer" or any combination of those terms.

28. Stirring Up Litigation, Directly or Through Agents

It is unprofessional for a lawyer to volunteer advice to bring a lawsuit, except in rare cases where ties of blood, relationship or trust make it his duty to do so. Stirring up strife and litigation is not only unprofessional, but it is indictable at common law. It is disreputable to hunt up defects in titles or other causes of action and inform thereof in order to be employed to bring suit or collect judgment, or to breed litigation by seeking out those with claims for personal injuries or those having any other grounds of action in order to secure them as clients, or to employ agents or runners for like purposes, or to pay or reward, directly or indirectly, those who bring or influence the bringing of such cases to his office, or to remunerate policemen, court or prison officials, physicians, hospital *attachés* or others who may succeed, under the guise of giving disinterested friendly advice, in influencing the criminal, the sick and the injured, the ignorant or others, to seek his professional services. A duty to the public and to the profession devolves upon every member of the Bar having knowledge of such practices upon the part of any practitioner immediately to inform thereof, to the end that the offender may be disbarred.

29. Upholding the Honor of the Profession

Lawyers should expose without fear or favor before the proper tribunals corrupt or dishonest conduct in the profession, and should accept without hesitation employment against a member of the Bar who has wronged his client. The counsel upon the trial of a cause in which perjury has been committed owe it to the profession and to the public to bring the matter to the knowledge of the prosecuting authorities. The lawyer should aid in guarding the Bar against the admission to the profession of candidates unfit or unqualified because deficient in either moral character or education. He should strive at all times to uphold the honor and to maintain the dignity of the profession and to improve not only the law but the administration of justice.

30. Justifiable and Unjustifiable Litigations

The lawyer must decline to conduct a civil cause or to make a defense when convinced that it is intended merely to harass or to injure the opposite party or to work oppression or wrong. But otherwise it is his right, and, having accepted retainer, it becomes his duty to insist upon the judgment of the Court as to the legal merits of his client's claim. His appearance in Court should be deemed equivalent to an assertion on his honor that in his opinion his client's case is one proper for judicial determination.

31. Responsibility for Litigation

No lawyer is obliged to act either as adviser or advocate for every person who may wish to become his client. He has the right to decline employment. Every lawyer upon his own responsibility must decide what employment he will accept as counsel, what causes he will bring into Court for plaintiffs, what cases he will contest in Court for defendants. The responsibility for advising as to questionable transactions, for bringing questionable suits, for urging questionable defenses, is the lawyer's responsibility. He cannot escape it by urging as an excuse that he is only following his client's instructions.

32. The Lawyer's Duty in Its Last Analysis

No client, corporate or individual, however powerful, nor any cause, civil or political, however important, is entitled to receive nor should any lawyer render any service or advice involving disloyalty to the law whose ministers we are, or disrespect of the judicial office, which we are bound to uphold, or corruption of any person or persons exercising a public office or private trust, or deception or betrayal of the public. When rendering any such improper service or advice, the lawyer invites and merits stern and just condemnation. Correspondingly, he advances the honor of his profession and the best interests of his client when he renders service or gives advice tending to impress upon the client and his undertaking exact compliance with the strictest principles of moral law. He must also observe and advise his client to observe the statute law, though until a statute shall have been construed and interpreted by competent adjudication, he is free and is entitled to advise as to its validity and as to what he conscientiously believes to be its just meaning and extent. But above all a lawyer will find his highest honor in a deserved reputation for fidelity to private trust and to public duty, as an honest man and as a patriotic and loyal citizen.

33. Partnerships—Names

Partnerships among lawyers for the practice of their profession are very common and are not to be condemned. In the formation of partnerships and the use of partnership names care should be taken not to violate any law, custom, or rule of court locally applicable. Where partnerships are formed between lawyers who are not all admitted to practice in the courts of the state, care should be taken to avoid any misleading name or representation which would create a false impression as to the professional position or privileges of the member not locally admitted. In the formation of partnerships for the practice of law, no person should be admitted or held out as a practitioner or member who is not a member of the legal profession duly authorized to practice, and amenable to professional discipline. In the selection and use of a firm name, no false, misleading, assumed or trade name should be used. The continued use of the name of a deceased or former partner, when permissible by local custom, is not unethical, but care should be taken that no imposition or deception is practiced through this use. When a member of the firm, on becoming a judge, is precluded from practicing law, his name should not be continued in the firm name.

Partnerships between lawyers and members of other professions or non-professional persons should not be formed or permitted where any part of the partnership's employment consists of the practice of law.

34. Division of Fees

No division of fees for legal services is proper, except with another lawyer, based upon a division of service or responsibility.

35. Intermediaries

The professional services of a lawyer should not be controlled or exploited by any lay agency, personal or corporate, which intervenes between client and lawyer. A lawyer's responsibilities and qualifications are individual. He should avoid all relations which direct the performance of his duties by or in the interest of such intermediary. A lawyer's relation to his client should be personal, and the responsibility should be direct to the client. Charitable societies rendering aid to the indigents are not deemed such intermediaries.

A lawyer may accept employment from any organization, such as an association, club or trade organization, to render legal services in any matter in which the organization, as an entity, is interested, but this employment should not include the rendering of legal services to the members of such an organization in respect to their individual affairs.

36. Retirement From Judicial Position or Public Employment

A lawyer should not accept employment as an advocate in any matter upon the merits of which he has previously acted in a judicial capacity.

A lawyer, having once held public office or having been in the public employ, should not after his retirement accept employment in connection with any matter which he has investigated or passed upon while in such office or employ.

37. Confidences of a Client

It is the duty of a lawyer to preserve his client's confidences. This duty outlasts the lawyer's employment, and extends as well to his employees; and neither of them should accept employment which involves or may involve the disclosure or use of these confidences, either for the private advantage of the lawyer or his employees or to the disadvantage of the client, without his knowledge and consent, and even though there are other available sources of such information. A lawyer should not continue employment when he discovers that this obligation prevents the performance of his full duty to his former or to his new client.

If a lawyer is accused by his client, he is not precluded from disclosing the truth in respect to the accusation. The announced intention of a client to commit a crime is not included within the confidences which he is bound to respect. He may properly make such disclosures as may be necessary to prevent the act or protect those against whom it is threatened.

38. Compensation, Commissions and Rebates

A lawyer should accept no compensation, commissions, rebates or other advantages from others without the knowledge and consent of his client after full disclosure.

39. Witnesses

A lawyer may properly interview any witness or prospective witness for the opposing side in any civil or criminal action without the consent of opposing counsel or party. In doing so, however, he should scrupulously avoid any suggestion calculated to induce the witness to suppress or deviate from the truth, or in any degree to affect his free and untrammeled conduct when appearing at the trial or on the witness stand.

40. Newspapers

A lawyer may with propriety write articles for publications in which he gives information upon the law; but he should not accept employment from such publications to advise inquirers in respect to their individual rights.

41. Discovery of Imposition and Deception

When a lawyer discovers that some fraud or deception has been practiced, which has unjustly imposed upon the court or a party, he should endeavor to rectify it; at first by advising his client, and if his client refuses to forego the advantage thus unjustly gained, he should promptly inform the injured person or his counsel, so that they may take appropriate steps.

42. Expenses of Litigation

A lawyer may not properly agree with a client that the lawyer shall pay or bear the expenses of litigation; he may in good faith advance expenses as a matter of convenience, but subject to reimbursement.

43. Approved Law Lists

It shall be improper for a lawyer to permit his name to be published in a law list the conduct, management or contents of which are calculated or likely to deceive or injure the public or the profession, or to lower the dignity or standing of the profession.

44. Withdrawal From Employment as Attorney or Counsel

The right of an attorney or counsel to withdraw from employment, once assumed, arises only from good cause. Even the desire or consent of the client is not always sufficient. The lawyer should not throw up the unfinished task to the detriment of his client except for reasons of honor or self-respect. If the client insists upon an unjust or immoral course in the conduct of his case, or if he persists over the attorney's remonstrance in presenting frivolous defenses, or if he deliberately disregards an agreement or obligation as to fees or expenses, the lawyer may be warranted in withdrawing on due notice to the client, allowing him time to employ another lawyer. So also when a lawyer discovers that his client has no case and the client is determined to continue it; or even if the lawyer finds himself incapable of conducting the case effectively. Sundry other instances may arise in which withdrawal is to be justified. Upon withdrawing from a case after a retainer has been paid, the attorney should refund such part of the retainer as has not been clearly earned.

45. Specialists

The canons of the American Bar Association apply to all branches of the legal profession; specialists in particular branches are not to be considered as exempt from the application of these principles.

46. Notice to Local Lawyers

A lawyer available to act as an associate of other lawyers in a particular branch of the law or legal service may send to local lawyers only and publish in his local legal journal, a brief and dignified announcement of his availability to serve other lawyers in connection therewith. The announcement should be in a form which does not constitute a statement or representation of special experience or expertness.

47. Aiding the Unauthorized Practice of Law

No lawyer shall permit his professional services, or his name, to be used in aid of, or to make possible, the unauthorized practice of law by any lay agency, personal or corporate.

AMERICAN BAR ASSOCIATION STANDING COMMITTEE ON ETHICS AND PROFESSIONAL RESPONSIBILITY

COMPOSITION AND JURISDICTION*

The Standing Committee on Ethics and Professional Responsibility, which consists of ten members, may:

(1) by the concurrence of a majority of its members, express its opinion on proper professional or judicial conduct, either on its own initiative or when requested to do so by a member of the bar or the judiciary;

(2) periodically publish its issued opinions to the profession in summary or complete form and, on request, provide copies of opinions to members of the bar, the judiciary, and the public;

(3) provide under its supervision informal responses to ethics inquiries the answers to which are substantially governed by applicable ethical codes and existing written opinions;

(4) on request, advise or otherwise assist professional organizations and courts in their activities relating to the development, modification and interpretation of statements of the ethical standards of the profession such as the Model Rules of Professional Conduct, the predecessor Model Code of Professional Responsibility and the Code of Judicial Conduct;

(5) recommend amendments to or clarifications of the Model Rules of Professional Conduct or the Code of Judicial Conduct; and

(6) adopt rules relating to the procedures to be used in issuing opinions, effective when approved by the Board of Governors.

RULES OF PROCEDURE

1. The Committee may express its opinion on questions of proper professional and judicial conduct. The Model Rules of Professional Conduct and the Code of Judicial Conduct, as they may be amended or superseded, contain the standards to be applied. For as long as a significant number of jurisdictions continue to base their professional standards on the predecessor Model Code of Professional Responsibility, the Committee will continue to refer also to the Model Code in its opinions.

2. The Committee may issue an opinion on its own initiative or upon a request from a member of the bar or the judiciary or from a professional organization or a court.

3. The Committee may issue opinions of two kinds: Formal Opinions and Informal Opinions. Formal Opinions are those upon subjects the Commit-

---

* As defined by the By–Laws of the American Bar Association, Article 30.7, as revised. For- merly called the Standing Committee on Professional Ethics.

766

tee determines to be of widespread interest or unusual importance. Other opinions are Informal Opinions. The Committee will assign to each opinion a non-duplicative identifying number, with distinction between Formal Opinions and Informal Opinions.

4. The Committee will not usually issue an opinion on a question that is known to be pending before a court in a proceeding in which the requestor is involved. The Committee's published opinions will not identify the person who was the requestor or whose conduct is the subject of the opinion. The Committee will not issue an opinion on a question of law.

5. The Committee may invite or accept written information relevant to a particular opinion from a person or persons interested in such an opinion before the Committee begins its work on an opinion. Ordinarily, the Committee will not invite anyone to make an oral presentation or argument in support of that position.

6. When a Committee or staff member receives an inquiry about the status of a draft opinion from anyone outside the Committee, the member may inform the inquirer that the Committee is considering the question. Draft opinions may, in appropriate circumstances, be shown to other interested ABA Committees and entities. Committee and staff members shall not, absent unusual circumstances, discuss the substance of pending opinions with the public, but may mention topics related to pending opinions in a general fashion.

7. Before issuing an opinion with respect to judicial conduct the Committee will submit the proposed opinion to the Judges' Advisory Committee and consider any objection or comment from the Judges' Advisory Committee and any member of it. The Committee may assume that the Judges' Advisory Committee and its members have no objection or comment if none is received by the Committee within 30 days after the submission.

8. If the Committee decides not to issue a requested opinion the requestor will be promptly notified.

9. The Committee will issue an opinion only with the concurrence of six members in a vote taken at a meeting or in a telephone conference call. When a Committee member votes against a position declaring a Committee policy, that vote may be recorded in the minutes, which may include the name of the dissenting Committee member. The minutes shall not reflect the names of Committee members voting for or against any non-Committee policy question except that a member's vote shall be recorded and identified at the member's request.

When drafting an opinion, policy statement or other document to be publicly disseminated, the Committee shall make every effort to reach a consensus. When, after a full examination of the issue and an exchange of views, the Committee cannot reach a consensus, a dissenting opinion may be appropriate to express the views of a Committee member or members. A member may place a statement of dissent in the Committee file or request that the dissent be published with the opinion.

10.   The Chair may assign to one or more members the responsibility of preparing a proposed opinion for consideration by the Committee. The Committee will issue a requested opinion as promptly as feasible.

11.   A Formal Opinion overrules an earlier Formal Opinion or Informal Opinion to the extent of conflict. An Informal Opinion overrules an earlier Informal Opinion to the extent of conflict but does not overrule an earlier Formal Opinion.

12.   Opinions of the Committee issued before the effective dates of the Model Rules of Professional Conduct, the predecessor Model Code of Professional Responsibility and the Code of Judicial Conduct continue in effect to the extent not inconsistent with those standards and not overruled or limited by later opinions.

13.   The Committee will make opinions and/or summaries of opinions available for publication in the *American Bar Association Journal.* The Committee will cause Formal Opinions and Informal Opinions to be published in loose-leaf form.

14.   The Committee may through its staff arrange to provide informal responses to ethics inquiries the answers to which are substantially governed by applicable ethical codes and opinions of this Committee or other ethics committees. The staff will maintain a log of such inquiries that will periodically be reviewed by the Committee.

15.   Information contained in Committee files relating to requests for opinions that would disclose the identity of the inquirer or the person whose conduct is the subject of the opinion will not voluntarily be disclosed by the Association without the consent of the affected persons.

MODEL COURT RULE ON INSURANCE DISCLOSURE (2004)

In August 2004, the ABA House of Delegates voted to adopt the following as a "Model Court Rule" but not as part of the Model Rules of Professional Conduct.

Rule ___. Insurance Disclosure

A. Each lawyer admitted to the active practice of law shall certify to the [highest court of the jurisdiction] on or before [December 31 of each year]: 1) whether the lawyer is engaged in the private practice of law; 2) if engaged in the private practice of law, whether the lawyer is currently covered by professional liability insurance; 3) whether the lawyer intends to maintain insurance during the period of time the lawyer is engaged in the private practice of law; and 4) whether the lawyer is exempt from the provisions of this Rule because the lawyer is engaged in the practice of law as a full-time government lawyer or is counsel employed by an organizational client and does not represent clients outside that capacity. Each lawyer admitted to the active practice of law in this jurisdiction who reports being covered by professional liability insurance shall notify [the highest court in the jurisdiction] in writing within 30 days if the insurance policy providing coverage lapses, is no longer in effect or terminates for any reason.

B. The foregoing shall be certified by each lawyer admitted to the active practice of law in this jurisdiction in such form as may be prescribed by the [highest court of the jurisdiction]. The information submitted pursuant to this Rule will be made available to the public by such means as may be designated by the [highest court of the jurisdiction].

C. Any lawyer admitted to the active practice of law who fails to comply with this Rule in a timely fashion, as defined by the [highest court in the jurisdiction], may be suspended from the practice of law until such time as the lawyer complies. Supplying false information in response to this Rule shall subject the lawyer to appropriate disciplinary action.

ABA MODEL COURT RULE ON PROVISION OF LEGAL SERVICES FOLLOWING DETERMINATION OF MAJOR DISASTER (2007)

RULE __. PROVISION OF LEGAL SERVICES FOLLOWING DETERMINATION OF MAJOR DISASTER

(a) DETERMINATION OF EXISTENCE OF MAJOR DISASTER. Solely for purposes of this Rule, this Court shall determine when an emergency affecting the justice system, as a result of a natural or other major disaster has occurred in:

(1) this jurisdiction and whether the emergency caused by the major disaster affects the entirety or only a part of this jurisdiction, or

(2) another jurisdiction but only after such a determination and its geographical scope have been made by the highest court of that jurisdiction. The authority to engage in the temporary practice of law in this jurisdiction pursuant to paragraph (c) shall extend only to lawyers who principally practice in the area of such other jurisdiction determined to have suffered a major disaster causing an emergency affecting the justice system and the provision of legal services.

(b) TEMPORARY PRACTICE IN THIS JURISDICTION FOLLOWING MAJOR DISASTER. Following the determination of an emergency affecting the justice system in this jurisdiction pursuant to paragraph (a) of this Rule, or a determination that persons displaced by a major disaster in another jurisdiction and residing in this jurisdiction are in need of pro bono services and the assistance of lawyers from outside of this jurisdiction is required to help provide such assistance, a lawyer authorized to practice law in another United States jurisdiction, and not disbarred, suspended from practice or otherwise restricted from practice in any jurisdiction, may provide legal services in this jurisdiction on a temporary basis. Such legal services must be provided on a pro bono basis without compensation, expectation of compensation or other direct or indirect pecuniary gain to the lawyer. Such legal services shall be assigned and supervised through an established not-for-profit bar association, pro bono program or legal services program or through such organization(s) specifically designated by this Court.

(c) TEMPORARY PRACTICE IN THIS JURISDICTION FOLLOWING MAJOR DISASTER IN ANOTHER JURISDICTION. Following the determination of a major disaster in another United States jurisdiction, a lawyer who is authorized to practice law and who principally practices in that affected jurisdiction, and who is not disbarred, suspended from practice or otherwise restricted from practice in any jurisdiction, may provide legal services in this jurisdiction on a temporary basis. Those legal services must arise out of and be reasonably related to that lawyer's practice of law in the jurisdiction, or area of such other jurisdiction, where the major disaster occurred.

(d) DURATION OF AUTHORITY FOR TEMPORARY PRACTICE. The authority to practice law in this jurisdiction granted by paragraph (b) of this Rule shall end when this Court determines that the conditions caused by the major disaster in this jurisdiction have ended except that a lawyer then representing clients in this jurisdiction pursuant to paragraph (b) is authorized to continue the provision of legal services for such time as is reasonably necessary to complete the representation, but the lawyer shall not thereafter accept new clients. The authority to practice law in this jurisdiction granted by paragraph (c) of this Rule shall end [60] days after this Court declares that the conditions caused by the major disaster in the affected jurisdiction have ended.

(e) COURT APPEARANCES. The authority granted by this Rule does not include appearances in court except:

(1) pursuant to that court's pro hac vice admission rule and, if such authority is granted, any fees for such admission shall be waived; or

(2) if this Court, in any determination made under paragraph (a), grants blanket permission to appear in all or designated courts of this jurisdiction to lawyers providing legal services pursuant to paragraph (b). If such an authorization is included, any pro hac vice admission fees shall be waived.

(f) DISCIPLINARY AUTHORITY AND REGISTRATION REQUIREMENT. Lawyers providing legal services in this jurisdiction pursuant to paragraphs (b) or (c) are subject to this Court's disciplinary authority and the Rules of Professional Conduct of this jurisdiction as provided in Rule 8.5 of the Rules of Professional Conduct. Lawyers providing legal services in this jurisdiction under paragraphs (b) or (c) shall, within 30 days from the commencement of the provision of legal services, file a registration statement with the Clerk of this Court. The registration statement shall be in a form prescribed by this Court. Any lawyer who provides legal services pursuant to this Rule shall not be considered to be engaged in the unlawful practice of law in this jurisdiction.

(g) NOTIFICATION TO CLIENTS. Lawyers authorized to practice law in another United States jurisdiction who provide legal services pursuant to this Rule shall inform clients in this jurisdiction of the jurisdiction in which they are authorized to practice law, any limits of that authorization, and that they are not authorized to practice law in this jurisdiction except as permitted by this Rule. They shall not state or imply to any person that they are otherwise authorized to practice law in this jurisdiction.

Comment

[1] A major disaster in this or another jurisdiction may cause an emergency affecting the justice system with respect to the provision of legal services for a sustained period of time interfering with the ability of lawyers admitted and practicing in the affected jurisdiction to continue to represent clients until the disaster has ended. When this happens, lawyers from the affected jurisdiction may need to provide legal services to their clients, on a temporary basis, from an office outside their home jurisdiction. In addition, lawyers in an unaffected jurisdiction may be willing to serve residents of the affected jurisdiction who have unmet legal needs as a result of the disaster or, though independent of the disaster, whose legal needs temporarily are unmet

because of disruption to the practices of local lawyers. Lawyers from unaffected jurisdictions may offer to provide these legal services either by traveling to the affected jurisdiction or from their own offices or both, provided the legal services are provided on a pro bono basis through an authorized not-for-profit entity or such other organization(s) specifically designated by this Court. A major disaster includes, for example, a hurricane, earthquake, flood, wildfire, tornado, public health emergency or an event caused by terrorists or acts of war.

[2] Under paragraph (a)(1), this Court shall determine whether a major disaster causing an emergency affecting the justice system has occurred in this jurisdiction, or in a part of this jurisdiction, for purposes of triggering paragraph (b) of this Rule. This Court may, for example, determine that the entirety of this jurisdiction has suffered a disruption in the provision of legal services or that only certain areas have suffered such an event. The authority granted by paragraph (b) shall extend only to lawyers authorized to practice law and not disbarred, suspended from practice or otherwise restricted from practice in any other manner in any other jurisdiction.

[3] Paragraph (b) permits lawyers authorized to practice law in an unaffected jurisdiction, and not disbarred, suspended from practice or otherwise restricted from practicing law in any other manner in any other jurisdiction, to provide pro bono legal services to residents of the affected jurisdiction following determination of an emergency caused by a major disaster; notwithstanding that they are not otherwise authorized to practice law in the affected jurisdiction. Other restrictions on a lawyer's license to practice law that would prohibit that lawyer from providing legal services pursuant to this Rule include, but are not limited to, probation, inactive status, disability inactive status or a non-disciplinary administrative suspension for failure to complete continuing legal education or other requirements. Lawyers on probation may be subject to monitoring and specific limitations on their practices. Lawyers on inactive status, despite being characterized in many jurisdictions as being "in good standing," and lawyers on disability inactive status are not permitted to practice law. Public protection warrants exclusion of these lawyers from the authority to provide legal services as defined in this Rule. Lawyers permitted to provide legal services pursuant to this Rule must do so without fee or other compensation, or expectation thereof. Their service must be provided through an established not-for-profit organization that is authorized to provide legal services either in its own name or that provides representation of clients through employed or cooperating lawyers. Alternatively, this court may instead designate other specific organization(s) through which these legal services may be rendered. Under paragraph (b), an emeritus lawyer from another United State jurisdiction may provide pro bono legal services on a temporary basis in this jurisdiction provided that the emeritus lawyer is authorized to provide pro bono legal services in that jurisdiction pursuant to that jurisdiction's emeritus or pro bono practice rule. Lawyers may also be authorized to provide legal services in this jurisdiction on a temporary basis under Rule 5.5(c) of the Rules of Professional Conduct.

[4] Lawyers authorized to practice law in another jurisdiction, who principally practice in the area of such other jurisdiction determined by this Court to have suffered a major disaster, and whose practices are disrupted by a major disaster there, and who are not disbarred, suspended from practice or otherwise restricted from practicing law in any other manner in any other jurisdiction, are authorized under paragraph (c) to provide legal services on a temporary basis in this jurisdiction. Those legal services must arise out of and be reasonably related to the lawyer's practice of law in the affected jurisdiction. For purposes of this Rule, the determination of a major disaster in another jurisdiction should first be made by the highest court of appellate jurisdiction in that jurisdiction. For the meaning of "arise out of and reasonably related to," see Rule 5.5 Comment [14], Rules of Professional Conduct.

[5] Emergency conditions created by major disasters end, and when they do, the authority created by paragraphs (b) and (c) also ends with appropriate notice to enable lawyers to plan and to complete pending legal matters. Under paragraph (d), this Court determines when those conditions end only for purposes of this Rule. The authority granted under paragraph (b) shall end upon such determination except that lawyers assisting residents of this jurisdiction under paragraph (b) may continue to do so for such longer period as is reasonably necessary to complete the representation. The authority created by paragraph (c) will end [60] days after this Court makes such a determination with regard to an affected jurisdiction.

[6] Paragraphs (b) and (c) do not authorize lawyers to appear in the courts of this jurisdiction. Court appearances are subject to the pro hac vice admission rules of the particular court. This Court may, in a determination made under paragraph (e)(2), include authorization for lawyers who provide legal services in this jurisdiction under paragraph (b) to appear in all or designated courts of this jurisdiction without need for such pro hac vice admission. If such an authorization is included, any pro hac vice admission fees shall be waived. A lawyer who has appeared in the courts of this jurisdiction pursuant to paragraph (e) may continue to appear in any such matter notwithstanding a declaration under paragraph (d) that the conditions created by major disaster have ended. Furthermore, withdrawal from a court appearance is subject to Rule 1.16 of the Rules of Professional Conduct.

[7] Authorization to practice law as a foreign legal consultant or in-house counsel in a United States jurisdiction offers lawyers a limited scope of permitted practice and may therefore restrict that person's ability to provide legal services under this Rule.

[8] The ABA National Lawyer Regulatory Data Bank is available to help determine whether any lawyer seeking to practice in this jurisdiction pursuant to paragraphs (b) or (c) of this Rule is disbarred, suspended from practice or otherwise subject to a public disciplinary sanction that would restrict the lawyer's ability to practice law in any other jurisdiction.

LAWYER'S CREED OF PROFESSIONALISM*

The ABA House of Delegates, at its August 1988 meeting, adopted as ABA policy a recommendation that state and local bar associations "encourage their members to accept as a guide for their individual conduct, and to comply with, a lawyers' creed of professionalism." The ABA Torts and Insurance Practice Section, which had sought and won the ABA's approval of such a policy, also set forth an example of such a "Lawyer's Creed of Professionalism." This document is published below in full text. The House of Delegates made clear that "nothing in such a creed shall be deemed to supersede or in any way amend the Model Rules of Professional Conduct or other disciplinary codes, alter existing standards of conduct against which lawyer negligence might be judged or become a basis for the imposition of civil liability of any kind."

At the same meeting, the House of Delegates authorized the dissemination to the profession of a "Lawyer's Pledge of Professionalism," which the ABA Young Lawyer's Section had proposed. This document is also published below in full text, and reprinted with permission.

Preamble

As a lawyer I must strive to make our system of justice work fairly and efficiently. In order to carry out that responsibility, not only will I comply with the letter and spirit of the disciplinary standards applicable to all lawyers, but I will also conduct myself in accordance with the following Creed of Professionalism when dealing with my client, opposing parties, their counsel, the courts and the general public.

A. With respect to my client:

1. I will be loyal and committed to my client's cause, but I will not permit that loyalty and commitment to interfere with my ability to provide my client with objective and independent advice;

2. I will endeavor to achieve my client's lawful objectives in business transactions and in litigation as expeditiously and economically as possible;

3. In appropriate cases, I will counsel my client with respect to mediation, arbitration and other alternative methods of resolving disputes;

4. I will advise my client against pursuing litigation (or any other course of action) that is without merit and against insisting on tactics which are intended to delay resolution of the matter or to harass or drain the financial resources of the opposing party;

5. I will advise my client that civility and courtesy are not to be equated with weakness;

6. While I must abide by my client's decision concerning the objectives of the representation, I nevertheless will counsel my client that a willingness to initiate or engage in settlement discussions is consistent with zealous and effective representation.

* Not adopted by the ABA House of Delegates. Not American Bar Association Policy.   Reprinted with permission. Copyrighted by the A.B.A.

B. With respect to opposing parties and their counsel:

1. I will endeavor to be courteous and civil, both in oral and in written communications;

2. I will not knowingly make statements of fact or of law that are untrue;

3. In litigation proceedings I will agree to reasonable requests for extensions of time or for waiver of procedural formalities when the legitimate interests of my client will not be adversely affected;

4. I will endeavor to consult with opposing counsel before scheduling depositions and meetings and before re-scheduling hearings, and I will cooperate with opposing counsel when scheduling changes are requested;

5. I will refrain from utilizing litigation or any other course of conduct to harass the opposing party;

6. I will refrain from engaging in excessive and abusive discovery, and I will comply with all reasonable discovery requests;

7. I will refrain from utilizing delaying tactics;

8. In depositions and other proceedings, and in negotiations, I will conduct myself with dignity, avoid making groundless objections and refrain from engaging in acts of rudeness or disrespect;

9. I will not serve motions and pleadings on the other party, or his counsel, at such a time or in such a manner as will unfairly limit the other party's opportunity to respond;

10. In business transactions I will not quarrel over matters of form or style, but will concentrate on matters of substance and content;

11. I will clearly identify, for other counsel or parties, all changes that I have made in documents submitted to me for review.

C. With respect to the courts and other tribunals:

1. I will be a vigorous and zealous advocate on behalf of my client, while recognizing, as an officer of the court, that excessive zeal may be detrimental to my client's interests as well as to the proper functioning of our system of justice;

2. Where consistent with my client's interests, I will communicate with opposing counsel in an effort to avoid litigation and to resolve litigation that has actually commenced;

3. I will voluntarily withdraw claims or defenses when it becomes apparent that they do not have merit or are superfluous;

4. I will refrain from filing frivolous motions;

5. I will make every effort to agree with other counsel, as early as possible, on a voluntary exchange of information and on a plan for discovery;

6. I will attempt to resolve, by agreement, my objections to matters contained in my opponent's pleadings and discovery requests;

7. When scheduling hearings or depositions have to be canceled, I will notify opposing counsel, and, if appropriate, the court (or other tribunal) as early as possible;

8. Before dates for hearings or trials are set—or if that is not feasible, immediately after such dates have been set—I will attempt to verify the availability of key participants and witnesses so that I can promptly notify the court (or other tribunal) and opposing counsel of any likely problem in that regard;

9. In civil matters, I will stipulate to facts as to which there is no genuine dispute;

10. I will endeavor to be punctual in attending court hearings, conferences and depositions;

11. I will at all times be candid with the court.

D. With respect to the public and to our system of justice:

1. I will remember that, in addition to commitment to my client's cause, my responsibilities as a lawyer include a devotion to the public good;

2. I will endeavor to keep myself current in the areas in which I practice and, when necessary, will associate with, or refer my client to, counsel knowledgeable in another field of practice;

3. I will be mindful of the fact that, as a member of a self-regulating profession, it is incumbent on me to report violations by fellow lawyers of any disciplinary rule;

4. I will be mindful of the need to protect the image of the legal profession in the eyes of the public and will be so guided when considering methods and content of advertising;

5. I will be mindful that the law is a learned profession and that among its desirable goals are devotion to public service, improvement of administration of justice, and the contribution of uncompensated time and civic influence on behalf of those persons who cannot afford adequate legal assistance.

CIVILITY CODES

State Bar of California Litigation Section's Model Code of Civility and Professionalism[1]

PREAMBLE

The practice of law should be an honorable and noble profession. In the State of California, it is undisputed that the vast majority of the members of the Litigation Section strive to practice law in a civil and professional manner. They diligently uphold the duties of civility and professionalism that are owed to their clients, other parties, third-party witnesses, opposing counsel, the Courts and other tribunals, and the public.

Due to the contentious nature of litigation, some lawyers occasionally resort to engaging in abusive, offensive, derogatory, uncivil and unprofessional conduct in an attempt to gain an unfair advantage. Such conduct not only is improper, it is detrimental to the legal profession as a whole, and counterproductive.

In order to address such inappropriate activities, and promote civil and professional conduct among litigators in this State, the Litigation Section has adopted this "Code of Civility and Professionalism" ("Code").

The guidelines contained in this Code are not intended to create new civil causes of action. Nothing in this Code should be deemed to create, augment, diminish, or eliminate any substantive legal duty of lawyers, or the non-disciplinary consequences of violating such a duty. Consequently, while this Code is not a set of legal rules or regulations that can be enforced in a Court of law, it is designed as a code of conduct for litigators to adhere to on a personal level, as they strive to succeed in their professional lives.

The Litigation Section welcomes comments from its members on ways in which the Code can be modified or improved, including the addition of guidelines to address specific problems that litigators regularly encounter.

SECTION 1

A Lawyer Should Adhere to the Highest Standards of Civility and Professionalism

A lawyer should adhere to the highest standards of civility and professionalism at all times and under all circumstances. Specifically, a lawyer should comply with the following guidelines to promote civil and professional conduct among litigators in the State of California:

(a) A lawyer should comply not only with the strict letter of the California Rules of Professional Conduct, but also the Rules' spirit.

(b) A lawyer should uphold the image of a lawyer as civil, professional and ethical in the eyes of the public at all times.

---

1. http://calbar.ca.gov/calbar/pdfs/sections/litigation/2006–01_model-code.pdf (accessed 28 September 2007).

(c) A lawyer should conduct himself/herself with honesty, integrity, courtesy, and a commitment to justice.

(d) A lawyer should honor all of his/her commitments, promises, and agreements, whether they are made orally or in writing.

(e) A lawyer should never knowingly or intentionally make untrue or misleading statements of fact or law.

(f) A lawyer should encourage and engage in pro bono or other civic, educational or volunteer activities to assist those who are poor, underprivileged, disadvantaged, or otherwise unable to afford legal services.

(g) A lawyer should never engage in, and should speak out against, any prejudice or discrimination against any person based on race, color, national origin, ancestry, sex, gender, sexual orientation, marital status, age, religious creed, medical condition, physical or mental disability, or pregnancy, childbirth or related medical conditions.

SECTION 2

A Lawyer Should Treat His/Her Clients With Courtesy and Respect, and Zealously Represent Such Clients in a Civil and Professional Manner

A lawyer should treat his/her clients with courtesy and respect, and zealously represent such clients in a civil and professional manner. Specifically, a lawyer should comply with the following guidelines to achieve each of his/her client's lawful and meritorious objectives:

(a) A lawyer should treat each of his/her clients with courtesy and respect at all times, and zealously represent each of the clients in a civil and professional manner.

(b) A lawyer should keep current in the areas of law in which the lawyer practices.

(c) A lawyer should strive to keep his/her clients informed about significant or noteworthy matters in a timely manner, including potentially damaging aspects of a client's case.

(d) A lawyer should ensure that copies of important correspondence and other documents are sent to his/her clients in a timely fashion, even if such correspondence or documents are unfavorable to the clients, or otherwise show that the Court has ruled against the clients on one or more issues.

(e) A lawyer should send complete and accurate billing statements to his/her clients on a regular basis.

(f) A lawyer should provide advance notice to his/her clients of all necessary appearances that the clients must make. A lawyer also should notify his/her clients as soon as is reasonably practicable of all hearings, depositions, meetings, conferences or other scheduled appearances that are cancelled or postponed.

(g) A lawyer should strive to promptly return or otherwise respond to all telephone calls, e-mail messages, faxes, letters and other communications received from his/her clients. If a lawyer is unable to personally respond to a client's communication in a prompt manner, to the extent possible, the lawyer should have someone from his/her office respond to the communication as promptly as possible, even if it is to simply acknowledge that the communication was received, and to inform the client of an approximate date or time when the lawyer will have an opportunity to respond to or otherwise contact the client.

(h) A lawyer should strive to achieve the best results for his/her clients in an efficient, expeditious and cost-effective manner.

(i) A lawyer should advise his/her clients that the lawyer will engage in professional and civil behavior while representing the clients' interests and handling the cases. A lawyer likewise should advise the clients that he/she expects the clients to engage in proper, non-abusive, and non-offensive behavior at all times and under all circumstances.

(j) A lawyer should advise his/her clients that the lawyer will not pursue any conduct or course of action that is without merit, intended solely for delay, or primarily designed to inflame, offend, harass, or drain the financial resources of the other party.

(k) A lawyer should never compromise the standards of civility or professionalism in any manner to achieve a litigation advantage over the other side.

(*l*) A lawyer should never allow any current or potential clients to insist or dictate that the lawyer, or any member of the law firm, including any partners, associates, or staff, engage in any uncivil or unprofessional behavior for any reason.

(m) A lawyer should advise his/her clients that, other than pursuing litigation, there are alternative methods of resolving their disputes with the other parties, including settlement negotiations, mediation, arbitration, or another form of alternative dispute resolution.

(n) A lawyer should provide his/her clients with an honest and straightforward analysis of the advantages or disadvantages of pursuing various strategies, courses of action, or methods of resolving their disputes with other parties, including whether they should proceed with litigation, settlement negotiations, mediation, arbitration, or another form of alternative dispute resolution.

(o) A lawyer should not foster or encourage unwarranted expectations or concerns for a client in connection with the merits of a client's case, including the probable chances of success or defeat relating thereto, in order to persuade a client to pursue an improper strategy, course of action, or method of resolving its disputes with another party, or to justify conducting unnecessary legal work in order to increase the amount of attorney's fees being charged to a client.

SECTION 3

A Lawyer Should Treat Other Counsel, and All Party and Third-Party Witnesses, in a Civil and Professional Manner

A lawyer should treat other counsel, and all party and third-party witnesses, in a civil and professional manner. Specifically, a lawyer should be courteous and respectful in communicating and interacting with other counsel, and all party and third-party witnesses, by complying with the following guidelines:

(a) A lawyer should be courteous and respectful in all of his/her oral and written communications. A lawyer should avoid hostile, demeaning, abusive, threatening or humiliating words in oral and written communications with other counsel, and with all party and third-party witnesses.

(b) A lawyer should not disparage the intelligence, integrity, morals, ethics, or personal behavior of other counsel, or of a party or third-party witness, unless such matters are relevant to the matters a lawyer is handling on behalf of his/her clients under the controlling substantive law.

(c) A lawyer should be truthful and accurate in all oral and written communications with or involving other counsel, and all party and third-party witnesses. A lawyer should not prepare a letter or other document which ascribes to other counsel or adversaries a position they have not taken, or which purports to create a "record" of events that have not occurred.

(d) A lawyer should not seek extensions or continuances for the purpose of harassment, or to improperly extend or delay litigation. When requesting an extension or continuance, a lawyer should explain to other counsel the specific reasons for the request. When requesting an extension or continuance of time, a lawyer should likewise grant a reciprocal extension or continuance of time to other counsel in connection with any deadlines that are impacted by the lawyer's request.

(e) Upon request, a lawyer should extend professional courtesies and grant reasonable accommodations to other counsel and their respective clients, unless to do so would substantially prejudice the lawful objectives of the lawyer's own client.

(f) A lawyer should agree, as a matter of courtesy, to a first request for a reasonable extension of time, unless time is of the essence, or agreeing to such a request would clearly be inconsistent with the legitimate interests of the lawyer's client. A lawyer should not refuse to grant an extension of time to other counsel simply because the same counsel had previously refused to grant an extension of time to the lawyer. Rather, the lawyer should strive to act in a civil and professional manner at all times irrespective of the prior activities or attitudes of other counsel.

(g) After agreeing to a first request for an extension of time, a lawyer should consider any additional requests for extensions of time by balancing the need for a prompt resolution of the matter against considerations involving the professional and personal schedule of other counsel or his/her client, the willingness of other counsel to grant reciprocal extensions, the anticipated time needed for the task, and whether it would be likely that a Court would grant the extension of time, if requested to do so.

(h) A lawyer should not, as a condition to granting a reasonable request for an extension of time, seek to eliminate or cut off the rights of other counsel or an opposing party. For example, a lawyer should not condition his/her agreement to grant a reasonable request for an extension of time to respond to a complaint on the basis that the opposing party will not challenge the sufficiency of a complaint by filing a demurrer or motion to strike.

(i) A lawyer should agree to reasonable requests for extensions of time when new counsel is substituted in for prior counsel, unless the substitution of new counsel is being done solely for the purpose of improperly extending or delaying the litigation, and granting such a request for an extension of time would substantially prejudice the lawful objectives of the lawyer's own client.

(j) A lawyer should make a reasonable effort to schedule all meetings, hearings, and discovery matters by agreement or consensus of other counsel, and should consider the scheduling interests of any opposing counsel, parties, witnesses, and/or the Court, to the extent that such persons are involved in such meetings, hearings or discovery matters. After an agreement has been reached concerning the scheduling of an event, a lawyer should send a notice to all counsel to avoid any future disputes or misunderstandings.

(k) A lawyer should not engage in unnecessary quarrels or disputes concerning the form or style of documents, but should only focus on matters of substance.

(l) To the extent a lawyer is engaged in negotiating and drafting the terms of a written document, the lawyer should clearly identify any and all changes he/she has made in any such document which is submitted to the lawyer's client, other counsel, or other parties, for their review and approval.

(m) A lawyer should not wait to return telephone calls until after it is likely that the other counsel has already left for the day, or otherwise is not in the office.

SECTION 4

A Lawyer Should Act in a Civil and Professional Manner in Connection With All Pre–Litigation Activities

A lawyer should act in a civil and professional manner in connection with all pre-litigation activities. Specifically, a lawyer should comply with the following guidelines:

(a) A lawyer should encourage negotiation of any and all disputes between parties prior to filing or otherwise commencing litigation, unless to do so would substantially harm the interests of the lawyer's own client, or would otherwise be considered futile under the circumstances at hand.

(b) If a lawyer knows the identity of counsel for a party, the lawyer should not cause a default or dismissal of a case to be entered against such party without first inquiring about the intent of such party's counsel to proceed and defend the case. A lawyer also should not seek an opposing party's default to obtain a judgment or substantive order without giving that opposing party sufficient advance written warning to allow the opposing party to cure the default.

SECTION 5

A Lawyer Should Act in a Civil and Professional Manner in Connection With All Discovery Proceedings

A lawyer should act in a civil and professional manner in connection with all discovery proceedings. Specifically, a lawyer should comply with the following guidelines:

General Guidelines Re Discovery:

(a) A lawyer should not seek Court intervention to obtain any discovery which is clearly improper, irrelevant, and not likely to lead to the discovery of admissible evidence.

(b) A lawyer should refrain from unnecessary, abusive, or excessive discovery.

Written Discovery (Including Document Demands, Interrogatories, and Requests for Admission):

(c) As provided in the applicable codes or rules, a lawyer should respond to all written discovery requests on behalf of his/her clients in a timely manner. In doing so, a lawyer should not make any unnecessary objections, or otherwise object to written discovery requests that are not objectionable. A lawyer should not make objections for the purpose of withholding relevant, non-privileged information, or otherwise obstructing or delaying the discovery process.

(d) In responding to written discovery requests, a lawyer should not interpret or decipher the categories of the written discovery requests in an artificially restrictive manner in an attempt to avoid disclosure, or to preclude the production of complete and accurate discovery responses. For example, in responding to a demand for production of documents, a lawyer should not interpret the request in an artificially restrictive manner in an attempt to preclude the production of all responsive and non-privileged documents. Similarly, in responding to interrogatories or requests for admission, a lawyer should not interpret the discovery requests in an artificially restrictive manner in an attempt to ensure that the answers are not truly responsive, and do not completely and accurately provide the information requested.

(e) In responding to written discovery requests, provided that counsel for the propounding party also provides the written discovery requests in an electronic form to the responding party, a lawyer for the responding party should set forth verbatim each of the requests, demands, interrogatories and/or questions presented by the propounding party, and following each such request, demand, interrogatory and/or question, provide the written response of his/her client thereto.

(f) In responding to a demand for production of documents, a lawyer should not knowingly or intentionally destroy, shred, lose, misplace, or withhold any responsive and non-privileged document(s) which are in his/her client's possession, custody or control for any reason, including the fact that such document(s) contain information that is damaging to the interests of the lawyer's client in the case. A lawyer also should advise his/her clients to diligently look for, locate and produce all documents that are responsive to a demand for production of documents, and not to shred, lose, misplace, hide, or withhold any such documents for any reason.

(g) In responding to a demand for production of documents, a lawyer should not adopt an expansive and invalid interpretation of the laws governing the various privileges and doctrines recognized in federal and state Courts, including attorney-client, attorney work product, physician-patient, marital communications, and trade secret privileges, in order to improperly withhold any of his/her client's documents from production to the requesting party.

(h) A lawyer should not delay producing any relevant, non-privileged documents in an attempt to prevent opposing counsel from inspecting such documents prior to the scheduled depositions of any party or third-party witnesses, or for any other tactical reason.

(i) If a lawyer inadvertently receives one or more document(s) which the lawyer knows are privileged, the lawyer should promptly contact counsel for the producing party and inform counsel that the privileged document(s) were produced. Upon request by counsel for the producing party, the lawyer should return any and all originals and copies of the privileged document(s) within one (1) week of receiving the request. The lawyer should not seek any further discovery, including asking any questions at depositions or through written discovery, concerning any privileged information contained in such privileged documents, unless the lawyer can demonstrate that he/she has obtained or learned the privileged information through other non-privileged sources.

Depositions:

(j) Before noticing the deposition of a party or third-party witness, a lawyer should make a good faith effort to consult with opposing and other counsel in an attempt to schedule the deposition on a date that is convenient for all counsel, parties and witnesses. Alternatively, if a lawyer fails to make a good faith effort to consult with opposing and other counsel before noticing a deposition, the lawyer should be willing to re-schedule the deposition to a date that is convenient for all counsel, parties and witnesses.

(k) Since an agreed-upon deposition date is presumptively binding, if a lawyer subsequently seeks to change the deposition date, the lawyer should attempt to coordinate a new date before changing the agreed-upon deposition date.

(l) When another party notices a deposition in the reasonably near future, a lawyer should not normally notice another deposition for an earlier date without the agreement of other counsel.

(m) A lawyer should notice and conduct a deposition of a witness only when actually needed to ascertain facts or information, or to perpetuate testimony. A lawyer should never use a deposition as a means of harassment or to generate expense.

(n) A lawyer should not engage in any conduct during a deposition that would be inappropriate in the presence of a judicial officer.

(o) A lawyer should remember that arguments or conflicts with other counsel during depositions are not personal, and vigorous advocacy is not inconsistent with professional courtesy. A lawyer should treat other counsel, other parties, and witnesses with courtesy and civility, and conduct himself/herself in a professional manner during depositions. A lawyer should not engage in discourtesies or offensive conduct at depositions, including, for example, disparaging the intelligence, integrity, ethics, morals or behavior of other counsel, other parties, and witnesses when those characteristics are not at issue, or disparaging a person based on race, color, national origin, ancestry, sex, gender, sexual orientation, marital status, age, religious creed, medical condition, physical or mental disability, or pregnancy, childbirth or related medical conditions.

(p) When conducting a deposition, a lawyer should only ask questions that are likely to lead to the discovery of admissible evidence and reasonably necessary for discovery in connection with the prosecution or defense of the action, and should not intentionally prolong or otherwise make the deposition last longer than necessary. A lawyer should not inquire into the personal affairs of the deponent when such questions are manifestly irrelevant to the subject matter of the action, and not likely to lead to the discovery of admissible evidence.

(q) When conducting a deposition, a lawyer should not repeatedly ask the same or a substantially-identical question of a deponent, if the question has already been fully and responsively answered by the deponent. Thus, unless the deponent's prior response was evasive or incomplete, a lawyers should not continue to ask the same or a substantially-identical question because a lawyer does not like or agree with the deponent's prior answer.

(r) When conducting a deposition, a lawyer questioning the deponent should provide to all other counsel present a copy of all documents shown to the deponent during the deposition. The copies should be provided either before the deposition begins, or contemporaneously with the showing of each document to the deponent.

(s) When defending a deposition, a lawyer should not make objections or statements which are designed to, or otherwise have the effect of, coaching a deponent as to what he or she should say, or otherwise suggest answers to a pending question. A lawyer should object to a question only when it is necessary under the applicable rules to preserve an objection (i.e., to the form of the question), or to preserve a privilege. A lawyer should state such objections in a concise manner, and not argue or otherwise attempt to explain the factual or legal basis for the objection during the deposition.

(t) When defending a deposition, a lawyer should not instruct a deponent to refuse to answer a question except (i) to protect a recognized privilege, (ii) to enforce a limitation on evidence previously directed by the Court, or (iii) to suspend the deposition and present a motion as provided by law or rule. If a prompt ruling as to the validity of such an instruction cannot be obtained, the instruction should stand and, upon agreement by counsel for the parties, the deposition should continue until a ruling is obtained, or the problem is resolved.

(u) When defending a deposition, if a lawyer or the deponent wish to take a break, for the comfort or convenience of the lawyer or the deponent, a request for such a break should be made on the record. Counsel should attempt to reasonably accommodate each other and the deponent in agreeing to take a break, including allowing the examining lawyer to come to a convenient juncture in his/her line of deposition questioning before such a break is taken.

(v) When defending a deposition, a lawyer and the deponent should be entitled to take a break and confer privately at any time during a deposition (including while a question is pending) for the purpose of determining whether a recognized privilege should be asserted, provided that, before any such break is taken, the examining lawyer should be given a reasonable opportunity to ask questions, and lay a foundation on the record concerning whether a legitimate issue of privilege does, in fact, exist. In addition, before any such break is taken, the examining lawyer should be entitled to rephrase or withdraw any questions implicating a privilege so as to eliminate the need for any break to be taken. Alternatively, the lawyer defending the deposition may simply instruct the deponent to answer the question(s) without revealing any privileged information, so as to eliminate the need for a break in the deposition.

(w) To the extent that a lawyer confers with a deponent while a question is pending to determine whether to assert a recognized privilege, the fact and duration of such a conference may be noted on the record and, in the event of abuse, an appropriate protective order may be sought. The details of any off-the-record conference between a lawyer and the deponent during a recess may be a subject for inquiry by the examining counsel, to the extent such information is not privileged.

(x) Absent a legitimate issue concerning privilege, neither a lawyer, nor the deponent, should unilaterally take a break in the deposition, while a question is pending or otherwise, for the purpose of allowing the lawyer to confer with the deponent, or vice versa.

Law and Motion:

(y) Prior to filing any law and motion matters, a lawyer should engage in good faith meet-and-confer discussions in an attempt to resolve any outstanding disputes.

(z) A lawyer should not file or serve a motion or other papers in any manner which would unfairly limit another party's opportunity to respond, including filing and serving a motion on the Friday before a holiday weekend, or during a time when a lawyer knows that the opposing attorney is out of town, on vacation, or engaged in another trial for an extended period of time, or is otherwise unavailable to review the motion and prepare a timely response thereto, unless the lawyer is required to file and serve the papers on a specific date or time based on the rules governing the specific law and motion matter.

SECTION 6

A Lawyer Should Act in a Civil and Professional Manner in Connection With All Mediation Proceedings or Settlement Discussions

A lawyer should act in a civil and professional manner in connection with all mediation proceedings or settlement discussions. Specifically, a lawyer should comply with the following guidelines:

(a) During mediation or settlement discussions, a lawyer should not act to protect his/her own personal interests, but should strive to achieve a resolution that is in the best interests of his/her own clients. A lawyer should not interfere with or object to a client's desire to settle the dispute quickly and in a cost-effective manner.

(b) During mediation or settlement discussions, a lawyer should provide his/her client with an honest and straightforward analysis of the settlement demands or offers made by the other parties, and the advantages and disadvantages of accepting such demands or offers in lieu of taking the case to trial.

(c) During mediation or settlement discussions, a lawyer should do his/her best to provide the mediator or settlement officer with all of the necessary facts, law, theories, opinions and arguments which would assist the mediator or settlement officer in reaching a resolution of the dispute with the other parties.

(d) A lawyer should not falsely hold out the possibility of settlement as a means for terminating discovery or delaying trial.

(e) When preparing settlement agreements, a lawyer should attempt to prepare documents which completely and accurately reflect the agreement reached between the parties. A lawyer should not knowingly or intentionally include provisions which have not been agreed upon, or omit provisions which have been agreed upon, by the parties.

SECTION 7

A Lawyer Should Act in a Civil and Professional Manner in Connection With All Trial Proceedings

A lawyer should act in a civil and professional manner in connection with all trial proceedings. Specifically, a lawyer should comply with the following guidelines:

(a) A trial lawyer should conduct himself/herself so as to preserve the right to a fair trial, which is one of the most basic of all constitutional guarantees. This right underlies and conditions all other legal rights, constitutional or otherwise. In administering justice, a trial lawyer should assist the Courts in the performance of two difficult tasks: (i) discovering where the truth lies between conflicting versions of the facts so that the lawyer does not knowingly advocate a position on behalf of his/her client that is based on false or misleading facts or evidence, and (ii) applying the relevant legal principles to the facts at issue. These tasks are demanding and cannot be performed in a disorderly environment. Unless order is maintained in the courtroom and disruption prevented, reason cannot prevail and constitutional rights to liberty, freedom and equality under the law cannot be protected. The dignity, decorum and courtesy, which have traditionally characterized the Courts of civilized nations, are not empty formalities. They are essential to an atmosphere in which justice can be done.

(b) During a trial, a lawyer should always display a courteous, dignified and respectful attitude toward the judge presiding, not for the sake of the judge's person, but for the maintenance of respect for and confidence in the judicial office. The judge, to render effective such conduct, has reciprocal responsibilities of courtesy to and respect for the lawyer who also is an officer of the Court. A trial lawyer should vigorously present all proper arguments against rulings or judicial demeanor that the lawyer deems erroneous or prejudicial, and see to it that a complete and accurate case record is made. In this regard, the trial lawyer should not be deterred by any fear of judicial displeasure or punishment.

(c) During a trial, a lawyer has a professional obligation to represent every client courageously, vigorously, diligently and with all the skill and knowledge the lawyer possesses. It is both the right and duty of the trial lawyer to present the client's cause fully and properly, to insist on an opportunity to do so, and to see to it that a complete and accurate case record is made without being deterred by any fear of judicial displeasure or punishment. However, the obligations of the trial lawyer are to be performed within, and not outside, the bounds of the law. The office of the attorney does not permit, much less does it demand, of a lawyer for any client a violation of law or any manner of fraud or chicanery. A trial lawyer must obey his/her conscience and not that of the client.

(d) In performing these duties, a trial lawyer should conduct himself/herself according to the law and standards of professional conduct as defined in codes, rules and canons of the legal profession, and in such a way so as to avoid disorder or disruption in the courtroom. A trial lawyer should advise the client appearing in the courtroom of the kind of behavior expected and required of the client there, and prevent the client, so far as lies within the lawyer's power, from creating disorder or disruption in the courtroom.

(e) During a trial, a lawyer should refrain from raising frivolous objections, or otherwise making improper comments or statements about other counsel, parties, third-party witnesses, the Court, or members of the Court's staff, including during voir dire, opening statement, the direct or cross examinations of any witnesses, or closing argument.

(f) During a trial, a lawyer should refrain from engaging in any conduct or using any body language which is designed to ridicule, poke fun of, mock, demean, or otherwise embarrass or humiliate other counsel, parties, third-party witnesses, the Court, or members of the Court's staff, including rolling his/her eyes, throwing up his/her hands, shrugging his/her shoulders, shaking his/her head, sighing deeply, or any combination thereof.

(g) During a trial, a lawyer should not: (i) unlawfully or improperly obstruct another party's access to evidence, unlawfully alter, destroy or conceal a document or other material having potential evidentiary value, or counsel or assist another person to do any such act; (ii) falsify evidence, counsel or assist a witness to testify falsely, or offer an inducement to a witness that is prohibited by law; (iii) knowingly disobey an obligation under the rules of the tribunal; or (iv) allude to any matter that the lawyer does not reasonably believe is relevant or that will not be supported by admissible evidence, or assert personal knowledge of facts in issue except when testifying as a witness.

SECTION 8

A Lawyer Should Uphold the Integrity and Independence of the Courts

A lawyer should uphold the integrity and independence of the Courts. Specifically, a lawyer should comply with the following guidelines:

(a) A lawyer should strive to be punctual at all times, and should notify the Court as soon as is reasonably practicable if the lawyer anticipates that he/she will be delayed for a hearing or other matter pending before the Court.

(b) Subject to the presumption of privilege for all communications with a lawyer's client and all work product of the lawyer, a lawyer should strive to fully answer all questions posed by the Court in an honest, complete, and straightforward manner.

(c) A lawyer should not knowingly or intentionally misrepresent, mischaracterize, misquote or miscite facts or law to the Court in an attempt to gain an advantage over another party.

(d) A lawyer should file and submit papers to the Court which have been thoroughly and diligently researched and prepared by the lawyer or a member of his/her staff, and which do not contain any unnecessary, inflammatory or prejudicial material.

(e) A lawyer should file and submit declarations to the Court which are completely truthful, accurate and correct. A lawyer should not knowingly or intentionally omit, delete, withhold, leave out, or otherwise misstate important facts or information in an attempt to bolster the declarant's credibility, or otherwise support the client's case.

(f) Even if a lawyer disagrees with the analysis or rulings of a Court, a lawyer should continue to act in a civil and professional manner both before the Court itself, and in his/her subsequent dealings with the lawyer's clients, the media, and/or the public.

(g) When a lawyer is assigned to appear before a judicial officer with whom the lawyer has a social relationship or friendship beyond normal professional association, the lawyer should notify opposing counsel of the relationship.

THE NORTHAMPTON COUNTY BAR ASSOCIATION GUIDE TO CONDUCT AND ETIQUETTE AT THE BAR

These guiding principles comprise the considered opinion of the Bench and Bar of Northampton County concerning professional etiquette and are a result of suggestions made by the Bench at the request of the Bar.

1. Lawyers should dress in a fashion consistent with the respect they expect the public to have for their profession. Lawyers should not appear before the Court in overcoats or other wearing apparel designed for outdoor wear. Lawyers who are at the courthouse for reasons other than a Court appearance should nonetheless recognize the courthouse as the center and focus of their professional activity and dress accordingly. The same formality of dress that is appropriate for the courtroom is appropriate for an appearance before a Judge at the Judge's office or in the Judge's chambers.

2. Lawyers should ask permission to address the Court rather than just jumping up and starting to talk. The proper method of requesting such permission is to preface one's remark by the phrase: "May it please the Court ..."

3. Lawyers should request permission to approach the bench prior to doing so. While at sidebar, lawyers should not rest upon nor "drape themselves" over the bench.

4. Lawyers should first address the Court and opposing counsel before addressing the jury. The proper form of doing this is to first address the Court: "May it please the Court." The Court then acknowledges counsel. Counsel then addresses opposing counsel first: "Mr., Ms., Mrs., _____," and then "Ladies and Gentlemen of the Jury."

5. Lawyers should always stand when addressing the court. This should be done even at the call of the hearing list and the various trial lists.

6. Lawyers when making objections should stand and state a brief (one word if possible) reason for the objection, such as "Objection: Hearsay." If it is necessary to enlarge the record after an objection, lawyers should approach the bench and quietly, out of the hearing of the jury, state their reasons. They should not present their arguments to the jury but only to the Court.

7. In addressing a witness lawyers should stand behind their desk and if for any reason they want to approach the witness, they should only do so after obtaining the court's permission.

8. When marking exhibits for identification, it is suggested that the courteous way of doing this is to give the exhibit to the court reporter to have the exhibit marked, and to then exhibit it to the court and to opposing counsel. All of these actions should be performed before questions are again directed to the witness. The court reporter cannot possibly mark an exhibit and record testimony at the same time. Where there are a multitude of exhibits, they should be marked in advance by the court reporter or the lawyers. When possible and not too cumbersome, separate copies of exhibits should be provided for the Court. This permits the original to remain with the court reporter and avoids the problem of lawyers having to search for them on the bench or elsewhere.

9. Lawyers should always keep their voices up and remind their witnesses to do the same.

10. Lawyers should never directly address opposing counsel in Court. Lawyers should directly address only the Court, the jury, and the witnesses.

11. A lawyer should not call any witness, even his or her client, by the witness' first name.

12. Lawyers should limit voir dire questions to the proper purpose of voir dire and should not attempt to instruct the jury as to the law or to argue their case to the jury by means of voir dire questions.

13. As a tactical point, there is a great weight of authority to the effect that cases are won or lost on direct examination. Young lawyers uniformly have a tendency to overdo the cross-examination of witnesses.

14. Motion Court convenes at 9:00 A.M. every day except weekends and holidays. Except for rules to show cause, lawyers should supply to all opposing counsel a copy of the proposed motion and notice of the date the motion is to be presented at least three days prior to presenting the motion. A motion should not be presented to any Judge other than the Motion Judge, nor at any time other than during Motion Court, unless emergency relief is required.

15. Lawyers should be on time for all court appearances, including all calls of the list.

16. Lawyers who have cases on a miscellaneous hearing list should remain immediately available, so that when their case is called they are ready to begin promptly.

17. Lawyers should not initiate conversation with jurors who have served on a jury in a case they were trying.

18. If a lawyer has an uncontested motion or rule to show cause and cannot get to Motion Court, he or she may leave it with the Court Administrator who will present it to the Motion Judge and return it to the lawyer.

19. All lawyers, in accordance with the Court Rules and Rule 1.1 of the Rules of Professional Conduct, should be prepared at all times when they appear before the Court.

20. Lawyers should exhibit courtesy in the courtroom toward opposing counsel as well as to the court and to witnesses.

21. Lawyers should at all times deal with each other honestly and with respect. It is suggested that communication between counsel in the presence of clients and before the court shall be with respect and courtesy—"Treat others as you would have them treat you."

22. Lawyers should be cognizant of the effect of use of gender specific terms when addressing another lawyer. Such language tends to degrade the recipient in the eyes of clients and others.

23. By the very nature of our profession, heated exchanges occur. Threats of physical violence, however, cannot and should not be tolerated or condoned under any circumstances.

24. Whenever possible, trial counsel should include the authority relied upon in points for charge and refrain from unduly repetitious points.

25. Lawyers should wait until all of the assignments have been announced on a miscellaneous hearing or argument list before engaging others in conversation or gathering their briefcases, charts, and other paraphernalia and leaving the courtroom.

26. Lawyers should be available in their offices or at the Courthouse to respond to telephone civil status calls at least one-half hour prior to the designated time.

27. Trials or hearings may not be continued without Court approval. Discovery deadlines fixed by court order may not be extended without Court approval. The mere agreement of counsel to a continuance or to an extension is insufficient.

28. The Court's overall view is that it is pleased with the courtroom demeanor of the Northampton County Bar.

29. These guidelines should not be construed as being a criticism of the Bar in general, or of any lawyers in particular, but merely as suggestions to all members of the Bar who are perhaps not aware of these matters.

30. The Court has particularly expressed its satisfaction with the preparedness of counsel at pretrial conferences and will continue to insist that this level of preparedness be maintained.

Revised January 1994